ISSUES IN PEACE
AND
CONFLICT STUDIES

SELECTIONS FROM CQ RESEARCHER

SAGE

Los Angeles | London | New Delhi
Singapore | Washington DC

For information:

SAGE Publications, Inc.
2455 Teller Road
Thousand Oaks, California 91320
E-mail: order@sagepub.com

SAGE Publications Ltd.
1 Oliver's Yard
55 City Road
London, EC1Y 1SP
United Kingdom

SAGE Publications India Pvt. Ltd.
B 1/I 1 Mohan Cooperative Industrial Area
Mathura Road, New Delhi 110 044
India

SAGE Publications Asia-Pacific Pte. Ltd.
33 Pekin Street #02-01
Far East Square
Singapore 048763

Printed in the United States of America

Library of Congress Cataloging-in-Publication Data

Issues in peace and conflict studies : selections from CQ researcher.
    p. cm.
Includes bibliographical references and index.
ISBN 978-1-4129-9291-6 (pbk.)
  1. Conflict management. 2. Peace. 3. Arms control.

HM1126.I88 2011
303.6′9—dc22   2010034857

This book is printed on acid-free paper.

10 11 12 13 14   10 9 8 7 6 5 4 3 2 1

Acquisitions Editor:	Christine Cardone
Associate Editor:	Julie Nemer
Editorial Assistant:	Sarita Sarak
Production Editor:	Laureen Gleason
Typesetter:	C&M Digitals (P) Ltd.
Cover Designer:	Candice Harman
Marketing Manager:	Stephanie Adams

Contents

CRISES, CONFLICTS, AND PEACE PROSPECTS AROUND THE WORLD

Annotated Contents

POLITICAL AND PHILOSOPHICAL ISSUES

World Peacekeeping: Do Nation-States Have a "Responsibility to Protect"?

After the United Nations arose from the ashes of the Holocaust, the world's collective vow "Never again" seemed ironclad and irrevocable. As part of its effort to prevent future wars and genocides, the U.N. began to station peacekeepers around the globe, beginning in 1948 in Jerusalem. But the peacekeeping missions have had limited success. Now, prompted by the horror of the killings in Rwanda and Darfur, and before that in Bosnia, the world body has adopted a controversial new concept — the Responsibility to Protect — designed to stop future catastrophes. Known as R2P, it holds that the world community has a moral duty to halt genocide — even inside a sovereign country. But detractors call R2P legal imperialism, and even its defenders admit that the rhetoric has not yet translated into meaningful aid for Darfur. Other international alliances, meanwhile, have stepped up to provide military muscle to keep the peace in other hotspots, including NATO and the European and African unions.

Separatist Movements: Should Nations Have a Right to Self-Determination?

When Kosovo declared its independence on Feb. 17, 2008, thousands of angry Serbs took to the streets to protest the breakaway region's secession from Serbia. Less than a month later, Chinese authorities battled Buddhist monks in Lhasa, the legendary capital of Tibet, where separatist resentments have been simmering since China occupied the Himalayan region more than 50 years ago. The protests were the latest flashpoints in some two dozen separatist "hot spots" — the most active of roughly 70 such movements around the globe. They are part of a post-World War II independence trend that has produced a nearly fourfold jump in the number of countries worldwide, with 26 of those new countries emerging just since 1990. Some nations, like the far-flung Kurds and the Sri Lankan Tamils, are fighting fiercely to establish a homeland, while others — like Canada's Québécois — seem content with local autonomy. A handful have become de facto states that are as-yet-unrecognized by the U.N., including Somaliland, Taiwan, South Ossetia and Nagorno-Karabakh.

Nuclear Disarmament: Will President Obama's Efforts Make the U.S. Safer?

Peace activists have sought to eliminate nuclear weapons for decades, but now they have a new ally. President Barack Obama has pledged to negotiate new U.S.-Russian arms reductions, end U.S. nuclear testing and reduce the role of nuclear weapons in national defense policy. Obama argues that these steps, plus new measures to combat nuclear smuggling and theft, will make the United States safer. But critics say further nuclear cuts will embolden rogue countries like North Korea and Iran, which are widely thought to be seeking nuclear capabilities. Although the U.S. and Russia have drastically shrunk their Cold War arsenals, the United States still spends at least $52 billion annually on nuclear-related programs. Liberals and conservatives sharply disagree about addressing post-Cold War security threats with nuclear arms. But some experts warn that new, regional nuclear arms races could break out if the U.S. fails to rebuild global support for nuclear reductions.

Future of NATO: Is the Transatlantic Alliance Obsolete?

During the Cold War, the North Atlantic Treaty Organization (NATO) was the West's line of defense against possible Soviet aggression. But the end of the Soviet Union in 1991 and the disappearance of NATO's communist equivalent — the Warsaw Pact — raised doubts about NATO's relevance. Nearly 20 years later, the specter of obsolescence still hangs over the venerable 26-nation alliance. So-called "Atlanticists" in both the United States and Europe say NATO's role in keeping the United States tied strategically to Europe justifies the alliance's continued existence. Moreover, NATO makes Moscow uneasy, and that's a good thing, they say. Others feel NATO should "earn its keep" by assuming new military responsibilities, such as protecting global energy-supply routes. But one thing is certain: It's not your grandfather's alliance. Since the 1990s, nearly a dozen former Soviet states and Soviet-bloc nations have joined NATO, easing their transition to democracy. NATO also has expanded its operations beyond Europe to Afghanistan, which may become the 60-year-old alliance's ultimate testing ground.

CRISES, CONFLICTS, AND PEACE PROSPECTS AROUND THE WORLD

Anti-Semitism in Europe: Are Israel's Policies Spurring a New Wave of Hate Crimes?

A wave of anti-Jewish attacks on individuals and synagogues has beset Europe since 2000, when the second Palestinian uprising against Israel's occupation began. In France anti-Semitic youth gangs recently abducted and tortured two young Jewish men, one of whom was murdered. European soccer fans routinely taunt Jewish teams with Hitler salutes and chants, such as "Hamas, Hamas, Jews to the gas!" And while anti-Semitic attacks overall dipped slightly in some countries, violent assaults on individuals spiked last year, reaching a record high in Britain. Some scholars worry that the "new anti-Semitism" incorporates anti-Zionist language, which has become increasingly acceptable — particularly among Palestinian sympathizers in academia and the media. But Israel's critics — some of whom are Jewish — warn that calling people anti-Semitic because they oppose Israel's treatment of the Palestinians confuses the public. If the charge is made too often, they suggest, people will become cynical and won't recognize genocidal evil when it occurs.

Crisis in Darfur: Is There Any Hope for Peace?

More than two years after government and rebel fighters signed a peace agreement in Sudan, violence is still rampant in Darfur. At least 2.4 million people have been displaced and up to 400,000 have died since 2003. And observers say the situation is getting worse. Rebel groups have splintered into more than a dozen warring factions, bandits are attacking relief workers, and drought threatens to make next year among the deadliest in Darfur's history. Despite pressure from religious and human-rights groups, the international community seems unable — or unwilling — to find a lasting solution. A year after the U.N. authorized the world's largest peacekeeping force in Darfur, only 37 percent of the authorized personnel have been deployed, and no military helicopters have been provided. The International Criminal Court is considering genocide charges against Sudanese President Omar Hassan al-Bashir, but some fear an indictment would trigger more violence than justice. Some say China, Sudan's largest trading partner and arms supplier, should pressure Sudan to end the violence.

Crisis in Pakistan: Can the Fragile Democracy Survive?

South Asia experts warn that Pakistan — recently dubbed "the new center of the war against terrorism"— could become the world's first nuclear-armed "failed state." The Muslim country's new president faces a spike in terrorist bombings, rising Islamic fundamentalism, a weakened democracy and a faltering economy. Already, more people have been killed in suicide bombings in Pakistan during the first eight months of 2008 than in Iraq or Afghanistan. And Indian authorities suspect that Islamic terrorists from Pakistan-controlled Kashmir perpetrated the 2008 Mumbai terrorist attacks that killed 173 people. Another challenge for President Asif Ali Zardari and his relatively young nation: growing resentment about recent U.S. military incursions into terrorist-infested Pakistani tribal territories. Although the country has weathered many storms since its founding in 1947, experts wonder if recent developments threaten its survival. As the new administration tries to hold the disparate nation together, a strong military — with a long history of usurping civilian rule — is poised to take over once again. The world watches with growing concern to see if the fragile democracy can survive or if Pakistan — with its nuclear arsenal — will devolve into chaos.

Middle East Peace Prospects: Is There Any Hope for Long-Term Peace?

Three major events reshaped the political landscape of the Middle East during a seven-week period beginning in late 2008. Israel launched a devastating 22-day assault on Gaza to halt ongoing Palestinian rocket and mortar fire, Israeli parliamentary elections displayed growing disenchantment with the peace process and President Barack Obama moved into the White House promising to try to help resolve the Arab-Israeli conflict after more than six decades of violence. Obama's pledge raised hopes in some quarters for a revival of peace talks — in limbo since the controversial Gaza war began on December 27. But Israel's political shift to the right and deep, continuing Palestinian divisions raise the prospect of continued stalemate. Years of talks and several interim agreements have failed to encourage either side that they can eventually get what they want. Israelis, pursuing security, remain the target of militant attacks, while impoverished Palestinians — seeking a state of their own — remain under effective Israeli control.

The Troubled Horn of Africa: Can the War-Torn Region be Stabilized?

Plagued by conflict, poverty and poor governance, the Horn of Africa is arguably the most troubled corner of the world's poorest continent. In desperately poor Somalia, an 18-year civil war has forced more than a million people from their homes, leaving behind a safe haven for pirates and, possibly, Islamic terrorists. In Ethiopia, an increasingly authoritarian, Western-backed government has jailed opposition leaders and clamped down on the press and human rights activists. In tiny Eritrea, a government that once won the admiration of legions of Western diplomats and journalists for its self-sufficiency and discipline has become an isolated dictatorship. The recent withdrawal of Ethiopian troops from Somalia and the election of a moderate leader to the country's transitional government have raised international hopes that the lawlessness there will be brought under control. But Somalia's new government faces an insurgency from radical Islamists and worldwide pressure to stop the increasingly aggressive pirates who terrorize cargo ship crews off Somalia's coast and find refuge in its seaside villages.

U.S.-China Relations: Is a Future Confrontation Looming?

Disputes that have bedeviled relations between the United States and China for decades flared up again following President Obama's decision to sell weapons to Taiwan and receive Tibet's revered Dalai Lama. From the U.S. perspective, China's refusal to raise the value of its currency is undermining America's — and Europe's — economic recovery. Beijing also rebuffed Obama's proposal of "a partnership on the big global issues of our time." In addition, the Chinese insist on tackling their pollution problems in their own way, and have been reluctant to support U.S. diplomatic efforts to impose tough sanctions on nuclear-minded Iran. With the central bank of China holding more than $800 billion of the U.S. national debt in the form of Treasury notes, and their economy speeding along at a 9 percent growth rate, the Chinese are in no mood to be accommodating.

COPING WITH THE AFTERMATH

Aiding Refugees: Should the U.N. Help More Displaced People?

Some 42 million people worldwide have been uprooted by warfare or other violence, including 16 million refugees who are legally protected because they left their home countries. Most live in refugee camps and receive aid from the United Nations or other agencies but cannot work or leave the camps without special permission. Another 26 million people who fled violence are not protected by international treaties because they remained in their home countries. The number of such "internally displaced persons" (IDPs) has risen in the last decade, largely due to wars in Africa, Iraq, Afghanistan and Colombia. Millions of IDPs live in harsh conditions, and many receive no aid. Some critics say the U.N. High Commissioner for Refugees should do much more for IDPs, but the agency already faces severe budget shortfalls and bleak prospects for more donations from wealthy nations. Meanwhile, scientists warn that the number of people displaced by natural disasters — now about 50 million a year — could rise dramatically in coming years due to climate change.

Truth Commissions: Can Countries Heal After Atrocities?

After war and unspeakable violence, countries around the world face the challenge of moving forward while dealing with the past. But what should justice look like? From Bosnia to Burundi, from Argentina to Timor-Leste, millions of people around the world have been brutalized by genocide, torture, kidnappings and disappearances of loved ones — often at the hands of their own governments and countrymen. Today countries have a variety of legal options, known as transitional justice, including truth commissions — official panels that investigate atrocities and create authoritative records of past abuses. Truth-telling can foster social healing and reconciliation, supporters say, but early research suggests that results have been mixed. Other countries seek justice through international trials or tribunals. In the end, justice — however it is sought — seeks to expose the truth, protect human rights and pave a path to democracy.

Dangerous War Debris: Who Should Clean Up After Conflicts End?

Long after the guns of war have gone silent, people around the world are killed or maimed every day by the "silent killers" of warfare — the tens of millions of landmines, cluster bombs and other unexploded ordnance that litter abandoned battlefields, farmland and urban areas. Most of the victims are civilians, and many are children. Besides claiming more than 5,000 victims each year, dangerous war debris also prevents war refugees from returning to their homelands, stifles fragile economies and prevents farmers from planting crops or developers from investing in a nation's future. Many nations and organizations help the victims and work to ban, remove and disarm landmines and other "explosive remnants of war" (ERW). But questions are being asked about how best to help victims and whether enough is being done to destroy ERWs and stockpiles of banned chemical weapons.

Prosecuting Terrorists: Should Suspected Terrorists Be Given Military or Civil Trials?

President Obama is under fierce political attack for the administration's decision to try Khalid Sheikh Mohammed, the alleged mastermind of the Sept. 11 attacks, and Umar Farouk Abdulmutallab, the so-called Christmas Day bomber, in civilian courts instead of military tribunals. Republican lawmakers argue the defendants in both cases should be treated as "enemy combatants" and tried in the military commissions established during the Bush administration. Administration officials and Democratic lawmakers say criminal prosecutions are more effective, having produced hundreds of convictions since 9/11 compared to only three in the military system. And they insist that Abdulmutallab is providing useful information under interrogation by FBI agents. But the administration is reconsidering Attorney General Eric Holder's original decision to hold Mohammed's trial in New York City and considering making greater use of military commissions with other terrorism cases.

Caring for Veterans: Does the VA Adequately Serve Wounded Vets?

Battle-scarred veterans often spend more time waiting for decisions from the Department of Veterans Affairs (VA) on their disability claims than they spent at war. At least 500,000 veterans have waited an average of six months for a decision on a disability claim and another 200,000 have waited an average of five years for a decision on an appeal. New VA Secretary Eric Shinseki — himself a disabled Vietnam vet — vows to unblock the huge claims backlog, but it may take until 2015. That's partly because the VA has expanded the number of compensation-worthy illnesses from the Vietnam War. Veterans' organizations laud Shinseki but disagree over how deeply VA changes should run. Meanwhile, lawmakers in Congress are close to passing legislation to compensate relatives and friends caring for veterans with catastrophic, lifelong disabilities such as traumatic brain injuries arising from improvised explosive devices — the devastating homemade bombs that are the hallmark of the wars in Iraq and Afghanistan.

SPECIAL TOPICS

Attacking Piracy: Can the Growing Global Threat Be Stopped?

After centuries of inactivity, piracy has returned with a vengeance. Maritime marauders now operate across the globe from Peru to the Philippines, but they pose the biggest threat off the coast of Somalia — a failed state in the Horn of Africa. In the first six months of 2009, attacks by Somali pirates jumped sixfold over the same period last year. Piracy costs global shippers $10 billion to $50 billion a year in ransoms, lost cargoes, higher insurance premiums and disrupted shipping schedules — costs that are passed on to consumers. The world's largest navies have sent warships to the Horn of Africa in recent months and have captured more than 100 pirates. But it may be too costly to maintain the naval patrols over the long term. In addition, murky anti-piracy laws and jurisdictional issues are hampering prosecutions. Moreover, some security experts fear pirates may be exposing vulnerabilities that terrorists could exploit to disrupt global trade, raising the stakes in the fight to solve a growing international problem.

Terrorism and the Internet: Should Web Sites That Promote Terrorism Be Shut Down?

A decade ago, terrorist organizations operated or controlled only about a dozen Web sites. Today there are more than 7,000. Terrorist groups use the Internet for many activities, ranging from raising funds to explaining how to build a suicide bomb. They find the Internet appealing for the same reasons everyone else does: It's cheap, easily accessible, unregulated and reaches a potentially enormous audience. As terrorist content spreads to chat rooms, blogs, user groups, social networking sites and virtual worlds, many experts, politicians and law enforcement officials are debating how government and industry should respond. Some want Internet companies to stop terrorists from using the Web, while others say that is not the role of Internet service providers. As governments enact laws based on the belief that the Internet plays a significant role in promoting terrorism, critics say the new measures often overstep free-speech and privacy rights.

Climate Change: Will the Copenhagen Accord Slow Global Warming?

Delegates from around the globe arrived in Copenhagen, Denmark, for the U.N. Climate Change Conference in December hoping to forge a significant agreement to reduce greenhouse gas emissions and temper climate change. But despite years of diplomatic preparation, two weeks of intense negotiations and the clamor for action from thousands of protesters outside the meeting, the conferees adopted no official treaty. Instead, a three-page accord — cobbled together on the final night by President Barack Obama and the leaders of China, India, Brazil and South Africa — established only broad, nonbinding goals and postponed tough decisions. Yet defenders of the accord praised it for requiring greater accountability from emerging economies such as China, protecting forests and committing billions in aid to help poorer nations. But the key question remains: Will the accord help U.N. efforts to forge a legally binding climate change treaty for the world's nations?

Confronting Rape as a War Crime: Will a New U.N. Campaign Have Any Impact?

Rape has been a consequence of military defeat for millennia. But in the last 20 years — from Bosnia to Rwanda, from Colombia to the Democratic Republic of Congo — sexual violence against women, and sometimes even against men, has become a strategic military tactic designed to humiliate victims and shatter enemy societies. And increasingly, governments presiding over peaceful countries are using mass rape in deliberate and targeted campaigns to spread terror and humiliation among political dissenters, often during election seasons. The strategic use of rape has been recognized by international courts as an act of genocide and ethnic cleansing. The United Nations is working to change the mindset that wartime rape is inevitable, urging governments to end the violence and prosecute perpetrators. But silence and shame shroud the issue, and some governments that deny wartime rape occurs in their countries have banned international aid groups that treat their citizens who have been victimized. This spring, the United Nations' first special representative for sexual violence began a two-year campaign to help curb the crime. But experts say strategic rape won't be easy to eradicate.

Preface

D
o nation-states have a "Responsibility to Protect"? Can countries heal after atrocities? Who should clean up after conflicts end? These questions—and many more—are at the heart of peace and conflict studies. How can instructors best engage students with these crucial issues? We feel that students need objective, yet provocative examinations of these issues to understand how they affect society today and will for years to come. This collection aims to promote in-depth discussion, facilitate further research and help readers formulate their own positions on crucial issues. Get your students talking both inside and outside the classroom about issues in peace and conflict studies.

This first edition includes nineteen up-to-date reports by *CQ Researcher*, an award-winning weekly policy brief that brings complicated issues down to earth. Each report chronicles and analyzes executive, legislative and judicial activities at all levels of government.

CQ RESEARCHER

CQ Researcher was founded in 1923 as *Editorial Research Reports* and was sold primarily to newspapers as a research tool. The magazine was renamed and redesigned in 1991 as *CQ Researcher*. Today, students are its primary audience. While still used by hundreds of journalists and newspapers, many of which reprint portions of the reports, the *Researcher's* main subscribers are now high school, college and public libraries. In 2002, *Researcher* won the American Bar Association's coveted Silver Gavel award for magazine excellence for a series of nine reports on civil liberties and other legal issues.

Researcher staff writers—all highly experienced journalists—sometimes compare the experience of writing a *Researcher* report to drafting a college term paper. Indeed, there are many similarities. Each report is as long as many term papers—about 11,000 words—and is written by one person without any significant outside help. One of the key differences is that writers interview leading experts, scholars and government officials for each issue.

Like students, staff writers begin the creative process by choosing a topic. Working with the *Researcher's* editors, the writer identifies a controversial subject that has important public policy implications. After a topic is selected, the writer embarks on one to two weeks of intense research. Newspaper and magazine articles are clipped or downloaded, books are ordered and information is gathered from a wide variety of sources, including interest groups, universities and the government. Once the writers are well informed, they develop a detailed outline, and begin the interview process. Each report requires a minimum of ten to fifteen interviews with academics, officials, lobbyists and people working in the field. Only after all interviews are completed does the writing begin.

CHAPTER FORMAT

Each issue of *CQ Researcher,* and therefore each selection in this book, is structured in the same way. Each begins with an overview, which briefly summarizes the areas that will be explored in greater detail in the rest of the chapter. The next section chronicles important and current debates on the topic under discussion and is structured around a number of key questions, such as "Should suspected terrorists be given military or civil trials?" or "Is rape an inevitable consequence of war?" These questions are usually the subject of much discussion among practitioners and scholars in the field. Hence, the answers presented are never conclusive but detail the range of opinion on the topic.

Next, the "Background" section provides a history of the issue being examined. This retrospective covers important legislative measures, executive actions and court decisions that illustrate how current policy has

evolved. Then the "Current Situation" section examines contemporary policy issues, legislation under consideration and legal action being taken. Each selection concludes with an "Outlook" section, which addresses possible regulation, court rulings and initiatives from Capitol Hill and the White House over the next five to ten years.

Each report contains features that augment the main text: two to three sidebars that examine issues related to the topic at hand, a pro versus con debate between two experts, a chronology of key dates and events and an annotated bibliography detailing major sources used by the writer.

ACKNOWLEDGMENTS

We wish to thank many people for helping to make this collection a reality. Tom Colin, managing editor of *CQ Researcher,* gave us his enthusiastic support and cooperation as we developed this edition. He and his talented staff of editors and writers have amassed a first-class library of *Researcher* reports, and we are fortunate to have access to that rich cache. We also wish to thank our colleagues at CQ Press, a division of SAGE and a leading publisher of books, directories, research publications and Web products on U.S. government, world affairs and communications. They have forged the way in making these readers a useful resource for instruction across a range of undergraduate and graduate courses.

Some readers may be learning about *CQ Researcher* for the first time. We expect that many readers will want regular access to this excellent weekly research tool. For subscription information or a no-obligation free trial of *CQ Researcher,* please contact CQ Press at www.cqpress.com or toll-free at 1-866-4CQ-PRESS (1-866-427-7737).

We hope that you will be pleased by this edition of *Issues in Peace and Conflict Studies.* We welcome your feedback and suggestions for future editions. Please direct comments to Chris Cardone, Acquisitions Editor, SAGE Publications, 2455 Teller Road, Thousand Oaks, CA 91320, or christine.cardone@sagepub.com.

—The Editors of SAGE

Contributors

Irwin Arieff is a veteran journalist now freelancing in New York City. He served for 23 years as a correspondent for the Reuters news agency in Washington, Paris, New York and the United Nations. During more than four decades as a writer and editor — including five years writing for the *CQ Weekly* — Arieff covered subjects ranging from international affairs, the White House and U.S. politics to science and medicine, the television industry and financial market regulation. He has a masters degree in journalism from Northwestern University's Medill School.

Brian Beary, a freelance journalist based in Washington, D.C., specializes in European Union (EU) affairs and is the U.S. correspondent for *Europolitics,* the EU-affairs daily newspaper. Originally from Dublin, Ireland, he worked in the European Parliament for Irish MEP Pat "The Cope" Gallagher in 2000 and at the EU Commission's Eurobarometer unit on public opinion analysis. A fluent French speaker, he appears regularly as a guest international-relations expert on television and radio programs. Beary also writes for the *European Parliament Magazine* and the *Irish Examiner* daily newspaper. One of his recent reports for *CQ Global Researcher* was "Race for the Arctic."

John Felton is a freelance journalist who has written about international affairs and U.S. foreign policy for nearly 30 years. He covered foreign affairs for the *Congressional Quarterly Weekly Report* during the 1980s, was deputy foreign editor for National Public Radio in the early 1990s and has been a freelance writer specializing in international topics for the past 15 years. His most recent book, published by CQ Press, is *The Contemporary Middle East: A Documentary History*. He lives in Stockbridge, Massachusetts.

Roland Flamini is a Washington-based correspondent who writes a foreign-affairs column for *CQ Weekly*. Fluent in six languages, he served as *Time* magazine's bureau chief in Rome, Bonn, Beirut, Jerusalem and the European Common Market and later served as international editor at United Press International. He wrote "Afghanistan on the Brink" for *CQ Global Researcher*.

Karen Foerstel is a freelance writer who has worked for the Congressional Quarterly *Weekly Report* and *Daily Monitor, The New York Post* and *Roll Call,* a Capitol Hill newspaper. She has published two books on women in Congress, *Climbing the Hill: Gender Conflict in Congress* and *The Biographical Dictionary of Women in Congress.* She currently lives and works in London. She has worked in Africa with ChildsLife International, a nonprofit that helps needy children around the world, and with Blue Ventures, a marine conservation organization that protects coral reefs in Madagascar.

Sarah Glazer, a London-based freelancer, is a regular contributor to the *CQ Researcher.* Her articles on health, education and social-policy issues have appeared in *The New York Times, The Washington Post, The Public Interest* and *Gender and Work,* a book of essays. Her recent *CQ Researcher* reports include "Increase in Autism" and "Gender and Learning." She graduated from the University of Chicago with a BA in American history.

Alan Greenblatt is a staff writer at *Governing* magazine. He previously covered elections, agriculture and military spending for *CQ Weekly*, where he won the National Press Club's Sandy Hume Award for political journalism. He graduated from San Francisco State University in 1986 and received a master's degree in English literature from the University of Virginia in 1988. His recent *CQ Researcher* reports include "Sex Offenders" and "Pension Crisis."

Kenneth Jost graduated from Harvard College and Georgetown University Law Center. He is the author of

the *Supreme Court Yearbook* and editor of *The Supreme Court from A to Z* (both published by CQ Press). He was a member of the *CQ Researcher* team that won the 2002 ABA Silver Gavel Award. His recent reports include "Democracy in the Arab World" and "Religious Persecution."

Reed Karaim, a freelance writer living in Tucson, Arizona, has written for *The Washington Post, U.S. News & World Report, Smithsonian, American Scholar, USA Weekend* and other publications. He is the author of the novel *If Men Were Angels*, which was selected for the Barnes & Noble Discover Great New Writers series. He is also the winner of the Robin Goldstein Award for Outstanding Regional Reporting and other journalism awards. Karaim is a graduate of North Dakota State University in Fargo.

Peter Katel is a *CQ Researcher* staff writer who previously reported on Haiti and Latin America for *Time* and *Newsweek* and covered the Southwest for newspapers in New Mexico. He has received several journalism awards, including the Bartolomé Mitre Award for coverage of drug trafficking from the Inter-American Press Association. He holds an AB in university studies from the University of New Mexico. His recent reports include "The New Philanthropy" and "War in Iraq."

Lee Michael Katz has been a senior diplomatic correspondent for *USA Today*, the International Editor of UPI, and an independent policy journalist who has written lengthy articles on foreign policy, terrorism, and national security. He has reported from more than 60 countries. He holds an MS from Columbia University and has traveled frequently with the U.S. Secretary of State.

Robert Kiener is an award-winning writer whose work has appeared in the *London Sunday Times, The Christian Science Monitor, The Washington Post, Reader's Digest, Time Life Books, Asia Inc.* and other publications. For more than two decades he lived and worked as an editor and correspondent in Guam, Hong Kong, England and Canada and is now based in the United States. He frequently travels to Asia and Europe to report on international issues. He holds a MA in Asian Studies from Hong Kong University and an MPhil in International Relations from Cambridge University.

Barbara Mantel is a freelance writer in New York City whose work has appeared in *The New York Times,* the *Journal of Child and Adolescent Psychopharmacology* and *Mamm Magazine.* She is a former correspondent and senior producer for National Public Radio and has won several journalism awards, including the National Press Club's Best Consumer Journalism Award and the Front Page Award from the Newswomen's Club of New York. She holds a BA in history and economics from the University of Virginia and an MA in economics from Northwestern University.

Jason McLure is a correspondent for Bloomberg News and *Newsweek* based in Addis Ababa, Ethiopia. He previously worked for *Legal Times* in Washington, D.C., and in *Newsweek*'s Boston bureau. His reporting has appeared in *The Economist, Business Week,* the *British Journalism Review* and *National Law Journal.* His work has been honored by the Washington, D.C., chapter of the Society for Professional Journalists, the Maryland-Delaware-District of Columbia Press Association and the Overseas Press Club of America Foundation. He has a master's degree in journalism from the University of Missouri.

Jina Moore is a multimedia journalist who covers science, human rights and foreign affairs from the United States and Africa. Her work has appeared in *The Christian Science Monitor, Newsweek, The Boston Globe, Foreign Policy* and *Best American Science Writing,* among others. She was a 2009 Ochberg Fellow with the Dart Society for Journalism and Trauma and blogs at www.jinamoore.com.

Jennifer Weeks is a *CQ Researcher* contributing writer in Watertown, Massachusetts, who specializes in energy and environmental issues. She has written for *The Washington Post, The Boston Globe Magazine* and other publications, and has 15 years' experience as a public-policy analyst, lobbyist and congressional staffer. She has an AB degree from Williams College and master's degrees from the University of North Carolina and Harvard.

1

World Peacekeeping

Do Nation-States Have a
"Responsibility to Protect?"

Lee Michael Katz

A Polish soldier from the European Union Force supporting the U.N. mission in the Democratic Republic of the Congo participates in training for hostage-rescue operations at the EUFOR base in Kinshasa. A French helicopter hovers above.

From *CQ Global Researcher*,
April 2007.

As the United Nations marked Holocaust Commemoration Day this year, the world's failure to stop the deaths and devastation in Darfur made the occasion far more urgent than the usual calendar exercise.

New Secretary-General Ban Ki-moon had to deliver his remarks on videotape, pointedly noting he was on his way to Ethiopia for an African Union summit focusing on ending the carnage against black Africans in western Sudan. Just weeks after taking office, the head of the world body said he was strongly committed to this message: "We must apply the lessons of the Holocaust to today's world."[1]

Elderly Holocaust survivors in the audience served as visible witnesses before delegates of the international body that rose out of the ashes of World War II's Nazi evils. But it was clear that more than 60 years later, the lessons had not been fully learned.

"I still weep today" at the memories of those, including her father and brother, who were marched to the gas chambers at Auschwitz, said Simone Veil, a well known French Holocaust survivor.

But she also pointed to slaughter that happened decades afterward and is still happening today. While those who survived hoped the pledge "Never Again" would ring true, Veil said, sadly their warnings were in vain. "After the massacres in Cambodia, it is Africa that is paying the highest price in genocidal terms," she said, in a call for action to stop the killings in Darfur. An estimated 200,000 have been killed, countless women raped and 2 million made homeless as armed Arab militia known as janjaweed prey on vulnerable villagers.

Major Worldwide Peacekeeping Operations

The African Union, European Union Force, NATO and United Nations combine for 24 peacekeeping forces deployed around the world. The U.N. has 15 missions, with the most recent deployment being a police force in Timor-Leste in 2006.

Peacekeeping Missions

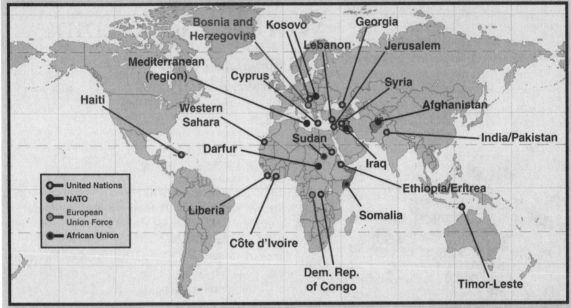

Sources: African Union, Delegation of the European Commission to the USA, NATO, United Nations Department of Peacekeeping Operations

The laments about a lack of lifesaving action continue despite the fact that the United Nations has endorsed, at least in principle, a new concept to keeping the peace in the 21st century called the Responsibility to Protect. At its heart is the fundamental notion that the world has a moral obligation to intervene against genocide.

This includes using military force if necessary, even when the deaths are taking place inside a sovereign nation as in the 1994 ethnic massacre in Rwanda. A reduced U.N. force in the African nation did not physically try to stop the slaughter by Hutus in Rwanda of 800,000 fellow Rwandans — mainly Tutsis but also moderate Hutus — in a matter of weeks. Traditionally, such intervention would be seen as off-limits inside a functioning state, especially a member of the United Nations.

So the notion of the Responsibility to Protect "is very significant because it removes an excuse to turn a blind eye to mass atrocities," says Lee Feinstein, a former U.S. diplomat and author of a 2007 Council on Foreign Relations report on R2P, as the concept is known.[2] Such excuses went "unchallenged" until recently, he says. "If the U.N. is serious about this — and there are questions — this is a big deal." But a decade after Rwanda, the deaths, displacement and widespread rapes in Darfur have been ongoing even after the Responsibility to Protect was endorsed by the U.N. General Assembly in 2005 and in a Security Council resolution a year later.

"Darfur is another Rwanda," said Paul Rusesabagina, whose actions to save 1,268 refugees from genocide were made famous by the movie "Hotel Rwanda."[3] "Many people are dying every day. The world is still standing by watching," he said. "History keeps repeating itself — and without teaching us a lesson."

Secretary-General Ban must make the Responsibility to Protect his top priority if there is hope to stem mass killings in the future, Feinstein argues. That contradiction between the promise of the Responsibility to Protect and the situation in Darfur is what Ban faces in leading the world body.

Ban has cited Responsibility to Protect as at least one of his priorities, noting its unfulfilled promise. "We must take the first steps to move the Responsibility to Protect from word to deed," Ban declared.[4]

But, like his predecessors, Ban wields only moral authority as the leader of the world body. There is no standing U.N. army to back up his pronouncements. "He doesn't have troops to send," says the Secretary-General's spokeswoman Michele Montas. "What the Secretary-General can do besides an advocacy role is limited."

Though U.N. peacekeeping forces have taken on an increasingly aggressive posture in recent years, the U.N. system of relying on donated troops doesn't offer the speed or military capability for invading a country to force an end to murders. Nor is it likely countries that traditionally contribute troops would rush to put their soldiers in harm's way, notes Jean-Marie Guéhenno, U.N. Undersecretary General in charge of peacekeeping operations. "If they feel they are going to have to shoot their way in, it's no more peacekeeping. Sometimes, it may be necessary," Guéhenno says candidly in an interview, "but it will have to be done by other organizations."

NATO, possibly the African Union (with outside logistical help and equipment) and ad hoc "coalitions of the willing" nations are the likely global candidates for any truly muscular interventions to stop the slaughter of innocents.

But even for U.N. peacekeepers, fast-moving events can foster a combat atmosphere. Today's peacekeeping faces the dangers of unrest or battle from Latin America to Africa.

Such threats have spawned a new term that has taken root in 21st-century U.N. operations: "robust peacekeeping." Modern U.N. forces may have attack helicopters and Special Forces, "the type of military capabilities

Ban Ki-moon, right, new secretary-general of the United Nations, gets a briefing in January 2007 at the United Nations Organization Mission in the Democratic Republic of the Congo in Kisangani, where he laid a wreath for fallen peacekeepers.

you would not have traditionally associated with peacekeeping operation, "Guéhenno notes.

"We're not going to let an armed group unravel a peace agreement that benefits millions of people," he says. The peacekeeping chief sounds more like a general threatening overwhelming force rather than a diplomat cautious of its implications. "So we'll hit hard on those spoilers," he promises. Guéhenno cited Congo as an example, but there are others.

Peacekeeping forces today face rapidly changing situations. In Somalia, Ethiopian troops conducted a successful invasion by New Year's 2007, well before peacekeepers could be deployed to stop the fighting. But attacks continued to rock Mogadishu, the capital, and emergency peacekeeping plans intensified.

In Lebanon last year, the deadly aftermath of Israel-Hezbollah battles brought the need for the U.N. to ramp up a large peacekeeping force extraordinarily quickly.

Guéhenno's U.N. peacekeeping department has its hands full as it is, trying to keep up with worldwide demand for troops, police and civilian advisors. Much like Microsoft dominates the computer world, the United Nations is by far the dominant brand in peacekeeping.

With more than 100,000 troops, police and civilian officials in 18 peace missions around the world, the United Nations has the largest amount of peacekeepers

U.N. Provides Half of Peacekeeping Forces

With 82,751 personnel spread among 15 missions worldwide, the United Nations contributes over 50 percent of the world's peacekeeping forces.

Organization	Personnel	Missions	Nations Contributing Personnel
United Nations	82,751	15	114
NATO	55,000	5	37 (includes 11 NATO allies)
African Union	15,000	2	10
European Union Force	8,500	2	34 (includes 10 non-EU nations)
Organization for Security and Co-operation in Europe	3,500	19	56
Multinational Force & Observers	1,687	1	11

Sources: African Union, Delegation of the European Commission to the USA, Multinational Force & Observers, NATO, OSCE, United Nations Department of Peacekeeping Operations

deployed since the organization's founding in 1945. That total could exceed 140,000 depending on the strength of any new missions in Somalia and Darfur. Former Secretary-General Kofi Annan warned before he left office: "U.N. peacekeeping is stretched as never before."

Traditionally, impoverished nations are major troop contributors, in part because the payments they receive help them economically. Bangladesh, Pakistan and India each had about 9,000-10,000 troops in U.N. peacekeeping forces in 2006. Jordan, Nepal, Ethiopia, Ghana Uruguay, Nigeria and South Africa were also major troop contributors.[5]

Although peacekeeping advocates argue peacekeeping is a bargain compared to the cost of all-out war, peacekeeping on a global scale does not come cheap. The approved U.N. 2006-2007 budget is more than $5 billion.

Peacekeeping is paid for by a special assessment for U.N. members weighted on national wealth and permanent Security Council member status. The United States pays the largest share of peacekeeping costs: 27 percent (though congressional caps on payment have resulted in lower payments in recent years).[6] Other top contributors include Japan, Germany, the United Kingdom, France, Italy, China, Canada, Spain and South Korea.[7]

But peacekeeping operations often are hampered by having to run deeply into the red. In November 2006, peacekeeping arrears totaled $2.2 billion.

U.N. peacekeeping is also hobbled by the built-in logistical problem of having to cobble each mission together after Security Council authorization. Plans for standing U.N. military forces have never gotten off the ground. But U.N. police are starting to take "baby steps," starting with dozens of officers for a permanent force, says senior U.N. police official Antero Lopes.

In recent years, U.N. peacekeeping officials have made inroads to daunting logistical problems by maintaining pre-positioned materiel in staging areas in Italy, notes former New Zealand Ambassador Colin Keating. But there is still a great need for equipment. "You can't just go down to Wal-Mart and buy a bunch of APCS [armored personnel carriers]," he says.

Other regional organizations involved in keeping the peace, with efforts ranging from armed intervention to watching over ballot boxes, include:

- **North Atlantic Treaty Organization (NATO):** The military alliance of 26 countries, including the United States, has 75,000 troops worldwide responsible for some of the more muscular interventions, such as the aftermath of the war in Afghanistan, where it has a force of 30,000.
- **African Union (AU):** Established in 2001, the 53-nation coalition has a 7,000-man force in Darfur, including many Rwandans. Another AU contingent of 8,000 has been in Mogadishu since March 6.
- **European Union (EU):** Its troops have taken over Bosnian peacekeeping with a force of 7,000. The EU's broader peacekeeping plans include creation of a long-discussed rapid-reaction force of 60,000. But EU foreign policy chief Javier Solana notes that despite those bold aims, the organization has been depending on a softer "mixture of civilian, military, economic, political and institution-building tools."[8]

- **Organization for Security and Co-operation in Europe (OSCE):** The 56-member group, working on a non-military level, has more than 3,000 OSCE officers in 19 locations from Albania to Uzbekistan. Their activities are aimed at encouraging political dialogue and supporting post-conflict resolution.[9]
- **Multinational Force and Observers (MFO):** It has about 1,700 troops from the United States and 10 other countries stationed on the Egyptian side of the Israeli-Sinai border.

As an abstract concept, global peacekeeping seems like a reasonable and virtuous response to global problems. Who better than neutral referees to keep fighters apart? Indeed, under the 1948 International Convention on the Prevention and Punishment of the Crime of Genocide, the United States and other participating countries are obliged "to prevent and punish" genocide. But forceful military intervention is clouded by questions that range from national sovereignty to international political will along with such practical issues as troop supply and logistics in remote corners of the world.

Increasingly, the Holocaust-related lesson seems to be the notion that the international community has a moral obligation — and indeed a right — to enter sovereign states to stop genocide and other human rights violations.

The Responsibility to Protect concept was detailed in a 2001 report by the International Commission on Intervention and State Sovereignty (ICISS), co-chaired by Algerian diplomat Mohamed Sahnoun and former Australian Foreign Minister Gareth Evans, now head of the non-governmental International Crisis Group, dedicated to stopping global conflict. "There is a growing recognition that the issue is not the 'right to intervene' of any State, but the 'Responsibility to Protect' of every State," the report said.[10]

By 2006, writes Evans in a forthcoming book, "the phrase 'Responsibility to Protect' was being routinely used, publicly and privately, by policymakers and commentators almost everywhere whenever the question was debated as to what the international community should do when faced with a state committing atrocities against its own people, or standing by allowing others to do so."[11]

More important, he points out, the concept was formally and unanimously adopted by the international community at the U.N. 60th Anniversary World Summit in September 2005. References to the Responsibility to Protect concept have also appeared in Security Council resolutions, including one calling for action in Darfur.

But R2P remains a sensitive concept, and the reference to U.N. military action in the 2005 World Summit document is very carefully couched: "We are prepared to take collective action, in a timely and decisive manner . . . on a case-by-case basis . . . as appropriate, should peaceful means be inadequate and national authorities are manifestly failing to protect their populations from genocide, war crimes, ethnic cleansing and crimes against humanity."[12]

As a rule, national sovereignty has been a hallowed concept at the United Nations, and what countries did within their own borders was considered their own business.

"The traditional view of sovereignty, as enabling absolute control of everything internal and demanding immunity from external intervention, was much reinforced by the large increase in U.N. membership during the decolonization era," Evans said at Stanford University on Feb. 7, 2007. "The states that joined were all newly proud of their identity, conscious in many cases of their fragility and generally saw the non-intervention norm as one of their few defenses against threats and pressures from more powerful international actors seeking to promote their own economic and political interests."

Given that history, if nations back up the R2P endorsement at the U.N. with action, it will represent a dramatic shift in policy.

Will the new "Responsibility to Protect" doctrine actually translate into international protection for the people of Darfur? That question has yet to be answered.

Meanwhile, in the wake of the international community's discussion of new powerful action, here are some of the questions being asked about the future of global peacekeeping:

Will the world support the Responsibility to Protect doctrine?

Judging by the inaction in Darfur in the face of highly publicized pleas from groups around world, the R2P is off to an inauspicious start. "Darfur is the first test of the Responsibility to Protect," says Feinstein, "and the world failed the test."

Echoes of the world's continuing failure to protect its citizens from mass murder reverberated off of the green marble podium in the cavernous U.N. General Assembly

An African Union peacekeeping soldier stands guard in the village of Kerkera in Darfur, a western province of Sudan, where government-sponsored troops and a militia of Arab horsemen known as "Janjaweed" have been conducting a campaign of devastation against black tribes.

Hall this year. "It is a tragedy that the international community has not been able to stop new horrors in the years since the Holocaust," General Assembly President Sheikha Haya Al Khalifa of Bahrain stated.[13] "This makes it all the more important that we remember the lessons of the past so that we do not make the same mistakes in the future."

Yet the Responsibility to Protect concept faces a number of daunting challenges, from potential Third World opposition to the appetite and physical ability of Western nations to intervene. Allan Rock, Canada's ambassador to the United Nations, who advanced the Responsibility to Protect resolution at the world body, said in 2001 that the doctrine was, "feared by many countries as a Trojan horse for the interveners of the world looking for justification for marching into other countries."[14]

Indeed, commented Hugo Chávez, president of Venezuela and nemesis of the United States, "This is very suspicious. Tomorrow or sometime in the future, someone in Washington will say that the Venezuelan people need to be protected from the tyrant Chávez, who is a threat. They are trying to legalize imperialism within the United Nations, and Venezuela cannot accept that."[15]

In Sudan, the shifting conditions of President Omar Hassan Ahmad al-Bashir to allow U.N. troops into Darfur has deterred them as of mid-April 2007.

Like Chávez, al-Bashir has said such a force would be tantamount to an invasion and warned that it could become a fertile ground for Islamic jihadists. Al Qaeda leader Osama bin Laden has already weighed in, urging resistance to any U.N. intervention in Sudan.[16]

And Libyan leader Muammar Qaddafi, far less of a pariah to the West than before, but still prone to inflammatory statements, told Sudanese officials last November, "Western countries and America are not busying themselves out of sympathy for the Sudanese people or for Africa but for oil and for the return of colonialism to the African continent. Reject any foreign intervention."[17]

With a lineup like that against U.N. deployment, cynics might say, there must be good reason to do so. In Darfur, however, the R2P doctrine has become bogged down by practical considerations: The geographical area to be protected is vast, and both the vulnerable population and predatory attackers are in close proximity.

But, says Chinua Akukwe, a Nigerian physician and former vice chairman of the Global Health Council, "The U.N. and its agencies must now think the unthinkable — how to bypass murderous governments in any part of the world and reach its suffering citizens in a timely fashion."[18]

Nicole Deller, program advisor for the pro-protection group Responsibility to Protect, says the careful wording of the R2P concept document has given pause to many countries. They remember the disastrous day when 18 Americans died in Mogadishu, Somalia in 1993 — memorialized in the book and movie "Black Hawk Down" — that gave both the United Nations and the United States a black eye. "A lot of that is still blowback from Somalia," she says.

But among African nations there appears an evolution of thinking about sovereignty. Ghana's representative to the United Nations, Nana Effah-Aptenteng, confirmed that change when he told a U.N. audience that African states "have an obligation to intervene in the affairs of another state when its people are at risk."[19]

This is further reflected in the AU Constitutive Act, which recognizes the role of African nations to intervene in cases of genocide.[20]

The Sudanese government, whose oil reserves have given them political and commercial leverage in resisting calls for an end to the slaughter, has reacted by changing the subject. When asked about his country facing possible international military action under The Responsibility to Protect for turning a blind eye to death and destruction in Darfur, Abdalmahmood Abdalhaleem, Sudan's U.N. ambassador, instead turns to resentment of the U.S. role in Iraq and Israel's actions in Lebanon last summer. "Why didn't they intervene when people in Iraq were slaughtered and people in Lebanon were bombarded and infrastructure destroyed?" he asks. "Why didn't they intervene there?"

The international community, either at the United Nations or elsewhere, is far from having a standard on when to intervene to stop violence or even genocide. But some attempts have been made to come up with questions that can help arrive at an answer. According to the International Commission on Intervention and State Sovereignty, five basic conditions are needed to trigger an intervention by U.N. or other multinational forces:

- **Seriousness of Harm** — Is the threatened harm to state or human security of a kind, and sufficiently clear and serious, to justify the use of military force? In the case of internal threats, does it involve genocide and other large-scale killing, "ethnic cleansing" or serious violations of international humanitarian law?
- **Proper Purpose** — Is the primary purpose of the proposed military action clearly to halt or avert the threat in question, whatever other motives may be in play?
- **Last Resort** — Has every nonmilitary option for meeting the threat in question been explored, with reasonable grounds for believing lesser measures will not succeed?
- **Proportional Means** — Are the scale, duration and intensity of the planned military action the minimum necessary to achieve the objective of protecting human life?
- **Balance of Consequences** — Is there a reasonable chance of the military action being successful . . . with the consequences of action unlikely to be worse than the consequences of inaction?

Certainly Darfur's miseries meet many of the conditions, but not all, Evans says. Questions remain whether all non-military options have been exhausted, and there are "hair-raisingly difficult" logistical concerns to

consider as well as high potential for civilian injuries, Evans says.

Thus, the R2P is not necessarily a green light for unfettered military action, according to Feinstein and others. "This is not a question of sending in the Marines or even the blue helmets" of the United Nations, he says, pointing out that the doctrine is most effective in bringing international political pressure to bear before conditions lead to mass killings.

Are regional peacekeepers effective?

While the United Nations leads peacekeeping forces around the world, it does not maintain a standing armed force designed to initiate military interventions. When robust military operations are needed, the U.N. can authorize other actors to respond, such as better-equipped or more willing regional organizations such as NATO, the European Union or the African Union, or a combination of those multinational forces. The R2P doctrine, in fact, specifies that U.N.-authorized military action be done "in cooperation with relevant regional organizations as appropriate."

"The U.N. culture is still very much against doing coercive types of operations," says French defense official Catherine Guicherd, on loan to the International Peace Academy in New York, "whereas the NATO culture goes very much in the other direction."

Two current regional operations — the NATO mission in Kosovo and the AU forces in Darfur — reflect the realities of such missions. NATO, working in its European backyard, has been largely effective. The AU, operating in a much larger area with fewer troops and less equipment and support, has been struggling.

At the beginning of 2007, there were 16,000 NATO troops from 36 mostly European nations stationed with the U.N. peacekeeping force in Kosovo, the Albanian-majority Serbian province seeking autonomy from Belgrade. There is a global alphabet of cooperation in Kosovo. The NATO "KFOR" forces coordinate closely with 2,700 personnel of the U.N. Interim Administration Mission — known as UNMIK — which in turn employs another 1,500 men and women from the EU and OSCE.

Two Israeli journalists who reported from Kosovo in 2002 described an atmosphere of tension and uncertainty and called the force of agencies "a massive and complex multinational presence signaling the commitment of the international community to restoring order

When Peacekeepers Prey Instead of Protect

U.N. seeking more women officers

The U.N. has been stung in recent years by reports that male peacekeeping soldiers have preyed on women — often girls under age 18 — in vulnerable populations.

In Congo, U.N. officials admit that a "shockingly large" number of peacekeepers have bought sex from impoverished young girls, including illiterate orphans, for payments ranging from two eggs to $5.

What's more, some peacekeeping missions reportedly covered-up the abuse, as well as the children that have been born as their result. Between January 2004 and November 2006, 319 peacekeeping personnel worldwide were investigated for sexual misconduct, U.N. officials say, with 144 military and 17 police sent home and 18 civilians summarily dismissed.[1]

"I am especially troubled by instances in which United Nations peacekeepers are alleged to have sexually exploited minors and other vulnerable people, and I have enacted a policy of 'zero tolerance' towards such offences that applies to all personnel engaged in United Nations operations," Secretary-General Kofi Annan said in March 2005. He also instituted a mandatory training course for all peacekeeping candidates to address the issues.

"You get [these abuses] not just with peacekeepers but with soldiers in general, and it gets worse the further they are from home and the more destitute the local population," says Richard Reeve, a research fellow at Chatham House, a London-based think tank. "The UN will never get rid of the problem, but they are really dealing with it and putting changes into practice."[2]

Now the U.N. is sending women instead of men on certain U.N. troop and police peacekeeping missions. The first all-female police unit, from India, recently was sent to Liberia, where peacekeepers had been accused of trading food for sex with teenagers.[3] Cases of misconduct by women police are "almost non-existent," says Antero Lopes, a senior U.N. police official.

The head of the new unit, Commander Seema Dhundia, says its primary mission is to support the embryonic Liberia National Police (LNP), but that the presence of female troops will also raise awareness of and respect for women in Liberia, and in peacekeeping. "Seeing women in strong positions, I hope, will reduce the violence against women," she says.[4]

"We plead for nations to give us as many woman police officers as they can," says Lopes. Another advantage of the all-female unit in Liberia is that it is trained in crowd control, Lopes says, shattering a barrier in what had been seen as a male domain. "It is also a message to the local society that women can perform the same jobs as men."

The U.N. is aggressively trying to recruit more female peacekeepers, from civilian managers to foot soldiers to high-ranking officers. "Our predominantly male profile in peacekeeping undermines the credibility of our efforts to lead by example," Jean-Marie Guéhenno, head of the U.N.

and rebuilding civil institutions in this troubled region."[21]

But NATO's toughest deployment has been in Afghanistan, with about 32,000 troops contributing to what is called the International Security Assistance Force (ISAF), which provides military support for the government of President Hamid Karzai. More than 100 peacekeepers died in Afghanistan in 2006. And 2007 brought more casualties.

"It's very bloody, much worse than NATO ever dreamed," says Edwin Smith, a professor of law and international relations at the University of Southern California and author of *The United Nations in a New World Order.*

"But this is a fundamental test of their ability to engage in peacekeeping and extraterritorial operations outside of their treaty-designated area," Smith continues. "If it turns out that they cannot play this function, then one wonders how do you justify NATO's continued existence?"

In Africa, European troops also may have to fight a psychological battle stemming from the colonial legacy. It is commonly held that many Africans resent non-African peacekeepers coming to enforce order. Perhaps a more pressing reason, observes Victoria K. Holt, a peacekeeping expert at the Stimson Center in Washington, is that a NATO or U.N. force under a powerful mandate "would be better equipped and thus, more effective and a challenge to what is happening on the ground."

peacekeeping department, told the Security Council.

That message was not always heard. A decade ago, peacekeeping consultant Judith Stiehm, a professor of political science at Florida International University, was hired by the U.N. to write a pamphlet on the need for women in peacekeeping. Today she says it was a show effort. "I don't think they even really distributed it," Stiehm says. But pushed by the only female peacekeeping mission head, the issue eventually became U.N. policy.

Security Council Resolution 1325, passed in 2000, "urges the secretary-general" to expand the role of women in field operations, especially among military observers and police.

"The little blue pamphlet and the impetus behind it brought about this very important resolution," Stiehm says, "which is not being implemented, but it's on the books." In fact, "less than 2 percent and 5 percent of our military and police personnel, respectively, are women," Guéhenno told the Security Council.

Beyond the issue of sexual abuse, the role of women soldiers is important in nations where substantial contact between unrelated men and women is prohibited by religion or custom. "Military men just cannot deal with Arab women — that's so culturally taboo," Stiehm notes, but military women can gather information.

Because the United Nations' peacekeeping forces represent more than 100 countries, cultural variations make a big difference in both the prominence of women and what

Bebiche is one of hundreds of internally displaced persons forced to flee warfare in eastern Democratic Republic of Congo. Countless women and girls there have been brutalized by unprecedented sexual violence, and they have few options for existence but to pursue survival sex.

behavior is acceptable, according to Stiehm. "It is very uneven," she says and "dependant very much on who heads the mission."

Stiehm points to Yasushi Akashi, a Japanese U.N. official in the early 1990s. When confronted with charges of sexual abuse of young girls by troops in his Cambodian mission, "Akashi's reaction was, 'Boys will be boys,' " she says.

In another case, Stiehm recalls arguing with her boss over trying to prevent troops from having sex with underage women. "He didn't see anything wrong with it," she says.

The U.N. is now trying to short-circuit the different-cultures argument with a "Duty of Care" code that pointedly states: "These standards apply to all peacekeepers irrespective of local customs or laws, or the customs or laws of your own country."

Moreover, Stiehm says, "Peacekeepers have an obligation to do better."

1 "U.N. will enforce 'zero tolerance' policy against sexual abuse, peacekeeping official says." U.N. News Centre, Jan. 5, 2007. www.un.org/apps/news/storyAr.asp?NewsID=21169&Cr=sex&Cr1=abuse&Kw1=SExual+Exploitation&Kw2=&Kw3=

2 Quoted in Tristan McConnell, "All female unit keeps peace in Liberia," *The Christian Science Monitor online*, March 21, 2005; http://news.yahoo.com/s/csm/20070321/ts_csm/ofemmeforce_1.

3 Will Ross, "Liberia gets all-female peacekeeping force," BBC News, Jan. 31, 2007, http://news.bbc.co.uk/2/hi/africa/6316387.stm.

4 *Ibid.*

The notoriously fickle government of Sudan has indicated it would be willing to accept only a hybrid AU-U.N. force. The U.N. should be limited to a "logistical and backstopping role," Ambassador Abdalhaleem says.

The AU can muster troops, but handling logistics and equipment in a huge and remote area such as Darfur is a major problem for even the best-equipped and trained forces. But the AU began 2007 with only 7,000 troops in Darfur, an area the size of France, and with limited equipment, according to Robert Collins, an Africa expert at the University of California-Santa Barbara, who has visited the war-torn nation over the past 50 years.

"They just don't have the helicopters," he says. "They don't have the big planes to fly in large amounts of

supplies. They're just a bunch of guys out there with a couple of rifles trying to hold off a huge insurgency. It doesn't work."

Besides Darfur, the AU has sent peacekeepers to a few other African hotspots, in effect adopting the underpinnings of the Responsibility to Protect by moving to establish its own African Standby Force. Slated to be operational by 2010, the force would have an intelligence unit and a "Continental Early Warning System" to monitor situations that can potentially spark mass killings. The force would be capable of responding to a genocidal situation within two weeks.[22]

Whether such an African force will be able to live up to its optimistic intent poses another big question:

AFP/Getty Images/Ermal Meta

A Swedish peacekeeper checks weapons seized in Kosovo. About 17,000 NATO-led peacekeepers in so-called KFOR missions are responsible for peace and security in the rebellious Albanian-dominated Serbian province. In 1999 NATO forces bombed the area to end ethnic cleansing by the Serbs.

Would it receive continuing outside financial help from the West?

African officials and experts report the biggest problem facing AU peacekeeping is funding, particularly in Sudan. "This is . . . one of the worst humanitarian disasters in the world, yet only five donors seem to be properly engaged," said Haroun Atallah, chief executive of Islamic Relief. "All rich countries must step up their support urgently if the disaster of Darfur isn't to turn into an even worse catastrophe."[23]

Should peace-building replace peacekeeping?

In the past, U.N. peacekeeping focused mainly on keeping warring nations apart while they negotiated a peace pact. Now, U.N. peacekeepers increasingly are being called in as part of complex cooperative efforts by regional military organizations, local military, civilians and police to rebuild failed governments.

Some say the shift is inevitable. More than military might is needed for successful peacekeeping, NATO Secretary-General Jaap de Hoop Scheffer noted last year. During a Security Council meeting to highlight cooperation between the United Nations and regional security organizations, he said he had learned "some important lessons," including the need for each organization to play to its strengths and weaknesses.

"NATO offers unparalleled military experience and capability," Scheffer said, "yet addressing a conflict requires a coordinated and coherent approach from the outset. Clearly defined responsibilities . . . are indispensable if we are to maximize our chances of success."[24]

So is post-conflict follow-through. The United Nations has set up a Peacebuilding Commission to follow up after conflicts have been quelled.

Because peacekeeping now often takes place inside nations rather than between them, the United Nations is typically charged not only with trying to keep the peace but also "with building up the basics of a state," notes Guéhenno. "That's why peacekeeping can never be the full answer. It has to be complemented by a serious peace-building efforts.

"Today, we have a completely different situation" from in the past, Guéhenno explains, referring to the world's growing number of so-called failed states. "You have a number of countries around the world that are challenged by internal divides. They don't have the capacity to maintain law and order."

But peacekeeping consultant Judith Stiehm, a professor of political science at Florida International University, sees a contradiction between peacekeeping and peacebuilding. "That's what gets them in trouble," she says. "You've got guys wearing military uniforms and their missions are very civilian. And once you add the mission of protection, you're not neutral anymore. Some people think of you as the enemy, and it muddies the waters. You can't have it both ways."

CHRONOLOGY

1940s-1950s *Founding of U.N. promises peace in the postwar world. First peacekeeping missions are deployed.*

1945 United Nations is founded at the end of World War II "to save succeeding generations from the scourge of war."

1948 First U.N. mission goes to Jerusalem following Arab-Israeli War.

1949 U.N. observers monitor the struggle over Kashmir following the creation of India and Pakistan.

1950 Security Council approves a U.N. "police action" in Korea.

1956 United Nations Emergency Force is established during the Suez Crisis involving Egypt, Israel, Britain and France.

1960s *Death of U.N. secretary-general in Congo causes U.N. to avoid dangerous missions.*

1960 U.N. Secretary-General Dag Hammarskjold dies in an unexplained plane crash during a U.N. intervention in Congo by U.N. peacekeepers; the mission fails to bring democracy.

1964 U.N. peacekeepers are sent to keep peace between Greeks and Turks on divided Cyprus; the mission continues.

1970s *Cambodian genocide occurs unhindered.*

1974 U.N. Disengagement Force is sent to the Golan Heights after fighting stops between Israel and Syria.

1975 Dictator Pol Pot kills more than 1 million Cambodians. U.N. and other nations fail to act.

1978 U.N. monitors withdrawal of Israeli troops from Lebanon.

1980s *Cold War barrier to bold U.N. actions begins to crumble.*

1988 U.N. peacekeeping mission monitors ceasefire between Iran and Iraq.

1989 Fall of Berlin Wall symbolizes collapse of Soviet empire and Cold War paralysis blocking U.N. agreement.

1990s *Security Council confronts Iraq. Failures in Bosnia, Somalia, dampen enthusiasm to stop Rwanda killing.*

1990 Iraqi leader Saddam Hussein invades Kuwait and defies Security Council demand for withdrawal.

1991 U.N.-authorized and U.S.-led international coalition expels Iraq from Kuwait. . . . U.N. peacekeeping mission is sent to El Salvador.

1992 U.N. Protection Force fails to stop killings in Bosnian civil war.

1993 Ambitious U.N. peace operation fails to restore order in Somalia.

1994 U.N. peacekeepers are unable to stop the massacre of more than 800,000 Rwandans.

1995 U.N. peacekeepers in the Bosnian town of Srebrenica are disarmed and left helpless by Serb forces.

1999 NATO takes military action against Serbia.

2000s-Present *U.N. mounts successful peace-building mission in Liberia.*

2003 U.N. peacekeeping mission in Liberia begins to keep peace.

2005 U.N. General Assembly endorses Responsibility to Protect concept at World Summit.

2006 Security Council endorses Responsibility to Protect but intervention in killings in Darfur region is stalled by Sudan's government.

April 9, 2007 U.N. Secretary-General Ban Ki-moon calls for "a global partnership against genocide" and upgrades the post of U.N. Special Adviser for the Prevention of Genocide — currently held by Juan E. Méndez of Argentina — to a full-time position.

U.N. Police Face Difficult Challenges

Small problems can escalate quickly

In Timor-Leste (formerly East Timor), a country still raw from decades of fighting for independence, Antero Lopes knew that promptly dealing with a stolen chicken was crucial.

As acting police commissioner for the U.N. mission in the tiny East Asian nation in 2006, he discovered that in such a tense environment, overlooking even a petty crime like a marketplace theft could have serious consequences. "Friends and neighbors are brought in, many of them veterans of Timor's bloody struggles, and suddenly you have an inter-community problem with 200 people fighting 200 people," he say from U.N. headquarters in Manhattan, where he is now deputy director of U.N. Police Operations.[1]

United Nations police were sent to the former Portuguese colony last year to restore order in the fledgling state. Timor-Leste gained independence from Indonesia in 2002 following a long struggle, but an outbreak of death and violence that uprooted more than 150,000 people prompted the Timorese government to agree to temporarily turn over police operations to the U.N., which called it "the first ever such arrangement between a sovereign nation and the U.N."[2]

The U.N.'s Timorese role reflects how U.N. police have become "a critical component" of the institution's peace-keeping efforts, notes Victoria K. Holt, a senior associate at The Henry L. Stimson Center in Washington and co-direc-tor of its Future of Peace Operations program. The U.N. now recognizes "you just can't go from military to civilian society. You have to have something in between."

A critical role for police wasn't always a given, says Holt, author of *The Impossible Mandate? Military Preparedness, the Responsibility to Protect and Modern Peace Operations.* For much of the United Nations' nearly 60-year peacekeeping history, she says, the lack of a major police role was "one of the biggest gaps. They actually now have a whole police division that didn't exist a number of years ago."

The role and size of the U.N. police effort has grown dramatically in recent years. "Peace operations are increasingly using significant numbers of police to handle security tasks," according to the U.N.'s 2006 Annual Review of Global Peace Operations. Led by the United Nations, the number of police peacekeepers worldwide has tripled since 1998 to about 10,000.

Lopes says that although he is a university-trained police manager with experience ranging from anti-crime to SWAT teams, he is also accustomed to operating in environments without the "same legal framework" one finds in Europe.

He was deployed in Bosnia, for example, while the civil war still raged there in the 1990's. "If you really like these kinds of [policing] challenges," he notes, "you can get addicted."

Roland Paris, an associate professor of political science at Canada's University of Ottawa, sees inherent cultural flaws, including Western colonialism, in peace-building. "Peace-building operations seek to stabilize countries that have recently experienced civil wars," he wrote. "In pursuing this goal, however, international peace-builders have promulgated a particular vision of how states should organize themselves internally, based on the principles of liberal democracy and market-oriented economics.

"By reconstructing war-shattered states in accordance with this vision, peace-builders have effectively 'transmitted' standards of appropriate behavior from the Western-liberal core . . . to the failed states of the periphery. From this perspective, peace-building resembles an updated (and more benign) version of the *mission civilisatrice,* the colonial-era belief that the European imperial powers had a duty to 'civilize' dependent populations and territories."[25]

But despite an ongoing debate, one part of the formula for the near future seems set: The U.N. has increasingly relied on deploying police to help rebuild a society as part of its peacekeeping efforts around the globe. In fact, as "an interim solution," the global U.N. cops have become the actual police force of such nations as East Timor and Haiti and in Kosovo. "We provide a measure of law and order and security that creates the political window to build up a state," Guéhenno says.

U.N. police realize they are operating in a very different environment. "Now we are a significant pillar in helping

Balkan violence may not be over, however. The U.N. mission in Kosovo — the Albanian-majority Serbian province seeking autonomy from Belgrade — is bracing for violence, with the disputed area's future set to be decided this year. Already, news of an impending Kosovo independence plan has triggered violent demonstrations. After U.N. police fired rubber bullets into a crowd of demonstrators in February, killing two people, the U.N. mission there pulled out.[3]

Outside of Kosovo (where the European Union plans to take over police responsibility), the major U.N. police presences are in Haiti and countries in Africa. In Africa, U.N. police missions are hampered by the African Union's lack of proper resources. "In many missions, we find even the lack of simple uniforms," Lopes says, not to mention operable radios, police cars or other basic police equipment.

In Sudan's troubled Darfur, any new police commitment would first focus on "stabilization" of the lawless situation, he says. However, he points out, while U.N. police must not compromise on basic law-enforcement tenets, they still must adapt to local customs in working with local authorities.

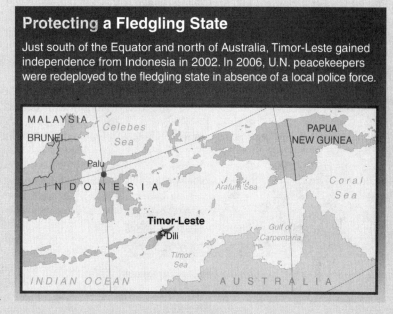

Protecting a Fledgling State

Just south of the Equator and north of Australia, Timor-Leste gained independence from Indonesia in 2002. In 2006, U.N. peacekeepers were redeployed to the fledgling state in absence of a local police force.

So Lopes finds it important to play the role of empathetic psychologist as well as tough global cop.

"This is an issue of local ownership," he says. "We must also read what is in their hearts and minds."

---

[1] U.N. News Service, December 2006.

[2] *Ibid.*

[3] The Associated Press, "Albanians protest UN Kosovo plan," *Taipei Times*, Feb. 12, 2007, p. 6.

the good-governance effort," says Lopes, deputy police advisor in the U.N. Department of Peacekeeping Operations, sounding like a bureaucrat as well as a sheriff.

The Portuguese-born Lopes, who has served as police commissioner for the U.N. mission in East Timor, calls such a heavy U.N. role "a revolution" in the way the United Nations intervenes in internal conflicts. "What we are actually doing is a mixture of peacekeeping and peace-building," he explains. "We are hoping that with good governance — promoting elections and democratized policing — problems will be reduced."

Now, Lopes says, "our role is really to restore the rule of law as opposed to the rule of might."

"It will increasingly be a necessary feature of peace operations," predicts activist Deller. "Just separating factions and establishing elections alone isn't a sustainable model."

But so far, the result in Timor-Leste (the former East Timor) has "been a real disappointment," Deller says. She cites the "re-emergence of conflict," with the U.N. having to come back to try and restore security in the fledgling nation. (*See sidebar, p. 12.*)

Keating, the former New Zealand ambassador to the U.N., believes that without peace-building, "it's very easy to have all these peacekeeping missions out there like Band-Aids," masking deep wounds underneath. He cites the example of "insufficient stickability" in Haiti, where six different U.N. peace operations have sought to hold together the fractured nation since 1995.[26]

U.N. Photo/Daniel Morel

Brazilian blue helmets of the United Nations' peacekeeping force in Haiti help Haitian police keep order in the capital, Port-au-Prince, after a fire that ravaged 50 stores in June 2004.

"You take your eye off the ball, and before you know it you're back where you started," Keating says.

The latest U.N. Stabilization Mission in Haiti began on June 1, 2004, with the mandate to provide a stable and secure environment, but some Haitian critics say the peacekeepers have behaved more like occupiers.

Alex Diceanu, a scholar at Canada's McMaster University, claims the Haiti operation "has become complicit in the oppression of Haiti's poor majority." For many Haitians, the operation has seemed more like "a foreign occupation force than a United Nations peacekeeping mission," he said. "The few journalists that have reported from these areas describe bustling streets that are quickly deserted as terrified residents hide from passing U.N. tanks."[27]

Armed battles are taking place in Haiti, where U.N. forces have taken casualties as they continue to battle heavily armed gangs for control of Haiti's notorious slums. Exasperated by an infamous warlord's hold on 300,000 people in a Port-au-Prince slum called *Cite Soleil*, U.N. troops took the offensive in February 2007. Almost one-tenth of the 9,000-man Haiti force took the battle to the streets, reclaiming control in a block-by-block battle. Thousand of shots were fired at the peacekeepers.[28]

U.N. troops and police are now willing to battle warlords to try and build a democratic political foundation in the impoverished Caribbean nation, Guéhenno says. "This notion of protection of civilians," he says, "that's a change between yesterday's peacekeeping and today's peacekeeping."

Impoverished Haiti is a tough case, but the United Nations can claim success in building democracy after civil wars in Liberia and Congo, Keating says, where missions are still ongoing. Finding a "sustainable solution" to get people to live together "ain't easy" for the United Nations, he adds. "They can make a huge difference, but it's a commitment involving many years" to rebuild civilian institutions.

Indeed, notes the legendary Sir Brian Urquhart, a former U.N. undersecretary-general and a leading pioneer in the development of international peacekeeping, "The challenges are far weightier than the U.N. peacekeeping system was ever designed for.

"It's a very ambitious thing," he says. "What they're really trying to do is take countries and put them back together again. That's a very difficult thing to do."

BACKGROUND

Late Arrival

The ancient Romans had a description for their effort to pacify their 3-million-square-mile empire: Pax Romana, the Roman Peace. It lasted for more than 200 years, enforced by the Roman legions.[29]

The Hanseatic League in the 13th and 14th centuries arguably was the first forerunner of modern peacekeeping. Without a standing army or police force, the German-based alliance of 100 northern towns stifled warfare, civic strife and crime within its domain, mostly by paying bribes.[30]

For French Emperor Napoleon Bonaparte, peacekeeping was subordinate to conquest, and the extensive colonial empires of the great powers in the 19th century were more intent on exploiting natural resources than on peacekeeping.

In one rare instance, France, inspired by a romantic age in Europe, sent "peacekeepers" to Greece during the Greek revolt against the Turks in 1831 and ended up in tenuous circumstances between two Greek factions competing to fill the power vacuum.[31]

Perhaps the first example of multi-national action against a common threat was in 1900 during the Boxer Rebellion in China, when a 50,000-strong force from Japan, Russia, Britain, France, the United States, German, Italy and Austro-Hungary came to protect the international community in Beijing from the Boxer mobs.[32]

The 20th century, ruptured by two world wars, saw few attempts at peace-making. In 1919, at the end of World War I — "the war to end all wars" — the international community established the League of Nations to maintain peace. But as World War II approached, the fledgling world body floundered, discredited by its failure to prevent Japanese expansion into China and by Italy's conquest of Ethiopia and Germany's annexation of Austria.[33]

The United Nations was born in 1945 from the rubble of World War II and the ultimate failure of the League of Nations. Britain's Urquhart notes that the U.N.'s most critical task was to prevent doomsday — war between the Soviet Union and the United States. "During the Cold War," he says, "the most important consideration . . . was to prevent regional conflict from triggering an East-West nuclear confrontation."

German Navy Captain Wolfgang Schuchardt joined his once-divided nation's military in the midst of the Cold War, in 1968. "We had a totally different situation then," he recalls. "We had [certain] positions and those were to be defended" against the Soviet Union. Now, priorities have changed and Schuchardt works on strategic planning for the U.N.'s peacekeeping operation in Lebanon, one of the Middle East's most volatile areas.

The United Nations established its first peacekeeping observer operation to monitor the truce that followed the first Arab-Israeli war in 1948. Based in Jerusalem, it proved ineffective in the long term, unable to prevent the next three major Arab-Israeli wars.

In 1949 the United Nations deployed a peacekeeping observer mission to a similarly tense India and Pakistan, then quarreling over a disputed area of Kashmir.

When communist North Korea invaded South Korea in 1950, the U.N.'s forceful response was unprecedented. The Korean War was actually fought under the U.N. flag, with troops from dozens of nations defending South Korea.

But the war was authorized through a diplomatic fluke. The Soviet Union, which would have vetoed the American-led invasion, was boycotting the Security Council when the vote to take U.N. action in Korea arose.[34]

As a child, Secretary-General Ban Ki-moon saw the U.N. in action. "As I was growing up in a war-torn and destitute Korea, the United Nations stood by my people in our darkest hour," he recalled. "For the Korean people of that era, the United Nations flag was a beacon of better days to come."[35]

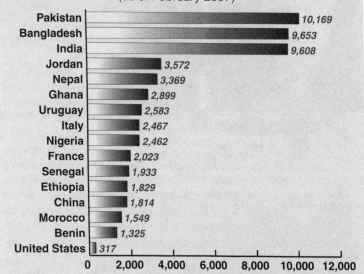

Developing Countries Provide Most Peacekeepers

Developing nations provide the most manpower to U.N. peacekeeping forces. Pakistan, Bangladesh and India were providing half of the U.N.'s nearly 58,000 personnel in early 2007.

U.N. Peacekeeping Forces by Country
(as of February 2007)

Pakistan	10,169
Bangladesh	9,653
India	9,608
Jordan	3,572
Nepal	3,369
Ghana	2,899
Uruguay	2,583
Italy	2,467
Nigeria	2,462
France	2,023
Senegal	1,933
Ethiopia	1,829
China	1,814
Morocco	1,549
Benin	1,325
United States	317

Source: "Ranking of Military and Police Contributions to UN Operations," Department of Peacekeeping Operations, United Nations, February 28, 2007

Sometimes they fight to keep the peace. In Marrakeh, Lebanon, a French soldier of the United Nations' peacekeeping contingent exchanges gunfire with insurgents of the Shiite militia movement, AMAL.

During the Suez Crisis in 1956, the U.N. deployed forces to Egypt, where President Gamal Abdel Nassar had nationalized the Suez Canal, an international waterway that had long been linked to British and French interests. An Israeli invasion and a secretly planned joint French-British air action combined to confront Egypt, then a client state of the Soviet Union. The move brought East-West tensions to a boil.

To cool the situation, Canada's secretary of state for external affairs, Lester Pearson, suggested sending a U.N. Emergency Force to Egypt. The troops had to be rounded up in a week, but their distinctive light-blue berets had not arrived. So Urquhart had surplus army helmets spray-painted. U.N. peacekeepers henceforth would be recognized around the world as "the blue helmets."[36]

Eventually, pressure from the United States forced Britain, France and Israel to withdraw from the canal. Pearson won the Nobel Prize for his efforts.

Congo Quagmire

In the early 1960s U.N. peacekeepers became embroiled in chaos in the fractious, newly created nation of Congo. After gaining independence from Belgium, Congo erupted when strongman Joseph Mobuto seized power, and Prime Minister Patrice Lumumba was assassinated. The struggle quickly turned into a proxy Cold War battle between the United States and the Soviet Union for influence in the region.[37]

Sweden's Dag Hammarskjold, then the U.N. secretary-general, saw in the Congo crisis "an opportunity for the United Nations to assert itself as the world authority in controlling and resolving major international conflicts," writes Poland's Andrzej Sitkowski. "It was his determination, personal commitment and effort which launched the clumsy ship of the organization full speed into the stormy and uncharted waters of Congo. He knew how to start the big gamble, but could not have known how and where it would end."[38]

While shuttling around Congo, a territory the size of Western Europe, Hammarskjold died in a plane crash that was "never sufficiently explained," Sitkowski continues. "It is a tragedy that his commitment and talents were applied, and, ultimately, laid waste in what he himself called a political bordello with a clutch of foreign madams."

The Congo mission cost the lives of 250 peacekeepers but yielded tepid results. Forty years later, U.N. peacekeepers would be back in the country, now known as the Democratic Republic of the Congo.

Other operations have successfully stabilized long-running disputes. In 1964 a U.N. force was deployed to stand between Greece and Turkey over a divided Cyprus. The operation began in 1964, but the island is still divided, and the U.N. force is still present.[39]

During the Cold War stalemate, U.N. peacekeeping had limited goals. As a result, however, it missed the opportunity (some would say moral duty) to stop Cambodian dictator Pol Pot's reign of genocidal terror against his own people. Well more than a million died in Cambodia's "killing fields," where piles of victims' skulls on display to visitors still mark that dark era. Yet the United Nations didn't enter Cambodia until years after the killing ended.[40]

During the 1980s, according to some observers, the United Nations was often stalemated while the Soviet Union and the United States fought over influence at the U.N., and peacekeeping's modest aims reflected the times.

Does the world community have a "responsibility to protect"?

YES — Gareth Evans

President, International Crisis Group
Former Co-Chair, International Commission on Intervention and State Sovereignty

From a speech at Stanford University, Feb. 7, 2007

While the primary responsibility to protect its own people from genocide and other such man-made catastrophes is that of the state itself, when a state fails to meet that responsibility . . . then the responsibility to protect shifts to the international community. . . .

The concept of the "responsibility to protect" [was] formally and unanimously embraced by the whole international community at the U.N. 60th Anniversary World Summit in September 2005 . . . reaffirmed . . . by the Security Council in April 2006, and begun to be incorporated in country-specific resolutions, in particular on Darfur. . . .

But old habits of non-intervention died very hard. Even when situations cried out for some kind of response — and the international community did react through the U.N. — it was too often erratically, incompletely or counter-productively, as in Somalia in 1993, Rwanda in 1994 and Srebrenica in 1995. Then came Kosovo in 1999, when the international community did, in fact, intervene as it probably should have, but did so without the authority of the Security Council. . . .

It is one thing to develop a concept like the responsibility to protect, but quite another to get any policy maker to take any notice of it. . . . We simply cannot be at all confident that the world will respond quickly, effectively and appropriately to new human catastrophes as they arise, as the current case of Darfur is all too unhappily demonstrating. . . .

As always . . . the biggest and hardest piece of unfinished business [is] finding the necessary political will to do anything hard or expensive or politically sensitive or seen as not directly relevant to national interests. . . . We can . . . always justify [the] responsibility to protect . . . on hard-headed, practical, national-interest grounds: States that can't or won't stop internal atrocity crimes are the kind of rogue . . . or failed or failing states that can't or won't stop terrorism, weapons proliferation, drug and people trafficking, the spread of health pandemics and other global risks.

But at the end of the day, the case for responsibility to protect rests simply on our common humanity: the impossibility of ignoring the cries of pain and distress of our fellow human beings. . . . We should be united in our determination to not let that happen, and there is no greater or nobler cause on which any of us could be embarked.

NO — Ambassador Zhenmin Liu

Deputy Permanent Representative
Permanent Mission of the People's Republic of China to the United Nations

Written for *CQ Global Researcher,* March 2007

The important Security Council Resolution 1674 . . . sets out comprehensive provisions pertaining to the protection of civilians in armed conflict. . . . What is needed now is effective implementation. . . .

First, in accordance with the Charter of the United Nations and international humanitarian law, the responsibility to protect civilians lies primarily with the Governments of the countries concerned. While the international community and other external parties can provide support and assistance . . . they should not infringe upon the sovereignty and territorial integrity of the countries concerned, nor should they enforce intervention by circumventing the governments of the countries concerned.

Second, it is imperative to make clear differentiation between protection of civilians and provision of humanitarian assistance. Efforts made by humanitarian agencies in the spirit of humanitarianism to provide assistance to the civilians affected by armed conflicts . . . should . . . at all times abide by the principles of impartiality, neutrality, objectivity and independence in order to . . . avoid getting involved in local political disputes or negatively affecting a peace process.

Third, to protect civilians, greater emphasis should be placed on prevention as well as addressing both symptoms and root causes of a conflict. Should the Security Council . . . manage to effectively prevent and resolve various conflicts, it would successfully provide the best protection to the civilians. . . . The best protection for civilians is to provide them with a safe and reliable living environment by actively exploring methods to prevent conflicts and effectively redressing the occurring conflicts.

While discussing the issue of protection of civilians in armed conflict, the concept of "responsibility to protect" should continue to be approached with caution by the Security Council. The World Summit Outcome last year gave an extensive and very cautious representation of "the responsibility to protect populations from genocide, war crimes, ethnic cleansing and crimes against humanity." . . . Since many member States have expressed their concern and misgivings in this regard, we believe, it is, therefore, not appropriate to expand, willfully interpret or even abuse this concept. . . .

Finally, we hope that . . . full consideration will be taken of the specific characteristics and circumstances of each conflict so as to adopt appropriate measures with a view to effectively achieving the objective of protecting civilians. This ensures that in the future, no matter how much moral authority the U.S. loses, its wagon is hitched firmly to the stars of these ascendant nations — and vice versa.

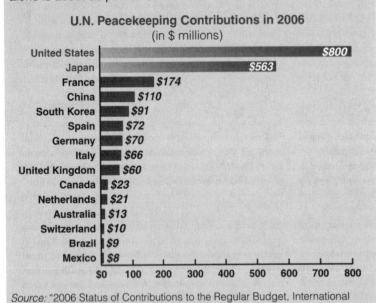

U.S., Japan Pay Most U.N. Peacekeeping Costs

The United States and Japan account for nearly two-thirds of the funds contributed by industrial nations to support the various peacekeeping missions at the United Nations. The U.S. share alone is about 38 percent of the total.

U.N. Peacekeeping Contributions in 2006
(in $ millions)

United States	$800
Japan	$563
France	$174
China	$110
South Korea	$91
Spain	$72
Germany	$70
Italy	$66
United Kingdom	$60
Canada	$23
Netherlands	$21
Australia	$13
Switzerland	$10
Brazil	$9
Mexico	$8

Source: "2006 Status of Contributions to the Regular Budget, International Tribunals, Peacekeeping Operations and Capital Master Plan," United Nations

"I don't think it was ever designed for victory," Urquhart says. "The peacekeeping business was designed to freeze a potentially very dangerous situation until you got around to negotiating. It was quite successful in that."

Failed Missions

The fall of the Berlin Wall in 1989 heralded the end of the Cold War between the United States and the Soviet Union, as well as an extraordinarily promising start for U.N. action.

In 1991, the Security Council authorized the Persian Gulf War coalition that dislodged Iraqi troops from Kuwait. Though it wasn't fought under a U.N. flag, as in Korea, the first Gulf War demonstrated the U.N.'s clear exercise of military action over words.

Saddam Hussein's 1991 invasion of Kuwait was an unprovoked action by a sovereign nation against another, and clearly prohibited by the U.N. charter. "I always tell my students," notes international law Professor Smith,

"that Saddam was the one guy on Earth dumb enough to do precisely the thing the United Nations was established to prevent."

Heady from that success, U.N. member states sought to transform the new post-Cold War cooperation into a dramatic expansion of United Nations peacekeeping. But its efforts were met by mixed results, and well-known bloody failures in the 1990s when it tried to intervene in critical situations in Africa and Bosnia.

In Somalia, on Africa's eastern horn, ultimately failed peacekeeping efforts led to the rise of warlord Mohamed Farah Aidid and the deaths of 18 U.S. soldiers in the infamous First Battle of Mogadishu. The book and film, "Black Hawk Down," told how a U.S. helicopter was shot down and the bodies of American soldiers were dragged through the streets. The battle left 700 Somalis dead along with a Malaysian and two Pakistanis.[41] Somalia would end up lapsing in lawlessness, and the psychological ramifications of the Somalia debacle still haunt the specter of tough peacekeeping operations.

The 1994 Rwandan genocide occurred in central Africa, far from the power centers and concerns of Western aid agencies. The international community, the Clinton administration and the United Nations were all slow to respond, and ineffectual when they did. Canada led U.N. peacekeeping troops in Rwanda, but the reduced force was not authorized or likely able to intervene to prevent the killings.

Former Canadian General Romeo Dallaire, who headed U.N. peacekeeping forces during the Rwandan genocide in 1994, has written the best-selling *Shake Hands with the Devil* in which he criticizes the U.N.'s approach to the conflict. "I have been taking the position from the start that the United Nations is nothing but the front man in this failure," Dallaire states in a BBC interview. "The true culprits are the sovereign states that influence the Security Council, that influence other nations into participating or not."[42]

Bosnia was also a symbol of peacekeeping helplessness. U.N. peacekeepers carved out what they called "safe havens" to protect civilians against the euphemistically called practice of "ethnic cleansing." "Unfortunately, that only created an illusion of safety in an area where there wasn't safety at all," says former New Zealand Ambassador Keating. "That's because there wasn't sufficient personnel."

International expert Smith argues the U.N.'s Bosnia effort was doomed from the start. "They planned it as a humanitarian exercise," he says. "They planned not to use force. And they hamstrung themselves."

The most public example of the United Nations' inability to bring protection or peace, he notes, was when lightly armed Dutch peacekeeping troops were held hostage by Bosnian Serb forces in Srebrenica in July 1995, and turned over thousands of Bosnian Muslims in exchange for the release of 14 Dutch soldiers. The Serbs eventually massacred some 8,000 Bosnian Muslim men and boys in Srebrenica. Photographs of the hapless Dutch were flashed around the world as visible proof that U.N. peacekeepers lacked the ability to defend even themselves.

The Somali and Bosnian experiences were diplomatic, military and humanitarian disasters. "There was no clear operational doctrine for the kinds of things they were doing," says Keating, who served on the U.N. Security Council during that bleak period. "So they made it up as they went along."

Successful Missions

A U.N. mission that helped bring Namibia to independence in 1989 is often cited as a major peacekeeping success story. The U.N. negotiated a protocol allowing the peaceful withdrawal of Marxist rebels from the South-West African Peoples Organization (SWAPO) and Cuban and South African troops.

"Never before had the U.N. devised a peace and independence plan supported by such a web of political agreements, institutional arrangements and administrative buildup," writes Sitkowski, who served with the operation.

In Liberia, a watershed election in 2005 — monitored by the United Nations, the European Union and the Economic Community of West African States — appears to have ended decades of turmoil and violence and translated "security gains into meaningful, political and economic progress," according to the U.N.-supported *Annual Review of Global Peace Operations.*[43]

Liberia's newly elected president, Ellen Johnson-Sirleaf, has become increasingly visible on the world stage. An

The first all-female U.N. force, more than 100 policewomen from India, arrives at Liberia's Roberts International Airport in Monrovia on Jan. 30, 2007. The women will spend at least six months in Liberia, a nation emerging from years of brutal civil war.

economist and former U.N. development official with a Harvard master's degree, she has earned the nickname "Iron Lady" for her ability to do tough jobs normally undertaken by "strongmen" in Africa.[44]

"Our peace is so fragile," she said, "that we need a continuation of the U.N. peacekeeping force for at least three to four years, until our own security forces have been restructured and professionalized."[45]

Since 2005 the United Nations' first all-female peacekeeping unit, 103 women from India, has been stationed in Liberia. (*See sidebar, p. 8.*) "The women have quickly become part of Monrovia's urban landscape in their distinctive blue camouflage fatigues and flak jackets," said *The Christian Science Monitor.* "They guard the Ministry of Foreign Affairs, patrol the streets day and night, control crowds at rallies and soccer games and respond to calls for armed backup from the national police who, unlike the Indian unit, do not carry weapons."[46]

CURRENT SITUATION

Force Expansion

The Security Council voted on Jan. 11, 2007, to set up a modest political mission in Nepal to oversee a disarmament and cease-fire accord between the government and former Maoist rebels.[47]

AFP/Getty Images/Eric Cabanis

Jasmina Zukic, a Muslim who lost 16 family members in the Balkans war, prays at the cemetery in Potocari, Bosnia, where she is waiting for the arrival and reburial of the remains of 610 Bosnian Muslim men, discovered in a mass grave on July 9, 2005. Local Serbs had killed more than 8,000 men and boys under the eyes of U.N. peacekeepers from The Netherlands.

The action came after a spate of significant growth for robust U.N. peacekeeping operations. During the last six months of 2006, the Security Council sent peacekeepers to maintain peace in southern Lebanon, prepare East Timor for reconciliation and stem the violence in Darfur. This built on rapid growth in the numbers and size of peace operations in recent years.

Secretary-General Ban wants to create a new office from the United Nations' 700-person peacekeeping department. It would focus entirely on supporting field operations and provide "a clear line of command, point of responsibility and accountability for field support," says U.N. spokeswoman Montas. That effort would bolster the R2P concept, she says, which is "to protect as rapidly as possible."

Montas points to the confusion and hesitation of the dark moments in the 1990s. "The U.N. had that painful experience of Rwanda and the former Yugoslavia," she says. "Things will have to be done better."

But Ban's peacekeeping reform efforts have been met with hesitation by the General Assembly, leading one European envoy to warn of "death by a thousand meetings."[48]

A major challenge looming for U.N. peacekeeping is the expansion of the force itself. With a potential 40 percent increase in the number of peacekeepers looming in 2007, the Security Council may have to cut short existing operations. That would be a mistake, says former

Ambassador Keating. "Leave too early," he says, "chances are you'll be back again in five years."

China and Sudan

In Sudan, mistrust has complicated efforts to get more peacekeeping troops to curb the horrors of Darfur. Sudan's regime, seen as both hostile and uncooperative by the West, is equally suspicious about U.N. involvement.

Sudan's U.N. Ambassador Abdalhaleem accuses Western nations of withholding support for the African Union in order to promote U.N. peacekeepers. "Their objective is to make it weak because their objective is to bring blue helmets in Darfur," he charges.

On Feb. 7, during the first visit ever by a Chinese leader to Sudan, President Hu Jintao asked Sudan's President Omar al-Bashir to give the United Nations a bigger role in trying to resolve the conflict in Darfur. Hu also said China wanted to do more business with its key African ally, according to Sudan state media reports.

Beijing has at least a two-fold strategy in courting Africa: political interest in influencing the 50-plus nations in Africa and a commercial interest in fueling its increasingly voracious economic engine with Sudanese oil and the continent's plentiful natural resources.[49]

Hu had been under Western pressure to do more to use his clout as Sudan's largest oil customer and international investor to push it to accept U.N. peacekeepers in Darfur.

A month later al-Bashir continued his defiance, telling an Arab League meeting in Riyadh, Saudi Arabia, that the proposed U.N.-AU force would be "a violation of Sudan's sovereignty and a submission by Sudan to outside custodianship."[50]

Arab leaders have been asked to step in to pressure Bashir. After a two-hour meeting with al-Bashir, Saudi Arabian King Abdullah and high-level Arab League and AU representatives, U.N. Secretary-General Ban told reporters, "I think we made progress where there had been an impasse. The king's intervention very much supported my position."

By April 4, as news broke that five AU peacekeepers had been killed in Darfur, Britain and the United States said they were drafting a U.N. resolution to impose financial sanctions and a possible "no-fly" zone over Darfur to punish Sudan's continued intransigence. Secretary-General Ban asked that a sanction vote be delayed to give him time for more negotiations planned in Africa and New York.[51]

On April 15, Saudi officials said Bashir told King Abdullah that an agreement had been reached for the hybrid AU-U.N. force. But given Bashir and Sudan's record of seeming to cooperate — and then pulling back after reports of agreement — the situation will be uncertain until more peacekeepers are actually in place in Darfur.

Meanwhile, China announced a new military cooperation deal with Sudan, a move one U.N. diplomat described as "pre-emptive." China appeared to be rushing to sign as many deals as possible with Sudan before economic and military sanctions are imposed on Khartoum, he said.[52]

Before Hu's February trip, Western observers, including Deller of the group Responsibility to Protect, had described China as "the great obstructer" in efforts to resolve the Darfur crisis.

Not surprisingly, Hen Wenping, director of African studies at the Chinese Academy of Sciences in Beijing, defended communist China's approach to Darfur: "China's strategy remains the same, and as always, it used quiet diplomacy to keep a constructive engagement, rather than waving a stick."[53]

Traditionally, none of the five permanent, veto-wielding members of the U.N. Security Council contributes many U.N. peacekeeping troops, since their influence in world affairs would compromise their neutrality. But China, one of the five, has emerged as a newly enthusiastic supporter of peacekeeping.

"China firmly supports and actively participates in U.N. peacekeeping operations," said Chinese Ambassador to the U.N. Zhang Yishan in late February. "Up till now, China's contribution in terms of personnel to 15 U.N. peacekeeping operations has reached the level of more than 5,000, and as we speak, there are about 1,000 Chinese peacekeepers serving in 13 mission areas."[54]

"China could flood the market of U.N. peacekeeping if they wanted to," French defense official Guicherd remarks. "Just like they are flooding other markets."

Afghanistan and Beyond

European nations responded tepidly last winter when the U.S.-led alliance in Afghanistan called for more NATO troops, frustrating the Bush administration and NATO officials. The alliance had sought more troops to combat an expected offensive by Taliban insurgents, and top officials warned of dire consequences if European nations didn't deliver. Frustrating NATO military efforts even more, Germany, France and Italy restricted the number of their troops taking part in the heavy fighting in southeastern Afghanistan, where the insurgency has shown its greatest strength.[55]

"I do not think it is right to talk about more and more military means," said German Defense Minster Franz Josef Jung. "When the Russians were in Afghanistan, they had 100,000 troops and didn't win."

Nonetheless, the German cabinet voted in February to send at least six Tornado jets to the front for surveillance operations against the Taliban. "Without security there is no reconstruction," said a chastened Jung, "and without reconstruction there's no security."[56]

The cost of continued combat duty in Afghanistan may influence the debate among NATO nations. Afghanistan has given the NATO organization "their very first taste of significant ground combat," says international law Professor Smith. "They're suffering casualties in ways they had not anticipated. NATO states are beginning to see people coming home in body bags and are wondering why they are involved at all."

Failure in Afghanistan could affect NATO's desire to project its military might in any new peacekeeping operations beyond Europe. "In the long run, there will be enough uncertainty in the world that members of NATO will understand that they must remain capable to some extent, but how far they are willing to stretch themselves will remain under consideration and debate," Smith adds.

Meanwhile, NATO intervention to serve as a buffer between Israel and the Palestinians remains a future possibility, but French defense official Guicherd says NATO is linked too closely with U.S. policy. Given the tension and the acute anti-Americanism in the region, she says, "it wouldn't be a very good idea for the time being."[57]

But NATO member Turkey could provide an entré into the Middle East, points out Smith. Turkey enjoys good relations with Israel and is a majority-Muslim country whose troops might be more acceptable to Arab populations. Smith calls it an "interesting idea. . . . Turkey has NATO [military] capabilities. They might actually play a meaningful role."

As *Turkish Daily News* columnist Hans De Wit put it, "The current situation in the Middle East is, in fact, a perfect chance for Turkey to show its negotiating skills, since its has good relations with all countries in this region.

"But somehow, its image as a former conqueror doesn't help. Turkey has done a terrible job in convincing the world that its intentions . . . are sincere; that it can bring mediation to the region and can be a stabilizer of importance."[58]

OUTLOOK

Is the World Ready?

As the still-uncertain response to Darfur indicates, countries around the world and at the United Nations are not rushing to every emergency call. "The international community has to prove that it is willing to step into difficult situations — and it may yet again," says former New Zealand Ambassador Keating. "But I wouldn't assume that it would every time."

The high ideals and bold aims articulated by the Responsibility to Protect doctrine may be tempered not only by whether the world has the will to send troops in to halt a massacre but also by whether there will be enough troops.

While it strives to play an increasing role around the world, NATO may be tied down at home. Kosovo is set to receive some form of U.N.-decreed independence from a reluctant Serbia, but the Balkans could again be rocked by the kind of bloody ethnic violence that marked the 1990s.

Such renewed ethnic hostility could challenge the NATO stabilization force, requiring the alliance to bolster its troop counts in Kosovo — and slow NATO efforts to export its peacekeeping influence elsewhere.

As the R2P concept takes root, however, pressure may increase for the kind of muscular intervention that only military forces like NATO troops can deliver.

"The right of an individual to live is a higher priority, at least in theory, than the right of states to do as they please," says former U.S. diplomat Feinstein. "Something important is happening in theory, and practice is lagging very far behind."

More than just words will be needed to make the Responsibility to Protect viable, says U.N. spokeswoman Montas. "The political will has to be there," she says, "and the political will has to come from the Security Council."

There is plenty of military might around the world to translate "theory into reality," according to former Australian foreign minister Evans. "The U.N. is feeling desperately overstretched . . . but with the world's armed services currently involving some 20 million men and women in uniform (with another 50 million reservists, and 11 million paramilitaries)," he observes, "it hardly seems beyond the wit of man to work out a way of making some of that capacity available . . . to prevent and react to man-made catastrophe."[59]

For many people, U.N. police official Lopes says, "We are the last port before Hell."

Having served on the Security Council during the Rwanda bloodbath, former Ambassador Keating knows all too well the limitations of U.N. action. Each case is weighed on "its own particular location in time as well as geography — and whether or not the resources are physically available to undertake the task that's envisaged," he says.

In Darfur, for example, there is the additional problem of mistakenly harming civilians, he says, so the council must weigh the "kind of scenario in which the bad guys and the good guys are almost stuck together." That's "one of the daunting things that's confronting any action with respect to Sudan — being 'realistic' about the situation," he says.

"It's unforgivable, really, when you think about the 'Never Again' statements" made after the Holocaust, Keating says, "but the reality is at the moment there's no willingness to do it."

Peacekeeping expert Holt, at the Stimson Center, calls peacekeeping "an enduring tool," even though "it's always criticized for falling short of our hopes. But we keep turning back to it.

"A lot of these lessons are learnable and fixable," she adds. Peacekeeping continues to evolve, it's a moving exercise," with very real global stakes. "Millions of people's lives remain in the balance if we don't get this right."

NOTES

1. Speech by Ban Ki-moon on Jan. 29, 2007, delivered as a video message.

2. Feinstein's comments on the civilian and military issues involved in the right to protect can be found at the Council on Foreign Relations Web site: www .cfr.org/publication/12458/priority_for_new_un_ secretarygeneral.html?breadcrumb=%2Fpublication %2Fby_type%2Fnews_release%3Fid%3D328.

3. Quoted in Lee Michael Katz, "The Man Behind The Movie," *National Journal*, April 22, 2006.

4. From U.N. Secretary-General Ban Ki-moon's address to the Center for Strategic and International Studies in Washington, D.C., Jan. 16, 2007.

5. U.N. Department of Peacekeeping Operations, "Fact Sheet," May 2006.

6. "Peacekeeping and Related Stabilization Operations," CRS Report for Congress, Congressional Research Service, July 13, 2006.

7. U.N. Department of Peacekeeping Operations, *op. cit.*

8. Quoted in "From Cologne to Berlin and Beyond — Operations, Institutions and Capabilities," address to European Security and Defense Policy Conference, Jan. 29, 2007.

9. Organization for Security and Co-operation in Europe (OSCE); www.osce.org/activities.

10. "The Responsibility to Protect," Report of the International Commission on Intervention and State Sovereignty, December 2001, p. VII.

11. Gareth Evans, *The Responsibility to Protect: The New Global Moral Compact* (forthcoming, 2007).

12. "World Summit Outcome," U.N. General Assembly, 60th Session, Sept. 20, 2005, Item 39, p. 31.

13. Quoted in United Nations summary of Holocaust Commemoration speeches, Jan. 29, 2007.

14. Quoted in Luiza Ch. Savage, "Canada's 'Responsibility to Protect' Doctrine Gaining Ground at the UN, *Maclean's*, July 18, 2005.

15. "Chávez Criticizes U.N. Reform in Speech," The Associated Press, Sept. 17, 2005.

16. Luiza Ch. Savage, *op. cit.*; and Paul Reynolds, "Western Pressure Fails to Move Sudan," BBC Online, Oct. 23, 2006; http://news.bbc.co.uk/2/ hi/ africa/6076698.stm.

17. Quoted in "Gadhafi: U.N. Darfur Force is Ruse to Grab Sudan's Oil," Reuters, Nov. 20, 2006, Global Research online; www.globalresearch.ca/index.php?co ntext=viewArticle&code=20061120&articleId=3934.

18. Chinua Akukwe, "Why the Darfur Tragedy Will Likely Occur Again," July 28, 2004, Worldpress.org; www.worldpress.org/Africa/1905.cfm.

19. William G. O'Neill, "The Responsibility to Protect," *The Christian Science Monitor*, Sept. 28, 2006; www .csmonitor.com/2006/0928/p0928/p09s01-coop .html. O'Neill is senior adviser to the Brookings Institution Project on Internal Displacement.

20. African Union, *Protocol Relating to the Establishment of the Peace and Security Council of the African Union* (Durban: African Union, July 2002).

21. David Newman and Joel Peters, "Kosovo as the West Bank, Macedonia as Israel," commentary, *Ha'aretz*, Oct. 30, 2002.

22. For an analysis of the problems and potential of an African peacekeeping force, see World Politics Watch; www.worldpoliticswatch.com/article .aspx?id=429.

23. "Aid Agencies Urge Donor Support for African Union Mission in Darfur," *Oxfam America* Online, July 20, 2006; www.oxfamamerica.org/.

24. See United Nations Security Council Meeting on cooperation with regional organizations, Sept. 20, 2006, http://daccessdds.un.org/doc/UNDOC/ PRO/N06/528/73/PDF/N065287.pdf?Open Element.

25. Roland Paris, from *Review of International Studies*, British International Studies Association (2002), pp. 637-656.

26. Center for International Cooperation, *Annual Review of Global Peace Operations*, February 2006; www.cic.nyu.edu.

27. Alex Diceanu, "For Many Haitians, MINUSTAH Has Been Closer to a Foreign Occupation Force than a U.N. Peacekeeping Mission," *Peace Magazine*, April 2006; www.globalpolicy.org/security/issues/ haiti/2006/04better.htm.

28. Marc Lacey, "U.N. Troops Fight Haiti Gangs One Battered Street at a Time," *New York Times*, Feb. 10 2007, p. A1.

29. See *World History*, McDougal Litell (2005).

30. *Encyclopedia Britannica* online; http://concise.britan-nica.com/ebc/article-9039167/Hanseatic-League.

31. David Brewer, *The Greek War of Independence: The Struggle for Freedom from Ottoman Oppression and the Birth of the Modern Greek Nation* (2001).

32. Naval Historical Center, "The Boxer Rebellion and the U.S. Navy, 1900-1901"; www. history.navy.mil/faqs/faq86-1.htm.

33. For background, see www.answers.com/topic/league-of-nations.

34. For background, see www.historylearningsite.co.uk/korea.htm.

35. Quoted in "Ban Ki-moon calls on new generation to take better care of Planet Earth than his own," U.N. News Centre, March 1, 2007; www.un.org/apps/news/story.asp?NewsID=21720&Cr=global&Cr1=warming.

36. James Traub, interviewed on "Fresh Air," National Public Radio, Oct. 31, 2006.

37. For a summary of the Congo's ongoing war, see Simon Robinson and Vivienne Walt, "The Deadliest War In The World," *Time*, May 28, 2006; www.time.com/time/magazine/article/0,9171,1198921-1,00.html.

38. Adrzej Sitkowski, *UN Peacekeeping Myth and Reality* (2006).

39. For background on the Congo crisis, see Justin Pearce, "DR Congo's Troubled History," BBC Online, Jan. 16, 2001; http://news.bbc.co.uk/1/hi/world/africa/1120825.stm.

40. The Cambodia Genocide Project at Yale University includes a definition of genocide as well as information on a Responsibility to Protect Initiative at Yale University Online; www.yale.edu/cgp/.

41. For a detailed account of the Somalia action, see Mark Bowden, "Black Hawk Down: An American War Story", *The Philadelphia Enquirer*, Nov. 16, 1997.

42. Interview with BBC, "Eyewitness: UN in Rwanda 1994," Sept. 6, 2000, news.bbc.co.uk.

43. *Annual Review of Global Peace Operations 2006, op. cit.*

44. For background, see http://africanhistory.about.com/od/liberia/p/Sirleaf.htm.

45. Quoted in "Liberia's New President," News Hour Online, March 23, 2006; www.pbs.org/news-hour/bb/africa/jan-june06/liberia_3-23.html.

46. Tristan McConnell, "All female unit keeps peace in Liberia," *The Christian Science Monitor* online, March 21, 2005; http://news.yahoo.com/s/csm/20070321/ts_csm/ofemmeforce_1.

47. Warren Hoge, "World Briefing: Asia: Nepal: U.N. Creating New Political Mission," *The New York Times*, Jan. 24, 2007.

48. Evelyn Leopold, "U.N. Chief's Reform Plans May Be Stalled in Meetings," Reuters, Feb. 5, 2007.

49. Alfred de Montesquiou, "Chinese president tells Sudan counterpart he must do more for peace in Darfur," The Associated Press, Feb. 2, 2007.

50. Quoted in Warren Hoge, "Arabs and U.N. Chief Press Sudan's Leader to End Darfur Crisis," *The New York Times*, March 29, 2007, p. A5.

51. See Colum Lynch, "U.N. Chief Seeks to Delay Sanctions Against Sudan," *The Washington Post*, April 3, 2007, p. A15.

52. *Ibid.*

53. Howard W. French, with Fan Wexin, "Chinese Leader to Visit Sudan for Talks on Darfur Conflict," *The New York Times* online, Jan. 25, 2007.

54. Statement by Ambassador Zhang Yishan at the 2006 Session of the Special Committee on Peacekeeping Operations, United Nations, Feb. 27, 2006. Full statement available at www.fmprc.gov.cn/ce/ceun/eng/xw/t237291.htm.

55. Michael Abramowitz, "Afghanistan Called 'Key Priority' For NATO," *The Washington Post*, Nov. 30, 2006.

56. Kate Connolly, "Germany beefs up Afghan presence with six fighter jets," *The Guardian* Online, Feb. 8, 2007; full story at www. guardian.co.uk/afghanistan/story/0,,2008088,00.html.

57. For background, see Samuel Loewenberg, "Anti-Americanism," *CQ Global Researcher*, March 2007, pp. 51-74.

58. Hans A. H.C. DeWit, "Turkey Needs Confidence, Not Fear," *Turkish Daily News* Online, Feb. 16, 2007; www.turkishdailynews.com.tr/article.php?enewsid=66304.

59. Evans, *op. cit.*

BIBLIOGRAPHY

Books

Cassidy, Robert, *Peacekeeping in the Abyss: British and American Peacekeeping Doctrine and Practice After the Cold War,* **Praeger, 2004.**
A Special Forces officer and international relations scholar examines and compares U.S. military efforts in Somalia and British operations in Bosnia in an effort to understand which military cultural traits and force structures are more suitable and adaptable for peace operations and asymmetric conflicts.

Danieli, Yael, *Sharing the Front Line and the Back Hills: Peacekeepers Humanitarian Aid Workers and the Media in the Midst of Crisis,* **Baywood, 2002.**
A clinical psychologist who is co-founder of the Group Project for Holocaust Survivors and Their Children gives voice to the victims of traumatic hotspots such as Kosovo, Haiti and Burundi.

Franke, Volker, ed., *Terrorism and Peacekeeping, New Security Challenges,* **Praeger, 2005.**
An associate professor of international studies at McDaniel College presents numerous case studies in order to examine the challenges to national security policymakers posed by peacekeeping and terrorism.

Johnstone, Ian, ed., *Annual Review of Global Peace Operations 2006,* **Lynne Rienner Publishers, 2006.**
A senior U.N. official and former senior associate at the International Peace Academy examines U.N. missions around the world; includes numerous statistics and also frank observations on peacekeeping's failures and limitations.

Luck, Edward, *The U.N. Security Council: Practice and Promise,* **Routledge, 2006.**
A Columbia University professor and longtime U.N. watcher examines the Security Council's roller-coaster history of military enforcement and sees a "politically awkward division of labor" between major powers and developing countries.

Sitkowski, Adrzej, *U.N. Peacekeeping Myth and Reality,* **Praeger Security International, 2006.**
A veteran U.N. official reflects on peacekeeping operations with a very critical eye; includes an inside look at serving in Namibia, regarded as a model of U.N. success.

Smith, Michael G., with Moreen Dee, *Peacekeeping in East Timor: The Path to Independence,* **International Peace Academy Occasional Series,** *Lynne Rienner Publishers,* **2003.**
"General Mike" Smith, who led the U.N. force in East Timor, concludes broadly there are no "templates" for peacekeeping and that lessons from previous missions were not fully learned.

Traub, James, *The Best Intentions: Kofi Annan and the UN in the Era of American World Power,* **Farrar, Straus and Giroux, 2006.**
A *New York Times* reporter critically portrays U.N. operations through the eyes and staff machinations of the recently departed secretary-general.

Articles

Dalder, Ivo, and James Goldgeiger, "Global NATO," *Foreign Affairs,* **September/October, 2006, p. A1.**
The authors argue that expanding NATO membership, even beyond Europe, can boost the security organization's new peacekeeping role.

Katz, Lee Michael, "The Man Behind the Movie," *National Journal,* **April 22, 2006.**
In an interview, Paul Rusesabagina, the real-life Hotel Rwanda manager, offers a witness to genocide's first-hand perspective, finding the U.N. "useless" in Rwanda.

Lacey, Marc, "U.N. Troops Fight Haiti Gangs One Battered Street at a Time," *The New York Times,* **Feb. 10 2007, p. A1.**
A look at "Evans," a gang leader who controls the slums and lives of 300,000 people in Haiti's Port-au-Prince — and U.N. peacekeeping troops' attempts to take him down.

Reports and Studies

"Darfur and Beyond: What Is Needed to Prevent Mass Casualties," *Council on Foreign Relations,* **January 2007.**

A carefully timed report suggests actions that should be taken by the new U.N. secretary-general, NATO, the European and African unions and the United States to prevent future genocides.

"The Responsibility To Protect," *Report Of The International Commission On Intervention and State Sovereignty,* **December 2001.**
Diplomats from Australia to Russia provide the intellectual underpinnings of The Responsibility to Protect in this landmark report. Because of the report's timing, it doesn't address the aftermath of the Sept. 11, 2001, attacks in depth.

"The Responsibility To Protect: The U.N. World Summit and the Question of Unilateralism," *The Yale Law Journal,* **March 2006.**
This cautious look at The Responsibility to Protect argues that it limits military action to narrow and extreme circumstances and can be used as a pretext to invade another nation.

For More Information

African Union, P.O. Box 3243, Addis Ababa, Ethiopia; (251)-11-551-77-00; www.africa-union.org. Promotes cooperation among the nations of Africa.

European Union Force, Rue de la Loi, 175 B-1048 Brussels, Belgium; (32-2)-281-61-11; www.consilium.europa.eu. Military detachments currently in Bosnia and Herzegovina and the Democratic Republic of the Congo.

International Commission on Intervention and State Sovereignty, 125 Sussex Dr., Ottawa, Ontario K1A 0G2; www.iciss.ca. Independent commission established by the Canadian government that promotes humanitarian intervention.

International Crisis Group, 149 Avenue Louise, Level 24, B-1050 Brussels, Belgium; +32-(0)-2-502-90-38; www.crisisgroup.org. Non-governmental organization using field-based analysis and high-level advocacy to prevent violent conflict worldwide.

Multinational Force and Observers, +39-06-57-11-94-44; www.mfo.org. International peacekeeping force on Sinai Peninsula monitoring military build-up of Egypt and Israel.

North Atlantic Treaty Organization, Blvd. Leopold III, 1110 Brussels, Belgium; +32-(0)-2-707-50-41; www.nato.int. Safeguards NATO member countries via military and political means.

Organization for Security and Co-operation in Europe, Kaerntner Ring 5-7, 1010 Vienna, Austria; +43-1-514-36-0; www.osce.org. World's largest regional security organization serves as a forum for political negotiations and decision-making in conflict prevention and crisis management.

Responsibility to Protect, 708 Third Ave., 24th Fl., New York, NY 10017; (212) 599-1320; www.responsibilitytoprotect.org. Advocacy group working to protect vulnerable populations from war crimes and crimes against humanity.

United Nations Department of Peacekeeping Operations, 760 U.N. Plaza, New York, NY 10017; (202) 963-1234; www.un.org/Depts/dpko/dpko. Responsible for all U.N. peacekeeping missions mandated by the Security Council.

2

Separatist Movements

Should Nations Have a Right to Self-Determination?

Brian Beary

The American Embassy in Belgrade is set ablaze on Feb. 21 by Serbian nationalists angered by U.S. support for Kosovo's recent secession from Serbia. About 70 separatist movements are under way around the globe, but most are nonviolent. Kosovo is one of seven countries to emerge from the former Yugoslavia and part of a nearly fourfold jump in the number of countries to declare independence since 1945.

From *CQ Global Researcher*, April 2008.

A ngry protesters hurling rocks at security forces; hotels, shops and restaurants torched; a city choked by teargas. The violent images that began flashing around the world on March 14 could have been from any number of tense places from Africa to the Balkans. But the scene took place high in the Himalayas, in the ancient Tibetan capital of Lhasa. Known for its red-robed Buddhist monks, the legendary city was the latest flashpoint in Tibetan separatists' ongoing frustration over China's continuing occupation of their homeland.[1]

Weeks earlier, thousands of miles away in Belgrade, Serbia, hundreds of thousands of Serbs took to the streets to vent fury over Kosovo's secession on Feb. 17, 2008. Black smoke billowed from the burning U.S. Embassy, set ablaze by Serbs angered by Washington's acceptance of Kosovo's action.[2]

"As long as we live, Kosovo is Serbia," thundered Serbian Prime Minister Vojislav Kostunica at a rally earlier in the day.[3] Kosovo had been in political limbo since a NATO-led military force wrested the region from Serb hands in 1999 and turned it into an international protectorate after Serbia brutally clamped down on ethnic Albanian separatists. Before the split, about 75 percent of Serbia's population was Serbs, who are mostly Orthodox Christian, and 20 percent were ethnic Albanians, who are Muslim.[4]

Meanwhile, war-torn Iraq witnessed its own separatist-related violence on Feb. 22. Turkish forces launched a major military incursion into northern Iraq — the first big ground offensive in nearly a decade — to root out Kurdish separatist rebels known as

Separatist Movements Span the Globe

Nearly two dozen separatist movements are active worldwide, concentrated in Europe and Asia. At least seven are violent and reflect ethnic or religious differences with the mother country.

Selected Separatist Hot Spots

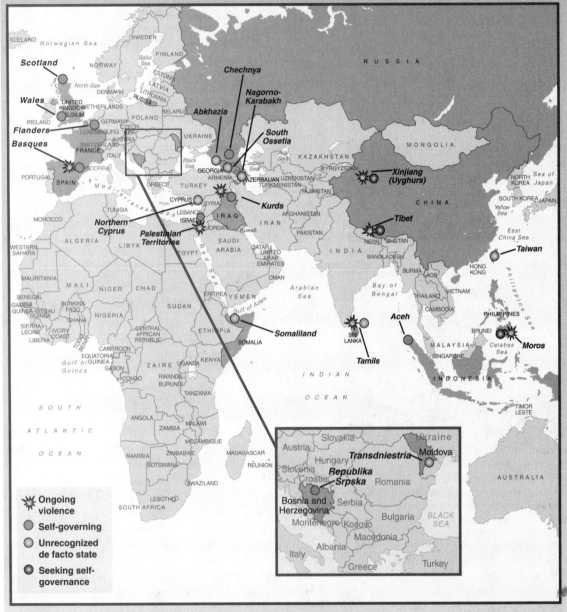

Sources: Unrepresented Nations and People's Organization, www.unpo.org; *Political Handbook of the World 2007*, CQ Press

Ongoing Separatist Movements

Africa

Somaliland — Militants in this northern Somalia territory established an unrecognized de facto state in the 1990s after the government of Somalia collapsed. The area was ruled by the United Kingdom from 1884 to 1960 and then became unified with the former Italian-ruled Somalia from 1960 to 1989.

Asia/Eurasia

Abkhazia — Independent Soviet republic briefly in 1921. Subsequently united with Georgia. Declared independence in 1992; war with Georgia ensued, which the Abkhaz won with Russian support. Since then, a stalemate has persisted. Up to 300,000 Georgians have fled since the 1990s, leaving an estimated 100,000 Abkhaz as the dominant force.

Aceh — One of the first places where Islam was established in Southeast Asia. Indonesia annexed the territory in 1949 upon becoming independent. Aceh was granted autonomy in 1959 and declared independence in 1976, with thousands dying in violence since then. A further 100,000 were killed in the 2004 Indian Ocean tsunami. A peace agreement was signed in 2005 granting autonomy.

Chechnya — A Muslim region in southern Russia, Chechnya was briefly independent in 1922. It declared independence after the collapse of the Soviet Union, but Russia opposed the secession and went to war with Chechnya from 1994-1996 and again in 1999. It became an autonomous Russian republic after a 2003 referendum.

Kurds — The world's largest ethnic group without its own country resides in Iraq, Iran, Turkey and Syria. The Iraqi Kurds have had autonomy since 1991. In Iran and Turkey they have no autonomy but are relatively free to speak Kurdish. The language is banned in Syria.

Moros — Muslims in the southern Philippines who live primarily on the island of Mindanao. Migration by Christian Filipinos from the north has diluted the Moro population. A militant Islamic fundamentalist group, Abu Sayyaf, is fighting the government to create a Moro Muslim state. Malaysia has committed the most international peacekeeping forces to stem the violence.

Nagorno-Karabakh — Declared independence from Azerbaijan in 1991, followed by a three-year war, during which most of the Azeris fled. A ceasefire has existed since 1994. It is now a de facto independent republic — unrecognized by the international community — populated mostly by ethnic Armenians.

Palestinian Territories — Since the largely Jewish state of Israel came into being in 1948, Arabs from the former Palestine have had no country of their own. The Palestinians live mainly in two non-contiguous areas, the Gaza Strip and West Bank, which Israel occupied in 1967 after a war with Egypt, Jordan and Syria. While the Palestinians have their own civilian administration and neither Israel nor neighboring Arab countries claim sovereignty over them, there is no independent Palestinian state yet because the terms cannot be agreed upon. A violent conflict between Israelis and Palestinians has persisted for decades.

South Ossetia — This region, which became part of Georgia in 1922, tried to become autonomous in 1989, but Georgia refused. After a war from 1990 to 1992 it became a de facto independent republic. Referenda in 1992 and 2006 confirming independence have not been recognized by any other country. Ossetian towns are governed by the separatist government; Georgian towns are overseen by Georgia.

Taiwan — The island off China's southeastern coast was established as a rival Chinese government in 1949 following the defeat of Chiang Kai-shek's Nationalists by Mao Tse-tung's communists. Between 1949 and 1971, it was recognized by most countries as the official government of China, but in 1971 mainland China replaced it as China's representative in the United Nations. In the 1990s, the Taiwanese government started a campaign to become a U.N. member again. Politics is polarized between those favoring unification with China — who won two recent elections — and those seeking official independence.

Tamils — Militant separatists known as the Liberation Tigers of Tamil Eelam (LTTE) have run a de facto state in northern Sri Lanka for many years. The LTTE assassinated Indian Prime Minister Rajiv Gandhi in 1991 for helping Sri Lanka crack down on the Tamils and Sri Lankan Prime Minister Ranasinghe Premadasa in 1993. A ceasefire was declared in 2002, but violence resumed in 2005. The Tamils are predominantly Hindu whereas the majority-Sinhalese community is Buddhist.

(Continued)

(Continued)

Asia/Eurasia (*Cont.*)

Tibet — China took over the Buddhist region in western China by force in the 1950s. Tibet's spiritual leader, the Dalai Lama, fled in 1959 and set up a government-in-exile in India. Recent separatist violence has been fueled by resentment over Chinese immigration into the autonomous region and the government's continued refusal to grant independence. The violence has prompted the Dalai Lama to consider resigning as the head of the exiled government.

Xinjiang — Known as East Turkestan or Chinese Turkistan, this vast region on China's northwest border with Central Asia — which comprises one-sixth of China's land mass — was annexed by China in the 18th century. Its 18 million inhabitants include 47 ethnic groups, including the Turkic-speaking Muslim Uyghurs — who once comprised 90 percent of the population. Today the Uyghurs make up only 40 percent of the inhabitants due to government policies that encourage Han Chinese to migrate there. Although the region has been officially autonomous since 1955, ethnic tensions have escalated in recent years. The U.S. State Department complains of serious human rights abuses against the Uyghurs due to Beijing's efforts to forcibly assimilate them and undermine their culture. China says Uyghur separatists are Islamic terrorists.

Europe

Basque Country — Basques in northeast Spain and southwest France have been pushing for greater autonomy or independence for more than a century. The militant separatist group ETA has killed about 1,000 people since 1968. Spain has granted its Basques extensive political and cultural autonomy but France has not.

Flanders — Flemish nationalism has grown in recent decades in Flanders, the northern part of Belgium where 60 percent of the population lives, most of them Dutch-speaking. Flanders, which has grown wealthier than French-speaking Wallonia to the south, already has extensive autonomy, but most Flemings would like more; many favor full independence.

Northern Cyprus — When Cyprus gained independence from British rule in 1960, relations between the Turks and Greeks on the island quickly deteriorated. Turkey's invasion in 1973 led to the Turkish Cypriots creating their own de facto state in the north that is only recognized by Turkey.

Republika Srpska — This self-governing territory within Bosnia, created in 1992, is populated mainly by ethnic Serbs who opposed Bosnia's secession from Yugoslavia. Moves to integrate it with the rest of Bosnia have failed so far.

Scotland and Wales — Demands by Celtic peoples in the northern and western corners of the United Kingdom for greater control over their affairs resulted in a devolution of power in 1999: A parliament was installed in Scotland and an assembly in Wales.

Transdniestria — First became a part of Moldova in 1812 when Russia captured both territories. From 1917 to 1939 it was part of the Soviet Union, while the rest of Moldova was ruled by Romania. From 1945 to 1991 both parts fell under Soviet rule. In 1992, when Moldova became an independent country Transdniestria seceded amid fear that Moldova would unify with Romania. The Moldovan army was repelled with the support of the Russian army. Its secession has not been recognized internationally. The area is dominated by Russian-speakers, with the Russian military also present.

The Americas (not shown on map)

Bolivia — After Evo Morales, Bolivia's first indigenous president, proposed changing the constitution last year to share more of the country's natural resources with the nation's indigenous highlanders, the mainly European-descended lowlanders have been threatening to secede.

Lakota Nation — This Indian nation of eight tribes living in South Dakota and neighboring states signed a treaty with the United States in 1851 granting them land rights. In 1989 they were awarded $40 million for losses incurred based on an 1868 land-rights treaty. In December 2007 a group of dissident Lakota delivered a declaration of independence to the State Department, which did not respond.

Québec — This majority French-speaking province has been threatening to secede from Canada since the 1960s. In two referenda on independence — in 1980 and 1995 — the Québécois voted to remain part of Canada. Today, they have a large degree of regional autonomy.

Sources: Unrepresented Nations and People's Organization, www.unpo.org; *Political Handbook of the World 2007,* CQ Press

the PKK, who have waged a bloody independence campaign against Ankara since 1984.[5]

The three hotspots reflect the same worldwide phenomenon — the almost inevitable conflict caused when a group of people want to separate themselves from a state that refuses to let them go. Despite today's oft-heard mantra that mankind is living in a global community where borders no longer matter, having a homeland of one's own clearly remains a dream for millions.

Out of more than 70 separatist movements around the globe, about two dozen are active, most in Europe and Asia, and seven of them are violent. And since 1990, more than two dozen new countries have emerged from separatist movements, mostly the result of the disintegration of the Soviet Union and the breaking apart of the former Yugoslavia.[6] Almost half of the 25 successful separatist movements were accompanied by some amount of violence, most of it ethnically based. (*See map and chart, pp. 28–30.*)

In fact, the number of independent countries around the globe has waxed and waned over the past 150 years. During the 19th century, the number declined as the European colonial powers gobbled up territories in Asia and Africa. Then after World War II the number mushroomed as those empires disintegrated. The United Nations has grown from 51 members when it was founded in 1945 to 192 members today (not counting Kosovo).[7] (*See graph, p. 39.*)

Among the groups fighting for independence today, the Kurds are the largest, with approximately 25 million dispersed in Turkey, Iraq, Iran and Syria.[8] Other separatist movements are microscopic by comparison: The South Ossetians — who have seceded from Georgia and formed a de facto but as-yet-unrecognized government — number just 70,000, for example. Some movements, like the Québécois in Canada and the Scottish in the United Kingdom, have been peaceful, while others, like the Tamils in Sri Lanka and Palestinians in Israel, have been violent. Indonesia has had two separatist movements with very different destinies: East Timor (Timor Leste) on Indonesia's eastern tip became independent in 1999 — although it is still struggling to fend for itself, relying on international aid to make up for its severe food shortages — while Aceh in the west has opted for autonomy within Indonesia.[9]

Separatism often triggers serious rifts between the world's major powers. In the case of Kosovo, the United

Protesters at a March rally in Tbilisi, Georgia, want Russia to stop supporting South Ossetia and Abkhazia, two Georgian regions that seceded and formed de facto states. Their placards — which say "Russia! Stop Dealing With the Fates of Small Nations!" — indicate how a separatist movement can become a pawn in a geopolitical tug-of-war. Russia supports the two breakaway states, while most of the international community does not recognize them.

States and its NATO allies — including the United Kingdom, France, Germany, Italy and Turkey — backed the secession. U.S. Assistant Secretary of State Daniel Fried has dubbed it "the last chapter in the dissolution of Yugoslavia," while acknowledging "many things can go wrong and probably will."[10] In stark contrast, Russia steadfastly opposes independence for Kosovo and is standing shoulder-to-shoulder with its historical ally, Serbia.

Outgoing Russian President Vladimir Putin has said, "If someone believes that Kosovo should be granted full independence as a state, then why should we deny it to the Abkhaz and the South Ossetians?" According to Matthew J. Bryza, U.S. deputy assistant secretary of State for European and Eurasian Affairs, Russia is covertly providing material support to South Ossetia and Abkhazia — two de facto states that have emerged from within Russia's political foe, the ex-Soviet Republic of Georgia.[11] The United States and the rest of the international community don't recognize the secession of either state.

Meanwhile, the Chinese government opposes the pro-independence movement among the ethnically

World's Newest Country Remains Divided

Kosovo is struggling to be recognized.

Delaware-size Kosovo grabbed the world's attention on Feb. 17 when its ethnic Albanian-dominated government declared its independence from Serbia, triggering street protests among some Serb citizens.

Because of fierce opposition from Serbs both inside Kosovo and in Serbia, a large international presence with armies from six "framework" nations keeps an uneasy peace: The United States controls the east, Ireland the center, Turkey and Germany the south, Italy the west and France the north.[1]

"Do not trust the apparent calm, it's the main difficulty of this mission," says Captain Noê-Noël Ucheida from the Franco-German brigade of the 16,000-strong NATO force in Kosovo. "It can be calm. But it becomes tense in the morning and ignites in the afternoon."[2]

The spotlight fell on Kosovo in 1999 — several years after the break-up of Yugoslavia — when Serbian leader Slobodan Milosevic's brutal campaign to forcibly remove Kosovar Albanians led to NATO having to step in and take the province out of Serb hands. Now Kosovo's 2 million Albanians seem determined to open a new chapter in their history by implementing a U.N. plan granting them internationally supervised independence. Not for the first time, the world's leading powers are divided over a conflict in the Balkans. The United States, Germany, United Kingdom, France and Italy back independence while Serbia, Russia and China oppose it.

Further complicating the issue are the 100,000 Serbs living in Kosovo, including 40,000 concentrated in a zone north of the Ibar River; the remainder are dispersed throughout the south. Just as Kosovo's Albanians fought tooth and nail to free themselves from Serb rule, so the Serbs in north Kosovo are equally resolved to be free of Albanian rule. "They already run their own de facto state," says Nicolas Gros-Verheyde, a French journalist who toured Kosovo just before the declaration of independence. "They are heavily subsidized by the Serbian government in Belgrade, which tops up the salaries of local police officers and supplies the electricity and mobile phone network."

The Ibar River is fast becoming yet another border in the Balkans. "Cars in the north have different registration plates. When Kosovar Serbs drive south, they remove them to avoid being attacked. Our translator, who was Serbian, would not even get out of the car," says Gros-Verheyde. He notes there was much greater contact between the Serb and Albanian communities during his previous visit to Kosovo in 1990, when the Serbian military patrolled the province. "But 15 years of ethnic conflict has bred mistrust and hatred," says Gros-Verheyde.

Daniel Serwer, vice president of the Center for Post-Conflict Peace and Stability Operations at the United States Institute of Peace (USIP), feels Serbia only has itself to blame for losing Kosovo. It drove the Kosovar Albanians to secede by excluding them from the Serbian government, he argues. "If Kosovars had been included — for example by being offered the presidency of Serbia — it might not have seceded. The Serbs want sovereignty over the territory of Kosovo, but they could not care less about the people," he says.

The economy of Kosovo has suffered terribly from two decades of strife throughout the region. With unemployment

Turkic Uyghur people, who live in the western Chinese autonomous region of Xinjiang. China has tried to stifle separatism in its western provinces by promoting mass migration of ethnic Chinese to both Tibet and Xinjiang to dilute the indigenous population. Critics say China used the Sept. 11, 2001, terrorist attacks in the United States as a pretext for clamping down on the Uyghurs, who are Muslim, by claiming they were linked to Islamic terrorist movements like al Qaeda.[12]

China's separatist woes are an embarrassment just four months before the start of the Summer Olympic Games in Beijing — China's chance to shine on the world stage. The Chinese call the Tibetan protests a "grave violent crime involving beating, smashing, looting and burning" orchestrated by the Dalai Lama, the Tibetan leader-in-exile.[13] But Western leaders are not buying Beijing's line. Nancy Pelosi, Speaker of the U.S. House of Representatives, traveled to India to meet with the Dalai Lama on March 21 and declared the Tibet situation "a challenge to the conscience of the world."[14]

Despite the international condemnation of China's treatment of the Tibetans, however, the international community and the United Nations (U.N.) — which in 1945 enshrined the right to self-determination in its

at 50 percent, thousands have migrated to Western Europe and the United States, sending money back to their families. Much of the country's income is derived from trafficking in drugs, weapons and women, claims Gros-Verheyde. Roads are dilapidated, and electricity is cut off several times a week.

Meanwhile, the international community is ever-present: The mobile phone network for Kosovar Albanians is provided by the principality of Monaco, the euro is the local currency and NATO soldiers' frequent the hotels and restaurants.

"The Albanian part is livelier than the Serbian," says Gros-Verheyde. "The birth rate among the Albanians is very high. They want to increase their population to ensure they are not wiped out."

Kosovo's future remains uncertain. Most of the world's nations have not yet recognized it as an independent country, and many are unlikely to do so, including Spain, Slovakia and Romania, which fear potential secessionist movements of their own.[3] Internally, tensions between the Albanian and Serb communities are unlikely to simply melt away. In fact, relations could further deteriorate over how to divide up the country's mineral resources, most of which lie in the Serb-controlled northern part.

Meanwhile, the world will keep a watchful eye and presence. The European Union (EU) is in the process of deploying a 1,900-strong police and rule-of-law mission to replace a U.N. police force.[4] Indeed, many observers think the EU may hold out the best hope of salvation: Under a plan proposed by the European Commission — and supported virtually across the board in Europe — all Balkan nations would be integrated into the EU, ultimately diminishing the significance of borders and smoothing out ethnic tensions.

Ethnic Albanians celebrate Kosovo's declaration of independence from Serbia on Feb. 17, 2008. The new state is backed by the United States and key European allies but bitterly contested by Serbia and Russia.

In the meantime, NATO holds the fort with a "high-visibility, low-profile" doctrine. "The soldiers have bullet-proof vests but keep them in the vehicles," says Gros-Verheyde. "They carry machine guns on their back but do not walk through villages with a weapon at their hip. A soldier told me the only exception to this was the American soldiers who have been traumatized by Iraq."

---

[1] Nicolas Gros-Verheyde, "One eye on Belgrade, the other on Pristina," *Europolitics*, (EU affairs subscription-based news service), Jan. 22, 2008, www.europolitics.info/xg/europolitique/politiquessectorielles/defense/217304?highlight=true&searchlink=true.

[2] Quoted in *ibid*.

[3] Joanna Boguslawska, *Europolitics*, Dec. 14, 2007, www.europolitics.info/xg/europolitique/politiquesexternes/relationsexterieures/215424?highlight=true&searchlink=true.

[4] For details, see Web sites of NATO and U.N. forces, respectively, at www.nato.int/KFOR and www.unmikonline.org.

---

founding charter — have provided little support to recent separatist movements. Many countries are wary of incurring the wrath of economic giants like China, and international law on separatism is ambiguous, leading to an inconsistent and non-uniform global reaction to separatist movements.

Though several international conventions reaffirm the right to self-determination, they also pledge to uphold the "principle of territorial integrity" — the right of existing states to prevent regions from seceding. "International law grows by practice," says Thomas Grant, a senior fellow and legal scholar at the United States Institute of Peace (USIP), an independent institution established and funded by the U.S. Congress that tries to resolve international conflicts. "The legal situation adapts itself to the factual situation." (*See box, p. 44.*)

Consequently, the international community's response to de facto separatist states varies widely. For example, most of the world refuses to deal with the Turkish Republic of Northern Cyprus, which has been punished with an economic embargo since 1973, when Turkish troops invaded Cyprus and permanently occupied the north, creating a Turkish-dominated de facto state there. Somaliland — which established a de facto state in northwestern Somalia in 1991 after the government in Mogadishu collapsed — has been largely ignored by the world community despite being a relative beacon of stability in the otherwise unstable horn of Africa.[15] The Tamils' campaign to gain independence from Sri Lanka attracts relatively little international diplomatic attention these days, in part, some say, because the area is not considered critical by the major powers.

Meanwhile, the island nation of Taiwan, off the coast of mainland China, is accepted as a global trading partner — the United States alone has 140 trade agreements with the Taiwanese — but not as an independent country. Few countries are willing to challenge Beijing's "one-China" policy, which denies any province the right to secede and sees Taiwan as its 23rd province.[16]

In addition, the world has done nothing — apart from occasionally condemning human rights violations — to prevent Russia from brutally repressing Chechnya's attempt to secede. While separatists there largely succeeded in creating their own state in the 1990s, Moscow has since regained control of it, although an insurgency continues.

The U.N. has no specific unit looking at separatism as a phenomenon. Instead, it usually waits for a conflict to break out and then considers sending a peacekeeping mission to restore law and order.

"U.N. member states are likely to be wary of separatism because of the knock-on effects it can have on themselves," says Jared Kotler, communications officer at the U.N.'s Department of Political Affairs. "Member states are very aware how one movement can encourage another — possibly in their own country."

"Thus far, territorial integrity has always won the debate," says Hurst Hannum, a professor of international law at Tufts University in Medford, Mass., and a specialist in self-determination theory. "This is why Kosovo will be an important precedent despite statements by all concerned that it should not be seen as such."

In Latin America, where most countries won wars of independence in the early 1800s, separatist movements are rare today, although one recently sprang up in Bolivia. Bolivians living in the lowlands, who are mostly of European ancestry, are threatening to secede to prevent the government from redistributing the profits from the nation's oil and gas reserves to the mainly indigenous highlanders. In North America, the United States has

not experienced a serious separatist threat since 1861 when 11 Southern states seceded, provoking the Civil War. And while few predict an imminent resurgence of such movements in the United States, diverse secessionist groups are beginning to coordinate their efforts.[17] (*See "At Issue," p. 49.*)

Some separatist movements have been highly successful. For example, since declaring independence from the Soviet Union in 1990, Lithuania has liberalized and grown its economy, consolidated democracy and joined the European Union (EU) and NATO.

Seth D. Kaplan, a foreign policy analyst and author of the forthcoming book *Fixing Fragile States*, has some advice for countries struggling to put out secessionist fires. "Countries that can foster sufficient social cohesion and a common identity while minimizing horizontal inequities are the most likely to stay whole," he says. "Those that don't and have obvious identity cleavages are likely to ignite secessionist movements."

While the world confronts growing separatism, here are some key questions being asked:

Should there be a right of self-determination?

"In principle, yes," says Daniel Serwer, vice president of the Center for Post-Conflict Peace and Stability Operations at the United States Institute of Peace. "But the real question is: What form should self-determination take?"

Self-determination is often interpreted to mean the right to secede and declare independence. But it can take other forms, too, such as local autonomy, similar to what Canada has granted to Québec, or a federal system with a strong central government that protects minority rights.

"In Kosovo, after nine years under U.N. control, young people expected independence," says Serwer. But other minorities have chosen a different path, he adds. For instance, "the Kurds in Iraq were thrown out of their homes" by Saddam Hussein. "They were even gassed. But so far they have not chosen the route of independence."

Gene Martin, executive director of the Philippine Facilitation Project at USIP, notes, "Local autonomy may not be enough for some people, who feel they just do not belong to a country." Plus, he adds, the government's ability or willingness to relinquish its authority also affects whether a minority will push for local autonomy or for full independence. Martin has been involved in brokering peace between the Philippine government and the Moro Islamic Liberation Front, which has for decades fought for an independent state for the Moros, a Muslim people living in southern Philippines.

Marino Busdachin — general secretary of the Hague-based Unrepresented Nations and Peoples Organization (UNPO), which represents 70 nonviolent movements pushing for self-determination — rails against the U.N. for not upholding that right. "Self-determination exists on paper only. It is a trap," he says. "We cannot apply to anyone for it. The U.N. member states block us."

Moreover, he says, seeking self-determination should not be confused with demanding the right to secede. "Ninety percent of our members are not looking for independence," he says.

That's a significant distinction, according to Diane Orentlicher, a professor of international law at American University in Washington, D.C. Although the U.N. has enshrined the right to self-determination, it has never endorsed a right of secession, and no state recognizes such a right. Such a step would be dangerous, she writes, because it would allow minorities to subvert the will of the majority. "Minorities could distort the outcome of political processes by threatening to secede if their views do not prevail," she writes.[18]

Dmitry Rogozin, Russia's ambassador to NATO, shares that view. "If the majority wants to live in a shared state, why does the minority have the right to break away?" he has asked.[19] "Look at Berlin. You could say it's the third-largest Turkish city [because of the large number of people of Turkish origin living there]. If tomorrow the Turks living in Berlin want to create a national state in the city, who can be against it?"

"The challenge for the West in Kosovo," says self-determination legal expert Hannum at Tufts, is to recognize its independence without implicitly recognizing its right to secede — just as "the West pretended that the former Yugoslavia 'dissolved' as opposed to recognizing the secession of its various parts."

The State Department's Bryza, who deals with conflicts in Abkhazia, South Ossetia and Nagorno-Karabakh, a separatist enclave in Azerbaijan, agrees. "It is unreasonable to have self-determination as the only guiding principle," he says. "If we did, the world would live in utter barbarity."

Fixing Fragile States author Kaplan believes separatism makes sense in a few cases, such as Kosovo and

AP Photo/Al Jacinto

The Moro Islamic Liberation Front — which for decades has fought for an independent state for the Moros, a Muslim group living in the south of the predominantly Catholic Philippines — are negotiating with the government to peacefully settle the dispute.

Somaliland. "But, generally, the international community is right to initially oppose separatism," he says.

So when should a group have the right to secede? "When you are deprived of the right to participate in government, and there are serious violations of human rights, such as genocide," says the USIP's Grant. "The bar is placed very high because you want to preserve the state, as that is the mechanism you use to claim your right of secession."

This is why, argues Serwer, ethnic Albanians in Macedonia, which borders Kosovo, do not have the right to secede. "If they called for independence — and I don't think they want this — I would say 'nonsense,' because they have their rights respected. It is only when other forms of self-determination — like local autonomy — are blocked that secession becomes inevitable."

Meto Koloski — the president of United Macedonian Diaspora, which campaigns for the rights of Macedonian minorities in Greece, Bulgaria, Albania, Serbia and

More Than Two Dozen New Nations Since 1990

Since 1990, 26 new countries have declared independence — 15 of them the result of the dissolution of the Soviet Union. Yugoslavia has separated into seven new states, the last one, Kosovo, declaring its independence in February.

Successful Separatist Movements Since 1990

Emerged from Ethiopia (1993)
Eritrea

Emerged from Indonesia (2002)
Timor Leste

Emerged from the Soviet Union (1991)

Armenia	Kazakhstan	Russia
Azerbaijan	Kyrgyzstan	Tajikistan
Belarus	Latvia	Turkmenistan
Estonia	Lithuania	Ukraine
Georgia	Moldova	Uzbekistan

Emerged from Czechoslovakia in 1993
Czech Republic
Slovakia

Emerged from Yugoslavia
Bosnia and Herzegovina (1992)
Croatia (1991)
Kosovo (2008, from Serbia)
Macedonia (1991)
Montenegro (2006)*
Serbia (2006)*
Slovenia (1991)

* For three years, Serbia and Montenegro existed as a confederation called Serbia & Montenegro, and then split into separate countries.

Sources: Unrepresented Nations and Peoples' Organization, www.unpo.org; *Political Handbook of the World 2007,* CQ Press, 2007; Tibet Government-in-exile, www.tibet.com.

Kosovo — says, "Everyone should have a right to self-determination, their own identity, language and culture but not to their own state."

Secession also is problematic — even if backed by a clear majority of those in the seceding region — because the minority opposed to secession could end up being oppressed. "Secession does not create the homogeneous successor states its proponents often assume," writes Donald Horowitz, a professor of law and political science at Duke University in Durham, N.C. "Guarantees of minority protection in secessionist regions are likely to be illusory; indeed, many secessionist movements have as one of their aims the expulsion or subordination of minorities in the secessionist regions.[20]

"There is an inevitable trade-off between encouraging participation in the undivided state and legitimating exit from it," he continued. "The former will inevitably produce imperfect results, but the latter is downright dangerous."[21]

Some would argue that certain separatist movements have no legal basis because the people concerned already exercised their right of self-determination when their country was first founded. "The whole self-determination theology is very slippery," says a U.S. government official with extensive knowledge of the separatist conflict in Aceh, Indonesia. "We support the territorial integrity of Indonesia. We never concluded that the human rights situation in Aceh was intolerable."

Jerry Hyman, governance advisor at the Center for Strategic and International Studies in Washington, highlights an often-overlooked point: "We have to ask how economically and politically viable are states like Transdniestria? If you apply this [right to secede] to Africa, it could explode. At best, Africa is a stained-glass window." Economic viability tends to be ignored when assessing separatist claims, he says, because the "we're special" argument usually prevails.

"If they are not viable, they will end up like East Timor, relying on the international community financially," he says.

Are globalization and regional integration fueling separatism?

Several organizations and treaties have emerged in recent years to encourage more regional integration and cross-border trade. The EU is the oldest and largest, but newer arrivals include the Association of Southeast Asian Nations (ASEAN), the African Union (AU), the Latin American trading blocs ANDEAN and MERCOSUR and the North American Free Trade Agreement (NAFTA). In addition, the World Trade Organization (WTO) is working to abolish trade barriers globally. Experts differ over whether these organizations promote or discourage separatism.

The Peace Institute's Grant believes they can encourage it. "What are the political impediments to independence?" he asks. The new states are not sustainable as a small unit, he says, adding, "If you reduce the significance of national borders and improve the free movement of people, goods and capital, you remove that impediment."

For instance, the possibility of being part of the EU's single market makes an independent Kosovo a more viable option and has seemingly suppressed Albania's desire to merge with the Albanians in Kosovo to create a Greater Albania. Asked if Albania had a plan to establish a Greater Albania, Foreign Minister Lulzim Basha said, "Yes, we do. It has a blue flag and gold stars on it," describing the EU flag. "Today's only goal is integration into NATO and the EU as soon as possible."[22]

Günter Dauwen, a Flemish nationalist who is director of the European Free Alliance political party in the European Parliament, says the EU fuels separatism by not adequately ensuring respect for regions. Dauwen is campaigning for more autonomy and possibly independence for Flanders, the mostly Dutch-speaking northern half of Belgium that already has a large degree of self-government. "The national capitals control the EU. They decide where funds for regional development go. This creates terrible tension."

Over-centralization of decision-making is particularly acute in Spain, he says, where it has triggered separatism in the region of Catalonia in the northeast and Galicia in the northwest. In addition, France suppresses regionalist parties in Brittany, Savoy and the French Basque country, he says. "When we complain to the EU, its stock answer is that only nation states can devolve power to the regions."

Dauwen points out that the European Court of Human Rights (ECHR) has condemned countries for not respecting the rights of ethnic minorities, but the EU doesn't force its members to comply with those rulings. For instance, he says, the ECHR condemned the Bulgarians for not allowing ethnic Macedonians to form their own political party. But the EU did nothing to force Bulgaria to abide by the ruling, further fueling the desire for separatism.

The State Department's Bryza disagrees. "The opposite works in my experience," he says. "As Hungary and Slovakia have deepened their integration into the EU, the desire of ethnic Hungarians who live in countries neighboring Hungary to become independent is receding. And the possibility for Turkish Cypriots in northern Cyprus [whose de facto state is only recognized by Turkey] to be part of the EU gives them an incentive to rejoin the Greek Cypriot government in the south, which is already in the EU."

Female Tamil Tiger fighters undergo training at a hideout deep in Tiger-controlled territory northeast of Colombo, Sri Lanka, in 2007. The Tamils, who comprise 18 percent of Sri Lanka's population, began fighting for independence in 1983 — a struggle that has resulted in the deaths of some 70,000 people. Tamils now control large swathes of the country.

Likewise, Ekaterina Pischalnikova — special assistant to the special representative of the secretary-general at the U.N. observer mission in Georgia, which is trying to resolve the Georgia-Abkhaz conflict — says EU regional integration has helped to "mitigate rather than fuel separatist movements."

Busdachin of the Unrepresented Nations and Peoples Organization says the EU "is helping to resolve separatist conflicts in many cases because it has the most advanced regime for protecting minorities." For example, the EU has consistently pressured Turkey, which wants to join the union, to grant the Kurds the right to express their language and culture more freely. Such a move could quell some Kurds' desire for full independence, he says, adding that he would like to see ASEAN, MERCOSUR and other regional organizations follow the EU model.

Author Kaplan — who has lived in Turkey, Nigeria, China and Japan — says regional integration "is only promoting separatism in the EU. Europe is peaceful and prosperous so there is no real need for states. But when you get into the wild jungle, the state is more important." For instance, he explains, "states in Africa and Central America do not want to give up their power, even though they would benefit the most from regionalism."

In Asia, ASEAN has no clearly defined policy on separatism, leaving it up to national governments to decide how to deal with separatist movements. The Shanghai Co-operation Organization (SCO) — set up in 2001 by Russia, China, Kazakhstan, Kyrgyzstan, Uzbekistan and Tajikistan to combat separatism, terrorism and extremism — strongly opposes separatist movements like that of China's Uyghurs.[23]

Ironically, separatism also can fuel regional integration. Many of the countries that have recently joined the EU or intend to do so — Lithuania, Slovakia, Slovenia, Montenegro and Macedonia — were formed from separatist movements. Too small to be economically self-sufficient, they see integration into the EU market as the only way to ensure continued prosperity and stability.

Does separatism lead to more violent conflict?

The recent developments in the Balkans provide strong evidence that separatism can provoke violent conflict — especially when countries divide along ethnic lines, as the former Yugoslavia has done.

Serbia's festering rage over Kosovo's declaration of independence is a prime example. "If this act of secession for ethnic reasons is not a mistake, then nothing is a mistake," said Serbia's Foreign Minister Vuk Jeremic, adding, "Serbia will not go quietly. We will fight, and we will not tolerate this secession."[24]

Serwer at the United States Institute for Peace says, "If you partition a state along ethnic lines, this almost inevitably leads to long-term conflict," especially if the central government resists the separatist movement.

"Secession converts a domestic ethnic dispute into a more dangerous one," according to Duke's Horowitz. "The recurrent temptation to create a multitude of homogeneous mini-states, even if it could be realized, might well increase the sum total of warfare rather than reduce it."[25]

The State Department's Bryza says separatism doesn't have to lead to violence "if leaders of national groups exert wise leadership and temper the ambitions of nationalist groups."

The campaign by Taiwanese separatists to obtain a seat for Taiwan at the U.N. — a March 22 referendum calling for this failed — shows how even nonviolent separatism can trigger conflict. "Bizarre as it may seem, a peaceful referendum in Taiwan may portend war," according to John J. Tkacik, a policy expert at the Heritage Foundation in Washington. He predicted China would invoke a 2005 anti-secession law to justify using "non-peaceful" means to counter Taiwanese separatism.[26] Fear of provoking a war with China is probably the main reason there is so little international support for the Taiwan independence movement.

As former U.S. Deputy Secretary of State Robert B. Zoellick said in 2006, "We want to be supportive of Taiwan, while we are not encouraging those that try to move toward independence. Because I am being very clear: Independence means war. And that means American soldiers."[27]

But independence does not always mean war. With a broadly homogeneous population, its own currency, flag, army, government and airline, Somaliland is an example of how a people can effectively secede without causing chaos and violence. Somaliland's isolation from the international community has not hindered its development — indeed it has helped, argues author Kaplan.

"The dearth of external involvement has kept foreign interference to a minimum while spurring self-reliance and self-belief," he says.

Martin at the Peace Institute points out that since the end of the Cold War, "most wars have been intra-state. Sometimes borders can be shifted to solve the problem and actually prevent war."

But separatist movements also are frequently manipulated by external powers as part of a geopolitical chess game that can become violent. "People want independence because of ethnic hatred and because it is in their economic interests to separate. But outside powers help separatists, too," says Koloski, of the United Macedonian Diaspora. For example, the United States, Britain and France support Kosovo's independence because they believe this will help stabilize the region, while Russia and China support Serbia's opposition because they fear it will encourage separatist movements elsewhere, including in their territories.

In some cases — notably Québec, Flanders, Wales and Scotland — separatist movements have not boiled over into violent conflict. In each, the central government granted some self-rule to the separatist region, preventing the situation from turning violent.[28] In addition, the movements were able to argue their case through elected political representatives in a functioning democratic system, which also reduces the likelihood of violence.

"When a country is too centralized and non-democratic, this produces separatist movements that can become violent," says Busdachin at the Unrepresented Nations and Peoples Organization. "The responsibility is 50-50."

But democracy does not always prevent separatism from escalating into conflict. From the 1960s to the '90s, extreme Irish Catholic nationalists in Northern Ireland waged a violent campaign to secure independence from the U.K., all the while maintaining a political party with elected representatives.

How the global community responds to one separatist movement can affect whether a movement elsewhere triggers a war. "Violence is not inevitable," says Flemish nationalist Dauwen. "But ethnic minorities do get frustrated when they get nowhere through peaceful means, and they see those who use violence — for example the Basque separatist movement ETA in Spain — attracting all the headlines."

As a Tamil activist notes, "Whatever we have achieved so far, we have got by force."

BACKGROUND

Emerging Nations

Throughout history separatism has manifested itself in various forms as groups grew dissatisfied with their

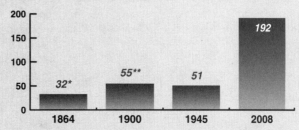

Number of Countries Reaches All-time High

The number of countries in the world has increased sixfold since the 1800s, when European colonization was at its peak. The greatest jump occurred after World War II, when Europe gave up its colonies amid a worldwide movement for independence. The United Nations, which includes nearly all of the world's countries, now has 192 members. The U.N. has not yet recognized Kosovo, which declared its independence in February.

Number of Countries Recognized Worldwide, 1864-2008

1864	32*
1900	55**
1945	51
2008	192

* Includes several states in Australia and New Zealand that were part of the British Empire; Finland and Poland were considered part of Russia; Africa is omitted entirely, since its interior was largely unmapped at that time. Since the U.S. Civil War was in progress, the Confederate States were counted as a separate country.

** The British Empire is counted as a single country, as are the French, German and Dutch empires; Austria-Hungary is considered one country and includes both Liechtenstein and Bosnia-Herzegovina; Finland and several Asian dependencies are counted as part of Russia; Turkey includes five states.

Sources: The Statesman's Year Book, 1864 and 1900; United Nations

governments. Even the Roman Empire — which was synonymous with order, peace and civilization in most of its conquered territories — had its Celtic resisters, the Britons and Gauls.[29]

In medieval Europe, the discontented sought to extricate themselves from kingdoms, feudal domains and churches. In the 18th and 19th centuries European colonies in the Americas, Australia and New Zealand began splitting off from the "mother" countries. By the 19th century, with the Hapsburg, Romanov and Ottoman empires on the decline, groups united by ethnicity, language or culture began to cast off their imperial shackles. Then in the late 1800s and early 20th century the major European powers — and the United States — began acquiring and consolidating colonies or territories.

Just three decades after its own war for independence from Great Britain, the United States had to weather its own secessionist storms. In 1814 a handful of New

CHRONOLOGY

1776-1944 *Nation states gradually eclipse multi-ethnic empires as the dominant form of government.*

1776 Britain's American colonies declare independence, triggering war.

Early 1800s Spanish and Portuguese colonies in Latin America become independent.

1861 Eleven Southern U.S. states secede, sparking Civil War. After four years of bitter fighting, the South loses and is reintegrated into the union.

1918 At the end of World War I new European states are created from the ashes of the Hapsburg and Ottoman empires.

1919 U.S. President Woodrow Wilson champions the "right of self-determination" but fails to get it adopted by the League of Nations.

1939 World War II breaks out. Borders shift as Germany, Japan and Italy occupy neighboring countries before being defeated by the Allies.

1945-1989 *More new states emerge as colonies gain independence, but borders are left largely intact.*

1945 U.N. charter includes the right of self-determination.

1949 China invades and occupies Tibet.

1960 U.N. General Assembly proclaims a Declaration on the Granting of Independence to Colonial Countries and Peoples, heralding the end of the colonial era.

1967 Biafra secedes from Nigeria; is reintegrated after a three-year war.

1975 World's leading powers sign the Helsinki Final Act, guaranteeing peoples the right of self-determination.

1984 A new, violent Kurdish separatist revolt breaks out in Turkey.

1990-2008 *Twenty-six new countries are created after the Soviet Union and Yugoslavia break apart.*

1990 Soviet republics begin resisting Moscow's central control. Lithuania on March 11 becomes the first republic to declare its independence, setting off a chain reaction that leads to the dissolution of the U.S.S.R.

1991 Slovenia and Croatia split from Yugoslavia, accompanied by violence, especially in Croatia. . . . New states emerge from the Soviet Union, as do unrecognized breakaway republics in Nagorno-Karabakh, Chechnya, South Ossetia, Abkhazia and Transdniestria. . . . In Africa, Somaliland separates itself from rapidly disintegrating Somalia.

1992 Bosnia splits from Yugoslavia, provoking a three-year war.

1993 Czechoslovakia splits peacefully into the Czech Republic and Slovakia. . . . Eritrea secedes from Ethiopia after a U.N.-monitored referendum.

1995 A referendum in Québec advocating secession from Canada is rejected by 50.6 percent of Québécois.

1999 North Atlantic Treaty Organization seizes Kosovo from Serbia in response to Serbia's persecution of Kosovar Albanians. . . . East Timor declares independence from Indonesia after 25 years of violence.

2004 The separatist region of Aceh is granted autonomy from Indonesia after a devastating Dec. 26 Indian Ocean tsunami creates a feeling of solidarity between Aceh's separatists and the Indonesian authorities.

2005 Chinese authorize use of force to prevent Taiwan from seceding.

2007 Belgium edges closer to disintegration. . . . In Bolivia, people of European descent threaten to secede in response to fears of losing control over the country's gas reserves.

2008 Taiwanese separatists are defeated in parliamentary elections on Jan. 12. . . . Kosovo declares independence from Serbia on Feb. 17, triggering violent protests among Serbs in Belgrade. Separatist protests in Tibet turn violent on March 14; Chinese send in troops to put down the rebellion.

England states opposed to the federal government's anti-foreign-trade policies and the War of 1812 organized a convention in Hartford, Conn., and produced a report spelling out the conditions under which they would remain part of the United States. The U.S. victory against the British in 1815 took the wind out of the initiative's sails, however, and secession negotiations never actually took place.

Then in 1861, largely in response to U.S. government efforts to outlaw slavery, 11 Southern states tried to secede from the union to form their own country. After a bloody, four-year civil war, the South was forcibly reintegrated into the United States in 1865.[30] The U.S. Supreme Court cemented the union with a ruling in 1869 (*Texas v. White*) that effectively barred states from unilaterally seceding.[31]

In 1914 nationalist opposition to imperialist expansionism in Europe sparked World War I. Aggrieved at the Austro-Hungarian Empire's annexation of Bosnia, home to many Serbs, 19-year-old Serbian Gavrilo Princip assassinated Archduke Franz Ferdinand, heir to the imperial throne. Many of the new countries created in the post-war territorial division, such as Lithuania and Poland, were constructed along broadly ethnic lines. At the same time the concept of "self-determination" — the right of a nation to determine how it should be governed — emerged, championed by President Woodrow Wilson.[32]

Wilson's effort to enshrine self-determination in the founding statute of the newly created League of Nations was defeated. The idea of holding a referendum to determine who should govern a disputed territory gained support in this period, too. And when the league set up a commission to determine the status of the Åland Islands (it determined Finnish sovereignty), the concept was developed that a people might have the right to secede when the state they belonged to did not respect their fundamental rights.[33]

One group, the Kurds, fared badly in the post-war territorial settlements. Emerging without a state of their own, Kurds repeatedly staged uprisings in Iraq, Iran and Turkey but were suppressed each time. The most recent and bloody of these has occurred in Turkey, where 40,000 people have been killed in an ongoing conflict that began in 1984. The Kurds in northern Iraq also suffered widespread massacres and expulsions in the late 1980s under Iraqi President Saddam Hussein, but when the United States and its allies defeated Saddam in the 1991 Gulf War, Iraqi Kurds effectively gained self-rule after the U.N. forced Saddam to withdraw from the region.[34]

The Palestinians were also dealt a poor hand in 1948 after their homeland became part of the new state of Israel, populated mainly by Jews fleeing post-war Europe. After winning the Six-Day War in 1967, Israel occupied Palestinian lands on the western bank of the Jordan River and in a narrow strip of land called Gaza. Ever since then, the Palestinians have been fighting to have a country of their own.[35]

Decolonization

The 20th century saw the number of independent countries around the globe more than triple — from the approximately 55 that existed in 1900 to the 192 that make up the United Nations today.[36] Most of the new nations were created in the post-World War II era, as the European powers shed their colonies in Africa and Asia. To ensure that the decolonization process was peaceful and orderly, the United Nations adopted the Declaration on the Granting of Independence to Colonial Countries and Peoples in 1960.[37]

But in practice the emergence of new states was often far from peaceful. Hundreds of thousands of people died in outbreaks of violence during the August 1947 partition of India and Pakistan, which within months went to war with each other over the disputed territory of Kashmir. In 1967 the Igbo people of Biafra tried to secede from Nigeria, triggering a devastating war and famine. Three years later the region was forcefully rejoined to Nigeria. Despite accusations that Nigeria was committing genocide on the Biafrans, the international community did not back Biafra's independence.

The former British colony of Somaliland in the horn of Africa became momentarily independent in 1960 but immediately chose to unite with its fellow Somalis in the newly constituted state of Somalia to the south created from Italy's former colony. When Somalia collapsed into violent anarchy in 1991, Somaliland seceded, and separatist militants installed a civil administration. In northern Ethiopia, Eritrea's 31-year secession struggle finally ended in independence in 1993 after passage of a U.N.-monitored referendum.

In Sri Lanka, which is dominated by Sinhalese people, the minority Tamils — who make up about 18 percent of the population — have been pushing for independence since the 1970s.[38] The Tamils had wielded considerable

Bye-Bye Belgium?

More prosperous Flanders wants autonomy.

Belgium experienced a surreal moment in December 2006 when a spoof news program on a French-speaking TV channel announced that Flanders, the country's Dutch-speaking region, had seceded. Footage of the king and queen of Belgium hastily boarding an airplane interspersed with shocked reactions from politicians convinced many viewers that their country was no more. Some even took to the streets to spontaneously rally for the Belgian cause.

But Dutch-speaking Flemings (as those who live in Flanders are called) were offended at how quickly their francophone compatriots (called the Walloons) believed Flanders had seceded. The incident triggered months of national soul-searching about the future of the country.

Fast-forward to the June 2007 general election, when the separatist-leaning Flemish Christian Democrats won the most seats in parliament and demanded that the constitution be amended to devolve more power to the regions, escalating an ongoing dispute between French and Dutch-speaking parties. The controversy became so fierce it took six months to form a government, and even then, it was only provisional, aimed at keeping the country united until the French- and Dutch-speaking communities could agree on a more long-term program. While a coalition pact was finally approved on March 18, bringing an end to the country's nine-month political limbo, the pact says nothing about devolution of powers, so the real battle has still to be fought.[1]

"If the French do not give us more autonomy, it's bye-bye Belgium," says Flemish nationalist Gunter Dauwen, director of the European Free Alliance, a political group that represents 35 nationalist parties in Europe.

Dauwen's party, Spirit, is demanding that unemployment benefits be paid for by the regional governments rather than the federal government. The jobless rate is higher in French-speaking Wallonia. Under Dauwen's plan, the Flemish would not have to subsidize the unemployed Walloons as they do now.

But such a lack of solidarity irks the Francophones. "We are a small country. We should all get the same benefits," says Raphael Hora, an unemployed Walloon. "You can't have a guy in Charleroi (Wallonia) getting less than a guy in Antwerp (Flanders)."

There is also a growing cultural chasm between Flemings and Walloons, he says. "I speak English, Italian, Spanish, Norwegian, German and Polish — but not Dutch. My father never wanted me to learn it."

Roughly 60 percent of Belgians speak Dutch, 39 percent speak French and the remaining 1 percent speak German. The Belgian constitutional system is Byzantine in its complexity, with powers dispersed between governments organized along municipal, linguistic, provincial, regional and national lines.

Hora, who recently moved to Berlin, sees Belgium's breakup as inevitable: "When it happens, I'll come back to Belgium and campaign for Wallonia to rejoin France. We'll be stronger then."

Dauwen insists independence for Flanders is not the goal for now. "My party is not campaigning for independence yet but for a confederation." Contrary to the widespread perception of Flemings as rampant separatists, Dauwen says, "We are all peaceful and not extreme." Flanders' largest pro-independence party, Vlaams Belang, actually lost support in last June's elections, although it remains a major force, garnering about 20 percent of Flemish voters.

According to Jérémie Rossignon, a landscape gardener from Wallonia living in Brussels, "Belgians are not very proud of being Belgian. They do not boast about their achievements and culture." He feels this is a pity, because Belgium has much to be proud of — from its world-renowned beers, chocolates and restaurants to its sports stars like tennis champ

---

influence when the island belonged to the British Empire but felt increasingly discriminated against after Sri Lankan independence in 1948. In the late 1970s and early '80s, when Indira Ghandi was India's prime minister, India — which is home to 70 million Tamils — supported the separatist "Tamil Tigers." But in the late 1980s her son and successor, Rajiv Ghandi, dispatched Indian troops to clamp down on the Tigers. He was later assassinated by a female Tamil suicide bomber, Thenmuli Rajaratnam.

Hopes of reconciliation were raised when Sinhalese and Tamil authorities agreed to rebuild areas devastated by the December 2004 Indian Ocean tsunami, which killed some 35,000 Sri Lankans. But the Sri Lankan Supreme Court struck down the agreement.

Justine Henin and the funky fashion designers of Antwerp to the eclectic euro-village that is Brussels.

"There is not much communication between the Francophones and Flemings any more," he continues. "Young Flemings speak English, not French, whereas their parents can speak French."

Meanwhile, he admits, the Francophones "are useless at foreign languages." Foreign-language movies and TV programs are dubbed into French, whereas in Flanders they are subtitled, he notes. The mostly French-speaking monarchy, which is supposed to unify the country, has become another cause of division. Belgium's Italian-born Queen Paola cannot speak Dutch, the language of 60 percent of her subjects, while Crown Prince Philippe has publicly slammed Flemish separatism.

Belgium's predominantly French-speaking capital, Brussels, is located in Flanders, and is seen alternately as a glue holding the country together or an obstacle preventing it from splitting apart. "The Walloons are trying to annex Brussels" by moving to the small strip of land in Flanders that separates Brussels from Wallonia, according to Dauwen. Elected representatives and residents in these municipalities squabble over which language should be used on official documents and street signs. And once a year the Flemings organize a bike ride — known as *Het Gordeel* (the belt) — around Brussels to send a symbolic message that Brussels must not extend itself further into Flanders.

The Francophones feel equally passionately. "The Romans conquered Brussels before the Germans did so we should stay French," says Marie-Paul Clarisse, a lifelong Bruxelloise, who works for an EU-affairs newspaper.

One compromise being floated would turn Brussels into Europe's Washington, D.C., and have it run by the EU, which is based in the city. An even wilder solution calls for tiny Luxembourg to annex Brussels and Wallonia.[2] And

Belgians Speak Three Languages

The Dutch-speaking portion of Belgium is called Flanders. The southern portion, Wallonia, includes both Francophones and German-speaking citizens. French is the predominant language of Brussels, the capital.

as if things were not complicated enough, Belgium also has an autonomous German-speaking community living in Wallonia. No one is quite sure what they want.

Even Rossignon, an ardent defender of Belgium, doubts its future: "The separatists will win out," he predicts, and the new government "will regionalize our country even more than it already is."

---

[1] "New Belgian Coalition Government Reaches Agreement," Agence France-Presse, March 18, 2008, http://afp.google.com/article/ALeqM5jhowUtJkHEsJRfNHhaSlnCb8-Zig.

[2] Laurent Lintermans, "Un Etat federal avec le Luxembourg?" *La Libre Belgique*, Aug. 18, 2007, www.lalibre.be/index.php?view=article&art_id=364931.

Dispersed across a vast plateau in the Himalayan mountains, Tibetans are a mostly Buddhist people with a 2,000-year written history and their own language, Tibetan, which is related to Burmese. China claims ownership of the region based on historical links with Tibetan leaders, which were especially strong in the 18th century. The Tibetans refute this claim and insist the

region was never an integral part of China and that from 1913 until 1949 Tibet existed as an independent state.

China invaded Tibet in 1949 and 1950, annexed it in 1951 and in 1965 created the Tibet Autonomous Region — a territory less than half the size of the region Tibetans consider their homeland.

Laws Are Ambiguous on Self-Determination

The right to self-determination — which allows people to secede from a mother state if they so choose — appears in various international conventions, including the founding document of the United Nations. But the international documents are ambiguous, because they also espouse the importance of "territorial integrity"— the right of countries not to have their territory dismembered.

International Texts Dealing with Self-determination and Territorial Integrity

U.N. Founding Charter (Article 1) — 1945

- One purpose of the United Nations is "to develop friendly relations among nations based on respect for the principle of equal rights and self-determination of peoples, and to take other appropriate measures to strengthen universal peace."

U.N. Resolution 2625 — 1970

- "Every State has the duty to refrain from any forcible action which deprives peoples referred to in the elaboration of the principle of equal rights and self-determination of their right to self-determination and freedom and independence."

- "Nothing in the foregoing paragraphs shall be construed as authorizing or encouraging any action which would dismember, or impair, totally or in part, the territorial integrity or political unity of sovereign and independent states conducting themselves in compliance with the principle of equal rights and self-determination of peoples and thus possessed of a government representing the whole people belonging to the territory without distinction to race, creed or color."

African Charter on Human and Peoples' Rights (Article 20) — 1981

- "All peoples shall have . . . the unquestionable and inalienable right to self-determination. They shall freely determine their political status and shall pursue their economic development according to the policy they have freely chosen."

Conference on Security and Co-operation in Europe's Charter of Paris for a New Europe — 1990

- "We affirm that the ethnic, cultural, linguistic and religious identity of national minorities will be protected."

- "We reaffirm the equal rights of peoples and their right to self-determination in conformity with the Charter of the United Nations and with the relevant norms of international law, including those related to territorial integrity of states."

Vienna Declaration and Program of Action adopted by World Conference of Human Rights — 1993

- The conference recognizes "the right of peoples to take any legitimate action, in accordance with the Charter of the U.N., to realize their inalienable right of self-determination."

Sources: Organization for Security and Co-operation in Europe, United Nations, University of Hong Kong, University of New Mexico, Unrepresented Nations and Peoples Organization

Over the past 60 years, according to the Tibetan government-in-exile, China has brutally repressed the Tibetans, killing 87,000 during the 1959 uprising against Chinese rule and destroying or closing down nearly all of the region's 6,259 monasteries by 1962. China unleashed more death and destruction against the Tibetans in 1966 during the Cultural Revolution, the Tibetans claim.[39]

In other regions, movements to allow ethnic minorities to express their cultures and govern their own affairs have flourished since the 1960s. Such efforts have succeeded among the Welsh in Scotland and the Basques in Spain. In Belgium divisions between Dutch-speakers in Flanders, who make up roughly 60 percent of the population, and the French-speakers of Wallonia widened as more power devolved from the central government to the regions. In Canada separatist aspirations among French-speakers, who make up about 80 percent of the population in the province of Québec, culminated in a 1980 referendum on independence that was rejected by 60 percent of the voters. A subsequent referendum in October 1995 failed by a smaller margin, with 50.6 percent voting No and 49.4 percent Yes.[40]

During the Cold War, the United States, the Soviet Union and others signed the Helsinki Final Act of 1975, which established, among other things, the principle of "equal rights and self-determination of peoples." Latvia, Lithuania and Estonia would later use this to justify seceding from the Soviet Union, according to a U.S. government official involved in overseeing implementation of the act. The 1977 Soviet constitution gave the constituent republics the right to leave the U.S.S.R., but the right was not exercised for fear of reprisals from Moscow.[41]

Mikhail Gorbachev — the Soviet leader from 1985 to 1991 whose "glasnost" policy of greater openness to the West proved to be a catalyst for the break-up the U.S.S.R. — had his doubts about self-determination. In his memoirs, he wrote that "the application by a community of its right to self-determination leads regularly to a corresponding attack on the other community. . . . It is obvious that the recognition of the rights of peoples to self-determination should not be absolute."[42]

Ethno-centrism Surges

The fall of communism in Eastern Europe in the late 1980s and early '90s unleashed a wave of nationalist sentiment that destroyed the two largest multi-ethnic states in the region — Yugoslavia and the Soviet Union. Lithuania got the ball rolling, declaring independence from the Soviets in March 1990. Within two years, 15 new states had emerged from the former Soviet Union and another four in the former Yugoslavia.[43]

Soon several of the new states were experiencing their own secession movements. Russia fought fiercely and successfully to suppress the independence aspirations of the Chechens, a Muslim people with a long history of resisting subjugation by Moscow. Largely Romanian-speaking Moldova saw its Russian-dominated Transdniestria region morph into a de facto yet unrecognized state with the help of the Russian military. Ethnic Armenians in Azerbaijan's Nagorno-Karabakh region set up their own

Yugoslavia Yields Seven New Nations

The former Yugoslavia has broken into seven new countries since 1991, and at least one additional province — the self-governing Republika Srpska in Bosnia and Herzegovina — is threatening to secede. Kosovo, on Serbia's southern border, declared its independence in February. The northern Serbian province of Vojvodina, populated by many Hungarians — is autonomous.

state in 1991, provoking a three-year war during which thousands of Azeris fled. Two regions — South Ossetia and Abkhazia — seceded from Georgia but have yet to be recognized by the international community.

Yugoslavia was torn asunder — eventually into seven new countries — due to the aggressive policies of nationalist leaders like Serbia's president, Slobodan Milosevic (1989-1997) and Croatia's president, Franjo Tudjman (1990-1999). The republics of Slovenia and Croatia in the northwest seceded in 1991, followed by Macedonia in the south and the triangular-shaped Bosnia and Herzegovina in 1992. The tiny republic of Montenegro seceded from Serbia in 2006. The province of Vojvodina in northern Serbia, populated by a substantial number of Hungarians, is autonomous but still part of Serbia.

Montenegro and Macedonia's splits were bloodless and Slovenia's relatively peaceful, but in Croatia and Bosnia

In northern Iraq's Qandil Mountains, recruits for a splinter group of the militant Kurdish PKK separatists are training to fight government troops across the border in Iran. Some 16-28 million Kurds are dispersed in Turkey, Iraq, Iran and Syria, making them the world's largest nation without its own country. The PKK wants a single Kurdish state; other Kurds seek either greater autonomy or independence from the countries where they live.

hundreds of thousands were either killed, fled persecution or were expelled, leading to the term "ethnic cleansing." NATO helped to take Kosovo, a province in Serbia whose autonomy was withdrawn in 1989, away from the Serbs in 1999 after Milosevic brutally cracked down on Kosovo Albanian separatists. Kosovo remained an international protectorate for the next nine years.

The Yugoslav experience highlighted the danger of using referenda to determine the status of territories. The Serbs living in Bosnia, who made up about a third of the population, did not want to secede from Yugoslavia so they boycotted the 1992 plebiscite. When it passed with the overwhelming support of the Bosnian Muslims and Croats, the Bosnian Serbs violently resisted integration into Bosnia, and a three-year war ensued. The EU had helped to trigger the referendum by imposing a deadline on the Yugoslav republics to request recognition as independent countries.[44]

In 1993, Czechoslovakia split into the Czech and Slovak republics even though no referendum was held, and opinion polls indicated most citizens wanted to keep the country together.[45] The split came about because the leading politicians decided in 1992 that a peaceful divorce was easier than negotiating a new constitution with the Czechs favoring a more centralized state and the Slovaks wanting more autonomy.

In August 1999 East Timor seceded from Indonesia after a U.N.-supervised referendum. East Timor's annexation by Indonesia in 1975 had never been recognized by the U.N., and the East Timorese were Catholic, unlike the predominantly Muslim Indonesians, since the area had been colonized by Portugal.

The path to independence was a bloody one. The Indonesian military supported anti-independence militias who killed some 1,400 Timorese, causing 300,000 to flee, and destroyed much of the country's infrastructure. Australian-led international peacekeepers helped restore order in September 1999, and Timor Leste became a U.N. member on Sept. 27, 2002.[46]

By contrast, the separatist movement in Aceh has never succeeded in gaining independence, despite a decades-long struggle. Instead, the Free Aceh Movement and the Indonesian government signed a peace treaty in 2005, granting Aceh autonomy. The rapprochement was facilitated by a feeling of solidarity that grew out of the December 2004 Indian Ocean tsunami, which killed more than 130,000 people in Aceh.

CURRENT SITUATION

Balkan Pandora's Box

The shock waves emanating from Kosovo's Feb. 17 declaration of independence show that separatism remains an explosive issue. For Prime Minister Hashim Thaçi, a former separatist guerrilla, "independence is everything for our country and our people. We sacrificed, we deserve independence, and independence of Kosovo is our life, it's our future."[47]

The Kosovars waited until Serbia's presidential elections were over before seceding in order to deny the more nationalistic Serb candidate, Tomislav Nikolic, the chance to make political hay out of the declaration. On Feb. 3, Nikolic narrowly lost to his more moderate opponent, Boris Tadiç. Kosovo also deliberately made its declaration before Russia assumed the presidency of the U.N. Security Council on March 1, knowing that Moscow opposes its independence.

At this stage, few expect Serbia to launch a military offensive to take back Kosovo, given the strong NATO presence in the region. The Serbs instead are vowing to diplomatically freeze out any countries that recognize

Kosovo. Russia's ambassador to the EU, Vladimir Chizhov, warned in February that such recognition would be "a thorn in our political dialogue."[48] This has not prevented more than 30 countries so far from endorsing Kosovo's independence, including the United States, Canada, Australia and much of Europe.

Some fear that recognizing Kosovo will open a Pandora's box of ethnically motivated separatism. For example, the ethnic Serbs in Bosnia and Herzegovina, who have already largely separated themselves from the rest of Bosnia by creating Republika Srpska, on Feb. 21 pledged to hold a referendum on secession. But the republic's chances of gaining acceptance as an independent country are slimmer than Kosovo's, because both the EU and the United States firmly oppose it.

Romania and Slovakia worry that their large Hungarian minorities could feel emboldened to demand more autonomy or even unification with Hungary. Hungarians in the Romanian region of Transylvania are already demanding that Romanian law recognize their ethnically based autonomy.[49]

Frozen Conflicts

Russia's heavy clampdown on separatists in Chechnya serves as a stark warning to other ethnic groups in the region with separatist leanings not to push for independence. The predominantly Muslim Chechens had managed to gain de facto independence from Moscow in their 1994-1996 war, but Russia recaptured the territory in 1999. Tens of thousands have been killed in these conflicts and hundreds of thousands displaced.

Ethnic violence has also spread to other neighboring republics in the North Caucasus like Dagestan, North Ossetia and Ingushetiya, where disparate rebel groups are fighting for more autonomy or independence. To prevent the Balkanization of Russia, the Putin government cracked down hard on the violence.

Meanwhile, the Central Asian republics of Kazakhstan, Tajikistan, Uzbekistan, Turkmenistan and Kyrgyzstan no longer are as economically integrated as they were during the Soviet era, fueling corruption. Reportedly officials

What Is a Nation?

The words nation, state and country are often used — incorrectly — as if they are interchangeable. But international law and usage today make clear distinctions in the concepts, as set out by U.S. lawyer and diplomat Henry Wheaton in his 1836 text Elements of International Law.

A "nation," he wrote, implies "a community of race, which is generally shown by community of language, manners and customs."

A country — or "state" — refers to "the union of a number of individuals in a fixed territory, and under one central authority," Wheaton explained. Thus a state "may be composed of different races of men" while a nation or people "may be subject to several states."

Wheaton noted that in ancient Rome, the philosopher and orator Cicero defined a state as "a body politic, or society of men, united together for the purpose of promoting their mutual safety and advantage by their combined strength."

Source: Henry Wheaton, *Elements of International Law,* 1836.

routinely demand bribes from traders and workers seeking to move goods or personnel across the new borders.[50] Some of the new states, like Kyrgyzstan, are weak and at risk of fragmenting or being subsumed by their neighbors.[51]

Transdniestria, Nagorno-Karabakh, South Ossetia and Abkhazia remain unrecognized de facto states, since Moldova, Azerbaijan and Georgia all lack the military or economic strength to recapture the four breakaway territories. The long, narrow valley of Transdniestria — which has a population of Russians, Moldovans and Ukrainians — is "like a Brezhnev museum," according to a U.S. government official involved in reconciliation efforts there, referring to the Soviet leader from 1964 to 1982 whose regime was characterized by stagnation and repression. "It is a nasty place: the rulers repress the Moldovan language, and the economy is largely black market." And Georgia's two secessionist regions — South Ossetia and Abkhazia — are egged on by Russia, according to the State Department's Bryza.

These so-called frozen conflicts have produced "an impasse of volatile stability [where] nobody is happy but nobody is terribly unhappy either, and life goes on, as neither central state nor de facto states have collapsed," writes Dov Lynch, author of a book on the conflicts and director of the U.S. Institute for Peace project. Up to a million people have been displaced, standards of living have dropped as economies barely function, organized

AP Photo/Martial Trezini

Wearing symbolic chains, a Uyghur protester in Geneva demands self-rule for the predominantly Muslim, ethnically Turkic Uyghurs in China's autonomous western region of Xinjiang. He also opposes China's one-child policy, which human rights advocates say forces some pregnant mothers to get abortions. China says recent separatist unrest in Tibet has triggered protests in Xinjiang, where some 500 Uyghurs held a demonstration in Khotan on March 23.

crime flourishes and a "profound sense of psychological isolation" prevails.[52]

In one of those ongoing conflicts, the militant Kurdish separatist organization, the PKK, has stepped up its violent campaign against Turkey, which has responded with a military strike into the PKK's base in northern Iraq.[53] The Kurds in northern Iraq already govern themselves. Some pragmatic Kurdish leaders feel their best solution would be to replicate this model in Iran, Syria and Turkey — where they do not have autonomy — instead of pushing for a single Kurdish state.

Meanwhile, the Israeli-Palestinian conflict seems to be edging towards a "two-state solution" under which the Palestinians would be given a state of their own in the West Bank and Gaza in exchange for acknowledgment of Israel's right to exist. However, the region's ongoing violence makes reaching a final agreement problematic.

In Africa, Somaliland looks to be creeping towards acceptance as a state, too. An African Union mission in 2005 concluded that Somaliland's case for statehood was "unique and self-justified" and not likely to "open a Pandora's box." Nevertheless, its neighbors continue to oppose recognizing it formally.[54]

Asian Disputes

The separatist movement in Sri Lanka remains strong. The Tamil Tigers run a de facto state in the northeast and are fiercely fighting the Sri Lankan government, which wants to regain control of the whole country. On Feb. 4 — the 60th anniversary of the country's independence — Sri Lankan President Mahinda Rajapaksa affirmed his commitment to "go forward as a single, unitary state."[55]

According to a Tamil activist who asked not to be identified, Sri Lanka is squeezing the Tamil-controlled area with an economic embargo and preventing international aid organizations from providing humanitarian supplies. Though Pakistan, India and China are helping the Sri Lankan government, the Tamils are holding onto their territory, he says, with the help of Tamils who have fled the country and are dispersed throughout the world. This "diaspora" community is providing funds for weapons that the guerrillas buy covertly from Asian governments, he says.

In Aceh, the 2005 self-rule pact with Indonesia "is working to some extent," according to a U.S. official in Indonesia. With rising crime, high unemployment, little trade with the outside world and little experience in spending public money, "the challenge for the ex-rebels is to become good governors. They need help from the international community," the official says.

Separatism in Taiwan received a blow in the January 2008 parliamentary and March 2008 presidential elections when the Kuomintang Party, which supports reunification with mainland China, trounced the separatist Democratic Progressive Party (DPP), which seeks U.N. membership for Taiwan.[56]

For its part, the United States continues to sit on the fence, reflecting the international community's ambivalence

Could separatism spread to the United States?

YES

Kyle Ellis
*Founder, Californians
for Independence*

Written for *CQ Global Researcher*, March 2008

Asking whether separatism will spread to the United States is a bit of an odd question to pose in a nation founded through an act of secession from the British Empire.

Secession is at the very foundation of what it means to be American, and over the years since the country was founded many secessionist organizations and movements have kept this American tradition alive.

If you think the Civil War ended the question of secession in the United States, any Internet search you run will show just how wrong you are. Dozens of groups in various states are organizing and agitating for secession.

These groups are getting larger, and more serious ones are being founded all the time. As the leader and founder of one of these new organizations, I would like to offer a little insight as to why I believe the idea of secession will become a lot more popular in the years to come.

Here in California, there is much resentment toward the federal government. People don't like how politicians who live thousands of miles away are able to involve themselves in the creation of California's laws and the allocation of local resources, not to mention the billions of tax dollars sent away each year that are never to be seen again.

Other states have other reasons for wanting independence: Vermonters see the federal government as fundamentally out of touch with their way of life; the Southern states believe their unique culture is being systematically destroyed by the actions of the federal government; and Alaska and Hawaii view the circumstances surrounding their admittance into the Union as being suspect, if not downright undemocratic.

All of these groups view the federal government as broken in such a way that it cannot be fixed from within the system — a valid view considering it is run by two political parties that are fundamentally statist in nature. The two-party system is not even democratic (as we know from the 2000 elections), because it effectively disenfranchises millions of third-party voters due to the winner-take-all nature of political contests.

The federal government also continues to encroach upon individual rights and liberties.

It is natural that marginalized and disenfranchised people will seek to break away from a system they are not a part of, just as the founders of the United States sought to break away from Britain.

NO

Seth D. Kaplan
*Foreign Policy Analyst and Business Consultant
Author,* Fixing Fragile States: A New
Paradigm for Development

Written for *CQ Global Researcher*, March 2008

Separatism requires a cohesive minority group that dominates a well-defined geographical area and possesses a strong sense of grievance against the central government. All three of these ingredients were present when the United States had its own encounter with separatism: the Confederacy's bid for independence in the 1860s. Southern whites possessed a unique identity, dominated a contiguous territory and were so aggrieved at the federal government that they were prepared to take up arms.

In recent decades, another disaffected and socioculturally distinct group in North America has waged a potent — but in this case nonviolent — campaign for independence: Canada's Québécois. Within the United States, however, no such groups exist today, and none seems likely to emerge in the foreseeable future. Puerto Rico does have a separatist movement, but Puerto Rico is already semi-autonomous and, more to the point, is only an unincorporated organized territory of the United States — not a full-fledged state. Some argue that California is close to reaching a level of economic self-sufficiency that would enable it to survive as an independent state. However, even if California could afford to be independent, neither its sense of difference nor of grievance seems likely to become strong enough to form the basis for a separatist movement.

Some Native American tribes, discontented with their circumscribed sovereignty, might wish to separate but — even if Washington raised no objections — their small populations, weak economies and unfavorable locations (inland, distant from other markets) would not make them viable as independent states.

The cohesiveness of the United States stands in marked contrast to most of the world's large, populous states. China, India, Indonesia and Pakistan all contend with separatist movements today.

Why has the United States escaped this danger? The answer lies in the impartiality of its institutions, the mobility of its people and the brevity of its history. Its robust and impartial institutions do not provide ethnic or religious groups with a strong enough sense of discrimination to ignite separatist passions. Its citizens migrate within the country at an unprecedented rate, ensuring a constant remixing of its population and tempering any geographically focused sense of difference. And its history as a relatively young, immigrant country — where people focus on the future far more than the past — means that few are fiercely loyal to any particular area.

toward Taiwan. According to Susan Bremner, the State Department's deputy Taiwan coordinating adviser, the United States has "not formally recognized Chinese sovereignty over Taiwan and [has] not made any determination as to Taiwan's political status."[57] In the past, however, the United States has said that if China were to bomb or invade Taiwan, it would help defend the island.[58]

In western China, the Uyghurs continue to see their proportion of the population decline as more ethnic Chinese migrate there. Chinese tourists are flooding in, too, as visiting EU official Fearghas O'Beara recently discovered in Kashgar. "The city was as foreign to the Chinese as it was to me," he said. "At times I felt a bit uneasy as well-to-do Chinese people took copious photos of the 'natives' with their quaint habits and clothing."[59]

Eclipsing all these movements are the newest round of protests by Tibetans that began in March, the 49th anniversary of a failed uprising against Chinese rule in Tibet. Protesters in Lhasa on March 14 burned, vandalized and looted businesses of ethnic Chinese immigrants, venting their seething resentment over the wave of immigration that has turned Tibetans into a minority in their capital city.[60] The Tibetans say 99 people were killed, but the Chinese put the figure at 22.[61] Though the Chinese riot police were initially slow to respond, Beijing is now cracking down hard on the protesters. It also is keeping monks elsewhere confined to their monasteries and forcing them to denounce the Dalai Lama. China accuses the exiled leader of orchestrating the violence — calling him "a vicious devil" and a "beast in human form" — even though he has condemned the violence and advocates autonomy rather than outright independence for Tibet.[62]

Before the outbreak of violence, a Chinese Foreign Ministry spokesman had urged the Dalai Lama to drop his "splittist" efforts to attain "Tibetan independence" and do more for average Tibetans. "The Dalai clique repeatedly talks about Tibetan culture and the environment being ruined. But in fact, the Tibetan society, economy and culture have prospered," said spokesman Qin Gang. "The only thing destroyed was the cruel and dark serfdom rule, which the Dalai clique wanted to restore."[63]

The 72-year-old Dalai Lama, Tibet's leader for 68 years, commands enormous respect around the world, as evidenced by U.S. President George W. Bush's decision to telephone China's President Hu Jintao on March 26 to urge the Chinese government "to engage in substantive dialogue" with the Dalai Lama.[64]

Tension over China's suppression of the Tibetans is mounting as some countries consider calling for a boycott of the Beijing Olympics in August to show solidarity with the Tibetans. European foreign ministers, meeting in Brdo, Slovenia, on March 28-29, came out against an outright boycott of the games, although the leaders of France and the Czech Republic are threatening to boycott the opening ceremony. And on April 1, U.S. House Speaker Nancy Pelosi, D-Calif., urged President Bush to reconsider his plans to attend the opening ceremony if China continues to refuse talks with the Dalai Lama.

But Bush at the time was becoming entangled in yet another separatist controversy. Stopping in Ukraine on his way to a NATO summit in Romania, Bush said he supports Georgia's entry into NATO, which Russia opposes. If Georgia were to join the alliance, the NATO allies could be forced to support any future Georgian military efforts to re-take South Ossetia and Abkhazia — also strongly opposed by Russia. That would put Georgia in the middle of the same geopolitical chess game that Kosovo found itself in.[65]

Secession in the Americas

Across the Americas, separatist movements are scarcer and weaker than in Europe, Africa and Asia. Perhaps the most significant is the recent flare-up in Bolivia, where the mainly European-descended lowlanders are pushing for greater regional autonomy and are even threatening secession.[66] They are wealthier than the mostly indigenous highlanders and fear that the centralization efforts of indigenous President Evo Morales will loosen the lowlanders' grip on Bolivia's natural resources. Already, Morales has proposed amending the constitution so that oil and gas revenues would be shared evenly across the country.[67]

There are also plans to redistribute a huge portion of Bolivia's land — beginning with its forests — to indigenous communities. Vice Minister of Lands Alejandro Almaraz, who is implementing the project, said recently the tension with the lowlanders was "very painful" and warned that "the east of Bolivia is ready to secede and cause a civil war" to thwart the government's redistribution plans.[68]

In the United States, separatism remains a marginal force, though the movement has never been more visible.

"There are 36 secessionist organizations now at work," including in New Hampshire, Vermont, California, Washington state, Oregon and South Carolina, says Kirkpatrick Sale, director of the Middlebury Institute, a think tank on secessionism that he established in 2004.

In Texas, Larry Kilgore — a Christian-orientated secessionist who wants to enact biblical law — won 225,783 votes or 18.5 percent in the March 4 primary for Republican candidate to the U.S. Senate.[69] "If the United States is for Kosovo's independence, there is no reason why we should not be for Vermont's independence," says Sale. "The American Empire is collapsing. It is too big, corrupt and unequal to survive."

Some Native American tribes with limited self-government continue to push for more autonomy. For example, a group of dissident Lakota Indians traveled to Washington in December 2007 to deliver a declaration of independence to the State Department, which did not respond.[70]

OUTLOOK

Ethnocentric Separatism

The growing tendency to construct states along ethnic lines does not necessarily bode well for the future. French philosopher Ernest Renan's warning, delivered in the era of empires and grand alliances, has as much resonance today as it did in 1882: "Be on your guard, for this ethnographic politics is in no way a stable thing and, if today you use it against others, tomorrow you may see it turned against yourselves."[71]

"The Kosovo case is not unique despite the many claims to that effect by European and American diplomats," says Serwer at the United States Institute for Peace. "If people worry about it being a precedent, they should have ensured its future was decided by the U.N. Security Council. That would have created a good precedent for deciding such things."[72]

Though some might support the creation of a U.N. body for assessing separatist claims, U.N. member states would most likely fear it would only serve to give more publicity to separatist causes, writes American University self-determination expert Orentlicher.[73]

The two Western European regions most likely to become independent within the next 10 years are Scotland and Flanders, says Flemish nationalist Dauwen. As for Transdniestria, "the more time that passes, the more likely it will become independent, because the military will resist rejoining Moldova," says a U.S. official working to promote peace in Eastern Europe. The passage of time usually increases the survival odds of unrecognized states, because entrenched elites who profit from their existence fight to preserve them regardless of how politically or economically viable the states are.[74]

The probability of separatist movements morphing into new states also depends on who opposes them. Nagorno-Karabakh, for instance, is more likely to gain independence from Azerbaijan than Chechnya is from Russia because the Azeris are weaker than the Russians.

Political leadership is another factor. When hardliners and extremists rise to power it triggers separatist movements, while the emergence of moderates willing to share power can entice separatist regions to be peacefully and consensually reintegrated into the mother country.

Ethnocentric separatism may also fuel irredentism — annexation of a territory on the basis of common ethnicity. For instance, the Albanians in Macedonia, Kosovo and Albania may push to form a single, unitary state. Ethnic Hungarians living in Romania, Serbia and Slovakia may seek to forge closer links with Hungary; Somalis scattered across Somaliland, Kenya, Ethiopia and Djibouti might decide to form a "Greater Somalia."

"The goal of attaining recognition is the glue holding it together," a State Department official said about Somaliland. "If recognized, I fear that outside powers will interfere more, and it could split."

Likewise, Kurds in Iraq, Turkey, Iran and Syria could rise up and push for a "Greater Kurdistan" encompassing all Kurds. While some countries might support the creation of a Kurdish state in theory, they would be reticent, too, knowing how much it could destabilize the Middle East.

In Southeast Asia, Myanmar (formerly Burma), Thailand and the Philippines are potential separatist hotbeds as tensions persist between the many different ethnic groups, with religious differences further aggravating the situation.[75] "If something moves in the region, it could have a tsunami effect, as happened in Eastern Europe in 1989," says Busdachin at the Unrepresented Nations and Peoples Organization. He adds that most of these groups are seeking autonomy, not independence.

Yet a U.S. official in Indonesia says of Aceh: "I would be very surprised if we would have a new country in

15 years. I don't see that dynamic. Things are moving in the other direction."

And in Taiwan, any push for U.N. membership would worry trading partners like the European Union and the United States, which are keen to maintain good relations with the island but reluctant to anger China.

As for the United States, the strong federal government that emerged during the Great Depression seems to be on the wane as state and local governments increasingly assert their powers. Yet the nation remains well-integrated, and outright secession of a state or group of states seems unlikely. Smaller changes are possible, however, such as the splitting of California into northern and southern states or the evolution of the U.S.-governed Puerto Rico into a new U.S. state or independent country.

In the long term, separatism will fade, author Kaplan believes. "Separatism always appears on the rise when new states are born because such entities do not have the deep loyalties of their people typical of older, successful countries," he says. But as states mature, he notes, the number of separatist movements usually declines.

A starkly different prediction is made by Jerry Z. Muller, history professor at The Catholic University of America in Washington. "Increased urbanization, literacy and political mobilization; differences in the fertility rates and economic performance of various ethnic groups and immigration will challenge the internal structure of states as well as their borders," he wrote. "Whether politically correct or not, ethnonationalism will continue to shape the world in the 21st century." Globalization will lead to greater wealth disparities and deeper social cleavages, he continues, and "wealthier and higher-achieving regions might try to separate themselves from poorer and lower-achieving ones." Rather than fight the separatist trend, Muller argues, "partition may be the most humane lasting solution."[76]

NOTES

1. For detailed accounts of the protests, see *The Economist*, "Trashing the Beijing Road," March 19, 2008, www.economist.com/opinion/displaystory .cfm?story_id=10875823 and Tini Tran, "Tibetan Protests Escalate into Violence," The Associated Press, March 14, 2008, http://news.yahoo.com/s/ap/20080314/ap_on_re_as/china_tibet.

2. Ellie Tzortzi, "US outrage as Serb protesters burn embassy," Reuters, Feb. 21, 2008, www.reuters.com/article/worldNews/idUSL2087155420080221?pageNumber=1&virtualBrandChannel=0.

3. See "In quotes: Kosovo reaction," BBC News, Feb. 17, 2008, http://news.bbc.co.uk/1/hi/world/europe/7249586.stm.

4. See European Commission's Web site for political and economic profiles of Serbia and Kosovo, http://ec.europa.eu/enlargement/potential-candidate-countries/index_en.htm.

5. Selcan Hacaoglu and Christopher Torchi, "Turkey launches ground incursion into Iraq," The Associated Press, Feb. 22, 2008, www.washingtontimes.com/apps/pbcs.dll/article?AID=/20080222/FOREIGN/297026899/1001.

6. For list of current U.N. member states, see the U.N.'s Web site, www.un.org/members/list.shtml.

7. To see growth in U.N. membership, go to www.un.org/members/growth.shtml.

8. See "Kurdistan — Kurdish Conflict," globalsecurity.org, www.globalsecurity.org/military/world/war/kurdistan.htm.

9. Lisa Schlein, "East Timor Facing Food Crisis," June 24, 2007, www.voanews.com/english/archive/2007-06/2007-06-24-voa8.cfm?CFID=213682651&CFTOKEN=33049644.

10. Fried was testifying at a hearing on the Balkans at the U.S. House of Representatives Committee on Foreign Affairs, March 12, 2008. For full testimony go to: http://foreignaffairs.house.gov/testimony.asp?subnav=close.

11. Gary J. Bass, "Independence Daze," *The New York Times*, Jan. 6, 2008, www.nytimes.com/2008/01/06/magazine/06wwln-idealab-t.html?ref=magazine.

12. Several Uyghurs were detained in the U.S. terrorist prison in Guantánamo Bay, Cuba. According to James Millward, history professor at Georgetown University, Washington, D.C., the Uyghurs' detention in Guantánamo became an embarrassment for the United States when it emerged they were pro-U.S. and anti-China. The U.S. administration decided it could not send them back to China because they would probably be mistreated. Although the United States asked more than 100 other countries to

take them, all refused except Albania, where some of the detainees were ultimately expatriated in 2006.

13. Chinese Foreign Ministry spokesperson Qin Gang at press conference, March 18, 2008, www .china-embassy.org/eng/fyrth/t416255.htm.

14. Jay Shankar, "Pelosi Urges Probe of Chinese Claim Dalai Lama Behind Unrest," Bloomberg News, March 21, 2008, www.bloomberg.com/apps/news? pid=20601101&sid=aDLLITUsmrIg&refer=japan.

15. Seth D. Kaplan, "Democratization in Post-Colonial States: The Triumph of a Societal-Based Approach in Somaliland," in *Fixing Fragile States: A new paradigm for development* (scheduled for publication July 2008).

16. Harvey Feldman, fellow in China policy for the Heritage Foundation, speaking at a discussion on Taiwanese elections in Washington, D.C., Jan. 15, 2008.

17. In November 2004, a group of about 50 secessionists, gathered for a conference in Middlebury, Vt., signed a declaration pledging to develop cooperation between the various secessionist groups in the United States, including setting up a think tank, The Middlebury Institute, devoted to studying separatism, secessionism and self-determination. See www .middleburyinstitute.org.

18. Diane Orentlicher, "International Responses to Separatist Claims: Are Democratic Principles Relevant," Chapter 1 of Stephen Macedo and Allen Buchanan, eds., *Secession and Self-Determination* (2003), p. 29.

19. Interview with Nicolas Gros-Verheyde, "Europe should develop its defence policy with Russia," *Europolitics* (EU affairs subscription-based news service), March 4, 2008, www.europolitics.info.

20. Donald L. Horowitz, "A Right to Secede," Chapter 2 of Macedo and Buchanan, *op. cit.*, p. 50.

21. *Ibid.*, p. 73.

22. Basha was speaking at the Center for Strategic and International Studies in Washington, D.C., on May 5, 2007.

23. Lecture on Shanghai Cooperation Organization by Professor Akihiro Iwashita, visiting fellow at the Brookings Institution, delivered at the Woodrow Wilson International Center for Scholars, Feb. 2, 2008.

24. Jeremic was addressing the European Parliament's Foreign Affairs Committee in Strasbourg, Feb. 20, 2008. See the press release at www.europarl.europa .eu/sides/getDoc.do?pubRef=-//EP//TEXT+IM-PR ESS+20080219IPR21605+0+DOC+XML+V0// EN&language=EN.

25. Horowitz, *op. cit.*, p. 56.

26. John J. Tkacik, "Dealing with Taiwan's Referendum on the United Nations," Heritage Foundation, Sept. 10, 2007, www.heritage.org/about/staff/ JohnTkacikpapers.cfm#2007Research.

27. Zoellick's remark, made at a U.S. congressional hearing on China on May 10, 2006, was quoted in John J. Tkacik, "America's Stake in Taiwan," Heritage Foundation, Jan. 11, 2007, www.heritage.org/Research/ AsiaandthePacific/bg1996.cfm.

28. For background, see "Nationalist Movements in Western Europe," *Editorial Research Reports*, April 16, 1969, available at *CQ Researcher Plus Archive*, www.library.cqpress.com.

29. Adapted quote from Ernest Renan, French philosopher and theoretician on statehood and nationalism, in his discourse "What is a nation?" widely viewed as the definitive text on civic nationalism (1882).

30. For more details, see Mark E. Brandon, Chapter 10, "Secession, Constitutionalism and American Experience," Macedo and Buchanan, *op. cit.*, pp. 272-305.

31. The case is 74 U.S. 700 (1868), available at http:// caselaw.lp.findlaw.com/scripts/getcase.pl?court= US&vol=74&invol=700.

32. See Patricia Carley, "Self-Determination: Sovereignty, Territorial Integrity, and the Right to Secession," *Peaceworks 7*, March 1996, p. 3, www.usip.org/ pubs/peaceworks/pwks7.html.

33. Orentlicher, *op. cit.*, p. 21.

34. For more details, see Washington Kurdish Institute, "The Territorial Status of Kirkuk," position paper, November 2007, http://71.18.173.106/pages/ WO-PositionPapers.htm#.

35. For background, see Peter Katel, "Middle East Tensions," *CQ Researcher*, Oct. 27, 2006, pp. 898-903.

36. Figures taken from *The Statesman's Yearbook*, an annual reference book on the states of the world that first appeared in 1864, and from the U.N. Web site, www.un.org/members/list.shtml.

37. For full text of the 1960 U.N. Declaration on the Granting of Independence to Colonial Countries and Peoples, go to www.un.org/Depts/dpi/decolonization/declaration.htm.

38. For background, see "Sri Lanka," *Political Handbook of the World*, CQ Press (2007).

39. According to the Central Tibetan Administration Web site, www.tibet.net/en/diir/chrono.html.

40. For background, see Mary H. Cooper, "Québec Sovereignty," *CQ Researcher*, Oct. 6, 1995, pp. 873-896.

41. Under Article 72 of the 1977 U.S.S.R. Constitution, "Each Union Republic retains the right freely to secede from the U.S.S.R," www.departments.bucknell.edu/russian/const/1977toc.html.

42. Mikhail Gorbachev and Odile Jacob, ed., *Avant Memoires* (1993), p. 30.

43. The 15 ex-Soviet states could have been 16. Karelia, a region now part of western Russia bordering Finland, used to be a separate Soviet republic until 1956 when its status was downgraded to an autonomous republic within Russia.

44. Orentlicher, *op. cit.*, p. 36.

45. *Ibid.*, p. 33.

46. See CIA, *The World Factbook*, https://www.cia.gov/library/publications/the-world-factbook/geos/tt.html.

47. Reported on CNN.com, Jan. 9, 2008, http://edition.cnn.com/2008/WORLD/europe/01/09/kosovo.independence/index.html.

48. Joanna Sopinska, "Russia in last-ditch bid to block Kosovo mission," *Europolitics* (EU affairs subscription-based news service), Feb. 7, 2008, www.europolitics.info.

49. See Medlir Mema, "Kosovo through Central European eyes," Jan. 2, 2008, Center for European Policy Analysis (CEPA), www.cepa.org/digest/kosovo-through-central-european-eyes.php.

50. From lecture by researchers Kathleen Kuehnast and Nora Dudwick at the Woodrow Wilson International Center for Scholars, Nov. 27, 2006.

51. From discussion with Professors Anthony Bowyer, Central Asia and Caucasus Program Manager at IFES, the International Foundation for Election Systems, Eric McGlinchey, associate professor at George Mason University, and Scott Radnitz, assistant professor at the University of Washington, at the School for Advanced International Studies, Dec. 12, 2007.

52. Dov Lynch, *Engaging Eurasia's Separatist States* (2004), pp. 91-93.

53. Al Jazeera, "Toll rises in Turkey-PKK conflict," http://english.aljazeera.net/NR/exeres/3E14DD15-F2D1-4C65-8148-5200DFB3E975.htm.

54. Kaplan, *op. cit.*

55. The president's speech can be viewed in English at www.priu.gov.lk/news_update/Current_Affairs/ca200802/20080204defeat_of_terrorism_is_victory_for_all.htm.

56. See "Opposition's Ma wins Taiwan poll," BBC News, March 22, 2008, http://news.bbc.co.uk/2/hi/asia-pacific/7309113.stm.

57. Letter from Susan Bremner, deputy Taiwan coordinating adviser at the U.S. State Department, June 26, 2007, quoted in article by Tkacik, "Dealing with Taiwan's Referendum on the United Nation," *op. cit.*

58. See Peter Brookes, "US-Taiwan Defense Relations in the Bush administration," Nov. 14, 2003, www.heritage.org/Research/AsiaandthePacific/hl808.cfm.

59. Travel diary of Fearghas O'Beara, media adviser to the president of the European Parliament, who toured the region in August 2007.

60. Jim Yardley, "As Tibet Erupted, China Security Forces Wavered," *The New York Times*, March 24, 2008, www.nytimes.com/2008/03/24/world/asia/24tibet.html?ex=1364097600&en=58a6edae8ae26676&ei=5088&partner=rssnyt&emc=rss.

61. *Ibid.*

62. See "Chinese Crackdown on Tibetan Protests," "The Diane Rehm Show," National Public Radio, March 20, 2008, http://wamu.org/programs/dr/08/03/20.php#19471; also see Pico Iyer, "A Monk's Struggle," *Time*, March 21, 2007, www.time.com/time/world/article/0,8599,1723922,00.html; also see Louisa Lim, "China's Provinces Feel Crush of Tibet Crackdown,"

National Public Radio, March 28, 2008, www.npr.org/templates/story/story.php?storyId=89160575&ft=1&f=1004.

63. "China urges Dalai Lama to drop splittist attempts," *Xinhua News Agency*, March 11, 2008.

64. See White House press release at www.whitehouse.gov/news/releases/2008/03/20080326-2.html.

65. Joanna Sopinska, "Ministers condemn Tibet crackdown, reject Olympic boycott," *Europolitics*, March 31, 2008, www.europolitics.info. See Peter Baker, "Bush Pushes NATO Membership for Ukraine, Georgia," *The Washington Post*, April 1, 2008.

66. See Kaplan, *op. cit.*, Chapter 9, "Bolivia: Building Representative Institutions in a Divided Country." Also see Roland Flamini, "The New Latin America," *CQ Global Researcher*, March 2008, pp. 57-84.

67. Flamini, *ibid.*, p. 79.

68. Almaraz was giving a presentation on his land reform proposals at the George Washington University in Washington on March 11, 2008.

69. Primary results posted on *The Austin Chronicle's* Web site, www.austinchronicle.com/gyrobase/Issue/story?oid=oid%3A599906.

70. Bill Harlan, "Lakota group secedes from U.S." *Rapid City Journal*, Dec. 21, 2007, www.rapidcityjournal.com/articles/2007/12/21/news/local/doc476a99630633e335271152.txt.

71. Renan, *op. cit.*

72. See Daniel Serwer, "Coming Soon to a Country Near You: Kosovo Sovereignty," *Transatlantic Thinkers*, December 2007, www.usip.org/pubs/usipeace_briefings/2007/1214_kosovo.html.

73. Orentlicher, *op. cit.*, p. 37.

74. Lynch, *op. cit.*, p. 119.

75. See Joseph Chinyong Liow, "Muslim Resistance in Southern Thailand and Southern Philippines: Religion, Ideology and Politics," East-West Center, Washington, 2006, www.eastwestcenter.org/fileadmin/stored/pdfs/PS024.pdf.

76. Jerry Z. Muller, "Us and Them: The Enduring Power of Ethnic Nationalism," *Foreign Affairs*, March/April 2008, www.foreignaffairs.org/20080301faessay87203/jerry-z-muller/us-and-them.html.

BIBLIOGRAPHY

Books

Kaplan, Seth D., *Fixing Fragile States: A New Paradigm for Development,* **Praeger Security International, 2008.**
A business consultant who has founded successful corporations in Asia, Africa and the Middle East uses various case studies from around the world to analyze what makes states function and why they become dysfunctional.

Lynch, Dov, *Engaging Eurasia's Separatist States — Unresolved Conflicts and De Facto States,* **United States Institute of Peace Press, 2004.**
The director of a U.S. Institute of Peace project describes the "frozen conflicts" in the breakaway republics of Transdniestra, Nagorno Karabakh, South Ossetia and Abkhazia.

Macedo, Stephen, and Allen Buchanan, *Secession and Self-Determination: Nomos XLV,* **New York University Press, 2003.**
In a series of essays, different authors debate whether there should be a right to secede and analyze specific secessionist cases, notably Québec and the pre-Civil War Southern U.S. states.

Articles

"The Territorial Status of Kirkuk," *Washington Kurdish Institute,* **November 2007, http://71.18.173.106/pages/WO-PositionPapers.htm#.**
The institute argues that Kirkuk should be unified with the Kurdish region of northern Iraq.

Mema, Medlir, "Kosovo Through Central European Eyes," *Center for European Policy Analysis,* **Jan. 2, 2008, www.cepa.org/digest/kosovo-through-central-european-eyes.php.**
A Balkans scholar explains how many of the countries near Kosovo that have sizeable ethnic minorities are wary of the precedent set by an independent Kosovo.

Muller, Jerry Z., "Us and Them: The Enduring Power of Ethnic Nationalism," *Foreign Affairs,* **March/April 2008, pp. 18-35.**
A professor of history at Catholic University argues in the magazine's cover story that ethnic nationalism will drive global politics for generations.

Ponnambalam, G. G., "Negotiation with Armed Groups: Sri Lanka and Beyond," *Tufts University symposium*, April 6, 2006, http://fletcher.tufts.edu/news/2006/04/ponnambalam.shtml.
An academic paper by a member of the Sri Lankan parliament charts the unsuccessful efforts by the Sri Lankan authorities and Tamil separatists to end their conflict.

Renan, Ernst, "What is a Nation?" March 11, 1882, www.tamilnation.org/selfdetermination/nation/renan.htm.
This classic lecture by a French philosopher and theoretician on statehood and nationalism at the Sorbonne University in Paris is viewed as the definitive text on civic nationalism.

Serwer, Daniel, "Coming Soon to a Country Near You: Kosova Sovereignty," *Bertelsmann Stiftung Transatlantic Thinkers series*, December 2007, www.usip.org/pubs/usipeace_briefings/2007/1214_kosovo.html.
A conflict resolution expert argues for Kosovo's independence.

Tkacik, John J., "Dealing with Taiwan's Referendum on the United Nations," *Heritage Foundation*, Sept. 10, 2007, www.heritage.org/about/staff/JohnTkacikpapers.cfm#2007Research.
A China policy scholar assesses how the international community should respond to the ongoing campaign by Taiwanese separatists to obtain a U.N. seat for Taiwan.

Reports and Studies

Carley, Patricia, "Self-Determination: Sovereignty, Territorial Integrity, and the Right to Secession," *United States Institute of Peace, Peaceworks 7*, March 1996, www.usip.org/pubs/peaceworks/pwks7.html.
A conflict resolution expert outlines the main issues in the self-determination debate, including the uncertainty over what the right entails and who is entitled to claim it.

Gutierrez, Eric, and Saturnino Borras, Jr., "The Moro Conflict: Landlessness and Misdirected State Policies," *East-West Center Washington*, 2004, www.eastwestcenter.org/fileadmin/stored/pdfs/PS008.pdf.
The authors explain how resentment over not having control of their land has fueled separatism among the Muslim Moros in the southern Philippines.

Millward, James, "Violent Separatism in Xinjiang: A critical assessment," *East-West Center Washington*, 2004, www.eastwestcenter.org/fileadmin/stored/pdfs/PS006.pdf.
A history professor at Georgetown University in Washington highlights the plight of the Uyghurs, a Turkic people living in western China, where separatist tensions are simmering.

Schulze, Kirsten E., "The Free Aceh Movement: Anatomy of a Separatist Organization," *East-West Center Washington*, 2004, www.eastwestcenter.org/fileadmin/stored/pdfs/PS002.pdf.
A senior history lecturer at the London School of Economics discusses the history of the separatist movement in the Indonesian province of Aceh since 1976. The paper was published just prior to the brokering of a peace agreement in 2005.

For More Information

Center for Strategic and International Studies, 1800 K St., N.W., Washington, DC 20006; (202) 887-0200; www.csis.org. Think tank focused on regional stability, defense and security.

Centre for the Study of Civil War, P.O. Box 9229, Gronland NO-0134, Oslo, Norway; +47 22 54 77 00; www.prio.no/cscw. An autonomous center within the International Peace Research Institute, Oslo, that studies why civil wars break out, how they are sustained and what it takes to end them.

Commission on Security and Co-operation in Europe (Helsinki Commission), 234 Ford House Office Building, Washington, DC 20515; (202) 225-1901; www.csce.gov. An independent agency of the U.S. government created to promote democracy, human rights and economic development.

European Free Alliance, Woeringenstraat 19, 1000 Brussels, Belgium; +32 (0)2 513-3476; www.e-f-a.org/home.php. A political alliance consisting of regionalist and nationalist parties in Europe seeking greater autonomy for regions and ethnic minorities through peaceful means.

Middlebury Institute, 127 East Mountain Road, Cold Spring, NY 10516; (845) 265-3158; http://middlebury institute.org. Studies separatism, self-determination and devolution, with a strong focus on the United States.

United Nations Observer Mission in Georgia, 38 Krtsanisi St., 380060 Tbilisi, Georgia; (+995) 32 926-700; www.un.org/en/peacekeeping/missions/past/unomig/. Established by the U.N. in 1993 to verify that the Georgian and Abkhaz authorities are complying with their ceasefire agreement.

United States Institute of Peace, 1200 17th St., N.W., Washington, DC 20036; (202) 457-1700; www.usip.org. An independent agency funded by Congress to prevent and resolve violent international conflicts and to promote post-conflict stability and development.

Unrepresented Nations and Peoples Organization, P.O. Box 85878, 2508CN The Hague, the Netherlands; +31 (0)70 364-6504; www.unpo.org. An umbrella organization that promotes self-determination for various indigenous peoples, occupied nations, ethnic minorities and unrecognized states.

Washington Kurdish Institute, 611 4th St., S.W., Washington, DC 20024; (202) 484-0140; www.kurd.org. Promotes the rights of Kurdish people and awareness of Kurdish issues.

Nuclear Disarmament

3

*Will President Obama's Efforts
Make the U.S. Safer?*

Jennifer Weeks

President Barack Obama called for new efforts to stop the spread of nuclear weapons during an address before the U.N. General Assembly on Sept. 23. The next day the Security Council called for nuclear reductions and disarmament and tighter controls on nuclear technology. Many experts warn that abolishing nuclear weapons would make the world less safe, in part by enabling terrorists and rogue states to threaten other nations.

AFP/Getty Images/Stan Honda

From *CQ Researcher*,
October 2, 2009.

S peaking to the United Nations General Assembly on Sept. 23, President Barack Obama pledged his administration would work with other nations to strengthen world peace and prosperity.

"First, we must stop the spread of nuclear weapons, and seek the goal of a world without them," Obama said. "If we fail to act, we will invite nuclear arms races in every region, and the prospect of wars and acts of terror on a scale that we can hardly imagine."[1]

It is an ambitious goal, especially for the United States. Nuclear weapons have been integral to U.S. defense policy since the end of World War II. Even today, nearly 20 years after the Cold War ended, the United States still spends more than $50 billion every year on nuclear armaments and related programs, including weapons systems, missile defenses and environmental and health costs from past nuclear weapons production.[2]

Many civilian and military experts say abolishing nuclear weapons is impossible. Moreover, they argue, doing so would make the world less safe, because rogue states and terrorists would feel freer to threaten other countries.

But in 2007, four men who had shaped U.S. national security policy for decades — both Democrats and Republicans — warned that relying on nuclear weapons to keep the peace was "becoming increasingly hazardous and decreasingly effective." The problem, said former secretaries of state Henry Kissinger and George Shultz, former Defense Secretary William Perry and former Senate Armed Services Committee Chairman Sam Nunn, was that countries like India, Pakistan, North Korea and Iran were seeking the bomb, and a global black market in nuclear materials was expanding. Instead,

Nuclear Weapons Network Spans Seven States

Eight nuclear facilities in seven states make up the U.S. nuclear weapons complex. Responsibilities at each site range from the design and production of the nation's nuclear arsenal to testing and improving bomb yield.

The U.S. Nuclear Weapons Network

① Pantex: Tests, retrofits and repairs weapons in the stockpile and dismantles surplus nuclear weapons.

② Kansas City Plant: Produces non-nuclear components for nuclear weapons.

③ Y-12: Produces and reworks nuclear weapon components and stores enriched uranium and plutonium.

④ Savannah River: Produces radioactive tritium to boost the yield of nuclear weapons.

⑤ Los Alamos National Laboratory: Designs and certifies the safety and reliability of the explosive cores of nuclear weapons; oversees refurbishment of all weapons in the stockpile.

⑥ Lawrence Livermore National Laboratory: Designs and certifies safety and reliability of nuclear weapons; conducts research on weapons physics.

⑦ Sandia National Laboratory: Designs the non-nuclear components of nuclear weapons.

⑧ Nevada Test Site: Performed nuclear tests until 1992; conducts underground sub-critical tests and maintains the capability to resume testing if so directed.

Source: "Nuclear Matters: A Practical Guide," Office of the Under Secretary of Defense for Acquisition, Technology and Logistics, 2008

his predecessor, George W. Bush, had argued were needed to replace older weapons in the U.S. arsenal. On April 5, in Prague, Czechoslovakia, Obama laid out a broad agenda for moving toward nuclear abolition. First, he said, the U.S. would reduce the role of nuclear weapons in its own security strategy by:

- Negotiating new strategic (long-range) arms reductions with Russia;
- Ratifying a treaty ending nuclear weapons testing; and
- Seeking a new international treaty to end production of fissile materials for nuclear weapons.[4]

Obama also proposed strengthening the Nuclear Non-Proliferation Treaty (NPT), under which 188 nations have pledged not to seek nuclear weapons, by:

- Giving international inspectors more authority;
- Agreeing on consequences when nations break the rules; and
- Creating an international nuclear-fuel bank so countries with nuclear power reactors would not need nuclear technology to produce their own fuel.

Finally, Obama announced new actions to keep nuclear weapons away from terrorists, including measures to secure vulnerable nuclear materials worldwide and stronger programs to detect nuclear smuggling.

"I'm not naïve. This goal will not be reached quickly — perhaps not in my lifetime," Obama said. "But now we, too, must ignore the voices who tell us that the world cannot change."[5]

Obama took another important step in mid-September, canceling Bush administration plans to deploy antimissile

they argued, the best way to reduce nuclear dangers was to work toward completely eliminating nuclear weapons.[3]

President Obama agrees. His proposed fiscal 2010 budget eliminates funds for designing new nuclear warheads, which

defense systems in Poland and the Czech Republic. The installations were intended to defend Europe against missile strikes from Iran. But Russian leaders saw them as a provocative intrusion into Eastern Europe and argued that the system might be expanded and reconfigured to threaten Russia. Instead, the Obama administration said it would field shorter-range interceptors, initially based on ships, which could be targeted more easily against Iranian threats.[6]

Russian Prime Minister Vladimir Putin called Obama's move a "correct and brave decision."[7] But conservatives said Obama was undermining U.S. security commitments to European allies. "Given the serious and growing threats posed by Iran's nuclear and missile programs, now is the time when we should look to strengthen our defenses, and those of our allies," said Republican senator and former presidential candidate John McCain of Arizona. "I believe the decision to abandon [the land-based system] unilaterally is seriously misguided."[8]

On Sept. 24 the Security Council unanimously passed a resolution urging all countries to work toward nuclear reductions and disarmament and to put tighter controls on nuclear technologies and materials.[9] U.N. Secretary-General Ban Ki-Moon welcomed the council's new resolve and urged states to follow through on the resolution. "Together we have dreamed about a nuclear-weapon-free world. Now we must act to achieve it," he said.

Other heads of state who had long supported faster nuclear reductions echoed the secretary-general. "While we sleep, death is awake. Death keeps watch from the warehouses that store more than 23,000 nuclear warheads, like 23,000 eyes open and waiting for a moment of carelessness," said Oscar Arias Sanchez, president of Costa Rica.[10]

The world has lived with nuclear threats for more than 60 years, but today's challenges differ dramatically

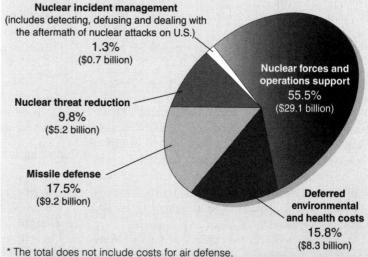

Budget on Nuclear Weapons Exceeds $52 Billion

At least $52 billion was appropriated for nuclear weapons and related expenses in fiscal 2008.* Most of the money was allocated for nuclear forces and operations support.

U.S. Nuclear Weapons-Related Appropriations, FY 2008 (includes nuclear delivery systems, warheads and bombs)

Nuclear incident management
(includes detecting, defusing and dealing with the aftermath of nuclear attacks on U.S.)
1.3%
($0.7 billion)

Nuclear threat reduction
9.8%
($5.2 billion)

Missile defense
17.5%
($9.2 billion)

Nuclear forces and operations support
55.5%
($29.1 billion)

Deferred environmental and health costs
15.8%
($8.3 billion)

* The total does not include costs for air defense, antisubmarine warfare, classified programs and most nuclear-weapons-related intelligence programs.

Note: Figures do not total 100 due to rounding.

Source: Stephen I. Schwartz and Deepti Choubey, "Nuclear Security Spending: Assessing Costs, Examining Priorities," Carnegie Endowment for International Peace, 2009

from those during the Cold War, when the greatest global security risk was war between the United States and the Soviet Union. Under the doctrine of "mutual assured destruction," each country fielded tens of thousands of nuclear weapons to ensure that it could survive a first strike and still inflict catastrophic damage on its enemy. The policy kept the peace, advocates argued, by making each side afraid to start a war.

But accidents and misread signals nearly caused nuclear explosions more than once, when nations came close to nuclear exchanges or troops mishandled their own nuclear weapons. (*See sidebar, p. 70.*) Many experts still worry that too many nuclear weapons are on high alert, and that U.S. or Russian leaders might misinterpret an accidental launch as a planned strike and respond by launching more missiles and killing millions of people.

Now the threat of terrorism has compounded the danger. "The greatest threat to our security is that al Qaeda will acquire a nuclear weapon from Pakistan's or Russia's arsenal, or the material to build one from any of a dozen countries that don't guard their material adequately," says Joseph Cirincione, president of the Ploughshares Fund, which supports efforts to prevent the spread of nuclear weapons. "Another risk is that nuclear weapons could be used in a regional war — for example, between India and Pakistan."

The United States and Soviet Union (succeeded by Russia) have always possessed nearly all the nuclear weapons in the world. Together they have about 24,500 nuclear weapons today, down from a peak of roughly 64,000 in 1986.[11] (*See graph, p. 64.*) More than half of these weapons are held as spares, in reserve, or are awaiting dismantlement. But advocates say the U.S. and Russia should make further cuts, both to reduce the risk of a nuclear exchange and to build support for strong, global nonproliferation policies.

"The NPT requires the nuclear powers to move toward disarmament," says Daryl Kimball, executive director of the nonprofit Arms Control Association. "If we don't, other countries will be less willing to support tough controls on nuclear bomb material and sanctions on countries that try to develop nuclear weapons. Treading water is not a feasible option. And nuclear weapons aren't practical tools to deal with terrorist threats or conventional conflicts. Their only defensible purpose is to deter use of nuclear weapons by another country, and only Russia has an arsenal as big as ours."

Most advocates agree the U.S. should maintain a strong deterrent force as long as other countries have nuclear weapons. Earlier this year, a congressionally appointed bipartisan commission concluded the United States could make more nuclear reductions jointly with Russia, but it recommended retaining bombers, land-based missiles and submarines to deliver them. The report also left open an option for developing new warheads, and commission members disagreed over ending U.S. nuclear testing.[12]

Defense hawks argue that treaties constrain the U.S. but do nothing to reduce threats from countries determined to acquire nuclear weapons. One of their prime examples, Iran, made headlines less than 24 hours after the Security Council's disarmament resolution, when it was revealed that Iran was building a secret underground plant to enrich uranium.[13]

Obama and his British and French counterparts accused Iran — a member of the NPT — of flouting its non-nuclear pledges. Obama warned that if Iran did not disclose all of its nuclear activities immediately, it would face "sanctions that bite." But critics said negotiations would not curb Iran's alleged bomb program.

"In the bitter decades of the Cold War, we learned the hard way that the only countries that abide by disarmament treaties are those that want to be disarmed," *The Wall Street Journal* argued in an editorial.[14]

In the debate over U.S. nuclear policies, here are some issues under consideration:

Can all nuclear weapons be eliminated?

The United States has officially supported abolishing nuclear weapons ever since President Lyndon B. Johnson signed the Non-Proliferation Treaty in 1968. Article VI requires the five countries that then possessed nuclear weapons (United States, Soviet Union, Britain, France and China) to "negotiate in good faith on effective measures relating to the cessation of the nuclear arms race at an early date and to nuclear disarmament."[15] But advocates disagreed then and now about how quickly that should happen.

Today, arms reduction advocates say key steps to nuclear abolition include:

- Ending nuclear testing so that nations cannot develop new weapons;
- Ceasing production of fissile material for military use;
- Setting up a global civilian nuclear fuel bank so nations won't need to build plants that can produce bomb-usable material; and
- Drastically reducing U.S. and Russian nuclear arsenals.

Disarmament advocates argue that once the superpowers have made major cuts, perhaps below 1,000 warheads each, other nations with nuclear weapons would join the disarmament process. As arsenals shrink toward zero, they say, all countries then would have to accept intrusive inspections and monitoring to show that they were keeping their pledges.

Some supporters envision such a scenario within several decades. For example, Global Zero, an international coalition led by more than 100 former political and military leaders from the United States, Russia, China, Britain, and other countries, issued a plan last June to eliminate nuclear weapons by 2030.[16] "It's in the national interest of every country to live in a world free of nuclear weapons," says former U.S. Air Force nuclear weapons launch officer Bruce Blair, president of the World Security Institute in Washington and a Global Zero coordinator.

As evidence of worldwide support for abolition, Blair notes that 188 countries have signed the NPT, and only nine nations worldwide — the five recognized in the treaty plus India, Pakistan, Israel and North Korea — possess nuclear weapons.[17] What's more, a number of countries have abandoned once-secret nuclear weapons programs since the 1970s, including South Korea, Brazil, Argentina, Taiwan, South Africa and, most recently, Libya.[18]

In Blair's view, serious efforts to eliminate nuclear weapons will make it increasingly hard for the four hold-out nations to keep going against the tide. "All other countries are currently members of the NPT, which obligates them to remain nuclear weapons-free. So they would have no reason not to sign a Global Zero accord, and strong reason to support the trend toward zero," Blair says.

Others believe disarmament will take more than political pressure. "You would have to believe that there will be a time when Russia doesn't feel beleaguered and dependent on nuclear weapons, that Israel feels at peace with its neighbors and that India isn't at war with Pakistan," says Linton Brooks, who headed the National Nuclear Security Administration during George W. Bush's administration. "Then you have to ask how we'll know that people have given up nuclear weapons. Then you have to figure out what to do if you discover somebody is cheating."

In Brooks's view, the solution will take many decades and should not divert attention from current nuclear challenges. "Abolition has focused a lot of intellectual energy in the think-tank community on something that will happen in 40 and 50 years, instead of current problems like what we'll do if we can't keep Iran from producing nuclear

weapons," he warns. "I think we're not spending enough intellectual time on near-term problems."

Another argument often raised against going to zero points out that the basics of how nuclear weapons work are widely known. "Proliferating states, even if they abandoned these devices under resolute international pressure, would still be able to clandestinely retain a few of their existing weapons — or maintain a standby, break-out capability to acquire a few weapons quickly, if needed," wrote former Defense Secretary Harold Brown and former Energy Secretary and CIA Director John Deutch in 2007.[19]

But others say a breakout nation could not achieve very much with a handful of nuclear bombs. "Nuclear weapons make it harder for other people to threaten you and conquer you, but they're not good for blackmailing or getting your way in many international political situations," says Stephen Walt, a professor of international affairs at Harvard University.

Going nuclear actually may be counterproductive for would-be regional powers like Iran, Walt contends, because their neighbors will arm in response. "Iran will have more influence in the Persian Gulf if no one has nuclear weapons, so I think it's in their interest not to develop nuclear weapons," he says. "The way we make that point is to stop holding a gun to their heads and try to persuade them that they're better off not weaponizing their technology. They should know that if they produce weapons they'll go to the top of our potential terrorist source list. Our goal should be persuading them to be more like Japan and less like Pakistan."

Making disarmament viable for countries like Pakistan with enemies next door will require creative strategies for taming regional conflicts. "Pakistani leaders are worried about an attack from India, so giving them enough political will to abandon nuclear deterrence may mean creating a demilitarized zone between Pakistan and India," says Sharon Squassoni, a senior associate at the Carnegie Endowment for International Peace. "The weakest nation with nuclear weapons will have to feel comfortable letting go of that safety net and believe that it will be better off without it."

Should the United States end nuclear testing?

From 1945 through 1992 the United States detonated more than 1,000 nuclear weapons. Most other nuclear

Global Stockpiles on the Decline

The United States has a little more than 5,200 nuclear weapons stockpiled this year, about one-sixth of the amount it had in the mid-1960s when stockpiles were at their highest. Similarly, stockpiles have steadily declined for Russia since the collapse of the Soviet Union.

U.S., Russian Nuclear Stockpiles, 1945-2009

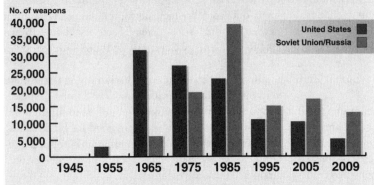

Note: France, China and the United Kingdom have a few hundred nuclear weapons each.

Source: Natural Resources Defense Council

and reliable over time, and that ending U.S. tests would have little impact on proliferator countries.[22]

In 1999 Senate Republicans forced a quick debate and rejected the CTBT on a 51-48 vote. Support fell far short of the 67 votes required under the Constitution to ratify a treaty, even though the Energy and Defense departments and Joint Chiefs of Staff urged approval. In his Prague speech earlier this year, President Obama promised to try again.

"After more than five decades of talks, it is time for the testing of nuclear weapons to finally be banned," Obama said.

But critics argued that without testing the nation's nuclear deterrent would be weakened. Sen. Jon Kyl, R-Ariz., and former Assistant Secretary of Defense Richard Perle asserted that ending nuclear testing, together with Obama's decision not to fund new nuclear warhead designs, amounted to "unilateral disarmament by unilateral obsolescence."[23]

CTBT supporters predict that all Senate Democrats will support ratification and that some Republicans who voted no in 1999 will reconsider their positions, including Sens. Richard Lugar of Indiana and Arizona's McCain. (As a presidential candidate in 2008, McCain promised to keep an open mind on the issue.) But others still believe the treaty undercuts U.S. security interests.

"I know of no information that suggests that the matters that led the Senate to reject the treaty have changed for the better," said Sen. Kyl earlier this year. "CTBT, a bad idea shrouded in good intentions, would not even be capable of detecting political tantrums like the North Korean test [in May], even when the international monitoring system is told where and when to look."[24]

In fact, the CTBT's international monitoring system — with 130 seismic monitoring stations worldwide — detected North Korea's first test in 2006 as well as last May's test, which registered as far away as Texas. On the day of the test, CTBT officials said the system could pinpoint the location of the explosion to an area the size of

nations, including Russia, Britain, France, China, India, Pakistan and North Korea, are known to have also carried out nuclear tests.

Arms control advocates have long sought a global ban on nuclear testing to keep nations from developing and validating new warhead designs. Since 1996, 148 countries have signed and ratified the Comprehensive Test-Ban Treaty (CTBT), which bars members from carrying out or helping with nuclear explosions and sets up an international monitoring system to detect clandestine tests. If a member country is suspected of conducting a test, other countries can request on-site inspections of its facilities.[20] But for the CTBT to enter into force, it must be ratified by nine more states: the U.S., China, North Korea, Egypt, India, Indonesia, Iran, Israel and Pakistan.[21]

President Bill Clinton signed the CTBT in 1996, but the Republican-controlled Senate delayed action on ratifying the treaty. Although the United States had adopted a moratorium on nuclear tests five years earlier (initiated by a Democratic Congress), many conservative critics argued the treaty was not verifiable because cheaters could easily hide low-level nuclear tests. They also contended tests were essential to assure that U.S. nuclear weapons remained safe

Berlin, and would be able to make that estimate much more precise with further analysis.[25]

Such findings indicate the CTBT can detect cheaters, advocates say. "The design objective for the monitoring system was to be able to detect explosions measuring one kiloton or less in any medium anywhere in the world, and it looks as though we're doing better than that," says Princeton University physicist Frank von Hippel, a former arms control adviser during the Clinton administration. "North Korea's test was a fraction of a kiloton. Seismologists have become very sophisticated at discriminating between explosions and other signals like earthquakes. A nuclear test is a sudden expansion of a gas in all directions, and that creates a very different signal from two sides of a fault shifting against each other." (*See "At Issue," p. 76.*)

Advocates of continued testing question whether the Department of Energy can maintain a robust nuclear weapons stockpile without conducting tests, in part because some of the precisely engineered materials in nuclear weapons change over time, including plutonium cores and the chemical explosives that compress bomb cores to critical mass. A 2002 National Academy of Sciences study acknowledged that aging would make stewardship of the U.S. stockpile increasingly challenging, but said, "[W]e see no reason that the capabilities of those mechanisms . . . cannot grow at least as fast as the challenge they must meet."[26]

The directors of the three DOE laboratories that design and build nuclear weapons (Los Alamos and Sandia in New Mexico and Lawrence Livermore in California) must certify annually to Congress that U.S. nuclear weapons are safe and reliable. (*See map, p. 60.*) So far they have made that certification each year, but questions persist. "[A]s the weapons age, a thing that is referred to as margins begins to decrease," said Gen. Kevin Chilton, head of the U.S. Strategic Command, early last year. "A simple way to think of [margin] is the likelihood it's going to work the way you want it to work the day you need it. . . . And margin, because of shelf life and chemistry, is decreasing."[27]

Siegfried Hecker, a professor of management science and engineering at Stanford University and former director of Los Alamos National Laboratory, argues that stockpile stewardship creates some uncertainty and is a slower and more expensive way to resolve certain questions than testing. But Hecker nonetheless supports

ratifying the CTBT because, in his view, other nations need nuclear tests more than the U.S. does.

"The single most important reason to ratify the CTBT is to stop other countries from improving their arsenals — China, India, Pakistan, North Korea, and Iran if it ever progresses that far," says Hecker. "We gain substantially more from limiting other countries than we lose by giving up testing — even with a gradual loss of confidence, which stockpile stewardship has held to an acceptable level. The U.S. has carried out more than 1,000 nuclear tests, and the Chinese have done about 45. You can see the difference in the sophistication of our arsenals."

Does the United States need new nuclear weapons?

The United States built its last nuclear weapon in 1992 — nearly 20 years ago — and today experts sharply disagree over whether new weapons are needed. New-construction advocates say the thousands of weapons in the current stockpile were not designed for shelf lives longer than about 20-30 years, and that simply refurbishing them would leave uncertainty about how they will perform. Opponents say the stockpile is reliable and can be kept that way through regular maintenance, and that producing new models would signal an expanding role for nuclear weapons in U.S. security policy.

After the Persian Gulf War in 1991, when air strikes failed to destroy many of Iraq's underground military facilities, some defense planners proposed developing low-yield nuclear weapons that could destroy buried targets. Congress rejected the idea in 1993, barring work on "mini-nukes" with explosive yields of five kilotons or less. But conservative legislators and weapon designers continued to press the issue of usable nuclear weapons to destroy "very hard targets."[28]

Spurred by its search for al Qaeda leader Osama bin Laden in the caves of Afghanistan, the Bush administration sought funding from Congress starting in 2003 for a Robust Nuclear Earth Penetrator (RNEP). But critics, led by Rep. David Hobson, R-Ohio, argued the so-called "bunker buster" would cause too much damage in the area surrounding a target, and that building it would undermine U.S. nonproliferation policy. "It gave people a lot of reason to build their own weapons," Hobson later said.[29]

After Congress zeroed out bunker buster funding in 2004 and 2005, Hobson urged the Bush administration instead to develop what became known as the Reliable Replacement Warhead (RRW) program to design safer, more durable replacements for the most problematic weapons in the stockpile. But when DOE responded by proposing an entire new generation of nuclear warheads, Hobson and other critics zeroed funding for RRW, arguing that first the U.S. needed to develop post-Cold War deterrence strategies and decide how many weapons it needed to carry them out.[30]

Although Obama did not include RRW in his fiscal 2010 budget request, some senior administration officials are on record supporting new nuclear weapons. In October 2008, Defense Secretary Robert Gates described the long-term outlook for the U.S. nuclear stockpile as "bleak," thanks to aging weapons and an aging nuclear work force. RRW, said Gates, "is not about new capabilities — suitcase bombs or bunker busters or tactical nukes. It is about safety, security and reliability. It is about the future credibility of our strategic deterrent, and it deserves urgent attention."[31]

At a congressional hearing last March, the Strategic Command's Gen. Chilton said, "We do not need a new weapon with new capabilities. But I do believe we have a great opportunity here to develop modern nuclear weapons . . . that have 21st-century requirements put into their designs," such as higher reliability and better security features in case a weapon is stolen by terrorists.

Then-Rep. Ellen Tauscher, D-Calif., who is now Under Secretary of State for Arms Control and International Security, agreed, "as long as the [constraints] include no testing; no new capabilities for the weapons in the sense that we're not increasing yield . . . and that it is all done in a context of ratifying [the CTBT] and taking down weapons and dismantling them."[32]

Opponents counter that warheads in the stockpile are safe and reliable. The 2002 National Academy of Sciences study on technical issues associated with the CTBT concluded that thanks to investments in nuclear weapons science that do not involve testing, "confidence in the reliability of the stockpile is better justified technically today than it was [in 1992 when the U.S. stopped testing]."[33]

More recently, studies released in 2006 by the JASON group, a panel of high-level experts that provides independent scientific advice to the U.S government, and by the Livermore and Los Alamos national laboratories, concluded that plutonium "pits," or cores, for most U.S. nuclear weapons would be reliable for at least 85 years — about twice as long as scientists had previously estimated. The JASON report concluded that the weapons laboratories "have also made significant progress in prioritizing the unresolved questions regarding the aging of stockpile weapons" and have "identified key metrics to assess the effects of aging."[34]

In addition to studying scientific problems like plutonium aging, the DOE is carrying out "life extension" programs on each of the major weapon types in the U.S. stockpile. Designed to extend the lives of warheads by 20 to 30 years, the programs involve refurbishing some components and replacing others that have degraded or pose technical problems. As of mid-2009, DOE had completed a life extension on the B61, an air-delivered bomb, and was working on the W76 warhead, which is carried on submarine-launched ballistic missiles.[35]

Debate over building new nuclear weapons is part of a larger discussion about the future of the aging DOE nuclear complex and the increasing challenge of recruiting talented scientists to maintain the U.S. nuclear stockpile and develop new weapons if they ever are needed (a stated U.S. policy goal).[36] "The U.S. is experiencing a serious brain drain in the loss of veteran nuclear weapons designers and technicians," Gates said last October. "Half of our nuclear lab scientists are over 50 years old, and many of those under 50 have had limited or no involvement in the design and development of a nuclear weapon."[37]

But it is less obvious that U.S. military leaders want new nuclear weapons. In a 2008 poll of more than 3,400 senior active-duty and retired military officers, only about 2 percent of respondents thought the U.S. needed to develop a new generation of nuclear weapons.[38] "Nuclear weapons don't factor into the kinds of missions that most military officers perform day to day, and it's civilian leaders who make the decision about pressing the button," says Carnegie Endowment analyst Squassoni. "Military leaders are much more focused on issues like getting their forces to the theater and communicating with them."

Many observers predict that to win votes for CTBT ratification, Obama may strike a deal that increases funding and activities related to nuclear weapon design (but not production). "There are a lot of things you can do to ensure the safety and reliability of the arsenal in between nothing and developing new warheads, and that's where the discussion is happening now," says the Ploughshares Fund's Cirincione. "You can already see the outlines of a compromise around robust research and development at the labs. We need to find a balance between making sure that our nuclear weapons work as intended and avoiding activities that make other countries think we're improving our capabilities while we tell them to reduce theirs."

BACKGROUND

Dawn of Arms Race

The United States made the world's first nuclear weapons, drawing on work by researchers in England, Italy, France and Germany. Through the 1930s and early 1940s these scientists solved pieces of the central challenge — splitting the atom and releasing huge quantities of energy. But only the United States, its research ranks swelled by top European physicists fleeing the Nazi government, undertook a full-scale effort to build the bomb.

In October 1941, with the nation on the brink of war, President Franklin D. Roosevelt ordered advisers to find out whether an atomic bomb could be built and what it would cost. Three months later, after Japan's surprise attack on Pearl Harbor, Roosevelt approved the Manhattan Project — a crash program to develop nuclear weapons. Working in secret, the Army Corps of Engineers built a nuclear production complex by 1945 that was as large as the U.S. auto industry. At its peak the Manhattan Project employed some 130,000 people from Washington state to South Carolina.[39]

On July 16, 1945, the world's first nuclear test lit up the desert at Alamogordo, New Mexico. Describing it, J. Robert Oppenheimer, the Manhattan Project's scientific director, recalled a statement in Hindu scripture by the god Vishnu: "Now I am become Death, the destroyer of worlds." A month later U.S. bombers dropped two atomic bombs in three days on the Japanese cities of Hiroshima and Nagasaki, killing more than 100,000 people immediately, and perhaps twice that number within weeks from radiation poisoning.[40]

Although scientists urged Roosevelt and his successor, President Harry S. Truman, to tell the Soviet Union about the bomb program, Truman only told Premier Josef Stalin

that the U.S. was working on "a new weapon of great force" 12 days before the Hiroshima bombing.[41] In 1946 U.S. negotiator Barnard Baruch presented a plan to the United Nations to destroy all existing atomic bombs and put atomic energy technology under international control. But the Soviet Union, which by then had launched its own atomic bomb program, rejected the plan.

In 1949 the Soviets tested their first atomic bomb. Truman then approved development of even more powerful thermonuclear, or hydrogen, bombs. By 1953 both superpowers had tested H-bombs and were expanding their nuclear stockpiles rapidly, each seeking the ability to respond instantly and massively to a sudden nuclear attack.

President Dwight D. Eisenhower renewed the idea of international control in his 1953 "Atoms for Peace" speech, which urged the United Nations to promote peaceful uses of atomic energy. The proposal led to establishment of the International Atomic Energy Agency in 1957 but did not slow the growth of nuclear arsenals. Emulating the United States and Soviet Union, Britain had tested a nuclear weapon in 1952. France and China would follow in the 1960s.

The arms race intensified in 1957, when the Soviet Union launched its *Sputnik* satellite into orbit, demonstrating that it could build a long-range ballistic missile.[42] *Sputnik* raised U.S. fears of falling behind and becoming vulnerable to nuclear blackmail. Concerns about a "missile gap" persisted until 1961, when satellite photographs showed that the U.S.S.R. had deployed only four long-range ballistic missiles.[43] The United States had more than 24,000 nuclear weapons — roughly 10 times as many as the Soviets.[44]

Early Agreements

Democratic President John F. Kennedy (1961-1963) came to office supporting limits on nuclear testing, but friction with the Soviet Union obstructed progress. In 1962 the superpowers came to the brink of nuclear war when U.S. satellite photographs revealed that Russians were installing nuclear missiles in Cuba that could reach U.S. territory.[45]

Some advisors recommended conventional air strikes on the Cuban missile sites, but instead Kennedy imposed a naval quarantine on Cuba and insisted that the weapons be removed. After a 13-day standoff, Soviet Premier Nikita

CHRONOLOGY

1940s-1960s *Atomic Age begins.*

August 1945 U.S. drops atomic bombs on Hiroshima and Nagasaki, Japan, killing 250,000 people.

1949 Soviet Union tests atomic bomb.

1952 Britain tests first nuclear bomb; U.S. tests hydrogen bomb.

1957 International Atomic Energy Agency (IAEA) is created to promote peaceful uses of nuclear energy.

1960 France tests nuclear bomb.

1962 Cuban Missile Crisis brings U.S., Soviet Union to brink of nuclear war.

1963 Limited Test Ban Treaty bars tests in atmosphere, space, and underwater.

1964 China tests its first nuclear bomb.

1968 Nearly 100 countries sign Nuclear Non-Proliferation Treaty (NPT).

1970s-1980s *Developing countries start acquiring nuclear arms.*

1972 U.S. and U.S.S.R. conclude Strategic Arms Limitation Talks (SALT I).

1974 India carries out "peaceful" underground nuclear explosion.

1979 U.S. and U.S.S.R. sign SALT II, cutting long-range missiles.

1983 U.S. deploys nuclear missiles in Western Europe, triggering widespread protests.

1986 President Ronald Reagan and Soviet Premier Mikhail Gorbachev discuss eliminating nuclear weapons at summit in Reykjavik, Iceland. Talks collapse but lay base for 1987 Intermediate-Range Nuclear Forces Treaty.

1989 Pakistan is revealed to be developing "nuclear capability."

1990s-2000s *U.S., Russia reduce Cold War arsenals; other proliferation threats increase.*

July 31, 1991 President George H. W. Bush and Gorbachev sign Strategic Arms Reduction Treaty (START I). . . . Inspectors begin destroying Iraq's nuclear weapons research sites. . . . Soviet Union collapses; U.S. provides aid to safeguard nuclear weapons.

1993 U.S., Russia sign START II treaty, reducing number of deployed strategic warheads by end of 2007. Russia conditions ratification on preservation of ABM Treaty's limits on development of missile defense systems.

1994 North Korea agrees to stop producing plutonium in return for food and energy aid. . . . START I enters into force for 15 years.

1996 Comprehensive Test Ban Treaty (CTBT) signed by 71 nations.

1998 India, Pakistan test nuclear weapons.

1999 U.S. Senate votes 51-48 against CTBT.

2002 U.S. withdraws from ABM Treaty, which President George W. Bush says prevents protection of Americans from rogue or terrorist attacks. Russia repudiates START II. The two countries conclude Strategic Offensive Reduction Treaty (SORT).

2003 U.S. invades Iraq, claiming it is developing weapons of mass destruction; no nuclear weapons program is found. . . . North Korea withdraws from NPT. . . . Libya agrees to dismantle clandestine nuclear weapons program.

2006 North Korea conducts nuclear test. . . . U.N. Security Council learns Iran has uranium enrichment program.

2008 Poland, Czech Republic agree to host U.S. missile defense systems; Russia says it will deploy missiles near Poland.

2009 President Barack Obama pledges steps toward nuclear-free world, including new nuclear reduction agreements with Russia and CTBT ratification and cancels missile defense deployment in Eastern Europe. . . . North Korea conducts second nuclear test. . . . Obama and Russian President Dmitry Medvedev sign joint understanding on treaty to reduce nuclear forces.

Khrushchev agreed to remove the missiles. In return the U.S. promised not to invade Cuba (a fear that had spurred the Soviets to install the missiles), and also agreed confidentially to remove its own nuclear missiles from Turkey.

After the Cuban Missile Crisis, Kennedy renewed efforts to limit nuclear testing, hoping to make it harder for other countries to develop nuclear weapons. In March 1963 Kennedy said, "I see the possibility in the 1970s of the president of the United States having to face a world in which 15 or 20 or 25 nations may have these weapons. I regard that as the greatest possible danger and hazard." And he argued that even if a test ban constrained the U.S., it would still make the nation safer.[46]

The Limited Test Ban Treaty, signed later that year, banned nuclear tests in the atmosphere, outer space and under water, but allowed underground tests to continue.[47]

Under Kennedy's successor, Lyndon B. Johnson, the U.S. and Russia joined with other countries to negotiate the Nuclear Non-Proliferation Treaty, which barred members other than the current nuclear powers (the U.S., Soviet Union, Britain, France, and China) from acquiring nuclear weapons. In return signatories were guaranteed access to peaceful nuclear energy technologies, and the five nuclear states agreed to negotiate toward disarmament, although without any time frame.[48] Ninety-eight countries signed the NPT when it was completed in 1968, and many more joined later.

By this time the United States had more than 28,000 nuclear weapons, down from a peak of 31,700 in 1966, and the Soviet Union had nearly 10,000. [49] Both sides were developing weapons that could deliver multiple warheads to different targets, known as MIRVs (multiple independently targetable reentry vehicles), and anti-ballistic missile defense systems that could shoot down attacking missiles.

Unable to agree on a broad nuclear disarmament plan, the superpowers shifted to a more modest goal in the late 1960s: setting some upper limits on their arms race. In 1972 U.S. and Soviet leaders signed an interim agreement (referred to as SALT I because it was negotiated during the Strategic Arms Limitation Talks) freezing the number of each side's long-range ballistic missiles, bombers and submarines, and also the Anti-Ballistic Missile (ABM) Treaty, which limited each country to a single defensive system around its capital and another at a missile launch area.[50] By preventing either country from developing a nationwide missile defense system, the ABM Treaty sought to maintain the so-called "balance of terror" that kept the superpowers from attacking each other.

Negotiations during the Ford and Carter administrations produced the SALT II treaty in 1979, which set permanent limits on many types of nuclear weapons but did not require any existing weapons to be destroyed. After the Soviet Union invaded Afghanistan in 1980, President Jimmy Carter asked the Senate to put SALT II ratification on hold and signed a directive that stated, "To continue to deter in an era of strategic nuclear equivalence . . . we must be capable of fighting [a nuclear war] successfully," so that the enemy would recognize that it could not possibly benefit from attacking.[51]

New Directions

President Ronald Reagan (1981-1989) ran on a platform that called for rebuilding U.S. military power, and some of his senior advisers alarmed the public with statements about planning for nuclear war. For example, in 1981 Deputy Under Secretary of Defense T. K. Jones argued that with a robust civil defense program, most Americans could survive a nuclear attack. "Dig a hole, cover it with a couple of doors and then throw three feet of dirt on top," Jones said.[52]

Many Americans rejected such views and supported proposals to freeze and reduce nuclear arsenals. One of the biggest anti-nuclear rallies, in New York's Central Park in 1982, drew 700,000 people.[53] When the U.S. started deploying medium-range nuclear missiles in Western Europe in 1983 (a step approved during the Carter administration to balance new Soviet missiles), protests spread to European capitals. The U.S. Conference of Catholic Bishops weighed in with a pastoral letter that argued, "The arms race is one of the great curses on the human race; it is to be condemned as a danger, an act of aggression against the poor, and a folly which does not provide the security it promises."[54]

Reagan opposed a nuclear freeze and argued that increasing U.S. military power was the best way to preserve peace. But he also believed that once Soviet leaders saw that they could never win an arms race, nuclear weapons could be eliminated. In 1983 Reagan further complicated

What If an Armed Nuclear Bomber Crashed?

Potentially catastrophic accidents have occurred.

The terms are vaguely military, but innocent-sounding: "bent spears" and "broken arrows." But they refer to a dreadful reality: potentially catastrophic incidents involving nuclear weapons.

"Broken arrows" are the most serious, such as the accidental or unauthorized launch of a nuclear weapon that could lead to nuclear war, an explosion of nuclear or non-nuclear weapon components, radioactive contamination or loss or seizure of a nuclear weapon. To date, the U.S. military has logged 32 such incidents — all before 1983 and none resulting in a nuclear detonation.[1]

But some came close. In 1966 an American B-52 bomber carrying four hydrogen bombs collided with a tanker plane during mid-air refueling off the coast of Spain. The bomber broke apart, and three of the bombs fell on land near a small fishing village; the bombs didn't detonate, but non-nuclear explosives in two of the bombs did go off, contaminating a square mile with radioactive material. The fourth bomb landed in the Mediterranean Sea and was recovered intact two months later.[2]

"Bent spears" involve the mishandling of nuclear weapons or incidents that pose a risk of explosion, radioactive contamination or damage to the weapon.[3] The most recent bent spear occurred in 2007, when crewmen loaded what they thought were 12 unarmed cruise missiles onto a bomber at Minot Air Force Base in North Dakota. The airmen and the officer in charge didn't realize that six of the missiles carried nuclear warheads. The loaded plane stood unguarded on the runway for 15 hours before flying to a base in Louisiana, where the nuclear missiles were discovered nine hours later.[4]

Afterward, seven officers at Minot were reassigned, and 90 service members temporarily lost authority to handle nuclear weapons.[5] In 2008, after it was disclosed that another Air Force unit had mislabeled fuses for nuclear

missiles and accidentally shipped them to Taiwan, Defense Secretary Robert Gates ordered an investigation of the Air Force's problems handling nuclear weapons. In June, the Air Force's military chief of staff and civilian secretary were forced to resign.[6]

Many security experts say the risk of accidental nuclear war has grown since the end of the Cold War, largely because the United States and Russia still maintain hundreds of nuclear weapons at a high stage of alert. In addition, Russia's computer systems degraded after the Soviet Union disintegrated, raising concerns that leaders might misinterpret a malfunction or false signal as an attack and launch weapons in response. Indeed, false alarms indicating a Soviet attack occurred in the United States in 1979 and 1980, and in 1995 Russian leaders almost launched a nuclear attack on the U.S. in response to what turned out to be a Norwegian research rocket.[7]

"About 800 to 900 U.S. warheads, and a comparable number of Russian warheads, are launch ready — fuelled, armed, targeted and will instantly fire if they receive a very short stream of computer launch signals," says Bruce Blair, president of the World Security Institute and a former Air Force nuclear missile launch officer. "Nothing has been done to change these legacy postures, except for a cosmetic detargeting agreement between [President Bill] Clinton and [Soviet President Boris] Yeltsin in 1994." The U.S. and Russia agreed not to target each other, but nuclear weapons can be retargeted in seconds.

Military leaders maintain that launch-ready warheads are under rigorous controls, including design features, safety rules and procedures, accident prevention or mitigation measures, physical security and coded control systems.[8] U.S. Strategic Command head Gen. Kevin Chilton said in 2008 that nuclear weapons are "in the holster" with two combination locks, which must be opened by two people

arms control discussions when he called for "rendering nuclear weapons impotent and obsolete" by developing a national missile defense system.

Reagan envisioned sharing missile defense technology with the Soviet Union, but Soviet leaders and U.S. critics argued that the Strategic Defense Initiative (SDI), popularly known as "Star Wars," would escalate the nuclear

arms race and make cuts in offensive weapons impossible. Many scientists also argued that it was technically impossible to build effective defenses against a large-scale nuclear attack.[55] In a 1986 summit meeting at Reykjavik, Iceland, Reagan and Soviet General Secretary Mikhail Gorbachev nearly agreed on a proposal to eliminate nuclear weapons but deadlocked over missile defense.

who can only act under authenticated orders from the president.[9]

Nonetheless, former Senate Armed Services Committee Chairman Sam Nunn, D-Ga., has urged the United States and Russia to remove all nuclear weapons from high-alert status. "We are running the irrational risk of an Armageddon of our own making," Nunn said in 2004.[10]

During the 2008 presidential campaign, President Barack Obama pledged to "work with Russia to take U.S. and Russian ballistic missiles off hair-trigger alert." That issue will be addressed during the congressionally mandated Nuclear Posture Review, a study of U.S. nuclear forces and policies scheduled for completion by the end of this year.

Cyber-intrusion by computer hackers could also pose a risk.[11] "If outside actors, perhaps with insider collusion that provides passwords and other access information, manage to break into 'closed' nuclear communications and computer networks, then this risk could become high as long as nuclear missiles remain on launch-ready alert," Blair warns.

In fact, since 2006 hackers have breached the networks at the Defense, Commerce and State departments, the Federal Aviation Administration and the military's U.S. Central Command, according to the Center for Strategic and International Studies, a Washington think tank.[12] The Defense Department is creating a new military command to manage offensive and defensive computer warfare, in coordination with a new civilian cyber-security initiative announced by President Obama last May.[13]

No other countries keep their forces on launch-ready alert, according to Blair, and other nations usually keep warheads separated from delivery vehicles. However, he worries that India, Pakistan and China may start mating warheads with missiles and adopting quick-launch postures.

"If there's a crisis, they will be more likely to assemble weapons and bombs, mate them to delivery vehicles and prime them for use," Blair says. "That's the context in which mistaken or unauthorized launch becomes a concern."

To avoid that scenario, Blair recommends that all countries with nuclear weapons agree to prohibit launch-ready postures except in extreme circumstances and require pre-notification and information exchange about steps governments take to alert their forces.

"A joint warning center with multinational crews from all of the nuclear weapons countries (except North Korea) and links to all their national early warning centers would also help to minimize misinterpretation of missile launches," he says.

— Jennifer Weeks

[1] Office of the Deputy Assistant to the Secretary of Defense (Nuclear Matters), *Nuclear Matters: A Practice Guide* (2008), p. 183, www.acq.osd.mil/ncbdp/nm/nmbook/index.htm.

[2] For details see Barbara Moran, *The Day We Lost the H-Bomb: Cold War, Hot Nukes, and the Worst Nuclear Weapons Disaster in History* (2009).

[3] Office of the Assistant to the Secretary of Defense for Nuclear and Chemical and Biological Defense Programs, Nuclear Weapons Accident Response Procedures, Feb. 22, 2005, pp. 28-29, www.dtic.mil/whs/directives/corres/pdf/315008m.pdf.

[4] Joby Warrick and Walter Pincus, "Missteps in the Bunker," *The Washington Post*, Sept. 23, 2007.

[5] Marc V. Schanz and Suzann Chapman, "No More Bent Spears," *Air Force Magazine.com*, Feb. 15, 2008.

[6] Kristin Roberts, "U.S. Mistakenly Sent Nuclear Missile Fuses to Taiwan," Reuters, March 25, 2008; "Moseley and Wynne Forced Out," *Air Force Times*, June 9, 2008.

[7] Lachlan Forrow, *et al.*, "Accidental Nuclear War — A Post-Cold War Assessment," *New England Journal of Medicine*, vol. 338, no. 18 (April 30, 1998), pp. 1326-32; Geoffrey Forden, "False Alarms on the Nuclear Front," NOVA, updated December 2001, www.pbs.org/wgbh/nova/missileers/falsealarms.html.

[8] E-mail from U.S. Strategic Command to Arms Control Association, Nov. 28, 2007, www.armscontrol.org/interviews/20071204_STRATCOM.

[9] Elaine M. Grossman, "Top U.S. General Spurns Obama Pledge to Reduce Nuclear Alert Posture," Global Security Newswire, Feb. 27, 2009.

[10] "Nunn Urges U.S. and Russia to Remove All Nuclear Weapons from Hair-Trigger," Nuclear Threat Initiative, June 21, 2004.

[11] See Peter Katel, "Homeland Security," *CQ Researcher*, Feb. 13, 2009, pp. 129-152.

[12] James Andrew Lewis, "Cyber Events Since 2006," Center for Strategic and International Studies, June 11, 2009, http://csis.org/publication/cyber-events-2006.

[13] David E. Sanger and Thom Shanker, "Pentagon Plans New Arm to Wage Cyberspace Wars," *The New York Times*, May 29, 2009.

Gorbachev insisted that the U.S. should adhere to the ABM Treaty, but Reagan refused, saying that would constrain SDI.[56]

A year later, however, Reagan and Gorbachev signed the Intermediate Nuclear Forces (INF) Treaty, the first agreement to eliminate an entire class of nuclear weapons (ground-launched missiles with ranges of 500 to 5,500 kilometers).[57] Negotiations continued, and in 1991 Gorbachev and President George H. W. Bush signed the Strategic Arms Reduction Treaty (START I) — the first agreement to require each side to make major cuts in long-range nuclear weapons. START I limited each side to 6,000 "accountable" (deployed) warheads and set up an intrusive verification system.

U.S. Seeks New Roles for Bomb Builders

Nation's science leadership faces "precipitous decline."

As the United States downsizes its nuclear arsenal and makes cutbacks at its nuclear weapons laboratories, managers are finding it harder and harder to recruit and retain top-level nuclear scientists and engineers.

"We've slowly but steadily lost the capabilities that have made these places incredibly good scientific institutions," says former Los Alamos Director Siegfried Hecker.

More broadly, "Our nation is witnessing a precipitous decline in global science and technology leadership," warned a task force last spring convened by the Henry L. Stimson Center think tank in Washington, D.C. To start reversing that decline, members called for diversifying the labs' core mission so they can "address an array of 21st-century national security challenges."[1]

The nation's three nuclear weapons laboratories — Los Alamos and Sandia in New Mexico and Livermore in California — face both budget challenges and bureaucratic red tape, says Hecker. While other agencies use the labs' world-class facilities and technology in joint non-nuclear projects — such as developing advanced conventional munitions — those initiatives have not provided steady funding for the labs. "Other agencies have typically come into the labs as users of the technologies, not builders of it," he says, "so they've never supported the underlying science and technology base." Furthermore, he adds, "It's hard to do anything experimentally because the labs have been driven toward a zero-risk environment."

Still, the labs have made important contributions to non-weapons initiatives. In the 1980s, for instance, Los Alamos created the human DNA libraries that laid the groundwork for the Human Genome Project, which identified all of the genes in human DNA. And both Los Alamos and Livermore have developed strong climate-modeling programs.

To expand the labs' core mission, the task force recommended moving them from the Energy Department's National Nuclear Security Administration (NNSA) to a new, independent Agency for National Security Applications. The agency's mission would still be nuclear-related but also would include verifying compliance with arms control treaties; nuclear forensics (analyzing recovered nuclear materials to identify their sources); counter-terrorism research; and analysis of intelligence information on foreign nuclear weapons programs.

"Almost everyone understands the labs' role poorly," says Stimson Center senior fellow and study director Elizabeth Turpen. "They have been servicing broader national security needs beyond the nuclear stockpile since before the end of the Cold War, and they're huge in the nuclear nonproliferation arena. But they should be bigger."

The challenge is most urgent for Los Alamos and Livermore, which were created to design nuclear weapons and today are primarily focused on ensuring the safety and reliability of those weapons. Sandia, which designs and produces non-nuclear components of nuclear weapons, "has already turned the corner," says Turpen. "Only about 42

Opportunities and Threats

In December 1991, a few months after START I was signed, the Soviet Union dissolved. Now Russia posed a new kind of nuclear threat: with its economy in crisis and its borders no longer secured, many leaders worried that nuclear weapons and materials from former Soviet republics might be stolen or sold on the black market.

In response the U.S. started providing aid for so-called Cooperative Threat Reduction (CTR) — joint work by the superpowers to secure weapon-usable nuclear materials and destroy the Soviet Union's surplus nuclear weapons.

Starting at $400 million in 1991, the initiative (popularly known as Nunn-Lugar after its lead Senate sponsors, Sens. Sam Nunn, D-Ga., and Indiana Republican Richard Lugar), grew into a multi-agency, multi-year program. Through fiscal 2008 the U.S. had provided about $15 billion to help other countries destroy or improve controls over nuclear, chemical, biological and missile technologies, weapons and materials.[58]

The end of the Cold War and Russia's economic collapse undercut many of the assumptions underlying U.S. nuclear policies. Just before leaving office, President Bush and Russian President Boris Yeltsin took another big step by

percent of their current budget comes from defense programs, so they already think of themselves as a national security laboratory."

In 2000 the NNSA was split off as an autonomous agency within the Department of Energy (DOE) after security lapses and alleged Chinese spying at the labs raised congressional concerns that DOE was not overseeing the weapons complex effectively.[2] But that made it harder to broaden their portfolios, partner with other agencies and attract talented young scientists, the Stimson task force concluded.

"NNSA has never achieved the autonomy that Congress intended, just an overlay of bureaucracy," says Turpen. "And DOE's bureaucratic culture is very risk-averse in all of its decisions about the labs. There are lots of stovepipes, and anyone can stop a decision."

Early this year the Office of Management and Budget (OMB) asked for a cost-benefit analysis of putting the labs under the control of the Pentagon or another agency. Housing them within DOE "hasn't been a good marriage," said former Sandia Director C. Paul Robinson.[3] But others point out that the United States has had a longstanding policy of civilian control.

"For the past 63 years non-military control over the development of nuclear weapons technology has ensured independence of technical judgment over issues associated with our nuclear arsenal, has attracted the best scientific and technical talent to these important programs and has served to underline the crucial differences between nuclear weapons and conventional military munitions," a bipartisan group of U.S. senators wrote to OMB in March.[4]

The future of the labs is part of a larger debate over what kind of nuclear weapons complex the U.S. needs to support a post-Cold War arsenal. Some former production sites

have been closed for cleanup, but the DOE still conducts weapons-related activities at eight sites. (*See map, p. 60.*) A Bush administration plan — originally called Complex 2030 and later renamed Complex Transformation — would have modernized many facilities and equipped them to produce a new stockpile of Reliable Replacement Warheads and maintain sizeable nuclear reserves.[5]

Now, however, the replacement warhead is off the table, and President Obama has called for further nuclear reductions. Many observers say the United States should complete its ongoing Nuclear Posture Review before deciding what goals nuclear weapons will serve. Then the size and scope of the nation's nuclear weapons infrastructure can be shaped accordingly.

— *Jennifer Weeks*

[1] "Leveraging Science for Security: A Strategy for the Nuclear Weapons Laboratories in the 21st Century," Henry L. Stimson Center, March 2009, p. 9, www.stimson.org/cnp/pdf/Leveraging_Science_for_Security_FINAL.pdf.

[2] "Congress Approves DOE Reorganization; Clinton Leaves Control with Energy Secretary," *Arms Control Today,* September/October 1999.

[3] Sue Vorenberg, "Feds Ponder Switching Labs to Military Agency," *Santa Fe New Mexican,* Feb. 4, 2009.

[4] "Senators Ask Obama Administration to End Study of Proposal to Move DOE Weapons Labs to Defense Department," Senate Energy and Natural Resources Committee, March 18, 2009. The senators were Sens. Jeff Bingaman (D-NM), Lisa Murkowski (R-AK), Byron Dorgan (D-ND), Robert Bennett (R-UT), and Bill Nelson (D-FL).

[5] For details see National Nuclear Security Administration, "Complex Transformation SPEIS," www.complextransformationspeis.com/index.html, and Philip Coyle III, "The Future of the DOE Complex Transformation Program," testimony before the House Committee on Appropriations, Subcommittee on Energy and Water, March 17, 2009, www.cdi.org/pdfs/CoyleHouseDOE3.09.pdf.

signing the START II treaty, which called for each side to reduce its deployed strategic warheads to between 3,000 and 3,500 by 2007. START II also set other limits, such as barring multiple warheads on land-based missiles.

To assess what these changes meant for U.S. security policy, Congress ordered the Clinton administration to carry out an assessment of U.S. nuclear forces and policies in a post-Cold War world. The first Nuclear Posture Review, completed in 1994, stuck to the status quo in many ways. It endorsed continued reliance on a triad of nuclear delivery systems (bombers, land-based missiles and submarine-launched missiles). And it recommended that the U.S. should

"lead but hedge" on arms control by supporting nuclear reductions but keeping warheads removed from service in storage, where they could be reloaded quickly onto missiles and bombers if U.S.-Russian relations deteriorated.[59]

Clinton was the first world leader to sign the Comprehensive Test Ban Treaty (CTBT) when it was completed in 1996. But a Republican-led Senate rejected the treaty in 1999, with opponents arguing it would not keep other countries from going nuclear (India and Pakistan had each tested nuclear weapons a year earlier), and that ending U.S. nuclear testing would make it harder to ensure that U.S. nuclear weapons were safe and reliable.

President George W. Bush's administration (2001-2009) was cooler toward nuclear arms control and argued that the U.S. needed many options to deter rogue countries or terrorist groups with nuclear weapons. In 2002 a second Nuclear Posture Review by Bush's Defense Department argued that the ABM Treaty and the CTBT were not applicable to current security conditions.[60]

A leaked version of the study named countries against which the U.S. should be ready to use nuclear weapons — including Russia, China, Iran, Iraq, Libya, North Korea, and Serbia — and proposed developing new warheads, spurring charges that Bush was expanding U.S. reliance on nuclear weapons.[61] But the administration rejected that view. "We were trying to make nuclear weapons less usable, not more usable," says Brooks, the former National Nuclear Security Administration director under Bush.

In 2002 Bush traveled to Moscow and with Russian President Vladimir Putin signed the Strategic Offensive Reduction Treaty (SORT), a pact to reduce U.S. and Russian deployed strategic warheads to between 1,700 and 2,200 each by 2012. The agreement superseded START II, which had never been enacted because Russia's legislature conditioned its approval of that agreement on the U.S. adhering to the ABM Treaty. Unlike START II, the Moscow treaty did not specify how each side's pledges would be verified or dictate what would be done with warheads removed from service.[62] A few weeks later the U.S. withdrew from the ABM Treaty and pledged to deploy missile defenses against growing threats from countries like North Korea and Iran.

Russia's response was subdued at first, but the issue heated up in 2007 when the Bush administration started negotiating to put missile interceptors and radar in Poland and the Czech Republic. U.S. officials said they were needed to counter Iranian attacks on European and American targets, but Russian leaders argued the new sites could become part of a defensive network against Russian missiles. Putin said the U.S. defense system would lead to "an inevitable arms race" and suggested Russia might target its own weapons on Poland and the Czech Republic.[63]

CURRENT SITUATION

Reshaping U.S. Forces

The Obama administration is currently carrying out the third U.S. Nuclear Posture Review (NPR) since the end of the Cold War. This study, due in December, will establish policies for the next five to 10 years governing U.S. nuclear deterrence doctrine, strategies, and the makeup of U.S. nuclear forces. Congress, executive branch officials, and many advocacy groups expect the NPR to define how nuclear weapons fit into President Obama's foreign and military agendas.

"The most important measure of whether President Obama is serious about pursuing a nuclear-free world will be how the NPR defines the future role of U.S. nuclear weapons," says Kimball of the Arms Control Association. "The president ought to articulate that nuclear weapons no longer play a useful role in deterring or fighting wars that start as conventional conflicts. They're not useful to deter or counter chemical and biological warfare threats. Mission statements dictate targets and requirements, so if the Obama administration crafts that kind of nuclear vision, the U.S. and Russia will be able to reduce their stockpiles to 1,000 warheads or fewer apiece. That will let us engage other countries in a discussion about multilateral nuclear disarmament."

To conservatives, however, nuclear weapons serve many important security functions, including reassuring U.S. allies that they are protected under a strong nuclear umbrella. "The key elements of a robust deterrent are under extreme stress today and will be imperiled further by a presidential determination to pursue a 'world without nuclear weapons' and the attendant policy of not investing in modernization of the stockpile," a group of former U.S. security officials warned in July.[64] The authors, with years of service in mainly Republican administrations, argued that modernizing U.S. nuclear weapons and delivery systems and developing national missile defenses should take priority over negotiating any new nuclear reduction agreements with Russia.

In that same month, however, Obama and Russian President Medvedev agreed on new warhead reduction targets for a follow-on treaty to START I, which expires in December. Under the new targets the United States and Russia pledge to reduce their deployed strategic nuclear warheads from the current limit of 2,200 each by 2012 to between 1,500 and 1,675 each by 2016. Both sides would also make some cuts in nuclear bombers and missiles.[65]

Alarmed over these new proposed reductions, Senate conservatives attached several non-binding resolutions to a defense spending bill stating that the new treaty should not limit missile defenses, space capabilities or advanced conventional weapons, and endorsing the Bush administration's proposed missile defense system based in Poland and the Czech Republic. "I have yet to hear a convincing strategic rationale that would justify going this low [on warheads and delivery vehicles]," said Sen. Jeff Sessions, R-Ala., who warned that he would condition his support for any START follow-on agreement on "a serious commitment by the administration to modernize our nuclear deterrent."[66]

Some observers predict that with hawks pushing back, President Obama may have trouble making radical policy changes in the Nuclear Posture Review. "There are a lot of Bush administration holdovers in the nuclear bureaucracy, so the NPR may not end up being all that pathbreaking," says Carnegie Endowment analyst Squassoni. "The real question is whether the president will step in and make a difference."

North Korea and Iran

As the U.S. reexamines its own nuclear weapons policies, it is also working to limit options for proliferators, especially North Korea and Iran. North Korea expelled international inspectors and withdrew from six-nation denuclearization talks in April, then conducted its second nuclear test in May. Although security experts estimate North Korea has produced enough plutonium for perhaps four to eight bombs, they mainly fear Pyongyang will sell nuclear materials and technology to other countries or groups.[67]

Because North Korea is diplomatically isolated, the U.S. has little direct leverage over its behavior. In the short term, U.S. leaders want to keep the North from spreading nuclear technology abroad. "You can't do anything about North Korea until it wants to have a different kind of relationship with the world, so the problem is to contain its impact," says Harvard's Walt.

Other nations also support containment of North Korea. In June the U.N. Security Council unanimously condemned its May nuclear test, tightening trade sanctions and calling on member countries to inspect and destroy all banned cargo coming to or from North Korea. China and Russia, both former allies of North Korea, both condemned the test.[68]

"We still want North Korea to come back to the negotiating table, to be part of an international effort that will lead to denuclearization," said Secretary of State Hillary Rodham Clinton in July. "But we're not going to reward them for doing what they said they would do in 2005 and 2006."[69]

Defense Secretary Gates said after the May test that the U.S. "will not accept North Korea as a nuclear state."[70] However, many observers believe North Korea hopes the U.S. will ultimately do just that — much as it opposed but ultimately recognized India's and Pakistan's nuclear programs.[71]

The challenge is different with Iran, which still belongs to the Nuclear Non-Proliferation Treaty and maintains that its nuclear research activities are strictly for peaceful purposes. But that position rings hollower than ever after last month's disclosure that Iran had built a second secret uranium enrichment plant.[72] President Obama's emphasis on diplomatic engagement and enforcing international treaties will be tested as the United States works to rally a strong international response.

The United States wants Iran to suspend enrichment activities, declare all of its nuclear activities, and open its nuclear facilities to international inspections.

"[I]f the U.S. extends a defense umbrella over the region, if we do even more to support the military capacity of those in the [Persian] Gulf, it's unlikely that Iran will be any stronger or safer, because they won't be able to intimidate and dominate, as they apparently believe they can, once they have a nuclear weapon," Secretary Clinton said in July. Officials in Washington said this was the first time the U.S. had publicly discussed offering defensive support to other Middle Eastern countries like Saudi Arabia and Egypt if Iran continued to pursue a nuclear capability.[73]

One of Obama's major diplomatic goals will be persuading Russia and China to support strong international sanctions on Iran if its leaders refuse to disclose their nuclear activities. Both countries have trade relationships with Iran and have resisted sanctions in the past. However, they also supported the Security Council resolution, which reaffirms the need to strengthen the NPT.

"It's all very well and good for the U.N. to condemn proliferator countries, but state actions supporting those measures determine whether they'll work or not," says Squassoni. "We can't be the global nuclear weapons policemen on our own. We need collaboration from our allies and Russia and China and a lot of other states."

Can we detect Nuclear Test Ban cheaters?

YES
Richard L. Garwin
Fellow Emeritus, Thomas J. Watson Research Center, IBM

Written for *CQ Researcher*, September 2009

I have been involved in detecting clandestine nuclear explosions since before December 1958, when I had a role in the U.N. Conference of Experts in Geneva devoted to seismic detection. The weapons that destroyed Hiroshima and Nagasaki were in the 10-kiloton range, but stockpile nuclear weapons today range to considerably more than a megaton yield (1 million tons of TNT equivalent).

Now 247 of the 337 facilities planned for the International Monitoring System (IMS) have been certified. These include primary and auxiliary seismic stations, infrasound sensors, hydroacoustic detectors and radionuclide laboratories.

The seismic sensors in particular are augmented by thousands of university seismometers in cooperative networks, with advancing capabilities to detect earthquakes. These networks can be focused even after the fact on nuclear test sites or suspect locations. The technology of detection has continuously improved, as well as the ability to distinguish underground explosions from background earthquakes. There has been no such evolution in means of hiding nuclear explosions.

According to a 2002 National Academy of Sciences study that analyzed the planned capability for Comprehensive Test Ban Treaty (CTBT) verification and possible military advances by any foreign testing that might evade detection, "[T]he only evasion scenarios that need to be taken seriously at this time are cavity decoupling and mine masking." The IMS network readily meets its goal of confident detection of a one-kiloton explosion non-evasively tested anywhere in the world, and has sensitivity a thousand times greater to explosions in the oceans.

In general, advanced nuclear weapon states that could hide a one-kiloton explosion would have little to gain from successfully doing so, and much to lose if concealment failed. Emerging nuclear powers are unlikely to be successful in such concealment and would also have little benefit, because the test explosive would have to be so modified to limit its yield as to bear little resemblance to an actual weapon.

The CTBT provides for on-site inspections (OSI) following a questionable seismic detection, allowing the search of 1,000 square kilometers of terrain. An OSI exercise of similar size was practiced in Kazakhstan in August 2008, with good results.

Former U.S. arms control negotiator Paul Nitze wrote in 1999 that the CTBT can be verified "with great confidence," more than meeting his prior general requirement that an arms control agreement be "adequately verifiable." I am now involved in a reassessment of this question.

NO
Thomas Scheber
Vice President, National Institute for Public Policy

Written for *CQ Global Researcher*, March 2007

To be effective, a CTBT detection and verification regime would need to be highly intrusive and guarantee timely on-site inspections to resolve indications of cheating. The planned treaty regime is incapable of doing that.

First, there cannot be confidence in verification if major parties to the treaty don't agree on what is banned and permitted. The treaty is not clear. The CTBT prohibits all nuclear explosions. The U.S. interprets this prohibition strictly as zero-yield. Apparently Russia and possibly China do not accept the U.S. criterion and conduct low-yield nuclear tests.

Second, a zero-yield treaty poses an unattainable verification challenge. Evasion techniques can reduce the signature of a nuclear explosion by factors of 50 to 100; evidence can be obscured by natural geologic activity or man-made explosions. A National Academy of Sciences report on the CTBT addressed testing techniques to evade detection or attribution and concluded that, with evasive techniques, verification of testing below a kiloton could be problematic. These techniques include cavity decoupling, masking, or testing in an environment that makes attribution difficult. A CIA assessment concluded: "an evader could successfully contain a decoupled test in hard rock, using a cautious experimental approach, and thereby avoid detection by sensors external to its country."

Third, nuclear tests below a kiloton can provide valuable data — perhaps more valuable for the Russians than for the U.S. Russia has extensive experience with low-yield nuclear testing and a system to fully contain very low-yield tests. When U.S. personnel helped clean up a former Soviet test site in Kazakhstan, they discovered that 20 percent of the tests conducted there had escaped detection. These tests were low-yield and designed for special weapon effects. Recently, Russia has gone to great expense to restore its nuclear testing infrastructure.

Fourth, even the planned, inadequate verification provisions won't be fully implemented because CTBT cannot enter into force until it is ratified by North Korea, Iran, China, India, Pakistan, Israel, and Egypt.

Finally, verifying compliance would require timely on-site challenge inspections to investigate evidence of cheating. The CTBT requires that 30 of 51 members of an Executive Council consider the evidence and vote for inspection. Only 10 of the 51 member-states would be from North America or Western Europe; the U.S. is not even guaranteed a vote. This is a prescription for inaction.

Bottom line: A "zero-yield" nuclear test ban treaty is not verifiable.

New START with Russia

President Obama's administration came into office determined to "press the reset button with Russia," in Vice President Joseph Biden's words, and restore cooperation with Moscow on many issues — particularly arms control — where cooperation had deteriorated under President Bush.[74]

"We can and should cooperate to secure loose nuclear weapons and materials to prevent their spread, to renew the verification procedures in the START Treaty, and then go beyond existing treaties to negotiate deeper cuts in both our arsenals," Biden said in February. "The United States and Russia have a special obligation to lead the international effort to reduce the number of nuclear weapons in the world."[75]

Obama and Russian President Medvedev issued a joint statement in April affirming that they had committed both nations to "achieving a nuclear free world" through steps including a follow-on agreement to the START Treaty and efforts to strengthen international nuclear non-proliferation policies, bring the Comprehensive Test Ban Treaty into force and negotiate a fissile production cutoff treaty. They also noted the possibility of U.S.-Russian cooperation on missile defense issues — no longer a far-fetched prospect in the wake of Obama's decision not to base mid-range defenses in Eastern Europe.[76]

But putting these agreements into action will require much more work. For example, the July agreement on post-START reductions identified ranges, not final numbers. Nuclear warheads would be limited to between 1,500 and 1,650 on each side, while delivery vehicles (bombers and missiles) would be reduced to between 500 and 1,100 each. Russia reportedly favors the lower numbers, while U.S. negotiators pushed for the higher figures. Nonetheless, observers saw the targets as a good first step.

"Russia is eager to do a START follow-on because its nuclear forces are coming down anyway," says former NNSA administrator Brooks. "And the transparency measures in the new treaty will be important, because we're still deeply suspicious of Russia's technology efforts, and they're suspicious of ours."

Since 1992 the United States and Russia have worked together under the Cooperative Threat Reduction (CTR) partnership, popularly known as the Nunn-Lugar initiative, to deactivate more than 7,000 warheads and destroy hundreds of bombers and long-range ballistic missiles.[77]

CTR has also greatly improved security at many sites that store warheads and nuclear materials, although much remains to be done to consolidate the former Soviet Union's sprawling nuclear complex.[78]

"This work is essential in preventing nuclear terrorism and deserves greater support and government resources," said Nunn last May after the United States, Russia and the International Atomic Energy Agency helped remove 162 pounds of weapon-grade uranium (enough for about three bombs) from Kazakhstan.[79]

But even the popular Nunn-Lugar program faces constant budget pressures. Indeed, while Obama announced a new international effort in his Prague speech to "secure all vulnerable nuclear material around the world within four years," his 2010 budget request for nuclear threat reduction and related programs totals about $2.8 billion, about $150 million below the current level.[80]

OUTLOOK

Tipping Point?

In April 2010, members of the Nuclear Non-Proliferation Treaty (NPT) will hold their next five-year review conference to assess how well the pact is working. Most observers see the meeting as a critical decision point. If governments agree that progress is being made toward international arms control goals, they will be likely to make new commitments to support it. Conversely, if nations cannot agree on how to achieve key nonproliferation goals — as happened at the 2005 review conference — some experts worry that more proliferation, not less, could be the result.

"The 2005 review conference was a total disaster," says the Arms Control Association's Kimball. "The nonproliferation regime was in crisis: North Korea was withdrawing from the NPT and producing plutonium, Iran had been discovered to be developing a nuclear capability and the Bush administration had rejected the Comprehensive Test Ban Treaty as counter to U.S. interests. It was an important time for the world to come together and strengthen the treaty, and it didn't, partly because the United States didn't lead."

The tone has been more optimistic in preparatory meetings for the 2010 conference, and progress toward new U.S. and Russian reductions will help to demonstrate that the nuclear superpowers are serious about their disarmament commitments. "Obama's new approach is already producing some results," says Kimball, "but the U.S. and other countries will have to work hard to build consensus for an action plan that sets new limits on nuclear weapon development."

Many steps could be taken to strengthen the NPT regime. For example, says the Carnegie Endowment's Squassoni, states could endorse limits on reprocessing plutonium and enriching uranium. In addition, supporting the creation of an international nuclear fuel bank to replace national facilities would take the moral high ground away from countries like Iran that use civilian nuclear programs as cover for military activities.

"In 2005 countries like Iran talked about their rights to enrichment, reprocessing and peaceful use of nuclear energy under the NPT, and a lot of nonaligned states bought it," she says. "The debates were very polemical, not constructive."

Other helpful steps could include agreement on how NPT members should react if another state emulates North Korea and withdraws from the treaty, or more states adopt so-called additional protocols (intrusive inspections and monitoring) to their basic nuclear safeguard agreements with the International Atomic Energy Agency. As of mid-2009, 42 countries had not brought additional protocols into force, including Iran.[81]

Either as part of the review conference or separately, many experts would like to see cooperative threat reduction (CTR) programs expanded globally, as President Obama pledged in Prague. "I'd like to see it extended to all countries that have fissile materials," says Stanford University's Hecker, who has discussed protection, control and accounting for nuclear materials with officials in countries including Russia, India and North Korea. "There's very little uniformity across the world in how countries handle these materials or what they think needs to be done to provide a comprehensive safeguards system."

Some observers say that CTR programs could be much more effective. Rens Lee, an independent security consultant and author of a book on nuclear smuggling, argues that Obama needs a more proactive strategy that includes sharing intelligence with Russia about nuclear trafficking. "[A]ctual sharing remains woefully inadequate, both bilaterally and with international organizations such as the International Atomic Energy Agency," Lee wrote in July.[82]

But the basic concept of CTR has broad support. A congressionally mandated National Academy of Sciences study, released earlier this year, called for dramatically scaling up CTR programs to reduce threats from weapons of mass destruction in regions including the Middle East and Asia.

"The world is smaller than it was in 1992," the study said. "Ignoring globalization is not an option, whether in economics, public health, combating terrorism, or reducing the threat of WMD [weapons of mass destruction]. While our technological and military capabilities will continue to play an essential role, engagement is also one of the most important tools in the national security arsenal."[83]

NOTES

1. "Text of Obama's speech to the United Nations General Assembly," *The New York Times*, Sept. 23, 2009.

2. Stephen I. Schwartz with Deepti Choubey, *Nuclear Security Spending: Assessing Costs, Examining Priorities* (2009), p. 7, www.carnegieendowment.org/files/nuclear_security_spending_low.pdf.

3. George P. Shultz, *et al.*, "A World Free of Nuclear Weapons," *The Wall Street Journal*, Jan. 4, 2007.

4. Nuclear weapons get their explosive power from materials that are fissile, meaning that their atoms can be split by certain types of sub-atomic particles (neutrons). The main fissile materials are uranium-233, uranium-235, and plutonium-239.

5. Remarks by President Barack Obama, Prague, Czech Republic, April 5, 2009, www.whitehouse.gov/the_press_office/Remarks-By-President-Barack-Obama-In-Prague-As-Delivered/.

6. "U.S. Scraps Missile Defense Shield Plans," CNN.com, Sept. 17, 2009.

7. Clifford J. Levy and Peter Baker, "Putin Applauds Brave U.S. Decision on Missile Defense," *The New York Times*, Sept. 19, 2009.

8. "Statement of Senator John McCain," Sept. 17, 2009, http://mccain.senate.gov/public/.

9. "Historic Summit of Security Council Pledges Support for Progress on Stalled Efforts to End

Nuclear Weapons Proliferation," United Nations, Sept. 24, 2009.

10. *Ibid.*

11. Natural Resources Defense Council, "Archive of Nuclear Data: Table of Global Nuclear Weapons Stockpiles, 1945-2002," www.nrdc.org/nuclear/nudb/datab19.asp.

12. America's Strategic Posture: Final Report of the Congressional Commission on the Strategic Posture of the United States (2009), chapters 2, 5 and 9, www.usip.org/files/file/strat_posture_report_adv_copy.pdf.

13. David E. Sanger and Helene Cooper, "Iran is Warned Over Nuclear Deception," *The New York Times*, Sept. 26, 2009.

14. "The Disarmament Illusion," editorial, *The Wall Street Journal*, Sept. 26, 2009.

15. For the treaty's history and full text, see www.state.gov/www/global/arms/treaties/npt.html.

16. www.globalzero.org/files/pdf/gzap_3.0.pdf.

17. For background see Mary H. Cooper, "Nuclear Proliferation and Terrorism," *CQ Researcher*, April 2, 2004, pp. 297-320.

18. Joseph Cirincione, *Bomb Scare: The History & Future of Nuclear Weapons* (2007), pp. 126-127.

19. Harold Brown and John Deutch, "The Nuclear Disarmament Fantasy," *The Wall Street Journal*, Nov. 19, 2007.

20. Treaty text is at www.state.gov/www/global/arms/treaties/ctb.html.

21. Annex 2 of the treaty lists 44 countries that must sign and ratify the treaty for it to enter into force. As of mid-2009, 35 of these countries had done so.

22. Damien J. LaVera, "Looking Back: The U.S. Senate Vote on the Comprehensive Test Ban Treaty," Arms Control Today, October 2004.

23. Jon Kyl and Richard Perle, "Our Decaying Nuclear Deterrent," *The Wall Street Journal*, June 30, 2009.

24. Congressional Record, June 8, 2009, p. S6238.

25. Comprehensive Nuclear Test Ban Treaty Organization, "CTBTO's Initial Findings on the DPRK's 2009 Announced Nuclear Test," May 25, 2009, www.ctbto.org/press-centre/press-releases/2009/ctbtos-initial-findings-on-the-dprks-2009-announced-nuclear-test/.

26. National Academy of Sciences, Technical Issues Related to the Comprehensive Nuclear Test Ban Treaty (National Academy Press, 2009), p. 5.

27. Speech at Strategic Weapons in the 21st Century Conference, Washington, D.C., Jan. 31, 2008, pp. 2-3, www.lanl.gov/conferences/sw/docs/chilton-speech-SW21-31Jan08.pdf.

28. Charles D. Ferguson, "Mini-Nuclear Weapons and the U.S. Nuclear Posture Review," Monterey Institute of International Studies, April 8, 2002, http://cns.miis.edu/stories/020408.htm.

29. James Sterngold, "Failure to Launch," *Mother Jones*, January 2008.

30. Jonathan Medalia, "The Reliable Replacement Warhead Program: Background and Current Developments," Congressional Research Service, Sept. 12, 2008, pp. 45-46, www.fas.org/sgp/crs/nuke/RL32929.pdf.

31. Robert Gates, "Nuclear Weapons and Deterrence in the 21st Century," speech at Carnegie Endowment for International Peace, Oct. 28, 2008, p. 5, www.carnegieendowment.org/files/1028_transcrip_gates_checked.pdf.

32. Hearing before House Armed Services Committee, March 17, 2009, www.stratcom.mil/speeches/21/.

33. *Technical Issues Related to the Comprehensive Nuclear Test Ban Treaty*, National Academy of Sciences (2002), p. 5.

34. "Pit Lifetime," MITRE Corporation, Nov. 20, 2006, p. 16, www.nukewatch.org/facts/nwd/JASON_ReportPuAging.pdf; National Nuclear Security Administration, "Studies Show Plutonium Degradation in U.S. Nuclear Weapons Will Not Affect Reliability Soon," Nov. 29, 2006.

35. National Nuclear Security Administration, "Life Extension Programs," http://nnsa.energy.gov/defense_programs/life_extension_programs.htm.

36. For details see U.S. Government Accountability Office, "Nuclear Weapons: Annual Assessment of the Safety, Performance, and Reliability of the Nation's Stockpile," Feb. 2, 2007, p. 14.

37. Gates, *op. cit.*, p. 5.

38. "The U.S. Military Index," *Foreign Policy*, March/April 2008, p. 77.

39. U.S. Department of Energy, Office of History and Heritage Resources, "The Manhattan Project: An Interactive History," www.cfo.doe.gov/me70/manhattan/retrospect.htm.

40. *Ibid.*

41. McGeorge Bundy, *Danger and Survival: Choices About the Bomb in the First Fifty Years* (1988), p. 113.

42. A ballistic missile is powered during the launch phase of its flight and then falls freely toward its target.

43. Bundy, *op. cit.*, p. 350.

44. Natural Resources Defense Council, "Table of Global Nuclear Weapons Stockpiles, 1945-2002," www.nrdc.org/nuclear/nudb/datab19.asp.

45. For an account and analysis of the crisis, see Bundy, *op cit.*, pp. 391-452. Bundy was President Kennedy's national security advisor during the missile crisis.

46. News conference 52, March 21, 1963, www.jfklibrary.org/Historical+Resources/Archives/Reference+Desk/Press+Conferences/.

47. Text and background at www.state.gov/www/global/arms/treaties/ltbt1.html.

48. *Ibid.*

49. Natural Resources Defense Council, *op. cit.*

50. Text and background at www.state.gov/www/global/arms/treaties/salt1.html and www.state.gov/www/global/arms/treaties/abm/abm2.html.

51. Presidential Directive 59, July 25, 1980, www.fas.org/irp/offdocs/pd/pd59.pdf.

52. Robert Scheer, *With Enough Shovels: Reagan, Bush and Nuclear War* (1983), p. 20.

53. Michael Goodwin, "Antinuclear Protest Cost the City $1.8 Million," *The New York Times*, July 25, 1982.

54. U.S. Catholic Bishops' Pastoral Letter on War and Peace, May 3, 1983, www.nuclearfiles.org/menu/key-issues/ethics/issues/religious/us-catholic-bishops-pastoral-letter.htm.

55. For background see Mary H. Cooper, "Missile Defense," *CQ Researcher*, Sept. 8, 2000.

56. Nikolai Sokov, "Reykjavik Summit: the Legacy and a Lesson for the Future," Nuclear Threat Initiative, December 2007.

57. Text and background at www.state.gov/www/global/arms/treaties/inf1.html.

58. Compiled from Nuclear Threat Initiative, "Threat Reduction Budgets," www.nti.org/e_research/cnwm/overview/cnwm_home.asp.

59. Nuclear Threat Initiative, "U.S. Nuclear Posture Reviews," www.nti.org/f_wmd411/f2c.html.

60. *Ibid.*

61. Philipp C. Bleek, "Nuclear Posture Review Leaks: Outlines Targets, Contingencies," *Arms Control Today*, April 2002.

62. Arms Control Association, "START II and Its Extension Protocol at a Glance," January 2003, www.armscontrl.org/print/2562; Nuclear Threat Initiative, "The SORT Treaty," updated July 2009www.nti.org/f_wmd411/f2b2_1.html.

63. Steven A. Hildreth and Carl Ek, "Long-Range Ballistic Missile Defense in Europe," Congressional Research Service, June 22, 2009, p. 17, www.fas.org/sgp/crs/weapons/RL34051.pdf.

64. New Deterrent Working Group, "U.S. Nuclear Deterrence in the 21st Century: Getting It Right," Center for Security Policy, July 2009, p. 12, http://204.96.138.161/upload/wysiwyg/center%20publication%20pdfs/NDWG-%20Getting%20It%20Right.pdf.

65. Clifford J. Levy and Peter Baker, "U.S.-Russia Nuclear Agreement is first Step in Broad Effort," *The New York Times*, July 7, 2009.

66. Congressional Record, July 22, 2009, p. S7850.

67. Siegfried S. Hecker, "The Risks of North Korea's Restart," Bulletin of the Atomic Scientists, May 12, 2009; David E. Sanger, "Tested Early by North Korea, Obama Has Few Options," *The New York Times*, May 26, 2009. For background see Mary H. Cooper, "North Korean Crisis," *CQ Researcher*, April 11, 2003, pp. 321-344.

68. United Nations Department of Public Information, "Security Council, Acting Unanimously, condemns

in Strongest Terms Democratic People's Republic of Korea Nuclear Test, Toughens Sanctions," June 12, 2009.

69. Interviewed on Meet the Press, July 26, 2009, www.msnbc.msn.com/id/32142102/ns/meet_the_press/.

70. Neil Chatterjee, "U.S. Says Will Not Accept N. Korea as Nuclear State," Reuters, May 30, 2009.

71. See Martin Fackler, "Test Delivers a Message for Domestic Audience," *The New York Times*, May 26, 2009,

72. David E. Sanger and Helene Cooper, "Iran Is Warned Over Nuclear Deception," *The New York Times*, Sept. 26, 2009.

73. Mark Landler and David E. Sanger, "Clinton Speaks of Shielding Mideast from Iran," *The New York Times*, July 23, 2009.

74. For background see Roland Flamini, "Dealing with the 'New' Russia," *CQ Researcher*, June 6, 2008, pp. 481-504.

75. "Biden's full remarks at the Munich conference," *Politico.com*, Feb. 7, 2009, www.politico.com/news/stories/0209/18535.html.

76. "Joint Statement by President Obama and President Medvedev," The White House, April 1, 2009.

77. Office of Sen. Richard G. Lugar, "The Nunn-Lugar Scorecard," http://lugar.senate.gov/nunnlugar/scorecard.html.

78. Matthew Bunn, "Securing the Bomb 2008," Harvard University, November 2008, pp. vi-xi, www.nti.org/e_research/STB08_Executive_Summary.pdf.

79. "NTI Co-chairman Sam Nunn Commends Successful Removal of Dangerous Nuclear Material from Kazakhstan," Nuclear Threat Initiative, May 19, 2009.

80. Kingston Reif and Cuyler O'Brien, "Obama Nuclear Nonproliferation Budget Disappointing," Center for Arms Control and Non-Proliferation, June 2, 2009.

81. International Atomic Energy Agency, "Strengthened Safeguards System: Status of Additional Protocols," July 9, 2009, www.iaea.org/OurWord/SV/Safeguards/sg_protocol.html.

82. Rens Lee, "Toward an Intelligence-Based Nuclear Cooperations Regime," Foreign Policy Research Institute, July 2009.

83. Committee on International Security and Arms Control, National Academy of Sciences, *Global Security Engagement: A New Model for Cooperative Threat Reduction* (2009), p. 9.

BIBLIOGRAPHY

Books

Allison, Graham, *Nuclear Terrorism: The Ultimate Preventable Catastrophe*, Times Books, 2004.
A Harvard professor and former Defense Department official explores the risk of terrorist nuclear attacks on the U.S.

Bundy, McGeorge, *Danger and Survival: Choices About the Bomb in the First 50 Years*, Vintage, 1990.
A national security adviser to presidents Kennedy and Johnson examines factors that led nations to pursue or forswear nuclear weapons during World War II and the Cold War.

Moran, Barbara, *The Day We Lost the H-Bomb: Cold War, Hot Nukes, and the Worst Nuclear Weapons Disaster in History*, Presidio Press, 2009.
Journalist Moran revisits the 1966 collision of a U.S. B-52 bomber carrying four hydrogen bombs with a refueling plane over Spain.

Shultz, George P., *et al.*, eds., *Reykjavik Revisited: Steps Toward a World Free of Nuclear Weapons*, Hoover Institution Press, 2008.
National security experts examine the steps required to reduce threats from nuclear weapons and move toward their elimination.

Articles

Bender, Bryan, "Obama Seeks Global Uranium Fuel Bank," *The Boston Globe*, June 8, 2009.
Bender outlines an idea advocated by many arms control specialists: creating an international nuclear fuel supply so that countries would not need to build fuel production systems that could produce weapon-grade nuclear material.

Broad, William J., and David E. Sanger, "Obama's Youth Shaped His Nuclear-Free Vision," *The New York Times*, **July 5, 2009.**
President Obama's support for nuclear abolition dates back to his college years.

DeSutter, Paula A., "The Test Ban Treaty Would Help North Korea," *The Wall Street Journal*, **June 1, 2009.**
A former Bush administration official argues that ending nuclear testing would erode U.S. nuclear credibility.

Kimball, Daryl, "Change Nuclear Weapons Policy? Yes, We Can," *Foreign Policy in Focus*, **Nov. 25, 2008.**
The director of the Arms Control Association contends that without action by the Obama administration to shrink nuclear arsenals and transform U.S. nuclear policy, global risks of nuclear proliferation and terrorism will increase.

Suri, Jeremi, "The Nukes of October: Richard Nixon's Secret Plan to Bring Peace to Vietnam," *Wired*, **Feb. 25, 2008.**
A professor details how in 1969 President Richard M. Nixon sent nuclear-armed bombers to the edge of Soviet airspace to convince Soviet leaders and their North Vietnamese allies that unless they joined talks to end the Vietnam War, the United States might end it with nuclear weapons.

Reports and Studies

"Leveraging Science for Security: A Strategy for the Nuclear Weapons Laboratories in the 21st Century," *Henry L. Stimson Center*, **March 2009, www.stimson .org/cnp/pdf/Leveraging_Science_for_Security_ FINAL.pdf.**
A task force co-chaired by former senior officials from the Clinton and Bush administrations recommends moving nuclear weapons laboratories in the United States into a new agency that would maintain the nuclear arsenal and analyze national security problems.

"U.S. Nuclear Weapons Policy," *Council on Foreign Relations*, **Independent Task Force Report No. 62, 2009, www.cfr.org/content/publications/attach- ments/Nuclear_Weapons_TFR62.pdf.**
Nuclear security experts recommend how to reshape U.S. nuclear forces and policies to address nuclear proliferation and other post-Cold War security threats.

"White Paper on the Necessity of the U.S. Nuclear Deterrent," *National Institute for Public Policy*, **Aug. 15, 2007, www.nipp.org/Publication/Downloads/ Publication%20Archive%20PDF/Deterrence%20 Paper%20-%20version%202.pdf.**
Conservative security scholars and former government officials contend the United States still needs nuclear weapons for deterring attacks, destroying strategic military targets and stemming nuclear proliferation.

Perkovich, George, *et al.*, **"Abolishing Nuclear Weapons: A Debate,"** *Carnegie Endowment for International Peace*, **February 2009, www.carnegieendowment.org/ files/abolishing_nuclear_weapons_debate.pdf.**
Security experts in 13 countries examine what would be required to achieve nuclear disarmament.

Schwartz, Stephen I., with Deepti Choubey, *Nuclear Security Spending: Assessing Costs, Examining Priorities* **(2009), p. 7, www.carnegieendowment.org/ files/nuclear_security_spending_low.pdf.**
A review of U.S. funding for programs related to nuclear weapons finds that the nation is still spending more than $50 billion annually in this area nearly two decades after the Cold War.

For More Information

Alliance for Nuclear Accountability, 903 West Alameda St., #505, Santa Fe, NM 87501; (505) 473-1670; www .ananuclear.org. A network of local, regional and national organizations working to control pollution from nuclear weapons production.

Arms Control Association, 1313 L St., N.W., Suite 130, Washington, DC 20036; (202) 463-8270; www.armscontrol .org. A nonprofit, nonpartisan organization that promotes public understanding of and support for effective arms control policies.

Atomic Heritage Foundation, 910 17th St., N.W., Suite 408, Washington, DC 20006; (202) 293-0045; www .atomicheritage.org. A nonprofit organization to preserve and interpret the Manhattan Project and its legacy.

Center for International Security and Cooperation, 616 Serra St., E200, Stanford University, Stanford, CA 94305-6055; (650) 723-9265; http://cisac.stanford.edu. Studies nuclear weapons strategy and proliferation.

National Institute for Public Policy, 9302 Lee Hwy., Suite 750, Fairfax, VA 22301-1214; (703) 293-9181; www .nipp.org. A nonprofit education organization focusing on foreign and defense policy from a conservative perspective.

National Nuclear Security Administration, U.S. Department of Energy, 1000 Independence Ave., S.W., Washington, DC 20585; (800) 342-5363; http://nnsa.energy.gov. Manages the nation's nuclear stockpile and related laboratories and production plants.

Nuclear Threat Initiative, 1747 Pennsylvania Ave., N.W., 7th Floor, Washington, DC 20006; (202) 296-4810; www .nti.org. Works to strengthen global security by preventing the spread of weapons of mass destruction.

Ploughshares Fund, Fort Mason Center B-330, San Francisco, CA 94123; (415) 775-2244; www.ploughshares.org. Opposes the spread of nuclear weapons.

4

Future of NATO

Is the Transatlantic Alliance Obsolete?

Roland Flamini

With global energy resources heavily concentrated in countries with unstable or unpredictable governments and terrorism on the rise, protecting energy supplies has become a legitimate security issue. NATO is debating whether its 21st-century mandate should include protecting oil pipelines — like these transporting Russian oil to Germany — and global energy-supply routes, including ocean shipping lanes.

AFP/Getty Images/Katja Buchholz

From *CQ Global Researcher*, January 2009.

For weeks, Germany's special forces and Afghan intelligence had been secretly spying on a notorious Taliban commander known only as the Baghlan bomber. They had pieced together his behavior patterns and followed him whenever he left his safe house in northern Afghanistan.

The insurgent leader was linked to a long list of terrorist acts, including the shocking November 2007 raid on the ceremonial reopening of a new sugar factory in Baghlan province, which killed 79 people, including dozens of children and several high-ranking officials and politicians.

Last March, German and Afghan commandos moved in to arrest him. Clad in black and wearing night-vision goggles, they came within a few hundred yards of the house when lookouts raised the alarm. In the ensuing confusion, their quarry got away, though several marksmen had him in their sights.

In fact, said *Der Spiegel*, Germany's most popular news magazine, "It would have been possible for the Germans to kill him," but the notorious terrorist was allowed to escape — and subsequently returned to carry out further attacks.[1] He got away because German troops are among the national contingents serving in Afghanistan with North Atlantic Treaty Organization (NATO) forces who are not allowed to shoot unless they are being fired upon. Troops from France, Italy, Spain, Portugal and several other countries are similarly restricted. Because the Baghlan bomber was fleeing instead of attacking, he could not be shot.

As a result of these "selective participation" policies, most of the casualties among the 50,000 troops serving in the alliance's International Security and Assistance Force (ISAF) in Afghanistan

NATO in Europe Has Doubled in Size

The North Atlantic Treaty Organization (NATO) — the postwar defense alliance that originally linked the United States and Western Europe — now has 26 members, with additional participants from the fragments of the collapsed Soviet Union, including most of Eastern Europe and the Baltic states, making it twice its original size within Europe. In North America, the United States, Canada and Greenland — a self-governing Danish province — are part of NATO. Croatia and Albania are expected to join in April — and possibly Macedonia. Ukraine and Georgia are involved in intense talks with NATO about joining the alliance someday, as are Bosnia and Herzegovina and Montenegro. Although Turkey — on the southern border of the former Soviet Union — had joined the alliance in 1952, NATO's inclusion of Romania, Bulgaria and the three former Baltic states (Lithuania, Latvia, and Estonia) in 2004 brought the alliance smack up against Russia's northern and eastern borders, stirring Kremlin objections.

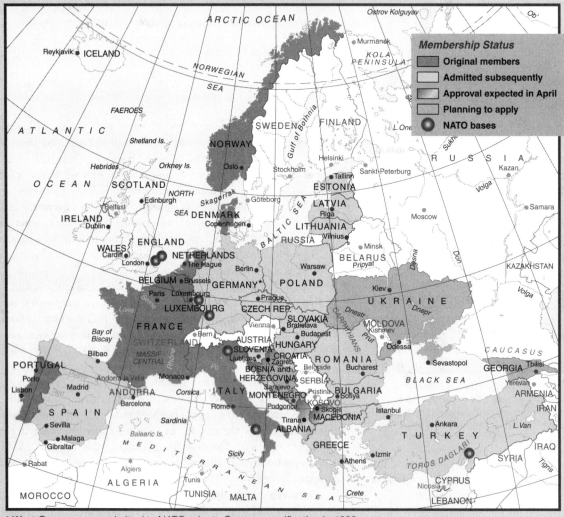

* West Germany was admitted to NATO prior to German reunification in 1990.

Source: North Atlantic Treaty Organization

are being suffered by U.S., British and Canadian soldiers, who are fully engaged in combat operations against insurgents. The United States has lost 630 troops in its NATO contingent in Afghanistan since 2001, Britain 138 and Canada 106; but Italy had only 13 deaths, Germany 28 and Portugal 2.[2]

The restrictive rules of engagement for some NATO participants reflect the widely divergent views about the alliance's goals in Afghanistan. But the dispute is only one of the many contentious issues plaguing NATO as it celebrates its 60th year at a summit in April. Others include:

• **How best to help Afghanistan** — The United States and Britain see NATO as being engaged in a full-scale conflict against the Taliban insurgency. But most Europeans eschew the idea of achieving a military victory and focus more on helping the Afghan people become self-sufficient in security and democratic governance. The ongoing debate has stymied ISAF's efforts to formulate a unified strategy in Afghanistan and has allowed the Taliban to continue its attacks from within safe havens in Pakistan's largely uncontrolled frontier territory.[3]

• **How to deal with global terrorism** — After the Sept. 11, 2001, terrorist attacks in the United States, NATO responded to President George W. Bush's appeal for support in invading Afghanistan and hunting down 9/11 mastermind Osama bin Laden and his al Qaeda terrorist organization. The Bush administration at first opted to go it alone, but once the Taliban were driven out of Afghanistan, the alliance deployed the ISAF. But European governments generally view terrorists as criminals — rather than as jihadist fighters — and

U.S. Provides Most Funds, Troops

NATO's 24 European members contributed about half of the alliance's $1.2 trillion budget for military operations in 2007, while the United States alone contributed 45 percent. Most of the money was used for the war in Afghanistan and to maintain NATO troops in Kosovo. NATO doesn't maintain a standing force. Its troops come from the armies of member nations, and all 3.8 million troops in NATO's member countries are considered potentially available for a NATO deployment. The United States maintained 1.3 million troops in its armed forces in 2007, more than twice the amount maintained by Turkey, the NATO member with the second-largest army. Iceland does not maintain an army or contribute to NATO's military budget.

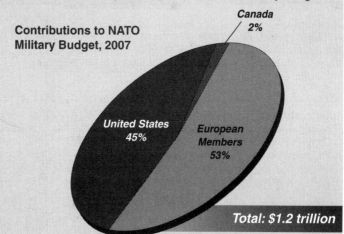

Contributions to NATO Military Budget, 2007

Canada 2%
United States 45%
European Members 53%

Total: $1.2 trillion

Number of Troops Maintained by NATO Members, 2007
(in thousands)

Belgium	39	Hungary	20	Portugal	41
Bulgaria	41	Iceland	0	Romania	76
Canada	65	Italy	298	Slovakia	18
Czech Republic	25	Latvia	6	Slovenia	7
Denmark	18	Lithuania	10	Spain	132
Estonia	5	Luxembourg	1.6	Turkey	496
France	354	Netherlands	51	United Kingdom	190
Germany	247	Norway	20	United States	1,346
Greece	142	Poland	150	**Total:**	**3,799**

Source: North Atlantic Treaty Organization

disagree with the Bush administration's declaration of a global "war on terror."[4]

"Europe is not at war," European Union foreign policy chief Javier Solana famously declared dismissively,

AFP/Getty Images/Elvis Barukcic

Belgian soldiers from the NATO-led peacekeeping mission (KFOR) in newly independent Kosovo patrol Mitrovica last March. NATO has been monitoring the area since the late 1990s, when the alliance launched air strikes against the former Yugoslavia to halt ethnic cleansing in Kosovo.

adding that Europeans do, however, "energetically oppose terrorism."[5]

- **Sharing the burden** — The United States has borne the brunt of funding and arming NATO, despite efforts to persuade the Europeans to invest more in defense. NATO members promise to earmark at least 2 percent of their annual gross domestic product (GDP) for defense, but over the years many members have come to regard that minimum as a ceiling. (*See graph, p. 87.*)

In fact, while the United States spends 4 percent of its GDP on defense, only five European members — Bulgaria, Britain, France, Greece and Turkey — allocate even 2 percent for defense. Other European governments spend less, in part because of peacetime complacency and the high cost of their social programs. France and Britain accounted for 48 percent of Europe's defense spending in 2008, while Germany — NATO's largest European member — spent only 1.2 percent of its GDP on defense in 2008 (scheduled to increase to 1.4 percent this year through 2012). Overall, NATO's 24 European members have budgeted $280 billion in military expenditures in 2009, but the impact of those expenditures is dissipated since they are spread out over dozens of separate national programs.[6]

The gap between the United States and its European allies in military technology is also widening, making it increasingly difficult for forces to work together. When NATO intervened to prevent ethnic strife in the Balkans in 1998, for instance, only the United States could conduct precision strikes and airborne refueling and had high-tech surveillance and command-and-control systems. And the situation hasn't changed much since then. (*See sidebar, p. 94.*)

- **Selective participation** — During the Cold War, members of the alliance agreed on the threat NATO faced from the Soviet Union and how to address it. While consensus remains the cornerstone of the alliance, in today's more complex, post-Cold War world agreeing on strategy is more difficult, which puts a constant strain on relations. It is generally agreed that if NATO is to survive it must be willing to act "out of area" — or outside of members' territories. Indeed, "out of area or out of business" is a popular refrain at NATO headquarters in Brussels, Belgium, nowadays. Yet European nations are increasingly cautious about committing forces to non-self-defense missions.

As a result, the "coalition of the willing" approach — in which individual members decide which missions they will participate in — has become the norm. Though the alliance dutifully closed ranks in the case of Afghanistan, NATO refused to become involved in the Iraq conflict, even though several alliance members joined the U.S.-initiated attack. And in April 2009, when incoming President Barack Obama is expected to ask U.S. allies to match projected U.S. troop increases in Afghanistan, Europe will probably balk. With both military and civilian deaths rising in Afghanistan, opposition to what Europeans once regarded as the "good" war — as opposed to the "bad" one in Iraq — is increasing in some European countries.

- **NATO enlargement** — After the fall of the Soviet Union, NATO survived — and even grew from 15 members to 26 — because it became "a great tool to transform Cold War countries into democracies," observes Henning Riecke, a security specialist at the German Foreign Policy Institute in Berlin. Former communist states in Eastern Europe and the Baltics were offered membership in the alliance if they became more democratic. Countries like the Czech Republic, Poland and Lithuania eagerly complied, attracted by the implied promise — through NATO — of American protection from their old nemesis Russia.

Too battered economically and politically to protest, the Russians were allowed to participate in the alliance by joining the specially created NATO-Russia Permanent Joint Council, in which Russia has military-observer status in Brussels. But when in 2007 the Bush administration began pressing the alliance to extend membership to Georgia and Ukraine, a newly prosperous, oil-rich Russia began to raise strong objections.

"The emergence of the powerful military bloc at our borders will be seen as a direct threat to Russia's security," Russian Prime Minister Vladimir Putin declared in October 2008, referring to NATO. "I heard them saying . . . that the expansion is not directed against Russia. But it's the potential, not the intention that matters."[7] Led by France and Germany — both heavily dependent on Russian energy supplies — NATO has stalled on admitting Russia's two southern neighbors.

Then last August, Russia's massive incursion into Georgia in response to a botched Georgian bid to invade its separatist province of South Ossetia stirred new fears in Eastern Europe that Moscow might overrun its democratic neighbors in an effort to reclaim the old Soviet empire.[8] President Bush has continued to push for NATO membership for Georgia and Ukraine despite Europe's coolness to the idea, and President-elect Obama supported Georgia's membership during the election campaign.

But perhaps the biggest arguments within NATO today focus on the alliance's future. "The end of the USSR . . . destroyed any rationale for the United States to continue defending Europe," argued Doug Bandow, a former Reagan administration senior policy analyst.[9]

Moreover, Europeans have "a growing lack of enthusiasm for defense spending and far-flung military commitments," says Elizabeth Sherwood-Randall, an expert on alliance relations at the New York-based Council on Foreign Relations think tank.

Allied leaders must do some "careful bricklaying" if NATO is to stay in business for another 60 years — or even 10 more years, says Sherwood-Randall. Until now, they have based their commitments "on past understandings but now need to renew the effort to reach a joint threat assessment, set allied expectations for behavior and prepare militarily for future scenarios."

The problem may be that NATO has too many roles in the 21st century. "Today, three NATOs co-exist," says Riecke. "There's the NATO of the Cold War, there's the exporter of stability to ex-Soviet countries and there's the NATO directed against new threats. East Europeans favor the first NATO because it offers protection from Russia; Western Europeans want the second because it has brought democratic stability; the United States favors the third because of its commitment to the war on terrorism. But which is the real NATO? It's hard to reconcile the three."

To mark its 60th anniversary this April, NATO is updating its strategic concept — a document second in importance only to the alliance's 1949 founding treaty. Alliance officials hope the end product will become the basis for NATO's post-Cold War strategic role — a discussion many believe is long overdue.

With little likelihood of a new war in Europe, the alliance's political and military objectives are expected to continue to concentrate on scenarios that involve NATO action outside of members' territory. Officials also may decide that NATO's goals include protecting the global energy infrastructure, responding to the rise of China and fighting global terrorism.

As NATO member states discuss the future of the alliance, here are some of the questions being debated:

Is NATO obsolete?

"NATO is an interesting paradox because normally alliances disappear when they win the war," says Josef Joffe, publisher-editor of the German intellectual weekly *Die Zeit* and a highly respected specialist on defense issues. "Yet this one is still alive for all the old reasons. You want to be allied to the United States because the United States is a kind of security lender of last resort. You never know what might happen, especially with Russia coming back, point No. 1.

"Point No. 2, NATO is the most important thing that stands between us and the renationalization of our defense policies" — that is, the return to nationalism in Europe, which he argues has historically led to weapons escalations and eventually to conflict.[10]

The debate over whether the North Atlantic Alliance should remain in existence has been going on since the Soviet Union — the threat that sparked NATO's creation — collapsed in 1991.

American critics of the alliance argue that NATO no longer serves any strategic purpose yet ties up U.S. troops, financially burdens the United States and alarms and alienates Russia. In addition, some Americans say that

AFP/Getty Images

AP Photo/Allauddin Khan

Death and Rebuilding

Residents of Afghanistan's Helmand province display the bodies of some of the 17 civilians they say were killed by misguided U.S. or NATO air strikes on Oct. 16, 2008. NATO's International Security Assistance Force (ISAF) said reports of enemy air strikes in the region that day make it difficult to determine what happened. At least 321 Afghan civilians were killed in air strikes in 2007 — three times as many as in the previous year — feeding Afghan resentment toward U.S. and NATO forces. To avoid such unintended consequences, some European governments promote non-military "soft" power, such as the work provided by NATO's Provincial Reconstruction Teams (PRTs). An Afghan military official, (below, left) and a Canadian ISAF member (right) inaugurate a road-building project funded by the Canadian Provincial Reconstruction Team in Kandahar province, in April 2008.

reliance on the U.S.-led organization discourages Europe from assuming responsibility for its own defense.

"NATO has become absurd in the post-Cold War world, with global warming and food shortages transcending the antiquated security notions associated with armies," Saul Landau, a fellow at the Institute for Policy Studies, a liberal Washington think tank, wrote recently.[11]

With Albania and Croatia about to join NATO, "It's not clear against whom these countries need to be defended. It's even less clear why America should do the defending," says Bandow, the former Reagan analyst.[12]

A conservative American critic of NATO, E. Wayne Merry, said U.S. domination of the North Atlantic Alliance, with the Europeans relegated to junior partner roles, has stunted Europe's growth by preventing "the evolution of European integration to include full responsibility for continental security." Merry, a former senior U.S. State Department and Pentagon official and now a senior associate at the American Foreign Policy Council in Washington, contends that, "The growth of European identity and European integration makes this approach obsolete."[13]

Advocates of preserving NATO point out that it embodies multilateralism in an increasingly interdependent world. "Bush quickly discovered [in Iraq] that unilateralism didn't work, and when NATO let him down, he had to create an ad hoc NATO of his own," observes Massimo Franco, a leading political commentator and columnist at the Italian paper *Corriere della Sera*. Bush's so-called coalition of the willing in Iraq fell apart, he says, "because it didn't have the underpinnings of a true alliance."

Or, as Riecke of the German Foreign Policy Institute points out, "Only NATO is capable of mustering the forces for a very complex operation; no other organization can do it. NATO is the stability actor in Europe."

Responding to a proposal by Russian President Dmitry A. Medvedev that NATO consider a new "security architecture" for Europe, NATO Secretary General Jaap de Hoop Scheffer of the Netherlands said in early December that NATO members are "quite happy" with the existing security structure in Europe and that there is "not a shimmer of a chance that . . . NATO could or would be negotiated away."[14]

NATO is also a built-in customer for the multibillion-dollar U.S. weapons industry, and American arms manufacturers are avid supporters of NATO expansion. NATO expansion into Eastern Europe and the Baltic nations has been a boon for weapons sales.[15] The boom began in the 1990s, when former Soviet states wishing to join the alliance were required to modernize their armed forces. Many replaced their dated Soviet arms with new Western weapons.[16]

As the number of new NATO countries has increased, arms sales have kept pace. In 2006, U.S.

government-to-government arms sales were valued at $16.9 billion, including $6.6 billion with NATO countries and Japan and the balance to developing countries. By 2008, the overall amount of such transactions had almost doubled, to $32 billion, with the United States capturing 52 percent of the world arms market.[17] These numbers do not include private arms sales to different countries by U.S. companies without government involvement — rare in the case of major sales of combat hardware. Such sales are impossible to calculate with any accuracy.

Polish Foreign Minister Radek Sikorsky says the downside of dismantling NATO far outweighs any advantages. He identifies five reasons for keeping NATO in existence:

- The transition costs "would be problematic," he says. U.S. withdrawal from NATO would deprive the European economy of billions of dollars, not counting the cost of extracting and relocating the U.S. troops.
- With no power to check them, Germany and France would dominate Europe, which other countries would dread — especially Eastern and Central European countries like Poland.
- As a full-fledged power with a bigger population and economy than the United States, Europe would begin to see itself more as a competitor with America, especially with the U.S. arms industry. And once "divorced" from the United States, Europe could align itself with other powers. "A Europe with its own independent military capability will more frequently say 'no' to America" on a wide range of international issues, Sikorsky says.
- If the United States and Europe subsequently had to fight alongside each other, "they would no longer be a workable coalition," he says. "Pretty soon, they would be working to reinvent NATO."

Should energy security become a new NATO responsibility?

European members of NATO import 50 percent of their energy needs — 25 percent of it from Russia. Thus, as demand rises for oil and gas, and with much of the world's energy resources in countries with unstable or unpredictable governments, energy has become a legitimate security issue.[18]

In 2006, a NATO forum on energy-security technology was told that the global oil market loses a million barrels a day to politically motivated sabotage.[19] Later that year at a NATO summit in Riga, Latvia, alliance leaders decided to add energy security to its agenda.

"Alliance security interests can also be affected by the disruption of the flow of vital resources," said the summit's final declaration. "We support a coordinated, international effort to assess risk to energy infrastructure and to promote energy infrastructure security." Member states were charged to "consult on the most immediate risks in the field of energy security."[20]

Precedents for protecting member states' energy supplies date back to the Cold War, when NATO created and maintained 10 storage and distribution facilities across Europe, primarily for military use. During the Iran-Iraq War in the 1980s, NATO ships protected Saudi Arabian and Gulf state oil tankers from attack by either side in case they tried to cut off supplies to the West. And in 1990, although NATO did not participate as an organization in the first Gulf War, France, Italy, Britain and the Netherlands joined the United States in liberating Kuwait from Iraqi occupation — thus ensuring that Kuwait retained its oil fields.

The alliance has yet to make public any plan of action, but analysts say NATO could help protect energy sources, including oil fields, pipelines and sea routes used for transporting unrefined oil — especially vital sea routes like the Panama and Suez canals and the straits of Hormuz in the Persian Gulf and Malacca between Malaysia and Indonesia. Terrorist attacks on these strategic routes would have drastic consequences for energy supplies. Moreover, pipelines deliver 40 percent of the oil and gas to world markets and are even more susceptible to terrorist action.[21]

The idea of expanding NATO's tasks to include protecting global energy supplies has its problems. For example, guarding the thousands of miles of pipelines carrying Russian oil and gas across Central Asia and the Caucasus, if it were even possible, could lead to tension with the Russians.

The size of the undertaking is daunting. "NATO cannot really protect pipelines, but it can control the maritime 'choke' points where traffic is heavy, such as the Gulf, and key drilling points," observes Riecke at the German Foreign Policy Institute. The involvement of an

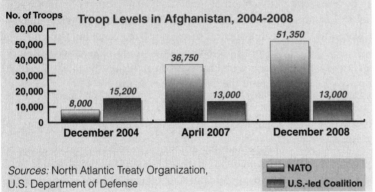

NATO Troop Levels in Afghanistan Jumped Sixfold

Over 51,000 NATO troops are serving in the war in Afghanistan — more than a sixfold jump over 2004 levels. About 40 percent of the NATO troops are Americans. Another 12,000 Americans are serving in the U.S.-led coalition in Afghanistan. President-elect Barack Obama has vowed to send additional U.S. troops and is expected to ask NATO countries to deploy more troops as well.

Troop Levels in Afghanistan, 2004-2008

No. of Troops

- December 2004: NATO 8,000; U.S.-led Coalition 15,200
- April 2007: NATO 36,750; U.S.-led Coalition 13,000
- December 2008: NATO 51,350; U.S.-led Coalition 13,000

Sources: North Atlantic Treaty Organization, U.S. Department of Defense

■ NATO
■ U.S.-led Coalition

according to NATO.[22] Leaders recognized the challenge of international terrorism as a new role for the alliance, even though there was no consensus among members about the nature of the threat and how to deal with it.

Former Spanish Prime Minister José María Aznar even calls on NATO to break out of its transatlantic mold and become a global antiterrorist force. NATO needs what he calls a "bold transformation . . . to build a "strategic [antiterrorist] partnership," he says. He would like to see the alliance open its doors to Japan, Australia and Israel in order "to better reflect the nations that are willing and able to cooperate in eliminating the threat of Islamist terror."[23]

essentially Western alliance in global energy security could make other countries feel uneasy as well. For example, an energy role would extend NATO's reach into Asia, and the Chinese will almost certainly object, he says.

In addition, argues Turkish commentator and oil executive Sohbet Karbuz, if NATO deploys in Gulf waters, non-NATO countries might decide to do the same, adding to regional tensions. "What if China now wants to patrol the Strait of Hormuz?" asks Karbuz. "After all, China imports more oil from the region than the United States or the European Union."

Can NATO effectively address international terrorism?

On Sept. 12, 2001, less than 24 hours after terrorists attacked the World Trade Center and the Pentagon, NATO invoked Article 5 of the alliance charter, which commits all members to aid any member that is attacked. Thus the first time the article came into play was not against the Soviet Union — for whom it was originally intended — but against jihadist terrorists.

In 2002, at a summit in Prague, Czech Republic, NATO retroactively included antiterrorism as "a permanent agenda item and priority for the alliance,"

Although the alliance has not taken Aznar's advice, it did launch a major antiterrorist program, including developing expertise in detecting chemical, biological and nuclear weapons and establishing specialist teams to deal with the after-effects of such attacks. An alliance-wide, fail-safe cyber system to protect the NATO computer network from terrorist hackers has also been implemented. And in 2004, NATO agreed to establish a Terrorism Threat Intelligence Unit to analyze and distribute terrorist intelligence throughout the alliance.[24]

Since 9/11, NATO has also carried out Operation Active Endeavour to "detect and deter" terrorist activity in the Mediterranean, through which 65 percent of Europe's oil and gas imports pass.[25] The continuous maritime surveillance operation escorts oil supertankers and other ships and inspects ships on the high seas, looking for illegally transported nuclear materials. The operation was initially limited to the eastern Mediterranean but in 2004 was extended to cover the entire Mediterranean.

In 2004, NATO provided Greece with a massive, protective blanket — in the form of navy patrols and air surveillance — around Athens and other Summer Olympics venues to protect the games from terrorists. In 2006, NATO did the same for the Soccer World Cup in Germany. But militarily NATO's biggest antiterrorist engagement to date has clearly been Afghanistan, where nearly all member states are deployed.

"NATO has brought essential value to the fight against terrorism, and Afghanistan is the best example of this," says Secretary General de Hoop Scheffer.

It is widely agreed that NATO needs to succeed in Afghanistan if its role in the fight against terrorism is to have credibility. "The mission is vital for NATO," says Bastian Giegerich, a research fellow on European Security at the London-based International Institute of Security Studies. "If the alliance fails in Afghanistan, its appetite to engage in that kind of operation will become very limited."

But the strong differences that persist over how the International Security and Assistance Force should approach its mission in Afghanistan are seen as fundamental flaws in NATO's commitment. Rather than defeating the Taliban and al Qaeda, Europeans generally perceive ISAF's role as "counterinsurgency coupled with helping to improve governance," says Giegerich. Europeans focus on beefing up the effectiveness of Afghan troops and police and strengthening democratic institutions.

Germany's Gen. Egon Ramms, until recently overall commander of ISAF operations in Afghanistan, defined NATO's role in Afghanistan as "to help the people of the country . . . protect the Afghan people" against insurgents.[26]

Britain, Canada and the Netherlands — on the other hand — follow the U.S. approach, which entails armed engagement with the insurgents. The result of this double standard, as an unnamed Pentagon consultant told the *London Daily Telegraph*, is "frustration [and] irritation. . . . The mistake was handing it over to NATO in the first place. For many countries being in Afghanistan seems about keeping up appearances, rather than actually fighting a war that needs to be won."[27]

What does not seem in dispute throughout the alliance is that NATO should be involved in the war on terror. But as U.S. Army Gen. Bantz John Craddock, NATO's supreme commander, says, "Each NATO nation has its own internal issues that it must address."

On the other hand, he added, "a completely resourced force sends a clear message to our adversary . . . that NATO is committed to achieving success."

A military funeral is held for U.S. Army Pfc. Joseph A. Miracle, 22, on July 14, 2007, in Waterford, Mich. He was one of the 630 Americans killed during NATO operations in Afghanistan since 2001. About 60 percent of the NATO's casualties in Afghanistan have been Americans, followed by British and Canadian forces. German, French, Italian and other NATO troops are only allowed to shoot in self-defense, so their troops are not stationed in heavy combat areas.

BACKGROUND

Internal Differences

Differences over Afghanistan are hardly the first time NATO members have run into internal dissent. In fact, the alliance's 60-year history is full of spirited debates, but all of them have been peacefully overcome — a testament to the institution's resilience and adaptability. Meanwhile, the fact that the Soviet Union never attacked defines NATO's success as a mutual defense alliance between the United States and Western Europe.

At the start of the alliance's often querulous existence, NATO's first secretary general, Britain's Lord Ismay, said the alliance was designed "to keep Russia out, the Germans down and the Americans in."

Technology Gap Separates U.S. and NATO Forces

Combat interoperability is still a long way off.

Working together effectively in combat has always been a key objective of the North Atlantic Treaty Organization (NATO). So far, however, so-called interoperational cooperation among NATO allies remains more an earnest desire than military reality.

A wide technology gap exists not only between the United States and Eastern Europe's armed forces, which for the most part are still switching from Soviet-era arms to Western versions, but also with its more modern Western European allies.

The gap is partly a legacy of the Cold War, when Europeans were forced to concentrate on defensive equipment against a possible invasion, such as armor and heavy artillery, while the United States — worried more about a long-distance war on another continent — devoted more resources to long-range air transport and missile development.

During the Balkan conflict in the 1990s, the Europeans suddenly realized that without U.S. support they could never have sustained their participation in the conflict. The Americans carried out 75 percent of the combat and support sorties and fired 95 percent of the cruise missiles and other precision-guided devices. Americans also had the only satellite-supported system that guides so-called "smart" bombs and tactical missiles. The U.S. Air Force also had

several hundred aircraft equipped with electronic systems that protect planes from enemy air-defense systems and can perform in-flight refueling.[1]

In recent years Europe's aircraft industry has been closing the technology gap. NATO forces began using German-made in-flight refueling aircraft in 2004. But completion of a European-made equivalent of the U.S. C-17 Globemaster military transport, originally due for delivery in late 2008, has been delayed more than a year due to production hold-ups.

As for high-tech combat, Europeans are far from becoming interoperational with their U.S. counterparts because they lag behind in technology. In Iraq and Afghanistan U.S. forces use spy satellites, airborne intelligence-gathering units and software that analyzes combat options — all linked via satellite to troops on the ground.

However, all this precision technology hasn't always been able to avoid killing Afghan civilians, and NATO's image has suffered badly as a result. Yet, without U.S. involvement, the Europeans could not conduct such modern warfare. Experts also say Europe's annual $150 billion defense expenditures would be more effective if they were pooled. But Europeans find collective decision-making difficult.

Once Russia was out and Germany was no longer regarded as a threat to European peace, many predicted NATO would dissolve. The alliance has done just the opposite, evolving into an expanded security and peacekeeping organization. And its aggressive recruitment effort across Central and Eastern Europe has resulted in a doubling in the alliance's size in Europe.

When NATO was formed in 1949, a shattered, vulnerable postwar Europe still sought a continued U.S. presence, both out of fear of a possibly resurgent Germany and as protection from the often unpredictable Soviet Union. The Soviets had at least 700,000 troops capable of overrunning Western Europe. European poverty made Moscow-backed communist parties attractive — posing a viable political threat to take power democratically. Fearing that if Moscow somehow took control of industrial Europe it

could threaten U.S. interests and even the United States itself, Washington pumped billions of dollars into shattered European economies (through the massive Marshall Plan), and committed itself to the defense of Europe through NATO.[28]

The original signatories of the NATO treaty were Belgium, Denmark, France, Iceland, Luxembourg, the Netherlands, Norway, Canada, Portugal, Italy, the United Kingdom and, of course, the United States. (*See map, p. 86.*) The French, seeking greater influence, were difficult partners from the start. "The French attitude seems pretty hopeless: they still fear the Germans and still want our money, but not our advice," U.S. Navy Adm. Forrest Sherman complained in his diary in 1950.[29]

But there were other strains as well. In 1950 Sherman warned British negotiators that the United States might

European NATO members also spend a smaller percentage of their income on defense than the United States. Although under NATO rules all members vow to spend at least 2 percent of their gross domestic product (GDP) on defense, most European members now treat the 2 percent minimum as a ceiling instead, spending about 1.4 percent of their GDPs on defense. The United States spends about 4 percent of its GDP on defense.

American critics of NATO say that with a productive population of 445 million and a combined GDP of about $11 trillion, Europeans can afford to look after themselves militarily. But by spending less on defense — and refusing to pool their resources on most joint projects — the Europeans create resentment across the Atlantic about the unfair financial burden borne by the United States. The situation also undermines efforts to create a common defense policy within the military organization.

Aside from technological coordination issues, basic cooperation also needs to improve among the allies. "Considerations of competition and security, proliferation fears and numerous laws, especially on the U.S. side, often still obstruct the path toward a joint allied 'plug and fight' architecture," wrote German security specialist Henrik Enderlein.[2]

Coordinating the alliance's military efforts bogs down for two other key reasons, according to Dag Wilhelmsen, manager of NATO's Consultation and Command and Control Agency, which strives to increase interoperability. The greatest challenge, he said, "is the desire of individual nations to safeguard information and technology from their allies." It is

A helicopter is loaded aboard a huge U.S. C-17 Globemaster military transport plane. Europe's NATO members rely on U.S. cargo planes as they try to close the military technology gap between U.S. and other NATO forces.

also difficult to bring together systems "designed to address national needs, which often differ widely among member nations."[3]

---

[1] Hendrik Enderlein, "Military Interoperability," *IP Internationale Politik*, www.ip-global.org/archiv/2002/winter2002/military-interoperability .html.

[2] *Ibid.*

[3] Quoted in Robert Ackerman, "In NATO, technology challenges yield to political interpolarity handles," *Signal Communications*, Jan. 17, 2006, www.imakenews.com/signal/e_article000509437.cfm?x=b11,0,w.

change its mind about joining NATO if London didn't withdraw its insistence on appointing a British supreme commander over the U.S. fleet in the Mediterranean. The British "demanded exclusive control in the Mediterranean of our fleet plus their odds and ends," Sherman fumed.[30]

By 1952, the alliance had expanded to include Greece and Turkey. In 1955, after a long debate, West Germany was allowed to re-arm and was brought into the pact. The Soviets responded by forming the Warsaw Pact alliance with seven Eastern and Central European satellite states.

Guarding the Gap

NATO's anti-Soviet line of defense extended from the Turkish border with Russia in the south to Norway in the north. But the major threat was in divided Germany, where

watchful U.S. and European forces were concentrated along the Fulda Gap in the Bavarian mountains, which created a natural divide between communist East Germany and the West German Federation. In the event of hostilities, it was there on the broad, flat plain that a potential Soviet tank invasion was most likely.

In 1952, NATO members agreed to deploy 100 divisions within two years. But by 1954 it was obvious that the alliance didn't have the economic strength or the political will to achieve that target. In any case, by 1953 the United States had begun deploying strategic nuclear weapons at friendly bases in Europe, and Washington — and eventually NATO — opted for a strategy of massive retaliation in defense of Europe, which entailed the almost exclusive use of nuclear weapons regardless of the size and nature of the attack. By the late 1950s, Moscow also

C H R O N O L O G Y

1940s *The North Atlantic Treaty Organization (NATO) emerges as an alliance of democracies in Europe and North America.*

1945 World War II ends.

1949 Twelve Western countries sign the North Atlantic Treaty, promising mutual defense.

1950s-1960s *NATO deploys forces along Iron Curtain to prevent Soviet attack on Western Europe*

1950 U.S. Gen. Dwight D. Eisenhower becomes first NATO commander.

1952 Greece and Turkey join NATO.

1955 West Germany joins NATO; Soviet Union and seven Eastern European states form the Warsaw Pact.

1966 France withdraws from NATO's military structure, evicts NATO troops.

1967 NATO headquarters moves from Paris to Brussels. NATO agrees
to work to improve East-West
relations.

1970s-1980s *U.S. and Soviet Union negotiate on nuclear arms control. Soviets invade Afghanistan.*

1972 Interim arms limitation and anti-ballistic missile treaties are signed.

1979 NATO deploys medium-range missiles — but continues arms-control diplomacy — after Moscow deploys intermediate-range nuclear missiles aimed at Western Europe. . . . Soviets invade Afghanistan.

1982 Spain joins NATO.

1990s *Soviet Union collapses; Warsaw Pact dissolves. East European nations begin joining NATO. Alliance launches its first military operation.*

1991 Soviet Union collapses; Warsaw Pact dissolves.

1995 NATO flies 3,515 missions to defend civilians in Bosnia from Serb attacks and . . . deploys troops to enforce cease-fire in Bosnia.

1999 Hungary, Czech Republic, Poland become first former Soviet-bloc states to join NATO. . . . Alliance launches air strikes against Yugoslavia to halt ethnic cleansing in Kosovo.

2000-Present *NATO continues eastward expansion, deploys troops in Afghanistan. Members debate NATO's 21st-century role.*

2001 NATO declares the Sept. 11 terrorist attack on the United States an attack on all NATO members. U.S.-led coalition — including some NATO members — attacks Taliban and al Qaeda in Afghanistan.

2002 NATO-Russia Council is launched, allowing joint consultations.

2003 NATO deploys forces to Kabul, its first major operation outside Europe.

2004 Estonia, Latvia, Lithuania, Bulgaria, Romania and Slovakia join NATO.

2005 NATO enlarges its force in Afghanistan.

2006 NATO takes over from U.S.-led coalition in southern Afghanistan.

2007 Many European governments limit their troops in Afghanistan to self-defensive actions.

2008 At summit in Bucharest, Romania, NATO puts off U.S. request for immediate membership for Georgia and Ukraine but endorses American plan to deploy missile shield in Poland and Czech Republic. In August, Russia invades Georgia after surprise Georgian attack on separatist South Ossetia. NATO condemns Russia's "disproportionate" use of force. In December, NATO agrees to delay Georgia and Ukraine membership. To counter U.S. missile plan, Russian President Dmitry A. Medvedev vows to deploy intermediate-range missiles in Kaliningrad in 2009.

April 2009 NATO holds 60th-anniversary summit in Strasbourg, France.

had developed intercontinental ballistic missiles, making the United States itself vulnerable to nuclear attack.[31]

It took NATO nearly a decade of debate to develop and adopt a new, more rational, defensive approach — so-called flexible response. President John F. Kennedy outlined the strategy in 1962, but it didn't become official NATO policy until five years later. It relied on a sequence of three escalating responses: conventional, tactical nuclear and strategic nuclear. The first involved conventional defense against attack, also called direct defense. If that failed, tactical nuclear weapons (short-range missiles for use on the battlefield) were to be used to force the attacker to stop the conflict and withdraw from NATO territory. The third line of defense was a strategic nuclear response using intercontinental rockets, which shifted the focus of the conflict from the European battlefield to a direct U.S.-Soviet nuclear confrontation.

Flexible response worried Washington's European allies because it "decoupled" the United States from the conflict until the third option. They felt the United States would be prepared to brave Soviet retaliation as a last resort, after Europe had taken a lot of punishment. In fact, U.S. strategists did envision a long conventional war before moving to the second option.[32] Meanwhile, several efforts were made to integrate U.S. and European forces, such as the U.S.-proposed Multilateral Force of the early 1960s. The 25-ship seaborne force was to be equipped with 200 Polaris ballistic missiles, manned by European sailors from NATO powers under U.S. control. But NATO member states had no enthusiasm for mixed crews, and the project was quietly dropped.

France Pulls Out

In 1966, French President Charles de Gaulle pulled France out of NATO's military command structure, complaining that France had been relegated to a secondary role in the alliance. At de Gaulle's insistence, NATO's headquarters moved from Paris to Brussels.

France's departure reflected internal uncertainties about NATO's continued role, especially given that the Soviets had never invaded. East-West tension began to relax, and the alliance began to broaden its political role. In 1967, NATO adopted recommendations from a report by Belgian Foreign Minister Pierre Harmel that its future military posture combine defense and détente. In other words, defense programs were to be combined with efforts to establish better relations with the Soviet Union and its Eastern European satellites.

The decision would greatly influence NATO in subsequent years.[33] At the time, some member states were improving their bilateral relations with Moscow. The Harmel Report helped reconcile the different diplomatic approaches of the American and European leaders in the face of the Soviet challenge. It also eventually led to NATO-Soviet negotiations beginning in 1973 to reduce ground forces in Central Europe — the Mutual and Balanced Force Reduction talks, and to the Conference on Security and Cooperation in Europe in 1975.

In the late 1970s the Soviet Union introduced the medium-range SS-20 missile, capable of carrying nuclear warheads to European cities. NATO responded in the early 1980s with a "dual track" strategy: plans to deploy 108 U.S.-supplied Pershing II missiles and 462 ground-launched cruise missiles in Europe while pressuring Moscow to negotiate the mutual removal of medium-range arsenals from Europe.

What quickly became known as Euromissiles stirred strong public opposition, with violent protests breaking out in West Germany and Italy. Meanwhile, Moscow worked hard to open a rift between the United States and its European allies. Ailing Soviet leader Leonid Brezhnev flew to Bonn in an attempt to persuade Chancellor Helmut Schmidt to reject the American missiles. However, faced with a critical test of the alliance's political resolve and cohesion, European governments stood firm.

Enlarging NATO

After the collapse of the Soviet Union in 1991, NATO began expanding its membership to include former Soviet satellite countries, starting with Poland, Hungary and the Czech Republic in March 1999, followed by Bulgaria, Romania, Estonia, Lithuania, Latvia, Slovakia and Slovenia in 2004.

Aspiring nations were required to show progress towards democratization and improve their military effectiveness. NATO enlargement thus became a catalyst for quick change in the former communist states, under close Western guidance. Eastern Europeans and the Baltic nations, still nervous about the intentions of their Russian neighbor, welcomed NATO's (i.e. America's) protective shield.

"What we're doing here is hoping for the best and creating the conditions for the best but also being prepared for the possibility of Russia's reasserting itself," President Bill Clinton told members of Congress on

NATO-Russia Relations Are Strained

Alliance enlargement and U.S. missile defense system alarm Russia.

When the Russian missile frigate *Pytlivy* steamed into the Mediterranean in the summer of 2006, it was reversing history. Twenty years earlier, the presence of a Soviet vessel in the area would have triggered alarm bells at NATO's Sixth Fleet headquarters in Naples, Italy.

But that was then. The *Pytlivy* was reporting for duty as the first unit of the Russian Navy to take part in Operation Active Endeavour, NATO's permanent, post-9/11 counterterrorist patrol in the Mediterranean.[1]

Russian participation in Active Endeavour is one of the initiatives of the NATO-Russia Permanent Joint Council, an outgrowth of the cooperation agreement signed in 1997 by President Bill Clinton and President Boris Yeltsin to deepen and widen the scope of bilateral relations and — not incidentally — to offset the largely negative impact of NATO's decision to admit former Soviet republics and satellites into the alliance.[2] By participating in the council, Moscow has maintained a permanent presence at NATO headquarters and a military office at the alliance's military command headquarters since 2002. The council normally consists of military and diplomatic representatives from Russia and all 26 NATO members, but if the occasion calls for it, higher-ranking officials — up to heads of government — can participate in meetings.

Since creation of the council, NATO and Russia have initiated a slew of wide-ranging bilateral programs, including improvements in military-to-military interoperability (designed to enable respective armed forces to work together in joint military operations), cooperation in submarine-crew search and rescue and Active Endeavour. The Russians have also cooperated with NATO on counternarcotics operations, such as anti-drug training for Central Asian and Afghan personnel.[3]

In the 1990s, an economically weak Russia had been in no position to effectively oppose the earlier enlargements, but by 2000, enriched and emboldened by oil and gas exports, Russia began to draw the line. President — more recently Prime Minister — Vladimir Putin has raised strong objections, and President Dmitry A. Medvedev told the *Financial Times*, "No state can be pleased about having representatives of a military bloc to which it does not belong coming close to its borders."[4]

Col.-Gen. Nikolai Pishchev, first deputy-chief of the Russian general staff, took the same approach in the military newspaper *Krasnaya Zvezda*: "How would the public and government of any self-respecting state react to the expansion in the immediate proximity of its borders of what is already the world's biggest politico-military alliance? I believe that both the leadership and the citizens of that country would be quite

skeptical of any assurances of the purely peaceful character of such an alliance, and Russia in this sense is certainly no exception from the general rule."[5]

The NATO-Russian relationship survived and developed "even though Moscow's foreign policy from 2003 onward became more independent and assertive, and Russian relations with NATO began to sour," wrote Dmitri Trenin, senior associate at the Carnegie Institute for Peace in Moscow.[6]

But despite Russian protests, NATO continued to expand. In 2003 the three remaining Soviet satellites — Romania, Bulgaria and Slovakia — and the former Soviet republics of Latvia, Lithuania and Estonia joined NATO. The Bush administration was also pushing the candidacy of Georgia and Ukraine on Russia's southern border.

The Russians call their immediate neighbors the "near abroad" and consider them part of their sphere of influence. Indeed, Russia has been meddling in the politics of both Georgia and Ukraine ever since their independence in 1992. In the case of Georgia, Russia has backed militarily the separatist provinces of Abkhazia and South Ossetia. In Ukraine, Moscow backed candidates acceptable to the large Russian-speaking minority and even allegedly tried to fix the elections.

At a security conference in Munich in 2007, then-President Putin famously suggested that NATO's eastward expansion was directed against Russia. "NATO's expansion does not have any relation with the modernization of the alliance itself or ensuring security in Europe," Putin told an audience of defense officials and specialists that included U.S. Defense Secretary Robert Gates. "On the contrary, it represents a serious provocation that reduces the level of natural trust. And we have the right to ask: Against whom is this expansion intended?"[7]

NATO was divided over admitting Georgia, with Germany and France questioning the wisdom of accepting into the alliance a country with an unresolved territorial dispute. Then in August 2008 Russian troops invaded Georgia, sweeping aside the Georgian army and advancing across the country to the Black Sea port of Poti.[8] The Russians said they were reacting to a pre-emptive strike by Georgia on South Ossetia — which Georgian President Mikheil Saakashvili acknowledged in December. He said he had ordered the August attack in self-defense because of a build-up of Russian armor and troops on the Georgian border, which he believed could only mean that Moscow planned to invade his country.[9]

On Aug. 13, five days after Russian troops invaded, a cease-fire was brokered by French President Nicolas Sarkozy, then president of the European Union. NATO denounced Russia's "disproportionate" incursion and declared that while it was not breaking off all contact with Russia, it would not be "business as usual" in the NATO-Russia council. In December 2008, NATO foreign ministers agreed to resume what Secretary General Jaap de Hoop Scheffer called a "conditional and graduated re-engagement" with Russia.[10]

The Bush administration was not happy with the resumption of contact, but Secretary of State Condoleezza Rice went along with it to avoid a confrontation. Moreover, NATO remained adamant about withholding fast-track membership for Georgia and Ukraine, which the United States had sought. The two former Soviet states would join "some day," the alliance stated.[11]

The decision on Georgia and Ukraine sends a message to incoming President Barack Obama, who has publicly supported NATO membership for the two nations. Obama will also have to deal with the other major divisive issue in the complex relationship between Moscow and NATO: Washington's plan to deploy a missile defense shield in Poland and the Czech Republic. Although the Bush administration has insisted that the shield is intended to defend Europe from possible nuclear attack by Iran or North Korea, Russia is skeptical.

Russian officials say their country is the obvious target. "Since there aren't and won't be any [Iranian or North Korean] missiles, then against whom, against whom, is this [U.S.] system directed?" asked Russian Foreign Minister Sergei Lavrov. "Only against us!"[12]

As a result of the planned U.S. missile deployment and Russia's robust incursion into Georgia, Obama will inherit strained bilateral relations with Moscow. "Most analysts agree that relations between Washington and Moscow are not good," the Voice of America reported in November. "Some experts use 'poor,' 'tense,' and 'at a very low point,' to describe the relationship."[13] The Bush administration is blamed for pushing the missile shield and a hard line on the Georgia conflict.

For example, in September the administration insisted NATO cancel participation of the Russian ship *Ladno* in the Operation Active Endeavour anti-terrorism patrol. The *Ladno* was already off the coast of Turkey when the cancellation was transmitted to the Russians. Washington also blocked a request by the Russians for an emergency meeting of the NATO-Russia council to discuss the situation.[14]

Meanwhile, the Kremlin's level of protest also has been criticized within Russia as being too strident. Alexander Khramchikhin of the Institute of Political and Military Analysis in Moscow suggests the Kremlin is overstating the threat because the American ground-based interceptors "can hardly be said to exist, because many tests have failed. On top of that the bulky radar and launch pads are highly vulnerable to conventional tactical weapons."[15]

President-elect Obama appears to share this skepticism: He has said a case can be made for deploying the missile shield — if it works.

AFP/Getty Images/Dmitry Kostyukov

Russian troops invade South Ossetia in August 2008, shortly after Georgian forces entered the breakaway province. Georgian President Mikheil Saakashvili later said he invaded the province because he feared a Russian invasion. NATO quickly denounced Russia's "disproportionate" incursion.

[1] "Russian ship to join NATO exercise," *Eaglespeak*, May 19, 2006, www.eaglespeak.us/2006/05/russian-ship-to-join-nato-exercise.html.

[2] Jack Mendelsohn, "The NATO-Russian Founding Act," Arms Control Association, May 1997, http://legacy.armscontrol.org/act/1997_05/jm.asp.

[3] "NATO-Russia Relations," Topics Web page, North Atlantic Treaty Organization, Dec. 4, 2008, www.nato.int/issues/nato-russia/index.html.

[4] Newser.com, "Medvedev warns against NATO plans," March 28, 2008, www.newser.com/story/22487/medvedev-warns-against-nato-plans.html.

[5] Col. Gen. Nikolai Pishchev, "NATO Myths and Reality," *Krasnaya Zvezda*, Jan. 5, 2008, www.fas.org/man/nato/national/msg00006c.htm.

[6] Dmitri Trenin, "Partnerships Old and New," *NATO Review*, summer 2007, www.nato.int/docu/review/2007/issue2/english/art1.html.

[7] Yaroslav Butakov, "NATO against whom?" *Rpmonitor*, Feb. 12, 2007, www.rpmonitor.ru/en/en/detail.php?ID=3220.

[8] "Russian troops to patrol Georgian port — Gen. Staff," Novosti (Russian News and Information Agency), Aug. 23, 2008, http://en.rian.ru/russia/20080823/116235138.html.

[9] Mikheil Saakashvili, "Georgia Acted in Self-Defense," *The Wall Street Journal*, Dec. 2, 2008, http://online.wsj.com/article/SB122817723737570713.html?mod=googlenews_wsj.

[10] Reuters, "NATO, Russia to resume high-level contacts Friday," Dec 18, 2008, http://uk.reuters.com/article/latestCrisis/idUKLI401387.

[11] "NATO to resume Russian contacts," *Sky News*, Dec. 2, 2008, http://news.sky.com/skynews/Home/World-News/Nato-Agrees-To-Gradually-Resume-Contacts-With-Russia-In-Wake-Of-War-With-Georgia/Article/200812115171101?f=rss.

[12] M. K. Bhadrakumar, "In the Trenches of the New Cold War," *Asia Times*, April, 28, 2007, www.atimes.com/atimes/central_asia/ID28Ag01.html.

[13] Andre De Nesnera, "Obama to face strained U.S.-Russian relations after taking office," VOAonline, Nov. 20, 2008, www.voanews.com/english/archive/2008-11/2008-11-20-voa61.cfm?CFID=82992383&CFTOKEN=88186048.

[14] "NATO bars Russian ship from anti-terror patrol," *Javno*, Sept. 3, 2008, www.javno.com/en/world/clanak.php?id=172085.

[15] Alexander Khramchikhin, "Anti-ballistic missiles: menace or myth," *Space War*, www.spacewar.com/reports/Mutual_Destruction_Danger_In_US_Anti_Missile_Plan_Says_Putin_999.html.

Americans Suffer Most Casualties

Most of the 1,045 NATO troops killed in Afghanistan since 2001 have been American, British and Canadian, who are fully engaged in combat operations against Taliban and al Qaeda insurgents. Germany, France, Italy and other NATO governments only allow their soldiers to shoot at the enemy in self-defense, so their troops are not stationed in areas with heavy combat.

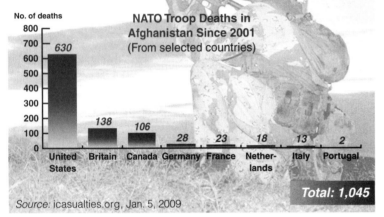

No. of deaths

NATO Troop Deaths in Afghanistan Since 2001
(From selected countries)

	No. of deaths
United States	630
Britain	138
Canada	106
Germany	28
France	23
Netherlands	18
Italy	13
Portugal	2

Total: 1,045

Source: icasualties.org, Jan. 5, 2009

the day of the first NATO enlargement. "We're walking a tightrope."[34]

As NATO's borders edged closer to Russia, the alliance tried to reassure Moscow by establishing the NATO-Russia council, with permanent military representation in Brussels, and — as Clinton said — "holding open a place for Russia in some future, evolved version of NATO."[35]

But Moscow's discomfort with NATO expansion grew as additional countries — including Croatia, Macedonia, Azerbaijan, Georgia and Ukraine — stood in line to join the alliance. Since 2006, Putin — first as president and more recently as prime minister — has issued several strong protests against NATO's continued enlargement into the "near abroad," as Moscow calls its closest neighbors.

The latest threat to NATO's survival, however, comes not from Russia but from a wild, rugged country where — ironically — 20 years ago, the Russians themselves learned the lesson of bitter defeat.

CURRENT SITUATION

Slowing Expansion

The war in Afghanistan, however, is not the only challenge facing NATO today.

At a NATO summit in Bucharest, Romania, in April 2008 — in the first known instance of NATO turning down a personal request by a U.S. president — the alliance rebuffed Bush's proposal that Georgia and Ukraine be given so-called Membership Action Plan (MAP) status, a period of preparation designed to improve an aspiring member's democratic credentials and military effectiveness. The alliance put the plan on the back burner and then reaffirmed its decision in early December at a meeting of the NATO foreign ministers in Brussels. Faced with strong protests from Prime Minister Putin, Germany and France led other member states in a maneuver acknowledging that the two Caucasian nations would become NATO members eventually but stopping short of giving them MAPs, saying further negotiations would be necessary.

The decision came after months of tense confrontation and rhetoric over the issue. In what many saw as a quid pro quo, NATO backed the Bush administration's plan to deploy interceptor missiles in Poland linked to a missile defense radar system in the Czech Republic. The United States says the system is intended to defend Europe from possible ballistic missile attacks by rogue states, such as Iran and North Korea, but Russia views it as a potential threat. Agreements on the deployment have since been signed with both NATO countries.

In retaliation, Moscow announced in November 2008 that it would begin installing its own intercontinental, nuclear-capable missiles within a year.[36] President Medvedev said newly developed RS24 missiles — with a range of 4,000 miles — would be sited in Kaliningrad, a Russian enclave awkwardly perched between NATO members Poland and Lithuania.[37]

The brief conflict between Russian and Georgian forces last August chilled relations between NATO and Russia. It also split the alliance, with the Bush administration continuing to champion Georgian President Mikheil Saakashvili despite his rash attempt to annex the breakaway province of South Ossetia — which Washington officials say they repeatedly warned him not to try — and the Europeans' more measured inclination to give Moscow at least some benefit of the doubt.[38]

The American position was complicated by the fact that a hotly contested presidential election was in full swing. Republican candidate Sen. John McCain of Arizona exploded in hawkish anti-Russian comments. Democratic candidate Sen. Obama of Illinois took a tough stance as well, saying Georgia's NATO aspirations should not be undermined by the August fighting.

South Ossetia (birthplace of Soviet dictator Josef Stalin) and the nearby region of Abkhazia have long sought to separate from Georgia and are supported by Russia.[39] Given the opportunity, the Russians retaliated in force, advancing across Georgia like a knife through butter as far as the Baltic port of Poti. NATO quickly censured Moscow's "disproportionate use of force" and expressed support for Tblisi, putting its relations with Moscow on hold. As Secretary General de Hoop Scheffer put it in August, there would be "no business as usual" in the NATO-Russia council for a while.[40]

The "while" lasted three months. At its December meeting NATO announced it was resuming a "conditional and graduated re-engagement" with Russia, which it said did not signify approval of Russia's incursion into Georgian territory or its continued presence in, and recognition of, the breakaway province of South Ossetia.[41] The decision represented a defeat for the tough line with Moscow that Washington wanted to maintain and a success for the European argument that NATO needed to engage the Russians rather than isolate them.

In fact, NATO support for either Georgian or Ukrainian membership has dwindled. "Even the position of friends of Georgia and Ukraine within the alliance has evolved," said Slawomir Debski, director of the Polish Institute of International Affairs in Warsaw, who believes no decision is likely until after the 60th-anniversary summit in April.[42] In Ukraine, he pointed out, the government had collapsed, and public opinion is deeply divided over NATO membership, with 60 percent of the population opposing joining the alliance.

"The political upheavals in Ukraine mean that there is no partner reliable enough to talk to," he said. "NATO should wait until the territorial conflict with Russia is resolved" before making a decision on Georgia's application. For instance, if Georgia had been able to invoke Article

"Yankees, Leave Your Radar At Home," say Czech communists to protest a radar base the United States wants to build in the Czech Republic as part of a global missile defense shield against a potential threat from Iran or North Korea. NATO's endorsement of the plan — which includes installing 10 interceptor missiles in neighboring Poland — has caused tension between the alliance and the Kremlin.

5 as a NATO member in August, the alliance would have been pulled into war with Russia, he pointed out.

Extending NATO membership to Ukraine and Georgia "borders on insanity," says Benjamin Friedman, a research fellow on security at Washington's Cato Institute, a libertarian think tank. "These countries are security consumers, not producers, and can provide little military benefit to the alliance. Both countries come with pre-existing conflicts with their stronger neighbor, Russia. . . . If you designed a country to be an uncomfortable ally, it would look something like Georgia — a weak nation with a territorial conflict with a nuclear-armed neighbor, led by a leader with a demonstrated capacity for recklessness."

That view is increasingly shared even in Washington, which has backed away somewhat from its position earlier in the summer, when outgoing Secretary of State Condoleezza Rice proposed that NATO consider dropping the MAP requirement and fast-tracking Georgia's and Ukraine's membership.

By December, faced with alliance opposition to circumventing the system, Rice had backtracked: "There should be no shortcuts," she declared, admitting that membership was "a long road ahead" for both countries.

'A Beast with 100 Heads'

The past year has been the deadliest yet for NATO forces in Afghanistan since the U.S.-led invasion. Financed by a flourishing opium trade, Taliban insurgents and al Qaeda

AT ISSUE

Has NATO become irrelevant?

YES — Fyodor Lukyanov

Editor, Russia in Global Affairs, a Moscow-Based Foreign-Policy Quarterly

Written for *CQ Global Researcher*, January 2009

It is difficult to find any institution besides the North Atlantic Treaty Organization (NATO) that would manifest such a wide gap between progress in form and lack of success in substance. Its public image is great: The alliance outlived its main enemy, the Warsaw Pact, and won the Cold War. The number of members has more than doubled, and other countries are queuing to join the most powerful and prestigious club in the world.

But this historic triumph brought a few existential challenges to which NATO can't respond — at least not yet. First, what, after all, is the new strategic mission of NATO? Twenty years after the end of the Cold War, it is still unclear what kind of tasks this alliance should address: The Euro-Atlantic area doesn't need protection from a Soviet threat any more. Attempts to turn NATO into a global alliance and main international security institution — which would be a natural continuation of post-Cold War logic — haven't been realized. European allies are far from enthusiastic to fulfill missions in distant parts of the world, where they don't see their clear interests. Afghanistan is evidence enough.

Second, why is transatlantic unity still necessary in the 21st century? Tradition? Sure. Common values? Yes, but Europe and the United States differ on how those should be implemented. Common threats? Unlikely. Neither China nor international terrorism provides a consolidating threat, while Russia is simply unable to pose it. Strategic horizons? Not at all. The United States, as a global superpower and Europe as a regional entity with a unique political culture have different views on world affairs.

Third, is NATO still able to spread stability and security? In the 1990s the West could transform the security system according to its own ideas. Russia was unable and unwilling to resist; China was completely focused on internal development.

Now, however, in an effort to export security NATO expansion has become a catalyst for serious conflict, provoking Russia by intruding into its historical domain. Since NATO is rooted in the previous Cold War epoch, it is unrealistic to expect Moscow to change its attitude *vis-à-vis* enlargement.

Conceptually, NATO is obsolete and unfit to address real threats, but political and bureaucratic inertia will keep it going and provoking new strategic misunderstandings.

NO — Bastien Giegerich

Research Fellow on European Security, International Institute of Security Studies, London

Written for *CQ Global Researcher*, January 2009

Since the end of the Cold War NATO has confounded regular predictions of its demise by demonstrating an impressive adaptive ability.

NATO's transformation is by no means complete, but it has mutated to reflect the myriad security threats posed in today's security environment, including international terrorism. Yet, at the same time, it has maintained its core capacity for collective defence, even though this latter capacity is no longer directed against a particular enemy.

The alliance provides a vital forum for transatlantic dialogue on security issues. It is also an invaluable tool to influence third countries through cooperation — a quick browse through NATO's various partnership programmes underlines this point.

The degree of pre-crisis military coordination among its member states remains unrivalled: NATO's defence planning system, commonly agreed goals and efforts to standardize procedures and equipment mean NATO member forces are much more interoperable than they would be otherwise. When NATO does deploy forces, there is a functional multilateral framework for doing so in which its members understand each other's strengths and weaknesses.

Being a coalition of democracies makes it necessary to build and maintain political consensus as a prerequisite for action, which is always time-consuming and sometimes tedious. However, the upside provided by being a genuine coalition of democracies means that once consensus exists, the international legitimacy of NATO's actions is high.

NATO remains the most promising tool for the United States to influence the security and defence policies of European countries, and thus an important instrument of leadership.

The United States does not have the capacity to deal with global security threats on its own. In eight out of 10 cases her NATO allies will remain the most capable and most reliable partners around.

This is not an argument for nostalgia: NATO must continue to adapt to stay relevant. The last two decades suggest that it can do both.

fighters have regrouped in Pakistan's lawless territories bordering Afghanistan, where fellow Pashtun tribes give them shelter and protection between their raids across the border.[43] The 294 allied military deaths in 2008 are the most ever in the seven years of the war. Reporters in Afghanistan say the conflict is "stalemated, at best."[44]

All 26 NATO countries and 13 non-NATO allies — which have small contingents, such as Sweden (with 85 personnel) and Austria (3) — have contributed troops to NATO's 50,000-strong International Security and Assistance Force (ISAF). The United States has 20,000 American troops serving under NATO command, plus another 12,000 in the U.S.-run Operation Enduring Freedom, which originally hunted for bin Laden — who is still at large — and his al Qaeda terrorists.

But terrorists are just one aspect of the challenge facing NATO forces. "We now have a country that's infested with everything from the Taliban and al Qaeda on the insurgency side, to bandits, warlords and narcotics traffickers," said former CIA officer Michael Scheuer in a recent PBS documentary. "We're really fighting a beast with 100 heads."[45]

U.S. Defense Secretary Robert Gates has called Afghanistan, "NATO's first ground war."[46] But that's not really true for troops from Germany, France and Italy, whose governments have imposed rules of engagement — so-called "caveats" — specifically prohibiting them from engaging in combat unless they come under attack.

The caveats are not just the result of domestic political pressure generated by the unpopularity of the Afghanistan mission. They also reflect differences in approach within NATO. While the United States plans to send in more troops for an Iraq-type "surge," the French attitude is more typical of the European position. France believes "the focus must be on transferring more power and responsibility to the Afghan authorities," says Shada Islam, senior program executive at the European Policy Centre think tank in Brussels. That's a tall order in a country where large areas have yet to be brought under the control of President Hamid Karzai's not-very-effective government.

French Foreign Minister Bernard Kouchner, Islam points out, has said he does not believe there will be a "military solution in Afghanistan." Instead, he and many European leaders say efforts should be focused on helping to develop Afghanistan's armed forces so the country can ultimately provide its own security.

A German military policeman (left) trains Afghan police officers in northern Afghanistan in September 2008. Many Europeans contend that rather than seeking a military solution in Afghanistan, NATO should focus on helping Afghan police and armed forces provide the country's own security. The army has improved in combat capability under NATO's guidance, but the police reportedly remain largely inefficient and corrupt.

So far, the 70,000-man Afghan army has improved in combat capability, say NATO leaders. But it's a small force in a country with a population of more than 32 million, and current plans are to expand it to 134,000 over the next five years. By contrast, the Afghan police, who are also being trained by ISAF, remain largely inefficient and corrupt.[47]

Provincial Reconstruction Teams (PRTs) — another non-combat project, made up of NATO military personnel and civilian aid workers — have had an uneven record of success, according to a 2008 report by specialists from the Woodrow Wilson School of International Affairs in Washington.[48] The German PRT operating in the northern province of Kunduz is the largest and one of the more successful, but its role was typical, albeit on a larger scale than most. Working with the provincial authorities, the report says, the PRT helped to restore drinking water to 850,000 inhabitants, constructed hundreds of elementary schools and clinics, conducted training for teachers, police and judges and provided security. But it has failed to convince the Afghans that the state had contributed to the effort.

"Kabul's authority continues to be regarded as more or less nonexistent," the report says. "Citizens are disappointed in the performance of the province's institutions."[49]

Meanwhile, the Pentagon is planning to deploy another 20,000-30,000 troops in Afghanistan this year, and incoming President Obama is expected to ask the NATO partners to send additional troops. But "European governments are likely to ignore Obama's demands that they assume greater responsibility by sending more troops," says Islam, which is expected to cast a pall over Obama's first official dealings with his NATO allies next April.

Many Europeans question whether a troop surge will work in Afghanistan's rugged terrain, which makes a heavy ground war nearly impossible, and air strikes mean heightened civilian casualties. In 2007, 321 Afghan civilians were killed in U.S. and NATO air strikes — three times as many as in the previous year — which has corroded Afghan views of U.S. and NATO forces as "liberators."

As an American soldier put it in the PBS documentary, "I don't think that even the little kids like us."[50]

OUTLOOK

New Strategic Concept

The upcoming NATO summit in April to celebrate the alliance's 60th anniversary would seem an obvious platform to begin reshaping its future. The French city of Strasbourg was chosen as the summit venue to mark the return of France to NATO's military command 40 years after President de Gaulle's withdrawal.

Former NATO Supreme Commander Gen. James L. Jones, who has been tapped to head President Obama's National Security Council, pinpoints one pressing change. "Most [NATO nations] understand that for NATO to survive as an institution in the 21st century, they need to start thinking about a new strategic concept," the former Marine commandant told *The New York Times* recently. "Unfortunately, NATO's mission is still rooted in the 20th-century, Cold War model of a defensive, static, reactive alliance instead of an agile, flexible and proactive 21st-century reality."[51]

But Poland's Debski doubts that the alliance will be able to produce a new strategic concept at the April summit. "The thinking about a new strategic concept is in progress; the machinery of consultation is moving," he says. But the summit will probably not discuss it in any depth in order "to give the Obama administration time to elaborate its own strategy towards NATO.

"The summit will be Obama's first NATO meeting, and . . . such a postponement seems likely," Debski continues. "With a new president in the White House we are at a point of departure." With a former NATO commander as national security adviser, however, the Obama administration might be in a position to articulate an alliance policy sooner than Europeans expect.

Equally important, say observers, NATO will want to see how U.S.-Kremlin relations develop with Obama in the Oval Office.

Oil-rich Russia's new determination to reshape its place in world affairs makes NATO members that are former Soviet satellites nervous. They want reassurance that NATO's security blanket is more than just rhetoric. If, for example, Russia attacks Latvia, will NATO come to its rescue under Article 5?

The 60th-anniversary summit is likely to reaffirm alliance guarantees because, as Giegerich of London's International Institute for Security Studies points out, "If there's an attack on a NATO member and the alliance doesn't respond to Article 5, then the alliance is dead." Debski calls the article "the essential fundament of the Alliance. If Article 5 is weakened, the whole institution may die very soon."

> "Today, three NATOs co-exist. There's the NATO of the Cold War, there's the exporter of stability to ex-Soviet countries and there's the NATO directed against new threats. . . . But which is the real NATO? It's hard to reconcile the three."
>
> — *Henning Riecke, security specialist German Foreign Policy Institute*

Developing NATO's role in protecting energy resources and transportation routes is also likely to be on the summit agenda. And it's not clear whether the new U.S. administration will continue President Bush's push for membership for Georgia and Ukraine. Giegerich foresees "a strategic pause" in the push for enlargement. "As long as the situation in Georgia is unsettled, it's not in NATO's interest to admit it."

However, Albania and Croatia are expected to be admitted.

Despite its problems, the alliance keeps the United States engaged in European security affairs. NATO enlargement has helped to unify a continent divided by 60 years of conflict and ease the entry of Eastern and Central European countries into the European Union. NATO has brought peace to the Balkans — and maintains that peace by keeping troops there. Through its Partnership for Peace, the alliance has established links with countries in other regions, such as Central Asia. Military cooperation between the allies promotes military interoperability and develops professional bonds and habits of cooperation that endure beyond an immediate deployment.[52]

Most observers say that if NATO is to remain an instrument for transatlantic security, it must be ready to take on more so-called out-of-area operations like the war in Afghanistan. But the alliance must establish parameters for such a commitment.

"In a world of 'globalized insecurity,' a regional Eurocentric approach simply no longer works," Secretary General de Hoop Scheffer declared recently. "We have to address security challenges where and when they emerge, or they will show up on our doorstep."[53]

NOTES

1. Suzanne Koelbl and Alexander Szander, "German Special Forces in Afghanistan Let Taliban Commander Escape," *Spiegel OnLine*, May 19, 2008, www.spiegel .de/international/world/0,1518,554033,00.html.

2. See http://icasualties.org/oef/.

3. For background, see Robert Kiener, "Crisis in Pakistan," *CQ Global Researcher*, December 2008, pp. 321-324.

4. Howard De Franchi, "US vs. Europe: two views of terror," *The Christian Science Monitor*, March 18, 2004, www.csmonitor.com/2004/0318/p01s01-usfp.html.

5. Tom Regan, "EU, U.S., differ on how to fight terrorism," *The Christian Science Monitor*, Feb. 2, 2004, www.csmonitor.com/2004/0329/dailyUpdate .html?s=entt.

6. "Forecast International Inc. News — Category Defence: A Frugal Pax Europa," Aerospace and Defence Network, Nov. 12, 2008, www .asd-network.com/press_detail/18416/A_Frugal_ Pax_Europa.htm.

7. Terence Hunt, "Bush, Putin at odds over NATO plans," *Oakland Tribune*, April 5, 2008, http:// findarticles.com/p/articles/mi_qn4176/is_/ai_ n25144063.

8. Vanessa Gera, "Polish Support for Missile Deal Soars," *Topix*, Aug. 18, 2008, www.topix.com/

forum/world/czech-republic/T1DPMN6G522MV 45HV.

9. Doug Bandow, "The NATO Alliance: Dangerous Anachronism," AntiWar.com, Oct. 17, 2008, www .antiwar.com/bandow/?articleid=13603.

10. Koelbl and Szander, *op. cit.*

11. Saul Landau, "The NATO Axiom: 2+2=5," *ukwatch*, May 22, 2008, www.ukwatch.net/article/the_nato_ axiom_2_2_5.

12. Bandow, *op. cit.*

13. E. Wayne Merry, "Therapy's End: thinking beyond NATO," *The National Interest*, Winter 2003, http:// findarticles.com/p/articles/mi_m2751/is_74/ai_ 112411717/pg_8?tag=outBody;col4.

14. Steven Erlanger, "NATO Chief Defends Opening to Russia," *The New York Times*, Dec. 4, 2008, www .nytimes.com/2008/12/04/world/europe/04nato .html?partner=rss&emc=rss.

15. Jeff Gerth and Tom Weiner, "Arms Makers See Bonanza in Selling NATO Expansion," *The New York Times*, June 29, 1999, http://query.nytimes.com/gst/ fullpage.html?res=9A06E4D81131F93AA15755C0 A961958260&sec=&spon=&pagewanted=2; see also Tom Lipton, "With White House Push, U.S. Arms Sales Jump," *The New York Times*, Sept. 18, 2008, www .nytimes.com/2008/09/14/washington/14arms .html?pagewanted=1&_r=1&hp.

16. Hendrik Enderlein, "Military Interoperability," *IP Internationale Politik*, www.ip-global.org/archiv/2002/ winter2002/military-interoperability.html.

17. Congressional Research Service reports to Congress for 2006 and 2008, respectively, www.fas.org/sgp/ crs/weapons/RL34187.pdf; and www.scribd.com/ doz/7788295/Arms-Sales-Transfers-2000-2007.

18. Federico Bordonaro, quoted from "Power and Interest News Report" in *ASAM Foreign Press Review*, May 19-20, 2005, www.avsam.org/fpr/rcs.htm, and Steve Clemons, "After Bucharest: Energy Security and Russia," *The Washington Note*, April 11, 2008, www.thewashingtonnote.com/archives/2008/04/ after_bucharest/.

19. "NATO Forum on Energy Security Technology," Institute for the Analysis of Global Security, Feb. 22, 2006, www.iags.org/natoforum.htm.

20. Sohbet Karbuz, "NATO and energy security," *Energy Bulletin*, Nov. 3, 2007, www.energybulletin.net/node/36716.

21. Johannes Varwick, "NATO's Role in Energy Security," *SpiegelOnline*, Jan. 7, 2008, www.spiegel.de/international/0,1518,563210,00.html.

22. "NATO and the fight against terrorism," NATO, www.nato.int/issues/terrorism/index.html.

23. Jose Maria Aznar, "Reforming NATO: The focus must be terrorism," *Europe's World*, spring 2006, www.europesworld.org/EWSettings/Article/tabid/191/ArticleType/ArticleView/ArticleID/21005/Default.aspx.

24. NATO, *op. cit.*

25. See "Operation Active Endeavour," www.nato.int/issues/active_endeavour/practice.html.

26. Alexander Kudascheff, "German NATO General: Most Afghans Back ISAF Mission," *Deutsche Welle*, Sept. 27, 2008, www.dw-world.de/dw/article/0,2144,3675301,00.html.

27. Tim Shipman, "US officials 'despair' at NATO allies' failings in Afghanistan," *Telegraph News*, June 22, 2008, www.telegraph.co.uk/news/worldnews/northamerica/usa/2170135/US-officials-%27despair%27-at-Nato-allies%27-failings-in-Afghanistan.html.

28. Benjamin Friedman and Justin Logan, "Don't Expand NATO: The Case Against Membership for Georgia and Ukraine," Cato Institute, Oct. 22, 2008, www.cato.org/pub_display.php?pub_id= 9738. For background on the Marshall Plan, see "Marshall Plan Home Page," U.S. Agency for International Development, www.usaid.gov/multimedia/video/marshall/.

29. Forrest P. Sherman, unpublished diary, Sept. 25, 1950 (quoted by permission of the Fitzpatrick family).

30. *Ibid.*, March 4, 1951.

31. "NATO's Strategy of Flexible Response and the Twenty-first Century," GlobalSecurity.org, www.globalsecurity.org/wmd/library/report/1986/LLE.htm.

32. *Ibid.*

33. For an analysis of the Harmel Report, see "NATO Strategy in 1967," www.db.niss.gov.ua/docs/nato/nato/sco32.html.

34. Strobe Talbott, *The Russia Hand: A Memoir of Presidential Diplomacy* (2002), p. 248.

35. *Ibid.*

36. "Russia Slams U.S., threatens missile deployment," CNN.com, Nov. 5, 2008, www.cnn/2008/WORLD/Europe/11/05/russia.missiles.

37. "Russia to deploy missile to counter US missile shield next year," *Daily Telegraph*, Nov. 28, 2008, www.telegraph.co.uk/news/worldnews/europe/russia/3533320/Russia-to-deploy-missile-to-counter-US-missile-shield-next-year.html. For background on Kaliningrad, see Brian Beary, "A Sliver of Russia Trapped in Europe," pp. 194-195, in "The New Europe," *CQ Global Researcher*, August 2007.

38. Lanny Davis, "Are we all Georgians? Not so fast," *Fox Forum*, Aug. 25, 2008, http://foxforum.blogs.foxnews.com/2008/08/25/are-we-all-georgians-not-so-fast/.

39. For background, see Brian Beary, "Separatist Movements," *CQ Global Researcher*, April 2008, pp. 85-114.

40. "NATO Agrees to Thaw in Contacts with Russia," *VOAnews*, Dec. 2, 2008, www.voanews.com/english/2008-12-02-voa58.cfm.

41. "NATO reopens talks with Russia, hold off on Ukraine and Georgia," *Deutsche Welle*, Dec. 2, 2008, www.dw-world.de/dw/article/0,2144,3843756.00.html.

42. Judy Dempsey, "U.S. presses NATO on Georgia and Ukraine," *The New York Times*, Nov. 25, 2008, www.nytimes.com/2008/11/26/world/europe/26nato.html?_r=1&ref=world.

43. See Kiener, *op. cit.*

44. Michael Gordon, "Strategy Shift for Afghan War Poses Stiff Challenge for Obama," *The New York Times*, Dec. 2, 2008, p. A1.

45. Marcela Gaviria and Martin Smith, "Frontline: The War Briefing," PBS, Oct. 28, 2008, www.pbs.org/wgbh/pages/frontline/warbriefing/view/.

46. Carol Bowers, "NATO grows with Afghanistan experience," U.S. Dept. of Defense, April 2, 2008, www.defenselink.mil/news/newsarticle.aspx?id=49433.

47. Gordon, *op. cit.*

48. Nima Abbaszadeh, *et al.*, "Provincial Reconstruction Teams: Lessons and Recommendations," January 2008, http://wws.princeton.edu/research/pwreports_f07/wws591b.pdf.

49. *Ibid.*

50. Gaviria and Smith, *op. cit.*

51. Helene Cooper and Scott L. Malcomson, "Welcome to My World, Barack," *The New York Times Magazine*, Nov. 16, 2008, www.nytimes.com/2008/11/16/magazine/16rice-t.html?ref=magazine&page wanted=all.

52. Elizabeth Sherwood-Randall, "Is NATO Dead or Alive?" *The Huffington Post*, April 1, 2008, www.huffingtonpost.com/elizabeth-sherwoodrandall/is-nato-dead-or-alive_b_94469.html.

53. See NATO Online Library, April 4, 2005, www.nato.int/docu/speech/2005/s050401b.htm.

BIBLIOGRAPHY

Books

Asmus, Ronald D., *Opening NATO's Door: How the Alliance Remade Itself for a New Era*, Columbia University Press, 2004.
The executive director of the Brussels-based Transatlantic Center provides an insider's account of the fierce divisions within the alliance over the Yugoslav wars and NATO enlargement.

Henricksen, Dag, *NATO'S Gamble: Combining Diplomacy and Airpower in the Kosovo Crisis, 1998-1999*, Naval Institute Press, 2007.
A Norwegian Air Force captain and military strategist who participated in NATO'S 78-day aerial-bombing campaign during the Kosovo conflict examines what happened.

Howorth, Jolyon, and John T. S. Keeler, (eds.), *Defending Europe: The EU, NATO, and the Quest for European Autonomy*, Palgrave Macmillan, 2003.
A professor of European politics at England's University of Bath (Howorth) and the dean of the School of Public and International Affairs at the University of Pittsburgh (Keeler) have compiled a variety of commentaries on the complex relationship between NATO and the European Union.

Kaplan, Lawrence S., *NATO 1948: The Birth of the Transatlantic Alliance*, 2007.
In his fourth book on NATO, a Georgetown University history professor examines the often-contentious 1948 negotiations about whether the United States should join the proposed alliance.

Kaplan, Lawrence S., *NATO Divided, NATO United: The Evolution of an Alliance*, 2004.
A leading NATO historian explores persistent differences between the United States and its European partners that quickly re-emerged after NATO rushed to support the United States following the Sept. 11, 2001, terrorist attacks.

Articles

Daalder, Ivo, and James Goldgeier, "Global NATO," *Foreign Affairs*, spring, 2006.
A senior fellow at the Brookings Institution (Daalder) and a professor of political science at The George Washington University (Goldgeier) argue that NATO must expand its membership beyond Europe in order to meet new security challenges.

Hulsman, John C., *et al.*, "Can NATO Survive Europe?" *The National Interest*, March 22, 2004.
Four distinguished scholars debate whether NATO can co-exist with the European Union.

Myers, Stephen Lee, and Thom Shanker, "NATO Expansion and a Bush Legacy Are in Doubt," *The New York Times*, March 18, 2008.
Disparities of might and will exist among NATO members.

Reports and Studies

Archick, Kristin, "The United States and Europe: Possible Options for U.S. Policy," *Congressional Research Service*, March 8, 2005, http://fpc.state.gov/documents/organization/41324.pdf.
An analyst of European affairs offers options for improving U.S.-European relations.

Gordon, Philip H., "NATO and the War on Terrorism: A Changing Alliance," *Brookings Institution*, Dec.

12, 2008, www.brookings.edu/articles/2002/
summer_globalgovernance_gordon.aspx.
A leading analyst wonders if NATO has an enduring role
but says writing off NATO would be "perverse and
mistaken."

Hunter, Robert E., Edward Gnehm and George
Joulwan, "Integrating Instruments of Power and
Influence: Lessons Learned and Best Practices,"
*National Security Research Division, RAND
Corporation*, 2008, www.rand.org/pubs/conf_
proceedings/2008/RAND_CF251.pdf.
A former U.S. ambassador to NATO (Hunter) leads a
prestigious group of "senior practitioners" in developing
a blueprint for post-conflict operations.

Hunter, Robert E., Sergei M. Rogov and Olga Oliker,
"NATO and Russia: Bridge-building for the 21st century, Report of the Working Group on NATO,"
RAND Corporation, 2002, www.rand.org/pubs/
white_papers/WP128/.

A former U.S. ambassador to NATO (Hunter) and
director of the Institute for U.S. and Canadian Studies at
the Russian Academy of Sciences (Rogov) — a Moscow-
based independent research organization — argue for
closer cooperation between NATO and post-communist
Russia.

Phillips, David, "Post-Conflict Georgia," *The Atlantic
Council of the United States*, Oct. 3, 2008, www.acus
.org/publication/post-conflict-georgia.
A visiting scholar at Columbia University's Center for
the Study of Human Rights examines the impact of the
Georgia conflict on U.S.-European relations within
NATO.

Rupp, Richard E., "NATO after 9/11: An Alliance in
Decline," March 2006, www.allacademic.com//
meta/p_mla_apa_research_citation/0/9/9/2/4/
pages99241/p99241-1.php.
A Purdue University history professor argues that NATO
is increasingly ineffective and cannot be reformed.

For More Information

Atlantic Council of the United States, 1101 15th St.,
N.W., 11th Floor, Washington, DC 20005; (202) 463-
7226; www.acus.org. Promotes constructive American
leadership in helping the Atlantic community meet the
challenges of the 21st century.

Brookings Institution, 1775 Massachusetts Ave., N.W.,
Washington, DC 20036; (202) 797-6000; www.brookings
.edu. A think tank that studies how to strengthen U.S.
democracy and promote a more cooperative international
system.

Cato Institute, 1000 Massachusetts Ave., N.W.,
Washington, DC 20001; (202) 842-0200; www.cato.org.
Seeks to increase understanding of public policies based on
the libertarian principles of limited government, free markets, individual liberty and peace.

Council on Foreign Relations, 58 East 68th St., New
York, N.Y. 10021; (212) 434-9400; www.cfr.org. Promotes
a better understanding of the foreign policy choices facing
the United States and other governments.

French Institute of International Affairs (IFRI), 27 rue
des Processions, Paris 75740, France; 33(0)1 40-61-60-00;
www.ifri.org. A leading European center for research,
meetings and debates on international issues.

International Institute for Strategic Studies, 13-15 Arundel
St. Temple Place, London WC2R 3DX, England; 44(0)20
7379-7676; www.iiss.org. Think tank focusing on international security with an emphasis on political-military conflict.

North Atlantic Treaty Organization, Blvd. Leopold III,
1110 Brussels, Belgium; 32(0)2 707-50-41; www.nato.int.
Headquarters of the North American-European mutual
defense alliance.

Polish Institute for International Affairs, 1a Warecka
Slwe, P.O. Box 1010, 00-950 Warsaw, Poland. Established
in 1996 to conduct research and provide unbiased expertise in international relations.

RAND Corporation, 1776 Main St., Santa Monica, CA
90401; (310) 393-0411; www.rand.org. Nonprofit organization that focuses on national security issues.

Russian Academy of Sciences, Leninskii Avenue, 14, Moscow,
Russia 119991; (495) 938-0309; www.ras.ru. Nonprofit organization researching policies that promote economic, social,
technological and cultural development in Russia.

Transatlantic Center, German Marshall Fund, Résidence
Palace, Rue de la Loi 155 Wetstraat, Brussels, Belgium
1040; +32-2-238-5270; www.gmfus.org. Promotes a more
integrated Europe and studies the impact on NATO.

Anti-Semitism in Europe

5

*Are Israel's Policies Spurring
a New Wave of Hate Crimes?*

Sarah Glazer

Ilan Halimi, a French Jew, was kidnapped and killed by a gang in Paris. He was found naked, handcuffed and covered with burn marks and died on the way to a hospital. The case spurred national outrage and huge marches protesting the rise of anti-Semitism in France.

From *CQ Global Researcher*, June 2008.

On Feb. 22, Mathieu Roumi, a 19-year-old French Jew, was tortured for nine hours in a basement in a Paris suburb by a group of young men, including several Muslims, who wrote "dirty Jew" on his face and forced him to eat cigarette butts and suck on a condom-covered stick.[1]

The incident bore eerie parallels to the 2006 murder of Ilan Halimi, a 23-year-old Jewish cell phone salesman who was kidnapped and killed by a gang in Paris after three weeks of torture. Halimi was found naked, covered in bruises, knife slashes and burns; he died on the way to the hospital.[2]

Both Halimi and Roumi were abducted in their own neighborhoods in Paris' low-income Bagneux quarter. Halimi had been abducted by a gang calling itself the Barbarians, which had tried unsuccessfully to extort a ransom of 3 million Euros ($4.5 million) from Halimi's family. Unlike Halimi, however, Roumi knew his attackers and was ultimately released.

When police raided the apartments of gang leader Youssouf Fofana and other gang members charged with Halimi's killing, they discovered anti-Semitic, neo-Nazi and radical Muslim, or Islamist, literature. Fofana continued to send anti-Semitic letters to the judge overseeing the case.

Gang members later admitted they selected Halimi assuming he was "one of these rich Jews" — although Halimi's family actually was of only modest means, defying the stereotype.[3]

The Halimi case spurred a storm of controversy about the state of anti-Semitism in France and was seen by the Jewish community as the culmination of a wave of anti-Jewish attacks on individuals and synagogues that has surged since 2000 — just after the start of

Individuals Targeted in Many Incidents

Forty percent of the 632 major attacks and violent incidents against Jews worldwide in 2007 targeted specific individuals, while 22 percent targeted cemeteries and memorials. More than half of the incidents were nonviolent — involving vandalism, graffiti or slogans.

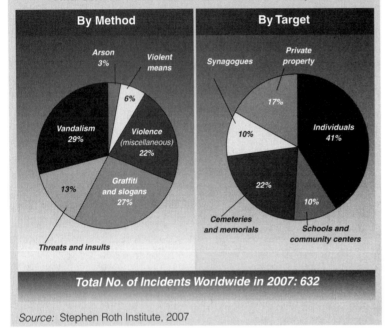

Anti-Semitic Attacks and Incidents Worldwide, 2007

Total No. of Incidents Worldwide in 2007: 632

Source: Stephen Roth Institute, 2007

violent incidents against Jews in Western Europe — including attacks on individuals and vandalizing of Jewish property — reached a new high — 352 incidents, or more than quadruple the number in 1999, according to the institute.[8] For instance, while France experienced a 33 percent drop in anti-Semitic acts of all kinds, major violent attacks on French individuals and property quadrupled from 2 to 8; violent, anti-Semitic offenses in Germany jumped more than 50 percent.[9]

A British parliamentary inquiry raised concern in 2006 about a "widespread change in mood and tone when Jews are discussed" in the media, at universities and in other public settings.

"We are concerned that anti-Jewish themes and remarks are gaining acceptability in some quarters in public and private discourse in Britain, and there is a danger that this trend will become more and more mainstream," the report warned.[10]

Many young people in the Jewish community tolerated living with verbal and physical assaults — so much so, the report found, that many incidents weren't even reported, particularly in orthodox Jewish neighborhoods. "The routineness of anti-Semitism was most shocking — how it became accepted as a normal part of life," says John Mann, chair of the Parliamentary Committee Against Anti-Semitism.

A month before the report's release on Aug. 9, 2006, Jasmine Kranat — a 13-year-old Jewish girl riding home from school on a bus — was asked by teenagers demanding money whether she was Jewish. The teenagers punched her in the face until she lost consciousness, and no one on the bus offered her assistance.[11]

Middle East or Muslim-related news events — such as the 9/11 terrorist attacks in the United States or the 2006 Lebanon war between Israel and Hezbollah — appear to trigger anti-Jewish violence in Europe, notes Mark Gardner, a spokesman for the Community Security Trust,

the second Palestinian intifada, or uprising, against Israel's occupation — according to the Stephen Roth Institute for the Study of Contemporary Anti-Semitism and Racism in Tel Aviv.[4] It also raised questions about a new source of anti-Semitism in Europe — radical, anti-Zionist Muslims.

In fact, the institute's latest report on global anti-Semitism found mixed trends in 2007: Anti-Jewish incidents of all kinds slowed and even declined a bit from the previous year in a handful of countries, and it was the quietest year the French Jewish community has known since the rise in attacks began in 2000.[5] But violent attacks on individuals continued to rise, causing some Jewish groups and experts to worry that Europe appears to be adjusting to a new, high level of violent hate incidents and blatant anti-Jewish rhetoric.

Although anti-Semitic incidents overall declined last year in Britain,[6] Belgium and Germany,[7] major attacks and

a London-based group that tracks anti-Semitic incidents in Britain.

"Our fear is that since 2000 there have been so many trigger events that the net effect is a considerable increase in underlying anti-Semitic incidents," contributing to a high, ongoing base level, says Gardner. "In 2007 there were no trigger events, yet it was still the second-worst year on record" since his organization began recording them in 1984. Even with the slight drop in anti-Jewish incidents in Britain last year, the 547 incidents that did occur — which included assaults, hate mail, anti-Semitic graffiti and verbal abuse — amounted to twice as many as in 1999. And, disturbingly, 114 of the 2007 incidents were violent assaults — the highest number since 1984.[12]

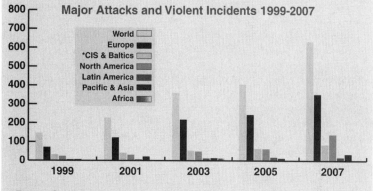

Most Anti-Semitic Attacks Occur in Europe

Major anti-Semitic attacks and violent incidents worldwide jumped more than fourfold between 1999 and 2007. North America saw more than a fivefold increase — from 25 in 1999 to 140 in 2007 — but more than half of the 632 major attacks worldwide last year occurred in Europe.

Major Attacks and Violent Incidents 1999-2007

Legend: World, Europe, *CIS & Baltics, North America, Latin America, Pacific & Asia, Africa

* Former Soviet bloc countries

Source: Stephen Roth Institute, 2007

Last year many religious Jews, identifiable by their dress, were attacked and injured by Arabs or North Africans, according to the Roth Institute. For example, on Sept. 7, Rabbi Zalman Gurevitch was stabbed in the stomach in Frankfurt am Main, Germany, by someone he described as an Arab speaker who shouted "[Pig] Jew, I will kill you."[13]

A great deal of this violence apparently is stimulated by opposition to the existence of Israel, or anti-Zionism, which is shared both by Muslims and by much of Europe's intellectual elite, according to the Roth Institute's latest report on anti-Semitism worldwide. "The fact that anti-Zionism has become politically correct in some sectors encourages not only anti-Semitic activists of the left and right but also young, second- or third-generation Muslims who have been exposed (via satellite TV and the Internet) to hate preachers from the Arab world," the report says.[14]

Franco Frattini, the European Union (EU) commissioner responsible for combating racism and anti-Semitism in Europe, has attributed half of all documented anti-Semitic incidents in Europe to "radical Islamic elements."[15]

The U.S. State Department calls anti-Zionist political cartoons and news commentary that appear after Israeli-Palestinian flareups the "new anti-Semitism," a term adopted by critics of the European left and even included in a working definition of anti-Semitism agreed to by EU states in January 2005.[16] These critics have savaged the liberal European media and leftist activists for what they consider their one-sided sympathizing with the Palestinians.

"Zionism is now a dirty word in Britain, and opposition to Israel has become a fig leaf for a resurgence of the oldest hatred," Melanie Phillips, a commentator for the British *Daily Mail*, recently charged.[17]

Some find this new type of anti-Semitism particularly disturbing because they fear it arouses European racial canards that existed before and during World War II. Political cartoons in newspapers and on the Internet have revived caricatures reminiscent of medieval beliefs in the Jew as child-killer and employed Nazi-like imagery to portray Jewish Israelis as cruel and bloodthirsty in countries as varied as Norway, Greece and England.[18]

So many familiar anti-Jewish stereotypes appeared in the mainstream media during the Lebanon war in 2006 that British scholar David Hirsch described the period as "the summer in which anti-Semitism entered the mainstream."[19]

Hate rhetoric coming out of the Middle East is often beamed into Europe via Syrian and Egyptian satellite TV

Who Are Israel's Harshest Critics?

Liberal British Jews oppose Palestinian occupation.

At a March meeting in London of activists opposed to Israel's occupation of Palestinian territories, attendees could buy fair-trade, organic Palestinian olive oil soap, with revenues going to widows in Ramallah.

But this was not a meeting directed at London's large Muslim population. It featured a panel of Israeli protesters who have come to view their nation's treatment of the Palestinians as incompatible with a democratic, racially equitable society. And it was organized primarily by liberal-left British Jewish groups critical of Israel, such as Jews for Justice for Palestinians.

About 200 mostly middle-aged Jews crowded into the room, the kind of rumpled, intellectual audience one might expect at a talk at New York's famous 92nd Street Y. Palestinian psychiatrist Eyad El-Sarraj, director of the Gaza Community Mental Health Program, described on a live phone line how Israel's blockade had left Gazans so short of bottled water and water filters that they were forced to drink salty, polluted tap water.

"Imagine living in a prison that you're not allowed to leave, and the prison is bombed," he told the hushed room. As for the violence, he said, "I cry for the children killed in Gaza," but also "I cry when my people celebrated in the streets" over the killing of children in Jerusalem.

Parallels to apartheid South Africa were frequently drawn by the speakers as photos flashed across a screen of impoverished Palestinians confronting armed soldiers at checkpoints and standing dwarfed by Israel's security wall dividing it from Palestinian villages. The overwhelmingly sympathetic crowd applauded calls for a boycott of Israeli academics and of companies that benefit from the occupation of Palestinian territories.

Michael Kustow, a British writer and organizer of the event, anticipated criticism from the British Jewish community. "Those of us who criticize Israel do not think we're disloyal or self-hating," he maintained. "We're trying to return Israel to . . . its own values."

Harsh criticism of Israel is common on campuses in Great Britain, which often comes as a shock to visiting American Jewish students. "I've been very surprised at the amount of anti-Israel programming at the institutional level," says Naomi Berlin, a student at Tufts University in Medford, Mass., spending her junior year at Oxford. "When you say Israel, you get words like 'occupation,' 'apartheid,' 'racist.'"

Berlin cited two highly controversial debates organized this academic year by the eminent Oxford Union Debating Society. One, a November forum on free speech featuring Holocaust denier David Irving, was picketed by Jewish students. Another, a debate on whether Israel should exist, invited two prominent critics of Israel to argue in favor of Israel's existence. One of them actually switched sides during the debate and argued against Israel's right to exist.

stations and the Internet, but it has been getting less attention from the liberal press than it once did, says Charles Small, director of the Yale Initiative for the Interdisciplinary Study of Antisemitism. As an example, Small cites the lack of coverage for a recent speech by Iranian President Mahmoud Ahmadinejad calling Israel "filthy bacteria," in language reminiscent of Nazi demands for eradication of Jews.[20]

"On the one hand, you have a genocidal movement" coming out of the Muslim world, says Small, "and on the other you have acquiescence in Europe. . . . I think increasingly because of anti-Semitism among the elite in Europe, particularly in the U.K. and France, you have this dual-loyalty issue coming in. As Israel becomes more and more tarnished as an apartheid, Nazi-like state, you also have the accusation that Jews are loyal to this entity."

In England, the majority of perpetrators identified in connection with anti-Semitic incidents are not disaffected Muslims but white youths, according to criminologist Paul Iganski of Britain's Lancaster University. Although he agrees the Middle East conflicts serve as trigger events, incidents often start with a mundane irritation such as road rage or a dispute over a parking spot — which "becomes aggravated by deep-seated anti-Semitic feeling," he says. "There is a reservoir of anti-Semitic bigotry there simmering below the surface."

Adam Parker, a first-year student from Manchester who co-founded the Israeli Cultural Society at Oxford this year, helped organize a protest against the Irving event. "I think it was a disgrace," he says.

Yair Zivan, campaigns director for the Union of Jewish Students, claims anti-Zionism on campus "often spills over into anti-Semitism." According to Zivan, three anti-Semitic incidents were reported at Manchester University when Jewish students protested a resolution to "twin" their student union with Palestinian An-Najah University, where some students have become suicide bombers, Zivan says.

The harshest critics of Israel at places like Oxford are Jewish professors, notably Israeli Professor of International Relations Avi Shlaim, who charges that Israel's aim in its current blockade of Gaza is "to starve the people of Gaza into submission."[1]

Seth Anziska, an American Oxford graduate student in Middle Eastern studies, says, "Europeans — and the British in particular — have a much more pessimistic outlook" about the peace process between Israel and the Palestinians than Americans. But he adds, "In some ways, it's more realistic."

Yet some prominent British Jews aren't buying it. Shalom Lappin, a professor of computational linguistics at King's College, London, who has written on the history of British Jews, dismisses groups like Jews for Justice for Palestinians. He sees them as part of a long tradition of what he calls "a survival strategy" among British Jews to gain acceptance from the British establishment by not provoking anger.

"I don't doubt their sincerity," he says, "but they're celebrated with open access to *The Guardian* and the *London*

Demonstrators outside England's famed Oxford Union Debating Society protest the presence of British writer David Irving, a notorious Holocaust denier, at a debate on freedom of speech.

Review of Books and paraded across campuses as 'the good Jews,' not the 'tribal and bad Jews.' "

"I'm proud to be Jewish," responds the organization's chair, Dan Judelson, who said he became active after his daughter was born. "That sense of Jewish injustice and treating people equitably was something I wanted to pass on to my daughter."

---

[1] Avi Shlaim, "Free Speech? Not for Critics of Israel," *The Jewish Chronicle*, Feb. 29, 2008.

For example, anti-Semitic taunts now ring out at soccer stadiums throughout Europe, where so-called soccer hooligans have traditionally sympathized with the extreme right, according to two recent reports. In the Netherlands, supporters of the traditionally Jewish soccer team Ajax Amsterdam are regularly taunted by fans of opposing teams with Hitler salutes and chants of "Hamas, Hamas, Jews to the gas!"[21]

In a recent report, British MP Mann found that anti-Semitic cheers and paraphernalia are proliferating at Europe's soccer stadiums in part because of the increasing tendency of fans to travel across borders and share anti-Jewish attitudes on the Internet. "We're not prepared to

tolerate that; we're meeting with football authorities to take action to stamp this out," Mann says.

However, some experts downplay such concerns, noting that Jews no longer face discriminatory laws in Europe, while Muslims and other minorities are far more likely to face prejudice in employment and housing.

And liberal critics of Israel are leery of what they see as a tendency to equate criticism of Israel's policies with anti-Semitism. "This redefining devalues the word [anti-Semitism] itself. You desensitize people — they become confused," objects Antony Lerman, executive director of the Institute for Jewish Policy Research, a London-based think tank.[22] (*See "At Issue," p. 131.*)

Vandals spray-painted a star of David hanging from a gallows on this gravestone at the only remaining Jewish cemetery in Bialystok, Poland. Defacing Jewish gravestones is a frequent outlet for expressions of anti-Semitism.

"I'm critical of what is done [by Israel] in the occupied territories, but I've never seen myself as an anti-Semite," says Lerman. "I feel as if I'm being bracketed in with anti-Semites."

Here are some of the questions about anti-Semitism and other forms of prejudice being debated across Europe:

Is anti-Semitism on the rise in Europe?

Some Jewish groups and experts point to the surge in reported anti-Semitic incidents since 2000, particularly violent attacks on individuals and anti-Jewish imagery in the press, as a sign that anti-Semitism is growing.[23]

In addition, the European Union's Agency for Fundamental Rights (FRA) and other Europe-wide groups have documented increases in anti-Semitism.[24]

In June 2007, the Parliamentary Assembly of the Council of Europe issued a resolution noting "the persistence and escalation of anti-Semitic phenomena. . . . [F]ar from having been eliminated, anti-Semitism is today on the rise in Europe. It appears in a variety of forms and is becoming commonplace."[25]

The data are somewhat problematic, however, because Jewish communities that are best organized and living in open, democratic societies tend to report the highest number of incidents. Assiduous reporting by Jewish groups in

Britain, for instance, makes that country look worse than nations that are less transparent, such as those in Eastern Europe with a long tradition of anti-Semitism in both the church and government. For example, in Belarus, government enterprises produce and distribute anti-Semitic material, but the nation does not rank high on comparative international charts. In addition, figures compiled by law-enforcement agencies or community groups often do not measure anti-Semitic attitudes, such as those captured in political cartoons.[26] (*See graph, p. 110.*)

A recent State Department report makes a distinction between traditional anti-Semitism — which draws on older ideas of Jews as racially inferior, bloodthirsty or Christ killers — and the "new anti-Semitism," which relies primarily on anti-Zionist language but sometimes also incorporates older stereotypes such as Jews as world conspirators.

Eastern European countries tend to specialize in older forms of anti-Semitism. According to a June 2007 report by Human Rights First, extreme, nationalist political groups in Eastern Europe recently have adopted 19th-century anti-Semitic language. The group singled out Poland, Ukraine and Hungary as countries where certain Orthodox and Roman Catholic institutions have encouraged anti-Semitism.[27] (*See "Background" and sidebar, p. 118, for more detail on Poland.*)

In Poland, recent attention has focused on anti-Semitic remarks broadcast on Catholic Radio Maryja, part of the Polish media empire run by the Rev. Tadeusz Rydzyk of the Catholic missionary order Redemptorists. Rydzyk was quoted most recently calling Jews greedy and responsible for lobbies that control the Polish president.[28]

The Rydzyk empire's audience is estimated to be approaching 3 million mostly elderly Poles. Polls show Polish seniors are more likely than young people to hold anti-Semitic views, such as the belief that Jews killed Christ, observes Michal Bilewicz, a social psychologist at Warsaw University's Centre for Research on Prejudice. "We have demography on our side," he says.

Polls also suggest that many traditional stereotypes are commonly held in both Western and Eastern Europe. Anti-Defamation League polls show substantial percentages in many countries believe traditional conspiracy theories about Jews, such as that they have too much power in the business world or in international financial markets.[29]

The most heated debate in Europe, however, has focused on the new anti-Semitism, which often emanates from radical Muslims, relies on anti-Zionism and is concentrated in Western European countries like Great Britain and France, according to advocates of the term.

These experts say they are most concerned about the type of anti-Semitism promoted by radical Muslims known as Islamists, who often appeal to left-leaning European intellectuals for support of the Palestinian liberation movement.

In a 2005 interview, French philosopher and political scientist Pierre-André Taguieff, who helped coin the term "the new anti-Semitism," said all Jews have come to be seen as "more or less hidden Zionists; Zionism equals colonialism, imperialism and racism; therefore the Jews are colonialists, imperialists and racists, openly or not." Zionism, says Taguieff, "became the incarnation of absolute evil."[30]

Like Taguieff, critics in England and Germany have charged that anti-Semitic comments by Muslim groups are often ignored by the liberal media and by leftist academics who support the Palestinians' liberation movement.

For example, in a recent book, *Jihad and Jew-Hatred*, political scientist Matthias Küntzel reports trial testimony showing that 9/11 leader Mohammed Atta and fellow plotters were convinced that "the Jews" sought world domination. The plotters saw New York City as the center of world Jewry, making it their obvious target.[31]

Yet that testimony was widely ignored in the German and international media, according to Küntzel. "If we had the same quotes by the Oklahoma [City] bomber — by far-right white perpetrators — I think it would have made headlines. But if the very same anti-Semitism is displayed by Muslims, people think perhaps this is Israel's fault, and we just have to tackle the Middle East problem and it will vanish again," says Küntzel, a research associate at the Vidal Sassoon International Center for the Study of Antisemitism at Hebrew University in Jerusalem.

It's no accident, he says, that al Qaeda leader Osama bin Laden quotes left-leaning American intellectual Noam Chomsky, a strong critic of Israel's Palestinian politics. "This is the most dangerous aspect of this Islamism ideology," Küntzel says. In an effort to appeal to the European

Demonstrators in Paris protest racism and anti-Semitism in February 2006. The sign says "Anti-Semitic barbarism. Our child murdered." The photograph is of Ilan Halimi, the Jewish Frenchman murdered in Paris.

left, he maintains, Islamist leaders "put themselves in the same role as communism [once played] — as the only potent force against global capitalism. They want to build a broad alliance in order to fight against America and Israel."

Leftist criticism of Israelis as powerful oppressors with Nazi-like characteristics can spur anti-Semitic violence, suggests British journalist Phillips. For example, in a widely reported incident in 2005, when a Jewish reporter approached London's former far-left Mayor Ken Livingstone with a question, the mayor snapped, "What did you do before? Were you a German war criminal?" When the reporter said he was Jewish, Livingstone compared him to a "concentration camp guard."

Later, several perpetrators of anti-Semitic attacks mentioned those comments, according to the Community Security Trust, which tracks anti-Semitic incidents in Britain and provides security advice to Jewish schools and other institutions.[32]

"The Jewish organizations — particularly Jewish-defense organizations — are highlighting how these themes on campuses, Web sites and classrooms have physical manifestations: That can be a swastika on a wall or a physical attack like the one in Paris," says Ben Cohen, the American Jewish Committee's associate director for tackling anti-Semitism and extremism and the editor of a new Web site, www.z-word.com, focusing on anti-Zionism.

However, some observers think the significance of anti-Semitic acts counted by Jewish groups is often overplayed. "Every time someone smears anti-Semitic graffiti on a synagogue wall in France we are warned that 'the unique evil' is with us once more, that it is 1938 all over again," New York University historian Tony Judt recently wrote. "We are losing the capacity to distinguish between the normal sins and follies of mankind — stupidity, prejudice, opportunism, demagogy and fanaticism — and genuine evil. . . . After all, if we see evil everywhere, how can we be expected to recognize the real thing?"[33]

In a similar vein, a prominent French historian, Patrick D. Weil, of the National Center for Scientific Research (CNRS) at the University of Paris, downplays the significance of the recent kidnapping in Paris and paints a positive picture of the general climate in France. "It is in France that you have the most open society with respect to Jews," he says, citing surveys that find French Muslims and French people generally rate at the top of European countries when asked if they have a favorable view of Jews. "But it doesn't mean at the local individual level or at the margin you won't have activist anti-Semitism from some very small segments of the population," he adds.

Bagneux, the poor suburb where Roumi lived and was kidnapped, is integrated, with Jews living alongside Arabs, and Roumi apparently knew his attackers. News reports indicate he was "not a saint," Weil points out, but was involved in some petty criminality like his attackers. "The fact that people [of different ethnic origin] live all together is perhaps good for the integration of society, but it can also produce these extreme attitudes and acts," says Weil. Such assaults may stem as much from the rising tendency of people in France to identify with their own ethnic group, he suggests, which affects other minorities as well.

Experts critical of Israel downplay the levels of anti-Semitism in Europe. "I don't think the evidence is there to suggest that the growth is as bad as many people do claim," says Lerman, at the Institute for Jewish Policy Research. "Quite a few research institutions in Europe and the U.S. have spoken of anti-Semitism as being so extreme it's like being back at *Kristallnacht* on the eve of the Holocaust — which I find unnecessary. I personally would say in the last year or so it's reached a plateau."

Is anti-Zionism a cover-up for anti-Semitism?

Increasingly, groups such as the American Jewish Committee charge that inflammatory anti-Zionist language is being used in Europe as a pretext for anti-Semitism. Anti-Defamation League Director Abraham Foxman has charged that in Britain, hostility towards Jews often "is camouflaged as criticism of Israel."[34]

"The canard," in Foxman's words, that Israel resembles apartheid-era South Africa — reflected in February's "Israel Apartheid Week" organized on British campuses by Muslim students — is "fueling dislike, distrust, hatred of Jews," Foxman has written.[35]

Critics in Britain and France have charged that members of the liberal intelligentsia, in their eagerness to make common cause with the Palestinians, have turned a blind eye to the anti-Semitism that is part of Islamist rhetoric.

"Essentially, you see the movement into the mainstream of ideas that until 10 years ago were confined to the far left and the far right," says Shalom Lappin, a professor at King's College in London and one of the founders of a group of academics, the Euston Manifesto, which has protested against British anti-Semitism. "They place Israel and Jews at the center of the Jewish conspiracy, part of the lobby used to subvert foreign policy. . . . It's sweeping campuses; it lends toxicity to public debate."

French philosopher and political scientist Taguieff contends that anti-Jewish stereotypes and accusatory themes originally drawn from Palestinian nationalism "have become more and more widespread since the 1970s in the French public arena . . . as well as in the West more generally." This new anti-Semitism, he said, often relies on anti-Zionist themes, using metaphors like "cancer" to describe Israel and creating what he called the most recent form of "eliminationist" anti-Semitism.[36]

Weil of CNRS is skeptical of the concept. "I think what we call a new anti-Semitism resembles the old one — the same kind of theory of the plot of the *Protocols of the Learned Elders of Zion*," says Weil, referring to the infamous anti-Semitic literary hoax alleging a Jewish plot to achieve world domination. "Some people call it new because it comes from Arabs."

British journalist Phillips has charged that "Language straight out of the lexicon of medieval and Nazi Jew-hatred has become commonplace in acceptable British discourse, particularly in the media." For her, "the most striking evidence that hatred of Israel is the latest muta-tion of anti-Semitism is that it resurrects the libel of the world Jewish conspiracy, a defining anti-Semitic motif that went underground after the Holocaust."[37]

For example, she cites the left-leaning *New Statesman* magazine's investigation into the "Zionist" lobby in Britain, which it headlined the "Kosher Conspiracy" and illustrated on its Jan. 14, 2002, cover with a gold Star of David piercing the Union Jack.[38] *The Guardian*, Britain's leading liberal daily, published a cartoon on July 19, 2006, depicting a huge fist, armed with brass knuckles shaped like Stars of David, hammering a bloody child.[39] A cartoon in *The Independent* in 2003 showing former Israeli leader Ariel Sharon biting the head off a Palestinian baby won first prize in the British Political Cartoon Society's annual competition for that year.[40]

Some critics say such drawings of Jews killing chil-dren are reminiscent of the imagery of the "blood libel," the medieval European belief that Jews murdered Gentile children to obtain their blood for religious rituals — sparking massacres of Jews throughout history.

But not all Jews see these media images as intention-ally ill-motivated. "What that proves is there's a great deal of criticism of Israel, some of which spills over into odious anti-Semitism," says Dan Judelson, chair of Jews for Justice for Palestinians, a British group. "It's not a type of deep-seated, visceral hatred of the Jews; it's just intellectual laziness."

Judelson's is one of several groups of generally left-leaning Jews who have been active in criticizing Israel's actions towards the Palestinians. He says Israel's defend-ers equate criticism of Israel with anti-Semitism as a way of "de-legitimizing" sincere criticism. And he takes issue with a commonly used definition of anti-Semitism from the European Union's monitoring arm, which encom-passes "denying the Jewish people their right to self-determination, e.g. by claiming that the existence of a State of Israel is a racist endeavor."[41] Not all Jews define self-determination as having a Jewish state, he points out. (*See sidebar, p. 112.*)

Groups like Judelson's have been criticized for march-ing for Palestinian liberation with Muslim activists who carried placards linking a swastika to a Star of David with an equal sign. Judelson says whenever he's con-fronted Muslim marchers about this kind of imagery, they have responded by changing their symbols.

But other observers, including a former Islamist, say liberal Jewish groups are naïve about the ultimate motives of such Muslim activists. Rashad Ali, a former director in the command structure of the radical Islamist group Hizb-ut-Tahrir Britain, says the group would capitalize on sentiments against Israel for its own political ends.

During the conflict between Israel and Lebanon, he says, "We'd always know we can get a Jewish rabbi to talk about the atrocities in Israel; then we'd take over and say what we need is the Caliphate" — which Ali describes as a dictatorship in which laws would be based on Islamic religious interpretation. (When asked which groups such a rabbi would come from, Ali mentioned Neturei Karta, an orthodox Jewish group that opposes the establish-ment of the state of Israel before the coming of the Messiah.)

At least one radical Islamist group has been careful to replace the word "Jew" with "Zionist" in its leaflets and Web sites in order to appeal to more mainstream critics of Israel, says Ali, now head of research and policy at the Quilliam Foundation, a new London-based group aimed at fighting extremist forms of Islam. He has printed out an online leaflet that he said Hizb had recently removed from its Web site following wide distribution. Entitled "The Muslim Ummah will never submit to the Jews," the leaflet is replete with anti-Semitic stereotypes such as "The Jews are cowards, they are a people of money and not a people of fighting."

Formerly, anti-Semitic language was used heavily "because it has a lot of currency in Islamist crowds," Ali says. But after then-Prime Minister Tony Blair declared he wanted to ban Hizb, the group underwent a public re-imaging. "They didn't change any of their ideas, but they realized the need to re-brand them-selves for public media consumption. They started to tailor their language to say the 'Zionist state,' not 'the Jewish state.' "

But is anti-Zionism always anti-Semitism? NYU his-torian Judt, a British Jew and an outspoken critic of Israel, recently argued that by "shouting anti-Semitism every time someone attacks Israel or defends the Palestinians, we are breeding cynics" and risk losing the attention of those who need to recognize genuine genocidal evil.

"When people chide me and others for criticizing Israel too forcefully, lest we rouse the ghosts of prejudice,

Confronting the Past in Poland

Accounts of pogroms rouse anti-Semitic ghosts.

Anti-Semitism in Poland today is almost entirely about history. Unlike France and England, where Israel's treatment of the Palestinians is often the source of anti-Jewish feeling, the most recent debates in Poland have centered on Poles' responsibility for the deadly fate of their Jewish neighbors during and after the Holocaust.

In Poland today, "The problem of the Jews is the problem of the past," says Anna Bikont, a Polish journalist with the leading daily newspaper *Gazeta Wyborcza*, who has written about Polish reactions to the revelations that Poles in the town of Jedwabne killed Jewish neighbors during the war.

The most prominent Jewish issue in the Polish media since the fall of communism in 1989 has been the infamous massacre. On July 10, 1941, about 400 people were forced into a barn on the town's outskirts and burned alive by their Polish neighbors. During the communist era, the incident was blamed on the Nazis; even the monument at the site made no mention of Poles' part in the massacre.

But in 2001, the publication of the book *Neighbors*, by Jan T. Gross, a Polish Jewish historian now at Princeton University, revealed documentary evidence that residents of the town were primarily to blame for the deaths of up to 1,600 of their Jewish neighbors.[1] When news reports made clear that Poles had carried out the deadly pogrom, with only a little encouragement from the Nazis, the "bombshell" shocked the Polish public, according to Hanna Kwiatkowska, who has analyzed anti-Semitism in the right-wing Polish press for her doctoral thesis at University College, London.

The ensuing discussion encouraged the press, which denied that Poles ever participated in the crime, to launch a full-blown anti-Semitic campaign. Seven years later Jedwabne continues to serve as an anti-Semitic tool and litmus test of "real Poles," according to Kwiatkowska.[2]

The newspaper *Nasz Dziennik*, which is part of a conservative Catholic media empire in Poland, charged that Jews were using "lies" about the massacre to blackmail Poland into paying them "billions of dollars" in restitution. The theme of "Jewish profiteers" has persisted several years later in the paper's coverage.[3] While such views were confined mainly to the right-wing press, skepticism about Poles' guilt in the event was surprisingly widespread in Poland. In 2002, 35 percent of respondents said the Germans had murdered the Jews in Jedwabne, while 38 percent believed the townspeople had been forced by the Germans to launch the pogrom.[4]

"We have an old and strong tradition of anti-Semitism," which Poles use to define their national identity, says Bikont. "To be very Polish you have to be different from the Jew." She cites typical stereotypes: "The Jews are so intelligent, they like to manipulate other people; the Polish people are honest and supported one another. The Jews didn't fight in the diaspora; the Poles were always very brave."

But Bikont says views about responsibility for the past seem to be changing among young people. In a recent poll, *Gazeta Wyborcza* asked if Poles should examine their conscience in connection with actions against Jews in the past. Only 14 percent of respondents old enough to have been alive in World War II answered yes, but 37 percent of 18- to 24-year-olds answered in the affirmative, Bikont reports. (The audience for the most anti-Semitic newspapers and radio programs is composed largely of elderly pensioners, who have been forced into reduced circumstances since the fall of communism.)

Shortly after the revelations about Jedwabne, residents in their forties, most with family links to the original murderers, clung angrily to the town's innocence and blamed the new account on Jewish journalists or Jews seeking money or political power, Bikont reported.

When Bikont questioned residents about Jews who had lived on their street, a typical response was, "Now, don't you try to threaten us. We have all the papers proving our ownership of this house."[5] (Gross suggests that Poles' attacks on Jews during and after the war were partly motivated by Poles' coveting and subsequent confiscation of Jewish property.)

The family of a resident who revealed more details to the press about the residents' part in the massacre was forced to move away after they were ostracized, called "Jewish lapdogs" and received death threats, according to Bikont. Some elderly residents who concurred in Gross's account were told by the local priest they would not be buried in the Catholic cemetery, she adds.[6]

Gross's latest historic revelation describes how a few Jewish survivors of the Holocaust, destitute and emaciated, returned to their Polish hometowns after the war, only to be attacked and sometimes murdered by residents, who often had occupied former Jewish homes.[7] In the most horrifying instance, an estimated 42 people, including a mother with her baby and a pregnant woman, were shot or stoned to death by residents of Kielce in 1946. Until the release of Gross' account in January, many people in Poland believed the Kielce massacre had been provoked by the communists.

At a recent meeting in Kielce to discuss Gross's book, Bikont said only a few people spoke in virulently anti-Semitic tones. "Many people talked about feelings of guilt about things in Kielce" — a contrast from her interviews in Jedwabne several years ago, where she met mainly denial.

"I think Jedwabne opened up something in Poland," she says. "It's really changed."

Poland's chief rabbi, Michael Schudrich, has a different take on Kielce. "People forget that in the postwar period the Nazis had so succeeded in destroying morality in society that one of the normal options to resolve a conflict was killing the other person."

In a recent U.S. State Department report, Poland is criticized for desecrations last year at one of the country's largest Jewish cemeteries. Vandals in Czestochowa spray-painted about 100 gravestones with swastikas, "SS" and "Jews out."[8]

The report doesn't say, Schudrich notes, that "the mayor of the town was out there with me and teens scrubbing off the swastikas" shortly afterwards. "Yeah, bad things happen," but the question is, "How does the rest of society react?" Harking back to the Holocaust, he observes, "Genocide happens when the good are silent."

Neglect, rather than vandalism, is the main threat to Jewish cemeteries in communities where no Jews remain, says Bikont. Some have been used to dump garbage, while others have been dug up for building sites. In a few towns, Polish Jews are trying to restore crumbling cemeteries. Bikont also points out that it's no longer dangerous to be a Jew in Poland.

At the same time, however, Kwiatkowska finds it "a worrying sign" that Poland's second-most-popular daily newspaper, *Rzeczpospolita*, gave a platform to right-wing voices in response to Gross's recent revelations about Kielce. It could be a nod towards the current, conservative government, which partially owns the paper.[9]

But Schudrich has a more optimistic outlook. In May 2006, he was attacked in the most serious anti-Semitic incident in Poland in years. Schudrich, who wears a kepah (Jewish skullcap), was walking on the street after Sabbath prayers when a man, later identified with right-wing causes,

Then-Polish President Aleksander Kwasniewski lays a wreath at a new monument to mark the place where Poles massacred Jews from the town of Jedwabne, Poland, in 1941. Kwasniewski addressed relatives of the victims and apologized in the name of Poland.

yelled "Poland for Poles," a well-known anti-Semitic slogan from before the war, historically followed by "Jews to Palestine!"

When Schudrich confronted the man and asked why he had yelled that, the rabbi was punched and pepper-sprayed. After the incident, Schudrich received a call from the prime minister and an invitation to the presidential palace, where government officials condemned the incident before the Polish media. His attacker served two months in jail.

"It did happen," but "much more important was the response — universal condemnation," Schudrich said in an interview last year.[10]

Asked about the incident recently, he added, "And no such attack has happened again. If anti-Semitism is rampant, it should be happening every other day."

[1] Jan T. Gross, *Neighbors: The Destruction of the Jewish Community in Jedwabne, Poland* (2002). In 2002, the Institute of National Memory (IPN) in Poland disputed Gross's figure of 1,600 deaths (the pre-war Jewish population in Jedwabne) after an investigation, suggesting it was only in the hundreds, but concluded the real figure would never be known. See "'Fear'": An Exchange," *The New York Times*, Aug. 20, 2006. For an estimate that half of adult men, plus some women and children, witnessed or participated in the massacre and an estimate that some 400 were killed in the barn, see, Peter S. Green, "Polish Town Still Tries to Forget its Dark Past," *The New York Times*, Feb. 8, 2003.

[2] Hanna Kwiatkowska, "Conflict of Images. Conflict of Memories. Jewish Themes in the Polish Right-Wing Nationalistic Press in the Light of Articles from Nasz Dziennik 1998-2007," unpublished doctoral thesis.

[3] *Ibid.*

[4] *Ibid.*

[5] Anna Bikont, "Seen from Jedwabne," www1.yadvashem.org/download/about_holocaust/studies/bikont.pdf.

[6] *Ibid.*

[7] Jan T. Gross, *Fear: Anti-Semitism in Poland after Auschwitz* (2007).

[8] "Contemporary Global Anti-Semitism: A Report Provided to the United States Congress," U.S. State Department, March 2008, p. 17, www.state.gov/g/drl/rls/102406.htm.

[9] Hanna Kwiatkowska, "Book Reviews: Jan T. Gross, *Fear*," East European Jewish Affairs, April 1, 2007, pp. 119-121, www.informaworld.com.

[10] "Insight: Interview with Michael Schudrich, chief rabbi of Poland," *San Francisco Chronicle* podcast, May 4, 2007, www.sfgate.com/cgi-bin/blogs/sfgate/detail?blogid=5&entry_id=16203.

Young Poles Turn to Judaism

"People treat it like something exotic."

If you walked into the only active synagogue in Warsaw during morning prayers, many of those praying would probably have been brought up as Catholics. Most would have discovered only as adults that they had Jewish family roots.

In a country where over 90 percent of its more than 3 million Jews perished under the Nazis, where Jewish concentration camp survivors who returned to their villages were murdered by their Polish neighbors and where communist oppression reigned for decades, it was for many years dangerous to reveal one's Jewish heritage.[1]

But since 1989, as the collapse of communism in Poland made it safe for families to reveal their Jewish ties to their children and as interest in their lost culture has grown, a growing number of young Poles have been drawn to Judaism, even some with no known Jewish heritage.

"It's a fun thing . . . oriental. People treat it like something exotic with a secret language no one understands," says Krzystof Izdebski, 27, a lawyer and secretary of Zoom, a Warsaw cultural group aimed at bringing young Jewish Poles together. "Also, there are people who have empathy for the Jews; they are taught about the *Shoah* [Holocaust] in school and want to pay tribute. The majority of Zoom's 126 members, ages 16-35, only discovered their Jewish heritage in their teens, or even later, according to Izdebski.

Of an estimated 5,000-10,000 Jews who participate in Jewish religious life in Poland today, more than 60 percent did not discover they were Jewish until adulthood, estimates Michael Bilewicz, a social psychologist at Warsaw University who studies Polish Jewish identity. (Some estimates place the number of Jews in Poland much higher, around 20,000, as a result of the growing number discovering they have Jewish roots.[2])

The discovery of Jewish roots is often problematic, especially if it breaches a deeply held family secret. Anna Bikont, a 54-year-old Warsaw journalist, was 35 when she discovered that her mother was Jewish but had survived the war on "the Aryan side" in Poland, married to a Christian.

When Bikont decided to raise her children as Jews and send them to a Jewish school, her mother at first refused to have any contact with her. "She was anxious and furious," Bikont recalls. "All her life she did all she could [to make sure] that my sister and I wouldn't be Jews." Today, Bikont's 19-year-old daughter Ola identifies strongly with Judaism, is a member of Zoom and has applied for Israeli citizenship.

The variety of reasons for this enduring secrecy reflects the historical difficulty of being Jewish in Poland. During the war, many Jewish children were given to Christian families by parents who would not survive the Holocaust. Some Jewish families passed as Christians with false identity papers and after the war were still afraid to reveal their true identity. Those Jewish families who stayed after the war or returned as communists from the Soviet Union were more likely to be secular or atheistic in a Catholic country known for its hostility toward Jews. And some children of Jewish communists rebelled against their parents' generation by participating in the Catholic opposition that gave rise to the Solidarity anti-communist movement. (Adam Michnik, editor of Warsaw's *Gazeta Wyborcza*, a leading Polish newspaper, is the most famous Solidarity leader with Jewish roots.)

In an attempt to curry favor with the Soviet Union, the communist government in Poland responded to the 1967 Six-Day Israeli war with an anti-Semitic campaign in 1967-68, accusing Jews of loyalty to the Zionist state, blaming Jews for student protests against the regime, firing Jewish workers and confiscating property. Of Poland's 30,000 remaining Jews, about 20,000 emigrated in 1968-69.[3]

What's driving young Poles to reconnect with Jewish culture or religion — especially if their link is as tenuous as a grandparent they never knew? "The need to belong to a defined and exotic ethnic group is very common," Bilewicz found in an ongoing study of young Polish Jews.[4] Poland's homogeneous population is 90 percent ethnically Polish, white and Christian, he points out, so "being Jewish gives a sense of being distinctive."

I tell them that they have the problem exactly the wrong way around. It is just such a taboo that may itself stimulate anti-Semitism," Judt recently asserted.[42]

But British MP Mann argues that anti-Zionism in the press and public discussion stirs up deeper hatred than criticism of other countries because it is fundamentally racist, not just making a political point.

"Why are young Jewish kids abused in the streets when there's conflict in Lebanon?" he asks. "Young Chinese kids are not abused when there's conflict in Tibet. People feel free

The desire to get in touch with a family tradition broken during the Holocaust is also important, he says. Ironically, it's often religious Catholics who feel most comfortable making the switch to religious Judaism, he notes, because they already believe in God. Indeed, Zoom has some members who consider themselves Jews but also attend Catholic church, according to Izdebski.

Chief Rabbi of Poland Michael Schudrich says he knows of a handful of Poles with no Jewish family heritage who have converted to Judaism. "They simply believe Judaism helps them find God and brings morality into their lives."

The movement may also reflect a growing curiosity among Poles generally about a people that virtually disappeared. Many Poles have never laid eyes on a Jew, notes Bikont. "In Poland, many young people are now interested in Jewish history," she says. "It's very new, and it's very strong. We have five or six new plays about Jews written by young people this year." A Jewish cultural festival attracts thousands to Krakow every year.

The recent Jewish revival dates back to the early 1990s, when young Poles who had just discovered their Jewish family connections found the elderly regulars at Polish synagogues less than welcoming toward people who knew nothing about the faith, according to Bilewicz.

Schudrich, then a dynamic young American rabbi, started to offer "a new way of being Jewish," Bilewicz says — organizing Shabbat dinners, translating prayers into Polish and introducing guitar music to services.

Today, Rabbi Schudrich estimates that thousands of Jews have discovered they have Jewish roots since the fall of

Members of Czulent, a group for young Polish Jews in Krakow, pose in front of graffiti referring to "Jude Gang" (literally "Jewish Gang"), the name taken by fans of Krakow's soccer team. The team's fan club protected Jews during the Nazi era and represents a positive link with Jews in Poland. "We decided to take the photo here to show we are not afraid to tell people we are Jewish," says Czulent's Anna Makowka.

communism. "The question is, what are they going to do about it? That's what we do: Try to create programming and an environment that will empower them to look into their Jewish heritage."

In this vein, cultural associations like Zoom in Warsaw and Czulent* in Krakow — organized by young Poles who returned from Israel wanting to know more about their newfound Judaism — organize Jewish holiday parties, seminars on Judaism and multicultural dialogues. These gatherings offer a way for young Poles to connect to Judaism as a culture — not necessarily by conversion. They also offer companionship for new entrants to a tiny minority group that has lost most of its communal memory.

Young people who suddenly discover their Jewish background often have to overcome a feeling of alienation from Poles around them, Czulent's Web site acknowledges. "Sometimes it's better to have a beer together than to go to lectures," says Izdebski. "Or go for Shabbat dinner to someone's home, so you don't feel so alone in Polish society."

---

* Czulent is the name of a traditional Sabbath dish of slow-cooking meat and beans, http://czulent.org.

[1] See Tony Judt, *Postwar* (2007), p. 804. According to Judt, 97.5 percent of Poland's Jews were exterminated.

[2] See Stephen Roth Institute for the Study of Antisemitism and Racism, "Poland 2006," p. 1, and "Poland" 1997, p. 1, at www.tau.ac.il/Anti-Semitism/asw2006/poland.htm. The 2006 report estimates 5,000-10,000 Jews in Poland.

[3] Judt, *op. cit.*, pp. 434-435.

[4] Cohen Center for Modern Jewish Studies, Brandeis University, "Taglit-Birthright Israel International," http://cmjs.org/Project.cfm?idProject=18.

---

to criticize China or Israel, but the consequences are very different. That is because of the language used. . . . There is a difference: It's stoked by anti-Semitic discourse, and the language used in attacking Israel is a big part of that," he says. "It creates this legitimacy for racist abuse."

Recently, Small at Yale's Initiative for the Interdisciplinary Study of Antisemitism and a colleague decided to test whether there is a statistical correlation between Israel-bashing and anti-Semitic attitudes in a survey of 500 people in 10 European countries.[43] The results,

CHRONOLOGY

Middle Ages *Ritual-murder rumors incite pogroms; Jew are persecuted during Spanish Inquisition.*

1144 Blood-libel charge emerges in England.

1218 English Church requires Jews to wear special badges to identify them as non-Christians.

1247 Pope declares ritual-murder allegations fraudulent.

1290 Jews expelled from England.

1492-1498 Jews expelled from Spain, then Portugal and France.

18th Century *Some European Jews are emancipated during Enlightenment.*

1791 France gives Jews equal rights.

19th Century *Ottoman Empire declares religious tolerance; Russian pogroms scatter Jews to Western Europe; "Dreyfus affair" spurs Zionism.*

1839 Ottoman sultan decrees equality for Jews, Christians.

1879 German journalist Wilhelm Marr coins term "anti-Semitic."

1880 First wave of Russian Jews arrives in England.

1894-99 Capt. Alfred Dreyfus, a French Jew, is falsely accused of treason. Affair radicalizes Austrian Jewish journalist Theodor Herzl, who later leads Zionist movement.

Early 20th Century *Britain restricts Jewish immigration, declares support for Jewish homeland.*

1903 "Protocols of the Learned Elders of Zion" — an anti-Semitic literary hoax — appears in Russia.

1906 Britain's Aliens Act of 1905 limits Jewish refugees.

1917 Balfour Declaration states British support for Jewish homeland in Palestine.

1930s *Nazis begin persecuting Jews, followed by systematic eradication.*

1933 Nazis begin restricting Jews' rights; Dachau concentration camp opens.

Nov. 9-10, 1938 A night of mob attacks on German Jews, known as *Kristallnacht* ("Night of Broken Glass") destroys Jewish businesses and synagogues. Some 30,000 Jews are sent to concentration camps, launching the Nazi plan to eradicate Europe's Jews.

1940s *Six million Jews die in Nazi concentration camps; Vichy French hand over Jews to Nazis; Allied propaganda and press barely mention Jews.*

July 1940 Vichy regime initiates anti-Jewish laws.

July 10, 1941 Poles kill Jewish neighbors in Jedwabne.

1942 Mass gassings begin at Auschwitz-Birkenau camp; Polish Jews are deported to concentration camps; Vichy government deports 13,000 French Jews to Auschwitz.

Postwar 1940s *Anti-Semitism continues.*

1945 Soviet troops liberate Auschwitz-Birkenau; Nuremberg war trials begin.

1946 Jews returning to Poland are murdered by former neighbors.

1960s-1980s *Holocaust enters public consciousness; fall of communism opens door for Eastern European Jews to reveal family roots.*

1962 Israel kidnaps former Nazi official Adolf Eichmann in Argentina, prosecutes and later hangs him for his role in killing Jews.

1968-1969 Polish communist regime invokes anti-Semitism to suppress student protests.

January 1979 "Holocaust" TV series raises awareness of war-time atrocities among millions of West Germans.

1985 Documentary "Shoah" raises awareness in France.

1989 Communist regimes fall in Eastern Europe.

1990s-2000s *Anti-Jewish crimes surge in Europe as Arab-Israeli tensions escalate; anti-Israel resolutions are debated in international, national arenas.*

1991 U.N. General Assembly overturns 1975 resolution declaring Zionism "racism."

1995 President Jacques Chirac acknowledges French responsibility in sending Jews to concentration camps.

2000 Second Palestinian uprising spurs anti-Semitic crimes; European Union begins tracking anti-Jewish incidents.

2004 Organization for Security and Co-operation in Europe declares that events in the Middle East do not justify anti-Semitism.

Feb. 13, 2006 Kidnapped French Jew Ilan Halimi dies after being found tortured in Paris suburb; national outrage ensues.

Sept. 7, 2006 British report finds anti-Semitism increasing.

Feb. 14, 2008 Report shows anti-Semitic incidents in Britain dropped slightly in 2007.

Feb. 22, 2008 French Jew Mathieu Roumi is kidnapped and tortured in Paris.

May 2008 British professors' union revives debate over boycotting Israel.

published in the *Journal of Conflict Resolution*, showed an "off-the-charts" correlation with beliefs that Israel purposely kills children or that Israel is an apartheid state, he says. "In many countries, people who hold such beliefs are 13 times more likely to be anti-Semitic than the average population," reports Small.

Is anti-Semitism as severe as racial discrimination against other minorities in Europe?

"Would you feel safe, accepted [and] welcome today as a 'Paki' in parts of England? A black in Switzerland? Or would you not feel safer more integrated, more accepted as a Jew?" historian Judt recently asked.[44]

Although attacks like the recent kidnappings of two young French Jews are disturbing, young Arabs and Africans frequently face harassment in France — often several times a day — including interference from police, according to Weil of CNRS. Most people concede that European Jews — largely assimilated, educated and middle class — do not face the kinds of job, housing or personal discrimination faced by darker-skinned immigrants.

Those most concerned about the state of anti-Semitism today concede it does not approach the social discrimination faced by other minorities. But some experts contend that anti-Semitism has always been different in nature from other kinds of racial discrimination. Since the 19th

century, anti-Semitism has not just been about looking down on Jews as an inferior race, notes Ruth Wisse, a professor of Yiddish and comparative literature at Harvard University and author of the 2007 book *Jews and Power*. It's also been the polar opposite: attributing great power to Jews as a global conspiracy controlling government, banks and the media. As such, Jews often served as a convenient scapegoat for a society's social ills, she says.

Following this logic, the Nazis called for killing all Jews as a way of cleansing society of all evil, something Iran's Ahmadinejad has repeatedly called for, notes historian Küntzel. By contrast, no head of state today calls for the killing of all blacks as a way to solve society's ills, he notes. "Therefore anti-Semitism is the most dangerous" of these phenomena and the threats of Ahmadinejad are to be taken seriously, he says.

Yet, while assaults on individual Jews have clearly risen in recent years in Britain, the Institute for Jewish Policy Research's Lerman says the attacks against other groups, especially Muslims, are far worse. They are rarely captured in statistics, however, because other ethnic communities are less organized in collecting the data, according to Lerman.

In London, a Jewish person is three times as likely to be the subject of racial attack as a non-Jewish white person, but Arabs, blacks and Asians are 9 to 12 times more

Some Poles Hid Jews From the Nazis

More than 70 people are alive today thanks to Jerzy Kozminski.

Editor's note: During a recent trip to Poland, CQ Global Researcher contributing writer Sarah Glazer interviewed 83-year-old Jerzy Kozminski, whose family in Warsaw had helped hide several members of her own family during the Nazi occupation.

In the winter of 1942, a gas company meter reader — a member of the underground Council for Aid to Jews — approached a Christian Polish family living in a small house in German-occupied Warsaw and asked if they would be willing to hide three Jews.

The family agreed, even though it was widely known that Poles who hid Jews would be executed by the Nazis — along with their entire families. The Kozminskis had just enough room to house the two men, watchmakers, and one of their wives, recalls 83-year-old Jerzy Kozminski — then a 17-year-old living with his father, stepmother and 2-year-old stepbrother. But the family could not afford to feed three more people.

So when the two watchmakers ran short of watch parts — essential for buying their food on the black market — they asked young Jerzy to seek help from an acquaintance in the Jewish ghetto, Samuel Glazer — a cousin of mine — who had owned a shirt factory in Lodz before the war.

Donning a yellow Jewish armband, which the Nazis required all Jews to wear, Jerzy crept into the Jewish ghetto for the first of numerous trips as a courier. Once, a guard sprayed him with submachine fire as he began scaling the ghetto wall; another time, as he emerged on the "Aryan" side of the wall, he was grabbed by an undercover officer, whom he paid off with a small bribe.

Samuel asked if Jerzy's family would hide his large extended family of seven. Jerzy's father agreed, and the Kozminskis rented a larger house on the outskirts of Warsaw and dug a basement bunker where the family could hide.

The Glazers paid smugglers to get them out of the ghetto on April 19, 1943, the day the Warsaw ghetto uprising began, just as residents were being ordered to gather for the fateful transfer to the Treblinka death camp. Only one family member didn't make it out: Samuel's sister-in-law, Anda Herling, the mother of a 10-year-old daughter, was caught by guards while escaping, and the family never saw her again.

Later, Jerzy led another four members of the Glazer family to a safe hiding place in Warsaw, where he continued to look after them. The Kozminskis also took in other groups of Jews for varying periods of time.

Eleven members of the Glazer family survived the war hidden in the Kozminski house and their Warsaw hiding place until liberation by the Russians. All told, Kozminski is credited with saving more than 20 Jews.[1] He has been honored by the Yad Vashem Institute in Jerusalem as one of the Righteous Among the Nations — non-Jews who risked life or liberty to rescue Jews during the Holocaust.

Today, the retired engineer with a keen, blue-eyed gaze and a smile playing around his lips remembers many of his close calls with a sense of humor. After three residents of the Warsaw apartment where Samuel's elderly father was hiding were arrested on the street, the Glazers feared he was in danger of being discovered by police. It was vital to move the old man to a new hiding place. But his long beard would instantly identify him as an Orthodox Jew. Kozminski remembers with a chuckle that the old man's son Sewek shaved off the beard over his father's vigorous protests. Then, disguised as a peasant with a handlebar mustache in an old-fashioned cap and boots, the old man followed Kozminski to his home through the streets of Warsaw without being discovered.

It was difficult to hide the fact that so many people were living in the house, especially since large amounts of food had to be purchased. On at least one occasion, Kozminski remembers his little brother blurting out cheerfully at the local store, "There is no one living in our basement."

"The neighbors knew someone was there, but they didn't know who," Kozminski believes. If those hidden had been Polish underground partisans, he points out, the neighbors knew that denouncing the family would put them at risk of being killed by the Polish resistance.

Kozminski says he does not like the word "hero" and tends to brush off the idea that he did anything out of the ordinary. Indeed, in his view, "This rescue was a patriotic act" at a time when Poles were suffering under Nazi occupation. "Many people in Poland did things against the Germans."

In his modesty, Kozminski is typical of other Poles who saved Jews, of whom more than 6,000 have received the Righteous award.[2] In their insistence that they did nothing unusual, "I sense a stubborn belief in human decency being not the exception but the rule," suggests Konstanty Gebert, founder of the Polish-Jewish monthly *Midrasz*. "[A]nd were the Righteous to be considered exceptional, this belief would fail."[3]

Simple humanity may be another explanation. Kozminski's father had many Jewish friends while a student in Switzerland, the son recalls, and had once been in love with a Jewish girl — or so his wife used to tease him.

Moreover, Kozminski's stepmother, "was a woman who couldn't say 'No'" if someone came to her door seeking help, recalls Gita Baigelman, 86, of New York City, one of Samuel's surviving sisters, who met the Kozminski family after the war.[4]

When asked about the Poles who murdered their Jewish neighbors in notorious pogroms during and after the war, Kozminski displayed his only flare of anger during a recent interview, declaring, "The pope said that a Christian, if an anti-Semite, is not a Christian."

After joining the Polish resistance, Kozminski was caught by the Nazis in October 1943 while on a gun-buying run. When he failed to return home, the Glazers feared their hiding place would be revealed, Baigelman recalls. What they didn't know was that Jerzy had been questioned by the Gestapo but had kept their secret.

After his interrogation, Kozminski was sent to Auschwitz and then to the Mauthausen concentration camp. Upon the camp's liberation by the Americans in May 1945, he emerged emaciated, unable to eat, his health broken by starvation. By happy coincidence, he located Samuel, who was once again running a clothing factory in Lodz. The Glazers sent him to a doctor, who gradually restored his health.

One theme that is often overlooked in rescue accounts is the extent to which Jewish families aided those who hid them. As Kozminski remembers it, the Glazers "promised to help me recover; they delivered on their word."[5]

In 1964, Samuel and his family, who had moved to Israel, invited Jerzy's stepmother Theresa to stay with them. Then a widow, she took them up on their invitation, married a Jewish man, converted to Judaism and lived out the rest of her life in the Jewish homeland. She was made an honorary citizen of Tel Aviv and buried in a cemetery for distinguished citizens.

In 1996, when the Anti-Defamation League honored Kozminski for the rescue, it estimated that more than 70 people around the world — the descendants of those he saved — were alive because of his efforts.[6]

Halinka Herling, the 10-year-old whose mother did not survive the escape from the ghetto, is now a grandmother living in Israel.

Jerzy Kozminski, now 83, helped hide several members of the author's family in Warsaw during the Nazi occupation.

Kozminski proudly displays a photograph of Halinka surrounded by her smiling grandchildren, which he received after he was reunited with her two years ago. This, he declares, is his reward. "God gave me the present of the grandchildren of Halinka on my 81st birthday," he says, adding he could not imagine a better gift.

— Sarah Glazer

[1] Jerzy Kozminski, "The Memories of a Righteous Man" (unpublished memoir, undated). Those rescued include 11 members of the extended Glazer family, the three-member Seifman family and eight Jews housed for three weeks.

[2] A total of 6,066 people from Poland were honored with the award, more than any other nation. However, Poland also had the largest number of Jews of any country in Europe before the Holocaust, www1.yadvashem.org/righteous_new/statistics.html.

[3] "Recalling Forgotten History: For Poles Who Rescued Jews During the Holocaust," album prepared to accompany a ceremony honoring the Righteous at the Polish National Opera in cooperation with the Museum of History of Polish Jews, Oct. 10, 2007, published by the Chancellery of the President of the Republic of Poland.

[4] Gita Baigelman was living in the Lodz ghetto, from where she was transferred to Ravensbrück concentration camp and a labor camp in Germany. She met the Kozminskis after the war.

[5] Kozminski, *op. cit.*

[6] Anti-Defamation League, press release, "ADL Honors Christian Rescuers of Jews During the Holocaust Who Had the Courage to Care," Nov. 22, 1996, www.adl.org/PresRele/ChJew_31/2857_31.asp.

likely to be attacked, according to police authorities cited by Lerman. A recent speech by the Archbishop of Canterbury proposing adoption of sharia law for Muslims in England for personal matters like marriage was followed by a storm of hostile protest, including some 500 incidents against Muslims in Britain ranging from verbal abuse to attacks on mosques, according to Lerman.

Lerman sees these attacks, like anti-Semitic crimes, as part of "the rise of racism generally. More has to be done to combat racism."

But some scholars of anti-Semitism think there's something unique that distinguishes it from other forms of racism. Hitler, of course, spoke of the inferior racial nature of Jews and their need to be eliminated in his quest for Aryan racial purity. "People love to talk about that form of anti-Semitism — that was the only form that was defeated," says Wisse.

It's more important, she suggests, to defend against the tendency to use Jews as a scapegoat for everything that's wrong with capitalism and modernity.

"It's an anti-modernist ideology that says, 'You think emancipation, democracy, is such a terrific force, but it's only a vehicle for the Jews to take us over.'" In Wisse's view, "The horror is that this organization of politics against the Jews is much more important to the Arabs than it ever was to Europe" because anti-Semitism has become the "glue" that ties disparate Muslim countries together.

Meanwhile, discrimination against Muslims — dubbed "Islamophobia" — has been garnering growing government and press attention. A 2006 report by the EU's European Monitoring Centre on Racism and Xenophobia said that while discrimination and incidents against European Muslims remain underdocumented and underreported, Muslims in the European Union "frequently suffer different forms of discrimination which reduce their employment opportunities and affect their educational achievement."[45]

Indeed, several columnists have recently described Muslims as "the new Jews" of Britain in connection with events seen as discriminatory against Muslims. After several Muslims were arrested in connection with an alleged terrorist plot, Mohammad Naseem, chairman of the Birmingham Central Mosque, told the press that Britain was becoming a "police state" and compared the police raids to the persecution of Jews in Germany.[46]

But when the EU's racism-monitoring arm investigated incidents of Islamophobia following 9/11, it found very few incidents of physical assaults on Muslims in most countries. (Only in the U.K. was a significant rise in attacks on Muslims reported.)[47] Historian David Cesarani of Royal Holloway, University of London, says this is a significant contrast from the spikes in attacks on Jews following events like the invasion of Afghanistan and Israeli incursions into the West Bank and Gaza Strip.

In addition, while Muslim immigrants may experience poverty and social discrimination, as Jewish immigrants once did, Muslims today are often connected to powerful foreign governments, while diaspora Jews historically had no homeland. When Muslims in Denmark were offended in September 2005 by cartoons depicting the Prophet Mohammed, for example, they could appeal to governments of Muslim countries, triggering an international wave of protests.

In addition, Cesarani notes, Jews historically never constituted a rival military or economic force to Europe, whereas Europeans rightfully feared Muslim power during the Ottoman Empire. Today, European reactions to Muslims are to some degree accurate perceptions of the real menace of Islamic terrorism, according to Cesarani.

"Islamophobia is incommensurable with anti-Semitism because Jews as Jews never espoused the attitudes ascribed to them by anti-Semites" or threatened a state in the name of Judaism, he argues. "Islamophobia may be an inappropriate . . . reaction to a grossly inflated 'threat,' but the danger of terrorism by Islamists is real, and there are several conflicts in the world in which Islamic militants are at war in the name of Islam."[48]

BACKGROUND

'Blood Libel' Slander

The accusation that Jews killed Christians, usually children, to obtain their blood for religious rituals originated in England in 1144, when Jews were accused of a ritual murder during the Passover period. This fabricated slander would become one of the most common incitements to anti-Jewish riots and killings throughout Europe during the Middle Ages, despite a papal bull in 1247 that declared such accusations false.[49]

The blood libel accusation lasted well into the 20th century, providing the ostensible cause for a pogrom as late as 1946 against Jewish survivors returning to their homes in Kielce, Poland. The accusation: The Jews planned to use the blood from the murder of a small boy to bake matzo for Passover.

In England and other European countries these seemingly spontaneous riots occurred as Jews were being denied equal rights with Christians. Restrictions imposed on Jews owning land and their exclusion from craft guilds made them dependent upon money lending and other forms of commerce, providing a historical basis for the stereotype of the Jew as greedy money-lender, notably the character of Shylock in Shakespeare's "Merchant of Venice."[50]

In 1218 England became the first European country to implement a church decree that Jews wear a badge to distinguish them from Christians, a directive the Nazis revived when they required all Jews to wear a yellow Jewish star.[51]

In 1290, King Edward expelled all Jews from England, ending their official presence in Britain for the next 400 years — the first large-scale deportation of Jews from a country in Europe. In 1656, British political leader Oliver Cromwell achieved limited recognition for Jews in England, many of whom were descended from Spanish and Portuguese Jews, known as "Conversos," who had fled the Inquisition and been converted to Christianity to prevent discovery.

In a recent paper delivered at Yale, Lappin of Kings College argues that Britain mistakenly perceives itself as a society tolerant of Jews. While the year 1492 is infamous in history for Spain's expulsion of the Jews, notes Lappin, Britain's own expulsion is generally not mentioned in British school curriculum.

History, he says, reveals a "deeply rooted view of Jews as fundamentally alien to British life." For decades, if not centuries, Jews' social acceptability has been "conditional upon suppression of one's Jewish associations and cultural properties," Lappin argues.[52]

With each new influx of Jews, the British government imposed further legal restrictions, such as banning land ownership or citizenship — notably in 1753 and again in 1768 after pogroms in Poland and the Ukraine brought waves of impoverished East European Jews to London.

In the 19th century, while British reformers crusaded for abolition of the slave trade, giving women the vote and establishing workers' rights, no political movement

AFP/Getty Images/Ralf Succo

Exactly 68 years after a Nazi mob destroyed Munich's main synagogue, members of the city's Jewish community and Israeli Rabbi Mei Lau, left, deliver Torahs to a new Munich synagogue in 2006. Germany's growing Jewish community opened the synagogue amid a resurgent debate about rising anti-Semitism in Germany.

supported Jewish emancipation, according to Lappin. Rather, Anglo-Jewish leaders pursued a strategy of "quiet diplomatic engagement."[53]

For example, between 1847 and 1852, banker Lionel Rothschild was prevented three times from taking the House of Commons seat to which he was elected. Rothschild was only allowed to enter the House 11 years after his first election and only after the Commons made an exception — suspending the required Christian oath for members of Parliament. Then, from 1880 to 1905 a large wave of Jewish immigrants escaping pogroms in Russia stimulated a strong anti-immigrant sentiment. The Aliens Act of 1905 was the first of several 20th-century measures aimed at limiting entry into the country.

Restricting Jewish Refugees

Britain's attitude towards Jewish refugees during the Nazi regime was more hostile than sympathetic, Lappin argues, in contrast to the country's reputation as a welcoming refuge. After the Nazis took power in Germany in 1933, British officials, like other Western governments, were flooded with requests from German Jews seeking to escape the regime. However, throughout the pre-war period, Britain maintained its system of rigorous controls on immigration, keeping Jewish immigration to a minimum except for those who could fill jobs in which labor was needed — notably female servants.

Nazis Exported Anti-Semitism to the Middle East

Hitler repackaged anti-Semitism as anti-Zionism.

On Nov. 2, 1917, Britain's foreign minister, Lord Balfour, announced Britain's support for the establishment in Palestine of a national home for the Jewish people.

The Balfour Declaration is often cited as the start of the Jewish-Arab conflict — and some would say it was the original source of anti-Israel sentiment in Europe.[1] But as political scientist Matthias Küntzel points out in his recent book, *Jihad and Jew-Hatred*, it wasn't clear that it would turn out that way. Some Arab leaders initially supported Zionist settlements, hoping Jewish immigration would bring economic development.

Before 1937, when the German government first decided it needed to turn the Arabs against the Jews, Jews held prominent positions in business and government in Egypt.[2] Indeed, in 1839 the sultan of the Ottoman Empire had decreed equality for Jews and Christians, and in 1856 such equality was established in law, motivated partly by the Ottoman elite's desire to draw closer to European civilization and to modernize.[3]

But some Arab leaders violently opposed Jewish immigration and the prospect of a Jewish homeland. In the decade leading up to 1936, the mufti of Jerusalem, Amin al-Husseini, the highest religious authority in Palestine, incited Palestinian Arabs to violence against Jews with the aim of ending Jewish immigration and destroying the prospect of a Jewish majority ruling the area. This movement culminated in the 1936-39 Arab revolt, which included anti-Semitic demonstrations, riots, bombings and raids on Jewish villages.[4]

As perhaps the leading inciter of hatred against Jews in the Arab world, the mufti became the region's most committed supporter of Nazism and "a local henchman of the Nazis," according to Küntzel, a research associate at the Vidal Sassoon International Center for the Study of Antisemitism at Hebrew University, Jerusalem.[5]

By 1938, amid mounting tension in Europe, the continuing flight of Jews from Germany to Palestine was provoking renewed Arab violence, including attacks against British fortifications, attacks on Jews and Jewish reprisals. The mufti fled Palestine in 1938 to avoid arrest by the British for his part in the Arab revolt. He spent most of the war in Berlin, recruiting Bosnian Muslims for the SS, the semi-military Nazi organization that oversaw Hitler's extermination of the Jews. From 1939 to 1945, the mufti's Arabic radio broadcasts, which mixed anti-Semitic propaganda with quotes from the *Koran*, made his station the most popular in the Arab world.[6]

The mufti also agreed with the Nazi policy of exterminating the Jews. In 1943, as a propaganda stunt, SS leader Heinrich Himmler wanted to permit 5,000 Jewish children to emigrate to Palestine, in exchange for 20,000 German prisoners. The mufti fought against the plan, and the children were sent to the gas chambers.[7]

The Nazis funded the burgeoning growth of Muslim fundamentalism, helping the radical Muslim Brotherhood distribute Arabic translations of *Mein Kampf*, Hitler's autobiographical political treatise, and the forged *Protocols of the Learned Elders of Zion* and helped fan anti-Zionist flames in the Arab world.[8]

In Germany, a mutual-admiration society appeared to have developed between the mufti and Hitler, who described the mufti inaccurately as having blond hair and blue eyes, to emphasize that he was not a member of an inferior race. Hitler had also expressed his antagonism to Zionism in *Mein Kampf.*

Küntzel argues that the idea of Jews as an all-powerful, dominating world force was essentially a Western idea exported to the Middle East by the Nazis in an effort to turn Muslims against Jews and Zionism. After all, the *Koran* portrays Jews primarily as a defeated force, and for centuries

In 1938, the "Kindertransports" brought about 10,000 Jewish children from Germany and Austria to Britain. These efforts often are cited as proof of British efforts to help the Jews. However, because of British immigration rules — not German restrictions — the children were forced to come without their parents, according to Lappin. As a result, many of these children became orphans at the end of the war.

Jews were treated as second-class citizens in most Arab countries.

But in a recent review of Küntzel's book, Jeffrey Goldberg, a journalist who writes about the region for *The Atlantic*, disagrees, arguing that plenty of anti-Jewish ideas were organic to Muslim thought. And he doesn't buy Küntzel's view that this history explains much Arab hostility towards Israel today. "Jews today have actual power in the Middle East, and Israel is not innocent of excess and cruelty," he writes.[9]

In Europe, Hitler's propaganda machine didn't begin waging a public war on Zionism until 1944, according to Michael Berkowitz, a professor of modern Jewish history at University College, London. In his 2007 book *The Crime of My Very Existence*, Berkowitz argues that Nazi leaders refashioned anti-Semitism as anti-Zionism as part of a broader tactic of painting Jews as criminals. Zionism was painted as the guise for a criminal conspiracy to create a Jewish world government. The Nazis often concocted specific charges against Jews based on technical aspects of tax laws and currency-exchange regulations in addition to charges of petty criminality.[10]

The criminality charges, Berkowitz argues, were chosen because Nazis feared their project of wiping out the Jews for racial reasons would not be universally compelling among German citizens who might be friendly with Mr. Stern the baker or Mrs. Morgen the neighbor. By contrast, the "law and order" motive for assailing an ethnic group was much more persuasive and survives today in stereotypical attitudes toward other ethnic groups, like blacks in the United States or West Indians in Britain, Berkowitz observes.

By 1944, as Nazis feared they were losing the war and would face international outrage at the genocide of the Jews, Zionism "was reconfigured as the apex of Jewish evil and organized criminality to rationalize the decimation of 6 million" Jews, he writes.[11]

Toward the end of the war, when the Nazis had nearly annihilated European Jews, they were searching for new enemies. As a Nazi propagandist put it at the time, once the Jews were all gone, momentum and sympathy for anti-Semitism would be lost: "When asked, young 20-year-old officers say that they have never yet knowingly seen a Jew.

Adolf Hitler meets with Grand Mufti Amin el-Husseini.

Therefore they find no interest . . . in the Jewish problem as it has been presented to them up to now."[12]

Most significantly for today, the Nazis' anti-Zionism represented "a new form of anti-Jewish discourse," Berkowitz writes, one that "contributed to the evil brew of post-1948 Arab anti-Semitism."[13]

[1] See www.yale.edu/lawweb/avalon/mideast/balfour.htm.

[2] The stimulus for Nazi support of Arabs was the British Peel Commission's 1937 partition plan, providing for a Jewish state, which the Germans feared would increase power for world Jewry. See Matthias Küntzel, *Jihad and Jew-Hatred* (2007), p. 29.

[3] *Ibid.*, p. 33.

[4] Martin Gilbert, *Churchill and Jews* (2007), p. 102.

[5] Küntzel, *op. cit.*, p. 101.

[6] *Ibid.*, pp. 34–35.

[7] *Ibid.*, p. 36.

[8] See www.hitler.org/writings/Mein_Kampf/.

[9] Jeffrey Goldberg, "Seeds of Hate," *New York Times Book Review*, Jan. 6, 2008, www.nytimes.com/2008/01/06/books/review/Goldberg-t.html?_r=1&oref=slogin.

[10] Michael Berkowitz, *The Crime of My Very Existence: Nazism and the Myth of Jewish Criminality* (2007), p. xviii.

[11] Berkowitz, *op. cit.*, pp. 112–113, xix.

[12] *Ibid.*, p. 133.

[13] *Ibid.*, p. 113.

By then, approximately 60,000 Jewish refugees remained in Britain, while another 10,000-20,000 had entered and then re-emigrated or were deported. Lappin notes that while the U.S. government's attitude towards aiding Jews shifted in early 1944 due in part to public pressure from American Jewish groups, the British Jewish community consistently refrained from publicly challenging the government on its handling of refugees.

AP Photo

In a dramatic gesture that helped to raise Europe's consciousness about the Holocaust, West Germany's Chancellor Willy Brandt kneels before the Jewish Heroes' monument in Warsaw, Poland, on Dec. 6, 1970.

In addition, the postwar Labor government refused to accept survivors beyond token numbers. Fewer than 5,000 survivors were admitted from 1945-50 under a family-reunification program, even as Britain was admitting 365,000 non-Jewish immigrants to solve its severe labor shortage. Foreign Secretary Ernest Bevin insisted Jews would not be easily assimilated into British life and that admitting large numbers would aggravate anti-Jewish sentiment stemming from Britain's conflict with Zionists in Palestine.[54]

Ironically, many of the most vocal anti-Zionists among today's British leftists insist that a solution to the Jewish refugee problem during the Holocaust should have been found in European countries rather than in Palestine — "obtuse to the fact that their own political precursors" helped to block Jewish immigration to Britain, Lappin observes.[55]

Forged 'Protocols'

The forgery known as the "Protocols of the Learned Elders of Zion" is the most famous document to libel the Jews. The tract purportedly comprises the minutes from 24 sessions of a conference supposedly held by representatives from the 12 tribes of Israel and led by a Grand Rabbi, whose apparent purpose is to lay out a plan for Jewish world conquest.

It first appeared in Russia in 1903 and again in 1905, inspired partly by the first Zionist congress, held in 1897 under the leadership of Theodor Herzl, an Austro-Hungarian Jewish journalist considered the father of Zionism. The protocols initially were used to blame the Jews for the 1905 Russian Revolution, but the tract soon proved adaptable to other situations where Jews were the target of blame.

"The Nazis saw its value immediately," writes Stephen Eric Bronner, a professor of political science at Rutgers University. The document provides a glimpse into what makes anti-Semitism unique by presenting the Jew as a kind of "chameleon," in Bronner's words. "The Jew is not simply a capitalist or a communist revolutionary, but the Jew is now any enemy required by the anti-Semite."[56]

Herzl, Paris correspondent for the liberal Viennese daily newspaper *Neue Frei Presse*, covered the notorious 1894 trial of Capt. Alfred Dreyfus, a French Jew falsely accused of spying for the Germans. During the trial Herzl witnessed anti-Jewish demonstrations in which cries of "Death to the Jews" were common. The Dreyfus Affair, as it is known, became a watershed event for Jews in France, who felt increasingly vulnerable to anti-Semitism — even though Dreyfus was pardoned in 1899 and his innocence officially recognized in 1906.

A secular Jew, Herzl decided that if anti-Semitism was so entrenched in the capitals of the European Enlightenment, Jews had no hope of assimilating in Europe. In 1896, he published *Der Judenstaat* (The Jewish State), in which he argued that Jews needed to create their own state. In 1897 he organized the First Zionist Congress in Basel, Switzerland, which voted to establish a "publicly and legally secured home" for the Jews in Palestine.[57]

Herzl had a utopian vision of the future homeland, imagining in his 1902 novel *Altneuland* (Old-New Land) an Israel much like his home city of Vienna, an intellectual café society of opera-going, German-speaking Jews. He also imagined that Arabs in Palestine would welcome the gifts of science and improved hygiene brought by the Jews.[58] But Arab opposition to the influx of Jews only hardened over time, leading to the development of the Palestine national liberation movement. (*See sidebar, p. 128.*)

Numerous theories have been put forward in trying to explain the success of anti-Semitism during the Nazi period, some reaching back to much earlier historical

Is anti-Zionism a cover-up for anti-Semitism?

YES
Ben Cohen
Associate Director, Department on
Anti-Semitism and Extremism, American
Jewish Committee; editor, www. z-word.com

Written for *CQ Global Researcher*, June 2008

Anti-Zionism has gained greater visibility over the last decade, but it is not an unknown phenomenon historically. In communist Europe, remnants of Jewish communities that perished during the Nazi Holocaust were frequently persecuted in the name of anti-Zionism.

These days, anti-Zionist views are heavily concentrated among the educated elite. If you regard anti-Zionism as one more expression of hatred towards Jews, this is somewhat puzzling, because anti-Semitism — particularly after the Holocaust — is widely perceived to be more beer hall than bistro.

Anti-Semites regard Jews as a malign social force that controls the banks, media and governments. But most of Zionism's mainstream critics say they are only concerned with the Jewish state, not demented fantasies about what Jews are up to.

So can we construct an unbreachable partition between anti-Semitism and anti-Zionism? The answer is "No," and here is why:

- You can't disavow anti-Semitism as a vulgar form of bigotry and then invoke the age-old themes of anti-Semitic conspiracy theory. After assuring us their arguments were not anti-Semitic, U.S. academics John Mearsheimer and Stephen Walt upended decades of political science research by advancing a monocausal theory of U.S. foreign policy in the Middle East: The powerful "Israel Lobby" cajoles the United States into doing things it otherwise wouldn't do.
- Anti-Zionism is founded upon a caricature of Israel as the apartheid-like child of a colonial enterprise. But Zionism's goal is to guarantee, after centuries of horrendous persecution, the freedom and security of Jews, not the subjugation of non-Jews.
- Before Israel's creation in 1948, there was a vibrant debate about the desirability of a Jewish state. But to be an anti-Zionist now is to question the legitimacy of only Israel, out of nearly 200 states worldwide. In a world of disintegrating polities from Iraq to the Democratic Republic of Congo, why should only Israel's existence be subject to debate?

No serious supporter of Israel claims that mere criticism is anti-Semitism. There is, however, a vital distinction between a rational critique of Israeli policies and demonization, which too often is stimulated by or evokes anti-Semitism.

NO
Antony Lerman
Director, Institute for Jewish
Policy Research

Written for *CQ Global Researcher*, June 2008

Anti-Zionism and hostility to Israel can be anti-Semitic if they are expressed using the symbols of the anti-Semitic figure of the Jew or of Jewry as a whole. For example, if Zionism is characterized as a worldwide Jewish conspiracy, or a plan straight out of the forged, anti-Semitic "Protocols of the Learned Elders of Zion," that is anti-Semitism.

But to believe that anti-Zionism and anti-Semitism are one and the same ignores the history of Zionism.

For decades Zionism was supported only by a minority of Jews. The rest were either indifferent or manifestly opposed to the whole idea of the establishment of a Jewish state. Anti-Zionism was therefore a perfectly respectable position to hold, and one that continues to be held today by hundreds of thousands of strictly orthodox Jews and many secular Jews with left-liberal perspectives.

Equating anti-Zionism and anti-Semitism — what has become known as the "new anti-Semitism" — fundamentally subverts the shared understanding of what anti-Semitism is, built up painstakingly through research and study by scholars over many years: It drains the word anti-Semitism of any useful meaning. The advocates of the concept of a new anti-Semitism argue that it is anti-Semitic to either criticize Israeli policies or deny Israel's right to exist, even if one does not hold beliefs historians have traditionally regarded as an anti-Semitic view: hatred of Jews per se, belief in a worldwide Jewish conspiracy, belief that Jews created communism and control capitalism, belief that Jews are racially inferior and so on.

Those who argue that anti-Zionism and anti-Semitism are one claim they don't say criticism of Israeli policies is illegitimate. However, in practice this view virtually proscribes any such thing.

As the Oxford academic Brian Klug has written, anti-Zionism and hostility to Israel — if based on a political cause or moral code that is not anti-Jewish per se — is not anti-Semitic. And arguing that it is harms the all-important struggle to combat anti-Semitism. If people feel unfairly stigmatized as anti-Semitic simply for speaking out about the plight of the Palestinians and the Israeli government's role in causing their suffering, they could become cynical and alienated whenever the problem of anti-Semitism is raised.

roots. Austrian-born American historian Raul Hilberg contends the Germans greeted Nazi anti-Semitism without suspicion as to its ultimate goal because it drew on old forms of anti-Semitism that had been part of Christian writings since the 16th century, when Martin Luther railed against what he saw as recalcitrant Jews because of their resistance to Christianity.[59]

The term "anti-Semitism" was coined in 1879 by German journalist and Jew-hater Wilhelm Marr, who wished to emphasize the "scientific," ethnic character of his opposition to Jews. Like the Nazis that followed him, Marr saw the Jews as a threatening race, incapable of assimilating, that had seized control of the German economy and society. "Semite" was his preferred term for Jews because it sounded scientific, neutral and modern.[60]

The Nazis, drawing on these ideas, believed exterminating Jews would cleanse humanity and save the world from a lethal threat to European morality and culture. Jews were allegedly a satanic race involved in a conspiracy for world domination that would lead to extinction of so-called "Aryan" civilization.

Holocaust Denial

By the end of 1942, Allied governments were aware of concentration camps holding thousands of Jewish prisoners across Europe and that six camps were devoted exclusively to killing. But in 1943, Jews were barely mentioned in Allied propaganda.[61]

Nor were Jews discussed much in the press. In Britain, where the photo of British troops liberating the Nazi camp Bergen-Belsen became a familiar image, the skeleton-like survivors shown on cinema newsreels were not generally identified as Jews.[62]

Not until Israel captured and tried Nazi official Adolf Eichmann in the early 1960s did the horrifying nature of European Jewry's fate enter public consciousness. For example, there is no mention of genocide in the charter under which the major Nazi war criminals were tried at Nuremberg. The term Holocaust did not come into use to describe the extermination of the Jews until several years after the war.

"Today we find this difficult to understand, but the fact is that the Shoah — the attempted genocide of the Jews of Europe — was for many years by no means the fundamental question of postwar intellectual life in

Europe.... Indeed most people — intellectuals and others — ignored it as much as they could," writes historian Judt.[63]

However, it was no mystery that 6 million Jews had been put to death during World War II — a fact widely accepted within a few months of the war, Judt notes in *Postwar: A History of Europe Since 1945.*[64]

In France, less than 3 percent of the 76,000 Jews deported in 1940-44 survived. In the Netherlands, which had 140,000 Jews before the war, fewer than 5,000 returned. In Germany, just over 21,000 of the country's 600,000 Jews remained after the war.[65]

But even the remnants of returning Jews were "not much welcomed," Judt notes. "After years of anti-Semitic propaganda, local populations everywhere were not only disposed to blame 'Jews' in the abstract for their own suffering but were distinctly sorry to see the return of men and women whose jobs, possessions and apartments they had purloined."[66]

In Paris in 1945, hundreds of people protested when a returning Jewish deportee tried to reclaim his occupied apartment, screaming "France for the French!"[67]

Postwar Poland's Anti-Semitism

Poland was perhaps the most dangerous country for returning Jews. Although it had the largest concentration of Jews before the war — more than 3 million — 97.5 percent of them had been exterminated under the Nazis.[68]

In his recent book, *Fear*, Princeton historian Jan T. Gross estimates that after the war, 500-1,600 Jews returning to their hometowns in Poland — sick, traumatized and destitute, often from concentration camps — were killed by Poles upon their arrival.[69] (*See sidebar, p. 118.*)

Why did Poles attack their returning neighbors after the war? During the Nazi persecution and following the Jews' deportation to concentration camps, many Poles benefited materially, moving into Jewish homes and seizing their possessions. (Sometimes the property was pitiful: Gross describes a 1945 letter from a surviving Polish Jew asking a Polish court to make his neighbor return the two eiderdown quilts and pillows he had left in his safekeeping.[70])

As Jews returned, Poles often feared this property would be reclaimed. The Poles' "widespread collusion" in Nazi plunder and murder of the Jews — and suppressed guilt about it — generated virulent anti-Semitism after the war, in Gross' view.[71] "Jews were perceived as a threat to the material status quo, security and peaceful conscience of their Christian fellow-citizens," he writes.[72]

More people witnessed the death of Jews in Poland than in any other country, since it was the site of Auschwitz and other major concentration camps. But in some cases, Poles also participated in the killings.

During the Soviet occupation of Poland, many Poles believed the Jews had betrayed Poland, collaborating with the Russians while the Poles were fighting and being deported to Siberia. In recent years, some Poles cited this version of history, which Gross discredits, as the reason behind the massacres.[73]

In addition, Polish national identity depended to some extent on stories Poles told about their own suffering during the war, and "comparative victimhood" continued to poison relationships with the few remaining Jews after the war.[74]

In fact, the communist period became yet another period in which the memory of the Jews' suffering was suppressed in official accounts, and many Jews were afraid to reveal their origins. In the 1960s, a student uprising against the communist regime was denounced as being perpetrated by Zionist agents. The 1968 campaign also drew on the myth of "Judeo-communism," in which Jews were believed to have cooperated with the Stalinists. By the end of 1968, two-thirds of Poland's Jews had been driven away.[75]

Facing the Holocaust

The trials of Eichmann and of Auschwitz guards in the early 1960s triggered renewed interest in the Holocaust in countries like Germany and the Netherlands, where silence had reigned. The postwar baby boomers were curious about recent history and skeptical of the story told by the "silent generation" of their parents, Judt notes.

During the 1960s and '70s, several events helped to put the Jews' suffering in the German spotlight, according to Judt: The Six-Day Arab-Israeli War of 1967, Chancellor Willy Brandt dropping to his knees at the Warsaw Ghetto memorial and the telecast in Germany in 1979 of an American miniseries, "Holocaust."[76]

Twenty million German viewers saw the series — well over half the population. From then on, writes Judt,

English Football Association Chief Executive Brian Barwick (left) and Noel White (2nd-left), chairman of the association's International Committee, and representatives of fans lay wreaths on March 23, 2007, at the "Hall of Remembrance" at the Yad Vashem Holocaust Memorial in Jerusalem commemorating the 6 million Jews killed by the Nazis during World War II. The association says it is committed to reducing anti-Semitism at soccer matches.

"Germans would be among the best-informed Europeans on the subject of the Shoah and at the forefront of all efforts to maintain public awareness of their country's singular crime." Compared to 1968, when a little over 400 school groups visited Dachau, by the 1970s more than 5,000 a year were visiting the former concentration camp, located 10 miles outside of Munich.[77]

As Judt notes, some major European countries — the Netherlands, Belgium, Norway, Italy — could claim that their orders to deport and execute Jews came from the Germans. The exception was France. Marshal Philippe Petain's Vichy regime, elected in July 1940 by the French parliament, initiated its own anti-Jewish laws in 1940 and 1941. French authorities rounded up the country's Jewish population; most Jewish deportees from France never saw a foreign uniform until they were handed over to Germans for the final shipment to Auschwitz.

Not until 1995 did President Jacques Chirac break a 50-year silence and acknowledge for the first time that the French were responsible for rounding up nearly 13,000 Jews — more than 4,000 of them children — for deportation to Auschwitz in July 1942.[78]

Chirac's acknowledgement followed publication in the late 1960s and mid-'70s of several books by foreign historians demonstrating that the Vichy crimes were French, not German initiatives.

President Charles de Gaulle's 1967 press conference after Israel's victory in the Six-Day War, when he referred to Jews as "a people sure of themselves and domineering" provoked outrage among French Jews and contributed to a new level of awareness of French Jews.[79] Marcel Ophuls's film "The Sorrow and the Pity," about the trials of high-ranking French officials, and a 1985 documentary film, "Shoah," by the French director Claude Lanzmann, also had a dramatic impact.

Anti-Semitism Re-emerges

Immediately after World War II, Austria and West Germany, led by anti-Nazi parties, barred Nazis from political participation and banned overt support of Nazi ideology. On May 8, 1948, the Austrian government banned Nazi activities. West Germany prohibited public expression of Nazi beliefs, banned Nazis from the political process and outlawed swastikas.

In the 1960s, however, extremist, neo-Nazi groups re-emerged in both countries. After German reunification in the 1990s, the groups gained followers among disaffected teenagers from the former East Germany. Such groups tended to merge with skinheads, a far-right youth subculture that developed in Britain during the "rude boy" music scene of the 1960s.[80] Skinheads re-surfaced in the late 1970s with white-power, racist, anti-Semitic overtones. The term "skinhead" described the close-cropped hairdo adopted by its adherents, sometimes accompanied by leather boots and tattoos. Skinheads were known for creating violent confrontations with non-whites, Muslims, Jews and gays — a movement that soon spread to the rest of Europe and North America.

The German National Democratic Party (NPD) is Germany's oldest and most influential right-wing party. In 2006, after receiving 7.3 percent of the vote in the regional parliamentary elections for Mecklenburg-Western Pomerania, the party launched an online news show on its Web site featuring videos, for example, of a memorial march in honor of Hitler's deputy Rudolf Hess.[81] The party holds weekly demonstrations and meetings of extreme-right sympathizers, including neo-Nazis and skinheads, according to the Stephen Roth Institute. To get around the legal bans on Nazi activity, the groups recruit East German youth using music — including music videos and far-right music portals on the Web — sponsoring trips to concerts and offering free beer. At a 2006 NPD event, an Iranian flag was hoisted to demonstrate the party's solidarity with the Iranian government's denial of the Holocaust — a way to express that view without violating German law against Holocaust denial.[82]

Between 2001 and 2005 anti-Semitic incidents increased in eight European countries — Austria, Belgium, Denmark, France, Germany, Netherlands, Sweden and Britain. At the same time, anti-Jewish crimes increased significantly in France between 2001 and 2006, but only slightly in Germany and Sweden.[83]

Although many perceive that today's anti-Semitic hate crimes are perpetrated by disaffected Muslims instead of right-wing skinheads, the European Union's monitoring agency says the shift is "difficult to substantiate," noting that several countries prohibit investigating ethnic or religious backgrounds of criminal suspects.[84]

According to the EU Agency for Fundamental Rights, the most troubling development in European attitudes has been the increase since 2005 in the number of respondents questioning the loyalty of Jewish citizens, as recorded in surveys by the Anti-Defamation League. Last year, the percentage of those believing Jews are "more loyal to Israel than to this country" rose in the United Kingdom, Austria, Belgium, Hungary, the Netherlands and Switzerland.[85]

Today there is no single hand directing anti-Semitic propaganda worldwide, as there was under the Nazis or under the Soviet Union in the 1970s or '80s. Anti-Semitism today generally does not have the power of the state behind it, except for governments in the Muslim world like Iran with its official discrimination against Jews.

International Action

Since the beginning of its upsurge in 2000, anti-Semitism in Europe has been monitored and surveyed continually, and analyzed at international conferences and by Europe-wide organizations. Since 2003, the 56-nation Organization for Security and Co-operation in Europe (OSCE) has held six major conferences on anti-Semitism. A conference in April 2004 produced the "Berlin Declaration," which stated that "international developments . . . including those in Israel or elsewhere in the Middle East, never justify anti-Semitism."[86]

In 2003 the OSCE recommended that member states actively collect data on hate crimes, including anti-Semitic incidents, and it has established a special envoy to combat anti-Semitism.

On March 1, 2007, the EU established the Agency for Fundamental Rights, to collect reliable and comparable data on racism and anti-Semitism. In 2000, its forerunner agency, the European Monitoring Centre on Racism and Xenophobia, established a system to help states collect and analyze data. However, only four out of 27 member states — Germany, France, the Netherlands and Great Britain — have mechanisms for accurate data collection on anti-Semitic incidents, the agency reported last year.[87]

In April 2007, the Council of the European Union agreed that member states should harmonize their minimal criminal provisions against racist agitation, including Holocaust denial. The final document, if adopted, would give countries two years to incorporate these provisions into their national laws.[88]

On June 27, 2007, the Parliamentary Assembly of the Council of Europe issued a resolution noting that it "remains deeply concerned about the persistence and escalation of anti-Semitic phenomena."[89]

In response to the Iranian government's sponsorship of an international conference aimed at denying the Holocaust, the U.N. General Assembly in January 2007 declared Holocaust denial "tantamount to approval of genocide in all its forms."[90]

In 1991, the General Assembly had overturned a 1975 resolution declaring Zionism "a form of racism." However, according to a recent State Department report, the assembly has established bureaucracies "with the sole mandate of singling out Israel as a violator of the human rights of others." In its first 16 months, which ended on Sept. 30, 2007, the U.N. Human Rights Commission adopted 15 anti-Israel decisions but has taken little action against notorious human-rights violators like Myanmar, complains the State Department. The report also charges that Muslim countries have used the U.N. system to "demonize Israelis implicitly, and Jews generally," an approach, the department warns, which may be "fueling anti-Semitism."[91]

In response to rising anti-Semitism worldwide, the U.S. Congress passed the Global Anti-Semitism Review Act of 2004, which requires the State Department to document and combat anti-Semitic acts internationally.

The act also established a special envoy to combat anti-Semitism.

CURRENT SITUATION

Britain Reacts

Countries today vary widely in their legal approaches to combating anti-Semitism. Six European countries, including France and Germany, impose criminal penalties on certain forms of anti-Semitic expression, such as denial of the Holocaust. British MP Mann, chair of the committee on anti-Semitism in Parliament, says he wants to shut down Web sites spewing anti-Semitic ideas, several of which originate in the United States. So far, the U.S. government has resisted these efforts because they would conflict with constitutional protection for freedom of speech.

A British parliamentary inquiry produced a report in September 2006 finding that "violence, desecration of property and intimidation directed towards Jews is on the rise."

The report found that only a minority of police forces in Britain can record anti-Semitic incidents. According to Mann, a new national data-gathering and reporting system will shortly be in place to correct this.[92]

The panel also complained that only a few anti-Semitic incidents are being prosecuted as racial harassment, which carries increased penalties, and called on the Crown Prosecution Service to address the problem. The Service released an investigation in May that found the low number of prosecutions resulted from the inability to identify suspects and the unwillingness of victims to pursue prosecution. To reverse the trend, the Service is encouraging the Jewish community and police to pursue these crimes.[93]

Noting that anti-Semitic incidents in Britain declined by 8 percent in 2007 from the previous year, Mann says, "We're bringing the problem down to more reasonable levels, where it can be dealt with more routinely."

A campaign for an academic boycott of Israel, the focus of much campus-based anti-Zionism in Britain, died last year after a legal opinion found that the movement would violate discrimination laws. The proposed boycott by the University and College Union — which would have barred Israeli academics from coming to British universities and prevented British academics from participating in Israeli conferences — provoked international outrage and charges of anti-Semitism.

However, it appears the debate is being re-ignited. In May, delegates to the union's annual congress passed a motion asking members "to consider the moral and political implications of educational links" with Israel in light of Israel's policies towards the Palestinians.[94] Union leaders said the motion's goal was "to provide solidarity with Palestinians," not to boycott Israel.[95] But Stop the Boycott Coalition, formed of academics and Jewish and non-Jewish groups, fought the motion, saying it constituted a thinly veiled illegal boycott.

Whatever the motion's impact, observers say boycott proposals are likely to come back in the form of "divestment" resolutions on campuses vowing not to purchase Israeli products. In February, the student union of the London School of Economics was one of the first to pass such a resolution, which called for students to lobby the school to divest from Israel and from companies that "provide military support for the occupation."[96]

In February, a report on the continued presence of anti-Semitic soccer chants came out just as Avram Grant, the Israeli manager of the Chelsea soccer team, received a package said to contain a lethal white powder and a threatening note describing him as "a backstabbing Jewish bastard" who would die "a very slow and painful death."[97]

French Anti-Semitism?

While overall anti-Semitic incidents in France decreased 32 percent for the first eight months of 2007 compared to the same period the previous year, several troubling developments have led to government action.

The 2006 kidnapping and death of the 23-year-old Halimi led to a government report to then-Prime Minister Dominique de Villepin stressing the gravity of anti-Semitic propaganda. The Education Department also ratified inclusion of Holocaust studies, anti-Semitism and Jewish-Arab relations in the 2007 school curriculum.[98]

In February President Nicolas Sarkozy proposed making every 10-year-old French student honor one of the 11,000 Jewish children from France killed in the Holocaust, by learning about the selected child's background and fate. The proposal provoked a storm of protests from experts, including some prominent Jews, who said it would be too traumatic for young children. France's education minister later softened the proposal so that entire classes would adopt one child.

But Sarkozy defended the plan, saying "We must tell a child the truth."[99]

Sarkozy had been toying with this idea since serving as interior minister under President Chirac, when he was astonished by the high number of anti-Semitic incidents.[100]

Many are particularly disturbed by the growing popularity of French comedian Dieudonné M'bala M'bala, who claims the African slave trade was a Jewish enterprise and that France is ruled by Zionists and neo-Zionists.

After Halimi's death, French groups monitoring anti-Semitism said the words of the comedian, who made an abortive bid for the presidency, had influenced the killers. Dieudonné (as he is known), is of Afro-Caribbean descent and is a folk hero among black and Arab immigrants. A great many attacks against Jews occur in their neighborhoods.[101]

Jean-Marie Le Pen, leader of the right-wing National Front Party, wooed Muslim immigrants by receiving Dieudonné at his party convention in 2006. (In February, Le Pen, widely known for his anti-Semitism, received a suspended prison sentence for saying that the Nazi occupation of France was "not particularly inhumane.")[102] Last March, a Paris court fined Dieudonné 5,000 euros for saying Jews had been slave traders and were now bankers and terrorists.[103]

However, in the presidential balloting in May, Le Pen won only 10 percent of the vote — his worst showing since 1974 — and failed to qualify for a second round. In June, his party failed to win a single seat in the legislative elections.[104]

In February, 21 people were charged in Halimi's kidnapping and murder, including Muslim immigrants from North Africa and immigrants from Congo and the Ivory Coast. The gang's self-proclaimed leader, Fofana, who was eventually found and arrested in the Ivory Coast, told police he organized Halimi's kidnapping but has denied killing him. No trial date has been set.[105]

Meanwhile, six people are being held in connection with Roumi's February kidnapping and torture, also in the Bagneux quarter.[106] In both cases, money appears to have been a substantial part of the motive.

In Bagneux, following Halimi's murder, a social worker said the belief that "all Jews are rich is an anti-Semitic prejudice that didn't exist in the neighborhood 20 years ago."[107]

OUTLOOK

Growing Discomfort

By many measures, life for Jews in Europe has never been better. They no longer fear any political party agitating for discrimination against them or for their deportation, as in past centuries.

But Jews also maintain a historical consciousness that a comfortable middle-class life can suddenly become a mirage, as it did in Germany, France and Poland in the late 1930s. To one another, Jews often speak of having, at least metaphorically, a bag packed under the bed, "just in case." Indeed, Jews increasingly are emigrating from France to Israel — 2,400 in 2004; 3,000 in 2005 — indicating a growing sense of discomfort as attacks on Jews and religious property have risen.[108]

As the Middle East conflict continues, anti-Jewish and anti-Zionist attitudes are likely to gain even more force. A conference last month in Jerusalem marking the 60th anniversary of Israel's creation treated global threats like terrorism and Iran as especially harmful to Israel and Jews.

"Cataclysms always seem to affect Jews first," said Stuart E. Eizenstat, a senior official in the Clinton and Carter administrations and author of an essay that formed the basis for the conference. "Go back to the Black Plague. It was not a Jewish issue, but it had particular impact on Jews because they were blamed for it."[109]

Some fear that European leftists will continue to court the growing population of young Muslims — who are often hostile to Jews — as the new working class, contributing to the new anti-Semitism. By contrast, the French Jewish population is small and aging, and many French Jews adhere to the traditional stance of "being Jewish at home and a citizen outside," making them a less strident political faction.

Nevertheless, the French left appears to be "turning away from the unholy alliance with Islamic fundamentalism," especially as the anti-Semitic content of Islamic ideology is exposed, noted a 2005 analysis from the Stephen Roth Institute.[110] Indeed, French historian Weil suggests this alliance is no longer a problem, though it's understandable how it happened.

"There was a cognitive impossibility for some people, especially some Jews who fought against racism and colonialism in the past, to suddenly acknowledge that anti-Semitism could come from the people they were defending for so many years," who themselves suffered from racism, he observes. "It took time for some people on the left. It was, 'Oh my God, how can this happen?'"

In Eastern Europe, notably Poland, while the older generation continues to battle with its Jewish ghosts, the younger generation is showing greater curiosity and openness toward Jewish culture, and some are even returning to Jewish roots. (*See sidebar, p. 120.*) Many hope that will change the overall climate for the better.

Meanwhile, in Central and Eastern Europe left-wing anti-Semites are joining right-wing nationalists to protest globalization, which they blame on Jewish financiers.[111]

Officials in Europe and in international bodies have become more conscious of anti-Semitism, arguing that where it is tolerated other forms of racism will follow. "We're making it less acceptable by challenging it and doing things about it," says British MP Mann. But he adds, "We're not complacent."

NOTES

1. Brett Kline, "Echoes of Halimi in French Suburb," *JTA*, March 6, 2008, www.jta.org.

2. "The Terrible Tale of Ilan Halimi," *The Economist*, March 4, 2006.

3. Stephen Roth Institute for the Study of Contemporary Antisemitism and Racism, "Antisemitism Worldwide 2006," p. 6, www.tau.ac.il/Anti-Semitism/asw2006/gen-analysis.pdf.

4. Stephen Roth Institute, "France 2006," p. 12, www.tau.ac.il/Anti-Semitism/asw2006/france.htm.

5. Daniel Ben Simon, "Anti-Semitism in France/Calm Interrupted," *Haaretz*, March 6, 2008, www.haaretz.com/hasen/spages/961302.html.

6. Community Security Trust, press release, "Antisemitic hate incidents remain at unacceptably high level," Feb. 14, 2008, www.thecst.org.uk.

7. Stephen Roth Institute, "Antisemitism Worldwide 2007," 2008, p. 1.

8. *Ibid.*, Appendices: "Major Attacks and Violent Incidents 1999-2007." Major attacks are defined as attacks and attempted attacks by violent means such as shooting, arson, or firebombing. Major violent incidents include harassment of individuals,

vandalizing Jewish property and street violence not involving a weapon.

9. *Ibid.*, pp. 1, 7.

10. All-Party Parliamentary Group Against Antisemitism, "Report of the All-Party Parliamentary Inquiry into Antisemitism," September 2006, www.thepcaa.org/report.pdf.

11. Office of the Special Envoy to Monitor and Combat Anti-Semitism, U.S. Department of State, "Contemporary Global Anti-Semitism: A Report Provided to the United States Congress," March 2008, p. 77. See "Action Heroes," *Telegraph Magazine*, June 2, 2007, www.telegraph.co.uk.

12. Community Security Trust, "Antisemitic Incidents Report 2007," 2008, www.thecst.org.uk.

13. Stephen Roth Institute, "Antisemitism Worldwide, 2007," *op. cit.*, p. 6.

14. *Ibid.*, p. 6.

15. *Ibid.*, p. 6. Frattini is EU Commissioner for Justice, Freedom and Security.

16. Stephen Roth Institute, *op. cit.*, p. 12.

17. Melanie Phillips, "Britain's Anti-Semitic Turn," *City Journal*, autumn 2007, www.city-journal.org/html/17_4_anti-semitism.html.

18. U.S. Department of State, *op. cit.*, pp. 28-35. See p. 35 for cartoons in *Guardian* and Norwegian press.

19. Stephen Roth Institute, "Antisemitism Worldwide 2006," *op. cit.*, p. 5.

20. *Jerusalem Post* staff and Michael Lando, "Amadinejad: Israel Filthy Bacteria," *Jerusalem Post*, Feb. 20, 20008, www.jpost.com/servlet/Satellite?pagename=JPost%2FJPArticle%2FShowFull&cid=1203343707673.

21. Yves Pallade, *et al.*, "Antisemitism and Racism in European Soccer," American Jewish Committee Berlin Office, May 2007, p. 10.

22. www.jpr.org.uk.

23. U.S. Department of State, *op. cit.*, p. 3.

24. European Agency for Fundamental Rights, "Anti-Semitism: Summary Overview of the Situation in the European Union 2001-2007," January 2008, *FRA Working Paper*, http://fra.europa.eu.

25. U.S. Department of State, *op. cit.*, p. 3.

26. *Ibid.*, p. 3.

27. *Ibid.*, p. 31.

28. Vanessa Gera, "Israel Urges Poland, Catholic Church to Condemn Polish Priest for Anti-Semitic Comments," The Associated Press, July 30, 2007.

29. U.S. Department of State, *op. cit.*, pp. 22, 28.

30. "Pierre-André Taguieff on the New Anti-Zionism," interview in *Observatoire du Communautarisme*, Sept. 7, 2005, www.zionism-israel.com/ezine/New_Antizionism.htm. Taguieff's 2002 book published in France *La nouvelle judeophobie* (The New Judephobia) was published in English translation in 2004 under the title *Rising from the Muck: The New Anti-Semitism in France.*

31. Matthias Küntzel, *Jihad and Jew Hatred: Islamism, Nazism and the Roots of 9/11* (2007), p. 129.

32. Phillips, *op. cit.*

33. Tony Judt, "On the 'Problem of Evil' in Postwar Europe," *New York Review of Books*, Feb. 14, 2008, pp. 33-36, www.nybooks.com/articles/21031.

34. Abraham H. Foxman, "Britain's Jewish Problem," *New York Sun*, May 18, 2005, at www.adl.org/ADL_Opinions/Anti_Semitism_Global/20050518-NY+Sun.htm.

35. *Ibid.*

36. Pierre-André Taguieff, *Rising from the Muck: The New Anti-Semitism in Europe* (2004), pp. 12-17.

37. Phillips, *op. cit.*

38. See Dennis Sewell, "A Kosher Conspiracy," newstatesman.com, Jan. 14, 2002, www.newstatesman.com/200201140009.

39. U.S. Department of State, *op. cit.*, p. 35.

40. "Report of the All-Party Parliamentary Inquiry into Antisemitism," *op. cit.*, p. 35.

41. "EUMC Working Definition of Anti-Semitism," *ibid.*, p. 6.

42. Judt, *op. cit.*, pp. 33-36.

43. Edward H. Kaplan and Charles A. Small, "Anti-Israel Sentiment Predicts Anti-Semitism in Europe," *Journal of Conflict Resolution*, August 2006, www.h-net.org/~antis/papers/jcr_antisemitism.pdf.

44. Judt, *op. cit.*

45. "EUMC Presents Reports on Discrimination and Islamophobia in the EU," European Monitoring Centre on Racism and Xenophobia, Dec. 18, 2006, www.fra.europa.eu/fra/index.php?fuseaction=content.dsp_cat_content&catid=43d8bc25bc89d&contentid=4582ddc822d41. The report found only one member state, the United Kingdom, publishes criminal justice data that specifically identify Muslims as victims of hate crimes.

46. "Cameron to Meet Mosque Leaders," *Birmingham Daily Mail*, Feb. 5, 2007, www.birminghammail.net/news/tm_headline=cameron-to-meet-city-mosque-leaders&method=full&objectid=18577092&siteid=50002-name_page.html.

47. David Cesarani, "Are Muslims the New Jews? Comparing Islamophobia and Anti-Semitism in Britain and Europe," draft discussion paper delivered to the Yale Initiative for the Interdisciplinary Study of Antisemitism, March 27, 2008, www.yale.edu/yiisa/Cesarani_Paper.pdf.

48. *Ibid.*, p. 12.

49. Jan T. Gross, *Fear* (2007), p. 149.

50. Shalom Lappin, "This Green and Pleasant Land: Britain and the Jews," delivered to the Yale Initiative for the Interdisciplinary Study of Anti-Semitism, Nov. 29, 2007, p. 7, at www.yale.edu/yiisa/lappin_yiisa072.pdf.

51. *Ibid.*, p. 6.

52. *Ibid.*, p. 12.

53. *Ibid.*

54. Lappin, *op. cit.*, p. 18. In the period immediately following the war, the British government kept legal restrictions on the 60,000 refugees still in the country — as aliens without full rights to seek employment until 1948. This group included people who had served in the British army or worked for the war effort in other ways.

55. *Ibid.*, p. 19.

56. Stephen Eric Bronner, "Libeling the Jews: Truth Claims, Trials and the Protocols of Zion," in Debra Kaufman, *et al.*, eds., *From the Protocols of the Learned Elders of Zion to Holocaust Denial Trials* (2007), pp. 15-17.

57. David Remnick, "Blood and Sand," *The New Yorker*, May 5, 2008, p. 72.

58. Jeffrey Goldberg, "Unforgiven: Israel Confronts its Existential Fears," *The Atlantic*, May 2008, pp. 34-51, p. 42. Also See Martin Gilbert, *Churchill and the Jews* (2007).

59. Michael Berkowitz, *The Crime of My Very Existence: Nazism and the Myth of Jewish Criminality* (2007), p. xvii.

60. Robert S. Wistrich, "European Anti-Semitism Reinvents Itself," American Jewish Committee, May 2005, www.ajc.org. Originally, the term Semite referred to peoples from ancient southwestern Asia who spoke Hebrew, Aramaic, Arabic or Amharic.

61. Henry Feingold, "The Surprising Historic Roots of Holocaust Denial," in Debra Kaufman, *et al.*, *op. cit.*, pp. 66-79.

62. Tony Judt, *Postwar: A History of Europe since 1945* (2007), p. 807. Also see B. W. Patch, "Anti-Semitism in Germany," in *Editorial Research Reports*, Aug. 2, 1935, available in *CQ Researcher Plus Archive*, www.library.cqpress.com.

63. Judt, *New York Review of Books, op. cit.*, p. 33.

64. Judt, *Postwar, op. cit.*, p. 804.

65. *Ibid.*

66. *Ibid.*

67. *Ibid.*, p. 805.

68. *Ibid.*, p. 804.

69. Gross, *op. cit.*, p. 35.

70. *Ibid.*, p. 42.

71. *Ibid.*, p. xiv.

72. *Ibid.*, p. 247.

73. See Gross, *op. cit.*, and Peter S. Green, "Polish Town Still Tries to Forget its Dark Past," *The New York Times*, Feb. 8, 2003.

74. Judt, *op. cit.*, p. 823.

75. *Ibid.*

76. *Ibid.*, p. 811.

77. *Ibid.*

78. Tom Reiss, "Letter from Paris: Laugh Riots," *The New Yorker*, Nov. 19, 2007, pp. 44-50, www.newyorker.com/reporting/2007/11/19/071119fa_fact_reiss.

79. Judt, *Postwar, op. cit.*, p. 817.

80. For background, see R. L. Worsnop, "Neo-Nazism in West Germany," *Editorial Research Reports*,

April 12, 1967, available at *CQ Researcher Plus Archives*, www.library.cqpress.com. See "Neo-Nazi Skinheads," Anti-Defamation League, www.adl .org/hate-patrol/njs/neonazi.asp.

81. Stephen Roth Institute, "Germany 2006," at www .tauc.il/Anti-Semitism, p. 2.

82. *Ibid.*, pp. 4, 6, 7.

83. European Agency for Fundamental Rights, *op. cit.*, p. 18. The report specifies that only these three countries collect sufficient criminal data to analyze a trend, www.libertysecurity.org/IMG/pdf_ Antisemitism_Overview_Jan_2008_en.pdf.

84. *Ibid.*, p. 21.

85. *bid.*, p. 17.

86. U.S. Department of State, *op. cit.*, p. 3.

87. Stephen Roth Institute, *op. cit.*, 2007, p. 18.

88. *Ibid.*, p. 16.

89. U.S. Department of State, *op. cit.*, p. 68.

90. *Ibid.*, p. 69.

91. *Ibid.*, pp. 47, 48-50.

92. All-Parliamentary Group against Anti-Semitism, *op. cit.*

93. The Crown Prosecution Service, press release, "CPS Publishes Response to All-Party Parliamentary Inquiry into Antisemitism," May 6, 2008, www .cps.gov.uk/news/pressreleases/134_08.html.

94. Francis Beckett, "Israel, administration or pay?" *The Guardian*, May 27, 2008, http://education .guardian.co.uk.

95. University and College Union, press release, "UCU Delegates vote for International Solidarity," May 28, 2008, www.ucu.org.uk.

96. Simon Rocker, "LSE Student Union in New Drive to Encourage Divestment from Israel," *The Jewish Chronicle*, Feb. 22, 2008, p. 5, http://education.guardian .co.uk/higher/worldwide/story/0,2268513,00.html.

97. Dana Gloger and Simon Griver, "Racist Death Threats Don't Scare Us, Say Avram's Family," *The Jewish Chronicle*, Feb. 22, 2008, p. 2, www.thejc .com/home.aspx?ParentId=m11&SecId=11&AId =58231&ATypeId=1.

98. European Agency for Fundamental Rights, *op. cit.*

99. The Associated Press, "French Government Softens Sarkozy Plan to Honor Holocaust Victims," *Haaretz*, Feb. 18, 2008, www.Haaretz.com.

100. Daniel Ben-Simon, "Analysis: Sarkozy's Holocaust Education Plan Baffles Jews," *Haaretz*, Feb. 19, 2008, www.Haaretz.com.

101. Reiss, *op. cit.*

102. Reuters, "France's Le Pen Gets Suspended Jail Term for Comments on Nazi Occupation," *Haaretz*, Feb. 20, 2008, www.haaretz.com/hasen/ spages/952527.html.

103. Stephen Roth Institute, "France 2006," *op. cit.*

104. *Ibid.*

105. Daniel Ben-Simon, "21 Charged with Kidnap, Murder of Jewish Man," *Haaretz*, Feb. 20, 2008, www.haaretz.com/hasen/spages/955962.html.

106. Ingrid Rousseau, "6 Held in Anti-Semitic Attack in France," *USA Today*, March 5, 2008, www.usatoday .com/news/world/2008-03-05-2346559257_x.htm.

107. Reiss, *op. cit.*

108. Stephen Roth Institute, "France 2006," *op. cit.*

109. Ethan Bronner, "At 60, Israel Redefines Roles for Itself and for Jews Elsewhere," *The New York Times*, May 8, 2008, p. A23.

110. Jean-Yves Camus, "The French Left and Political Islam: Secularism Versus the Temptation of an Alliance," Stephen Roth Institute, 2005, p. 13, www .tau.ac.il/Anti-Semitism/asw2005/camus.html.

111. Stephen Roth Institute, 2007, *op. cit.*, p. 35.

BIBLIOGRAPHY

Books

Berkowitz, Michael, *The Crime of My Very Existence: Nazism and the Myth of Jewish Criminality,* **University of California Press, 2007.**
A professor of modern Jewish history at University College, London, traces how the Nazis used accusations of criminality and a Zionist conspiracy to justify murdering the Jews.

Gross, Jan T., *Fear: Anti-Semitism in Poland after Auschwitz,* **Random House Trade Paperbacks, 2007.**
A Princeton University historian analyzes why Poles killed their Jewish neighbors returning to Poland after the war.

Judt, Tony, *Postwar: A History of Europe Since 1945,* **Pimlico, 2007.**

This history of postwar Europe by a New York University historian contains an excellent epilogue cataloguing the hostility to Jews who remained in Europe after the war.

Kaufman, Debra, *et al.*, *From the Protocols of the Learned Elders of Zion to Holocaust Denial Trials: Challenging the Media, Law and the Academy*, *Valentine Mitchell*, 2007.
This collection of essays on Holocaust denial and anti-Semitism grew out of a conference at Northeastern University in 2001.

Küntzel, Matthias, *Jihad and Jew-Hatred: Islamism, Nazism and the Roots of 9/11*, *Telos Press Publishing*, 2007.
Anti-Semitism in today's jihadist movement and its Nazi roots are discussed in this account by a German political scientist.

Taguieff, Pierre André, *Rising from the Muck: The New Anti-Semitism in Europe*, *Ivan R. Dee*, 2004.
A French philosopher and historian of ideas at France's Center for Scientific Research (CNRS) charges that anti-Zionist rhetoric in France has become the "New Anti-Semitism."

Articles

Judt, Tony, "The 'Problem of Evil' in Postwar Europe," *New York Review of Books*, Feb. 14, 2008, pp. 33-35.
Historian Judt asks whether the threat of anti-Semitism today is exaggerated, especially when linked to criticism of Israel.

Kline, Brett, "Echoes of Halimi in a French Suburb," *JTA* (Jewish Telegraphic Agency), March 6, 2008, www.jta.org.
Jews in Paris respond to the torture of a young Jewish man in the Paris suburbs in February.

Phillips, Melanie, "Britain's Anti-Semitic Turn," *City Journal*, autumn 2007, www.city-journal.org.
A British journalist claims that anti-Semitism is growing and that anti-Israel actions like the proposed academic boycott of Israel are inherently anti-Semitic.

Reiss, Tom, "Letter from Paris: Laugh Riots," *The New Yorker*, Nov. 19, 2007, pp. 44-50.
Some experts fear that the popularity of French comedian Dieudonné M'Bala M'Bala, whose routines have become increasingly anti-Jewish, may be tapping a reservoir of anti-Semitic feeling in France.

Reports and Studies

All-Party Parliamentary Group against Antisemitism, "Report of the All-Party Parliamentary Inquiry into Antisemitism," September 2006, www.thepcaa.org/report.html.
A parliamentary investigation calls on the British government to tackle a disturbing rise in anti-Semitism.

European Union Agency for Fundamental Rights, "Anti-Semitism: Summary Overview of the Situation in the European Union 2001-2007," updated version January 2008, http://fra.europa.eu/fra/material/pub/AS/Antisemitism_Overview_Jan_2008_en.pdf.
The arm of the European Union responsible for monitoring racism and anti-Semitism compiled data on anti-Semitic incidents from government and community organizations within EU countries. The most recent data for most countries were from 2006.

Mann, John, and Johnny Cohen, "Antisemitism in European Football: A Scar on the Beautiful Game," *The Parliamentary Committee Against Antisemitism*, 2008, www.johnmannmp.com/publications.
A report lists examples of anti-Jewish behavior at soccer stadiums as well as "good practices" aimed at curbing the behavior.

Pallade, Yves, *et al.*, "Antisemitism and Racism in European Soccer," *American Jewish Committee Berlin Office*, May 2007.
The problem of anti-Semitic incidents and chanting continues in soccer stadiums, according to this report, which also describes some initiatives to counteract them.

Stephen Roth Institute for the Study of Contemporary Antisemitism and Racism, "Antisemitism Worldwide."
The institute's annual report contains statistics and analysis on anti-Jewish incidents around the world.

U.S. Department of State, "Contemporary Global Anti-Semitism: A Report Provided to the United States Congress," March 2008, www.state.gov/documents/organization/102301.pdf.
The State Department's mandated report on anti-Semitism worldwide shows anti-Jewish incidents are increasing.

For More Information

American Jewish Committee, 165 E. 56th St., New York, NY 10022; (212) 751-4000; www.ajc.org. Monitors anti-Semitism in Europe through offices in Berlin, Brussels, Geneva and Paris.

Anti-Defamation League, 605 Third Ave., New York, NY 10158; (212) 692-3900; www.adl.org. Monitors anti-Semitism around the world.

Community Security Trust; 020-8457-9999; www.thecst .org.uk. A U.K.-based group that provides physical security for British Jews and monitors anti-Semitism in Britain.

Engage; www.EngageOnline.org.uk. A British group that challenges anti-Semitism in unions and universities and opposes an academic boycott of Israeli academics.

European Jewish Congress, 78 Avenue des Champs-Elysées, 75008 Paris, France; 33-1-43-59-94-63; www.eurojewcong .org/ejc. A Paris-based group that coordinates 40 elected Jewish leaders in Europe to represent their concerns, including anti-Semitism.

Institute for Jewish Policy Research, 79 Wimpole St., London W1G 9RY, United Kingdom; +44-20-7935-8266; www.jpr.org.uk. A think tank promoting multiculturalism and the role of Jews in Europe.

Jews for Justice for Palestinians, P.O. Box 46081, London W9 2ZF, United Kingdom; www.jfjfp.org. Opposes the Israeli occupation.

Middle East Media Research Institute, P.O. Box 27837, Washington, DC 20038; (202) 955-9070; www.memri.org. A Washington-based group with offices in London and Rome

that translates messages coming from the Middle East in Arabic, Persian and Turkish.

Office of Special Envoy to Monitor and Combat Anti-Semitism, U.S. Department of State, 2201 C St., N.W., Washington, DC 20520; (202) 647-4000; www.state.gov/g/drl/seas. Advocates for U.S. policy on global anti-Semitism.

Parliamentary Committee Against Antisemitism, P.O. Box 4015, London W1A 6NH, United Kingdom; 020-7935-8078; www.thepcaa.org. A committee of the British Parliament that monitors anti-Semitism in Britain and issues annual reports on the subject.

Quilliam Foundation; 020-7193-1204; www.quilliamfoundation.org. London-based think tank created by former activists of radical Islamic organizations that aims to counter extremism among Muslims in the West.

Stephen Roth Institute, Tel Aviv University, P.O. Box 39040, Ramat Aviv, Tel Aviv 69978, Israel; 972-3-6408779; www .tau.ac.il/Anti-Semitism. Publishes annual reports on anti-Semitism worldwide.

Yale Institute for the Interdisciplinary Study of Anti-semitism, Yale University, 77 Prospect St., New Haven, CT 06520; (203) 432-5239; www.yale.edu/yiisa. A center for research on anti-Semitism that presents papers on European anti-Semitism by prominent experts.

The Z-word, 165 E. 56th St., New York, NY 10022; (212) 751-4000; www.z-word.com. Independent online journal created by the American Jewish Committee focusing on the link between anti-Zionism and anti-Semitism.

6

Crisis in Darfur

Is there any hope for peace?

Karen Foerstel

Courtesy of Brian Steidle

Villages continue to be attacked and burned in Darfur by the notorious Arab *janjaweed* militia — aided by aerial bombing by the Sudanese government — despite a two-year-old peace agreement between the government and rebel groups. The prosecutor for the International Criminal Court recently said the government's "scorched earth" tactics amount to genocide, but others say there is insufficient evidence that civilians have been targeted because of their ethnicity.

From *CQ Global Researcher*, September 2008.

It was mid-afternoon when helicopters suddenly appeared and opened fire on the terrified residents of Sirba, in Western Darfur. Then hundreds of armed men riding horses and camels stormed the village, followed by 30 military vehicles mounted with weapons.

"The cars . . . were shooting at everyone, whether a woman, man or child," said Nada, one of the survivors. "They were shooting at us even when we were running away."[1]

Almost simultaneously, another attack was taking place a few miles away in the town of Abu Suruj. Witnesses say Sudanese soldiers and members of the notorious *janjaweed* militia shot people, set homes on fire and stole livestock. Many died in flames inside their huts. Three-quarters of the village was burned to the ground, as government planes bombed the town and surrounding hills where residents had fled for cover.

But that wasn't all. In a third nearby village, Silea, women and girls were raped and two-thirds of the town was destroyed by fire. Among the victims was Mariam, 35, who was shot as she tried to stop looters.

"They told me to leave and not to take anything, and then one of the men on a Toyota shot me, and I fell down," she said. Her father found her and took her by horse-drawn cart to a regional clinic. "I was pregnant with twins, and I lost them while we made the trip," she said. "I lost so much blood."[2]

In all, nearly 100 people were killed and 40,000 civilians driven from their homes in a single day, according to Human Rights Watch (HRW), a global advocacy group. The Sudanese military said the strikes were in retaliation against the Justice and Equality

Conflict Continues Despite Cease-Fire Accords

Darfur is an ethnically diverse area about the size of France in western Sudan — Africa's largest country. It has been wracked by decades of tension — and more recently open warfare — over land and grazing rights between the nomadic Arabs from the arid north and predominantly non-Arab Fur, Masalit and Zaghawa farmers in the more fertile south. A third of the region's 7 million people have been displaced by the conflict, which continues despite numerous cease-fire agreements. The United Nations has set up several camps inside Darfur and in neighboring Chad for those fleeing the violence.

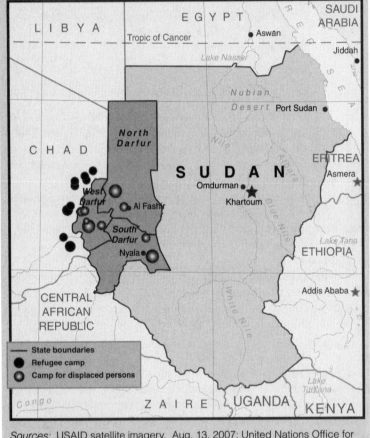

Sources: USAID satellite imagery, Aug. 13, 2007; United Nations Office for the Coordination of Humanitarian Affairs, June 2, 2008 .

While HRW criticized the rebels for operating around populated areas, it strongly condemned the Sudanese government for targeting civilians and using a "scorched earth" policy to clear the region and make it easier to go after JEM positions.[3]

Indeed, civilians have been targeted and terrorized throughout the long and bloody fighting in Darfur between non-Arab rebel groups who want to overthrow the Sudanese government and government troops backed by Arabic *janjaweed* militias.* During the peak fighting between 2003 and 2005, from 200,000 to 400,000 people — mostly civilians — died from armed attacks as well as famine and disease. More than 2.4 million Sudanese — about a third of the population — have been forced to flee their homes since 2003; tens of thousands now live in refugee camps across the region.[4]

But the same-day attacks in the three villages did not occur during the period of peak fighting. They occurred on Feb. 8 of this year, nearly two years after rebels and the government signed the Darfur Peace Agreement (DPA) in May 2006.

The continuing conflict has sparked the world's largest humanitarian mission, with more than 17,000 aid workers now stationed in Darfur.[5] And the situation is deteriorating. Observers predict next year will be one of the worst ever.

Growing banditry and lawlessness have made much of Darfur — a region in western Sudan as large as France — inaccessible to aid workers.[6] Rising food prices, drought and

Movement (JEM), an anti-government rebel group that had recently launched a military offensive in the region, attacking a police station, killing three civilians and detaining local officials.

---

* The word *janjaweed*, which means devil on a horse, is used to describe horsemen from the nomadic Arab tribes in Darfur that have been armed and supported by the Sudanese government.

a poor cereal harvest also are combining to form what Mike McDonagh, chief of the U.N. Office for Coordination of Humanitarian Affairs, described as a "perfect storm."[7]

Already, conditions are dire:

- In the first five months of this year, 180,000 Darfuris were driven from their homes.[8]
- More than 4.2 million people in Darfur now rely on humanitarian aid for food, water and medical care.[9]
- Attacks against aid workers have doubled since last year.[10] (*See chart, p. 152.*)
- The U.N. World Food Program was forced to cut its food rations in Darfur by 40 percent this year because of repeated attacks by armed gangs.[11]
- About 650,000 children — half of the region's children — do not receive any education.[12]

While attacks on civilians have decreased since the peace deal was signed, international watchdog groups say the drop has little to do with increased security. "A third of the population has been displaced, so the targets are fewer," says Selena Brewer, a researcher with Human Rights Watch. "But there are far more perpetrators."

The fighting between non-Arab rebels and the Arab-led government's forces — backed by the *janjaweed* — has morphed into all-out lawlessness. The two main rebel groups — the JEM and the Sudanese Liberation Army/Movement (SLA/M) — have splintered into more than a dozen factions that fight among themselves as much as against the government. Moreover, some disaffected *janjaweed* fighters have joined the rebels, and skirmishes between ethnic tribes are increasing. Bandits attack civilians, aid workers and international peacekeepers almost at will.[13]

Lack of Resources Hampers Peacekeepers

More than a year after the U.N. authorized the largest peacekeeping force in the world in Darfur, the joint U.N.-African Union (UNAMID) force has received only 37 percent of the nearly 32,000 military, police and civilian personnel that were authorized and 72 percent of the funds. Much of the force's equipment has been delayed by Sudanese customs, hijacked by bandits or simply not provided by international donors. For instance, by the end of May not a single military helicopter had been donated to the force.

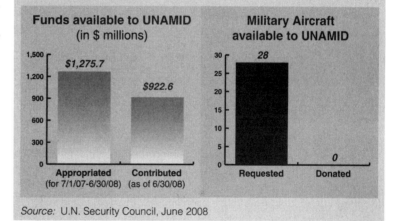

Source: U.N. Security Council, June 2008

"We no longer know who is attacking," says Denise Bell, a Darfur specialist with Amnesty International USA.

To make matters even more complicated, Darfur has become the staging ground for a proxy war between Sudan and its western neighbor Chad. The two governments support opposing groups in the region with the goal of launching coup attempts against one another. As arms pour into the area, civilians are the primary victims.

Many describe the conflict as Arabs vs. non-Arabs. "The *janjaweed* . . . would tell us that the black Africans

During a 2007 visit to Sudan, Chinese President Hu Jintao reviews Sudanese troops with President Omar Hassan al-Bashir. In the run-up to the Beijing Olympics this summer, China came under intense international pressure to use its economic clout as Sudan's biggest oil buyer and weapons supplier to convince Bashir to stop the slaughter in Darfur. Hu convinced Bashir to allow joint U.N.-African Union peacekeeping forces to enter Darfur, but critics say China could do much more.

were a lesser race and that they shouldn't be there . . . and that they would drive them out or kill them," said former U.S. Marine Capt. Brian Steidle, whose book about his six months as an unarmed military observer in Darfur was made into an award-winning documentary.[14]

But most observers say the situation is more complicated than that. Nearly all Darfuris speak Arabic, and nearly all are Muslims. Generations of intermarriage have resulted in little physical difference between the groups, and not all Arab tribes have joined the *janjaweed* while some Arab groups have even been targeted themselves — although most of the victims are from the non-Arab Fur, Masalit and Zaghawa ethnic groups.

But poverty, drought and the ongoing conflict have led to increased tensions between Arab groups, who are mainly nomadic, and non-Arabs, who are mainly farmers, as they compete for dwindling land and water resources.[15] The Sudanese government is widely accused of doing all it can to inflame these historical tensions and grow support among its Arab political base in Darfur by arming and recruiting the *janjaweed* to clear the region of non-Arabs.

But most agree race has little to do with government motives. "It's all about divide to rule. It's just the government using one lot of poor people against another lot of

poor people," says Gillian Lusk, associate editor of the London-based newsletter *Africa Confidential.* "It's not about ethnic supremacy. If the so-called Arabs don't help the government, it will kill them, too. It's just renting them."

Although Sudan says its attacks in Darfur comprise a "counterinsurgency" campaign, the prosecutor for the International Criminal Court (ICC) refuted that claim in July when he sought an indictment against Sudanese President Omar Hassan Al-Bashir for genocide and crimes against humanity.[16]

"The most efficient method to commit genocide today in front of our eyes is gang rapes, rapes against girls and rapes against 70-year old women," Chief ICC Prosecutor Luis Moreno-Ocampo said as he described the brutality of the war in Darfur. "Babies born as a result have been called *janjaweed* babies, and this has led to an explosion of infanticide." In addition, he said, "Al-Bashir is executing this genocide without gas chambers, without bullets and without machetes. The desert will do it for them. . . . Hunger is the weapon of this genocide as well as rape."[17]

Many hope the prosecutor's action will pressure Sudan to halt its attacks in Darfur. But others fear an indictment would prompt Bashir to prevent peacekeepers and Western aid organizations from working in Darfur.

"[An indictment] would have very serious consequences for peacekeeping operations, including the political process," U.N. Secretary-General Ban Ki-moon said. "I'm very worried. But nobody can evade justice."[18]

While the ICC is considering charging Bashir with genocide, many aid groups, governments and the United Nations have avoided using the "G-word" to describe the situation in Darfur. Some say the reluctance stems from the fact that international law requires countries to take action to "prevent and punish" genocide. But others, including Amnesty International, say that despite the obvious atrocities, there is insufficient evidence civilians were targeted because of their ethnicity.[19]

The international community also disagrees on how to solve the crisis. While the United States and the United Nations have sanctioned the Bashir government, the move has largely been opposed by China, Russia, Arab nations and the African Union (AU) — a political and economic coalition of African countries.

"China is uniquely positioned to fix this," says Alex Meixner, director of government relations for the Save

Darfur Coalition. "They have a fair amount of leverage over Bashir." China buys two-thirds of Sudan's petroleum — much of which comes from the south — and is its largest supplier of weapons. But as a member of the U.N.'s Security Council, China repeatedly has used its veto threat to block action against Sudan.[20]

Over the past year, however, as the Beijing Olympics brought international attention to China's human-rights policies — its government has played a more active role in trying to solve the crisis. It appointed a special envoy to help negotiate a peace settlement and helped convince Sudan to allow a joint U.N.-African Union peacekeeping force — known as UNAMID — to enter Darfur. In July China sent 172 engineers to join the peacekeeping force, bringing China's participation in the mission to more than 300 personnel.[21]

Nearly a year into their mission, however, the force is severely undermanned, underequipped and under constant attack. Although authorized to have 26,000 military and police peacekeepers — the largest deployment in the world — fewer than half that number have been deployed and not a single military helicopter has been donated to the force. (*See graph, p. 145.*)[22]

Darfur is "a test case for international response — or the inability of the international community to respond — to this type of situation," says Imani Countess, senior director for public affairs at TransAfrica Forum, which campaigns for human rights in Africa. "It's a damning indictment against the government of Sudan, because it refuses to end the violence. But it's also a pretty damning indictment of the international community."

And while the international community stands by, the situation in Darfur threatens to destabilize the entire region. Millions of refugees from the area are creating economic and political chaos in Sudan and neighboring countries, and the region's porous borders have turned Darfur into the headquarters for rebels from Chad and the Central African Republic.

The growing crisis also threatens to undo the precarious 2005 Comprehensive Peace Agreement (CPA) that ended the bloody 20-year civil war between North and South Sudan — Africa's longest civil war.

"A lot of attention has been diverted to Darfur," causing backsliding and insufficient funding for implementing the peace agreement, says Bell of Amnesty International. "Darfur threatens to overshadow the CPA.

AFP/Getty Images/Khaled Desouki

AFP/Getty Images/Ashraf Shazly

Defying the Court

Surrounded by security guards, Sudanese President Omar Hassan al-Bashir (center, top), greets supporters in North Darfur just days after the chief prosecutor at the International Criminal Court accused him of masterminding genocide in the region. Bashir dismissed the accusations as lies and vowed not to cooperate with the court. Soon after the accusation, the Sudanese government convicted and sentenced to death more than three dozen rebels — including these prisoners (bottom) — in connection with a daring attack last May on Khartoum, the capital, in which more than 200 people were killed.

If the CPA falls, the country falls. The international community needs to be much more aware of that."

In June, Jan Eliasson — the U.N.'s special envoy to Darfur — resigned, blaming himself, the U.N. and the international community for not doing enough to bring peace to the region. He said attention has been too narrowly focused on Darfur alone and that a more comprehensive strategy — addressing the many tensions and conflicts across the region — must now be pursued.

Climate Change Blamed for Darfur Conflict

Nomads and farmers battle for scarce water and arable land.

For generations, Arab nomads in Darfur enjoyed a symbiotic relationship with their farming non-Arab neighbors. As the seasons changed, the nomads would bring their livestock from the arid north to the greener lands to the south during the dry season and then lead them back north during the rainy season. The non-Arabs, who came from several different ethnic groups, would allow the nomads to graze camels, sheep and goats on their farmlands, and in exchange the livestock would provide fertilizer for the farmers' crops.[1]

That relationship, however, began to change about 75 years ago. And today, what had once been a convenient alliance between nomads and farmers has exploded into a bloody war between Darfur's Arabs and ethnic African tribes.

While many blame the bloodshed on political or ethnic divisions, others say climate change lies at the root of the devastation. "It is no accident that the violence in Darfur erupted during the drought," U.N. Secretary-General Ban Ki-moon said. "Until then, Arab nomadic herders had lived amicably with settled farmers."[2]

Most people use "a convenient military and political shorthand" to describe Darfur as an ethnic conflict between Arab militias fighting black rebels and farmers, Ban explained. And, while the conflict involves a complex set of social and political causes, it "began as an ecological crisis, arising at least in part from climate change," he said.

According to the U. N., average precipitation in Sudan has declined 40 percent since the early 1980s.[3] Signs of desertification began emerging as far back as the 1930s. A lake in El-Fashir in northern Darfur reached its lowest water level in 1938, after which wells had to be drilled to tap into underground water supplies. Villages in northern Darfur increasingly were evacuated because of disappearing water supplies.[4]

In the 1980s a severe drought and famine made the northern areas nearly impossible to cultivate, forcing nomadic tribes to migrate even further south and increasingly encroach upon their farming neighbors' more fertile lands.[5] To prevent damage from the nomad's passing herds, the farmers began to fence off their shrinking fertile plots. Violent land disputes grew more and more common.

"Interestingly, most of the Arab tribes who have their own land rights did not join the government's fight," said David Mozersky, the International Crisis Group's project director for the Horn of Africa.[6]

"This simply cannot go on," Eliasson said. "A new generation in Sudan may be doomed to a life in conflict, despair and poverty. The international community should have learned enough lessons from other conflicts where the populations were left to stagnate and radicalize in camps."[23]

As the situation deteriorates in Darfur, these are some of the questions being asked:

Has genocide occurred in Darfur?

In July 2004, the U.S. Congress declared the violence in Darfur "genocide" and urged President George W. Bush to do the same. But for months afterward, Secretary of State Colin L. Powell studiously avoided using the word, on the advice of government lawyers.

Under the International Convention on the Prevention and Punishment of Genocide, any signatory country — including the United States — which determines that genocide is occurring must act to "prevent and punish" the genocide. However, while some believe the 1948 treaty requires military intervention to stop the killing, others believe economic sanctions alone are permitted.[24]

The Bush administration used the word to describe what is happening in Darfur only after religious groups launched a lobbying and media campaign condemning the Sudanese government for "genocide." In May 2004, the U.S. Holocaust Memorial Museum issued a "genocide alert" for Darfur, and two months later the American Jewish World Service and the Holocaust Museum founded the Save Darfur Coalition — an alliance of secular and religious groups calling for international intervention to halt the violence.[25] That August, 35 evangelical Christian leaders said genocide was occurring in Darfur and asked the administration to consider sending troops.[26]

A new report by the European Commission predicts that increasing drought and land overuse in North Africa and the Sahel — the semi-arid swath of land stretching from the Atlantic Ocean to the Horn of Africa — could destroy 75 percent of the region's arable land. As land and water resources disappear, the report said, such violent conflicts will increase around the world.[7]

"Already today, climate change is having a major impact on the conflict in and around Darfur," the report said.[8]

Economist Jeffrey Sachs, director of the Earth Institute at Columbia University, said Darfur is an example of the conflicts that increasingly will erupt because of climate change.

"What some regard as the arc of Islamic instability, across the Sahel, the Horn of Africa, Yemen, Iraq, Pakistan and Afghanistan, is more accurately an arc of hunger, population pressures, water stress, growing food insecurity and a pervasive lack of jobs," Sachs wrote earlier this year, using Darfur as an example of a conflict sparked by climate change.[9]

But others say climate change is just an excuse used by the Sudanese government to relieve itself of responsibility. Politics is the real cause of the bloodshed in Darfur, many say, with President Omar Hassan al-Bashir's government bearing full blame for the ongoing violence.

"Jeffrey Sachs and Ban Ki-moon said it's essentially environmental. How dare they?" says Gillian Lusk, associate editor of the London-based newsletter *Africa Confidential*. "The essential issue is the Sudan government went in there and killed people." And any attempts "to turn it into a primary ethnic or environment issue are dangerous."

Still, many international leaders say Darfur is a warning sign of growing environmental degradation. "Climate change is already having a considerable impact on security," French President Nicolas Sarkozy told an international governmental conference in April. "If we keep going down this path, climate change will encourage the immigration of people with nothing towards areas where the population does have something, and the Darfur crisis will be only one crisis among dozens."[10]

---

[1] Stephan Faris, "The Real Roots of Darfur," *The Atlantic*, April 2007, www.theatlantic.com/doc/200704/darfur-climate.

[2] Ban Ki-moon, "A Climate Culprit in Darfur," *The Washington Post*, June 16, 2007, p. A15.

[3] *Ibid.*

[4] M. W. Daly, *Darfur's Sorrow* (2007), pp. 141-142.

[5] Gerard Prunier, *Darfur: The Ambiguous Genocide* (2005), pp. 49-50.

[6] Faris, *op. cit.*

[7] "Climate Change and International Security," The High Representative and the European Commission, March 14, 2008, p. 6, http://ec.europa.eu/external_relations/cfsp/doc/climate_change_international_security_2008_en.pdf.

[8] *Ibid.*

[9] Jeffrey Sachs, "Land, Water and Conflict," *Newsweek*, July 14, 2008.

[10] "Climate change driving Darfur crisis: Sarkozy," Agence France-Presse, April 18, 2008, http://afp.google.com/article/ALeqM5h7l_NjlMjZF-QWDOwxIbibX5AeuA.

A month later, Powell finally capitulated, telling the Senate Foreign Relations Committee, "We concluded — I concluded — that genocide has been committed in Darfur and that the government of Sudan and the *janjaweed* bear responsibility — and genocide may still be occurring."[27] Powell then called on the U.N. to take action for the "prevention and suppression of acts of genocide."[28] A week later, the United States pushed a resolution through the General Assembly threatening Sudan with economic sanctions if it did not protect civilians in Darfur.[29]

But most other governments and international humanitarian groups — including Amnesty International — say genocidal intent has not been proven.

"There is a legal definition of genocide, and Darfur does not meet that legal standard," former President Jimmy Carter said last year. "The atrocities were horrible, but I don't think it qualifies to be called genocide. If you read the law textbooks . . . you'll see very clearly that it's not genocide, and to call it genocide falsely just to exaggerate a horrible situation — I don't think it helps."[30]

Not surprisingly, Sudan denies targeting ethnic groups in Darfur, instead blaming the massive deaths on tribal conflict, water disputes and collateral military damage. "We do not deny that atrocities have taken place," says Khalid al-Mubarak, a media counselor at the Sudanese Embassy in London. "We do deny that they have been planned or systematic. They happened in an area out of reach of the central government. The government could not have planned or controlled it."

A U.N. commission investigating the conflict also said genocidal intent has not been proven, but it did say Sudanese forces working with *janjaweed* militias had "conducted indiscriminate attacks, including killing of civilians, torture, enforced disappearances, destruction of villages, rape and other forms of sexual violence, pillaging and forced displacement."[31]

"I don't think it matters [whether you call it genocide or not]," says *Africa Confidential's* Lusk. "In terms of legitimizing intervention, it might be important. But no one wants to get involved anyway."

In a joint statement in May, the three leading American presidential candidates at the time — Sens. Barack Obama, D-Ill., Hillary Rodham Clinton, D-N.Y., and John McCain, R-Ariz., — called the situation in Darfur "genocide" and promised, if elected, to intervene.[32]

Some other U.S. politicians — including Democratic vice presidential nominee and Foreign Relations Committee Chairman Sen. Joseph R. Biden, of Delaware — have called for military intervention to halt the mass killings.[33] Susan Rice, a foreign policy adviser to Obama, has called for legislation authorizing the use of force.[34]

But experts say the international backlash against the Iraq War — including the abuse of Muslim prisoners at Abu Ghraib prison by U.S. soldiers — makes intervention in another Muslim country unlikely anytime soon, whether the word genocide is used or not. "Sudan can say all this 'genocide' stuff is a conspiracy to steal [their] oil," says Peter Moszynski, a writer and aid worker with 25 years of experience in Sudan. "With the Iraq backlash, Bashir became bulletproof."

Sudan is Africa's fifth-largest oil producer, with proven reserves of 5 billion barrels. Experts say in the next few years Sudan's daily production could reach 700,000 barrels — enough for nearly 30 million gallons of gasoline a day — about 10 percent of U.S. daily needs.[35]

The United States is also in the awkward position of balancing its national-security interests against calls to end the genocide. Since the Sept. 11, 2001, terrorist attacks in the United States, Sudanese officials have worked closely with the CIA and other intelligence agencies to provide information on suspected terrorists. Although Sudan is on the U.S. list of "state sponsors of terrorism," a 2007 State Department report called Sudan "a strong partner in the War on Terror."[36]

"I am not happy at all about the U.S. working with Sudan," says El-Tahir El-Faki, speaker of the JEM legislative assembly. "Definitely it is genocide in Darfur. They are targeting ethnic people with the aim of eliminating people. . . . It will be contrary to American interest supporting a government that is killing people."

Regardless of what the violence is called, most agree the label is meaningless if nothing is done to stop the killing. "It's like walking down the street and you see someone being beaten up. You don't stop and think whether it's bodily harm or not. You stop and help and let the lawyers figure out the legal side later," says James Smith, head of the Aegis Trust, a British group that works to halt genocide. "Stopping genocide is more of a political and moral question than a legal one."

"The legal framework exists to prevent or mitigate genocide if the political will is sufficient," he continues. "However, politicians and diplomats create legal ambiguity to mask their disinterest in protecting lives in certain far-away countries."

Would arresting Sudanese President Bashir do more harm than good?

In July, when he asked the International Criminal Court to charge Bashir with genocide and other war crimes, the ICC prosecutor cast aside all the debate over how to label the violence in Darfur. Bashir's motives were "largely political," ICC prosecutor Luis Moreno-Ocampo said. "His pretext was a 'counterinsurgency.' His intent was genocide. . . . He is the mastermind behind the alleged crimes. He has absolute control."[37]

The court is expected to decide this fall whether to accept the charges and issue an arrest warrant. Many heralded the prosecutor's unprecedented request — the first genocide indictment sought for a sitting head of state — as a critical first step to peace in Darfur.

"Darfur has had very little justice of any kind. They've been let down by the African Union, by the U.N. peacekeeping force, by other countries," says *Africa Confidential's* Lusk. "It's about time a small sign of justice appeared on the horizon. Impunity has reigned for 19 years. This action says this is not a respectable government."

But others fear an indictment could spark reprisal attacks against foreign peacekeepers and aid workers by the Sudanese government and could block a peace settlement. Sudan's U.N. ambassador, Abdalmahmood Abdalhaleem Mohamad, said the charges would "destroy" efforts toward a peace agreement in Darfur. "Ocampo is playing with fire," he said. "If the United Nations is serious about its engagement with Sudan, it should tell this man to suspend what he is doing with this so-called indictment. There will be grave repercussions."[38]

Sudanese officials said that while they would not retaliate with violence, they could not guarantee the safety of any individual. "The U.N. asks us to keep its people safe, but how can we guarantee their safety when they want to seize our head of state?" asked Deputy Parliament Speaker Mohammed al-Hassan al-Ameen.[39]

The Sudanese government, which refused to hand over two other officials indicted for war crimes last year by the ICC, said it would not cooperate with the ICC's latest efforts either.

The United Nations evacuated staff from the region shortly after Ocampo made his announcement.[40] Representatives from the five permanent members of the U.N. Security Council — Britain, China, France, Russia and the United States — met with U.N. officials to discuss the safety of the peacekeeping force in Darfur, which evacuated non-essential staff and cut back on operations that could endanger civilian staff.[41]

Meanwhile, the African Union (AU), the Arab League and others asked the U.N. to delay the ICC legal action, which some say could be used as a bargaining chip to force Bashir to end the killing. "We are asking that the ICC indictment be deferred to give peace a chance," Nigerian Foreign Affairs Minister Ojo Maduekwe said after an emergency meeting on the issue by the African Union's Peace and Security Council in July. China and Russia also support deferring ICC action.[42]

Others fear the request for delay could produce its own backlash — among the rebels. Leaders of JEM and one of the SLA's factions said they will no longer recognize AU efforts to mediate peace because of its request for a deferral. "The African Union is a biased organization and is protecting dictators and neglecting the African people," said Khalil Ibrahim, president of JEM.[43]

Former U.S. Special Envoy for Sudan Andrew Natsios agrees an indictment could derail peace negotiations and make it impossible to hold free and fair elections, scheduled next year. "The regime will now avoid any compromise or anything that would weaken their already weakened position, because if they are forced from office they'll face trials before the ICC," Natsios wrote. "This indictment may well shut off the last remaining hope for a peaceful settlement for the country."[44]

The United States — which, like Sudan, has never ratified the treaty creating the ICC — nevertheless said Sudan must comply with the ICC. But the U.S. envoy to

Lynsey Addario

After years of fighting the Sudanese government, rebels in Darfur — like these from the Sudanese Liberation Army/ Movement (SLA/M) — have splintered into more than a dozen factions that fight among themselves as much as against the government. Meanwhile, bandits are attacking civilians, aid workers and international peacekeepers almost at will, contributing to rampant lawlessness in the region.

the United Nations has been vague on whether the United States would support a deferral. "We haven't seen anything at this point that could have the support of the United States," said U.S. Ambassador to the United Nations Zalmay Khalilzad. "We certainly do not support impunity for crimes."

But he added, "As you know also, we're not a member of the ICC. So there are various factors in play here. And as I said, I don't see any action on this in the council that would provide impunity anytime in the foreseeable future."[45]

Others point out that efforts to solve the crises diplomatically were faltering long before the ICC prosecutor's recommendations. "The process hasn't gotten anywhere," says veteran aid worker Moszynski. "If we're going to say 'never again,' we've got to do it. Someone must be held accountable.

In any case, he added, the pending ICC charges — and potential indictments — have turned Bashir into an international "pariah," making it nearly impossible for him to play any leadership role on the international stage.

Is China blocking peace in Darfur?

In the year leading up to the Beijing Olympics, U.S. government leaders, human-rights activists and Hollywood's elite used the international sporting event as a platform to criticize China's policy toward Darfur.

Aid Workers Face Danger

Eight humanitarian workers in Darfur were killed and 117 kidnapped within the first five months of 2008. Rising lawlessness has made parts of Darfur inaccessible to the 17,000 aid workers stationed in Darfur to help the more than 4 million people affected by the ongoing fighting between government and rebel forces, militia attacks and inter-tribal fighting.

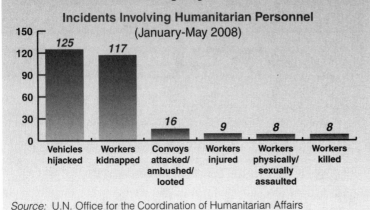

Incidents Involving Humanitarian Personnel (January-May 2008)

Source: U.N. Office for the Coordination of Humanitarian Affairs

China is Sudan's biggest trading partner, weapons supplier and oil-industry investor. It has built a 957-mile-long pipeline in Sudan — one the largest foreign oil projects in China's history. It also has constructed three arms factories in Sudan and provided small arms, anti-personnel mines, howitzers, tanks, helicopters and ammunition. China also has done more than any other country to protect Khartoum from U.N. sanctions.[46]

China "potentially has the most influence with Sudan," says Amnesty International's Bell. "People who are the main [economic] players are able to dictate the rate of progress that is made."

American actress Mia Farrow last year branded the Beijing Olympics the "Genocide Olympics," and Hollywood producer Steven Spielberg stepped down as one of the event's artistic advisers, citing the ongoing violence in Darfur.[47] Last May, a bipartisan group of 108 members of Congress warned the Chinese government that if China did not pressure Sudan to do more to help Darfur, protests and boycotts could destroy the Olympics.

"[We] urge you to protect your country's image from being irredeemably tarnished, through association with a genocidal regime, for the purpose of economic gains," the group wrote. "[U]nless China does its part to ensure that the government of Sudan accepts the best and most reasonable path to peace, history will judge your government as having bank-rolled a genocide."[48]

The day after the letter was sent, China appointed a special envoy for Darfur and since then has made several moves to mitigate the crisis.[49] In addition to sending 315 engineers to join the UNAMID peacekeeping force to build roads, bridges and wells, China last May donated more than $5 million in humanitarian aid and in February handed over a $2.8 million package of financial and development aid.[50] According to China's official news agency, China has given a total of $11 million in humanitarian aid to Darfur, and Chinese companies have spent about $50 million on development projects in the region, including 53 miles of water pipelines.[51]

"We have done as much as we can," said China's assistant foreign minister Zhai Jun. "China remains committed to resolving the Darfur issue and has made unremitting efforts."[52]

But many say China could do much more, and that its millions of dollars in arms sales to Sudan feed the continuing violence. "They've taken some action, but not nearly enough," says Meixner of the Save Darfur Coalition. "They sent engineers to UNAMID, but they're kind of milking that. I look at that as China's having kept these engineers in their back pocket until right before the Olympics."

More meaningful, he says, would be an immediate halt or reduction in China's arms sales to Sudan. According to Amnesty International, China sold Sudan $24 million worth of arms and ammunition in 2005, plus $59 million worth of parts and aircraft equipment.[53]

In March 2005, the U.N. banned the sale of weapons to any combatants for use in Darfur.[54] But earlier this year the BBC reported that China had been providing trucks being used by the Sudanese military in Darfur. China admitted that 212 trucks were exported to Sudan in 2005 but said all were for civilian use and were only later equipped with guns in a defensive move by the government to stave off rebel attacks.[55]

"The Western media and in particular the activities of some nongovernmental organizations have caused China's role to be distorted," said China's Special Envoy to Darfur, Liu Guijin.[56]

China, which repeatedly has opposed or abstained from U.N. votes to sanction or condemn Sudan's actions in Darfur, says diplomacy and humanitarian support are the best path to peace. It has expressed "great concern" over the ICC prosecutor's request for an arrest warrant against Bashir and is considering supporting an effort to delay further action by the court.[57]

Some say such "subtle diplomacy" has persuaded Sudan to reduce military attacks in Darfur and improved conditions for civilians. Former U.S. Envoy Natsios told a Senate hearing last year that Beijing complemented rather than undercut Washington's sanctions-based policy and said China had convinced Sudan to accept UNAMID peacekeepers. "There has been a lot of China-bashing in the West, and I'm not sure, to be very frank with you, that . . . it's very helpful," he told the committee.[58]

Others say that while China is a powerful player in Sudanese affairs, Beijing alone cannot be blamed for the continuing violence. "The finger is pointed first at the Sudan government, and then China . . . and then many other countries," says *Africa Confidential's* Lusk.

John Prendergast, co-chair of the anti-genocide ENOUGH Project, agreed. "Unless China and the U.S. are both exerting much more pressure on Sudan, the crisis will continue to spiral out of control," he said. "China has unique economic leverage, while the U.S. retains leverage based on its ability to confer or withdraw legitimacy."[59]

BACKGROUND

Ostrich Feathers, Ivory and Slaves

The name Darfur comes from the Arabic word "dar," meaning home, and the name of the principal ethnic group of the region, the non-Arab Fur. For centuries, however, Darfur has been home to a wide range of people — both Arab and non-Arab. Darfur is at the crossroads of Africa

and the Middle East, and Islamic traders as well as pilgrims traveling to Mecca have long traversed the province — leaving their cultural and religious imprint.[60] Today, around 90 percent of all Darfuris are Muslim.[61] After generations of intermarriage between Arabs and non-Arabs, it is nearly impossible to discern the ethnic ancestry of the people of Darfur, other than through cultural traditions: "Arabs" tend to be nomadic and "non-Arabs" tend to be farmers. Blurring the lines even further, it is not uncommon for people to call themselves Arab one day and non-Arab another.[62]

Around 1650, a Fur sultanate was established, and the region became a prosperous trading center for such goods as ostrich feathers, ivory and black slaves.[63] Over the next two centuries, the sultanate spread across 80 percent of the area known today as Darfur, encompassing 40 to 90 different ethnic groups or tribes.[64] The sultanate was considered one of the region's most powerful kingdoms, wholly separate in culture and heritage from the rest of modern-day Sudan.

In 1899, Egypt and Britain — which had occupied Egypt since 1882 — assumed joint authority over Sudan with the British taking the South and Egyptians taking the North. Even before Sudan came under joint control, Egyptian rulers had for decades occupied northern Sudan, amassing great wealth, largely from kidnapping black Africans from the South and selling them into slavery. Southern resentment against the North for the brutal slave trade remains today.[65]

Sudan's division between Britain and Egypt set the stage for the clashing cultures and religions that would later lead to the Sudanese civil war that raged for more than 20 years. The Egyptian North — with a higher concentration of Arabic population — was predominantly Islamic, while those in the South were animists or Christians. British missionaries were dispatched to spread the Christian faith in the South.

In 1916, Darfur was annexed by Sudan, merging two states with vastly different cultures and political structures.[66] "There was the problem of differential integration: Darfur is not the Sudan," says Gerard Prunier, author of the book *Darfur: The Ambiguous Genocide*. "Darfur was the easternmost sultanate in Africa, not part of the Nile Valley" as is the rest of Sudan.

And the colonial authorities did nothing to help integrate Darfur into their new state, largely ignoring the

CHRONOLOGY

1899-1956 *Colonization sows seeds of poverty and division.*

1899 Britain takes control of mostly Christian southern Sudan; Egypt takes the predominantly Muslim north.

1916 Sudan annexes Darfur.

1956 Britain and Egypt turn control of Sudan over to northern Arab elites.

1957-Early 1970s *Multiple coups switch control of Sudan between military and civilian governments; Darfur remains neglected as civil war rages in the east.*

1964 Civilians overthrow Sudan's military government.

1965 Chadian fighters establish bases in Darfur after civil war breaks out in neighboring Chad.

1969 Gen. Jaafar al-Nimeiri takes control of Sudan in military coup.

1972 Sudan's civil war ends when peace agreement is signed in Addis Ababa.

Late 1970s-1980s *Darfur serves as staging ground for Chadian rebels; Libya arms Darfuri rebels; rising Islamic extremism sparks renewed civil war in eastern Sudan; famine and drought devastate Darfur.*

1976 Libyan-backed Darfuri rebels attack Khartoum, are defeated. Government tracks down and kills alleged sympathizers in Darfur.

1983 Nimeiri imposes sharia law and nullifies peace agreement, triggering new civil war in eastern Sudan.

1984 Drought devastates Darfur; Arabs and non-Arabs fight over land, water.

1985 Civilian uprising overthrows Nimeiri.

1989-1999 *Civil war intensifies; U.S.-Sudanese tensions increase.*

1989 Gen. Omar Hassan al-Bashir seizes power, embraces militant Islam and hosts al Qaeda's Osama bin Laden.

1993 U.S. lists Sudan as a state sponsor of terrorism.

1996 Sudan expels bin Laden under U.S. pressure.

1997 China agrees to build oil refinery in Khartoum, becomes Sudan's leading weapons supplier.

1998 U.S. bombs Khartoum pharmaceutical factory, claiming it produces chemical weapons, which is never proven.

2000-2005 *War breaks out in Darfur. U.S. says genocide is occurring in Darfur. Civil war in eastern Sudan ends.*

2001 President George W. Bush appoints former Sen. John C. Danforth, R-Mo., as special envoy to Sudan to try to settle the civil war.

2003 Darfur rebels attack North Darfur's capital, marking start of war in Darfur. A cease-fire is reached in the civil war between northern and southern Sudan.

2004 U.S. House of Representatives labels the fighting in Darfur as "genocide." . . . U.N. imposes arms embargo on Darfur and endorses deployment of African Union (AU) peacekeepers.

2005 Sudan's 20-year civil war in the east ends with signing of peace accord.

2006-Present *Darfuri peace deal dissolves; rebel groups splinter; peacekeepers fail to control chaos.*

2006 Darfur Peace Agreement is signed by government and one rebel group.

2007 U.N. creates joint U.N.-AU peacekeeping force.

2008 During run-up to Beijing Olympics, human-rights activists accuse China of abetting genocide in Darfur. . . . International Criminal Court considers indicting Bashir for genocide and war crimes.

former sultanate and giving various tribes semi-autonomous rule over their individual lands. But tribal leaders were often illiterate and corrupt and did little to help Darfur. By 1935, only four government primary schools existed in all of Darfur.[67] Health care and economic development also were non-existent under the colonial rulers, who actually boasted of keeping Darfur poor and powerless.

"We have been able to limit education to the sons of chiefs and native administration personnel," wrote Philip Ingleson, governor of Darfur from 1935 to 1944, "and we can confidently look forward to keeping the ruling classes at the top of the educational tree for many years to come."[68]

Independence and Instability

After World War II, Britain began withdrawing from Sudan and reconnecting the North and South. The British handed power over to northern Arab elites in Khartoum, which became the center of government.[69] Once again, Darfur was ignored.

"Darfur had no say whatsoever over the structure or features of an independent Sudan," Prunier says.

In fact, much of the conflict in Darfur has its roots in the post-independence history of eastern Sudan, which involved a long-running civil war between the Arab- and Muslim-dominated North and the oil-rich, Christian and animist South. Darfur also became a political pawn in strategic maneuverings by Sudan, Chad and Libya, with each country arming rebel groups in the region to further their parochial interests.

Within months of Sudan's independence in January 1956, the consolidation of power in the Arab North sparked rebellion in the South. Over the next 10 years, a series of political coups alternated the government in Khartoum between military and civilian power, as civil war continued between the North and the South. Yet successive administrations continued to ignore growing poverty and dissent in Darfur. In 1972 the military government of Gen. Jaafar Nimeiri signed a peace agreement in Addis Ababa, Ethiopia, providing substantial power- and wealth-sharing between the North and South but offering nothing to the Darfuris.

However, the North-South tensions remained, and growing conflict in neighboring Chad created even more instability in Sudan. Arab rebels from Chad who opposed their country's Christian government used Darfur as a home base for their own civil war. Libyan leader Muammar Qaddafi — hoping to create a powerful Arab belt stretching into central Africa — supported the Chadian rebels and proposed a unified Arab state between Libya and Sudan, but Nimeiri rejected the offer. Angered by Nimeiri's rejection and Sudan's agreement to end the civil war with the Christians in South Sudan, Qaddafi labeled Nimeiri a traitor to the Arab cause and began arming militant Arab organizations in Darfur who opposed the governments of both Chad and Sudan.

In 1976, Libyan-backed rebels attacked Nimeiri's government in Khartoum but were defeated in three days. The Sudanese military then hunted down and killed Darfuri civilians accused of sympathizing with the insurgents.[70]

Suddenly, after years of neglect, Darfur was getting the attention of Sudan's political leaders — but not the kind it had wanted. The ongoing violence also catapulted Darfur's various local tribes into the broader polarized conflict between "Arabs" and "non-Arabs," depending on which regime they supported.[71]

Making matters worse, a drought and famine in the early 1980s plunged Darfur deeper into poverty and desperation. For the next two decades, the nomadic "Arabs" and the farming "non-Arabs" increasingly fought over disappearing land and water resources. (*See sidebar, p. 148.*) The Arab-led government in Khartoum frequently intervened, providing arms to its nomadic Arab political supporters in Darfur, who in turn killed their farming neighbors.[72]

Another Civil War

After the failed coup by Libyan-backed Arab rebels in 1976, Nimeiri tried to appease radical Islamic groups who felt he was disloyal to the dream of a united Arab front. He named leading Islamist opposition leaders to important government posts, including extremist Hassan al-Turabi as attorney general.[73]

The discovery of oil in Southern Sudan in the late 1970s added to the pressure from the increasingly Islamic government to back away from the Addis Ababa peace agreement, because the Arab authorities in the North did not want to share the profits with the Christian South, as the peace deal stipulated. In 1983, Nimeiri ordered the 11-year-old agreement null and void, began imposing

Arabs Criticized for Silence on Atrocities

Islamic countries also lag in donations, troop support.

The thin, white-haired man living in a U.N. refugee camp in Chad was soft-spoken but fervent as he thanked Americans "and the free world" for the food, medicine and other donations sent to the victims of the conflict in Darfur.

But, he asked a visiting filmmaker intently, tears trickling down his face, "Where are the Arab people? I am Muslim. We receive nothing from Islamic people."[1]

While nations around the world have criticized the Arab-dominated Sudanese government for not halting the rapes and murders of Muslims in the beleaguered region, other Arab governments have been largely silent about the atrocities being committed against Muslims by other Muslims.

"The Islamic world's response to the daily killings and suffering of millions of Muslims in Darfur has been largely silent — from both civil society as well as the institutions and majority of Islamic governments," said the newly formed Arab Coalition for Darfur, representing human-rights groups from 12 Muslim countries. "The Islamic world must decide to end its wall of silence, before it is too late."[2] The coalition made its statement in June before the Organization of the Islamic Conference, an intergovernmental organization of 57 Muslim nations.

Moreover, among the world's Arab governments — many of them awash in petrodollars — only the United Arab Emirates (UAE) earmarked any money ($100,000) specifically for aid to Darfur this year.* The rest of the international community donated more than $100 million, according to ReliefWeb, run by the U.N. Office for the Coordination of Humanitarian Affairs, including $28 million from the European Commission and $12 million from the United States.[3]

Moreover, only 587 of the 12,000 U.N. peacekeepers in Darfur have come from nations belonging to the 22-member Arab League. Of those, 508 were from Egypt, and the rest came from Jordan, Mauritania, Yemen and Libya.[4]

Amjad Atallah, senior director for international policy and advocacy with the Save Darfur Coalition, charges that the Arab League is more worried about protecting Arab leaders than about representing ordinary Arabs. "They seem to have a more compelling need to come to the defense of Arab states than for the people suffering under the regimes," says Atallah.

For its part, the Arab League did help convince Sudan to allow peacekeepers from the joint U.N.-AU peacekeeping mission into Darfur. And in 2004, an Arab League Commission of Inquiry into Darfur publicly condemned military attacks against civilians as "massive violations of human rights." But after Sudan complained, the statement was removed from the Arab League Web site.[5]

And in July, when the International Criminal Court prosecutor sought to indict Sudanese President Omar Hassan al-Bashir for genocide and war crimes, the Arab League expressed "solidarity with the Republic of Sudan in confronting schemes that undermine its sovereignty, unity and stability." The group said the charges would undermine ongoing negotiations to stop the violence in Darfur, and that Sudan's legal system was the appropriate place to investigate abuses in Darfur.[6] The league

---

* The UAE and Saudi Arabia, however, did contribute a total of $44 million to Sudan as a whole — about 3 percent of the $1.3 billion contributed to Sudan by the international community.

---

strict Islamic law, or sharia, across the country and transformed Sudan into an Islamic state.[74] Southern opposition groups formed the Sudan People's Liberation Army (SPLA) and civil war broke out again.

In 1985 civilians overthrew Nimeiri, and hopes began to emerge for a new peace settlement. But in yet another coup in 1989, Bashir seized power with the help of the National Islamic Front (NIF) and its leader, former Attorney General Turabi.[75]

Then-Gen. Bashir and the NIF embraced militant Islam and welcomed foreign jihadists, including Osama bin Laden. In 1993, the United States added Sudan to its list of state sponsors of terrorism, and President Bill Clinton imposed economic sanctions against Sudan in 1996 and 1997. In 1998, after U.S. embassies were bombed in Kenya and Tanzania, the United States bombed a Khartoum pharmaceutical factory claiming it was producing chemical weapons. The allegation was never proven.[76]

Meanwhile, Bashir and the NIF launched a bloody counterinsurgency against the South, which became one of the deadliest wars in modern history. An estimated 2 million people died before the fighting ended in 2003.

turned down several requests to be interviewed for this article.

While Arab governments have been muted in their criticism of the situation in Darfur, the citizens of Arab countries are more outspoken. According to a poll last year, a vast majority of the public in Morocco, Egypt, Saudi Arabia, the UAE, Turkey and Malaysia think their countries should do more to help Darfur. And more than three-quarters of the Muslim respondents said Arabs and Muslims should be as concerned about the situation in Darfur as they are about the Arab-Israeli conflict.

"The poll shatters the myth that Arabs and Muslims don't care about Darfur," said James Zogby, president of the Arab American Institute, which commissioned the poll. "While they fault news coverage for not being extensive enough, Arabs and Muslims feel compelled by the images and stories they see coming out of Darfur. The poll clearly illustrates a great degree of concern among Muslims, even rivaling that of another longstanding issue to Arabs and Muslims, the Arab-Israel conflict."[7]

Last year, the institute launched an Arabic-language television advertising campaign calling for increased action to help the people of Darfur. The commercial, which featured first-hand accounts in Arabic from victims of the violence in Darfur, concluded by saying, "Palestine, Lebanon, Iraq — Darfur. We must pray for them all."[8]

Darfuri refugees pray at an improvised mosque in a refugee camp in Chad. Arab governments have been largely silent about the Muslim-on-Muslim violence in Darfur and have contributed little aid to the victims.

[1] Quoted from "The Devil Came on Horseback" documentary film, Break Thru Films, 2007.

[2] "Arab Panel Scolds Islamic World for Darfur Silence," Agence France-Press, June 20, 2008, http://news.yahoo.com/s/afp/20080620/wl_mideast_afp/sudandarfurunrestrightsislamoic_080620190222. The coalition represents human-rights groups from Egypt, Jordan, Bahrain, Algeria, Iraq, Yemen, Syria, Libya, Mauritania, Kuwait, Saudi Arabia and the Palestinian territories.

[3] "Sudan 2008: List of all commitments/contributions and pledges as of 18 August 2008," U.N. Office for the Coordination of Humanitarian Affairs, http://ocha.unog.ch/fts/reports/daily/ocha_R10_E15391_asof__08081816.pdf.

[4] "UN Mission's Contributions by Country," United Nations, June 2008, www.un.org/Depts/dpko/dpko/contributors/2008/jun08_5.pdf.

[5] Nadim Hasbani, "About The Arab Stance Vis-à-vis Darfur," Al-Hayat, March 21, 2007, International Crisis Group, www.crisisgroup.org/home/index.cfm?id=4722.

[6] "Arab League Backs Sudan on Genocide Charges," The Associated Press, July 19, 2008, www.usatoday.com/news/world/2008-07-19-Sudan_N.htm.

[7] "Majorities in six countries surveyed believe Muslims should be equally concerned about Darfur as the Arab-Israeli conflict," Arab American Institute, press release, April 30, 2007, www.aaiusa.org/press-room/2949/aaizogby-poll-muslims-across-globe-concerned-about-crisis-in-darfur.

[8] "AAI Launches Darfur Ads Aimed at Arabic-Speaking International Community," Arab American Institute, press release, Jan. 8, 2007, www.aaiusa.org/press-room/2702/aai-launches-darfur-ads-aimed-at-arabic-speaking-international-community.

At least one out of every five Southern Sudanese died in the fighting or from disease and famine caused by the war. Four million people — nearly 80 percent of the Southern Sudanese population — were forced to flee their homes.[77]

Throughout the war, China sold arms to Sudan, and in 1997 China — whose domestic oil-production capacity had peaked — agreed to build an oil refinery near Khartoum and a massive pipeline from southern Sudan to Port Sudan on the Red Sea in the north.[78] Bashir declared that the "era of oil production" had begun in Sudan and that the country would soon become economically self-sufficient despite the U.S. sanctions.[79]

Darfur Erupts

Darfur, meanwhile, was suffering from economic neglect, and numerous non-Arab tribes faced repression from government-supported militias. In 2000, the non-Arabs began to fight back, especially after the so-called *Black Book* circulated across the region describing how a small group of ethnic northern tribes had dominated Sudan since independence, at the expense of the rest of the country — especially Darfur.

Human-rights advocates in London call on the international community to stop the violence in Darfur. The conflict erupted in 2003, when ethnic Africans in western Sudan took up arms against the central government in Khartoum, accusing it of marginalizing them and monopolizing resources.

"When we were writing the book, we were not thinking of rebellion. We wanted to achieve our aims by democratic and peaceful means," said Idris Mahmoud Logma, one of authors and a member of the rebel Justice and Equality Movement. "Later, we realized the regime would only listen to guns."[80]

But international attention remained focused on peace prospects between the North and South, overshadowing the book's impact. The first peace talks began in Nairobi, Kenya, in January 2000. At about the same time, Bashir pushed his former ally, the radical Islamist Turabi, out of power — a move away from religious extremism in the view of the international community.[81]

In 2001, President Bush dispatched former Sen. John C. Danforth, R-Mo., as a special envoy to Sudan to help bring the North and South toward a peace agreement.[82] Just days after the appointment, terrorists attacked the World Trade Center and the Pentagon, prompting Sudan to cooperate with the United States to avoid retaliatory strikes. The two countries soon began sharing intelligence on terrorists, including information about al Qaeda, bin Laden's terrorist organization.[83]

For the next 18 months, as peace negotiators debated splitting wealth and power between the North and South, they never considered sharing any of the pie with Darfur. Moreover, an international community focused on ending the civil war ignored the increasing repression in Darfur and the rebel groups preparing to fight.

In April 2003, just months before a North-South ceasefire was signed in Naivasha, Kenya, Darfuri rebels attacked the airport in El-Fashir, the capital of North Darfur, killing 30 government soldiers and blowing up aircraft. Rebels killed more than 1,000 Sudanese soldiers in the following months.[84]

"The Darfuris saw they had no shot at being part of the process," says Prendergast of the ENOUGH Project. "Leaving these guys out helped reinforce their desire to go to war. Darfur was completely ignored during the first term of the Bush administration, allowing Khartoum to conclude it could do whatever it wanted to in Darfur."

Indeed, Khartoum counterattacked, enlisting the brute force of the desperately poor Arab *janjaweed* militias the government had armed years earlier to settle internal land disputes. Over the next two years, up to 400,000 people died in the conflict by some estimates, and nearly 2.4 million people were displaced.[85] Civilian populations primarily from the Fur, Zaghawa, and Masalit ethnic groups — the same ethnicities as most of the rebel SLA/M and JEM groups — were the main targets.

Through most of the early fighting, global attention remained focused on negotiations to stop the North-South civil war, which officially ended in January 2005 when the government and the SPLA signed the Comprehensive Peace Agreement.

But by then Darfur had already spun out of control. The U.N. human rights coordinator for Sudan the previous April had described the situation in Darfur as "the world's greatest humanitarian crisis," adding "the only difference between Rwanda and Darfur is the numbers involved."[86] Human rights and religious groups had launched a media and lobbying campaign demanding that the international community act. In July 2004, the U.S. House of Representatives called the violence in Darfur "genocide."

A few days later, the U.N. passed its first resolution on Darfur, imposing an arms embargo on militias in the region and threatening sanctions against the government if it did not end the *janjaweed* violence. It also endorsed the deployment of African Union peacekeeping troops.[87] The resolution, the first of a dozen the U.N. would pass regarding Darfur over the next four years, was approved by the Security Council with 13 votes and two abstentions — from China and Pakistan.[88]

"What they've done is produce a lot of pieces of paper," says Brewer, of Human Rights Watch. "But they haven't been reinforced. Khartoum has played a very clever game. They stop aggression just long enough for the international community to look away, and then they start all over again."

Over the past four years rebel groups and Sudanese officials have agreed to a variety of ceasefires and settlements, which one or all sides eventually broke. The most recent — the Darfur Peace Agreement — was reached in May 2006, but only the government and one faction of the SLA/M signed the deal; JEM and another SLA/M faction refused to participate.[89] The SLA/M soon splintered into more than a dozen smaller groups, and fighting grew even worse.[90]

The African Union peacekeepers — under constant attack from rebels and bandits — proved ineffective. So in 2006, the U.N. voted to send international troops to bolster the AU mission. Bashir initially blocked the proposal as a "violation of Sudan's sovereignty and a submission by Sudan to outside custodianship."[91]

But after extended negotiations with China, the AU and the U.N., Bashir finally agreed. In July 2007, the Security Council unanimously voted to send up to 26,000 military and police peacekeepers as part of the joint U.N.-AU force. U.N. Secretary-General Ban heralded the unanimous vote as "historic and unprecedented" and said the mission would "make a clear and positive difference."[92]

But just three months before the peacekeepers began arriving in January 2008, hundreds of rebels in 30 armed trucks attacked a peacekeeping base in the Darfur town of Haskanita, killing at least 10 soldiers, kidnapping dozens more and seizing supplies that included heavy weapons.

"It's indicative of the complete insecurity," said Alun McDonald, a spokesman for the Oxfam aid organization in Sudan. "These groups are attacking anybody and everybody with total impunity."[93]

CURRENT SITUATION

Indicting Bashir

The summer's Olympic Games in Beijing thrust Darfur back into international headlines. Movie stars, activists and athletes have criticized China's continued cozy relationship with the Bashir government and called on the world to stop the violence. Olympic torch-carrying ceremonies in cities around the world were interrupted by

protesters complaining about China's support for Sudan and its recent crackdown on dissenters in Tibet.[94]

But even bigger news in the weeks leading up to the Games was the ICC prosecutor's effort to charge Bashir with genocide and war crimes. While, the ICC is not expected to decide until later this year whether to indict and arrest Bashir, the decision could be delayed even further if the Security Council agrees with the AU and others that the indictment should be deferred. The council can defer for 12 months — and indefinitely renew the deferral — any ICC investigation or prosecution.[95]

The ICC's move was not its first against Sudanese officials. On March 31, 2005, the United Nations passed a resolution asking the ICC prosecutor to investigate allegations of crimes against humanity and war crimes in Darfur. After a 20-month investigation, the prosecutor presented his evidence to the court in February 2007 and the court agreed two months later to issue arrest warrants for Sudan's former Interior Minister Ahmad Harun and *janjaweed* leader Ali Kushayb.[96] Bashir has refused to hand over either man, and Harun has since been named head the Ministry of Humanitarian Affairs and oversees the government's activities to aid the victims of the atrocities.[97]

This July, just days after the court's announcement about Bashir, the Sudanese president traveled to Darfur and met with 600 refugees from various tribes, including those he is accused of inflicting war crimes against. He promised to send them farming equipment and to free more than 80 rebels imprisoned last May after an attack on Khartoum's twin city Omdurman. Bashir called the prisoners "boys" and said they would be freed and pardoned — although he did not say when.[98]

Sudan also appointed its own prosecutor to investigate war crimes in Darfur and said it was sending legal teams to the region to monitor the situation. Sudan, which is not a signatory of the treaty that created the ICC, said its legal system was adequate to look into alleged abuses in Darfur and that it would pass legislation making genocide a punishable crime in Sudan.[99]

International Betrayal

Despite Secretary-General Ban's confidence in the new UNAMID peacekeeping force, deadly assaults against the mission have occurred almost non-stop. The first

More Than 4.2 Million Affected by Crisis

Continued violence forced nearly 180,000 Darfuris to abandon their homes in the first five months of this year, bringing to 4.2 million the number affected by the ongoing conflict. While from 200,000 to 400,000 have been killed, nearly 2.4 million have been displaced. Many now live in U.N. camps inside Sudan — set up for so-called internally displaced persons (IDPs) — or have fled to refugee camps in neighboring Chad.

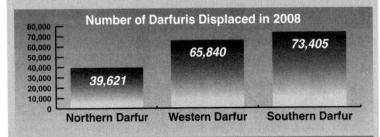

Number of Darfuris Displaced in 2008

Northern Darfur	Western Darfur	Southern Darfur
39,621	65,840	73,405

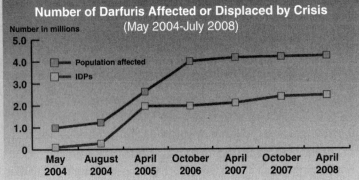

Number of Darfuris Affected or Displaced by Crisis (May 2004-July 2008)

Sources: Sudan — Darfur: Humanitarian Profile, June 2, 2008, U.N. Office for the Coordination of Humanitarian Affairs; United Nations Sudan Information Gateway

feel UNAMID itself needs some protection, because UNAMID is not at full strength."[101]

More than a year after the UNAMID force was authorized, only a third of the 26,000 troops are on the ground, and not a single military transport or tactical helicopter among the 28 requested has been deployed to patrol the area — which is the size of France.

On July 31, the day UNAMID's mandate was to expire, the Security Council extended it for a year.[102] Meanwhile, 36 human rights groups — along with Nobel Peace Prize laureate Desmond Tutu and former President Carter — issued a report revealing that countries were not donating helicopters that are desperately needed by UNAMID to restore order.[103] The report said a handful of NATO countries and others that typically contribute aircraft to peacekeeping missions — specifically India, Ukraine, Czech Republic, Italy, Romania and Spain — could easily provide up to 70 helicopters for the mission. (*See graphic, p. 145.*)

"Many of these helicopters are gathering dust in hangars or flying in air shows when they could be saving lives in Darfur," said the report, entitled "Grounded: the International Community's Betrayal of UNAMID."[104]

UNAMID peacekeeper — a civilian police inspector from Uganda — was killed in May, just four months after the new force began arriving.

On July 9, seven peacekeepers were killed and dozens more injured when their convoy was ambushed by hundreds of horsemen and 40 trucks mounted with machine guns and antiaircraft weapons. The two-hour firefight marked the first time UNAMID had to use force to protect itself, and some observers described it as being near the point of "meltdown."[100]

"The effort being achieved so far is not enough," said, Fadallah Ahmed Abdallah, a Sudanese city official in Darfur working with the peacekeepers. "Sometimes we

"It's really shameful," says Brewer of Human Rights Watch. "But it's not just helicopters. They need water, trucks, everything. I don't know whether it's because countries don't have faith in UNAMID, or they don't want to put their troops as risk or if it's fear of being involved in something that will fail."

Brewer also blames the Sudanese government for delaying delivery of peacekeepers' equipment and refusing to accept troops from Western countries. Aside from peacekeepers, aid workers also are being targeted by rebel factions and bandits searching for food and supplies. Eight aid workers were killed in the first five months of 2008, and four times as many aid vehicles were hijacked during the first quarter of this year compared to the same period last year.[105] Armed gangs also attacked 35 humanitarian compounds during the first quarter — more than double the number during the same period last year.[106]

"We are now in the worst situation ever" — even worse than when the government-rebel conflict was at its peak, says Hafiz Mohamed, Sudan program coordinator with Justice Africa, a London-based research and human rights organization. "At least in 2004 we only had two rebel movements. Now we have more than 12 SLA factions and more than four JEM factions. Security-wise, Darfur is worse than in 2004."

In May, SLA Unity rebels arrested a dozen Sudanese government employees in Darfur gathering census information for next year's national elections. The rebels, who believe the census will be inaccurate — depriving Darfur of political representation — vowed to try the census takers in military courts as "enemies," which carries the death penalty.[107]

Rebel attacks also are increasing outside Darfur. Last year JEM — which wants to overthrow the Sudanese government — attacked government positions and kidnapped two foreign workers at a Chinese-run oil field in neighboring Kordofan province. "This is a message to China and Chinese oil companies to stop helping the government with their war in Darfur," said JEM commander Abdel Aziz el-Nur Ashr.[108] JEM has said oil revenues are being used to continue the fighting in Darfur.

JEM rebels made their most audacious push against the government in May, when they reached suburban Khartoum before being repelled by Sudanese forces. Sudan immediately cut off diplomatic ties with Chad, which it accused of sponsoring the attack. Chadian officials denied any involvement but accused Sudan of launching a similar attack against their capital three months earlier.[109]

"The entire region is affected by what is happening in Darfur," says Mohamed of Justice Africa. "It's a proxy war. Unless we resolve the relationship between Chad and Sudan, we will not have an agreement for peace in Darfur."

Meanwhile, relations between North and South Sudan are worsening. Both sides remain deadlocked over some of the most contentious issues of the 2005 peace treaty, including how to draw the North-South border and how to split oil profits. The South has a large portion of the country's oil reserves while the North has most of the

AFP/Getty Images/Mustafa Ozer

AFP/Getty Images/Jose Cendon

Life in the Camps

About a third of the Darfuri population has been forced to flee their homes since 2003, with many now living in refugee camps in Darfur or neighboring Chad. Conditions in the camps, like these near Nyala, are harsh. Children (bottom) attend class at a makeshift outdoor school, but about 650,000 don't attend school at all.

infrastructure. The South has repeatedly accused the North of not sharing oil revenue fairly, while the North has charged the South with mishandling their portion of the funds.[110]

Under the Comprehensive Peace Agreement (CPA), a referendum is scheduled for 2011 on whether the South will secede from the North. Some wonder if tensions between the two sides will hold until then.

"There are real prospects of another North-South war," says Sudan expert Moszynski. "South Sudan is spending 40 percent of their budget on military. They're preparing

An African Union (AU) peacekeeper offers bread to two women near the West Darfur town of Murnei. The women said they were raped, beaten and robbed by *janjaweed* militiamen when they left their refugee camp to gather firewood — a common occurrence in Darfur. After being criticized as ineffective, the AU force has been beefed up this year with 10,000 U.N. military and police peacekeepers. Another 16,000 have been authorized.

for the next war with the North. There are a lot of problems in Sudan. In between all of that, they're not going to sort out Darfur."

Mission Impossible?

While the U.N. has been slow to send in troops and materiel, individual governments and private organizations have provided billions of dollars' worth of food, water, housing, medicine and other humanitarian aid to Darfur and the nearby refugee camps in Chad.

In 2004, when the war between rebels and government forces was at its peak, only 230 relief workers were stationed in the region.[111] Today, there are more than 17,000 national and international aid workers from some 80 NGOs, 14 U.N. agencies and the Red Cross/Red Crescent Movement.[112]

"The humanitarian response has been incredible," providing "a staggering amount of money, a staggering number of people," says Brewer. However, she says she sometimes wonders if people are substituting aid for serious "political engagement to find a solution."

And most agree that only political engagement — coming from a unified global community — can solve the ongoing conflict.

"We need more coordinated diplomacy. We can't have different messages coming from France, China, the U.N.,

the U.S. and African nations," says Meixner of the Save Darfur Coalition. "Bashir can thwart one or two, but if there's a united front, including China and African nations, it's not so easy."

Specifically, he says, multilateral sanctions should be adopted. "Sudan is the test case for multilateralism," he says.

But others say "regime change" is the only viable solution. "I don't think we'll find a political solution for the Darfur crisis if the current government stays in power," says Mohamed of Justice Africa. "Since 1997 we've had six agreements, the CPA, the DPA. This regime will never honor any agreement. . . . If [the international community] managed to overthrow the regime, there is the possibility of a permanent solution."

But Alex de Waal, a program director at the Social Science Research Council in New York and author of *Darfur: A Short History of a Long War*, says global and Arab anger sparked by the Iraq War leaves "zero chance" that the international community will launch any military action against another Muslim country.

However, Obama foreign affairs adviser Rice — a former Clinton-era State Department official — said the U.N. should not let the experience in Iraq deter military action. "Some will reject any future U.S. military action, especially against an Islamic regime, even if purely to halt genocide against Muslim civilians," Rice told a Senate committee in April 2007. "Sudan has also threatened that al Qaeda will attack non-African forces in Darfur — a possibility, since Sudan long hosted bin Laden and his businesses. Yet, to allow another state to deter the U.S. by threatening terrorism would set a terrible precedent. It would also be cowardly and, in the face of genocide, immoral."[113]

Meanwhile, the U.N. has unsuccessfully tried to resurrect peace talks between the Bashir government and rebel groups. Talks in Libya were called off last October after rebel factions refused to participate.[114]

"The last six months have seen some very negative developments," former U.N. Special Envoy Eliasson said upon his resignation in June. If the international community's energy is not mobilized to halt the fighting, he continued, "we risk a major humanitarian disaster again. The margins of survival are so slim for the people of Darfur."[115] The U.N. could start showing its commitment, he said, by stationing his replacement full time

AT ISSUE

Would military intervention solve the crisis in Darfur?

YES
Hafiz Mohamed
Sudan Program Coordinator
Justice Africa

Written for *CQ Global Researcher*, August 2008

The current crisis in Darfur has claimed more than 200,000 lives and displaced millions — due primarily to the Sudanese government's counterinsurgency policy, which uses the *janjaweed* as proxy fighters and bombs villages with government aircraft.

Despite more than 16 U.N. Security Council resolutions and authorization of a joint U.N.-African Union peacekeeping mission in Darfur (UNAMID), the mass killing and displacement of civilians continues. The parties to the conflict have signed many cease-fire agreements since 2004, but all of them have been violated, and even the mechanisms for monitoring the cease-fires have failed. Early last month, peacekeepers were attacked in Darfur, primarily because they were outmanned and outgunned. No country has provided them even with helicopters.

Hardliners within Sudan's National Congress Party still believe in a military solution to the crisis and use any means to defeat the Darfuri armed movements. All their rhetoric about being committed to a peaceful solution is just for public opinion and not a genuine endeavor to achieve a peaceful settlement to the conflict. They will only accept peace if they are pressured to do so or feel the war is unwinable.

The regime is in its weakest position since taking power in 1989 and will only cave when it feels threatened. For example, after the International Criminal Court prosecutor initiated proceedings recently to indict the Sudanese president, the government began mobilizing the public to support the president and seek a peaceful resolution.

There is strong evidence that military intervention is needed to stop the killing of civilians and force the Sudanese government to seriously seek a peaceful solution for the crisis. This could start by imposing a no-fly zone on Darfur, which would prevent the government from using its air force to bomb villages and give air support to the *janjaweed's* attacks; the normal sequences for the attacks on the villages is to start an attack from the air by using the government bombers or helicopter machine guns, followed by attacks by militia riding horses or camels.

A no-fly zone will stop this, and many lives will be saved. The no-fly zone can start by using the European forces based in neighbouring Chad. The UNAMID forces then can be used to monitor movement on the ground and intervene when necessary to stop the ground attacks on villages.

NO
Imani Countess
Senior Director for Public Affairs
TransAfrica Forum

Written for *CQ Global Researcher*, August 2008

For the sake of the 2 million displaced peoples and 200,000 killed, the international community should mount a military force that would protect and restore the dignity and livelihoods to those raped, tortured and maimed by the Sudanese government. But whatever peace comes to Sudan will be the result of those who brought the issue to the world stage: Darfurians supported by millions around the globe who are standing in the breach created by the failures and inaction of the nations of the world.

Truth be told, not one major military or economic power is willing to expend the political capital required to solve the crisis in Darfur.

For the United States, Darfur has become "collateral damage" in the global war on terror. The administration states that genocide is occurring, yet it continues to share intelligence with key Sudanese officials implicated in the tragedy in Darfur — sacrificing thousands of Darfuri lives in exchange for intelligence and extraditions of suspected terrorists.

Other Western nations provide plenty of rhetoric and limited sanctions. But they have failed miserably where it counts: providing adequate support for the joint African Union-U.N. peacekeeping force in Darfur. According to AfricaFocus, UNAMID is "understaffed, underequipped, underfunded and vulnerable to attacks." The U.N. authorized up to 19,555 military personnel for the mission, plus 6,432 police and more than 5,000 civilians. But so far fewer than 8,000 troops and 2,000 police have been deployed, along with just over 1,000 civilians. Critical equipment is lacking, and more than half of the $1.3 billion budget was unpaid as of the end of April.

For the international community as a whole — particularly China and India — continued access to Sudan's oil is the major interest.

If military intervention is not the answer, then what will work? Continued pressure from below. In the United States, the Bush administration was compelled to name the crisis "genocide" because of pressure from faith-based, human-rights and social-justice groups. Across the country, divestment activity — modeled after the anti-apartheid campaigns of the 1970s and '80s — has forced U.S. monies out of Sudan. The transnational human-rights movement will continue to pressure governments, businesses and multilateral institutions to move beyond rhetoric to effective human-centered engagement.

in Sudan. Eliasson had been headquartered in Stockholm.

The new U.N. special envoy, Burkino Faso's foreign minister Djibril Bassole, is hopeful. "This will be a difficult mission," he said after his first visit to Sudan in July. "But it's not mission impossible."[116]

OUTLOOK

Bleak Future

As unstable and violent as the past four years have been for Darfur, the next three could be even more tumultuous — for the entire country.

Under Comprehensive Peace Agreement provisions, elections must be held next year — the first in 23 years. In preparation Sudan conducted its first census since 1993 earlier this year, but many doubt that either the census results — or the vote count — will be accurate.[117]

Displaced Darfuris in refugee camps don't trust the government to take an accurate headcount. Indeed, the huge numbers of displaced persons seem to make both an accurate census and democratic elections nearly impossible.

"It's hard to see how elections can take place in a fair and free way in Darfur," says Lusk of *Africa Confidential.* "Half the people are dead, and the other half are in camps."

"The [displaced] people are concerned that if they register to vote while living in the camps, . . . they will lose their land," says Brewer. "There is great lack of clarity in land law."

Some wonder if the Bashir government will back out of the elections altogether, but Sudanese officials insist the polling will be held. "Rebels said the census should not take place, but it did take place," says Mubarak of the Sudanese Embassy in London. "The elections will go ahead."

But elections will at best do little to help the people of Darfur and at worst prompt further violence from those who oppose the results, say some observers. "The elections will have no impact on Darfur — if they happen," says former U.S. Rep. Howard Wolpe, D-Mich., who directs Africa programs at the Woodrow Wilson Center. "At the end of the day, elections have no impact . . . if you haven't built a sense of cohesion or a way of moving forward."

After the elections, the Sudanese people must brace themselves for another potential upheaval — caused by a planned 2011 referendum on Sudanese unity. While the South appears ready to vote for secession, many say Khartoum will never let that happen.

Others say secession could spell dark times for Darfur. "If the South secedes, [Bashir's National Congress Party] will have greater power in the North, and that is worse for Darfur," says Brewer. "If they vote for power sharing, it could be good for Darfur."

Meanwhile, all eyes are waiting to see whether the ICC will give in to pressure to defer action on Bashir's indictment and how Bashir and the rebel groups will respond to either an indictment or a delay.

The November U.S. presidential election could also bring about some changes. Both McCain and Obama have said they will pursue peace and security for Darfur with "unstinting resolve." And Obama's running mate, Foreign Relations Committee Chairman Biden, was unequivocal last year when he advocated U.S. military intervention. "I would use American force now," Biden said during hearings before his panel in April 2007. "It's time to put force on the table and use it." Biden, who had also pushed for NATO intervention to halt anti-Muslim genocide in Bosnia in the 1990s, said 2,500 U.S. troops could "radically change" the situation on the ground in Darfur. "Let's stop the bleeding. I think it's a moral imperative."[118]

Given the uncertainties of the Sudanese elections, the growing North-South acrimony, the continued fighting between Chad and Sudan and the upcoming ICC decision, most experts say it is nearly impossible to predict what will happen in Darfur in the future.

"Even five years is too far to predict what will happen," says author Prunier. "You have to take it in steps. First look at what happens in 2009, then what happens leading up to the referendum, then what happens after that."

Most agree, however, that whatever future lies ahead for Darfur, it will likely be bleak.

"Sudanese politics is like the British weather: unpredictable from day to day but with a drearily consistent medium-term outlook," de Waal of the Social Science Research Council wrote recently. "There are few happy endings in Sudan. It's a country of constant turbulence, in which I have come to expect only slow and modest improvement. Sometimes I dream of being wrong."[119]

NOTES

1. "They Shot at Us as We Fled: Government Attacks on Civilians in West Darfur," Human Rights Watch, May 2008, p. 18, www.hrw.org/reports/2008/darfur0508/.

2. *Ibid.*, p. 19.

3. *Ibid.*, p. 2.

4. "Darfur Crisis: Death Estimates Demonstrate Severity of Crisis, but Their Accuracy and Credibility Could Be Enhanced," Government Accountability Office, November 2006, pp. 1-2, 7. The U.S. State Department puts the death toll for the period 2003-2005 at between 98,000 and 181,000.

5. "Sudan — Darfur: Humanitarian Profile," United Nations Office for the Coordination of Humanitarian Affairs, June 2, 2008, www.unsudanig.org/library/mapcatalogue/darfur/data/dhnp/Map%201226%20Darfur%20Humanitarian%20Profile%20June%203%202008.pdf.

6. *Ibid.*

7. Sarah El Deeb, "UN warns of bad year in Darfur," The Associated Press, June 22, 2008, www.newsvine.com/_news/2008/06/16/1581306-un-warns-of-bad-year-in-darfur.

8. "Darfur faces potential food crisis unless action taken now, warn UN agencies," UN News Centre, United Nations, June 23, 2008, www.un.org/apps/news/story.asp?NewsID=27114&Cr=darfur&Cr1=.

9. "Darfur 2007: Chaos by Design," Human Rights Watch, September 2007, p. 20.

10. El Deeb, *op. cit.*

11. "Darfur faces potential food crisis," *op. cit.*

12. "Almost Half of All Darfur Children Not in School, Says NGO," BBC Monitoring International Reports, Feb. 29, 2008.

13. Stephanie McCrummen, "A Wide-Open Battle For Power in Darfur," *The Washington Post*, June 20, 2008, p. A1, www.washingtonpost.com/wp-dyn/content/article/2008/06/19/AR2008061903552_pf.html.

14. Quoted from "The Devil Came on Horseback" documentary, Break Thru Films, 2007.

15. Julie Flint and Alex de Waal, *Darfur: A Short History of a Long War* (2005), p. 10.

16. Colum Lynch and Nora Boustany, "Sudan Leader To Be Charged With Genocide," *The Washington Post*, July 11, 2008, p. A1, www.washingtonpost.com/wp-dyn/content/article/2008/07/10/AR2008071003109.html. Also see Kenneth Jost, "International Law," *CQ Researcher*, Dec. 17, 2004, pp. 1049-1072.

17. Quoted in Hussein Solomon, "ICC pressure shows some result; An arrest warrant for Sudan's President Al-Bashir has resulted in a flurry of activity for change in Darfur," *The Star* (South Africa), Aug. 21, 2008, p. 14.

18. "Court Seeks Arrest of Sudan's Beshir for 'genocide,' " Agence France-Presse, July 14, 2008.

19. For background, see Sarah Glazer, "Stopping Genocide," *CQ Researcher*, Aug. 27, 2004, pp. 685-708.

20. For background, see Karen Foerstel, "China in Africa," *CQ Global Researcher*, January 2008, pp. 1-26.

21. Alexa Olesen, "China Appoints Special Envoy for Darfur," The Associated Press, May 11, 2007; "China paper decries Sudan's Bashir arrest move," Reuters, July 17, 2008; "China boosts peacekeepers in Darfur," Agence France-Presse, July 17, 2008, http://afp.google.com/article/ALeqM5jxVo9_9z2jJm2wxZW65dyP8CflEw.

22. Neil MacFarquhar, "Why Darfur Still Bleeds," *The New York Times*, July 13, 2008, www.nytimes.com/2008/07/13/weekinreview/13macfarquhar.html.

23. "Darfur's Political Process in 'Troubled State of Affairs,' " U.N. Security Council press release, June 24, 2008, www.un.org/News/Press/docs/2008/sc9370.doc.htm.

24. Glazer, *op. cit.*, p. 687.

25. Neela Banerjee, "Muslims' Plight in Sudan Resonates with Jews in U.S.," *The New York Times*, April 30, 2006, www.nytimes.com/2006/04/30/us/30rally.html.

26. Alan Cooperman, "Evangelicals Urge Bush to Do More for Sudan," *The Washington Post*, Aug. 3, 2004, p. A13, www.washingtonpost.com/wp-dyn/articles/A35223-2004Aug2.html.

27. Glenn Kessler and Colum Lynch, "U.S. Calls Killings in Sudan Genocide," *The Washington Post*, Sept. 10, 2004, p. A1, www.washingtonpost.com/wp-dyn/articles/A8364-2004Sep9.html.

28. "The Crisis in Darfur: Secretary Colin L. Powell, Written Remarks Before the Senate Foreign Relations Committee," Secretary of State press release, Sept. 9, 2004.

29. "Security Council Declares Intention to Consider Sanctions to Obtain Sudan's Full Compliance With Security, Disarmament Obligations in Darfur," U.N. Security Council press release, Sept. 18, 2004, www.un.org/News/Press/docs/2004/sc8191.doc.htm.

30. Opheera McDoom, "Statesmen Say Darfur Violent and Divided," Reuters, Oct. 4, 2007, http://africa.reuters.com/wire/news/usnMCD 351991.html.

31. "UN Report: Darfur Not Genocide," CNN.com, Feb. 1, 2005, http://edition.cnn.com/2005/WORLD/africa/01/31/sudan.report/. See also Marc Lacey, "In Darfur, Appalling Atrocity, but Is That Genocide?" *The New York Times*, July 23, 2004, p. 3, http://query.nytimes.com/gst/fullpage.html?res=9B04E0DC163DF930A15754C0A9629C8B63.

32. Hillary Rodham Clinton, John McCain and Barack Obama, "Presidential Candidates' Statement on Darfur," May 28, 2008, www.cfr.org/publication/16359/presidential_candidates_statement_on_darfur.html?breadcrumb=%2Fregion%2F197%2Fsudan.

33. George Gedda, "Biden Calls for Military Force in Darfur," The Associated Press, April 11, 2007.

34. Susan E. Rice, "The Escalating Crisis in Darfur," testimony before the U.S. House Committee on Foreign Affairs, Feb. 8, 2007, www.brookings.edu/testimony/2007/0208africa_rice.aspx.

35. Opheera McDoom, "Analysis — Darfur Scares European Investors Off Sudan's Oil," Reuters, Aug. 3, 2007. One barrel of oil produces 42 gallons of gasoline. Also see Energy Information Administration database, at http://tonto.eia.doe.gov/dnav/pet/pet_cons_psup_dc_nus_mbblpd_a.htm.

36. "US Sanctions on Sudan," U.S. Department of State fact sheet, April 23, 2008, www.state.gov/p/af/rls/fs/2008/103970.htm. Also see "Country Reports on Terrorism," U.S. Department of State, April 30, 2007, Chapter 3, www.state.gov/s/ct/rls/crt/2006/82736.htm.

37. "Situation in Darfur, The Sudan: Summary of the Case," International Criminal Court, July 14, 2008, www.icc-cpi.int/library/organs/otp/ICC-OTP-Summary-20081704-ENG.pdf.

38. Colum Lynch and Nora Boustany, "Sudan Leader To Be Charged With Genocide," *The Washington Post*, July 10, 2008.

39. *Ibid.*

40. Stephanie McCrummen and Nora Boustany, "Sudan Vows to Fight Charges of Genocide Against Its Leader," *The Washington Post*, July 14, 2008, www.washingtonpost.com/wp-dyn/content/article/2008/07/14/AR2008071400112_pf.html.

41. Mohamed Osman, "Sudan Rejects Genocide Charges Against President," The Associated Press, July 14, 2008.

42. Anita Powell, "AU to Seek Delay in al-Bashir Indictment," The Associated Press, July 21, 2008.

43. Opheera McDoom, "Darfur Rebels Condemn AU on ICC Warrant," Reuters, July 22, www.alertnet.org/thenews/newsdesk/L22832812.htm.

44. Andrew Natsios, "A Disaster in the Making," The Social Science Research Council, Making Sense of Darfur blog, July 12, 2008, www.ssrc.org/blogs/darfur/2008/07/12/a-disaster-in-the-making/.

45. "Media Stakeout with Ambassador Zalmay Khalilzad," Federal News Service, July 22, 2008.

46. Foerstel, *op. cit.*, pp. 7, 13. Also see "Sudan," *Political Handbook of the World*, CQ Press (2008).

47. Danna Harman, "Activists Press China With 'Genocide Olympics' Label," *The Christian Science Monitor*, June 26, 2007, www.csmonitor.com/2007/0626/p13s01-woaf.html.

48. "Letter to Chinese President Hu Jintao," Rep. Steven Rothman Web site, May 7, 2007, http://foreignaffairs.house.gov/press_display.asp?id=345.

49. Alexa Olesen, "China Appoints Special Envoy for Darfur," The Associated Press, May 11, 2007.

50. See Jason Qian and Anne Wu, "Playing the Blame Game in Africa," *The Boston Globe*, July 23, 2007, www.iht.com/articles/2007/07/23/opinion/edqian .php; "China boosts peacekeepers in Darfur," *op.cit.*

51. "China envoy: more humanitarian aid to Darfur," Xinhua, Feb. 26, 2008, www.chinadaily.com.cn/ china/2008-02/26/content_648 3392.htm.

52. Robert J. Saiget, "China says can do no more over Darfur," Agence France-Presse, June 26, 2008, http://afp.google.com/article/ALeqM5g D2S4zFfzj6CZfnluWi5Kq4eFrgw.

53. Danna Harman, "How China's Support of Sudan Shields A Regime Called 'Genocidal,'" *The Christian Science Monitor*, June 26, 2007, www .csmonitor.com/2007/0626/p01s08-woaf. html.

54. Security Council Resolution 1591, United Nations, March 29, 2005, www.un.org/Docs/sc/ unsc_resolutions05.htm.

55. "China says BBC's accusation on arms sales to Sudan 'ungrounded,'" Xinhua, July 18, 2008, http://news.xinhuanet.com/english/2008-07/18/ content_8570601.htm.

56. Saiget, *op. cit.*

57. Audra Ang, "China urges court to rethink Sudan arrest warrant," The Associated Press, July 15, 2008.

58. Harman, *op. cit.*

59. Lydia Polgreen, "China, in New Role, Presses Sudan on Darfur," *International Herald Tribune*, Feb. 23, 2008, www.iht.com/articles/2008/02/23/ africa/23darfur.php.

60. M. W. Daly, *Darfur's Sorrows* (2007), p. 1.

61. "Crisis Shaped by Darfur's Tumultuous Past," PBS Newshour, April 7, 2006, www.pbs.org/newshour/ indepth_coverage/africa/darfur/political-past .html.

62. Gerard Prunier, *Darfur: The Ambiguous Genocide* (2007), pp. 4-5.

63. Daly, *op. cit.*, p. 19.

64. Prunier, *op. cit.*, p. 10. Also see Flint and de Waal, *op. cit.*, p. 8.

65. Prunier, *op. cit*, p. 16.

66. *Ibid.*, pp. 18-19.

67. *Ibid.*, p. 30.

68. *Ibid.*

69. Don Cheadle and John Prendergast, *Not On Our Watch* (2007), p. 53.

70. Prunier, *op. cit.*, pp. 45-46.

71. *Ibid.*

72. Cheadle and Prendergast, *op. cit.*, p. 73.

73. *Ibid.*, p. 55.

74. *Ibid.*, p. 56.

75. *Ibid.*, p. 57.

76. Polgreen, *op. cit.*

77. "Sudan: Nearly 2 million dead as a result of the world's longest running civil war," The U.S. Committee for Refugees, April 2001.

78. "Sudan, Oil and Human Rights," Human Rights Watch, September 2003, www.hrw.org/ reports/2003/sudan1103/index.htm; "Sudan's President Projects the Export of Oil," *Africa News*, July 13, 1998.

79. "President's Revolution Day Address," BBC Worldwide Monitoring, July 5, 1998.

80. "Crisis Shaped by Darfur's Tumultuous Past," *op. cit.*

81. Prunier, *op. cit.*, p. 88.

82. "President Appoints Danforth as Special Envoy to the Sudan," White House press release, Sept. 6, 2001, www.whitehouse.gov/news/releases/2001/ 09/20010906-3.html.

83. Polgreen, *op. cit.*

84. Prunier, *op. cit.*, pp. 95-96.

85. "Darfur Crisis," *op. cit.*, p. 1. Also see Sheryl Gay Stolberg, "Bush Tightens Penalties Against Sudan," *The New York Times*, May 29, 2007, www.nytimes .com/2007/05/29/world/africa/29 cnd-darfur.html.

86. Gerard Prunier, "The Politics of Death in Darfur," *Current History*, May 2006, p. 196.

87. Security Council Resolution 1556, United Nations, July 30, 2004, www.un.org/Docs/sc/ unsc_resolutions04.html.

88. "Security Council Demands Sudan Disarm Militias in Darfur," U.N. press release, July 30, 2004, www.un.org/News/Press/docs/2004/ sc8160.doc.htm.

89. "Background Notes: Sudan," U.S. State Department press release, April 24, 2008, www.state.gov/r/pa/ei/bgn/5424.htm.

90. Scott Baldauf, "Darfur Talks Stall After Rebels Boycott," *The Christian Science Monitor*, Oct. 29, 2007, www.csmonitor.com/2007/1029/p06s01-woaf.html.

91. Lydia Polgreen, "Rebel Ambush in Darfur Kills 5 African Union Peacekeepers in Deadliest Attack on the Force," *The New York Times*, April 3, 2007.

92. "Secretary-General Urges All Parties to Remain Engaged, As Security Council Authorizes Deployment of United Nations-African Union Mission in Sudan," U.N. Security Council press release, July 31, 2007, www.un.org/News/Press/docs/2007/sgsm11110.doc.htm.

93. Jeffrey Gettleman, "Darfur Rebels Kill 10 in Peace Force," *The New York Times*, Oct. 1, 2005, www.nytimes.com/2007/10/01/world/africa/01darfur.html.

94. For background, see Brian Beary, "Separatism Movements," *CQ Global Researcher*, April 2008.

95. "Arab League Backs Recourse to UN on Sudan War Crimes," Agence France-Presse, July 21, 2008.

96. "The Situation in Darfur, the Sudan," International Criminal Court fact sheet, www.icc-cpi.int/library/organs/otp/ICC-OTP_Fact-Sheet-Darfur-20070227_en.pdf.

97. "Arrest Now!" Amnesty International fact sheet, July 17, 2007, http://archive.amnesty.org/library/Index/ENGAFR540272007?open&of=ENG-332.

98. Sarah El Deeb, "Sudan's President Pays Visit to Darfur," The Associated Press, July 24, 2008.

99. Abdelmoniem Abu Edries Ali, "Sudan Appoints Darfur Prosecutor," Agence France-Presse, Aug. 6, 2008.

100. Stephanie McCrummen, "7 Troops Killed in Sudan Ambush," *The Washington Post*, July 10, 2008, www.washingtonpost.com/wp-dyn/content/article/2008/07/09/AR2008070900843.html.

101. Jennie Matthew, "Darfur hopes dim six months into UN peacekeeping," Agence France-Presse, June 25, 2008.

102. "Security Council extends mandate of UN-AU force in Darfur," Agence France-Presse, July 31, 2008.

103. "Aid groups urge helicopters for Darfur," Agence France-Presse, July 31, 2008, http://afp.google.com/article/ALeqM5i2aYTRiEePGRmbRqVQbByF28X_RQ.

104. "Grounded: the International Community's Betrayal of UNAMID — A Joint NGO Report," p. 4, http://darfur.3cdn.net/b5b2056f1398299ffe_x9m6bt7cu.pdf.

105. "Sudan — Darfur: Humanitarian Profile," *op. cit.*

106. "Darfur Humanitarian Profile No. 31," Office of U.N. Deputy Special Representative of the U.N. Secretary-General for Sudan, April 1, 2008, p. 4, www.unsudanig.org/docs/DHP%2031_1%20April%202008_narrative.pdf.

107. Opheera McDoom, "Darfur rebels say they arrest 13 census staff," Reuters, May 4, 2008, www.reuters.com/article/homepageCrisis/idUSL04471626._CH_.2400.

108. "Darfur rebels say they kidnap foreign oil workers," Reuters, Oct. 24, 2007, www.alertnet.org/thenews/newsdesk/MCD470571.htm.

109. Shashank Bengali, "Darfur conflict stokes Chad-Sudan tensions," McClatchy-Tribune News Service, June 14, 2008, www.mcclatchydc.com/160/story/40518.html.

110. Jeffrey Gettleman, "Cracks in the Peace in Oil-Rich Sudan As Old Tensions Fester," *The New York Times*, Sept. 22, 2007, www.nytimes.com/2007/09/22/world/africa/22sudan.html?fta=y.

111. "Sudan — Darfur: Humanitarian Profile," *op. cit.*

112. "Darfur Humanitarian Profile No. 31," *op. cit.*, p. 6.

113. Susan E. Rice, Testimony before Senate Foreign Relations Committee, April 11, 2007.

114. "Darfur envoys end visit without date for peace talks," Agence France-Presse, April 19, 2008.

115. Steve Bloomfield, "Negotiators quit Darfur, saying neither side is ready for peace," *The Independent*

(London), June 27, 2008, www.independent.co.uk/news/world/africa/negotiators-quit-darfur-saying-neither-side-is-ready-for-peace-855431.html.

116. "Darfur mediator arrives for a 'difficult mission,' " *The International Herald Tribune*, July 21, 2008.

117. Opheera McDoom, "Counting begins in disputed Sudan census," Reuters, April 22, 2008, www.reuters.com/article/homepageCrisis/idUSMCD 246493._CH_.2400.

118. Presidential Candidates' Statement on Darfur, *op. cit.* Gedda, *op. cit.*

119. Alex de Waal, "In which a writer's work — forged in the heat of chaos — could actually save lives," *The Washington Post*, June 22, 2008, p. BW 11, www.washingtonpost.com/wp-dyn/content/article/2008/06/19/AR2008061903304_pf.html.

BIBLIOGRAPHY

Books

Cheadle, Don, and John Prendergast, *Not On Our Watch*, Hyperion, 2007.
Cheadle, who starred in the African genocide movie "Hotel Rwanda," and human-rights activist Prendergast explore the Darfur crisis, with tips on how to impact international policy. Forward by Holocaust survivor and Nobel Peace Prize-winner Elie Wiesel, and introduction by Sens. Barack Obama, D-Ill., and Sam Brownback, R-Kan.

Daly, M. W., *Darfur's Sorrow*, Cambridge University Press, 2007.
An historian and long-time observer of Sudan traces the complex environmental, cultural and geopolitical factors that have contributed to today's ongoing conflict. Includes a timeline of events in Darfur since 1650.

Flint, Julie, and Alex de Waal, *Darfur: A Short History of a Long War*, Zed Books, 2005.
Two longtime observers of Sudan and Darfur explore the genesis of today's bloodshed and describe the various actors in the conflict, including the region's many ethnic tribes, the *janjaweed* militia, Libyan leader Muammar Qaddafi and the current Sudanese government.

Prunier, Gerard, *Darfur: The Ambiguous Genocide*, Cornell University Press, 2007.
A French historian who has authored several books on African genocide provides a comprehensive account of the complex environmental, social and political roots of the ongoing fighting in Darfur.

Articles

"Timeline: Conflict in Darfur," *The Washington Post*, June 19, 2008, www.washingtonpost.com/wp-dyn/content/article/2008/06/19/AR2008061902905.html.
This brief narrative outlines the fighting in Darfur and various efforts to find peace over the past five years.

Faris, Stephan, "The Real Roots of Darfur," *The Atlantic Monthly*, April 2007, p. 67.
Climate change and shrinking water supplies have motivated much of the fighting between Darfur's nomadic Arabs and ethnic African farmers.

Macfarquhar, Neil, "Why Darfur Still Bleeds," *The New York Times*, July 13, 2008, p. 5.
A veteran foreign correspondent discusses the many factors fueling the fighting in Darfur and how international leaders now recommend a comprehensive solution.

McCrummen, Stephanie, "A Wide-Open Battle for Power in Darfur," *The Washington Post*, June 20, 2008, p. A1.
The rebellion in Darfur has devolved into chaos and lawlessness that threatens civilians, aid workers and peacekeepers.

Natsios, Andrew, "Sudan's Slide Toward Civil War," *Foreign Affairs*, May/June 2008, Vol. 87, Issue 3, pp. 77-93.
The former U.S. special envoy to Sudan says that while attention is focused on Darfur another bloody civil war could soon erupt between Sudan's north and south.

Prunier, Gerard, "The Politics of Death in Darfur," *Current History*, May 2006, pp. 195-202.
The French historian discusses why the international community has been unable to solve the crisis in Darfur.

Reports and Studies

"Darfur 2007: Chaos by Design," *Human Rights Watch*, **September 2007, http://hrw.org/reports/2007/ sudan0907/.**
Through photographs, maps, first-hand accounts and statistics, the human-rights group summarizes the events that led to the conflict and describes Darfuris' daily struggles.

"Darfur Crisis," *Government Accountability Office*, **November 2006, www.gao.gov/new.items/d0724 .pdf.**
The report analyzes the widely varying estimates on the number of deaths caused by the Darfur conflict and reviews the different methodologies used to track the casualties.

"Displaced in Darfur: A Generation of Anger," *Amnesty International*, **January 2008, www.amnesty .org/en/library/info/AFR54/001/2008.**

Using interviews and first-hand accounts, the human-rights group vividly describes the death and destruction in Darfur and recommends ways to end the fighting.

"Sudan — Darfur: Humanitarian Profile," *United Nations Office for the Coordination of Humanitarian Affairs*, **June 2, 2008, www.unsudanig.org/.../darfur/ data/dhnp/Map%201226%20Darfur%20 Humanitarian%20Profile%20June%203%202008 .pdf.**
This frequently updated U.N. Web site provides maps and charts illustrating areas hit worst by the crisis, the number of attacks on humanitarian workers and the number of people affected by the fighting.

"They Shot at Us As We Fled," *Human Rights Watch*, **May 2008, www.hrw.org/reports/2008/darfur0508/.**
Using first-hand accounts from victims, the report describes how attacks against Darfuri villages in February 2008 violated international humanitarian law.

For More Information

Aegis Trust, The Holocaust Centre, Laxton, Newark, Nottinghamshire NG22 9ZG, UK; +44 (0)1623 836627; www .aegistrust.org. Campaigns against genocide around the world and provides humanitarian aid to genocide victims.

African Union, P.O. Box 3243, Addis Ababa, Ethiopia; +251 11 551 77 00; www.africa-union.org. Fosters economic and social cooperation among 53 African nations and other governments.

Amnesty International, 1 Easton St., London, WC1X 0DW, United Kingdom; +44-20-74135500; www.amnesty.org. Promotes human rights worldwide, with offices in 80 countries.

Council on Foreign Relations, 1779 Massachusetts Ave., N.W., Washington, DC 20036; (202) 518-3400; www.cfr .org. A nonpartisan think tank that offers extensive resources, data and experts on foreign policy issues.

Human Rights Watch, 350 Fifth Ave., 34th Floor, New York, NY 10118-3299; (212) 290-4700; www.hrw.org. Investigates human-rights violations worldwide.

Justice Africa, 1C Leroy House, 436 Essex Road, London N1 3QP, United Kingdom; +44 (0) 207 354 8400; www .justiceafrica.org. A research and advocacy organization that campaigns for human rights and social justice in Africa.

Save Darfur Coalition, Suite 335, 2120 L St., N.W., Washington, DC 20037; (800) 917-2034; www.savedarfur .org. An alliance of more than 180 faith-based, advocacy and humanitarian organizations working to stop the violence in Darfur.

Social Science Research Council, 810 Seventh Ave., New York, NY 10019; (212) 377-2700; www.ssrc.org. Studies complex social, cultural, economic and political issues.

TransAfrica Forum, 1629 K St., N.W., Suite 1100, Washington, DC 20006; (202) 223-1960; www.transafricaforum .org. Campaigns for human rights and sustainable development in Africa and other countries with residents of African descent.

7

Crisis in Pakistan

Can the Fragile Democracy Survive?

Robert Kiener

Asif Ali Zardari became Pakistan's new president in September after the resignation of Pervez Musharraf in August. The widower of slain former Prime Minister Benazir Bhutto (in portrait), Zardari faces a multitude of challenges, including a spike in terrorist bombings, rising Islamic fundamentalism, a weakened democracy, a faltering economy and growing anger over U.S. anti-terrorist strikes into Pakistani tribal territories.

From *CQ Global Researcher*, December 2008.

Credit (vertical): AFP/Getty Images/Aamir Qureshi

Just after 8 p.m. on September 20 a large truck crashed into the security gates in front of the heavily guarded Marriott Hotel in Islamabad. Seconds later, suicide bombers in the truck detonated its tarpaulin-covered cargo — more than 1,200 pounds of TNT and RDX explosives — killing at least 54 people, injuring hundreds and destroying much of the luxurious landmark.[1]

For visitors and residents alike, the Marriott had been more than a hotel. It was the meeting place for Westerners as well as Pakistan's elite, attracting businessmen, government officials and journalists. Located in the heart of Pakistan's capital — just a few hundred yards from Parliament and the homes of the president and prime minister — the well-guarded Marriott had been a secure and quiet oasis in a boisterous city. Indeed, newly elected President Asif Ali Zardari and other top leaders had reportedly been scheduled to dine there on the night of the attack, changing their plans only at the last minute.[2]

The blast — quickly dubbed Pakistan's 9/11 — came on the very day of President Zardari's maiden address to Parliament, in which he promised to banish terrorists from Pakistan: "We must root out terrorism and extremism wherever and whenever they may rear their ugly heads."[3]

Shortly after the bombing, Interior Minister Rehmam Mali echoed other Pakistani officials and Western diplomats when he claimed the attack had been organized by Taliban militants associated with al Qaeda based in Pakistan's vast, mountainous region known as the Federally Administered Tribal Areas (FATA), which borders Afghanistan.[4]

Between a Rock and a Hard Place

Sandwiched between Afghanistan and India, Pakistan has been battered by growing terrorism and Islamic fundamentalism, a weakening democracy and a faltering economy. Some observers question whether the fledgling democracy — the size of Texas and Tennessee combined and the world's second-largest Muslim nation — could become a failed state. Taliban militants linked to the al Qaeda terrorist organization are based in the lawless mountain region of Pakistan bordering Afghanistan known as the Federally Administered Tribal Areas, where terrorist leader Osama bin Laden is thought to be hiding. Conflict with India over Kashmir adds to Pakistan's growing instability.

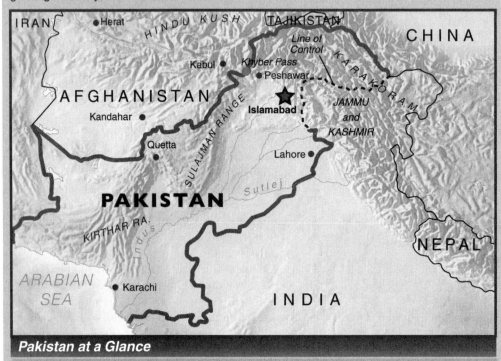

Pakistan at a Glance

Area: 310,402 sq. miles, or about the size of Texas and Tennessee combined; excludes disputed areas of Jammu and Kashmir.

Population: 156.9 million (2006), excluding Jammu and Kashmir; growing at 2% (2008 estimate)

Unemployment rate: 5.6% (2007)

Religion: Muslim — 95%, other (Christian and Hindu) — 5%

Government: The president is elected for a five-year term by the provincial assemblies and the Parliament, which consists of the Senate and the National Assembly. The prime minister — elected by the National Assembly — is head of the ruling party or coalition and is considered the head of government. The president — who is the head of state — oversees the military and can dissolve the National Assembly, effectively dismissing the prime minister and triggering new elections.

Economy: Decades of internal political disputes and an ongoing confrontation with India, primarily over Jammu and Kashmir, have discouraged foreign investment. Since 2001, economic recovery has been bolstered by significant foreign assistance, renewed access to global markets and reforms recommended by the International Monetary Fund — notably, privatization of the banking sector. Gross domestic product grew by 6-8 percent from 2004 to 2007, and poverty levels decreased by 10 percent since 2001.

Sources: Political Handbook of the World 2008, CQ Press, 2008; *The World Factbook*, Central Intelligence Agency

"All roads lead to FATA," said Mali, referring to the remote, lawless area where many believe Osama bin Laden — mastermind of the 9/11 terrorist attacks in the United States — is hiding.[5]

Ever since Pakistani troops stormed Islamabad's Red Mosque in mid-2007 to root out militants who had occupied it, killing an estimated 100 people during the takeover, a coalition of Taliban groups known as Tereek Taliban-e-Pakistan has declared war on the Pakistani government. Many experts see Pakistan's handling of the Red Mosque incident as a turning point that eventually led to the September attack on the Marriott.

The horrific blast left nearly 60 people dead and a smoldering 40-foot-wide by 25-foot-deep crater in front of the burned-out hotel. It also delivered a chilling message. "The bombing sent a signal to the fragile government and authorities that militants had muscle and could extend that muscle into the very heart of the capital," explains Farzana Shaikh, the Pakistani author of the forthcoming *Making Sense of Pakistan* and an associate fellow at London's Royal Institute of International Affairs. "They were telling the government they are a force to be reckoned with."

Since the Sept. 11, 2001, terrorist attacks on the United States, more and more militants have sought safe haven in FATA and in the equally rugged North-West Frontier Province (NWFP), the smallest of the country's four provinces. (*See map, p. 175.*) "Militants are launching attacks on Afghanistan and Pakistan itself from these regions," says Hassan Abbas, a former Pakistani government official and now a fellow at Harvard University's John F. Kennedy School of Government. "Years of neglect, incompetent governance and failure to effectively fight religious extremism have allowed the Taliban and other extremist groups to expand their influence there."

As many observers have confirmed, Taliban warlords have taken near-total control inside the tribal areas, effectively replacing Pakistani government control with their own strict form of Islam.[6] In addition, say American officials, al Qaeda has hundreds of terrorist training camps throughout FATA.[7] Many believe that former Prime Minister Benazir Bhutto's December 2007 assassination was ordered by Taliban leader Baitullah Mehsud, who is based in the region. (*See sidebar, p. 180.*) In a recent Council on Foreign Relations report, former State Department official Dan Markey wrote, "Should another

9/11-type attack take place in the United States, it will likely have its origins in this area."[8]

Almost overnight, the growth and influence of the terrorists has put Pakistan on the radar screens of leaders around the world. Many point to the world's second-most-populous Muslim nation as a "safe haven" for terrorists and home to a growing militant movement that threatens its stability. The late November terrorist attacks in Mumbai that killed more than 173 people underscored that point. India has blamed the deadly assaults on a Pakistani militant group, Lashkar-e-Taiba, dedicated to ending Indian rule in Kashmir. (*See story, p. 186.*) The attacks are expected to harm Indo-Pakistan relations, since India has complained bitterly in the past that Islamabad allows militants to strike India from within Pakistan's borders.

As tensions between the two countries rise, the security of Pakistan's nuclear weapons also is being questioned. With a weakening economy and social unrest spreading within its borders, many are asking whether Pakistan could soon become a "failed state" with a deadly arsenal at risk.

"Pakistan may be the single, greatest challenge facing the next American president," contends Pakistan expert Stephen Philip Cohen, a fellow at the Brookings Institution think tank in Washington, D.C.[9]

Along with the Taliban, other extremist movements are on the rise across the nation. For example, Balochistan Province, which covers 44 percent of Pakistan, is home to burgeoning nationalistic insurgencies. And a secular separatist movement has taken root in Sindh Province, the backbone of Pakistan's economy.

As a result, terrorism-related violence has racked up grim statistics. During the first eight months of 2008, 324 blasts, including 28 suicide attacks, killed more than 619 people throughout the country.[10] In fact, more people were killed in suicide bombings in Pakistan during the first eight months of 2008 than in Iraq or Afghanistan, according to Pakistan's Inter Services Intelligence agency, the ISI. But last year was even bloodier: Some 2,100 citizens, soldiers and police died in terrorism-related violence, plus nearly 1,500 terrorists, according to the South Asia Terrorism Portal, run by the Institute for Conflict Management in Delhi, India.[11] The U.S. government's National Counterterrorism Center puts the non-terrorist toll at 1,335. (*See graph, p. 174.*)

Terror Attack Fatalities Jump Five-Fold

Attacks by al Qaeda and other terrorist groups killed more than 1,300 security personnel and civilians in Pakistan in 2007 — a fivefold increase from just three years earlier. Most of the victims, by far, have been civilians — with nearly 1,000 killed in 2007.

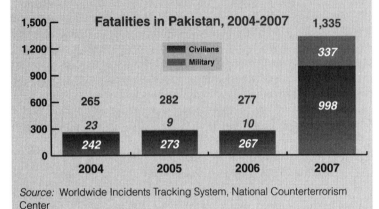

Fatalities in Pakistan, 2004-2007

Source: Worldwide Incidents Tracking System, National Counterterrorism Center

The brutality of the attacks has been staggering. For instance, this past summer:

- In Waziristan, a mountainous region in the FATA, Mehsud's followers slaughtered 22 government negotiators who had come to discuss a cease-fire pact.[12]
- In July a terrorist killed 19 people when he blew himself up near the Red Mosque, marking the one-year anniversary of the July 2007 siege there.[13]
- Two suicide bombers in August killed more than 60 people outside Pakistan's largest weapons factory in Wah, some 20 miles north of Islamabad.[14]

As the many al Qaeda and Taliban-inspired attacks show, Pakistan has become ground zero in global terrorism. But militants' attacks are only part of Pakistan's troubles. "Terrorism, militancy and separatism are symptoms of Pakistan's bigger problem," explains Akbar Ahmed, Pakistan's former high commissioner to Great Britain and the holder of the Ibn Khaldun chair in Islamic Studies at American University in Washington, D.C. "The nation is in crisis. Many are beginning to call it a 'failed state.'"

Amid the turmoil, President Zardari, Bhutto's widower, is scrambling to unify his splintered nation. But he faces massive challenges. He must balance relations with the United States — which is urging him to step up attacks on militants in FATA — with the concerns of many Pakistanis who believe the war on terror has nothing to do with Pakistan. According to a recent Pew survey, nearly two-thirds of Pakistanis feel the United States is one of the countries posing the greatest threat to Pakistan.[15]

Zardari cannot be seen as being "Washington's puppet," but that increasingly is the perception, especially since the U.S. military recently has been crossing into Pakistan to attack terrorist strongholds. And on Nov. 18 American troops in Afghanistan fired an artillery barrage at insurgents in Pakistan's tribal region.[16] Meanwhile, the new president must appease opposition parties — especially the powerful wing of the Pakistan Muslim League headed by former Prime Minister Nawaz Sharif that dropped out of the coalition government this year — and the military, which fell from power when unpopular Gen. Pervez Musharraf resigned the presidency on Aug. 18, 2008.

"Political stability is a key to Pakistan's survival," explains Shaikh at the Royal Institute of International Affairs. "But the present leaders are at a disadvantage. Years of military rule have stunted the development of political rule."

And with the recent weakening of Pakistan's formerly robust economy — gross domestic product grew on average nearly 7 percent annually under Musharraf — the outlook appears even more forbidding. The rupee has hit an all-time low against the dollar, and inflation — about 30 percent — is the highest in 30 years. In October Standard & Poor's cut Pakistan's credit rating for the second time this year; foreign investors are pulling out of the stock market; and foreign-exchange reserves are running out.[17]

According to *The Economist* magazine's Intelligence Unit, the economy is in a "state of crisis."[18] With economic woes come higher taxes and higher costs on staples like food and power. Electricity shortages are soaring, along with food prices, which jumped more than 20 percent last March.[19] In October protesters in Lahore, the country's second-largest city, ransacked a power company's offices and burned their electric bills. Phasing out government subsidies on imported fuel has led to skyrocketing prices for everything from gasoline to cooking oil.

"Every day that passes, things get worse. . . . The economy is in a downspin," said Zubair Iqbal, a Pakistani economist retired from the International Monetary Fund and now an adjunct scholar at the Middle East Institute in Washington.[20]

Relations with India, recently on the mend after years of conflict over Kashmir and other issues, received a huge setback after the recent terrorist attacks in Mumbai. Although Zardari has labeled Kashmiri guerrillas as "terrorists" and says Pakistan will not continue its "nuclear first-strike option," the Mumbai attacks have damaged that progress.

Pakistan's myriad woes threaten to further fragment an already splintered nation. The weak economy and a notoriously anemic education system make young, dissatisfied Pakistanis more susceptible to recruitment by insurgents. "The more people become socially and economically marginalized, the greater the risk for instability," explains Harvard's Abbas. "Chaos — with the streets full of angry, violent protesters — is a real possibility unless these problems are addressed."

Since its founding in 1947, Pakistan has survived despite constantly lurching between democracy and military dictatorships, but some wonder if the oncoming "perfect storm" of insurrection, political fragility, a weakening economy and an increasingly disenfranchised populace may finally topple

A Diverse Linguistic Landscape

Pakistan's numerous tongues reflect the country's ethnic and religious diversity (top). Although Urdu is the official language, only 8 percent of the population uses it as their primary language, while 48 percent speak Punjabi. Balochistan is the largest of Pakistan's four provinces (bottom).

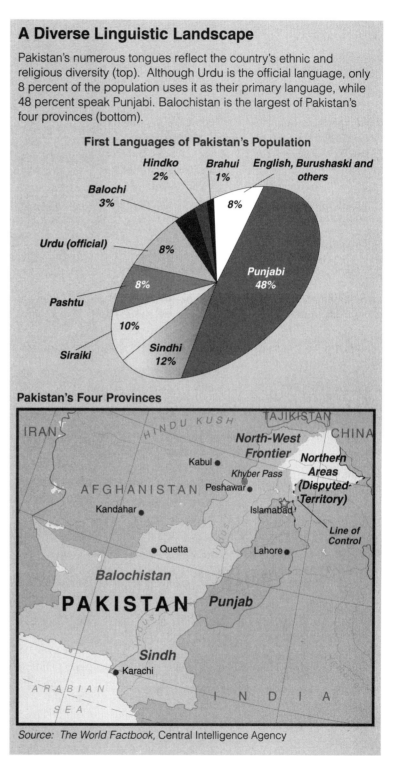

First Languages of Pakistan's Population

Hindko 2%
Brahui 1%
English, Burushaski and others
Balochi 3%
8%
Urdu (official) 8%
Punjabi 48%
Pashtu 8%
Siraiki 10%
Sindhi 12%

Pakistan's Four Provinces

Source: The World Factbook, Central Intelligence Agency

the nation. The situation in Pakistan is "very bad," with the country itself "on the edge," according to U.S. officials who recently drafted a top secret National Intelligence Estimate. One official portrayed the situation in Pakistan as: "No money, no energy, no government."[21]

"Pakistan is in even scarier shape than most of the so-called experts are willing to admit," wrote Sumit Ganguly, a longtime Pakistan watcher and director of research at the Center on American and Global Security at Indiana University. "Pakistan is facing an existential crisis — on its streets and in its courts, barracks and Parliament."[22]

As Pakistan fights for its survival, here are some of the questions being asked:

Can Pakistan control its radical militants?

When Adm. Mike Mullen, chairman of the U.S. Joint Chiefs of Staff, addressed the powerful House Armed Services Committee in September, he sent a clear message to both Pakistan and the militants that operate within its borders. He called for "a new, more comprehensive military strategy for the region that covers both sides of that border," adding that the United States must work with Pakistan to "eliminate safe havens." Until then, he continued, "the enemy will only keep coming."[23]

In marked contrast to previous U.S. comments, analysts say, Mullen was expressing America's impatience with Pakistan's lack of control over its border regions and the resulting effect on the U.S. war in Afghanistan. "In the past, Washington has listened to Pakistan's explanations of [its] inability to control the militants in these areas and subsequently refrained from pushing the Pakistani leadership harder for fear of disrupting bilateral relations," noted Lisa Curtis, senior research fellow on South Asia at the conservative Heritage Foundation.[24]

But times have changed. The United States has lost confidence in Pakistan's ability to control the militancy within its borders. And with U.S. forces in Afghanistan coming under attack from al Qaeda and Taliban militants operating from safe havens in Pakistan, the United States is pushing Zardari to step up Pakistan's anti-insurgent campaign. Many experts say the United States has a right to be frustrated, having sent more than $11 billion to Pakistan since 9/11, primarily in military aid intended to help combat the militants.[25]

Is the "gloves off" approach working? Pakistan's Army Chief of Staff, Gen. Ashfaq Parvez Kayani, claims his campaign against the Taliban and al Qaeda in the tribal area of Bajaur has killed 1,500 insurgents over the last year. But he strongly criticized a cross-border raid by U.S. troops on Sept. 4, vowing to defend Pakistan's "sovereignty and territorial integrity" at all costs.[26] Meanwhile, analysts say it is still too early to tell whether Pakistan's military is fully behind the battle against Islamic extremists.

It's also unclear whether Pakistan has the political will to clean out the terrorists. According to Husain Haqqani, Pakistan's ambassador to the United States, "The great majority of Pakistan's elected leaders believe firmly that fighting terrorism is Pakistan's own war."[27]

But experts disagree on this point. Recent parliamentary proceedings showed little evidence that Pakistani politicians have the will to battle the terrorists.[28] This potential impasse highlights a recurring problem with what President Zardari has called "Pakistan's war."

"If Pakistan ever wants to control the militants, it needs to have the political will and the [military] capacity to succeed," says former State Department official Markey. "Right now, it has problems with both."

Convincing Pakistan's people and politicians that going to war against the militants is in the nation's best interest is proving to be a tough sell.

"Many members of Parliament are reluctant to come out in support of a war on militants," explains Shuja Nawaz, a Pakistani political analyst and author of *Crossed Swords: Pakistan, Its Army and the Wars Within.* "Some are concerned that the present government may not be stable, and they are also reluctant to advocate violence against fellow Muslims. But the government has to convince all interested parties that a new, much broader, insurgency is affecting the man on the street, and that it is penetrating to the very heart of the country."

Some believe Pakistan needs a "national consensus" to curb the militants. "The recent program to curb militancy that the Parliament has drawn up is a first step," says the Royal Institute of International Affairs' Shaikh. "But Pakistan is a divided Muslim state, and many will never agree to fight what is seen as war against other Muslims."

For example, the Jamiat Ulema-e-Islam-Fazl, a religious party that is part of the ruling coalition with the Pakistan Peoples Party, recently proposed that the army immediately stop fighting the militants in FATA. "This is not a war we want to be part of," said Jehangir Tareen, a Pakistan Muslim

League politician, expressing the feeling of many in his party. "There is a sentiment that we are being pushed to do this by the United States. We want this war to end."[29]

Clearly, the government has a long way to go to convince more Pakistanis that the war against terrorists operating in Pakistan is their war, not just America's.

The political will to back such a fight is important, but having the military capacity to carry out that battle is even more important. Although Pakistan's military has lost more than 2,000 soldiers in battles against the militants, some wonder if the military is firmly convinced of the need for the conflict.

"The army has to come out and support Zardari's strong statements in deed and word," pointed out Pakistan expert Cohen at the Brookings Institution. So far, however, it has been silent, he noted.[30]

The military's silence may have more to do with politics than strategy. "The army wants the government to lead and take the political responsibility for going after the extremists so that the army's present unpopularity does not get worse," noted Lahore-based journalist and author Ahmed Rashid.[31]

The military has also been criticized for not having a credible approach to the fight against extremists, particularly since the military oversaw the buildup of lawless militancy during Musharraf's rule. "The army lacks strategy or coherence — one day bombing villages in FATA, the next day announcing ceasefires and offering compensation to the militants," noted Rashid. "It has failed to protect the people of FATA — some 800,000 of a population of just 3.5 million have fled the region since 2006 — terrified of both the army and the Taliban."[32]

The military also needs fundamental operational and structural changes, including — first — retooling itself for counterinsurgency. "The army has long been fixated on war with India," notes Markey. "It needs to change its culture and retrain its members in counterinsurgency methods."

Harvard's Abbas believes Pakistan needs a new "central command" to wage war on the militants. "Presently, there is no coordination, no planning with the civilian outfits. No agency is in complete control of this war," he says. Law enforcement also needs to be modernized and brought into the war, he contends. "Historically, where terrorism was defeated it was by law enforcement. Police have had successes in Pakistan at this, why not empower them?"

Terrorists Target Luxury Hotels

Two hotels popular with foreigners — Islamabad's luxurious Marriott (top) in Pakistan and the Taj Mahal in Mumbai, India (bottom) — were attacked recently by Pakistani terrorists, according to intelligence officials. Pakistan officials say the Sept. 20 Marriott attack, which killed nearly 60 people and has been dubbed "Pakistan's 9/11," was organized by al Qaeda-linked Taliban militants based in Pakistan's Federally Administered Tribal Areas. Indian officials say the three days of savage assaults in late November at several locations in Mumbai, which killed 173 and have been called "India's 9/11," were carried out by Islamic extremists from Pakistani-controlled Kashmir. The same group has attacked India on several previous occasions, aggravating tensions between the two nuclear-armed neighbors.

In the end, though, guns alone are not enough to defeat militancy. Economic, educational and social infrastructure improvements in the region will help win hearts and minds, say many experts. "A closer look into Pakistan's counterinsurgency strategy since the launch of

Lawless Tribal Areas Harbor Terrorists

Pakistan's Federally Administered Tribal Areas, stretching along the Pakistan-Afghanistan border, consist of seven Pashtun-dominated "agencies": Khyber, Kurram, Orakzai, Mohmand, Bajaur, North Waziristan and South Waziristan. The British created the enclave to give maximum autonomy to the fiercely independent Pashtuns and to serve as a buffer between then-undivided India and Afghanistan. Smuggling, drug trafficking and gun-running flourish in the region, which has become a safe haven for Taliban and al Qaeda insurgents.

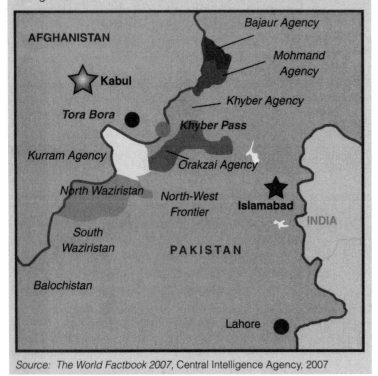

Source: *The World Factbook 2007,* Central Intelligence Agency, 2007

operations in 2003 reveals a policy focused entirely on a military approach, wholly ignoring the prospect of winning hearts and minds of local Pashtun tribesmen," wrote Pakistani journalist Imtiaz Ali. "For that reason more than any other, the seven-year-long counterinsurgency strategy pushed single-handedly by former President Musharraf has proved ineffective, if not downright disastrous."[33]

In the end, it is likely that only a modernized, coordinated and multilateral approach to combating militancy will work. As Gen. Kayani has noted, "There are no quick fixes in this war. Falling for short-term gains while

ignoring our long-term interest is not the right way forward."[34]

Can democracy survive in Pakistan?

How important is democracy to some Pakistanis? If last February's election — after nearly 10 years of rule by military dictatorship — was anything to go by, it can be a matter of life and death.

On Feb. 9, 2008, a suicide bomber killed 27 and injured more than 30 attending a political rally near Charsadda in the NWFP. A week later another suicide bomber killed 47 and injured 109 outside a candidate's residence in the FATA town of Parachinar. In March alone, 37 workers from different political parties were killed.[35]

But committed voters were not deterred. Waiting her turn to vote in Rawalpindi on Feb. 18, 57-year-old Sakina Bibi spoke for many when she said, "I am not worried. It is up to God. If I am meant to die, I will die here."[36]

Such courage speaks to the point made by American University's Ahmed: "Pakistanis know the nation was founded on democracy. If democracy fails, Pakistan fails. Remember how we returned to democracy this time. It wasn't thanks to the Americans who preached democratic ideals while supporting a dictator. Lawyers, activists and people marching peacefully in the streets fought for it. Democracy is the lifeblood of Pakistan."

But democracy is more than just free elections. In order to work, elections must be supported by a free press, an unfettered judiciary and a viable opposition, say experts. Before being toppled, President Musharraf attacked some in the West for its "obsession" with democracy. Give Pakistan time, was his message.

But Pakistan's front pages loudly disagreed. "No, not an obsession!" blared a typical headline.[37] When asked recently how important it was to live in a democratic country, 8.4 out of 10 Pakistani respondents ranked it very high.[38]

Nonetheless, the country has been plagued by a "revolving-door democracy," with civilian governments regularly being replaced by military dictatorships. In fact, no elected government has ever completed its term in office. The military has ruled Pakistan for more years than civilians have, severely stunting democratic institutions. "History shows that dictatorships destroy the social fabric of societies and diminish the capacity of state institutions to function effectively," says Abbas of Harvard.

How, then, can democracy survive? For starters, Pakistan's political parties must become more representative of the nation's diversity, says former State Department official Markey. "Pakistan has elections and aspirations to democracy, but it needs effective, representative political parties for it to grow and prosper," he contends.

For too long Pakistan's major political parties have been dynastic, feudal, family-run and representative of the small ruling elite, say Pakistan analysts. Many are merely "affinity groups of the rich and famous," according to Brookings's Cohen. Real political parties, unlike interest groups or nongovernmental organizations, "will aggregate diverse and even conflicting interests."[39]

Most democracy experts also say a democracy needs an informed, educated populace, newspapers that are free to report what they want and an independent judiciary. No Pakistani politician denies that the country needs a better education system in order for democracy to grow and survive. But those same politicians seem to have done little to help the Pakistanis who cannot read or write — nearly half of the adult population — or the 40 percent of children who don't attend school.

Furthermore, the military inhibits democracy's survival in Pakistan. As an old Pakistani joke goes, "All countries have armies, but here, an army has a country." Although the army is no longer in power, it still has a strong influence on political matters. Experts say Pakistan's government must establish ways it can work with the military without being dominated by it. To foster democracy, "Pakistan needs a policy process that integrates civilian activities with military activities," says Markey.

Although Gen. Kayani assures the government he has no desire to return the military to the "governing business," history makes many Pakistanis skeptical. "To ensure that, the military needs to be contained," says Shaikh, of

Militants from the Tereek Taliban-e-Pakistan group in South Waziristan guard some of the 38 police and security personnel they kidnapped in September. The group has declared war on the Pakistani government. Since then 25 of the hostages have been released.

the Royal Institute of International Affairs. Many experts agree that the military needs to take a back seat while Pakistan finds a workable model of democracy.

"Pakistan has been ruled by military regimes for over half its existence," wrote the Heritage Foundation's Curtis. "The military's pervasive involvement in civilian affairs has stifled the development of civil society and democratic institutions. The time has come to reverse this trend. Pakistan's future stability depends on it."[40]

With few exceptions — such as Pakistan's founder Mohammad Ali Jinnah — the nation's democratic leaders have been less than stellar. Civilian leaders who followed in the wake of military dictator Gen. Mohammad Zia ul-Haq have been especially criticized. "Most Pakistanis believe that post-Zia politicians have been self-seeking, corrupt and unprincipled," wrote Owen Bennett Jones, a BBC journalist and author of *Pakistan: Eye of the Storm*.[41] *The Economist* was even blunter: "In truth, both Miss Bhutto and Mr. [Nawaz] Sharif were lousy prime ministers."[42]

Some of the blame for weak democratic leadership can be laid at the doorstep of autocratic and dictatorial military governments. "Civilian successor governments acquire and retain these powers from the military regime," explains Pakistani political analyst Nawaz. "These mitigate against free-flowing democracy." President Zardari, for example, has retained many

Deadly Taliban Commander Stays in the Shadows

Baitullah Mehsud is linked to scores of suicide attacks in Pakistan.

For someone who has been called "The Newest Enemy No. 1 in the War on Terror," and "al Qaeda's newest triggerman," remarkably little is known about Baitullah Mehsud, the powerful commander of Taliban forces in South Waziristan, part of Pakistan's mountainous and lawless Federally Administered Tribal Areas.[1]

He is said to have planned scores of suicide attacks on government and military targets in Pakistan, and many believe he ordered the Dec. 27 assassination of former Prime Minister Benazir Bhutto. But, according to *Jane's Terrorism and Insurgency News*, although he has become "the most powerful militant commander in Pakistan, he remains a shadowy figure with perhaps a larger-than-life reputation."[2]

After fighting for the Taliban in Afghanistan in the 1990s, the black-bearded jihadist leader first popped up on anti-terrorist radar screens after being promoted to a Taliban command position following the death of militant leader Nek Mohammad, who was killed in a missile attack in June 2004.[3]

Since then, Mehsud's rise to power reflects the transformation of Pakistan into al Qaeda's main battleground and safe haven. In December 2007 he was appointed to head the Pakistan Taliban movement, known as Tereek Taliban-e-Pakistan. Operating under Afghan Taliban commander Jalaluddin Haqqani, Mehsud is believed to command some 20,000 fighters.[4]

Mehsud shuns publicity and refuses to have his photograph taken. During those rare occasions when he gives interviews, he covers his face with a black cloth.[5] He reportedly rarely sleeps in the same bed two nights in a row and travels in a convoy surrounded by armed guards. A Pashtun tribesman, Mehsud was born in the South Waziristan village of Landidog and is said to be in his mid-30s. According to one analyst, Mehsud is "not well educated" but is famous for his political acumen and military skills. His colleagues say he's "a natural leader who has great ability to infuse vitality among his followers."[6]

Mehsud once admitted to an interviewer that he has crossed into Afghanistan to fight foreign troops. It is, he claims, the duty of Muslims to wage jihad against "the infidel forces of America and Britain." As he told the BBC last year, "Only jihad can bring peace to the world."[7]

Last year Mehsud said his aim was to target London and New York City.

powers more associated with a dictator than a democratic leader, such as immunity from prosecution and the power to dissolve Parliament and to select Supreme Court judges.

Zardari also must live down his reputation as "Mr. Ten Percent" — a reference to his alleged involvement in kickback schemes while serving as investment minister during his wife's second term. Another hurdle: Because the president is appointed by the Parliament instead of having to face a popular vote, Zardari, like Musharraf before him, has absolute power without a mandate from the electorate.

He does have determination, however. Referring to the 11 years he spent in jail on various charges (he was never convicted of anything), he has written: "Those years made me a stronger person and hardened my resolve to fight for democracy. I wish I could do it at my wife's side. Now I must do it in my wife's place."[43] Only time will tell if he can nurture democracy in such harsh surroundings.

There may be some within the military as well as militants who do not see democracy as a necessity for Pakistan, but most analysts agree it is a prerequisite for the nation's survival. "Democracy must survive," says American University's Ahmed, "It is crucial to Pakistan's existence."

Ambassador Haqqani is optimistic. "Like all transitions, the transition from one-man rule to a pluralist system will be tough," he said. "But Pakistanis have proven their commitment to the democratic idea after four failed military dictatorships in 60 years."[44]

Perhaps the last words on the importance of democracy's survival in Pakistan should go to the dynamic Bhutto, who gave her life for it. As she reportedly told her son Bilawal, who may one day inherit her mission,

Intelligence sources cite reports of a Mehsud-dispatched terrorist cell recently arrested in Spain as proof of his global ambitions. He and his troops are skilled fighters. In August 2007 they captured more than 250 Pakistani soldiers, who reportedly surrendered without a fight. Mehsud then demanded that the military pull out of the tribal area and the government release 30 imprisoned militants. To emphasize his demands he had three of the soldiers beheaded. President Pervez Musharraf soon released 25 of the jailed militants.

Given Mehsud's penchant for secrecy, it's not surprising that Pakistani papers and television news reports have been full of reports that he was gravely ill, dying or already dead from illnesses ranging from diabetes to typhoid or attacks by the Pakistani military. In October 2008, however, a Taliban spokesman in Pakistan said he was "fit and well."[8]

Apparently Mehsud knows it is only a matter of time before he falls victim to a Pakistan army bullet or a U.S. drone missile. As he reportedly told a Taliban leader, "The Angel of Death is flying over our heads all the time."[9]

Pakistan's top Taliban leader Baitullah Mehsud, center, with back to camera, talks to reporters in South Waziristan. Mehsud reportedly masterminded recent suicide attacks on government and military targets in Pakistan and may have ordered the assassination of former Prime Minister Benazir Bhutto last year.

[4] Syed Shoaib Hasan, "Profile: Baitullah Mehsud," BBC News, Dec. 28, 2007.

[5] "Where is Baitullah Mehsud," *The Nation*, Sept. 28, 2008, www.nation.com.pk/pakistan-news-newspaper-daily-english-online/Regional/Karachi/29-Sep-2008/Where-is-Baitullah-Mehsud.

[6] Sohail Abdul Nasir, "Terrorism Focus: Baitullah Mehsud: South Waziristan Unofficial Amir," Jamestown Foundation, www.jamestown.org, July 5, 2006.

[7] Hasan, *op. cit.*

[8] "Top Pakistan militant not dead," BBC News, Oct. 1, 2008.

[9] Yousafzai and Moreau, *op. cit.*

[1] Sami Yousafzai and Ron Moreau, "Al Qaeda's newest triggerman," *Newsweek*, Jan. 14, 2008.

[2] "Pakistan's Most Wanted," *Jane's Terrorism and Insurgency News*, Feb. 12, 2008.

[3] See David Rohde and Mohammed Khan, "Ex-Fighter for Taliban Dies in Strike in Pakistan," *The New York Times*, June 19, 2004, p. A6.

"Democracy is the best revenge." And just before returning to Pakistan last year, she said, "This is the beginning of a long journey for Pakistan back to democracy, and I hope my going back is a catalyst for change. We must believe that miracles can happen."[45]

Are Pakistan's nuclear weapons secure?

Pakistanis could not believe their eyes. On Feb. 4, 2004, a national hero broke down in tears as he confessed his crime, broadcast on millions of television screens across the nation. But this was no mere politician begging for forgiveness. It was Abdul Qadeer Khan, the Pakistani nuclear scientist who had achieved cult status for his role in creating the nation's first nuclear bomb. "A.Q. Kahn," as he is known, confessed to masterminding and running a global, black-market operation trading in nuclear weapon-making materials.

For 15 years, Kahn had sold designs and technology necessary to manufacture the fuel for nuclear weapons to Iran, North Korea and Libya. He was arrested after the United States discovered a shipment of parts for centrifuges that were believed to have been manufactured in Malaysia to his design and were being shipped from Dubai to Libya.[46] An official of the International Atomic Energy Agency dubbed Khan's operation the "Wal-Mart of private-sector proliferation."[47]

How did Khan carry out his illicit operation for so long? Although he claimed to have received no help from Pakistan's military, few believe he could have acted without its assistance. The day after his tearful confession, President Musharraf pardoned him and put him under house arrest, where he remains to this day.

Khan's global operation caused many to question the safety of Pakistan's nuclear arsenal. With militancy and political and religious unrest threatening the world's only nuclear-armed Islamic nation, one question has special relevance today: Could al Qaeda or another terrorist group gain control of one of Pakistan's nuclear weapons?

"The Pakistanis have an enormous national interest in making their nuclear weapons secure, because they see them as a guarantee against Indian aggression or destruction," says former State Department official Markey. "So they have devoted a lot of resources to safeguard them."

Intelligence sources estimate that Pakistan, which tested its first nuclear weapon in 1998, has an estimated 50-120 nuclear warheads, held in secret locations. Various nuclear components reportedly are stored in heavily guarded underground bunkers at military bases around the country. After the 9/11 terrorist attacks, at the urging of the United States, Pakistan agreed to upgrade the security of its nuclear weapons. The United States has spent almost $100 million on a secret program to help Pakistan secure the weapons, according to *The New York Times*.[48]

"I don't see any indication right now that security of those weapons is in jeopardy, but clearly we are very watchful, as we should be," said Joint Chiefs Chairman Mullen last November.[49]

Harvard's Abbas, who has studied the system, notes, "Experts say the command-and-control system is very advanced. The army has taken the best from the U.S. and the UK." The personnel guarding the facilities reportedly were trained in the United States. In addition, a multilayered system of safeguards surrounds the weapons, and officials in charge are screened for everything from mental instability to having sympathies for al Qaeda or the Taliban.

Pakistan also protects the weapons' integrity by isolating the triggers (the fissile core) from the rest of the weapons. Thus, thieves would have to take over several bunkers to get a complete bomb. "Although the U.S. experts may not have visited the bunkers, because the Pakistanis jealously guard their exact location, the U.S. has offered its most advanced safeguards," says political analyst Nawaz.

However, "There is a concern that pro-Islamist military officers could gain access to the weapons in the future," says Shaikh, at London's Royal Institute of International Affairs. And some experts worry about renegade or rogue scientists helping militants acquire or design a bomb.

There is reason for such concern. In 2001 two Pakistani nuclear scientists were detained on suspicion of passing secrets to the Taliban. One of them, Sultan Bashiruddin Mahmood, had met several times with bin Laden in 2000 and 2001. Bin Laden reportedly asked the deeply conservative Muslim two chilling questions: "How can a nuclear bomb be made? Can you help us make one?" Both meetings occurred before 9/11. Mahmood claims he turned bin Laden down.[50]

Another scenario keeps analysts up at night: Workers inside a nuclear facility smuggle out and sell "fissile" material — the enriched uranium or plutonium needed to build a nuclear bomb. As former U.N. weapons inspector David Albright told *The Washington Post*, "They may look for an opportunity to make a quick buck. You may not be able to get the whole weapon, but maybe you can get the core."[51]

Retired Brig. Gen. Shaukat Qadir, a Pakistani nuclear expert, disagrees. "Both the weapons and the fissile material are accorded the same level of security," he told the BBC. "The material therefore has the same chance of being stolen as the weapons."[52]

Despite all the recent concerns — Khan, the Marriott and World Trade Center bombings, domestic political turmoil and recent militant uprisings — Pakistan claims its weapons are secure.

"I am confident of two things," said former Deputy Director of the CIA John E. McLaughlin, who helped expose Khan's nuclear perfidy. "That the Pakistanis are very serious about securing this material, but also that someone in Pakistan is very intent on getting their hands on it."[53]

BACKGROUND

Early Beginnings

Pakistan's history can be traced back 8,000 years to the Mehgarh settlement in what is now Balochistan. But its roots are more easily followed from the flourishing Indus civilization, which peaked around 2500-1500 B.C. on the banks of the Indus River in what is now Pakistan and India.

Ruins of the civilization's two major cities — Harappa and Mohenjo Daro — can still be seen in Pakistan. This advanced society, which boasted a sophisticated bureaucracy, collapsed around 1500 B.C. — possibly due to catastrophic floods or because the river changed its course — and was replaced by a series of foreign invaders.[54]

The Aryans, whose Vedic beliefs would evolve into Hinduism, came into the region from Central Asia about that time, followed by the Persians, who conquered the Punjab in around 500 BC. Alexander the Great came over the Hindu Kush mountains and took over most of what is now Pakistan in 326 BC. The region changed hands frequently, becoming part of the Mauryan Empire, then falling to Greeks from Bactria, Scythians from Afghanistan, Parthians, the Kushans, Guptas and the Huns, who invaded the region from their base in central Asia in the 5th century.[55]

Islam arrived via Muslim traders in the early 8th century. By the 11th century Muslims invaded Pakistan from Persia, and eventually a Muslim kingdom was established along the Indus Valley. The Mughals — under fabled rulers Babur, Akbar, Shah Jahan and Aurangzeb — dominated the subcontinent during the 16th and 17th centuries. Remnants of their artistic legacy can be seen today in the Taj Mahal in India and numerous examples in Pakistan.

Eventually, the Mughal Empire weakened, and local rulers replaced its rulers. Persians, Afghans, Sikhs and others controlled the region that is modern Pakistan. Officially, the Mughals were finally toppled in 1857, when the British ousted their last ruler, Bahdur Shah II, who had been controlled by the British East India Company. By the early 20th century the British, thanks to inroads first made by the company, controlled all of what is now Pakistan and India or, as they dubbed it, "British India."

British educational reforms exacerbated already strained relations between the Hindus and Muslims in the region. While Hindus saw school attendance as a way to advance within the colonial system, most Muslims favored their own schools. Then, as more and more Hindus earned jobs in business and government, the Muslims — many of whom were working as farmers and laborers — began to feel disenfranchised.

Not wanting to be left out in a growing bid for autonomy from the British and wanting to make sure their rights were secured, Muslims in 1906 formed the All India Muslim League to balance the Hindu-dominated India National Congress Party. Eventually, inspired by poet and philosopher Allama Mohammed Iqbal, a movement for a Muslim state took hold. By 1940 the Muslim League, headed by Muhammad Ali Jinnah, was demanding a separate state for Muslims in the Muslim-majority areas of northwestern and northeastern India. The name, "Pakistan" was chosen because it means "land of the pure" in Urdu, and its letters stand for the states it would include: Punjab, the Afghan States (NWFP), Kashmir, Sind and Tan (for Balochistan).

But when the British and Indians rejected the plan for Pakistan's independence (both were reluctant to divide the subcontinent), violence broke out between Hindus and Muslims. Britain finally agreed to partition the subcontinent in 1947, and a mass migration involving nearly 20 million people ensued — with Hindus and Sikhs heading east and Muslims heading west to their new homelands. More than half a million were killed in religious-based violence in the process. On Aug. 14, 1947, Pakistan declared independence, as did India a day later.

As the etymology of its name suggests, Pakistan is a complex mix of ethnic groups. The Punjabis comprise the largest ethnic group followed by the Pashtuns, Sindhis, Saraikis, Muhajirs (Muslim migrants from India) and the Balochs. The Punjabis are considered the most powerful, with Punjab being the richest and most populous province. While the country is ethnically diverse, it is religiously homogeneous: 95 percent Muslim.

Quest for Democracy

Shortly after independence, India and Pakistan went to war over the ownership of the states of Jammu and Kashmir — on Pakistan's northeastern border with India — which was 85 percent Muslim, but whose former Hindu ruler had decided to join India during the partition. The United Nations interceded and brokered a cease-fire in 1948, but both India and Pakistan retained control over portions of Kashmir. The two nations have been battling over control ever since, a feud that has blocked closer relations and even led in part to both countries obtaining nuclear arsenals. (*See map and story, p. 186.*)

The Kashmir dispute remains highly sensitive. "Obtaining justice for Muslim Kashmiris living in the India-administered parts of the state has been a central goal of Pakistan's foreign and security policy for five decades," wrote Cohen of Brookings. "Pakistan has tried diplomatic, military and low-level military pressure on

India to hold a plebiscite (as recommended in several U.N. resolutions) or to negotiate a change in the status quo, all to no avail."[56]

With independence, the question of whether Pakistan should become a democracy or an Islamic theocracy was hotly debated. Instead of choosing a strictly secular democratic or purely Islamic model, early leaders tried to blend the two, leaving many to wonder: "Was Pakistan a Muslim state or a state in which Muslims live?" Like the Kashmir problem, the uncertainty has caused repercussions throughout Pakistan's short history.[57]

Jinnah seemed to contradict his earlier democratic yearnings in 1948, when he summarily dismissed the Congress-led government of North-West Frontier Province and dictated to the Bengali-speaking residents of East Pakistan that Urdu would be the nation's official language. Both decisions would have serious consequences.

In 1953, after Jinnah's death, Governor-General Ghulam Muhammad dismissed the country's first civilian government. It was the first of many such upheavals and set in motion Pakistan's destructive cycle of democratic civilian governments replaced by military dictatorships. In 1954 the Supreme Court justified Muhammad's actions with the "theory of necessity" — which has been used by the judiciary to justify "nearly every dismissal of a civilian government and every military takeover" since then, wrote BBC correspondent M Ilyas Khan.[58]

In 1956 Pakistan became the Islamic Republic of Pakistan. But after two years of civilian rule, Gen. Mohammed Ayub Khan ousted the civilian government. Khan would be the first in a long line of military leaders to command the country. The military would seize power again in 1969 under Gen. Agha Muhammad Yahya Khan and in 1977, when Gen. Muhammad Zia ul-Haq ousted Zulfikar Ali Bhutto. In 1999 Gen. Musharraf overthrew Muhammad Nawaz Sharif, who had been elected for the second time in 1997.

The army's fondness for governing follows a recurring pattern. First, the army warns the citizenry, which it regards as incompetent or foolish, that the government is not functioning properly, wrote the Brookings Institution's Cohen. "Second, a crisis leads to army intervention, which is followed by the third step: attempts to 'straighten out' Pakistan, often by introducing major constitutional changes. Fourth, the army, faced with growing civilian discontent, 'allows' civilians back into office; and fifth, the army reasserts itself behind a façade of civilian government, and the cycle repeats itself."[59]

Although the army held power throughout the 1960s, a military failure eventually ushered in a civilian government. For years Bengali speakers in East Pakistan had been feeling disenfranchised by what they saw as Islamabad's lack of recognition. After the December 1970 election, disgruntled East Pakistanis won a majority of seats in Parliament and sought full autonomy. When negotiations on a new political arrangement failed, the Pakistani army cracked down in March 1971. A harsh martial law was imposed, and many East Pakistanis were killed; millions fled to India. A bitter insurgency began, and ultimately in December 1971 India intervened militarily. Outgunned and outmanned, 90,000 Pakistani soldiers surrendered after two weeks of fighting, and East Pakistan became independent Bangladesh.

India's actions left deep wounds. "India's decision to invade East Pakistan in support of the Bengali independence movement inflicted on Pakistan a humiliation from which it has still not recovered," wrote the BBC's Jones. "India's victory left a wound that festers to this day."[60]

The loss also propelled a civilian government, led by President Zulfikar Bhutto, into power. But six years later the military ousted Bhutto; he was convicted of ordering the murder of a political opponent (a charge many say was untrue) and was executed in 1979. The next civilian government came to power in 1988, and two parties shared rule for the next 10 years — a rare, 10-year democratic interregnum led by Benazir Bhutto, the daughter of the late president, and Pakistan Muslim League-N leader Sharif. Each served two terms. Pakistan would not see its next civilian government until 2008, after Benazir Bhutto's assassination.

But even though the military was officially out of power for a decade, from 1988-1998, it did not relinquish control of the government. Pakistan's civilian rule is usually the result of "a masterful manipulation of the political stage," with the military and intelligence agencies playing a major role in "rigging polls, underwriting political parties and dismissing prime ministers," according to political analyst Seth Kaplan, author of *Fixing Fragile States*.[61]

During the 1980s, the U.S. Central Intelligence Agency worked closely with the Pakistan intelligence services, funneling up to $3 billion worth of weapons to Afghan fighters, called mujahedin, to help them oust the Soviets.

CHRONOLOGY

1940-1950s *Pakistan becomes independent; constitution adopted. The first of many military dictatorships declares martial law.*

1947 Pakistan gains independence, with Muhammad Ali Jinnah — leader of the All India Muslim League — as governor-general. First Indo-Pakistan war over Kashmir begins.

1948 Jinnah dies.

1951 The nation's first prime minister, Liaquat Ali Khan, is assassinated; Governor-General Khawaja Nazimuddin succeeds him.

1956 The first constitution is adopted, declaring Pakistan the world's first Islamic republic; Governor-General Iskander Mirza becomes Pakistan's first president.

1958 Mirza is sent into exile and Gen. Mohammed Ayub Khan assumes presidency after a military coup.

1960s *Pakistan goes to war with India over Kashmir for second time; martial law is declared.*

1965 Second Indo-Pakistan war over Kashmir lasts for six weeks.

1969 Gen. Agha Muhammad Yahya Khan becomes president.

1970s *Pakistan goes to war with India again; East Pakistan secedes; martial law is declared again.*

1971 Civil war erupts after East Pakistan tries to secede; Pakistan goes to war with India; East Pakistan becomes Bangladesh. . . . President Khan resigns; former Foreign Minister Zulfiqar Ali Bhutto becomes president.

1973 A new constitution is adopted; Bhutto resigns presidency to become prime minister.

1977 Gen. Muhammad Zia ul-Haq overthrows Bhutto, proclaims martial law.

1979 Bhutto is hanged for ordering the assassination of a political rival.

1980s *With U.S. aid, Pakistan supports the Northern Alliance's eight-year struggle to expel Soviets from Afghanistan.*

1988 Zia dies in plane crash. . . . Bhutto, 37, daughter of Zulfiqar Ali, becomes Pakistan's first female prime minister.

1990s *Nawaz Sharif becomes prime minister. Gen. Pervez Musharraf takes power after military coup.*

1990 Bhutto's government is dismissed; Sharif, leader of the Pakistan Muslim League, becomes prime minister.

1993 Bhutto becomes prime minister again. She is dismissed three years later.

1997 Sharif becomes prime minister again.

1998 Pakistan tests its first nuclear weapon.

1999 Musharraf overthrows Sharif in a military coup. Bhutto and her husband are sentenced to five years in prison for alleged money laundering; the convictions are set aside in 2001.

2000-Present *Military returns to power. U.S. invades Afghanistan after 9/11 terror attacks; fleeing terrorists settle in Pakistan's tribal areas. Musharraf resigns; Bhutto is assassinated; elections held.*

2004 Nuclear scientist A.Q. Khan confesses to international nuclear weapons trading; Musharraf pardons him.

2005 Earthquake kills up to 80,000 people in northern Pakistan.

2007 Musharraf removes chief justice, sparking huge demonstrations by lawyers; Musharraf declares state of emergency. . . . 100 people die when army attacks Red Mosque in Islamabad; Bhutto returns from exile and is assassinated.

2008 Musharraf resigns; Bhutto's widower Asif Ali Zardari becomes president. Islamabad Marriott Hotel is attacked by terrorists. Terrorists, allegedly from Pakistan, kill 173 people in Mumbai, India.

Truck Convoy Sparks Hope in Kashmir

Reopening trade route links Pakistani and Indian sectors.

A convoy of 16 trucks — each piled high with apples, walnuts, spices, honey and other items — recently rumbled west across the "Peace Bridge" from the India-controlled sector of Kashmir into the Pakistani sector. Onlookers waved banners and cheered the smiling drivers. After six decades of hostility in Kashmir, the two nations had finally re-opened trade links.

"Today marks the beginning of the dismantling of the border," said Mubeen Shah, president of the Kashmir Chamber of Commerce and Industries, reflecting the hopes of many. "I am sure this trade will grow and help bring peace in the region."[1]

India and Pakistan have been fighting for control of the mountainous, rugged Himalayan region of Kashmir ever since Pakistan was partitioned from India in 1947. Muslim Pakistanis saw the mostly Muslim state as logically theirs; India claimed it for its Hindu populace because it had been ruled by a Hindu maharaja who chose to join India after partition. On April 21, 1948, the United Nations Security Council, via Resolution 47, called for a national referendum on Kashmir's future. Pakistan was willing, but India has continued to object.[2]

The 60-year-long battle for Kashmir — punctuated by two additional wars — has impeded political and economic relations between India and Pakistan and made life for Kashmiris intolerable. Pakistan occupies about one-third of the region, and India occupies most of the rest, with China holding a small area. The so-called 463-mile long Line of Control (LOC) running through the Himalayas separates the Pakistani and Indian sectors.

While the 1948 war between India and Pakistan initially divided Kashmir, they again fought over the region in 1965. A U.N.-negotiated cease-fire ended that war. But rugged Kashmir has rarely been peaceful for long, and the two went to war again in 1971.

Pakistan wants control of Kashmir not just because of its Muslim population. The region also contains the headwaters of several key rivers that flow through Pakistan's farming regions. India doesn't want to lose face and fears that if Kashmir is allowed to secede, other Indian states could follow suit.

Since 1989 a growing Islamist separatist movement against Indian rule in Kashmir has added fuel to the

AP Photo/Mukhtar Khan

For the first time in six decades, trade between India and Pakistan resumes in the Himalayan region of Kashmir on Oct. 21. A convoy of trucks festooned with flags and decorations and laden with fruit, honey, garments and spices crosses the fortified frontier.

long-simmering conflict. While some of the separatists seek independence, others want Kashmir united with Pakistan. Tens of thousands of lives have been lost as Kashmiri Muslims — joined by Islamic militants with backing from Pakistan and others — have tried to force the Indians out of Kashmir. India claims Pakistan supports the insurgents, calling its aid "cross-border terrorism."

Kashmiri militants have attacked India on numerous occasions. In December 1999, a group hijacked an Indian airliner and a year later attacked Indian citizens inside New Delhi's Red Fort. In December 2001 terrorists said to be sympathetic to Kashmiri separatists attacked the Indian Parliament.[3]

Although it was unclear who was responsible for the horrific terrorist attacks in Mumbai last week, many claimed it was organized by Lashkar-e-Taiba, the largest Islamic separatist group in Kashmir, also said to be responsible for the 2001 assault on India's Parliament.[4]

In 1999 Gen. Pervez Musharraf of Pakistan sent troops into Indian-occupied Kashmir and took control of several hundred square miles, including the mountainous, mostly Muslim region of Kargil. Occupying the high, fortress-like region would give Pakistan an offensive advantage over the Indian army. In response, India flooded Kargil with troops. Suddenly, what had been a regional, traditional border spat looked like it might escalate into a terrifying nuclear confrontation as the two nuclear powers battled one another.

When the United States learned Pakistan was preparing covertly to deploy nuclear weapons against India, President Bill Clinton insisted that its ally retreat from the region and cancel all plans to use the weapons against India. In early July, after Pakistani Prime Minister Nawaz Sharif asked Clinton to intervene on Pakistan's behalf against India, Clinton told him he would but sternly warned Sharif that he was "messing with nuclear war." Sharif agreed to remove Pakistan's forces from the disputed region.[5]

Despite the pullback, Clinton famously described Kashmir as "the most dangerous place on earth." That was borne out in May 2002 when India accused Pakistan of backing Islamic militant incursions into the Indian section of Kashmir. The two powers amassed nearly a million troops on their borders, and Pakistan again rattled its nuclear sword by test firing nuclear-capable missiles. Indian Defense Minister George Fernandes responded by declaring, "India can survive a nuclear attack but Pakistan cannot." Both sides eventually backed down.[6]

In 2004, Pakistan and India entered into ongoing peace negotiations. Among the sticking points: India wants the Line of Control to become the official border, but Pakistan lays claim to additional Muslim-majority areas. Many insurgents reject both claims and want independence.

The cross-border truck convoys grew out of an agreement by Pakistan's newly elected President Asif Ali Zardari and Indian Prime Minister Manmohan Singh during a recent U.N. meeting.[7]

Does the reopened trade route signal a thaw? "The roots of the Kashmir conflict remain; Kashmiris seek self-determination; India and Pakistan each claim to be the rightful owners," writes Rajon Manon, professor of International relations at Lehigh University and author of *The End of Alliances.* "But commerce that continues and expands can create mutual gains that widen benefits and build trust. And trust is what's needed for any advances — however incremental — on the Kashmir dispute. That's why those trucks are so important."[8]

Disputed Kashmir

Pakistan and India have fought three wars over Kashmir, a beautiful, mountainous region the size of Kansas located between the two nuclear-armed countries, and Muslim militants from Kashmir have made repeated terrorist attacks inside India. Many regard Kashmir as the globe's most likely nuclear flashpoint.

Source: Indo American Kashmir Forum

[1] Sudip Mazumdar, "Some Thawing of Relations in Kashmir," *Newsweek*, Oct. 23, 2008, http://blog.newsweek.com/blogs/ov/archive/2008/10/23/some-thawing-of-relations-in-kashmir.aspx.

[2] Owen Bennett Jones, *Pakistan: The Eye of the Storm* (2003), pp. 56-70.

[3] See Neil MacFarquhar, "3rd Attempt to Free Pakistani Militant," *The New York Times*, Dec. 29, 1999, p. A14; Barry Bearak, "Gunmen Kill 3 at Garrison in New Delhi's Center," *The New York Times*, Dec. 23, 2000, p. A5; and Rama Lakshmi, "Indians Blame Attacks On Pakistan-Based Group," *The Washington Post*, Dec. 15, 2001, p. A23.

[4] "Mumbai probe focuses on Pakistan-based militants" Agence France-Presse, Dec. 1, 2008, www.google.com/hostednews/afp/article/ALeqM5hSh98EQFTH33W9oGoMskBm0x2ZeA.

[5] "Pakistan 'prepared nuclear strike,' " BBC News, May 16, 2002, http://news.bbc.co.uk/2/hi/south_asia/1989886.stm.

[6] Michael Richardson, "India and Pakistan are not 'imprudent' on nuclear option; Q&A/George Fernandes," *The International Herald Tribune*, June 3, 2002.

[7] Somini Sengupta, "India and Pakistan open Kashmir trade route," *The New York Times*, Oct. 22, 2008, www.nytimes.com/2008/10/22/world/asia/22kashmir.html.

[8] Rajan Menon, "Progress in Kashmir," *Los Angeles Times*, Oct. 25, 2008, www.latimes.com/news/opinion/commentary/la-oe-menon25-2008oct25,0,809573.story.

One of the militant anti-Soviet leaders to receive U.S. funds was bin Laden. While up to 1 million Afghans died during the struggle, nearly 3 million — including many Taliban and al Qaeda fighters — fled to neighboring Pakistan's border areas, where many have remained. The Soviets, who had invaded Afghanistan on Christmas Eve in 1979, were finally expelled in late 1989.[62]

After that, the Afghan communists held onto power for three more years, and were finally ousted in 1992. Then a series of warlords — many corrupt and oppressive — seized power until challenged and overthrown by the next one, paving the way for a strong, religiously conservative military force to come in and take over the country.

Taliban Gathers Strength

It is some of the most inhospitable terrain in the world. Known officially as the Federally Administered Tribal Areas (FATA), the mountainous, mostly lawless stretch of land between Afghanistan and Pakistan's North-West Frontier Province is home to some of the world's most fiercely independent fighters, including the tough, much-feared Pashtun warriors who have resisted rule by outsiders — and their own government — for centuries. Today, it is now home for a newer, equally notorious fighter: the Taliban.

The Taliban (which means "religious students") were Pashtun students educated in Pakistani madrassas, or Muslim religious schools, who first rose to prominence in 1994 after being assigned by Pakistan security forces to protect truck convoys in Afghanistan. They proved to be capable fighters. Within two years, with the help of the Pakistanis, they had kicked out the Kabul government and controlled much of Afghanistan.

The Taliban set up a repressive Islamic government headed by Mullah Mohammed Omar, the group's spiritual and military leader, which enforced strict Islamic law, or sharia, and banned music and television, which they considered "non-Islamic" and "frivolous."

Following the Afghan war against the Soviets, bin Laden resettled in Sudan. But in 1996 — under pressure from Egypt, Saudi Arabia and the United States — Sudan expelled him, and he returned to Afghanistan. The Taliban offered him and his al Qaeda fighters a refuge, and allowed him to set up training camps. He seemed to have found a safe haven in Afghanistan.

However, all this changed after 9/11, when the United States demanded that the Taliban turn over bin Laden and his followers. When the Taliban refused, the United States began bombing Afghanistan and supporting the Northern Alliance resistance movement. By December 2001 the Taliban, bin Laden and his followers all had fled to the mountainous border region between Afghanistan and Pakistan.[63]

Since then, the Taliban has regrouped, operating training camps in the Pakistan regions of North and South Waziristan and Balochistan. Beginning in 2003 they began counter-attacking against Afghan, U.S. and NATO forces in Afghanistan. Their presence also influenced the build-up of a home-grown "Pakistani Taliban" movement, comprised mainly of local Pashtuns sympathetic to Taliban causes, leading to the area being nicknamed Talibanistan.[64]

Although the government has consistently denied that it aids the Taliban, a recent RAND Corporation report accused Pakistani intelligence agents and paramilitary forces of helping train the insurgents and informing them about U.S. troop movements in Afghanistan. The think tank identified several insurgent groups that, along with the Taliban, "regularly ship weapons, ammunition and supplies into Afghanistan from Pakistan, and a number of suicide bombers have come from Afghan refugee camps based in Pakistan."[65]

The Taliban continued to launch attacks into Afghanistan. Indeed, 2006 was the deadliest year of fighting since the 2001 war. In 2005 there were 25 suicide bombings in Afghanistan; in 2006 there were 139.[66] Throughout the spring, Taliban militants swept into southern Afghanistan, launching attacks on Afghan and U.S. troops. That September, Musharraf brokered a peace agreement with the Pakistani Taliban, which critics claimed offered the militants a safe haven.

But once Musharraf held up his end of the deal by scaling back military operations in the tribal areas, suicide bombings and cross-border raids into Afghanistan picked up. "The state has withdrawn and ceded this territory," said Samina Ahmed of the Brussels-based International Crisis Group. "[The Taliban] have been given their own little piece of real estate."[67]

With the Taliban and al Qaeda fighters safely ensconced in Pakistan's tribal areas, terrorism now threatens to infiltrate Pakistan proper. Recently, "Militants began moving out of the FATA and into the rest of Pakistan, taking control of the towns and villages in North-West Frontier Province. Militants began attacking Pakistani police and soldiers," wrote *New York Times* correspondent Dexter Filkins. "Inside the FATA, Mehsud was forming the Tehreek Taliban-e-Pakistan, an umbrella party of some 40 Taliban groups that claimed as its goal the domination of Pakistan. Suddenly, the Taliban was not merely a group of militants who were useful in extending Pakistan's influence into Afghanistan. They were a threat to Pakistan itself."[68]

Within a relatively short time, homegrown terrorists would be blamed for both the assassination of Bhutto, the Marriott Hotel suicide bombing and the attacks in Mumbai, India. The war being waged by the Taliban, bin Laden, al Qaeda and others was getting deadlier and deadlier. As Pakistan's Interior Minister Mali would say shortly after the Marriott tragedy, "All roads lead to FATA."

CURRENT SITUATION

Fighting Intensifies

Since August, remotely operated U.S. Predator "drone" missiles have been striking inside Pakistan. At least 20 attacks have occurred, sometimes in conjunction with raids by American commandos on the ground.[69]

For instance, on Sept. 3 helicopter-borne Special Forces soldiers killed 20 people in a raid on a suspected militant hideout in South Waziristan.[70] Soon afterwards, a U.S. drone launched five missiles at a compound thought to belong to Afghan Taliban commander Jalaluddin Haqqani. Although it missed Haqqani, it allegedly killed several al Qaeda operatives, along with women and children.

Meanwhile, the United States continues to pressure the Pakistani army to confront the militants more aggressively. The Pakistanis have been battling the insurgents in remote places like Bajaur, Dera Adam Khel and Swat.[71] In late October the army claimed to have captured Loi Sam in the Bajaur tribal region, killing 1,500 militants after a two-month battle. The town had been described as a "mega-sanctuary" for militants.[72]

When confronted, the militants fight back with intimidation, weapons and suicide bombers. Since July 2007 more than 90 suicide attacks on civilian, military and Western targets have killed nearly 1,200 people.[73]

With battles raging around them, many residents have fled. In Bajaur alone, more than 200,000 people have abandoned their homes, cattle and crops for makeshift camps near Peshawar or in Afghanistan.[74] "Every day, their lives are threatened by the pounding [Pakistani] jets that sweep into the valleys on bombing runs and by the clattering helicopter gunships that the Pakistan military is using to spearhead its assaults," reported London's *Independent*. "The people sitting in the dust are the so-called 'collateral damage' of Pakistan's own war on terror."[75]

In other efforts to appease Washington, the Pakistan government recently banned the umbrella militant group Tehreek Taliban-e-Pakistan based in South Waziristan and headed by Taliban warlord Mehsud, who is blamed for planning numerous suicide attacks. (*See sidebar, p. 180.*)[76]

However, a recent move to encourage tribal militias — lashkars — to fight the Taliban and al Qaeda has been "far from promising," according to *The New York Times*.[77] The lashkars are lightly armed and are vulnerable to suicide bombers. In early November, a suicide bomber killed 23 lashkars as they prepared to attack Taliban hideouts near Bajaur. Several weeks earlier, more than 50 Bajaur tribesmen were killed while discussing plans to attack the Taliban.[78]

Without military backing the lashkars have little hope of effectively combating the militants. A case in point: After being promised military backing, some men in Hilal Kel, a village in a Taliban-dominated region of Bajaur, formed a lashkar. The Taliban responded by bringing in 600 reinforcements from Afghanistan, a resident told *The New York Times*.[79]

"The Taliban sowed terror by kidnapping and executing four tribal leaders of the lashkar, leaving their bodies on the roadside, their throats slit," wrote *Times* reporters Jane Perlez and Pir Zubair Shah. Villagers then fled or surrendered.[80]

Opposing the U.S.

Some U.S. experts remain unconvinced that Pakistan is committed to confronting the militants. Many, for example, have accused Pakistan's Inter Services Intelligence (ISI) agency of supporting al Qaeda and Taliban operatives. Last summer, for instance, CIA Deputy Director Stephen Kappes reportedly handed Islamabad evidence that ISI officials were involved in the Taliban's suicide bombing of the Indian embassy in the Afghan capital of Kabul on July 7, 2008, in which 54 people were killed.[81]

Pakistan has begun recruiting tribal militias — lashkars — to fight Islamic extremists, but the militias are lightly armed and vulnerable to suicide bombers, so the results have been disappointing. The Taliban have responded by bringing in reinforcements from Afghanistan and executing four tribal leaders as a warning to others.

Meanwhile, some experts are pushing the United States to step up its cross-border incursions into Pakistan, despite protests from Pakistan over the forays. "Decisions to take decisive action will be Pakistani, but the U.S. should make it openly clear that the U.S. cannot wait for Pakistan to make such decisions and will have to treat Pakistani territory as a combat zone if Pakistan does not act," wrote Anthony Cordesman, a defense expert at the Center for Strategic and International Studies in Washington. "Pakistan cannot both claim sovereignty and allow hostile non-state actors to attack Afghanistan, U.S., and NATO . . . forces from its soil. Pakistan must understand that use of [unpiloted aircraft], limited Special Forces and hot-pursuit/defense operations in Pakistani territory will continue until Pakistan takes action to secure its own territory and borders."[82]

Such sentiments help to wedge President Zardari's infant government even more firmly between a rock and a hard place. "America has to realize its actions and rhetoric are increasing anti-American sentiment among the Pakistanis," explains Harvard's Abbas. Indeed, in a stern signal to Washington, Pakistan's Parliament in October passed a resolution calling for dialog with militants and ending military action against them.

Raza Rabbani, a member of the ruling Pakistan Peoples Party, said, "We need to prioritize our own national-security interests. As far as the U.S. is concerned, the message that has gone with this resolution will definitely ring alarm bells, *vis-à-vis* their policy of bulldozing Pakistan."[83]

Another member of Parliament was even blunter. "Our country is burning," he told *The Guardian.* "We don't want Bush to put oil on the fire. We want to extinguish this fire."[84]

The next week Pakistan protested to U.S. Ambassador Anne W. Patterson about U.S. missile strikes in the border region. "It was emphasized that such attacks were a violation of Pakistan's sovereignty and should be stopped immediately," said a Foreign Ministry spokesman.[85] And when Gen. David Petraeus, new head of the U.S. Central Command, recently met Pakistani officials, he heard widespread criticism of the U.S. missile strikes.

"Continuing drone attacks on our territory, which result in loss of precious lives and property, are counterproductive and difficult to explain by a democratically elected government," President Zardari said after meeting with Petraeus. "It is creating a credibility gap."[86]

As the gap widens, pressure mounts on Zardari to distance himself and his government from the United States. Meanwhile, Sharif, a former prime minister and head of the second-biggest party in Pakistan's coalition, pulled out of the coalition and stepped up verbal attacks on the United States. Thus, Zardari's fragile, new democracy must now fend off the United States, the opposition, an enraged populace and militants.

Ahmed, the former high commissioner to Great Britain now at American University, echoes many in Pakistan when he says the United States must change its military policy. "Bombing tribal people has not solved anything. If the United States carries on as it has, it risks losing Pakistan. And if you lose Pakistan, you lose Afghanistan, and your war on terror collapses!"

Obama Optimism

After Barack Obama's inauguration on Jan. 20, his administration should reassess Pakistan's strategic importance, says Seth Jones, a terrorism expert at the RAND Corporation think tank. "Pakistan should be No. 1," Jones contends. "The most serious homeland threat to the United Sates from abroad comes from militant groups operating in Pakistan."[87]

Moreover, having sent at least $11.2 billion in overt aid to Pakistan since 9/11, most of which was for military spending, experts agree the United States should provide more help for Pakistan's people and infrastructure.[88] Many see a pending proposal — co-sponsored by newly elected

Should the United States pursue militants inside Pakistan?

YES

Malou Innocent
Foreign Policy Analyst,
Cato Institute

Written for *CQ Global Researcher*, November 2008

Militants use Pakistan's lawless, highly porous western frontier with Afghanistan, known as the Federally Administered Tribal Areas (FATA), to slip into and out of Afghanistan and attack U.S. and NATO troops. To complicate matters, FATA lies within the territorial confines of Pakistan but remains formally outside of its constitution. Thus, U.S. policy makers must carefully consider how to approach this unpoliced region without further destabilizing a nuclear-armed, Muslim-majority, front-line state in America's "war on terror."

Ideally, the United States, NATO and Pakistan should work together to meet shared challenges in the region. But over the past several years, Pakistan's army has proven unable — and at times unwilling — to uproot militant havens and has lost thousands of soldiers in confrontations with insurgents. In FATA, many soldiers lack proper training, equipment and communication gear, rendering vulnerable villages even more susceptible to militant attacks.

Even worse, Islamabad and Washington are on different pages strategically. Elements of the Inter Services Intelligence Directorate (ISI), Pakistan's national intelligence agency, still support the Afghan Taliban. The ISI supported pro-Taliban insurgents allegedly responsible for the July 7, 2008, bombing of the Indian Embassy in Kabul, according to U.S. intelligence. And many Pakistani defense planners admit their country has turned a blind eye to the Taliban's depredations in order to use them as a proxy force against the Afghan government, which they say is pro-India.

Thus, the United States has no choice but to attack militants inside Pakistan. A judicious approach would be to employ low-level, clear-and-hold operations along the Afghan-Pakistan frontier to limit cross-border movement and respond aggressively to attacks against troops and civilians.

It might even be necessary to deploy up to a few hundred U.S. Special Forces personnel within Pakistan as part of a larger operation in support of local Pakistani security forces — but nothing more. Large-scale military action would further radicalize FATA's indigenous population and push wavering tribes further into the Taliban camp.

Meanwhile, on a strategic level, America should engage in vigorous regional diplomacy with all countries surrounding land-locked Afghanistan. Overall, U.S. policy toward Pakistan is complicated and imperfect. But achieving success in Afghanistan requires a judicious campaign against militant sanctuaries inside Pakistan.

NO

Shuja Nawaz
Political analyst, author, Crossed Swords:
Pakistan, Its Army, and the Wars Within

Written for *CQ Global Researcher*, November 2008

Pakistan is in the midst of a series of crises. A fledgling civilian government is trying to gain control of the country and its army after eight years of military rule. Its economy is in free fall, with depleted reserves, roaring inflation and shortages of power and food. Increasing militancy threatens security, especially in the tribal areas along the Afghan border, which has become a base for attacks on U.S. forces in Afghanistan.

The continuation of unilateral U.S. drone attacks on militant targets inside the Pakistani tribal belt has already angered the local population and embarrassed the government and army. It exposes Pakistan's inability to protect its own borders or to rein in the United States, a country with whom Pakistan has chosen to ally itself in the so-called war on terror. If anything could help coalesce opposition to the shaky civilian regime and perhaps upend it, it would be yet another incursion by U.S. forces against militant targets inside Pakistan.

By trying to draw Pakistan into fighting the war on U.S. terms, the United States has undermined Pakistan's effectiveness. Rather than giving Pakistani forces the intelligence and capacity to undertake military operations, the United States has been tardy in giving Pakistan the wherewithal to fight the insurgents. And it has taken it upon itself to execute a policy of hot pursuit into Pakistan to defend its own troops in Afghanistan. While this policy may have achieved some results, the process has alienated a non-NATO ally and its population.

The United States could help control militancy inside Pakistan by speeding up the supply of modern, night-vision goggles and helicopters to Pakistani forces on the border so they can better track and interdict militants hiding or traveling in or out of Afghanistan. And it could collaborate more closely on intelligence, allowing Pakistanis themselves to fight militancy inside their own country.

To underpin these military relationships, the United States needs to accelerate the flow of economic assistance to Pakistan, to allow it to recover from the effects of global inflation. These funds could help provide employment, health care and better education to the Pakistanis, especially the impoverished 3.5 million in the border region that the militants call home. Attacking the roots of militancy in a fragile democracy is better than bombing it at will.

Vice President Joseph Biden and Sen. Richard Lugar — to commit $1.5 billion per year in non-military spending as an excellent first step.

During his campaign for president, Sen. Obama expressed support for the Biden-Lugar aid bill, which he co-sponsored, and most analysts think there is enough bipartisan support for it to pass during the next Congress. If there is one stumbling block, it may be financial: Will the United States be willing to spend the funds the bill has earmarked for aid?

"We need to redefine the terms of engagement between Pakistan and the United States," said former Pakistani Ambassador to the United States Tariq Fatmi. "Our importance should not be confined merely to the war on terror." Fatmi said many believe Obama will move the United States away from policies pursued by the Bush administration.[89]

Brookings's Cohen agrees. "Washington needs to rethink its approach to Pakistan," he said.[90] In fact, the new administration is expected to reexamine U.S. policy toward both Afghanistan and Pakistan. After deciding on the size of the U.S. military buildup in Afghanistan and how to strengthen that government, the Obama administration also must decide how to deal with militant sanctuaries inside Pakistan and whether or not it can reconcile with the Taliban and help to stabilize Pakistan.

As former Assistant Secretary of State Richard C. Holbrooke recently wrote in *Foreign Affairs*, "Getting policy toward Islamabad right will be absolutely critical for the next administration — and very difficult. . . . The continued deterioration of the tribal areas poses a threat not only to Afghanistan but also to Pakistan's new secular democracy, and it presents the next president with an extraordinary challenge."[91]

The Center for American Progress recently published a report that summarizes the need for a revamped U.S. policy toward Pakistan: "A fundamental strategic shift in U.S. policy on Pakistan should occur away from a narrow focus on military and intelligence cooperation. Pakistan's problems will not be solved by military means alone. Long-term stability in Pakistan depends not only on curtailing extremism and militancy in Pakistan but on strengthening Pakistan's economy and democracy and on reducing tensions between Pakistan and its neighbors."[92]

"Pakistanis now eagerly await change in Washington's policy towards their country," wrote Nasim Zehra, a fellow at Harvard's Asia Center and a former special envoy from Pakistan on U.N. reforms. "With Barack Obama in the White House and a democratic government in Pakistan, they look forward to greater cooperation within the framework of genuine dialogue, greater trust and mutual respect."

Especially among Pakistanis in North-West Frontier Province, there is hope for a lessening of conflict and, in turn, fewer drone missile attacks. As Zehra noted, "Perhaps as a sign of this region's clamor for peace, last month a group of young students in Peshawar collected $200 to contribute to Obama's election campaign. Their message, broadcast throughout Pakistan, was: 'We are sending Obama this money for his campaign so that when he becomes president he will not attack our homeland.' "[93]

OUTLOOK
Doomsday Scenarios

Pakistan is often described as "fragile." But these days that may be too optimistic. Buffeted by Islamic uprisings, a weakened government, a faltering economy and pressure from abroad, Pakistan faces an uncertain future.

"There are few other countries where you could say things could so totally implode or turn out OK, because we are not seeing any pattern yet," says former U.S. State Department official Markey. "There's so much uncertainty."

The "Whither Pakistan?" question has been vexing experts for decades as the nation has veered between "emerging democracy" and "failed state." Analysts sketch out three possible scenarios for Pakistan's future.

In the first, democracy survives with an improved balance between the military and civilian sectors. More capable civilian leaders emerge and Pakistan, helped by the international community, becomes more integrated with the global economy, especially with neighboring India and Afghanistan. "The situation in Afghanistan may change and lead to discussions with the militants; a strong center could emerge in Pakistani politics; and the government and the military could achieve a balanced relationship," says Pakistani political analyst Nawaz.

In the second scenario, Pakistan continues to alternate between civilian and military rule, which has played out since independence in 1947. "I don't see anything that suggests this pattern is going to shift in any fundamental way," says Shaikh, at London's Royal Institute of International Affairs. Some believe that if control of the country continues to flip-flop between ineffective civilian governments and dictatorial military rulers, the populace will become even more alienated than in the past. "That's one way you could envision an Iran-style revolution or a civilian strongman coming to power," says Markey. "It could lead to Pakistan becoming an extremist or an authoritarian state."

In the most chilling scenario, Pakistan gradually falls apart. Institutions weaken and disappear. Militants, extremists and even criminals take over. Eventually, the country spirals down into a failed state that threatens the region and the world.

Indeed, the term "failed state" is heard more and more regarding Pakistan. According to *Foreign Policy* magazine's "Failed States Index," Pakistan moved to ninth from the top this year, from 12th last year.[94]

To prevent a further descent into chaos, Pakistan must first curb militancy within its borders and then address social, economic and political shortcomings, experts say. Cease-fire negotiations reportedly are already underway with some militants. It is the rare Pakistan expert who doesn't stress that the United States must stop attacks on Pakistani soil while the government enters into talks with militants.

"The U.S., meanwhile, should end direct military strikes in the area, even if these are conducted with the knowledge and cooperation of Pakistan's military," writes Harvard's Abbas. "Force has never worked with the Pashtun tribes, and there is no evidence that this has changed. There are real signs that the new government is considered a credible partner in the tribal areas. It needs to be given time to find a way out of the endless cycle of violence."[95]

Establishing better relations with India, especially in light of the recent Mumbai terrorist attacks, is also seen as crucial. If this year's reopening of the Kashmir border to trade is any indication, the region will breathe easier.

As Benazir Bhutto once wrote, "It is time for new ideas. It is time for creativity. It is time for bold commitment. And it is time for honesty, both among people and between people."

She also believed deeply in Pakistan and its future, predicting shortly before she was assassinated, "Time, justice and the forces of history are on our side."[96]

Getty Images/Jeff J. Mitchell

More than 200,000 people were forced to abandon their homes — and at least 800 were killed — during a major Pakistani military assault in August on militants in the troubled Bajaur district. Many took refuge in makeshift camps near Peshawar (above). "The people sitting in the dust are the so-called 'collateral damage' of Pakistan's own war on terror," wrote reporters for London's Independent.

But not everyone is optimistic. In his much-admired analysis of Pakistan's future, the Brookings Institution's Cohen wrote, "In summary, the human material is there to turn Pakistan into a modern state, but it has been systematically squandered for three generations by an elite persuaded that Pakistan's critical strategic location would be enough to get it through critical times. Now, the distant future has arrived, with Pakistan unequipped to face a fast-changing world while coping with new and mounting domestic problems."[97]

NOTES

1. "How to beat the terrorists?" *The Economist*, Sept. 23, 2008, www.economist.com/research/articlesBy Subject/displaystory.cfm?subjectid=1604388&story_id=12284547.

2. Carlotta Gall, "Bombing at hotel in Pakistan kills at least 40," *The New York Times*, Sept. 21, 2008, www.nytimes.com/2008/09/21/world/asia/21islamabad.html.

3. "Address of President of Pakistan Asif Ali Zardari to the Parliament," Sept. 20, 2008, www.satp.org/satporgtp/countries/pakistan/document/papers/speechpresident.htm.

4. Jane Perlez, "Pakistan's faith in its new leader is shaken," *The New York Times*, Sept. 27, 2008, www.nytimes .com/2008/09/27/world/asia/27pstan.html?em. Also see Roland Flamini, "Afghanistan on the Brink," *CQ Global Researcher*, June 2007, pp. 125-150.

5. The Associated Press, "Change of Plans saved Pakistani leaders from blast," *USA Today*, Sept. 22, 2008, www.usatoday.com/news/world/2008-09-22-pakistan-change-of-plans_ N.htm.

6. Dexter Filkins, "Right at the edge," *The New York Times Magazine*, Sept. 7, 2008, www.nytimes .com/2008/09/07/magazine/07pakistan-t.html.

7. Quoted in Paul Wiseman and Zafar Sheikh, "Militants flourish in Pakistan's tribal areas," *USA Today*, Oct. 1, 2008, www.usatoday.com/news/world/2008-10-01-tribes_N.htm.

8. See Daniel Markey, "Hotbed of Terrorism," Council on Foreign Relations, Aug. 11, 2008, www.cfr.org/publication/16929/hotbed_of_terror.html?breadcrumb=%2Fbios%2F13611%2Fjayshree_bajoria%3Fpage%3D2.

9. Stephen P. Cohen, "The Next Chapter," Brookings Institution, Oct. 10, 2008, www.brookings .edu/reports/2008/09_pakistan_cohen.aspx?rssid=cohens.

10. "Pakistan Assessment 2008," *South Asian Terrorism Portal*, www.satp.org/satporgtp/countries/pakistan/.

11. *Ibid.*

12. Aryn Baker, "Dangerous Ground," *Time*, July 10, 2008, www.time.com/time/magazine/article/0,9171,1821495,00.html?iid=digg_share.

13. *Ibid.*

14. Jane Perlez, "64 in Pakistan die in bombing at arms plant," *The New York Times*, Aug. 21, 2008, www .nytimes.com/2008/08/22/world/asia/22pstan .html?_r=1&hp&oref=slogin.

15. "Musharraf's Support Shrinks, Even As More Pakistanis Reject Terrorism . . . and the U.S.," http:// pewresearch.org/pubs/561/pakistan-terrorism.

16. The Associated Press, "Afghanistan: Attack in Pakistan," *The New York Times*, Nov. 18, 2008, www.nytimes.com/2008/11/19/world/asia/19briefs-ATTACKINPAKI_BRF.html?partner=rss&emc=rss.

17. "The Last Resort," *The Economist*, Oct. 23, 2008, www.economist.com/world/asia/displaystory.cfm?story_id=12480386.

18. "China to Pakistan's rescue?" *The Economist*, Oct. 16, 2008, www.economist.com/agenda/displaystory .cfm?story_id=12445315.

19. Baker, *op. cit.*

20. David Lynch, "Global financial crisis may hit hardest outside U.S.," *USA Today*, Sept. 30, 2008, www .usatoday.com/money/economy/2008-10-29-global-financial-crisis_N.htm.

21. Jonathan Landay, "New intelligence report says Pakistan is 'on Edge,'" McClatchy Newspapers, Oct. 14, 2008, www.mcclatchydc.com/world/story/53926.html.

22. Sumit Gangult, "Danger ahead for the most dangerous place in the world," *The Washington Post*, Oct. 12, 2008, www.washingtonpost.com/wp-dyn/content/article/2008/10/09/AR2008100901206.html.

23. "Secretary Gates and Admiral Mullen testify," Institute for the Study of War, Sept. 11, 2008, www .understandingwar.org/print/315.

24. Lisa Curtis, "Combating terrorism in Pakistan: going on the offensive," Heritage Foundation, July 15, 2008, www.heritage.org/research/AsiaandthePacific/wm1991.cfm.

25. See Caroline Wadhams, *et al.*, "Partnership for Progress: Advancing a new strategy for prosperity and stability in Pakistan and the region," Center for American Progress, November 2008, p. 63, www.americanprogress.org/issues/2008/11/pdf/pakistan.pdf.

26. "US to focus on Pakistani border," BBC, Sept. 10, 2008, http://news.bbc.co.uk/2/hi/south_asia/7609073.stm.

27. Husain Haqqani, "The Capital Interview: Fighting terrorism is Pakistan's own war," Council on Foreign Relations, Oct. 21, 2008, www.cfr.org/publication/17567/.

28. Jane Perlez, "Pakistani legislators show little appetite for a fight," *The New York Times*, Oct. 21, 2008, www.nytimes.com/2008/10/21/world/asia/21pstan .html.

29. *Ibid.*

30. Stephen Philip Cohen, "A Pakistani response to the Marriott Attack," Brookings Institution, Sept. 22, 2008, www.brookings.edu/opinions/2008/0922_pakistan_cohen.aspx?rssid=LatestFromBrookings.

31. Ahmed Rashid, "Pakistan's New Stage of Struggle," BBC News, Aug. 20, 2008, http://news.bbc.co.uk/2/hi/south_asia/7571085.stm.

32. Ahmed Rashid, "Pakistan on the Brink," *Yale Global Online*, Sept. 19, 2008, http://yaleglobal.yale.edu/display.article?id=11350.

33. Imtiaz Ali, "Foreign policy challenges for new US president," *Yale Global Online*, Oct. 31, 2008, http://yaleglobal.yale.edu/display.article?id=11538.

34. B. Raman, "PAK-US SNAFU," *International Terrorism Monitor: Paper No. 442*, South Asia Analysis Group, Sept. 13, 2008, www.southasiaanalysis.org/papers29/paper2843.html.

35. Faraz Khan, "10 months, 10 parties, 100 killed," *Daily Times*, Oct. 31, 2008, www.dailytimes.com.pk/default.asp?page=2008%5C10%5C31%5Cstory_31-10-2008_pg12_1.

36. Aryn Baker, "Pakistan votes amid tension," *Time*, Feb. 18, 2008, www.time.com/time/world/article/0,8599,1714206,00.html.

37. Lyce Doucet, "Pakistan ponders meaning of democracy," BBC News, Feb. 17, 2008, http://news.bbc.co.uk/2/hi/programmes/from_our_own_correspondent/7247096.stm.

38. "Pakistanis want larger role for both Islam and democracy," USIP.org, Jan. 7, 2008, www.usip.org/newsmedia/releases/2008/0107_pakistan_opinion.html.

39. Stephen Philip Cohen, *The Idea of Pakistan* (2004), p. 278.

40. Lisa Curtis, "Pakistan: Stumbling Towards Democracy," Heritage Foundation, Aug. 10, 2007, www.heritage.org/press/commentary/ed081007b.cfm.

41. Owen Bennett Jones, *Pakistan: The Eye of the Storm* (2003), p. 230.

42. "The World's Most Dangerous Place," *The Economist*, Jan. 5, 2008, www.economist.com/opinion/displaystory.cfm?story_id=10430237.

43. Asif Ali Zardari, "Democracy within our reach," *The Washington Post*, Sept. 4, 2008, www.washingtonpost.com/wp-dyn/content/article/2008/09/03/AR2008090303131.html.

44. Husain Haqqani, "America is better off without Musharraf," *The Wall Street Journal*, Aug. 21, 2008, http://online.wsj.com/article/SB121927727332058621.html?mod=googlenews_wsj.

45. Benazir Bhutto, *Reconciliation: Islam, Democracy, and the West* (2008), p. 2.

46. Paul Reynolds, "On the trail of the black market bombs," BBC News, Feb. 12, 2004, http://news.bbc.co.uk/2/low/americas/3481 499.stm.

47. Jonathan Manthorpe, "Pakistani scientist ran a nuclear Wal-Mart," *Vancouver Sun*, Aug. 26, 2006, www.canada.com/vancouversun/columnists/story.html?id=328861ae-88b1-46f7-b14c-89f7fbd78239.

48. David E. Sanger and William J. Broad, "US secretly aids Pakistan in guarding nuclear arms," *The New York Times*, Nov. 18, 2007, www.nytimes.com/2007/11/18/washington/18nuke.html.

49. *Ibid.*

50. "Osama Wanted Nuke Help," The Associated Press, Dec. 30, 2002, http://uttm.com/stories/2002/12/30/world/main534727.shtml.

51. Joby Warrick, "Lack of knowledge about arsenal may limit US options," *The Washington Post*, Nov. 11, 2007, www.washingtonpost.com/wp-dyn/content/article/2007/11/10/AR2007111001684_pf.html. Also see Roland Flamini, "Nuclear Proliferation," *CQ Global Researcher*, January 2007, pp. 1-26.

52. Syed Shoaib Hasan, "Are Pakistan's nuclear weapons safe?" BBC News, Jan. 23, 2008, http://news.bbc.co.uk/2/hi/south_asia/7190033.stm.

53. Sanger and Broad, *op. cit.*

54. Ahmad Hasan Dani, "Pakistan: History through the centuries," www.geocities.com/pak_history/pak.html.

55. "History of Pakistan," www.geocities.com/pak_history/.

56. Cohen, *op. cit.*, p. 6.

57. Jones, *op. cit*, p. 11.

58. M. Ilyas Khan, "Pakistan's circular history," BBC News, Aug. 11, 2007, http://news.bbc.co.uk/2/hi/south_asia/6940148.stm.

59. Cohen, *op. cit.*, p. 124.

60. Jones, *op. cit.*, p. xiii.

61. Seth Kaplan, *Fixing Fragile States* (2008), p. 151.

62. For background, see Flamini, "Afghanistan on the Brink," *op. cit.*

63. For background, see David Masci and Kenneth Jost, "War on Terrorism," *CQ Researcher*, Oct. 12, 2001, pp. 817-848; and Kenneth Jost, "Rebuilding Afghanistan," *CQ Researcher*, Dec. 21, 2001, pp. 1041-1064.

64. Hassan Abbas, "A profile of Tehrik-I-Taliban Pakistan," *CTC Sentinel*, January 2008.

65. "US Think tank: Pakistan helped train Taliban, gave info on US troops," The Associated Press, June 9, 2008, www.iht.com/articles/ap/2008/06/09/asia/AS-GEN-Afghan-Pakistan.php.

66. Brian Glyn Williams and Cathy Young, "Cheney attack reveals suicide bombing patterns," Jamestown Foundation, Nov. 21, 2008, www.jamestown.org/news_details.php?news_id=222.

67. Aryn Baker, "The truth about Talibanistan," *Time*, April 2, 2007, www.time.com/time/magazine/article/0,9171,1601850,00.html.

68. Dexter Filkins, "Right at the edge," *The New York Times*, Sept. 7, 2008, pp. 52-61, 114-116, www.nytimes.com/2008/09/07/magazine/07pakistan-t.html.

69. Candace Rondeaux, "Suspected US airstrike kills 6 fighters in Pakistan," *The Washington Post*, Nov. 19, 2008, www.washingtonpost.com/wp-dyn/content/article/2008/11/19/AR2008111903714.html?hpid=sec-world.

70. Aryn Baker, "US stepping up operations in Pakistan," *Time*, Sept. 10, 2008 www.time.com/time/world/article/0,8599,1840383,00.html.

71. Jane Perlez, "Confronting Taliban, US finds itself at war," *The New York Times*, Oct. 3, 2008, www.nytimes.com/2008/10/03/world/asia/03pstan.html.

72. "Pakistan captures militant stronghold," The Associated Press, Oct. 26, 2008, http://news.yahoo.com/s/ap/20081025/ap_on_re_as/as_pakistan.

73. "Missile attacks, apparently by US, kill 27 in Pakistan, including Qaeda operative," The Associated Press, Oct. 31, 2008, www.nytimes.com/2008/11/01/world/asia/01drone.html?ref=world.

74. Jane Perlez, "As Taliban overwhelm police, Pakistanis hit back," *The New York Times*, Nov. 2, 2008, www.nytimes.com/2008/11/02/world/asia/02pstan.html; "Pakistanis flee into Afghanistan," BBC News, Sept. 29, 2008, http://news.bbc.co.uk/2/hi/south_asia/7642015.stm.

75. Andrew Buncombe and Omar Waraich, "Exclusive dispatch: Pakistan's Hidden War," *The Independent*, Oct. 23, 2008, www.independent.co.uk/news/world/asia/exclusive-dispatch-pakistans-hidden-war-969784.html.

76. Huma Yusuf, "Pakistan bans Taliban outfit amidst military campaign," *The Christian Science Monitor*, Aug. 26, 2008, www.csmonitor.com/2008/0825/p99s01-duts.html.

77. Jane Perlez and Pir Zubair Shah, "Pakistan uses tribal militias in Taliban war," *The New York Times*, Oct. 23, 2008, www.nytimes.com/2008/10/24/world/asia/24militia.html?hp.

78. Jane Perlez and Pir Zubair Shah, "Pakistan's tribal militias walk a tightrope in fight against Taliban," *The New York Times*, Oct. 24, 2008, www.nytimes.com/2008/10/24/world/asia/24militia.html?hp.

79. Zahid Hussain and Matthew Rosenberg, "Bombing targets Pakistan militia," *The Wall Street Journal*, Nov. 6, 2008.

80. Perlez and Shah, *op. cit.*

81. Mark Mazzetti and Eric Schmitt, "Pakistanis aided attack in Kabul," *The New York Times*, Aug. 1, 2008, www.nytimes.com/2008/08/01/world/asia/01pstan.html?_r=1&hp&oref=slogin.

82. Anthony Cordesman, "US Security interests after Musharraf," Center for Strategic and International Studies, Aug. 21, 2008, www.csis.org/component/option,com_csis_pubs/task,view/id,4810/.

83. Saeed Shah, "US risks overplaying hand with Pakistan strikes," *The Guardian*, Oct. 24, 2008.

84. *Ibid.*

85. Jane Perlez, "Pakistan tells US to stop strikes in tribal zones," *The New York Times*, Oct. 29, 2008, www.nytimes.com/2008/10/30/world/asia/30pstan.html.

86. Jane Perlez, "Petraeus in Pakistan, hears complaints about missile strikes," *The New York Times*, Nov. 4, 2008, www.nytimes.com/2008/11/04/world/asia/04pstan.html?partner=rssnyt&emc=rss.

87. Aryn Baker, "Pakistan: Negligent on terror?" *Time*, June 30, 2008, www.time.com/time/world/article/0,8599,1819125,00.html.

88. Wadhams, *et al., op. cit.*

89. Nick Schifrin and Habibullah Khan, "Will Obama change US Pakistan policy?" ABC News, Nov. 5, 2008, http://abcnews.go.com/International/story?id=6189479&page=1.

90. Cohen, *op. cit.*

91. "An expanding war in Afghanistan awaits next US president," Agence France-Presse, Nov. 1, 2008, http://afp.google.com/article/ALeqM5iwbu3EDjze-Li-CDAI-yx8VzqBrw.

92. Wadhams, *et al., op. cit.*

93. Nasim Zehra, "Obama and Pakistan: Mutual Trust, Respect and Understanding," Asia Society, Nov. 5, 2008, http://asiasociety.org/resources/081105_obama_pakistan.html.

94. "The Failed States Index 2008," *Foreign Policy*, 2008, www.foreignpolicy.com/story/cms.php?page=1&story_id=4350.

95. Hassan Abbas, "Exorcising General's Ghost," *Khaleed Times*, July 13, 2008, www.khaleejtimes.com/DisplayArticleNew.asp?section=opinion&xfile=data/opinion/2008/july/opinion_july54.xml.

96. Bhutto, *op. cit.*

97. Cohen, *op. cit*, p. 299.

BIBLIOGRAPHY

Books

Abbas, Hasaan, *Pakistan's Drift into Extremism: Allah, the Army and America's War on Terror*, 2004.
A Harvard fellow and former member of Pakistan's anti-corruption police force explores how radicalism has shaped and influenced the nation's development.

Ahmed, Akbar, *Journey Into Islam: The Crisis of Globalization, Brookings Institution Press*, 2007.
A noted Islamic studies professor, joined by several non-Muslim students, sets out on an international trip to numerous Muslim countries to explore the importance of improved dialog between the Muslim and non-Muslim worlds.

Bhutto, Benazir, *Reconciliation: Islam, Democracy, and the West, Harper Collins*, 2008.
The former prime minister finished writing this gripping account of her return to Pakistan just days before her assassination. She explores the complex relationship between the Middle East and the West and shows how democracy and Islam can coexist.

Cohen, Stephen Philip, *The Idea of Pakistan, The Brookings Institution*, 2004.
A respected historian examines the military, religious, political and other factors that make Pakistan one of the world's least understood countries.

Haqqani, Husain, *Pakistan: Between Mosque and Military, Carnegie Endowment for International Peace*, 2005.
Pakistan's ambassador to the United States (former journalist and academic) examines the relationships between Pakistan's military and religious sectors.

Jones, Owen Bennett, *Pakistan: Eye of the Storm, Yale University Press*, 2002.
A BBC correspondent formerly based in Pakistan offers an excellent examination of the complex relationships between the country's society, military and political sectors.

Kaplan, Seth D., *Fixing Fragile States: A New Paradigm for Development, Praeger Security International*, 2008.
In this wide-ranging study, the author examines Pakistan and six other countries that appear to be teetering on the brink of "failed state" status.

Kux, Dennis, *The United States and Pakistan 1947-2000: Disenchanted Allies, Woodrow Wilson Center Press*, 2001.
A retired State Department South Asia specialist and career diplomat offers a detailed, informative survey of post-independence U.S.-Pakistan relations.

Nawaz, Shuja, *Crossed Swords: Pakistan, Its Army and the Wars Within, Oxford University Press,* **2008.**
A Pakistani journalist with impeccable contacts inside Pakistan's military provides a landmark study of the military's role in aiding — and hampering — Pakistan's development.

Rashid, Ahmed, *Descent into Chaos: The United States and the Failure of Nation Building in Pakistan, Afghanistan and Central Asia, Viking,* **2008.**
The Pakistani author of *Taliban* examines domestic and foreign forces that have helped turn Pakistan into a volatile flashpoint.

Talbot, Ian, *Pakistan: A Modern History, Palgrave Macmillan,* **2005.**
A British academic provides a thorough, well-researched account of the founding of Pakistan and its political history.

Articles

Filkins, Dexter, "Right at the Edge," *The New York Times,* **Sept. 7, 2008, pp. 52-61, 114-116, www.nytimes .com/2008/ 09/07/magazine/07pakistan-t.html.**
A seasoned foreign correspondent interviews militants, security forces and civilians in Pakistan's tribal areas.

Moreau, Ron, and Mark Hosenball, "Pakistan's Dangerous Double Game," *Newsweek,* **Sept. 22, 2008.**
A first-hand exploration of the U.S. military's recent, more aggressive approach to attacking militants inside Pakistan.

Reports and Studies

"The Next Chapter: The United States and Pakistan," *Pakistan Policy Working Group, Brookings Institution,* **September 2008.**
A group of experts on U.S.-Pakistan relations offers suggestions on how Washington can rethink its approach to Pakistan.

Grare, Frederic, "Rethinking Western Strategies Toward Pakistan: An action agenda for the United States and Europe," *Carnegie Endowment for International Peace,* **2007.**
A leading expert on South Asia calls for a new strategy to encourage the Pakistan military to promote civilian rule.

Markey, Dan, "Securing Pakistan's Tribal Belt," *Council on Foreign Relations,* **July/August 2008.**
A noted South Asia expert and former State Department officer examines issues shaping modern-day Pakistan.

Reidel, Bruce, "Pakistan and Terror: The Eye of the Storm," *The Annals of the American Academy,* **July 2008.**
A former CIA official and NATO adviser provides an overview of the present security situation in Pakistan.

For More Information

Carnegie Council, 170 E. 64th St., New York, NY 10021; (212) 838-4120; www.cceia.org. Think tank that advocates ethical decision-making in international policy.

Council on Foreign Relations, 58 E. 68th St., New York, NY 10021; (212) 434-9400; www.cfr.org. Promotes a better understanding of the foreign-policy choices facing the United States and other governments.

Human Rights Commission of Pakistan (HRCP), Secretariat/Punjab Chapter, Aiwan-I-Jamjoor, 107-Tipu Block, New Garden Town, Lahore 54600, Pakistan; (92) (042) 5838341; www.hrcp-web.org. Nongovernmental organization that acts as a clearinghouse for information on human rights abuses throughout Pakistan.

International Crisis Group, 149 Ave. Louise, Level 24, B-1050 Brussels, Belgium; +32-(0)-2-502-90-38; www.crisisgroup.org. Nongovernmental organization that uses field-based analysis and high-level advocacy to prevent violent conflict worldwide.

International Institute for Strategic Studies, 13-15 Arundel St., Temple Place, London WC2R 3DX, United Kingdom; +44-(0)-20-7379-7676; www.iiss.org. Think tank focusing on international security with emphasis on political-military conflict.

Islamabad Policy Research Institute, House No. 2, Street No. 15, Margella Rd., Sector F-7/12, Islamabad, Pakistan; +92-51-921-3680-2; www.ipripak.org. Evaluates national and international political-strategic issues and developments affecting Pakistan and surrounding countries.

Pakistan Institute of Legislative Development and Transparency, # 7, 9th Ave., F-8/1 Islamabad — 44000, Pakistan; +92-51-111 123 345; www.pildat.org. An independent, nonpartisan, nonprofit research and training institution that aims to strengthen democracy and democratic institutions in Pakistan.

Middle East Peace Prospects

Is There Any Hope for Long-Term Peace?

Irwin Arieff

8

AP Photo/Hatem Moussa

Palestinian militants stand guard during an Islamic Jihad rally in Bureij, Gaza, on Dec. 26, 2008 — the day before Israel launched its deadly, three-week assault on the Hamas-governed Palestinian territory. Israel says the invasion was necessary to stop persistent Palestinian shelling of Israeli territory from the Gaza Strip. Despite a six-month cease-fire that began last June, at least 1,750 rockets and 1,520 mortar shells landed in Israeli territory in 2008 — more than double the number in 2007.

From *CQ Global Researcher*, May 2009.

Ezzeldeen Abu al-Aish is a Palestinian physician and media personality well known in Israel. He speaks Hebrew, champions Israeli-Palestinian reconciliation and during Israel's controversial assault on Gaza earlier this year regularly briefed Israeli broadcast audiences on the fighting.

He was at home in Gaza giving a phone interview to Israeli television in mid-January when two Israeli tank shells suddenly struck his house — killing three of his eight children and a niece.

"My daughters, they killed them," sobbed Abu al-Aish on the broadcast. "Oh God. They killed them, Allah. . . . They died on the spot."[1]

The wrenching interview dramatically drove home for Israelis the impact their government's brutal 22-day assault against Gaza was having on innocent Palestinian civilians.

"I cried when I saw this," then-Israeli Prime Minister Ehud Olmert said later. "How could you not? I wept."[2]

The Israeli military later defended the tank-fire as "reasonable" because it was the result of mistaken intelligence that militants were using the doctor's home to fire on Israeli troops.[3]

Israel has justified its deadly Dec. 27 invasion into Hamas-governed Gaza on the grounds that it needed to stop Palestinian militants in the Gaza Strip from firing rockets into Israeli territory. Some 1,750 rockets and 1,520 mortar shells landed in Israel in 2008, killing eight people, according to Israel's nonprofit Intelligence and Terrorism Information Center. That was more than double the number in 2007, the center says, despite a six-month cease-fire that began in mid-June of 2008.[4]

Neighbors, But Worlds Apart

Israel's economy is flourishing compared to the territories it occupied after the 1967 Six-Day War. Israel's gross domestic product (GDP) of $28,000 per capita makes it among the world's wealthiest nations, while the West Bank and Gaza Strip are two of the world's poorest areas. Similarly, the unemployment rate in Israel is a relatively low 6 percent compared with 16 in the West Bank — and a staggering 41 percent in Gaza.

Israel

Area: 8,019 square miles (slightly smaller than New Jersey)

Population: 7,233,701 (July 2009 est., including Israeli settlers in the West Bank, Golan Heights and in East Jerusalem

Religion: Jewish 76%, Muslim 16%, Christians 2%, Druze 2%, unspecified 4%

GDP per capita: $28,200 (2008 est.)

Unemployment rate: 6.1% (2008 est.)

West Bank

Area: 2,263 square miles (slightly smaller than Delaware)

Population: 2,461,267 (July 2009 est.)

Religion: Muslim 75%, Jewish 17%, Christian and other 8%

GDP per capita: $2,900 (2008 est.)

Unemployment rate: 16.3% (June 2008)

Gaza Strip

Area: 139 square miles (about twice the size of Washington, D.C.)

Population: 1,551,859 (July 2009 est.)

Religion: Muslim 99%, Christian 1%

GDP per capita: $2,900 (2008 est.)

Unemployment rate: 41.3% (June 2008)

Note: Statistics for Israel include the Golan Heights — a hilly, 444-square-mile strip of land in northeastern Israel occupied during the Six-Day War and unilaterally annexed by Israel in 1981.

Source: The World Factbook, Central Intelligence Agency

"We wanted to stop the rockets on our cities," says Asaf Shariv, Israel's consul general in New York City. "The goal was to change the security reality on the ground — meaning that they won't shoot without paying a price for that."

During a visit to southern Israel five months before the Gaza war started, then-presidential candidate Barack Obama appeared to support Israel's reasoning. "If somebody was sending rockets into my house where my two daughters sleep at night, I'm going to do everything in my power to stop that. And I would expect Israelis to do the same thing," Obama had said in July 2008.[5]

Palestinian militants say their rockets were fired in retaliation for Israel's continuing stranglehold on Gaza, including regular military raids and tight control over the movement of goods and people in and out of the territory.

But as the deaths of Abu al-Aish's children tragically demonstrated, Middle East violence produces other innocent victims than just Israelis killed by Palestinian rocket fire. According to the Palestinian Centre for Human Rights in Gaza City, of the 1,417 Palestinians killed during Israel's 22-day assault on the densely populated territory, 926 were civilians, including 313 children.[6]

The Israel Defense Forces (IDF) dispute those figures, putting the total at 1,166 Palestinians killed, 709 of them Hamas militants and fewer than 300 of them innocent civilians — including 89 children.[7] The military said it had tried hard to avoid civilian casualties but that the militants often chose to fight in heavily populated areas, effectively using civilians as human shields.

Hamas, one of the two main Palestinian political groups along with Fatah, is a hard-line Islamic organization backed by Iran and Syria that refuses to recognize Israel's right to exist. It also embraces violence — including rocket launches and suicide attacks against Israel — in its fight for what it sees as Palestinian land.

"When we are fired upon, we need to react harshly," then-Foreign Minister Tzipi Livni said on March 9 in Jerusalem after discussing the Gaza war with visiting U.S. Secretary of State Hillary Rodham Clinton.[8]

Ultimately, however, only 13 Israelis died in the conflict — 10 soldiers in combat and three civilians to rocket fire. The disparity in casualties triggered widespread international criticism of Israel's use of fighter jets, tanks and other heavy weapons to target poorly armed urban

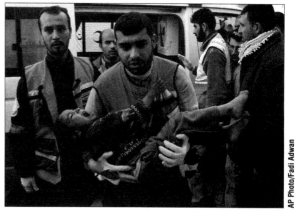

AP Photo/Fadi Adwan

A Palestinian medic rushes an injured child to the hospital during the Israeli invasion of Gaza on Jan. 4, 2009. According to the Palestinian Centre for Human Rights, 926 of the 1,417 Palestinians killed during the three-week assault on the densely populated territory were civilians, including 313 children. Israel Defense Forces estimated that 1,166 Palestinians were killed, fewer than 300 of them civilians, including 89 children.

guerrillas in a densely populated enclosed territory — and accusations of war crimes.[9]

Israel's initial air campaign unleashed 88 attack aircraft on 100 targets in three minutes and 40 seconds. "It was intense, probably more so than any conflict since the January 1991 start of the Iraq War," said Paul Rogers, an international security expert for the London-based Oxford Research Group. The degree of destruction "far exceeded what Hamas planners had anticipated."[10]

"There is a feeling in the Arab world that this kind of disproportionality has been used in the electoral process — that the [then-governing] Kadima and Labor parties were using [harsh military tactics] to increase their chances in the Israeli election," says Maged Abdelaziz, Egypt's ambassador to the United Nations.

Indeed, Israel's invasion occurred just before a major election on Feb. 10 for Israel's single-chamber parliament, the Knesset. Israeli frustration over the rocket launches and the lack of progress from years of peace efforts resulted in a sharp shift to the right, and the installation of conservative Benjamin Netanyahu as prime minister. (*See sidebar, p. 216.*)

During the several weeks it took for Netanyahu to assemble his governing coalition, former Prime Minister Olmert's caretaker government continued its tight rein on the flow of humanitarian and commercial goods into

Jewish state's creation in May 1948. But a glimmer of hope that change might be in the wind appeared on Jan. 20, when Barack Obama moved into the White House pledging to court global Muslim public opinion and personally strive for a comprehensive Middle East peace. Within days of his inauguration, he named former Sen. George Mitchell, D-Maine, a veteran international mediator, as his special Middle East peace envoy.

"We're not going to wait until the end of my administration to deal with Palestinian and Israeli peace, we're going to start now," Obama said.[12]

His pledge underlined the reality that, despite years of talks and numerous military clashes, Israelis are fed up with years of fruitless peace negotiations while they remain under attack from Palestinian militants, and the Palestinian population bridles at continued Israeli restrictions and sees little hope for a homeland of their own.

Further complicating peace efforts, right-wing fundamentalists are pressuring each side not to accept a two-state solution: Militant Jewish settlers insist that all of the occupied territories rightfully belong to the Jews, while radical Muslims believe Israel itself occupies land wrongfully taken from them.

Moreover, the entire region's geopolitical landscape has been reshaped in recent years by the growing strategic importance of its vast oil reserves, the 2003 U.S. invasion of Iraq, the Muslim world's widening Shiite-Sunni schism and simmering tensions between Syria and Lebanon. In addition, the U.S. toppling of strongman Saddam Hussein's Sunni regime in Iraq unintentionally strengthened predominantly Shiite Iran next door, which worries other Sunni neighbors, such as Saudi Arabia, Jordan and Egypt.

Tehran is also accused by the West of seeking nuclear weapons — a charge it denies — and is openly hostile toward Israel, which is widely presumed to have its own nuclear arsenal. Israel now sees Tehran, not the Palestinians, as its greatest threat, particularly after Iranian President Mahmoud Ahmadinejad repeatedly called for Israel to be "wiped off the map."[13] Iran also supports Hamas as well as Hezbollah, an anti-Israeli militant group that is now a part of the government of Lebanon, Israel's northern neighbor.

In a bold challenge to President Obama's often-stated hopes for swift progress toward Palestinian statehood, a top Israeli official announced in April that Israel's new

Suffering on Both Sides

Israeli air strikes on Jan. 9, 2009, turned entire blocks of the Jabalia refugee camp in the Gaza Strip (top) into piles of rubble. Throughout Gaza, the U.N. estimates that 4,000 Palestinian homes were destroyed and 20,000 severely damaged during the three-week war — about 20 percent of the territory's housing stock. In the Israeli city of Ashdod, a man surveys a house (bottom) damaged by a Palestinian rocket on Jan. 18, 2009.

war-torn Gaza, fueling tensions in the territory just as the international community was trying to calm things down.[11] Although both sides unilaterally agreed to stop fighting in January — and Egypt is mediating long-term cease-fire talks — Palestinian militants quickly resumed their rocket fire, and Israel continued to block full access to Gaza — stirring fresh anguish in southern Israel and Palestinian pleas for international help to rebuild a shattered Gaza. The rocket fire also triggered retaliatory Israeli strikes, leading to more Palestinian casualties.

The developments were only the latest in a seemingly endless cycle of Israeli-Palestinian violence since the

government would condition entering peace talks with the Palestinians on Washington first making progress in derailing Iran's suspected pursuit of nuclear weapons and curtailing Tehran's regional ambitions.[14]

"It's a crucial condition if we want to move forward," Israeli Deputy Foreign Minister Daniel Ayalon said. "If we want to have a real political process with the Palestinians, then you can't have the Iranians undermining and sabotaging."

Obama has repeatedly warned against delay in addressing the Israeli-Palestinian conflict, and since taking office on Jan. 20 his administration has been simultaneously working to resolve both that crisis and that of Iran — although the global recession has gotten top priority.

Because the United States is Israel's closest ally and arms supplier, the ongoing Israeli-Palestinian conflict continues to fuel anti-American sentiment in the Arab world, perhaps energizing Washington to try harder to resolve the conflict. As part of his post-9/11 war on terror, U.S. President George W. Bush strongly supported Israel's aggressive campaign against Palestinian militants, even though in June 2002 he became the first U.S. leader to publicly embrace the goal of Palestinian statehood.[15]

Nevertheless, the combination of America's pro-Israel stance and its invasion of Iraq have been interpreted by many Muslims as a thinly veiled war on Islam rather than a war on "terrorists." As a result, Islamic militants in Iraq and elsewhere declared holy war against the United States.

After a fruitless year of Middle East diplomacy launched in 2007 in Annapolis, Md., the Bush administration in its final days put the blame squarely on Hamas for the harsh Israeli attack on Gaza, even as many U.S. allies — including moderate Muslim states with normally friendly ties to Israel like Egypt and Turkey — called for Israeli moderation.[16]

In a dramatic moment at this year's World Economic Forum in Davos, Switzerland, Turkish Prime Minister Recep Tayyip Erdogan lashed out at Israeli President Shimon Peres: "When it comes to killing, you know well how to kill."[17]

Some analysts accused Washington of undermining its own interests by blindly supporting Israel.[18] Former President Jimmy Carter drew fire from both U.S. and Israeli officials by meeting with representatives of Hamas,

which the United States and Israel shun because it refuses to renounce violence, acknowledge Israel's right to exist and uphold previous Palestinian agreements.[19]

The war, its ratcheting up of regional and international tensions plus the possibility of change have reopened the debate on virtually all aspects of the peace process. Among them: whether Palestinian statehood remains a desirable goal, whether the internationally crafted "roadmap" to peace needs revising and whether the so-called Quartet of international mediators can help the parties along the path to peace.

The Quartet — representing the United States, the United Nations, the European Union and Russia — was pulled together in 2002 by former U.N. Secretary-General Kofi Annan and Spanish Foreign Minister Miguel Angel Moratinos, former European Union (EU) special envoy for the Middle East. The next year the Quartet published its "roadmap" to peace, aimed at Palestinian statehood by the end of 2005.[20]

The roadmap was meant to build on the landmark 1993 Oslo Accords. In those agreements and in accompanying letters, Palestinian leaders recognized Israel's right to exist, Israel recognized the Palestinians' right to eventual self-government and they both agreed to negotiate a final, comprehensive peace agreement gradually over a five-year period.[21]

As it turned out, neither plan did the trick. Six years after the roadmap and 16 years after Oslo, Arab-Israeli peace and Palestinian statehood appear as elusive as ever.

As the search for a peaceful solution in the Middle East continues, here are some questions being debated:

Is a two-state solution still a viable possibility?

Palestinian statehood was not widely accepted as a central focus of the Middle East peace process until recently. The 1993 Oslo Accords did not even mention statehood. (*See box, p. 210.*) And although the idea was central to the failed 2000 Camp David Two peace talks, President Bill Clinton — the host of the summit — didn't publicly acknowledge that fact until January 2001, his final month in office.

Palestinian statehood was formally affirmed as a U.S. goal in June 2002, when President Bush declared in a White House speech, "My vision is two states, living side by side, in peace and security."[22] Since then, both sides

Expanding Israeli Settlements Undermine Peace Efforts

The continuing growth of Israeli settlements in Palestinian territories occupied by Israel during the 1967 Six-Day War poses a major barrier to Middle East peace. Although Israel has evacuated its Gaza Strip settlements and repeatedly promised to cap growth in West Bank and East Jerusalem settlements, they have grown steadily. Israel has also been walling off many settlements to bar suicide bombers but also blocking Palestinian access to the land. The Israelis also have built more than two dozen settlements in the Golan Heights, which was abandoned by the Syrian population when the Israelis invaded in 1967.

Source: Foundation For Middle East Peace

have endorsed the idea, and the U.N. Security Council has incorporated it in several resolutions. But the lack of progress over the last seven years has prompted questions about the viability and desirability of statehood.

In fact, in a reflection of growing Arab impatience with the peace process, Libyan leader Muammar Qaddafi recently has called for a single state, on the grounds that a two-state solution would neither satisfy Israeli security concerns nor give Palestinians the borders they desire. "In absolute terms, the two movements must remain in perpetual war or a compromise must be reached. The compromise is one state for all, an 'Isratine' that would allow the people in each party to feel that they live in all of the disputed land, and they are not deprived of any one part of it," he argued.[23]

In time, he predicted, "these two peoples will come to realize, I hope sooner rather than later, that living under one roof is the only option for a lasting peace." Years before Qaddafi's article, the idea had caught on with some Palestinians and liberal Israelis, who argue that Israel will never actually allow a separate Palestinian state — despite past commitments.

But Israeli leaders say the one-state idea is a nonstarter due to changing demographics. Within about a decade Jews will comprise a minority in "Greater Israel" — the original state plus the lands it acquired in the 1967 Six-Day War — because its Arab population is growing faster than the Jewish population. Thus, a single state would be run, eventually, by Arabs rather than by Jews.

The demographic trend leaves Israel precious little time to negotiate Palestinian statehood, Prime Minister Olmert warned a Knesset committee in September. "Ever-growing segments of the international community are adopting the idea of a binational state," he said. "[But] I see a Jewish state as a condition for our existence."[24]

Israeli concerns about a single state strengthened during the Gaza invasion, after many Israeli Arabs participated in anti-Israel demonstrations.

And while some Palestinians may dream of controlling a greater Israel, the idea that "Israel would give equal rights to Palestinians in such a model is a bit of an illusion," says Dutch diplomat Robert H. Serry, the U.N. special coordinator for the Middle East peace process.

For the Palestinian Authority, the internationally acknowledged administrator of the Palestinian territories, the two-state plan remains the best option, but the

two sides cannot close a deal on their own, says Riyad Mansour, Palestine's non-voting observer at the United Nations. "They need a third party that they know and trust, and if that third party could act decisively, then the deal could be closed," he says. "And we hope that President Obama is the third party that will help us to reach that conclusion."

Since taking office, the Obama administration has repeatedly reaffirmed the two-state model. "The inevitability of working toward a two-state solution seems inescapable," Secretary of State Clinton said during a visit to Israel in March. "We happen to believe that moving toward the two-state solution, step by step, is in Israel's best interest."[25]

But following the Israeli elections, many diplomats and analysts began wondering whether the parties might instead end up with what some call the "non-state" solution — a continuation of the status quo in which the peace process is indefinitely frozen. Netanyahu, Israel's new prime, has consistently refused to express support for Palestinian statehood, preferring instead to focus on Palestinian economic development and security issues and giving a higher priority to the potential nuclear threat from Iran.

Moreover, despite Palestinian efforts to form a national unity government that could include Hamas, Netanyahu insists he would not negotiate with a Palestinian government that includes Hamas — a movement he sees as an enemy of the Jewish state that must be defeated. "We won't negotiate with Hamas, because we won't negotiate with people who only want to negotiate our funeral arrangements," says Israeli Consul General Shariv.

But, he adds, if Hamas agrees to the three key principles set out by the Quartet as a prerequisite for Hamas to be accepted by the international community, "we negotiate with Hamas. It's as simple as that."

A Quartet statement issued after Hamas won the 2006 Palestinian election advised all world governments against dealing with any new Palestinian administration that did not reject violence, recognize Israel and accept all prior Palestinian commitments and obligations — including the roadmap.[26]

Hamas has so far refused to honor those principles, leaving it and Gaza increasingly isolated. After the 2006 elections, the isolation fueled a fierce rivalry between Hamas and Fatah, the other main Palestinian political

Israeli Settlements Continue to Grow

Despite repeated calls for Israel to withdraw its settlers from the West Bank and East Jerusalem and freeze further settlement expansion, the population in West Bank settlements rose 61 percent from 1999 to 2008. The Israeli population in East Jerusalem in 2006, the latest year for which data are available, was 8 percent more than in 2000. Israel withdrew all settlers from Gaza in 2005.

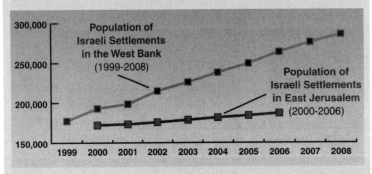

Source: Foundation for Middle East Peace, based on data from Israel's Central Bureau of Statistics and The Jerusalem Institute for Israel Studies.

grew out of the lack of progress that followed the Oslo Accords. The Quartet was set up in 2002 when its members concluded the Israelis and Palestinians could not work together on their own to reach a final peace agreement. The Quartet then gave them a "roadmap" to follow.

"They saw that the parties were not capable of producing any peace agreement. You needed the U.S. and the Quartet to hold the hand of both parties," says Norwegian diplomat Terje Roed-Larsen, a former U.N. special coordinator for the Middle East peace process and an architect of the Quartet. "So the roadmap was negotiated between the European Union, the United Nations, the United States and Russia, and then presented to the parties."

organization, leading to a civil war that left Hamas in control of the Gaza Strip and Fatah running the West Bank.

Hamas believes Israel was established on land belonging to the Palestinians, regardless of what this or any other Israel government believes about an eventual Palestinian state. But Palestinian President Mahmoud Abbas, whose Fatah party is more moderate than Hamas, said the shared goal of Palestinian statehood — as embraced by past Israeli governments — should not be affected by elections. "We respect the choice of the Israeli people, and we respect the elections that took place in Israel," he said when Secretary Clinton visited the West Bank on March 4. "But we demand that the Israeli government also commits itself to the roadmap plan and the two-state vision."[27]

But Shariv says it is not Netanyahu who is blocking Palestinian statehood but the deep divisions between Hamas and Fatah. "The Palestinians understand that they cannot go to a Palestinian state without Gaza," he says. "They don't want to have a three-state solution."

Has the "roadmap for peace" become a fig leaf for inaction?

The idea of an international overseer — the Quartet — that would push Israelis and Palestinians toward peace

The roadmap set out parallel paths for each side to pursue simultaneously, in three phases, culminating in a permanent and comprehensive peace agreement in 2005. "Both parties accept this vision. But we can reach it only if we move rapidly and in parallel on all fronts. The so-called 'sequential' approach has failed," U.N. chief Annan explained at the time.[28] (*See box, p. 210.*)

But in practice the roadmap didn't work. While the Quartet monitored the process and met on an irregular basis to comment on developments and appeal to the parties, there was no mechanism to enforce or even document the parties' performance. And Israel quickly announced that it viewed its obligations under the plan as conditioned on an immediate end to Palestinian violence.

"Full performance will be a condition for progress between phases and for progress within phases," the Israeli cabinet said in attaching 14 reservations to its acceptance of the plan.[29]

The roadmap made its debut during one of the lowest points of the peace process. The 2000 Camp David Two summit — attended by Palestinian leader Yasser Arafat and Israeli leader Barak — had failed to produce a peace agreement, instead triggering a Second Intifada, or Palestinian uprising against Israeli occupation. The violence lasted more than four years and caused the deaths of more than 4,000 people, three-quarters of them Palestinians.[30]

With the Intifada raging, President Clinton asked former Sen. Mitchell to look for ways to bring the violence to an end. Mitchell's first foray into high-stakes Middle East diplomacy called for a freeze on Israeli settlements in occupied territories and a Palestinian crackdown on terrorism. The roadmap later built on Mitchell's 2001 recommendations.[31]

But progress stalled when each side argued that its actions should be contingent on the other side's performance, rather than occur simultaneously. Israel insisted that Palestinian attacks end before Israel would take such required political steps as dismantling settlements erected since March 2001 and easing restrictions on the movements of people and goods; the Palestinians have said the attacks would not end until Israel honors its commitments.

While the Quartet called on both sides to take specific steps, some analysts and diplomats say the Quartet has been softer on Israel overall, due to the United States' close ties to the Jewish state.

"Even though there has developed a generally agreed approach on some aspects of what should be demanded of the Palestinian side, this is not the case as regards Israel," wrote Peruvian diplomat Alvaro de Soto, who served as the chief U.N. Middle East peace envoy from 2005 to 2007, in his confidential end-of-mission report. The report, which cited Washington's "very serious qualms about exerting pressure on Israel," was quickly leaked and ended up on the Internet.[32]

Harvard University professor Stephen Walt, a critic of Israel's outsized political influence in the United States, has argued that, because the roadmap is unevenly enforced, "defending the two-state solution has become a recipe for inaction, a fig leaf that leaders can utter at press conferences while ignoring the expanding settlements and road networks on the West Bank that are rendering it impossible."[33]

Egypt's U.N. ambassador Abdelaziz agrees. "There was a period of calm for about two years immediately after the roadmap was introduced, but during this entire time settlement activities continued, roadblocks continued, confiscation of land continued."

According to the most recent statistics, the number of Israeli settlers living in the Palestinian West Bank grew from 223,954 in 2003 — the year the roadmap was issued — to 276,462 in 2007.[34]

"The Israelis argue that calm is required before steps along the roadmap can be taken," Abdelaziz says. "We need to prove the contrary: If there is to be calm, we want the political process to move forward."

U.N special Middle East coordinator Serry hopes Sen. Mitchell's appointment will be just one part of Obama's strategy. "I very much hope also that the Americans will be using the Quartet a bit more, and a bit more effectively, in a determined international role here," he says.

"Quartet meetings have so far been very much ad hoc. They need to be more structured. And top envoys need to be present more on the ground [in the region] rather than just meeting in capitals," adds Serry, who is based in Jerusalem. Other Quartet members agree the group should be more effective and not be abandoned.

The Obama administration believes "the Quartet remains the most effective instrument for advancing the international community's engagement in the effort to bring lasting peace to the Middle East," Susan Rice, Washington's new U.N. ambassador, told the Security Council in February.[35]

"This is one of the best things we have," says Russia's U.N. ambassador, Vitaly Churkin.

"It is easy to blame the Quartet for not having made peace in the Middle East in so many years. But nobody else has, or has even tried," adds the EU ambassador to the Middle East, Marc Otte, a Belgian. "The Quartet has been useful in harmonizing and coordinating action and has been a plus for EU-U.S. cooperation."

Can the Palestinians form a national unity government?

Hamas's 2006 election victory, its takeover of Gaza in 2007 and the recent Israeli assault on Gaza have left Palestinians deeply divided at a time when they face enormous domestic and international challenges.

To restore its economy, for instance, postwar Gaza must obtain basic food, medicine and commercial goods and rebuild its institutions and shattered housing. The U.N. estimates that 4,000 Palestinian homes were destroyed and 20,000 severely damaged during the three-week war — about 20 percent of the housing stock.[36] In March, at a conference in the Egyptian resort town of

Major Milestones in Israeli-Palestinian Peace Process

The Israeli-Palestinian conflict began immediately after Israel declared itself a state in May 1948, but progress toward peace has been painfully slow and elusive. The U.S.-mediated Camp David Accords led to the first peace treaty between Israel and an Arab state. The Oslo Accords, negotiated secretly between Israeli and Palestinian officials in Norway, set out a plan for a Palestinian Authority to gradually take over administration of lands seized by Israel in the 1967 Six-Day War. The 2003 Roadmap for Peace was drafted by the United States, the United Nations, the European Union and Russia — a self-proclaimed Quartet of international mediators — to guide Israelis and Palestinians to establishment of a Palestinian state as part of a comprehensive peace agreement. While Israel and Egypt remain at peace today, the Oslo Accords and the Roadmap were never carried out.

Here are three major milestones reached along the way:

Camp David Accords (1978)

- Negotiated in secret at the Camp David, Md., U.S. presidential retreat under the guidance of then-President Jimmy Carter.
- Signed at the White House by Egyptian President Anwar El Sadat and Israeli Prime Minister Menachem Begin.

- Led to the Israel-Egypt Peace Treaty of 1979, in which both countries agreed to mutual recognition.
- Established a framework for Egyptian-Israeli relations and for an autonomous, self-governing authority in the West Bank and Gaza Strip.
- Deliberately excluded the fate of Jerusalem.
- Established U.S. economic and military aid packages for each country that over the past 30 years have totaled $142 billion.
- Led to Sadat and Begin winning 1978 Nobel Peace Prize.

Oslo Accords (1993)

- Signed by Israeli Prime Minister Yitzhak Rabin and PLO Chairman Yasser Arafat on Sept. 13, 1993, in the White House Rose Garden with President Bill Clinton. Highlight of the ceremony was the first public handshake between Israeli and Palestinian leaders.
- Called for withdrawal of Israeli forces from certain parts of West Bank and Gaza Strip; creation of a transitional Palestinian Authority to administer the territories under its control, and democratic election of a transitional representative council.
- Called for the two sides to negotiate a comprehensive and permanent peace agreement within five years,

Sharm el-Sheikh, international donors pledged nearly $4.5 billion in aid for the Palestinians.

But Israel and Egypt tightly control all access to Gaza, including financial flows. And under the Quartet principles, none of the aid can pass through Hamas. Since the Palestinian Authority is not present on the ground in Gaza, that effectively leaves only international agencies in charge of reconstruction.

To address the problem, Egypt has pressed Fatah and Hamas to try to form a government of national unity. If the talks succeed, some U.N. and European diplomats have said such a government might also be accepted by Israel and the international community as a negotiating partner in peace talks.

"If we succeed in having a national unity govt., the U.S. and the Quartet should accept that," says Palestinian U.N. envoy Mansour.

To U.N. Secretary-General Ban Ki-moon, unity is crucial. "For any sustainable political progress to occur, and for Gaza to properly recover and rebuild, Palestinians must engage in reconciliation," Ban told a Feb. 10 news conference.[37] He appealed to Palestinians to "overcome divisions and to work toward one Palestinian government within the framework of the legitimate Palestinian Authority."

But how can a unity government include Hamas, which has refused to accept the Quartet principles that all Palestinian factions must renounce violence, recognize Israel and accept past Palestinian peace deals?

Looking back, it was a mistake for the international community to isolate Hamas after its 2006 election victory, argued de Soto, who was the U.N. Middle East envoy at that time. Hamas "has become a formidable political player. They cannot be ignored in the search

based on principles previously established by the U.N. Security Council.

- Divided the West Bank and Gaza into three zones, pending a final agreement: Areas under complete control of the Palestinian Authority; areas under Palestinian civil control and Israeli security control and areas under complete Israeli control.

- Established a framework for future relations between the two parties, with particular emphasis on regional development and economic cooperation. In side letters (agreements) to the accords, Arafat said the Palestine Liberation Organization (PLO) recognized Israel's right to exist in peace and security and renounced the use of terrorism and other acts of violence, and Rabin said Israel recognized the PLO as the representative of the Palestinian people and would begin negotiations with the PLO within the Middle East peace process.

President Bill Clinton gleams with pride as Palestinian Liberation Organization leader Yasser Arafat (right) and Israeli Prime Minister Yitzhak Rabin (left) shake hands in the White House Rose Garden on Sept. 13, 1993. It was the first direct, face-to-face meeting between Israeli and Palestinian political representatives.

Roadmap for Peace (2003)

Set out a performance-based and goal-driven roadmap to a comprehensive and final settlement of the Israeli-Palestinian conflict by 2005, in three phases:

- **Phase I** (to be completed by May 2003): end Palestinian violence; implement Palestinian political reform; Israeli withdrawal and freeze on expansion of settlements in the West Bank and Gaza Strip; Palestinian elections.
- **Phase II** (to be completed by December 2003): hold international conference on Palestinian economic

recovery; establish a process leading to an independent Palestinian state.

- **Phase III** (to be completed by the end of 2005): Israel and Palestinians conclude a permanent agreement that ends their conflict, ends the Israeli occupation that began in 1967, defines Palestinian refugees' right to return to their former homes, establishes Jerusalem's borders and status and fulfills the vision of two states — Israel and Palestine — living side by side in peace and security. Arab states agree to establish full diplomatic relations and make peace with Israel.

for peace with Israel," he wrote recently. "And yet ignore them, and beyond, undermine them and sidestep them, is precisely what the international community has done since their election to a majority in the Palestinian legislature. . . . It should not surprise us that many in Hamas have interpreted this as meaning that there is no interest in a move by them toward democracy and peace, leaving no other recourse but continued armed struggle."[38]

For the time being, however, Israel and most of the key international players, including most Arab donors, appear to be sticking with the three principles and ensuring their aid bypasses Hamas. The three principles are "not the United States talking. That is the Quartet and the Arab League," Secretary of State Clinton said in March during a tour of the region. "Everyone knows what Hamas must do, and it is up to Hamas."[39]

While Egypt has said the unity talks show that Hamas and Fatah want a unity deal, Israeli Consul General Shariv says: "They have been saying that for approximately two years now." The talks will drag on, he says, because "the hate between Fatah and Hamas is bigger than the hate between the Palestinians and Israelis."

Egypt has an uneasy relationship with Hamas, due in part to its repression of the Muslim Brotherhood in Egypt, with which Hamas is allied. But Egypt argues that isolating Hamas unfairly harms all Gazans, most of whom are not Hamas supporters. "We deal with Hamas as part of the Palestinian population. Whether we believe that this national unity government is going to be successful or not, we must first achieve some kind of reconciliation among the Palestinian people themselves," says Egypt's U.N. envoy Abdelaziz.

Obama's Middle East Troubleshooter Gets Mixed Reception

Arab-American George Mitchell is expected to take an even-handed approach.

President Barack Obama's appointment of George Mitchell as his special envoy to the Middle East was widely greeted as a potential game-changer in one of the world's most enduring trouble spots. But he is certainly not the first special envoy to be dispatched to the region.

Former British Prime Minister Tony Blair currently fills that bill for the Quartet — the "pressure group" of diplomats from the United States, Russia, the European Union and the United Nations — with a mandate to focus on beefing up the Palestinian economy. Veteran U.S. diplomat Dennis Ross spent years shuttling between Washington and the region and remains a special envoy to the Obama administration, although this time for Iran.

Mitchell, a 14-year veteran of the U.S. Senate representing Maine, has gained a global reputation as a skilled international troubleshooter for helping tame violence in Northern Ireland and expose steroid use among U.S. Major League Baseball players. His mother migrated to the United States from Lebanon at 18 and he identifies himself as an Arab-American.

After a previous stint in the Middle East at the request of President Clinton, Mitchell in 2001 called on Palestinians to reform their security forces and end violence and for Israel to halt the expansion of settlements on land seized in the 1967 Six-Day War. Clinton had asked Mitchell to investigate the causes of the Second Intifada, or Palestinian uprising, which began in mid-2000 after a Clinton-hosted peace initiative failed.

Mitchell's recommendations had little impact, however, and the Intifada raged on for years, resulting in thousands of Palestinian and Israeli deaths. Palestinian rockets and mortars remain a top international concern, as do Israel's ever-expanding West Bank settlements. Israel withdrew its settlers from Gaza when it pulled out of the territory in 2005.

Obama's appointment of Mitchell was greeted warmly in the Arab world while Israel has reacted more coolly. "George Mitchell has rich experience in solving conflicts — in Northern Ireland, for example — and he has a lot of respect among parties in the region," says Palestinian U.N. Ambassador Riyad Mansour.

But Asaf Shariv, Israel's consul general in New York, stopped short of praising the former senator. Asked if Mitchell made Israel nervous, he responded: "If Sen. Mitchell can help us reach a peace agreement, we would be the most happy people in the world. That is what we want. We know who our friends are, and the United States is the best friend we have, and we want to have peace."

The Mitchell appointment is significant for three reasons, said Paul Rogers, a global security expert with the Oxford Research Group in London. "Mitchell has family knowledge of the Middle East combined with a reputation for evenness in his work in Northern Ireland," Rogers said. "He is not regarded as close to the Israel lobby in Washington, and . . . President Obama made it clear that this was his [personal] initiative" rather than the action of an underling.[1]

However, many Israelis warn that even if the Palestinian Authority led the unity government initially, Hamas could soon end up in control, because President Abbas's four-year term expired in January. He is calling for new presidential and legislative elections by Jan. 24, 2010.[40]

A recent poll showed Hamas gaining popularity after the Gaza war, the opposite of what Israel had hoped. The survey of 1,270 people in the West Bank and Gaza, conducted March 5-7 by the Palestinian Center for Policy and Survey Research, showed Hamas leader Ismail Haniyeh defeating Abbas in a hypothetical election for Palestinian president, which could give Hamas a political foothold in the West Bank and East Jerusalem as well as Gaza.[41] The Fatah leadership has been plagued for years by criticism that the party is corrupt and resists needed financial and security reforms, and this is undoubtedly hurting Fatah among Palestinian voters.

"According to Palestinian public-opinion experts, Hamas emerged from the recent Gaza war stronger than

"For the Arabs, the Americans are the only ones who can actually deliver the Israelis," says a U.N. Middle East analyst, who spoke on condition of anonymity because he is not authorized to speak for the world body. During the George W. Bush administration, "the U.S. appeared to them to be more and more wedded to the Israeli side. So the Arab world is so enthralled with Obama because they see him as a change."

But Egyptian U.N. Ambassador Maged Abdelaziz warns that, while he is "cautiously optimistic" about the role Sen. Mitchell can play, it will take him a while to learn the terrain and identify openings to a solution. "The Americans are still learning to drive, and for them, it is a new car," he says.

He adds, however, "We don't want to repeat the experience of those other envoys, who come every month and have the same round of discussions with everybody, and then go back to Washington, and then come back the next month, and nothing moves forward. We need a time-bound plan, that we are going to do this now, and then that the next month."

EU Middle East envoy Mark Otte also advises caution. "Mitchell is held in very high regard in the region, and also in Europe, due to his involvement in resolving the Northern Ireland conflict. And true statesmanship actually occasionally happens, even in the Middle East," he says. "But I think there is a delusion that just because we — the U.S., the Europeans — want a problem to be solved, that people are ready to solve it.

"There is a new opportunity in that the U.S. government is willing to deal up-front with the problem," he continues. "But there is also a negative side, in that time is running out for a number of strategic problems of the region, including the confrontation with Iran on the nuclear issue and its regional ambitions that are scaring off the Arab governments. There is a potential for a deal between Arabs and Israelis. But the opportunity should not

President Barack Obama's envoy to the Middle East, former Democratic Sen. George Mitchell (left), has a global reputation as a skilled international troubleshooter. A Lebanese-American, Mitchell is expected to take an even-handed approach to discussions with both sides, including hard-line Israeli Foreign Minister Avigdor Lieberman (right).

be lost before something else maybe more radical or catastrophic happens."

[1] Paul Rogers, "Gaza — The Aftermath," Oxford Research Group, January 2009, www.oxfordresearchgroup.org.uk/publications/monthly_briefings/index.html.

ever, especially in the West Bank, where the Fatah party has been neither reformed nor rebuilt," said Yossi Alpher, an Israeli blogger and former director of the Jaffee Center for Strategic Studies at Tel Aviv University. "This means a unity government could quickly confront Israel with the challenge of Hamas rule rather than 'unity' rule in the West Bank as well as Gaza."[42]

"Then Hamas takes over, and then we will see rockets landing on Tel Aviv, certainly on Ben Gurion Airport, and of course where I live in the center of Jerusalem,"

adds Amnon Lord, an Israeli writer and former editor of the *Makor Rishon* newspaper.

International diplomats say that unity could be achieved without Hamas by establishing a government of technocrats — skilled administrators without political affiliations — such as the current Palestinian Authority cabinet.

That may be the only way to keep Israel on board, predicts a veteran European diplomat with long experience in the Middle East. To include Hamas in a unity government "would be the perfect cover for those in Israel who do not want a two-state solution, who want a non-state solution," he says, speaking on condition of anonymity due to his continued involvement in the matter.

"They will never agree to a Hamas role," he continues. "Given that thousands of rockets have flown into Israel, given that those rockets continue to fly, public opinion in Israel is so strong on these issues that there is no government in Israel that could engage with a Palestinian government like that and survive."

BACKGROUND

Decades of Deadlock

While the Israeli-Palestinian conflict has continued for years, the broad outlines of a plan for ending the conflict have long been known to the parties. At one time or another, both sides have endorsed most of the major elements of an agreement.[43]

"All the issues have been negotiated so many times before that we know what the solutions will be," says Palestinian U.N. Ambassador Mansour.

Yet a final resolution remains elusive, say Middle East peacemakers, in part because the two sides view virtually every issue and every development in a fundamentally different way, and thus discussions tend to proceed in endless circles of blame and retribution.

Outside mediators say they try to steer the parties to focus on the future and avoid eternal debate over events long past. But the two sides seem to prefer to dwell on past wrongs: on how to interpret them and how to correct them.

The result has been decades of deadlock.

"It is a conflict over a very small piece of land, and it is a conflict between two rival nationalist movements, with all the rancor and violence that can come with nationalism," says U.N. Middle East specialist Markus Bouillon, a German. "The divergent points of view are fueled by historical experience: For the Jewish people, there is the Holocaust, having no home, the diaspora. And that completely clashes with the Palestinian perspective — that 'this is our land, we have always been here, everybody else has their state, why did you come and steal our land?' These arguments are driven by morality and emotion, making for a powerful argument on both sides."

So the parties in effect end up pitting the Arab grandmother living in a Palestinian refugee camp and still clutching the keys to the family home abandoned in 1948 against the Jewish grandmother with the concentration camp number tattooed on her arm, Bouillon says.

In search of the roots of the conflict, a convenient starting point is the surge in Jewish immigration to the Middle East shortly after the start of the 20th century. Starting in 1904, Jews escaping Russia's anti-Semitic massacres — called pogroms — began creating a state-within-a-state in a region of the Ottoman Empire known as Palestine, where an Arab population was already long established.

Earlier, in the 19th century, Austro-Hungarian journalist Theodor Herzl, considered the father of Zionism, and other Jews began calling for Jews to settle in "Zion," their historic homeland. They argued that Europe had never accepted their presence and never would. The Zionists based their claim to Palestine on the Jews' ancient presence there, which had ended when the Romans destroyed Jerusalem and dispersed most of the Jews in 70 A.D.

The nascent state grew even stronger after a fresh wave of immigration following World War I, when Great Britain took over Palestine under a mandate from the League of Nations, the predecessor of the United Nations. The new arrivals further stoked tensions with the longtime Arab population. Under the so-called Balfour Declaration of 1917, Britain committed itself to allowing the establishment of a Jewish "national home" in Palestine, with the proviso that "nothing shall be done which may prejudice the civil and religious rights of existing non-Jewish communities in Palestine." The measure was endorsed by France, Italy, Japan and, in principle, by the U.S. Congress in 1922.[44]

After the genocide of 6 million Jews by the Nazis in World War II, thousands of Holocaust survivors flooded into Palestine, many joining the ranks of a determined and effective underground army called the Haganah and other similar militias. Their guerrilla-style attacks on British and Arab targets and Palestinian Arab violent resistance to growing Zionist strength prompted the United Nations General Assembly to vote in November 1947 to partition the Palestinian territory into separate countries for Arabs and Jews — Israel and Palestine.

CHRONOLOGY

1948-1977 *Israel becomes a nation, opening new era regularly punctuated by war with its Arab neighbors.*

1948 Israel declares statehood on May 14; Arab armies attack a day later. Israel emerges as victor within months, but 750,000 Palestinians are uprooted.

1965 Exiled Fatah leader Yasser Arafat, now heading new Palestine Liberation Organization (PLO), declares armed struggle against Israel to reclaim former Arab lands.

1967 In Six-Day War, Israeli troops repulse Arab attack, enter Jerusalem and occupy west bank of Jordan River, Gaza Strip along Mediterranean.

1973 Egypt and Syria launch initially successful surprise attack on Israel on Oct. 6, the Jewish holiday of Yom Kippur. Israel makes major territorial gains in the Golan Heights and in the Sinai desert before a U.N.-sponsored cease-fire takes effect, just weeks after the conflict started.

1978-2000 *Peace attempts alternate with periods of heightened violence.*

1978 After secret talks hosted by President Jimmy Carter at Camp David, Egyptian President Anwar Al-Sadat and Israeli Prime Minister Menachem Begin sign agreement leading to 1979 peace treaty, the first between Israel and an Arab neighbor.

1987 Palestinians rise up against Israeli occupation in first Intifada ("uprising"); violence continues for six years.

1993 In secretly negotiated Oslo Accords, Israel agrees to gradually transfer administration of West Bank and Gaza to Palestinians; PLO, in accompanying letter, recognizes Israel's right to exist.

2000 President Bill Clinton fails in push for final Palestinian-Israeli peace deal at second Camp David summit. Second Intifada erupts. Clinton appoints former Sen. George Mitchell, D-Maine, to lead an international inquiry into how to end it.

2001-2007 *Bush administration initially steers clear of involvement in Middle East peace efforts.*

2001 Mitchell tells President George W. Bush Israel should freeze its settlements and the Palestinians end terrorism. Arab terrorists attack United States on Sept. 11, prompting Bush's global war on terror and increasing Muslim-Western tensions.

2002 U.S., European Union, Russia and U.N. form Quartet of global mediators to help resolve Arab-Israeli differences. Bush endorses Palestinian statehood.

2003 United States and allies topple Saddam Hussein in a move widely seen as a grab for Iraqi oil. Quartet's two-year plan (roadmap) calls for Palestinian state.

2005 Israel abandons its Gaza settlements and withdraws from the area.

2006 Hamas wins Palestinian elections. Arab guerrillas capture Israeli soldier Gilad Shalit and demand release of imprisoned Palestinians. Israel invades southern Lebanon on July 12 after Hezbollah guerrillas capture two Israeli soldiers.

2007 Hamas defeats Fatah in Palestinian civil war and takes full control of Gaza on June 15. Bush convenes conference in Annapolis, Md., to seek Israeli-Palestinian peace deal.

2008-Present *Israelis elect new conservative government after controversial invasion of Gaza.*

2008 Palestinian militants in Gaza fire thousands of rockets and mortars into southern Israel. Mid-year truce ends on Nov. 4 after Israeli and Hamas forces clash along Gaza border. On Dec. 27 Israel launches 22-day invasion of Gaza. Annapolis conference ends without a deal.

2009 Barack Obama becomes U.S. president, says time is ripe for new Middle East negotiations and names Mitchell his special Middle East envoy. In Feb. 10 elections, Israel elects Likud Party leader Benjamin Netanyahu to head new right-leaning government. Obama plans to meet with Netanyahu on May 18 and later with Palestinian and Egyptian leaders.

Israel's New Government Could Block Quick Peace

Netanyahu: No peace talks until progress is made on Iran.

While the Palestinian Authority, President Barack Obama and most world governments are calling for a quick, new push for Palestinian statehood, Israel has signaled through its votes in Feb. 10 parliamentary elections that it is not in any hurry.

What's more, even as critics express concern over Israel's aggressive tactics in Gaza, some Israeli officials are warning of fresh military action over the rocket fire still raining down on southern Israel from Gaza. Sporadic rocket attacks resumed within days of the end of the Gaza operation in January, undermining initial Israeli boasts about the success of its initial assault, launched mainly to stop the attacks.

Continuing rocket fire "will be answered with a painful, harsh, strong and uncompromising response from the security forces," caretaker Prime Minister Ehud Olmert warned on March 1, a month before turning power over to his successor, conservative Likud Party leader Benjamin Netanyahu.[1]

But Hamas — the militant political party that governs Gaza and refuses to recognize Israel's right to exist — was not firing the rockets launched in the months after the Gaza operation, Israeli government and private experts say. "It is only independents — very small and extreme groups — that are shooting. It is not Hamas. We can tell by the rocket and who manufactured it who is shooting," Asaf Shariv, the Israeli consul general in New York and one-time media spokesman for former Prime Minister Ariel Sharon, said in late March. Should Hamas later resume fire, Israel could "go back in" to Gaza, he added.

But the lull continued in April, says Reuven Erlich, head of the Intelligence and Terrorism Information Center, a private organization in Ramat Hasharon, Israel. "It is in Hamas' interest to keep a low profile and calm down the situation at this time. But this won't necessarily continue for the long run," he continues, speculating that Hamas may be using the lull to rebuild its military or enable the reconstruction of Gaza to get under way.

The threat of renewed military action in Gaza is just one sign of Israelis' unhappiness with the peace process. Judging by the election results, "Israel realizes that the so-called peace process has led it to the brink of great peril for its own existence," says Amnon Lord, an Israeli writer and former newspaper editor.

Netanyahu argues that now is not the time for a Palestinian state. He wants to focus instead on Palestinian economic development and security issues. He also champions Israeli settlements in the West Bank and East Jerusalem, despite multiple U.N. Security Council demands to freeze all settlement activity.

Netanyahu also wants to focus above all on the threat from Iran. Israel's deputy foreign minister, Daniel Ayalon, said in April that his country's new government would not begin peace talks with the Palestinians until Washington first made progress in ensuring that Tehran does not develop nuclear weapons.[2]

But the Obama administration has been pushing for a comprehensive approach that aims for progress on the

But borders were never established for the two separate states, and Palestine's Arabs and Jews engaged in a spiral of deadly clashes in the months following the U.N. vote. When Britain's mandate to administer Palestine ran out, Israel simply declared itself an independent nation on May 14, 1948. Immediately, the Arab League went to war to reclaim the land. But Israel defeated the league — made up of Egypt, Syria, Lebanon, Transjordan (now Jordan), Iraq, Saudi Arabia and Yemen — in what Israelis call the "War of Independence." Palestinians call it "the catastrophe" ("al-Naqba") because it led to the departure or expulsion of hundreds of thousands of Arabs from the new country of Israel — creating the

root of today's conflict. Debate over whether the Palestinians were forced out or fled on their own has since become part of the two sides' divergent historical narratives.[45]

Israel's founding triggered a succession of Middle Eastern wars that essentially continues to this day. The 1948 War of Independence was followed by the Six-Day War of 1967 against the region's major Arab countries — led by Syria and Egypt — and the Yom Kippur War of 1973. After the Six-Day War Israel occupied lands now known as the Palestinian territories — the West Bank (of the Jordan River) and the Gaza Strip, which runs along the Mediterranean.

Palestinian and Syrian peace tracks as well as Iran. "The United States is committed to a comprehensive peace between Israel and its Arab neighbors, and we will pursue it on many fronts," Secretary of State Hillary Rodham Clinton said during a March Middle East visit that included trips to Jerusalem, the West Bank city of Ramallah and the Egyptian resort town of Sharm el-Sheikh.[3]

During her tour of the region, Clinton made it clear that, unlike the previous U.S. administration, Washington would press Israel on its commitments to freeze settlement activities and speak out when it disagreed with Israeli leaders.[4]

In elections for the 120 seats in Israel's single-chamber parliament, the Knesset, Likud won 15 additional seats — for a total of 27 — but still finished in second place behind the centrist Kadima Party's 28 seats, despite months of polls suggesting Likud would end up leading the pack. The biggest surprise was the right-wing Yisrael Beitenu Party of Avigdor Lieberman, which captured four new seats — for a total of 15 — putting it in third place.

While Kadima normally would have been tasked with assembling a coalition government supported by more than half of Knesset members, the job in this case went to Netanyahu because right-wing and religious parties enjoyed an overall strong majority.

As coalition talks dragged on, Netanyahu managed to cut deals with the center-left Labor Party as well as with Yisrael Beitenu that assigned the post of foreign minister to Lieberman, whose campaign was widely seen by Israelis as extremist, racist or advocating ethnic cleansing of the Palestinians.[5]

Netanyahu's new government took power on March 31.

Analysts saw the agreement with Labor as helping to shield Netanyahu from U.S. criticism that the government was too right-wing and too opposed to the peace process.

But Lieberman has called for all Israeli citizens — including Israeli Arabs, who make up a fifth of the population — to swear an oath of loyalty to the state in order to retain their rights. Critics said the proposal was aimed at driving Israeli Arabs out of the country. Others, however, have painted Lieberman as more difficult to categorize.

"Lieberman is an enigma for me," says one international diplomat, speaking on condition he not be identified because he will have to work with the Israeli politician. "If you look at what he is saying, it is very, very dangerous to talk of an ethnic Jewish state with no place at all for Israeli Arabs. But on the other hand, Lieberman is for a two-state solution, he wants a Palestinian state. He even wants to think about parts of Jerusalem being part of it."

Adds Israel's Shariv: "It is true that he had a very interesting campaign that made everyone in the world raise some questions about him, but he is a very practical person."

---

[1] Matti Friedman, "Israeli leader vows 'painful' response to rockets," The Associated Press, March 1, 2009, http://news.yahoo.com/s/ap/20090301/ap_on_re_mi_ea/ml_israel_palestinians;_ylt=Aizxs6J4fCD8EJDs_WfT2RRI2ocA.

[2] Howard Schneider and Glenn Kessler, "Israel Puts Iran Issue Ahead of Palestinians," The Washington Post, April 22, 2009, www.washingtonpost.com/wp-dyn/content/article/2009/04/21/AR2009042103998.html?hpid=topnews.

[3] Hillary Rodham Clinton, "Intervention at the International Conference in Support of the Palestinian Economy for the Reconstruction of Gaza," Sharm el-Sheikh, Egypt, March 2, 2009, www.state.gov/secretary/rm/2009a/03/119900.htm.

[4] "Secretary Clinton, Palestinian President Abbas in Ramallah," March 4, 2009, www.america.gov/st/texttransEnglish/2009/March/20090304125709eaifas0.3768885.html?CP.rss=true.

[5] See for example, Lily Galili, "Avigdor Lieberman said to be ex-member of banned radical Kach movement," Haaretz.com, Feb. 3, 2009, www.haaretz.com/hasen/spages/1061172.html.

During the second half of the 20th century, nationalism grew among Palestinian Arabs, who demanded the return of their homeland. By 1964, a group of exiles that included Fatah leader Arafat founded the Palestine Liberation Organization (PLO), which brought together religiously oriented political activists and left-wing Arab nationalists. The following year, they declared an armed struggle against Israel to reclaim the formerly Arab lands.

Peace Accords

Just as there was a series of Arab-Israeli wars, there has been a series of peace summits to settle the intractable conflict.

The first Camp David summit, hosted by President Carter in 1978, led to a formal peace treaty between Israel and Egypt in 1979. As part of the deal, the United States agreed to provide $7.5 billion in economic and military aid to the two countries that year, with the lion's share going to Israel. Over the following three decades, seeking to encourage continued friendly ties, Washington has funneled an average of $4.3 billion a year in aid (three-quarters of it to Israel) to the two Middle East neighbors — a costly arrangement that could well be repeated in future Middle East agreements mediated by the United States.[46]

Support for the Palestinian cause eroded, however, with the collapse of the Eastern European bloc — a strong financial and political backer of the Arab world — as the Cold War began to wind down in the late 1980s. Palestinians, frustrated by the continued Israeli occupation of their lands, rose up in 1987 in what is now called the First Intifada, an uprising that lasted until 1993.

In response to the violence, a secret peace initiative was launched in Oslo with the help of Norwegian diplomat Roed-Larsen, leading to the first face-to-face negotiations between Israel and the PLO and ultimately to the so-called 1993 Oslo Accords.[47] The agreements were signed on Sept. 13, 1993, in an historic White House Rose Garden ceremony in which Arafat and Israeli Prime Minister Yitzhak Rabin shook hands as a beaming President Clinton looked on.

Under the accords, the parties committed themselves to negotiate the final details of a comprehensive peace agreement by 1999. The final details — concerning such crucial issues as borders, the disposition of Jerusalem and Palestinian refugees' "right of return" to their former home — became known as the "final status" or "permanent status" issues and remain unresolved today.

The accords also provided for Israel to gradually transfer power and responsibility for the West Bank and Gaza to the Palestinians, and to recognize Arafat's Palestine Liberation Organization as the representative of the Palestinian people and as a negotiating partner.

For its part, the PLO in a letter accompanying the accords formally recognized Israel's right to exist and renounced the use of "terrorism and other acts of violence." The agreement also divided up security responsibilities among the two parties.

But extremists on both sides were unhappy with the accords and in 1995 essentially sabotaged the negotiations toward a comprehensive peace: Palestinian militants stepped up their attacks against Israel, and a Jewish extremist assassinated Rabin.

Five years after that, in May 2000, Israel withdrew its forces from southern Lebanon, which it had first invaded in 1978 in hopes of ending cross-border guerrilla attacks on civilians in northern Israel. Years of occupation and low-intensity warfare between the Israeli occupiers and Hezbollah militia had taken a political toll on Israel, and most Israelis saw the conflict with Palestinians in the West Bank and Gaza as a more pressing concern.[48]

Two months later, the Clinton administration came the closest ever to a broad agreement ending the Israeli-Palestinian conflict by luring Arafat and then-Israeli Prime Minister Barak to the Camp David presidential retreat near Washington.

Their talks, known as Camp David Two, convened on July 11, 2000, and at first made significant progress. But they ran out of steam and ended after two weeks without a deal.[49]

Blame for the failure of Camp David Two has since been hotly debated, with each side blaming the other for failure to go the final mile.[50] Following the talks' collapse, Palestinian frustration boiled over, leading to the popular uprising in September 2000 that became known as the Second Intifada. Dismayed by the deadly violence, Clinton asked former Sen. Mitchell to chair a commission to identify its causes and recommend how to end the uprising.

Clinton left office in January 2001, and Mitchell turned over his findings to President George W. Bush, whose administration avoided direct involvement in the conflict even as it offered strong support for Israeli policies. Mitchell's May 4, 2001, report split the blame, calling for an end to Palestinian violence and a freeze on Israeli settlements. Mitchell saw the settlements as undermining Israel's earlier commitments to the general principle of "land for peace," under which Israel would cede land gained in the Six-Day War in exchange for peace with the Palestinians.[51]

But both sides largely ignored Mitchell's recommendations.

War on Terror

Less than four months after Mitchell's report was published, Islamic extremists hijacked airliners and crashed them into the World Trade Center and the Pentagon, radically altering Washington's relationship with the Middle East and greatly complicating peace efforts while drawing the United States more deeply into the region's political woes.

Bush declared a global war on terror in which the United States vowed to use all its power against radical Islamists. The campaign started with a coalition-led invasion of Afghanistan to oust the ultraconservative Taliban regime, which was harboring al Qaeda leader Osama bin Laden, the architect of the 9/11 attacks. At the same time, Israel adapted Washington's war on terror to its own ends, citing it to defend a crackdown on Palestinian militants.

Following a deadly suicide bombing in the northern town of Netanya during the Jewish Passover holiday in 2002, Prime Minister Ariel Sharon sent the military into the West Bank to reoccupy towns evacuated as part of the Oslo Accords. Israeli forces surrounded Arafat, confining him to his Ramallah offices.[52]

As Middle East violence picked up, U.N. Secretary-General Annan convened a meeting of top diplomats from the United States, the European Union and Russia, urging them to join the United Nations in a pressure group of four, which they dubbed the Quartet. The group began drafting a roadmap to peace to present to the Israelis and Palestinians.

To counter accusations that he was biased against the Arab world, Bush in a June 24, 2002, White House address became the first U.S. president to publicly embrace the so-called two-state solution — separate Palestinian and Israeli states, existing side by side within secure borders.[53] Palestinian statehood was included as a provision of the roadmap, which became international law upon adoption by the U.N. Security Council on Nov. 19, 2003.[54]

But Bush inflamed the Arab world anew with his March 2003 invasion of Iraq to rid it of alleged chemical, biological and nuclear weapons. The weapons were never found, and Washington ended up occupying the oil-rich country. The invasion, building on Bush's war on terror and his unwavering support for Israel, prompted fresh Arab accusations that Washington was waging a war on Islam.[55]

With violence persisting in Gaza, Sharon pushed through a domestically unpopular plan to shut down Israeli settlements there and withdrew from the territory in September 2005. The pull-out initially was widely hailed as a fulfillment of Israeli commitments to end its occupation of Palestinian areas.

But Israel, worried that weapons and fighters would enter Gaza through Egypt, continued to clamp down on border crossings into Gaza from Israel and Egypt. That severely limited the commerce on which Gaza's economic future depended.[56]

Within months, Israel was attacking militants inside Gaza with artillery and air strikes. Militants in Gaza in turn continued their attacks on the Jewish state, arguing they remained under occupation despite the withdrawal.[57]

Getty Images/Yoray Liberman

A Jewish settler cries out in despair when Israeli policemen tell her she must abandon her home in the Atzmona settlement in Gaza Strip on Aug. 21, 2005. All Israeli settlers were forced to leave Gaza under an unpopular plan engineered by Prime Minister Ariel Sharon. Although the pull-out was widely hailed as a fulfillment of Israeli commitments to end its occupation of Palestinian areas, Israel has continued to expand its settlements in other occupied areas.

In the January 2006 elections, the militant Gaza-based Hamas movement defeated long-dominant Fatah to win a majority of the seats in the Palestinian Legislative Council. Bush had been promoting Middle East democracy, but when Hamas won power, Israel and the Quartet refused to deal with it or recognize its authority. To gain recognition, the Quartet declared, Hamas would have to recognize Israel's right to exist, foreswear violence and honor all agreements reached by previous Palestinian administrations.[58] The Quartet principles, presented as recommended policy to all world governments, ended up isolating the Gazan population as well as Hamas from the international community.

Growing tension between Hamas and Fatah soon led to intermittent civil war that ended in the seizure of Gaza by Hamas fighters in mid-2007. That left the Palestinian Authority effectively in charge only of the West Bank, although in international eyes it remains the leader of both territories.[59]

To the north, meanwhile, Lebanon's Hezbollah para-military forces resumed targeting Israel from a second front, launching rockets at northern Israeli towns and then kidnapping two Israeli soldiers in a daring cross-border raid. In July 2006 Israel responded by sending troops back into southern Lebanon with orders to wipe out Hezbollah forces. Like Sharon's 2002 reoccupation of the West Bank and the December 2008 incursion into Gaza, the 34-day operation started out with great fanfare but soon began rolling up heavy civilian casualties even as it fell short of its goals, triggering international criticism of the Israeli military's tactics.[60]

Although Hezbollah ended up suffering militarily, it was politically strengthened by the Israeli assault in Lebanon. Within a year, a new Lebanese government had been formed in which the group and its allies held effective veto power over government actions.[61]

With time running out on his presidency, Bush in November 2007 gave a final try to advancing the Israeli-Palestinian peace process from Washington, convening an international peace conference in Annapolis, Md. But even as the conference began, participants played down expectations of a dramatic result, and Bush — shying from specifics — called on the parties only to try to finish whatever they chose to accomplish by the end of 2008.[62]

In line with expectations, the Annapolis initiative produced no agreement before time ran out 13 months later. The U.N. Security Council on Dec. 16, 2008, adopted a resolution supporting the failed initiative's attempt at peace and welcoming the idea of another international conference, as yet unscheduled, in Moscow in 2009.[63] On Dec. 27, four days before the deadline for an Annapolis deal, Israel sent its troops into Gaza.

CURRENT SITUATION

U.S. Role

With new U.S. and Israeli governments settling in, and Palestinian leaders crippled by internal divisions, the Middle East peace process seems on hold for now. In the region and around the world, interested governments are standing on the sidelines, putting off any initiatives until they hear what the Obama administration has in mind.

Meanwhile, Israel, the Palestinians and outsiders involved with the region all agree on at least one thing: The United States must continue to play a central role in Middle East diplomacy.

Washington's key role, of course, can cut both ways. Washington's disinterest has nipped some initiatives in the bud, while U.S. support has breathed life into other proposals. Washington is Israel's closest and most trusted ally and the world's lone superpower. International diplomats say Washington alone has the power to influence — although not necessarily alter — Israeli policy, and Washington's deep pockets will make it a necessary partner in any agreement.

"U.S. commitment to the resolution of this conflict is indispensable," says Otte, the EU's Middle East ambassador.

For his part, President Obama appears eager to get involved but cautious about the outcome. "I am a strong supporter of a two-state solution, and I think that there are a lot of Israelis who also believe in a two-state solution," he told reporters on April 21 during a visit to Washington by King Abdullah of Jordan. "Unfortunately, right now what we've seen not just in Israel but within the Palestinian territories, among the Arab states, world-wide, is a profound cynicism about the possibility of any progress being made whatsoever.

"What we want to do is to step back from the abyss," he continued, "to say, as hard as it is, as difficult as it may be, the prospect of peace still exists, but it's going to require some hard choices, it's going to require resolution on the part of all the actors involved, and it's going to require that we create some concrete steps that all parties can take that are evidence of that resolution. And the United States is going to deeply engage in this process to see if we can make progress."[64]

Obama's caution is understandable. Months of Palestinian negotiations on a national unity government have gone nowhere. Because of Hamas's pariah status with the Quartet, most international donors refuse to provide it with direct funding, and it can only participate indirectly in the multibillion-dollar international program to rebuild Gaza.

Meanwhile, Egyptian-led talks between Israel and the Palestinians seeking a long-term Gaza cease-fire are at an impasse. Hamas's refusal to release kidnapped Israeli soldier Gilad Shalit, held by Gaza militants since June 2006, has been a major stumbling block. And Israel, furious over continued rocket fire from Gaza, has maintained a tight rein on the movement of people and goods in and out of the area. Despite Israel's insistence that it is not slowing the shipment of food and medicine into Gaza, U.N. officials say otherwise.[65]

Since the 2007 Hamas takeover of Gaza, both before and after its invasion of the territory, Israel has pursued a policy "of near-total closure of the Gaza Strip," Lynn Pascoe, the U.N. undersecretary-general for political affairs, told the Security Council on April 20.[66] Israeli officials say vital supplies are not being blocked. But Pascoe pointed out that while basic emergency needs such as food and blankets have been met, broader humanitarian and reconstruction aid has been "impossible" due to restrictions on the flow of fuel, cash and construction materials.

"The lack of access to Gaza is deeply frustrating," he continued. "Without the materials for recovery and reconstruction, the process cannot begin, and that requires a substantial easing by Israel of its policy of closure of the Gaza Strip."

Besides promoting negotiations between Israel and the Palestinians, the Obama administration also hopes to revive the so-called Syrian track of the Middle East peace process, which centers on the Golan Heights. Israel captured the tract of Syrian land in the 1967 Six-Day War, and Syria wants it back.

Despite being neighbors, Syria and Israel have no diplomatic relations. They held secret, indirect peace talks under Turkish mediation in 2008, but Damascus put the talks on hold after Israel invaded Gaza in December. But in February President Bashar al-Assad told a visiting U.S. official that an agreement with Israel was still possible and that Syria was prepared to resume the talks if Washington joined them.[67]

Syria — a close ally of Iran and a backer of Hamas and Hezbollah — has been listed as a state sponsor of terrorism by the United States since 1979.[68] But Secretary of State Clinton in March dispatched two U.S. envoys to Damascus to explore bilateral and regional issues. "We have no way to predict what the future with our relations concerning Syria might be," she said. "But I think it is a worthwhile effort to go and begin these preliminary conversations."[69]

Israel's Role

The new coalition government formed by Israeli Prime Minister Netanyahu teams right-wing parties cool to Palestinian statehood and the peace process with the Labor Party, which supports negotiations for a Palestinian state. Netanyahu assembled a cabinet after his Likud Party finished first in the Feb. 10 parliamentary elections.

Global Reaction

Israel's harsh three-week campaign against Hamas militants in the Gaza Strip sparked demonstrations around the world, both in support of the assault and in condemnation. Demonstrators outside the Israeli embassy in Madrid (top) show their support for Israel on Jan. 18, 2009, while protesters in Ankara, Turkey, on Jan. 3, 2009, show their outrage (bottom).

Netanyahu said during the campaign that he would continue negotiating with the Palestinians, but not about statehood. Instead, he would grant the Palestinians some degree of sovereignty over any territory they govern while maintaining Israeli control over their borders and airspace.

"Netanyahu has already announced that he will continue the negotiations, especially in the West Bank, about these issues, and to strengthen what he calls the economic peace — to make the Palestinian economy much stronger, to build infrastructure, to encourage companies to work there, to make life better," says Shariv, the Israeli consul general.

Under its coalition agreement with the Labor Party, Likud agreed to respect all of Israel's international agreements — which presumably would include the roadmap to Palestinian statehood.

But Netanyahu thus far has avoided the word "statehood," seemingly seeking to divert international attention from peace talks with the Palestinians and keep it focused instead on containing Iran. While some observers worry that Tehran may be just months away from being able to make nuclear weapons, the timetable on Palestinian statehood "is open-ended," Israeli Deputy Foreign Minister Daniel Ayalon said in April, defying President Obama's insistence that ending the Israeli-Palestinian conflict is an urgent global priority.[70]

"The Palestinians should understand that they have in our government a partner for peace, for security and for rapid economic development of the Palestinian economy," Netanyahu said in late March. "If we have a strong Palestinian economy, that's a strong foundation for peace."[71]

Israelis are also heatedly debating whether a second military thrust into Gaza might be needed to halt the renewed rocket fire into southern Israel. While the continued attacks on Israeli civilians show the 22-day military campaign fell short of its goals, the invasion also prompted a flood of international criticism of aggressive Israeli tactics in Gaza's densely populated urban area as well as of Hamas's rocket fire at Israeli civilians.

Within days after the war ended, New York-based Human Rights Watch called for an international investigation into allegations of war crimes by both Hamas and Israel.[72] A U.N. human rights investigator issued a similar appeal several weeks later. Gaza's civilian population was subjected to "an inhumane form of warfare that kills, maims and inflicts mental harm," said Richard Falk, the U.N. special rapporteur on human rights in the Palestinian territories. "As all borders were sealed, civilians could not escape from the orbit of harm." Israel has prevented Falk — who is a professor emeritus on international law at Princeton — from visiting Gaza, so he based his findings on "preliminary evidence" that was available.[73]

The Geneva-based U.N. Human Rights Council announced in April that famed South African judge Richard Goldstone, who has been involved in human-rights investigations and prosecutions in South Africa, Yugoslavia and Rwanda, would lead an investigation into the allegations on both sides.[74]

International efforts to promote peace in the region will also focus in the coming months on the steady growth of Israeli settlements, diplomats said. All settlements in Gaza were dismantled in 2005, when Israel withdrew from the area. But despite repeated Israeli commitments to freeze them, settlements in the West Bank and East Jerusalem have grown steadily, reaching a combined population of at least 472,657 by the end of 2008, according to the latest available Israeli figures.[75]

"Illegal settlement activity continues, prejudicing final status negotiations and undermining Palestinians who seek a negotiated peace," U.N. envoy Serry told the Security Council in February. "The approach taken since Annapolis to secure implementation of roadmap commitments to freeze settlement activity, including natural growth, and remove outposts, has not worked. This is a clear challenge that must be addressed," Serry said, adding that in 2008, there were 69 percent more new structures built in settlements than in 2007.[76]

"When the Quartet repeatedly states that Israel must freeze all settlement activity and dismantle all outposts, and the Quartet does not do anything, then the Quartet is marginalizing itself," says Mansour, the Palestinian U.N. observer.

But Israel's Shariv dismisses the settlement concerns as overwrought. "When the Palestinians completely stop the terror, we are going to take a few bulldozers or tractors and soldiers, and we are going to evacuate according to the agreement," he says. Israel "should do a better job" of meeting its commitments on settlements, "but you cannot compare terror to settlements."

Discussion of the future of the settlements almost certainly will be on the agenda in May, when Obama meets for the first time with Netanyahu, Abbas and Egyptian President Hosni Mubarak to discuss new U.S. priorities for the region. Obama and Netanyahu are scheduled to meet May 18.[77]

Palestinians' Role

While Israel's political divisions represent an enormous challenge to international peacemakers, Palestinian disunity — specifically the intense hatred between Fatah and Hamas — seems far more untenable.

International donors have offered to pour billions of dollars into Gaza's reconstruction, but tight Israeli border controls and Quartet restrictions on Hamas prevent the people of Gaza from reaping the benefits. Palestinian leaders demand evidence of good faith from the Israelis on fulfilling their commitments, including freezing settlement activities, easing access to Gaza and pursuit of a Palestinian state. But the Israelis say the Palestinians must prevent militants from firing rockets into Israel.

Talks among Palestinians on a national unity government drag on in a fitful way without result. Palestinian Authority bureaucrats scramble to clean up the West Bank's finances and reform their security forces, only to come under fire from hardliners who either question their competence or say they don't deserve to govern because they are cozying up to Israel. Talks aimed at ensuring a lasting cease-fire between Gaza and Israel have stalled over a Hamas plea for the release of some of the 11,000 Palestinian prisoners — a mix of criminals, alleged terrorists and political prisoners — held in Israeli jails in exchange for the freeing of kidnapped Israeli soldier Shalit.

In early April, nearly two weeks passed without violence in Gaza and southern Israel. But during the previous four-week period, 30 rockets and mortar rounds were launched into southern Israel by Palestinian militants, according to Pascoe, the U.N. undersecretary-general for political affairs. The Israeli military retaliated by carrying out two air strikes on the Gaza Strip.[78]

In addition, the Israeli army reported that a Palestinian ship loaded with explosives had blown up in the vicinity of an Israeli naval vessel in mid-April, though without causing injury to the Israeli ship. Egyptian police seeking to prevent the smuggling of arms into Gaza — whether by underground tunnel, the sea or donkey cart — found nearly 2,000 pounds of explosives along Egypt's border with Gaza, Pascoe reported.

While Palestinian Authority security forces stepped up their activity in the West Bank in April — bearing down on criminal gangs and shutting down a suspected explosives manufacturing lab in the West Bank city of Qalqilia — a Palestinian wielding an axe killed a 13-year-old boy and injured a 7-year-old in the Israeli settlement of Bat Ayin, triggering clashes between Israeli settlers and Palestinians that ultimately was halted only after Israeli military intervention, Pascoe told the U.N. council.

The sprawling Ramot housing development in East Jerusalem is built on land Israel captured from Jordan during the 1967 Six-Day War. Despite repeated Israeli commitments to freeze expansion of such settlements in the West Bank and East Jerusalem, they have continued to grow in recent years — undermining peace talks.

Such violence makes a durable end to the war in Gaza just one of peacemakers' many priorities, Secretary of State Clinton said during her early March visit to the region.

"That can only be achieved if Hamas ceases the rocket attacks. No nation should be expected to sit idly by and allow rockets to assault its people and its territories," she said. "These attacks must stop and so must the smuggling of weapons into Gaza."

There have been recent indications that Hamas leaders may be softening their refusal to participate in the peace process, although probably not enough to fully satisfy the Quartet principles. Hamas leader Khaled Meshal said in early May that the group had made a conscious decision to curtail militants' rocket fire into southern Israel.

"Not firing the rockets currently is part of an evaluation from the movement which serves the Palestinians' interest," he said. "After all, the firing is a method, not a goal."[79]

OUTLOOK
'Mammoth Job'

With so little progress in the Middle East peace process, how can the search for peace emerge headed in the right direction? Much will depend on Sen. Mitchell's recommendations and President Obama's resolve to carry them out, say international diplomats.

Did Israel's military action in Gaza make Israel more secure?

YES Yoaz Hendel
Security and Military Affairs Analyst and Research fellow, Begin-Sadat Center for Strategic Studies Bar-Ilan University, Israel

Written for *CQ Global Researcher*, April 2009

The Israeli operation in Gaza started too late and ended too early. For the past eight years, southern Israeli citizens have been under a continuous rain of rockets from Gaza. Repeated threats of military action have done nothing to deter Gaza terror organizations from strikes on Israeli civilians.

The fighting between the Israel Defense Forces (IDF) and Gaza terrorist groups is different from other conflicts pitting conventional armies against guerrilla groups. Intelligence reports show deep Iranian involvement in Gaza. Right under Israel's nose, Iran has established a foothold with the potential to threaten most IDF southern bases, including major air force facilities.

When the IDF withdrew from Gaza in summer 2005, then-Prime Minister Ariel Sharon warned of a strong reaction to any violation of Israeli sovereignty. But Palestinian groups including Hamas only intensified their attacks.

Last summer, the Israeli government — then led by Ehud Olmert — approved a six-month cease-fire with Gaza despite continued attacks on Israeli civilians. During the cease-fire, intelligence reports warned that the terrorists intended to use new weapons from Iran to alter the power balance in the area. The rockets kept falling, even as Hamas prepared for renewed war with Israel.

Part of any state's responsibility is to protect its citizens. But the IDF, established to provide this protection, was not deployed for this purpose until last December.

The basic assumption for Israel in fighting terror across borders is that its forces will pay a heavy price for attacking. The IDF had assumed since its 2005 withdrawal from Gaza that it risked significant casualties by sending its forces back across the border to fight terror. This assumption had been upheld in the 2006 war between Israel and Hezbollah, when 119 Israeli soldiers and 44 Israeli civilians were killed.

But the decisive military tactics in Gaza forced the terrorists to retreat and go into hiding, with just one Israeli soldier killed by a direct Hamas attack. The IDF was just a step short of absolute victory when the fighting was halted. The Israeli military was on the verge of a historic opportunity to alter the basic conditions that had allowed Hamas to steadily increase its military might.

The Israeli government decision to end the operation was a mistake that will lead us in the near future to another war in Gaza — but this time with a higher price in lives for both Israelis and Palestinians.

NO Paul Rogers
Global Security Consultant, Oxford Research Group, and Professor of Peace Studies, University of Bradford, United Kingdom

Written for *CQ Global Researcher*, April 2009

Israel's military assault on Gaza had the stated aim of so weakening Hamas' paramilitary capabilities that it could no longer fire unguided rockets into Israeli territory.

As the war began, senior Israeli sources made it clear that the aim extended beyond this, toward destroying Hamas' political and administrative infrastructure in order to weaken and possibly destroy the movement as a functioning entity. The actual conduct of the war suggests that this more extensive operation was indeed being implemented.

Indeed, the war started with a remarkably intensive and sudden air assault in which 88 aircraft attacked 100 targets in under four minutes. The initial assault included an attack on a police graduation ceremony in which 60 people reportedly were killed.

Four hundred more targets were hit during the first week, including numerous police stations and agricultural facilities, government offices and the main campus of the Islamic University.

At the end of the three-week war, the United Nations estimated that 1,300 Gazans had been killed, including 412 children. More than 5,000 people were injured, 4,000 homes were destroyed and 20,000 severely damaged — about 20 percent of the entire housing stock.

Although Hamas' paramilitary was undoubtedly caught by surprise in the initial assault, it reacted very quickly, and most of the personnel went to ground. There was some limited engagement with Israeli ground troops, but for the most part Hamas' military wing recognized the futility of engaging the vastly superior Israeli firepower and escaped with little damage. Rockets continued to be fired into Israel throughout the war. Afterward, Hamas quickly resumed control, returning police and security personnel to the streets and repairing smuggling tunnels to Egypt.

Claims of Israeli attacks on civilians were persistently rebutted by the Israeli Defense Force, but sources within the Israeli Army have recently provided evidence to support the claims. Israel might have expected a strong Arab public reaction to the war, but what was much less expected was considerable antagonism across much of Europe. With Hamas still in control of Gaza and substantially more popular among Palestinians, with rockets still being fired and with Israel losing public support in the wider world, the end result has been counterproductive to Israel's long-term security interests. It may, however, have some impact in persuading Israelis that a state of permanent war is not the best way to ensure the country's long-term survival.

"In spite of all the wars and the difficulties and the rise of extremists on both sides, I still believe that, if there is a decisive political will in Washington, D.C. — and potentially there is one — then . . . a peace deal could be reached between the two sides in a relatively short period of time," says Palestinian U.N. envoy Mansour.

"Honestly I really don't know if it is five minutes before 12, or five past," adds U.N. envoy Serry. "An early engagement of the Americans will be very much needed."

But even then, a deal is likely to remain out of reach for now, diplomats caution. "We face serious difficulties," says EU envoy Otte. "Nobody has really concentrated on the ability of the parties to implement such an agreement."

For example, any deal likely would require the Palestinians to give up the right of refugees to return home to what is now Israel. Its two feuding factions would have to agree to work closely together in governing their new state. At the same time, given the current realities, such a state's economy and security likely would remain heavily dependent on Israel.

Meanwhile, Israel would have to evacuate as many as hundreds of thousands of settlers from the West Bank and East Jerusalem and find a place for them to live and work. It also would have to accept the reality of the Palestinians, former foes, as permanent neighbors and friends.

"It's not something that is done easily," Otte says. "It's not impossible, but it would take years to implement."

Each side also must have the confidence that what it offers will be politically acceptable to its people. Is a new Israeli government capable of delivering on the two-state solution? Is the institutional chaos on the Palestinian side capable of accepting it?

"Both are highly unlikely," laments a veteran Middle East mediator, speaking on condition of anonymity on grounds that his grim view could damage future negotiations. "That is why any kind of significant diplomatic breakthrough at this time — I wish it had happened yesterday — is totally unrealistic." Doing the necessary groundwork, he continues, "is a mammoth job, and it will take time."

With those difficulties in mind, the Israeli approach during the year-long Annapolis discussions was to consider peace talks as only theoretical. The process was aimed at reaching what was referred to as a "shelf agreement" because it would, if reached, be put aside until conditions were right for it to take effect.

Since nothing was changing on the ground, "Prime Minister Olmert said, 'Let's change the sequence. Let's start with negotiation on a final status agreement,' " explains Israel's Shariv. "If we reach an agreement, we'll put it on a shelf. . . . This will show the Palestinians something they can wish for."

But Rashid Khalidi, a prominent U.S. scholar of Arab descent at Columbia University's Middle East Institute, sounds a more urgent note. "Current discussions of whether [to seek] a one-state or a two-state solution . . . have an unrealistic quality at the present moment," says Khalidi. "What has to be devised is how to reverse — very rapidly — the current dynamic, which is a highly inequitable, de facto, one-state solution that looks more and more entrenched — and will become more and more untenable as time goes on."

NOTES

1. "Israeli TV airs Gaza doctor's pleas after children killed," Israel's Channel 10 via YouTube, www.youtube.com/watch?v=OLUJ4fF2HN4.

2. " 'I wept,' Olmert says of death of Gaza children," Reuters, Jan. 23, 2009, www.reuters.com/article/latestCrisis/idUSLN571480.

3. "Agency Says Hamas Took Aid Intended for Needy," *The New York Times*, Feb. 5, 2009, www.nytimes.com/2009/02/05/world/middleeast/05mideast.html?ref=world.

4. "Summary of Rocket Fire and Mortar Shelling in 2008," Intelligence and Terrorism Information Center, Jan. 1, 2009, www.terrorism-info.org.il/malam_multimedia/English/eng_n/pdf/ipc_e007.pdf.

5. "Obama's Speech in Sderot, Israel," *The New York Times*, July 23, 2008, www.nytimes.com/2008/07/23/us/politics/23text-obama.html?ref=politics.

6. "PCHR Contests Distortion of Gaza Strip Death Toll," Palestinian Centre for Human Rights, press release 44/2009, March 26, 2009, www.pchrgaza.org/files/PressR/English/2008/44-2009.html.

7. "Israel challenges Palestinian claims on Gaza death toll," Ynetnews, March 26, 2009, www.ynetnews.com/articles/0,7340,L-3692950,00.html.

8. "Remarks With Israeli Foreign Minister Tzipi Livni: Hillary Rodham Clinton, Secretary of State," Jerusalem, March 3, 2009, U.S. Department of State transcript, www.state.gov/secre tary/rm/2009a/03/119956.htm.

9. Dan Williams, "Israel fends off censure over Gaza civilian deaths," Reuters, Jan. 19, 2009, http://uk.reuters.com/article/usTopNews/idUKTRE50I2LU20090119.

10. Paul Rogers, "Gaza — The Aftermath," Oxford Research Group, January 2009, www.oxfordresearch-group.org.uk/publications/monthly_briefings/2009/02/gaza-aftermath.html.

11. "Gaza: situation at border crossings 'intolerable,' Ban says," U.N. Department of Public Information, March 10, 2009, www.un.org/apps/news/story.asp?NewsID=30138&Cr=gaza&Cr1=.

12. "Transcript: Obama's interview with Al Arabiya," Al Arabiya News Channel, Jan. 27, 2009, www.alarabiya.net/articles/2009/01/27/65096.html.

13. "Iranian President Stands by Call to Wipe Israel Off Map," *The New York Times*, Oct. 29, 2005, www.nytimes.com/2005/10/29/international/middleeast/29iran.html.

14. Howard Schneider and Glenn Kessler, "Israel Puts Iran Issue Ahead of Palestinians," *The Washington Post*, April 22, 2009, www.washingtonpost.com/wp-dyn/content/article/2009/04/21/AR2009042103998.html?hpid=topnews.

15. "Text of U.S. President George W. Bush's Middle East speech," June 24, 2002, www.bitterlemons.org/docs/bush.html.

16. Robert Pear, "White House Puts Onus on Hamas to End Violence," *The New York Times*, Dec. 28, 2008, www.nytimes.com/2008/12/28/world/middleeast/28diplo.html.

17. Katrin Bennhold, "Leaders of Turkey and Israel Clash at Davos Panel," *The New York Times*, Jan. 29, 2009, www.nytimes.com/2009/01/30/world/europe/30clash.html.

18. See, for example, John J. Mearsheimer and Stephen M. Walt, *The Israel Lobby and U.S. Foreign Policy* (2007).

19. "Israel's U.N. envoy calls Jimmy Carter 'bigot,' " Reuters, April 24, 2008, www.reuters.com/article/politicsNews/idUSN2448131520080425.

20. "A Performance-Based Road Map to a Permanent Two-State Solution to the Israeli-Palestinian Conflict," the Quartet (of the United States, the European Union, the United Nations and Russia), April 30, 2003, www.bitterlemons.org/docs/roadmap3.html.

21. "Declaration of Principles on Interim Self-Government Arrangements," Government of the State of Israel and the P.L.O. Team, Sept. 13, 1993, www.bitterlemons.org/docs/dop.html. Also see "Israel-PLO Recognition: Exchange of Letters between PM Rabin and Chairman Arafat — Sept. 9, 1993," Israel Ministry of Foreign Affairs, www.mfa.gov.il/MFA/Peace+Process/Guide+to+the+Peace+Process/Israel-PLO+Recognition+-+Exchange+of+Letters+betwe.htm.

22. "Text of U.S. President George W. Bush's Middle East speech," *op. cit.*

23. Muammar Qaddafi, "The One-State Solution," *The New York Times*, Jan. 22, 2009, www.nytimes.com/2009/01/22/opinion/22qaddafi.html.

24. Shahar Ilan and Barak Ravid, "Olmert warns of binational state if no peace deal reached," *Haaretz.com*, Sept. 16, 2008, *Haaretz.com*, www.haaretz.com/hasen/spages/1021689.html.

25. "Remarks With Israeli Foreign Minister Tzipi Livni: Hillary Rodham Clinton, Secretary of State," *op. cit.*

26. "Quartet Statement," *London*, Jan. 30, 2006, www.un.org/news/dh/infocus/middle_east/quartet-30jan2006.htm.

27. "Secretary Clinton, Palestinian President Abbas in Ramallah," transcript of joint press conference, March 4, 2009, www.america.gov/st/texttrans-english/2009/March/20090304125709eaifas0.3768885.html?CP.rss=true.

28. "Kofi Annan's speech to the General Assembly," *The Guardian*, Sept. 13, 2002, www.guardian.co.uk/world/2002/sep/13/iraq.united nations1.

29. "Israel's road map reservations," *Haaretz.com*, May 27, 2003, www.haaretz.com/hasen/pages/ShArt.jhtml?itemNo=297230.

30. "Intifada toll 2000-2005," BBC News, Feb. 8, 2005, http://news.bbc.co.uk/2/hi/middle_east/3694350.stm.

31. "The Sharm el-Sheikh Fact-Finding Committee," April 30, 2001, www.al-bab.com/arab/docs/pal/mitchell1.htm.

32. "Secret UN report condemns US for Middle East failures," *The Guardian*, June 13, 2007, www .guardian.co.uk/world/2007/jun/13/usa.israel.

33. Stephen Walt, "What do we do if the 'two-state' solution collapses?" *ForeignPolicy.com*, Feb. 10, 2009, http://walt.foreignpolicy.com/posts/2009/02/10/what_do_we_do_if_the_two_state_solution_collapses.

34. "Settlement population," based on figures obtained from Israel's Central Bureau of Statistics and the Jerusalem Statistical Yearbook, *B'tselem*, www .btselem.org/English/Settlements/Settlement_population.xls.

35. "Statement by Ambassador Susan E. Rice, U.S. Permanent Representative, Middle East Consultations in the Security Council," Feb. 18, 2009, www.usun newyork.usmission.gov/press_releases/20090218_031.html.

36. See Rogers, *op. cit.*

37. Transcript of press conference by Secretary-General Ban Ki-moon, U.N. headquarters, Feb. 10, 2009, www.un.org/News/Press/docs/2009/sgsm12092.doc.htm.

38. Alvaro de Soto, "Few will thank UN when this war ends," *The Independent*, Jan. 16, 2009, www .independent.co.uk/opinion/commentators/alvaro-de-soto-few-will-thank-un-when-this-war-ends-1380408.html.

39. Hillary Rodham Clinton, "Press Availability at the End of the Gaza Reconstruction Conference," Sharm el-Sheik, Egypt, March 2, 2009, www.state .gov/secretary/rm/2009a/03/119929.htm.

40. "Secretary Clinton, Palestinian President Abbas in Ramallah," *op. cit.*

41. "Hamas's popularity rises after Israel's Gaza war," Reuters, March 9, 2009, www.reuters.com/article/worldNews/idUSTRE52841Q20090309.

42. Yossi Alpher, "Not now," bitterlemons.org, March 2, 2009, www.bitterlemons.org/previous/bl020309ed9.html#isr1.

43. For background, see the following *CQ Researchers*: Peter Katel, "Middle East Tensions," Oct. 27, 2006, pp. 889-912; Nicole Gaouette, "Middle East Peace,"

Jan. 21, 2005, pp. 53-76; and David Masci, "Prospects for Mideast Peace," Aug. 30, 2002, pp. 673-696.

44. This section is drawn from Reinhard Schulze, *A Modern History of the Islamic World* (2002); Thomas L. Friedman, *From Beirut to Jerusalem* (1989); Ali M. Ansari, *Confronting Iran: The Failure of American Foreign Policy and the Next Great Conflict in the Middle East* (2006); and Walter Laqueur, *A History of Zionism* (2003).

45. See, for example, Daniel Williams, "New Conflicts of Historic Interest Rack the Heart of the Holy Land," *Los Angeles Times*, May 14, 1989, Part 5, p. 2; Joel Greenberg, "Israel's History, Viewed Candidly, Starts a Storm," *The New York Times*, April 10, 1998, p. A8.

46. Figures from Jeremy M. Sharp, author of two Congressional Research Service reports: "Egypt: Background and U.S. Relations," March 26, 2009, and "U.S. Foreign Aid to Israel," Feb. 3, 2009.

47. "Declaration of Principles on Interim Self-Government Arrangements," *op. cit.*

48. "Q & A: Leaving Lebanon," BBC, May 23, 2000, http://news.bbc.co.uk/1/hi/world/middle_east/636594.stm.

49. Jane Perlez and Elaine Sciolino, "High Drama and Hard Talks at Camp David, Against Backdrop of History," *The New York Times*, July 29, 2000, www .nytimes.com/2000/07/29/world/high-drama-and-hard-talks-at-camp-david-against-backdrop-of-history.html.

50. See, for example, Hussein Agha and Robert Malley, "Camp David: The Tragedy of Errors," *The New York Review of Books*, Aug. 9, 2001, www.nybooks .com/articles/14380.

51. "The Mitchell Report," May 4, 2001, www.jewish-virtuallibrary.org/jsource/Peace/Mitchellrep.html.

52. Yoav Peled, "Dual War: The Legacy of Ariel Sharon," *Middle East Report Online*, March 22, 2006, www .merip.org/mero/mero032206.html.

53. Text of U.S. President George W. Bush's Middle East speech, *op. cit.*

54. "Security Council Adopts Resolution Endorsing Road Map Leading Towards Two-State Resolution

of Israeli-Palestinian Conflict," U.N. Security Council press release SC/7924, Nov. 19, 2003, www.un.org/News/Press/docs/2003/sc7924.doc.htm.

55. See, for example, "Bush Says US Not At War With Islam," *Sky News*, Sept. 20, 2006, http://news.sky.com/skynews/Home/Sky-News-Archive/Article/20080641234424.

56. See, for example, Greg Myre, "Envoy in Mideast Peace Effort Says Israel Is Keeping Too Tight a Lid on Palestinians in Gaza," *The New York Times*, Oct. 25, 2005, www.nytimes.com/2005/10/25/international/middleeast/25mideast.html.

57. Greg Myre, "Because of Attacks, Israel Declares Part of Gaza Off Limits," *The New York Times*, Dec. 29, 2005, www.nytimes.com/2005/12/29/international/middleeast/29mideast.html.

58. "Quartet Statement," *op. cit.*

59. "Hamas takes full control of Gaza," BBC, June 15, 2007, http://news.bbc.co.uk/2/hi/middle_east/6755299.stm.

60. "Why They Died: Civilian Casualties in Lebanon during the 2006 War," Human Rights Watch, Sept. 5, 2007, www.hrw.org/en/reports/2007/09/05/why-they-died-0.

61. Laila Bassam, "Lebanon forms unity government with Hezbollah," Reuters, July 11, 2008, www.reuters.com/article/homepageCrisis/idUSL1159875._CH_.2400.

62. Sheryl Gay Stolberg, "Peace? Sure, I'll See What I Can Do," *The New York Times*, Dec. 2, 2007, http://query.nytimes.com/gst/fullpage.html?res=9802E5D61638F931A35751C1A9619C8B63.

63. "Adopting Text on Middle East Conflict, Security Council Reaffirms Support for Annapolis Outcomes, Declares Negotiations 'Irreversible,' " press release SC/9539, U.N. Department of Public Information, Dec. 16, 2008, www.un.org/News/Press/docs/2008/sc9539.doc.htm.

64. "President Obama Discusses Mideast During Visit of Jordan's King Abdullah," CQ Transcriptswire, April 21, 2009, www.cqpolitics.com/wmspage.cfm?parm1=5&docID=news-000003099340.

65. "Efforts to end current Gaza 'impasse' imperative — UN political chief," U.N. News Centre, March 25, 2009, www.un.org/apps/news/story.asp?NewsID=30290&Cr=gaza&Cr1=.

66. U.N. Undersecretary-General for Political Affairs Lynn Pascoe, "Briefing to the Security Council on the Situation in the Middle East," April 20, 2009, http://domino.un.org/UNISPAL.NSF/e872be638-a09135185256ed100546ae4/b24712e38d4c2a0a8525759f004bc662!OpenDocument.

67. "Peace with Israel possible, says Syria's Assad," Reuters, March 9, 2009, www.reuters.com/article/worldNews/idUSTRE5281NL20090309.

68. "Background Note: Syria," U.S. Department of State Web site, www.state.gov/r/pa/ei/bgn/3580.htm. Also see "State Sponsors of Terrorism Overview," U.S. Department of State, April 30, 2008, www.state.gov/s/ct/rls/crt/2007/103711.htm.

69. "Remarks With Israeli Foreign Minister Tzipi Livni: Hillary Rodham Clinton, Secretary of State," *op. cit.*

70. Schneider and Kessler, *op. cit.*

71. Jeffrey Heller, "Netanyahu says will negotiate peace with the Palestinians," Reuters, March 25, 2009, www.reuters.com/article/middleeastCrisis/idUSLP254174.

72. "Israel/Gaza: International Investigation Essential," Human Rights Watch, Jan. 27, 2009, www.hrw.org/en/news/2009/01/27/israelgaza-international-investigation-essential.

73. Stephanie Nebehay, "U.N. rights envoy sees Israeli war crimes in Gaza," Reuters, March 20, 2009, www.reuters.com/article/middleeastCrisis/idUSLJ155314.

74. "Richard J. Goldstone Appointed to Lead Human Rights Council Fact-Finding Mission on Gaza Conflict," U.N. Human Rights Council, press release, April 3, 2009, www.unhchr.ch/huricane/huricane.nsf/view01/2796E2CA43CA4D94C125758D002F8D25?opendocument.

75. "Settlement Population," *op. cit.*

76. "The situation in the Middle East, including the Palestinian question," U.N. Security Council, Feb. 18, 2009, http://domino.un.org/UNISPAL.NSF/e872be638a09135185256ed100546ae4/44906205538f760085257562004be029!OpenDocument.

77. See Barak Ravid, "Netanyahu aides fear 'surprise' demands from Obama," *Haaretz.com*, May 2,

2009, www.haaretz.com/hasen/spages/1082144.html.

78. "Briefing to the Security Council on the situation in the Middle East," April 20, 2009, http://domino.un.org/UNISPAL.NSF/e872be638a09135185256ed100546ae4/b24712e38d4c2a0a8525759f004bc662!OpenDocument.

79. Quoted in Taghreed El-Khodary and Ethan Bronner, "Addressing U.S., Hamas says it Grounded Rockets," *The New York Times*, May 5, 2009, p. A5, www.nytimes.com/2009/05/05/world/middleeast/05meshal.html?_r=1&ref=world.

BIBLIOGRAPHY

Books

Hirst, David, *The Gun and the Olive Branch: The Roots of Violence in the Middle East,* **Nation Books, 2003.**

The Middle East correspondent for the *Manchester Guardian* traces the history of the Israeli-Palestinian conflict from the 1880s through the Sept. 11, 2001, terrorist attacks in the United States.

Indyk, Martin, *Innocent Abroad: An Intimate Account of American Peace Diplomacy in the Middle East,* **Simon & Schuster, 2009.**

A former U.S. ambassador to Israel dissects the successes and failures of President Bill Clinton's intensive and highly personal pursuit of a peace deal.

Khalidi, Rashid, *Sowing Crisis: The Cold War and American Dominance in the Middle East,* **Beacon Press, 2009.**

The director of Columbia University's Middle East Institute explores how George W. Bush's global war on terror spilled over into the Middle East.

Kurtzer, Daniel, and Scott Lasensky, *Negotiating Arab-Israeli Peace,* **United States Institute of Peace Press, 2008.**

A veteran U.S. diplomat and lecturer in Middle Eastern policy at Princeton University's Woodrow Wilson School of Public and International Affairs (Kurtzer) and a researcher at the U.S. Institute of Peace analyze two decades of U.S. peace efforts in the Middle East.

Miller, Aaron David, *The Much Too Promised Land: America's Elusive Search for Arab-Israeli Peace,* **Bantam, 2008.**

A former adviser on Middle East negotiations to six U.S. secretaries of state (1978-2003) provides a frank, insightful walk through decades of diplomacy in the region.

Oz, Amos, *A Tale of Love and Darkness,* **Harcourt, 2004.**

An Israeli writer traces his family history from 19th-century Ukraine to the Palestine of the 1930s to Jerusalem in the 1940s and '50s, illuminating some of the human drama leading to Israel's birth.

Tolan, Sandy, *The Lemon Tree: An Arab, A Jew, and the Heart of the Middle East,* **Bloomsbury, 2007.**

A journalist and producer of radio documentaries views the Middle East crisis through the eyes of two families — one Arab and one Jewish — that lived at different times in a house near Tel Aviv with a lemon tree in its garden.

Articles

"Timeline: Israel, the Gaza Strip and Hamas," *The New York Times,* **Jan. 4, 2009, www.nytimes.com/interactive/2009/01/04/world/20090104_ISRAEL-HAMAS_TIMELINE.html.**

This interactive Web-based timeline traces the history of Israel and the Gaza Strip from Israel's statehood to the withdrawal of Israeli troops from Gaza on Jan. 21, 2009.

Qaddafi, Muammar, "The One-State Solution," *The New York Times,* **Jan. 22, 2009, www.nytimes.com/2009/01/22/opinion/22qaddafi.html.**

The Libyan leader argues that Israelis and Palestinians will never find peace until they band together in a single state he calls "Isratine."

Walt, Stephen, "What do we do if the 'two-state' solution collapses?" *ForeignPolicy.com,* **Feb. 10, 2009.**

A professor of international relations at Harvard University argues that U.S. support for Palestinian statehood makes it sound reasonable and moderate without actually having to do anything to bring about that goal.

Reports and Studies

"Israeli settlements in the Occupied Palestinian Territory, including Jerusalem, and the occupied

Syrian Golan: Report of the Secretary-General," *U.N. General Assembly*, Nov. 5, 2008.
This annual report documents Israeli settlement activity through mid-2008 and recommends steps for both Israel and the Palestinians to comply with international law.

"The Middle East Quartet: A Progress Report," *CARE, Christian Aid, Oxfam, Save the Children Alliance, World Vision, et al.*, Sept. 25, 2008, www .reliefweb.int/rw/rwb.nsf/db900sid/VDUX-7JSSZD.
This report by a consortium of nongovernmental relief organizations finds that the Quartet of international Middle East mediators falls short in addressing an ongoing humanitarian crisis in Palestinian areas.

"The Six Months of the Lull Arrangement," *Intelligence and Terrorism Information Center*, December 2008, www.terrorism-info.org.il/malam_ multimedia/English/eng_n/pdf/hamas_e017.pdf.
This report by an Israeli nongovernmental organization documents Palestinian rocket and mortar fire into southern Israel from Gaza during 2008. Includes many color photos and charts.

Migdalovitz, Carol, "Israeli-Arab Negotiations: Background, Conflicts, and U.S. Policy," *Congressional Research Service*, updated March 9, 2009.
A Middle East expert documents decades of efforts to find a peaceful solution to the region's longest-running conflict.

For More Information

American Israel Public Affairs Committee, 440 First St., N.W., Suite 600, Washington, DC 20001; (202) 639-5200; www.aipac.org. Widely known as AIPAC, the leading lobbying group for Israel in the United States.

Bitterlemons.org; www.bitterlemons.org. Presents weekly commentary from both the Palestinian and Israeli point of view on key developments in the Middle East conflict; features a helpful archive of key historic documents dating back to 1947.

B'Tselem, 8 HaTa'asiya St. (4th Floor), P.O. Box 53132, Jerusalem 91531, Israel; (972-2) 673-5599; www.btselem .org/English. Leading Israeli human-rights organization that seeks to document human-rights violations in the occupied territories and to promote the protection of Palestinians' human rights.

Intelligence and Terrorism Information Center, Maj. General Aharon Yariv Blvd., P.O. Box 3555, Ramat Hasharon 47134, Israel; (972-3) 760-3579; www.terrorism-info.org.il/. A private organization focuses on issues linked to terrorism and intelligence; reports available on its Web site on a broad range of related topics including Palestinian policies concerning terrorism, Palestinian groups it considers terrorist groups, terrorism-related activities in other countries including Syria and Iran and global terrorism financing mechanisms.

J Street, Washington, D.C.; (202) 248-5870; http://jstreet .org/. Launched in April 2008; a nongovernmental organization that represents Americans who support both a secure Jewish homeland and a sovereign Palestinian state; advocates strong U.S. leadership to end the Arab-Israeli and Israeli-Palestinian conflicts through diplomatic rather than military means.

Jerusalem Center for Public Affairs, Beit Milken, 13 Tel Hai St., Jerusalem 92107, Israel; (972-2) 561-9281; http:// jcpa.org. A private, nonprofit Israeli think tank that focuses on analysis of various global challenges facing Israel, including Islamic extremism and global anti-Semitism. The group's president, Dore Gold, is a close associate of Israel's new prime minister, Benjamin Netanyahu.

Oxford Research Group, Development House, 56-64 Leonard St., London EC2A 4LT; (44-20) 7549-0298; www.oxfordresearchgroup.org.uk. Independent British think tank that promotes nonviolent resolution of international conflicts, with a special focus on the Middle East.

Palestinian Centre for Human Rights, P.O. Box 1328, Gaza City; (972-8) 282-4776 or (972-8) 282-5893; www .pchrgaza.org. Private nonprofit organization dedicated to protecting human rights and promoting the rule of law and democratic principles in the occupied Palestinian territories. It has branch offices in the West Bank town of Ramallah and three in the Gaza Strip.

United Nations, First Avenue at 46th St., New York, NY 10017; (212) 963-1234; www.un.org/english. Supports Middle East programs ranging from economic development and humanitarian aid to human rights, peacekeeping and diplomacy. Its Web site has two main sections devoted to the region, on U.N.-related Middle East news (www.un.org/apps/news/ infocusRel.asp?infocusID=22&Body=middle&Body1=east) and on Palestinian programs (http://un.org/Depts/dpa/qpal/).

The Troubled Horn of Africa

9

Can the War-Torn Region Be Stabilized?

Jason McLure

A Somali woman wounded in fighting between government soldiers and Islamist insurgents last June is among thousands of civilians killed or wounded in Somalia's 18-year civil war. The conflict has destabilized the entire region, forcing nearly 1.3 million people from their homes and creating a lawless safe haven for pirates and terrorists.

AFP/Getty Images/Mustafa Abdi

From *CQ Global Researcher*, June 2009.

alima Warsame's husband and son were killed two years ago after a mortar shell landed on their shop in Mogadishu, the war-torn capital of Somalia. But the impoverished nation's long civil war wasn't finished with her yet.

After living in a camp for people who had fled the fighting, she returned home in April. But in mid-May renewed fighting forced her to return to the camp.

"I thought with the Ethiopian troops gone and the new government [in place] everything would be alright, only it got worse," she says. "I don't see any hope that our situation will ever improve."[1]

Indeed, there is little reason for optimism. During just two weeks in May, at least 67,000 people were driven from their homes in the beleaguered seaside capital by clashes between the country's U.N.-backed transitional government and Islamist extremists. But they are just the latest victims. Somalia's 18-year civil war has killed tens of thousands, forced nearly 1.3 million people from their homes and created a lawless safe haven for pirates and suspected terrorists.[2]

Once a gem of Italian colonial architecture overlooking the Indian Ocean, parts of Mogadishu have been reduced to a moonscape of gutted buildings where warring militias wielding shoulder-fired grenade launchers and AK-47s periodically wreak havoc, sending civilians fleeing to dozens of primitive camps surrounding the city.

The fighting has continued despite more than a dozen attempts to establish a central government — including the latest, in January, when moderate Islamist Sheikh Sharif Sheikh Ahmed became

Grinding Poverty Afflicts Most of Africa's Horn

The four nations in the Horn of Africa cover an arid swathe about three times the size of Texas. More than 100 million people live in the war-torn region — 85.2 million of them in landlocked Ethiopia, Africa's second-most populous country. Tiny Djibouti is the smallest with half a million people. Ethiopia and Eritrea are near the bottom on the U.N.'s 179-nation Human Development Index, which ranks countries by life expectancy and other factors. Somalia doesn't even make the list, since it has no way to collect statistics. Some analysts say the area's poverty and weak or corrupt governments make it a safe haven for Islamic terrorists and pirates.

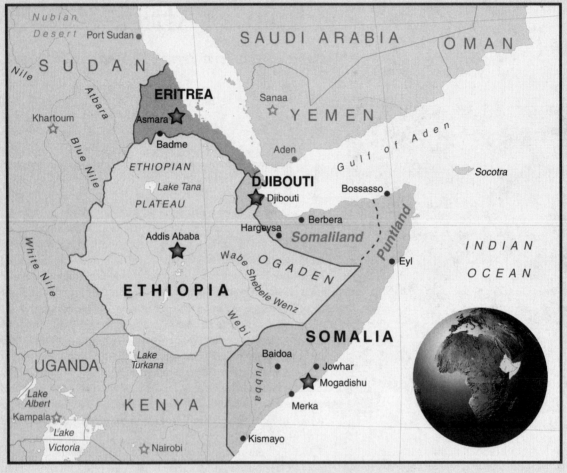

Source: The World Factbook, Central Intelligence Agency; U.N. Development Programme

president. In fact, Ahmed's government is said to have, at best, a tenuous hold on just a few blocks of the capital itself. The ongoing security vacuum has encouraged the clan violence and anarchy that make Somalia a global poster child for a "failed state."

But the fighting in Somalia is only part of an inter-related web of conflicts plaguing the Horn of Africa — one of the most benighted corners of the world's poorest continent. Archrivals Ethiopia and tiny Eritrea have backed factions in Somalia's civil war and continue to arm rebel groups destabilizing the region. And both nations have kept tens of thousands of troops dug in along their mutual border since the end of a 1998-2000 border war that killed 70,000.

In January, Ethiopia ended a two-year occupation of Mogadishu, where it initially succeeded in ousting an Islamist alliance that U.S. officials feared was courting links with the al Qaeda terrorist group. Western nations have showered Ethiopia with billions of dollars in aid and avoided criticizing the regime's recent clampdown on opposition parties, journalists and human rights activists.

Eritrea, once admired for its self-sufficiency and discipline, has become an isolated dictatorship facing possible international sanctions for having backed the Islamist insurgents in Somalia. Meanwhile Eritrea's effort to build a military counterweight to much-larger Ethiopia has kept more than a third of its productive population serving in the military.[3]

"Eritrea and Ethiopia are battling to determine which will be the dominant power in the region," says Dan Connell, a former adviser to the Eritrean government and author of the book *Against All Odds: A Chronicle of the Eritrean Revolution.* "The border issue is more excuse than cause."

Thus beleaguered by poor governance, conflict and poverty, Ethiopia and Eritrea rank near the bottom on the United Nations' 179-country Human Development Index, which ranks countries by life expectancy, literacy and other factors. Somalia, with no functioning central government to collect statistics, doesn't even make the list.[4] But with 40 percent of the population needing emergency aid, U.N. officials describe Somalia as the world's worst humanitarian and security crisis.[5]

Horn of Africa at a Glance

Somalia

Area: 246,201 sq. miles (slightly smaller than Texas)
Population: 9.8 million (July 2009 est.)
GDP per capita: $600 (2008 est.)
Unemployment rate: n/a
UN Human Development Index rank: not included
Religion: Sunni Muslim
Government: Sheikh Sharif Sheikh Ahmed was elected president in January 2009; Somaliland in the north remains autonomous, having declared its own local government in 1991 but has not been recognized internationally. Puntland, in the northeast, declared itself the Puntland State of Somalia in 1998 but has refrained from making a formal bid for independence.

Ethiopia

Area: 435,186 sq. miles (about twice the size of Texas)
Population: 85.2 million (July 2009 est.)
GDP per capita: $800 (2008 est.)
Unemployment rate: n/a
UN Human Development Index rank: 169 (out of 179)
Religion: Christian, 61%; Muslim, 33%; other 6%
Government: Federal republic, bicameral Parliament; Prime Minister Meles Zenawi was elected in 2000.

Eritrea

Area: 46,842 sq. miles (slightly larger than Pennsylvania)
Population: 5.6 million (July 2009 est.)
GDP per capita: $700 (2008 est.)
Unemployment rate: n/a
UN Human Development Index rank: 164 (out of 179)
Religion: Muslim, Coptic Christian, Roman Catholic, Protestant
Government: Provisional government since independence from Ethiopia in 1991, constitutional options presented but none yet implemented; single-party state run by the leftist People's Front for Democracy and Justice; President Isaias Afwerki elected by National Assembly in 1993 in country's only election so far.

Djibouti

Area: 8,880 sq. miles (about the size of New Jersey)
Population: 516,055 (July 2009 est.)
GDP per capita: $3,700 (2008 est.)
Unemployment rate: 59% in urban areas, 83% in rural areas (2007 est.)
UN Human Development Index rank: 151 (out of 179)
Religion: Muslim 94%, Christian 6%
Government: Republic; President Ismail Omar Guelleh has held office since 1999.

Source: The World Factbook, Central Intelligence Agency; U.N. Development Programme

"The region seems to be going backwards fast," says Ioan Lewis, a retired professor at the London School of Economics who has written several books on Somalia. "Whether it can change gear and change course, I really don't know."

The region's human rights record worries the international community as much as its dire economic

Death and Demonstrations

The remains of Somalis killed during Ethiopia's two-year occupation are recovered near a former Ethiopian military camp in Somalia (top). More than 10,000 people reportedly were killed during the occupation, which ended in January. Ethiopia also has come under international criticism for a recent crackdown on opposition leaders, the press and human rights organizations. Protesters demonstrate against Prime Minister Meles Zenawi during the April meeting of world leaders in London (bottom).

conditions. The European Parliament on Jan. 15 expressed its "great concern" for the state of "human rights, the rule of law, democracy and governance in all countries of the Horn of Africa," where there were "credible reports of arbitrary arrests, forced labour, torture and maltreatment of prisoners, as well as persecution of journalists and political repression."[6]

The chaos has provided refuge to suspected al Qaeda terrorists and allowed pirates to wreak havoc on international shipping. The conflict and poverty have sent millions of refugees fleeing to neighboring countries or to camps in Somalia for internally displaced persons (IDPs) where they depend on international aid agencies for food and shelter — aid that is often blocked by violence, theft or piracy. (*See graph, p. 238.*)[7]

Somalia's civil war has been fuelled in large part by distrust and competition between the country's Byzantine network of clans and subclans and by warlords with a vested interest in instability. A brief flicker of hope accompanied the withdrawal of Ethiopian troops in January and the accession of Sheikh Ahmed to the presidency of the country's Transitional Federal Government. But that hope was dimmed by fierce fighting in April and May and the capture of key towns by Islamist insurgents. Even veteran observers of Somalia marvel at the seeming senselessness of the fighting.

"All I can say now is that I have felt it a privilege to observe a people who shot themselves in the foot with such accuracy and tumbled into the abyss in such style," Aidan Hartley, a Kenyan-born Reuters correspondent who covered Somalia in the early 1990s, wrote in a 2003 book.[8]

Such sentiments are still echoed today. "We are all . . . shocked that Somalis keep finding reasons to kill Somalis," said Ahmedou Ould-Abdallah, a Mauritanian diplomat who is the U.N. special envoy to Somalia, during a Feb. 2 press conference.

The four nations of Africa's Horn — Somalia, Ethiopia, Eritrea and the micro-state Djibouti — cover an arid swathe about three times the size of Texas. About 100 million people live in the region — 85.2 million of them in Ethiopia, Africa's second-most populous country after Nigeria. To the north, tiny Eritrea — which split away from Ethiopia in 1993 — maintains Africa's largest army in an effort to deter its southern neighbor from invading.

Conflict is not new to the Horn of Africa, where the predominately Christian highlanders of the Ethiopian plateau have been fighting with the Muslim lowlanders of eastern Ethiopia (known as the Ogaden) and Somalia for centuries. But the region is also periodically plagued by famine, due to a rapidly growing population and increasingly unpredictable rainfall. This year the warfare and drought will force about 15.5 million people in Somalia and Ethiopia to seek humanitarian aid.[9]

And the long-term trends are equally worrying. About 80 percent of Ethiopians and Eritreans are subsistence farmers or herders. Agricultural production per capita has declined in Ethiopia since the 1960s, while the population has more than tripled.[10] Eritrea's government-controlled economy has eliminated nearly all private enterprise, and its farmers don't produce enough food to feed the country, a situation exacerbated by the government's decision not to demobilize tens of thousands of farmers from the military.[11] Somalia, which imports about 60 percent of the grain needed to feed its estimated 8 to 10 million people, has little prospect of feeding itself anytime soon.

"Ethiopia adds to its population between 1.5 to 2 million people a year," says David Shinn, U.S. ambassador to the country from 1996 to 1999. "That is not sustainable for a country that has been unable to feed itself for more than three decades."

While Somalia's humanitarian disaster is the region's most pressing issue, a longer-term question is whether the war-wracked country as presently configured can survive. Its northwestern region, known as Somaliland, has declared independence after building a functional administration and maintaining a comparatively peaceful, democratic existence for the last decade.

"The hard questions have not been asked as to what sort of a nation-state Somalia should look like," says Rashid Abdi, a Nairobi-based analyst for the International Crisis Group, a conflict-resolution think tank. "The focus has been on creating a national government. Unfortunately, in spite of a lot of investment in the last 15 years, we are nowhere near a functioning, credible nation-state."

Western policy in the region has been influenced largely by the perception that Somalia's lawlessness provides a safe haven for al Qaeda. Somalia's radical Islamist al-Shabaab militia, the most powerful group battling the transitional government, has links to al Qaeda and reportedly has been recruiting jihadists in the United States.[12] And while recent reports indicate that hundreds of foreign fighters from the Middle East and Muslim communities in North America and Europe have arrived in Somalia, analysts disagree over whether Somalia's Islamic radicals pose any real threat outside of the Horn.[13] Some blame the George W. Bush administration in particular for fomenting chaos in Somalia by arming warlords whose sole virtues were their willingness to fight Islamic groups.

"Violent extremism and anti-Americanism are now rife in Somalia due in large part to the blowback from policies that focused too narrowly on counterterrorism objectives," writes Kenneth Menkhaus, an American Horn of Africa specialist from Davidson College who worked as a U.N. official in Somalia in the 1990s.[14]

If there is reason for optimism, it is that the new Obama administration in Washington has signaled its willingness to focus more on human rights and stability and less on waging war against radical Islamists and their allies. Such a move would involve both pressing Ethiopia to resolve its border dispute with Eritrea and showing a greater willingness to work with moderate Islamists in Somalia, who many believe are the only force capable of bridging the divide between the country's constantly warring clans.

As analysts and diplomats discuss the Horn of Africa's future, here are some of the questions being debated:

Is there a real threat of international terrorism from Somalia?

When 17-year-old Burhan Hassan didn't come home from school in Minneapolis last Nov. 4, his mother thought he was at a local mosque. Unfortunately he wasn't. Although his family had fled Somalia when he was a toddler, Hassan — it turned out — had embarked that day for the southern Somali port town of Kismayo, a stronghold of al-Shabaab, the military wing of the Islamic Courts Union (ICU) that briefly controlled southern Somalia in 2006 before being ousted by Ethiopian troops.

U.S. law enforcement and counterterrorism officials fear Burhan is one of about 20 young Somali-Americans who may have left the United States since mid-2007 to join the group, which the State Department considers a terrorist organization.[15] The fear is that they may return to the United States or Europe as part of a sleeper cell, sent by a group that is increasingly vociferous about its links to international terrorism. Since 2007 some American generals have considered Somalia a "third front in the war on terror,"[16] and U.S. military planes are a common sight over the nation.[17]*

A spokesman for al-Shabaab said it began seeking links with al Qaeda after it was listed as a terrorist group

---

* In 2003, the U.S. opened a military base in Djibouti, less than 30 miles from the border of Somalia. Camp Lemonier houses about 2,000 U.S. personnel who monitor suspected terrorists in the Horn of Africa and train the militaries of Ethiopia and other U.S. allies.

AFP/Getty Images/Simon Maina

Newly elected Somalia President Sheikh Sharif Sheikh Ahmed is regarded by many as one of the few men whose clan base and political skills might bring peace to the war-ravaged country. Somalia has had no effective central authority since former president Mohamed Siad Barre was ousted in 1991, touching off an endless cycle of war between rival factions.

by the Bush administration in 2008. Before that, Shabaab "had no official links with al Qaeda," Sheikh Mukhtar Robow, a spokesman for the group, said in 2008. Now, however, "we're looking to have an association with them. Al Qaeda became more powerful after it was added to the list; we hope that it will be the same with us."[18]

Experts differ on whether the links are substantive. Those who worry that Somalia has become a safe haven for terrorists point out that several Somali Islamist leaders were trained in al Qaeda camps in the Afghanistan-Pakistan border regions in the 1990s before returning to Somalia to help form al-Ittihad al-Islamiya, a forerunner of al-Shabaab.

"We face a very serious counterterrorism challenge in Somalia, with extremists affiliated with al Qaeda training and operating in substantial portions of southern Somalia," said Susan Rice, the Obama administration's U.N. ambassador, during confirmation hearings in January. "And that has the potential to pose a serious and direct threat to our own national security."

Those concerned about the terrorism threat from Somalia often cite Gouled Hassan Dourad, a Somali national who was trained in Afghanistan, captured in Somalia in 2004 and held in the CIA's secret prison system before being transferred to Guantánamo Bay in 2006. The United States claims he supported al Qaeda's

East Africa cell and was privy to plots to attack an Ethiopian airliner and the U.S. military base in Djibouti in 2003.[19] Likewise, Fazul Abdullah Mohammed — a Comoran national accused of involvement in the 1998 bombings of U.S. embassies in Kenya and Tanzania and suspected in the 2002 truck bombing of the Paradise Hotel in Mombasa that killed 15 — is also thought to have taken refuge in Somalia.[20] A third figure, Hassan al-Turki, is said to run a training camp for Islamist militants in southern Somalia, and, like Mohammed, has been the target of an unsuccessful U.S. air strike in Somalia.[21]

"Definitely you have the al Qaeda East Africa cell that has only been able to function in Somalia with the protection of Somali Islamist movements," says Andre LeSage, an American Horn of Africa specialist at the Pentagon's National Defense University. "Previously, it had been with the protection of al-Ittihad, now it's with the protection of al-Shabaab."

But others say the international terrorism threat from Somalia has been exaggerated, both by al Qaeda and by the United States and its allies. "There is very strong documentation, using declassified al Qaeda documents, indicating that it was in and out of Somalia starting in 1992-1993," says Shinn, the former ambassador to Ethiopia. "They had relatively little success, however. They thought it was going to be relatively easy pickings until they learned Somalis could be just as obstreperous with them as with everyone else. It was very tough sledding.

"Over time they've had increasing success. But I think there is a certain amount of hype here," he says, especially when the West compares al-Shabaab to the ultraconservative Taliban in Afghanistan. "The idea that the Taliban is moving into Somalia is just utter nonsense."

Indeed, some argue that U.S. support for Ethiopia's 2006 invasion of Somalia and subsequent U.S. air strikes in Somalia that have often mistakenly killed civilians have been counterproductive and have helped to radicalize the population — increasing the terrorism threat. But so far, these analysts point out, no Somali-born citizens have been involved in successful acts of international terrorism.

"The Ethiopian invasion was totally negative," says Lewis, the Somali historian. "The terrorist threat is much more real now than before the interventions."

Coordinated suicide attacks last October on five separate targets in the autonomous Somali regions of Somaliland and Puntland — apparently carried out by

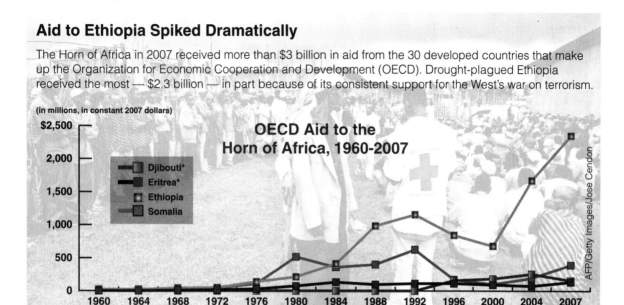

Aid to Ethiopia Spiked Dramatically

The Horn of Africa in 2007 received more than $3 billion in aid from the 30 developed countries that make up the Organization for Economic Cooperation and Development (OECD). Drought-plagued Ethiopia received the most — $2.3 billion — in part because of its consistent support for the West's war on terrorism.

OECD Aid to the Horn of Africa, 1960-2007

(in millions, in constant 2007 dollars)

Legend:
- Djibouti*
- Eritrea*
- Ethiopia
- Somalia

AFP/Getty Images/Jose Cendon

* Djibouti was a French colony until 1977. Eritrea declared its independence from Ethiopia in 1993.

Source: Organization for Economic Cooperation and Development

al-Shabaab — have raised fears the group's capacity for such tactics is growing.[22]

"The suicide bombings in Puntland and Somaliland were clear evidence that these guys have the capacity to work outside their comfort zone," says Menkhaus. "They've also demonstrated their capacity to induce some young men to commit suicide, which is fairly new to Somalia.

"Where will the next threat present itself? Kenya, Ethiopia, Djibouti? Shabaab has every reason to keep this conflict internationalized," he adds.

Is Somalia a viable state?

In the 18 years since the fall of dictator Mohamed Siad Barre, Somalia's foundations have steadily crumbled, with two large northern swathes of the country declaring themselves autonomous or independent entities.

In some ways, the Somalia that existed in the three decades before 1991 — a unified Somalia with a capital in Mogadishu — was an historical anomaly. It never existed previously and has not existed since. Though some analysts express optimism about the newest U.N.-backed Transitional Federal Government (TFG) formed

in February, the fact remains that its 14 predecessors since 1991 have all failed.[23]

The TFG struggles to control the port of Mogadishu, which is its main source of revenue, and has authority over just a tiny fraction of Somali territory. Though the current government has 36 cabinet ministers, most of the ministries have no employees and no budget.[24] The situation is so chaotic that businessmen print their own currency, and educated Somalis seek passports from neighboring countries to facilitate international travel.

Despite a string of U.N.-funded peace-and-reconciliation conferences in neighboring countries, a constantly shifting array of militia groups has defied outside attempts at reconciliation. In 2008, World Food Programme convoys bringing aid from Mogadishu to refugee camps 18 miles away needed to pass through more than a dozen checkpoints controlled by different militia groups, according to Peter Smerdon, a spokesman for the program.

"There are too many separate interests on the ground in Somalia," says LeSage, of the National Defense University. "You have so many different power centers there, and each one is being held by a different faction

Somali War Refugees Burden Neighboring States

Nearly a half-million Somalis have fled into neighboring countries to escape the country's 18-year civil war. Most have gone to Kenya and Yemen. Only 10 percent have remained in other Horn of Africa countries.

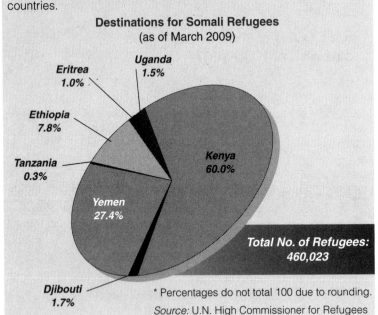

Destinations for Somali Refugees
(as of March 2009)

Uganda 1.5%
Eritrea 1.0%
Ethiopia 7.8%
Tanzania 0.3%
Kenya 60.0%
Yemen 27.4%
Djibouti 1.7%

Total No. of Refugees: 460,023

* Percentages do not total 100 due to rounding.
Source: U.N. High Commissioner for Refugees

"We don't know who to talk to now in Somalia," he continues. "There is no central government. They are so fragmented. They have been killing and killing and killing and oppressing. The people of Somaliland have enjoyed peace, security and democracy, and they're confident they can continue."

Because of the lack of international recognition, however, the region has not garnered needed development aid or political support. Many countries are reluctant to recognize break-away states unless it is politically expedient to do so, and there is no coherent international policy for recognizing separatist states.[25]

"There is no way Somaliland will rejoin Somalia, not in my lifetime," says Abdi, the International Crisis Group analyst. "They are dead-set on independence. If we don't reward Somaliland with some form of recognition, they risk sliding back. I think they are the most democratic administration in the Horn of Africa."

Neighboring Puntland also has functioned largely autonomously from both the Islamist militias and the Western-backed transitional government in the south. Dominated by the Majerteyn subclan of Somalia's Darod clan, the region declared itself the Puntland State of Somalia in 1998 but has refrained from making a formal independence bid.[26] That's in part because Abdullahi Yusuf, a native of Puntland, served as president of the TFG in Mogadishu for four years until being pressured to resign in December.

Puntland also has made democratic strides. The regional president was ousted in a parliamentary election in January by Abdirahman Mohamed Farole, a former finance minister.[27] But the area's reputation has been harmed by its status as a launching point for dozens of pirate attacks in 2008 and 2009. In December a U.N. report expressed concern "about the apparent complicity in pirate networks of Puntland administration officials at all levels" — a charge Puntland officials have disputed.[28] (*See sidebar, p. 244.*)

leader. They don't all share the same agenda for the way forward for the government. . . . You've already got 30-odd political groups just in Mogadishu."

The notable exception is Somaliland, formerly controlled by Britain. It declared independence from Somalia in 1991, ratified a national constitution in 2001 and has remained relatively peaceful since then. Its autonomous government, based in Hargeysa, prints money, operates a police force and issues passports. The region's combination of electoral democracy and clan-based power-sharing has drawn widespread praise, though so far no other government has recognized its independence.

"Somalia hasn't been functioning as a unified state at all, and Somaliland is virtually a separate state that really requires international recognition," says historian Lewis. "I don't think Somalia needs to exist in its present fashion."

Mohamed Hassan, Somaliland's ambassador to Ethiopia, says his homeland's independence was inevitable: "It was a bad marriage, and when a marriage is bad you have to separate.

"They are somewhere between secession and union with the rest of Somalia," says Abdi. "Depending on how things evolve in the next few months, Puntland is just hedging its bets. If they think union with Somalia is a dead-end, they will go their own way."

Recognition for either autonomous region would likely have to come first from Ethiopia, the regional power and a close ally of both administrations, or from the African Union (AU). So far both have refrained from doing so. "Those areas are pretty well-secured," Jean Ping, the Gabonese chairman of the African Union Commission, told a Jan. 27 press conference. "But the AU is characterized by respect for the territorial integrity of Somalia."

The United States has said it prefers a unified Somalia. "We will stay in line with the AU; that was the Bush administration's policy," says Jendayi Frazer, the U.S. assistant secretary of state for African affairs from 2005 to 2008. And it's a policy the Obama administration is likely to continue.

Most analysts say a unified Somalia would need a decentralized administrative system in order to be effective. "Our insistence that Somalis remake themselves in our image with ministries of this and this and this isn't realistic," says Menkhaus, the former U.N. official in Somalia. "A state that could emerge in a more organic way is possible. That might include a full array of local Islamic courts, municipalities and hybrid arrangements involving professional groups and clerics."

Should the United States reconsider its policies toward Ethiopia?

Ethiopia's human rights record is among the worst on the continent. But because the predominantly Christian nation — Africa's second-most populous country — cooperates in counterterrorism efforts, the United States and its European allies rarely criticize Prime Minister Meles Zenawi's government.

"There has been full support largely because they view the region through the counterterrorism lens, and Ethiopia has been considered the primary partner in the region," says Leslie Lefkow, a researcher at Human Rights Watch. "This has been problematic because it's ignored the very serious downward trajectory of Ethiopia's human rights record."

Indeed, the Zenawi government has become increasingly repressive in recent years:

- During an ongoing offensive against insurgents in eastern Ethiopia's Somali-speaking Ogaden region, Ethiopian troops have been accused of burning villages, raping women and summarily executing civilians suspected of supporting the separatist Ogaden National Liberation Front.[29]
- Opposition leader Birtukan Mideksa has been held in solitary confinement since December, when she was jailed for life for disputing terms of a pardon agreement that freed her and other opposition leaders from prison in 2007.[30]
- In April 2008, the ruling party and its allies swept to victory in local elections after major opposition parties withdrew, citing government intimidation.
- In January Ethiopia's parliament effectively banned foreign aid agencies from funding groups that promote democracy and human or women's rights.[31]

Lefkow also points out that U.S. support for Ethiopia's invasion of Somalia has not been rewarded by the death or capture of major terrorist suspects. "The small number of people that the U.S. was interested in have not been detained," she says. "The scores of people who were detained in 2007 were either not implicated at all in anything or were very minor people."

Western support for Ethiopia's 2006 invasion of Somalia — as well as Ethiopia's continued occupation of territory awarded to Eritrea in 2002 by the Eritrea-Ethiopia Boundary Commission — have led to growing resentment toward the West among Ethiopia's rivals.

"Sovereign Eritrean territories are still under Ethiopian occupation," Eritrean President Isaias Afwerki said in April 2008.[32] "This is basically the problem of the United States. Ethiopia doesn't have the power to occupy Eritrean territory without the support and encouragement of the U.S. administration. And this is the core of the problem."

"U.S. support for the Ethiopian invasion and pursuit of terrorist targets in Somalia in the name of the war on terrorism have further weakened Washington's credibility in the Horn of Africa and galvanised anti-American feeling among insurgents and the general populace," says a December 2008 report from the International Crisis Group.[33]

Connell, the former adviser to Eritrea, says Ethiopia has manipulated U.S. support to its own ends. "Ethiopia

Ethiopia Takes On Malaria

New effort attacks a deadly foe.

When malaria swept through the green hills of his village in southwest Ethiopia three years ago, Biya Abbafogi was lucky. The 35-year-old coffee farmer and three of his children were stricken with the deadly, mosquito-borne disease, but they all survived. Thirteen neighbors and friends in Merewa didn't.

"We would take one child to the hospital and come back and another one would be sick," he says.

The treatment Abbafogi and his family received was cheap by Western standards — just $40. But that was about a third of his annual coffee earnings, and the bills from the medical clinic — located two hours away by foot — forced Abbafogi to sell one of the oxen he used to plow his small corn field.

But today things are much better for Merewa's 4,335 residents, thanks to two young women trained to treat and prevent malaria and other common ailments. They're not doctors or nurses, and they haven't been to college. But with just one year of training they've cut malaria rates during the infectious season from 15 to 20 new cases per day to one to three.

Merewa's success has been replicated all across Ethiopia, where the government has dispatched an army of up to 30,000 "health extension workers" in the past four years. With money from donors like the Geneva-based Global Fund and the Carter Center in Atlanta, the women have distributed 20 million mosquito-repelling nets and offered basic malaria testing and treatment in isolated villages dozens of miles from the nearest paved road.

Every year 4 million Ethiopians contract malaria, which is particularly deadly for children. As many as one in five youngsters under age 5 who get the disease die from it. In response, Ethiopia is at the forefront of two major public-health initiatives in poor countries. The first, known as task-shifting, trains lower-skilled health professionals — who are cheaper to pay and easier to retain — to provide basic treatments and teach prevention. The second aims to distribute anti-malarial bed nets to 600 million Africans living in mosquito-infested regions by 2011.

Ethiopia's poverty helped drive the new approach. As one of the world's poorest countries, Ethiopia has trouble keeping doctors from moving to better-paying jobs overseas, says Tedros Adhanom, Ethiopia's health minister. "Right now, 50 percent of the doctors Ethiopia trains will emigrate," he says. To compensate, he says, Ethiopia is training more doctors — medical schools admitted 1,000 students in 2008, four times more than in 2007 — and shifting as much work as possible to nurses and health extension workers.

Lower-skilled extension workers don't emigrate, and they're also willing to work for less and to serve in rural areas, Adhanom says. "To tackle our health problems, the solutions are simple," he says. "You don't need highly skilled people to tell you how to prevent malaria."

Health workers learn 16 different health-education and treatment interventions, including midwifery, malaria treatment and hygiene education. They also make sure villagers are vaccinated and organize insecticide spraying to kill malaria-transmitting mosquitoes.

The mosquito net distribution program faces many obstacles in a country where many of the 85 million citizens live miles from paved roads. But improved technology offers hope the new anti-malaria effort will succeed where earlier attempts failed.

Bed nets not only provide a physical barrier against malaria-bearing mosquitoes but also kill the pests with insecticide sprayed on the nets. In the past, bed nets had to be dipped in chemicals annually to retain their potency. But newer nets are treated with long-lasting chemicals that require re-dipping only once every three to four years.

Dipping the older nets every year posed "a huge logistical problem" in rural places, Adhanom says. "Fewer than 40 percent of villagers would show up to have their old nets dipped. That really compromised the whole program."

So far, the combined initiatives seem to be working. Malaria prevalence dropped by 67 percent in Ethiopia between 2001 and 2007, according to a World Health Organization study, while the number of deaths of children under 5 has dropped 56 percent.[1]

---

[1] "Impact of the Scale-Up of Anti-Malarial Interventions Measured Using Health Facility-Based Data in Ethiopia," World Health Organization, Feb. 1, 2008.

is embroiled in a self-interested effort to promote its interests at the expense of its neighbors," he says. "We cannot build relations with so-called anchor states under such circumstances. Tamp down the regional confrontations, however, and the relationship again makes sense from our perspective. Let it fester and we will again and again be drawn into fights that are not of our own making and not in our interests."

Others say the United States won't offend Ethiopia because it has contributed peacekeepers to help monitor the conflicts in Sudan's Darfur region and Burundi and supports the Comprehensive Peace Agreement between north and south Sudan. And despite human rights abuses, Ethiopia's governance looks good in comparison with neighboring Eritrea, Sudan and Somalia.

"What you have is a very difficult balancing act where you try to push Ethiopia to open up on human rights . . . without jeopardizing Ethiopia's help on regional issues," says Shinn, the former ambassador to Ethiopia. "I don't take the opinion that you should just hammer them on human rights and let the other side drop off. On the other hand, I don't think their help in counterterrorism and peacekeeping is so important you ignore human rights."

While some critics of the regime say the United States and other Western countries should cut economic aid to Ethiopia over concerns about rising oppression, others say that would be naïve. (*See "At Issue," p. 251.*)

The Bush administration's top diplomat for Africa agrees. "Obviously, we have a lot of interests in Ethiopia," says Frazer. "Ethiopia has one of the largest, best-trained militaries in Africa. There are many Ethiopians in the United States, and Ethiopia is a major player within the African Union."

The Obama administration is still formulating its policy toward the region but has suggested that democratic reforms will have a higher priority than counterterrorism cooperation.

"It is extremely important that Ethiopia . . . not close down its democratic space, that it allow its political opposition — its civil society — to participate broadly in the political life of that country," Johnnie Carson, Obama's assistant secretary of state for African affairs, told a Senate subcommittee on April 29. "We have our strongest relationships among our democratic partners where we share ideals and values together, rather than

where we share common enemies together. A balanced relationship is absolutely essential."

BACKGROUND

Christian Kingdoms

Christianity arrived in Ethiopia in the early 4th century A.D., about 300 years before it arrived in England. According to tradition, two shipwrecked Syrian sailors brought the religion to what the Romans called Abyssinia.[34] A series of Christian kingdoms would rise and fall in the Ethiopian highlands until the 14th century, when feudalism descended over the country.

The dark ages lasted until the 1850s, when central authority was resurrected by the emperors Tewodros II, Yohannes IV and Menelik II. By the 1890s, Italy — a latecomer to the race for colonies in Africa — had conquered much of present-day Eritrea, which had only sporadically been under Ethiopian rule. But Italy's colonial ambitions were checked when Menelik's troops resoundingly beat back an Italian invasion from its Eritrean colony in 1896, ensuring that Ethiopia would remain the lone African nation never colonized by Europeans.

After becoming emperor in 1930, Haile Selassie, a former noble from the eastern city of Harar, barely had time to consolidate his rule before facing another challenge from Italy. In 1935 up to 100,000 Italian troops invaded northern Ethiopia. Selassie appealed to the League of Nations for help, but was rebuffed by France and the United Kingdom. Backed by bombers and tanks, the Italians had conquered most of Ethiopia's main cities by 1936, forcing Selassie into exile in Britain.[35]

But the Fascist Italians never controlled the countryside, and by 1941 a British-backed Ethiopian insurgency had ousted them.[36] Selassie reasserted the country's sovereignty in 1942 and turned to a new patron, the United States, to escape falling into Britain's colonial sphere.[37]

Compared with Ethiopia's rich history of ancient lords and kings ruling over peasant farmers in the cool highlands, Somalia's history is one of desert nomads who appeared in the Horn of Africa relatively late. Newly Islamized Somalis first began expanding south from the coastal area near the modern port of Berbera in northwestern Somalia in the 10th century. Fiercely independent camel and goat herders, Somalis have only rarely been brought under

CHRONOLOGY

1850s-1940s *Britain, France, Italy and Ethiopia divvy up the Horn of Africa, setting the stage for later ethnic disputes.*

1950s-1970s *Emperor Haile Selassie's grip on Ethiopia and Eritrea weakens as Somalia gains independence.*

1952 U.N. panel rules Eritrea should become part of a federation with Ethiopia rather than gain independence.

1960 Somalia gains independence, uniting British Somaliland with Italian Somalia, but not Somali-speaking regions of Kenya, Ethiopia and Djibouti. . . . Eritrean exiles in Egypt found Eritrean Liberation Front to fight for independence, beginning a three-decade-long struggle.

1969 Somalia's democratically elected president is assassinated. Military seizes power under Gen. Siad Barre, who proclaims Somalia a socialist state.

1974 Coup deposes Ethiopia's Selassie. Military group called the Derg takes control under Col. Mengistu Haile Mariam, establishing communist government.

1977-1978 Somalia conquers much of southeastern Ethiopia before Soviet Union enters war on Ethiopia's side. Barre turns away from communist bloc.

1980s-1990s *Civil wars overthrow authoritarian rulers across the Horn, but Somalia fails to recover.*

1983-1985 Drought triggers massive famine in Ethiopia, exacerbated by Mengistu's efforts to block food supplies to northern areas held by Eritrean and Tigray rebels. . . . Up to a million people die.

1991 As Soviet Union collapses, Ethiopia's Derg is overthrown by Eritrean and Tigrayan rebels from the North. Clan militias oust Barre regime in Somalia and then turn on one another. Somalia's civil war begins.

1992-1995 U.N. and U.S. try to help Somalia after up to 300,000 die from famine due to civil war and drought. U.S. withdraws in 1994 after U.S. troops die in "Black Hawk Down" incident.

1993 Eritreans vote for independence.

1998-2000 Ethiopia and Eritrea go to war over economic and border disputes. Ethiopia advances into Eritrea by 2000, capturing disputed town of Badme. U.N. peacekeepers begin patrolling border zone.

2000s *U.S. focus on anti-terrorism in the Horn leads to realigned loyalties.*

2001 Somaliland, which declared independence in 1991, ratifies constitution that endorses independence from southern Somalia, still mired in civil war. . . . Sept. 11 terrorist attacks on U.S. put focus on fighting al Qaeda threats in Somalia. Eritrean President Isaias Afwerki arrests Eritrean dissidents and closes private press.

2002 Eritrea-Ethiopian Boundary Commission awards Badme to Eritrea, but Ethiopia continues occupation.

2005 Ethiopia's first multiparty elections end badly as opposition leaders protest government claims of victory. At least 193 protesters are killed by Ethiopian security forces in Addis Ababa and thousands more injured. Government jails more than 120 opposition leaders, journalists and human rights activists.

2006 Islamic Courts Union (ICU) defeats U.S.-backed warlords in Mogadishu to take control of southern Somalia. Eritrean-armed ICU threatens jihad against Ethiopia.

December 2006 U.S.-backed Ethiopian troops invade Somalia, eventually ousting ICU. Efforts to install U.N.-backed Transitional Federal Government (TFG) amid Islamist insurgency fail due to resentment of Ethiopian occupation and intransigence of TFG President Abdullahi Yusuf.

December 2008-Present Ethiopian troops withdraw from Somalia; Islamist militias still control much of the south. Yusuf resigns. Sheikh Sharif Sheikh Ahmed, former ICU chairman, becomes president of U.N.-backed Somali government. . . . Shabaab and hardline militias declare war on Sheikh Ahmed's new government. Islamists capture additional towns in southern Somalia.

the control of a central state. A notable exception occurred during the holy wars against Ethiopia in the 13th-16th centuries, which culminated in the mid-16th century, when a predominantly Muslim army under Ahmed Gragn — "Ahmed the Left-Handed" — conquered much of the Ethiopian highlands.

The clan is the foundation and defining feature of Somali society. It is also at the root of the nation's problems, fostering factionalism and competition for resources rather than a sense of nationhood. The four major clan groups — Darod, Hawiye, Isaq and Dir — are each divided into sub-clans and sub-sub-clans, defined by shared ancestors going back hundreds of years.[38]

By the 19th century, France, Britain and Italy were competing with the rulers of Zanzibar, Egypt, Oman and Ethiopia for control of Somali lands. By the 1890s, the French had taken control of what is now Djibouti; Britain had established a protectorate in Somaliland; the Italians controlled central and southern Somalia and the Ethiopians ruled the Ogaden — now eastern Ethiopia.[39]

After World War II Italy was given "trusteeship" of its Somali territory, where it had developed banana and mango plantations using forced labor during the colonial era. But as independence movements swept the continent in the 1950s, the U.N. decided to unify British and Italian Somalia into a single independent state.[40] The move dashed nationalists' hopes for a Greater Somalia encompassing Somali-speaking populations in Djibouti, northern Kenya and the Ogaden.

Rise of Dictatorships

In the 1960s Somalia's young, democratically elected government unsuccessfully tried to expand its territory through a brief war with Ethiopia and by sponsoring Somali rebels in Kenya's Somali-speaking Northern Frontier District.[41] The assassination of President Abdirashid Ali Sharmarke in 1969 by one of his bodyguards heralded the end of those aspirations and of the country's nine-year-old democracy.

The army seized power under Gen. Barre, who quickly moved the government toward communism. On the first anniversary of the coup in 1970, Barre announced that his nation of nomadic herders henceforth would pursue "Scientific Socialism," Barre's own strain of Marxism.

"The Big Mouth," as he was known colloquially, soon established internal-security services and security courts

to prosecute political crimes and "Victory Pioneers," modeled on China's Red Guards, to defend the revolution.[42] Exerting unprecedented political authority over the people, he tried to quell tribalism by prohibiting citizens from referring to their clan affiliations and by building rural schools and clinics.[43]

Meanwhile, Ethiopia's Selassie won a major diplomatic victory after World War II, when he persuaded the U.N. to unite Eritrea and Ethiopia, dashing the hopes of Eritrea's fledgling independence movement. But by the 1960s, the emperor's reign — backed by the landowners who ruled millions of peasants like medieval serfs — was chafing at the currents of the 20th century. His Amhara-dominated government faced rebellion from Tigrays in Eritrea and Oromos in southern Ethiopia. He also faced war with Somalia, which still sought control of the Ogaden.[44]

By 1973 the imperial regime's denial and botched response to a famine in northern Ethiopia, combined with soaring inflation and pressure from the Somali and Eritrean rebellions, led to a military revolt. The next year, "His Imperial Majesty Haile Selassie I, King of Kings, Lord of Lords, Conquering Lion of the Tribe of Judah, and Elect of God" was ousted.[45]

The new military government — headed by Lt. Col. Mengistu Haile Mariam and calling itself the Derg, the Amharic word for committee — aligned itself with the communist bloc and nationalized all private land, giving each peasant family 10 hectares (25 acres). The aging Selassie mysteriously died the same year. Many Ethiopians believe he was smothered with a pillow by Mengistu himself.

In 1977, the Derg was still struggling to consolidate its rule. To eliminate civilian Marxist rivals, it launched the so-called Red Terror, during which tens of thousands of students, businessmen and intellectuals suspected of disloyalty to the military government were murdered.[46] Meanwhile, with rebellions widening in the southeast and north, Somalia seized the opportunity to invade the Ogaden in hopes of fulfilling the grand dream of a Greater Somalia.

Although the Ogaden War pitted two of the Soviet Union's client states against each other, the U.S.S.R. eventually supported Ethiopia. Reinforced with Cuban troops and Soviet airpower, the Derg's army drove the Somalis out of the Ogaden in early 1978.[47]

Somali Pirate Attacks on the Increase

Sophisticated gangs rake in millions in ransoms, thwart navy patrols.

"I will never go back to sea," 25-year-old seaman Jiang Lichun told the *China Daily* after being held hostage for seven months by Somali pirates in the Gulf of Aden.[1]

During his harrowing 2007 ordeal, a shipmate was murdered after ship owners initially refused to pay a $300,000 ransom. "We heard six gunshots, but no one could believe Chen was dead," he said. Later, when the hostages were allowed up on deck, it was covered with blood.[2]

More recently, American sea captain Richard Phillips did not have to wait seven months to escape the clutches of Somali pirates. After his U.S.-flag ship carrying humanitarian aid for Africa was attacked in April, he gave himself up as a hostage so his shipmates could go free. He spent several days in a lifeboat with the pirates before U.S. Navy snipers killed his captors and freed Phillips.[3] Since then the pirates have seized several more ships with dozens of hostages.

The uptick in piracy in the Gulf of Aden has become the face of the lawlessness that engulfs Somalia. Until recently, the chaos had been largely contained within Somalia's borders. But in recent years what began as the occasional attack by local fishermen, angry at foreign vessels vacuuming their coastal waters, has morphed into one of Somalia's biggest sources of revenue, with sophisticated criminal gangs ramping up the hunt for ransoms.

Attacks on commercial ships off Somalia's coast increased from 20 to 111 between 2006 and 2008. Last fall, a vessel was attacked on average once every other day. Though killings have been rare, about 300 seamen and 18 vessels were being held by Somali pirates in late April. Ransoms paid in 2008 alone amounted to between $50 million and $80 million.[4]

The growth of Somali piracy was an unforeseen consequence of the 2006 U.S.-backed Ethiopian invasion of Somalia. The invasion ousted Somalia's governing Islamic Courts Union (ICU), which had effectively stamped out

French soldiers take suspected Somali pirates into custody on the French warship Le Nivose on May 3, 2009. Attacks on commercial ships increased from 20 in 2006 to 111 in 2008. Last fall, a vessel was attacked on average once every other day.

piracy during its brief reign in 2006. "The Islamic Courts, for some reason known only to themselves, decided to take action against maritime piracy," says Pottengal Mukundan, director of the International Maritime Bureau. "They made a public announcement saying those guilty of piracy would be punished in 2006. During the summer of 2006, there were no attacks at all."

Since the ICU was ousted, piracy has exploded. Armed with rocket launchers and machine guns, Somalia's buccaneers prowl the seas in small vessels that can range as far as 200 miles off shore. Often they'll approach a boat disguised as fishermen or traders, then fire weapons at the bridge and attempt to climb aboard using ropes and grappling hooks. Once aboard there is little foreign militaries can do. The pirates quickly take the crew hostage and steam the hijacked ship back to Eyl and other pirate bases along Somalia's Indian Ocean coast to await ransom payments.

The pirate gangs have become highly organized and intertwined with Somalia's various militias. "They have

Civil Wars

The 1983-1984 famine that would make Ethiopia synonymous with images of emaciated children resulted not just from drought but also from government policies

intended to starve rebel-held areas.[48] With the Derg preoccupied with preparations for a lavish 10th anniversary celebration of the communist revolution, up to a million Ethiopians died in the famine as the government

spies," says Gérard Valin, a vice admiral in the French navy, who led a successful raid on pirates in April 2008 after the payment of a ransom to free a French yacht. "They have people in Djibouti, Nairobi and the Gulf giving them intelligence about the good ships to take. It's a business. They have people for taking ships, and they have people for negotiations."

The millions of dollars flowing into Somali fishing villages from piracy have overwhelmed the local economy. Pirates have built luxurious new homes and support hundreds of others who supply food, weapons and khat leaf, a stimulant popular with the pirate gangs. Ilka Ase Mohamed lost his girlfriend to a pirate who wore a black cowboy hat, drove a Land Cruiser and paid a $50,000 dowry to his girlfriend's mother.

"This man was like a small king," the 23-year-old Mohamed told *The Washington Post*. "He was dressed like a president. So many people attended him. I got so angry, I said, 'Why do they accept this situation? You know this is pirate money!' "[5]

The wave of attacks in late 2008 climaxed with the hijacking of the *Sirius Star*, a Saudi supertanker carrying $100 million worth of crude oil. Since then, foreign navies, which had largely ignored the problem, have rallied to the cause. As of late March as many as 30 warships from 23 countries were patrolling the area in a loose anti-pirate alliance that includes the United States, Iran, India and Pakistan.[6] Still, the problem won't be solved at sea, says Valin. Even with two dozen warships on patrol, he says, it's often difficult to distinguish between a fishing boat and a pirate skiff until the pirates are nearly aboard a commercial vessel, and many countries struggle with how to prosecute pirates picked up in international waters.

What's needed, experts say, is a functioning government on land that will shut down pirate safe havens. That's no easy task for either the newly elected Somali government of Sheikh Sharif Sheikh Ahmed — which controls just a few small areas in southern and central Somalia — or the Puntland regional government, which is the nominal authority over the

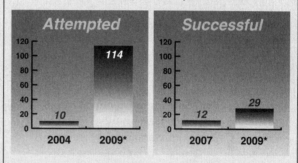

Somali Piracy Up Sharply

The 114 pirate attacks in the Gulf of Aden and Indian Ocean so far this year represent an 11-fold jump over 2004. This year 29 of the attacks were successful, more than twice the 2007 number.

Somali Pirate Attacks, 2004-2009

Attempted — 2004: 10; 2009*: 114

Successful — 2007: 12; 2009*: 29

* Through May 12, 2009

Source: International Maritime Bureau

areas where most of the pirates operate. Pirate ransom revenues last year were greater than either government's budget, and a U.N. report in December accused the Puntland administrators of complicity with pirate gangs.[7]

[1] "Chinese Sailor Recalls Terror of Somali Kidnapping," Agence France-Presse, Jan. 4, 2009.

[2] *Ibid.*

[3] Josh Meyer, "Snipers kill pirates in dramatic rescue," *Chicago Tribune*, April 13, 2009, p. 1.

[4] "Somalia: Anti-pirate Alliance," *Africa Confidential*, March 20, 2009, p. 8.

[5] Stephanie McCrummen, "Somalia's Godfathers: Ransom-Rich Pirates; Coastal Villagers Find Blessings and Ruin at Hands of Sea Robbers," *The Washington Post*, April 20, 2009, p. A1, www.washingtonpost.com/wp-dyn/content/article/2009/04/19/AR2009041902236.html.

[6] "Somalia: Anti-pirate Alliance," *op. cit.*

[7] "Report of the Monitoring Group on Somalia," United Nations, Dec. 10, 2008, www.un.org/sc/committees/751/mongroup.shtml.

systematically tried to hide images of starving peasants from the outside world while using aid to buttress government control rather than to alleviate suffering.[49] In an effort to undermine support for the rebels, entire regions of Tigray peasants in the north were forcibly moved to government camps — a policy known as villagization.[50]

Meanwhile, the humiliation of the Ogaden War led to an unsuccessful coup attempt in Somalia against Barre,

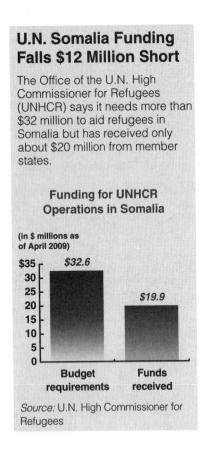

U.N. Somalia Funding Falls $12 Million Short

The Office of the U.N. High Commissioner for Refugees (UNHCR) says it needs more than $32 million to aid refugees in Somalia but has received only about $20 million from member states.

Funding for UNHCR Operations in Somalia

(in $ millions as of April 2009)

Source: U.N. High Commissioner for Refugees

led by officers from the Darod's Majerteyn sub-clan. From then on Barre maintained power by playing off the clans against each other. After the war, 700,000 Ethiopian Somalis poured across the border into Somalia, swelling the population by up to 20 percent. The collapse of the banana and mango plantations under socialism made Somalia's economy increasingly dependent on foreign aid.

The result was a widening civil war. By 1990, with government control of the countryside collapsing, Barre's enemies referred to him as the "Mayor of Mogadishu." In January 1991 he was chased from Mogadishu by a Habar Gida (a subgroup of the Hawiye clan) militia headed by a former heroin smuggler and police chief, Gen. Muhammad Farah "Aideed," whose nickname means "one who does not take insults lying down."[51] After a long sickness, the Somali state was now dead.

In Ethiopia, Mengistu's demise came the same year. By 1988 the Ethiopian Army was demoralized by the failure to win a military victory or reach political compromise with Isaias Afwerki's Eritrean People's Liberation Front. With Eritrean rebels controlling access to the Red Sea and Zenawi's Tigrayan rebels pushing south into central Ethiopia, Mengistu fled to Zimbabwe, and rebels occupied Asmara and Addis Ababa.[52]

Somalia's Descent

Back in Mogadishu, Barre's 1991 ouster led to an orgy of bloodshed. A period of "ethnic cleansing" ensued, mostly along clan lines. The Darod were especially targeted for their links with the hated Barre. Individual militia groups took control of the port, the airfield and major intersections.

At checkpoints, travelers were asked to recite the names of their ancestors — a Somali ritual that identifies people by clan and sub-clan. Those with the wrong lineage were often shot on the spot.[53] Darod militias retreated south, laying waste to the villages of smaller clans and killing and terrorizing civilians and stealing their grain. The ensuing famine claimed some 300,000; a million more were forced from their homes in search of food.

In reaction, the United States sent 28,000 troops to join 5,000 international peacekeepers under the optimistic banner Operation Restore Hope.[54] Though the mission initially succeeded in delivering aid to tens of thousands, it quickly became bogged down in street battles with militias and efforts to capture Aideed. In October 1993 several U.S. helicopters sent on a mission to arrest two of Aideed's top lieutenants were shot down over Mogadishu. In the ensuing effort to rescue trapped U.S. pilots and commandos, 18 American soldiers were killed and 84 injured in fighting that left hundreds of Somalis dead. Afterwards, the naked bodies of American soldiers were dragged through the streets as residents celebrated.

Immortalized by Mark Bowden's book *Black Hawk Down*, the battle led U.S. forces to withdraw by March 1994 and the remaining U.N. peacekeepers to leave a year later.[55] The stinging humiliation suffered by the U.S. military in Somalia is widely credited with leading to America's hesitancy in 1994 to intervene in a month-long genocidal rampage in Rwanda that left nearly a million people dead.[56]

After the U.S. withdrawal Aideed's militias expanded their control of southern Somalia, allying themselves with Islamists aligned with hard-line Saudi and Egyptian clerics. Aideed declared himself "interim president" but was killed in 1996 in fighting with rival Hawiye militias from the Abgal subclan.[57] Thereafter, the international community largely ignored Somalia until the terrorist attacks on New York and the Pentagon on Sept. 11, 2001, led to a renewed focus on Somalia as a haven for Islamic terrorists.[58]

One-Party Rule

Ethiopia embarked on a new path after 1991. The Derg had been defeated primarily by the separatist Eritrean People's Liberation Front. Zenawi's Tigray People's Liberation Front (TPLF) claimed power in Addis Ababa and agreed that Eritreans should be allowed a national referendum on independence. By 1993, Eritrea was independent, and Afwerki was in power in Asmara.

To expand his base, Zenawi reconstituted the TPLF as the Ethiopian People's Revolutionary Democratic Front (EPRDF) during the last years of the civil war. The party, still dominated by Tigrayans from the north, became the foundation of a one-party state. Opposition parties faced harassment, intimidation and imprisonment while politically favored businessmen were given control of economic assets. Tension over economic disputes soon emerged between former allies Zenawi and Afwerki: Eritrea raised port fees on its landlocked southern neighbor and destabilized the Ethiopian birr, still used by both countries, by establishing its own currency market.[59]

The friction erupted into warfare in 1998 in the town of Badme. An estimated 70,000 were killed and 750,000 displaced by the fighting before the Organization of African Unity helped arrange a cease-fire in 2000. By then Ethiopian troops had conquered Badme, and a 25-kilometer demilitarized buffer zone had been established inside Eritrean territory, patrolled by U.N. peacekeepers.

After the war, Afwerki quashed dissent in Asmara, arresting those who questioned his war strategy and abolishing the private press. Rule by the increasingly isolated Afwerki has evolved into a personality cult, and the economy has stagnated as military conscription decimated the labor force. Although an independent boundary commission awarded Badme to Eritrea in 2002, Ethiopia has never fully accepted the decision, and Eritrea — lacking both diplomatic support and military equipment — lacked the power to enforce it.

Ethiopia then briefly moved toward democracy. During political campaigning in 2005, the opposition Coalition

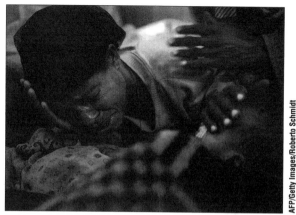

A mother in the Ethiopian town of Kuyera grieves over her sick child at a medical center run by Doctors Without Borders on Sept. 3, 2008. Earlier that day two children in nearby beds had died of malnutrition. Food shortages caused by a 2008 drought left at least 75,000 Ethiopian children under age 5 at risk, according to the U.N.'s Office for the Coordination of Humanitarian Affairs.

AFP/Getty Images/Roberto Schmidt

for Unity and Democracy (CUD) debated ruling party officials on state television and was allowed to stage large rallies in several cities.

After the election, the ruling party claimed an outright victory in parliament, but the CUD disputed the claim. In ensuing demonstrations, 193 people were killed by government security forces, and 127 top opposition leaders, journalists and human rights activists were jailed. Since then democratic freedoms in Ethiopia have been steadily scaled back. In 2008 local and parliamentary elections, opposition parties managed to win just three of 3.6 million races.[60]

In Somalia, the roots of the country's latest attempt at governance trace to 2004, when the Transitional Federal Government was formed with Ethiopian support under the leadership of President Abdullahi Yusuf, a Darod warlord from the Puntland semi-autonomous region. Yusuf's government was viewed skeptically from the beginning by many Somalis, who saw it as a puppet of Ethiopia.[61]

The fledgling TFG largely stayed in exile in its initial years, and by 2006 all-out war had erupted in Mogadishu between a group of CIA-backed anti-Islamist warlords calling themselves the Alliance for the Restoration of Peace and Counterterrorism and supporters of the Islamic Courts Union (ICU), a group of Islamists that sought to bring order to the lawless country by settling disputes and

AFP/Getty Images /Khaled Fazaa

The increasingly harsh government of Ethiopian Prime Minister Meles Zenawi has triggered calls for Western governments to withhold aid from the regime. But in part because Ethiopia has staunchly supported the West's anti-terror campaign, international aid to Ethiopia has grown dramatically in recent years.

bringing criminals to trial under Islamic law. By mid-2006 the alliance, widely despised by ordinary Somalis for its corruption and criminality, was defeated and replaced by the ICU — which ended fighting in much of southern Somalia while instituting a strict form of sharia law.[62]

But the ICU, openly supported by Ethiopia's nemesis Eritrea, laid claim to Ethiopia's Ogaden region. By December 2006 it had succeeded in provoking an Ethiopian invasion. The United States, hoping to capture al Qaeda suspects linked to ICU radicals, gave the Ethiopians intelligence and logistical support, and U.S. Special Forces accompanied Ethiopian troops in the invasion.[63]

Ethiopia's technologically superior army quickly smashed the ICU's militia. But it soon found controlling Mogadishu more difficult than invading it. Within weeks remnants of the ICU's military wing — al-Shabaab — had

allied with disaffected local clans to begin a bloody guerrilla campaign against the Ethiopian occupation. Ethiopia sought African Union peacekeeping troops to replace its forces in Mogadishu, but less than a quarter of the 8,000 authorized AU troops arrived in the first year after the Ethiopian invasion.[64]

Meanwhile the TFG under Yusuf's leadership proved both corrupt and inept. Reliant on Ethiopian soldiers for security in Mogadishu, it failed to bring functioning schools or clinics to the areas of southern Somalia nominally under its control. As the insurgency grew in Mogadishu, hundreds of thousands of people fled the fighting for makeshift refugee camps west of the city. Members of the government were accused of looting food aid from World Food Programme trucks. Radio stations that broadcast critical news were shuttered, and journalists were arrested.

Two years after Yusuf returned to Mogadishu, a U.N. report found that his government's central bank and finance ministry appeared to exist "in name only" and that Yusuf kept a printing press inside his presidential compound to print Somali shillings.

Ethiopian efforts to train a Somali security force to bolster the TFG failed dramatically. By October 2008, an estimated 14,000 of the 17,000 troops trained by the Ethiopians had deserted.[65] The Islamists recruited hundreds of the armed deserters by paying them $200 a month and playing on resentment of the Ethiopian occupation.[66]

By late 2008 Islamists and other opposition militias controlled most of southern Somalia, including the key ports of Kismayo and Merka. Disillusioned with Yusuf's failure to make peace with moderate Islamists, Ethiopia gave notice that it would withdraw troops even if that meant the Islamists would reclaim control.

Yusuf resigned in December 2008 after neighboring states threatened to freeze his assets. Ethiopian troops headed for the exit within weeks, opening the door for a new attempt at peace in the Horn of Africa.

CURRENT SITUATION

Fledgling Government

On May 24, a suicide bomber driving a Toyota Land Cruiser exploded a bomb at the gates of a TFG military compound in Mogadishu, killing six soldiers and a civilian.[67] The bombing was just the latest incident in a new spasm of violence between the TFG and Shabaab insurgents that has seen the Islamist militants tighten their grip over southern and central Somalia.

It wasn't supposed to be this way. After Ethiopian troops, widely despised by ordinary Somalis, pulled out of Mogadishu in January, Yusuf was replaced as president of the TFG by Sheikh Ahmed, the moderate Islamist who had chaired the Islamic Courts Union before the Ethiopian invasion and, from exile in Djibouti, had opposed both the occupation and Yusuf's corrupt government. Though 14 previous U.N.-backed Somali governments had failed to bring peace and stability to the country, it was hoped that Ahmed, as a Hawiye clan leader with previous links to some of the insurgent groups' leaders, could make peace with the Hawiye and Islamist militias opposed to the TFG.

Instead, bolstered by as many as 300 foreign fighters and arms from Eritrea, al-Shabaab has rejected Ahmed's overtures and moved from strength to strength, capturing Ahmed's hometown of Jowhar and neighboring Mahaday, cutting government links with central Somalia.[68] Ahmed has been forced to take refuge in a compound in Mogadishu, protected by foreign troops from the African Union. The growing chaos has led the TFG's new prime minister, Omar Abdirashid Ali Sharmarke, to all but rule out peace talks with insurgents.

"I don't think there is a chance to just sit with them and discuss issues with these people," Sharmarke told Reuters in late May. "The only way to deal with them that they can understand is to fight, and we are prepared to eradicate them."[69]

As fighting intensified in May, Ethiopia launched an apparent strike into Somalia, raising the specter of a possible re-invasion should the TFG collapse and al-Shabaab take control.[70] "Ahmed and the new TFG face an increasing challenge from al-Shabaab and an allied organization known as Hizbul Islam," says Shinn, the former ambassador to Ethiopia. "Al-Shabaab, although not centrally controlled, is well financed from outside and relying on a growing number of foreign fighters."

"The euphoria with which Sheikh Sharif's government was greeted has evaporated," says Abdi, of the International Crisis Group. "Things are very difficult. Unless something happens to unlock this logjam, this is just one of those cycles of transitions that will end up in a failure."

The TFG's reliance on 4,000 Ugandan and Burundian troops in Mogadishu — operating under the African Union — also hurts the fledgling government's legitimacy. "As foreigners [the AU troops] are also resented," says Shinn. "They are keeping the port and the airport out of the hands of al-Shabaab and protecting the presidency. The TFG probably could not accomplish this on its own."

Additional outside help seems remote. The U.N. has repeatedly declined requests from African nations to send a force to stabilize the country, while the AU has struggled to find more countries willing to contribute to the force. An uptick in attacks on AU peacekeepers last year has raised fears that the mission could end in a debacle as the U.S.-U.N. mission did 15-years ago.

"The AU peacekeepers haven't kept any peace because there is no peace to keep," says historian Lewis. "They're just useless."

Still, al-Shabaab also faces risks, especially since its brand of Islam is more radical than Somalia's traditional Sufi Islam. Among the moves that have provoked public revulsion: the amputation of the hands of accused thieves, public flogging of criminals and desecration of the graves of Sufi saints. Most dramatically, in October Islamist clerics in Kismayo ordered the public stoning of a young woman who may have been as young as 13 for committing adultery. Human rights groups said the woman, who was killed in a stadium in front of as many as 1,000 onlookers, had been raped.[71] More recently, al-Shabaab's decision to continue its war after Ethiopia withdrew has also tarnished its identity as a liberation movement fighting Ethiopian occupiers.

"In Mogadishu, public disappointment towards al-Shabaab militants is growing," says Faizal Mohammed, a Somali columnist for the Addis Ababa-based *Sub-Saharan Informer.* "Hawiye elders and some religious leaders have criticized al-Shabaab's move to continue the war after the Ethiopian withdrawal and to target AU peacekeepers."

The TFG also received a recent boost when Islamist warlord Yusuf Indahaadde, the former ICU defense minister, decided to support Ahmed and the TFG after Ahmed announced his government would implement Islamic law.[72]

"It will be messy and slow and it will be subject to reversals, but there is no reason why the right coalition of political and religious and business interests could not

AFP/Getty Images/Abdirashid Abdulle

Somalis displaced from their homes in war-torn Mogadishu prepare a meal at the Dayniile camp — one of dozens that surround the Somali capital. The ongoing civil war and poverty have sent more than a million refugees fleeing to neighboring countries or to camps inside Somalia, where they depend on international assistance for food and shelter — aid that is often blocked by violence, theft or piracy.

pull something together," says Menkhaus, the former U.N. official. "This new coalition government, it's the type of government that could work."

Meanwhile, the country continues to be a source of terrorism. On March 15 a suicide bomber allegedly trained in Somalia killed four South Korean tourists in Yemen. Three days later a second bomber attempted to kill a group of Koreans investigating the attack.[73]

Some analysts say the U.S. and Ethiopian intervention in Somalia has worsened the threat of terrorism by radicalizing the Islamists. "The problem has grown into a much bigger, hydra-headed problem because of that policy," says Lefkow, of Human Rights Watch. "That was a very ill-judged strategy on the part of both the Ethiopians and the U.S."

Ethiopia has a different view. "Ethiopia successfully neutralized" the Islamic Courts, says Ethiopian Foreign Minister Seyoum Mesfin. "Today there is only al-Shabaab and a few terrorist groups working as small units without any formidable organization. Their military backbone [and] organizational structure have been completely shattered."

Frazer, the former Bush administration diplomat, says the Ethiopian intervention had little effect on the threat. "When Ethiopia wasn't there, they were opening the country to jihadists," she says. "When Ethiopia was there, they were continuing to do it. After Ethiopia left, the country is still open to jihadists."

Standoff Continues

In February Ethiopian state-run television was filled with images of troops parading through Ethiopian cities, celebrating their withdrawal from Somalia. Though the two-year occupation of Somalia began with the ouster of one anti-Ethiopian Islamist group and ended with a more radical anti-Ethiopian group taking control of much of the country's south, Ethiopia's foreign ministry declared "Mission Accomplished."[74]

"We believe a great victory has been secured," Prime Minister Zenawi said on March 19. But the withdrawing troops have not had much time to rest. Despite official denials from Zenawi's government, Somali residents along the border between the two countries have reported repeated Ethiopian incursions since January.[75] In March the Ogaden National Liberation Front — an Eritrean-backed ethnic Somali separatist group in eastern Ethiopia — claimed it killed 24 Ethiopian troops near the town of Degehebur, not far from the Somalia border.[76]

Meanwhile, the standoff between Ethiopia and Eritrea continues to feed regional instability. Throughout 2008 Eritrea delivered up to $500,000 a month to a faction that was battling both Ethiopian troops and TFG security forces inside Somalia. And Eritrea regularly delivers arms and ammunition by small boat to Somali insurgents. It has also supplied arms and funding to the militia of Mohamed Sai'd "Atom," whose Shabaab-affiliated fighters have battled Puntland security forces. Atom's militia was also implicated in the kidnapping of a German aid worker in 2008 and a bombing that killed 20 Ethiopian migrants waiting for transport to Yemen in the Puntland port of Bossasso.[77]

"The Eritreans, under Isaias, are pursuing the same sort of strategy they followed in winning their independence: setting out to weaken Ethiopia from as many directions as possible," says Connell, the former adviser to the Eritrean government. "This results in steady support for all of Ethiopia's enemies, within Ethiopia's borders and without. Hence the support for Islamists in Somalia, whom you might least expect Eritrea to favor."

Eritrea's support of such groups has hindered its diplomatic efforts to get international enforcement for the

Should the West cut aid to Ethiopia over human rights concerns?

YES

Berhanu Nega

Exiled former mayor, Addis Ababa
Leader of opposition group Ginbot 7
Professor of economics, Bucknell University

Written for *CQ Global Researcher*, May 2009

The West's policy toward Ethiopia has been a disaster, and President Barack Obama and European leaders must reconsider their support to its government. Ethiopia received more than $1 billion in U.S. aid last year plus generous support from the United Kingdom and European Union. However, the country's human rights record is among the worst on the continent and getting worse by the day.

The possibility of a peaceful transition to democracy vanished in 2005 after Prime Minister Meles Zenawi's security forces killed 193 innocent civilians for peacefully protesting a stolen election and jailed tens of thousands of democracy activists, including 127 opposition leaders, journalists and civil society activists — including me.

Ethiopia is now a totalitarian police state with a human rights record comparable to that of Robert Mugabe's Zimbabwe. Meles and his inner circle have cowed the parliament, the courts and the press. Human rights groups claim the government has killed civilians in several regions. The government held local elections last year with more than 95 percent of the candidates from the ruling party; passed a restrictive new press law; jailed opposition leader Birtukan Mideksa and banned most human rights, democracy and gender-equality organizations.

Why shore up such a brutal dictatorship? Ethiopia is one of the poorest nations in the world, and Western policy makers say aid helps the poor more than the government. But after 18 years in power, Meles' regime still cannot feed its people: Some 14 million Ethiopians required foreign food aid last year. Donors have little control over how aid is delivered, and the government deliberately withholds foreign food aid to punish villages sympathetic to ethnic-Somali rebels.

The West's aid props up an anti-democratic regime and is ineffective in helping the poor. But proponents say Ethiopia — bordered by war-torn Sudan, a belligerent Eritrea and lawless Somalia — needs aid to remain stable in one of the world's toughest neighborhoods. But that's hard to swallow, given that Ethiopia's disastrous, two-year occupation of southern Somalia ended up ejecting a moderate Islamist government while empowering radicals; its nine-year border dispute with Eritrea remains unresolved; and numerous, armed indigenous groups wage domestic attacks with increasing ferocity.

U.S. and European economic pressure could make Meles' government negotiate a peaceful settlement to the country's explosive political problems.

NO

Patrick Gilkes

Adviser to Ethiopia's Ministry of Foreign Affairs; Author, The Dying Lion, Conflict in Somalia and Ethiopia; *and, with Martin Plaut,* Conflict in the Horn: Why Eritrea and Ethiopia Are at War

Written for *CQ Global Researcher*, May 2009

Activists who call for cuts in foreign aid to Ethiopia are seriously misguided. Ethiopia's government is far from perfect, but those who pressure the U.S. Congress and other Western governments to slash assistance to Ethiopia should remember it has averaged economic growth of 11 percent from 2003 to 2008, nearly double Africa as a whole and comparable to that of the Asian "tiger" economies in the 1990s.

The country launched a five-year Sustainable Development and Poverty Reduction Program in 2006 and is devoting about 60 percent of its federal budget to "pro-poor spending," as defined by the World Bank. This is one of the best rates in Africa.

The government has held defense spending to less than 1.5 percent of gross domestic product, even as it has fought a two-year anti-terrorism engagement in Somalia and strives to deter Eritrean aggression. Ethiopia remains a desperately poor nation, but there have been massive investment and major advances in infrastructure, education and health.

Despite the opposition's failure to take up seats in the first multi-party federal elections in 2005 and ensuing violence, local elections took place last year without incident. Ethiopia's federal structure has produced widespread acceptance of self-rule and meaningful fiscal and political devolution. Ethiopia provides a very clear demonstration of the effective use to which aid can and should be put. These must be developments well worth nurturing.

Much has been done in human rights — despite exaggerated opposition claims and poor research by Human Rights Watch and other groups. This includes major training programs for the judiciary, armed forces and police as well as the recent establishment of a government ombudsman and a Human Rights Commission. The recently enacted law regulating nongovernmental organizations (NGOs) has been controversial, but its critics wildly overstate its ramifications. The goal is protection and transparency for NGO humanitarian and development activity.

Ethiopia's long and close relations with the United States and Europe have been enormously important to development. Amidst international financial crisis and climate change, Ethiopia needs support to ensure development efforts don't falter, as it successfully implements its long-term strategy of democratization and poverty reduction. There's still much to do. This is certainly not the time to interrupt the process or threaten regional stability.

AP Photo/Farah Abdi Warsameh

A Somali insurgent holds a rocket-propelled grenade launcher in Mogadishu in January 2009, shortly after Ethiopian troops ended a two-year occupation of parts of Somalia. Some analysts say U.S. support for Ethiopia's 2006 invasion of Somalia radicalized many Somalis and increased the threat of anti-U.S. terrorism from Somalia.

Ethiopia-Eritrea Boundary Commission's 2002 decision awarding Badme to Eritrea.[78] With a strong push from Ethiopia, the African Union's Peace and Security Council in May called for international sanctions against Eritrea for its role in arming Somali militants.

Ethiopia also backs proxies. In May 2008 it hosted a conference of Eritrean rebel groups and opposition parties in Addis Ababa.[79] Last August, Ethiopia delivered 3,000 to 5,000 AK-47 assault rifles to the Puntland semi-autonomous government and has provided weapons and training to at least one other anti-Islamist militia in Somalia.[80]

Tens of thousands of troops from the two armies remain dug in across their shared border, sometimes only meters apart. And without U.N. peacekeepers, who were forced to withdraw in February 2008, the border skirmish could again flare up into all out war.

But many analysts believe such an outcome is unlikely. "Eritrea doesn't have diplomatic might or military strength to challenge the status quo," says Shinn, the former U.S. ambassador to Ethiopia. "It's not in either of their interests to resume that war, and they both know it."

However, both regimes have used the continuing presence of an external threat to sharply reduce democratic freedoms. "The stalemate on the border feeds and in turn is fed by growing authoritarianism in both states," said a

June 2008 International Crisis Group report. "The ruling regimes rely on military power and restrictions on civil liberties to retain their dominant positions."[81]

However, it continued, "Both regimes have an interest in keeping the conflict at a low simmer rather than resolving it."

OUTLOOK

Unresolved Conflicts

Few analysts are optimistic that the Horn of Africa's political and economic status will be vastly improved over the next decade.

For the moment, Ethiopia's future looks the brightest. The government says economic growth averaged 11 percent between 2003 and 2008, bolstered by large inflows of aid and debt forgiveness. Some independent economists say the figure is overstated, and that real growth has been around 7 or 8 percent — still a remarkable figure for a land-locked country with no significant oil or mineral reserves.

But, problems abound. The global financial crisis will undoubtedly slow growth. Exports of coffee, Ethiopia's largest foreign-exchange earner, appear likely to decline for the second consecutive year while hospitals and factories face shortages of key supplies. And with dim prospects for a breakthrough with Eritrea, Ethiopia will probably face continuing conflict on at least three fronts: in Somalia, in the Ogaden and along its northern border with Eritrea.

"The future is impossible to predict so long as this simmering confrontation remains unresolved," says former Eritrean adviser Connell. Ethiopia and Eritrea "have enormous potential for growth, but the conflict between them and attendant repression of rights within each country hold both back."

Ethiopia's government, dominated by ethnic Tigrayan Christians from the northern highlands, remains unpopular with the ethnic Amharas and Oromos from central, southern and western Ethiopia, who together make up nearly two-thirds of the population. And the recent crackdown on opposition leaders, the press and human rights groups casts a pall over upcoming 2010 elections.

"I'm not optimistic that 2010 is going to be a breakthrough," says former U.S. Ambassador Shinn. "The tip-off was the local elections in 2008. I think that's a pity."

The government's failure to improve food self-sufficiency also leaves the ongoing threat of drought and famine, which helped trigger the demise of both the communist Derg regime and the Selassie government. "Ethiopia has a relatively high population growth rate," says Shinn. "If you can't feed your people and you're constantly at the mercy of foreign handouts, you've got to do something about it."

In Eritrea the outlook is decidedly dim. The economically and politically isolated government offers few prospects for improving its citizens' lives. "Eritrea is a one-man dictatorship masquerading as a one-party state," says Connell, who formerly worked for the Afwerki government. "The ruling party is little more than a cabal of Isaias Afwerki loyalists, whom he plays off against one another to maintain his iron-fisted rule. The closest analog I can imagine is North Korea." Afwerki's repressive rule, he adds, "is far more effective and all-encompassing than that of, say, [President Robert] Mugabe in Zimbabwe."

In April Human Rights Watch accused Eritrea of becoming a "giant prison" and issued a 95-page report detailing government atrocities against dissidents and evangelical Christians. Thousands of Eritreans risk the government's shoot-to-kill policy to flee to neighboring Sudan and Ethiopia each year, the report said.[82]

"The country is hemorrhaging," said an independent analyst, who asked that his name not be used so that he can continue traveling to Eritrea. "It's largely a police state. I don't see how the regime can survive in the long term. The government has control at the moment, but at some point something will give way."

In Somalia, analysts say probably only an Islamist government can reach across clan divisions to bring a semblance of order to the country's south. "It wouldn't surprise me if an Islamist movement took hold," says the historian Lewis. "How severe it will be and how rigorous is up for grabs."

Unfortunately, he continues, "the radical Islamist movement that they have now developed is particularly poorly educated and poorly informed about the world. It's taking the Somalis really back almost to colonial times."

Rebuilding the country after 18 years of civil war will be a long and difficult task.

"The best-case scenario is that [TFG President] Sharif may succeed in bringing in the hardline groups and — after a bumpy five to six years of transition — we may see a moderate Islamist government take control and become a regional player," says Abdi, of the International Crisis Group. "The worst-case scenario is Sharif's government will collapse, and insurgents will step up their attacks and Ethiopia will invade Somalia again. Somalia is by no means out of the woods."

If the radicals succeed, the threat from terrorism is likely to grow. The recent recruitment of Somali-American jihadis to fight in Somalia raises the question of whether radical Islamists in Somalia might be able to export suicide bombers to Western countries with Somali immigrant communities.

"Would they be able to use U.S. passport holders from places like Minneapolis as sleepers?" asks Menkhaus, the former U.N. official in Somalia. "It's something we need to pay attention to."

The Obama administration should take a more low-key, comprehensive strategy in helping Somalia than the short-term counterterrorism goals followed by the Bush administration, according to Menkhaus. "In fighting terrorism on land and piracy at sea, U.S. national security interests will be better secured if we aligned ourselves more with the interest of most Somalis in better security and effective governance," he writes. "Helping to build the house and using the back door will be much more effective than barging into the front door of a house that has yet to be built."[83]

NOTES

1. "Somalia: Exodus Continues Despite Lull in Mogadishu Fighting," IRIN News, May 21, 2009, www.irinnews.org/report.aspx?Reportid=84483.

2. "Escalating Violence Displaces Somalis," U.N. High Commissioner for Refugees, summary of briefing by spokesman Ron Redmond, May 26, 2009, www.unhcr.org/news/NEWS/4a1bbefb2.html. See also "Some 45,000 Somali Civilians Flee Mogadishu in Past Two Weeks," U.N. High Commissioner for Refugees, May 20, 2009, www.unhcr.org/cgi-bin/texis/vtx/news/opendoc.htm?tbl=NEWS&id=4a140e5b2, May 26, 2009.

3. "Beyond the Fragile Peace Between Ethiopia and Eritrea: Averting New War," International Crisis Group, June 17, 2008, p. 10, www.crisisgroup.org/home/index.cfm?id=5490&l=4.

4. "United Nations Human Development Indices: A Statistical Update 2008," U.N. Development Programme, http://hdr.undp.org/en/statistics.

5. "Consolidated Appeal for Somalia 2009," U.N. Office for the Coordination of Humanitarian Assistance, Nov. 19, 2008, www.relief web.int/rw/dbc.nsf/doc104?OpenForm&rc=1&cc=som. See also "Somalia is Worst Humanitarian Crisis: U.N. Official," Global Policy Forum, Jan. 30, 2008, www.globalpolicy.org/component/content/article/205/39493.html.

6. See "European Parliament resolution of 15 January 2009 on the situation in the Horn of Africa," European Parliament, www.europarl.europa.eu/document/activities/cont/200901/20090122ATT46879/20090122ATT46879EN.pdf.

7. For background, see John Felton, "Aiding Refugees," *CQ Global Researcher*, March 1, 2009, pp. 59-90.

8. Aidan Hartley, *Zanzibar Chest* (2003), p. 187.

9. "Horn of Africa Media Briefing Note," U.N. Development Programme, Feb. 11, 2009, www.reliefweb.int/rw/rwb.nsf/db900sid/EDIS-7P6MR3?OpenDocument. Note: The U.N. does not have statistics for those in need of emergency aid in Eritrea, which evicted most foreign aid organizations following the 1998-2000 Ethiopia-Eritrea war.

10. Derek Byerlee and David Spielman, "Policies to Promote Cereal Intensification in Ethiopia: A Review of Evidence and Experience," International Food Policy Research Institute, June 2007.

11. "Eritrea," *CIA World Fact Book*, Central Intelligence Agency, www.cia.gov/library/publications/the-world-factbook/geos/er.html.

12. Dina Temple-Raston, "Al Qaeda Media Blitz Has Some on Alert," National Public Radio, April 8, 2009, www.npr.org/templates/story/story.php?storyId=102735818.

13. Lolita C. Baldor, "Terrorists Moving from Afghan Border to Africa," The Associated Press, April 28, 2009, http://abcnews.go.com/Politics/wire Story?id=7445461.

14. Ken Menkhaus, "Somalia After the Ethiopian Occupation: First Steps to End the Conflict and Combat Extremism," Enough Project, www.enoughproject.org/

publications/somalia-after-ethiopian-occupation-first-steps-end-conflict-and-combat-extremism.

15. Dan Ephron and Mark Hosenball, "Recruited For Jihad?" *Newsweek*, Feb. 2, 2009, www.newsweek.com/id/181408.

16. Alex Perry, "Somalia's War Flares Up Again," *Time*, Nov. 12, 2007, www.time.com/time/world/article/0,8599,1682877,00.html.

17. Scott Johnson, "An Unclenched Fist: Barack Obama Has a Unique Opportunity to Bring Something Resembling Stability to Africa's Horn," *Newsweek*, Feb. 2, 2009, www.newsweek.com/id/181313.

18. Scott Johnson, "Dilemmas of the Horn," *Newsweek*, April 21, 2008, www.newsweek.com/id/131836.

19. "Biographies of High Value Terrorist Detainees Transferred to the U.S. Naval Base at Guantánamo Bay," Office of the Director of National Intelligence, Sept. 6, 2006, www.dni.gov/announcements/content/DetaineeBiographies.pdf.

20. Lloyd de Vries, "Elusive Al Qaeda Suspect Was Real Deal," CBS News, Jan. 10, 2007, www.cbsnews.com/stories/2007/01/10/world/main2347258.shtml.

21. Alisha Ryu, "US Airstrike in Somalia Targets al-Qaida Suspect," Voice of America, March 3, 2008, www.voanews.com/english/archive/2008-03/2008-03-03-voa15.cfm?CFID=141624149&CFTOKEN=26521211&jsessionid=de308dbc94966565a9d81e432739512c471d.

22. Hamsa Omar and Jason McLure, "Somali Breakaway Regions Targeted by Suicide Bombers (Update1)," Bloomberg News, Oct. 29, 2008.

23. Jeffrey Gettleman, "The Most Dangerous Place in the World," *Foreign Policy*, March/April 2009, www.foreignpolicy.com/story/cms.php?story_id=4682.

24. Akwei Thompson, "Somali's New 36-Member Cabinet Larger Than Speculated," Voice of America, Feb. 22, 2009, www.voanews.com/english/Africa/2009-02-22-voa20.cfm, March 14, 2009.

25. For background, see Brian Beary, "Separatist Movements," *CQ Global Researcher*, April 2008, pp. 85-114.

26. I. M. Lewis, *A Modern History of the Somali Nation and State in the Horn of Africa* (2002), p. 289.

27. Alisha Ryu, "New Puntland President Faces Stiff Challenges," Voice of America, Jan. 15, 2009, www .voanews.com/english/archive/2009-01/2009-01-15-voa51.cfm.

28. "Report of the Monitoring Group on Somalia," United Nations, Dec. 10, 2008, www.un.org/sc/committees/751/mongroup.shtml.

29. Jason McLure, "Caught in Ethiopia's War," *Newsweek.com*, Jan. 22, 2008, www.newsweek.com/id/98033. See also Jeffrey Gettleman, "In Ethiopia, Fear and Cries of Army Brutality," *The New York Times*, June 18, 2007, and "Collective Punishment: War Crimes and Crimes Against Humanity in the Ogaden Area of Ethiopia's Somali Retion," Human Rights Watch, June 11, 2008, www.hrw.org/en/node/62175/section/1.

30. Jason McLure, "Ethiopian Police Re-arrest Opposition Leader Mideksa," Bloomberg News, Dec. 29, 2008.

31. "Clean Sweep for Ethiopian Party," BBC News, May 19, 2008, http://news.bbc.co.uk/2/hi/africa/7408185.stm. Also see Jason McLure, "Ethiopian Law Curbs Promotion of Rights, Critics Say," Bloomberg News, Jan. 6, 2009, www .bloomberg.com/apps/news?pid=20601116&sid=ah IahjCUZMz0&refer=africa.

32. "President Isaias Afwerki's Interview with Al-Jazeera Television," Eritrean Ministry of Information, April 24, 2008, www.shabait.com/cgi-bin/staging/exec/view.cgi?archive=17&num=8190.

33. "Somalia: To Move Beyond the Failed State," International Crisis Group, Dec. 23, 2008, p. 26, www.crisisgroup.org/home/index.cfm?id=5836 &l=1.

34. Graham Hancock, *The Sign and the Seal* (1992), pp. 12-13.

35. Harold G. Marcus, *A History of Ethiopia* (2002), pp. 99-104, 138-142.

36. Sebastian O'Kelly, *Amedeo: The True Story of an Italian's War in Abyssinia* (2003).

37. Marcus, *op. cit.*, pp. 150-152.

38. Lewis, *op. cit.*, pp. 22-23.

39. *Ibid.*, p. 48.

40. *Ibid.*, p. 181.

41. *Ibid.*, pp. 201-202.

42. Ayaan Hirsi Ali, *Infidel* (2007), p. 55.

43. Lewis, *op. cit.*, pp. 210-212, 224.

44. For a first-person account of the student ferment that led to Haile Selassie's ouster, disillusionment under the succeeding Derg regime and the 1977 Ogaden War, see Nega Mezlekia, *Notes From The Hyena's Belly* (2000).

45. Marcus, *op. cit.*, pp. 173-178, 180.

46. Mezlekia, *op. cit.*, p. 295.

47. John Lewis Gaddis, *The Cold War* (2005), pp. 207-208.

48. See Robert Kaplan, *Surrender or Starve: Travels in Ethiopia, Sudan, Somalia and Eritrea* (2003).

49. See Myles F. Harris, *Breakfast in Hell: A Doctor's Eyewitness Account of the Politics of Hunger in Ethiopia* (1987).

50. Marcus, *op. cit.*, pp. 208-209.

51. Lewis, *op. cit.*, pp. 245-246, 259-263.

52. Michela Wrong, *I Didn't Do It For You: How the World Used and Abused a Small African Nation* (2005), pp. 349-352.

53. Hartley, *op. cit.*, p. 184.

54. Lewis, *op. cit.*, pp. 264-265, 268-269.

55. See Mark Bowden, *Black Hawk Down: A Story of Modern War* (1999).

56. For background, see Sarah Glazer, "Stopping Genocide," *CQ Researcher*, Aug. 27, 2004, pp. 685-708.

57. Lewis, *op. cit.*, p. 280.

58. *Ibid.*, pp. 305-306.

59. Marcus, *op. cit.*, pp. 237, 242, 249-250.

60. "2008 Human Rights Report: Ethiopia," U.S. Department of State, April 24, 2009, www.state.gov/g/drl/rls/hrrpt/2008/af/119001.htm.

61. Ken Menkhaus, "Somalia: A Country in Peril, A Policy Nightmare," Enough Project, Sept. 3, 2008, www.enoughproject.org/files/reports/somalia_rep090308.pdf.

62. *Ibid.*

63. Gettleman, *op. cit.*

64. Jason McLure, "Nigeria Needs Helicopters, Tanks to Send Troops to Somalia," Bloomberg News, June 28, 2008.

65. "Report of the Monitoring Group on Somalia," *op. cit.*

66. "Somalia: To Move Beyond the Failed State," *op. cit.*

67. Mustapha Haji Abdinur, "Suicide Attack on Somali Military Camp Kills Seven," Agence France-Presse, May 25, 2009.

68. Derek Kilner, "Somali Insurgents Take Another Town North of Capital," Voice of America, May 18, 2009, www.voanews.com/english/2009-05-18-voa18.cfm.

69. Abdiaziz Hassan, "Somali PM: Little Hope of Talks with Insurgents," Reuters, May 21, 2009.

70. "Ethiopian Forces Return to Somalia: Witnesses," Agence France-Presse, May 19, 2009.

71. "Stoning Victim 'Begged for Mercy,'" BBC News, Nov. 4, 2008, http://news.bbc.co.uk/2/hi/africa/7708169.stm. See also: "Somali Justice — Islamist Style," BBC News, May 20, 2009, http://news.bbc.co.uk/2/hi/africa/8057179.stm.

72. "Residents: Islamic Insurgents Seize Somalia Town," The Associated Press, May 20, 2009.

73. "Man Blows Himself Up in Failed Yemen Attack," Reuters, March 18, 2009, www.reuters.com/article/latestCrisis/idUSLI290474.

74. Jason McLure, "Ethiopia Quits Somalia, Declares 2-Year 'Mission Accomplished,'" Bloomberg News, Jan. 5, 2009, www.bloomberg.com/apps/news?pid=20601116&sid=aJqblcQ0bUCo.

75. Abdi Sheikh and Abdi Guled, "Ethiopia Denies Its Troops Enter Somalia," Reuters, Feb. 3, 2009. See also: "Ethiopian Forces Return to Somalia: Witnesses," Agence France-Presse, May 19, 2009.

76. Ogaden National Liberation Front Military Communique, March 7, 2009.

77. "Report of the Monitoring Group on Somalia," *op. cit.*, p. 33.

78. "Beyond the Fragile Peace Between Ethiopia and Eritrea: Averting New War," *op. cit.*

79. Jason McLure, "Eritrean Group Calls for 'Popular Uprising' Against Government, Bloomberg News, May 8, 2008.

80. "Report of the Monitoring Group on Somalia," *op. cit.*

81. "Beyond the Fragile Peace Between Ethiopia and Eritrea: Averting New War," *op. cit.*

82. "Service for Life: State Repression and Indefinite Conscription in Eritrea," Human Rights Watch, April 16, 2009. See also Jason McLure, "Eritrea a 'Giant Prison,' Human Rights Watch Says (Update 1)," Bloomberg News, April 16, 2009.

83. Ken Menkhaus, "Beyond Piracy: Next Steps to Stabilize Somalia," Enough Project, www.enough-project.org/publications/beyond-piracy-next-steps-stabilize-somalia.

BIBLIOGRAPHY

Books

Ali, Ayaan Hirsi, *Infidel,* **Free Press, 2007.**
This coming-of-age tale of a Somali girl living in Somalia, Saudi Arabia, Ethiopia, Kenya, the Netherlands and, finally, the United States explores how Somali culture and Islamic codes subordinate women.

Hartley, Aidan, *The Zanzibar Chest,* **Harper Perennial, 2003.**
A Reuters correspondent's memoir of covering wars in Somalia, Ethiopia and Rwanda in the early 1990s is interlaced with his family's British colonial history in East Africa and Yemen. Highlights include his eyewitness account of entering Addis Ababa in 1991 with Tigrayan rebels for the fall of the communist Derg regime and witnessing the U.S. military's "Black Hawk" assault on Mogadishu.

Lewis, I. M., *A Modern History of the Somali,* **James Currey Ltd., 2002.**
One of the few Western academics to have spent his career studying Somalia, anthropologist Lewis focuses on how clan identities have shaped Somalis' history.

Marcus, Harold G., *A History of Ethiopia,* **University of California Press, 2002.**
This brief history begins with the famed fossil of Lucy, a human ancestor who roamed eastern Ethiopia 4 million years ago, and ends shortly after the 1998-2000 Ethiopia-Eritrea war.

Mezlekia, Nega, *Notes from the Hyena's Belly: An Ethiopian Boyhood, Picador USA*, **2000**.

An Ethiopian writer's memoir of growing up during the 1970s provides a first-person account of the country's communist revolution and the ethnic tensions between Somalis and Ethiopian highlanders that still shape regional politics.

Wrong, Michela, *I Didn't Do It For You: How the World Used and Abused A Small African Nation, Harper Perennial*, **2005**.

Mixing history and travelogue, a British journalist traces Eritrea's four-decade battle for independence after World War II. Wrong shows how the stubborn and resourceful Eritrean resistance becomes a pawn of Cold War powers and documents post-independence disillusionment under the dictatorial regime of former rebel leader Isaias Afwerki.

Articles

Ephron, Dan, and Mark Hosenball, "Recruited for Jihad?" *Newsweek*, Feb. 2, 2009, www.newsweek.com/id/181408.

Two Washington journalists uncover efforts by Somali Islamists to recruit fighters from U.S. refugee communities.

Gettleman, Jeffrey, "In Ethiopia Fear and Cries of Army Brutality," *The New York Times*, June 18, 2007, www.nytimes.com/2007/06/18/world/africa/18ethiopia.html.

The only Western journalist to enter Ethiopia's Somali region without being accompanied by Ethiopian security forces in recent years gives an account of atrocities by Ethiopian soldiers. Gettleman was arrested by the Ethiopian government during the trip.

Gettleman, Jeffrey, "The Most Dangerous Place in the World," *Foreign Policy*, March/April 2009, www.foreignpolicy.com/story/cms.php?story_id=4682.

The New York Times East Africa correspondent gives a short history of how Ethiopia and the United States exacerbated Somalia's civil war between 2005 and 2008.

Perry, Alex, "Somalia's War Flares Up Again," *Time*, Nov. 12, 2007, www.time.com/time/world/article/0,8599,1682877,00.html.

Perry outlines the motivations of the various actors in Somalia's civil war, including the transitional government, Islamist militias, Ethiopia and the United States.

Reports and Studies

"Beyond the Fragile Peace Between Ethiopia and Eritrea: Averting New War," *International Crisis Group*, June 17, 2008, www.crisisgroup.org/home/index.cfm?id=1229.

The continuing cold war between Ethiopia and Eritrea after their 1998-2000 war is fueling a host of regional conflicts.

"2008 Human Rights Report: Ethiopia," *U.S. Department of State*, Feb. 25, 2009, www.state.gov/g/drl/rls/hrrpt/2008/af/119001.htm.

Despite its close ties with Ethiopia's government, the U.S. State Department provides one of the most rigorous and detailed reports on human rights violations under Prime Minister Meles Zenawi.

"Report of the Monitoring Group on Somalia," *United Nations*, Dec. 10, 2008, www.un.org/sc/committees/751/mongroup.shtml.

The U.N. team that monitors Somalia's arms embargo describes the various militias and their links to foreign governments, piracy and other illicit activities.

Menkhaus, Kenneth, "Somalia: A Country in Peril: A Policy Nightmare," *Enough Project*, Sept. 3, 2008, www.enoughproject.org/files/reports/somalia_rep090308.pdf.

A former U.N. official in Somalia dissects the missteps by Somali regional and international powers that led Somalia to the brink and suggests how to bring peace to the troubled country.

For More Information

African Union, P.O. Box 3243, Addis Ababa, Ethiopia; (251) 11 551 77 00; www.africa-union.org. Seeks political and economic cooperation among the 53 member nations.

Amnesty International, 1 Easton St., London, WCIX 0DW, United Kingdom; (44) 20 74135500; www.amnesty .org. Advocates for human rights around the globe and publishes periodic reports on abuses.

Council on Foreign Relations, 1779 Massachusetts Ave., N.W., Washington, DC 20036; (202) 518-3400; www.cfr .org. Nonpartisan think tank that offers extensive resources, data and experts on foreign policy issues.

Enough Project, 1225 I St., N.W., Suite 307, Washington, DC 20005; (202) 682-1611; www.enoughproject.org.

Lobbies for ending genocide and crimes against humanity.

Human Rights Watch, 350 Fifth Ave., 34th Floor, New York, NY 10118-3299; (212) 290-4700; www.hrw.org. Investigates human rights abuses worldwide with a team of lawyers and researchers.

Institute for Security Studies, P.O. Box 1787, Brooklyn Square, Tshwane (Pretoria) 0075, South Africa; (27) 012 346 9500; www.iss.co.za. African foreign policy think tank that provides a range of views on African issues.

International Crisis Group, 149 Avenue Louise, Level 24, B-1050 Brussels, Belgium; (32) 2 502-9038; www.crisisgroup .org. Provides independent research on international relations and the developing world.

10

U.S.-China Relations

Is a Future Confrontation Looming?

Roland Flamini

Bustling Shanghai — with twice the number of high rises as Manhattan — reflects China's phenomenal growth. Some economists worry that China holds nearly $900 billion in U.S. Treasury securities, refuses to fairly value its currency and maintains an annual trade advantage over the U.S. of more than $230 billion.

From *CQ Researcher*,
May 7, 2010.

President Bill Clinton's trip to China in July 1998 was a splashy, 10-day display of America's power and prestige. Clinton arrived in Beijing with an entourage that included his wife, Hillary, and daughter Chelsea, five Cabinet secretaries, more than 500 White House staffers, members of Congress and security personnel, plus a swarm of journalists. His meetings with China's leaders turned into vigorous and lively debates. At Beijing University, Clinton delivered a forthright speech on human rights and answered questions from Chinese students, all of which was televised live nationwide. The authorities released a number of dissidents, and as the American visitors toured China's landmarks large crowds turned out to greet them.[1]

But that was then. President Obama's China visit in November 2009 was a low-key, four-day affair, part of a swing through Southeast Asia. Wife Michelle and daughters Malia and Sasha remained at home in Washington. His one direct contact with the Chinese public, a town meeting with 500 Chinese students in Shanghai, was deemed a local event and not broadcast nationwide. Throughout his stay, Obama made no public statement on human rights — although he did criticize China's Internet censorship, without mentioning China by name. In Beijing, his joint press appearance with his Chinese host, President Hu Jintao, was limited to a statement from each leader, with no press questions taken. Like Clinton, Obama visited the Forbidden City, but only after it was emptied of tourists.

In the years between the two presidential visits, China has emerged as the world's third-largest economy after the United States and Japan, and a force to be reckoned with in global affairs.

Trigger Points in the East and the West

China shares a western border with pakistan, which buys 36 percent of all China's arms exports — the largest share. Security experts worry that some of those arms may end up in the hands of anti-American Insurgents in Afghanistan. In the east, concern focuses on the buildup of China's naval fleets and its bellicose comments about U.S.-supported Taiwan.

Chinese Fleets

- North Sea HQ
- East Sea HQ
- South Sea HQ

Sources: The World Factbook, Central Intelligence Agency

And while the United States and Europe continue their uphill struggle to recover from the world recession, China is back on track, posting a phenomenal 11.9 percent growth rate for the first quarter of 2010 — well above the annual 8 percent its leaders consider crucial to keeping unemployment and social unrest at bay.[2]

Last year, China overtook Germany as the world's top exporter. China is now America's second-biggest trading partner after Canada, with $62.3 billion in trade to date in 2010 (up from $52.5 billion during the same period in 2009).³ But China is also the leading trading partner of the European Union, Japan, Brazil and India, reflecting the global reach of its burgeoning commercial activity. It is second only to the United States in energy consumption, has overtaken the U.S. as the biggest producer of greenhouse gasses on the planet and is also the No. 1 market for automobile sales.

The string of accomplishments has tilted the balance of the world's most important bilateral relationship in favor of the Chinese. With America's economy weakened, its military mired in two long and costly wars and its trade imbalance with China heavily in the red (-$238 billion) Obama's trip was fashioned to Beijing's specifications — brief and businesslike. Because China holds more than $877 billion of U.S. Treasury securities, commentators likened the visit to a debtor meeting with his bank manager.

Persuading the Chinese to increase the value of their currency was high on Obama's talks agenda. Concerned American manufacturers and unions say China deliberately keeps the renminbi (also referred to as the yuan) low against the dollar, giving China's goods an unfair advantage in U.S. and other foreign markets. China's refusal to adopt a floating currency system, according to experts, leads to so-called goods "dumping" by Chinese exporters — making their goods cheaper and undercutting foreign manufacturers.

The dispute over pricing has led to a tit-for-tat tariff battle. The United States currently imposes special tariffs and duties on 95 categories of goods imported from China — the highest for any country.⁴

When — shortly before Obama's visit — the United States announced stiff penalties on $3.2 billion in steel pipe from China for use in oil and gas fields, the Ministry

China at a Glance

Area: *9.6 million sq. km. (slightly smaller than the U.S.)*

Population: *1.34 billion (July 2009 est.); U.S.: 308 million*

Birth rate: *14 births/1,000 population (2009 est.); United States: 13.82 births/1,000 population (2009 est.)*

Ethnic groups: *Han Chinese 91.5%; Zhuang, Manchu, Hui, Miao, Uyghur, Tujia, Yi, Mongol, Tibetan, Buyi, Dong, Yao, Korean, and other nationalities 8.5% (2000 census)*

Religions: *Mainly Daoist (Taoist) and Buddhist; Christian 3%-4%, Muslim 1%-2%*

Languages: *Standard Chinese or Mandarin (Putonghua, based on the Beijing dialect) about 70%; Yue (Cantonese), Wu (Shanghainese), Minbei (Fuzhou), Minnan (Hokkien-Taiwanese), Xiang, Gan, Hakka dialects, minority languages*

Government: *Communist state. President and vice president elected by National People's Congress for five-year terms. Unicameral National People's Congress with 2,987 seats; members elected by municipal, regional and provincial people's congresses and People's Liberation Army to five-year terms.*

Economy: *GDP: $8.8 trillion (2009 est.); United States: $14.43 trillion (2009 est.)*

Exports: *mining and ore processing, iron, steel, aluminum, other metals, coal; machine building; armaments; textiles and apparel; petroleum; cement; chemicals; fertilizers; consumer products, including footwear, toys, and electronics; food processing; transportation equipment, including automobiles, rail cars and locomotives, ships and aircraft; telecommunications equipment, commercial space launch vehicles, satellites.*

Unemployment rate: *4.3% (Sept. 2009 est.); United States: 9.3% (2009 est.)*

Military expenditures: *4.3% of GDP (2006); United States: 4.06% of GDP (2005 est.)*

Source: *The World Factbook*, Central Intelligence Agency

of Commerce denounced the move as "protectionist" and said it was looking into whether American sedans and big sport utility vehicles on sale in China were subsidized by the United States government. "By not recognizing China as a market economy, the U.S. is acting in a discriminatory manner," stated ministry spokesman Yao Jian.⁵

Not so, said U.S. Steelworkers Union president Leo Gerard. "We're fed up with [the Chinese] cheating on our trade laws. Penalties for these transgressions are long overdue."⁶

On the foreign-policy front, the Obama administration needs China's help in containing Iran's nuclear ambitions. The next planned step in Washington's high-priority attempt

AFP/Getty Images/STR

A February meeting between the Dalai Lama — Tibet's exiled leader — and President Obama miffed the Chinese government, which maintains that Tibet is an inherent part of China and refuses to recognize Tibetan independence.

to stymie the ruling ayatollahs' efforts to produce nuclear weapons is tight U.N. sanctions to block Iran from acquiring any more of the technology it still needs. As one of the five veto-wielding, permanent members of the U.N. Security Council, China possesses an indispensable vote needed to pass any U.N. sanctions resolution. (The other members are the United States, Russia, Britain and France.)

But Iran is China's third-largest crude oil supplier, shipping 460,000 barrels a day in 2009 and about the same this year. China's National Petroleum Corp. also has sizable investments in Iranian oil production.[7] In Beijing, the Chinese shared Obama's concern that Iran should become a nuclear power but resisted his pressure to cooperate. Since then they have agreed to help in drafting a U.N. resolution — but have said nothing about voting for it. The president also raised U.S. concern over China's lack of respect for copyright laws and patent rights — a perennial Western complaint. Despite some new legislation to protect intellectual property, the production of knock-offs of famous brand names and the piracy of music, films and electronic game software remains a full-blown industry.[8]

In China's latest copyright scandal, the embarrassed organizers of Shanghai's $40 billion Expo 2010, which opened on May 1, recently withdrew the trade fair's promotional theme song after being deluged with protests that it had been plagiarized from a Japanese pop song.[9]

Such controversies are hardly new, but as China's economy and military have become more robust, so has its belief that it is operating from a position of strength, and the United States from growing weakness. "I think it is a common perception in the region that U.S. influence has been on the decline in the last decade, while Chinese influence has been increasing," Jeffrey Bader, director of Asian affairs at the National Security Council, declared prior to Obama's Asian trip. "And one of the messages that the president will be sending in his visit is that we are an Asia-Pacific nation and we're there for the long haul." Coming from a senior White House adviser the admission was revealing.[10]

In the end there was very little give by the Chinese leadership on either trade or Iran. Obama also made a pitch to the Chinese for what he described as "a positive, constructive and comprehensive relationship that opens the door to partnership on the big global issues of our time: economic recovery, development of clean air energy, stopping the spread of nuclear weapons and the surge of climate change, the promotion of peace in Asia and around the globe."[11]

Zbigniew Brzezinski, a former U.S. national security adviser who advised the Obama election campaign, described Obama's proposal more succinctly as a Washington-Beijing G-2 partnership. But the Chinese seemed lukewarm to Obama's power-sharing offer. "China fundamentally has not promoted the idea that China and the U.S. will form the two major powers," says Feng Zhongping, the head of the European section of the Beijing-based Chinese Institute of Contemporary International Relations. "China believes that the idea that [China and the United States] could undertake the responsibility of administering the world is incorrect."[12]

As experts try to read the tea leaves on the future of U.S.-China relations, here are some of the questions being asked:

Is a U.S.-China partnership actually possible?

Until the early 1970s, when President Richard M. Nixon made his historic trip to China, the two countries were virtual enemies — militarily and ideologically. Today, as China becomes a global powerhouse and a challenge to U.S. commercial and political interests, the relationship is deeply complex.

"It may be a cliché, but there are issues on which the United States and China have a common interest, and other issues with divergent interests, and difficulties are going to persist for some time, and occasionally there will be some friction," says China specialist Bonnie Glaser at Washington's Center for Strategic and International Studies. "But China does not want to have an unstable, unhealthy relationship with the United States. It's extremely important to the Chinese to have good relations."

To underline this, Chinese officials pointed out to the author that in Beijing Obama signed 11 bilateral agreements, including those on nuclear proliferation, economic cooperation, climate change, participation in multinational anti-pirate patrols in the Horn of Africa, visits between U.S. and Chinese forces (the U.S. carrier *USS Nimitz* visited Hong Kong in February), plus a joint commitment to strengthen people-to-people exchanges. As part of an enlarged U.S. academic-exchange program, Obama has promised to send 100,000 American students to China — roughly the same number of Chinese currently studying in the United States.[13]

The Chinese leadership's determination to avoid even the impression of giving in to pressure is almost a conditioned reflex because this would mean a dreaded loss of face.

Thus when Obama in Beijing held out the prospect of a closer partnership to tackle the major global issues, the response was noncommittal. Four months later, President Hu came to Washington to attend the Nuclear Security Summit. In a one-on-one with Obama, according to the official Xinhua news agency, he put forward a five-point proposal "to establish a partnership to jointly deal with common challenges."

Hu's overture covered much the same ground as Obama's, but only up to a point: The second of his five points stressed that each country "would respect the other's core interests and major concerns," a point not specifically made by Obama, and one that left wide latitude for divergence. Two of these interests were Tibet and Taiwan, which "concern China's sovereignty and territorial integrity and its interests," Xinhua stated, and which the United States should "handle with caution."[14]

This balance-of-interests approach by the Chinese is typically — and almost cryptically — expressed by Kaiser Kuo, an associate researcher at Beijing's World Politics Institute. "Sino-American competition and cooperation are increasingly intertwined," Kaiser says. "There is cooperation within competition, and competition within cooperation. There is no absolute cooperation or competition.

Therefore, we should not completely reject competition — and we should strengthen cooperation."[15]

In Washington, President Hu also hinted that China might be considering a revaluation of its currency, "based on its own economic and social-development needs." In other words, not because Washington is pressing for it.[16]

Hu also agreed that Beijing should cooperate on the wording of an Iran sanctions resolution. But in Beijing, Chinese Foreign Ministry spokeswoman Jiang Yu repeated China's position that "dialogue and negotiations are the best way."[17]

But some analysts think U.S.-Chinese relations may be less about cooperation and more about an ascendant China challenging the United States in areas once firmly in America's sphere of influence. "Obama and his policy makers are required to face up to a new reality," commented the Seoul-based English-language *Korean Times*, "in which China is jockeying for the world's No. 2 position while the U.S., the world's sole superpower, is waning, especially in the aftermath of the global financial and economic crisis."[18]

Unlike U.S.-Soviet relations during the Cold War, the challenge is not ideological. Still, according to the Congressional Research Service, "China's growing 'soft power' — primarily diplomatic and economic influence in the developing world — has become a concern among many U.S. policy leaders, including members of Congress."[19]

Because of its voracious demand for raw materials, Chinese trade with Latin America — the United States' back yard — grew tenfold between 2002 and 2007. In 2008, Chinese trade with Latin America ($142 billion) was a sixth of U.S. trade with the region — but growing at a faster rate. China's footprint in Africa is even larger in terms of both financial aid and investments.[20] But more significant from Washington's point of view is Beijing's increasing involvement in the Middle East.

In 2009, exports of Saudi Arabian crude to China were higher than to the United States, as Beijing courted the world's largest oil producer — and longtime U.S. ally.

"Saudi Arabia used to be very much an American story, but those days are over," said Brad Bourland, head researcher at Jadwa Investment in Riyadh, Saudi Arabia. The Saudis "now see their relationship with China as very strategic, and very long term."[21]

In a recent interview, Xu Xueguan, director of North American affairs at the Chinese Foreign Ministry's huge

China Sells Most Arms to Pakistan

Pakistan purchased more than a third of all Chinese conventional arms from 2003-2007 — by far the largest share. The second-largest buyer was Sudan, followed by Iran, Saudi Arabia and Egypt.

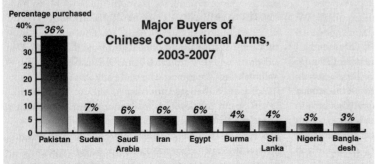

Source: "Military Power of the People's Republic of China, 2009," Office of the Secretary of Defense

China hands like Elizabeth Economy, director of Asia Studies at the Council on Foreign Relations think tank in Washington, downplay the new "Red Scare." Economy argues that the West — particularly the United States — has "completely lost perspective on what constitutes reality in China today." Economy concedes that "there is a lot that is incredible about China's economic story, but there is a lot that is not working well on both the political and economic fronts," distorting the real picture.

In other words, China has enough problems without provoking the challenge of an international nemesis. The Chinese leadership appears to worry about a fragile society: A persistent nightmare is that a sudden significant spike in unemployment, officially kept at 4 percent (but possibly higher because of the huge, hard-to-track migrant-worker population) could lead to widespread unrest.[24]

Still, looking at the Chinese as the potential aggressors, does China have the capacity for a military confrontation with the United States?

In the past five years China has spent hundreds of billions of dollars modernizing its armed forces, with special emphasis on the navy. China's 1.7 million Chinese under arms is considerably more than the 1.4 million in the U.S. armed forces, but in 2009 the U.S. defense budget was $738 billion and China's estimated at between $69.5 billion and $150 billion.[25]

The government insists it seeks a peaceful solution to the issue of uniting Taiwan to the mainland, but the Chinese have built up a formidable fleet of submarines and developed anti-ship missiles to counter a possible U.S. defense of the Taiwan Strait. The Americans will be ready for them. In its annual report to Congress on China's military power, the Pentagon said it was "maintaining the capacity to defend against Beijing's use of force or coercion against Taiwan."

Beyond the strait, the Pentagon reported, "China's ability to sustain military power . . . remains limited."[26] The Pentagon's annual report is a source of irritation to the Chinese, who routinely denounce it. This year, the Xinhua news agency dismissed the assessment as "a

headquarters in Beijing, told the author he couldn't understand why China had not been included in the so-called Quartet, the coalition of the United Nations, European Union, United States and Russia that is seeking a peaceful solution to the Israel-Palestine confrontation. When the Quartet was set up eight years ago, China did not yet have the clout to insist on being included. More recently, Beijing has expressed interest in becoming the fifth member of the U.N.-sponsored peace effort, without success — at least so far.

Is a confrontation with China inevitable, as some predict?

The Chinese leadership is "gunning for a paradigm shift in geopolitics. In particular, Beijing has served notice that it won't be shy about playing hardball to safeguard what it claims to be 'core national interests,' " writes Willy Lam, a China specialist at the Washington-based Jamestown Foundation think tank.[22] At the top of those national interests is Taiwan which, *The Economist* magazine said recently, "has been where the simmering distrust between China and America most risks boiling over."[23]

The chance of a war between China and the United States is generally regarded as remote. The Chinese threat to the United States is indirect — for example, if China should decide to use force to annex Taiwan, and America intercedes — as it is committed to do even though the United States does not recognize the island as an independent state.

largely subjective report with distorted facts and groundless speculation."[27]

Less hypothetical is the threat to the U.S. government's computer system. The Pentagon's 2009 report said U.S. government computers had been the target of "intrusions that appear to have originated" in China, although not necessarily from the military.[28] And in his annual "Threat Assessment" to the Senate Select Committee on Intelligence, Director of National Intelligence Dennis C. Blair warned in February that "malicious cyber activity is occurring on an unprecedented scale with extraordinary sophistication."

As a result, Blair added, the United States "cannot be certain that our cyberspace infrastructure will remain available and reliable during a time of crisis." Blair did not refer to China directly at that point. However, later in his assessment he called "China's aggressive cyber activities" a major concern.[29]

In January, after Google reported that hackers in China had targeted the computers of more than 30 U.S. corporations, including its own, and that the e-mail accounts of human rights activists had also been hacked, Secretary of State Hillary Rodham Clinton called on the Chinese government to investigate and to make its findings public.[30] (*See sidebar, p. 270.*)

U.S. officials and business executives warn that a trade war could also erupt if the Chinese don't yield to international pressure and raise the aggressive undervaluation of the renminbi, kept artificially low to favor Chinese exports. China's cheap currency is a serious problem for the global economy by undercutting exports throughout the industrial world, including the United States, and contributing to the trade imbalance. (President Obama has contended that if China lets the renminbi appreciate, U.S. exports would increase.)

The Obama administration has so far avoided picking a public fight with China over its currency — even

U.S. Trade Deficit With China Has Surged

The United States imports far more from China than it exports, causing a significant and growing trade gap. U.S.-China trade rose rapidly after the two nations reestablished diplomatic relations and signed a bilateral trade agreement in 1979 and provided mutual most-favored-nation treatment beginning in 1980. In recent years, China has been one of the fast-growing U.S. export markets, and it is expected to grow even further as living standards continue to improve and a sizable Chinese middle class emerges.

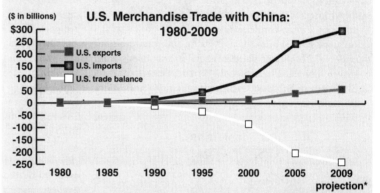

U.S. Merchandise Trade with China: 1980-2009

($ in billions)

- U.S. exports
- U.S. imports
- U.S. trade balance

* Based on actual data for January-April 2009

Source: Wayne M. Morrison, "China-U.S. Trade Issues," Congressional Research Service, June 23, 2009

to the extent of postponing indefinitely a Treasury Department report on worldwide currencies originally due out on April 15. Without any movement by Beijing on the currency front, the report could well label China a "currency manipulator." If that happens, Sen. Charles E. Schumer, D-N.Y., is ready with draft legislation that would place more tariffs on Chinese goods.

Chinese Commerce Minister Chen Deming recently told *The Washington Post* that the United States would lose a trade war with China. "If the United States uses the exchange rate to start a new trade war," he said, "China will be hurt. But the American people and U.S. companies will be hurt even more."[31]

One way for America to increase its exports, said Chen, would be to remove the restrictions on high-tech goods with possible military applications, which the United States imposed following Beijing's repressive crackdown on student demonstrations in 1989 in Tiananmen Square — something the Obama administration shows no signs of doing.

China's U.S. Holdings Greatly Increased

Since the early 2000s, China's holdings of U.S. securities — including U.S. Treasury securities and corporate stocks and bonds — have risen above $1.2 trillion — an increase of more than 500 percent. While China's U.S. holdings have helped the United States meet its investment needs, some policymakers worry they could give China increased leverage over the U.S. on political and economic issues.

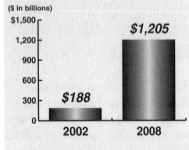

China's Holdings of U.S. Securities (June 2002-June 2008)

($ in billions)

2002: $188
2008: $1,205

Source: Wayne M. Morrison, "China-U.S. Trade Issues," Congressional Research Service, June 23, 2009.

Has China's "market authoritarian" model of government emerged as an alternative to Western democracy?

Despite predictions, China's emergence from isolation and its spectacular economic growth have not led to democratization. Instead, China has developed what Stefan Halper, director of the Atlantic Studies Program at Cambridge University, calls "a market authoritarian form of government, in which the free market is allowed to operate, but the government holds a very firm hand on political activity in the country."

In so doing, says Halper, author of the recent book *The Beijing Consensus*, the Chinese have produced an alternative to the Western democratic system that is thought to go hand in hand with a free-market economy. Non-democratic countries around the world like Egypt, Indonesia, Myanmar and Malaysia must find much to envy in a country that has achieved a 9 percent growth rate yet "managed to control its media, the legislature and the dissident voices, and has achieved global prominence," Halper adds.

The Chinese system "offers a seductive model that is eagerly taken up by the leaders of countries that have not yet settled on democratic structures," writes Australian China hand Rowan Callick in *The American*, the magazine of the American Enterprise Institute, a conservative Washington think tank. The Chinese model attracts autocrats because "their broader populations become content and probably supportive because their living standards are leaping ahead."[32]

China, however, has no interest in exporting its form of government. Its dealings with the rest of the world are dominated by the single-minded pursuit of one objective: economic development. As a ubiquitous lender and financial aid donor, China finds the door open in developing countries because Beijing's money comes with no strings attached about human rights and democracy — which is hardly the case with financial assistance from either the United States or the European Union.

Chinese money "is made available relatively easily and quickly without the political, economic, social and environmental conditions . . . that U.S. and European donors typically impose," says the Congressional Research Service report on China's foreign trade.[33]

But envious autocratic leaders should take note: Authoritarian capitalism may only work up to a point, writes Thomas P.M. Barnett, author of the recent book *Great Powers: America and the World after Bush*. He argues that when an economy starts to mature and needs to become more efficient, productive and innovative-based —"then we're talking intensive growth . . . something that nobody ever has been able to plan, because it lives and breathes on fierce competition, which only a true free market, accompanied by democracy, can supply."[34]

Moreover, under closer scrutiny, China's economic success has fragile underpinnings, with some doubting its long-term sustainability. For example, for all its progress, China's per capita income is still $6,546, compared

C H R O N O L O G Y

1970s-1980s *After Mao's death Deng institutes sweeping reforms, including relations with the United States.*

1972 President Richard M. Nixon makes historic trip to China, meets Mao Zedong and signs Shanghai Joint Communiqué declaring Taiwan part of mainland China.

1975 President Gerald R. Ford visits China, meets the ailing Mao, who dies the next year.

1978 Deng Xiaoping emerges as new leader, launches economic and social reforms.

1979 U.S. and China establish diplomatic relations. . . . Congress passes Taiwan Relations Act pledging to continue to supply Taiwan with weapons. . . . Deng visits United States.

1982 In joint U.S.-Chinese communiqué, United States pledges to gradually reduce arms sales to Taiwan.

1984 President Ronald Reagan visits China and meets Deng, who says that Taiwan remains a crucial problem in bilateral relations.

1989 President George H. W. Bush visits Beijing, invites dissidents to dinner. . . . People's Liberation Army crushes student-led pro-democracy demonstration in Beijing's Tiananmen Square, killing hundreds of protesters. . . . White House National Security Adviser Brent Scowcroft holds secret meeting in Beijing with Chinese leaders following the Tiananmen Square massacre.

1990s-2000s *China's economy welcomes Western investors; U.S.-China relations continue to warm.*

1992 Reversing a decade of U.S. policy, President George H. W. Bush decides to sell Taiwan F-16 combat planes, infuriating the Chinese.

1993 Newly elected President Bill Clinton establishes policy of "constructive engagement" with China, meets President Jiang Zemin in Seattle.

1996 China tests missiles off Taiwan to discourage vote for separatist Lee Teng-hui in the presidential election; U.S.

sends two aircraft carrier battle groups to area to support Taiwan.

1997 Britain hands Hong Kong back to China after 156 years. . . . Clinton is first U.S. president to visit China in a decade; criticizes Tiananmen massacre but strengthens U.S. commitment not to support Taiwan independence.

2000 U.S. Senate passes Permanent Normal Trade Relations bill (PNTR) giving China the same low-tariff access to the American market as other trading partners.

2001 China seizes U.S. spy plane after midair collision with Chinese fighter, hands over 24 American crewmembers after President George W. Bush apologizes for the Chinese pilot's death. . . . Bush makes first trip to China. . . . China joins World Trade Organization.

2002 Bush makes second visit to China to mark the 30th anniversary of Nixon's historic trip. . . . Future leader Hu Jintao visits White House for talks. . . . President Jiang Zemin visits Bush at his Texas ranch; they agree to cooperate on crisis following North Korea's announcement that it has nuclear weapons.

2003 With U.S. participation, Beijing hosts six-party talks on a unified approach to North Korea's nuclear weapons program.

2006 China's Great Firewall, or Golden Shield, Internet censorship system goes into service.

2008 China closes down Twitter, YouTube to block discussion on 20th anniversary of Tiananmen massacre.

2009 President Obama visits Shanghai and Beijing, makes no headway in persuading Chinese to raise value of their currency or to back sanctions against Iran.

2010 President Hu attends summit on nuclear security in Washington, despite tense U.S.-China relations over Iran sanctions, currency issues and imminent American weapons sale to Taiwan. . . . Expo 2010 opens in Shanghai. . . . Annual "strategic dialogue" between U.S. and China set for late May. . . . U.S. and China to attend G20 summit in Seoul, South Korea, in late June.

Is China Less Welcoming to U.S. Investors?

As Chinese know-how grows, opportunities diminish for foreigners.

It's one of the ironies of the U.S. trade deficit with China that a sizable portion of the goods exported to America are made by Chinese workers for U.S. firms. Earlier this year, the state-run Xinhua news agency reported that of the 200 top exporting firms last year, 153 were "foreign funded firms" — up from 141 in 2008.[1]

It's estimated that at least a third of those companies are U.S.-owned. For example, Shanghai alone has about 3,600 American expatriate business executives — although it was around 4,000 before the 2008 economic downturn. Chongqinq, China's largest city, with a population of 32 million, lists 41 foreign firms operating there, including Lear, Du Pont, Delphi Packard and Pepsi. General Motors, the largest auto maker in China, expects to sell 3 million vehicles in the Asian market by 2015 from its Chinese plants. In 2009, the 665,000 foreign firms in China accounted for 28 percent of the nation's industrial output, 56 percent of its exports and 45 million of its workers. In the first quarter of this year, foreign investment rose 12.1 percent, to $9.4 billion, according to *Business Week*.[2]

Even so, Google's recent difficulties with hackers in China may be an indication that as the Chinese economy matures the investment climate may no longer be as welcoming as it once was. One American executive doing business in Beijing says industrial espionage is rife and that the Chinese are experts at copying products. A foreign firm has at most a two-year window to establish itself on the Chinese market before it is challenged by an emerging local competitor.

As Chinese industrial know-how grows, the opportunities for foreign investors continue to diminish, according to business executives in Shanghai and Beijing. Recently, the Chinese authorities issued a directive encouraging government agencies to buy Chinese goods.

In a country where the state is still a major customer, this is a disturbing measure. But investors remain attracted by China, argues writer Zachary Karabell, author of the 2009 book *Superfusion: How China and America Became One Economy and Why the World's Prosperity Depends on It*. Says Karabell, "There's really nowhere else to go where you have 10 percent growth, 300-600 million emerging middle class Chinese who want to buy stuff and an environment where the rule of law is increasingly at least adequate in enforcement of contracts and getting your investments out of the country."

Google quit China after its servers were hacked, adds Karabell, partly because it wasn't doing very well in the Chinese market, and because it could afford not to do business with China.

The continued uncertain global environment has focused the Chinese government's attention on generating a domestic consumer market, so far with mixed results. Parting older-generation Chinese with their money means reversing a

to $40,208 in the United States. China's gross domestic product barely reaches $9 trillion, whereas allowing for the recent volatility of exchange rates, U.S. GDP exceeds $14 trillion.

Because China's economic development is export driven, the world recession caused 23 million Chinese workers to be laid off as Chinese exports dropped by 15-18 percent, says Stephen Green, chief economist at the SunTrust Bank in Shanghai. By the end of 2009, however, 98 percent of those had found other work, as the Chinese economy bounced back quicker than Western economies, boosted by a 4 trillion renminbi ($586 billion) stimulus package. (The U.S. economic stimulus was $874 billion.)

But the lesson to Beijing was that China can't export itself to growth. Though exports have picked up, the

Chinese have turned their attention to trying to develop a domestic market. For example, to stimulate sales of domestic appliances in rural areas, the government offered 13 percent rebates to farmers who buy refrigerators, TV sets and even mobile phones. In 2009, Beijing also spent $755 million to push car sales, cutting the purchase tax from around 15 percent to 5 percent. The result was a record 770,000 sales in March alone, a 27 percent jump over the previous month. Banks had instructions to increase mortgage lending, but the government reined them in again when they started granting loans for third homes.[35]

Though officials in China say 250 million Chinese were lifted out of poverty between 1980 and 2005, about 70 percent of China's population of 1.3 billion still lives in rural areas, often in villages with few paved roads and frequent

culture of saving, but the younger generations are avid shoppers. In the modern high rise that houses the Standard Chartered Bank in Shanghai — one of the thousands that crowd the city's skyline — Stephen Green, head of research, says older Chinese stubbornly stick to the "rainy day" syndrome — but "anyone born after 1980 behaves like an American."

In the past decade, for example, Starbucks has opened more than 350 coffee shops in China, where it is flourishing at the same time its U.S. business has been hammered by recession. Starbucks' success is puzzling because the Chinese really don't drink coffee; China produces about 30,000 tons of beans a year but exports most of it.

Caren Li, Starbucks' spokeswoman at the company's downtown Chinese headquarters in Shanghai, says Green Tea Frappuccino is a predictably steady seller, but "we're promoting a coffee culture, offering the Chinese more choices besides tea." Even so, it's not really about coffee: The coffee houses with the round green logo have become trendy meeting venues (there's even one in Beijing's Forbidden City), the chic place to be seen.

In 2009, a former Starbucks executive in China, Eden Woon, launched Toys Я Us in China (locally called Toy LiFung), and today the American retailer has 15 stores in the country. China may be the world's leading toy manufacturer, but its citizens buy mainly for very young children. "There's no toy culture in China because parents think toys distract children from their studies," Woon says over breakfast in a bustling hotel restaurant offering acres of dishes ranging from American pancakes and waffles to wonton soup. So Woon launched a campaign in this nation of overachievers with the message: "Toys are an important part of growing up."

Chinese flock to the 350 Starbucks coffee shops in China, including this one in Shanghai, but customers come for tea, not coffee, and because Starbucks is considered cool.

Mary Kay Inc., the Texas-based home-sales cosmetics firm, began operating in China in 1995. Headquartered in Shanghai, it marshals about 200,000 independent beauty "consultants," thanks to a skin-care line tailored to the local market, including a four-week "whitening cream" treatment that sells for the equivalent of $120.

— *Roland Flamini*

1 Xinhua news agency, http://news.xinhuanet.com/english2010/business/2010-04/20/c_13260044.htm.

2 "Foreign Investment in China Jumped in First Quarter," *Business Week/ Bloomberg*, April 14, 2010, www.businessweek.com/news/2010-04-14/foreign-investment-in-china-jumps-in-first-quarter-update1-.html.

water and power shortages. An ambitious and costly urbanization program is trying to shift people to the cities.

State-controlled media limit reports about unrest, but "bottom-up pressures for change in China are intense, spontaneous and multifaceted," according to a report by Ying Ma, a visiting fellow at the Hoover Institution at Stanford University. "Every day, Chinese leaders worry about the challenge to regime stability, but they have responded by continuing to exert brutal and sophisticated top-down control."[36]

"Riots take place in China every day," Ying says. The Chinese authorities reported 10,000 protests throughout the country in 1994, and 87,000 in 2005. Mobile phones and the Internet have given protesters and activists effective new weapons, which the regime is battling tooth and nail. Using the new technology the Chinese people

clamor for the government to address their grievances on the local level in increasing numbers: 10 million petitions in 2004 jumped to 30 million the following year.[37]

BACKGROUND

Presidential Challenges

Shortly after Mao Zedong's death in 1976, Chinese leaders took a hard look at their country and didn't like what they saw. China was just emerging from the Cultural Revolution, a decade of mob-led extremism started by Mao himself that had kept the country in chaos. China was desperately poor, deliberately isolated from the world economy and aloof from or opposed to nearly every international institution, including — until 1971 — the

'Harmonizing' the Internet in China

China's love affair with the Net is increasing along with censorship.

When a website is censored in China, the screen usually doesn't reveal that the government has blocked it. Instead, either a fake error message appears or an announcement about the site being unavailable, with an invitation to "Please try again."

By now, most of China's estimated 384 million "netizens" (nearly a quarter of the world's Internet users) are not taken in: They know the site has been "harmonized."[1]

In China, Internet censorship is often ironically called "harmonizing" because "harmony" — the absence of public dissent — is a key phrase in the government's propaganda. So as China's love affair with the Internet increases so does the Communist regime's censorship effort intensify — possibly because there is so much more material online for the government to worry about.

"China's blocking of overseas websites — including Facebook, Twitter and thousands of other sites is more extensive and technically more sophisticated than ever," Rebecca MacKinnon, a Hong Kong-based university journalism professor and China Internet expert, tells me via e-mail from Princeton's Center for Information Technology Policy, where she is currently a visiting fellow. "Controls over domestic content have also been tightening."

The Chinese authorities use a filtering system nicknamed The Great Firewall of China, but officially referred to as Golden Shield, to scan Internet content for specific key words and then block, or try to block, Web pages in which such words are used.

A list of blacklisted terms compiled by ConceptDoppler, a tool developed for the purpose by the universities of California, Davis, and New Mexico includes triggers such as "eighty-nine" and "June 4", the year and date of the Tiananmen Square protests, "massacre," "political dissident," "Voice of America," "*Playboy* magazine" and "Xinjiang independence" — a reference to the restive, predominantly Muslim province in northwestern China. Any one of these terms sends a series of three reset commands to both the source and the destination, effectively breaking the connection, says Jed Crandall, a professor of computer science at the University of New Mexico and one of the developers of ConceptDoppler, in an e-mail message.

A more recent addition to the list is "Charter 08," a lengthy manifesto calling on the Communist regime to relinquish its monopoly of power and introduce democratic reforms. Originally, Charter 08 was signed by 300 intellectuals and activists. After the document appeared briefly on the Internet — and before Chinese censors banned it — some 10,000 other signatures were added.

U.S. computer giants like Google entered the market knowing that they would have to comply with the regime's policy and exercise content censorship. Ultimately, Google found the controls too constricting to live with and earlier this year shifted its operations to less restrictive Hong Kong, at the same time complaining of Chinese hacking into the e-mail accounts of human rights activists and U.S. corporations.

Other U.S. Internet companies still operating in China, including Microsoft and Yahoo!, now face even tougher censorship restrictions. A new law, adopted on April 29 and set to take effect Oct. 1, requires them to stop the transmission of "state secrets" over the Internet, if they "discover" them — effectively requiring them to act as police informers.[2]

Some analysts maintain that while flowers were placed outside Google's Beijing office by users sorry to see it go, the impact of Google's departure is limited because the majority of China's netizens prefer to use homegrown Internet servers that exercise self-censorship rather than jeopardize their access.

Besides, the analysts point out, even with the constraints that grow daily the Internet has given Chinese citizens an unprecedented voice in the country's affairs.

"We should measure protest in China not by protests on the streets or availability of news on protests, but by the involvement of the Chinese citizens in policy decisions," says Yasheng Huang, a China expert at MIT's Sloan School. "By the latter yardstick, China had made huge progress, thanks largely to the Internet."[3]

United Nations. Under Deng Xiaoping, China's leaders reversed course and embraced globalization.

Since then successive U.S. presidents have wrestled with the challenge of how to deal with China's rapid rise. The Clinton administration fashioned a policy of "constructive engagement," calling for close bilateral economic and political cooperation, at the same time urging democratization and human rights.

"Seeking to isolate China is clearly unthinkable," President Bill Clinton declared in July 1998, defending

In recent years, Internet-based campaigns have pressured the Chinese government to release political prisoners, launch investigations into scandals, such as kidnapping boys for slave labor in mines, and convict corrupt officials.[4] China's version of Facebook, called Douban, and YouTube, called YouKu, as well as thousands of Internet bulletin boards teem with debate on current events.

Still, the censorship is not well defined, and some well-known dissident bloggers don't know when they have crossed the line until there is a knock at the door.

But mainly, it works by suggestion: "Many Internet users only have access to public computers at Internet cafes or universities, and just the existence of censorship might cause them to avoid topics they know they're not supposed to access, changing their online behavior," says Crandall.

The government maintains that censorship is partly a security measure and partly a responsibility to protect the public from what it sees as the negative side of the Internet's rapid growth.

Qian Xiaoqian, vice minister at the Chinese State Council information office, whose functions include deciding what gets blocked, says that while the government intervenes when a site is seen as plotting to overthrow the state, on another level it is also responding to public worry about the addictive nature of the Net.

"There is a discussion going on in this country about the potential negative influences of the Internet," Qian said last December over cups of tea, invariably served to visitors to any Chinese office. "Chinese parents are worried about the pornography; but not just the pornography." The government blames "Internet addiction" for youthful alienation.

A recently published survey by the Chinese National People's Congress found that 10 percent of Chinese youth were addicted to the Internet, Qian says. Many Chinese parents are sending their children to "boot camp" to cure them of "internetitis" — a solution which the government first encouraged but later seemed to back away from, warning against too much brutality in rehab methods.[5]

Critics of Chinese Internet censorship, including MacKinnon, say the regime uses such arguments to justify tightening control over the Net.

Mounting concerns over security and censorship by the government led Google to leave mainland China in March and relocate in Hong Kong.

But Qian claims "the Chinese government assumes a very important responsibility in managing the Internet. America is a mature society. At this stage Chinese society is still not — and besides, different people have different interpretations of freedom."

For those who prefer the Internet censor-free, the United States is leading the effort to produce circumvention software that connects to blocked websites via proxy computers outside the country. Programs like Psiphon, Tor and the Global Internet Freedom Consortium have been increasingly successful at breaching the wall.[6]

— *Roland Flamini*

---

[1] David Talbot, "China's Internet Paradox," *MIT Technology Review*, May/June 2010, www.technologyreview.com/web/25032/page1/.

[2] Mike Elgan, "New Chinese law may force Microsoft, Yahoo, to follow Google," *ITWorld*, April 29, 2010, www.itworld.com/internet/106191/new-chinese-law-may-force-microsoft-yahoo-follow-google-out, and Jonathan Ansfield, "Amendment Tightens Law on State Secrets in China," *The New York Times*, April 30, 2010, p. A9.

[3] Quoted in Talbot, *op. cit.*

[4] *Ibid.*

[5] The information is from a Chinese television news "magazine" show, with a translation provided to the author.

[6] For example, www.FreeGate.com, the Freedom Consortium's software developed by a group of Chinese expatriates in the United States.

---

his approach. "We would succeed instead in isolating ourselves and our own policy."[38]

The George W. Bush administration used the catchphrase "responsible stakeholder," pressing China to become a responsible member of the international community and to embrace democracy. Prior to President Obama's November China trip, Deputy Secretary of State James B. Steinberg mapped out a policy of "strategic reassurance" toward Beijing, and the phrase — as intended — has stuck.

"Just as we are prepared to accept China's arrival as a prosperous and successful power," Steinberg explained, the Chinese must "reassure the rest of the world that its development and growing global role will not come at the expense of the security and well-being of others."[39]

Whatever the label, the fundamental underpinning of American policy toward China has been economic engagement. In 2000, for example, Congress granted China permanent normal trade relations (PNTR) with the United States. In 2001, the United States backed China's entry into the World Trade Organization, thus placing the Chinese under international business rules, which was reassuring for would-be foreign investors.

All Business

In his inaugural address last year, Obama echoed Clinton's 1997 statement that communist China stood "on the wrong side of history." The conventional wisdom about China was that the market forces unleashed by global trade and investment would inevitably give more people a stake in the economy and open up China politically, leading to the creation of political parties and more democracy and respect for human rights.

Only it hasn't happened. In China, the party's far from over. China calls its authoritarian capitalism a "socialist market system," and the ruling Chinese Communist Party (CPC) appears more entrenched than ever — helped by a large, efficient and pervasive police organization.

In 2009, the party celebrated its 60th anniversary, and the state-controlled media took care to trumpet the regime's economic and political achievements.

Yet how much is left of communist ideology is open to question: As the author discovered during a reporting trip to China last November, the huge portrait of Mao still looks out over Tiananmen Square, and Marxist theory is still taught at the party school for senior officials. But the old party slogans praising the proletariat class and condemning capitalism have disappeared from the walls and factories.

The party has opened membership to entrepreneurs and business people, and the state-held shares of the country's 1,300 companies, many of which are listed on the Beijing stock exchange, are publicly traded.

Challenged to explain exactly how Marxism-Leninism fits into the "socialist market system," Chinese officials quote Deng Xiaoping's famous observation that it doesn't matter whether the cat is black or white as long as it kills the mouse.

Officials today will even quote Confucius without first cautiously looking over their shoulder. The great Chinese sage has had his ups and downs. In the Cultural Revolution he was reviled as an imperial lackey because of his position as adviser to the emperor.

But Confucius has been rehabilitated as a symbol of China's glorious past. The Chinese have set up hundreds of Confucius institutes worldwide, including 25 in the United States. The institutes promote Chinese language and culture, just as the Goethe institutes promote German culture, and the Dante Alighieri institutes do the same for Italy.

Even so, "China did not take a missionary approach to world affairs, seeking to spread an ideology or a system of government," writes Robert D. Kaplan, a senior fellow at the Center for a New American Security. "Moral progress in international affairs is an American goal, not a Chinese one. China's actions abroad are propelled by its need to secure energy, metals and strategic materials in order to support the living standards of its immense population."

In Kaplan's view, Beijing "cares little about the type of regime with which it is engaged. It requires stability, not virtue as the West conceives it."[40]

As early as 2005, when China for the first time was included in the annual economic survey of the Organization for Economic Cooperation and Development (OECD), it noted, "Well over half of China's GDP is produced by privately controlled enterprises."[41] But while the trend has continued, communications, transport, infrastructure, banking and energy remain under tight state supervision.

In late November 2009, Xu Kuangdi, a senior adviser to the Chinese Communist Party, told this reporter and other visiting U.S. journalists that it would be dangerous to hold free elections because China was "not ready," and some demagogue might win by promising to take the money from the new rich and give it to the poor! "The ultimate goal is common prosperity," he said, "but we have to let a group of people get rich first."

In 2003, looking for places to put its growing export revenue, China began buying U.S. Treasury bills on a large scale. By 2005, China had acquired $243 billion worth of the U.S. debt, second only to Japan. In 2006, China overtook Japan when its holdings climbed to $618 billion. In 2009, possibly fearing that the global recession would undermine the dollar, China sold some $34 billion of its Treasuries — but was soon back on a buying spree. By February 2010, China held a whopping $877.5 billion in Treasuries.[42] Meanwhile, a well-heeled middle class has emerged in China. Cars create traffic jams in Chinese cities, and the once ubiquitous bicycles are now kept by many Chinese for week-end country excursions.

In Beijing, a five-star hotel is flanked by two glass-fronted dealerships, one for Maseratis, the other for Lamborghinis. Four years ago, the China branch of HSBC Bank launched a credit card: It now boasts 11 million cardholders, said D.G. "Dicky" Yip, of the Bank of Communications in Shanghai last November.

China's new rich have acquired a taste for art as well as luxury cars. First it was contemporary art by artists who a decade earlier had been suppressed or even jailed because of their avant garde works. More recently, classic traditional paintings and Chinese calligraphy have been sold at auction for millions of RMB. In a crowded auction hall in Beijing filled with Chinese bidders in November, a scroll painting by the Ming Dynasty landscape master Wu Bin sold for the equivalent of $24.7 million to a Chinese bidder.

The bad news for the government has been the widening gap between the urban prosperous and the rural impoverished. China's poor are a restive majority running into the hundreds of millions. In 2008, the average income of a rural worker was $690, compared to a city average of $2,290 — and higher in Shanghai and Beijing.[43] But the annual salary of a chief executive in China is around $100,000, a fraction of corporate salaries in the United States but still astronomical in Chinese terms.

To make matters worse for the poor, the government has been slow to reform a social system that cuts off the medical and other benefits of China's millions of internal migrant workers once they quit their hometowns. As things now stand many immigrants are left to fend for themselves — even when they find employment.

The social system also needs to catch up with the aging Chinese population, which is getting older faster than in the United States. The problem is exacerbated by a relatively high life expectancy — about 73 — versus 77 in the United States. By 2040 demographers say that each Chinese worker will be forced to support two parents and four grandparents.

An 'Edgy' Game

With the economic boom unfolding against a background of frequent unrest, "The No. 1 challenge for China is to maintain domestic stability and at the same time

More than 150 nations and 50 international organizations have registered for the Shanghai World Expo, and 70 million visitors are anticipated, making the six-month-long world's fair the largest ever. The Expo's theme — "Better City — Better Life" — is intended to showcase Shanghai as the next great world city in the 21st century.

sustainable economic development," says Yang Jiemian, director of the Shanghai Institute of International Studies.

The Internet, which has gone from 620,000 users in China in 1997 to 370 million users today — more people than the entire U.S. population — has become a forum for online dissent. The authorities crack down on the deluge of cyber-dissent using a (patchy at best) online censorship, ironically known as the Great Firewall of China — which also tries to block pornographic sites. (*See sidebar, p. 270.*) Persistent blogging about subjects deemed subversive can lead to imprisonment. (There are 20 million bloggers in China.) For example, Chinese writer Liu Xiaobo was jailed for 11 years on Dec. 25 after co-drafting and posting "Charter '09," a lengthy manifesto calling on the government to introduce democratic reforms.

The regime's biggest nightmare remains large-scale unemployment. To keep it at the current 4 percent level China needs to ensure continued growth generating 24 million new jobs every year.[44] Hence the need to buttress its current dependence on exports by boosting consumer demand at home. But the Chinese are not only great savers but also traditionally have an aversion to being in debt. For example, no doubt to the chagrin of HSBC officials, 80 percent of the bank's credit card holders avoid interest charges by paying their whole bill every month — compared to the national U.S. average of 20 percent.

Commenting on the government's combination of a market economy and tight control, Halper at Cambridge University says, "This is an edgy game, and things could

Is today's China a communist country?

YES
Xu Kuangdi
President, Chinese Academy of Engineering in Beijing, former Shanghai mayor

Written for *CQ Researcher*, May 2010

The Chinese Communist Party (CPC) has never done things by the book. In the early days, some party members, following the lead of the Soviet Union, launched the workers' movement in the cities. But the party shifted its focus to the rural areas where government control was relatively weak. We mobilized the peasants; we developed land reform.

Today, we don't do things according to what Karl Marx wrote or Vladimir Lenin said 80 years ago. We're doing things to advance the development of productive forces, and we are doing things to serve the interests of the vast majority of people.

Marx is still widely respected by the party. He is a great mind and a very great thinker on the development of civilization. His theories on capitalism inspired us on how to overcome the current financial crisis. But Marx lived 100 years ago; he couldn't predict how science and technology would develop. That is why our new ideology is to keep pace with the times. That doesn't mean we have forgotten Marx. Marxism is still our long-term goal.

The CPC is committed to building a society in which property and well-being can be enjoyed by all, a society of harmony between rich and poor. Today, we have a problem of a widening gap between rich and poor, which we are trying our best to narrow. But it will not be solved by dividing the property of the rich among the poor.

Our previous lessons showed us that the division of property is not the answer. Nor is Western democracy the answer. If we introduced Western democracy, we may have turbulence in the society.

A Western friend told me that he would only go to church three times in his lifetime. The first time is to be baptized, the second for his marriage and the third for his funeral. It doesn't follow that he doesn't have God in his heart. It's the same for us with Communism.

To live up to our beliefs we sometimes have to take different paths. As [former CPC leader] Deng Xiaoping has put it: The ultimate goal is common prosperity, but we have to let some people get rich first.

NO
Stefan Halper
Director, Atlantic Studies Program, Cambridge University, author, The Beijing Consensus: How China's Authoritarian Model Will Dominate the Twenty-First Century

Written for *CQ Researcher*, April 2010

There's a wonderful comment by the legendary U.S. diplomat and Russia expert George F. Kennan, who said, "Let's not ask what communism has done to Russia, but rather what Russia has done to communism." Much the same didactic is applicable to today's China.

Mao and Stalin would be spinning in their graves if they saw what was happening in China in the name of communism. China has shed any remnants of Marxist ideology, even to the point of directly addressing the question of who owns the land, a serious point of contention in the recent People's Congress. It is now accepted that land can be privately owned and houses built on it.

China is not expansionist, it does not seek to undermine the Western system: instead, its market-authoritarian system provides an example for the world beyond the West where growing numbers of leaders admire China, see China as a Third World nation at the pinnacle of world power and wish to emulate China's progress.

So while China may continue to call itself communist, it certainly isn't communism as we know it, but more of a form of state capitalism; the role of state is market authoritarian, not Marxist-Leninism. A Marxist economy is the polar opposite of the dynamic market economy China is developing today.

The Chinese leadership is highly practical, opportunistic and focused on economic growth and stability. The only remnants of communism are the single party rule of the party, a general embrace of socialist principles and the various structures that the party employs to govern the country: a politburo, a people's congress and a central committee.

Of course, it still calls itself communist, but it's just as much a corporatist state, even a form of fascism in its classical, Mussolini-type form, which is to say a process that coordinates the interest of the state and large corporations. Put another way, the business of China is business.

go seriously wrong. Just trying to control the Internet is really tough work. The glue that holds the whole thing together is a ferociously powerful security service."

CURRENT SITUATION

Tense Beginning

This is a period of waiting for the other shoe to drop in U.S.-China relations following a tense first quarter of 2010.

There is unresolved business on the currency front, on Iran sanctions, on the issue of U.S. weapons sales to Taiwan and on the broader question of how the two countries should engage in the future.

The Obama administration has put a lot of effort into trying to convince the Chinese government that it is in both sides' interest to move toward what Obama calls "a more market-oriented exchange rate" for the renminbi. Following a meeting between President Obama and President Hu Jintao in Washington in April, during the Nuclear Security Summit, it seemed clear that the Chinese had not budged on revaluing their currency. Any change would not come from U.S. pressure, Hu said.[45]

In New York, the five permanent members of the U.N. Security Council are working on an Iran-sanctions resolution. "The Chinese were very clear they share our concern about the Iranian nuclear program," said Bader at the National Security Council.[46] Still, the Chinese government has not said that it will vote for a U.N. resolution and still insists publicly that diplomacy and negotiation are the way to go.

Cooperation on climate control seems at a stalemate after Hu told the December Copenhagen summit that China's own emissions control program would not be subject to U.N. supervision. For its part, the United States rejected a Chinese request that developing countries should be compensated for cutting carbon emissions.

Yu Qintgou, the official responsible for climate change at China's Ministry of Foreign Affairs, explained the familiar Chinese position in an interview in Beijing on Dec. 1. Simply put, Yu said, the world's climate change problem was not the making of China or India but of the developed countries. The United States and the other industrialized nations should "acknowledge their historic responsibility" as emitters of greenhouse gases and not put so great a burden on the emerging nations that it would set back their development, he said.

The latest tension had its origins in November, when Obama's Chinese hosts insisted on a low-key visit that minimized his contact with the public.

"It's a mystery," David Shamburgh, a professor of Chinese studies at Georgetown University, told *The Wall Street Journal* during the presidential visit. "[Obama is] a populist politician, but he's not getting any interaction with Chinese people."[47] It's not such a mystery, perhaps, when one considers Obama's popularity worldwide, in contrast to a Chinese leadership with limited contact with its own people.

Indeed, on the morning following Obama's arrival in Shanghai, the city's government-controlled English-language paper carried a large front-page photo of Hu with the prime minister of Canada, who was in China at the time. A one-column photo of Obama appeared below the fold. In a country where much importance is attached to not losing face, such signals matter.

The tension had escalated two months later when Obama made two moves calculated to anger the Chinese. First, in February the president received Tibet's exiled spiritual leader, the Dalai Lama, after Beijing had expressly asked him not to do so.

The meeting drew a protest from Beijing even though the White House kept the visit private and carefully avoided showing pictures of Obama and the Dalai Lama together.

In a second affront, Obama approved a long-delayed $6.4 billion weapons sale to Taiwan, which China continues to threaten with hundreds of missiles while at the same time insisting that it wants a peaceful solution to the island's claims of independence. The package includes 114 Patriot missiles worth $2.2 billion, and 60 Blackhawk helicopters worth $3.1 billion.

Beijing promptly ratcheted up its rhetoric, and U.S.-Chinese relations took "a nosedive," *The Washington Post* said.[48] A senior Chinese Defense Ministry official, Huang Xueping, said China was resolved to punish the United States if the weapons were delivered and that the U.S. could expect even greater consequences if Washington added advanced F-16 jet fighters to the sale.[49]

The Chinese went still further. Beijing threatened to sanction U.S. firms involved in the deal. And then it showed off its military prowess by successfully testing — without warning — an advanced missile interception system. The timing also seemed a further demonstration of Beijing's ire. "The people who tied the knot should untie the knot," said Chinese Foreign Ministry spokesman Qin Gang.[50]

China spends more than 4 percent of its gross domestic product (GDP) on its military, about the same ratio as the United States. The country's rising military spending, including the beefing up of key naval bases near Taiwan, has caused concern in Washington.

Commentators attributed China's new tough and uncompromising attitude to more than one factor. They said China's seemingly quick recovery from the global financial crisis while the West continues to struggle has vindicated the Chinese development model in Chinese eyes and the weakness of the less-disciplined Western approach.

A second explanation, though, was the jostling for position in the leadership in advance of the 2012 Communist Party Congress, an event that spurs aspiring candidates to display their nationalist credentials. Behind the united front China's leadership shows to the world, deep divisions exist between the hard-line "realists" and those who favor openness in China's international dealings — and the hard-liners currently have the upper hand. According to another explanation, the regime's aggressiveness toward the outside world stems from the government's desire to find a distraction from socioeconomic problems at home.

After all, this is the Year of the Tiger — always turbulent and often unpredictable.[51]

OUTLOOK

The Taiwan Question

It remains to be seen how the Chinese will react, if or when the United States begins delivery of the weapons sold to Taiwan.

Analysts say the recently proposed (but not finalized) additional sale of F-16s would raise the level of China's objections even further. Although the original weapons deal drew protests, it had initially been negotiated by the Bush administration and was well known to the Chinese. But Jean-Pierre Cabestan, a professor of international studies at Hong Kong Baptist University, predicts that "if an F-16 sale moves forward, we can expect another wave of difficulties between the U.S. and China."

The outlook is hard to forecast with any accuracy because of the ongoing cooperation-competition dance between China and the U.S. For example, despite its protests over Taiwan, Beijing at the same time is committed to working with Washington and other governments in securing vital sea lanes and enforcing regional stability. Early in 2010, China agreed to take a lead role in anti-piracy patrols off Somalia. Chinese navy units had not strayed outside Chinese waters for centuries, but today 80 percent of China's oil imports are shipped through the narrow Straits of Malacca that connect the Indian Ocean and the South China Sea.

There is no indication that China would actually support sanctions against Iran. In the past, China had signed on to three previous U.N. sanctions resolutions — and the Chinese eventually delayed and weakened every one of them, said Iran expert Flynt Leverett, a senior fellow at the centrist New America Foundation think tank.[52]

Also casting a shadow over the next few months is the thorny question of China's undervalued renminbi. Foreign-policy issues are rarely prominent in U.S. elections, but at a time of high unemployment and economic uncertainty, some analysts believe China's currency seems set to become a thorny question in November's mid-term elections, possibly creating anti-Chinese public sentiment.

Given the upcoming elections, some analysts say a slight currency revaluation designed to take the dispute out of the campaign is in the offing. But, says Glaser at the Center for Strategic and International Studies, "The Chinese are not going to revalue their currency because we tell them to. They will choose their own time."

One reason: Chinese leaders cannot afford seeming to act in response to pressure from the "foreign devils" (*qwai lo*) — which to the Chinese is just about everybody including the United States — without serious loss of face in the eyes of their own people.

The United States has a risky card of sorts to play in the shape of the annual U.S. Treasury analysis (mandated by the 1988 Omnibus Trade and Competitiveness Act) of the currencies of foreign countries to determine whether they are manipulating the currency to gain unfair trade advantage. To Congress' exasperation, the Treasury has so far not labeled China a "currency manipulator."

If and when it does, New York's Sen. Schumer has a draft bill waiting that would impose stiff penalties on countries that manipulate their currencies, including possible tariffs. "China's currency manipulation would be unacceptable even in good economic times," Schumer said in a recent statement. "At a time of 10 percent unemployment, we simply will not stand for it."

There is an obvious political edge to Schumer's bill: The senator is up for re-election. But others also feel the time has come to confront the Chinese. The Obama administration "needs to draw a line in the sand, and say to the Chinese: 'You're exporting unemployment by undervaluing your currency by 20 percent to 40 percent,'" says Cambridge University's Halper. If the Chinese don't revalue, "we should impose similar tariffs."

> Despite its protests over Taiwan, Beijing at the same time is committed to working with Washington and other governments in securing vital sea lanes and enforcing regional stability.

It was out of consideration for Hu's visit in April that Treasury Secretary Timothy Geithner postponed publication of the Treasury report, which is normally released on April 15. No new date has been announced, but analysts say the delay is strategic, giving the Chinese more time for further reflection.

Two important dates are coming up for possible further discussion — the U.S.-China yearly "strategic dialogue" in late May, and the broader forum of the G20 summit in Seoul, South Korea, in late June.

The Chinese, however, are focused on another event they hope will boost their prestige, much as the 2008 Summer Olympics had done: The Shanghai Expo 2010, which the city expects will attract over 70 million visitors. Its theme reflects China's hopes and aspirations — "Better city, better life."

NOTES

1. "Clinton in China," BBC Special Report, July 3, 1998, http://news.bbc.co.uk/2/hi/special_report/1998/06/98/clinton_in_china/118430.stm. Also Lin Kim, "Sino-American Relations: a new stage?" *New Zealand International Review*, Vol. 23, 1998, www.questia.com/googleScholar.qst;jsessionid=LY2JTpnRvl29qyD1Byf HwVQxJtmVQQ7bcyJ6RW47LJJnw6WmnYwg!555 708061!-1331918248?docId=5001372599.

2. "China's economy grew 11.9 pct y/y in Q1 — sources," *The Guardian*, April 14, 2010. www.guardian.co.uk/business/feedarticle/9031081.

3. U.S. Census Bureau, www.census.gov/foreign-trade/balance/c5700.html#2010.

4. Howard Schneider, "U.S. sets tariff of up to 90 percent on imports of Chinese oilfield pipes," *The Washington Post*, April 10, 2010.

5. Wang Yanlin and Jin Jing, "Trade dispute heats up while Obama visit nears," *ShanghaiDaily.com*, Nov. 7, 2009, www.shanghaidailycom/sp/article/2009/200911/20091107/article_418781.htm.

6. Schneider, *op. cit.*

7. "China, India, Japan Iran's Top Partners in Crude Oil Trade," Moinews.com, April 14, 2010, www.mojnews.com/en/Miscellaneous/ViewContents.aspx?Contract=cms_Contents_I_News&r=485205.

8. For background see Alan Greenblatt, "Attacking Piracy," *CQ Global Researcher*, August 2009, pp. 205-232.

9. "China Must Protect Intellectual Property," *Korea Herald*, April 22, 2010, www.koreaherald.co.kr/national/Detail.jsp?newsMLId=20100422000363.

10. White House transcript, Nov. 9. 2009, www.whitehouse.gov/the-press-office/briefing-conference-call-presidents-trip-asia.

11. "Commentary: China, U.S. sail in one boat amid global issues," Xinhua news service, Nov. 16, 2009; http://news.xinhuanet.com/english/2009-11/16/content_12463881.htm.

12. Martin Walker, "Walker's World: Haiku Herman's G2," United Press International, Dec 7, 2009, www.spacewar.com/reports/Walkers_World_Haiku_Hermans_G2_999.html.

13. U.S.-China Joint Statement, U.S. Embassy, Beijing, http://beijing.usembassy-china.org.cn/111709.html.

14. "Hu presents 5-point proposal for boosting China-U.S. ties," Xinhua, April 13, 2010, http://english.cctv.com/20100413/102277.shtml.

15. Kaiser Kuo, "The Intertwining of Sino-American Cooperation and Competition," China Geeks Translation and Analysis of Modern China, February 2010, http://chinageeks.org/2010/02/the-intertwining-of-sino-american-competition-and-cooperation/.

16. Edwin Chen and Rob Delaney, "Hu Tells Obama China Will Follow Its Own Path on Yuan," Bloomberg, April 13, 2010, www.bloomberg.com/apps/news?pid=20601070&sid=a07psM9uKD6g.

17. "China-U.S. agreement sends warning to Iran," *The National*, April 13, 2010, www.thenational.ae/apps/pbcs.dll/article?AID=/20100413/FOREIGN/704139996/1014.

18. "Obama's Asia Visit," editorial, *Korea Times*, Nov. 10, 2009, www.koreatimes.co.kr/www/news/opinon/2010/04/202_55210.html.

19. Thomas Lunn, *et al.*, China's Foreign Aid Activities in Africa, Latin America, and Southeast Asia, Feb. 25, 2009, www.fas.org/sgp/crs/row/R40361.pdf. Report is based largely on research by New York University's Robert F. Wagner Graduate School of Public Service.

20. *Ibid.*

21. Jad Mouawad, "China's Growth Shifts the Geopolitics of Oil," *The New York Times*, March 19, 2010, www.nytimes.com/2010/03/20/business/energy-environment/20saudi.html.

22. Willy Lam, "Beijing Seeks Paradigm Shift in Geopolitics, "The Jamestown Foundation, March 5, 2010, www.jamestown.org/programs/chinabrief/single/?tx_ttnews%5Btt_news%5D=36120&tx_ttnews%5BbackPid%5D=25&cHash=a9b9a1117e.

23. "Facing up to China," *The Economist*, Feb. 4, 2010, www.economist.com/PrinterFriendly.cfm?story_id=15452821.

24. Nicholas D. Kristof, "China, Concubines, and Google," *The New York Times*, March 31, 2010, www.nytimes.com/2010/04/01/opinion/01kristof.html.

25. Drew Thompson, "Think Again: China's Military," *Foreign Policy*, March/April 2010, www.foreignpolicy.com/articles/2010/02/22/think_again_chinas_military.

26. "Annual Report to Congress: Military Power of the People's Republic of China, 2009," Department of Defense, www.defense.gov/pubs/pdfs/China_Military_Power_Report_2009.pdf.

27. "Pentagon issues annual report on China's military power," Xinhuanet, March 26, 2009, www.news.xinhuanet.com/english/2009-08/26/content_11079173.htm.

28. Pentagon report to Congress, *op. cit.*

29. Dennis Blair, "Annual Threat Assessment of the U.S. Intelligence Community for the Senate Select Committee on Intelligence," February 2010, www.dni.gov/testimonies/20100202_testimony.pdf.

30. Cecilia Kang, "Hillary Clinton calls for Web freedom, demands China investigate Google attack," *The Washington Post*, Jan. 22, 2010, www.washingtonpost.com/wp-dyn/content/article/2010/01/21/AR2010012101699.html.

31. John Pomfret, "China's Commerce Minister: U.S. has most to lose in a trade war," *The Washington Post*, March 22, 2010, www.washingtonpost.com/wp-dyn/content/article/2010/03/21/AR2010032101111.html.

32. Rowan Callick, "The China Model," *The American*, November/December 2007, www.american.com/archive/2007/november-december-magazine-contents/the-china-model.

33. Lunn, *et al.*, *op. cit.*

34. Thomas P.M. Barnett, "The New Rules: Why China Will Not Bury America," *World Politics Review*, Feb. 1, 2010, www.worldpoliticsreview.com/articles/5031/the-new-rules-why-china-will-not-bury-america.

35. Wieland Wagne, "How China is battling global economic crisis," *San Francisco Sentinel*, May 23, 2009, www.sanfranciscosentinel.com/?p=28287.

36. Ma Ying, "China's Stubborn Anti-Democracy," Hoover Institution Policy Review, February/March 2007, www.hoover.org/publications/policyreview/5513661.html.

37. *Ibid.*

38. Brian Knowlton, "Citing 'Constructive Engagement,' He Acts to Counter Critics in Congress: Clinton Widens Defense of China Visit," *The New York*

Times, July 12, 1998, www.nytimes.com/1998/06/12/news/12iht-prexy.t.html?pagewanted=1.

39. Evan Osnos, "Despatches from Evan Osnos: Strategic Reassurance," *The New Yorker Online,* Oct 6, 2009, www.newyorker.com/online/blogs/evanosnos/2009/10/strategic-reassurance.html.

40. Robert D. Kaplan, "The Geography of Chinese Power," *Foreign Affairs,* May/June 2010.

41. "China could become World's largest exporter by 2010," Organization for Economic Cooperation and Development, Sept. 16, 2005, www.oecd.org/document/29/0,3343,en_2649_201185_35363023_1_1_1_1,00.html.

42. U.S. Department of Treasury, www.ustreas.gov/tic/mfh.txt.

43. http://news.bbc.co.uk/2/hi/asia-pacific/7833779.stm.

44. Li Beodong, head of China's delegation to the United Nations in Geneva, official transcript of speech in 2009.

45. The Associated Press, "China's Hu rebuffs Obama on yuan," *Minneapolis Star Tribune,* April 13, 2010, www.startribune.com/business/90728804.html.

46. Transcript of White House press briefing, April 12, 2010, www.whitehouse.gov/the-press-office/press-briefing-jeff-bader-nsc-senior-director-asian-affairs.

47. Ian Johnson and Jonathan Wiseman, "Beijing limits Obama's exposure," *The Wall Street Journal* Online, Nov. 17, 2009, http://online.wsj.com/article/SB125835068967050099.html.

48. John Pomfret and Jon Cohen, "Many Americans see U.S. influence waning as that of China grows," *The Washington Post,* Feb. 25, 2010, p. A11.

49. Andrew Jacobs, "China Warns U.S. Against Selling F-16s to Taiwan,"

50. *Ibid.*

51. David Shambaugh, "The Year China Showed its Claws," *Financial Times,* Feb. 16, 2010, www.ft.com/cms/s/0/7503a600-1b30-11df-953f-00144feab49a.html.

52. Corey Flintoff, "Will China Help Sanction Iran's Nuke Program?" NPR, April 14, 2010, www.npr.org/templates/story/story.php?storyId=125991589&ft=1&f=1004.

BIBLIOGRAPHY

Books

Halper, Stefan, *The Beijing Consensus, Basic Books,* **2010.**
A Cambridge University professor analyzes the economic and strategic sides of U.S.-China relations.

Jacques, Martin, *When China Rules the World: The Rise of the Middle Kingdom and the End of the Western World, Penguin,* **2010.**
A British commentator predicts that history is about to restore China to its ancient position of global power.

Karabell, Zachary, *Superfusion: How China and America Became One Economy and Why the World's Prosperity Depends on It, Simon & Schuster,* **2009.**
An economist and historian writes that despite an increasingly less hospitable business environment, foreign investors keep flocking to China.

Mann, James, *The China Fantasy: How Our Leaders Explain Away Chinese Repression, Viking,* **2007.**
A veteran China reporter files a passionate complaint that U.S. elites are misleading the American public to boost trade with a hostile regime.

Shirk, Susan, *China: Fragile Superpower: How China's Internal Politics Could Derail Its Peaceful Rise, Oxford University Press,* **2007.**
A former top State Department official says understanding the fears that drive China's leadership is essential to managing the U.S.-China relationship without military confrontation.

Tyler, Patrick, *A Great Wall: Six Presidents and China, Public Affairs,* **1999.**
An investigative reporter describes the struggles of six presidential administrations in shaping a sustainable China policy.

Articles

Mufson, Stephen, and John Pomfret, "There's a New Red Scare, but is China Really So Scary?" *The Washington Post,* **Feb. 28, 2010, www.washingtonpost.com/wp-dyn/content/article/2010/02/26/AR2010022602601.html.**
Two *Post* correspondents argue that America's reading of China is an insight into America's collective psyche.

Talbot, David, "China's Internet Paradox," *MIT Technology Review*, May-June 2010, www.technology review.com/web/25032/.
China's Internet usage is not as restricted as the regime would wish despite intense censorship efforts.

Wong, Edward, "Chinese Military to Extend its Naval Power," *The New York Times*, April 23, 2010, www .nytimes.com/2010/04/24/world/asia/24navy.html.
The Chinese military is building a deepwater navy to protect its oil tankers.

Xue, Litai, and Jiang Wenran, "Debate Sino-U.S. Ties," *China Daily*, April 20, 2010, www.chinadaily .net/opinion/2010-04/26/content_9772895_2.htm.
Two U.S.-based Chinese scholars debate the state of the U.S.-China relationship.

Ying, Ma, "China's Stubborn Anti-Democracy," *Hoover Institution Policy Review*, February-March 2007, www.hoover.org/publications/policyreview/ 5513661.html.
An American Enterprise Institute fellow examines why China's economic development hasn't led to democratization.

Reports and Studies

"Annual Report to Congress: Military Power of the People's Republic of China — 2009," *Office of the Secretary of Defense*, 2009, www.defense.gov/pubs/ pdfs/China_Military_Power_Report_2009.pdf.
The Pentagon's annual assessment of the People's Liberation Army invariably draws criticism from Beijing.

Godement, Francois, *et al.*, "No Rush to Marriage: China's Response to the G2," *China Analysis, European Council on Foreign Relations and the Asia Center of the Sciences Po*, June 2009, http://ecfr.3cdn.net/ d40ce525f765f638c4_bfm6ivg3l.pdf.
An East Asian historian and analyst says that while Europeans worry about an emerging U.S.-Chinese global duopoly, the Chinese are still examining their options.

Green, Michael J., *"U.S.-China Relations Under President Obama,"* July 14-15, 2009, Brookings Institution, http://iir.nccu.edu.tw/attachments/news/ modify/Green.pdf.
A scholar at the centrist think tank examines whether the administration's cooperative China policy will work.

Huang, Ping, *et al.*, "China-U.S. Relations Tending Towards Maturity," *Institute of American Studies, Chinese Academy of Social Sciences*, June 2009, http:// ias.cass.cn/en/show_project_ls.asp?id=1012.
Four analysts offer a Chinese perspective on relations between the United States and their country.

Lunn, Thomas, "Human Rights in China: Trends and Policy Implications," *Congressional Research Service*, Jan. 25, 2010, www.fas.org/sgp/crs/row/RL34729.pdf.
The nonpartisan research agency offers the most current periodic report to Congress on human rights in China.

For More Information

American Enterprise Institute, 1150 17th St., N.W., Washington, DC 20036; (202) 862-5800; www.aei.org. A nonpartisan think tank dedicated to research and education on government, politics, economics and social welfare.

Brookings Institution, 1775 Massachusetts Ave., N.W., Washington, DC 20036; (202) 797-6000; www.brookings .edu. Non-profit public policy institution working for a more cooperative international system.

Center for a New American Security, 1301 Pennsylvania Ave., N.W., Suite 403, Washington, DC 20004; (202) 457-9400; www.cnas.org. An independent, nonpartisan think tank established in 2007 dedicated to developing strong, pragmatic and principled national security and defense policies that promote and protect American interests and values.

Center for Strategic and International Studies, 1800 K St., N.W., Washington, DC 20006; (202) 887-0200; www .csis.org. A nonpartisan think tank that provides strategic insights and policy solutions to decision-makers in government, international institutions, the private sector and civil society.

Center for U.S.-China Relations, Tsinghua University, Beijing, China 100084; (86-10) 62794360; www.chinausa.org .cn. First research institute specializing in U.S.-China relations established by a Chinese institute of higher education.

China Institute, 125 E. 65th St., New York, NY 10065; (212) 744-8181; www.chinainstitute.org. Promoting a better understanding of China through programs in education, culture and business.

China Institute of International Studies, 3 Toutiao, Taijichang, Beijing, China 100005; (86-10) 85119547; www .ciis.org.cn. Think tank and research institution arm of the Chinese Ministry of Foreign Affairs.

China-United States Exchange Foundation, 15/f Shun Ho Tower, 24-30 Ice House Street, Hong Kong; (852) 25232083; www.cusef.org.hk. Fostering dialogue between Chinese and U.S. individuals from the media, academic, think tank and business environments.

Confucius Institute, 0134 Holzapfel Hall, University of Maryland, College Park, MD 20742; (301) 405-0213; www.international.umd.edu/cim. One of more than 60 Chinese cultural institutes established on U.S. campuses by the Chinese government, offering language courses and cultural programs.

National Security Council, www.whitehouse.gov/administration/eop/nsc. The NSC is the president's principal forum for considering national security and foreign policy matters with his senior national security advisors and Cabinet officials.

Nottingham University China Policy Institute, International House, Jubilee Campus, Nottingham NG8 1B8, England, United Kingdom; (44-115) 8467769; www.nottingham.ac.uk/cpi. Think tank aimed at expanding knowledge and understanding of contemporary China.

Shanghai Institute for International Studies, 195-15 Tianlin Rd., Shanghai, China 200233; (86-21) 54614900; www.siis.org.cn. Research organization focusing on international politics, economy, security strategy and China's international relations.

U.S.-China Policy Foundation, 316 Pennsylvania Ave., S.E., Suites 201-203, Washington, DC 20003; (202) 547-8615; www.uscpf.org. Works to broaden awareness of China and U.S.-China relations within the Washington policy community.

11

Aiding Refugees

Should the U.N. Help More Displaced People?

John Felton

Residents struggle to maintain normalcy in Kenya's Eldoret camp, home to 14,000 Kenyans who fled their homes during post-election rioting in December 2007. But they are the lucky ones. Many of the world's 26 million internally displaced people (IDPs) receive no aid at all or live in crude huts made of sticks and plastic sheeting, without reliable access to food or clean water. The U.N. High Commissioner for Refugees provided aid to some 13.7 million IDPs in 2007.

From *CQ Global Researcher,*
March 2009

For more than two decades, the guerrilla group known as the Lord's Resistance Army (LRA) has been terrorizing villagers in Uganda — forcibly recruiting child soldiers and brutally attacking civilians. In recent years, the dreaded group has crossed the border into the Democratic Republic of Congo.

Last October, LRA marauders attacked Tambohe's village in northeastern Congo. They shot and killed her brother-in-law and two others, then torched the houses, even those with people inside.

Tambohe and her surviving family members — five adults and 10 children — fled into the forest, briefly returning five days later to bury the bodies after the raiders had left. The family then walked north for three days until they found safety in a village just across the border in southern Sudan, living with several hundred other Congolese displaced by the LRA.

"We have built a hut, and we live there," the 38-year-old Tambohe later told the medical aid group Doctors Without Borders. "The children sleep badly due to the mosquitoes and because we sleep on the ground. I sleep badly because I dream of the stench of burnt flesh. I dream they [the LRA] come and . . . take us to their camp."[1]

LRA violence is only one aspect of ongoing conflict in Congo that has killed 5 million people in the past decade and forced millions from their homes — including more than 400,000 last year, according to Human Rights Watch.[2]

Many, like Tambohe, fled their homes and crossed into another country, making them legally refugees. Under international law, she and her family should be able to remain in Sudan and receive

Most Displaced People Are in Africa and the Middle East

The U.N. High Commissioner for Refugees (UNHCR) monitors nearly 32 million people around the world who have been uprooted for a variety of reasons, including 25 million who fled their homes to escape war or conflict, mostly in Africa and the Middle East. Among those are 11 million refugees — those who have crossed borders and thus are protected by international law — and nearly 14 million internally displaced people (IDPs) who remain in their home countries. Some critics want the UNHCR to monitor and assist the world's other 12.3 million IDPs now being aided by other agencies.

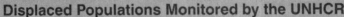

Displaced Populations Monitored by the UNHCR

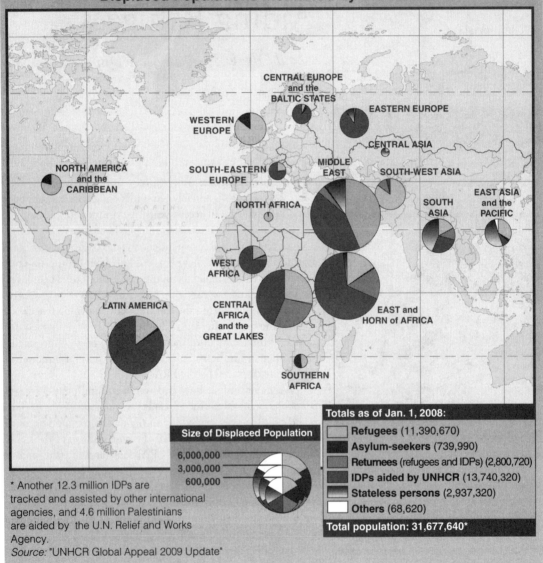

Totals as of Jan. 1, 2008:

- Refugees (11,390,670)
- Asylum-seekers (739,990)
- Returnees (refugees and IDPs) (2,800,720)
- IDPs aided by UNHCR (13,740,320)
- Stateless persons (2,937,320)
- Others (68,620)

Total population: 31,677,640*

Size of Displaced Population

6,000,000
3,000,000
600,000

* Another 12.3 million IDPs are tracked and assisted by other international agencies, and 4.6 million Palestinians are aided by the U.N. Relief and Works Agency.

Source: "UNHCR Global Appeal 2009 Update"

humanitarian aid, shelter and protection because they have a "well-founded fear" of persecution if they return home.[3]

If Tambohe had fled her home but remained in Congo, she would have been considered an "internally displaced person" (IDP), and the Congolese government would be legally responsible for aiding and protecting her. But in the Democratic Republic of the Congo and many other countries, international law is little more than a theory. The Kinshasa government is weak, and the army itself has been accused of abusing civilians.[4] So helping the Tambohes of the world falls primarily to the United Nations (U.N.) and nongovernmental aid agencies.

Today, there are more than 90 million refugees, displaced persons and disaster victims around the world. More than 40 million have fled conflict or violence, according to Antonio Guterres, U.N. High Commissioner for Refugees (UNHCR), who leads international efforts to aid the displaced.[5] Of those, about 16 million are refugees (including 4.6 million Palestinians) and 26 million are IDPs. (*See map, p. 284.*) Up to 50 million more people are victims of natural disaster, according to the U.N.'s Office

U.N. Serves About Half the World's Displaced

The U.N. High Commissioner for Refugees (UNHCR) has provided aid to an average of about 5.7 million of the globe's 11 million refugees each year — mostly in developing countries — over the past decade (dark gray lines). Meanwhile, the world's population of internally displaced persons (IDPs) has risen from 19 million in 1998 to 26 million in 2007. Individual governments are responsible for IDPs. But since 2005 the UNHCR has more than doubled the number of IDPs it serves each year — from 6.6 million in 2005 to 13.7 million in 2007 (light gray lines).

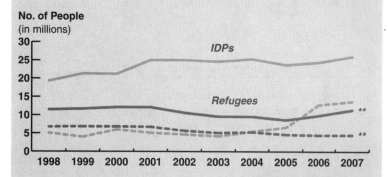

Total Refugees and IDPs vs. Those Receiving UNHCR Aid
(1998-2007)

* Does not include 4.6 million Palestinians assisted by the U.N. Relief and Works Agency in 2007.

** 2007 figures include people "in refugee-like situations" who were not included in previous years and excludes some 822,000 resettled refugees previously included in refugee statistics. Thus the 2007 data are not comparable with previous years.

Sources: 2007 U.N. High Commissioner for Refugees, Statistical Yearbook; "Global IDP Estimates (1990-2007)," Internal Displacement Monitoring Centre

for the Coordination of Humanitarian Affairs. In China's Sichuan Province, for example, many of the 5 million people who lost their homes last May in an earthquake remain homeless, and thousands of Americans are still displaced from Hurricane Katrina, which struck New Orleans in 2005.[6]

Millions of displaced people overseas live in sprawling camps or settlements established by governments or the United Nations, often in harsh desert or jungle environments. A large but unknown number of others, like Tambohe, find their own temporary

shelter — sometimes living with friends or relatives but more often building makeshift tents and huts or moving into crowded rental housing in urban slums.

Food insecurity — or even starvation — rank among the most serious consequences of displacement. In Kenya, for example, last year's post-election bloodshed caused so many farmers from key food-producing areas to flee their homes — leaving crops unplanted or unharvested — that an estimated 10 million Kenyans now face starvation.[7]

Sudan Hosts Most Displaced People

Of the millions of refugees and internally displaced persons (IDPs) monitored by the U.N. High Commissioner for Refugees, Sudan houses nearly 4 million — more than any other country. Four of the top 10 host countries are in Africa. Most refugees and IDPs come from Iraq, Afghanistan, Colombia and five African countries.

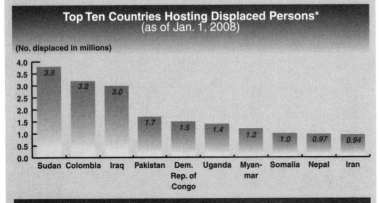

Top Ten Countries Hosting Displaced Persons*
(as of Jan. 1, 2008)

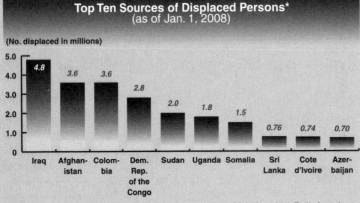

Top Ten Sources of Displaced Persons*
(as of Jan. 1, 2008)

* Does not include 4.6 million Palestinians assisted by the U.N. Relief and Works Agency.

Source: "UNHCR Global Appeal, 2009 Update," U.N. High Commissioner for Refugees, January 2009

Some experts predict the world increasingly will be forced to deal with massive displacements — potentially involving hundreds of millions of people — caused by natural disasters intensified by climate change. Elisabeth Rasmusson, secretary general of the Norwegian Refugee Council, which aids and advocates for the displaced, warned last December that the world faces a potential vicious cycle: As climate change degrades the environment, it triggers more civil conflicts as people fight for access to water and other resources, further damaging the environment — displacing more people at each stage.[8]

Long before concern about climate change, however, international agencies were overwhelmed by the magnitude of conflict-caused displacements, which have been rising dramatically over the past decade.[9] And while the UNHCR's budget has nearly doubled since 2000 — from under $1 billion to $1.8 billion this year — the agency struggles to protect and care for refugees and IDPs in 116 countries around the world. As of Jan. 1, 2008, the agency was aiding 4.5 million of the world's 11.4 million refugees and 13.7 million of the world's 26 million IDPs. (*See graph on p. 285.*) Because the UNHCR and other aid agencies often operate in or near conflict zones, the delivery of humanitarian relief can be dangerous and, at times, impossible. In the Darfur region of western Sudan, for example, aid groups repeatedly have been forced to halt aid shipments because of attacks on relief convoys.[10]

But the lack of security is only one of a daunting litany of challenges faced by the UNHCR and its dozens of partner agencies, including chronic shortages of funds and reliance on "emergency" appeals to wealthy countries, the hostility of local governments, bureaucratic turf battles and indifference among world leaders.

And, despite promises to the contrary, the U.N. Security Council often has been unable or unwilling to take effective action — such as in Rwanda in 1994 and in Darfur since 2003 — to halt horrific death and displacement tolls. In both situations, ill-equipped and undermanned U.N. peacekeepers were unable to prevent what some have called the genocidal slaughter of hundreds of thousands of people. Yet some critics question whether the U.N. is trying to do either too much or too

Refugees Fall into Eight Categories

When people flee their homes and seek aid, they can be assigned to one of eight classifications, each of which conveys unique legal rights or restrictions. For instance, some are entitled under international law to receive humanitarian aid, shelter and protection because they have a "well-founded fear" of persecution if they return home. Here are the key definitions under international law and commonly accepted practice of the various categories of people who are seeking, or in need of, assistance:

Asylum-seeker: A person who has applied (either individually or as part of a group) for legal refugee status under national and international laws. If refugee status is denied, the asylum-seeker must leave the country (and could face expulsion) unless he or she is given permission to stay on humanitarian grounds.

Internally displaced person (IDP): Someone who has been forced to flee his home due to armed conflict, generalized violence, human-rights violations or natural or man-made disasters but has not crossed an international border.

Migrants: In the absence of a universally accepted definition of a migrant, the International Organization on Migration says the term is "usually understood" to cover all cases in which "the decision to migrate is taken freely by the individual concerned for reasons of 'personal convenience' and without intervention of an external compelling factor. An "economic migrant" is someone who leaves his home country in search of better economic opportunities elsewhere.

Persons in "IDP-like" situations: This relatively new term developed by the U.N. High Commissioner for Refugees (UNHCR) describes "groups of persons who are inside their country of nationality or habitual residence and who face protection risks similar to those of IDPs, but who, for practical or other reasons, could not be reported as such." For example, the UNHCR has used the term to describe displaced people in Georgia (including former residents of the breakaway provinces of Abkhazia and South Ossetia) and Russia.

Persons in "refugee-like" situations: Another relatively recent term used by the UNHCR to describe people who are outside their country or territory of origin "who face protection risks similar to those of refugees, but for whom refugee status has, for practical or other reasons, not been ascertained." In many cases, these are refugees who have settled more or less permanently in another country on an informal basis. The largest single population in this group is the estimated 1.1 million Afghans living outside formal refugee camps in Pakistan.

Refugee: Under the 1951 Refugee Convention (as amended in 1967), a refugee is someone who, due to a "well-founded fear of being persecuted for reasons of race, religion, nationality, membership of a particular social group or political opinions," has left his home country and is unable or, owing to fear, "unwilling to avail himself of the protection of that country." A person becomes a refugee by meeting the standards of the Refugee Convention, even before being granted asylum (*see above*), which legally confirms his or her refugee status.

Returnee: A refugee or IDP who has returned to his home — or home country or region.

Stateless person: Anyone who is not recognized as a citizen of any country. Stateless persons lack national or international legal protections and cannot legally cross international borders because they don't have and cannot obtain a valid passport or other identity papers. Between 3 million and 12 million people worldwide are stateless; the wide range results from a lack of information in some countries and conflicting assessments about which groups actually are stateless.

Sources: "Glossary on Migration," International Migration Law, International Organization for Migration, Geneva, Switzerland, www .iom.int/jahia/webdav/site/myjahiasite/shared/shared/mainsite/ published_docs/serial_publications/Glossary_eng.pdf; and "Glossary," U.N. High Commissioner for Refugees, Geneva, Switzerland, www .unhcr.org/publ/PUBL/4922d4390.pdf

little, and others say international refugee law needs to be updated to take into account recent trends, such as the rapid increase in IDPs.

Those living in refugee and IDP camps have more immediate concerns, including overcrowded conditions; inadequate housing, food and medical care; and the refusal of local governments to allow them to work (or even to leave the camps). Negash, an Ethiopian who has lived in Kenya's sprawling Kakuma refugee camp for nearly four years, says aid officials often don't understand how their

IRIN/Manoocher Deghati (both)

Camp Life

Tents patched together from scraps of cloth house Afghans living in a camp near Kabul, Afghanistan (top). The government helps Afghans uprooted by decades of war, but many face overcrowded conditions and inadequate housing, food and medical care. Typically, internally displaced persons cannot work for wages in order to preserve jobs for local residents, so some set up their own small businesses inside the camps, such as a Kenyan seamstress at the Eldoret camp in Kenya (bottom).

decisions affect the camp's 50,000 residents every day. "There are people who work for agencies here that don't know what is happening in the camp," he says. "They live in their own compounds and don't really communicate with the refugees to find out what is happening to them."

The United Nations began reforming its humanitarian system in 2005, partly to address concerns about its inability to deliver timely and effective aid to internally displaced people. Jeff Crisp, director of policy and

evaluations for UNHCR, says the U.N.'s reforms are having "a solid and positive impact" on the lives of displaced people even though revamping such a large-scale system of delivering aid "clearly is a work in progress."

The rise in refugees and IDPs is the direct result of dozens of small wars between rebels and government soldiers during the last 50 years, particularly in Africa and Asia. Some have dragged on for decades, creating generations of displaced families. For instance, Sudan's 20-year-long civil war displaced 400,000 people, but at least 130,000 remain in neighboring countries, according to the U.N.[11] Colombia's ongoing civil conflict has displaced nearly 10 percent of the country's population.[12]

Even when the wars end, civilians often remain displaced because they fear returning home, their homes have been destroyed or they have become settled elsewhere. In Afghanistan, for example, more than 5 million Afghan refugees have returned home since the United States ousted the Taliban regime seven years ago, but some 3 million remain in neighboring Pakistan and Iran — a large number of whom probably never will go back.[13]

The Afghan refugees represent what experts call a "protracted situation," which is defined as when at least 25,000 people are displaced from their homes for five years or more. (*See sidebar, p. 298.*) More than 30 protracted situations exist around the world, according to Elizabeth Ferris, director of the Brookings-Bern Project on Internal Displacement, run by the Brookings Institution in Washington, D.C., and the University of Bern (Switzerland) School of Law.

As governments, international agencies and specialists in the field seek better ways to protect and aid refugees and internally displaced people, here are some of the questions being debated:

Is the U.N. meeting refugees' needs?

Since its founding in 1951, the UNHCR has been the world's frontline agency for aiding and protecting refugees. Working with other U.N. agencies and nongovernmental agencies — such as CARE and the International Federation of Red Cross and Red Crescent Societies — the Geneva, Switzerland-based agency is spending $1.8 billion this year to provide housing, food, medical care and protection for millions of refugees and displaced persons in 116 countries.[14] The agency also decides the legal status of refugees in 75 countries that can't, or won't, make those determinations themselves. In 2007, the UNHCR determined the status of 48,745 people.[15]

Both critics and its defenders, however, say the agency often falls short of its official mandate to safeguard "the rights and well-being of refugees."[16] Barbara Harrell-Bond, the founder and former director of the Refugee Studies Center at Oxford University and a harsh critic of the UNHCR, says one of her biggest concerns is how aid programs are funded.

"The funds . . . always come from emergency budgets and are allocated to UNHCR by governments at their discretion," she says. As a result, agency programs are "at the mercy of the whims of international politics."

If world leaders become fixated on a particular crisis that is making headlines in Western countries — such as the situation in Sudan's Darfur region — refugees elsewhere suffer, Harrell-Bond says. In addition, education and job training programs designed to help refugees lead dignified lives once they leave the camps are considered "development" programs, she says, which "come from a completely different budget . . . and never the twain shall meet."

Moreover, local governments rarely receive international aid for hosting refugees and usually are anxious for refugees to go home, she says, so they have little incentive to improve camp conditions. As a consequence, refugees are "just warehoused" in camps for years and years. Furthermore, she adds, the UNHCR and its partner agencies routinely deny refugees' basic rights, including the right to leave the camps. Most host governments want refugees to be contained in camps, and the U.N. complies "by putting them in what amounts to gigantic cages," Harrell-Bond says.

In her 2005 book, *Rights in Exile: Janus Faced Humanitarianism*, Harrell-Bond and a co-author argue that "the rights of refugees cannot be protected in camps and settlements." They harshly criticize the UNHCR for not protecting refugees' rights, based on extensive research into the treatment of Kenyan and Ugandan refugees during the late 1990s — treatment the authors say continues today in many refugee camps.

For instance, refugees usually are not allowed to leave the camps and are not allowed to work. Harrell-Bond says the UNHCR should push governments harder to accept refugees into the local community. "Refugees can contribute to the societies where they have taken refuge and not simply live on handouts from the U.N.," she

Most Refugees Flee to Neighboring Countries

Contrary to the perception that refugees are flooding into developed countries in Europe and other regions, most find asylum in neighboring countries and remain there. Only between 10 percent and 17 percent leave the countries where they were granted asylum.

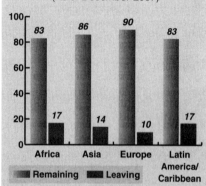

Refugees Remaining in or Leaving Their Asylum Regions
(As of December 2007)

Source: "2007 Global Trends: Refugees, Asylum-seekers, Returnees, Internally Displaced and Stateless Persons," U.N. High Commissioner for Refugees, June 2008

says, citing examples in Uganda and Zambia where so-called "local integration" has worked.

UNHCR Policy Director Crisp acknowledges the agency sometimes fails to meet refugees' needs but says decisions to "warehouse" refugees are made by the host countries. "In many cases, refugees are admitted to countries on strict condition that they be accommodated in camps and provided with their basic needs by UNHCR and other agencies," he says. UNHCR tries to get governments to improve refugees' situations, "but this is not always possible."

Despite such constraints, Crisp says the UNHCR is trying new approaches, particularly for those trapped in

Chaos in Somalia Puts Nation at Risk

Humanitarian aid feeds nearly half the population

Mohamed Abdi, his wife, and five children fled the never-ending violence in Somalia's capital city of Mogadishu last October, finding safety — but not much more — in the breakaway region of Somaliland to the north. The trip took nine days, and all along the way they feared being attacked by the opposing sides in the most recent round of conflict in Somalia.

Once they reached Somaliland, Abdi and his family found very little in the way of services, but the local government welcomed them as refugees. "We don't have much, and we depend on the kindness of these people; some days we eat, some we don't," he told the United Nations' IRIN news service in October. "But at least we have peace and security. That is what we want and the chance to make a living for our families without being afraid of being killed."[1]

Displaced people like Abdi never have it easy, often living in crude shelters and on starvation rations. But the situation is especially grave in Somalia — the only country in the world that for nearly two decades has been without even a functioning government — where a fatal combination of internal conflict and natural disaster has generated hundreds of thousands of refugees, migrants and internally displaced people (IDPs).

Ever since the last real government — a harsh dictatorship — was overthrown in 1991, hundreds of thousands of refugees settled in Kenya and other neighboring countries. Thousands of others have crossed the dangerous Gulf of Aden to equally impoverished Yemen.

Meanwhile, an estimated 1.3 million Somalis have become IDPs — displaced but living within their own country.[2] Most had fled Mogadishu, decimated by years of fighting among warlords, rebel groups, failed temporary governments and the Ethiopian army, which invaded in late 2006 and withdrew in January.

But IDPs escaping violence are not the only Somalis suffering. The U.N. Food and Agriculture Organization reported in October 2008 that 3.2 million people — 43 percent of the population — regularly need humanitarian assistance to survive.[3] While armed conflict has created most of the dislocations among Somalis, frequent droughts and floods have also caused recurrent famines that sent rural families fleeing to urban areas, often to be displaced by fighting.

Waves of conflict and displacement have swept over Somalia ever since the military dictatorship of Major General Mohamed Siad Barre was pushed from power in 1991. The most severe recent displacement occurred in August 2007, just eight months after Ethiopia invaded Somalia to oust a short-lived Islamist regime. Some 400,000 people were displaced by fighting in Mogadishu; most of them ended up in one of 200 camps that cropped up along a nine-mile stretch of the main road outside of the capital — "the most congested IDP nexus in the world," according to a refugee official.[4]

The U.N. High Commissioner for Refugees (UNHCR) and other aid groups provide limited food and medical aid to the camps, but little in the way of shelter. Patrick Duplat, an advocate for Refugees International who visited the camps twice in 2008, describes them as "mostly a sprawl of makeshift shelters — twigs and cloth, and sometimes plastic sheeting, whatever people are able to find."

Since Ethiopia withdrew its army in January, some 40,000 IDPs have returned to several Mogadishu neighborhoods, apparently with the intention of staying, according to the UNHCR.[5] Even so, continued fighting in the city has displaced an unknown number of others. The UNHCR said on Feb. 27 it is still discouraging IDPs from returning to what would be "ruined homes and livelihoods."[6]

In recent years nearly 500,000 people have fled Somalia to neighboring countries, but they have encountered daunting hazards along the way, including bandits, security forces protracted situations. For instance, in 2008 the high commissioner set deadlines for getting people out of five specific protracted situations:

- Afghan refugees in Iran and Pakistan;
- Bosnian and Croatian refugees in Serbia;
- Eritrean refugees in eastern Sudan;
- Burundians in Tanzania; and
- Members of Myanmar's Rohingya minority who fled to Bangladesh.[17]

More broadly, as part of its 2005 reform program, the U.N. established clear guidelines for which U.N. agency should provide services in specific situations.[18] The

demanding bribes and even possible death on the high seas.[7] Those who avoid violence and persecution may be eligible for refugee status and entitled to return home someday; others probably would be considered migrants because they are searching for economic opportunities overseas.

Thousands of Somalis have risked crossing the Gulf of Aden or the Red Sea by boat to reach Yemen. On Feb. 28, 45 Somalis drowned when their boat capsized as they were crossing the gulf. Those who arrive safely generally are given *de jure* refugee status, even

AFP/Getty Images/Radu Sigheti

An estimated 1.3 million people have been uprooted by the ongoing conflict in Somalia but are still living inside the country. Persistent violence, drought and flooding have created one of the world's longest ongoing humanitarian crises.

they had tried to register as refugees but had given up because of the lack of space in the camps. "After risking their lives to flee appalling violence in Somalia and make it to the relative safety of Kenya, they end up with nothing: no food, no shelter, and incredibly difficult access to water and health care," Simpson said.[12]

though many might be considered migrants because they never plan to return to their homes. About 82,000 Somalis were registered as refugees in Yemen in late 2008, but the UNHCR said the total could be closer to 150,000.[8]

Most Somali refugees, however, have fled into neighboring Kenya, even though it closed its borders to Somalis in 2007. According to the U.N., some 250,000 Somali refugees are in Kenya, including at least 45,000 who entered in 2008.[9]

At the border, would-be refugees often set out on foot to the U.N.'s official transit camps at Dadaab, 50 miles inside Kenya, frequently traveling at night to evade Kenyan police. As of late January the camps held 244,127 people — nearly triple their capacity. "Trying to squeeze 200,000-plus people into an area intended for 90,000 is inviting trouble," said Craig Johnstone, deputy U.N. high commissioner for refugees, after visiting on Feb. 5.[10] The UNHCR has been trying to raise $92 million from international donors to build two new camps for 60,000 more refugees.[11]

Human Rights Watch researcher Gerry Simpson, who visited the camps in late 2008, said many people told him

[1] "Fleeing from the frying pan into the fire," IRIN news service, Oct. 29, 2008, www.irinnews.org/Report .aspx?ReportId=81164.

[2] "Displaced Populations Report," U.N. Office for the Coordination of Humanitarian Affairs, Regional Office for Central and East Africa, July-December 2008, p. 5.

[3] "Poor rains intensify human suffering and deprivation — report," IRIN news service, Oct. 17, 2008, www.irinnews.org/Report .aspx?ReportId=80971.

[4] "Somalia: To Move Beyond the Failed State," International Crisis Group, Dec. 23, 2008, pp. 12, 18.

[5] "Thousands of Somalis Return to Mogadishu Despite Renewed Fighting," U.N. High Commissioner for Refugees, Feb. 27, 2009, www.unhcr.org/news/NEWS/49a7d8bb2.html.

[6] *Ibid.*

[7] "Somalia Complex Emergency: Situation Report," Jan. 15, 2009, U.S. Agency for International Development, www.usaid.gov/our_work/ humanitarian_assistance/disaster_assistance/countries/somalia/ template/fs_sr/fy2009/somalia _ce_sr04_01-15-2009.pdf.

[8] "2009 Global Update for Yemen," U.N. High Commissioner for Refugees, p. 1, www.unhcr.org/publ/PUBL/4922d4240.pdf.

[9] "Displaced Populations Report," *op. cit.*, p. 6.

[10] "Camp resources stretched by influx of Somali refugees," IRIN news service, Feb. 6, 2009, www.irinnews.org/Report.spx?ReportId=82792.

[11] "Somali refugees suffer as Dadaab camp populations swell to 230,000," UNHCR, www.unhcr.org/news/NEWS/4950ef401.html.

[12] "Kenya: Protect Somali Refugees. Government and Donors Should Urgently Address Refugee Crisis," Human Rights Watch, Nov. 13, 2008, www.hrw.org/en/news/2008/11/13/kenya-protect-somali-refugees.

so-called cluster approach made the UNHCR responsible for managing camps for IDPs displaced by natural disasters and providing emergency shelter and protection for IDPs displaced by conflict.[19]

A 2007 evaluation found the new approach had improved humanitarian responses in Chad, the Democratic Republic of the Congo, Somalia and

Uganda.[20] Ramesh Rajasingham, head of the Displacement and Protection Support Section for the U.N.'s humanitarian affairs office, says giving UNHCR a "clear leadership" role in managing displacement camps and emergency shelters has fostered "an improved IDP response."

But some non-U.N. experts say the bureaucratic changes have produced only modest benefits. Implementation has

Most Funds Go to Africa, Come From U.S.

More than one-third of U.N. refugee aid in 2009 will go to programs in Africa, more than any other region. In 2007, the United States contributed nearly one-third of the funds for the Office of the U.N. High Commissioner for Refugees (UNHCR) — four times more than No. 2-donor Japan.

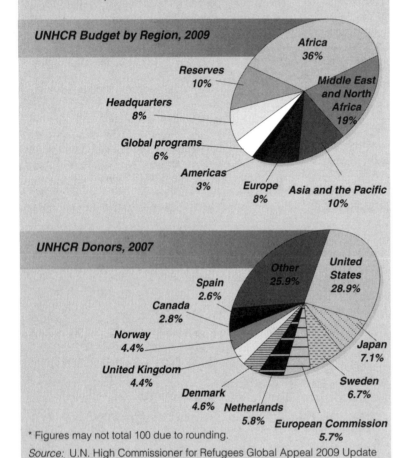

UNHCR Budget by Region, 2009

- Africa 36%
- Middle East and North Africa 19%
- Asia and the Pacific 10%
- Europe 8%
- Americas 3%
- Global programs 6%
- Headquarters 8%
- Reserves 10%

UNHCR Donors, 2007

- United States 28.9%
- Other 25.9%
- Spain 2.6%
- Canada 2.8%
- Norway 4.4%
- United Kingdom 4.4%
- Denmark 4.6%
- Netherlands 5.8%
- European Commission 5.7%
- Sweden 6.7%
- Japan 7.1%

* Figures may not total 100 due to rounding.

Source: U.N. High Commissioner for Refugees Global Appeal 2009 Update

been "half-hearted," especially in protecting IDPs, says Roberta Cohen, a senior fellow at the Brookings Institution and prominent IDP advocate. The UNHCR is not "playing the robust leadership role" she had hoped for in protecting IDPs.

Likewise, Joel Charny, vice president for policy at Refugees International, says the UNHCR's protection of IDPs remains "problematic." Ferris, Cohen's successor at the Brookings-Bern Project on Displacement,

recommends a rewards structure that would give agencies and individuals an incentive to better aid and protect displaced persons.

"Agencies need to internalize their work with IDPs and not see it as something separate from their missions or a burden they have to carry," she says.

James Milner, a refugee policy analyst at Carleton University in Ottawa, Ontario, Canada, and former UNHCR consultant, says the agency "does a good job in some places and a bad job in some places." While it has saved millions of lives during civil wars, the agency also ends up "warehousing" refugees for long periods, he says, causing them to abandon hope for better lives and become totally dependent on aid.

Like Harrell-Bond, Milner — who coauthored a 2008 book sympathetic to the agency's successes and failures — traces most of UNHCR's problems to its funding procedures. In effect, he says, industrialized countries that provide the bulk of UNHCR's money "earmark" where they want the money to go.[21]

"The United States, for example, gives funding to emergencies it considers important" but gives less to other situations, Milner says. "When I worked in Cameroon, each October we simply ran out of funding to provide health care for nursing mothers, because that was not a priority for the people in Washington. You can criticize UNHCR for not being more aggressive in some of these situations, but when you recognize the constraints placed on UNHCR, it places the challenges in a broader context."

Should the Refugee Convention be updated?

The 1951 Convention Relating to the Status of Refugees — known as the Refugee Convention — is the basic underpinning of refugee law. Created to protect European refugees during and after World War II, the treaty was amended in 1967 to apply worldwide.

The treaty grants "asylum" to refugees, or groups of them, who can demonstrate a "well-founded fear of being persecuted" because of race, nationality, religion or political beliefs. Those who flee their country because of such a fear are considered refugees. The process of demonstrating that fear and seeking permission to stay in the country of refuge is called seeking asylum. However, in many places — including the United States — asylum seekers may be imprisoned for months or even years while their cases are reviewed. Once asylum is granted, refugees can stay in the host country until it is safe to return home. Refugees who are denied asylum often are deported, usually back to their home countries.

Even with the 1967 amendment, the convention does not apply to the vast majority of people who flee from their homes. For example, IDPs do not have legal protection because they do not cross international borders, nor do those who flee across borders to escape natural disasters.[22] Being covered by the treaty might have little significance for people forced from their homes by violent groups like the Lord's Resistance Army. Even so, some advocates say applying the treaty to IDPs might, in some cases, pressure the governments involved to take better care of their citizens.

The treaty has critics across the ideological spectrum. Some refugee advocates, including Harrell-Bond, complain that it lacks universal standards for granting asylum, so Western countries, in particular, "are free to turn away asylum-seekers on no basis whatsoever."

Some Western officials say the treaty is being misused by "economic migrants" — would-be immigrants from poor countries simply seeking a better life — who claim to be refugees but do not qualify for asylum on the basis of a fear of persecution.

The treaty "is no longer working as its framers intended," then British Home Secretary Jack Straw said in 2001, citing the large increase in displaced people worldwide. "Too much effort and resources are being expended on dealing with unfounded claims for asylum, and not enough on helping those in need of protection."[23] He called for "radical thinking" on a better way to determine who is a refugee and who is not.

Despite such concerns, many experts say the convention will not be amended or updated any time soon. The U.N.

AP Photo/Eranga Jayawardena

More than 250,000 Sri Lankans have been forced from their homes, often repeatedly, in the latest — and possibly final — round of the 26-year war between government forces and separatist Tamil Tiger guerrillas. Above, internally displaced Tamil civilians wait to enter a government shelter near Colombo.

treaty-making process is cumbersome and takes years to complete. Moreover, global interest in new treaties has dwindled in recent years, and even IDP advocates aren't willing to risk having the treaty watered down instead of strengthened.

Carleton University's Milner notes the current treaty was negotiated shortly after World War II, "when notions of human justice were quite powerful because of what happened during the war, particularly in Nazi Germany." Nearly six decades later, Western countries — the desired destination for many refugees — are increasingly reluctant to open their borders. "If we reopened the Refugee Convention, we likely would see a race to the lowest common denominator — protecting borders — rather than refugees," Milner says. "That's a risk I'm not willing to take."

Khalid Koser, an analyst specializing in refugee affairs at the Geneva Center for Security Policy, agrees. "At least the current convention has 150-odd signatories, most of whom abide by it," Koser says.

The UNHCR has expressed similar concerns. In a recent paper exploring whether those fleeing natural disasters should be given legal status under the treaty, the agency warned that any attempt to modify the convention could lower refugee-protection standards "and even undermine the international refugee-protection regime altogether."[24]

Meanwhile, Europe is engaged in a spirited debate over implementation of the treaty; since 2001 the European Union (EU) has been developing a common system for granting asylum among its 27 member countries. The European Pact on Immigration and Asylum, adopted by EU leaders on Oct. 16, 2008, promises that EU countries will speed up asylum determinations, eliminating delays that often stretch into months or years.[25] Refugee rights advocates, however, worry the EU is trying to close its doors to legitimate refugees, not just economic migrants who are not entitled to asylum under the treaty.

At Human Rights Watch, refugee policy Director Bill Frelick says the new European pact also does little to relieve unequal burden-sharing. Most migrants and refugees from Africa and the Middle East enter Europe through the poorest countries in southeastern Europe, which have been rejecting refugees at very high rates. For instance, since 2004 Greece has granted asylum to fewer than 1 percent of the refugees from Iraq, Afghanistan and other countries, according to the European Council on Refugees and Exiles, a coalition of 69 nongovernmental organizations.[26] By contrast, some other European countries, particularly in Scandinavia, accept upwards of 90 percent of asylum-seekers, Frelick notes.

"There has been an utter failure to share the refugee burdens," Frelick says. "The richer countries have done an effective job of deflecting the burden off onto the poor countries, which are responding by turning people away, even those who are legitimate refugees."

Should the United States admit more Iraqi refugees?

Fearing that some could be terrorists, the United States has been slow to accept Iraqis who have fled to neighboring countries — notably Syria and Jordan — since the U.S. invasion in 2003.

Through the middle of 2008, the Bush administration accepted only about 10,000 Iraqi refugees out of the 1-2 million who have fled, according to Refugees International and other nongovernmental organizations.[27] But under pressure from Congress and advocacy groups, it stepped up Iraqi admissions last year and admitted more than 13,800 Iraqis as permanent residents — slightly more than the administration's 12,000 annual goal for fiscal 2008, which ended on Oct. 1. The administration's 2009 goal is 17,000 Iraqi admissions.[28]

Several major refugee and human-rights groups want the U.S. quota raised to 105,000 Iraqis in 2009. Among the Iraqi refugees in Syria and Jordan are thousands who worked directly with the U.S. military and other government agencies, American contractors and the news media. Some served as translators or even intelligence operatives, while others filled jobs such as drivers and cooks.

"Their stay in neighboring states remains extremely precarious, and many live in fear of being forcibly returned to Iraq, where they face death threats and further persecution," said a joint statement by Refugees International and a dozen other organizations on July 31, 2008. Helping these Iraqis resettle in the United States "will demonstrate America's dedication to protecting the most vulnerable and our commitment to peace and security in the region."[29]

The U.S. Department of Homeland Security said in September it was "committed to streamlining the process for admitting Iraqi refugees to the U.S. while ensuring the highest level of security."[30] However, the Obama administration has not announced plans for a dramatic increase in admissions. A State Department spokesman said in early February a decision was pending.

A report released in January by the Center for American Progress, a liberal think tank in Washington, D.C., said 30,000 to 100,000 Iraqis have been "affiliated" with the United States in one way or another during the war, and many would be "in imminent danger" of assassination if they returned home.[31]

The group advocates bringing up to 25,000 of those Iraqis and their families to the United States over the next five years. Natalie Ondiak, lead author of the proposal, says the United States "has a moral obligation to the Iraqis who have worked for the government, were loyal to us and now fear for their lives because of the stigma of having been associated with the United States."

However, Ann Corcoran — a Maryland blogger who runs the Refugee Resettlement Watch blog — is a vocal critic of such proposals. She cites cases in which church groups and other agencies bring refugees to the United States but fail to help them adjust to their new lives.

"These organizations are not taking very good care of the refugees who are already here, and they say they don't have the resources to do the job," she says. "So, if we are talking about another 25,000 or 100,000 refugees, where do they think these people will be cared for? Who is going to make sure they have housing and jobs and education for their children? It's just insane."[32]

A better alternative, she says "is to keep them in the region, to keep them comfortable and proceeding with their lives in the Middle East until the situation in Iraq is safe enough for them to return."

Congress in 2006 created a program to speed up admissions for up to 500 Iraqi and Afghan translators per year. In 2008 Congress added another program allowing up to 5,000 Iraqis who worked in various capacities for the U.S. government or contractors to enter the United States in each of the five fiscal years, beginning in 2008. However, Ondiak says only about 600 translators gained admission in 2008.

BACKGROUND

Refugee Rights and Needs

Although the forced displacement of people from their homes is as old as human history, the idea that society has a moral obligation to come to their aid is relatively new.

After World War I, the newly formed League of Nations created the post of High Commissioner for Refugees but gave the office little authority and few resources. The league (the forerunner of the U.N.) also adopted two treaties in the 1930s offering limited legal protection to refugees, but only a handful of countries ratified them.[33]

The displacement of millions of people during World War II finally brought significant action on refugees. As the war was winding down, the United States and its allies created the United Nations Relief and Rehabilitation Agency, which gave emergency aid to 7 million displaced people. After the war, a successor organization, the International Refugee Organization, helped some 1 million dislocated Europeans find new homes.[34]

The modern era of international aid to refugees began in 1950-51, when the United Nations created the office of the U.N. High Commissioner for Refugees and held

a special conference in Geneva to draft the treaty that became known as the Refugee Convention. Both the UNHCR and the treaty were aimed at aiding European war refugees or those who fled Eastern Europe after the Soviet Union imposed communist rule across the region. In fact, the treaty applied only to those who had become refugees before Jan. 1, 1951, and the text made clear the drafters had Europeans in mind. Moreover, the U.N. General Assembly gave the UNHCR only a three-year mandate, assuming the refugee problem would be quickly solved.[35]

In 1949, before the UNHCR started work, the U.N. Relief and Works Agency for Palestine Refugees in the Near East (known as UNRWA) was created to assist the 700,000 Palestinians who fled or were driven from their homes in what is now Israel during the 1948 Arab-Israeli war.[36] The UNRWA also was considered short-lived. But nearly 60 years later the ultimate status of the Palestinians remains unresolved, and the UNRWA is still providing food, medical care and other aid to a Palestinian population that has grown to 4.6 million. About 1.4 million Palestinians live in UNRWA camps in Jordan, Lebanon, Syria, the West Bank and Gaza Strip; the rest live on their own.[37]

Conflicts continued across the globe after World War II, some of them widely seen as proxy wars among governments and rebel groups backed by the two Cold War superpowers, the Soviet Union and the United States. In each case, dislocated civilians crossed international borders and created a new generation of refugees.

The U.N. General Assembly officially recognized the new refugee trend in 1967, adopting an amendment, or protocol, to the refugee convention. The Protocol Relating to the Status of Refugees dropped the pre-1951 limitation, giving legal protection to refugees worldwide, not just in Europe.[38] The convention and its protocol are now among the most widely adopted U.N. treaties; each has been ratified by 144 countries.[39]

The collapse of the Soviet Union in 1991 brought new hope for peace. But bloody sectarian conflicts in the Balkans and Africa's Great Lakes region shattered such dreams. Some conflicts dislocated enormous populations, but many people, for one reason or another, stayed in their own countries, where as IDPs they were not covered by the international refugee treaties.

In the 1990s international agencies and human-rights advocates began demanding aid and legal protections for

CHRONOLOGY

1940s-1950s *Newly created United Nations (U.N.) aids refugees after World War II ends.*

1949 U.N. Relief and Works Agency is established to aid Palestinians pushed from their homes during the 1949 Arab-Israeli war.

1950 Office of U.N. High Commissioner for Refugees (UNHCR) is created.

1951 Special U.N. conference adopts Convention Relating to the Status of Refugees (the Refugee Convention) to protect those who fled their countries before Jan. 1, 1951, to escape persecution due to "race, religion, nationality or membership of a particular social group." Generally viewed as applying only to Europeans, the treaty goes into effect in 1954.

1960s-1980s *Cold War conflicts and upheavals create waves of new refugees.*

1967 U.N expands Refugee Convention to cover all refugees fleeing persecution as described in the treaty, not just Europeans who left their home countries before 1951.

1969 Organization of African Unity broadly defines a refugee in Africa as anyone who flees his country because of "external aggression, occupation, foreign domination or events seriously disturbing public order in either part or the whole of his country of origin."

1984 The Colloquium on the International Protection of Refugees in Central America, Mexico and Panama adopts the Cartagena Declaration, defining refugees as anyone fleeing their country because their "lives, safety or freedom" are threatened by "generalized violence, foreign aggression, internal conflicts, massive violation of human rights or other circumstances." Although not official policy, many regional governments adopt the declaration.

1990s-2000s *New wave of civil conflicts forces policy makers to pay more attention to the needs of people displaced within their own borders.*

1992-1995 Civil conflicts in the former Yugoslavia displace several hundred thousand people.

1994 Genocidal rampage in Rwanda kills 800,000 Hutus and Tutsis; hundreds of thousands of others flee their homes, many into neighboring countries.

1997 Government-backed rebels oust longtime dictator Mobutu Sese Seko of Zaire (later the Democratic Republic of the Congo), triggering years of civil war in Africa's Great Lakes region; an estimated 5 million people die, and thousands are displaced during fighting that continues today.

1998 The Guiding Principles on Internal Displacement establish rules for aiding and protecting internally displaced persons (IDPs); the guidelines eventually are incorporated into U.N procedures but are not legally binding.

2002 About 2 million Afghan refugees return home (mostly from Pakistan and Iran) after a U.S.-led invasion topples the Taliban government. Some 6 million had fled during three decades of war — the largest number of refugees generated by any conflict since World War II.

2004 In a landmark decision, Colombia's Constitutional Court orders the government to increase aid to about 2 million people displaced by conflict.

2005 U.N. adopts "responsibility to protect" doctrine, which holds every government responsible for protecting the rights of its citizens and says the international community has a responsibility to intervene if a government abuses its own citizens. . . . U.N. gives UNHCR more responsibility for helping IDPs.

2008 U.N. launches a year-long publicity campaign to focus international attention on the needs of IDPs. . . . UNHCR starts a campaign to help end long-term displacements of those forced from their homes in Afghanistan, the Balkans, Burundi, Eritrea and Myanmar.

2009 African Union is scheduled in April to adopt a treaty recognizing the rights of internally displaced people, based on the 1998 Guiding Principles.

these large groups. In 1992, U.N. Secretary-General Boutros Boutros-Ghali appointed Francis Deng, a former Sudanese diplomat, as the U.N.'s first special representative on internally displaced people.

Deng, who held the post until 2004, was largely responsible for drafting the Guiding Principles on Internal Displacement.[40] Although the document has never been put into international law, U.N. agencies and a dozen countries have incorporated its principles into their laws and policies. (*See box, p. 306.*)

However, says refugee specialist Koser at the Geneva Center for Security Policy, "there is very little political will to formalize [the principles] into a binding convention, and few states would ratify it."

Rising Displacements

U.N. officials and policy experts count more than four dozen countries — most in Africa and Asia — with significant populations displaced by civil wars or other violence. When the consequences of natural disasters are considered, however, the displacement problem becomes nearly universal. Thousands of Gulf Coast residents in the United States remain displaced by Hurricane Katrina in 2006, and millions in China's Sichuan Province are homeless nearly a year after a major earthquake.

Colombia has one of the world's largest IDP populations, and hundreds of thousands of people are still displaced in Chechnya and Georgia in the Caucuses and in Bosnia, Croatia, Kosovo and Serbia as a result of the Balkan wars. Thousands more have been displaced by ongoing conflict and instability in Somalia. (*See sidebar, p. 290.*)

Here are some of the displacements that are high on the international agenda:

Afghanistan — At least 6 million Afghans fled — mostly to Pakistan and Iran — between the Soviet Union's December 1979 invasion and the U.S. ousting of the Taliban government in late 2001. During periods of relative calm in the 1980s and '90s, hundreds of thousands of Afghan refugees returned home, but many fled again when fighting resumed.[41]

Shortly after a new Western-backed government took office in Kabul at the end of 2001, refugees began returning home in large numbers. Between 2002 and late 2008, about 5.6 million refugees returned, of whom nearly 4.4 million received UNHCR aid (the rest returned on their own).[42] Since 2007, thousands of refugees have returned because Pakistan closed some refugee camps, and Iran deported thousands of mostly undocumented Afghan men seeking work.[43]

By late 2008, the UNHCR estimated that about 2 million Afghan refugees were still in Pakistan and nearly 1 million in Iran.[44] Worried about its inability to provide housing, jobs and other services for returning refugees, the Afghan government in 2008 began discouraging large-scale returns. "We don't have the means to provide an encouraging environment for refugees to repatriate," Shir Mohammad Etibari, minister of refugees and returnees, said in September. The U.N. and other international agencies "only make promises but do little."[45]

Another 235,000 Afghans are displaced but still in Afghanistan. Some were forced to return to Afghanistan against their will, only to find that they had no place to live and could find no jobs. Among the most vulnerable are several thousand returnees who were forced out of Pakistan and now live at a camp in the Chemtala desert, about 15 miles west of Jalalabad. Last winter they struggled to survive in mud huts and tents provided by the UNHCR and the Norwegian Refugee Council. "I wish we hadn't left Pakistan," said elderly returnee Golam Shah. "Life was much better there."[46]

A similar complaint came from 18-year-old Wali, who grew up in Pakistan's Jalozai refugee village. Forced out last May, he now lives in a tent in Balkh Province in northern Afghanistan. "I didn't expect to face such problems or to end up in such a place," he said. "There is nothing here — no shelter, not enough water, no trees for firewood, no electricity and no work."[47]

Colombia — A long-running rebel insurgency and the government's aggressive, U.S.-backed war against narcotics cartels have created what the U.N. calls the worst humanitarian crisis in the Western Hemisphere. Up to half a million Colombians have fled to neighboring countries, and thousands have emigrated to the United States. At least 2.8 million mostly rural people are internally displaced in the nation of 45 million.[48]

Since the 1960s the military has brutally suppressed two leftist guerrilla groups claiming to be fighting for land reform and other social causes — the Revolutionary Armed Forces of Colombia (FARC) and the National Liberation Army (ELN). Right-wing paramilitary armies formed by major landowners and elements of the military aided the anti-insurgency campaign.

Millions Remain in Exile for Decades

"Whole generations of kids grow up in refugee camps."

Miljo and Milica Miljic grabbed their two children and fled Tuzla, Bosnia, in 1992, at the beginning of a nearly four-year civil war that tore their country apart. "We didn't take anything with us because we didn't have time," Miljo told a representative of the U.N. High Commissioner for Refugees (UNHCR) this past January. "We had to run for our lives. The only thing that comes to mind in such a situation is to save your children and your own life. You don't think about the photographs, about personal documents, clothes, whatever."[1]

The Miljics are among nearly 97,000 refugees from Bosnia and Croatia who have not returned to their homes, even though the war ended in late 1995. They are still in Serbia, where the refugee population has slowly dwindled down from more than 500,000 in 1996.[2]

The words "refugees" and "displaced persons" conjure up images of short-term emergencies: people fleeing their homes temporarily because of wars, hurricanes or earthquakes, only to return home a few weeks, or at most a few months, later. While many do return home once a crisis has passed, most refugees and internally displaced persons (IDPs) remain displaced long after the emergency is over.

In fact, refugees fleeing conflict end up staying away from their homes an average of 18 years, and many IDPs are displaced for comparable periods. James Milner, a refugee expert at Carleton University in Ottawa, Canada, says some situations last even longer: The Palestinians who fled Israel during the 1948-49 Arab-Israeli war have been in exile ever since.

In recent years experts have begun focusing on "protracted situations" involving refugees and IDPs displaced for at least five years, and numerous conferences have been held to discuss the problem of long-term displacements. U.N. High Commissioner Antonio Guterres said more than 30 situations around the world involve a total of about 6 million refugees who have been living in long-term exile.

"Many are effectively trapped in the camps and communities where they are accommodated," Guterres said. "Their home countries are caught in endless conflict or afflicted by political stalemate or human-rights violations, and most are not allowed to hold jobs, work the land where they live or integrate into the local communities."[3]

Most of the long-term displaced are children and youth, says Elizabeth Ferris, director of the Brookings-Bern Project on Internal Displacement. "You have whole generations of kids who grow up and live in refugee camps, where typically you have a breakdown of normal social institutions," she says.

From 11 million to 17 million people have been displaced for at least five years but are still living inside their own countries, Ferris says. "Unfortunately, the world has paid very little attention to these situations, which are allowed to fester for years and years," she says.

Aside from the Palestinians, perhaps the best-known protracted refugee situation involves the estimated 6 million people who have fled their homes during three decades of warfare in Afghanistan, which began with the Soviet Union's invasion in 1979. Most went to neighboring Iran or Pakistan, where they settled in formal camps or moved into cities. Millions of Afghan refugees returned home after the U.S. invasion in 2001, but nearly 3 million are still refugees.[4]

Many scholars and aid officials worry that another long-term refugee situation is developing among the 2 million or more Iraqis who have fled their homeland. Although the Baghdad government has encouraged some to return, the U.N. and private aid groups say it is still too unsafe, especially for Sunni Muslims or members of other minority groups.[5]

Other protracted refugee situations prioritized by the UNHCR include:

- **Myanmar/Bangladesh.** Some 200,000 Rohingya, a Muslim ethnic group in North Rakhine state in Myanmar, fled to neighboring Bangladesh in 1991 to escape persecution by the military junta in Myanmar. Thousands have since returned to Myanmar, but the majority remain in Bangladesh and are classified by the U.N. as "stateless" persons because Myanmar no longer considers them as citizens.[6]

- **Eritrea/Sudan.** Some 90,000 Eritreans are long-term refugees in eastern Sudan, many since the late 1960s when Eritrean rebels launched a 30-year-long war against Ethiopia. (Eritrea gained its independence in 1993, but the two countries fought another bloody war from 1998 until 2000.) Additional Eritrean refugees continue to arrive in Sudan, joined by refugees from Ethiopia and Somalia. Most live in camps and lack any rights or protections but have increasingly begun to move into Khartoum and other Sudanese cities, over the government's objection.[7]

- **The Balkans.** Like the Miljics, hundreds of thousands of people dislocated by war in the former Yugoslavia during the 1990s have not returned to their home regions. Some 200,000 refugees, mostly ethnic Serbs, became naturalized citizens in Serbia rather than return to Bosnia or Croatia, where Serbs are in the minority.[8]

- **Burundi/Tanzania.** Violent civil conflict in Burundi in 1972 forced thousands to flee into neighboring Tanzania, where the government created three settlements in central and western Tanzania and provided land and other services for them. In 2007, about 218,000 refugees were still in the settlements. Under an agreement that many experts consider historic, Burundi and Tanzania decided in 2008 to resolve the status of these so-called "old settlement" refugees from 1972. Tanzania agreed to grant citizenship to, and fully integrate into local communities, some 176,000 of the remaining refugees. Those wanting to return to Burundi were to be allowed to do so by September 2009.[9]

Protracted IDP Situations

Globally, about half of the estimated 26 million IDPs displaced by violence are stuck in protracted situations, according to Neill Wright, the UNHCR's senior coordinator for IDPs. And some who were forced from their homes by natural disasters also remain displaced after five years.

Both types of protracted situations exist in Kenya, where about 350,000 people have been displaced long-term by conflict, unresolved land disputes and natural disasters.[10] Post-election violence displaced another 500,000 Kenyans in late 2007 and early 2008, but about half of those had returned home by late 2008.[11]

Ferris, of the Brookings-Bern project, says at least three-dozen countries have long-term displacement situations, and people are still being displaced in about a dozen others, such as Colombia, the Democratic Republic of the Congo and Somalia. In most other countries, the fighting has ended, but thousands remain displaced because peace agreements were never negotiated or the IDPs there are afraid, or unwilling, to return to their homes for other reasons.

Experts say no single solution will solve the protracted-displacement problem. Even negotiating peace agreements does not guarantee that displaced people can or will return home.

But policy makers have identified several essential elements that would help create "durable solutions" for protracted situations. One element, they say, is recognizing that forcing or encouraging people to return to their original homes may not always be the best solution, particularly when people have been displaced for many years, and they no longer have reasons for returning home.

An alternative to repatriation is "local integration" — allowing displaced people to become part of the local communities where they have taken refuge. This route is often politically difficult because local communities usually don't

The U.N. Relief and Works Agency, which for 60 years has aided Palestinian refugees, was stretched thin during prolonged Israeli military strikes earlier this year. More than 1,000 Palestinians were killed and many homes were destroyed, such as this woman's house in the Jabalia refugee camp in northern Gaza.

AFP/Getty Images/Mohammed Abed

want to absorb large numbers of outsiders. Milner says he hopes Tanzania's willingness to accept Burundians displaced for nearly four decades as citizens will become a model for other countries.

"This creates a significant strategic opportunity for the international community to demonstrate that local integration can work," he says. "Now, the next step is for the donor community to meet its responsibilities to help countries, like Tanzania, that might be willing to resolve these situations."

The UNHCR also acknowledged in November 2008 that its policy of providing only short-term humanitarian aid to refugees in camps had failed to help them develop personal independence and job skills that would allow them to live on their own. Too often, a UNHCR report said, "refugees were left to live in camps indefinitely, often with restrictions placed on their rights, as well as their ability to support themselves by means of agriculture, trade or employment."[12]

Under the U.N.'s "humanitarian reform" program adopted in late 2005, the agency is changing its approach, says Jeff Crisp, director of UNHCR's policy and evaluation service.

[1] "The continuing struggle of Europe's forgotten refugees," U.N. High Commissioner for Refugees, Jan. 12, 2009, www.unhcr.org/news/NEWS/496b6ad12.html..

[2] *Ibid.*

[3] "Protracted Refugee Situations: High Commissioner's Initiative," U.N. High Commissioner for Refugees, December 2008, p. 2, www.unhcr.org/protect/PROTECTION/4937de6f2.pdf.

[4] "Protracted Refugee Situations: Revisiting The Problem," U.N. High Commissioner for Refugees, June 2, 2008, pp. 5-6, www.unhcr.org/excom/EXCOM/484514c12.pdf.

[5] "NGOs warn against encouraging large-scale refugee returns," IRIN news service, Nov. 3, 2008, www.irinnews.org/Report.aspx?ReportId=81258.

[6] "Protracted Refugee Situations: The High Commissioner's Initiative," *op. cit.*, pp. 9-11.

[7] *Ibid.*, p. 14.

[8] *Ibid.*, p. 32.

[9] *Ibid.*, pp. 25-29.

[10] "Frequently Asked Questions on IDPs," U.N. Office for the Coordination of Humanitarian Affairs, Dec. 4, 2008, p. 4.

[11] *Ibid.*, p. 2.

[12] "Protracted Refugee Situations: A discussion paper prepared for the High Commissioner's Dialogue on Protection Challenges," Nov. 20, 2008, p. 13, www.unhcr.org/protect/PROTECTION/492ad3782.pdf.

Colombia's long-running rebel insurgency and the government's aggressive, U.S.-backed war against narcotics cartels have created the worst humanitarian crisis in the Western Hemisphere, according to the U.N. This family living in a tent in a Bogotá park is among at least 2.8 million displaced Colombians.

Both the guerrillas and paramilitaries eventually became deeply involved in the drug trade, turning an ideological war over land reform and other social issues into a battle for control of illegal cocaine production. The government's war against cocaine — most of which is consumed in the United States — has been funded largely by Washington.

Colombia is now the hemisphere's major source of refugees, most of whom have fled to Ecuador and Venezuela; others sought refuge in Brazil, Panama and Costa Rica.[49] About 460,000 Colombians are in "refugee-like situations" — they've fled Colombia but are not officially considered refugees and receive little if any official aid.[50] The flow of refugees has worsened Colombia's relations with left-leaning Ecuador and Venezuela.

Colombia estimates it has 2.8 million registered IDPs — among the world's highest for an individual country.[51] But nongovernmental agencies say the real number is much higher. The Catholic Church-affiliated Consultancy for Human Rights and Displacement puts the number at more than 4.3 million.[52] Many displaced people do not register for fear of retaliation or being forced to return to unsafe areas. The displacement rate has escalated in recent years, according to both the government and private agencies: About 300,000 people were displaced in 2007, but 270,000 were displaced in just the first six months of 2008.[53]

Colombia's IDPs have received serious attention since the country's Constitutional Court in 2004 ordered the government to provide aid — one of the few instances where an activist court has significantly helped IDPs.

Andrea Lari, a senior advocate at Refugees International, says the government helps IDPs survive on a daily basis but does virtually nothing to enable them to escape from urban shantytowns. The government provides "too much social welfare and not enough . . . job training or education beyond primary schools — the help needed to sustain themselves where they now live," he says. Going home "is not a serious option" for most because they have lost their land and are afraid to return.

Democratic Republic of the Congo — Hundreds of thousands of civilians continue to suffer from fighting in the eastern provinces of Africa's second-largest country — a war that officially ended more than five years ago. At least 400,000 Congolese were displaced in 2008 and early this year by continuing violence, bringing the total displaced to about 1.25 million.[54]

Two major wars — involving five other African countries at one point — raged in Congo from 1997 until peace agreements hammered out in 2002-03 ended most of the fighting and led to elections in 2006. More than 5 million people may have died during the wars — the largest toll by far of any post-World War II conflict, according to the International Rescue Committee.[55]

Lingering conflicts still plague several areas, including North Kivu Province on the borders with Rwanda and Uganda. There, remnants of the Hutu extremist forces responsible for Rwanda's genocide in 1994 have battled a rebel force claiming to support the Congolese Tutsis, members of the same ethnic group targeted by the Hutus in the Rwandan genocide. Until recently, the Congolese army had not curbed either faction.

In January, however, the Congolese and Rwandan armies launched an unusual joint military operation targeting both the Hutu and Tutsi forces in North Kivu. And in a potential step toward peace, the Rwandan army on Jan. 22 arrested the self-styled Tutsi general Laurent Nkunda, whose rebels had wreaked havoc in the region.[56] The arrest — coming on the heels of a related international campaign against the Lord's Resistance Army — offered the first tangible hope in many years that the region's troubles might some day come to an end.[57]

Online Newspaper Fights for Refugees in Kenya

'We need to be able to help ourselves'

Problems with the water supply, inadequate health inspections of food suppliers, indifferent officials. Such issues would be the meat-and-potatoes of any local newspaper. But who draws attention to such concerns in a refugee camp as big as a mid-size city?

Most refugee camps have community organizations that present residents' concerns to camp officials, but they rarely receive wide attention locally. Since last December, however, the problems faced by the 50,000 refugees at the Kakuma camp in northwest Kenya have been exposed not only to local residents but to people around the world via the camp's Internet newspaper, *Kanere* (KAkuma NEws REflector).

The paper (http://kakuma.wordpress.com) is run by staff of volunteer journalists aided by Bethany Ojalehto, a 2008 Cornell University graduate who is studying the rights of refugees at the camp on a Fulbright research scholarship. She says several refugees interested in starting a newspaper approached her for help when she arrived at the camp last October, and she agreed because their interests and her research "blended seamlessly and have now been channeled into this project."

So far *Kanere* is published only in English, which is a common language for many of the camp's residents, who can read it at computer stations in several locations. The paper's editors say they hope to expand into other languages once they get more help.

Twenty-four-year-old Qabaata, one of the paper's editors, says he fled Ethiopia in 2003 after being targeted by government security forces for writing an article supporting a student strike. A journalism student at the time, he went with other students to Kakuma after being arrested and released by authorities in Addis Ababa, Ethiopia's capital. He is seeking asylum status from the UNHCR because he says he cannot return to Ethiopia. "It is not safe for me there," he says. He hopes to win a scholarship to finish his journalism studies but has no immediate prospects for attaining that goal.

Kakuma has one of the most diverse camp populations in Africa. Opened in 1992 to aid refugees from the long civil war in southern Sudan, Kakuma now houses about 25,000 Sudanese, 18,000 Somalis, 4,500 Ethiopians and 1,800 other Africans.[1] Since mid-2008 the U.N. High Commissioner for Refugees (UNHCR) has transferred thousands of Somali refugees to Kakuma from three over-crowded camps at Dadaab, Kenya, about 700 miles to the east. (*See Somalia box, p. 290.*)

Qabaata says *Kanere* provides a unique opportunity to share concerns across the camp's different ethnic and national communities and to voice grievances to camp officials. "The refugees here don't have access to the people who are governing them," he says. "They only have access through their community leaders, but even their leaders do not always have access."

Negash, another Ethiopian refugee who works on *Kanere*, notes that one crucial issue is water. All water for the camp comes from underground aquifers and is rationed at about 20 liters per refugee per day. And some refugees have to walk long distances to get it. The paper's first issue, in December 2008, pointed out that refugees in one section of the camp had recently gone without adequate water for three days while a broken pump was being fixed. Why is water rationed for refugees, the paper asked, while U.N. and other aid agencies' staff members living nearby "are given unlimited water?"

Kanere also deals with UNHCR budget cutbacks, long food-distribution lines, the lack of job opportunities, low pay for refugees compared to local Kenyans and the "poor performance" of the camp's 14 primary and two secondary schools.

Above all, say Qabaata and Negash, *Kanere* advocates on behalf of refugees' basic human rights. "As refugees, we are told we have rights, but in reality we have no rights here in the camp," Negash says. "We hope *Kanere* will empower the refugee community, help it to be self-reliant. As it is, the humanitarian community is just making us dependent, reliant on them. We need to be able to help ourselves."

---

[1] "Kenya: Population of Concern to UNHCR," November 2008, p. 6, www.unhcr.org/partners/PARTNERS/4951ef9d2.pdf.

Permanent Solutions Sought for the Displaced

Aid agencies turning away from short-term solutions

In the past, the U.N. High Commissioner for Refugees (UNHCR) and other aid agencies have focused primarily on short-term fixes — such as providing emergency food, medical care and other aid — for those displaced by war, conflict or natural disaster. They also generally assumed that displaced people wanted to return to their homes, and encouraging them to do so was easier than resettling them elsewhere.

But in recent years aid agencies have begun paying more attention to moving displaced people out of camps and makeshift shelters and back into normal lives.

Three so-called durable solutions have been proposed for refugees as well as internally displaced persons (IDPs), or those still living in their own countries:

- **Return or repatriation** — Returning either to their past residence or to their home neighborhood or region.
- **Local integration** — Settling permanently in the locality or country where the person has sought temporary refuge.
- **Resettlement elsewhere** — For refugees, moving to a willing third country; for IDPs, moving to a different part or region of their home countries.

In the absence of universally accepted standards for deciding when an IDP is no longer displaced, the Brookings-Bern Project on Internal Displacement in 2007 created a "Framework for Durable Solutions" for IDPs, which has been officially "welcomed" by the U.N.[1] It says IDPs' displacement should be considered ended when one of the three durable solutions occurs, and they "no longer have needs specifically related to their displacement." Although former IDPs may still have humanitarian needs, at this point "their needs are basically the same as other people in the local population, and it's the government's responsibility to help them," says project director Elizabeth Ferris.

In 2007, about 2 million IDPs and 731,000 refugees returned to their home countries, their actual homes or to their home regions, according to the UNHCR.[2] About half were in the Democratic Republic of the Congo, although conflict displaced another 500,000 Congolese that same year.[3] More than half of the returning refugees — some 374,000 — were Afghans.[4]

Barbara Harrell-Bond, a veteran advocate for refugees and leading critic of the UNHCR, faults the agency for continuing to focus on repatriation for refugees, because she says integration in asylum countries "often is the only solution." UNHCR officials, however, say local integration and resettlement are difficult because host countries are not inclined to accept refugees and displaced people on a permanent basis.

But resettlement efforts are occurring, albeit on a small scale, say the UNHCR and refugee advocacy groups. In 2007, the UNHCR recommended 99,000 refugees for resettlement in third countries, nearly double the previous year, but only 70,000 were able to resettle — less than 1 percent of the total refugees.[5] Historically, the United States has accepted more refugees than any other country; in 2006, the last year for which comparative figures are

Iraq — The 1991 Persian Gulf War and sectarian violence following the 2003 U.S. invasion of Iraq have swelled the ranks of displaced Iraqis to between 3 million and 5 million — out of a total population of around 28 million. Most have remained in the country but fled their home regions, usually to escape sectarian violence.[58]

Many of the Iraqi IDPs live with friends or relatives and receive government food rations. For those who cannot get rations, the World Food Program on Jan. 3 announced a one-year program to aid about 750,000 Iraqis inside Iraq and 360,000 in Syria.[59]

Many IDPs live in informal camps inside Iraq. The Iraqi government early in 2008 had announced an ambitious plan to build IDP housing, but falling oil prices have forced budget cuts that endanger the effort.[60] Then in late 2008 the government moved to close some of the camps by giving families one-time $4,250 stipends to return to their homes or find new places to live.[61] The UNHCR plans to help about 400,000 Iraqi IDPs this year.[62]

Some 300,000 displaced Iraqis have returned home, and nearly two-thirds of those still displaced want to return to their original home regions, according to a

available, the United States accepted 41,300 refugees — more than half of the 71,700 resettlements that occurred that year.[6]

Local integration sometimes occurs informally, particularly when displaced people are not confined to official camps or settlements. For instance, in Pakistan, many of the estimated 1.8 million remaining Afghan refugees have established new lives in Peshawar, Quetta and other cities. Many had been refugees for more than 20 years, and more than half were born outside Afghanistan; a substantial number were ethnic Pashtuns, which also is the dominant ethnic group in the border areas of Pakistan. As a result, remaining in Pakistan has been a natural solution for them.[7]

In contrast, official agreements allowing large numbers of refugees or IDPs to move permanently from camps into local communities are rare. An exception is Tanzania, where more than 200,000 Burundians have been refugees since 1972. Seeking to resolve a situation that had dragged on so long, and with U.N. help that included limited financial aid, Burundi and Tanzania agreed in 2007 that 172,000 refugees could remain in Tanzania as citizens, while 46,000 would return to Burundi. The agreement is expected to be implemented by late 2009.[8]

James Milner, of Canada's Carleton University, says Tanzania's willingness to accept long-term refugees as permanent refugees "creates a strategic opportunity for the

Afghan refugees who have just returned from Pakistan wait to register at a transition center in Kabul in June 2008. Aid agencies have begun focusing on moving displaced people out of camps and back into normal lives, often by returning them to their home countries.

international community to show that there are alternatives to warehousing refugees forever in camps."

The only missing element, he says, is a willingness by the major donor nations to put their money and diplomatic leverage to work to encourage other countries to follow Tanzania's example. "The United States is the hegemon in the global refugee regime," he says. "If the United States were to support more of this kind of action, eventually we could see real solutions for refugees."

---

[1] "When Displacement Ends: A Framework for Durable Solutions," Brookings-Bern Project on Internal Displacement, June 2007, www.brookings.edu/reports/2007/09displacementends.aspx.

[2] "Note on International Protection," U.N. High Commissioner for Refugees, June 2008, p. 2, www.unhcr.org/publ/PUBL/484807202.pdf.

[3] *Ibid.*, p. 15.

[4] *Ibid.*

[5] *Ibid.*, p. 17.

[6] "Global Trends for 2006: Refugees, Asylum-seekers, Returnees, Internally Displaced and Stateless Persons," U.N. High Commissioner for Refugees, June 2007, p. 8, www.unhcr.org/statistics/STATISTICS/4676a71d4.pdf.

[7] "Afghanistan — The Challenges of Sustaining Returns," U.N. High Commissioner for Refugees, www.unhcr.org/cgi-bin/texis/vtx/afghan?page=intro.

[8] "Protracted Refugee Situations: The High Commissioner's Initiative," U.N. High Commissioner for Refugees, December 2008, pp. 25-29, www.unhcr.org/protect/PROTECTION/4937de6f2.pdf.

---

survey released on Feb. 22 by the International Organization for Migration.[63]

Since 2003 at least 2 million Iraqis have fled to several neighboring countries: Syria (1.2 million), Jordan (450,000), the Gulf states (150,000), Iran (58,000), Lebanon (50,000) and Egypt (40,000).[64]

Some experts question the government estimates. Amelia Templeton, an analyst at Human Rights First, suggests only about 1 million Iraqi refugees are living in neighboring countries, based on school registrations and the number of refugees receiving UNHCR aid.

In contrast to many other refugee situations, nearly all of the Iraqi refugees live in or near major cities, such as Damascus, Syria, and Amman, Jordan, because Iraq's neighbors don't permit refugee camps. A high proportion of Iraqi refugees are lawyers, doctors, professors and other well-educated professionals.

National Public Radio journalist Deborah Amos tells the stories of Iraqi refugees in Syria and Lebanon in a soon-to-be-published book. She says many of the professionals belonged to the Sunni elite or Christian minority groups (such as Chaldeans), who for centuries were tolerated in

Iraq but suddenly were targeted with violence. Many have spent their life savings during the years in exile and now rely on U.N. handouts. As in much of the world, local governments will not allow the refugees to work, forcing some female refugees in Damascus to turn to prostitution to support their families, Amos writes.

Myanmar — Cyclone Nargis struck on May 2, 2008, killing 140,000 people — mostly by drowning — and forcing up to 800,000 from their homes.[65] Humanitarian agencies pressed the government to allow international aid workers into the vast Irrawaddy Delta, but the secretive generals who run Myanmar resisted the appeals for several weeks until U.N. Secretary-General Ban Ki-moon finally persuaded the top general, Thwan Shwe, to accept outside aid.

Aid agencies and foreign governments donated emergency relief supplies and began helping rebuild homes and communities. But about 500,000 people remained displaced at year's end.[66] Many of those displaced by cyclone-caused floods have faced severe water shortages in recent months due to the recent onset of the dry season and water contamination caused by the cyclone.[67] Full recovery from the cyclone could take three to four years, a senior U.N. aid official said in January.[68]

Meanwhile, members of the Muslim Rohingya minority, from the northern state of Rakhine, are officially stateless. According to Amnesty International, thousands of Rohingyas flee Myanmar each year because of land confiscation, arbitrary taxation, forced eviction and denial of citizenship.[69] Since 1991, more than 250,000 have fled, mostly to neighboring Bangladesh, where the UNHCR runs two camps housing 28,000 refugees; another 200,000 unregistered Rohingyas live outside the camps.[70]

In early 2009, the Thai navy reportedly intercepted boats carrying hundreds of Rohingya trying to cross the Andaman Sea. The action generated international outrage after CNN published a photo purportedly showing armed forces towing refugee boats out to sea and leaving the occupants to die, but the Thai government denied the reports. Some were later rescued off the coasts of India and Indonesia, but many went missing.[71]

In early February actress and U.N. goodwill ambassador Angelina Jolie visited refugee camps in Thailand housing 110,000 Karen and Kareni ethnic refugees from Myanmar. She called on the Thai government to lift its

ban on refugees working outside the camps and asked the government to extend hospitality to the Rohingyas.[72]

Prime Minister Abhisit Vejjajiva had said earlier that Thailand would not build a camp for the Rohingyas and will continue to expel them. "They are not refugees," he said. "Our policy is to push them out of the country because they are illegal migrants."[73]

Leaders of the Association of Southeast Asian Nations agreed on March 2 to discuss the status of the Rohingyas at a mid-April summit in Bali. Malaysian Prime Minister, Abdullah Ahmad Badawi said the Rohingya problem "is a regional issue that needs to be resolved regionally."[74]

Sudan — Two major internal conflicts plus other conflicts in central and eastern Africa have displaced millions of Sudanese in the past three decades. At the beginning of 2009, more than 3.5 million were still displaced, including about 130,000 in neighboring countries. Sudan hosts more than 250,000 refugees from nearby countries.[75]

Sudan's two-decade civil war between the government in Khartoum and a separatist army in south Sudan ended with an uneasy peace in January 2005. More than 300,000 refugees who had fled the violence have returned to their home regions, but UNHCR has estimated that about 130,000 remain in Egypt, Ethiopia, Kenya and Uganda.[76] And more conflict could erupt if, as expected, the southerners vote in 2011 for full independence.

Elsewhere in Sudan, a series of inter-related conflicts between the Khartoum government and rebel groups in western Darfur have displaced about 2.7 million people and killed an estimated 300,000.[77] Although Darfur has generally faded from world headlines, the conflict continues, with about 1,000 people fleeing their homes every day.[78] Complicating the refugee crisis, 243,000 Darfuris have fled into Chad, while some 45,000 Chadians have crossed into Darfur to escape a related conflict.[79]

More than 200,000 other refugees also are in Sudan, mostly from Eritrea, having fled the long war between Eritrea and Ethiopia.[80]

CURRENT SITUATION

'Responsibility to Protect'

Since last fall, 26-year-old Kandiah and his family have moved eight times to avoid the long-running civil war

Should the U.N. High Commissioner for Refugees help more displaced people?

YES
Joel R. Charny
Vice President for Policy
Refugees International

NO
Guglielmo Verdirame
Professor, International Human Rights
and Refugee Law, Cambridge University

Co-author, Rights in Exile: Janus-Faced
Humanitarianism

Written for *CQ Global Researcher,* February 2009

Current efforts to help displaced populations do not reflect the fact that twice as many people displaced by conflict remain inside their own borders rather than crossing an international one, thus failing to become refugees protected under international law. With the U.N. High Commissioner for Refugees (UNHCR) focusing primarily on legal protection for refugees, the current system is outmoded. A bold solution is needed to prevent further unnecessary suffering.

Internally displaced people (IDPs) suffer when their governments don't aid and protect their own citizens. They also suffer from the lack of a dedicated international agency mandated to respond to their needs when their states fail. With IDP numbers growing, expanding the UNHCR's mandate to include IDPs is the best option available to fill this gap.

A dedicated agency would be more effective than the current system, characterized by the "cluster leadership" approach, under which international agencies provide help by sectors, such as health, water and sanitation and shelter. For example, in the 1990s the U.N. secretary-general mandated that UNHCR respond to the needs of IDPs displaced by the civil war in Sri Lanka. Over the years, the agency effectively fulfilled this responsibility with donor support, and the entire U.N. country team — as well as the Sri Lankan government — benefited from the clarity of knowing that the agency was in charge. Moreover, carrying out this exceptional mandate did not undermine either the UNHCR's work with refugees in the region or the right of Tamil Sri Lankans to seek asylum in southern India.

Giving one agency responsibility for an especially vulnerable population is more effective than patching together a response system with multiple independent agencies. Because the circumstances and needs of IDPs are so similar to those of refugees, and because UNHCR has a proven capacity to respond holistically to displacement, it is best suited to take on this responsibility.

Having a formal mandate for IDPs would triple UNHCR's caseload and pose an immense challenge. The agency already has difficulty fulfilling its current mandate and perpetually lacks sufficient funds. Taking the lead on internal displacement would require new thinking, more advocacy work with governments and flexible approaches to programming outside of camp settings. But the alternative is worse: Maintain the status quo and perpetuate the gap in protection and assistance for some of the world's most vulnerable people.

Written for *CQ Global Researcher,* February 2009

Forced displacement is a human tragedy even when it occurs within the boundaries of a state. But the test for deciding whether it would be appropriate for the U.N. High Commissioner for Refugees (UNHCR) to add internally displaced people (IDPs) to its current mandate on a permanent basis is not one of comparability of suffering. Rather, the proper test is whether UNHCR is the right institution for dealing with this problem. I think it is not, for several reasons.

First, crossing an international boundary continues to make a difference in today's world. By virtue of being outside their country of nationality, refugees are in a different position than the internally displaced.

Second, the international legal regime for refugees was established as an exception to the sovereign prerogatives enjoyed by states over admission and expulsion of aliens in their territory. While most refugees were the victims of a human-rights violation in their home country, the focus of the refugee legal regime is not on the responsibility of the country of nationality but on the obligations of the country where they take refuge. Because internally displaced persons are still inside their home countries, protecting their rights will require different strategies and methods.

Third, human-rights bodies, including the office of the U.N. High Commissioner for Refugees, are better-placed to deal with what are, in essence, violations of human rights against citizens.

Finally, the rationale for getting the UNHCR involved with IDPs is premised on a distinctly problematic view of the organization as a provider of humanitarian relief rather than as the international protector of refugees. UNHCR's work with refugees has already greatly suffered from the sidelining of the agency's role as legal protector: The warehousing of refugees in camps is just one example. It would not help the internally displaced if the UNHCR's involvement resulted in their being warehoused in camps, as refugees already are.

In a world where asylum is under serious threat, the real challenge for UNHCR is to rediscover its protection mandate, to act as the advocate of refugees and as the institutional overseer of the obligations of states under the 1951 Refugee Convention. It is a difficult enough task as it is.

Legal Protections for Displaced Populations

A 1951 treaty gives refugees the most protection

International law protects some — but not all — refugees who cross international borders, while the non-binding Guiding Principles on Internal Displacement cover internally displaced people (IDPs), or those forcibly displaced within their home countries.

Here are the main laws protecting refugees and IDPs:

1951 Refugee Convention

The Convention Relating to the Status of Refugees — the basic international treaty concerning refugees — was adopted by a United Nations conference on July 28, 1951, and became effective on April 22, 1954. It defines a refugee as someone who, "owing to well-founded fear of being persecuted for reasons of race, religion, nationality, membership of a particular social group or political opinion, is outside the country of his nationality and is unable or, owing to such fear, is unwilling to avail himself of the protection of that country; or who, not having a nationality and being outside the country of his former habitual residence as a result of such events, is unable or, owing to such fear, is unwilling to return to it."

Excluded are those who flee their countries because of generalized violence (such as a civil war) in which they are not specifically targeted, or those who flee because of natural disasters or for economic reasons, such as a collapsing economy. The convention also prohibits a host country from expelling or returning refugees against their will to a territory where they have a "well-founded" fear of persecution.

The 1967 Protocol

Because the 1951 convention applied only to people who became refugees before Jan. 1, 1951, it was widely considered to apply only to European refugees from World War II. To aid those displaced by subsequent events, the United Nations adopted a new treaty, known as a Protocol, which eliminated the pre-1951 limitation. It took effect on Oct. 4, 1967.[1]

As of October 2008, 144 countries were parties to both the convention and the Protocol, though the two groups are not identical.[2]

Regional Treaties

Two regional documents expanded refugee protections of the convention and Protocol to Africa, Mexico and Central America. The 1969 Convention Governing the Specific

between the Sri Lankan army and rebels known as the Tamil Tigers. By late February they had joined several dozen people sleeping on a classroom floor in Vavuniya, in northern Sri Lanka.

At one point, Kandiah (not his real name) and his family stayed in an area that was supposed to be safe for civilians. For more than a week, he said, "We stayed in the open air with scores of other families . . . but the shelling was intense. There was shelling every day. We barely escaped with our lives."[81]

Kandiah and his family are among more than 250,000 people forced from their homes, often repeatedly, in the latest — and possibly final — round of the 26-year war. Claiming to represent the ethnic Tamil minority, the Tigers have been fighting for independence in the eastern and northern portions of the island.

Although the conflict has been among the world's most violent, international pressure to end it has been modest, at best. The U.N. Security Council, for example, considered it an "internal" affair to be resolved by Sri Lankans themselves, not by the international community and has never even adopted a resolution about it. Norway took the most significant action, mediating a cease-fire in 2002 that lasted nearly three years.

The plight of people like Kandiah illustrates the international community's failure to follow through on promises world leaders made in September 2005. At a summit marking the U.N.'s 60th anniversary, world leaders adopted the "responsibility to protect" philosophy, which holds every government responsible for protecting its own citizens.[82] Moreover, if a government fails to protect its citizens, it cannot prevent the international community

Aspects of Refugee Problems in Africa — adopted by what is now the African Union — defined refugees in Africa, while the 1984 Cartagena Declaration on Refugees is an informal statement of principles drafted by legal experts from Mexico and Central America.[3]

Guiding Principles on Internal Displacement

The U.N. has never adopted a treaty specifically aimed at establishing legal rights for IDPs. However, in 1998 the organization endorsed a set of 30 nonbinding guidelines intended to heighten international awareness of the internally displaced and offer them more legal protection. Known as the Guiding Principles on Internal Displacement, they have been presented to the various U.N. bodies but never formally adopted.

Based on the Universal Declaration of Human Rights and other treaties and agreements, the principles provide legal and practical standards for aiding and protecting displaced people. For example, the first principle states that displaced persons should enjoy "the same rights and freedoms under international and domestic law as do other persons in their country. They shall not be discriminated against . . . on the ground that they are internally displaced."

Regional bodies (including the European Union and the Organization of American States) and numerous nongovernmental organizations have endorsed the principles, and the UNHCR has treated them as official policy since world leaders — meeting at the U.N. in September 2005 — endorsed them. Nearly a dozen countries also have incorporated all or some of the principles into national legislation. In one case, the Colombian Constitutional Court in 2001 placed them into the country's "constitutional block," effectively making them a binding part of national law. Other countries that have adopted the principles into national laws or policies include the Maldives, Mozambique, Turkey and Uganda.

IDP advocates say the most significant potential use of the Guiding Principles is in Africa, where the African Union since 2006 has been working on a plan to incorporate a version of them into a binding regional treaty. This treaty — to be called the Convention for the Prevention of Internal Displacement and the Protection of and Assistance to Internally Displaced Persons in Africa — is expected to be adopted by African leaders at a summit meeting in Kampala, Uganda, in April.[4]

[1] Text of the Convention and Protocol is at www.unhcr.org/protect/PROTECTION/3b66c2aa10.pdf.

[2] "States Parties to the Refugee Convention," U.N. High Commissioner for Refugees, www.unhcr.org/protect/PROTECTION/3b73b0d63.pdf.

[3] Text of Refugee Convention in Africa is at www.unhcr.org/basics/BASICS/45dc1a682.pdf; Text of the Cartegena Declaration is at www.unhcr.org/basics/BASICS/45dc19084.pdf.

[4] Text of the Guiding Principles is at www3.brookings.edu/fp/projects/idp/resources/GPEnglish.pdf.

from intervening on their behalf. World leaders at the summit declared the U.N.'s right to take "collective action, in a decisive and timely manner," when governments failed to protect their own citizens.[83]

The U.N. has not followed through on that ringing declaration, however, usually because of dissension within the Security Council — the only U.N. body authorized to take forceful action. In addition, major countries with large, well-equipped armies — notably the United States and many European countries — have been unwilling to contribute sufficient troops to U.N. peacekeeping forces. The U.N.'s inability to protect displaced people has been most evident in eastern Congo and Darfur, where peacekeeping forces, mainly from African Union countries, are ill-equipped and undermanned.[84]

Early in February, for example, Doctors Without Borders bitterly denounced the U.N. peacekeeping mission in Congo for its "inaction" in response to the recent LRA attacks. Laurence Gaubert, head of mission in Congo for the group, said the U.N. peacekeepers "are just based in their camp, they don't go out of their camp, they don't know what is happening in the area."[85] Gaubert noted that the Security Council last Dec. 22 adopted Resolution 1856 demanding protection for civilians in Congo.[86] "This is something they have signed," she said, "but is not something you can see in the field that they have put in place."[87]

U.N. Under-Secretary-General for Humanitarian Affairs John Holmes acknowledged that the peacekeepers could do more to protect civilians but said the harsh criticism of them was "unreasonable and unjustified."

Serb refugees stage a demonstration along the Kosovo border in April 2007 to urge the U.N. to return them to their home provinces. Hundreds of thousands of people dislocated by war in the former Yugoslavia during the 1990s have not yet returned to their home regions.

Only 250-300 troops were in the area at the time, he said, and most were engineers, not combat forces.[88]

The U.N. has faced similar hurdles in trying to protect the millions of civilians displaced in Darfur since 2003. African Union peacekeepers began limited operations in Sudan in 2004 but lacked either the mandate or the resources to prevent government-backed militias or rebel groups from attacking civilians in camps and settlements. The Sudanese government agreed in 2006 and 2007 to allow beefed up U.N. peacekeeping missions, but — as in Congo — the U.N. has been unable to deploy adequate forces over such an enormous area. In Sudan, the government dragged its feet in following through on its agreement, and other countries have failed to provide the necessary money and manpower. The UNHCR operates in seven displaced-persons camps in Darfur (and in six camps in eastern Chad) but must rely on the peacekeeping mission for security.[89]

U.N. officials have repeatedly called for more forceful action to protect Darfuri civilians, only to be stymied by the Security Council — largely because of resistance from China, which has economic interests in Sudan — and delaying tactics by Sudan. The Khartoum government on Feb. 17 signed an agreement with the largest Darfur rebel group, the Justice and Equality Movement, calling for negotiation of a formal peace accord within three months.[90] The hurdles to such an accord were evident the very next day, when government forces reportedly bombed some of the rebel group's positions. The future of the peace agreement was further complicated by the International Criminal Court's (ICC) landmark decision on March 4 to issue an arrest warrant for Sudanese President Omar al-Bashir, charging him with directing the mass murder of tens of thousands of Darfuri civilians and "forcibly transferring large numbers of civilians, and pillaging their property." It was the first time the Hague-based court has accused a sitting head of state of war crimes. Unless he leaves Sudan, there is no international mechanism for arresting Bashir, who denies the accusations and does not recognize the court's jurisdiction. Some aid organizations fear the ICC ruling could trigger more violence — and thus more displacements.[91]

Focusing on IDPs

The number of people displaced by violence who remain within their own countries has been averaging more than 20 million per year, according to the Internal Displacement Monitoring Center, an arm of the Norwegian Refugee Council. More than a third of them are in just three countries: Colombia (up to 4.3 million), Sudan (3.5 million) and Iraq (up to 2.8 million).[92] Tens of millions more have been driven from their homes by natural disasters.

In December 2008, to give IDPs more international attention, the U.N.'s Office for the Coordination of Humanitarian Affairs launched a series of events focusing on IDPs, including workshops, panel discussions, a Web site and high-level conferences.

The agency is particularly concerned about displaced people who languish for years without help from their governments. "For millions of IDPs around the world, an end to their years of displacement, discrimination and poverty seems to be of little concern for those in power," said the U.N.'s Holmes. The U.N. also is encouraging governments to adopt the Guiding Principles on Internal

Displacement for dealing with IDPs. And, it is pressing for "more predictable, timely and principled funding" for programs that help IDPs return home or find new homes, he said.[93]

In recent years, displaced people, usually from rural areas, have tended to head for cities. Experts say it is difficult to calculate the number of urban IDPs, but the monitoring center put the 2007 figure at 4 million, and the UNHCR estimated in 2008 that about half of the 11.4 million refugees were in cities.[94]

Urban IDPs and refugees pose logistical problems for local and international agencies charged with helping them. "In a camp, you have all these tents lined up in a row, and so it's easy to know how many people are there, and how much food and medicine you need every day," says Patrick Duplat, an advocate for Refugees International. "In an urban setting, it's much more complicated to reach people. Who is a refugee, who is an IDP and how are they different from the local population?"

U.N. High Commissioner Guterres acknowledged in a speech last October that global efforts to aid and protect urban refugees and IDPs have been "weak."[95] The approximately 2 million Iraqi refugees living in Damascus and Amman represent "a completely new and different challenge in relation to our usual activities in encampment situations," he told a conference in Norway.[96]

Last year the UNHCR tried handing out cash coupons and ATM cards to several thousand Iraqi refugees in Damascus, enabling them to buy food and other goods at local markets. The UNHCR and the World Food Program also gave food baskets or rice, vegetable oil and lentils to Iraqi refugees considered most in need, aiding about 177,000 Iraqis in 2008.[97] But some refugees reportedly were selling their rations to pay for housing and other needs.[98]

A major step toward legally protecting African IDPs could come in April at a planned special African Union (AU) summit meeting in Uganda. Experts have been working for nearly three years on a Convention for the Protection and Assistance of Internally Displaced Persons in Africa. This treaty would incorporate some, but not all, of the 1998 Guiding Principles on Internal Displacement, which sets nonbinding standards for protecting IDPs.[99]

If a treaty is produced, ratified and implemented, it could be an important step in protecting IDPs, because so

many are in Africa, says Cohen from Brookings. But she is concerned that the final treaty, which already has been revised several times, might not be as strong in protecting human rights as the voluntary Guiding Principles. "We'll have to wait and see what the leaders agree to, and even if they adopt it," she says.

Guterres strongly endorses the AU's plan for a binding treaty. He also says that because the treaty has been developed by Africans, not imposed by outsiders, it "will not be subject to questions about the legitimacy of its objectives."[100]

OUTLOOK

Environmental Refugees

Environmental deterioration caused by climate change could force up to 1 billion people from their homes in coming decades, according to a paper presented to a high-level U.N. meeting last October.[101] Small island nations, notably the Maldives in the Indian Ocean and Kiribati and Tuvalu in the Pacific, could be inundated — causing mass evacuations — if sea levels rise to the extent predicted by many scientists.[102]

Rising seas also endanger several hundred million people in low-lying coastal regions. Many of these areas are in developing countries — such as Bangladesh and the Philippines — that already are prone to cyclones, floods, earthquakes or volcanic eruptions.[103] Many scientists believe that climate change will increase the severity and frequency of weather-linked disasters, particularly cyclones and floods, thus displacing even more people in the future.

L. Craig Johnstone, deputy U.N. High Commissioner for Refugees, said "conservative" estimates predict that up to 250 million people could be displaced by the middle of the 21st century due to climate change. The minority of scientists who doubt the impact of climate change dismiss such estimates as overblown.[104] But aid officials at the U.N. and other international agencies say they have no choice but to prepare for the worst.

Regardless of the impact of climate change on displacements, experts across the spectrum say it is becoming increasingly important for the international community to decide how long to provide humanitarian aid for displaced people. Decades-long displacements are difficult for both the IDPs and refugees as well as the aid groups and host countries involved. (*See sidebar, p. 302.*)

"When can they stop being vulnerable as a result of their displacement and simply be compared to any other poor person in their country?" asks Koser, at the Geneva Center for Security Policy. He cites the 4.6 million Palestinians still being aided by the United Nations six decades after their original displacement.

UNHCR officials acknowledge that international aid programs are not always equitable but say addressing the vulnerability of the world's poor and ending the causes of displacement depend on the political will of global leaders. In his annual remarks to the Security Council on Jan. 8, High Commissioner Guterres said global displacement issues won't be solved until the conflicts that force people from their homes are ended.

"While it is absolutely vital that the victims of armed conflict be provided with essential protection and assistance, we must also acknowledge the limitations of humanitarian action and its inability to resolve deep-rooted conflicts within and between states," he said. "The solution, as always, can only be political."[105]

NOTES

1. "Only after five days we dared to bury the bodies," Doctors Without Borders, Jan. 19, 2009, www.condition-critical.org/.

2. "Congo Crisis" fact sheet, International Rescue Committee, p. 1, www.theirc.org/resources/2007/congo_onesheet.pdf; also see "World Report 2009," Human Rights Watch, www.hrw.org/en/world-report/2009/democratic-republic-congo-drc.

3. "Convention and Protocol Relating to the Status of Refugees," U.N. High Commissioner for Refugees, www.unhcr.org/protect/PROTECTION/3b66c2aa10.pdf.

4. "World Report 2009," *op. cit.*

5. "Statement by Mr. Antonio Guterres, United Nations High Commissioner for Refugees, to the Security Council, New York," U.N. High Commissioner for Refugees, Jan. 8, 2009, www.unhcr.org/admin/ADMIN/496625484.html.

6. "Internally Displaced People: Exiled in their Homeland," U.N. Office for the Coordination of Humanitarian Affairs, http://ochaonline.un.org/News/InFocus/InternallyDisplacedPeopleIDPs/tabid/5132/language/en-US/Default.aspx; also see "China Earthquake: Facts and Figures," International Federation of Red Cross and Red Crescent Societies, Oct. 31, 2008, www.ifrc.org/Docs/pubs/disasters/sichuan-earthquake/ff311008.pdf.

7. Jeffrey Gettleman, "Starvation And Strife Menace Torn Kenya," *The New York Times*, March 1, 2009, p. 6.

8. "Top UNHCR official warns about displacement from climate change," U.N. High Commissioner for Refugees, Dec. 9, 2008, www.unhcr.org/news/NEWS/493e9bd94.html.

9. "2007 Statistical Yearbook," U.N. High Commissioner for Refugees, p. 23, www.unhcr.org/cgi-bin/texis/vtx/home/opendoc.pdf?id=4981c3252&tbl=STATISTICS; "Statement by Mr. Antonio Guterres," *op. cit.*

10. For background, see Karen Foerstel, "Crisis in Darfur," *CQ Global Researcher*, September 2008, pp. 243-270.

11. "2009 Global Update: Sudan," U.N. High Commissioner for Refugees, pp. 1-3, www.unhcr.org/publ/PUBL/4922d4130.pdf.

12. "Millions of Hectares of Land Secured for Internally Displaced," International Organization for Migration, Jan. 9, 2009, www.iom.int/jahia/Jahia/pbnAM/cache/offonce;jsessionid=29AD6E92A35FDE971CDAB26007A67DB2.worker01?entryId=21044.

13. "Afghanistan — The Challenges of Sustaining Returns," U.N. High Commissioner for Refugees, www.unhcr.org/cgi-bin/texis/vtx/afghan?page=home.

14. See "UNHCR Global Appeal, 2009"; "2009 Global Update, Mission Statement," U.N. High Commissioner for Refugees, www.unhcr.org/publ/PUBL/4922d43f11.pdf; "Statement by Mr. Antonio Guterres," *op. cit.*; "2009 Global Update, Working with the Internally Displaced," U.N. High Commissioner for Refugees, www.unhcr.org/publ/PUBL/4922d44c0.pdf.

15. The Refugee Status Determination (RSD) Unit, U.N. High Commissioner for Refugees, www.unhcr.org/protect/3d3d26004.html.

16. "2009 Global Update, Mission Statement," *op. cit.*

17. "Protracted Refugee Situations: High Commissioner's Initiative," U.N. High Commissioner for Refugees, December 2008, www.unhcr.org/protect/PROTECTION/4937de6f2.pdf.

18. "Humanitarian Reform," United Nations, www.humanitarianreform.org.

19. "The Global Cluster Leads," U.N. Office for the Coordination of Humanitarian Affairs, http://ocha.unog.ch/humanitarianreform/Default.aspx?tabid=217.

20. "Cluster Approach Evaluation 2007," United Nations, www.humanitarianreform.org/Default.aspx?tabid=457.

21. The book Milner co-authored is *The United Nation's High Commissioner for Refugees (UNHCR): The Politics and Practice of Refugee Protection into the 21st Century* (2008).

22. "Convention and Protocol Relating to the Status of Refugees," *op. cit.*

23. "Full Text of Jack Straw's Speech," *The Guardian*, Feb. 6, 2001, www.guardian.co.uk/uk/2001/feb/06/immigration.immigrationandpublicservices3.

24. "Climate change, natural disasters and human displacement: a UNHCR perspective," www.unhcr.org/protect/PROTECTION/4901e81a4.pdf.

25. "European Pact on Immigration and Asylum," www.immigration.gouv.fr/IMG/pdf/Plaquette_EN.pdf.

26. "ECRE calls for suspension of Dublin transfers to Greece," European Council on Refugees and Exiles, April 3, 2008, www.ecre.org/resources/Press_releases/1065.

27. "NGO Statement Addressing the Iraqi Humanitarian Challenge," July 31, 2008, www.refugeesinternational.org/policy/letter/ngo-statement-addressing-iraqi-humanitarian-challenge.

28. "Fact Sheet: USCIS Makes Major Strides During 2008," U.S. Citizenship and Immigration Services, Nov. 6, 2008, www.uscis.gov/portal/site/uscis/menuitem.5af9bb95919f35e66f614176543f6d1a/?vgnextoid=2526ad6f16d6d110VgnVCM1000004718190aRCRD&vgnextchannel=68439c7755cb9010VgnVCM10000045f3d6a1RCRD.

29. "NGO Statement: Addressing the Iraqi Humanitarian Challenge," *op. cit.*

30. "Fact Sheet: Iraqi Refugee Processing," U.S. Citizenship and Immigration Services, Sept. 12, 2008, www.dhs.gov/xnews/releases/pr_1221249274808.shtm.

31. "Operation Safe Haven Iraq 2009," Center for American Progress, www.americanprogress.org/issues/2009/01/iraqi_airlift.html.

32. Her blog site is http://refugeeresettlementwatch.wordpress.com/.

33. "The 1951 Refugee Convention," U.N. High Commissioner for Refugees, www.unhcr.org/1951convention/dev-protect.html.

34. *Ibid.*

35. *Ibid.*

36. "Establishment of UNRWA," www.un.org/unrwa/overview/index.html.

37. "UNRWA Statistics," www.un.org/unrwa/publications/index.html.

38. "A 'Timeless' Treaty Under Attack: A New Phase," U.N. High Commissioner for Refugees, www.unhcr.org/1951convention/new-phase.html.

39. "States Parties to the Convention and the Protocol," U.N. High Commissioner for Refugees, www.unhcr.org/protect/PROTECTION/3b73b0d63.pdf.

40. "Guiding Principles on Internal Displacement," www3.brookings.edu/fp/projects/idp/resources/GPEnglish.pdf.

41. "FMO Research Guide: Afghanistan," Teresa Poppelwell, July 2007, pp. 17-19, www.forcedmigration.org/guides/fmo006/.

42. "Afghanistan — The Challenges of Sustaining Returns," U.N. High Commissioner for Refugees, www.unhcr.org/cgi-bin/texis/vtx/afghan?page=home.

43. "Jalozai camp closed, returnees face difficulties at home," IRIN news service, June 2, 2008, www.irinnews.org/Report.aspx?ReportId=78506; also see "Iran called upon to halt winter deportations," IRIN news service, Dec. 18, 2008, www.irinnews.org/PrintReport.aspx?ReportId=82007.

44. "Afghanistan — The Challenges of Sustaining Returns," *op. cit.*

45. "Minister disputes call to boost refugee returns," IRIN news service, Sept. 10, 2008, www.irinnews.org/Report.aspx?ReportId=80218.

46. "Cold tents for returnees in east," IRIN news service, Jan. 15, 2009, www.irinnews.org/Report.aspx?ReportId=82373.

47. "Afghanistan at the crossroads: Young Afghans return to a homeland they never knew," U.N. High Commissioner for Refugees, Nov. 14, 2008, www.unhcr.org/cgi-bin/texis/vtx/afghan?page=news&id=491d84c64.

48. "2009 Global Update, Colombia situation," U.N. High Commissioner for Refugees, www.unhcr.org/publ/PUBL/4922d43411.pdf.

49. "Colombia Situation," U.N. High Commissioner for Refugees 2008-09 Global Appeal for Colombia, p. 2, www.unhcr.org/home/PUBL/474ac8e814.pdf.

50. *Ibid.*

51. "Millions of Hectares of Land Secured for Internally Displaced," International Organization for Migration, Jan. 9, 2009, www.iom.int.

52. *Ibid.*

53. *Ibid.*

54. "2009 Global Update," Democratic Republic of the Congo, U.N. High Commissioner for Refugees, www.unhcr.org/publ/PUBL/4922d4100.pdf.

55. "Congo Crisis" fact sheet, *op. cit.*

56. "A Congolese Rebel Leader Who Once Seemed Untouchable Is Caught," *The New York Times*, Jan. 24, 2009, www.nytimes.com/2009/01/24/world/africa/24congo.html?_r=1.

57. "An arresting and hopeful surprise," *The Economist*, Jan. 29, 2009, www.economist.com/displayStory.cfm?story_id=13022113. For background, see David Masci, "Aiding Africa," *CQ Researcher*, Aug. 29, 2003, pp. 697-720; John Felton, "Child Soldiers," *CQ Global Researcher*, July 2008.

58. "2009 Global Update: Iraq," U.N. High Commissioner for Refugees, p. 2, www.unhcr.orgpubl/PUBL/4922d4230.pdf.

59. "WFP to help feed one million displaced Iraqis," World Food Program, Jan. 3, 2009, www.wfp.org/English/?ModuleID=137&Key=2732.

60. "Budget cuts threaten IDP housing projects," IRIN news service, Jan. 6, 2009, www.irinnews.org/Report.aspx?ReportId=82209.

61. "IDPs enticed to vacate southern camp," IRIN news service, Dec. 15, 2008, www.irinnews.org/Report.aspx?ReportId=81963.

62. "2009 Global Update: Iraq," *op. cit.*, p. 2.

63. "Three Years of Post-Samarra Displacement in Iraq," International Organization for Migration, Feb. 22, 2009, p. 1, www.iom.int/jahia/webdav/shared/shared/mainsite/published_docs/studies_and_reports/iom_displacement_report_post_samarra.pdf.

64. *Ibid.*

65. "Post-Nargis Periodic Review I," Tripartite Core Group, December 2008, p. 4, www.aseansec.org/22119.pdf.

66. "2009 Global Update: Myanmar," U.N. High Commissioner for Refugees, p. 2, www.unhcr.org/publ/PUBL/4922d42b0.pdf.

67. "Cyclone survivors face water shortages," IRIN news service, Dec. 29, 2008, www.irinnews.org/Report.aspx?ReportId=82129.

68. "Cyclone recovery 'will take up to four years,' " IRIN news service, Jan. 15, 2009, www.IRINnews.org/Report.aspx?ReportId=82383.

69. Michael Heath, "Angelina Jolie, U.N. Envoy, Asks Thailand to Aid Myanmar Refugees," Bloomberg News, www.bloomberg.com/apps/news?pid=20601080&sid=aL5VlfM46aAc&refer=asia#.

70. "2009 Global Update: Bangladesh," U.N. High Commissioner for Refugees, p. 1, www.unhcr.org/publ/PUBL/4922d42818.pdf.

71. "Myanmar Refugees Rescued at Sea," *The New York Times*, Feb. 3, 2009, www.nytimes.com/2009/02/04/world/asia/04indo.html?ref=world.

72. "Angelina Jolie voices support for Myanmar refugees in northern Thailand camps," U.N. High Commissioner for Refugees, Feb. 5, 2009, www.unhcr.org/news/NEWS/498ab65c2.html.

73. *Ibid.*

74. "ASIA: Regional approach to Rohingya boat people," IRIN news service, March 2, 2009, www.irinnews.org/Report.aspx?ReportId=83232.

75. "2009 Global Update: Sudan," U.N. High Commissioner for Refugees, pp. 1-3, www.unhcr.org/publ/PUBL/4922d4130.pdf.

76. "Number of returnees to South Sudan passes the 300,000 mark," U.N. High Commissioner for Refugees, Feb. 10, 2009, www.unhcr.org/news/NEWS/4991a8de2.html; "2009 Global Update," *op. cit.*, p. 1.

77. "Darfur remains tense after recent eruption of fighting, U.N. reports," IRIN news service, Jan. 28, 2009, www.un.org/apps/news/story.asp?NewsID=29699&Cr=darfur&Cr1=.

78. "Report of the Secretary-General on the deployment of the African Union-United Nations Hybrid Operation in Darfur," United Nations, Oct. 17, 2008, p. 11, http://daccessdds.un.org/doc/UNDOC/GEN/N08/553/95/PDF/N0855395.pdf?OpenElement.

79. "2009 Global Update: Sudan," *op. cit.*; "2009 Global Update: Chad," U.N. High Commissioner for Refugees, www.unhcr.org/publ/PUBL/4922d41214.pdf.

80. "2009 Global Update: Sudan," *op. cit.*, p. 3; "World Refugee Survey, 2008," Sudan chapter, U.S. Committee for Refugees and Immigrants, www.refugees.org/countryreports.aspx?id=2171.

81. "Kandiah: 'There was shelling every day. We barely escaped with our lives,'" IRIN news service, Feb. 19, 2009, www.IRINnews.org/Report.aspx?ReportId=83015.

82. For background, see Lee Michael Katz, "World Peacekeeping," *CQ Global Researcher*, April 2007, pp. 75-100.

83. "World Summit Outcome 2005," U.N. General Assembly, Resolution A/RES/60/1, paragraphs 138-139, September 2005, www.un.org/summit2005/documents.html.

84. See Foerstel, *op. cit.*

85. "DRC: MSF denounces the lack of protection for victims of LRA violence in Haut-Uélé," Doctors Without Borders, Feb. 4, 2009, www.msf.org.

86. Security Council Resolution 1856, Dec. 22, 2006, http://daccessdds.un.org/doc/UNDOC/GEN/N08/666/94/PDF/N0866694.pdf?OpenElement.

87. *Ibid.*

88. "Press Conference by Humanitarian Affairs Head on Recent Trip to Democratic Republic of Congo," U.N. Department of Public Information, Feb. 13, 2009, www.un.org/News/briefings/docs/2009/090213_DRC.doc.htm.

89. "2009 Global Update: Sudan," *op. cit.*

90. "Sudan and Darfur Rebel Group Agree to Peace Talks," *The New York Times*, Feb. 18, 2009, www.nytimes.com/2009/02/18/world/africa/18sudan.html?_r=1&ref=todayspaper.

91. "Sudan bombs rebels day after Darfur deal: rebels," Agence France-Presse, Feb. 18, 2009. See Mike Corder, "International court issues warrant for Sudan president on charges of war crimes in Darfur," The Associated Press, March 4, 2009.

92. "2009 Global Update," *op. cit.*; "Global Overview of Trends and Developments: 2007," Internal Displacement Monitoring Centre, Norwegian Refugee Council, p. 12, April 2008, www.internal-displacement.org/idmc/website/resources.nsf/(httpPublications)/0F926CFAF1EADE5EC125742E003B7067?OpenDocument.

93. "UN launches year-long campaign to highlight, and solve, plight of displaced," IRIN news service, Dec. 18, 2009, www.un.org/apps/news/story.asp?NewsID=29358&Cr=IDPs&Cr1.

94. "Addressing Urban Displacement: A Project Description," Internal Displacement Monitoring Centre, Norwegian Refugee Council, 2007, p. 2; also see "2007 Global Trends," U.N. High Commissioner for Refugees, June 2008, p. 2, www.unhcr.org/statistics/STATISTICS/4852366f2.pdf.

95. "Ten years of Guiding Principles on Internal Displacement: Achievements and Future Challenges," statement by Antonio Guterres, Oslo, Oct. 16, 2008, www.unhcr.org/admin/ADMIN/48ff45e12.html.

96. *Ibid.*

97. "WFP to help feed one million displaced Iraqis," World Food Program, Jan. 3, 2008, www.wfp.org/English/?ModuleID=137&Key=2732.

98. "Iraqi refugees selling some of their food rations," IRIN news service, Jan. 28, 2009, http://one.wfp.org/english/?ModuleID=137& Key=2732.

99. "From Voluntary Principles to Binding Standards," *IDP Action*, Jan. 9, 2009, www.idpaction.org/index.php/en/news/16-principles2 standards.

100. "Ten Years of Guiding Principles on Internal Displacement," *op. cit.*

101. "Climate Change, Migration and Displacement: Who will be affected?" Working paper submitted by the informal group on Migration/Displacement and Climate Change of the U.N. Inter-Agency Standing Committee, Oct. 31, 2008, http://unfccc.int/resource/docs/2008/smsn/igo/022.pdf.

102. "Climate Change and Displacement," *Forced Migration Review*, p. 20, October 2008, www.fmreview.org/climatechange.htm; for background see Colin Woodard, "Curbing Climate Change," *CQ Global Researcher*, February 2007, pp. 27-50, and Marcia Clemmitt, "Climate Change," *CQ Researcher*, Jan. 27, 2006, pp. 73-96.

103. "Climate Resilient Cities: A Primer on Reducing Vulnerabilities to Disasters," World Bank, 2009, pp. 5-6.

104. "Top UNHCR official warns about displacement from climate change," *op. cit.*

105. "Statement by Mr. Antonio Guterres," *op. cit.*

BIBLIOGRAPHY

Books

Evans, Gareth, *The Responsibility to Protect: Ending Mass Atrocity Crimes Once and For All, Brookings Institution Press*, 2008.
A former Australian foreign minister and current head of the International Crisis Group offers an impassioned plea for world leaders to follow through on their promises to protect civilians, even those abused by their own governments.

Loescher, Gil, Alexander Betts and James Milner, *The United Nations High Commissioner for Refugees (UNHCR): The Politics and Practice of Refugee Protection Into the 21st Century, Routledge*, 2008.
Academic experts on refugee issues offer a generally sympathetic but often critical assessment of the UNHCR's performance as the world's main protector of refugees.

Verdirame, Guglielmo, and Barbara Harrell-Bond, with Zachary Lomo and Hannah Garry, *Rights in Exile: Janus-Faced Humanitarianism, Berghahn Books*, 2005.
A former director of the Refugee Studies Center at Oxford University (Harrell-Bond) and an expert on refugee rights at Cambridge University offer a blistering critique of the U.N. and nongovernment agencies that protect refugees.

Articles

"Managing the Right of Return," *The Economist*, Aug. 4, 2008.
The practical implications of refugees' legal right to return to their home countries are examined.

Cohen, Roberta, and Francis Deng, "The Genesis and the Challenges," *Forced Migration Review*, December 2008.
This is the keystone article in an issue devoted to the Guiding Principles on Internal Displacement 10 years after their creation. Cohen and Deng were prime movers of the document.

Feyissa, Abebe, with Rebecca Horn, "Traveling Souls: Life in a Refugee Camp, Where Hearts Wander as Minds Deteriorate," *Utne Reader*, September-October 2008, www.utne.com/2008-09-01/Great Writing/Traveling-Souls.aspx.
An Ethiopian who has lived in northwestern Kenya's Kakuma refugee camp for 16 years writes about life in the camp.

Guterres, Antonio, "Millions Uprooted: Saving Refugees and the Displaced," *Foreign Affairs*, September/October 2008.
The U.N. High Commissioner for Refugees lays out an ambitious agenda of action to aid and protect the displaced.

Harr, Jonathan, "Lives of the Saints: International Hardship Duty in Chad," *The New Yorker*, Jan. 5, 2009, www.newyorker.com/reporting/2009/01/05/090105fa_fact_harr.
A frequent *New Yorker* contributor offers a sympathetic portrait of idealistic aid workers at refugee camps in Chad.

Stevens, Jacob, "Prison of the Stateless: The Derelictions of UNHCR," *New Left Review*, November-December 2006, www.newleftreview.org/?page=article&view=2644.

A review of the memoirs of former High Commissioner Sadako Ogata becomes a strongly worded critique of the U.N. refugee agency. A rebuttal by former UNHCR special envoy Nicholas Morris is at www.unhcr.org/research/RESEARCH/460d131d2.pdf.

Reports and Studies

"2009 Global Update," *U.N. High Commissioner for Refugees,* **November 2008, www.unhcr.org/ga09/index.html.**
Published in November, this is the most recent summary from the UNHCR of its operations, plans and budget for 2009.

"Future Floods of Refugees: A comment on climate change, conflict and forced migration," *Norwegian Refugee Council,* **April 2008, www.nrc.no/arch/_img/9268480.pdf.**
The refugee council surveys the debate over whether climate change will worsen natural disasters and force untold millions of people from their homes.

"Protracted Refugee Situations: High Commissioner's Initiative," *U.N. High Commissioner for Refugees,* **December 2008, www.unhcr.org/protect/PROTECTION/4937de6f2.pdf.**
The UNHCR offers a plan of action for resolving several long-term situations in which refugees have been trapped in camps or settlements for decades.

"When Displacement Ends: A Framework for Durable Solutions," *Brookings-Bern Project on Internal Displacement,* **June 2007, www.brookings.edu/reports/2007/09displacementends.aspx.**
This detailed blueprint for how international agencies can help IDPs find "durable solutions" to their displacements is the product of conferences and other studies.

Cohen, Roberta, "Listening to the Voices of the Displaced: Lessons Learned," *Brookings-Bern Project on Internal Displacement,* **September 2008, www.brookings.edu/reports/2008/09_internal_displacement_cohen.aspx.**
The author recommends better ways to aid and protect displaced people around the world, based on interviews with dozens of IDPs.

For More Information

Brookings-Bern Project on Internal Displacement, The Brookings Institution, 1775 Massachusetts Avenue, N.W., Washington, DC, 20036; (202) 797-6168; www.brookings .edu/projects/idp.aspx. A joint project of the Brookings Institution and the University of Bern (Switzerland) School of Law; conducts research and issues reports on policy questions related to internally displaced people (IDPs).

Institute for the Study of International Migration, Georgetown University, Harris Building, Third Floor, 3300 Whitehaven St. N.W., Washington, DC, 20007; (202) 687-2258; www12.georgetown.edu/sfs/isim/index.html. An academic research center focusing on all aspects of international migration, including refugees.

Internal Displacement Monitoring Centre, Chemin de Balexert, 7-9 1219 Chatelaine Geneva, Switzerland; 41-22-799-07 00; www.internal-displacement.org. Provides regular reports on IDPs globally; the major source of information about the numbers of people displaced by conflict.

International Organization for Migration, 17 Route des Morillons, CH-1211, Geneva 19, Switzerland; 41-22-717-9111; www .iom.int. A U.N. partner (not officially within the U.N. system) that aids refugees and migrants and studies migration trends.

Norwegian Refugee Council, P.O. Box 6758, St. Olavs Plass, 0130 Oslo, Norway; 47-23-10 9800; www.nrc.no. A prominent nongovernmental organization that provides aid programs for displaced persons and advocates on their behalf.

Refugee Studies Centre, Queen Elizabeth House, University of Oxford, Mansfield Road, Oxford OX1 3TB, United Kingdom; 44-1865-270-722; www.rsc.ox.ac.uk/index .html?main. A prominent research center on refugees and the displaced. Publishes the *Forced Migration Review*, a quarterly journal written by experts in the field.

Refugees International, 2001 S St., N.W., Suite 700, Washington, DC, 20009; (202) 828-0110; www.refugees international.org. Advocates on behalf of refugees and IDPs and publishes regular reports based on site visits to key countries.

U.N. High Commissioner for Refugees, Case Postale 2500, CH-1211, Geneva 2 Depot, Switzerland; 41-22-739-8111; www.unhcr.org/cgi-bin/texis/vtx/home. The U.N. agency with prime responsibility for aiding and protecting refugees; increasingly has taken on a similar role in regard to IDPs.

U.S. Committee for Refugees and Immigrants, 2231 Crystal Dr., Suite 350, Arlington VA 22202-3711; (703) 310-1130; www.refugees.org. An advocacy group that publishes reports focusing on human-rights abuses and other problems encountered by refugees and immigrants.

12

Truth Commissions

Can Countries Heal After Atrocities?

Jina Moore

GENOCID 1992 – 1995

ZVORNIK - LIPLJE
Prvi logor u Bosni i Hercegovini
danas izgleda ovako

Survivors of Bosnian-Serb war crimes protest on Sept. 16, 2009, at U.N. headquarters in Sarajevo, the capital of Bosnia and Herzegovina. The demonstrators said the International Criminal Tribunal for the Former Yugoslavia in The Hague was not being tough enough on former Serbian leader Radovan Karadzic, who is charged with genocide, war crimes and crimes against humanity for his part in the four-year siege of Sarajevo and the 1995 massacre of 8,000 Muslim men in Srebrenica. Such tribunals can impose jail sentences and are an alternative to nonprosecutorial truth commissions.

From *CQ Global Researcher*, January 2010.

I
n Bomaru, a dusty Sierra Leonean village along the Liberian border, nearly 800 residents gathered in early 2008 for an unusual ceremony — one they hoped would help them come to terms with their past and each other.

Up to 50,000 people were killed during the country's decade-long civil war, 200,000 women were raped and tens of thousands of others were brutally maimed, including children, after rebels hacked off their hands or arms for refusing to join the cause. All told, the fighting displaced roughly 1 million people.[1]

The Bomaru residents had come to participate in a ritual of reconciliation that included confessions by the perpetrators and forgiveness from the victims. After music and dancing, the villagers presented a gift to their ancestors to cleanse the village and bring back the harvests.

It wasn't Bomaru's first attempt at reconciliation. The Sierra Leone Truth and Reconciliation Commission had arrived years before to gather some of the 7,000 statements it would use to write a definitive history of the conflict, which started over control of the region's diamonds.[2] But the commission hadn't healed the village, elders said. Something more was needed.

During the 2008 reconciliation attempt, residents gathered to recall what had happened, but froze when a visiting American film crew moved in with its video cameras. The ceremony came to a halt. "They are afraid that if they talk," one leader explained, "they will be prosecuted."[3]

Bomaru's concerns are echoed in countries around the world recovering from massive human rights abuses. The fear of prosecution often prevents "the truth" about past atrocities from emerging.

317

Many Countries Seek Truth After Past Atrocities

Since 1976, at least 58 countries have set up truth commissions — nonjudicial panels that establish official records of human rights abuses by former regimes. Three commissions are currently operating or just getting organized: in Canada, Kenya and the Solomon Islands. The commissions are one method used by emerging democracies to obtain post-conflict "transitional justice." Wartime crimes against humanity also have been prosecuted in 11 countries by international tribunals — ad hoc judicial bodies, usually established by the United Nations. The International Criminal Court (ICC), given universal jurisdiction over war crimes and crimes against humanity, is pursuing investigations in four countries: Sudan, Uganda, the Democratic Republic of the Congo and the Central African Republic. In November, the ICC prosecutor asked for permission to open a preliminary investigation into ethnic-based violence following Kenya's 2007 election.

Major Truth Commissions or War Crimes Trials
(Past or Ongoing)

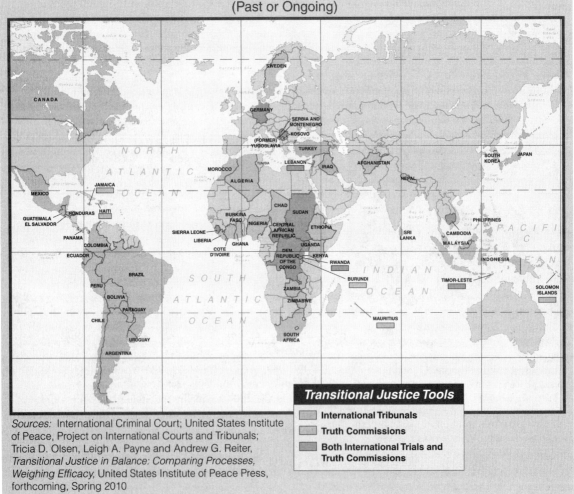

Transitional Justice Tools

- International Tribunals
- Truth Commissions
- Both International Trials and Truth Commissions

Sources: International Criminal Court; United States Institute of Peace, Project on International Courts and Tribunals; Tricia D. Olsen, Leigh A. Payne and Andrew G. Reiter, *Transitional Justice in Balance: Comparing Processes, Weighing Efficacy,* United States Institute of Peace Press, forthcoming, Spring 2010

And when there are thousands of perpetrators, some of whom remain powerful, it is difficult for victims to tell their stories and offenders to be brought to justice.

In the last three decades, several dozen countries — from Argentina to Zimbabwe — have chosen an innovative answer: truth commissions. The panels are organized by national governments, usually with the help of the international community, to create official records of human rights abuses committed by past governments. The panels typically spend one to two years recording statements from thousands of victims and perpetrators, sometimes offering perpetrators immunity if they cooperate.

While the commissions uncover crimes, they are not trials: They do not corroborate facts, cross-examine witnesses or judge individual guilt like the 11 international tribunals — such as the famous Nuremberg trials after World War II — established in the past 100 years to investigate war crimes and other human rights abuses. Rather than indictments and verdicts, truth commissions issue final reports that function as official histories of what happened and offer a series of recommendations, often focused on reparations and on nurturing democracy, transparency and human rights. A handful of commissions, however, have recommended certain individual prosecutions.

In some countries, most famously in South Africa, truth commissions are also asked to foster reconciliation. Such "truth and reconciliation commissions" usually recommend how the government can promote peaceful coexistence among formerly warring factions or even individuals.

"Truth commissions are supposed to reconcile what are seen as two big, conflicting goals for a society coming out of a dark period of war and human rights violations — peace on the one hand and justice on the other," says Martin Flaherty, a founder and director of the Leitner Center for International Law and Justice at Fordham Law School in New York City.

Those goals first clashed in Latin America in the 1980s, as countries emerging from abusive authoritarian rule struggled to democratize. In Argentina, the first country to successfully hold a truth commission, the outgoing leaders of a brutal military dictatorship had granted themselves immunity from prosecution for their crimes before the commission was established. Challenging the amnesty law was impossible: The

Sudanese President Omar al-Bashir defiantly holds a rally on April 7, 2009, shortly after he was indicted for war crimes in Darfur by the International Criminal Court (ICC). The Sudanese president responded to his ICC arrest warrant by evicting 13 Western aid agencies — fueling criticism that internationally imposed justice can backfire, further harming the victims.

judiciary was too weak — and the people too cowed — to take on the junta.[4]

Instead, Argentina's new president launched a commission to gather testimony on the prior regime's behavior. In just nine months the panel interviewed more than 7,000 Argentines and documented nearly 9,000 stories of the "disappeared" — civilians who were kidnapped, tortured and murdered by the junta. In a country that had long suffered in fear and silence, the 1984 truth commission report, *Nunca Más* ("Never Again"), became an instant best seller.[5]

Truth commissions since then have emerged as a popular tool of "transitional justice" — a variety of legal options for countries coping with past human rights abuses. "A generation ago, there wasn't even a phrase," says Martha Minow, dean of Harvard University Law School and an expert on transitional justice. "Now, in places all over the world, you hear people saying, 'Maybe we should have a truth commission.'"

Truth commissions aren't the only option for societies recovering from rights abuses. In 2002, the world community set up a permanent global court in The Hague, Netherlands — the International Criminal Court (ICC) — to replace the ad hoc international tribunals, most of which had been mandated by the United Nations. The ICC — which prosecutes genocide, crimes against humanity and war crimes — has opened four investigations so far: in Sudan, Uganda, the Democratic Republic of the Congo and the Central African Republic.

Some countries use a hybrid approach to justice. Cambodia set up a U.N.-backed national-international court in Phnom Pehn, which in November concluded its first trial of a former Khmer Rouge official charged with mass murder during the notorious 1970s regime.[6] A verdict is expected in March in that case. Meanwhile, genocide charges were filed on Dec. 18 against three other former Khmer Rouge officials, including president Khieu Samphan, the most senior Khmer Rouge leader indicted in connection with the deaths of 1.7 million people during the 1975-79 "killing fields" reign of terror.[7]

But truth commissions have been far more popular than international trials or tribunals; they're cheaper and don't require as much international assistance. So far, nearly 60 truth commissions have been established around the world, mostly in Latin America and sub-Saharan Africa, though that's beginning to change.[8] In 2002, Timor-Leste's truth commission reported on 30 years of violent and repressive Indonesian rule, and in 2004 Morocco opened the Arab world's first truth commission, which focused on disappearances and arbitrary detentions over a 43-year period beginning in 1956. (*See map, p. 318.*)

Truth commissions often cast themselves in transformative terms. "We believe . . . that there is another kind of justice — a restorative justice, which is concerned not so much with punishment as with correcting imbalances, restoring broken relationships — with healing, harmony and reconciliation," wrote Archbishop Desmond Tutu, chair of the South African Truth and Reconciliation Commission, in the panel's final report. "Such justice focuses on the experience of the victims."[9]

Sweeping goals aside, truth exercises are not unlike the commissions of inquiry common in Western democracies, such as the Warren Commission that investigated the Kennedy assassination or the 9/11 Commission. Like them, truth commissions are temporary bodies, official but independent, mandated to create an official record of the past.

Truth commissions, however, focus on patterns of abuse over time, not on single events, and they usually are established during moments of regime change, particularly during a country's transition to a democratic or open society.[10]

In fact, it is during such fragile transition periods that truth commissions are most needed — and, some say, most effective. Indeed, creating a public record of secret state crimes represents more than a historical exercise.

"In countries like Chile or Argentina, commissions have successfully made it impossible to deny that the crimes took place," says Eduardo Gonzalez, director of the truth and memory program at the International Center for Transitional Justice (ICTJ) in New York. Consequently, says Gonzalez, a Peruvian who served on the staff of his own country's commission, "truth commissions have been fundamental to cement allegiance to democracy and the rule of law."

But most truth commissions don't exist long enough to see that change blossom. Some succumb to infighting or political pressure before their terms expire. Others are followed by renewed violence, like the 1993 commission in Rwanda — where ethnic violence among Tutsis and Hutus erupted later, killing about 800,000 people.

And truth commissions face incredible financial and logistical hurdles. The panels need qualified commissioners — universally respected by all sides — to conduct the investigations. They also need money to travel across the country and take thousands of statements from victims and perpetrators and sustained political will to weather fatigue and controversy.[11]

Still, truth commissions can be a pragmatic way for young states to handle large numbers of perpetrators. They also are lauded for giving voice to victims, which some say promotes psychosocial healing.[12]

There are, predictably, spoilers in the truth-telling process. Perpetrators often want to maintain their silence. In 1995, 46 percent of white South Africans called the just-established truth and reconciliation commission a "witch-hunt" designed to discredit the former apartheid government.[13]

In other countries, perpetrators often refuse to apologize for their crimes.

"I sleep good," said Prince Johnson, one of Liberia's most notorious warlords and now a senator, when he was investigated by Liberia's Truth and Reconciliation Commission. "I snore."[14] When the panel recommended prosecuting him for war crimes, Johnson threatened to return to the bush and renew the country's civil war.[15]

Even victims themselves don't universally support truth-telling. Some don't believe that sharing their stories will lessen their pain or nudge their countrymen toward reconciliation. More than 90 percent of Rwandan genocide survivors thought the country's truth-telling mechanism would renew trauma; more than half thought truth-telling would make it difficult to live with the perpetrators.[16]

Other countries worry that focusing on the past will open old wounds. Yet the other option — doing nothing — may be equally problematic, say scholars and experts.

"People want acknowledgment. Before they can get on with their lives they need that acknowledgment," says Richard Goldstone, a renowned former South African judge and the former chief prosecutor of the international criminal tribunals for both Rwanda and the former Yugoslavia. "If they don't get it, then you get calls for revenge. That's how cycles of violence are born."

As governments, victims and human rights advocates try to heal the wounds of the past, here are some of the questions they are debating:

Do truth commissions produce accurate records of the past?

Truth commissions are designed to provide countries and their people with a single, official version of a controversial past, based on thousands of interviews. But experts say getting an official version of the truth is not always the same as getting an accurate picture of the past.

"They should be called 'fact and fiction commissions,' or 'some-of-the-truth commissions,'" quipped a long-time observer of truth commissions.[17]

There are limitations on what truth commissions can discover. They give higher priority to fairness and honesty than to culpability and thereby attempt to arrive at a definitive — but not necessarily complete — picture of the past. "Truth commissions are meant to provide a national narrative of a conflict, but they can be debated, discussed, challenged and contested," says Elizabeth Goodfriend, a program associate at the International Center for Transitional Justice in Liberia. "There's no one truth."

When the South African Truth and Reconciliation Commission was set up in 1995 to examine abuses by the former apartheid governments, it acknowledged four versions of the truth: the forensic truth of numbers and facts; the narrative truth of personal experience; the social truth of publicizing thousands of personal stories and the restorative truth of acknowledging a dark history before moving forward.[18]

Those truths can compete in any public process, and the South African commissioners didn't say which truth should trump others.[19] But even when there is no outright conflict among them, each version has its limits, and one version can sometimes require another in order to uncover the complete scope of what happened.

"Interviewing 8,000 people doesn't tell you how many victims there were over a 25-year period; it just tells you the stories of those particular individuals," says David Cohen, director of the War Crimes Studies Center at the University of California-Berkeley. Whether a truth commission gets an accurate picture of the past, he says, "depends on which truth you're looking for."

Truth commissions also risk recording untruths, especially if they encourage witnesses to come forward by offering them an incentive that looks a lot like immunity. South Africa offered outright amnesty if individuals confessed fully and truthfully. In Liberia, the truth commission promised it wouldn't recommend prosecution for anyone who offered a full confession and genuine regret for crimes committed during the 14-year civil war.

Such an incentive, critics say, may be a temptation to lie. "If you tie up admissions of guilt and expressions of repentance with provisions of amnesty, you of course have a recipe for pretending," says Thomas Brudholm, a Danish scholar of transitional justice and co-editor of the book *Religious Responses to Mass Atrocities.*

Whatever version of the truth emerges, it may be just a start. "It's better to understand any of these transitional devices as contributing to a multigenerational struggle over truth, rather than any one of them producing a definitive truth," says Harvard's Minow.

The messy debates over recent Balkan history suggest a truth commission can be a healthy start to that process. Although an international tribunal in The Hague is prosecuting Balkan war criminals, the region has never had a truth commission. Every generation of schoolchildren learns a different version of history, depending on their ethnicity. "There should be a recorded history," said a Bosnian civil society leader, when asked if a truth

Former Liberian warlord Prince Johnson has refused to apologize for his role in Liberia's long civil war. When the country's truth and reconciliation commission recommended prosecuting Johnson for war crimes, he threatened to return to the bush and resume fighting.

and reconciliation commission could establish a historical record of what happened. "It is not good that different people are hearing different histories. It is bad for future generations."[20]

Criminal justice, meanwhile, is limited. It requires hard, physical evidence and a perpetrator who is present in the courtroom. "There were thousands upon thousands of incidents the prosecutor would never get to," says Goldstone, the tribunal's former chief prosecutor. Were there a truth commission, "the prospects for permanent peace would be a lot better."

Whether a truth commission can get an accurate record of the past, or even the best record, may soon become a secondary argument. A growing movement seeks to establish the "right to truth" as a universal human right that — like other rights — governments must protect and fulfill.

"The state has an obligation to explore the truth to the best of its abilities and to disclose it publicly," Juan Méndez, an Argentinean who was the first United Nations special advisor on the prevention of genocide, has argued. "Whether we call it a right or not, the obligation of the state very honestly to explore every detail of human rights abuses is now so well established that almost nobody denies it anymore."[21]

Can truth commissions reconcile individuals and societies?

Few people considered reconciliation a component of truth-telling until 1995, when South Africa mandated creation of a truth and reconciliation commission. It has become the gold standard of truth commissions for its ability to avoid violence and reunite South Africans after the fall of apartheid. Today, many people — both inside and outside of conflict countries — expect truth commissions to produce reconciliation.

However, there is no universally accepted definition of reconciliation. Priscilla Hayner, a co-founder of the ICTJ and an expert on truth commissions, calls reconciliation a "hazy concept" that can describe everything from the cessation of hostilities to the co-existence of social groups to forgiveness between victims and their perpetrators.

Others agree the conversation can be confusing. Charles Griswold, author of *Forgiveness: A Philosophical Exploration* and a philosophy professor at Boston University, says, "You've really got three moving parts: forgiveness, truth and reconciliation, and the relation of the three of them is debated."

Reconciliation is generally defined as a process that acknowledges the past and repairs the relations it has destroyed. But there's a debate about culture and context.[22]

In Rwanda, where local courts function as a kind of hybrid truth commission and trial chamber, forgiveness plays a major role in the social and political process of reconciliation, which is a national priority. "The committed sins have to be repressed and punished, but also forgiven," Rwandan President Paul Kagame has said. "I invite the perpetrators to show courage and to confess, to repent and to ask forgiveness."[23]

In Latin America, on the other hand, reconciliation was an unpalatable goal, according to Gonzalez of the International Center for Transitional Justice. After a decades-long official silence that covered up state crimes, reconciliation was seen as a cover that allowed political elites to get away with abuses.

Hayner and others doubt that truth commissions can produce individual reconciliation, so they recommend that commissions and the societies they serve distinguish between individual and national (political) reconciliation.[24]

Forgiveness and reconciliation can be especially difficult if the perpetrator's identify is unknown. In Liberia, more than 80 percent of 85,000 victims didn't know who committed a crime against them.[25]

"Forgiveness is really a relation between two individuals — a way of repairing that relation," says Griswold. If the perpetrator's identity is unknown, there is no relationship to restore.

And in the few instances where victims and perpetrators did cross paths at Liberia's Truth and Reconciliation Commission (TRC) hearings, it didn't go well. "The perpetrators were condescending," says Aaron Weah, a Liberian civil society advocate and co-author of the book *Impunity Under Attack — Evolutions and Imperatives for the Liberian TRC.* "They were very rude."

Moreover, "To expect survivors to forgive is to heap yet another burden on them," wrote Harvard's Minow in *Between Vengeance and Forgiveness: Facing History After Genocide and Mass Violence.* "The ability to dispense, but also to withhold, forgiveness is an ennobling capacity and part of the dignity to be reclaimed by those who survive the wrongdoing."[26]

Others find the notion of forgiveness downright impossible. "If it is difficult for some individuals to forgive during a family dispute, why would it be easy for a victim of torture to reconcile with a perpetrator?" asks Gonzalez. "No institution can be expected to reconcile in a matter of a few years a society that has been divided by violent conflict."

Gonzalez faced that expectation himself as a core staff member of the Peruvian Truth and Reconciliation Commission, established in 2001 to investigate assassinations, disappearances and torture under previous presidents. "We were given the mandate to reconcile," says Gonzalez, "but the question was, at what level? We

Trials and Amnesties Are Used Most Often

Since the early 1990s, criminal trials have been used most often in seeking justice following human rights abuses, usually perpetrated by authoritarian governments. Amnesty laws, which absolve perpetrators, have been the second most popular option, followed by truth commissions. The use of all three approaches jumped dramatically in the early 1990s, with the end of the Cold War and the dissolution of the Soviet Union. Since 1993, more than 90 countries have transitioned from authoritarian rule.

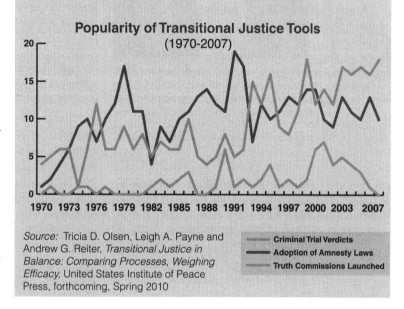

Popularity of Transitional Justice Tools (1970-2007)

Source: Tricia D. Olsen, Leigh A. Payne and Andrew G. Reiter, *Transitional Justice in Balance: Comparing Processes, Weighing Efficacy,* United States Institute of Peace Press, forthcoming, Spring 2010

— Criminal Trial Verdicts
— Adoption of Amnesty Laws
— Truth Commissions Launched

decided it would be impossible — it would be too much to ask of the victims — to push for individual reconciliation between them and their perpetrators."

Instead, the commission tried to "reconcile the individual with the state," the only relationship it felt a government body could repair, he says. To do that, the commission analyzed the causes of the violence and the breakdown in citizen-state relations underlying the violence. Proposals for governmental reform thus shared center stage with collecting individual stories.

Moreover, truth commissions appear to be better at supporting peaceful coexistence between individuals than at full-fledged reconciliation. "You might cease hostilities," says Griswold, "but continue to hate each other. That's perfectly possible."

Finding Out What Really Happened

Statistician separates fact from fiction for truth commissions.

Patrick Ball is used to being the odd guy out. When he walks into the headquarters of most truth commissions, he finds himself surrounded by lawyers. As a statistician and a self-professed data geek, Ball is there to crunch numbers and "hack code," as he puts it.

Ball heads the Human Rights Data Analysis Group (HRDAG) at Benetech, a Palo Alto, Calif.-based non-profit technology consulting firm with a social justice focus. His team brings quantitative analysis to truth commissions, which otherwise rely on anecdotes from victims, survivors and alleged perpetrators of war crimes and genocide. It's an unusual application of technology — few college students solving problem sets in statistics labs imagine they're learning skills useful in defending human rights. But when the challenge is to find patterns of violence amid conflicting claims and denials, a statistician like Ball is an invaluable ally.

"Human rights violations don't occur one at a time," says Ball. His job is to help clarify whether violent incidents number in the thousands or the tens of thousands.

The essence of Ball's job is the ability to see ordinary material as statistical data. "Everything is data to us," he says. "A pile of scrungy paper from border guards — 690 pages — that's data." His team finds it, codes it, analyzes it, interprets it. But statistics is a world of careful hypotheses, not bold proclamations. Data, he says, "is what we're able to observe. That's not the same as what is true."

Still, data that Ball and his team observe — and quantify — have changed our ideas about what's true in places around the globe. In Peru, for example, Ball's team estimated that the number of dead or "disappeared" in that country's 1980s war against terrorists was twice as high as the estimate by a human rights commission in Lima. In Guatemala, the group helped prove that genocide had been committed against the indigenous Mayans. And in Kosovo, the data they collected and analyzed unraveled Slobodan Milosevic's defense during his trial at an international tribunal.

In that case, Ball used hundreds of pages of border-crossing reports, analyzing who moved across the Kosovo-Albanian border and when. The pattern that emerged from that data, combined with 11 other sources on civilian deaths in Kosovo, cast doubt on Milosevic's claim that Kosovars were fleeing NATO bombings, not Serb violence. Ball's work helped prosecutors make a case that the deaths amounted to "ethnic cleansing."

HRDAG grew out of Ball's independent consultations with truth commissions in South Africa, Haiti, Guatemala, Timor-Leste and Peru. The group also has worked with commissions in Ghana and Sierra Leone, as well as non-governmental human rights groups in Cambodia, Sri Lanka and Burma (also called Myanmar) and with the International Criminal Tribunal for the Former Yugoslavia.

Peaceful coexistence can still succeed, however, if the victims and their aggressors mutually foreswear vengeance or violence. "If reconciliation means what I heard in South Africa — simply that 'When I'm walking down the street, and I see someone I know is part of the secret police and they see me, we just keep walking' — if that's reconciliation, then I think a truth commission can be very helpful," says Minow.

Forgiveness, on the other hand, seems far more unlikely. As one Rwandan genocide survivor told a French journalist, "A man may ask forgiveness if he had one Primus [beer] too many and then beats his wife. But

if he has worked at killing for a whole month, even on Sundays, whatever can he hope to be forgiven for?"[27]

Are truth commissions more effective than trials?

Human rights advocates often warn that failing to hold perpetrators accountable for their deeds perpetuates a "culture of impunity." Unless we try war criminals like Sudanese President Omar al-Bashir, the argument goes, future heads of state won't think twice about committing crimes against humanity.

As former U.S. Secretary of State Madeleine Albright remarked, "Adolf Hitler once defended his plan to kill

Much of the work can be tedious, and some of the victories minor. At times, though, Ball's work surpasses even his most ambitious expectations. For a truth commission in El Salvador, for instance, he wrote software to aggregate and analyze the human rights records of army officers; the results forced a quarter of the military leadership to retire. The issue was so politically sensitive, Ball remembers, "We figured they were going to blow our office up." Instead, the officers sued the commission — an unexpected recourse to the very rule-of-law principles that truth commissions try to enshrine.

Today, Ball's team is working on its most sensitive project yet: analyzing the 80-million-page archive of the Guatemalan National Police. Human rights advocates have long blamed them for much of the rampant kidnapping, torture and murder during the country's 36-year civil war, but there was no proof until four years ago. Then tons of police records — stacks upon stacks of musty, molding paper — were found in an abandoned ammunitions depot.

Although the team has gone through only about 10 percent of the archive, a new picture already is emerging. There is "no doubt that the police participated in the disappearances and assassinations," says Carla Villagran, former adviser to the Project to Recover the Historic Archives of the National Police.[1]

Changing the picture of a nation's horrific experiences can help give atrocity victims' suffering "meaning in some bigger story," Ball says. The science of numbers can help victims separate painful histories from destructive mythologies of violence.

Still, for all the good that analyzing patterns can do, Ball knows that numbers and graphs don't say everything

Ann Harrison

Statistician Patrick Ball examines some of the 80 million pages of the Guatemalan National Police archives — discovered by accident — that show the police participated in kidnapping, torture and murder during the country's 36-year civil war.

about the bigger story. "Statistics define the limits of what's plausible and what's not plausible," he says. "Statistics do not tell us how it felt to be there."[2]

---

[1] Julian Smith, "A Human Rights Breakthrough in Guatemala; A chance discovery of police archives may reveal the fate of tens of thousands of people who disappeared in Guatemala's civil war," *Smithsonian*, October 2009, www.smithsonianmag.com/history-archaeology/Digs-Paper-Trail.html?c=y&page=1.

[2] See Jina Moore, "A human rights statistician finds truth in numbers," *The Christian Science Monitor*, Feb. 7, 2008.

Jews by asking the rhetorical question: 'Who, after all, remembers the Armenians?' "[28] He was referring to the allegation by Armenians that the Ottoman Turks slaughtered hundreds of thousands of Armenians during World War I.[29]

Truth commissions and trials both counter impunity, but in different ways. In the Latin America of the 1980s, where military dictators wrote their own immunity into the laws, "prosecution was pretty much off the table," says former South African Judge Goldstone. "In that context, truth commissions were the best one could hope for. Since then, the world has changed dramatically."

Today, international law prohibits amnesty for crimes against humanity, and the ICC is required to prosecute large-scale abuses in the 110 countries that have given it jurisdiction if their own governments fail to pursue trials or prosecution. That means truth commissions have fewer options for offering amnesties to encourage cooperation.

"I think South Africa just scraped by with the amnesties," says Goldstone. "By today's standards, I would find it difficult to amnesty crimes against humanity. In 1995, it was a little different."

Truth commissions can seem, deceptively, like a simpler alternative to courtroom justice. "There is often this sort of sentiment, 'Let's have a truth commission, and let's not really deal with everything else.' It does feel like the easier route toward accountability, without really putting anyone in jail," says International Center for Transitional Justice co-founder Hayner. "But it doesn't play out that way." The Chilean truth commission's files helped indict former Chilean leader Gen. Augusto Pinochet, nearly 10 years later, despite an amnesty law.[30]

In Sierra Leone, an international criminal tribunal and a truth and reconciliation commission operated simultaneously, with occasional cooperation and complications, according to William Schabas, a professor of human rights law at the National University of Ireland and a member of Sierra Leone's commission. A majority of Burundians want both mechanisms for the country's 30-year ethnic conflict: Nearly 8 out of 10 support a truth and reconciliation commission and nearly 7 in 10 want to see perpetrators tried and punished.[31]

Méndez, the former U.N. special advisor on genocide, thinks countries like Burundi need, and can have, commissions and courts. "Both aspects, truth-telling and prosecutions of perpetrators, are obligations of the state in transitional justice, and both have to be conducted in good faith," he has said. "What I reject is the notion that the state can say it will not prosecute anyone but it will give the victims a report on what happened. That is a travesty, because it tries to exchange the demands for justice for a truth-telling exercise."[32]

But good faith doesn't help post-conflict countries solve a pressing public-policy dilemma: If justice, truth and reconciliation are all national priorities, which takes precedence? "If reconciliation is the goal, truth commissions probably do a better job than criminal prosecutions," says Schabas. "In Sierra Leone, most of the people didn't know who the perpetrators were," he explains, making prosecution impossible for all but the leaders of the warring factions.

Even when individual perpetrators' identities are known, truth-telling has advantages over trials. "Truth commissions often come up with a grand narrative that is more plausible, or at least more visible, than an individual trial, which telescopes all the issues through an individual defendant," says Harvard Law School dean Minow. "There, the grand narrative is often in the background."

But some trials can create records that rival, or even surpass, those of truth commissions. The War Crimes Studies Center's Cohen, an adviser to the Timor-Leste commission, points to the International Criminal Tribunal for the Former Yugoslavia. "No truth commission could have possibly compiled all the documents they did, or examined individual cases in the exhaustive manner the court did."

Ultimately, trials and truth commissions are not mutually exclusive, and each achieves advantages the other can't. "I see all of these things as tools of transitional justice," says Judge Goldstone, "and you've got to use the best tools for the situation."

BACKGROUND

From Constantinople to The Hague

Truth commissions and their emphasis on accountability have roots in an earlier era of human rights innovation.

Behind the bloody battlefields of the 20th century's two world wars, genocide raged. The Armenians, a religious and ethnic minority, allege that the Ottoman Empire committed genocide by killing hundreds of thousands of Armenians during World War I. (The Turks don't deny the deaths occurred, but they vehemently deny it was genocide.) And more than 6 million Jews and others considered "undesirable" by the Nazi regime were put to death during World War II.[33]

Immediately after World War I two commissions began investigating the Armenian deaths, though both panels were largely thought marred by corruption and politics. In British-ruled Constantinople in 1919, the British insisted that the Turkish political elite be tried for crimes against the Armenians. The British were eager to punish the Turks for the suffering of both the Armenians and British prisoners of war. The effort faltered after British politicians demanded the Turks release the British prisoners, claiming due-process violations. A year after it was established, the Constantinople court crumbled.[34]

That legacy helped to shape the future of international human rights law, while the Constantinople proceedings set the stage for the post-World War II war crimes trials in Nuremberg. In the capital of German history and culture, 22 senior Nazi officials were tried in 1945 for "crimes against humanity" — language borne out of the

Armenian experience 25 years before. Nuremberg marked the first time such crimes ever reached a courtroom.[35]

Yet the Nuremberg trials were far from perfect. Run by the wartime Allied powers, the trials were criticized as retaliatory victors' justice. Twelve of the 19 men convicted at Nuremberg were executed; two of those indicted committed suicide in their cells.[36]

Crimes of war weren't new, but trials for crimes against humanity — against civilians — were, and retroactively applying these new charges raised concerns. Halfway around the world, the Tokyo tribunals, where the United States tried 28 Japanese military leaders for war crimes and human rights atrocities, raised similar critiques, according to Minow.[37]

Today, the Nuremberg trials are remembered as a watershed event for human rights and international justice. And yet, the judicial precedents they established lay untouched for decades, while the Pol Pot regime in Cambodia murdered nearly 2 million people in the mid-1970s, the Guatemalan government killed nearly 200,000 Mayans during a 36-year internal conflict that began in 1960 and Saddam Hussein slaughtered 50,000 Kurds in 1988.[38]

"There was Nuremberg and Tokyo, and then there's nothing for 60 years," says the Leitner Center's Flaherty.

But when the U.N.-run international criminal tribunals for the former Yugoslavia (ICTY) and for Rwanda (ICTR) were established in the early 1990s they followed the Nuremberg precedents. Launched in 1993, the ICTY was directed to investigate war crimes committed after 1990 in the Balkans during the dissolution of the republic, where a genocidal campaign, mostly against Muslims, gave the world the term "ethnic cleansing."

Two years later, the ICTR was established to try the masterminds of the 100-day-long Rwandan genocide, in which more than 800,000 people, mostly Tutsis, were killed.[39] Although slow and fraught with political and bureaucratic difficulties, the tribunals for Rwanda and Yugoslavia have completed the trials of 170 people (and indicted nearly 70 others) and established important human rights law precedents that paved the way for similar tribunals in Sierra Leone and Cambodia.[40]

But at the beginning of the 21st century, policy makers decided international justice needed a more permanent solution. The International Criminal Court (ICC) was created in 2002 by adoption of the so-called Rome Statute. The ICC prosecutes those responsible for massive human rights violations committed in countries that are unable or unwilling to prosecute such crimes themselves. So far, the ICC has filed cases against Congolese and Ugandan rebels and Sudanese government officials — including the president — and rebels.

Normally, the ICC can only try individuals for crimes committed in the 110 countries that have ratified the 2002 Rome Statute. When abuses happen in non-ratifying countries — such as Sudan — an investigation can begin only if the U.N. Security Council refers the case to the ICC. That's when international justice gets complicated by world politics: The United States and China — veto-wielding members of the Security Council — have refused to ratify the Rome Statute. When it came to a vote, the ICC worried the two powers would oppose a referral, blocking the court from investigating crimes in Darfur. They didn't, and the court's investigations led to indictments against Sudanese President al-Bashir.

Truth vs. Justice

For all the progress made by modern war crimes tribunals, some remain vulnerable to a poignant, longstanding criticism.

"There is a critique of Nuremberg and Tokyo for not giving enough air time to the victims and survivors," says Harvard Law School's Minow. "It says, 'Why is all this attention being paid to the banality of evil? What about the people who died, or who survived?' "

Beginning in 1980s Latin America, citizens began experimenting with truth commissions as they threw off the chains of military dictatorships and groped towards democracy. "Justice was just impossible because the army was so powerful," says Cohen, of the War Crimes Studies Center in Berkeley. "They were saying, 'We're not going to be able to get justice, so let's get as much truth as possible.' "

The Argentinian commission's hands were tied when it came to recommending punishment of particular individuals, primarily because of the junta's self-awarded immunity. The protection was later repealed, mostly because of the commission's report.[41]

The 1990 Chilean commission also inherited amnesty laws passed by and for the previous government. Nonetheless, Gen. Pinochet was arrested in Europe almost

CHRONOLOGY

1910s-1940s *After atrocities in two world wars, "crimes against humanity" becomes a legal precedent.*

1915 The term "crimes against humanity" is coined by a Russian minister in a declaration by World War I allies vowing to hold Turkey accountable for the Ottoman Empire's massacre of hundreds of thousands of Armenians.

1918 Two Ottoman fact-finding commissions look into malfeasance during the war, including the Armenian massacres.

1919-1920 *Setting precedents for the later Nuremberg trials, the Ottoman Empire holds a court-martial and an international tribunal to investigate Turkish officials' behavior during World War I, including the ordering of the Armenian massacres.*

1945 World War II allies, led by the United States, launch war crimes trials in Nuremberg, Germany, against 22 former Nazi officials. Twelve were executed; some committed suicide in their cells.

1946 International tribunal begins in Tokyo for Japanese military and government officials charged with atrocities during World War II. Together with Nuremberg, the trials set precedent for future international justice.

1980s-1990s *Truth commissions emerge as a new method of transitional justice, while ad hoc war crimes tribunals carry on the legacy of Nuremberg.*

1982 Bolivia opens Latin America's first truth commission; it disbands before completing its work, but the country later tries former officials and paramilitary officials for civilian murders and "disappearances."

1984 Argentina publishes *Nunca Más* ("Never Again") — a landmark truth commission report that documented nearly 9,000 reports of the "disappeared," ordinary citizens kidnapped, tortured and murdered by the military junta. Report becomes instant best seller.

1993 U.N. creates International Criminal Tribunal for the Former Yugoslavia to try Balkan officials for war crimes.

1995 South Africa opens its Truth and Reconciliation Commission, the first to include reconciliation in its mandate. . . . U.N. empowers International Criminal Tribunal for Rwanda to try leaders of the 1994 Rwandan genocide. . . . Sri Lanka opens Asia's first truth commission.

1997 Guatemala opens a truth commission to investigate 36 years of state repression and violence, including the genocide of more than 150,000 indigenous Mayans.

2000s *International Criminal Court (ICC) is established, creating a new legal option for post-conflict justice.*

2002 Rome Statute establishes the International Criminal Court (ICC).

2003 U.N.-sponsored Special Court for Sierra Leone begins trials of those responsible for atrocities during that country's long civil war.

2005 ICC indicts Joseph Kony and other leaders of the Lord's Resistance Army, a Ugandan rebel group. Kony demands immunity from prosecution in exchange for surrender. Local leaders suggest using traditional reconciliation rituals instead, but the issue remains stalemated.

2008 The Extraordinary Chambers in the Courts of Cambodia is given a U.N. mandate to try five Khmer Rouge leaders for genocide from 1974 to 1979.

2009 ICC indicts its first sitting head of state, Sudanese President Omar al-Bashir, for war crimes; he retaliates by evicting aid groups from the country. . . . ICC opens its first trial, of Congolese warlord Thomas Lubanga, accused of using child soldiers. . . . Liberia's Truth and Reconciliation Commission recommends banning President Ellen Johnson Sirleaf from public office for 30 years for her past support of former warlord and indicted President Charles Taylor. . . . Kenya sets up a truth commission to examine violence after its 2007 elections; ICC asks for permission to conduct preliminary investigation of the ethnically tinged Kenyan election violence. . . . First Khmer Rouge trial ends in Cambodia in November with verdict expected in 2010.

10 years later, when a Spanish judge, Baltasar Garzón, insisted he had universal jurisdiction to try anyone from anywhere who committed crimes against humanity, thereby overriding Chile's amnesty law.[42]

South Africa's TRC is perhaps the most well-known example of trading amnesty for truth. The commission agreed to take applications for amnesty from perpetrators, provided they fully confessed their crimes and the crimes were politically motivated. Those who confessed to "gross violations of human rights" had to answer questions in public. More than 7,000 witnesses asked for amnesty, but fewer than 10 percent received it.[43]

Truth commission expert Hayner says the idea that justice must take a back seat to truth may be an outdated concept. "Ten years ago that tension was very present," she says. "Now, that's changed." Most human rights lawyers today say it's legally impossible to offer amnesty for testimony, thanks to changes in international law.

Yet the carrot of amnesty may be critical to truth commissions. In one of the most sweeping empirical comparisons of truth commissions, political scientists Jack Snyder and Leslie Vinjamuri say that on the rare occasions when truth commissions have been successful, they have been accompanied by amnesties.[44]

El Salvador, on the other hand, is a cautionary example of how the process can unravel. In 1993, a truth commission report on the country's decade-long civil war named high-level military and government officials as human rights abusers. Five days later, after threats of a coup, the legislature granted general amnesty for all crimes committed during the conflict.[45]

"Justice on the Grass"

Virtually every day for the last four years, a community somewhere in Rwanda has gathered to confront the nation's 1994 genocide. Survivors offer testimony, and the accused — often wearing pink prison uniforms — respond. Often, they deny having participated; sometimes they confess. Nine *inyangamugayo*, or "persons of integrity," preside over the process. They interrogate defendants and witnesses alike, ultimately determining guilt or innocence. There is copious truth-telling here, but this is also a court, and the guilty go to jail.[46]

The process — called *gacaca*, or "justice on the grass" — is a modern adaptation of a conflict resolution ritual the government says stretches back to Rwanda's

precolonial days. While celebrated as a "traditional" approach to Rwanda's atrocities, *gacaca* is also expedient: By turning trials over to local communities, it has brought justice to nearly a million genocide suspects, according to Denis Bikesha, director of training, sensitization and mobilization services at the National Service of Gacaca Courts in Kigali, Rwanda.

But Human Rights Watch argues that *gacaca* trials violate defendants' due process rights and exclude crimes committed during and after the genocide by the military — which at the time was led by current Rwandan President Paul Kagame. A Spanish court, invoking universal jurisdiction for crimes against humanity, in 2008 indicted 40 former Rwandan army officers in 1994 and said it would have indicted Kagame, except that as a head of state he has immunity.[47]

But those shortcomings may reflect the same violence *gacaca* investigates. After genocide, the Rwandan government thought, Western justice wasn't necessarily the best answer, says Stephen Kinzer, author of *Thousand Hills: Rwanda's Rebirth and the Man Who Dreamed It.* "*Gacaca* tries to combine the two necessities [Rwandans] see in the reconciliation process. One is justice, that is, the punishment of the guilty, and the other is reconciliation."

As thousands of prisoners trade truth for jail time, survivors are finally learning where their families were killed and have been able to retrieve their remains. Every April 7, on the anniversary of the beginning of the genocide, families rebury the bones at the national memorial, "with dignity and honor," in the words of one survivor.

If Rwanda is an example of a society choosing to remember, Mozambique has chosen to forget. Nearly a million people died in Mozambique's 16-year war that ended in 1992. Ten days after a peace agreement was signed, the parliament passed a general amnesty. But unlike Latin America, where survivors rallied for justice, Mozambique has never had a truth commission, and it's difficult to find anyone there who wants one.

"Today, if we opened up the idea of the past, it would be to restart the hate," said Brazao Mazula, who once headed the country's electoral commission."[48]

Others share his preference for official silence, but for a different reason. "I don't believe in truth commissions," a Mozambiquan journalist has said. "People need the right to their own interpretations of the past. I don't want to

Do Truth Commissions Work?

The jury is still out, experts say

Is transitional justice working? So far, experts say they can't tell for sure. Too few researchers have studied the impact of truth commissions and related human rights tools, and almost no one can say for certain where and when reconciliation actually has occurred in post-conflict countries.

"There have been a lot of claims about whether truth commissions can provide — fill in the blank — human rights, democracy, reconciliation, the list goes on," says Eric Wiebelhaus-Brahm, a senior researcher at the International Human Rights Law Institute at DePaul University and author of the new book *Truth Commissions and Transitional Justice: The Impact on Human Rights and Democracy.* "The broader research community is really only beginning to scratch the surface in terms of coming up with compelling, empirically based evidence to support any of those contentions."

The complexity of the social science underpinning such studies makes them especially difficult, and often too little time has passed since the end of the war or conflict. But a picture is beginning to emerge about how trials and truth commissions help secure human rights and encourage democracy.

The picture is surprisingly bleak. Most studies produce no evidence that truth commissions make much difference, according to James Ron, an associate professor at the Norman Paterson School of International Affairs at Carleton University in Ottawa, Canada, who co-authored a paper on transitional justice.[1] And one study found that truth commissions can exacerbate the very tensions they seek to quell.[2]

Leigh Ann Payne, a professor of political science at the University of Wisconsin at Madison, has just completed a forthcoming comprehensive study on the effectiveness of truth commissions. She and her two co-researchers found that the commissions by themselves are actually bad for human rights and democracy. However, when combined with trials and amnesties, truth commissions are likely to improve democracy and human rights.[3]

Payne says it's too early to say, with empirical confidence, why the combination of approaches works. "It's probably not that amnesties work because of the threat of trials," she says. In fact, most of the amnesties they examined were followed by trials. "Our hunch is that amnesties provide a way for fragile democracies to get through that very vulnerable moment."

Payne says many of the potential benefits of truth commissions can't be captured by even the most rigorous research. "The measures that are standard in social sciences tend to look at institutional changes. They may not pick up on some of the societal changes taking place," says Payne.

But it's the desire for precisely those societal changes — namely, democracy — that spurs truth commissions. "Truth commissions do a whole lot of other things, particularly giving voice to the victims and acknowledging the violent past, that may not show up" in the variables analysts look at, says Payne.

---

[1] Oskar N. T. Thomas, James Ron and Roland Paris, "The Effects of Transitional Justice Mechanisms," working paper, University of Ottawa Centre for International Policy Studies, April 2008, www.isn.ethz.ch/isn/Digital-Library/Publications/Detail/?ord588=grp1&ots591=0C54E3B3-1E9C-BE1E-2C24-A6A8C7060233&lng=en&id=103597.

[2] Jack Snyder and Leslie Vinjamuri, "Trials and Errors: Principle and Pragmatism in Strategies of International Justice," *International Security*, winter 2003/04, p. 20.

[3] Tricia D. Olsen, Leigh A. Payne and Andrew G. Reiter, *Transitional Justice in Balance: Comparing Processes, Weighing Efficacy*, United States Institute of Peace Press, forthcoming, spring 2010.

---

reconcile myself with the horrendous crimes against the people."[49]

There may be a bias among human rights activists for more truth telling, but some say the option to forget must be given due consideration. "You have to put on the table, as well, doing nothing," says Harvard's Minow, who notes that Cambodia managed its transition successfully without formal transitional justice mechanisms. Today, the country is stable and moving steadily toward economic prosperity.

Others are not so sure. Survivors of the Khmer Rouge's killing fields have rarely talked about the past; when they do, Cambodian youths — who make up more than half of the country — don't believe them.[50] A U.N.-sponsored national/international trial of five Khmer Rouge leaders began in 2008 — 35 years after the Cambodian genocide took nearly 2 million lives and a decade after Pol Pot died.

So far, it's unclear whether the power of truth is opening more wounds in Cambodia than it's healing — and whether it's worth passing the trauma on to a generation that doesn't know it. "It reminds me of my experiences then, how my parents were killed," survivor Yim Somlok told a U.N. agency. "It's good to show everyone, but it's also difficult for me to see the children watching such terrible things."[51]

A high-level Cambodian diplomat said Cambodia just needs a little more time to process its painful past. Perhaps the country's best hope, he said, is that the generation traumatized by the Khmer Rouge — both its perpetrators and its victims —"die off and with them gone, the country might start over again, afresh."[52]

Compensation

Together with justice and reconciliation comes an urge for restitution. Rwanda forces perpetrators of genocide to build roads or terrace hillsides, and in dozens of villages they have volunteered to build homes for genocide survivors.[53] Other governments, on the basis of truth commission recommendations, have compensated victims.

Chile offered a free college education to the children of the "disappeared," and family members receive a monthly pension check; Argentina gave each survivor $220,000 in state bonds.[54]

Most truth commissions recommend monetary reparation as both a literal and symbolic restitution. But getting the money isn't easy. Once a commission's final report is published, the panel is disbanded, and the government may have no interest in or budget for even symbolic payments.

Sierra Leonean human rights activist John Caulker, for instance, spent nearly 10 years lobbying the government to make good on the truth commission's recommendation, and the government's subsequent promise, to provide financial redress for victims of the country's decade-long war.[55]

Not making reparations can be more than a matter of simple political inaction. South Africa's truth commission recommended a "wealth tax" on those who benefited from apartheid as a way to address the poverty of those who suffered in the segregated system. But the government did not institute a formal reparations program, leading to cynicism about the supposed success of a commission that offered some perpetrators amnesty, while victims got only rhetoric.[56] "Reparations," suggests an expert on South Africa's truth commission, "can perhaps correct for amnesty" by making the scales of truth and justice feel more balanced.[57]

But exchanging cash for suffering is equally complicated. International law demands that governments provide restitution for wrongs committed by states, but from whose pocket should the money come?

"The irony is you'd be having the Nelson Mandela regime literally paying for the misdeeds of Bothe," the last president of the apartheid regime, says Flaherty of the Leitner Center for International Law and Justice.

And the compensation should not be too small, says Gonzalez at the International Center for Transitional Justice, who worked on the Peruvian commission. "Reparations need to have an element of magnanimity," he says. "It's nice to have recognition, but if the government says, 'The life of your husband is worth $50,' that's a slap in the face."

CURRENT SITUATION

Publicizing Results

Even in the midst of a global communications revolution, truth commissions have trouble publicizing their work. While they may generate attention in capital cities, the details — including the conclusions — don't always reach the rural areas, especially in undeveloped countries.

Indeed, it's a safe bet that few people read truth commissions' voluminous final reports.

"The report we wrote was nine volumes long," says Gonzalez. "Who reads a report of 4,000 pages?"

Schabas, of the Sierra Leone TRC, admits, "There is a tradition with the published reports of truth commissions of 'mine is longer than yours,' " which can make their findings all but inaccessible.

But even the shorter reports don't always reach rural areas, where many people can't read, in part due to the years of education lost during the very conflicts the reports cover.

Some groups have used multimedia techniques to spread the word. Peru's commission hosted a photography exhibition. In Sierra Leone, the United Nations Children's Fund commissioned a children's version of the report, and WITNESS, a video-oriented human rights organization, produced a companion video version of the commission's final document. But even with these innovations, says

Schabas, "there are limits to how far you can go in a country like that because of the level of literacy and education. You're not going to get very much profound thinking and concern about deep issues of governance."

Still, spreading the word can produce concrete results. The Peruvian commission's "very expensive recommendations on reparations" unexpectedly created "an interesting alliance between victims and one local government," who realized they could use reparations funds to force national leaders to help their impoverished province, Gonzalez says.

Traditional vs. International Justice

The hillsides of northern Uganda are slowly emerging from 30 years of violence, but today there's a new battle raging. This time, the fight is over peace.

The International Criminal Court in 2005 indicted the three top leaders of the Lord's Resistance Army (LRA) — a rebel group that has fought a generation-long insurgency in Uganda — for some of its brutal crimes. Among other things, the group kidnapped hundreds of children, often after forcing them to murder their own parents, and then impressed them into service as child soldiers.[58]

But LRA founder Joseph Kony and his two deputies are hiding in the Democratic Republic of the Congo (DRC), where they are terrorizing civilians already traumatized by a long-running civil war. Some local leaders in Uganda are willing to give Kony the amnesty he wants, if he submits to *mato oput* — "drinking the bitter herb" — a conflict resolution ritual of the Acholi people, the ethnic group primarily targeted by the LRA. The ritual requires offenders to provide details about their crimes, victims to forgive and both parties to share a drink of the herb.[59] Both Uganda's president and the Ugandan Amnesty Act, which recognizes traditional mechanisms as legitimate forms of justice, support the use of such rituals.[60]

The two processes aren't necessarily mutually exclusive, but local leaders say a choice must be made about which should come first.

"At the international level they say, 'There is no justice without peace, there is no peace without justice,' an argument that is a bit ridiculous to me as an international lawyer," says Fabius Okumu-Alya, director of the Institute for Peace and Strategy Studies at Gulu University in northern Uganda. "At least one of the two comes first.

The Acholi are not saying we don't want Kony to be prosecuted. They are not supporting impunity. But what they want is prioritization."[61]

The LRA indictments have thus produced a stand-off in Uganda. ICC indictments in the DRC and Sudan have created similar tensions. When Chief Prosecutor Luis Moreno-Ocampo indicted al-Bashir for genocide in Darfur, the Sudanese president responded by evicting 13 international aid agencies, including those offering food aid and assistance for rape survivors.[62]

In the DRC, on the other hand, the indictments of three rebels on charges including recruitment of child soldiers, have been viewed as an unfair gesture of accountability. One ex-child soldier, after watching a video of the trial of Congolese warlord Thomas Lubanga, wondered how he ended up in the dock in The Hague when "others who did the same thing are working within the government?"[63]

Moreno-Ocampo, the Argentinian lawyer who was named ICC prosecutor in 2003, insists his hands are tied. "I can't make allowances for politics," he has said. "I have to apply and implement the law."[64]

But American lawyer Adam Smith, author of the 2009 book *After Genocide: Bringing the Devil to Justice*, says the court should incorporate the expertise of more than just lawyers. "The decision to indict people in the LRA is a decision made in The Hague by international lawyers, but other people should be involved, such as anthropologists or sociologists or psychologists, people who are better able than I am or Ocampo is" to determine the wisdom of prosecution, Smith says.

"Everything is embedded," he continues. "If you don't see where it's coming from, where it's going and what's around it," he continues, "you're not going to have resonance on the ground [and prosecution] won't have a sustainable benefit."

Future TRCs?

The International Institute for the Rule of Law, backed by the Washington-based U.S. Institute of Peace, is courting public support for a truth commission on the atrocities committed by the former Saddam Hussein regime in Iraq.[65]

Some ground for a truth commission has been laid by the Iraq History Project, a three-year collaboration between the Iraqi Ministry of Human Rights and DePaul University's

Can the International Criminal Court bring justice to Darfur?

YES

Pamela Yates
Documentary Filmmaker
"The Reckoning: The Battle for the
International Criminal Court"

Written for *CQ Global Researcher,* January 2010

Nothing has caught the attention of Sudan's President Omar al-Bashir more than the arrest warrant issued for him by the International Criminal Court (ICC) on charges of war crimes and crimes against humanity in Darfur. The ICC warrant — the first ever issued against a sitting head of state — caused al-Bashir to curtail his travel to regional and global summits and raised questions about the legitimacy of a national leader with a war crimes indictment hanging over his head.

Since the crisis in Darfur began, Darfuris have pleaded with the world to stop the murders, rapes and forced dislocations and to bring the perpetrators to account. Despite harrowing photos, filmed evidence, survivor testimonies, copious hand-wringing and speech-making on the part of the international community and claims of a peace process by the Sudanese government, the Darfuris continue to be victimized by these massive crimes. Only after the U.N. Security Council referred the case to the ICC in 2005 did a serious criminal investigation into the alleged crimes begin.

The meticulous ICC investigation involved 17 countries, and the evidence led back to President al-Bashir. The ICC's decision to issue an arrest warrant was not made without a look at Sudan's own institutions; the ICC found that there were no credible prospects for justice in Sudan, despite the government setting up courts that purportedly investigated crimes in Darfur.

Halima Bashir, a young Sudanese woman who has been a victim of and witness to numerous barbaric acts in Darfur, has spoken out against the government in Khartoum with a hard-hitting book about the tragedy: "I can't explain how happy I am for the ICC case," she said. "It is now more than five years this has been going on, and very little has been done. It's as if we've been talking to deaf people. For me this is a step for justice."

Darfuri refugees and the international diaspora overwhelmingly supported the International Criminal Court. In fact, more than 100 babies born this year to Darfuris in Sudan have been named Ocambo — in honor of ICC prosecutor Luis Moreno-Ocampo.

Now it is time for the international community, in particular the Security Council, to support bringing al-Bashir to face justice in The Hague. Otherwise, our work to create the International Criminal Court — and raise awareness about Darfur — will be for naught.

NO

Adam M. Smith
International Lawyer and Author
After Genocide: Bringing the
Devil to Justice

Written for *CQ Global Researcher,* January 2010

ICC prosecutions are unlikely to provide real, enduring justice, consistent with the peace Darfuris deserve. The roots of the present crisis stretch far beyond the recent violence. The ICC's mandate, however, is restricted — temporally, to the last seven years; geographically, to the "situation in Darfur"; personally, to those whom it deems "most responsible" and, punitively, to the courtroom.

Nonetheless, the court dominates and limits justice discourse throughout Sudan, reducing prospects for more comprehensive solutions and disempowering the real stakeholders: the Sudanese. Bosnian and Rwandan experiences demonstrate that narrow top-down justice cannot quell longstanding inter-ethnic conflict, nor build institutions needed for sustainable peace.

Given Khartoum's lack of political will, it may appear fanciful to argue that justice for Darfur must come from Sudan itself. Yet this is no more unlikely than Khartoum extraditing its ICC-indicted president to The Hague. Both international and domestic justice require Sudan to investigate Darfur crimes, and absent such a choice, neither can be pursued.

The African Union's Panel on Darfur recommends a hybrid court. Operating alongside nonprosecutorial tools like truth commissions, homegrown approaches have greater chances of coming into being, imparting justice and establishing the conditions required for security and meaningful reconciliation.

The ICC may yet compel Sudan to address Darfur, but at what cost? The court has already distorted political debate (with unknown risks), and pursuit of ICC justice imperiled millions when President al-Bashir criminally (but predictably) responded to his indictment by evicting aid agencies from Darfur.

More concerted international action — from the U.N. Security Council or otherwise — could have similarly cajoled Khartoum, without the negative consequences of an indictment. As we have seen in Uganda, where the possibility of ICC prosecution keeps indictee Joseph Kony in the bush, threats of Hague justice may limit leaders' willingness and ability to guarantee peace.

Many Darfuris dream of an al-Bashir trial. Many also rightly worry that such proceedings will radicalize his supporters, unleash more crimes and catalyze violence surrounding the 2010 elections and 2011 referendum, which will likely approve the contentious secession of the oil-rich South.

There need not be debate about "peace versus justice." Sudan needs both. If ICC action leads to more violence, or impedes genuine security, neither will emerge.

International Human Rights Law Institute. Though not a formal truth commission, the program — which has recorded more than 7,000 stories from both victims and perpetrators — was designed to pave the way for an official truth-telling process.[66]

"People here ... have been through so much: the Iraq-Iran war, 35 years under Saddam, civil war in Kurdistan," said Kurda, a 26-year-old Iraqi who ran the project's local office in Iraq. "So people sometimes forget they are human."[67]

But observers warn the time may not yet be right for a truth commission in Iraq. "One of the requirements [of a commission] is that it looks at past abuses with a new regime," says Kevin Avruch, a professor of conflict resolution and anthropology at George Mason University in Fairfax, Va. "The Sunni and Shia and the Kurds are still working things out, so to speak."

Many say the same is true in Afghanistan, where the war between coalition forces and the Taliban is still raging. "At the moment, there's not the political will" for a truth commission, "neither by the Afghan government nor by the international community," says Huma Saeed, an Afghan human rights activist. "The model in South Africa came from within parliament; in El Salvador, it came with a U.N. mandate. We have neither of these."

Even if there were local or international support for a commission, it's unclear how much truth it would uncover. In 2007, Afghan President Hamid Karzai signed a bill, passed by both houses of parliament, granting blanket amnesty to anyone who fought in the 25 years of violence that preceded U.S. operations in 2002.[68] Human rights lawyers challenge the law's validity, arguing that under international law there can be no amnesty for war crimes. But local human rights activists say the damage is done.

"Even if the amnesty bill legally has not taken this right from us, socially and politically it has created problems in the mind of people," an activist says.[69]

OUTLOOK

Jurisdictional Battles

International courts, truth commissions and local processes will continue to compete for attention among the options available in the transitional justice system, say experts in international justice.

Last fall, Kenya approved a truth, justice and reconciliation commission to examine the violence that erupted after the 2007 elections. But the government also has promised to prosecute those responsible, and the ICC prosecutor is pushing for indictments, which could land current senior officials in The Hague.[70]

But it's simplistic to view the friction between the judicial tools as a turf war. After all, the 110-signatory Rome Statute of 2002 gives the ICC the jurisdiction — indeed, the obligation — to investigate crimes against humanity in states that are unwilling or unable to prosecute.

"The question is, does a domestic procedure that is a truth commission, or for that matter a traditional process, count as an adequate domestic response that deprives the ICC of jurisdiction?" says Harvard's Minow.

The answer can be complicated. Rwanda's *gacaca* system highlights the problem: Hailed by some as an effective and efficient adaptation of tradition to deal with crimes on a massive scale, critics say it violates the due process rights of the accused.

At the same time, political realities complicate the post-conflict picture in ways no one yet understands. Aside from social reconciliation, difficult matters of statecraft must be considered. For instance: Are truth commissions good for state building, or are tribunals better? Do either prevent the recurrence of violence?

"We don't know," says Minow.

Today's justice scales are weighted in favor of the ICC. The court has near-universal jurisdiction and more resources than most truth commissions. But its real strength is in its founding statute: States that ratified the statute, and thereby gave the court its power, must now adopt its terms into their national laws. They cannot offer even limited amnesties, which have been the underlying incentive truth commissions have held out to would-be witnesses.

"I fear that the ICC's international justice is perverting the situation on the ground," says international lawyer Smith. "If the ICC continues this way, it will further infuse the importance of prosecutions, which will in turn make it difficult to use other tools."

While nothing technically makes an ICC trial and a local truth commission incompatible, trials and commissions have not exhibited a stellar track record when it comes to collaboration. Smith prefers that the ICC dupli-cate a different model — bolstering local judicial systems' capacities to investigate and make domestic prosecutorial decisions. Two years ago, for example, ICC staff members helped Senegal prepare to try exiled Chadian president Hissine Habre, accused of torture and crimes against humanity.[71] In a historic action, the African Union had referred the case from Chad to Senegal.

The possibility of collaboration addresses a common critique among Africans of international justice: that tribunals and truth commissions are "white man's justice" imposed on the developing world. "The white man will come and take over our leaders and do whatever they want with them," says Sarrfo Amoakohene, a small busi-ness operator in Ghana.

"To the extent that we say these issues apply just to [those in developing countries], that's the end," warns James A. Goldston, executive director of the Open Society Institute's Justice Initiative, a global law reform program with offices in five world capitals and New York City. "These ideas are very much applicable to the developed world."

Among developed countries, Canada is learning just how complicated transitional justice can be. It established a truth commission in 2008 after Prime Minister Stephen Harper apologized to Canada's First Nations for more than 100 years of "residential education" — a program that forcibly removed more than 100,000 aboriginal children from their homes and put them in often abusive boarding schools.[72] After some controversy and political battles, the commission began its work in December.

And in the United States, Sen. Patrick Leahy, D.-Vt., chairman of the Judiciary Committee, has called for a truth commission to investigate alleged abuses during the George W. Bush administration, including the use of coercive interrogation techniques generally considered to be torture. The proposal is seen as a compromise between critics demanding criminal prosecutions of those involved in authorizing so-called enhanced interrogation techniques and others, who want to move on.[73] Because the United States has not signed the Rome Statute, the ICC has no jurisdiction over the case. But an Italian court in November convicted in absentia 22 Central Intelligence Agency operatives for a kidnapping that led to the "extraordinary rendition" of an Italian citizen.[74] And the same Spanish judge who indicted former Chilean leader Pinochet opened

Post-election violence ravages Kibera, a slum in Nairobi, Kenya, in December 2007, leaving more than 1,000 people dead and hundreds of thousands of people homeless. Although the Kenyan government's Truth and Reconciliation Commission — set up in 2008 to investigate human rights violations during the rampage — has yet to release its final report, the International Criminal Court has expressed interest in conducting its own independent investigation of the violence.

a criminal investigation into alleged Bush administration involvement in the torture of five Spanish citizens or residents.[75]

President Barack Obama has said he is "more interested in looking forward than in looking back." But Leahy insists, "It's a lot easier to look forward if you know what happened in the past."[76]

The debate echoes those in dozens of other countries, where the push for peace collides with the need for acknowledgement and accountability for past abuses.

NOTES

1. "We Will Kill You If You Cry: Sexual Violence in the Sierra Leone Conflict," Human Rights Watch, Jan. 16, 2003, p. 25; "Sierra Leone: Getting Away with Murder, Mutilation and Rape," Human Rights Watch, July 1999.

2. "Statistical Appendix to the Report of the Truth and Reconciliation Commission of Sierra Leone," Human Rights Data Analysis Group, Oct. 5, 2004, www.cbc.ca/canada/story/2008/06/11/pm-statement.html.

3. Jina Moore, "Sierra Leoneans look for peace through full truth about war crime," *The Christian Science Monitor*, July 8, 2009.

4. Priscilla Hayner, *Unspeakable Truths: Facing the Challenge of Truth Commissions* (2002), pp. 33-34.

5. *Ibid.*

6. Seth Mydans, "Moving Beyond Khmer Rouge's Ghosts," *The New York Times*, Nov. 30, 2009, p. A8, www.nytimes.com/2009/11/30/world/asia/30 cambodia.html.

7. See Jared Ferrie, "New genocide charge in Cambodian Khmer Rouge trial," Reuters, Dec. 18, 2009.

8. Several countries have had more than one truth commission. For a list, see "Truth Commissions Digital Collection," U.S Institute of Peace Margarita S. Studemeister Digital Collections in International Conflict Management, International Center for Transitional Justice.

9. "South Africa Truth and Reconciliation Commission Final Report," Vol. 1, p. 9.

10. Mark Freeman and Priscilla B. Hayner, "Truth-Telling," in *Reconciliation After Violent Conflict: A Handbook* (2002), p. 125.

11. Hayner, *op. cit.*, p. 222.

12. Martha Minow, *Between Vengeance and Forgiveness: Facing history after genocide and mass atrocity* (1999), pp. 61-62.

13. Nahla Valiji, "Race and Reconciliation in Post-TRC South Africa," paper presented at the conference, "Ten Years of Democracy in Southern Africa," Queens University (Canada), May 2004.

14. Glenna Gordon, "An Interview with Senator Prince Johnson of Liberia," *ForeignPolicy.com*, July 7, 2009, www.foreignpolicy.com/articles/2009/07/07/you_cant_look_back.

15. "Prince Johnson's Threat Worries America," *Liberian Observer*, July 6, 2009, http://orgtema.org/July_2009/Prince%20Johnson's%20Threat%20Worries%20America.htm.

16. "Opinion survey on gacaca and national reconciliation," National Unity and Reconciliation Commission of Rwanda, Kigali, January 2003, p. 92.

17. Hayner, *op. cit.*, p. 222.

18. Don Foster, "Evaluating the Truth and Reconciliation Commission of South Africa," *Social Justice Research*, vol. 19, no. 4, December 2006, p. 533.

19. *Ibid.*

20. Kristen Cibelli and Tamy Guberek, "Justice Unknown, Justice Unsatisfied? Bosnian NGOs Speak about the International Criminal Tribunal for the Former Yugoslavia," Education and Public Inquiry and International Citizenship Program, Tufts University, undated, p. 20, www.hrdag.org/resources/publications/justicereport.pdf.

21. "Human Rights and the Future: Advancing Human Rights in a Dangerous World," Remarks at the American Bar Association's annual meeting, Sept. 17, 2008, www.ictj.org/en/news/features/1982.html. For background, see Alan Greenblatt, "Rewriting History," *CQ Global Researcher*, December 2009.

22. Karen Fogg, preface to *Reconciliation after Violent Conflict: A Handbook*, *op. cit.*, p. i.

23. Quoted in Thomas Brudholm and Valerie Rosoux, "The Unforgiving: Reflections on the resistance to forgiveness after mass atrocity," *Law and Contemporary Problems*, spring 2009, p. 41.

24. Hayner, *op. cit.*, p. 155.

25. Kristen Cibelli, Amelia Hoover and Jule Kruger, "Descriptive Statistics from Statements to the Liberian Truth and Reconciliation Commission," Human Rights Data Analysis Group, 2009, p. 40, www.trcofliberia.org/reports/final/final-report/descriptive-statistics-from-statements-to-the-liberian-trc-benetech.

26. Minow, *op. cit.*, p. 17.

27. Jean Hatzfeld, *Into the Quick of Life: The Rwandan Genocide — The Survivors Speak,* (2005), p. 26 in Thomas Brudholm, *Resentment's Virtue: Jean Amery and the refusal to forgive* (2008).

28. "Address to the Symposium on Human Rights and the Lessons of the Holocaust," Oct. 17, 1995, http://dosfan.lib.uic.edu/ERC/democracy/releases_statements/951017.html.

29. For background, see Greenblatt, *op. cit.*

30. USIP Studemeister Digital Collection, *op. cit.*

31. "Ready to talk about the past: A survey of knowledge and attitudes toward transitional justice in Burundi," BBC World Service and Search for Common Ground, December 2008.

32. Interview with Juan Méndez, in "Justice for a Lawless World: Rights and reconciliation in a new era of international law," IRIN News, June 2006, Part II, p. 9.

33. "Armenians remember 1915 killings," BBC, April 24, 2009, http://news.bbc.co.uk/2/hi/europe/8017316.stm; United States Holocaust Memorial Museum.

34. Gary Bass, *Stay the Hand of Vengeance* (2000), pp. 106-127.

35. M. Cherif Bassiouni, "Crimes Against Humanity," in *Crimes of War Project: A-Z Guide*, undated.

36. "International Military Tribunal at Nuremberg," *Holocaust Encyclopedia*, United States Holocaust Memorial Museum, www.ushmm.org/.

37. Richard Overy, "Making Justice at Nuremberg," BBC online, www.bbc.co.uk/history/worldwars/wwtwo/war_crimes_trials_01.shtml.

38. An exception is the Israeli trial of Adolph Eichmann, the "architect" of the Holocaust, whose 1961 hearing was largely considered a political show trial. Also see "Cambodia: Coming to terms with a violent past," IRIN, Nov. 11, 2009; Human Rights Data Analysis Group's Guatemala Project, www.hrdag.org/about/guatemala.shtml; and Edward Wong, "Saddam charged with genocide of the Kurds," *The New York Times*, April 5, 2006, www.nytimes.com/2006/04/05/world/05iht-saddam.html.

39. Gerard Prunier, *The Rwanda Crisis* (1997), p. 265.

40. ICTR Status of Cases, www.ictr.org/default.htm; ICTY "Key Figures" fact sheet, Nov. 12, 2009, www.icty.org/sid/24.

41. Hayner, *op. cit.*, p. 222.

42. "Strategic Choices in Designing Truth Commissions," Search for Common Ground, Program on Negotiation at Harvard University and the European Centre for Common Ground, www.truthcommission.org.

43. Hayner, *op. cit.*, pp. 43-45.

44. Jack Snyder and Leslie Vinjamuri, "Trials and Errors: Principle and Pragmatism in Strategies of International Justice," *International Security*, winter 2003/04, p. 20.

45. United States Institute of Peace, digital archive; the amnesty has been challenged by the Inter-American Commission on Human Rights as a violation of international law.

46. Jina Moore, "Rwandans: A re-education in how to live together," *The Christian Science Monitor*, April 8, 2009.

47. "Rwanda gacaca criticized as unfair for genocide trials," Voice of America News, April 9, 2009; *ibid.*; also see Tracy Wilkinson, "Spain indicts 40 Rwandan officers; Jurist charges officials in massacres after 1994 genocide. President Kagame is accused, but he has immunity," *Los Angeles Times*, Feb. 7, 2008, p. A6.

48. Hayner, *op. cit.*, p. 190.

49. *Ibid.*, p. 195.

50. Adam Saltsman, "Hate to Remember and Remember to Hate," report for the International Center for Conciliation, January 2007, www.centerforconciliation.org/ReadingRoom/HatetoRememberJan07.htm; "New Year Baby," a documentary film by Socheata Poeuv.

51. "Coming to terms with a violent past," IRIN, Nov. 11, 2009, www.IRINnews.org/report.aspx?Reportid=86980.

52. Michael Paterniti, "Never Forget," *GQ*, July 2009, www.gq.com/news-politics/big-issues/200907/cambodia-khmer-rouge-michael-paterniti.

53. "As We Forgive," a documentary film by Laura Waters Hinson, www.asweforgivemovie.com.

54. Hayner, *op. cit.*, pp. 328-331.

55. Jina Moore, "Fambul Tok Heals Scars of War," *The Christian Science Monitor*, July 7, 2008.

56. Hayner, *op. cit.*, p. 330.

57. James Gibson, *Overcoming Apartheid* (2004), p. 262.

58. For background, see John Felton, "Child Soldiers," *CQ Global Researcher*, July 2008, pp. 183-211.

59. "Traditional drink unites Ugandans," BBC, Sept. 29, 2006, http://news.bbc.co.uk/2/hi/africa/5382816

.stm; and "Forgiveness for ex-Ugandan rebel starts on an egg," Reuters, Sept. 28, 2008, www.reuters.com/article/worldNews/idUSTRE48R26P20080928.

60. *Ibid.*

61. Fabius Okumu-Alya, "Why mato oput system should come before ICC," *New Vision*, Dec. 4, 2006.

62. Rebecca Hamilton, "Left Behind: Why aid for Darfur's rape survivors has all but disappeared," *The New Republic*, Oct. 14, 2009.

63. Adam Hochschild, "The Trial of Thomas Lubanga," *The Atlantic*, December 2009, p. 80.

64. Thomas Darnstaedt, "A Dangerous Luxury: The International Criminal Court's Dream of Global Justice," *Der Spiegel*, Jan. 14, 2009, www.spiegel.de/international/world/0,1518,601258-3,00.html.

65. "In Iraq, truth commission idea gains traction," CNN, March 25, 2009, http://edition.cnn.com/2009/WORLD/meast/03/25/iraq.reconciliation/index.html.

66. Louis Bickford, "Informal truth telling," *Human Rights Quarterly 29* (2007), p. 1004.

67. "Iraqi Daily Lives: Kurda," BBC News, Nov. 20, 2006, http://news.bbc.co.uk/2/hi/talking_point/6151460.stm.

68. "War crime immunity law gets green light," IRIN, March 11, 2007, www.irinnews.org/Report.aspx?ReportId=70637.

69. Unpublished work of Huma Saeed, Afghan human rights activist.

70. USIP Studemeister Digital Collection, *op. cit.*; David McKenzie, "ICC prosecutor: Suspects in Kenya violence will be tried," CNN, Nov. 5, 2009, http://edition.cnn.com/2009/WORLD/africa/11/05/kenya.icc.trials/index.html.

71. "Former Chadian president will be tried in Senegal, says ICC registrar," Hirondelle News Agency, Feb. 27, 2008, www.hirondellenews.com/content/view/10683/180/.

72. "Prime Minister Stephen Harper's Statement of Apology" and "Indian Residential Schools: An FAQ," Canadian Broadcasting Corporation, May 15 and June 11, 2008, www.cbc.ca/canada/story/2008/06/11/pm-statement.html; and www.cbccacanadastory/2008/05/16/f-faqs-residential-schools.html.

73. For background, see Seth Stern, "Torture," *CQ Global Researcher*, September 2007, pp. 211-236.

74. Annie Lowry, "Italian court convicts CIA agents in absentia," *Foreign Policy*, Nov. 4, 2009, http://blog.foreignpolicy.com/posts/2009/11/04/italian_court_convicts_cia_agents_in_absentia.

75. "Spain considers prosecuting U.S. officials for torture," *Los Angeles Times*, May 6, 2009, http://articles.latimes.com/2009/may/06/opinion/oe-miller6.

76. Bobby Ghosh, "Leahy's Plan to Probe Bush-Era Wrongdoings," *Time*, Feb. 17, 2009, www.time.com/time/nation/article/0,8599,1879810,00.html#ixzz0YM6vqfPN.

BIBLIOGRAPHY

Books

Bass, Gary J., *Stay the Hand of Vengeance: The Politics of War Crimes Tribunals, Princeton University Press,* **2000.**
A Princeton professor draws connections between the Armenian trials and the Rwandan and Yugoslavian tribunals.

Hatzfeld, Jean, and Linda Coverdale, *The Antelope's Strategy: Living in Rwanda After the Genocide, Farar, Strauss and Giroux,* **2009.**
A French journalist spends nearly a decade in Rwanda talking to genocide survivors and perpetrators.

Hayner, Priscilla, *Unspeakable Truths: Facing the Challenge of Truth Commissions, Routledge,* **2002.**
This comprehensive overview of truth commissions around the world, by the co-founder of the International Center for Transitional Justice, is being updated in 2010.

Nettelfield, Lara J., *Courting Democracy in Bosnia and Herzegovina: The Hague Tribunal's Impact in a Postwar State, Cambridge University Press,* **2010.**
A Balkans scholar examines the effect of international justice on regions with some of the worst battlefields of the 1990s.

Rice, Andrew, *The Teeth May Smile But the Heart Will Not Forget, Metropolitan Books*, 2009.
A journalist traces one family's efforts to find justice for a father's murder during Idi Amin's reign of terror in Uganda.

Roht-Arriaza, Naomi, and Javier Mariezcurrena, *Transitional Justice in the Twenty-First Century: Beyond Truth Versus Justice, Cambridge University Press*, 2006.
Expert authors look at the second generation of truth commissions and how they provide both truth and justice.

Tutu, Desmond, *No Future Without Forgiveness, Image, Doubleday*, 1999.
The chairman of South Africa's truth and reconciliation commission explains why forgiveness is necessary.

Wiebelhaus-Brahm, Eric, *Truth Commissions and Transitional Justice: The Impact on Human Rights and Democracy, Routledge*, 2009.
A senior human rights researcher from DePaul University examines data to see if truth commissions work.

Articles

Gourevitch, Philip, "The Life After," *The New Yorker*, May 4, 2009.
A reporter who has written about Rwanda's genocidal rampage returns to the country 15 years later.

Hochschild, Adam, "The Trial of Thomas Lubanga," *The Atlantic*, December 2009.
The author of *King Leopold's Ghost* returns to the Democratic Republic of the Congo to ask whether justice can be achieved in the violence-ridden country.

Moore, Jina, "Forgive and Forget?" *The Christian Science Monitor*, July 7-9, 2008.
A Sierra Leonean human rights activist brings traditional reconciliation rituals back to rural communities, after a truth and reconciliation commission disappoints villagers victimized by the nation's wrenching civil war.

Paterniti, Michael, "Never Forget," *GQ Magazine*, July 2009.
As aging Khmer Rouge leaders go on trial, Cambodia finally faces its past.

Reports and Studies

Ball, Patrick, "Policy or Panic? The Flight of Ethnic Albanians from Kosovo, March-May 1999," *American Association for the Advancement of Science*, 2000.
The world's foremost human rights statistician provides an analysis on migration patterns in the Balkans, used to help prosecute Serb president and accused warlord Slobodan Milosevic.

Carranza, Ruben, "The Right to Reparations in Situations of Poverty," *International Center for Transitional Justice*, September 2009.
A former Philippine defense ministry official involved in the United Nations takeover of East Timor argues for the importance of reparations and examines their use in impoverished countries.

Greiff, Pablo de and Roger Duthie, *Transitional Justice and Development: Making Connections, Social Science Research Council*, June 2009.
The editors build a thorough look at the relationship between justice and development, two fields that often operate in isolation.

Olsen, Tricia D., Leigh A. Payne and Andrew G. Reiter, "Transitional Justice in Balance: Comparing Processes, Weighing Efficacy," *U.S. Institute of Peace*, 2010.
Researchers provide a cross-national analysis of the effectiveness of transitional justice mechanisms in every post-conflict country since 1970.

Thomas, Oskar N. T., James Ron and Roland Paris, "The Effects of Transitional Justice," working paper, *Center for International Policy Studies, University of Ottawa*, April 2008.
The researchers distill current social science research on truth commissions, concluding that there's not yet enough research to determine whether truth commissions work.

For More Information

Acholi Religious Leaders Peace Initiative, P.O. Box 200, Gulu, Uganda; (256) 471-32-484; www.km-net.org.uk/about/partners/arig/intro.htm. Religious and community conflict-resolution leaders work to end the war in northern Uganda.

Center for the Study of Violence and Reconciliation; P.O. Box 30778, Braamfontein, Johannesburg, South Africa; +27 (11) 403-5650; www.csvr.org.za. A research and advocacy organization devoted to peace and reconciliation in South Africa and beyond.

Fambul Tok International; Freetown, Sierra Leone, and Portland, Maine. www.fambultok.org. A West African organization focused on identifying traditional rituals for post-conflict healing across Africa.

Human Rights Data Analysis Group; Benetech HRDAG, 480 S. California Ave., Suite 201, Palo Alto, CA 94306-1609; (650) 644-3400; www.hrdag.org. A consulting group that designs scientific research and analysis methods for human rights projects.

Institute for Historical Justice and Reconciliation, Laan van Meerdervoort 70, The Hague, 2517AN Netherlands; +31 (0) 70 361 5530; www.historyandreconciliation.org. Organization that brings together local historians and other stakeholders to work through disputes about historical truth.

Institute for Justice and Reconciliation, 10 Brodie Road, Wynberg, Capetown 7800, South Africa; (21) 763-7128; www.ijr.org.za. A research institute that examines the lessons of South Africa's TRC and looks at how to apply them across Africa.

International Center for Transitional Justice; offices worldwide and New York Headquarters, 5 Hanover Street, Floor 24; New York, NY 10004; (917) 637-3800; www.ictj.org. A research and consulting group offering help to countries transitioning from eras of human rights abuse.

Leitner Center for International Law and Justice, Fordham University, 33 West 60th St., New York, NY 10023; (212) 636-6862; LeitnerCenter@law.fordham.edu. An early pioneer of law and human rights studies; sponsors hundreds of programs a year open to the public.

Open Society Institute; worldwide offices and headquarters at 400 West 59th St., New York, NY 10019; (212) 548-0600; www.soros.org. Oversees programs on transitional justice, rule of law and open societies in the Americas, Asia, Eastern Europe and Africa.

United Nations Peacebuilding Commission, United Nations Plaza, New York, NY; www.un.org/peace/peacebuilding/pbso.shtml. An intergovernmental advisory body that supports holistic approaches to peace in post-conflict countries, including providing consultations on truth commissions.

13

Dangerous War Debris

Who Should Clean Up After Conflicts End?

Robert Kiener

Hussein Ahmed lost his hands in a landmine explosion in Mogadishu, Somalia. Experts say more than 250,000 landmines and other unexploded artillery shells, hand grenades, mortars, cluster bombs and rockets are scattered throughout war-torn Somalia. Tens of millions of live munitions threaten people in more than 70 nations around the world, and some 5,200 people worldwide were killed or maimed by landmines and other explosive war debris in 2008.

From *CQ Global Researcher,*
March 2010.

AP Photo/Mohamed Sheikh Nor

Martine Niafouna, a rice farmer in Senegal, was walking down a path near her village when she stepped on a landmine. The explosion threw her into the air, blew off the lower part of her right leg and horrifically burned her left leg.

Unable to work, she wonders how she will ever support her two children and 10 siblings. "It's ruined my life," she said recently, sitting in her one-room hut, her eyes filling with tears. "I can't do anything anymore. Anything at all."[1]

Niafouna, 36, is one of 748 people killed or seriously injured by landmines left over from a 27-year conflict in the Casamance region of southern Senegal, home to rice fields and beautiful beaches.[2]

But the West African nation is only one of more than 70 countries endangered by tens of millions of antipersonnel landmines covering nearly 750,000 acres — an area the size of Rhode Island.[3] (*See map, p. 342.*) Left behind by warring armies and insurgents, landmines are often called "silent killers," because they lie in wait to kill or maim, often years after a conflict ends. After more than a decade of conflict, the Iraqi government claims that at least 25 million landmines have already been left in Iraq by warring factions.[4]

Worldwide, about 5,200 people were wounded or killed by landmines during 2008 — or about 14 people per day.[5] Adding to the misery they cause, landmines also hamper economic development by keeping large tracts of land off limits for agriculture or other uses.

Across the continent from Niafouna, on Africa's East Coast, Mohamed Olhaye Nour, 60, is a typical subsistence farmer in the war-torn Horn of Africa who can't earn a living due to landmines.

341

War Debris Affects 70 Nations

Civilians in some 70 countries — mainly in Africa, Asia and the Middle East — were killed or injured in 2008 by land mines or unexploded grenades and other explosive remnants of war (ERW) left over from conflicts.

Countries with Casualties from Dangerous War Debris, 2008

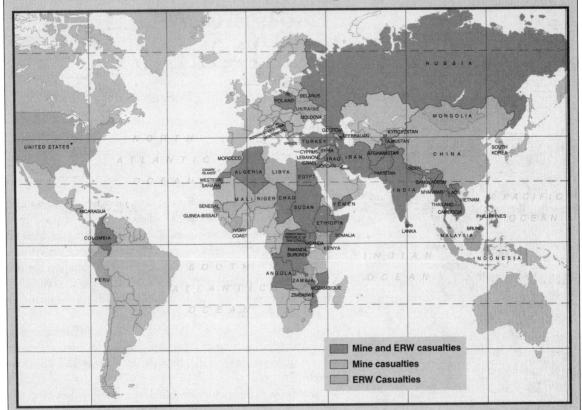

* U.S. casualties occurred when two men were fatally wounded after ordnance exploded at a metal recycling plant in Raleigh, N.C., and a man died while restoring a Civil War-era cannonball he had found.

Source: "Mines and Explosive Remnants of War (ERW) Casualties in 2008," *Landmine Monitor,* 2009

His village of Abuda — 15 miles southwest of Somaliland's capital, Hargeisa — was mined during both the 1977-1978 war between Somalia and Ethiopia and the decade-long war between the Somali National Movement and the Somali National Army that ended in 1991.[6]

"Before the war, our life was good; we did not worry about making ends meet," he said recently. Since the wars ended, Nour and others have been too terrified to

return to their land. Two people who did return paid heavily: Both were injured by landmines; one lost both arms. Nour, who now ekes out a living keeping livestock, has lost 36 of his animals to the mines. Nour's story is not unusual; experts say more than 250,000 landmines and other unexploded ordnance (UXO) — artillery shells, hand grenades, mortars, cluster bombs and rockets — lie in wait throughout Somalia.[7]

Many of the most heavily mined countries are among the poorest on the globe and can least afford to lose territory to the deadly weapons. For instance:

- In Cambodia, 40 percent of the population lives near explosive remnants of war (ERW). Over a three and a half year period from January 2006 to June 2009, more than 1,200 men, women and children were either maimed or killed by the weapons.[8]

- In Mozambique, from 500,000 to several million landmines were laid in 123 of the nation's 128 districts during the country's 25 years of revolution and civil war. Although more than 173,000 mines (plus 133,000 other items of unexploded ordnance) were removed between 1993 and 2006, today 9 percent of the population still lives in mine-affected areas. Removing them costs about $4.2 million per year — a sum the impoverished nation can ill afford and must get from foreign donations.[9]

- In Sri Lanka, although the civil war has recently ended, more than 1 million landmines contaminate about 100,000 acres in the northern part of the country, preventing thousands of displaced residents from returning to their homes and livelihoods.[10]

"Landmines are insidious," says Richard Moyes, director of policy and research at Action on Armed Violence, formerly called Landmine Action — a London-based nongovernmental organization working to reduce armed violence around the world. "They can lay dormant for decades until an innocent person treads on one with horrific results." They also are indiscriminate: 60 to 80 percent of landmine victims are innocent civilians, usually farmers working in fields or children playing.[11] Valued farm animals, such as sheep or cows, also fall victim to landmines.[12] (*See graphic, p. 344.*)

Landmines as we know them today were first used widely in the Civil War but were used much more

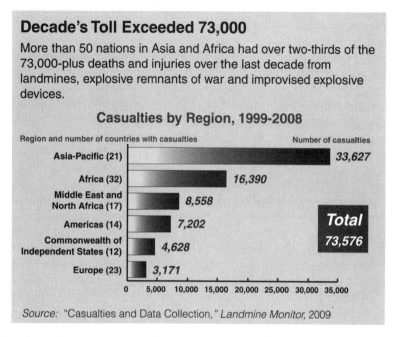

Decade's Toll Exceeded 73,000

More than 50 nations in Asia and Africa had over two-thirds of the 73,000-plus deaths and injuries over the last decade from landmines, explosive remnants of war and improvised explosive devices.

Casualties by Region, 1999-2008

Region and number of countries with casualties — Number of casualties

Region and number of countries with casualties	Number of casualties
Asia-Pacific (21)	33,627
Africa (32)	16,390
Middle East and North Africa (17)	8,558
Americas (14)	7,202
Commonwealth of Independent States (12)	4,628
Europe (23)	3,171

Total 73,576

Source: "Casualties and Data Collection," *Landmine Monitor*, 2009

extensively during World War II. They are relatively cheap to manufacture (costing as little as $3) and generally range from the size of a hockey puck to a dinner plate. The pressure-sensitive devices contain an inner core of explosives and a detonator and a fuse encased in rubber, metal, plastic or even wood.[13]

Landmines are especially insidious because they are designed to maim, rather than kill. "Designers of landmines reasoned that an enemy had to spend more time caring for a wounded soldier than a dead one," says Rupert Leighton, former director of Cambodia operations for the international mine-clearing organization Mines Advisory Group (MAG).

They are also designed to spread fear throughout the enemy's ranks. It's easy to imagine how terrifying it is to watch a fellow soldier lose a leg to a landmine just yards away. Because they can be planted ahead of time and explode on contact, they also free up soldiers for fighting elsewhere.

As British officer Col. J. M. Lambert wrote in 1952, "Mine warfare is an unpleasant business. It is foreign to our character to set traps cold-bloodedly, or to kill a man a fortnight in arrears so to speak, when you yourself are out of harm's way; and most British soldiers who have experienced it will own a rooted dislike of mine warfare

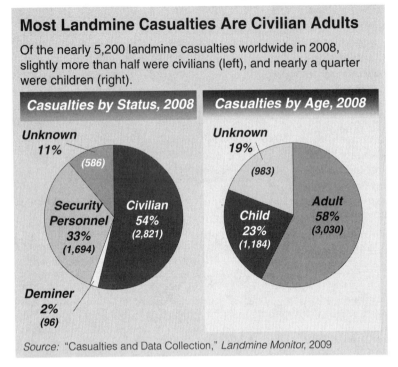

Most Landmine Casualties Are Civilian Adults

Of the nearly 5,200 landmine casualties worldwide in 2008, slightly more than half were civilians (left), and nearly a quarter were children (right).

Casualties by Status, 2008

Unknown
11%
(586)

Security
Personnel
33%
(1,694)

Civilian
54%
(2,821)

Deminer
2%
(96)

Casualties by Age, 2008

Unknown
19%
(983)

Child
23%
(1,184)

Adult
58%
(3,030)

Source: "Casualties and Data Collection," *Landmine Monitor,* 2009

in principle and in practice."[14] American Civil War General William Tecumseh Sherman called the use of landmines "Not war, but murder."[15]

While landmines remain widely used, their civilian toll helped to spawn a coordinated, international anti-mine campaign in the late 1980s, spurred by the Soviet Union's planting of mines throughout Afghanistan. The campaign was led largely by nongovernmental organizations (NGOs) such as the International Red Cross, the Vietnam Veterans of America and the International Campaign to Ban Landmines (ICBL). In 1997 the late Princess Diana helped generate publicity for the cause by visiting landmine victims in Angola.

Eventually, on Dec. 3, 1997, 122 nations signed the Ottawa Convention, also known as the Mine Ban Treaty (MBT), a landmark agreement banning the use, manufacture and sale of landmines. Since then 34 more countries have signed the treaty, but 39 states — including the United States, Russia, China and Pakistan — have not ratified it.

The United States, however, abides by many of the treaty's provisions. For example, it retains its stockpiles of landmines but has not used them since the 1991 Persian

Gulf War and has not exported them since 1992, according to the ICBL. And no American company has manufactured landmines since 1997.[16] However, India, Pakistan and Burma (also called Myanmar) and some insurgent groups still build landmines. But there is no identifiable international trade in landmines.

The United States has not joined the treaty despite persistent lobbying by anti-landmine activists, largely because the U.S. military says landmines can be important weapons and officials don't want to be prohibited from ever using them again.

Rebuffed by the George W. Bush administration, many treaty advocates felt fortunes would change with the election of Democrat Barack Obama. However, just days before last November's MBT meeting in Cartagena, Colombia, the U.S. State Department announced that the Obama administration had decided not to change the Bush-era policy and sign the treaty.[17]

That decision was "a default of U.S. leadership and a detour from the clear path of history," said an angry Sen. Patrick Leahy, D-Vt., a longtime proponent of the treaty. "The United States took some of the earliest and most effective steps to restrict the use of landmines. We should be leading this effort, not sitting on the sidelines."[18]

Jeff Abramson, deputy director of the Arms Control Association, a nonpartisan arms control policy group in Washington, also was amazed when the Obama administration affirmed the Bush administration's policy. "It seemed like a no-brainer for the new administration," he says. Human rights groups and NGOs echoed their comments. A day later the administration said it would review the decision, a process that is still ongoing.

While landmine activists continue to pressure other nations to ratify the MBT, few believe any of them will do so until the United States reconsiders. When confronted, non-signatories such as China, Israel, Russia and Pakistan point in their defense to the U.S. government's reluctance to sign the treaty. China has repeatedly said it opposes a total ban on landmines, and it — like Russia and Israel — prefers to deal with the landmine issue within the framework of the Convention on Certain Conventional Weapons (CCW). That 1980 treaty, eventually signed by 109 countries, regulated the use and transfer of landmines but fell short of banning them outright.

While landmines may be the best-known and most notorious Explosive Remnants of War, there is a growing concern about other dangerous war debris like cluster bombs and other types of unexploded ordnance. "Large numbers of civilians are killed or injured each year by ERW," said the ICRC. These are the unexploded artillery shells, hand grenades, mortars, cluster bomblets, rockets and other explosive ordnance that remain after the end of an armed conflict. Like antipersonnel mines, the presence of these weapons has serious consequences for civilians and their communities."[19]

Cluster munitions are deployed either by aerial bombs or artillery shells that can release hundreds of smaller explosive devices, or bomblets, which can blanket an area as large as several football fields. Although most bomblets explode on impact, up to 10 percent don't. Like landmines, the bomblets can explode years later, maiming and killing indiscriminately. (For a Human Rights Watch video demonstration of a cluster bomb, go to www.youtube.com/watch?v=TpGMiAlVM6g.)

NATO estimates that 10 percent of the cluster bombs dropped in Kosovo in the late 1990s did not explode, leaving some 30,000 unexploded "submunitions," as they are called, on the ground.[20] Civilians, especially inquisitive children, are often the unintended victims. According to Brussels-based Handicap International, 85 percent of the victims of landmines and unexploded ordnance are civilians and 23 percent children.[21]

Cluster munitions have been used since World War II, and by some estimates unexploded cluster bombs have caused up to 100,000 civilian casualties over the last 40 years.[22] However, after Israel dropped some 4 million cluster bombs over southern Lebanon during the 2006 Israel-Hezbollah war, the negative publicity it generated helped to re-ignite a three-decade-old movement to ban cluster bombs.[23]

After the MBT, activists and concerned governments began to campaign against cluster bombs, and in December 2008 more than 90 countries signed the

AP Photo/Sergey Ponomarev

Bomb expert Frank Masche, technical field manager from the Mine Advisory Group, studies a cluster bomblet found in southern Lebanon after the 2006 war with Israel. Israel dropped an estimated 4 million cluster bombs during the brief war, generating a wave of negative publicity that helped to reignite a three-decade-old movement to ban the weapons, which scatter lethal debris over a wide area.

Convention on Cluster Munitions (CCM), which bans cluster bombs and provides assistance to affected communities to help with removal and victim assistance. But as with the MBT, some of the world's major military powers and biggest users of cluster bombs have not signed the treaty, including the United States, Russia, Pakistan, Israel, India and China.

Many military experts describe cluster bombs as valuable weapons against entrenched forces. "With cluster bombs, they can take out a lot of your enemy at once," said Lawrence Freedman, a professor of war studies at King's College London. "And they can . . . make it hard for your enemy ground forces to operate."[24]

The United States last used cluster bombs in 2003 in Iraq. Although President Obama joined 29 other U.S. senators in voting in 2006 to restrict the sale and use of cluster munitions, his administration has not yet decided whether to sign the CCM. "From a humanitarian point of view it is completely unacceptable that the USA continues to opt out of the cluster bomb treaty," says Stephen Goose, director of the arms division of the New York City-based Human Rights Watch.

But the armed forces of the United States and other nonsignatory nations see cluster bombs as useful, effective weapons. Russia, for example, has repeatedly described cluster bombs as legitimate weapons of war if targeted correctly.

Meanwhile, other remnants of war — including more than 70,000 tons of stockpiled chemical weapons of which 95 percent belong to Russia and the United States — must be destroyed or decommissioned. And debate surrounds the question of what effects, if any, using depleted uranium in armor-piercing tank rounds may have on military troops and civilians.[25] While only the United States and the U.K. have admitted using depleted uranium weapons, up to 20 other countries are thought to have them. The Defense Department claims the depleted uranium weapons "pose no known" health risk, but many question those findings.[26]

As officials continue to debate what to do about toxic and dangerous war debris, here are some of the questions being asked:

Should the United States join the landmine and cluster bomb treaties?

Just two weeks before President Obama accepted the Nobel Peace Prize in Oslo, Norway, for his commitment to "disarmament and arms control" last year, his administration shocked activists around the world when it announced it would continue with the Bush administration's stance on landmines and not sign the international treaty banning them.

"It was painful that President Obama chose to reject this treaty just before he was to join the ranks of Nobel Peace laureates, a group that includes the International Campaign to Ban Landmines," says Human Rights Watch's Goose. "This decision lacks vision, compassion and basic common sense and contradicts the administration's professed emphasis on multilateralism, disarmament and humanitarian affairs."

Furthermore, said Jody Williams, the founding coordinator of the International Campaign to Ban Landmines (ICBL) and co-winner (with the ICBL itself) of the Nobel Peace Prize for her role in banning landmines, "This decision is a slap in the face to landmine survivors, their families and affected communities everywhere."[27]

Many argue that the United States should sign the treaty both for tactical reasons and on humanitarian and moral grounds. "Every member of NATO has joined the treaty," says Tim Rieser, an aide to Sen. Leahy. "They recognize that mines pose unacceptable risks to innocent civilians and to their own troops. The U.S. should follow

their example. By joining, we would strengthen the treaty and eliminate the excuse that some countries use for not doing so: 'The U.S. hasn't, why should we?' "

Yet opponents of the treaty argue the global status of the United States requires it to reject the treaty. "Because of our unique role in the world, the United States needs to have certain strategic and tactical weapons available to it," says Steven Groves, a fellow at the conservative Heritage Foundation. "It is very easy for countries like Norway to pressure us to sign this treaty and the cluster bomb ban. However, when it comes time to bring armed force into a situation, it's not going to be the Norwegian Special Forces that are called upon; it will be U.S. forces. And if they need landmines to protect them from incursion or cluster munitions for protection or assault, these weapons need to be available."

The treaty's proponents point out that the United States has not used landmines in nearly 20 years. "Simply put, landmines aren't very good weapons, and the military is aware of how stigmatized they have become," says Goose. "Politically, it's poison to use them."

Moreover, says Rieser, "It would be a serious mistake to use landmines in Afghanistan, where the U.S. military is doing its utmost to reduce civilian casualties. Afghanistan has joined the treaty, as have our coalition partners. How would it look if innocent civilians, or United States soldiers, were blown up by a U.S. landmine in Afghanistan, the world's most heavily mined country, where the United States, the U.N. and others have spent hundreds of millions of dollars to remove the mines and help the injured?"

Groves counters: "War is terrible. Any civilian death is tragic. But anti-personnel mines and cluster munitions have legitimate purposes, and when used responsibly by the United States they can be effective on the battlefield. Signing these treaties would limit our strategic options."

Richard Garwin, a fellow at the Council on Foreign Relations think tank in New York, agreed, arguing that signing the MBT would "gravely increase the risk to our ground forces during combat, and to those civilians they may be sent to protect."[28]

Opponents of both landmines and cluster bombs point to their "indiscriminate" effects as reason enough to ban them. "Neither weapon can discriminate between a 2-year-old kid and an enemy combatant," says Rieser. "Besides, if landmines were so important strategically, why haven't we used them in two decades, and why have our allies banned them?"

Historically, the Pentagon has described antipersonnel landmines (APLs) as an "essential capability." As a Pentagon spokesman noted, "Should an operational commander determine that APLs are required to support operations or to protect U.S. men and women in uniform, he can request authority to use them in accordance with pre-established rules."[29]

Many landmine and cluster bomb opponents compare them to poison gas, which also does not differentiate between friend, foe or civilian. And, they remind landmine advocates, it took a U.S. president agreeing to outlaw poison gas before the Defense Department agreed to stop using it.

Casualties Rise in Some Countries, Fall in Others

Among countries with high rates of casualties from landmines and other unexploded ordnance, five countries — Afghanistan, Myanmar (Burma), Pakistan, Iraq and Somalia — saw casualties increase from 2007 to 2008. Casualties declined in Cambodia, Chad and Colombia.

Casualty Trends for Selected Countries,* 2007-2008

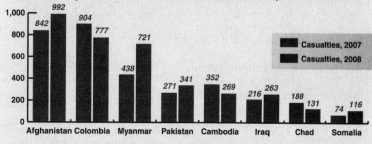

* Countries with more than 100 landmine casualties in 2008.

Source: "Casualties and Data Collection," *Landmine Monitor*, 2009

What about the so-called "smart" cluster bombs, which are designed to self-destruct after a set period of time? Could they justify the U.S. refusal to sign the CCM?

Human rights activists say some smart bombs fail to self-destruct up to 16 percent of the time. Moyes, at London's Action on Armed Violence, says, "With high failure rates and the inability to discriminate between combatant and civilian, these bomblets could never be termed 'smart.' "

"These are not the laser guided weapons the Pentagon showed destroying their targets during the invasion of Baghdad," says Sen. Leahy. "The cluster munitions that fail to explode as designed . . . remain as active duds, like landmines, until they are triggered by whoever comes into contact with them. Often it is an unsuspecting child or a farmer."

Leahy, a champion of assistance for landmine victims, is adamant the United States should ratify both treaties: "Victim-operated weapons should be a thing of the past. Period."

Is enough being done to destroy banned toxic weapons?

Amid much fanfare last May, Russia opened a new facility in Shchuchye, Siberia, dedicated specifically to neutralizing chemical weapons. Tons of deadly nerve agents,

a single drop of which could kill a person, sat locked tightly behind a sturdy barbed-wire fence. Russia's chemical weapons arsenal — the world's largest — includes the nerve agents sarin, mustard gas, phosgene and soman.[30]

Although long delayed, the facility's opening was welcome news to activists, who had been frustrated by Russia's tardiness in destroying its chemical weapons. Russia, like the United States and 188 other states, had signed the 1997 Chemical Weapons Convention (CWC), which bans chemical weapons and requires their destruction within a specified period of time.

Under the treaty, chemical stockpiles and production facilities were to have been destroyed by 2007. But so far, the seven treaty signatories known to have chemical weapons — the United States, Russia, India, Albania, South Korea, Iraq and Libya — have only destroyed 43 percent of their 70,000 metric tons of munitions.

Several years ago Russia and the United States — which has destroyed 70 percent of its 31,500-ton chemical arsenal — were given until April 29, 2012, to finish neutralizing their weapons. The United States now claims it needs another decade.

"Some of the delay in the U.S. can be attributed to bungling by the military," noted Jonathan B. Tucker, a senior fellow at the James Martin Center for Nonproliferation

Studies in Washington. In addition, residents near the new disposal sites were worried about possible harmful effects from the incineration activities. Added Tucker: "The army was not prepared for the resistance from communities located near several of the . . . sites." Tucker is also skeptical that Russia will meet its new 2012 deadline.[31]

The U.S. disposal process has been hampered by delays, work stoppages, environmental issues and shortages of funds.[32] "During the Bush administration funds earmarked for chemical weapons disposal were often shifted over to the Iraq and Afghanistan war budgets," notes Tucker.

Craig Williams, executive director for the Kentucky-based Chemical Weapons Working Group, a coalition of citizen groups who live near stockpile sites, said: "To intentionally put tens of thousands of Americans at an unnecessary risk by continuing to store these weapons is reprehensible. Not only are they ignoring our international treaty obligations, they are undermining the military's obligation . . . to protect U.S. citizens."[33]

In April 2008 Iran rebuked the United States and Russia for insufficient progress in destroying the banned weapons, claiming the delay "is a matter of serious concern" because it indicates a state's intention to retain chemical weapons for military purposes.[34]

The Army claims it is working as fast as it can. The disposal program "is a tremendous success story," said Carmen Spencer, deputy assistant secretary of the Army for elimination of chemical weapons. "Not only is the U.S. doing all it can to meet its international commitments, but, more importantly, the [agency responsible for disposal] is contributing to the national security of the United States in the process. These weapons in the wrong hands can do harm. They are safely and securely storing and destroying them while providing maximum protection to the public and environment."[35]

Admittedly, disposal is a complex and costly exercise. U.S. costs alone will top $20 billion. "The dismantlement challenge is enormous," said Rogelio Pfirter, head of the U.N.'s Organization for the Prohibition of Chemical Weapons. "The financial crisis certainly doesn't help."[36]

Some experts criticize the CWC itself, saying it should include "non-lethal" chemical agents such as riot control and incapacitating agents. Others claim the treaty does not set up a suitable framework to allow on-site inspections of stockpiled chemical weapons.[37]

Until all nations sign the CWC treaty, chemical weapons continue to be a threat, say some critics. They note that of the seven nonsignatory nations — Angola, Egypt, Israel, Myanmar, North Korea, Somalia and Syria — Egypt is known to have used chemical weapons in conflict, while North Korea and Syria are suspected of maintaining chemical weapon stockpiles.

Libya, a treaty signatory that admitted having more than 25 metric tons of mustard gas in 2004, has not destroyed any of its stockpiles. It pulled out of an agreement for the United States to help build an incinerator for the weapons, citing environmental complaints from nearby residents, a claim few experts believe. Libyan leader "Quaddafi is mercurial, and we just don't know if he is serious about destroying his chemical weapons," says Tucker. "The jury is still out."

In addition to the chemical agents being destroyed under the CWC, another even more ominous source of chemical weapons exists: older, non-stockpiled arms that were abandoned — often dumped — after earlier wars. For example, after World War II, the U.S. Army secretly dumped 64 million pounds of nerve and mustard agents off the coasts of 11 states, along with 400,000 chemical-filled bombs, land mines and rockets.[38] According to some estimates more than 300 tons of chemical weapons were dumped into the world's oceans by the United States and other nations between 1946 and 1972.[39] (See map, p. 358.) And according to the Chinese government, Japan left some 2 million chemical weapons — including shells, bombs and barrels of mustard gas, phosgene and hydrogen cyanide — in China after they were defeated in 1945.[40]

There are countless other chemical weapons rotting away in fields or hidden in long-forgotten stockpiles, some from as long ago as World War I. Accidental discoveries are common. About 500 chemical weapons are found in Belgium every year. Danish fishermen have pulled up more than 200 mustard gas shells in their nets since the end of World War II. In 2006 the U.S. Army found 15 million pounds of chemical weapons dumped off the shores of Hawaii.[41] And in the affluent Spring Valley section of Washington, D.C., crews have been excavating caches of World War I nerve gas from neighborhood yards for several years.

While the CCW treaty dictates that signatories work to recover these long-forgotten weapons, no one is pressuring governments to identify and collect "inaccessible" disposed chemical weapons. As one U.S.-based chemical weapons removal expert recently noted, these non-stockpiled chemical weapons will continue to plague generations to come.

"Our kids and grandkids will be finding them," he said.[42]

Is the world doing enough to help ERW victims?

Landmine and cluster bomb treaty activists agree that over the last decade much progress has been made to rid the world of these two "silent killers." Since 1999 a total area twice the size of London has been cleared in more than 90 countries. More than 2.23 million landmines and 17 million ERW have been destroyed, and annual casualties have dropped from around 20,000 a year to 5,200.[43]

International funds for mine clearing and victim assistance totaled $4.27 billion between 1992 and 2008.[44] As impressive at those numbers are, however, activists say much more must be done, particularly in the area of victim assistance.

"Despite this high level of overall funding, over the past decade victim assistance has made the least progress of all the major sectors of mine action, with funding and action falling far short of what was needed," said the International Campaign to Ban Landmines. "Most efforts remained focused on medical care and physical rehabilitation, often only when supported by international organizations and funding, rather than on promoting economic self-reliance for survivors, their families and communities."[45]

Brussels-based Handicap International recently reported that two-thirds of the 1,645 ERW victims surveyed in 25 countries said "their needs are not taken into account by national victim assistance plans."[46] Unemployment among the hundreds of thousands of survivors is high — 70 percent in Afghanistan — and fully 90 percent of those surveyed said they had little chance of getting a job.[47]

In addition to their often horrific injuries and the loss of income, ERW victims can also suffer from depression, psychological trauma and social ostracism. Among the HI survey's respondents was Rosa Jose Njango, from Mozambique's Maputo province. She was 13 when she stepped on a landmine in 1981 and lost both her legs.

She eventually married and had two children. However, when her husband died her relatives took her children, claiming she is unable to care for them. "She now lives alone in a humble hut," said the report.

Like many landmine and ERW victims, Rosa never received any psychological, economic reintegration or financial assistance. When asked what she would like to tell potential donors, she replied, "Enough words, now let's move to concrete actions."[48]

Only about 5 percent of the more than $4 billion spent on mine action over the last decade has gone to victim assistance. Dismayed by funding shortfalls at last year's Cartagena Convention, Christine Beerli, vice president of the Swiss-based ICRC, said: "Despite our efforts, the hopes that most landmine survivors had for this convention have not yet been fulfilled."[49]

Paul Vermeulen, director of Handicap International, was blunter about the need for change. "The first thought of landmine victims is suicide," he noted.[50]

More countries must increase their aid to ERW victims, say many activists. "I'm proud of the fact that the U.S. is the largest contributor to demining programs and assistance for landmine survivors," says Sen. Leahy. "But other countries could and should do more."

Some say countries are doing enough for landmine victims but that the manufacturers should offer more aid. "The focus ought to be to bind armament manufacturers to develop cleanup programs for their products that fail during military deployment," says James Shikwati, the Kenya-based founder and director of the Inter Region Economic Network, an African think tank. "More money devoid of tying responsibility to weapon manufacturers and suppliers will not prevent an increase in people falling victim to armaments left over from wars."

Marc Joolen, director general of Handicap International, said, "It is not enough for countries to destroy stockpiles and clear the land; they must also help the people who survived the explosions." Most survivors still have to fall back on their friends and families for support. Jobs and educational opportunities are the biggest needs.[51]

After reaching a peak in 2008, funding for mine neutralization has dropped off. Although 27 countries and 95 agencies last year submitted proposals to the United Nations for 227 projects costing $589 million, only $24

America's 'Secret War' Still Kills and Maims

Laos, the world's most bombed nation, still suffers from war debris

Even from the air the decades-old destruction in Laos is obvious. Flying into the Southeast Asian nation, visitors often marvel at the pockmarked moonscape below. The countryside is dotted with countless craters, many filled with water and resembling small, serene ponds or reservoirs. But their origin is far from peaceful.

The craters were formed during the 1960s and '70s, when U.S. aircraft unleashed planeload after planeload of bombs onto the lush, landlocked nation. The aim was to stop the North Vietnamese troops who were using Laos to infiltrate South Vietnam. Between 1966 and 1975 American forces flew some 80,000 missions over all but two of Laos' 17 provinces, dropping a staggering 2 million tons of bombs — the equivalent of one B-52 bomb load every eight minutes, around the clock, for nearly a decade.[1]

More ordnance was dropped on tiny Laos during what came to be known as the "Secret War," than was dropped on all of Europe by all combatants during World War II — giving Laos the dubious distinction of being the most bombed nation on Earth.[2] The U.S. bombings of Laos were called the "Secret War" because Laos was officially neutral, so the bombings were covered up by the U.S. government.

Up to a third of the tens of millions of bombs dropped on Laos failed to explode, turning the country into a vast minefield. Most of those 84 million unexploded weapons are cluster bomblets, or "bombies" as Laotians call them. Many failed to detonate either because they malfunctioned or were cushioned by lush trees or rice fields. Whatever the reason, Laos cannot afford the massive unexploded ordnance (UXO) cleanup operation it faces.

The bomblets lying in wait have left fully one-third of the country lethally contaminated.[3] Numerous mine-clearing groups such as the British group MAG (Mine Advisory Group), UXO Lao and others have been clearing mines, bomblets and other ordnance in Laos for decades.

But using present resources, experts say, it will take nearly a century to complete the cleanup. In the 15 years of demining operations ending in 2007, only 131 of the 87,000 square kilometers of contaminated land had been cleared.[4]

With so much live ordnance lying in wait, Laotians — 80 percent of whom are farmers — are at great risk. Between 1964 and 2008 more than 30,000 Laotians died from UXO and 20,000 were injured.[5] UXO-contaminated land stifles the economy and forces many farmers to risk clearing their lands themselves.

"In the end Lao people regard lack of food as much greater threat than unexploded bombs," said David Hayter, the Laos country director of the Mines Advisory Group. "Each UXO death is marked by a big bang, but deaths from lack of food or poor water are less noticeable."[6]

The link between unexploded ordnance and the economy is well documented. "UXO contamination continues to be an obstacle to agriculture production, thus reducing the potential livelihood outcomes," said a World Food Programme report. The study showed that 17 percent of households in UXO-affected villages have poor or borderline food consumption compared with 12 percent in other villages.[7]

In a nation where many live on less than $1 a day, the temptation to gather unexploded weapons for their scrap metal value is hard to resist. Adults and children in the risky business sell the high-end steel, aluminum and copper they gather to dealers from Vietnam and China. With prices of up to 35 cents a kilogram (about two pounds), it is tempting to those earning as little as $5 a month.[8]

Although rarely a day goes by without a serious UXO casualty in Laos, some good news is on the horizon. With the Convention on Cluster Munitions entering into force on Aug. 1, Laos will the host the treaty's first meeting of participating nations this November, the first time the country has taken such a leading international role in the cluster munitions treaty.

"For such a heavily bombed — and too-long ignored — nation to be hosting this event is momentous," says Richard Moyes, policy and research director of Action on Armed Violence, a London-based advocacy group. "The world is sure to take notice."

— Robert Kiener

---

[1] "Wartime cluster bombs still reap deadly harvest in Laos," Agence France-Presse, April 27, 2008. For a video about the Laos bombing aftermath, see "Bombies," Parts 1 and 2, at www.youtube.com/watch?v=Vru9c_ffQ5A and www.youtube.com/watch?v=NPdRpFZIBBQ&NR=1.

[2] Ian MacKinnon, "Forty years on, Laos reaps bitter harvest of the secret war," *The Guardian*, Dec. 3, 2008.

[3] "Laos: deadly cost of unexploded cluster munitions," IRIN, May 29, 2008.

[4] *Ibid.*

[5] "Survey reveals 50,000 victims of unexploded ordnance in Laos," *Korea Herald*, Feb. 6, 2010, www.koreaherald.co.kr/NEWKHSITE/data/html_dir/2010/02/06/201002060002.asp.

[6] Mackinnon, *op. cit.*

[7] Marwaan Macan-Markar, "Unexploded cluster bombs hold up farming," IPS, Feb. 5, 2010.

[8] "Laos: scrap metal income courts UXO danger," IRIN, Nov. 12, 2009.

million had been secured as of December 2009.[52] The global recession has affected funding. Canada, for instance, recently announced it would slash funds for demining in Afghanistan from $77 million to $40 million for the next four years.[53]

In some cases, aid has been criticized as "too little and too late." For instance, the U.S. military sprayed about 12 million gallons of the toxic defoliant dioxin (known as Agent Orange) over nearly 10 percent of the Vietnamese countryside in the 1960s and 1970s to expose enemy hideouts during the Vietnam War.

"One scientific study estimated that between 2.1 million and 4.8 million Vietnamese were directly exposed to Agent Orange," noted a recent U.S. congressional study. And Vietnamese advocacy groups claim there are more than 3 million Vietnamese "suffering from serious health problems caused by exposure to the dioxin in Agent Orange."[54]

Those health problems, which range from multiple cancers to birth defects to diabetes, are similar to the health problems suffered by American Vietnam War veterans. For decades the U.S. government denied that the illnesses were caused by dioxin exposure but in 2009 allowed Vietnam veterans to claim disability and receive healthcare from the Veteran's Administration for more than a dozen diseases, ranging from Parkinson's disease to hairy-cell leukemia to ischemic heart disease.[55]

However, while the U.S. government has funded cleanup of dioxin-contaminated sites in Vietnam, it has not admitted responsibility for alleged dioxin-caused illnesses among the Vietnamese population, despite consistent lobbying by nations and activist groups. Between 2007 and 2009 the U.S. Congress allocated only $6 million to clean up dioxin-contaminated sites in Vietnam. Hardly any of this will help Vietnamese suffering from what they claim are dioxin-related illnesses.[56]

"It's appreciated that the U.S. Congress has twice agreed to allocate [money] for the [cleanup] work," said Ngo Quang Xuan, vice chair of the foreign relations committee of the Vietnamese National Assembly. But the money does not reach those who have suffered from dioxin-related illnesses, he complained.[57]

As for landmine cleanup, says Human Rights Watch's Goose, unless the aid money is spent wisely, increasing assistance won't solve victims' problems.

Reuters/Peter Andrews

Demining teams in 2008 cleared a record 62 square miles of landmines and other unexploded ordnance, including cluster bomblets (above). Since 1999 more than 2.2 million antipersonnel mines have been found and neutralized, and more than 44 million stockpiled landmines have been destroyed. Eleven nations have cleared all their known mine areas.

"Lots of money was wasted on things in the past like general surveys of lands that produced incorrect results," he says. Money also was wasted on "super-costly, high-tech landmine clearing machines that didn't work. Much of that $4 billion [allocated so far] could have been better spent."

Finally, noted Dennis Barlow, director of the Mine Action Information Center at James Madison University in Harrisonburg, Va., the victims must be treated like human beings and not just casualty statistics.

"The solution — easy to state, hard to implement — is to use what we know now about landmine victims to individually design programs for each victim [and] to apply them locally, realistically and cost effectively," he said.[58]

BACKGROUND

Ancient 'Landmines'

Among the oldest form of arms, mines have their origins in such early weapons as spikes and stakes used 2,500 years. And some military experts link the mine to the ancient caltrop, which resembles a larger version of a child's jack. Made of four iron spikes (the earliest were made of bone) joined at the center, the caltrop was

CHRONOLOGY

1910s–1920s *World War I combatants use chemical weapons, landmines.*

1914 French use tear gas; Germans retaliate.

1918 British Royal Engineers design and deploy anti-tank landmines; Germans attack U.S. forces with toxic gases phosgene and chloropicrin; United States begins chemical weapons program.

1930s–1940s *Widespread use of landmines by all forces turns them into "new form of warfare;" cluster bombs are developed.*

1939 Germans begin widespread use of landmines, planting more than 8 million a year by 1944. Allies also use mines widely.

1942 Nazis begin using Zyklon B in concentration camp gas chambers for mass murders of prisoners.

1943 Soviet Union uses air-dropped cluster munitions against Germany; Germans drop more than 1,000 butterfly bombs on the British port of Grimsby.

1960s–1970s *United States uses landmines and cluster bombs in Southeast Asia; Israel and others use cluster bombs in the Middle East.*

1960s United States drops millions of cluster bombs during Vietnam War. Landmines widely used by U.S. and Viet Cong forces; United States sprays "Agent Orange" defoliant in Vietnam.

1978 Israel drops cluster bombs in southern Lebanon.

1980s *Soviets use cluster munitions and landmines in Afghanistan, sparking campaign to ban their use; international treaty restricts landmine use. Iraq uses chemical weapons.*

1980 Convention on Certain Conventional Weapons (CCW) (Protocol II) restricts the use of landmines but doesn't ban them.

1987 Iraq attacks Kurds with mustard gas, hydrogen cyanide and other chemicals, killing thousands.

1990s *United States and its allies drop cluster munitions in first Persian Gulf War. International movement to ban landmines gathers strength.*

1991 United States, France, Great Britain and Saudi Arabia drop 61,000 cluster bombs during Gulf War.

1992 Activists establish International Campaign to Ban Landmines. . . . U.N. adopts Chemical Weapons Convention (CWC) banning chemical weapons.

1994 Russia uses cluster bombs against insurgents in Chechnya; President Bill Clinton calls for "eventual elimination" of landmines.

1996 CCW is amended to ban nondetectable antipersonnel mines and require some mines to have self-destruct devices.

1997 Mine Ban Treaty (MBT) is signed by 122 nations, excluding the Unites States, Russia, China and others.

2000s *Thirty more nations sign MBT. Pressure mounts to ban cluster bombs.*

2001–2002 United States drops 1,228 cluster bombs in Afghanistan.

2003 United States and U.K. use nearly 13,000 cluster munitions during Iraq War. Anti-cluster bomb activists form Cluster Munitions Coalition.

2006 Israel drops more than 4 million cluster bomblets against Hezbollah in Lebanon, according to U.N.

2008 Nearly 100 nations sign Convention on Cluster Munitions (CCM).

2009 Chemical Weapons Convention Coalition forms to press for a ban.

2010 CCM enters into force in August after ratification by 30 countries; Laos plans to host first meeting of participating nations in November.

designed so that when thrown on the ground, one of the spikes would always be pointing upwards.

"One may imagine the efficiency of concealed caltrops," wrote Mike Croll, author of *The History of Landmines.* "Massed ranks of soldiers rushing towards an enemy, skewering their feet on unseen spikes . . . while the enemy launches spears at the wounded and prostrate bodies. An attack would rapidly turn into disarray, the front ranks being pressed forward by the rear, who would not see what was happening ahead of them."[59]

China's Song Dynasty used explosive landmines in 1277 A.D. to stop invading Mongol warriors. A 14th-century Chinese text, the Huolongjing, describes "self-trespassing" landmines, one of the first references to pressure-activated explosive devices. Europe's first landmine was created in the 16th century in Sicily and Southern Italy. Called a fougasse, the device resembled a cannon placed underground and showered rocks upon invaders when detonated.

By the 18th century Europe was using improvised mines: bombs buried under scrap metal or other hard objects that served as shrapnel. The word "mine" comes from the Latin word *mina*, which means "vein of ore." This refers to the early military tactic of tunneling into an enemy's territory, filling the tunnel with explosives and detonating them from a distance.[60]

Mechanically fused antipersonnel mines were used during the Civil War in the Battle of Yorktown, after being invented and first used by Confederate Army Brigadier-Gen. Gabriel J. Rains. He used the devices to blow up a horse and its rider on May 4, 1862 — an act his commanding officer condemned as neither "a proper nor effective method of war."

Union Gen. George B. McClellan called the Confederates' use of the mines "murderous and barbarous conduct."[61]

Although only a few dozen men were killed or injured, the mines had a lasting effect on the troops. "The psychological damage was sufficient," Croll noted. "Soldiers would have imagined every conceivable place to be booby-trapped. An atmosphere of fear would have pervaded the abandoned Yorktown."[62] A century later, five live Confederate landmines were discovered in Alabama.[63]

Although landmines were used in some 19th-century colonial campaigns and the Russo-Japanese War (1902-1906),

they weren't widely used until World War I. Anti-tank mines were developed to combat tanks, and antipersonnel mines were widely deployed to prevent the removal of those anti-tank mines. The Germans also developed pipe bombs, among the first mines designed to maim rather than kill. Reportedly, South Africans fighting the Germans in Africa were so outraged by such devices that many soldiers had to be restrained from killing prisoners for using them.[64]

New Warfare

The "golden age" of landmines occurred during World War II, when most of the mines we know today were developed. Mines were used extensively in battle theaters in dozens of countries as "force multipliers" or "silent soldiers," to deter the advancing enemy and free soldiers for combat.

During the war the Germans went from having only two types of anti-tank mines and one type of antipersonnel mine to 16 and 10, respectively. One of the most-feared antipersonnel mines was the "bouncing Betty." When stepped on, an initial charge would send it about three feet into the air; a second charge then would scatter up to 350 steel balls over more than 100 yards.

The Germans favored smaller anti-personnel mines because they used fewer explosives and were easier to lay than larger mines. But there were other, more horrific reasons. As historian Croll noted, "For attacking forces, small mines are more difficult to locate, and the wounded are a greater burden on medical and transport resources than the dead, [and] the sight of a limbless soldier in agony is more demoralizing to his comrades than a dead one, thus inhibiting aggressiveness."[65]

Landmines played a vital role in North Africa and on the Eastern front, where the Soviet Union used them to block the German advance. The Soviets deployed an estimated 222 million landmines in Europe during the war.[66] By the end of the war, the U.S. Army reported that landmines had caused 2.5 percent of combat fatalities and 20.7 percent of tank losses.

Cluster bombs were also used widely during World War II. German forces dropped so-called "butterfly bombs" that could detonate on impact or be set to explode later. During the Korean War about 4 percent of U.S. causalities were caused by landmines, some of which had been deployed by the United States. Landmines

Women Help Rid the World of Deadly Mines

All-female teams excel at formerly all-male job.

It is just before noon on a blistering hot day in western Cambodia, and Poy Ing is lying on the hard-baked ground, perspiring under 11 pounds of protective body armor and a blast-proof helmet. The sparse bamboo and mango tree forest is alive with the buzz of cicadas, mosquitos and biting black flies.

Like a surgeon probing a wound, the veteran deminer gingerly slips a 10-inch blade into the rich red soil in front of her as she hunts for a deadly landmine. Again and again she pushes the razor-sharp knife into the ground, carefully keeping the blade at a 30-degree angle, away from the sensitive top of any powerful landmine.

One wrong move, one slip, and she could be killed or seriously maimed.

Inch by inch, Ing, 54, explores the ground in an ever-widening arc. Suddenly, she feels the blade hit something. It could be a stone, a root or a discarded scrap of metal. Beads of sweat drip down her forehead as she begins to peel back the thick, dry grass around the object. Her body tenses as she uses the knife to carve away more earth.

There, lying just a few feet in front of her, and only inches below the surface, she sees the green, circular outline of a long-buried K5 landmine, packed with enough explosive to rip her body in half. Instinctively, she recoils and blows a loud blast on her whistle; a signal to the rest of the team that she has found a landmine, which could have been planted by any of the Khmer Rouge, Cambodian or Vietnam forces that have fought in the area over the last three decades.

As a member of an all-female demining team, Ing is part of a growing trend from Sudan to Lebanon to Laos. It's an idea that has caught on, for several reasons.

"Demining statistics throughout the world have shown that, while female deminers may be slower than their male counterparts, their work is more thorough," noted Stephen Bryant, a demining manager in Jordan.[1]

"Men are stronger and sometimes quicker than women deminers," echoed Seng Somla, another female Cambodian deminer, "but women are more patient, and they try harder so they easily make up."[2]

Other experts describe woman as "more reliable" and more effective than men. "They don't get drunk as the men often do," said a demining program manager in Sudan. "Over the past two years they are the teams that have found the most mines."[3]

Women also have proven to be more "team-oriented" than men. As one report noted, "There are no 'Rambos' amongst women deminers."[4]

Women team members also find it easier to talk with local women to get information about landmine locations, while all-male teams usually speak just to the men in a community about their knowledge of the mine threat in the area.[5]

were used by both sides and many were deployed to prevent entry into the south from northern forces. Since the fighting stopped in 1953, U.S. and South Korean forces have maintained a minefield along the demilitarized zone separating North and South Korea. (The United States officially transferred ownership of the landmines to South Korea.)

Landmines also featured heavily in the Vietnam War. Up to 30 percent of the American ground soldiers killed in battle in Vietnam were landmine victims. The Viet Cong used them against both civilian and military targets, the South Vietnamese used them to protect bases and villages and the United States laid them as perimeter defenses and to deter infiltration. The Viet Cong were adept at both stealing U.S.-laid mines and fabricating their own. About 90 percent of the mines that killed American forces were U.S. made or contained American components.[67]

The United States also dropped millions of cluster bombs on Vietnam, Laos and Cambodia during the 1960s and '70s, and many of the bomblets never exploded. (*See sidebar, p. 350.*)

In the mid-1980s the U.S. Air Force replaced the Vietnam-era cluster bomb with the 1,000-pound CBU

David Hayter, director of the Laos office of the MAG (Mine Advisory Group), points out that women are more likely to focus on clearing mines in forests and along paths to water sources, because they are usually the ones collecting firewood and water. "Men and women have different roles in Laos, [so] their UXO clearance needs might be different. For example, women and children usually collect water, but men undertake construction tasks," he said.[6]

By working in what has long been a traditionally male-only position, female deminers are not just breaking down gender barriers. They're also bringing much-needed income to their families. In Cambodia, for example, some women deminers earn almost 10 times the national average wage.[7]

How does Cambodia deminer Somala feel about breaking into a previously male-only career? "This is a real example of what women in Cambodia can achieve," she said. "It will improve the profile of women and promote our position in society."[8]

— *Robert Kiener*

CQ Press/Robert Kiener

Female deminers, like this predominantly female team in Cambodia, are valued as more careful and effective workers than their male counterparts.

[1] "Jordan: First all-female demining team in Middle East," IRIN, Dec. 1, 2008, www.irinnews.org/Report.aspx?ReportId=81741.

[2] Sean Sutton, "Cambodian women clear mines," *Alert Net*, Dec. 19, 2003, www.alertnet.org/thenews/photogallery/KHmag.htm.

[3] "Demining not just a man's job," IRIN, June 23, 2009, www.relief-web.int/rw/rwb.nsf/db900SID/MYAI-7VF9YD?OpenDocument.

[4] "The Hidden Impact of Landmines: Points of Enquiry for a Research into the Significance of Gender in the Impact of Mines and of Mine Action," Swiss Campaign to Ban Landmines, January 2007, www

.wilpf.int.ch/PDF/DisarmamentPDF/ClusterMunitions/WILPF-Women-and-Cluster-Munitions.pdf.

[5] Leah Young, "NPA's All-female Demining Team in Sudan," *The Journal of ERW and Mine Action*, Issue 12.2, Winter 2008/2009, http://maic.jmu.edu/journal/12.2/focus/young/young.htm.

[6] Fran Yeoman, "Women at the deadly end of the cluster-bomb debate," *The* [London] *Times*, Feb. 23, 2003, www.women.timesonline.co.uk/tol/life_and_style/women/article7036794.ece.

[7] Sutton, *op. cit.*

[8] *Ibid.*

87, which holds more than 200 bomblets that can blanket an area the size of several football fields with hundreds of small but deadly explosions.

The weapon uses an intricate delivery method. "As the CBU-87's soda can-sized bomblets fall, a 'spider' cup is stripped off the body, releasing a spring which pushes out a nylon 'parachute' (called the decelerator)," says a Human Rights Watch description of the weapon. "[That] inflates and then stabilizes and arms the bomblet. The bomblets orient perpendicular to the ground for optimal top attack, and the descent is slowed to approximately 125 feet per second. On impact the primary firing mechanism detonates

the bomblet. A secondary firing system [detonates] if the bomblet impacts other than straight on, or if the bomblet lands in soft terrain or water."[68]

Cluster bombs also were dropped during the first Gulf War, in Kosovo in 1999, in Afghanistan in 2001 and Iraq in 2003. Of the more than 13 million bomblets dropped during the first Gulf War, 400,000 failed to explode. Weather was a common cause of failure.

NATO forces used cluster bombs during the air campaign in the former Yugoslavia from March to June 1999. U.S., British and Dutch aircraft dropped more than 1,765 cluster bombs containing more than 295,000 bomblets.

Life After Landmines

Landmine victims warm up for volleyball practice at a rehabilitation center in Phnom Penh, Cambodia (top). Although deminers have destroyed some 2.7 million landmines and unexploded ordnance over the last two decades, there are still an estimated four to six million explosives in almost half of the nation's villages. Landmine victims eat lunch at a prosthetic rehabilitation program in Kabul, Afghanistan, run by the International Committee of the Red Cross (bottom). In recent decades, thousands of Afghans have been injured by mines and other war debris left behind by various conflicts. Recently, a new danger has appeared — improvised explosive devices, or IEDs, used by the Taliban in their fight with coalition forces.

After the war more than 20,000 unexploded bomblets littered the area.

Up to 150 civilians died during these cluster bombings. On May 7, 1999, NATO forces dropped cluster bombs on the Nis Airfield, killing 14 civilians and injuring 28.[69] The casualties led to the United States restricting their use by American forces, which reduced civilian deaths.

Banning 'Silent Killers'

Nations have been encouraged over the last half-century to ban landmines. Protocol II of the 1980 Convention on Certain Conventional Weapons regulated the use and transfer of landmines. That section of the convention, which entered into force in December 1998, prohibited non-detectable mines but fell short of banning landmine use outright.

The CCW is seen as a "minimum international norm" for parties that have not agreed to ban landmines. It prohibits the use of "dumb" antipersonnel mines — those without self-destructing and self-deactivating mechanisms. It also restricts placement of mines, requires mines to be detectable, prohibits transfers of non-detectable mines and obliges parties to clear landmines after hostilities have ended. The United States, while not a party to the Ottawa Treaty, adheres to the CCW.

Present-day successes at banning landmines are attributed to the birth in 1992 of the International Campaign to Ban Landmines (ICBL). Worried that the 1980 conventional weapons treaty did not go far enough, six NGOs came together to work for a total ban on the use, production, stockpiling, sale, transfer and export of landmines. *They also lobbied for more victims' assistance and landmine awareness programs.

Within a year, the European Parliament had passed a five-year moratorium on the trade in antipersonnel mines, and Sen. Leahy had co-sponsored a bill calling for a one-year moratorium on U.S. landmine use and establishing a victims' aid program. After a conference to review the CCW in 1995 failed to produce any further changes, campaigners decided that a total ban, via a completely separate treaty, was the only solution.

In October 1996 Canada hosted an international conference to devise a global ban on antipersonnel mines, supported by 50 governments, the United Nations, the ICBL, the ICRC and other organizations. Nobel Peace Prize winner Williams, a treaty proponent, remembers

---

* The six groups were the Mines Advisory Group, the Vietnam Veterans of America Foundation, Human Rights Watch, Handicap International, Medico International and Physicians for Human Rights.

that Canada's foreign minister, Lloyd Axworthy, "challenged the world to return to Canada in a year to sign an international treaty banning antipersonnel landmines. Members of the International Campaign to Ban Landmines erupted in cheers. . . . It was really breathtaking."[70]

The U.N. General Assembly then passed a resolution calling on all countries to agree to prohibit landmines "as soon as possible," and a draft text was drawn up. In September the final text of the treaty was negotiated and adopted. It defined antipersonnel mines as devices that are placed under, on or near the ground and detonated by the presence, proximity or contact of a person. Excluded from the treaty were anti-vehicle or anti-tank mines, including those with "anti-handling devices" that detonate when it's tampered with or otherwise intentionally disturbed.

The resultant Convention on the Prohibition of Anti-Personnel Mines, also known as the Ottawa Convention, required signatories to:

- Ban the use, production, transfer and stockpiling of landmines;
- Destroy existing stockpiles within four years of signing;
- Clear minefields under its jurisdiction within 10 years (unless they can justify an extension);
- Cooperate with a compliance regime; and
- Support mine clearance and victim assistance.

On Dec. 2, 1997, a month after Williams and the ICBL had been awarded the Nobel Peace Prize, delegates from 125 governments came to Ottawa for a treaty-signing conference.

The treaty was remarkable on several counts: It was the first time nations agreed to completely ban a weapon already widely used; it was drafted and signed within a few years and it was the first time such a wide-ranging treaty was negotiated outside of the United Nations process.

"The final treaty emerged from the negotiating process stronger than when negotiations started," said Williams. That would have been "essentially impossible inside the U.N. process, where reaching consensus, and therefore generally the lowest common denominator, is the rule."[71]

By going outside the U.N., the MBT activists did not need the support of the major powers, such as the United States or Russia, to achieve their ends. "The success of the Mine Ban Treaty shows that ordinary citizens can change the world without the support of superpowers," says Moyes, of London's Action on Armed Violence.

The movement to ban cluster munitions took its cue from the success of the landmine activists and worked outside of the United Nations to campaign for a similar ban. Like landmines, the 1980 conventional weapons treaty had restricted the use of cluster munitions, but activists felt the treaty's restrictions were inconsequential. In 2003, Protocol V — the Protocol on Explosive Remnants of War — was adopted, regulating the clearance of cluster munitions but not regulating or banning their use. So in November 2003, more than 200 organizations joined together to establish the Cluster Munition Coalition (CMC) at The Hague in the Netherlands.

Israel's 2006 war with Hezbollah, in which both sides were accused of dropping huge amounts of cluster munitions, further galvanized support for a cluster bomb ban. According to some estimates, Israel dropped so many cluster bombs in the last 72 hours of the war that a million unexploded bomblets lay scattered across southern Lebanon.[72]

"When hundreds of thousands of civilians displaced by the fighting began to return to the area, they found thousands of cluster bomblets in gardens, houses and streets, orange orchards, banana plantations and olive groves, often hanging from the branches," *Time* reported. At least 30 civilian deaths and 180 injuries were blamed on the bomblets.[73]

Alarmed by the Lebanese casualties and frustrated by the CCW's ineffectiveness, Norway announced an alternative effort to negotiate a cluster bomb treaty. At a meeting in Oslo in 2007 attended by 49 governments, the "Oslo Declaration" was hashed out. It aimed to "prohibit the use, production, transfer and stockpiling of cluster munitions that cause unacceptable harm to civilians."

After the Oslo meeting, 140 countries and members of the anti-cluster bomb coalition met repeatedly to discuss terms of a treaty. In May 2008 more than 100 countries met in Dublin and approved the final wording, which banned cluster weapons. The United States, Russia, China, Israel and Pakistan did not participate.

"While the United States shares the humanitarian concerns of those in Dublin, cluster bombs have demonstrated military utility, and their elimination from U.S. stockpiles would put the lives of our soldiers and those of our coalition partners at risk," explained a Pentagon spokesman.[74]

U.S. Dumped Thousands of Tons of Chemicals

Following World War II, thousands of tons of toxic chemical weapons were dumped in oceans around the world, most of it by the U.S. military.

1, 2, 3 —Thousands of tons of mustard agent, Lewisite, hydrogen cyanide, nerve gas and other chemicals were dumped at numerous sites off Alaska, Hawaii, the West and East Coasts and the Gulf of Mexico.

4 North Sea —U.S. dumps about 4,500 tons of German chemical munitions (1948).

5 Norway/Denmark —U.S. and Britain dump about 170,000 tons of German mustard and nerve gas in Skagerrak area of North Sea (1945-1947). About 150 fishermen have been killed or seriously burned after accidentally pulling up gas containers.

6 Italy — U.S. dumps unknown quantities of chemical bombs and mustard gas off the coast (1945-1946).

7 France — About 3,400 chemical bombs are dumped into Mediterranean Sea off French Riviera by U.S. (1946).

8 Pakistan — Unknown quantities of mustard gas bombs are dumped in only 250 feet of water off coast of Karachi (1943).

9 Bay of Bengal — U.S. dumps about 16,000 chemical bombs off the coasts of India, Pakistan and Bangladesh (1945). Mustard gas, phosgene gas and cyanogen chloride bombs also are dumped.

10 Philippines — U.S. dumps unknown number of mustard gas bombs in Manila Bay (1941) and near Asunción (1945). About 1,000 pounds of white phosphorous shells and six tons of chlorine are dumped in Marveles Bay near oyster beds (1942).

11 Japan — U.S. dumps American and Japanese chemical weapons off coast after war. During the past 50 years, 52 people have been injured in 11 incidents at one of eight dumpsites alone.

12 Australia — U.S. dumps 30,400 tons of chemical weapons off Cape Moreton (1945). Since then fishing trawlers have pulled up two one-ton containers of mustard gas and another washed ashore.

13 New Caledonia — More than 4,200 tons of unidentified "toxic artillery ammunition" from Guadalcanal is dumped offshore (1945).

Sources: U.S. and Australian government data compiled by John M. R. Bull, "The Deadliness Below," *Daily Press* (Newport News, Va.), Oct. 31, 2005.

The United States has also argued that the proper forum to discuss cluster munitions is within the Convention on Certain Conventional Weapons framework. While the United States has not used cluster bombs since the 2003 invasion of Iraq, it wants to keep them in its arsenal for defensive use. It also says new cluster bombs with a failure rate of less than 1 percent are being developed.

In 2008 Congress limited the sale of cluster munitions to those with a 1 percent or lower failure rate and said other nations could use them only against military targets where no civilians are present.

The Convention on Cluster Munitions was signed by 94 states in Oslo in December 2008. So far, 104 parties have signed and 30 have ratified the treaty.

CURRENT SITUATION

Global Success

Demining work continues successfully worldwide today, changing lives for the better in communities around the globe.

For instance, in northwest Cambodia's Battambang province, the Mines Advisory Group recently removed or neutralized 3,000 antipersonnel mines and about 80 unexploded shells in the village of Ou Chamlong. Today the former minefields are rich with tapioca, beans and sweet corn. Farmers do a brisk trade selling their produce to nearby Thailand, and the standard of living for the village's 225 households has soared.

"Development here has doubled," said village chief Kim Chin, noting

Should the United States sign the Mine Ban Treaty?

YES
Richard Moyes
Policy and Research Director
Landmine Action

Written for *CQ Global Researcher*, March 2010

The Obama administration's review of U.S. policies on land-mines represents a significant opportunity for the United States on the international stage. It is a chance to show strong commitment to protecting civilians from the effects of war — which is a fundamental strategic challenge in Afghanistan. Yet narrow thinking may cause the chance to be missed.

In 1997, as a response to the suffering of civilian men, women and children in many war-ravaged countries, an international agreement was reached prohibiting the use, production, stockpiling and sale of antipersonnel landmines. So far 156 countries have signed onto the agreement — 80 percent of the world's states — including all NATO members except Poland.

These nations joined not because they could imagine no circumstances in which antipersonnel mines might be useful weapons but because the limited military utility of these weapons was far outweighed by the suffering they caused.

Rather than joining the treaty, the United States has been keeping company with Russia, China, India, Pakistan, Israel and Iran — major powers whose military postures and actions will have a great influence on world affairs over the decades ahead.

It is in our common interest that these states develop a commitment to restraint in the use of force, and the United States should be pushing that commitment forward. If the United States were to join the Mine Ban Treaty, it would signal that self-imposed constraints, however small, have a role to play in achieving our greater security.

That signal also might strengthen U.S. forces, particularly in places such as Afghanistan, where they struggle to convince local populations that civilian protection is a priority.

The United States has not used antipersonnel mines since the treaty was established more that a decade ago, apparently constrained by its moral force yet unwilling to stand in support of it. In our globalized international society, it is a posture expressive of uncertainty about how to convert massive military power into positive political effects.

Accepting limitations on military capacity, even if of little or no operational significance now, is a serious matter and requires detailed analysis. Such analysis should look not only at whether a few hypothetical circumstances exist when antipersonnel mines would protect U.S. troops. It should also consider how commitment to civilian protection will also strengthen U.S. political and military authority — and which option will save more lives in the long run?

NO
Steven Groves
Bernard and Barbara Lomas Fellow
The Margaret Thatcher Center for Freedom, The Heritage Foundation

Written for *CQ Global Researcher*, March 2010

It is all well and good for most nations of the world to be party to the Ottawa Convention [the Mine Ban Treaty] and champion the absolute prohibition of antipersonnel landmines (APL). The United States, however, must balance its desire to promote humanitarianism with real-world military necessity.

The American military holds a unique position in the world: It is often called upon by U.S. national interests as well as the needs of the international community to engage in armed conflict. Unlike Ottawa Convention champions such as Norway, Switzerland and Belgium, the United States must retain the ability to deploy APL in ongoing and future conflicts. Properly deployed and responsibly removed at the end of hostilities, APL are essential to force protection, especially exposed positions and forward bases operating outnumbered in hostile territory.

Moreover, U.S. accession to the Ottawa Convention would undermine the existing international framework on landmines and other conventional weapons — the Convention on Certain Conventional Weapons (CCW) and Protocol II to the convention. Protocol II prohibits any use of nondetectable APL as well as the use of non-self-destructing and non-selfdeactivating mines outside fenced, monitored and marked areas. But the framework — which entered into force in 1983 — did not go far enough for landmine activist groups. Nothing short of an outright ban on APL of any kind was acceptable.

Stymied by an inability to ban APL outright, a group of 1,200 nongovernmental organizations (NGOs) calling itself the International Campaign to Ban Landmines convened its own treaty conference in 1996. One activist called the process "gently pushing aside the central feature of state sovereignty as the guide for all international relations."

And it is that lack of a multilateral process based on the consensus of sovereign nations that represents the fatal flaw of the Ottawa Convention. The CCW and Protocol II — whose members include China, India, Russia and the United States — have greater legitimacy than the Ottawa Convention, which counts none of those major nations among its members. The United States should not reward the transnationalist NGOs who birthed the "Ottawa Process" by ratifying its progeny.

The current U.S. policy on APL and other landmines — recently confirmed by the Obama administration and bolstered by the legitimacy of the CCW and Protocol II — strikes the proper balance between U.S. military needs and the threat of unexploded munitions.

that every bit of the land is now being used. "People's living conditions are now a lot better."[75]

In 2008 alone, demining teams cleared almost 62 square miles — the highest-ever annual total. Since 1999 more than 2.2 million antipersonnel mines have been found and destroyed, and more than 44 million stockpiled landmines have been destroyed. In fact, 11 nations have cleared all their known mine areas.[76]

But at least 70 states are still "mine affected," and more than 1,200 square miles need to be cleared.[77]

The task is massive. But at the Mine Ban Treaty's second five-year conference in Colombia late last year, attended by representatives from the more than 120 countries that signed the treaty, the mood was optimistic. In a little over a decade the effect of the MBT has been dramatic.

"Vast areas of previously contaminated land are now feeding some of the poorest communities on Earth instead of sowing fear in them," noted the ICRC's Beerli.[78]

Attendees learned that the number of countries that admit to still planting landmines has dropped from 15 in 1999 to just two today — Russia and Burma. In addition, three countries — India, Pakistan and Burma — produced the banned weapons in 2008, according to the ICBL, and 10 more countries have not yet renounced their right to produce them.[79] The MBT "has brought about a near halt to use of the weapons globally, the destruction of tens of millions of stockpiled mines and a huge expansion in mine clearance," said Human Rights Watch's Goose.[80]

Nongovernmental groups such as Taliban insurgents in Afghanistan and Pakistan, however, are planting new mines — known today as improvised explosive devices, or IEDs — with devastating results.[81] Recent figures from Afghanistan point to an increase in IED use by the Taliban. This January, 32 U.S. and allied troops were killed by IEDs, and 137 were wounded, compared with 14 killed and 64 injured last January.[82]

According to an Associated Press count, 40 percent of the U.S. fatalities in 2009 were caused by IEDs, and about three-quarters of all American deaths and injuries in Afghanistan are believed to have been caused by IEDs.[83] IEDs also were responsible for at least 40 percent of all coalition deaths in Iraq.

Nearly 60 insurgent groups — from Somalia to the Philippines — have stopped using landmines and, although

the United States has not joined the treaty, the Obama administration is reviewing it.[84] The United States attended the 2009 MBT conference for the first time and participated as an observer state, seen by treaty proponents as a positive sign. They also welcomed comments by James Lawrence, head of the U.S. delegation and director of the State Department's Office of Weapons Removal and Abatement: "The administration's decision to attend this conference is the result of an ongoing review of U.S. landmine policy initiated at the direction of President Obama."[85]

Nonsignatories China and Russia also attended the meeting as observers. Along with the United States, these nations hold some 145 million stockpiled antipersonnel landmines. The Chinese delegation leader repeated Beijing's commitment to forbid their export. So far, all three nations favor following Protocol II of the Convention on Certain Conventional Weapons rather than joining the MBT or, for that matter, the cluster bomb treaty.

Banning Cluster Bombs

Although supporters hope the cluster bomb treaty will garner as much international support as the 1997 Mine Ban Treaty, that hasn't happened yet. A total of 104 countries, including most NATO members, have signed the convention, and many have begun destroying their stockpiles, but major military powers like the United States, China, Russia, Israel, India and Pakistan haven't joined the treaty.

Nonetheless, advocates hope the use of cluster bombs will generate the same stigma attached to landmines. "The moral stigma is going to be so powerful we think cluster bombs will also become a thing of the past," said Thomas Nash, coordinator of the Cluster Munition Coalition.[86]

Pentagon spokesmen, however, repeatedly have described cluster munitions as "legitimate weapons when employed properly and in accordance with existing international law." The Bush administration viewed the cluster bomb treaty as superfluous and restrictive. Instead of an outright ban, the military prefers to use only cluster bombs with a failure rate of less than 1 percent.

In March 2009, Obama signed legislation banning the sale of cluster bombs if they are suspected of being used where civilians are present.[87] This effectively bans exports of the weapons because it is virtually impossible to guarantee they will be used in civilian-free zones.

In 2008, the Pentagon had asked to be allowed to export cluster bombs for another 10 years. Thus, the new legislation represents a "major turnaround in U.S. policy," said Human Rights Watch's Goose. "The passage of this measure is yet another indication the president should initiate a thorough review of U.S. policy with respect to cluster munitions. If it is unacceptable for foreign militaries to use these weapons, why would it be acceptable for the U.S. military to use them?"[88]

Few observers expect Obama to recommend joining either treaty in the immediate future. "With two wars raging, it's not likely he is about to antagonize the Pentagon and ask them to give up a weapon they claim they need," explains Goose.

Although it hasn't signed either treaty, the United States still ranks as a world leader in aiding ERW victims and weapons cleanup operations. In 2008 international funding for mine action from 23 countries and the European Union totaled $518 million, the highest ever total.[89] Of that, the United States allocated nearly $85 million for mine clearance and victim assistance.[90]

To focus more attention on chemical weapons and convince even more countries to join the chemical weapon treaty, dozens of the world's NGOs in December formed the Chemical Weapons Convention Coalition. The group hopes to persuade Libya, the United States and Russia to conduct safe, sound and timely destruction of chemical weapons.[91]

Yet, while many treaty members are eliminating their banned chemical weapons, they are largely ignoring the massive amounts of weapons that were dumped at sea, many of which may now be slowly leaking toxins. (*See map, p. 361.*) While research is underway to locate — and map — the abandoned chemicals and check on their condition, more needs to be done to examine the harmful effects they may be having on the environment. As a recent report for the U.S. Congress noted, "Incomplete historical records significantly limit the ability to identify and assess the condition of these weapons, particularly to determine whether chemical agents may have leaked, or are likely to do so."[92]

Just this year activists in Sweden accused the Russian military of dumping radioactive waste into the Baltic Sea in the early 1990s.[93] Although Russians deny the claim,

AFP/Getty Images/Georges Gobet

A female deminer checks a site in southern Senegal for the French organization Handicap International on May 10, 2008. Landmines planted during an armed insurrection that began in the region in the early 1980s still cause death and injury to the local population.

environmentalists point out that the world can no longer delay addressing the long-term effects of using the oceans as a waste disposal site. As some say, the clock is ticking.

OUTLOOK

Winning the War?

Attendees at last year's landmine conference in Cartagena had reason to celebrate. Landmines are well on their way to being confined to the dustbin of history. "Looking back, it's amazing to see how far we have come," says Leahy aide Rieser.

In the past decade, more than 2 million mines have been cleared, 156 nations have signed the Mine Ban Treaty and landmine use has been stigmatized. "There has been a growing acceptance that landmines are unacceptable," says Moyes, of London's Action on Armed Violence. "The world is winning the landmine war," the U.K.'s *Independent* recently trumpeted.[94]

The war is not over yet, however. Thirty-nine countries haven't signed the treaty, and massive stockpiles still exist. But many experts think time will change that.

"Ten years from now we will see more nations join the treaty," says the Human Rights Watch's Goose. "I think the Obama administration will do the right thing and come down on the humanitarian side of this issue."

"It is not a matter of if, but when, the United States joins the overwhelming majority of countries that have banned landmines," says Sen. Leahy. "We have by far the world's most powerful military. Landmines and cluster bombs — indiscriminate weapons that cause so many innocent casualties — have no place in our arsenal."

Once the United States signs the treaty, other nations will be under increasing pressure to join, say many landmine activists. "Twenty years ago there were dozens of nations using landmines; today almost no one does," explains Goose. He and others think landmines will largely disappear within decades.

Cluster bombs are another story. Efforts to ban them face more resistance. The U.S. military, for example, prefers developing higher-tech versions rather than banning them.

Few expect President Obama to pressure the Pentagon to change its mind anytime soon. "I think we are decades away from seeing similar progress," says Moyes.

But the Heritage Foundation's Groves sees "no reason for the USA to ban cluster munitions, now or 10 years down the road."

Both sides agree, however, that ERW victims will receive more help in the future. Treatment will improve as advancements, such as high-tech prostheses, become more widely available. And as ERW clearance operations wind down, more money can be available to help victims with psychological, social and economic problems.

Banned chemical weapons are being destroyed but more needs to be done to monitor those programs and convince countries such as Libya to speed up their disposal programs. Also, more research has to be done on possible side effects of depleted uranium when used on the battlefield.

Sadly, few expect wars and armed conflicts to cease in the near future. Remnants of war are the lethal legacy of armed conflict. Although a conflict may last only a few weeks, it can take years, even decades, to clean up and free civilians from the risk of death or injury. And although weapons will undoubtedly become more high-tech in the future, there will always be a risk to innocent civilians.

Landmines, cluster bombs, ERW and long-abandoned chemical weapons all share one characteristic in common: They all can take innocent lives and maim, long after peace has been made.

"The landmine cannot tell the difference between a soldier or a civilian — a woman, a child, a grandmother going out to collect firewood to make the family meal," said Nobel Prize winner Williams. "Once peace is declared the landmine does not recognize that peace. The landmine is eternally prepared to take victims."[95]

NOTES

1. "Senegal: Casamance still mined, still dangerous," International Committee of the Red Cross, Dec.12, 2009, www.icrc.org/web/eng/siteeng0.nsf/html/senegal-feature-231209.

2. *Ibid.*

3. "Landmine Monitor Report," (Executive Summary), International Campaign to Ban Landmines, 2009, http://lm.icbl.org/index.php/publications/display?url=lm/2009/es/toc.html.

4. "Local NGOs welcome cluster bomb ban," IRIN, Feb. 18, 2010, www.irinnews.org/Report.aspx?ReportId=88146; "Landmines in Afghanistan: a decades old danger," *Defense Industry Daily*, Feb. 1, 2009, www.defenseindustrydaily.com/Landmines-in-Afghanistan-A-Decades-Old-Danger-06143/.

5. "Casualties and Data Collection," *Landmine Monitor*, http://lm.icbl.org/index.php/publications/display?url=lm/2009/es/mine_casualties.html#1999-2009_overview.

6. For background, see Jason McLure, "Troubled Horn of Africa," *CQ Global Researcher*, June 2009.

7. "Somalia: "My land is full of mines," IRIN, Feb, 2, 2010, www.irinnews.org/report.aspx?Reportid=87953

8. David Randall, "The World is Winning the Landmine war," *The Independent*, Dec. 6, 2009, www.independent.co.uk/news/world/politics/the-world-is-winning-the-landmine-war-1835050.html.

9. "Mozambique: Demining is not a never ending story," IRIN, Oct, 27, 2009, www.irinnews.org/Report.aspx?ReportId=86758.

10. "Sri Lanka: landmines, unexploded ordnance a barrier to return," IRIN , Nov. 9, 2009 www.irinnews.org/Report.aspx?ReportId=86944.

11. "Landmine Monitor Report," *op. cit.*

12. *Ibid.*

13. "Explosive remnants of war and international humanitarian law," International Committee of the Red Cross, www.icrc.org/Web/eng/siteeng0.nsf/htmlall/section_ihl_explosive_remnants_of_war.

14. Quoted in Mike Croll, *The History of Landmines* (1998), p. x.

15. *Ibid.*

16. Randall, *op. cit.*

17. David Alexander, "U.S. will not join treaty banning landmines," Reuters, Nov. 24, 2009 www.reuters.com/article/idUSN24329250.

18. "Leahy hits US refusal to join landmine treaty," Office of Senator Leahy, Nov. 25, 2009. www.earthtimes.org/articles/show/leahy-hits-us-refusal-to-join-landmine-treaty,1062487.shtml.

19. International Committee of the Red Cross, *op. cit.*

20. "Explosive Remnants of War," International Committee of the Red Cross, July 2004, p. 9, www.icrc.org/Web/Eng/siteeng0.nsf/htmlall/p0828/$FILE/ICRC_002_0828.pdf.

21. "Cluster bomb treaty reaches 30th milestone," Handicap International, www.handicap-international.us/en/our-fight-against-landmines-and-cluster-bombs/cluster-bombs/.

22. "Cluster Munitions at a Glance," Arms Control Association, www.armscontrol.org/node/3125.

23. "Landmines and Explosives," *Alert Net*, Jan. 12, 2009, www.alertnet.org/db/topics/landmines.htm.

24. Kim Murphy, "Britain deals a setback to US," *Los Angeles Times*, May 29, 2008, http://articles.latimes.com/2008/may/29/world/fg-cluster29.

25. "Iraq: war remnants, pollution behind rise in cancer deaths?" IRIN, Oct. 14, 2009, www.irinnews.org/report.aspx?ReportId=86572. Also see "Current Issues: Depleted uranium weapons," Wise Uranium Project, December 2009, www.wise-uranium.org/diss.html.

26. *Ibid.*

27. Matthew Bolton, "Obama follows Bush on landmines," *The Guardian*, Nov. 26, 2009, www.guardian.co.uk/commentisfree/cifamerica/2009/nov/26/obama-landmine-ban-treaty.

28. Richard Garwin, "Bush sets the right course in control of land mines," *Los Angeles Times*, March 8, 2004, www.cfr.org/publication/6844/bush_sets_the_right_course_in_control_of_land_mines.html.

29. John Stanton, "Uncertainty remains about US landmine policy," *National Defense*, January 2004, www.nationaldefensemagazine.org/ARCHIVE/2004/JANUARY/Pages/Uncertainty3678.aspx.

30. Amanda Walker, "Russia to destroy 6,000 tons of nerve gas," *Sky News*, June 10, 2009, http://news.sky.com/skynews/Home/World-News/Chemical- Weapons-Russia-To-Destroy-6000-Tons-Of-Nerve- Gas/Article/200906215299439?lpos=World_News_Top_Stories_Header_4&lid=ARTICLE_15299439_Chemical_Weapons:_Russia_To_Destroy_6,000_Tons_Of_Nerve_Gas.

31. Rachel A. Weise, "Russia, U.S. lag on chemical arms deadline," Arms Control Association, July/August 2009, www.armscontrol.org/act/2009_07-08/chemical_weapons.

32. Breanne Wagner, "Buried poison: abandoned chemical weapons pose continual threat," *National Defense*, Aug. 1, 2007, www.thefreelibrary.com/Buried+poison:+abandoned+chemical+weapons+pose+continual+threat.-a0167430175.

33. Peter Eisler, "Chemical weapons' disposal delayed," *USA Today*, Nov. 20, 2006, www.usatoday.com/news/washington/2006-11-20-chemical-weapons_x.htm.

34. Weise, *op. cit.*

35. Kris Osborn, "US gains momentum destroying chemical weapons stockpiles," *AR News*, Feb. 4, 2010, www.globalsecurity.org/wmd/library/news/usa/2010/usa-100204-arnews01.htm.

36. Jonathan Tirone, "US, Russia plans to destroy chemical arms imperiled by crisis," Bloomberg, Feb. 24, 2009, www.bloomberg.com/apps/news?pid=20601087&sid=aghJzZXxi_FQ&refer=home.

37. Chris Schneidmiller, "New Coalition Aims to Promote Chemical Weapons Disarmament, Nonproliferation," Global Security Newswire, Jan. 22, 2010, www.globalsecuritynewswire.org/gsn/nw_20100122_8824.php.

38. John M. R. Bull, "Special Report, Part 1: The deadliness below," *Daily Press*, Oct. 30, 2005, www.dailypress.com/news/dp-02761sy0oct30,0,2199000.story.

39. "Dumped chemical weapons missing at sea," *New Scientist*, March 23, 2008, www.newscientist.com/article/mg19726482.800-dumped-chemical-weapons-missing-at-sea.html?haasFormId=f9768f0e-e55c-439a-b647-e3a56f64a4f7&haasPage=0.

40. Andrew Monahan, "Japan's China weapons cleanup hits a snag," *Time*, March 31, 2008, www.time.com/time/world/article/0,8599,1726529,00.html.

41. Wagner, *op. cit.*

42. *Ibid.*

43. "Landmine Monitor Report 2009," *op. cit.*

44. *Ibid.*

45. *Ibid.*

46. "Voices from the Ground," *Handicap International*, September 2009, www.handicap-international.us/our-fight-against-landmines-and-cluster-bombs/in-brief/?dechi_actus%5Bid%5D=68&cHash=5a6b6d36d8.

47. "Countries do little to help landmine victims: report," Reuters, Sept. 2, 2009, www.reuters.com/article/idUSTRE5814XZ20090902.

48. "Voices from the ground," *op. cit.*, p. 150.

49. Anastasia Moloney, "Governments plan to improve help for landmine victims," Reuters, Nov. 12, 2009, www.alertnet.org/db/an_art/59877/2009/11/4-113151-1.htm.

50. "Focus on victims at Mine Ban Treaty meeting," IRIN, Dec. 4, 2009, www.irinnews.org/Report.aspx?ReportId=87323.

51. *Ibid.*

52. "Money for mine action is hard to come by," IRIN, Dec. 4, 2009, www.irinnews.org/Report.aspx?ReportId=87325.

53. Rosie DiManno, "Canada bails on Afghanistan land mine duty," *The Star*, Feb. 3, 2010, www.thestar.com/news/canada/afghanmission/article/759735-dimanno-canada-bails-on-afghanistan-land-mine-duty.

54. James Dao, "Door opens to health claims tied to Agent Orange," *The New York Times*, Oct. 13, 2009, www.nytimes.com/2009/10/13/us/politics/13vets.html.

55. *Ibid.*

56. Martha Ann Overland, "Agent Orange Poisons New Generations in Vietnam," *Time*, Dec. 19, 2009, www.time.com/time/world/article/0,8599,1948084,00.html.

57. Jane Zhou, "Agent Orange War Legacy Attracts Aid," World Watch Institute, July 2009, www.worldwatch.org/node/6208.

58. Dennis Barlow, "Seven common myths about landmine victim assistance," *Journal of Mine Action*, December 2002, www.maic.jmu.edu/journal/6.3/editorial/editorial.htm.

59. Croll, *op. cit.*, p. 5.

60. "Laying landmines to rest? Humanitarian Mine Action," IRIN, Feb. 22, 2009, www.irinnews.org/InDepthMain.aspx?InDepthId=19&ReportId=62881.

61. Croll, *op cit.*, p. 17.

62. *Ibid.*

63. "Laying landmines to rest? Humanitarian Mine Action," IRIN, Feb. 22, 2009, www.irinnews.org/InDepthMain.aspx?InDepthId=19&ReportId=62881.

64. "The History of Landmines," http://members.iinet.net.au/~pictim/mines/history/history.html.

65. Croll, *op. cit.*, p. 43.

66. Mary H. Cooper, "Banning Landmines," *CQ Researcher*, Aug. 8, 1997, pp. 697-720.

67. *Ibid.*

68. "Cluster bombs in Afghanistan," Human Rights Watch, October 2001, www.hrw.org/legacy/backgrounder/arms/cluster-bck1031.htm#CBU-87.

69. Julie Hyland, "Human Rights Watch says NATO killed over 500 civilians in air war over Yugoslavia," *World Socialist*, Feb. 14, 2000, www.wsws.org/articles/2000/feb2000/nato-f14.shtml.

70. "Ban History," International Campaign to Ban Landmines, www.icbl.org/index.php/icbl/Treaties/MBT/Ban-History.

71. "A Nobel laureate looks back on the first 10 years of the Mine Ban Treaty," IRIN, Nov. 26, 2009, www.irinnews.org/Report.aspx?ReportId=87200.

72. "Cluster munitions at a glance," Arms Control Association, undated, www.armscontrol.org/node/3125.

73. Nicholas Blanford, "The 'toys' that kill in Lebanon," *Time*, Feb. 2, 2007, www.time.com/time/world/article/0,8599,1585565,00.html.

74. Kevin Sullivan and Josh White, "111 nations, minus the US, agree to cluster-bomb ban," *The Washington Post*, May 29, 2008, www.washingtonpost.com/wp-dyn/content/story/2008/05/28/ST2008052803176.html.

75. "Cambodia: development doubles after MAG clears land," Mines Advisory Group, Nov. 23, 2009, www.maginternational.org/news/cambodia-development-doubles-after-mag-clears-land/.

76. "Landmine Monitor Report," 2009, *op. cit.*

77. *Ibid.*

78. Randall, *op. cit.*

79. "Ban Policy: Overview 1998-2009," *Landmine Monitor*, International Campaign to Ban Landmines, http://lm.icbl.org/index.php/publications/display?url=lm/2009/es/ban.html.

80. *Ibid.*

81. C. J. Chivers, "Counterinsurgency: one stuck truck at a time," *The New York Times*, Feb. 1, 2010, www.atwar.blogs.nytimes.com/2010/02/01/counterinsurgency-one-stuck-truck-at-a-time/.

82. Tom Vanden Brook, "Roadside bombs taking bigger toll in Afghanistan," *USA Today*, Feb. 14, 2010, www.usatoday.com/news/military/2010-02-14-ieds-afghanistan_N.htm.

83. "US Troop surge combats top threat: IEDs," Associated Press, Feb. 2, 2010, www.foxnews.com/story/0,2933,584514,00.html.

84. Randall, *op. cit.*

85. Jeff Abramson, "In a first, US attends landmine meeting," Arms Control Association, Jan/Feb 2010, www.armscontrol.org/act/2010_01-02/Landmines.

86. Liz Sly, "Can the cluster bomb treaty be more than a symbol?" *Chicago Tribune*, Dec. 3, 2008, http://archives.chicagotribune.com/2008/dec/03/nation/chi-lebanon-cluster_slydec03.

87. Frida Berrigan, "Progress on cluster bombs," *Foreign Policy in Focus*, March 25, 2009, www.fpif.org/articles/progress_on_cluster_bombs.

88. Peter Beaumont, "Obama takes US closer to a total ban on cluster bombs," *The Guardian*, March 13, 2009, www.guardian.co.uk/world/2009/mar/13/us-national-security-obama-administration.

89. "Landmine Monitor Report," International Campaign to Ban Landmines, 2009, p. 2.

90. "Victim Assistance," *ibid.*, http://lm.icbl.org/index.php/publications/display?act=submit&pqs_year=2009&pqs_type=lm&pqs_report=usa&pqs_section=%23victim_assistance#victim_assistance.

91. Chris Schneidmiller, "New coalition aims to promote chemical weapons disarmament, nonproliferation," Global Security Newswire, Jan. 22, 2010, www.globalsecuritynewswire.org/gsn/nw_20100122_8824.php.

92. "U.S. Disposal of Chemical Weapons in the Ocean: Background and Issues for Congress," Congressional Research Service, Jan. 3, 2007, www.fas.org/sgp/crs/natsec/RL33432.pdf.

93. Damien McGuinness, "Sweden wants explanation on Baltic nuclear 'dumping,'" BBC News, Feb. 4, 2010, http://news.bbc.co.uk/2/hi/europe/8499762.stm.

94. Randall, *op. cit.*

95. "Landmine quotes," www.betterworld.net/quotes/landmines-quotes.htm.

BIBLIOGRAPHY

Books

Croll, Mike, *Landmines in War and Peace: From Their Origin to the Present Day, Pen and Sword,* 2009.
Updating his earlier history of landmines, a former British military bomb disposal officer provides a comprehensive history of landmines as they evolved from basic weapons in ancient times to today's modern weapons.

Sigal, Leon, *Negotiating Minefields: The Landmines Ban in American Politics, Routledge,* 2006.
The director of the Northeast Asia Cooperative Security Project at the Social Science Research Council in New York presents a detailed, absorbing history of efforts to ban landmines.

Tucker, Jonathan, *War of Nerves: Chemical Warfare From World War I to Al-Qaeda, Anchor,* 2007.
An arms control expert and a senior researcher at the Monterey Institute's Center for Non-proliferation Studies provides a detailed historical review of chemical warfare.

Williams, Jody, *et al.,* (eds.), *Banning Landmines: Disarmament, Citizen Diplomacy, and Human Security, Rowman and Littlefield,* 2008.
Nobel Peace Prize laureate Williams and other activists edited these essays by diplomatic negotiators, mine survivors, arms experts and human rights defenders, who describe progress since the 1997 landmine ban went into effect.

Articles

Bohaty, Rochelle F. H., "Lying In Wait: Researchers help U.S. Army search for chemical munitions dumped at sea," *Chemical & Engineering News,* March 30, 2009, http://pubs.acs.org/cen/government/87/8713gov1.html.
Authorities are investigating abandoned chemical weapons dumped off the coast of Hawaii by the U.S. military after World War II.

Bull, John M. R., "Special Report: The Deadliness Below," *Newport News Daily Press,* Oct. 30, 2005, www.dailypress.com/news/dp-2761sy0oct30,0,2199000.story.
This four-part series details the dumping of chemical weapons and unexploded ordnance in the world's oceans.

Eisler, Peter, "Chemical weapons disposal on fast track," *USA Today,* May 6, 2009, www.usatoday.com/news/military/2009-05-05-chemicalweapons_N.htm.
The Pentagon hopes to speed up destruction of its stockpile of banned chemical weapons.

Hart, John, "Looking Back: The Continuing Legacy of Old and Abandoned Chemical Weapons," *Arms Control Association,* March 2008, www.armscontrol.org/act/2008_03/Lookingback.
The writer examines the state of old and abandoned chemical weapons and the effectiveness of the Chemical Weapons Convention.

MacKinnon, Ian, "Forty years on, Laos reaps bitter harvest of the secret war," *The Guardian,* Dec. 3, 2008, www.guardian.co.uk/world/2008/dec/03/laos-cluster-bombs-uxo-deaths.
Landmines and unexploded ordnance have had a crippling effect on the Laotian people and countryside.

Randall, David, "The world is winning the landmine war," *The Independent,* Dec. 6, 2009, www.independent.co.uk/news/world/politics/the-world-is-winning-the-landmine-war-1835050.html.
As the Cartagena landmine conference wraps up, the author examines the state of the landmine treaty and progress on mine clearance and aid.

Reports and Studies

"Landmine Monitor Report," *International Committee to Ban Landmines,* 2009.
This annual survey takes a comprehensive look at developments in landmine-ban policy and provides current statistics on clearance, victim assistance and casualties.

"Voices from the Ground: Landmine and Explosive Remnants of War Survivors Speak Out on Victim Assistance," *Handicap International,* **September 2009.** An organization dedicated to raising awareness about disability and landmine issues describes the effects of explosive remnants of war from the victims' viewpoint.

"Weapon Contamination Manual," *International Committee of the Red Cross,* **2007.**

This comprehensive manual introduces the issues the ICRC thinks are needed to reduce the impact of ERW and landmines through field activities.

Bearden, David M., "U.S. Disposal of Chemical Weapons in the Ocean: Background and Issues for Congress," *Congressional Research Service,* **2007.** This detailed yet concise backgrounder provides the history and ramifications of chemical weapons dumped into the oceans.

For More Information

Action on Armed Violence (formerly Landmine Action), 2nd Floor, 89 Albert Enbankment, London, SE1 7TP, U.K.; +44 (0)20 7820 0222; www.landmineaction.org. Nongovernmental organization working to reduce the incidence and impact of armed violence around the world.

Arms Control Association, 1313 L St., N.W., Suite 130, Washington, DC 20005; (202) 463-8270; www.armscontrol .org. National nonpartisan organization dedicated to promoting public understanding and support for effective arms control policies.

Cluster Munitions Coalition, www.stopclustermunitions .org. A global network of organizations campaigning to ban cluster munitions.

Halo Trust, Carronfoot, Thornhill, Dumfries DG3 5BF, U.K.; +44 (0) 1848 331100; www.halotrust.org. International organization dedicated to clearing landmines and unexploded ordnance.

Handicap International, 67 Rue de Spastraat, B-1000 Brussels, Belgium; +32 2 280 16 01; www.handicap-international.be. International organization that offers help to those with disabilities.

Human Rights Watch, 350 Fifth Ave., 34th Floor, New York, NY 10118-3299; (212) 290-4700; www.hrw.org. Independent organization dedicated to defending and protecting human rights.

International Campaign to Ban Landmines, 9 Rue de Cornavin, CH-1201 Geneva, Switzerland; +41 (0)22 920 03 25; www.icbl.org. Nobel-prize winning group seeking complete ban on landmines; publishes *Landmine Monitor.*

International Committee of the Red Cross, Mine Action Sector, 19 Avenue de la Paix, 1202 Geneva, Switzerland; +41 22 734 60 01; www.icrc.org. Nonpartisan, independent humanitarian organization that provides assistance to victims of landmines and other unexploded ordnance.

Landmine Survivors Network, 2100 M St., N.W., Suite 302, Washington, DC 20037; (202) 464 0007; www.landminesurvivors.org. Helps mine victims and their families recover through peer counseling, sports and social and economic integration into their communities.

Mines Advisory Group, 47 Newton St., Manchester M1 1FT, U.K.; +44-161 236 4311; www.maginternational.org. Works to aid landmine-affected communities.

Prosecuting Terrorists

*Should Suspected Terrorists Be Given
Military or Civil Trials?*

Kenneth Jost

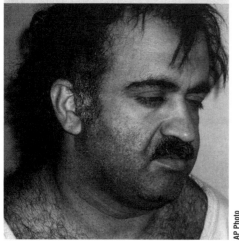

Republican lawmakers say al Qaeda terrorist Khalid Sheikh Mohammed, seen shortly after his capture in Pakistan in 2003, should be treated as an enemy combatant and tried in the military commissions established during the Bush administration. But administration officials and Democratic lawmakers say criminal prosecutions have produced hundreds of convictions since 9/11 compared to only three in the military system.

AP Photo

From *CQ Researcher*,
March 12, 2010.

H e has been described as Osama bin Laden's chief executive officer, the man who conceived the plan to crash hijacked airliners into buildings symbolic of America's political, military and financial power.

Some 18 months after the 9/11 attacks, Pakistani intelligence agents, working with the U.S. Central Intelligence Agency, captured Kuwait-born Khalid Sheikh Mohammed at an al Qaeda safe house in Rawalpindi. Rousted out of bed in the middle of the night, he looked like a street person — not the scion of a well-to-do Pakistani family once known for his expensive tastes and elegant dress.[1]

For the next three years, KSM — as U.S. officials and news media dubbed him — was held at a secret CIA site, reportedly in Poland, where interrogators waterboarded him 183 times in the first month of his captivity. In September 2006 he was transferred to the U.S. prison camp at the Guantánamo Bay naval base in Cuba, to be held awaiting trial.

The trial — on 2,973 counts of murder and other charges — began before a military judge on June 5, 2008, but was thrown into disarray six months later, when Mohammed announced that he and his four co-defendants wanted to plead guilty. A month later, the judge, Army Col. Stephen Henley, agreed to put the trial on hold in response to President Obama's decision, on his first full day in office, to suspend the military trials of all suspected "enemy combatants" being held at Guantánamo.

Now, a year after Obama's interim move, the proceedings against KSM remain in limbo thanks to the full-throttle controversy that erupted after Attorney General Eric Holder announced plans to try

Military Commissions Convicted Three

Three of the terrorism suspects who were detained at Guantánamo Bay — Ali Hamza Ahmad Suliman al Bahlul, Salim Ahmed Hamdan and David Hicks — have been convicted after trials before military commissions. Hicks, known as the "Australian Taliban," and Hamdan, identified as the driver for al Qaeda leader Osama bin Laden, have served their sentences already and been released to their home countries. Al Bahlul awaits a decision on his appeal to his life sentence before a U.S. military judge panel. Hamdan's appeal of his conviction is pending before the same panel; Hicks waived his right of appeal after pleading guilty.

Terrorists Convicted in Military Commissions at Guantánamo Bay

al Bahlul

Nationality:	Yemeni
Conviction date:	Nov. 3, 2008
Charges:	35 counts of solicitation to commit murder, conspiracy and providing material support for terrorism.
Current status:	Sentenced to life in prison; appeal pending before panel of military judges; argued Jan. 26.

AFP/Getty Images

Hamdan

Nationality:	Yemeni
Conviction date:	Aug. 6, 2008
Charges:	Providing material support for terrorism.
Current status:	Returned to Yemen and released; appeal pending before panel of military judges; argued Jan. 26.

AFP/Getty Images

Hicks

Nationality:	Australian
Conviction date:	March 30, 2007
Charges:	Providing material support for terrorism.
Current status:	Returned to Australia and released

Getty Images

Source: News reports

the five alleged 9/11 conspirators in a federal court in New York City. In announcing his decision on Nov. 13, Holder said the defendants would "answer for their alleged crimes in a courthouse just blocks away from where the twin towers [of the World Trade Center] once stood."[2]

New York City Mayor Michael Bloomberg and Police Commissioner Raymond Kelly welcomed Holder's decision, but many New Yorkers expressed concerns about the costs and risks of a sensational trial in Lower Manhattan. Some families of 9/11 victims also voiced criticism, saying enemies of the United States deserved military tribunals, not civilian courts.

Holder faced a buzz saw of criticism when he appeared before the Senate Judiciary Committee a week later to defend his decision — which he said he made without consulting the White House. Sen. Jeff Sessions of Alabama, the committee's ranking Republican, called the decision "dangerous," "misguided" and "unnecessary."[3]

Criticism of the decision intensified — and became even more overtly politicized — after the Christmas Day arrest of Umar Farouk Abdulmutallab for the attempted bombing of a Northwest Airlines flight bound from Amsterdam to Detroit. Republican lawmakers and former GOP officials, including former Vice President Dick Cheney and former Attorney General Michael Mukasey, strongly criticized the decision to treat Abdulmutallab as a criminal suspect instead of as an enemy combatant. A major focus of the criticism was the decision to advise Abdulmutallab of his Miranda rights not long after his arrest. (*See sidebar, p. 380.*)

GOP lawmakers raised the stakes on the issue by introducing legislation in Congress to prohibit the use of any funds to try KSM in civilian courts. With administration officials and Democratic lawmakers making little headway in quieting the criticism, the White House let it be known in early February that Obama was personally reviewing the planned location for the trial as part of the broader issue of where and how to try the remaining prisoners at Guantánamo.[4]

The trials have been delayed by controversies that began immediately after President George W. Bush decided to use the base to house alleged enemy combatants captured in the Afghanistan war or rounded up from other locations. Instead of using civilian courts or regular military courts — courts-martial — Bush used his power as commander in chief to create military commissions to try the detainees, with fewer procedural rights than courts-martial.[5]

Critics, including a wide array of civil liberties and human rights organizations, denounced the military commissions as a second-class system of justice. They also lent their support to legal challenges filed by some of the prisoners that eventually resulted in Supreme Court decisions guaranteeing judicial review of their cases and forcing some changes in the rules for the commissions.

Because of the legal uncertainties, the military commissions did not produce their first conviction until March 2007 when David Hicks, the so-called Australian Taliban, pleaded guilty to providing material support for terrorism. Two other Guantánamo prisoners were convicted on material-support counts the next year: Salim Ahmed Hamdan, former driver to bin Laden, and Ali Hamza Ahmad Suliman al Bahlul, an al Qaeda filmmaker and propagandist. (*See box, p. 370.*)

Even as the Guantánamo cases moved at a glacial pace, the Bush administration was using federal courts to prosecute hundreds of individuals arrested in the United States on terrorism-related charges. Among the first was Richard Reid, the so-called shoe bomber, who was charged with attempting to blow up a commercial aircraft en route to the United States on Dec. 22, 2001. Reid, an admitted al Qaeda supporter, is now serving a life sentence.

At various points, Bush himself touted the administration's record of convicting hundreds of individuals in terrorism-related cases in criminal courts. In a budget document in 2008, the Justice Department put the number of convictions or guilty pleas at 319 out of 512 individuals prosecuted.[6]

Guidelines Adopted for Detainee Prosecutions

The Justice and Defense departments adopted broadly written guidelines in July 2009 to be used in deciding whether a Guantánamo detainee was to be tried in a civilian court or before a military tribunal. The protocol begins with "a presumption that, where feasible, referred cases will be prosecuted in" federal criminal courts. The two-page agreement lists three categories of factors to be considered in deciding whether "other compelling factors make it more appropriate to prosecute a case in a reformed military commission":

Strength of interest, including where the offense occurred, where the defendant was apprehended and which agency or agencies investigated the case.

Efficiency, including protection of intelligence sources, foreign policy concerns and "legal or evidentiary problems that might attend prosecution in the other jurisdiction."

Other prosecution considerations, including the charges that can be brought and the sentences that can be imposed in one or the other forum.

Source: "Determination of Guantánamo Cases Referred for Prosecution," July 20, 2009, www.justice.gov/opa/documents/taba-prel-rpt-dptf-072009.pdf

---

More recently, a report written for Human Rights First counted 195 convictions or guilty pleas in al Qaeda- or Taliban-related terrorism cases through July 2, 2009, along with 19 acquittals or dismissals. The report, written by two lawyers who had previously served as federal prosecutors in New York, concluded that the criminal justice system "is well-equipped to handle a broad variety of cases arising from terrorism" associated with al Qaeda or similar groups.[7] (*See sidebar, p. 382.*)

Despite that record, GOP lawmakers, ex-Bush administration officials and conservative experts and advocates are arguing strongly for the use of military commissions to try Abdulmutallab and, apparently, most of the prisoners held at Guantánamo. "Wartime alien enemy combatants should be tried by military commissions in the safety of Guantánamo Bay," says Andrew McCarthy, a contributing editor with *National Review Online* and former federal prosecutor.[8]

While in the U.S. attorney's office in Manhattan, McCarthy was lead prosecutor in the 1995 trial of Omar Abdel Rahman, the so-called Blind Sheik, along with nine others for plotting to blow up various civilian targets in the New York City area. Rahman was convicted of seditious conspiracy and is now serving a life sentence.[9]

Human rights advocates, however, say military commissions have failed to produce results while tarnishing the United States' image both at home and abroad. "The only choice should be trial in civilian courts," says Laura Olson, senior counsel for the rule of law program at the Washington-based Constitution Project. "They're both tougher and more reliable than military commissions."

The Obama administration says civilian trials are the presumptive forum for terrorism cases but is continuing the use of what it calls "reformed" military commissions for some cases. A protocol adopted jointly by the Justice and Defense departments in July 2009 says forum selection will depend on a number of factors, including the agency or agencies involved in the investigation and the charges and sentences available in one or the other forum. Holder designated several Guantánamo prisoners for trial by military commissions on the same day he announced the decision to try KSM in New York City. (*See box, p. 375.*)

Meanwhile, administration officials also are saying that 50 or more Guantánamo prisoners may be held indefinitely without trial because they cannot be prosecuted successfully but are too dangerous to release.[10] Conservatives say the prolonged detentions are justifiable as long as the United States is effectively at war with al Qaeda. Civil liberties advocates strongly disagree.

President Obama cheered human rights groups with his initial moves on counterterrorism policies, especially his pledge to close the Guantánamo prison camp within a year. Now that the deadline has been missed and other policies recalibrated, Obama is drawing some complaints from liberal advocacy groups along with sharp criticism from Republicans and conservative groups for the planned use of federal courts to try enemy combatants.

Here are some of the major issues the administration faces:

Should suspected terrorists be tried in civilian courts?

When the FBI got wind of a group of Yemeni Americans who had trained at an al Qaeda camp in 2001 and returned to their homes in the Buffalo, N.Y., suburb of Lackawanna, Bush administration's officials were divided on what to do.

Vice President Dick Cheney and Defense Secretary Donald Rumsfeld wanted to use troops to arrest the men and treat them as enemy combatants to be tried before a military commission. President Bush, however, sided with Attorney General John Ashcroft and FBI Director Robert Mueller, who favored using federal agents to arrest the men and trying them in a federal court.

In the end, the men were arrested without incident on Sept. 14, 2002, and over the next year pleaded guilty and received prison sentences ranging from seven to 10 years for supporting a foreign terrorist organization. They also cooperated with authorities in providing information about al Qaeda, and three of them testified in the 2008 military commission trial of the al Qaeda filmmaker Bahlul.[11]

Supporters of criminal prosecutions — including but not limited to human rights and civil liberties groups — say prosecutions such as the Lackawanna Six case prove civilian courts can mete out effective, tough justice in terrorism-related cases without shortchanging constitutional rights.

"The criminal justice system is reasonably well-equipped to handle most international terrorism cases," New York attorneys Richard B. Zabel and James J. Benjamin Jr. wrote in the Human Rights First report in May 2008. A year later, the two former federal prosecutors reiterated that civilian court prosecutions had generally led to "just, reliable results" without causing security breaches or other harms to national security.[12]

National security-minded critics and some non-ideological experts counter that the rights accorded defendants in the criminal justice system do pose potential obstacles to successful prosecutions in some terrorism cases. "Civilian trials should be a secondary option," says David Rivkin, a former Justice Department official in the Bush administration now affiliated with the hawkish Foundation for the Defense of Democracies. Among other problems, Rivkin says classified information is harder to protect in a civilian court than in a military commission despite a federal law, the Classified Information Procedure Act (CIPA), which limits disclosure in federal trials.

"The federal courts have some real limitations," agrees Benjamin Wittes, a research fellow at the Brookings Institution and author of several influential reports about war-on-terror policies. He cites as examples the beyond-a-reasonable-doubt standard used in criminal prosecutions and the stricter standard on use of evidence obtained under coercive interrogation. Still, Wittes adds, the problems are "not as big as conservatives claim."

Critics assailed the decision to try the 9/11 conspiracy case in New York City in particular as a security risk. Rivkin complains of "the logistical nightmare" that would be created by a trial in a major metropolitan area such as New York.

When Holder visited New York to discuss plans for the trial in December, however, a Justice Department spokesman declared, "We have a robust plan developed by both federal and local officials to ensure that these trials can be safely held in New York, and everyone is committed to doing that."[13]

Above any practical considerations, however, critics such as Rivkin say simply that criminal prosecutions signal a wrong approach in the nation's fight against al Qaeda. "This is a long and difficult war," he says. "It is essential for any administration to inculcate the notion that this is a real war. And it is utterly jarring in that context to take enemy combatants, particularly high-value ones, and treat them as common criminals."

Benjamin counters that the criminal justice system in fact amounts to one of the United States' most effective weapons in the war on terror. "We are at war," he says. "One of the unique features of this particular war is that many of the people on the other side are violating our criminal law. If we can develop the evidence and successfully put them away, why in the world would we foreclose ourselves from doing that?"

Should suspected terrorists be tried in military tribunals?

Attorney General Holder's decision to try seven Guantánamo detainees in military commissions represents only a modest step toward resolving the cases of the remaining prisoners there. (*See box, p. 384.*) But the trials, if completed, would more than double the number of cases resolved by military tribunals since President Bush authorized them less than two months after the 9/11 attacks.

Supporters say history, law and national security justify the use of military tribunals to try enemy combatants. They blame opponents for the legal controversies that have limited their use so far.

"The record has been underwhelming," concedes ex-Justice Department attorney Rivkin. "Why should we be surprised? There has been a concentrated effort from day one to litigate against them."

Human rights and civil liberties groups counter that the military tribunals were flawed from the outset and, despite some recent reforms, still have significant problems and will face additional legal challenges.

"They remain vulnerable to constitutional challenge," says Olson of the Constitution Project. "We're going to have to go through this litigation for years and years."

In contrast to the three men convicted so far by military commissions, the prisoners that Holder designated in his Nov. 13 announcement for trial by military commissions include figures alleged to have played significant roles in al Qaeda operations. They include Abd al Rahim al Nashiri, a Yemeni accused of plotting the October 2000 attack on the *USS Cole*, and Noor Uthman Mohammed, a Sudanese alleged to have assisted in running an al Qaeda training center in Afghanistan.

The accusations against some of the others, however, depict them as hardly more than al Qaeda foot soldiers. The group includes Omar Khadr, the youngest Guantánamo detainee, who was captured at age 15 after a firefight in Afghanistan. Now 23, the Canadian citizen faces a charge of providing support for terrorism by throwing a grenade that killed a U.S. soldier. The charge goes against the United Nations' position that children should not be prosecuted for war crimes.[14]

In announcing his decisions on the legal forum to be used, Holder gave no explanation of the reasons for designating some of the prisoners for trial by military commissions. But he did say that recent changes approved by Congress for the commissions "will ensure that commission trials are fair, effective and lawful." Those changes include limits on use of hearsay and coerced testimony and greater access for defendants to witnesses and evidence.

Despite the changes, human rights advocates continue to oppose use of the military commissions. "We don't quarrel with military justice," says Ben Winzer, a staff attorney with the American Civil Liberties Union's (ACLU) national security project. "The problem is that even the modified military commissions are being used to paper over weaknesses in the government's evidence."

"Most of the growing pains have been alleviated," counters Rivkin. "The solution now is to stand them up,

AFP/Getty Images/Don Emmert

Omar Abdel Rahman, the so-called Blind Sheik, was convicted in a civilian criminal trial in 1995 along with nine others for plotting to blow up various civilian targets in the New York City area. Rahman is now serving a life sentence. Andrew McCarthy, the then-lead prosecutor for the U.S. attorney's office, is now a contributing editor with *National Review Online*, a conservative publication. He now says, "Wartime alien enemy combatants should be tried by military commissions in the safety of Guantánamo Bay."

make them work, give them the right resources and get out of the way."

For his part, Brookings Institution expert Wittes says the military commissions "have significantly underperformed to date" and continue to face a host of practical and legal difficulties. "We worry that the military commissions will present issues of their own, particularly with respect to challenges to the lawfulness and integrity of the system itself," he says. "And the rules have been used so little that there are a lot of issues about how the system works."

Among the most important pending issues is the question whether material support of terrorism — a mainstay of criminal prosecutions — is an offense that can be tried in a military tribunal. The review panel established to hear appeals from the military commissions currently has that issue under advisement after arguments in two cases in January.

"No one questions that these are crimes, but there are special rules that come into play when we start talking about what crimes military commissions can prosecute," says Stephen Vladeck, a law professor at American University in Washington. "I think there are far fewer cases in which the government realistically has a choice between civilian and military courts than we might think, if for no other reason than the jurisdiction of military commissions is actually tightly circumscribed by the Constitution."

Should some Guantánamo detainees be held indefinitely without trial?

In his first major speech on how to deal with the Guantánamo prisoners, President Obama called in May 2009 for "prolonged detention" for any detainees "who cannot be prosecuted yet who pose a clear danger to the American people." Obama said he would work with Congress to "construct a legitimate legal framework" for such cases, but added: "I am not going to release individuals who endanger the American people."[15]

In the nine months since, neither Congress nor the president has put any appreciable work into possible legislation on the issue. Now, administration officials are estimating 50 or more detainees will have to be held without trial, but they have not listed names or described procedures being used to designate individuals for that category.

The ACLU and other human rights groups immediately denounced Obama's remarks on the issue and continue to oppose detention without trial. The administration's conservative critics approve of holding some prisoners without trial but fault the administration for its efforts to transfer others to their home countries or other host nations because they might return to hostilities against the United States.

"The term is detention for the duration of hostilities," says Rivkin. "Those rules have been in place since time immemorial. They are not meant to punish anybody; they are designed to prevent someone from going back to the battlefield."

Rivkin says the policy of transferring prisoners to other countries — begun by the Bush administration and continued by Obama — amounts to "a revolving door" for terrorists. "We know for sure that they go back

Khalid Sheikh Mohammed and the 9/11 Attacks

Khalid Sheikh Mohammed, self-described mastermind of the Sept. 11 terrorist attacks, faces trial in federal court on 2,973 counts of murder and other charges along with his four co-defendants. Kuwait-born KSM first claimed to have organized the 9/11 attacks during interrogations in which he was waterboarded 183 times. In March 2007, at a hearing at the Guantánamo Bay prison, he said he was responsible for the attacks "from A to Z" — as well as for 30 other terrorist plots. The five co-defendants now face nine charges including conspiracy, terrorism, providing material support for terrorism and murder. Controversy erupted over Attorney General Eric Holder's plan to hold the trial in New York City, and the location of the trial is now being reconsidered. KSM's four co-defendants are:

- **Ramzi Bin al-Shibh (Yemen)** — Alleged "coordinator" of the attacks after he was denied a visa to enter the United States.
- **Walid bin Attash (Saudi Arabia)** — Charged with selecting and training several of the hijackers of the attacks.
- **Ali Abdul Aziz Ali (Pakistan)** — Allegedly helped hijackers obtain plane tickets, traveler's checks and hotel reservations. Also taught them the culture and customs of the West.
- **Mustafa Ahmed al-Hawsawi (Saudi Arabia)** — Allegedly an organizer and financier of the attacks.

to combat," Rivkin says. "This is the first war in human history where we cannot hold in custody a captured enemy. That's a hell of a way to run a war."

ACLU lawyer Winzer calls Obama's detention-without-trial proposal "an extraordinarily controversial statement in a country governed by the rule of law." Anyone "truly dangerous" should be and likely can be prosecuted, Winzer says. "Our material-support laws are so broad that if we don't have legitimate evidence to convict [detainees] under those laws, it's hard to accept that they are too dangerous to release."

Allegations that some of the released Guantánamo prisoners have returned to hostilities against the United States stem from studies released by the Pentagon during the Bush administration and sharply challenged by some human rights advocates. The final of three studies, released in January 2009 only one week before Bush was to leave office, claimed that 61 out of 517 detainees released had "returned to the battlefield."

But an examination of the evidence by Mark Denbeaux, a law professor at Seton Hall University in South Orange, N.J., and counsel to two Guantánamo detainees, depicts the Pentagon's count as largely unsubstantiated. In any event, Denbeaux says the Pentagon's count is exaggerated because it includes former prisoners who have done nothing more after their release than engage in propaganda against the United States.[16]

Supporters of detention without trial cite as authority the first of the Supreme Court's post-9/11 decisions, *Hamdi v. Rumsfeld*.[17] In that 2004 ruling, a majority of the justices agreed that the legislation Congress passed in 2001 to authorize the Afghanistan war included authority for the detention of enemy combatants. In the main opinion, Justice Sandra Day O'Connor said a detainee was entitled to some opportunity to contest allegations against him, but did not specify what kind of procedure.

The court rulings appear to support the government's power "to hold people indefinitely without charge if they are associated with al Qaeda or the Taliban in the same way that a solider is associated with an army," says Benjamin, coauthor of the Human Rights First report. Law professor Vladeck agrees, but says the number of people in that category is likely to be "small."

Brookings Institution expert Wittes defends the practice "philosophically" but acknowledges practical problems, including public reaction both in the United States and abroad. "The first risk is that it's perceived as the least legitimate option, domestically or internationally," he says. "It's not the way you like to do business."

The evidence needed to justify detention has been the major issue in the dozens of habeas corpus petitions filed by Guantánamo prisoners. Federal district judges in Washington who have been hearing the cases have mostly decided against the government, according to a compilation coauthored by Wittes.[18]

Wittes has long urged Congress to enact legislation to define the scope of indefinite detention. In an unusual interview, three of the judges handling the cases agreed. "It should be Congress that decides a policy such as this," Judge Reggie Walton told the online news site *ProPublica*.[19]

But David Cole, a law professor at Georgetown University in Washington and prominent critic of the detention policies, disagrees. The issues, Cole says, "require careful case-by-case application of standards. It's a job for judges, not Congress."[20]

BACKGROUND

Power and Precedent

The United States faced the issue of how to deal with captured members or supporters of al Qaeda or the Taliban with no exact historical parallel as guidance. The use of military tribunals for saboteurs, spies or enemy sympathizers dated from the American Revolution but had been controversial in several instances, including during the Civil War and World War II. After World War II, military commissions became — in the words of Brookings expert Wittes — "a dead institution." The rise of international terrorism in the 1980s and '90s was met with military reprisals in some instances and a pair of notable U.S. prosecutions of Islamist extremists in the 1990s.[21]

As commander of the revolutionary army, Gen. George Washington convened military tribunals to try suspected spies — most notably, Major John André, Benedict Arnold's coconspirator, who was convicted, sentenced to death and hanged. During the War of 1812 and the First Seminole War (1817-1818). Gen. Andrew Jackson was criticized for expansive use of his powers as military commander — most notably, for having two British subjects put to death for inciting the Creek Indians against the United States. During the occupation of Mexico in the Mexican-American War, Gen. Winfield Scott established — without clear statutory authority — "military councils" to try Mexicans for a variety of offenses, including guerrilla warfare against U.S. troops.

The use of military tribunals by President Abraham Lincoln's administration during the Civil War provoked sharp criticism at the time and remains controversial today. Lincoln acted unilaterally to suspend the writ of habeas corpus in May 1861, defied Chief Justice Roger Taney's rebuke of the action and only belatedly got Congress to ratify his decision. More than 2,000 cases were tried by military commissions during the war and Reconstruction. Tribunals ignored some judicial orders to release prisoners.

Lincoln, however, overturned some decisions that he found too harsh. As the war continued, the Supreme Court turned aside one challenge to the military commissions, but in 1866 — with the war ended — held that military tribunals should not be used if civilian courts are operating.[22]

During World War II, President Franklin D. Roosevelt prevailed in three Supreme Court challenges to expansive use of his powers as commander in chief in domestic settings. Best known are the court's decisions in 1943 and 1944 upholding the wartime curfew on the West Coast and the internment of Japanese-Americans. Earlier, the court in 1942 had given summary approval to the convictions and death sentences of German saboteurs captured in June and tried the next month before hastily convened military commissions. Roosevelt's order convening the seven-member tribunals specified that the death penalty could be imposed by a two-thirds majority instead of the normal unanimous vote. The Supreme Court heard habeas corpus petitions filed by seven of the eight men but rejected their claims in a summary order in the case, *Ex parte Quirin*, on July 31. Six of the men had been executed before the justices issued their formal opinion on Oct. 29.[23]

International law governing wartime captives and domestic law governing military justice were both significantly reformed after World War II in ways that cast doubt on the previous ad hoc nature of military commissions. The Geneva Conventions — signed in 1949 and ratified by the Senate in 1954 — strengthened previous protections for wartime captives by, among other things, prohibiting summary punishment even for combatants in non-traditional conflicts such as civil wars. The Uniform Code of Military Justice, approved by Congress in 1950, brought civilian-like procedures into a system previously built on command and discipline. The United States went beyond the requirements of the Geneva Conventions in the Vietnam War by giving full prisoner-of-war status to enemy captives, whether they belonged to the regular North Vietnamese army or the guerrilla Vietcong.

International terrorism grew from a sporadic problem for the United States in the 1970s to a major concern in the 1980s and '90s. The results of foreign prosecutions in two of the major incidents in the '80s left many Americans disappointed. An Italian jury imposed a 30-year sentence in 1987 on Magid al-Molqi after the Palestinian confessed to the murder of U.S. citizen Leon Klinghoffer during the 1985 hijacking of the cruise ship *Achille Lauro*; the prosecution had sought a life term. The bombing of

Pan Am Flight 103 over Scotland in 1988 — and the deaths of 189 Americans among the 270 victims — resulted in the long-delayed trial of Abdel Basset Ali al-Megrahi, former head of the Libyan secret service. Megrahi was indicted in 1991 in the United States and Scotland, extradited only after protracted diplomatic negotiations and convicted and sentenced to life imprisonment in 2001. He was released on humanitarian grounds in 2009, suffering from purportedly terminal pancreatic cancer.

Two prosecutions in the United States stemming from the 1993 bombing of the World Trade Center produced seemingly stronger verdicts. Omar Abdel Rahman, the so-called Blind Sheik, was convicted in federal court in New York City along with nine others in 1995 for conspiracy to carry out a campaign of bombings and assassinations within the United States. Abdel Rahman is now serving a 240-year prison sentence. Two years later, Ramzi Ahmed Yousef was convicted on charges of masterminding the 1993 bombing and given a life sentence. Even after the second verdict, however, questions remained about whether the plot had been sponsored by a foreign state or international organization.[24]

Challenge and Response

The Bush administration responded to the 9/11 attacks by declaring an all-out war on terrorism that combined separate strategies of detaining captured "enemy combatants" at Guantánamo outside normal legal processes and prosecuting hundreds of individuals in federal courts on terrorism-related charges. The improvised system of military tribunals at Guantánamo drew political and legal challenges that stalled their work, resulting in only three convictions late in Bush's time in office. Meanwhile, criminal cases proceeded in federal courts with relatively few setbacks and little hindrance from criticism by some civil libertarians of overly aggressive prosecutions.[25]

Even as the Guantánamo military tribunals were being formed, the administration was initiating criminal prosecutions in other al Qaeda or Taliban-related cases. In the most important, the government indicted Zacarias Moussaoui, sometimes called the 20th hijacker, on Dec. 11, 2001, on conspiracy counts related to the 9/11 attacks. The prosecution dragged on for more than four years, extended by Moussaoui's courtroom dramatics and a fight over access to classified information that ended with a ruling largely favorable to the government. The trial ended on May 3, 2006, after a jury that had deliberated for

seven days imposed a life sentence instead of the death penalty — apparently rejecting the government's view of Moussaoui as a central figure in the 9/11 attacks.

Two other early prosecutions ended more quickly. British citizen Richard Reid, the so-called shoe bomber, was charged in a federal criminal complaint on Dec. 24, 2001, two days after his failed explosive attack on American Airlines Flight 63. In January, Attorney General John Ashcroft announced that U.S. citizen John Walker Lindh, the so-called American Taliban captured in Afghanistan, would be tried in a civilian court in the United States. Both men entered guilty pleas in 2002; Lindh was given a 20-year sentence while Reid was sentenced in January 2003 to life in prison.

The government started two other early cases in the criminal justice system and moved them into the military system only to return later to civilian courts. Ali Saleh Kahlah al-Marri, a Qatari student attending college in Illinois, was detained as a material witness in December 2001 and indicted two months later on credit-card charges. Bush's decision in 2003 to designate him as an enemy combatant led to a protracted appeal that the Obama administration resolved in 2009 by indicting al-Marri on a single count of conspiracy to provide material support for terrorism. In a similar vein, U.S. citizen José Padilla was arrested at the Chicago airport on May 8, 2002, on suspicion of plotting a radioactive attack; designated an enemy combatant a month later and then indicted after drawn-out legal challenges that reached the Supreme Court. Padilla was convicted of terrorism conspiracy charges and given a 17-year prison sentence; al-Marri drew 15 years after pleading guilty.

Meanwhile, the military tribunals had been stymied by a succession of legal challenges before the Supreme Court and responses by the administration and Congress to the justices' rulings. In the pivotal decision in Hamdan's case, the court ruled in June 2006 that the military commissions as then constituted were illegal because the president had not shown a need to depart from established rules of military justice.[26] Reconstituted under the Military Commissions Act of 2006, the tribunals finally produced their first conviction in March 2007 when the Australian Hicks pleaded guilty to a single material-support count. Under a plea agreement and with credit for time served, he was allowed to return to Australia to serve the remaining nine months of a seven-year sentence.

Two more convictions followed in 2008, both after trials. Hamdan was convicted in August of conspiracy

C H R O N O L O G Y

1970s-2000 *International terrorism era begins, with attacks on civilian aircraft, facilities; prosecutions in foreign, U.S. courts get mixed results.*

1988 Bombing of Pan Am Flight 103 over Scotland kills 270, including 189 Americans; Scottish court later convicts and sentences to life former head of Libyan secret service; ill with cancer, he was released from Scottish jail in 2009.

1995 Civilian court convicts Omar Abdel Rahman and nine others for conspiring to blow up World Trade Center, other sites, in 1993.

1997 Ramzi Ahmed Yousef draws life sentence after 1997 conviction in civilian court for masterminding 1993 trade center bombing.

2000-Present *Al Qaeda launches 9/11 attacks; Bush, Obama administrations prosecute terrorism cases mainly in civilian courts.*

September-October 2001 Nearly 3,000 killed in al Qaeda's Sept. 11 attacks. . . . Congress on Sept. 14 gives president authority to use force against those responsible for attacks.

November-December 2001 President George W. Bush on Nov. 13 authorizes military commissions to try enemy combatants captured in Afghanistan, elsewhere. . . . U.S. Naval Base at Guantánamo Bay is chosen as site to hold detainees. . . . Zacarias Moussaoui indicted in federal court in Virginia on Dec. 11 for conspiracy in 9/11 attacks. . . . "Shoe bomber" Richard Reid arrested Dec. 21 for failed attack on American Airlines Flight 63.

2002 First of about 800 prisoners arrive in Guantánamo; first of scores of habeas corpus cases filed by detainees by mid-spring. . . . José Padilla arrested at Chicago airport May 8 in alleged radioactive bomb plot; case transferred to military courts. . . . John Walker Lindh, "American Taliban," sentenced Oct. 4 by a civilian court to 20 years in prison.

2003 Federal judge in Boston sentences Reid to life in prison on Jan. 31.

2004 Supreme Court rules June 28 that U.S. citizens can be held as enemy combatants but must be afforded hearing before "neutral decisionmaker" (*Hamdi v. Rumsfeld*); on

same day, court rules Guantánamo detainees may use habeas corpus to challenge captivity (*Rasul v. Bush*).

2006 Moussaoui is given life sentence May 3. . . . Supreme Court rules June 29 that military commissions improperly depart from requirements of U.S. military law and Geneva Conventions (*Hamdan v. Rumsfeld*). . . . Congress passes Military Commissions Act of 2006 in September to remedy defects.

2007 First conviction in military commission: Australian David Hicks sentenced on March 30 to nine months after guilty plea to material support for terrorism. . . . Padilla convicted in federal court Aug. 16 on material support counts; later sentenced to 17 years.

2008 Supreme Court reaffirms June 12 habeas corpus rights for Guantánamo detainees (*Boumediene v. Bush*). . . . Two more convictions of terrorists in military commissions: Hamdan convicted on material support counts Aug. 6, sentenced to a seven-and-a-half-year term; al Qaeda propagandist Ali Hamza al Bahlul convicted Nov. 3, given life sentence.

January-June 2009 President Obama pledges to close Guantánamo within a year, suspends military commissions pending review (Jan. 21). . . . Obama in major speech says some detainees to be held indefinitely without trial (May 21).

July-December 2009 Defense and Justice departments agree on protocol to choose civilian or military court (July 20). . . . Military Commission Act of 2009 improves defendants' protections (October). Attorney General Eric Holder announces plan to try Khalid Sheikh Mohammed (KSM), four others in federal court in Manhattan for 9/11 conspiracy (Nov. 13); other alleged terrorists designated for military commissions; plan for N.Y. trial widely criticized. . . . Umar Farouk Abdulmutallab arrested Dec. 25 in failed bombing of Northwest Flight 253; decision to prosecute in civilian court criticized, defended.

2010 Administration mulls change of plans for KSM trial. . . . U.S. appeals court backs broad definition of enemy combatant in first substantive appellate-level decision in Guantánamo habeas corpus cases (Jan. 5). . . . Military review panel weighs arguments on use of "material support of terrorism" charge in military commissions (Jan. 26).

and material support but acquitted of more serious charges and given an unexpectedly light sentence of 61 months. With credit for time served, he was transferred to his native Yemen in late November to serve the last month of his term. Earlier, a military tribunal on Nov. 3 had convicted Bahlul of a total of 35 terrorism-related counts after the former al Qaeda propaganda chief essentially boycotted the proceedings. The panel returned the verdict in the morning and then deliberated for an hour before sentencing the Yemeni native to life imprisonment.

As the Bush administration neared an end, the Justice Department issued a fact-sheet on the seventh anniversary of the 9/11 attacks touting its "considerable success in America's federal courtrooms of identifying, prosecuting and incarcerating terrorists and would-be terrorists." The report listed the Padilla and Moussaoui cases among eight "notable" prosecutions in recent years. It also briefly noted the department's cooperation with the Defense Department in developing procedures for the military commissions, defending against challenges to the system and jointly bringing charges against KSM and other high-value detainees.[27]

In an important post-election setback, however, a federal judge in Washington ruled on Nov. 20, 2008, in favor of five of the six Algerians whose habeas corpus petitions had led to the Supreme Court decision guaranteeing judicial review for Guantánamo detainees. Judge Richard Leon said the government had failed to present sufficient evidence to show that the six men, arrested in Bosnia in January 2002, had planned to travel to Afghanistan to fight against the United States. He found sufficient evidence, however, that one of the prisoners had acted as a facilitator for al Qaeda. Three of the five were returned to Bosnia in December; two others were transferred to France in May and November 2009.[28]

Change and Continuity

In his first days in office, President Obama began fulfilling his campaign pledge to change the Bush administration's legal policies in the war on terror. Obama's high-profile decisions to set a deadline for closing Guantánamo, shut down the secret CIA prisons and prohibit enhanced interrogation techniques drew support from Democrats and liberals and sharp criticism from Republicans and conservatives. By year's end, the roles were reversed, with support from the right and criticism from the left of Obama's decision to continue use of military tribunals

and claim the power to detain suspected terrorists indefinitely without trial. Meanwhile, the government was continuing to win significant terrorism-related convictions in federal courts but suffering setbacks in many habeas corpus cases brought by Guantánamo prisoners.

Even with the Guantánamo and interrogation policies under attack, the Justice Department was achieving some significant successes in prosecutions that carried over from the Bush administration. The new administration sidestepped a Supreme Court test of the power to detain U.S. residents by transferring al-Marri to civilian courts in late February and securing his guilty plea in April. Also in April, Wesam al-Delaema, an Iraqi-born Dutch citizen, was given a 25-year prison sentence for planting roadside bombs aimed at U.S. troops in his native country. Al-Delaema had fought extradition from the Netherlands and was to be returned there to serve what was expected to be a reduced sentence. The case marked the first successful prosecution for terrorist offenses against U.S. forces in Iraq.

In May, the government won convictions — after two prior mistrials — in its case against the so-called Liberty City Six (originally, Seven), who were charged with plotting to blow up the Sears Tower in Chicago and selected federal buildings. The jury in Miami convicted five of the men but acquitted a sixth. On the same day, a federal jury in New York City convicted Oussama Kassir, a Lebanese-born Swede, of attempting to establish a terrorist training camp in Oregon. Material-support charges were the major counts in both cases. Kassir was sentenced to life in September; of the six defendants in the Miami case, sentences handed down on Nov. 20 ranged from 84 to 162 months.

By summer, the Justice Department conceded that it would be late with an interim report on closing Guantánamo. In acknowledging the delay in a background briefing on July 20 — the eve of the due date for the report — administration officials claimed some progress in resettling some of the detainees but confirmed expectations to hold some of the prisoners indefinitely. The administration did release the two-page protocol from the Defense and Justice departments on prosecuting Guantánamo cases, with its stated "presumption" in favor of civilian prosecutions "where feasible." The memo outlined a variety of factors to consider in choosing between civilian courts or "reformed" military

The Case Against the 'Christmas Day' Bomber

Critics say prosecutors mishandled Abdulmutallab's arrest.

Caught in the act of trying to bomb a Northwest Airlines aircraft, Umar Farouk Abdulmutallab would appear to offer prosecutors a slam dunk under any of several terrorism-related charges. Indeed, there were dozens of witnesses to his capture.

But the case against the baby-faced Nigerian-born, Yemeni-trained al Qaeda supporter became enmeshed in post-9/11 American politics almost immediately after his Christmas Day flight landed in Detroit.[1]

President Obama invited the subsequent criticism by initially labeling Abdulmutallab as "an isolated extremist" on Dec. 26 before learning of his training in al Qaeda camps in Yemen and history of extreme Islamist views. Homeland Security Secretary Janet Napolitano compounded the administration's political problems by saying on Dec. 27 that Abdulmutallab's capture showed that "the system worked" — a statement she quickly worked hard to explain away, given that a U.S. airliner had nearly been bombed.

The administration also faced criticism for intelligence analysts' failure to block Abdulmutallab from ever boarding a U.S.-bound aircraft after having received a warning from the suspect's father, a prominent Nigerian banker, of his son's radicalization. Obama moved to stanch the criticism by commissioning and quickly releasing a review of the intelligence agencies' "failure to connect the dots" and by ordering other steps, including a tightening of airline security procedures.

The politicization of the case intensified, however, with a broadside from former Vice President Dick Cheney sharply attacking the administration's decision to treat Abdulmutallab as a criminal suspect instead of an enemy combatant to be tried in a military tribunal. Obama "is trying to pretend we are not at war," Cheney told *Politico*, the Washington-based, all-politics newspaper.

"He seems to think if he has a low-key response to an attempt to blow up an airliner and kill hundreds of people, we won't be at war. He seems to think if he gives terrorists the rights of Americans, lets them lawyer up and reads them their Miranda rights, we won't be at war."[2]

White House press secretary Robert Gibbs responded promptly by accusing Cheney of playing "the typical Washington game of pointing fingers and making political hay." But the response did nothing to stop Republican politicians and conservative commentators from keeping up a drumbeat of criticism for several weeks into the new year, focused in particular on the decision to advise Abdulmutallab of his right to remain silent and to confer with a lawyer.

The criticism appears to have been based in part on an erroneous understanding of when FBI agents advised the 21-year-old Abdulmutallab of his Miranda rights. For weeks, critics said he had been "Mirandized" within 55 minutes of his arrest. Only in mid-February did the administration release a detailed, materially different timeline.[5]

The administration's account showed that Abdulmutallab was questioned for 55 minutes and

commissions. With Guantánamo dominating the coverage, the memo drew little attention.[29]

Meanwhile, federal judges in Washington, D.C., were giving mixed verdicts as more of the long-delayed habeas corpus cases by Guantánamo detainees reached decision stage.[30] In the first of the rulings after Obama took office, Judge Leon ruled on Jan. 28 that evidence of serving as a cook for al Qaeda was sufficient to hold a prisoner for "material support" of terrorism. In 14 cases over the next year, however, the government lost more — eight — than it won (six). In five of the cases granting habeas corpus, judges found the government's

evidence either insufficient or unreliable. In one, the judge specifically found the government's evidence had been obtained by torture or under the taint of prior torture. In the two other cases, one of the detainees was found to have been expelled from al Qaeda, while the other was no longer a threat because he was cooperating with U.S. authorities.

In order to prevent leaks, Holder made his decision to try KSM in a federal court with little advance notice to New York City officials. He explained later to the Senate Judiciary Committee that a federal court trial would give the government "the greatest opportunity to

provided some information about his rights before being taken away for surgery. When he returned after the four-hour procedure — a total of nine hours after his arrest — Abdulmutallab declined to answer further questions.

Without regard to the precise timing, critics said Abdulmutallab should have been treated outside the criminal justice system to maximize his value as a source of intelligence. Former Attorney General Michael B. Mukasey said the administration had "no compulsion" to treat Abdulmutallab as a criminal defendant "and every reason to treat him as an intelligence asset to be exploited promptly." The administration claimed that Abdulmutallab did begin providing actionable intelligence after family members were brought to the United States from Nigeria, but Mukasey said the five-week time lag meant that "possibly useful information" was lost.[4]

Administration supporters noted, however, that the Bush administration handled all suspected terrorists arrested in the United States as criminal defendants with the concomitant necessity to advise them of their Miranda rights. The administration's defense was substantiated by John Ashcroft, Mukasey's predecessor as attorney general. "When you have a person in the criminal justice system, you Mirandize them," Ashcroft told a reporter for *Huffington Post* when questioned at the conservative Tea Party Conference in Washington in mid-February.[5]

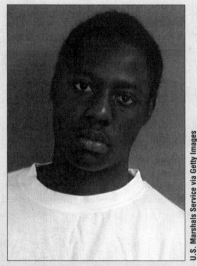

U.S. Marshals Service via Getty Images

Umar Farouk Abdulmutallab, a 23-year-old Nigerian, is charged with attempting to blow up a Northwest Airlines flight as it was landing in Detroit last Christmas Day.

Administration critics appeared to say little about the precise charges brought against Abdulmutallab. He was initially charged in a criminal complaint Dec. 26 with two counts: attempting to blow up and placing an explosive device aboard a U.S. aircraft. Two weeks later, a federal grand jury in Detroit returned a more detailed indictment charging him with attempted use of a weapon of mass destruction and attempted murder of 269 people. If convicted, he faces a life sentence plus 90 years in prison. No trial date is set.

— *Kenneth Jost*

[1] Some background drawn from a well-documented Wikipedia entry: http://en.wikipedia.org/wiki/Umar_Farouk_Abdulmutallab.

[2] Mike Allen, "Dick Cheney: Barack Obama 'trying to pretend,' " *Politico*, Dec. 30, 2009, www.politico.com/news/stories/1209/31054.html, cited in Philip Elliott, "White House Hits Back at Cheney Criticism," The Associated Press, Dec. 30, 2009.

[3] Walter Pincus, "Bomb suspect was read Miranda rights nine hours after arrest," *The Washington Post*, Feb. 15, 2010, p. A6.

[4] Michael B. Mukasey, "Where the U.S. went wrong on Abdulmutallab," *The Washington Post*, Feb. 12, 2010, p. A27.

[5] Ryan Grim, "Ashcroft: 'When You Have a Person in the Criminal Justice System, You Mirandize Them,' " *Huffington Post*, Feb. 19, 2010, www.huffingtonpost.com/2010/02/19/ashcroft-when-you-have-a_n_469384.html.

present the strongest case in the best forum." The explanation left Republicans, conservatives and many New Yorkers unconvinced of the benefits, dismayed at the potential costs and appalled at the idea of according full legal rights to a self-proclaimed enemy of the United States. Civil liberties and human rights groups applauded the decision while giving little attention to Holder's simultaneous move to try the alleged *USS Cole* plotter and others in military commissions that the groups had called for abolishing.

The political attacks over the administration's handling of Abdulmutallab's case added to the pressure

against trying KSM in New York City. Behind the scenes, Justice Department officials were looking for alternate, more remote sites for a possible civilian trial. And by February Holder was being deliberately ambiguous about whether the case would be tried in a civilian court at all.

"At the end of the day, wherever this case is tried, in whatever forum, what we have to ensure is that it's done as transparently as possible and with adherence to all the rules," Holder said on Feb. 11.[31] "If we do that, I'm not sure the location or even the forum is as important as what the world sees in that proceeding."

Material-Support Law Called Anti-Terror "Weapon of Choice"

Critics say the broadly written law criminalizes lawful speech.

Oussama Kassir never took up arms against U.S. forces in Afghanistan and never carried out a terrorist attack against Americans in the United States or abroad. But he is serving a life prison sentence today after a federal court jury in New York City found him guilty of attempting to establish a jihadist training camp in Oregon and distributing terrorist training materials over the Internet.

To put Kassir behind bars, federal prosecutors used a broadly written law that makes it a crime to provide "material support" — broadly defined — to any group designated by the government as a "terrorist organization." The law, first passed in 1994 and amended several times since, accounts for roughly half of the al Qaeda-related terrorism convictions since 2001, according to a study by two ex-prosecutors written for the Washington-based group Human Rights First.[1]

The material-support law is "the anti-terror weapon of choice for prosecutors," says Stephen Vladeck, a law professor at American University in Washington, D.C. "It's a lot easier to prove that a defendant provided material support to a designated terrorist organization than to prove that they actually committed a terrorist act."

Kassir, a Lebanese-born Swedish citizen, was convicted on May 12, 2009, after a three-week trial. The evidence showed he came to the United States in 1999 and bought a parcel of land in Oregon with plans to take advantage of lax U.S. gun laws to train Muslim recruits in assembling and disassembling AK-47 rifles. He also established six different Web sites and posted materials about how to make bombs and poisons.

The defense denied that Kassir conspired to train recruits and claimed the Web sites contained only readily available information. The jury deliberated less than a day before returning guilty verdicts on a total of 11 counts. U.S. District Judge John Keenan sentenced him to life imprisonment on Sept. 15.[2]

On the same day as the Kassir verdict, a federal court jury in Miami returned guilty verdicts against five of the so-called "Liberty City Six," who had been charged with plotting to blow up the Sears Tower in Chicago and selected federal buildings. In the Human Rights First report, New York lawyers Richard Zabel and James J. Benjamin Jr. note that the trial shows the importance of the material-support charge because prosecutors won convictions against only two defendants on an explosives charge and against only one defendant for seditious conspiracy.

Zabel and Benjamin, who both served in the U.S. attorney's office in New York City, say the material-support law has similarly been used to convict defendants for such actions as providing broadcasting services to a terrorist organization's television station or traveling to Pakistan for training in a jihadist camp. The law was also invoked against Lynne Stewart, a well-known defense lawyer, for transmitting messages to her terrorism-case client, Omar Abdel Rahman, the "Blind Sheik."

The law defines material support to include not only financial contributions but also any "property" or "service," including "personnel" and "training, expert advice or assistance." Medicine and religious materials are exempted.

CURRENT SITUATION

Watching Appeals

Lawyers for the government and for Guantánamo detainees are watching the federal appeals court in Washington and a specially created military appeals panel for the next major developments on the rules for prosecuting terrorism cases.

The government scored a major victory in early January when the U.S. Circuit Court of Appeals for the District of Columbia decisively backed the government's power to detain a low-level member of a pro-Taliban brigade captured during the Afghanistan war and held at Guantánamo for more than eight years.

Later in the month, the U.S. Court of Military Commission Review heard arguments on Jan. 26 from two

Some civil liberties and humanitarian groups contend the law sweeps too broadly. Material support is defined "so expansively and vaguely as to criminalize pure speech furthering lawful, nonviolent ends," the bipartisan Constitution Project says in a recent report. The report recommends amending the law to exempt "pure speech" unless intended to further illegal conduct. It also calls for giving groups the opportunity to contest designation as a terrorist organization.[3]

Appellate courts have generally upheld broad readings of the statute. In a decision in December 2007, however, the San Francisco-based U.S. Court of Appeals for the Ninth Circuit ruled that some of the law's terms — "training," "service," and "expert advice or assistance" — were impermissibly vague or overbroad.

The ruling came in a suit filed originally in 1998 by the Humanitarian Law Project on behalf of individuals or U.S.-based groups that sought to provide assistance to two designated terrorist organizations: the Kurdistan Workers' Party in Turkey or the Liberation Tigers of Tamil Eelam in Sri Lanka. The plaintiffs claimed they wanted to counsel both groups on use of international law and nonviolent conflict resolution.

The Supreme Court agreed to hear the government's appeal of the case as well as the plaintiffs' cross-appeal of the part of the ruling that upheld a broad construction of the term "personnel." The case was argued on Feb. 23; a decision is due by the end of June.[4]

Meanwhile, a military appeals panel is weighing challenges to the use of material-support counts in military commission proceedings. The United States Court of Military Commission Review heard arguments on Jan. 26 in appeals by two of the three men convicted so far in military commissions: Salim Ahmed Hamdan, former driver for al Qaeda

Oussama Kassir is serving a life sentence after a federal court jury in New York City found him guilty last year of attempting to establish a jihadist training camp in Oregon and distributing terrorist training materials over the Internet.

leader Osama bin Laden, and al Qaeda filmmaker and propagandist Ali Hamza Ahmad Suliman al Bahlul.

Hamdan, who was freed in late 2008 after about seven-and-a-half years in captivity, and al Bahlul, who was sentenced to life imprisonment, both contend that material support for terrorism is outside the military tribunals' jurisdiction because it is not a traditional war crime. The cases were argued before separate three-judge panels, which gave no indication when rulings would be expected.[5]

— *Kenneth Jost*

---

[1] Richard B. Zabel and James J. Benjamin Jr., "In Pursuit of Justice: Prosecuting Terrorism Cases in the Federal Courts," Human Rights First, May 2008, p. 32, www.humanrightsfirst .info/pdf/080521-USLS-pursuit-justice.pdf. See also by same authors "In Pursuit of Justice: Prosecuting Terrorism Cases in the Federal Courts: 2009 Update and Recent Developments," July 2009, www .humanrightsfirst.org/pdf/090723-LS-in-pursuit-justice-09-update.pdf. Background drawn from both reports.

[2] The press release by the U.S. Attorney for the Southern District of New York can be found at www.humanrightsfirst.org/pdf/090723-LS-in-pursuit-justice-09-update.pdf. See also "Man convicted in NY of trying to start terror camp," The Associated Press, May 12, 2009.

[3] "Reforming the Material Support Laws: Constitutional Concerns Presented by Prohibitions on Material Support to Terrorist Organizations,'" Constitution Project, Nov. 17, 2009, www.constitutionproject .org/manage/file/355.pdf.

[4] The case is *Holder v. Humanitarian Law Project*, 08-1498. For materials on the case, including links to news coverage, see SCOTUSWiki, www .scotuswiki.com/index.php?title=Holder_v._Humanitarian_Law_Project.

[5] Material in Bahlul's case can be found at www.defense.gov/news/ CMCRHAMZA.html/; materials in Hamdan's case at www.defense .gov/news/commissionsHamdan.html.

---

of the men convicted so far in the military tribunals challenging the government's power to prosecute material support for terrorism in military instead of civilian courts. Separate three-judge panels convened to hear the appeals by al Qaeda propagandist Bahlul and former bin Laden driver Hamdan gave no indication when they would rule on the cases.

With several other habeas corpus cases pending before the D.C. Circuit, the appeals court is likely to determine

both the direction and the pace of the next stage of the litigation from Guantánamo prisoners, according to Brookings Institution scholar Wittes.

If other judges follow the lead of the conservative-dominated panel in the Jan. 5 decision, many of the outstanding issues regarding the government's power to hold enemy combatants could be resolved quickly, Wittes says. But different rulings by panels in other cases could

Cole Bombing Case, Six Others Set for Tribunals

Abd al Rahim al Nashiri, the alleged mastermind of the October 2000 suicide attack on the *USS Cole*, is one of seven Guantánamo detainees designated by Attorney General Eric Holder for trial by military commissions. Seventeen U.S. sailors were killed in the attack on the warship as it lay docked in Aden, Yemen.

The Saudi-born al-Nashiri, now 45, allegedly served as al Qaeda's chief of operations in the Arabian peninsula before his capture in the United Arab Emirates in November 2002. He was held in a secret CIA prison (reportedly in Thailand) until being brought to Guantánamo in 2006.

The CIA has confirmed that al-Nashiri was waterboarded. He claims that he falsely confessed to the *Cole* attack and six other terrorist incidents as a result. It is also reported that he was the target of a mock execution by CIA interrogators.

The six other prisoners designated for trial by military commissions are:

- **Ahmed al Darbi (Saudi Arabia)** — Accused of plotting to bomb oil tankers in the Strait of Hormuz.
- **Mohammed Kamin (Afghanistan)** — Charged with planting mines in Afghanistan.
- **Omar Khadr (Canada)** — Accused of killing a U.S. soldier with a grenade in Afghanistan in 2002; Khadr was 15 at the time.
- **Noor Uthman Mohammed (Sudan)** — Charged with assisting in running al Qaeda training center.
- **Obaidullah (Afghanistan)** — Charged with possessing anti-tank mines.
- **Ibrahim al Qosi (Sudan)** — Accused of acting as Osama bin Laden's bodyguard, paymaster and supply chief.

add to what he calls the "cacophony" surrounding the habeas corpus cases and force the Supreme Court to intervene to resolve the conflicts.

The appeals court's decision rejected a habeas corpus petition by Ghaleb Nassar Al-Bihani, a Yemeni native who served as a cook for a Taliban brigade. He argued that he should be released because the war against the Taliban has ended and, in any event, that he was essentially a civilian contractor instead of a combatant.

In a 25-page opinion, Judge Janice Rogers Brown rejected both arguments. Brown, a strongly conservative judge appointed by President George W. Bush, said Bihani's admitted actions of accompanying the brigade to the battlefield, carrying a weapon and retreating and surrendering with the brigade showed that he was "both part of and substantially supported enemy forces."

As for the status of the war, Brown said, it was up to Congress or the president to decide whether the conflict had ended, not the courts. In a significant passage, Brown also said that U.S. instead of international law determined the president's authority to hold enemy combatants. "The international laws of war as a whole have not been implemented domestically by Congress and are therefore not a source of authority for U.S. courts," Brown wrote.

Judge Brett Kavanaugh, another Bush-appointed conservative, joined Brown's opinion. Judge Stephen Williams, who was appointed by President Ronald Reagan, agreed on the result but distanced himself from Brown's comments on the impact of international law. He noted that Brown's "dictum" — the legal term for a passage unnecessary to the decision in the case —"goes well beyond what the government has argued in the case."[32]

Wittes says the ruling is "a huge development if it stands." The appellate panel, he says, was "signaling" to the federal district court judges in Washington handling habeas corpus cases to "lighten up" on the government. District court judges have ruled against the government in somewhat over half of the cases decided so far.

The appeals court for the military commissions was created by the 2006 law overhauling the rules for the tribunals, but it had no cases to review until after Hamdan's and Bahlul's convictions in 2008.

In their appeals, both men claim that their convictions for material support for terrorism were improper because the offense is not a traditional war crime prosecutable in a military court. Bahlul also argues that the First Amendment bars prosecuting him for producing a video documentary for al Qaeda that recounts the bombing of

Should terrorism suspects ordinarily be tried in civilian courts?

YES
Laura Olson
Senior Counsel, Rule of Law Program
Constitution Project

Written for *CQ Researcher*, March 2010

Civilian courts are the proper forum for trying terrorism cases. Trial in our traditional federal courts is a proven and reliable way to provide justice, while ensuring our national security. This is in stark contrast to the new military commissions that were re-created for the third time in the Military Commissions Act (MCA) of 2009. Like their predecessors, these new commissions remain vulnerable to constitutional challenge.

We should not place some of the most important terrorism trials, and arguably the most important criminal trials, in our nation's history in the untested and uncertain military commissions system.

Since 2001, trials in federal criminal courts have resulted in nearly 200 convictions of terrorism suspects, compared to only three low-level convictions in the military commissions. Two of those three are now free in their home countries. This record demonstrates that prosecutions in our traditional federal courts are tough on terrorists.

To date, the rules to accompany the MCA of 2009 remain to be approved. Therefore, military commission judges are without guidance on how to proceed with these cases. Meanwhile, our traditional federal courts move ahead, applying long-established rules on procedure and evidence. For example, the Classified Information Procedures Act (CIPA) elaborates the procedures by which federal courts admit evidence while protecting national security information from improper disclosure. The MCA of 2009 incorporates CIPA procedures on dealing with classified information into the military commissions system, but military judges have little or no experience with these procedures. Federal judges have worked with CIPA for the last 30 years.

Our Constitution provides a safe and effective way to prosecute terrorism suspects. In fact, Ahmed Kfalfan Ghailani, a former Guantánamo detainee, is now being held in New York City for his trial in federal court there. The judge has issued a protective order on all classified information, and there have been no reports of any increased safety risks or expenses associated with this trial.

I agree with the nearly 140 former diplomats, military officials, federal judges and prosecutors and members of Congress, as well as bar leaders, national-security and foreign-policy experts, and family members of the 9/11 attacks that signed Beyond Guantánamo: A Bipartisan Declaration. This unique and bipartisan group is in favor of trying terrorism suspects in our traditional federal courts. Federal trials are the only way to ensure swift and constitutional trials of terrorism suspects.

NO
Sen. John McCain, R-Ariz.

From statement in support of the Enemy Belligerent Interrogation, Detention and Prosecution Act, March 4, 2010

This legislation seeks to ensure that the mistakes made during the apprehension of the Christmas Day bomber, such as reading him a Miranda warning, will never happen again and put Americans' security at risk.

Specifically, this bill would require unprivileged enemy belligerents suspected of engaging in hostilities against the U.S. to be held in military custody and interrogated for their intelligence value by a "high-value detainee" interagency team established by the president. This interagency team of experts in national security, terrorism, intelligence, interrogation and law enforcement will have the protection of U.S. civilians and civilian facilities as their paramount responsibility. . . .

A key provision of this bill is that it would prohibit a suspected enemy belligerent from being provided with a Miranda warning and being told he has a right to a lawyer and a right to refuse to cooperate. I believe that an overwhelming majority of Americans agree that when we capture a terrorist who is suspected of carrying out or planning an attack intended to kill hundreds if not thousands of innocent civilians, our focus must be on gaining all the information possible to prevent that attack or any that may follow from occurring. . . . Additionally, the legislation would authorize detention of enemy belligerents without criminal charges for the duration of the hostilities consistent with standards under the law of war which have been recognized by the Supreme Court.

Importantly, if a decision is made to hold a criminal trial after the necessary intelligence information is obtained, the bill mandates trial by military commission, where we are best able to protect U.S. national security interests, including sensitive classified sources and methods, as well as the place and the people involved in the trial itself.

The vast majority of Americans understand that what happened with the Christmas Day bomber was a near catastrophe that was only prevented by sheer luck and the courage of a few of the passengers and crew. A wide majority of Americans also realize that allowing a terrorist to be interrogated for only 50 minutes before he is given a Miranda warning and told he can obtain a lawyer and stop cooperating is not sufficient. . . .

We must ensure that the broad range of expertise that is available within our government is brought to bear on such high-value detainees. This bill mandates such coordination and places the proper focus on getting intelligence to stop an attack, rather than allowing law enforcement and preparing a case for a civilian criminal trial to drive our response.

FEMA News Photo/WireImage/Andrea Booher

Controversy erupted after Attorney General Eric Holder announced plans to try the five alleged 9/11 conspirators in a federal court "just blocks away from where the twin towers [of the World Trade Center] once stood." New York City Mayor Michael Bloomberg and Police Commissioner Raymond Kelly welcomed Holder's decision, but many New Yorkers expressed concern about the costs and risks of a sensational trial in Lower Manhattan.

the *USS Cole* and calls for others to join a jihad against the United States.

The government counters by citing cases from the Civil War and World War II to argue that providing support to unlawful enemy combatants has been prosecutable in military courts even if the term "material support for terrorism" was not used. As to Bahlul's free-speech argument, the government contends that the First Amendment does not apply to enemy "propaganda."[33]

Bahlul is also challenging the life sentence imposed in November 2008; Hamdan was freed later that month after being credited with the seven years he had already been held at Guantánamo.

Wittes says the government has "a big uphill climb" on the material-support issue. He notes that in the Supreme Court's 2006 decision in Hamdan's case, four of the justices questioned whether military tribunals could try a conspiracy charge, another of the generally phrased offenses the government has used in terrorism cases. Material support for terrorism would be harder to justify, he says.

Wittes adds that it is important to resolve the issue quickly if the military commissions are to be used in other cases. "What you don't want to happen is to have a whole lot of people sentenced in military commissions and then find out that the charges are invalid," he says.

Making a Deal?

The Obama administration may be on the verge of deciding to try Khalid Sheikh Mohammed and four other alleged 9/11 conspirators in a military tribunal in an effort to gain Republican support for closing the Guantánamo prison camp.

Administration officials are reportedly near to recommending that Obama reverse Attorney General Holder's Nov. 13 decision to hold the 9/11 conspiracy trial in federal court in hopes of securing support for closing Guantánamo from an influential Republican senator, South Carolina's Lindsey Graham.[34]

Graham, a former military lawyer, has strongly advocated use of military tribunals for detainees held at Guantánamo but has not joined other Republicans in attacking Obama's pledge to close the facility. GOP lawmakers have been pushing legislative proposals to block use of funds for closing Guantánamo or for holding the 9/11 conspiracy trial in federal court.

The administration's possible reversal on the KSM trial is drawing a heated response from civil liberties and human rights groups. The decision would "strike a blow to American values and the rule of law and undermine America's credibility," according to the ACLU.

Elisa Massimino, president and CEO of Human Rights First, says failure to support Holder's decision would set "a dangerous precedent for future national security policy."

In the wake of the strong criticism of holding the KSM trial in New York City, Justice Department lawyers and others had been reported to be holding onto the plan for a federal court trial, but in a different location. Among the sites reported to have been under consideration were somewhere else in southern New York, Northern Virginia and western Pennsylvania.[35]

Any of those sites would satisfy the constitutional requirement that trial of a federal criminal case be held in "the district wherein the crime shall have been committed." Besides the World Trade Center in New York City, the 9/11 hijackers also crashed a plane into the Pentagon in Northern Virginia and into a rural location in western Pennsylvania.

Graham, first elected to the Senate in 2002, argued during the Bush administration for a greater role for Congress in defining detention policies. Since Obama's election, he is widely reported to have formed a working relationship on several issues with White House chief of staff Rahm Emanuel, a former colleague in the House of Representatives. Emanuel was described in a flattering profile in *The Washington Post* and elsewhere as having disagreed with Obama's pledge to close Guantánamo and with Holder's decision to try KSM in federal court.[36]

Beyond the KSM trial and Guantánamo issue, Graham is continuing to call for congressional legislation to govern the handling of detention issues. "I want Congress and the administration to come up with a detainee policy that will be accepted by courts and so that the international community will understand that no one is in jail by an arbitrary exercise of executive power," Graham told *The New York Times*.[37]

As outlined, the legislation would authorize holding terrorism suspects inside the United States without charging them with a crime or advising them of Miranda rights; establish standards for choosing between military or civilian court for prosecution; and authorize indefinite detention under standards subject to judicial review. Civil liberties and human rights groups remain opposed to indefinite-detention proposals.

Administration officials were quoted in news accounts as saying Obama hopes to have the KSM trial issue resolved before he begins a trip to Asia on March 18. But officials quoted in *The Washington Post* cautioned against expecting a "grand bargain" with Graham on the full range of detention issues in the near future.

OUTLOOK

Bringing Justice to Bear

When he defended the administration's decision to try Khalid Sheikh Mohammed in a civilian court, deputy national intelligence director John Brennan made clear that he expected the trial would be fair and just, but the result certain and severe.

"I'm confident that he's going to have the full weight of American justice," Brennan said on NBC's "Meet the Press" on Feb. 7. Asked by host David Gregory whether Mohammed would be executed, Brennan initially skirted the question but eventually concluded, "I'm convinced and confident that Mr. Khalid Sheikh Mohammed is going to meet his day in justice and before his maker."[38]

Despite the assurance from Brennan, Attorney General Holder and other administration officials, Americans apparently lack the same confidence in the federal court system. An ABC/*Washington Post* poll conducted in late February showed Americans favoring military over civilian trials for terrorism suspects by a margin of 55 percent to 39 percent. In a similar poll in the fall, Americans showed a statistically insignificant preference for military trials: 48 percent to 47 percent.[39]

A survey by Democratic pollsters similarly finds a majority of respondents opposed to Obama's policy on interrogation and prosecution of terrorism suspects (51 percent to 44 percent). But the survey, conducted in late February for the Democratic groups Democracy Corps and Third Way, also found majority approval of Obama's handling of "national security" (57 percent to 40 percent) and "fighting terrorism" (54 percent to 41 percent).

In a memo, leaders of the two organizations advise Obama to move the issue away from "civilian" versus "military" trials. Instead, they say the administration should "place the debate over terrorism suspects into the broader context of tough actions and significant results."[40]

Even before the memo's release, civil liberties and human rights groups were following the strategy in public lobbying of Obama as the administration was weighing where to hold the KSM trial. In a March 5 conference call for reporters arranged by Human Rights First, three retired military officers all depicted the military commissions as an unproven forum for prosecuting terrorists. "This is not ready for prime time," said Human Rights First President Massimino.

The ACLU followed with a full-page ad in the Sunday edition of *The New York Times* that compared the 300 terrorism cases "successfully handled" in the criminal justice system to "only three" in military commissions. "Our criminal justice system will resolve these cases more quickly and more credibly than the military commissions," the March 7 ad stated.

Meanwhile, former prosecutor McCarthy conceded in a speech sponsored by a college-affiliated center in Washington, "I don't think the military commission system performed well. By and large, the civilian system has performed well."

Speaking March 5 at the Kirby Center for Constitutional Studies and Citizenship at Hillsdale College in Michigan, McCarthy nevertheless reiterated that discovery procedures available to defendants argued against use of criminal prosecutions. "When you're at war, you can't be telling the enemy your most sensitive national intelligence," the *National Review* columnist said. Massimino noted, however, that a new military commissions law passed in 2009 dictates that defendants are to have access to evidence "comparable" to that provided in civilian courts.

The White House now says a decision on the KSM trial is "weeks" away. On Capitol Hill, Sen. Graham is continuing to push for a deal that would swap Republican support for closing Guantánamo for the administration's agreement to try KSM and other high-level terrorism suspects in military commissions. But Graham has yet to gain any public support for the plan from GOP colleagues.

McCarthy mocks Graham's proposed deal. He says the White House has already "stood down" on the military commissions issues and is only deferring a decision in hopes of getting GOP support for closing Guantánamo. "It makes no sense to horse-trade when Obama was being pushed toward military commissions by reality," McCarthy writes.[41]

Fellow conservative Rivkin also expects military commissions to become the norm for terrorism suspects. "My hope is that we'll come to our senses," he says. The current policies "are not consonant with the traditional law-of-war architecture, and they're not consistent with prevailing in this war."

Liberal groups continue to strongly oppose use of military commissions, but acknowledge congressional politics may determine decision-making. "There's no question that Congress has been trying to hold hostage the president's national security agenda," Massimino says.

For his part, former Assistant U.S. Attorney Benjamin doubts that military commissions will prove as useful as conservatives expect. "It would be great if the military commissions develop into a forum that works," he says. "But I have my doubts about how quickly or how smoothly that will happen."

NOTES

1. Some background information drawn from Farhan Bokhari, *et al.*, "The CEO of al-Qaeda," *Financial Times*, Feb. 15, 2003. See also the Wikipedia entry on Khalid Sheikh Mohammed and sources cited there, http://en.wikipedia.org/wiki/Khalid_Sheikh_Mohammed.

2. Quoted in Devlin Barnett, "NYC trial of 9/11 suspects faces legal risks," The Associated Press, Nov. 14, 2009. For Holder's prepared remarks, see U.S. Department of Justice, "Attorney General Announces Forum Decisions for Guantánamo Detainees," Nov. 13, 2009, www.justice.gov/ag/speeches/2009/ag-speech-091113.html.

3. Quoted in Carrie Johnson, "Holder Answers to 9/11 Relatives About Trials in U.S.," *The Washington Post*, Nov. 19, 2009, p. A3. See also Charlie Savage, "Holder Defends Decision to Use U.S. Court for 9/11 Trial," *The New York Times*, Nov. 19, 2009, p. A18.

4. See Anne E. Kornblut and Carrie Johnson, "Obama to help pick location of terror trial," *The Washington Post*, Feb. 12, 2010, p. A1.

5. For background, see these *CQ Researcher* reports: Kenneth Jost, "Closing Guantánamo," Feb. 27, 2009, pp. 177-200; Peter Katel and Kenneth Jost, "Treatment of Detainees," Aug. 25, 2006, pp. 673-696; and Kenneth Jost, "Civil Liberties Debates," Oct. 24, 2003, pp. 893-916.

6. "FY 2009 Budget and Performance Summary: Part One: Summary of Request and Performance," U.S. Department of Justice, www.justice.gov/jmd/2009summary/html/004_budget_highlights.htm. See also Mark Hosenball, "Terror Prosecution Statistics Criticized by GOP Were Originally Touted by Bush Administration," *Declassified* blog, Feb. 9, 2010, http://blog.newsweek.com/blogs/declassified/archive/2010/02/09/terror-prosecution-statistics-criticized-by-gop-were-originally-touted-by-bush-administration.aspx.

7. Richard B. Zabel and James J. Benjamin Jr., "In Pursuit of Justice: Prosecuting Terrorism Cases in the Federal Courts: 2009 Update and Recent Developments," Human Rights First, July 2009,

www.humanrightsfirst.org/pdf/090723-LS-in-pursuit-justice-09-update.pdf. See also by the same authors, "In Pursuit of Justice: Prosecuting Terrorism Cases in the Federal Courts," Human Rights First, May 2008, www.humanrightsfirst.info/pdf/080521-USLS-pursuit-justice.pdf.

8. Andy McCarthy, "No Civilian Trial — In NYC or Anywhere Else," *Conservative Blog Watch*, Jan. 30, 2010, www.conservativeblogwatch.com/2010/01/30/no-civilian-trial-in-nyc-or-anywhere-by-andy-mccarthy.

9. See Benjamin Weiser, "A Top Terrorism Prosecutor Turns Critic of Civilian Trials," *The New York Times*, Feb. 20, 2010, p. A1.

10. See Del Quentin Wilber, " '08 habeas ruling may snag Obama plans," *The Washington Post*, Feb. 13, 2010, p. A2.

11. The defendants and their respective sentences were Mukhtar Al-Bakri and Yahya Goba (10 years each), Sahim Alwan (9-1/2 years), Shafal Mosed and Yaseinn Taher (eight years each) and Faysal Galab (seven years). For a full account, see Matthew Purdy and Lowell Bergman, "Where the Trail Led: Between Evidence and Suspicion, Unclear Danger: The Lackawanna Terror Case," *The New York Times*, Oct. 12, 2003, sec. 1, p. 1. See also Lou Michel, "Lackawanna officials say troops in city was bad idea," *Buffalo News*, July 26, 2009, p. A1.

12. *In Pursuit of Justice, op. cit.*, p. 2; *In Pursuit of Justice: 2009 Update, op. cit.*, p. 2.

13. Quoted in Bruce Golding, "Holder tours federal courthouse ahead of 9/11 terror trial," *The New York Post*, Dec. 9, 2009.

14. See Peter Finn, "The boy from the battlefield," *The Washington Post*, Feb. 10, 2010, p. A1.

15. "Remarks by the President on National Security," National Archives, May 21, 2009, www.whitehouse.gov/the_press_office/Remarks-by-the-President-On-National-Security-5-21-09/. For coverage, see Sheryl Gay Stolberg, "Obama Would Move Some Terror Detainees to U.S.," *The New York Times*, May 22, 2009, p. A1.

16. Department of Defense comments on the study are at www.defense.gov/Transcripts/Transcript

.aspx?TranscriptID=4340. See also Joseph Williams and Bryan Bender, "Obama Changes US Course on Treatment of Detainees," *The Boston Globe*, Jan. 23, 2009, p. A1. See Mark Denbeaux, Joshua Denbeaux and R. David Gratz, "Released Guantánamo Detainees and the Department of Defense: Propaganda by the Numbers?," Jan. 15, 2009, http://law.shu.edu/publications/GuantánamoReports/propaganda_numbers_11509.pdf.

17. The case is 542 U.S. 507 (2004). For an account, see Kenneth Jost, *Supreme Court Yearbook 2003-2004*, CQ Press.

18. Benjamin Wittes, Robert Chesney and Rabea Benhalim, "The Emerging Law of Detention: The Guantánamo Habeas Cases as Lawmaking," Brookings Institution, Jan. 22, 2010, www.brookings.edu/papers/2010/0122_Guantánamo_wittes_chesney.aspx. See Benjamin Wittes and Robert Chesney, "Piecemeal detainee policy," *The Washington Post*, Jan. 27, 2010, p. A17.

19. Chisun Lee, "Judges Urge Congress to Act on Indefinite Detention," *ProPublica*, Jan. 22, 2010, www.propublica.org/feature/judges-urge-congress-to-act-on-indefinite-terrorism-detentions-122. Walton, an appointee of President George W. Bush, was joined in the interview by Chief Judge Royce Lamberth, an appointee of President Ronald Reagan, and Judge Ricardo Urbina, an appointee of President Bill Clinton.

20. David Cole, "Detainees: still a matter for judges," *The Washington Post*, Feb. 9, 2010, p. A16.

21. Background drawn in part from Jennifer K. Elsea, "Terrorism and the Law of War: Trying Terrorists as War Criminals before Military Commissions," Congressional Research Service, Dec. 11, 2001, www.fas.org/irp/crs/RL31191.pdf. See also Louis Fisher, *Military Tribunals and Presidential Power: American Revolution to the War on Terrorism* (2005). Wittes's quote is from his book *Law and the Long War: The Future of Justice in the Age of Terror* (2008), p. 42.

22. The decision is *Ex parte Milligan*, 71 U.S. 2 (1866). *The New York Times'* contemporaneous account is reprinted in Kenneth Jost, *The New York Times on the Supreme Court 1857-2006* (2009), CQ Press, pp. 58-59.

23. The citation is 317 U.S. 1 (1942). The opinion was issued on Oct. 29, almost three months after the July 31 decision. The rulings on the curfew and internments are *Hirabayashi v. United States*, 320 U.S. 81 (1943), and *Korematsu v. United States*, 323 U.S. 214 (1944).

24. Joseph P. Fried, "Sheik Sentenced to Life in Prison in Bombing Plot," *The New York Times*, Jan. 18, 1996, p. A1, and Christopher S. Wren, "Jury Convicts 3 in a Conspiracy to Bomb Airliners," *The New York Times*, Sept. 6, 1996, p. A1. See also Benjamin Weiser, "Judge Upholds Conviction in '93 Bombing," *The New York Times*, April 5, 2003, p. A1.

25. Accounts drawn from *Pursuit of Justice* (2008), *op. cit.*, supplemented by Wikipedia entries or contemporaneous news coverage.

26. The decision is *Hamdan v. Rumsfeld*, 548 U.S. 557 (2006). For an account, see Kenneth Jost, *Supreme Court Yearbook 2005-2006*, CQ Press.

27. U.S. Department of Justice, "Fact Sheet: Justice Department Counter-Terrorism Efforts Since 9/11," Sept. 11, 2008, www.justice.gov/opa/pr/2008/September/08-nsd-807.html.

28. The Supreme Court decision is *Boumediene v. Bush*, 553 U.S. — — (2008). For an account, see Kenneth Jost, *Supreme Court Yearbook 2007-2008*, CQ Press. For Leon's decision granting habeas corpus to five of the six prisoners, see "Emerging Law of Detention," *op. cit.*, p. 99; William Glaberson, "Judge Declares Five Detainees Held Illegally," *The New York Times*, Nov. 21, 2008, p. A1.

29. See Peter Finn, "Report on U.S. Detention Policy Will Be Delayed," *The Washington Post*, July 21, 2009, p. A2.

30. For summaries of individual cases, see "Emerging Law of Detention," *op. cit.*, appendix II, pp. 88-105.

31. Quoted in Kornblut and Johnson, *op. cit.*

32. The decision is *Al Bihani v. Obama*, D.C. Cir., Jan. 5, 2010, http://pacer.cadc.uscourts.gov/docs/common/opinions/201001/09-5051-1223587.pdf. For coverage, see Del Quentin Wilber, "Court upholds ruling to detain Yemeni suspect," *The Washington Post*, Jan. 6, 2010, p. A3.

33. Material in Bahlul's case can be found at www.defense.gov/news/CMCRHAMZA.html/; materials in Hamdan's case had not been posted by the deadline for this report.

34. See Anne E. Kornblut and Peter Finn, "Obama aides near reversal on 9/11 trial," *The Washington Post*, March 5, 2010, p. A1; Charlie Savage, "Senator Proposes Deal on Handling of Detainees," *The New York Times*, March 4, 2010, p. A12.

35. Richard A. Serrano, "Experts make case for N.Y. terror trial," *Los Angeles Times*, March 3, 2010, p. A12.

36. Jason Horwitz, "Obama's 'enforcer' may also be his voice of reason," *The Washington Post*, March 2, 2010, p. A1.

37. Savage, *op. cit.* (March 4).

38. Transcript: www.msnbc.msn.com/id/35270673/ns/meet_the_press//.

39. http://blogs.abcnews.com/thenumbers/2010/03/911-and-military-tribunals.html

40. "The Politics of National Security: A Wake-Up Call," Democracy Corps/Third Way, March 8, 2010, www.democracycorps.com/strategy/2010/03/the-politics-of-national-security-a-wake-up-call/?section=Analysis. The memo was signed by Stanley B. Greenberg, James Carville and Jeremy Rosner of Democracy Corps, and Jon Cowan, Matt Bennett and Andy Johnson of Third Way.

41. Andrew McCarthy, "Hold the Champagne on Military Commissions — It's a Head Fake," *The Corner*, March 5, 2010, http://corner.nationalreview.com.

BIBLIOGRAPHY

Books

Fisher, Louis, *Military Tribunals and Presidential Power: American Revolution to the War on Terrorism, University of Kansas Press*, 2005.
The veteran separation-of-powers specialist at the Library of Congress examines the development of the president's wartime authority in legal matters. Includes chapter notes, 10-page bibliography and list of cases.

Wittes, Benjamin, *Law and the Long War: The Future of Justice in the Age of Terror, Penguin Press*, 2008.
A leading researcher on national security at the Brookings Institution provides a critical examination of detention and interrogation policies along with his arguments for

Congress to pass legislation to authorize administrative detention of suspected enemy combatants and to create a national security court to try terrorism cases. Includes detailed notes. Wittes is also editor of *Legislating the War on Terror: An Agenda for Reform* (Brookings, 2009).

Yoo, John, *War by Other Means: An Insider's Account of the War on Terror, Kaplan*, 2005.
Yoo, a law professor at the University of California-Berkeley who served as deputy assistant attorney general for the Office of Legal Counsel during the George W. Bush administration, provides a combative account of his role in detention and interrogation policies and a strong argument for presidential wartime powers vis-à-vis Congress and the courts. Includes detailed notes. Yoo's other books include *Crisis and Command: The History of Executive Power from Washington to George W. Bush* (Kaplan, 2009); and *The Powers of War and Peace: Foreign Affairs and the Constitution after 9/11 (University of Chicago* (2005).

Articles

Mayer, Jane, "The Trial," *The New Yorker*, Feb. 5, 2010, www.newyorker.com/reporting/2010/02/ 15/100215fa_fact_mayer.
The magazine's prolific staff writer details the legal reasoning behind, and political implications of, Attorney General Eric Holder's decision to prosecute Khalid Sheikh Mohammed and four other alleged 9/11 conspirators in a civilian court instead of a military tribunal.

Reports and Studies

Elsea, Jennifer K., "Comparison of Rights in Military Commission Trials and Trials in Federal Criminal Courts," *Congressional Research Service*, Nov. 19, 2009, http://assets.opencrs.com/rpts/R40932_20091119.pdf.
The 23-page report provides a side-by-side comparison of the rights accorded to defendants respectively in federal criminal courts under general federal law or in military commissions under the Military Commissions Act of 2009. Elsea, a legislative attorney with CRS, also wrote two previous reports on military commissions: "The Military Commissions Act of 2006 (MCA): Background and Proposed Amendments" (Sept. 8, 2009), http://assets.opencrs.com/rpts/R40752_2009 0908.pdf; and "Terrorism and the Law of War: Trying Terrorists as War Criminals before Military Commissions" (Dec. 11, 2001), www.fas.org/irp/crs/RL31191.pdf.

Laguardia, Francesca, Terrorist Trial Report Card: September 11, 2001-September 11, 2009, *Center on Law and Security, New York University School of Law*, January 2010, www.lawandsecurity.org/publications/TTRCFinalJan14.pdf.
The series of reports studies data from federal terrorism prosecutions in the post-9/11 years and analyzes trends in the government's legal strategies.

Wittes, Benjamin, Robert Chesney and Rabea Benhalim, "The Emerging Law of Detention: The Guantánamo Habeas Cases as Lawmaking," *Brookings Institution*, Jan. 22, 2010, www.brookings.edu/papers/2010/0122_guantanamo_wittes_chesney.aspx.
The comprehensive report examines and identifies unsettled issues in decisions by federal courts in Washington, D.C., in several dozen habeas corpus cases filed by Guantánamo detainees. Wittes is a senior scholar and Benhalim a legal fellow at Brookings; Chesney is a law professor at the University of Texas-Austin.

Zabel, Richard B., and James J. Benjamin Jr., "In Pursuit of Justice: Prosecuting Terrorism Cases in the Federal Courts: 2009 Update and Recent Developments," *Human Rights First*, July 2009, www.humanrightsfirst .org/pdf/090723-LS-in-pursuit-justice-09-update.pdf.
The 70-page report by two New York City lawyers who formerly served as federal prosecutors finds federal courts to have a "track record of serving as an effective and fair tool for incapacitating terrorists." The report updates the authors' original, 171-page report, "In Pursuit of Justice: Prosecuting Terrorism Cases in the Federal Courts" (May 2008), www.humanrightsfirst.info/pdf/080521-USLS-pursuit-justice.pdf.

On the Web

Two newspapers — *The New York Times* and *The Miami Herald* — maintain Web sites with comprehensive information on Guantánamo detainees: **http://projects .nytimes.com/guantanamo** and **www.miamiherald.com/ guantanamo/**. The Pentagon maintains a Web site on military commissions: **www.defense.gov/news/courtofmilitarycommissionreview.html**.

For More Information

American Civil Liberties Union, 125 Broad St., 18th Floor, New York, NY 10004; (212) 549-2500; www.aclu.org. Advocates for individual rights and federal civilian trials for suspected terrorists.

Brookings Institution, 1775 Massachusetts Ave., N.W., Washington, DC 20036; (202) 797-6000; www.brookings .edu. Public policy think tank focusing on foreign policy and governance.

Constitution Project, 1200 18th St., N.W., Suite 1000, Washington, DC 20036; (202) 580-6920; www.constitu-tionproject.org. Promotes bipartisan consensus on significant constitutional and legal issues.

Foundation for Defense of Democracies, P.O. Box 33249, Washington, DC 20033; (202) 207-0190; www.defend democracy.org. Nonpartisan policy institute dedicated to promoting pluralism, defending democratic values and opposing ideologies that threaten democracy.

Human Rights First, 333 Seventh Ave., 13th Floor, New York, NY 10001; (212) 845 5200; www.humanrightsfirst .org. Advocates for the U.S. government's full participation in international human rights laws.

National Institute of Military Justice, Washington College of Law, American University, 4801 Massachusetts Ave., N.W., Washington, DC 20016; (202) 274-4322; www.wcl.american .edu/nimj. Promotes the fair administration of justice in the military system.

15

Caring for Veterans

Does the VA Adequately Serve Wounded Vets?

Peter Katel

Eric Johnson, a scout from the 10th Mountain Division stationed at Fort Drum, near Watertown, N.Y., shares painful wartime experiences with friends at a coffeehouse catering to vets on April 16, 2008. Soldiers in Johnson's division have been deployed in Iraq and Afghanistan multiple times. Repeated deployments are creating an unprecedented number of cases of post-traumatic stress disorder, traumatic brain injury and associated mental-health conditions — overwhelming mental-health professionals in veterans' health care facilities.

From *CQ Researcher*,
April 23, 2010.

The car bomb exploded at dusk. Its target — a seven-ton U.S. Army personnel carrier — was blown about six feet by the force of the blast. Infantryman John Lamie came out alive, thanks to armor plating around his machine-gunner's cupola, but three of his buddies died in the Aug. 3, 2005, attack in Baghdad. Lamie went to Iraq a second time in 2007-2008, before the cumulative effects of combat eventually pushed him out of the Army.

Now he's fighting another kind of battle — with the Department of Veterans Affairs (VA). "I did two tours in Iraq and half my squad died," he says from his home in Cecil, Ga., only to "come home and get treated like a piece of crap in my own state."

Because of a series of complications over the validity of disability exams Lamie took for post-traumatic stress disorder (PTSD), traumatic brain injury (TBI) and other conditions, Lamie's most recent disability check amounted to $83.19. He and his wife have three children, and he's paying child support for a fourth child with his ex-wife.

Lamie says that when he tried to straighten out his case with staff of the VA's Veterans Benefits Administration (VBA), he ran into a wall of indifference. "The vet has no power, you are left to the wind," Lamie says. "You have to call and beg — I don't mean ask nicely, I mean beg — and I don't feel any vet should have to beg somebody to do their damn job."

However, by late April, Lamie had found a VA staffer who was trying to straighten out bureaucratic confusion involving multiple files shipped among multiple offices. "Fingers crossed," Lamie says. "Within another two months something might work itself out." He emphasizes "might."

Brain Injuries Put Strain on VA Benefits

Nearly 91,000 U.S. soldiers have either died, been wounded or medically evacuated for noncombat-related reasons thus far in the Iraq and Afghanistan wars (top). The 760,000 veterans who suffer from either post-traumatic stress disorder (PTSD) or traumatic brain injury (TBI), or both, have put the Veterans Benefits Administration under increasing pressure to meet the needs of the country's injured veterans.

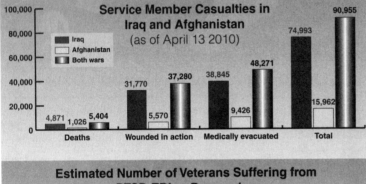

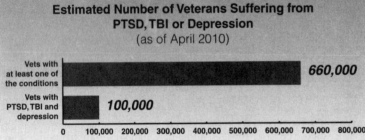

Sources: Veterans for Common Sense; RAND Center for Military Health Policy Research, 2008, www.rand.org/pubs/monographs/MG720

Veterans' advocates, the Government Accountability Office (GAO) and the VA's own inspector general have all reported similar communications breakdowns and wildly varying standards for evaluating disability claims among VBA regional offices, even as a steady stream of new claims pours into the VA.

Soldiers wounded while serving their country "are waiting — and waiting — for the help they have been promised," said Rep. Bob Filner, D-Calif., chairman of the House Veterans' Affairs Committee, after meeting with agency officials and veterans' organizations in March. "Frankly, it's an insult to our veterans and their service."[1]

About 1 million claims of all kinds are backlogged at the VA, according to veterans' organizations, some of which help veterans on behalf of the VA, which says the backlog of initial claims alone totals 500,000, using a different calculation method.

While VA medical care, delivered through the Veterans Health Administration, tends to earn high marks from vets, the VBA presents a different picture. In 2007-2008, staff at VBA regional offices compiled an overall accuracy record on initial claims decisions of only 77 percent, Belinda J. Finn, VA deputy inspector general, told the House Veterans' Disability Assistance and Memorial Affairs Subcommittee in early March. "This equates to approximately . . . 203,000 total claims where veterans' monthly benefits may be incorrect," Finn told the subcommittee.[2]

The VA's scramble to meet mounting demand for its services is occurring amid continuing warfare on two fronts: Since U.S. forces entered Afghanistan in 2001, at least 5,190 service members have been wounded, 425 of them this year. Since the 2003 U.S. invasion of Iraq, 31,176 service members have been wounded there.[3]

Yet the VA's difficulties providing adequate care for veterans got only sporadic attention until 2007, when a prize-winning *Washington Post* series pushed them to the top of the national agenda. (*See "Background," p. 401.*) With the issue in the spotlight, Congress in 2008 authorized free medical care for all Iraq and Afghanistan veterans for five years after leaving the military. And GI Bill educational benefits were expanded for veterans who entered the service after the Sept. 11, 2001, terrorist attacks.

Vets welcomed the new benefits, but questioned the VBA's ability to process all the new claims. The VA's new boss, retired Gen. Eric K. Shinseki, is vowing to shake up the agency. "2010 is my year to focus on finding and breaking the obstacles that deny us faster and better processing and higher quality outcomes," he told the Veterans of Foreign Wars in early March. To break the backlog while dealing with a rush of expected new claims, he proposes adding 4,000 claims examiners in the 2010-2011 fiscal year.[4]

His appointees aren't mincing words about what they found when they took over. "In my judgment, it cannot be fixed," Peter Levin, the VA's chief technology officer, said of the benefits claims system during a March meeting on Capitol Hill with veterans' organizations. (*See sidebar, p. 404.*) "We need to build a new system, and that is exactly what we are going to do."[5]

Veterans' advocates cheered Levin's comments and praise Shinseki's vision, but some wonder if he can put his stamp on the VA. A West Point graduate who lost most of a foot in Vietnam combat, Shinseki has earned a reputation for speaking out regardless of consequences. As Army chief of staff, he told the Senate Armed Services Committee in 2003 that securing Iraq after invading it would require "something on the order of several hundred thousand soldiers." Shinseki's civilian boss, Defense Secretary Donald Rumsfeld, contemptuously brushed that assessment aside and marginalized its author. But time proved Shinseki more accurate than Rumsfeld, who endorsed a forecast of 30,000-50,000 troops in Iraq after the invasion. By fiscal year 2008, U.S. troop strength had reached nearly 160,000.[6]

Now, Shinseki's leading an agency trying to adjust to the special demands created by 21st-century warfare. Vast advances in battlefield care are enabling thousands of vets to survive injuries that would have been fatal in the past. But those injuries, often caused by homemade bombs, or so-called improvised explosive devices (IEDs), can be crippling.

"IED blasts alone often cause multiple wounds, usually with severe injuries to extremities, and traumatic brain and other blast injuries, and they leave many . . . with serious physical, psychological and cognitive injuries," the government-funded Institute of Medicine (IOM) reported to Congress in a lengthy study published in March.[7]

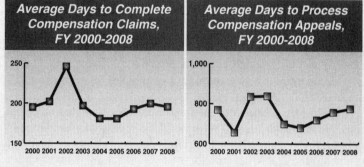

Appeals Take Longer Than Claims

The average processing time to complete a veteran's compensation claim in 2008 was nearly 200 days, more or less the same since 2003. Finalizing appeals, however, took nearly four times longer — a constant trend since 2000.

Average Days to Complete Compensation Claims, FY 2000-2008

Average Days to Process Compensation Appeals, FY 2000-2008

Source: "Veterans' Disability Benefits," Government Accountability Office, January 2010

Today's all-volunteer military is far smaller than past draftee-fed forces, requiring troops to be repeatedly recycled through combat zones. About a third of those who have been deployed to combat more than once have suffered from PTSD, TBI or major depression, and about 5 percent suffered from all three, according to the RAND Corp, a California think tank. Multiple deployments can double the risk of PTSD and other psychological problems, the Army surgeon general concluded in a 2008 report, which found mental health problems in 12 percent with one deployment and 27 percent with three or more deployments.[8]

Retired Army Capt. Anthony Kennedy, who attempted suicide after two tours in Iraq, described the nature of the fighting there and the psychological effects of the constant threat of being blown up by an IED. "One of my friends . . . had a friend whose arms and legs were blown off," Kennedy says. "All of us combat guys are thinking, 'Why do I want to go through life with no arms and no legs?' Our consensus: 'Can my battle buddy just put a bullet in me?' We talk about that."

Kennedy has had problems with the VA benefits system as well, but obtained a volunteer lawyer's help in pushing his PTSD rating from 30 percent to 70 percent disability. He says his 17 years in the service taught him how to deal with military-style bureaucracy. "I have the maturity and the knowledge to know that there's 100,000 applications out there, and I'm just one cog in the wheel," he says. "But I can imagine that if someone is completely disabled, and their father or mother comes in, the system can be a shock."

Even military reservists, accustomed to part-time service, can be taken aback by the VA system they encounter after active duty. Naval reservist Richard Sanchez of New York, a former paralegal for a Wall Street law firm, was discharged after his second deployment, which took him to Kuwait, where he was injured when an ammunition and weapons container fell on him in 2005.

After discharge, Sanchez began to suffer intense back pain, failing memory and depression. In his confused state, the VA system overcame him, he says. Eventually, he encountered a VA counselor who helped him straighten out a long series of bureaucratic complications, and in March received a letter from the VA apologizing for erroneous ratings and promising to reevaluate claims for PTSD, TBI and depression.

"I don't hate the VA," says Sanchez, who is attending college thanks to VA education benefits. "There are some faults there, but you can't blame the whole system."

That system is about to be tested even more forcefully. The VA is predicting that its claims workload will rise 30 percent next fiscal year, to about 1.3 million, in part because the department added three new ailments to the list of illnesses presumed to result from exposure to the Vietnam-era defoliant known as Agent Orange. And more "presumptive" illnesses associated with exposure to other battleground chemicals in more recent wars may be added later this year. (*See "Current Situation," p. 408.)*[9]

Still, it won't be easy to convince veterans that the VA has turned a new page. In Georgia, Iraq vet Lamie is trying to keep his family fed, his lights on and his car running on the small checks he receives now. "I've still got no faith in VA" — for now, he says.

As veterans' disability claims mount, here are some of the questions being debated:

Is the VA benefits system broken beyond repair?

Vietnam vet Elmer A. Hawkins filed a claim for disability benefits in 1990. Repeated errors by Regional Office (RO) staffers kept his case — based on exposure to Agent

Orange decades earlier while serving in Vietnam — bouncing between them and VA appeals boards.

Last year Hawkins tried to inject some urgency into the proceedings. He asked the Court of Appeals for the Federal Circuit to order the VA to finally decide his case. But the court rejected the request. After all, wrote Judge Haldane Robert Mayer, a decorated Vietnam combat veteran, "The RO may yet grant Hawkins VA benefits."[10]

However, the fact that the case has been pending for 20 years shocked U.S. District Judge Claudia Wilken of Oakland, Calif. — a stranger to the VA benefits system and its slow-moving clock. Serving temporarily on the federal circuit, Judge Wilken wrote in a dissenting opinion that the VA had "made repeated errors which have prolonged the decision-making process." These errors "cannot be excused as products of a burdened system."[11]

Hawkins' wait was unusually long. But years-long battles over claims aren't at all unusual, say experts on the system. Barton Stichman, joint executive director of the nonprofit National Veterans Legal Services Program, testified last year that the first step alone in the appeal process took an average of 563 days in fiscal 2007-2008. "Frustrated veterans have to wait many years before receiving a final decision on their claims," Stichman told the House Veterans' Disability Assistance and Memorial Affairs Subcommittee.[12]

Meanwhile, claims pile up in the system. "This massive backlog has resulted in a six-month average wait for an initial rating decision, and a two-year average wait for an appeal decision," Thomas J. Tradwell, commander in chief of Veterans of Foreign Wars, testified in March to a joint hearing of the Senate and House Veterans' Affairs committees. "That is completely unacceptable."[13]

Finn of the VA inspector general's office cited the 22 percent error rate in regional office disability assessments when she testified that even VA staffers assigned to identify mistakes compiled an imperfect record. "They either did not thoroughly review available medical and non-medical evidence or identify the absence of necessary medical information," Finn told the Disability Assistance and Memorial Affairs Subcommittee. "Without an effective and reliable quality assurance program, VBA leadership cannot adequately monitor performance to make necessary program improvements and ensure veterans receive accurate and consistent ratings."[14]

Getting a disability rating is the key to the process. Veterans like Hawkins who claim their illnesses or conditions were "service-connected" must prove that connection. The VBA's staff then state their conclusions in the form of ratings — such as that a veteran is 50 percent disabled because of an event that occurred while in the military.

"A vet fills out a 23-page claim form, then VHA sends it to the VBA office and it takes six months to get an answer," says Paul Sullivan, executive director of Veterans for Common Sense, which has sued the VA over the workings of the benefit system. "And the appeals process takes four to five years. That's unconscionable. VBA leaders failed, and they crashed the agency. It has suffered catastrophic meltdown."

A Gulf War veteran who worked at VBA in the 1990s, Sullivan praises the VA's new leaders but says even they cannot save the VBA without replacing it with an entirely new agency. With a war ongoing in Afghanistan, 98,000 troops still deployed in Iraq, the recent expansion of benefits for victims of Agent Orange and the proposed addition of other chemical exposures to the "presumptives" list, he says, "VBA is overwhelmed. It's broken beyond repair."[15]

Other veterans' advocates agree but not on Sullivan's proposed solution. "I got an e-mail yesterday from a vet who's been fighting with the VA for six years," says Tom Tarantino, legislative associate for Iraq and Afghanistan Veterans of America (IAVA). The organization is pressing for greater efficiency and accuracy in the benefits process.

But Tarantino says the current VA leadership is making great strides. "The VA has in the last year been incredibly aggressive in trying to address this issue" of claims processing, he says. "They have put in place a very solid, ambitious plan to upgrade the workflow, management, technology and customer service. Our challenge in the veterans' community is making sure that what we push and what Congress introduces do not interfere with actual progress at VA."

That big-picture perspective may not reassure veterans who are dealing with the current system. "When you contact people at these ROs [regional offices], they don't want to hear they did something wrong," says injured Iraq veteran Lamie, who has been disputing his 50 percent disability rating since shortly after retiring from the

AP Photo/Timothy Jacobsen

Double amputee Bradley Walker practices walking on his new prosthetic legs, using a moving sidewalk at Walter Reed Army Medical Center in Washington, D.C., on April 4, 2007. Wounded veterans' benefit claims are projected to rise 30 percent next fiscal year, to about 1.3 million, in part because additional illnesses are being classified as caused by military service, including ailments linked to the Agent Orange defoliant used during the Vietnam War.

Army late last year. "Instead of coming together with the vet and going through it page by page and seeing what went wrong, they blow you off, because you did something wrong — not them. You are left to the wind."

David E. Autry, deputy national communications director of Disabled American Veterans (DAV), agrees that some veterans encounter a lack of cooperation from some VA staffers. "It's clearly in the law that the VA has a 'duty to assist' the veteran," he says. "But in many cases we find that the VA is throwing up unnecessary roadblocks: 'You need to provide me with a documentary statement,' and you turn it in, and the VA loses it."

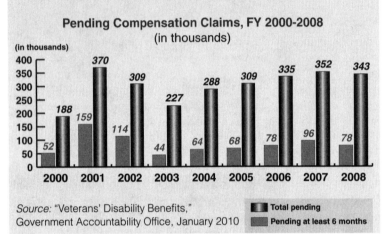

Backlog Claims Increase After Afghanistan, Iraq

After the war in Afghanistan began in 2001, compensation claims to the Veterans Administration nearly doubled. The pace picked up again after the start of the war in Iraq. Claims pending for more than six months have remained relatively constant.

Pending Compensation Claims, FY 2000-2008
(in thousands)

(in thousands)

Source: "Veterans' Disability Benefits,"
Government Accountability Office, January 2010

■ Total pending
■ Pending at least 6 months

The VA benefits system, Autry says, "has been approaching critical mass for some time." Still, he says, "The good news is that the VA seems to be committed to making things work differently."

Is the VA adjusting to the needs of 21st-century combat and technology?

The wars in Afghanistan ("Operation Enduring Freedom") and Iraq ("Operation Iraqi Freedom") have already lasted longer than World War II, which for the United States ran from 1941 to 1945. The wars also are presenting the VA with a new constellation of disabilities, along with heightened veteran expectations of government efficiency and attention.

Today's veterans grew up with the Web and with speedy online shopping. These experiences don't prepare them for dealing with the VA. "FedEx can track where your package is," Rep. Phil Roe, R-Tenn., ranking Republican on the House Veterans Affairs Oversight and Investigations Subcommittee, told VA technology officials last February. "You can order your coat from L.L. Bean and you know exactly where it is before it gets to you. Will it be possible when a veteran puts in for their benefits to track where their claim is with this current system that we're setting up?"[16]

"Absolutely," said Roger Baker, the VA's assistant secretary for information and technology, citing work on a system for tracking education benefits planned for release this fiscal year. The VA will eventually have "a Web site to which veterans can come and see the exact status of their claim from the point where it's received by the VA . . . to the point where the check is cut and sent to the veteran, and it will tell them everywhere along the process where they sit."[17]

But the technology gap is only part of the problem. The nature and severity of today's injuries also complicate the VA's job. Most casualties are caused by IEDs, the favorite enemy weapon in both conflicts. Victims of these powerful bombs may lose limbs, which typically aren't protected by torso-covering body armor. And even troops who avoid penetrating wounds may suffer harder-to-detect brain injuries.

Thanks to recent advances in battlefield care, "more service members survive to return home with severe combat-related injuries that require additional care," the Institute of Medicine concludes in a new research report.[18]

And repeated deployments are causing a growing incidence of PTSD and associated mental-health conditions, including depression. Veterans' demand for psychological services is outpacing the availability of mental-health professionals in areas with large vet populations, according to the IOM.[19]

Furthermore, family members increasingly must care full time for the growing number of vets who survive injuries that would have killed soldiers in earlier wars. The Wounded Warrior Project, a Jacksonville, Fla.-based nonprofit, estimates that the families of 2,000 severely disabled Iraq and Afghanistan veterans are now caring for them full time.[20]

"But the department has no systematic Family Caregiver Program," Anna Frese, sister of a severely brain-injured survivor of an IED attack in Iraq, told the House Veterans Affairs' Health Subcommittee last year. (*See sidebar, p. 406.*) "It has mounted some pilot programs. But overall, our experience is that very little institutional attention is being paid to family caregivers even though they are a vital link in the veteran's lifelong rehabilitation process. Families are coping largely on their own."[21]

The VA doesn't support the comprehensive caregiver support program that Frese, the Wounded Warrior Project and other nonprofits advocate, which would provide financial support and health coverage for caregivers. One point of dispute is the agency's insistence that family care be overseen by a VA staff member or contractor, who, an official implied, would be more objective in dealing with the disabled patient. "Health-care providers maintain their relationships on a professional level," Dr. Madhulika Agarwal, chief of patient care services for the VA's Veterans Health Administration, told the Health subcommittee.[22]

More recently, the VA has said it needs more information before proposing any policies and programs. "VA does not have adequate information on the number of caregivers, the number of family caregivers and the number of veterans receiving . . . services from family caregivers," says the agency's budget proposal for fiscal 2010-2011.[23]

The effects of intense combat during repeated deployments are showing up in another disturbing pattern. According to the most recent statistics available, suicides among young Iraq and Afghanistan veterans jumped 26 percent from 2005 to 2007, the VA reported early this year.[24]

Though the VA has strengthened its suicide-prevention programs, the agency's image among veterans lessens its effectiveness, according to M. David Rudd, dean of the University of Utah's College of Social and Behavioral Science. "It is important for the VA to recognize that they fight a longstanding image as an inflexible and unresponsive bureaucracy," Rudd told the Senate Veterans Affairs Committee in March.[25]

Seventy percent of veterans shun VA help, said Rudd, a specialist in military suicide. He urged the agency to establish partnerships with other mental-health providers. "Expansion of the existing VA system may not be the most effective expenditure of available funds," he testified.[26]

But, a top VA official countered at the same hearing, "Young veterans receiving VA care are significantly less likely to commit suicide than those not receiving VA care." Gerald M. Cross, acting principal deputy undersecretary for health, cited U.S. Centers for Disease Control and Prevention statistics showing a drop from 39 suicides per 100,000 in 2001 to 35 per 100,000 in 2007 among patients of VA health services, a decline equivalent to about 250 lives saved.[27]

Nevertheless, another VA mental health specialist said the VA is open to joining forces with other organizations, by contract or other arrangements. "We need to have partnerships," said Antoinette Zeiss, associate chief consultant for mental health. "We can't do it alone. If there is a level of care that VA is not able to provide in rural or in urban or suburban settings we should look for . . . well-tested programs."[28]

Before declaring that policy, Zeiss conceded that suicide-prevention programs have only recently been strengthened. For vets in danger of suicide, "We have instituted throughout the system far more intensive outpatient programs, so that instead of one, one-hour-a-week session," Zeiss said, "there are at least three hours a day, three days a week with an interdisciplinary team trying to deliver very complex and intensive services."[29]

Is the VA improving rapidly enough?

Debates about the quality of veterans' services are taking place amid a notable change in climate from the days of the Bush administration. Widespread agreement prevails that the VA's new leadership genuinely wants to make deep improvements and has the organizational competence to do so.

Under the Bush administration, even those who defended the VA against steadily increasing criticism from Iraq and Afghanistan vets didn't deliver more than pro-forma praise of top VA leaders. In October 2007, under the pressure of months of revelations of substandard and inadequate care from the VA, VA Secretary James Nicholson, who had headed the agency since 2005, resigned.[30]

Shinseki's experience with the Bush-era Defense Department and his Vietnam service gave him considerable credibility in the veteran community. And he named as one of his assistant secretaries L. Tammy Duckworth, a former Illinois Veterans Affairs director and Illinois National Guard helicopter pilot who lost both legs in Iraq in 2004.

IED Aftermath

Flames engulf a U.S. Army tank in Baghdad, Iraq, after it was struck by a homemade roadside bomb known as an improvised explosive device (IED) (top). Its crew escaped unharmed from the March 10, 2006, explosion, but Marine Sgt. Merlin German (bottom left), being promoted by Lt. Gen. James F. Amos (right) on May 21, 2007, suffered burns on 97 percent of his body after his vehicle struck an IED in Iraq. Blasts from IEDs — widely used by insurgents in both Iraq and Afghanistan — often cause multiple wounds, usually with severe injuries to extremities.

Measured by the size of his proposed new budget — an important gauge of intentions and administration support — Shinseki is planning to follow through on his modernization vows. He's asking for an increase of $9.4 billion in discretionary spending in fiscal 2011 — a 20 percent hike at a time of spending cutbacks and only modest increases elsewhere in government.[31]

Shinseki faced an early test in September 2009, when the VA failed to send out scheduled checks to about 277,000 college-bound vets who had qualified for GI Bill education benefits. As the VA showed itself incapable of processing the payments on time, some vets were forced to borrow money or take other emergency measures.[32]

Shinseki ordered the agency to issue emergency checks of up to $3,000 and to distribute them to veterans at VA offices around the country. The fast action and acknowledgement of the error struck many veterans' affairs specialists as a new approach. Shinseki explicitly endorsed that view. "We will change the [VA] culture," Shinseki told the House Veterans Affairs Committee three weeks later. "I assure you of that."[33]

Nevertheless, debate is still running strong on whether the agency's new leaders can transform the 300,000-employee department quickly enough to make a difference to the steadily growing ranks of veterans who depend on the VA.

Where benefits decision appeals are concerned, "The quality of decision-making hasn't improved," says Stichman of the National Veterans Legal Services Program. "It's in the same bad state."

Shinseki, he says, "does sound like he's intelligent and really wants to do something." But, the veterans-law expert says, "It's very difficult for a secretary to shake the bureaucracy. Can he get the lieutenants to follow orders?"

Autry of Disabled American Veterans acknowledges that giant institutions don't adapt to change easily or quickly. But the new leaders' determination is making a difference, he says. "The VA seems to be committed to making things work differently," he says.

To be sure, Autry, a Navy veteran of the Vietnam War, is also dissatisfied with the pace of transformation. "But this is an aircraft carrier," he says of the VA. "You don't just spin the wheel and turn it around."

But Sullivan of Veterans for Common Sense urges against accepting sluggishness as a given. "We're generally opposed to more layers of bureaucracy," he says. "But the agency has grown, and in order for Mr. Shinseki to leave his mark he is going to have to bring in new leaders."

Furthermore, growing pressures on the VA demand accelerated response, Sullivan says. The military is discharging a steady stream of combat veterans, at the same time as new data emerge that point to wartime conditions as causes of ailments suffered by Gulf War and Vietnam vets. "Right now is the pivotal moment," he says. "Will we repeat the mistakes of how horribly mistreated Vietnam and Gulf War veterans were when they came home?"

At least some of those veterans are still inclined to trust that Shinseki is moving as fast as possible, based on improvements already in place. "From my experience with the VA, from 2005 to now, there has been great change," says retired Capt. Kennedy, who served two tours in Iraq.

Kennedy won his fight to increase his PTSD disability rating to 70 percent, though he is still dealing with what he calls a VA error that cost him $13,000 in retirement pay — which he expects to recoup. He attributes part of his success to the free legal representation he received though the National Veterans Legal Services program.

However, he adds, "By hiring Gen. Shinseki as secretary, the Obama administration made a statement that they are committed to disabled veterans. People like me can see light at the end of the tunnel, but I know I'll never be part of it."

BACKGROUND

The Big Change

Victory in World War II, the biggest armed conflict by far in U.S. history, brought a monumental shift in veterans' care and compensation. For the first time, they were given a major opportunity to improve their lives, not just tend to their injuries or subsist on tiny pensions.

The new doctrine may have been inevitable. To achieve victory, the United States had mobilized more than 16 million men (and accepted 210,000 female volunteers) for military service — many of them for the entire four-year span of the war. More than 405,000 were killed, and more than 671,000 wounded.[34]

To be sure, veterans hadn't been ignored before World War II. Long before, Congress and the executive branch had established a series of institutions and systems designed to provide care and compensation. These included the Asylum for Disabled Volunteer Soldiers, created (under another name) in 1865, at the end of the Civil War, and the Consolidation Act of 1873, which set up a pension system based on the degree of disability, replacing a scale based on rank.

Of the 4.7 million men mobilized during World War I, 204,000 were wounded (and 116,000 were killed). But the veterans' system wasn't up to the challenge. In 1924, Congress made matters worse. Lawmakers created a bonus designed to make up the difference between military pay and the high wages earned by civilians who'd spent the war working in essential industries. But the money was granted in the form of a bond that would mature in 1945, and after the Great Depression began in 1929, vets needed their bonus immediately. Up to 40,000 veterans and their families — called the Bonus Marchers — set up an encampment in Washington in 1932, only to see it destroyed by Army troops, an event that shocked the nation.[35]

Fourteen years later, as World War II drew to a close, the Franklin D. Roosevelt administration and Congress were determined to prevent a repeat of the Bonus March disaster. Instead, the Servicemen's Readjustment Act of 1944 — known forever after as the "GI Bill of Rights" — created a broad range of opportunities for veterans.[36]

Under the bill, the Veterans Administration paid all or most of the costs of college or vocational training, provided guarantees for no-down-payment mortgages or business loans and granted unemployment compensation for up to a year. When the GI Bill expired in 1956, 7.8 million vets had received education or training, and the VA had guaranteed 5.9 million home mortgages worth a total of $50.1 billion.

The GI Bill, widely considered one of the most far-reaching pieces of social legislation ever enacted, "gave veterans from less-advantaged backgrounds chances they had never dreamed possible and a route toward the middle class," wrote Suzanne Metler, a political science professor at Syracuse University, author of a book about the law.[37]

In 1952, Congress passed a second version of the bill for veterans of the Korean War, which had begun in 1950. The new law was slightly less generous: For example, it covered only three years of college expenses instead of all four, and provided a smaller tuition subsidy.

Meanwhile, the magnitude of the veteran population created by World War II and the Korean conflict led to a vast expansion of the VA medical system, which by the early 1950s was caring for about 2.5 million vets.

Vietnam's Neglected Vets

The Vietnam War influenced veteran law and policy every bit as deeply as World War II, even though the conflict was much smaller than World War II.[38]

CHRONOLOGY

1944-1950s *GI Bill of Rights, enacted in final days of World War I, becomes the standard for all subsequent veteran care policy.*

1944 As World War II nears an end, Congress passes GI Bill to provide for education, home mortgages and business loans; allows millions of vets to move into the middle class.

1952 Korean War vets get their own, slightly downsized version of GI Bill.

1958 Veterans' unemployment insurance extended to peacetime draftees.

1967-1980s *Vietnam War gives rise to complaints of shoddy VA medical care; scientists begin evaluating evidence of psychological trauma from combat and physical damage from radiation and chemical exposure.*

1967 Six Vietnam veterans form Vietnam Veterans Against the War (VVAW), which grows into the thousands and directs much anger at VA.

1970 *Life* magazine reports on rat-infested VA hospital in the Bronx, N.Y.

1973 Paraplegic vet Ron Kovic leads takeover of Democratic Sen. Alan Cranston's office to call attention to deplorable conditions at VA hospitals.

1979 Accumulating evidence of psychological troubles among Vietnam vets leads Congress to authorize opening of 92 "Vet Centers" for counseling and other assistance. . . . Years-long debate among psychiatrists leads to inclusion of newly named post-traumatic stress disorder (PTSD) in the *Diagnostic and Statistical Manual of Mental Disorders.*

1981 U.S. District Court in Washington throws out VA regulation that effectively excludes 400,000 radiation-exposed World War II and postwar vets from claiming benefits for cancer and other disabilities.

1982 General Accounting Office reports that VA offices give short shrift to vets reporting physical symptoms from Agent Orange defoliant exposure.

1988 President Ronald Reagan signs law granting disability benefits to "atomic veterans" suffering from 13 (later 16) specific cancers.

1990s-2000s *VA benefits system begins to buckle under strain of disability claims arising from wars in the Persian Gulf and Afghanistan, as well as recognition of disabilities arising from Vietnam War.*

1991 VA recognizes two cancers are linked to Agent Orange.

1992 Persian Gulf War ends; reports emerge of physical and psychological symptoms among up to 100,000 veterans of the conflict.

1997 Medical researchers hypothesize that exposure to combinations of pesticide and nerve gas gave rise to "Gulf War syndrome." . . . VA begins providing benefits for Vietnam vets' children born with spina bifida.

2002 U.S. troops in Afghanistan report first enemy use of improvised explosive devices (IEDs).

2007 IEDs found to have caused two-thirds of 3,100 U.S. combat deaths in Iraq since U.S. invasion of 2003. . . . *Washington Post* publishes series on substandard conditions for outpatients at Walter Reed Army Medical Center in Washington.

2008 Congress authorizes free medical care for Iraq/Afghanistan veterans for five years after leaving military. . . . RAND Corp. reports that about one-third of service members deployed to combat suffered from PTSD, traumatic brain injury or major depression. . . . Delay in considering appeals of VA ratings rises to 563 days.

2009 VA issues emergency checks after agency fails to send education benefits to 277,000 college-bound vets. . . . IEDs reported to cause 55 percent of amputations among combat casualties.

2010 VA technology chief calls claims-management system "broken beyond repair." . . . Compromise reached on legislation to aid families caring for severely disabled vets. . . . Institute of Medicine reports shortage of mental health services for vets and "evidence of association" between Persian Gulf War service and multisymptom illness.

By the time the fighting ended with victory for the communist government of North Vietnam in 1975, 3.4 million service members had been deployed to Southeast Asia.[39]

U.S. society divided sharply over the war; so did the veterans' community. In 1967, six returnees founded Vietnam Veterans Against the War, which grew over the years and held a series of high-profile demonstrations, including one in 1971 in which several thousand veterans threw their service decorations over a fence at the U.S. Capitol.[40]

Debate over the rights and wrongs of the Vietnam War faded somewhat with its end, but anger and bitterness among veterans over shoddy VA services and treatment grew steadily. The discontent eventually transcended political views on the war itself, but challenges to the VA came at first from antiwar vets.

In 1973, paraplegic vet Ron Kovic (later portrayed by Tom Cruise in the 1989 film, "Born on the Fourth of July")[41] led other severely disabled vets in a 17-day hunger strike and occupation of the Los Angeles office of Sen. Alan Cranston, D-Calif. They were publicizing appalling conditions at VA hospitals in Southern California. A Senate hearing produced testimony about neglect of patients, brutal retaliation against those who complained and violations of basic hygiene. The testimony mirrored a 1970 *Life* magazine exposé about a VA hospital in the Bronx, N.Y., which was plagued by rats, filth and deficient medical care.

Meanwhile, with far less public attention, a group of psychiatrists with ties to antiwar veterans had started trying to describe and define a condition that they'd noticed in many Vietnam returnees. Symptoms included sleep disturbance, anxiety and depression. Eventually, the psychiatrists proposed that the American Psychiatric Association add the condition — which colleagues were also seeing in disaster survivors — to a new edition of the *Diagnostic and Statistical Manual of Mental Disorders*, the bible of the mental-health profession.

The fight to include what eventually became known as post-traumatic stress disorder went on for more than four years. Like the military and the VA, much of the psychiatric establishment initially dismissed the idea that intense combat or other wartime experiences could produce serious disturbances in a well-adjusted individual. Troubled veterans suffered from conditions that afflicted them before they joined the military, the skeptics argued.

But mounting evidence weakened their position. In 1979, PTSD was added to the manual. The move marked the beginning of a change in outlook, eventually of global dimensions, about the deep effects of war and disaster.

In a more immediate sense, the PTSD debate influenced Congress to pass in 1979 (shortly before the definition was formally added to the manual) a bill to create 92 Vet Centers, where Vietnam returnees could obtain psychological counseling. In 1991, the centers were opened to all combat veterans of any conflict.

Chemicals and Radiation

Meanwhile, a major issue affecting Vietnam vets' physical health — and that of their children — was also emerging. In 1970, journalist Thomas Whiteside reported in *The New Yorker* that dioxin — the main ingredient of a defoliant nicknamed "Agent Orange" used in large quantities by U.S. forces to strip jungle cover in Vietnam — was a carcinogen.[42]

The article led the Pentagon to ban Agent Orange (the nickname came from the orange-banded barrels in which it was stored). But by then hundreds of thousands of vets already had been exposed. As the decade wore on, many developed diseases, including leukemia and other cancers, and were also reporting an unusual number of birth defects in their children.

Initially, the VA resisted vets' claims that Agent Orange was the cause of their symptoms. In 1982, a congressionally commissioned study by the General Accounting Office, now the Government Accountability Office (GAO), concluded that the VA had neglected the issue, for instance, taking medical histories from only 10 percent of the 90,000 vets who had filed Agent Orange-based claims.

Not until 1991 did the VA recognize links between two cancers — soft-tissue sarcoma and non-Hodgkin's lymphoma — and Agent Orange exposure. Several more were added in 1993, and still more in later years. And in 1997 — 22 years after the war ended — the VA began a program to provide medical benefits, vocational training and a monthly allowance for veterans' children born with spina bifida, one of the birth defects associated with exposure to the chemical.

But the long-running Agent Orange dispute was only one of several controversies surrounding service members' exposure to dangerous substances and atomic radiation.

VA Benefits to Get High-Tech Overhaul

Current system is 'hopelessly broken.'

Members of today's tech-savvy military have grown up being able to buy virtually any product online and have it shipped overnight. Instantaneous communication by text, voice and video has been part of their everyday lives.

And it's now part of their military service as well. "I was battle captain for a unit that oversaw all the transportation into Iraq," says retired Army Capt. Anthony Kennedy about his second deployment there in 2007-2008. "Each night we had 3,000 trucks on the road. I needed to know where every truck was at every second."

Shortly thereafter, however, Kennedy retired from the military and encountered the VA benefits system. Suddenly, he was back in the mid-20th century, dealing with paper forms filled out by hand and sent by mail. His reaction: "Let's let Amazon run it," referring to the huge online retailer Amazon.com.

The VA recognizes the problem. "We have a manual, paper-bounded system; what we want is an automated electronic system," says Peter L. Levin, the VA's new chief technology officer. He has initiated several pilot projects designed to become the new system's backbone.

Levin became a "rock star" among veterans' organizations, says Tom Tarantino, legislative associate for Iraq and Afghanistan Veterans of America, by acknowledging at a March meeting organized by the House Veterans' Services Committee that the present system is hopelessly broken

and must be replaced. "He said some of the gutsiest things I've ever heard a VA person say in front of Congress," Tarantino adds.[1]

But Levin makes clear that he isn't promising the new system will be up and running tomorrow, or even next year. The deadline, set by VA Secretary Eric K. Shinseki, is 2015 (though parts of the system are scheduled to be online before then). "I come from the private sector, and I think I got this job based on a good reputation for on-time, on-budget deliveries," he says. "That is a reputation I intend to keep. I don't want to give unrealistic dates. The instructions are clear that if it is going to move in any direction it is going to be earlier, not later."

Levin was hired last year away from DAFCA Inc., which he cofounded and where he was CEO. The Framingham, Mass.-based firm designs software to test the reliability of computer chips and block malicious circuitry. Levin, who has a doctorate in electrical and computer engineering from Carnegie Mellon University in Pittsburgh, served as a White House fellow and as expert consultant in the Office of Science and Technology Policy in the Clinton administration.[2]

Paper won't entirely disappear from the redesigned system. Some records, Levin says, are too important to exist in purely digital form — birth and marriage certificates in the civilian world, for example. But medical scans and lists of medications should be digitized, he says.

World War II veterans, including thousands who had been assigned to clear rubble in Hiroshima and Nagasaki, Japan, after atomic bombs were dropped there, had filed about 1,500 claims for benefits, claiming adverse health consequences from the intense radiation they'd absorbed. Some survivors of deceased veterans also filed for death benefits. But the federal government long resisted paying for the claims; in 1979 the VA adopted a rule effectively rejecting 98 percent of claims by "atomic veterans." The group was substantial — 200,000 personnel who had been exposed to radiation in postwar Japan, and another 200,000 who had participated in atmospheric testing of atomic weapons.[43]

In 1981, U.S. District Judge June L. Green of Washington threw out that rule. Eventually, President Ronald W. Reagan signed a bill in 1988 establishing that atomic veterans suffering from 13 (later 16) specific kinds of cancers were automatically entitled to benefits.[44]

The Persian Gulf War of 1990-1991 prompted another wave of veteran medical concerns. About 100,000 of the 694,000 Gulf War veterans reported symptoms including fatigue, skin rash, headache, muscle and joint pain, memory loss, difficulty concentrating, shortness of breath, sleep disturbance, gastrointestinal problems and chest pain. Over the years, the number of vets reporting symptoms rose to 250,000.

Still, the planned improvements won't make dealing with the benefits system like dealing with Amazon. Kennedy notes that Amazon's customers get invited to buy specific books, music and other merchandise based on their records of past purchases. A VA version, he says, could tell a user, "Your account shows you've been treated for this, this and this — you should apply for this disability."

But Levin, while acknowledging the appeal of the Amazon model, argues that it's not a precise fit. Amazon sells mass-produced goods, with one copy of a book or CD, for instance, indistinguishable from another. "It turns out that every vet is a little different," he says. Nevertheless, a VA variant could produce data that allow a records examiner to see how vets with similar characteristics were treated.

For a veteran with a given list of claims, "I want to know what guys who are about your age and who served about where you served, and did things like you did while serving — I want to know what they're talking about that maybe you forgot," Levin says. And at some point, an examiner might be able to instantly access information on specific health and environmental conditions in given areas of operation.

Meanwhile, even the basic system is complicated enough to design and install that Levin is trying to improve the

Peter L. Levin, the Department of Veterans Affairs' new chief technology officer, became an instant "rock star" among some veterans' organizations when he told Congress the VA benefits system is hopelessly broken and must be replaced.

present system pending its replacement. "We do not have the option of turning off the system for six months and building a new one really quickly."

For vets, the bottom line is that paper documents are still indispensable to dealing with the VA. Indeed, Richard Sanchez, a U.S. Navy veteran, says he's on his way to resolving four years of miscommunications with the VA, partly because he heeded an old sailor's advice.

"He said, 'Make copies of everything; doesn't matter if it's not important, it might be important later, it might have a date on it. And then make a copy, and then another copy.' I did that," says Sanchez, "and it was true. I have an archive at home, another with relatives and another one in a safe-deposit box."

— *Peter Katel*

[1] Rick Maze, "VA official: Disability claims system 'cannot be fixed,' " *Federal Times*, March 18, 2010, www.federaltimes.com/article/20100318/DEPARTMENTS04/3180302/1055/AGENCY.

[2] "Executive Biographies," U.S. Department of Veterans Affairs, undated, www1.va.gov/opa/bios; "Carnegie-Mellon Engineering Alumnus Peter L. Levin Named as Chief Technology Officer at U.S. Veterans Affairs," Carnegie Mellon University, press release, Aug. 3, 2009; John Markoff, "F.B.I. Says the Military Had Bogus Computer Gear," *The New York Times*, May 9, 2008, p. C4.

Scientists and others advanced various hypotheses, including exposure to destroyed Iraqi stocks of sarin nerve gas, smoke from oil well fires or pesticides. Government-sponsored and private medical and environmental studies offered contradictory conclusions on whether an identifiable "Gulf War Syndrome" existed.

Nevertheless, Gulf War veterans continued to report ailments, some of them serious. And after President George W. Bush ordered troops into Afghanistan in 2001, and into Iraq, in 2003, veterans of both wars began reporting similar ailments, leading the VA and Defense Department to focus more closely on the possible effects of chemical exposure from "burn pits" on military bases, where plastics,

electronics, lubricants and medical waste were incinerated, among other things. (*See "Current Situation," p. 408.*)[45]

21st-Century Wounds

The nature of the wars in Afghanistan and Iraq, coupled with tremendous advances in battlefield medicine, produced significant increases in the numbers of severely disabled veterans. But some six years into the fighting, many began to question whether the military and VA were prepared for the consequences of the century's first two wars.

Initially, the focus was on the military. In 2007, *The Washington Post* published a devastating series of articles

Full-time Caregiving Challenges Families

Families make huge sacrifices to deal with soldiers' catastrophic injuries.

For the Edmundsons of New Bern, N.C., veteran care is a family mission. On Oct. 2, 2005, Eric Edmundson, then a 25-year-old sergeant in the 172nd Stryker Brigade, took the impact of a roadside bomb, which sent shrapnel shooting into his brain and elsewhere in his body.

After emergency surgeries in Baghdad, the young soldier's heart stopped, depriving his brain of oxygen for a full 30 minutes. "Eric can't walk, talk; he has cognitive memory issues," says his father, Ed, from the family home, which used to house Eric, his wife Stephanie and their daughter, Gracie Rose, 5. Now Ed and his wife Beth live there as well.

"We downsized our lives to be here for Eric and Stephanie," says Ed, 52, who had worked as a warehouse supervisor at ConAgra Foods. "I took my retirement, burned down our debt load, basically got rid of all our possessions. We live in a bedroom in my son's house."

Eric returned to North Carolina after six months of intensive care and training at the Rehabilitation Institute of Chicago. His parents quickly realized that Eric would need full-time care, and that the load was too much for Stephanie to handle alone.[1] "There's a high rate of divorce among the injured," Eric's father says. "We don't want to allow that to happen. Eric has a beautiful family. What my wife and I do is take care of Eric, dealing with rehabilitation and his doctor visits. That allows Eric and Stephanie and Gracie to have as much of a life as possible."

Eric has been able to function more fully than initially expected. He is working as a greeter two days a week in a sporting-goods store. In January he attended the opening of a photo exhibit at the University of North Carolina, Wilmington, of images he took in Iraq before being wounded. He addressed the crowd using a computer voice-generating device.[2] The young family is expecting a second child.

As Eric napped on a recent afternoon, his father spoke by phone, recounting in a matter-of-fact tone the realities of life as a full-time caregiver. For one thing, Edmundson says, "We don't have any retirement or financial future."

Last year, after two bouts of pneumonia, he was able to see a doctor only because of financial help from Wounded Warriors Project, a Jacksonville, Fla.-based nonprofit. Another nonprofit, Homes For Our Troops, built a fully accessible house for the family.[3] "I can't imagine what we would be going through if we didn't have nonprofits," he says.

The Edmundsons' daughter, Anna Frese, has testified in support of legislation to provide financial support and health care to family caregivers (*see "Current Situation"*), and Edmundson too would welcome some help. "Some small compensation would allow us to get a change of clothes or service our vehicle," he says, "and health care insurance would keep me moving forward." Under the pending legislation, health care would be available only for him or his wife, not both of them.

Meanwhile, the Edmundsons are aware that they may represent only the first wave of families dealing with the

about conditions for injured service members recovering at Walter Reed Army Medical Center outpatient facilities in Washington, D.C. The exposé led to the firings of Army Secretary Francis Harvey and of the Walter Reed commander, Lt. Gen. George W. Weightman. Lt. Gen. Kevin Kiley, Army surgeon general and a former Walter Reed commander who initially had minimized *The Post*'s accounts, was also forced to resign.[46]

The Walter Reed scandal focused media and political attention on the treatment of veterans in general. President George W. Bush appointed former Sen. Robert Dole, R-Kan., a disabled World War II vet, and former Health and Human Services Secretary Donna Shalala to co-chair a commission to examine the entire veterans' health care system. The commission recommended simplifying the ratings system and improving care for TBI and PTSD, among other steps.

The commission blamed much of the problem on the kind of war U.S. troops were fighting. Enemies in Iraq and Afghanistan were using IEDs as their major weapon. The bombs produce devastating effects without exposing the anti-American guerrillas to battlefield confrontations, in which U.S. forces held the advantage. Deployed as mines, packed into cars and trucks as well as bicycles and

after-effects of catastrophic wounds "The war wasn't supposed to last this long," he says. "The system hadn't been tested. But if they're going to take these young men and women and send them to war, they'd better be able to take care of them. They need to ramp up post-trauma care and rehabilitation."

Though the family is relying on Eric's VA benefit payments and on his VA-financed health care, the entire care mission otherwise has been independent of the VA. Edmundson says he's found the agency peopled with dedicated staff but somewhat snarled in its own procedures.

"For the first three years I spent almost 100 percent of my time dealing with VA red tape," Edmundson says. "We did a lot of self-education. We'd get up in the morning, take care of Eric and get on the computer and research and talk to people: Why were you able to do this or that? Why are we not able?"

Dealing with the VA isn't for the passive, Edmundson has concluded. "If you don't plead your case, you fall through the cracks." The Edmundsons located the Chicago Rehabilitation Institute on their own, for instance, and found it superior to the VA hospital where Edmundson had been previously. The VA did, however, finance the cost of the private rehab program.

The deeper issue, Edmundson says he's come to believe, is that the VA — and the government in general — are only now starting to adjust to advances in rehabilitative medicine. "For years, the answer was to institutionalize the soldier," he says. "But the soldiers of today don't want to be taken care of, they want to be rehabilitated, they want to go home."

— Peter Katel

U.S. Army Specialist Eric Edmundson (center), who suffered a severe traumatic brain injury in Iraq in 2005, and his father Ed (top) appear at a Nov. 10, 2009, news conference in Washington, D.C., to discuss legislation to provide financial support and health care for family members caring for wounded vets full time. The Edmundsons, who sold their house and moved in with their son and his family in order to care for him, may represent the first wave of families dealing with the after-effects of catastrophic wounds. Senate Majority Whip Dick Durbin (D-Ill.) (left) thanks Edmondson for his sacrifice.

[1] For a detailed account of Eric's stay at the Rehabilitation Institute, see "Eric Edmundson's Patient Story," Rehabilitation Institute of Chicago, undated, www.ric.org/aboutus/stories/EricEdmundson.aspx.

[2] Ashley White, "Photo collection at UNCW illustrates life as a soldier," News14 Carolina, Jan. 10, 2010, http://news14.com/triad-news-94-content/military/620344/photo-collection-at-uncw-illustrates-life-as-a-soldier.

[3] "Severely Wounded Army SGT Eric Edmundson Receives Specially Adapted Home from Homes for Our Troops," *Homes for Our Troops*, Nov. 5, 2007, www.homesforourtroops.org/site/News2?page=News Article&id=5743.

motorcycles, the bombs first appeared in Afghanistan in 2002 as radio-controlled roadside devices. But military officials planning the following year's invasion of Iraq didn't foresee the use of IEDs there, despite plentiful supplies of explosives.

By late 2007, IEDs were causing two-thirds of the 3,100 U.S. combat deaths registered through September of that year in Iraq. By then, IEDs had killed or wounded more than 21,000 Americans in Iraq. And by late 2009, the Pentagon calculated that the bombs accounted for up to 80 percent of U.S. and NATO casualties in Afghanistan.[47]

Aside from their appalling efficiency as killing machines, IEDs wrought damages on survivors that would have ended their lives in any previous war. Dramatic advancements in both the protective gear worn by soldiers and in military urgent care made the difference.

"This is the first war in which troops are very unlikely to die if they're still alive when a medic arrives," Dr. Ronald Glasser, who had treated troops wounded in Vietnam in 1968-1970, pointed out in *The Washington Post* in 2007.[48]

At that point, about 1,800 troops had survived brain injuries caused by penetrating wounds. But nearly a third of military personnel involved in heavy combat in Iraq or Afghanistan for at least four months were at risk of brain disorders from IED and mortar blasts. Symptoms of such shock-wave neurological disorders include memory loss, confusion, anxiety and depression, Glasser wrote.[49]

But the IEDs produced other types of injuries as well: As of mid-January, 2009, 1,184 U.S. personnel had suffered amputations, 55 percent of them the result of IED injuries.[50]

CURRENT SITUATION

'Presumptive' Diseases

In veterans' jargon, they're "presumptives" — certain diseases or conditions presumed by the VA to arise from military service in a certain time or place. In addition to having recently added to the list of ailments associated with exposure to Agent Orange in Vietnam, the agency is proposing to add nine new conditions that have developed among veterans of the 1990-91 Gulf War and the Afghan and Iraq conflicts.

Vets suffering from the following diseases or their after-effects would be presumed to have contracted them while serving: brucellosis, *Campylobacter jejuni, Coxiella burnetii* (Q fever), malaria, mycobacterium, tuberculosis, nontyphoid salmonella, shigella, visceral leishmaniasis and West Nile virus.

"We recognize the frustrations that many Gulf War and Afghanistan veterans and their families experience on a daily basis as they look for answers to health questions and seek benefits from VA," Shinseki said in announcing the proposed rule.[51]

In addition, the VA is proposing to add a presumption of service connection for Gulf-Iraq-Afghanistan vets suffering from "medically unexplained chronic multisymptom illness." Characteristics include fatigue, pain and inconsistent laboratory reports. That definition would cover Gulf War Syndrome, noted Sullivan of Veterans for Common Sense. "The proposed new VA rules may finally, after nearly two decades, open the door to a lifetime of free VA medical care for tens of thousands or more sick Gulf War veterans," he told *Military Times.*[52]

On the heels of the VA announcement, the Institute of Medicine issued the latest volume in its long study of Gulf War symptoms, finding that "sufficient evidence of association" exists between deployment to the Persian Gulf operations area and "multisymptom illness." That

conclusion falls one step short of establishing a causal relationship between the illness and Gulf War service. "There is some doubt as to the influence of chance, bias and confounding," the report said, using a statistical term for an element of an issue that mistakenly leads to associating exposure with outcome.[53]

Still, given the long and contentious history of Gulf War veterans' attempts to obtain scientific confirmation that they were suffering from something other than random, imagined or exaggerated symptoms, the institute's report marked an important milestone.

"The multisymptom illness that affects so many Gulf War veterans is a terrible, distinct illness," James E. Finn, chairman of a VA-appointed advisory committee on Gulf War illnesses, told *The Washington Post,* "and . . . this nation can and should launch a Manhattan Project-style research program to identify treatments and prevent this from happening again."[54]

Meanwhile, the VA is trying to pinpoint specific causes of Gulf War illness, including exposure to substances including "smoke and particles from military installation burn-pit fires that incinerated a wide range of toxic-waste materials," Bradley Mayes, director of the VBA Compensation and Pension Service, wrote in a February letter to VA medical personnel and claims examiners. *The Military Times,* which has no ties to the Defense Department, had reported on growing suspicions of burn-pit exposure as a cause of disease.[55]

Legal Benefits

The VA pipeline may be clogged for health and education claims, but vets facing criminal charges are getting a new form of assistance from federal and state court systems around the country.

At least 21 states, cities and counties have set up "veterans' courts." Modeled on "drug courts," which provide a chance at supervised addiction treatment — and in some cases a clean record — instead of jail time, the veterans' versions are designed to take into account the repercussions of military service, especially combat tours in Iraq and Afghanistan. PTSD, TBI and other after-effects have become widely acknowledged and, in the view of many in the criminal-justice system, deserve to be weighed when a vet is being prosecuted or sentenced.

In Buffalo, N.Y., where Judge Robert T. Russell Jr. pioneered the concept in 2008, the vets' court takes only those accused of nonviolent felonies and misdemeanors.

Should the VA's Veterans Benefits Administration be scrapped and rebuilt?

YES   Paul Sullivan
Executive Director, Veterans for Common Sense

Written for *CQ Researcher*, April 2010

VA's top leaders and auditors have confirmed that benefit claim processing at the Veterans Benefits Administration (VBA) cannot be fixed, as it represents an obsolete and unsustainable model. VBA leaders have no permanent solution for the 60-year-old system, and VBA should eventually be replaced using a careful plan.

This year, VA Secretary Eric Shinseki has a rare window of opportunity to build a new, high-tech, veteran-friendly VBA when he names a new under secretary for benefits. Fixing VBA is vital because an approved disability claim usually opens the door for both disability payments and health care. VBA's current woes include:

- 500,000 veterans now waiting an average of six months for a disability claim decision, plus 200,000 more veterans waiting five more years for an appealed decision.
- 70,000 new pages of paper clog up VBA every day.
- VBA makes an error in nearly one-in-four decisions.
- VBA improperly shredded claims, lost claims and backdated records.
- VBA leaders paid themselves millions in cash bonuses while rank-and-file employees struggled.
- Distraught veterans call VA's suicide prevention hotline out of frustration with endless VBA delays.

We urge the VA to begin a series of public meetings with Congress, veteran advocates and academic experts to pass new laws to design, build and deploy a new VBA with the shortest path possible between the veteran and VA benefits, including health care. Here are practical solutions for a new, high-quality VBA:

- Use a one-page claim form, a single, automated computer system and decide each claim within 30 days.
- Use easy-to-understand rules that presume more medical conditions are linked to military service.
- Use the new, robust lifetime military medical record.
- Move claims staff, currently isolated in a single office in each state, into medical facilities to help veterans set up claim exams as well as quickly and accurately decide claims.
- Allow veterans to hire an attorney before they file a claim, especially veterans with brain injuries or mental health conditions.

When these common sense solutions are adopted, then more of our veterans are welcomed home with the VA benefits and health care they need and earned after defending our freedom. Learn more at: www.FixVA.org.

NO   James B. King
National Executive Director, AMVETS; Marine Corps veteran of Vietnam

Written for *CQ Researcher*, April 2010

Since 2001, the Department of Veterans Affairs disability claims backlog has grown precipitously because of the ongoing conflicts in Iraq and Afghanistan and the establishment of new presumptive health conditions.

Thankfully, through constructive dialogue with the nation's top veterans' service organizations, the VA has implemented significant changes over the last few months that should help to alleviate strains on the system.

AMVETS is encouraged by the VA's recent steps to streamline the process, making a proposed scrapping of the current Veterans Benefits Administration (VBA) system duplicative and unnecessary. Today, VA has launched pilot programs at regional offices around the country, investigating ways to modernize the claims process, building on opinions and suggestions from leading veterans' groups. These pilot programs include the paperless claims process in Providence, the virtual regional office in Baltimore, team-based workload management in Little Rock and tiered case-management teams in Pittsburgh. AMVETS and other groups have had access to each of these programs, offering opinions and recommendations where necessary, based on decades of experience in the VA claims process. VA also recently implemented eight system-wide solutions to transform the mindset of all involved in the claims process — from the individual veteran to the VA adjudicator.

AMVETS will continue to monitor the progress of these initiatives to help find the best solutions to the daunting backlog. We encourage Congress to do the same before taking hasty legislative action. In AMVETS' opinion, plans to scrap the VBA would only exacerbate current benefits-delivery issues. Today, millions of veterans are entitled to care and compensation through their VBA ratings. By scrapping VBA, VA would need to develop a new corollary to deliver care and benefits to the millions of veterans already enrolled, dating back to World War II.

Plus, would veterans rated under the old system be entitled to reopen their claims? AMVETS believes that they must, which only creates more roadblocks to benefits. Forget the current 400,000-claim backlog — VA would be facing more than 3 million reopened claims and appeals.

AMVETS believes we are on the cusp of developing a modern VA claims process through constructive collaboration among VA and the veterans' groups that have helped our heroes navigate the system for decades. The proposed solutions could finally provide veterans with the timely and accurate claims processing they deserve. Thus, it's critical that the VBA be preserved.

But the Santa Ana, Calif., court is open to those charged with any offense. Judge Wendy Lindley, who established the program, told the *National Law Journal* that California criminal law specifically allows treatment instead of incarceration for a convicted veteran who has served in a combat zone and developed psychological or substance-abuse problems. Veterans' courts are also in session in Anchorage, Chicago, Pittsburgh and Tulsa.[56]

The VA started a program last year to work with veterans' courts, and VA Secretary Shinseki visited the Buffalo court in April to underline his support. "The secretary's purpose was to receive first-hand knowledge about how the program works in order to integrate and develop similar endeavors in other communities," the Erie County Veterans Service Agency said on its Web site.[57]

The VA formed its own Veterans' Justice Outreach Initiative last year. The program is designed in part to provide detailed reports to judges on a vet's medical history and on VA benefits and programs that might help him if he were sentenced to probation instead of jail. Staffers are also trained to work with vets serving jail time.[58]

As support grows, dissenters are making themselves heard. In Nevada, which along with Illinois and New York enacted statewide veterans' courts last year, the general counsel for the American Civil Liberties Union of Nevada argued that they represent a dangerous trend of creating different avenues of justice for certain kinds of people. Veterans' courts amount to establishing special courts for "police officers, teachers or politicians," Allen Lichtenstein told the Stateline.org news service.[59]

He also rejected the analogy to drug courts, which are open to defendants suffering from a condition. But all veterans are eligible for veterans' court, Lichtenstein pointed out.[60]

Nevertheless, federal judges are starting to take veterans' wartime experiences into account in sentencing. In Denver, Senior U.S. District Judge John Kane sentenced a federal prison guard to five years' probation, with mental-health treatment required, because of his Air Force service in Afghanistan and Iraq, where he dealt with seriously injured and dead service members and civilians. John Brownfield Jr. had pleaded guilty to accepting at least $3,000 in bribes for smuggling contraband to inmates.[61]

"It would be a grave injustice," Kane said in a written decision, "to turn a blind eye to the potential effects of multiple deployments to war zones on Brownfield's subsequent behavior."[62]

Sentencing guidelines aside, Kane's move seemed consistent with a U.S. Supreme Court decision in November, 2009, to throw out a death sentence for a Korean War veteran convicted of murdering his ex-girlfriend and her boyfriend. Ordering a new sentencing hearing, the justices cited "the intense stress and emotional toll that combat took" on George Porter Jr.[63]

Aiding Caregivers

Legislation is pending in Congress to channel aid to families and others who have become full time caregivers for catastrophically disabled Iraq and Afghanistan veterans.

In a unanimous vote in November, the Senate passed the Caregivers and Veterans Omnibus Health Services Act, sponsored by Senate Veterans Chairman Daniel Akaka, D-Hawaii. House action was held up while Akaka's staff negotiated changes with his counterparts. The resulting compromise is ready for action, which is expected some time in April or May.

The legislation represents the first comprehensive attempt to assist those suddenly thrust into the 24-hour-a-day caregiver role. Approximately $3.7 billion would be spent on stipends — amount unspecified — for caregivers, on temporary alternative care ("respite care") arrangements to give caregivers a breather, on training caregivers and on other forms of support, including expense reimbursement to accompany disabled vets to distant hospitals.[64]

Only those caring for veterans from Operation Enduring Freedom (OEF) — the Afghanistan war — and Operation Iraqi Freedom (OIF) would be covered by the bill. Yet, as veterans of other wars age, issues of round-the-clock care for them are beginning to weigh on families. "Veterans' service organizations would like to see the legislation open to all," says Barbara Cohoon, deputy director of government relations for the National Military Families Association. "But we recognize that OIF and OEF caregivers are experiencing the biggest hardship right now and that resources are limited. But this needs to be done for all at some point."

OUTLOOK

National Priority?

Researchers have been trying for the past several years to forecast the medium-term effects of the Iraq and

Afghanistan wars on veterans and, by extension, on the government agency that deals with them most closely.

Trend lines are exceptionally difficult to forecast, in part because fighting is still under way and may be for some time. Meanwhile, the VA "does not have the personnel, the funding, or the mandate from Congress to produce broad forecasts of service needs," the Institute of Medicine concluded in its recent report.[65]

The after-effects of past wars are of only limited usefulness, the institute noted, because so many more severely wounded service members are surviving combat now. The entire picture of the wounded veteran population has changed. "These survivors of very severe injuries need more intensive care than the most severely wounded service members from prior wars," the report said. "Extrapolating from past conflicts might result in an underestimation of the overall burden of need for persons impacted by OEF and OIF."[66]

What is clear, the institute reported, is that the needs of these veterans will be extensive. "The burden borne by wounded service members and their families, and thus the public responsibility to treat or compensate them, is large and probably will persist for the rest of their lives."[67]

Moreover, "peak demand for compensation" is likely to increase as veterans age, the institute said. "So the maximum stress on support systems for OEF and OIF veterans and their families might not be felt until 2040 or later."[68]

In the veterans' community, some express confidence in the VA's ability to keep up with an already growing demand for its services. "It has the potential to be as great as it needs to be," says Autry of Disabled American Veterans. "There are an awful lot of very dedicated people in the VA."

Their dedication is already being tested, and is certain to be tested even further, by the high incidence of PTSD, TBI and depression among Afghanistan and Iraq vets. "The prevalence of those injuries is relatively high and may grow as the conflicts continue," RAND has reported. Yet, both the Defense Department and the VA "have had difficulty in recruiting and retaining appropriately trained mental health professionals to fill existing or new slots."[69]

The RAND report urges that dealing with the trio of conditions be elevated to a "national priority." But even some relatively optimistic veterans say raising public concern to that level requires some heavy lifting. "We're

less than 1 percent of the population," says Kennedy, the retired Army captain.

For his own part, Kennedy is still "pretty sure" the VA will be "a lot better than it is" now, but he's not sure how it will have improved.

Sullivan of Veterans for Common Sense is a bit more skeptical. The VA is still trying to protect its reputation, he says, similar to shipping company officials who "were saying everything was fine while the *Titanic* was sinking."

But the potential exists to transform VA's benefits service into a smooth-running operation in which veterans have confidence. "A tremendous amount of effort must be invested in this moment of opportunity," Sullivan says. "We have a new administration, a Congress eager to help, veterans' groups who want to help and public understanding of an urgent need. We have a golden moment of opportunity now."

Sullivan's outlook is considerably sunnier than that of Lamie, the IED attack survivor. In 10 years, he says, "I think the situation will be worse. In 10 years, everybody is going to forget all about the Iraq war. If there's a war in 2020, those guys will probably be treated great. But if there's nobody dying on the TV screen nobody will care."

An outsider might say that Lamie's combat scars are still raw; his brother Gene, an Army sergeant, died in an IED attack in Iraq in 2007.[70] But dismissing his bleak outlook could be a mistake. The searing experiences that inform his forecast are shared by a growing number of young veterans.

NOTES

1. "Radical Change Needed for Veterans Disability Claims Process," House Committee on Veterans Affairs, press statement, March 18, 2010, http://veterans.house.gov/news/PRArticle.aspx?NewsID=559.

2. "Statement of Belinda J. Finn, Assistant Inspector General for Audits and Evaluations, Office of Inspector General, Department of Veterans Affairs," VA Office of Inspector General, March 24, 2010, www4.va.gov/OIG/pubs/VAOIG-statement-20100324-Finn.pdf.

3. lcasualties.org, updated regularly, http://icasualties.org/OEF/Index.aspx.

4. "Remarks by Secretary Eric K. Shinseki," Veterans of Foreign Wars National Legislative Conference, March 8, 2010, www1.va.gov/opa/speeches/2010/10_0308.asp; "Fiscal 2011 Budget: VA," Committee Testimony, Senate Veterans' Affairs Committee, Feb. 26, 2010; "FY 2011 Budget Submission," Department of Veterans Affairs, pp. 2B-4, 2C-2, www4.va.gov/budget/docs/summary/Fy2011_Volume_1-Summary_Volume.pdf.

5. Quoted in Rick Maze, "VA official: Disability claims system 'cannot be fixed,'" *Federal Times*, March 18, 2010, www.federaltimes.com/article/20100318/DEPARTMENTS04/3180302/1055/AGENCY.

6 Quoted in Philip Rucker, "Obama Picks Shinseki to Lead Veterans Affairs," *The Washington Post*, Dec. 7, 2008, www.washingtonpost.com/wp-dyn/content/article/2008/12/07/AR2008120701487.html; Bernard Weinraub and Thom Shanker, "Rumsfeld's Design for War Criticized on the Battlefield," *The New York Times*, April 1, 2003, p. A1; Amy Belaso, "Troop Levels in the Afghan and Iraq Wars," Congressional Research Service, July 2, 2009, Summary page, www.fas.org/sgp/crs/natsec/R40682.pdf; "US Forces Order of Battle," GlobalSecurity.org, undated, www.globalsecurity.org/military/ops/iraq_orbat.htm.

7 "Returning Home from Iraq and Afghanistan: Preliminary Assessment of Readjustment Needs of Veterans, Service Members, and Their Families," Institute of Medicine of the National Academies (2010), p. 52, http://books.nap.edu/openbook.php?record_id=12812&page=R1.

8. Terri Tanielian and Lisa H. Jaycox, eds., "Invisible Wounds of War: Psychological and Cognitive Injuries, Their Consequences, and Services to Assist Recovery," RAND Center for Military Health Policy Research, 2008, p. xxi, www.rand.org/pubs/monographs/MG720; U.S. Army Surgeon General study cited in Kline, Anna, *et al.*, "Effects of Repeated Deployment to Iraq and Afghanistan on the Health of New Jersey Army National Guard Troops: Implications for Military Readiness," *American Journal of Public Health*, February 2010, http://ajph .aphapublications.org/cgi/content/abstract/100/2/276.

9. The three are Parkinson's Disease, ischemic heart disease and B-cell leukemias. "FY 2011 Budget Submission," *op. cit.*, p. 1A-3; Gregg Zoroya, "VA to automate its Agent Orange claims process," *USA Today*, March 9, 2010, p. 4A.

10. *Hawkins v. Shinseki*, U.S. Court of Appeals for the Federal Circuit, 2009-7068, Dec. 7, 2009, www.cafc.uscourts.gov/opinions/09-7068.pdf.

11. *Ibid.*

12. "VA Appellate Processes," Committee Testimony, House Veterans' Affairs Committee, Subcommittee on Disability Assistance and Memorial Affairs, May 24, 2009.

13. "Legislative Presentations of Veterans' Organizations," House Veterans' Affairs Committee, Senate Veterans' Affairs Committee, March 9, 2010. For VA backlog figure, see "2010 Monday Morning Workload Reports," Department of Veterans Affairs, March 29, 2010, www.vba.va.gov/REPORTS/mmwr/index.asp.

14. Finn, *op. cit.*

15. "Iraq Index: Tracking Variables of Reconstruction and Security in Post-Saddam Iraq," Brookings Institution, updated March 30, 2010, p. 19, www.brookings.edu/~/media/Files/Centers/Saban/Iraq Index/index.pdf.

16. "The House Veterans' Affairs Subcommittee on Oversight and Investigations," *op. cit.*

17. *Ibid.*

18. "Returning Home from Iraq and Afghanistan . . .," *op. cit.*, pp. 29, 69.

19. *Ibid.*, p. 69.

20. *Ibid.*, p. 32.

21. "Needs of Family Caregivers," House Veterans' Affairs Committee, June 4, 2009.

22. *Ibid.*

23. "FY 2011 Budget Submission," Department of Veterans Affairs, p. 3A-7, www4.va.gov/budget/docs/summary/Fy2011_Volume_1-Summary_Volume.pdf.

24. Kimberly Hefling, "Increase in suicide rate of veterans noted," The Associated Press (*Army Times*), Jan. 12, 2010, www.armytimes.com/news/2010/01/ap_vet_suicide_011110.

25. "Veterans Suicide Prevention," Senate Veterans' Affairs Committee, March 3, 2010.

26. *Ibid.*

27. *Ibid.*

28. "Veterans Suicide Prevention," Senate Veterans' Affairs Committee, March 3, 2010, (Web video), http://veterans.senate.gov/hearings.cfm?action=release.display&release_id=d1a8548c-de2c- 49a8-b7f9-d0855265d435.

29. *Ibid.*

30. Walter F. Roche Jr., and James Gerstenzang, "Doctor picked to head VA," *Los Angeles Times*, Oct. 31, 2007, p. A11.

31. "FY 2011 Budget Submission," *op. cit.*, p. 1A-1; Jackie Calmes, "In $3.8 Trillion Budget, Obama Pivots to Trim Future Deficits," *The New York Times*, Feb. 1, 2010, www.nytimes.com/2010/02/02/us/politics/02budget.html?pagewanted=all.

32. James Dao, "Late Benefit Checks Causing Problems for Veterans Attending College On New G.I. Bill," *The New York Times*, Sept. 25, 2009, p. A16.

33. "House Veterans' Affairs Committee Holds Hearing on the State of the Department of Veterans Affairs," CQ Congressional Transcripts, Oct. 14, 2009.

34. Except where otherwise indicated, this subsection is drawn from "VA History in Brief," Department of Veterans Affairs, undated, www1.va.gov/opa/publications/archives/docs/history_in_brief.pdf. For number serving in the World War II military, male and female, "Facts for Features," U.S. Census Bureau, April 29, 2004, www.census.gov/Press-Release/www/2004/cb04-ffse07.pdf.

35. For background, see P. Webbink, "Veteran-aid Policies of the United States," *Editorial Research Reports*, Vol. IV, Oct. 6, 1930; and B. W. Patch, "The Bonus and Veterans' Pensions," *Editorial Research Reports*, Vol. I, Jan. 10, 1936, both available at *CQ Researcher Plus Archive*, www.library.cqpress.com.

36. For background, see R. McNickle, "Service Pensions for War Veterans," *Editorial Research Reports*, May 4, 1949, available at *CQ Researcher Plus Archive*, www.library.cqpress.com.

37. Suzanne Metler, "Why Skimp on GI Bill?" Military.com, Nov. 18, 2005, www.military.com/opinion/0,15202,80830,00.html. The book is Suzanne Metler, *Soldiers and Citizens: The GI Bill and the Making of the Greatest Generation* (2005).

38. Except where otherwise indicated, this subsection is drawn from Gerald Nicosia, *Home to War: A History of the Vietnam Veterans Movement* (2001), and "VA History in Brief," *op. cit.*

39. Neil Sheehan, *A Bright Shining Lie: John Paul Vann and America in Vietnam* (1988), p. 39; "Vietnam War," GlobalSecurity.org, undated, www.globalsecurity.org/military/ops/vietnam.htm; "America's Wars," Department of Veterans Affairs, updated November, 2009, www1.va.gov/opa/publications/factsheets/fs_americas_wars.pdf.

40. "VVAW: Where We Came From, Who We Are," Vietnam Veterans Against the War, undated, www.vvaw.org/about/; Jason Zengerle, "The Vet Wars," *The New York Times Magazine*, May 23, 2004, p. 30.

41. "Born on the Fourth of July," Internet Movie Database, www.imdb.com/title/tt0096969/.

42. Except as otherwise indicated, material in this section is drawn from "VA History in Brief," *op. cit.* For background, see Peter Katel, "Wounded Veterans," *CQ Researcher*, Aug. 31, 2007, pp. 697-720.

43. "Independent Review Could Improve Credibility of Radiation Exposure Estimates," GAO, January, 2000, p. 2, www.gao.gov/archive/2000/he00032.pdf; "Rules for Veterans' Radiation Benefits Voided," The Associated Press (*The New York Times*), Oct. 8, 1981, www.nytimes.com/1981/10/08/us/rules-for-veterans-radiation-benefits-voided.html.

44. "House Votes Bill Giving Benefits to Veterans Exposed to Radiation," The Associated Press (*The New York Times*), May 3, 1988, p. A26; "Independent Review . . .," *op. cit.*, p. 6; "Statement on Signing the Radiation-Exposed Veterans Compensation Act

of 1988," Ronald Reagan, May 20, 1988 the American Presidency Project, www.presidency.ucsb .edu/ws/index.php?pid=35855.

45. David Zucchino, "Veterans speak out against burn pits," *Los Angeles Times*, Feb. 18, 2010, http://articles.latimes.com/2010/feb/18/nation/la-na-burn-pits18-2010feb18.

46. Thom Shanker and David Stout, "Chief Army Medical Officer Ousted in Walter Reed Furor," *The New York Times*, March 13, 2007, p. A5.

47. Rick Atkinson, " 'The single most effective weapon against our deployed forces,' " *The Washington Post*, Sept. 30, 2008, p. A1; Ann Scott Tyson, "U.S. combat injuries rise sharply," *The Washington Post*, Oct. 31, 2009, p. A1.

48. Ronald Glasser, "A Shock Wave of Brain Injuries," *The Washington Post*, April 8, 2007, Outlook, p. B1.

49. *Ibid.*

50. "Returning Home from Iraq and Afghanistan . . . ," *op. cit.*

51. Quoted in "VA recognizes 'presumptive' illnesses in Iraq, Afghanistan," Veterans Administration, March 24, 2010, www.army.mil/-news/2010/03/24/36272-va-recognizes-presumptive-illnesses-in-iraq-afghanistan.

52. Quoted in Kelly Kennedy, "VA may designate 9 infectious diseases as service-connected," *Military Times*, April 5, 2010, p. A12; "Proposed Rule," Department of Veterans Affairs, *Federal Register*, Vol. 75, No. 52, March 18, 2010, www1.va.gov/ORPM/docs/20100318_AN24_PresumptionsPersian GulfService.pdf.

53. "Gulf War and Health, Vol. 8: Update of Health Effects of Serving in the Gulf War," Institute of Medicine, April 9, 2010, pp. 5-7, 25, www.iom.edu/Reports/2010/Gulf-War-and-Health-Volume-8-Health-Effects-of-Serving-in-the-Gulf-War.aspx.

54. David Brown, "Up to 250,000 Gulf War veterans have 'unexplained medical symptoms,'" *The Washington Post*, April 10, 2010, www.washingtonpost.com/wp-dyn/content/article/2010/04/09/AR2010040904712.html.

55. Quoted in Kennedy, *op. cit.*

56. Lynne Marek, "Courts for veterans spreading across U.S.," *National Law Journal*, Dec. 22, 2008, www.law.com/jsp/nlj/PubArticlePrinterFriendlyNLJ.jsp?id=1202426915992&hbxlogin=1; Carolyn Thompson, "Special court for veterans addresses more than crime," The Associated Press (*Boston Globe*), July 7, 2008, www.boston.com/news/nation/articles/2008/07/07/special_court_for_veterans_addresses_more_than_crime; John Gramlich, "New courts tailored to war veterans," Stateline.org, June, 18, 2009, www.stateline.org/live/details/story?contentId=407573.

57. Sergio R. Rodriguez, "VA Secretary Eric K. Shinseki visits the Buffalo Veterans Treatment Court," Veterans Service Agency, April 6, 2010, www.erie.gov/veterans/veterans_court.asp.

58. P. Solomon Banda, "Troubled Veterans Get a Hand," The Associated Press (*The Washington Post*), Aug. 7, 2009, p. A19.

59. Quoted in John Gramlich, *op. cit.*

60. *Ibid.*

61. Robert Boczkiewicz, "Veteran of Afghanistan, Iraq gets probation," *Pueblo Chieftain*, Dec. 19, 2009, www.chieftain.com/news/local/article_d2d823fb-19ee-5eb4-ac54-dca372dd75d4.html.

62. Quoted in *ibid.*

63. Quoted in John Schwartz, "Defendants Fresh From War Find Service Counts in Court," *The New York Times*, March 16, 2010, p. A14.

64. Leah Nylen and Jennifer Scholtes, "Senate Passes Vets' Package Despite Coburn's Concerns," *CQ Today*, Nov. 19, 2009; "S 1963 CRS Bill Digest Summary," March 10, 2010.

65. "Returning Home from Iraq and Afghanistan," *op. cit.*, p. 98.

66. *Ibid.*, p. 97.

67. *Ibid.*, p. 98.

68. *Ibid.*

69. "Invisible Wounds of War," *op. cit.*, pp. 452, 446.

70. "Sgt. Gene L. Lamie, United States Army, KIA 06 July 2007," www.ourfallensoldier.com/Lamie GeneL_MemorialPage.html.

BIBLIOGRAPHY

Books

Glantz, Aaron, *The War Comes Home: Washington's Battle Against America's Veterans*, University of California Press, 2009.
A journalist who covered the Iraq war reports critically on the state of VA services.

Nicosia, Gerald, *Home to War: A History of the Vietnam Veterans' Movement*, Crown, 2001.
The influence of the groundbreaking movement still resonates today, having helped to get post-traumatic stress disorder classified as a disability caused by military service.

Schram, Martin, *Vets Under Siege*, St. Martin's Press, 2008.
A veteran Washington reporter examines the VA's efforts to meet the demands placed on it by the Iraq and Afghanistan wars.

Articles

Cave, Damien, "A Combat Role, and Anguish, Too," *The New York Times*, Nov. 1, 2009, p. A1.
Women vets suffering from PTSD are more isolated than their male counterparts, because they are fewer in number and are expected to immediately jump back into household duties.

Chong, Jia-Rui, "Veterans' long-term ills linked to brain injuries," *Los Angeles Times*, Dec. 5, 2008, p. A25.
The first comprehensive report links TBI to long-term conditions including seizures and aggression.

Cullison, Alan, "On Battlefields, Survival Odds Rise," *The Wall Street Journal*, April 3, 2010, online.wsj.com/article/SB20001424052748704655004575114623837930294.html.
A journalist experienced in covering warfare in Afghanistan provides a close-in look at advances in battlefield medicine.

Dao, James, and Thom Shanker, "No Longer a Soldier, Shinseki Has a New Mission," *The New York Times*, Nov. 11, 2009, p. A21.
The VA's new boss as profiled by correspondents on the Pentagon and veterans' affairs beats.

Hefling, Kimberly, "The veterans hall is growing — online," *The Associated Press*, Dec. 7, 2008, p. A15.
The newest veterans are taking their postwar bonding to the Internet.

Kennedy, Kelly, "DoD concedes rise in burn-pit ailments," *Military Times*, Feb. 8, 2010, p. 10.
The Defense Department admits there are possible connections between waste-burning emissions and health problems.

Marcus, Mary Brophy, "Military families cry for help," *USA Today*, Jan. 27, 2010, p. 8B.
Families taking care of catastrophically wounded veterans struggle financially and emotionally, a medical correspondent reports.

Ungar, Laura, "Suicide takes growing toll among military, veterans," *The Courier-Journal* (Ky.), Sept. 13, 2009.
The health-affairs specialist for a newspaper situated near a big military base (Fort Knox) covers the rising tide of suicide.

Whitlock, Craig, "IED attacks soaring in Afghanistan," *The Washington Post*, March 18, 2010, p. A10.
A war correspondent for *The Post* charts the Taliban's growing use of the explosive devices.

Zoroya, Gregg, "Repeated deployments weigh heavily on troops," *USA Today*, Jan. 13, 2010, p. A1.
As repeat deployments continue, the newspaper's veterans-beat reporter covers the toll on service members.

Reports and Studies

"Gulf War and Health: Vol. 8: Update of Health Effects of Serving in the Gulf War," *Institute of Medicine*, 2009, www.nap.edu/catalog/12835.html.
The federally funded institute is finding evidence of a link between service in the Gulf and multisymptom illness.

"Returning Home From Iraq and Afghanistan: Preliminary Assessment of Readjustment Needs of Veterans, Service Members, and Their Families," *Institute of Medicine*, 2010, www.nap.edu/catalog/12812.html.
A massive examination and analysis of research data that attempts to portray the effects of the present wars on service members and society at large.

"Veterans' Disability Benefits: Further Evaluation of Ongoing Initiatives Could Help Identify Effective Approaches for Improving Claims Processing," *Government Accountability Office*, January 2010, www.gao.gov/new.items/d10213.pdf.

In the most recent of its reports on the VA claims system, Congress' investigative arm concludes that the backlog problem remains serious.

Mulhall, Erin, and Vanessa Williamson, "Red Tape: Veterans Fight New Battles for Care and Benefits," *Iraq and Afghanistan Veterans of America*, February 2010, media.iava.org/reports/redtape_2010.pdf.

The advocacy organization reports on delays and complicated procedures that still characterize the VA's disability claims system.

For More Information

AMVETS, 4647 Forbes Blvd., Lanham, MD 20706; (301) 459-9600; www.amvets.org. Originally formed for World War II vets; specializes in public policy and legislative work and aids vets with claims to the U.S. Department of Veterans' Affairs (VA).

Disabled American Veterans, P.O. Box 14301, Cincinnati, OH 45250; (859) 441-7300; www.dav.org. Specializes in VA claims work and other services for severely wounded vets.

Lawyers Serving Warriors, P.O. Box 65762, Washington, DC 20035; (202) 265-8305; www.lawyersservingwarriors .com. Provides free lawyers to veterans in disability and other cases, but is not accepting new clients; Web site remains a valuable source of information.

U.S. Department of Veterans Affairs, 810 Vermont Ave., N.W., Washington, DC 20420; (800) 827-1000; www.va .gov. Maintains a Web site that is a rich source of information on benefits and policy.

Veterans for Common Sense, 900 2nd St., S.E., Suite 216, Washington, DC 20003; (202) 558-4553; www.veterans forcommonsense.org. Advocacy organization focuses on VA reform.

Wounded Warrior Project, 7020 AC Skinner Pkwy., Suite 100, Jacksonville, FL 32256; (877) 832-6997; www.wound edwarriorproject.org. Provides aid to severely disabled veterans and their families.

16

Attacking Piracy

Can the growing global threat be stopped?

Alan Greenblatt

A Chinese destroyer escorts two Chinese freighters in the pirate-infested waters off the coast of Somalia. Warships from dozens of nations, including the United States, the European Union, China, India and Russia now patrol the region against a sudden upsurge in piracy, which costs the global shipping industry up to $50 billion a year. Despite the show of force, many experts argue that given Somalia's grinding poverty, eradicating piracy requires more than a naval solution.

From *CQ Global Researcher*, August 2009.

H assan Abdalla was on his way to deliver rice to starving Somalis when his freighter, the *Semlow*, was surrounded by small boats manned by pirates with AK-47 assault rifles and rocket-propelled grenades (RPGs).

Claiming to belong to the so-called Somali Marines — the largest of the many pirate gangs operating off the Somali coast — the hijackers took over the *Semlow* and began using it as a "mother" ship — for launching smaller, faster boats to attack other ships. Four months later Abdalla and his fellow mariners were released, after more than $500,000 in ransom was paid to the pirates.

"I knew they would hijack again, because ransom money is sweet," Abdalla told Daniel Sekulich, a reporter with *The Globe and Mail* in Toronto and author of a new book about piracy, *Terror on the Seas*. "Once you've tasted it, you want more."[1]

Indeed, the lure of easy money has turned the seas around the Horn of Africa into danger zones for commercial ships. Some 30,000 vessels per year use the region's shipping lanes to deliver oil and other goods between Europe, the Middle East and Asia.[2] In the first half of this year, armed Somali pirates attacked at least 150 oceangoing vessels in the area, a sixfold jump in attacks in that region over the same period in 2008.[3]

More than 250 years since the end of the so-called Golden Age of Piracy — the days of Blackbeard, Captain Kidd and other legendary figures — pirates have returned to the high seas, threatening maritime security, commerce and, some terrorism experts say, global security. "Piracy, the scourge of the 17th and 18th centuries, has emerged from the history books and has returned with deadly, terrifying results," writes John Burnett, a London-based maritime

Piracy Spans the Globe

Piracy occurs in most of the world's tropical oceans — including the Pacific waters off Peru, the east and west coasts of Africa and the seas of Southeast Asia. More than 60 percent of the 240 attacks in the first half of 2009 were attributed to heavily armed Somalis attacking ships in the Gulf of Aden and off the coast of Somalia. The second-largest number of pirate attacks this year occurred in the Southeast Asia/Far East region.

Successful and Attempted Pirate Attacks
(January–June, 2009)

Source: International Maritime Bureau

security consultant and former reporter, in his 2002 book *Dangerous Waters*.[4]

A record 889 crew members were taken hostage in 2008 — a 207 percent increase over 2007, according to Peter Chalk, a maritime security analyst with the RAND Corporation think tank. Although ransom negotiations are kept confidential, pirates collected an estimated $30 million to $150 million in booty last year. Many worry that such big — and rapidly growing — sums will only encourage, and fund, further attacks. Currently, Somali pirates are holding 10 foreign vessels hostage, awaiting ransom payments.[5]

Piracy costs the shipping industry overall — in ransoms, lost cargoes, higher insurance premiums and interrupted shipping schedules — from $10 billion to $50 billion a year, according to Sekulich. "Even the lowball estimates," he notes, are "well above the gross domestic product of numerous nations [and] virtually unprecedented in our global economic history."[6]

And, while no direct link has been established between the Somali pirates and terrorists, some worry the weaknesses in maritime security exploited by pirates will prove useful to those seeking to spread terror. (*See sidebar, p. 424.*) Martin N. Murphy, a senior research fellow at the Center for Strategic and Budgetary Assessments in Washington and author of a 2009 book on piracy and marine terrorism, says Web traffic and intelligence intercepts clearly indicate that Islamic extremist groups "are watching what's happening off Somalia. It reveals a clear weakness, and terrorists can exploit this."

While most pirate attacks today occur near Somalia, pirates also operate off the coasts of other countries, including Peru, Brazil and Nigeria. Private yachts in the Caribbean and Gulf of Mexico also have been attacked. For decades, pirates plagued Southeast Asia, especially the Malacca Strait — the strategic waterway that runs between Singapore, Indonesia and Malaysia and links

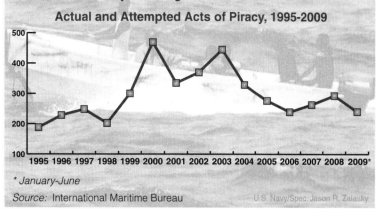

Piracy Could Set New Record This Year

In the first half of 2009 there were 240 attempted and successful pirate attacks worldwide — twice the number in the same period last year. The increase is due largely to attacks by Somali pirates in the Gulf of Aden and off the coast of Somalia. At the current rate, global piracy this year will surpass its modern peak of 469 attacks in 2000. Most of those attacks occurred in Southeast Asia and the Malacca Strait between Malaysia, Indonesia and Singapore. After those governments jointly cracked down, piracy declined dramatically in the region.

Actual and Attempted Acts of Piracy, 1995-2009

* January-June

Source: International Maritime Bureau   U.S. Navy/Spec. Jason R. Zalasky

northeast Asia with the Indian Ocean. But a tough, new, regional anti-piracy campaign has helped to control the attacks in recent years.

Recent pirate attacks have been concentrated off Somalia and in the Gulf of Aden/Red Sea area: Attacks by Somalis in the first six months of this year accounted for more than 60 percent of the world's 240 pirate incidents. At that rate, total attacks in 2009 could surpass the modern-day record of 469 incidents in 2000, when most piracy was occurring in Southeast Asia. But experts say shipowners only report about a third of actual attacks, because they don't want their voyages delayed further by criminal or insurance investigations.

One of the most dramatic attacks occurred in April, when Somali pirates boarded the *Maersk Alabama* — the first such incident against a U.S. vessel manned by an American crew. The captain, Richard Phillips, gave himself up as a hostage in exchange for the release of his crew and ship. Several days later he was dramatically rescued when three Navy SEAL snipers shot and killed his three captors.

Piracy Shifts From Asia to East Africa

The world's piracy hot spot has shifted dramatically from Southeast Asia to East Africa over the last decade. In 2000, nearly half of the 469 pirate attacks occurred in Southeast Asia, and only 5 percent in East Africa. But since Singapore, Malaysia and Indonesia jointly adopted a strong anti-piracy program in 2004, pirate attacks in the region have plummeted. In the first half of 2009, Southeast Asia experienced only 10 percent of the world's pirate attacks, and 60 percent occurred in Somalia, the Gulf of Aden and the Red Sea.

Location of Piracy Incidents, 2000 and 2009*

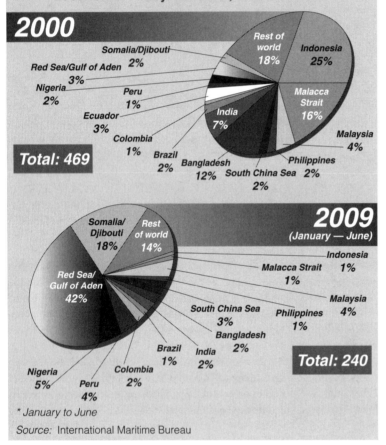

2000

Somalia/Djibouti 2%
Red Sea/Gulf of Aden 3%
Nigeria 2%
Peru 1%
Ecuador 3%
Colombia 1%
Brazil 2%
Bangladesh 12%
South China Sea 2%
India 7%
Rest of world 18%
Indonesia 25%
Malacca Strait 16%
Malaysia 4%
Philippines 2%

Total: 469

2009
(January — June)

Somalia/Djibouti 18%
Rest of world 14%
Red Sea/Gulf of Aden 42%
Nigeria 5%
Peru 4%
Colombia 2%
Brazil 1%
India 2%
Bangladesh 2%
South China Sea 3%
Philippines 1%
Malaysia 4%
Malacca Strait 1%
Indonesia 1%

Total: 240

* January to June

Source: International Maritime Bureau

Some in the shipping industry complained afterwards that killing pirates might endanger future hostages, who until now have mainly been unharmed. Some Somali pirates at the time boasted they would now target and kill American sailors, but that hasn't happened.[7]

The debate about the use of force reflected a larger point: Navies are uncertain how to handle the problem. They don't engage with pirates until after an attack has occurred, and, even when they do capture pirates, it's not always clear what they should do with them or who has jurisdiction over crimes committed in international waters. Because many Western nations lack clear anti-piracy statutes, dozens of captured pirates have been disarmed and released. Some have been taken to neighboring countries, especially Kenya, for prosecution. (*See sidebar, p. 430.*)

In the past year the ranks of Somali pirates have burgeoned, as more and more citizens of the failed state — lucky to earn $2 a day and attracted by the lucrative spoils — have joined their ranks. Today there are at least 3,000 Somali pirates, up significantly from the roughly 200 that were operating in early 2008, according to Burnett. Russian Vice Admiral Oleg Burtsev puts the number at 5,000 or more.[8]

"If you're young and able-bodied, what else can you do but join the pirates?" asks Peter Lehr, a terrorism-studies lecturer at the University of St. Andrews in Scotland. "It's like the California Gold Rush."

Regardless of the exact number, Somali pirates have grown bolder in recent months, targeting large container ships and even supertankers like the *Sirius Star*, which was carrying $100 million worth of oil and eventually was ransomed for an estimated $3 million.

Up to 90 percent of the world's goods travel by boat, making ships at sea the weak link in the global trading system. Given the threat, warships from nearly two-dozen countries, part of a "combined task force" set up by the United States in January, are now patrolling the area. The European Union is running a separate escort and patrol operation to protect food aid shipments like the one carried by the *Semlow*. It is the EU's first naval mission and the first time Britain's Royal Navy has been on an anti-piracy mission in nearly 200 years.[9] In addition, France, China, India, South Korea and Russia have sent their own vessels.

Despite the show of force, naval officials concede it's not enough. Patrolling more than half a million square miles of water would take hundreds of warships, not a couple dozen. "The weird thing is, piracy has increased while we have the heaviest presence of naval warships in that region that's ever been seen," says author Sekulich.

Many argue that ending piracy requires more than a naval solution. Piracy, particularly the Somali brand, reflects that country's poverty, limited opportunities and lack of a functioning central government. Since the fall of a dictatorial regime in 1991, Somalia has had a new government about once every 14 months, on average.[10] It's also awash in arms, after decades of civil war and Cold War efforts to play the Soviets off against the Americans.

But while Somalia has devolved into a failed state, its pirate gangs have become increasingly sophisticated, Sekulich points out. "Somalia has transformed itself, or rather the pirates have transformed themselves, into the most advanced and effective type of pirates we've seen in centuries."

The pirates often turn a portion of the ransom money over to their backers — sophisticated organized crime figures — who reinvest much of it in high-powered weaponry, faster boats, global positioning systems (GPS) and satellite phones. And the pirates now are apparently sharing intelligence about the movement of merchant ships.

"The most recent evidence shows that the mother vessels are telling each other about potential targets," British Rear Adm. Philip Jones, commander of the EU naval task force, said in May. "They are exchanging positional information, . . . information about ships they have seen or may have tried to attack. Obviously, that is a significant development."[11]

Given the enormous profits Somalis are pulling in, some analysts worry that the piracy problem will spread.

As the global community struggles to combat piracy, here are some of the questions people are debating:

Can navies defeat piracy?

Piracy has been a menace since ancient times. Cilician pirates from what is now Turkey disrupted commerce between cities and kidnapped important officials until 67 B.C., when a Roman commander, Gnaeus Pompeius Magnus ("Pompey the Great"), shut down the pirate operation in less than two months with a massive naval and land campaign.

Pompey divided his massive fleet into 13 naval squadrons responsible for various sections of the Mediterranean. He kept 60 ships under his direct command, using them to harass pirates into the areas patrolled by his commanders. Within 40 days, he cleared the western Mediterranean of pirates and chased them inland using tens of thousands of soldiers, attacking pirate strongholds in Turkey.

Similarly, the rise of modern-day piracy off Somalia has attracted the attention of the world's great navies, and their warships are having an effect. The United Nations had stopped sending food aid to Somalia for nearly three years due to pirate raids on the shipments. But since the EU launched its "Operation Atalanta" mission in December, not a single escorted U.N. shipment has been stopped, and 1.6 million Somalis are being fed by the U.N.'s World Food Programme (WFP) every day. In addition to protecting food shipments, Atalanta's ships and helicopters escort commercial vessels and provide aerial surveillance and other measures to deter piracy in the region.

"We hope very much that with this anti-piracy operation in the Horn of Africa — one of the busiest transit routes in the world — we can bring these piracy activities down," says Cristina Gallach, spokeswoman for the European Union's high Representative for the Common Foreign and Security Policy.

Although the EU recently extended the Atalanta mission for another year, Gallach says it's not a panacea. Pirates who can't hit ships along their accustomed corridors now attack ships as far south as the Seychelles. "It's just like any other criminal activity," says RAND's Chalk. "They'll exploit some other area where there isn't so much law enforcement."

Shippers want navies to disrupt piracy before attacks occur, says Pottengal Mukundan, director of the International Chamber of Commerce's International Maritime Bureau. Capturing or sinking the mother ships would be particularly helpful, he says.

Reuters/Crack Palinggi

Indonesian naval personnel guard pirates suspected of hijacking the palm oil tanker MT Kraton in the Strait of Singapore. Although the pirates changed the ship's name, a joint anti-piracy campaign by Indonesia, Malaysia and Singapore used a new international database to uncover the name change and apprehend the pirates in September 2007.

The Indian navy sank a mother ship last November, 325 miles southwest of Oman's port of Salalah. And in April, a French frigate sailing under the EU banner intercepted a mother ship in the Gulf of Aden, detaining 11 pirates.

"Navies have to increase their deterrent efforts — before pirates get on board," says Lee Willett, head of the maritime studies program at the Royal United Services Institute for Defence and Security Studies in London. "Stop them on shore, create exclusion zones bigger than the current corridors, stop any vessel out there with small engines, which are obviously out there for no good reason."

But aside from the "balloon effect" of pushing pirates out to new, unguarded areas, the battle against piracy ultimately must be won on land, says Gallach. "The problem of piracy is on land, not on the high seas."

Many observers agree the problem is "land-based," the result of Somalia's 18 years without a functioning government. Without law enforcement or any sense of order, Somali gangs and warlords have become increasingly sophisticated in their sponsorship of crimes extending out to the high seas. "Piracy is the maritime ripple effect of anarchy on land," wrote foreign policy journalist Robert D. Kaplan.[12]

Piracy has prospered because pirates have safe havens back home, and the ruined economy is not producing legitimate jobs for young Somalis. Since Somalia's 2,000-mile-long coastline sits near a key transit corridor — the Gulf of Aden — the country's problems have filtered far out to sea.

"You've got the most powerful naval armada assembled in recent history to fight the scourge of pirates who are really lightly armed in some puny boats, and they still can't stop them," says Burnett.

Historical battles against piracy have generally required action on land, from Pompey's use of 120,000 infantry to clemency deals cut with Chinese and Caribbean pirates. More recently, piracy in the Strait of Malacca and the surrounding region dropped from 187 attacks in 2003 to 65 in 2008 after Singapore, Indonesia, Malaysia and Thailand — with Japanese prodding and funding — launched a coordinated anti-piracy campaign.[13]

But without a functioning government in Somalia, "there's no way of controlling pirates internally," Burnett says. "There are efforts to build a coast guard there, but that's so far down the road."*

Chris Trelawny — head of maritime security for the U.N.'s London-based International Maritime Organization (IMO) — is more hopeful. He points out that 17 countries in the region drafted a code of conduct

---

* The Transitional Federal Government, formed in 2004, is the latest in a string of efforts to establish a central government in Somalia in the last 18 years. President Sheikh Sharif Sheikh Ahmed, elected in January, has not yet been able to provide essential services or maintain security. The externally funded, ultra-conservative jihadist al-Shabaab group controls much of the southern part of the country and some parts of the capital.

in January vowing to seize pirate ships and cooperate in the arrest and prosecutions of pirates.

Until a land-based solution can be instituted in Somalia, Trelawny says, "We welcome the work of the navies in carrying out what are essentially constabulary efforts."

The International Maritime Bureau's Mukundan disagrees. "It is a naval problem," he says. "In today's world, navies have the responsibility to protect maritime trade routes. They have stepped up to the mark splendidly." But he concedes that naval efforts are only a "temporary measure."

Willett concurs, saying naval action is needed to buy time for Somalia and other regional countries to get a handle on the problem. "While navies are a short-term element in the process," he says, "navies need to be there to keep a lid on it."

Despite the recent EU extension of its convoy program, some wonder whether the great powers will sustain their presence in the region for the years it undoubtedly will take for the Somali government to get its house in order enough to start prosecuting piracy.

The relatively low incidence of pirate attacks — only 240 so far this year on the tens of thousands of ships plying the world's oceans — has implications for how military resources are allocated, Michèle Flournoy, undersecretary of Defense for policy, told the Senate Armed Services Committee in May. She noted that merchant ship crews had thwarted 78 percent of the unsuccessful attacks, while military or law enforcement interventions had blocked only 22 percent.[14]

The millions being spent on naval patrols might even be counterproductive, suggests RAND's Chalk. "We're investing too much in naval solutions, to the detriment of long-term solutions."

"Navies cannot defeat piracy," insists EU spokeswoman Gallach. "Navies can . . . give protection to those

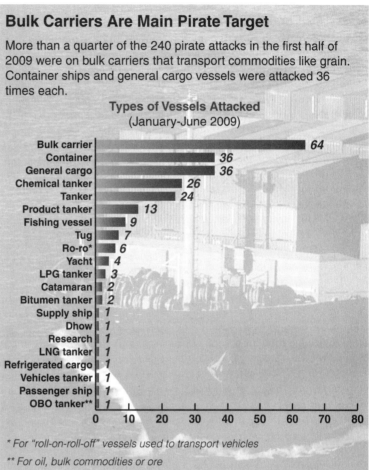

Bulk Carriers Are Main Pirate Target

More than a quarter of the 240 pirate attacks in the first half of 2009 were on bulk carriers that transport commodities like grain. Container ships and general cargo vessels were attacked 36 times each.

Types of Vessels Attacked
(January-June 2009)

Bulk carrier	64
Container	36
General cargo	36
Chemical tanker	26
Tanker	24
Product tanker	13
Fishing vessel	9
Tug	7
Ro-ro*	6
Yacht	4
LPG tanker	3
Catamaran	2
Bitumen tanker	2
Supply ship	1
Dhow	1
Research	1
LNG tanker	1
Refrigerated cargo	1
Vehicles tanker	1
Passenger ship	1
OBO tanker**	1

*For "roll-on-roll-off" vessels used to transport vehicles

** For oil, bulk commodities or ore

Source: "Piracy and Armed Robbery Against Ships," International Maritime Bureau, January-June 2009

who are in transit — the merchants, the ships that are transporting humanitarian aid."

Besides, as Flournoy and others suggest, chasing down pirates would divert their resources and attention from their fundamental strategic defense missions. "Prosecuting detained pirates . . . is simply not our business," said Cmdr. Achim Winkler, who heads an EU flotilla in the Gulf of Aden.[15]

Should shipping crews be armed?

A growing chorus of voices — including *Maersk Alabama* Capt. Phillips — are now convinced that maritime crews should be armed and trained to defend their ships.

No Link Seen Between Pirates and Terrorists

But some fear terrorists could adopt pirates' tactics.

Given the logistical difficulties involved, it's not surprising that terrorists have struck on land much more often than they've tried to strike at sea. Since the 1960s, there have been fewer than 200 maritime terror attacks worldwide, compared with over 10,000 terrorist incidents overall.[1]

But there is now some concern among defense analysts that the rapid growth of piracy might lead to more terror at sea. "Similar forces allow piracy and maritime terrorism to flourish," says Peter Chalk, a policy analyst with the RAND Corporation think tank. "The model of piracy could be mimicked by terrorists, including ransom demands."

Chalk notes that piracy can weaken political systems by encouraging corruption among public officials. And it's clear that piracy has been used as a fundraising tool by some terrorists, including the Free Aceh Movement in Indonesia and the Tamil Tigers in Sri Lanka. The two-decade-long Tiger insurgency was defeated by the Sri Lankan government in May.

"In the last year, we have seen structures related to al Qaeda that are taking advantage of the lawlessness that exists in Somalia," says Christina Gallach, a spokeswoman for the European Union.[2]

As Gallach and others point out, however, there appears to be no credible evidence of a direct link between pirates off the Somali coast and terrorists. "We are working very firmly in the belief that there is no proven link between piracy and al Qaeda-type terrorism," says Chris Trelawny, security chief of the International Maritime Organization. "What makes Somali piracy unique is that they are purely taking ships for kidnap and ransom."

In fact, pirates and terrorists work at cross-purposes, suggests Daniel Sekulich, author of the 2009 book, *Terror on the Seas: True Tales of Modern-Day Pirates.* Pirates' tools are subterfuge and anonymity, while terrorists want, more than anything else, to attract attention for their deeds.

"Pirates and terrorists have diametrically opposed goals," Sekulich says. "Pirates are seeking economic gain that comes from a steady supply of the world's shipping. They love all those container ships. Terrorists want to slow [or disrupt] shipping . . . for their own nefarious means."

Still, both piracy and terror are dangers because of the vulnerable nature of ocean-going trade. Piracy is a reflection of the fact that the weakest link in world trade is the lone vessel at sea, which could also be hit by politically motivated attackers.

"Arming the crew as part of an overall strategy could provide an effective deterrent under certain circumstances," Phillips told the Senate Foreign Relations Committee on April 30, just weeks after his spectacular rescue by Navy sharpshooters. But he doesn't think it would be "the best or ultimate solution to the problem."[16]

Vice Admiral James Winnefeld, director of strategic plans and policy for the Joint Chiefs of Staff, agrees. "It's a capacity issue," he told the Senate Armed Services Committee. "We believe this is something private industry needs to do for themselves."

The idea that shipowners should arm and train crew members — or hire private security forces to accompany ships or their escorts — appears to be gaining currency with U.S. defense officials. "It may be useful for Congress to consider developing incentives to encourage merchant ships to invest in security measures," Defense undersecretary Flournoy told the Armed Service Committee. "These could range from tax credits to reduced insurance rates for ships with enhanced security."

In other countries, however, proposals to arm crewmen or hire mercenaries remain highly controversial. Shipowners, insurers and seafarers all cite increased risks and legal and logistical complications posed by having firearms aboard merchant ships.

"Arming seafarers — that is totally out of the question," says Arild Wegener, chief of security for the Norwegian Shipowners Association.

Arming crews would trigger an arms race between the pirates and the crews and could increase the risk of serious harm and death onboard, even without a pirate attack, he says. So far, Somali pirates have shown little interest in harming their hostages, because they want to be able to collect ransom payments for them. But arming ship crews could change the equation.

"We believe the division between piracy and terrorism is much more blurred than some people seek to argue," says Andrew Linington, spokesman for the Nautilus International seafarers' union. "Certainly, our big worry is that a dozen guys in a fiberglass boat can take command of a ship like the *Sirius Star*, a massive vessel with millions of dollars of oil on board.

"We think that's an intolerable situation and should be sending huge warning signals out to governments about the fragility of safety at sea," he continues.

The deadliest terror attack at sea occurred in 2004, when 116 people were killed in the bombing of the Philippine *SuperFerry 14*. The ferry was blown up by 16 sticks of dynamite hidden in a hollowed out television set by members of the Abu Sayyaf Islamist separatist group. Such attacks worry security officials because they are so cheap and easy to carry out. Planning for the bombing took only a couple of months and cost no more than $400t.[3]

Marine terrorism is not new in the region of the world where piracy now dogs the shipping industry. In 2002, two suicide bombers attacked the oil tanker *Limburg* off Yemen, killing themselves and one crew member. The attack triggered a rise in the price of oil and area shipping insurance rates, causing a 93 percent drop in the container business at the Port of Aden.[4]

The disproportionate impact of such terrorist attacks is why some worry about the potential for piracy to lead to increases in maritime terrorism. Some experts worry, for example, that a liquefied natural gas tanker could be hijacked and turned into a massive bomb.

"No matter how well-protected, every ship afloat — and this includes those that carry enough reactor fuel to build a few nuclear devices — is physically highly vulnerable," writes maritime security consultant John Burnett.[5]

A more likely scenario, though, is that terrorists could take over or blow up a ship along one of the major shipping chokepoints, such as the Strait of Hormuz or the Suez Canal, disrupting the flow of oil or other crucial cargo. "With deliberate preparation and the occasional well-placed attack, a few men with small boats can keep the navies churning for years," writes journalist William Langewiesche in his 2004 book *The Outlaw Sea*.[6]

"If terrorists like al Qaeda want to keep Western powers tied up, would it not be logical for them to open another front to get attention off Afghanistan and Pakistan?" asks Lee Willett, a British naval security expert.

---

[1] Martin N. Murphy, *Small Boats, Weak States, Dirty Money* (2009), p. 185.

[2] For background, see Jason McLure, "The Troubled Horn of Africa," *CQ Global Researcher*, June 2009, pp. 149-176.

[3] Peter Chalk, "The Maritime Dimension of International Security: Terrorism, Piracy and Challenges for the United States," RAND Corporation, 2008, p. 26.

[4] *Ibid.*, p. 24.

[5] John S. Burnett, *Dangerous Waters* (2002), p. 288.

[6] William Langewiesche, *The Outlaw Sea* (2004), p. 39.

"Arming merchant sailors may result in the acquisition of even more lethal weapons and tactics by the pirates, a race that merchant sailors cannot win," John Clancey — chairman of the energy and shipping company Maersk Inc., which owns the *Maersk Alabama* — said during congressional testimony on April 30.[17]

"It has been our very strong policy that seafarers should not be armed," echoes Andrew Linington, a spokesman for Nautilus International, a British and Dutch seafarers' union. "It would be counterproductive and actually make things worse, partially because of the fear that in the wrong hands guns could actually inflame the situation."

For example, in a commonly cited case, New Zealander Sir Peter Blake, who had twice won the America's Cup, was anchored in the Amazon in 2001, when his ship was attacked by several armed men. Although Blake had a rifle and fired it in defense, he was shot and killed.[18]

Besides crew members being shot, Linington adds, gunfire could ignite a shipboard fire or cause other serious damage. Moreover, further problems would crop up when ships want to dock. Merchant ships are allowed to sail freely through territorial waters and come into port if they are not a threat to the security of the coastal state. That right of "innocent passage" could be forfeited if they were armed. The U.S. Coast Guard, for instance, considers armed vessels within U.S. territorial waters a threat.

"In many jurisdictions, a crew member could be arrested for possessing weapons," says John Bainbridge, who represents the International Transport Workers' Federation before the IMO on piracy issues. Most sailors also oppose having to undergo training and be responsible for protecting their workplaces along with their many other duties. "When asked, the overwhelming majority of seafarers have rejected this option," Bainbridge says.

United States Navy/SFC Eric L. Beauregard

Sailors from the guided-missile cruiser *USS Gettysburg* stop suspected pirates in the Gulf of Aden as part of the multinational task force conducting anti-piracy operations throughout the region. Since patrols began earlier this year, more than three times as many pirates have been interdicted as in all of 2008.

"The shipping industry is entirely against arming crews," says Neil Roberts, senior technical executive with Lloyd's Market Association, a London-based insurer.

But private security companies are anxious to offer their services. Blackwater Worldwide, a U.S. security firm, has offered dozens of shipping and insurance companies various options, such as a 181-foot long escort ship and certified mariners with small-arms training.

"The pirates are going after soft targets," said Jeff Gibson, vice president for international training and operations at Blackwater. "If a ship is being escorted by another boat, or some small boats or even a helicopter overhead, [the pirates] are going to decide, let's not make the effort."[19]

But hiring private security companies would be expensive — viable only for ships carrying the most valuable cargoes. And using private security companies "is fraught with difficulties," Roberts says, "not least because owners are unable to gauge the quality of various companies," since they are unregulated. If security guards kill someone, the shipping company could also be held liable.

And, many worry that hiring private security forces would ratchet up the potential for violence. Hiring armed security guards just escalates the situation "on both sides," says David M. Crane, a Syracuse University law professor. "Then you have a type of combat situation."

Despite such concerns, however, the rapid growth of piracy has led at least some analysts to rethink the long-standing prohibition against arming merchant ships. "Today's personnel, in signing up for a maritime career, do not wish to take upon themselves the responsibility and risk of providing for their own security in this way," says Graham Gerard Ong-Webb, a research fellow at the Centre for Defence and International Security Studies in London. "But I think these added responsibilities are inescapable today.

"We simply have to pay them more to do so," he continues. "I believe all maritime seafarers either have to undergo the requisite training to perform the basic defensive measures in deterring or staving off a pirate attack, or their employers should contract private security companies to do the job for them."

Those who argue that arming merchant ships will deter attackers rather than escalate the violence point out that Israeli and Russian merchant ships — which are assumed to be armed — are generally not attacked. For instance, in 2001, Burnett notes, no Russian or Israeli ships were attacked by pirates, compared to 27 attacks on U.S. and British ships.[20]

"It's very difficult to create a defense against armed pirates with unarmed ships," author Burnett says.

Nevertheless, he prefers that unarmed crew members use defenses such as water cannon, barbed wire around the decks or long-range acoustic devices that can destroy the eardrums of attackers — along with evasive maneuvers and general vigilance. "Guns aboard ships, unless they're military, just don't belong," he says.

Recalling the time when his own ship was boarded by pirates, Burnett says, "If I had been armed, if I had had my 12-gauge on board when I was attacked, I'd be dead today."

"If weapons are on board, they will get used," says Willett, of the Royal United Services Institute for Defence and Security Studies.

Should shipowners pay ransom?

Early pirate history is full of tales of extreme violence and even torture being used against captives. And earlier in this decade, when the greatest area of concern was in the Strait of Malacca, pirates generally stole the ships and cargo and killed crew members or set them adrift.

But Somali pirates are not out to kill: They need the crew alive for ransom from shipowners and insurance companies. The IMO's Trelawny points out that only two hostages have died in recent years while in pirate hands — one killed by a ricocheting bullet, another of a heart attack.[21]

"They were never nice to us and treated us the whole time as a potential threat," said Leszek Adler, an officer on the *Sirius Star*, the Saudi oil tanker taken by Somali pirates last November. But, "other than a few minor episodes, they weren't hostile toward us all, although there were a few of them that had a hotter temper."[22]

"Crew members are lots of money on two legs," says Lehr, the lecturer in terrorism studies at the University of St. Andrews.

A Congressional Research Service report points out that "while individual ransom payments can be significant," the payment of ransoms has kept Somali piracy violence "relatively low."[23] And because only a small percentage of ships in the area are successfully attacked and captured, some commercial entities view the overall risk of paying ransoms as low.

"What's the practical alternative?" asks Linington of Nautilus, the seafarers' union. "What are you going to do if you're not going to pay? Nobody seems to have a proper answer to that."

Indeed, once pirates control a ship, few alternatives remain. Navies can attempt rescues, but the casualty risk is high. French special forces storming a yacht taken by pirates in April may have killed its skipper during the firefight to rescue him and other hostages.[24]

But even the successful rescue of Capt. Phillips sparked criticism that it could lead pirates to greater violence. "Paying ransom certainly does encourage piracy, but they really don't have much alternative," says RAND's Chalk. "The amount of money paid for ransom is insignificant compared to the value of the ship.

"Shipowners remain concerned that should pressure be brought against them to not pay ransom, it will increase the danger that pirates might kill off a couple of crew members to establish the seriousness of their demands," he continues.

"The last people who want to pay a ransom are the industry," says the International Maritime Bureau's Mukundan. "They don't want to have to pay millions of dollars to get their ships and crews back. But . . . they don't have a choice. Inside Somali waters, no one else can help them. They have to do whatever they can. Today it means paying a ransom."

Governments don't pay ransoms. "We as a government do not condone the paying of ransom," said U.S. Defense undersecretary Flournoy. "We seek to end the paying of ransom."

But private shipping companies view paying ransom — or having their insurance companies pay — as the cheapest alternative and the most compassionate for the crew. "There is a concern that it sets a precedent, but ransoms do get paid," says Willett, of the Royal United Services Institute for Defence and Security Studies. "The amount tends to be only a small percentage of the value of the ship."

But even if paying ransoms is the more prudent course, is it the wisest? Trelawny feels it only exacerbates the situation. "Five years ago, the ransoms were in the tens of thousands, now they're in the millions," he says.

Though final payments are generally kept confidential, estimates of the total amount of ransoms paid to Somali pirates in 2008 range from $30 million up to $150 million.[25]

"At the moment, we seem to be approaching the worst of all possible worlds," wrote Bloomberg columnist Matthew Lynn. "Shipping companies either avoid the African coastline or . . . agree to pay what amounts to protection money for safe passage. Neither is satisfactory in the long term. Over time, the pirates will just grow stronger, the attacks will cover a wider area, and the ransom demands will get bigger."[26]

Little of the money stays with the pirates who carried out the crime. Usually, most of it goes to their backers — organized-crime syndicates or warlords. "In a typical ransom payment, 70 percent of that money is not returned to the pirates that undertake the operation. That goes to businessmen on land," Chalk writes.[27]

"To make matters worse, we know pirates use much of the ransom money paid to them to buy heavier and larger caliber weapons and bigger engines for their skiffs to make it even easier to overtake larger vessels," Senate Foreign Relations Committee Chairman John F. Kerry, D-Mass., said at the April 30 hearing. "They also use ransom money to arm and equip private militias. This is a dangerous and a vicious cycle, and it needs to be addressed."

Inevitably, the pirates' price comes down as negotiations drag on, sometimes for months. The pirates who took the *Sirius Star*, for instance, initially demanded $25 million but settled for an estimated $3 million after nearly two months of talks.

"What we want for this ship is only $25 million, because we always charge according to the quality of the ship and the value of the product," one of the hijackers told a reporter during the standoff.[28]

Delivering the ransoms has become another big business. Lawyers in London often handle the negotiations on behalf of shipowners, and private companies charge up to $1 million to deliver the ransoms, which are always paid in cash to avoid computer tracking. Bundled bills might be parachuted directly on board captured ships or delivered in suitcases to middlemen in cities such as Nairobi and Djibouti or to villages along the coast.

Recently, pirates have become more sophisticated, demanding only $50 and $100 bills and refusing easily traceable years of issue. The *Sirius Star*'s hijackers even brought a counting machine and a counterfeit-money detector on board with them.

However, the $3 million ransom they collected apparently was too much to carry away. The small getaway boat some of them took capsized. Five of the pirates drowned along with their shares, with one reportedly washing ashore with $153,000 in his pockets.[29] "The small boat was overloaded and going too fast," pirate leader Mohammed Said told the Agence France-Presse news agency. "The survivors told us they were afraid some foreign navies would attempt to catch them."[30]

Ong-Webb, of the Centre for Defence and International Security Studies, says it's perfectly understandable that shipping companies pay ransoms for their crews, but "it is not sustainable in the long term." Too much depends on global shipping to make payments to criminals a normal cost of doing business, he says.

Some countries, such as the United Kingdom, want to discourage private industry from paying ransom. But it will be difficult to come up with an alternative, since the decision about paying ransoms is made among shipping companies, insurers, national governments and captured crew members' families.

"Payment does encourage further attacks, and each one raises the bar, but unless shipowners pay ransoms they will be faced with a total loss of their ships," says Roberts, of Lloyd's Market Association.

But, he says, "While ships trade through such waters, there is no practical alternative to ransoms."

BACKGROUND

Piracy's 'Golden Age'

The poet Homer recorded an act of piracy in *The Odyssey*, written around 800 B.C., and in 75 B.C. the imperial barge carrying Roman Emperor Julius Caesar was apparently hijacked during a Mediterranean crossing.[31]

But piracy was tolerated — and even encouraged — by some rulers, who gave "letters of marque," or licenses, to privateers, legalizing their plundering so long as the ruler received a cut. "Piracy has always benefited from the support of unscrupulous great men only too happy to receive bribes and cheap pirated goods at no risk to themselves," writes British historian Peter Earle.[32]

Perhaps the most famous privateer was Francis Drake, who plundered gold and jewels from Spanish ships in the 1570s in support of Britain's Elizabeth I. Investors in Drake's voyage, including Elizabeth, received 47 British pounds for every pound they'd invested.[33]

"Elizabeth was not a weak monarch," writes Murphy of the Center for Strategic and Budgetary Assessments, "but she depended for the defense of her realm upon the sea power she could not afford."[34]

The most infamous pirates of all — Blackbeard, Captain Kidd and Henry Morgan — sacked towns in the Caribbean and North America and attacked ships during the so-called Golden Age of Piracy from the 1650s until the 1720s. Many were based in the lawless British colony of the Bahamas.

The pirates successfully eluded the British navy for years. Even when they were caught, the legal procedure for dealing with them, which dated from 1536, required them to be tried by an admiralty court in London. In 1700, Parliament passed the Act for the More Effectual Suppression of Piracy, which allowed trials outside England and authorized the death penalty outside of Great Britain.[35]

The new law allowed the British Navy to more aggressively dispatch armadas to drive pirates from their lairs and bring them to justice. Between 1716 and 1726 more than 400 men were hanged for piracy, effectively eliminating most of the leaders and decimating the general ranks.[36]

CHRONOLOGY

1700s-1800s *Rampant piracy in the Caribbean, Mediterranean and South China Sea is crushed.*

1700 Britain updates its piracy laws, enabling prosecution of pirates and use of the death penalty overseas. More than 400 men are hanged for piracy in the Atlantic and Caribbean.

Late 1700s U.S. builds a navy to fight state-sponsored piracy in North Africa. Two Barbary Wars ensue (1801-1805 and 1815-1816).

1810 China asks Western powers to help combat piracy in the South China Sea. Female pirate leader Cheng I Sao accepts amnesty deal, leading to surrender of hundreds of ships and more than 17,000 pirates.

1980s *Maritime piracy reemerges, especially in Southeast Asia.*

1985 Palestinian terrorists attack the Italian cruise ship *Achille Lauro*, prompting an international convention on maritime terrorism.

1988 Rome Convention makes seizing or endangering ships illegal.

1990s-2000s *Piracy and maritime terrorism grow in Asia and Africa.*

1990 In early example of "phantom ship" piracy, the *Marta* is hijacked en route to Korea, with pirates knowing all the details in advance about its whereabouts and cargo.

1991 *MV Naviluck* is attacked, ransacked and burned and the crew killed or thrown overboard on Jan. 12 — the first recorded modern piracy incident off Somalia. . . . Gen. Mohamed Siad Barre's dictatorship later collapses, triggering Somalia's "failed state" status and widespread piracy in the region.

1992 Oil tanker *Valiant Carrier* is attacked, sparking creation of the International Maritime Bureau's Piracy Reporting Centre. . . . Indonesia, Malaysia and Singapore begin anti-pirate patrols in Strait of Malacca; program is dropped due to cost.

1999 India captures and prosecutes hijackers of Japanese freighter *Alondra Rainbow*.

2000 Suicide bombers attack the *USS Cole* in Yemen, killing 17 sailors.

2002 In a post-9/11 security measure, President George W. Bush allows Navy to intercept merchant ships on high seas. . . . Al Qaeda suicide bombers damage the oil tanker *Limburg*, temporarily interrupting Gulf of Aden shipping.

2004 Terrorists bomb Philippine ferry, killing 116. . . . Singapore, Malaysia and Indonesia adopt coordinated anti-piracy policy.

2005 International Maritime Organization calls for action against piracy.

2006 Congress allows Pentagon to help other countries improve maritime security.

2008 Somali pirates seize French yacht *Le Ponant* and release the hostages; French commandos capture six of the pirates in the Djibouti desert (April 4). . . . Separatist attack forces Royal Dutch Shell to close its largest Nigerian offshore oil well (June 19). . . . Supertanker *Sirius Star* is hijacked near Kenya (Nov. 15). . . . Indian frigate destroys Somali pirate "mother ship" (Nov. 18). . . . U.N. authorizes all necessary measures to suppress Somali piracy (Dec. 16).

2009 International task force begins patrolling Gulf of Aden (Jan. 8), and capture more than 100 pirates in the first few months. . . . 17 nations adopt anti-piracy Code of Conduct (Jan. 29). . . . Capt. Richard Phillips of American freighter *Maersk Alabama* is taken hostage, freed by Navy sharpshooters off the Somali coast (April 8). . . . Pirate survivor of *Maersk Alabama* incident is indicted in New York (May 19). . . . International Maritime Bureau says pirates struck 240 times during first half of 2009 — more than double the rate in the same period of 2008 — with Somali pirates responsible for more than 60 percent of the attacks and 86 percent of the 561 hostages taken in 2009 (July 15). . . . Trials scheduled to resume in Yemen for more than 20 Somali

Countries Outsource Piracy Prosecutions

Western nations try pirates in Kenyan courts.

Francis Kadima has suddenly gotten very busy. The Kenyan defense attorney is taking on new clients by the dozen, brought to him by a variety of countries asking that Kenya become the venue of choice for Western countries wanting to bring captured pirates to trial.

Yemen has 30 alleged pirates awaiting trial in its courts, and Seychelles has 20, according to the International Maritime Organization. But Kenya has some 250 suspected pirates awaiting trial, sent there by the United Kingdom, United States and European Union. Those nations all signed memorandums of understanding offering Kenya — as one of Somalia's closest neighbors with a functioning judicial system — funding, computers and legal assistance if it would prosecute pirates.

Justice is being outsourced to Kenya largely because of the murkiness of the laws regarding piracy. According to maritime-law experts, under international law — including the U.N. Convention on the Law of the Sea — piracy is a universal crime and can be prosecuted by any country. However, because piracy had abated for centuries, few Western countries still have specific anti-piracy statutes on their books.

"In the majority of European Union states, piracy is not a crime," says Christina Gallach, an EU spokeswoman. "It's not in the criminal code anymore. It's something that happened many years ago."

Another obstacle: Pirates are jurisdictional orphans. Because of the multinational nature of global shipping, it is unclear who has jurisdiction to prosecute a pirate. For instance, if Somali pirates are captured in international waters by an Indian warship after they attacked a Panamanian-registered ship owned by a Japanese company and crewed by Filipinos, which country prosecutes the pirates?

Under current practice, the capturing country does the prosecuting. That's what India did in the scenario described above, when it caught pirates who had stolen goods from the *Alondra Rainbow* in 1999. But it's still a logistical and linguistic nightmare to bring foreign witnesses in to testify against foreign offenders. That's why several nations prefer to try the alleged pirates as close to the point of capture as possible, especially if the captor's home country has no anti-piracy statute.

Because of the legal limbo and logistical issues, many captured pirates are merely disarmed and released. Canadian and Dutch warships have caught pirates this year only to let them go, in what critics have mocked as "catch and release." "They can't stop us," Jama Ali, a pirate aboard a hijacked Ukrainian freighter, told *The New York Times* last December. "We know international law."[1]

"While nobody would advocate the ancient naval tradition of just making them walk the gangplank, equipment like GPS [receivers], weapons (and) ladders are often just tossed overboard and the pirates let go," said a Kenya-based diplomat.[2]

In fact, naval powers making up the combined international task force on piracy in the Gulf of Aden and Somalia have disarmed and released 121 pirates since it was established in January and turned 117 others over to Kenya for prosecution, U.S. Navy officials told Congress in March.

At one point the U.S. Navy held a piracy suspect for seven months because of confusion over where he would be prosecuted.[3]

And in the only modern piracy case being tried in the United States, an 18-year-old Somalians captured during the April attack on the *Maersk Alabama* was indicted in New York in May for piracy and conspiracy to seize a ship and take hostages. U.S. piracy laws are still on the books but haven't been used in 100 years. Once punishable by

"The Golden Age of Piracy . . . was conducted by a clique of 20 to 30 pirate commodores and a few thousand crewmen," writes journalist and author Colin Woodard.[37] Their trials and executions were highly public, with Captain Kidd's tarred body left to hang in a gibbet — an iron cage — over the Thames for years as a warning.

Barbary Piracy

About the same time, North Africa's Barbary corsairs — Muslim pirates and privateers who had long plagued the southern Mediterranean Sea — earned a special place in early U.S. naval history. In the late 1700s the pirates thought they had found easy pickings in merchant ships from the newly independent United States, which had lost the protection of the British Royal Navy. For years the Barbary pirates captured American ships and held the crews for ransoms and annual "tribute" payments from the U.S. government — just as they had traditionally extracted money from European governments. Signing treaties to buy off the pirates' state sponsors — Tripoli,

death, piracy has carried a mandatory life sentence in the United States since 1819.[4]

"It is a workable model," Pottengal Mukundan, director of the International Maritime Bureau, a London-based office of the International Chamber of Commerce, says of the Kenya prosecution contracts. He hopes to see more international arrangements to bring pirates to trial within the region, noting that countries such as China are not party to the agreements with Kenya.

Outsourcing piracy justice to Kenya, however, presents a major obstacle: Kenya's judicial system already has a backlog of 800,000 cases of all kinds in its courts. Suspects often spend a year or more in jail just waiting for a hearing.[5]

"What we would like to see is some measures coming from the International Maritime Organization or from the U.N., which allows for . . . all the countries with naval vessels in the region to hand over pirates for prosecutions to countries in the area," Munkundan says. "If the [navies] can't prosecute, then they might let them go or not pursue them with full vigor."

But Daniel Sekulich, a Canadian journalist and author of *Terror on the Seas*, says it's a mistake to outsource pirate justice. He prefers that nations update their laws and set up an international court.

"It is not going to result in the conviction of every captured suspect, but it is a reflection of the resolve of nations to not only dispatch warships but also prosecute suspects to the full extent of the law," he says.

The idea of an international court for piracy has received a fair amount of attention, but it remains controversial and would take years to implement. (*See "At Issue," p. 435*.)

In the interim, there are concerns that Kenya won't be able to handle the load. Aside from the heavy case backlog, there have been allegations that Kenya's courts are prone to corruption and questions about whether the country can provide western standards of due process.

"The problem is that Kenya itself cannot handle hundreds of pirate cases," Mukundan says, arguing for more

AFP/Getty Images/Tony Karumba

Suspected Somali pirates appear in court in Mombasa, Kenya, on April 23, 2009, after being apprehended by the French navy, which is part of Operation Atalanta, the EU anti-piracy effort.

international support. "It may grind down their own legal system." The critical question, then, is how much money and support rich nations will pour in to build judicial capacity there.

The fact that Kenya's parliament itself hasn't fully signed off on the international agreements is an issue Kadima has raised on behalf of his clients. "You can't just go around making up laws, you know," he said. "There is a process."[6]

---

[1] Jeffrey Gettleman, "Pirates in Skiffs Still Outmaneuvering Warships Off Somalia," *The New York Times*, Dec. 16, 2008, p. A6, www.nytimes.com/2008/12/16/world/africa/16pirate.html.

[2] Katharine Houreld and Mike Corder, "Navies ask: What do you do with a captured pirate?" The Associated Press, ABC News, April 17, 2009, http://abcnews.go.com/US/wireStory?id=7365467.

[3] Mike Corder, "Nations Look to Kenya as Venue for Piracy Trials," The Associated Press, April 17, 2009.

[4] Houreld and Corder, *op. cit.*

[5] *Ibid.*

[6] Jeffrey Gettleman, "Rounding Up Suspects, the West Turns to Kenya as Piracy Criminal Court," *The New York Times*, April 24, 2009, p. A8, www.nytimes.com/2009/04/24/world/africa/24kenya.html.

Tunis, Morocco and Algiers — was considered cheaper for the new country, still in debt from its Revolutionary War, than building its own navy.[38]

The ransoms and tributes prompted a debate that echoed today's controversy over whether paying ransom only encourages more piracy. Then-Ambassador to France Thomas Jefferson felt that paying ransom only invited more demands, so he tried to organize an international naval coalition to battle the pirates and their state sponsors.

"The states must see the rod," Jefferson wrote in an Aug. 18, 1786, letter to future president James Monroe, then a member of Congress. And in a letter to Yale College president Ezra Stiles, Jefferson wrote, "It will be more easy to raise ships and men to fight these pirates into reason, than money to bribe them."[39]

Although Jefferson was unable to establish a coalition, the payoffs were a blow to national pride. And in 1794, in response to Algerian seizures of American ships and crews, Congress appropriated $688,888 to build six frigates "adequate for the protection of the commerce of the United States against Algerian corsairs."[40]

After becoming president in 1801, Jefferson refused Tripoli's demands for $225,000, followed by annual payments of $25,000. Tripoli declared war, and the two Barbary Wars (1801-1805 and 1815-1816) ensued.

The first war involved a series of daring raids and bombardment of Tripoli. The turning point came in 1805, when a handful of U.S. Marines led 500 Greek, Arab and Berber mercenaries on a dramatic overland march across the desert from Alexandria, Egypt, to capture the Tripolitan city of Derna. When they raised the American flag in Derna, it was the first time the flag was raised in victory on foreign soil — an act memorialized in the "shores of Tripoli" line in the Marines' Hymn.

The Barbary nations were emboldened by the War of 1812, when the British chased U.S. ships from the Mediterranean. But eventually the Americans captured some Algerian ships, leading Algeria to foreswear further demands for tribute. In 1816, a massive bombardment of Algiers by an Anglo-Dutch fleet helped to end piracy in the Mediterranean.

Following their heyday, pirates were seen by some people as folk heroes. "Reason tells us that pirates were no more than common criminals, but we still see them as figures of romance," writes David Cordingly in *Under the Black Flag.*[41]

Part of that heroic image — at least to some — may have stemmed from the democratic way they ran their ships, unlike the navies of the time. Pirates elected their own captains and shared their booty according to set terms. "A hundred years before the French Revolution, the pirate companies were run on the lines in which liberty, equality and brotherhood were the rule rather than the exception," Cordingly writes.[42]

As piracy declined, the image of pirates as romantic buccaneers began to grow. In 1814, Lord Byron's poem "The Corsair" sold out seven editions in its first month of publication.[43] Pirates were further romanticized by novelists such as Walter Scott and Robert Louis Stevenson, whose *Treasure Island* in 1883 created the template for much pirate lore. (*See story, p. 434.*) In the 20th century, Hollywood also portrayed pirates as heroes — played by such romantic leading men as Errol Flynn, Douglas Fairbanks and Johnny Depp — whose playful portrayal of pirate Jack Sparrow in the "Pirates of the Caribbean" film series has grossed $2.7 billion worldwide for the Disney company.

Cold War's End

But portraying violent thieves as romantic or comedic characters was fundamentally misleading, argues author Murphy. It was "as if the period that began at the end of the 19th century, when piracy became a nursery story and later was thrown up on the silver screen, formed an impervious barrier through which the reality of maritime depredation could not seep into the modern era," he writes.[44]

In addition, he notes, the rise of sea power and the vast reach of Britain's Royal Navy led Westerners to believe by the early 20th century that piracy was obsolete.[45] "Piracy was seen as a problem out of history," with little relevance to the modern world, wrote Murphy.[46]

However, when the fall of the Soviet Union ended the Cold War, the super powers were no longer routinely patrolling the world's oceans. And merchant ships became more vulnerable as automation allowed shipowners to hire skeleton crews and rising fuel costs led to slower cruising speeds.

Meanwhile, modern pirates were gaining high-tech advantages, including satellite phones, GPS devices and faster fiberglass boats.

And, while piracy largely disappeared from the Atlantic and Mediterranean, it continued almost without interruption in Asia.

Asian Straits

Shih Fa-Hsien, a Buddhist monk from Sri Lanka, recorded cases of piracy in the Malacca Strait and South China Sea in 414 A.D. And 14th-century Moroccan traveler Ibn Battuta described being victimized by pirates off western India and commercial ships crossing the Indian Ocean in armed convoys for protection.[47]

"Slightly earlier," writes journalist Kaplan, "Marco Polo described many dozens of pirate vessels off Gujarat, India, where the pirates would spend the whole summer at sea with their women and children, even as they plundered merchant vessels."[48]

In the early 19th century, about 40,000 pirates on hundreds of junks dominated the South China Sea coastal waters. From 1807, they were led by Cheng I Sao — known as "Mrs. Cheng" — a former prostitute from Canton, who took command after her husband died. She enforced a stricter code than the West Indies pirates, with punishments including beheading for disobeying orders or stealing from the common treasury.

By 1809, she had amassed a fleet larger than most navies. The following year, the Chinese enlisted the help of Portuguese and British warships in their battle against the pirates. As it became clear that an all-out attack on piracy was imminent, Mrs. Cheng reportedly showed up unannounced at the governor-general's mansion in Canton — surrounded by women and children — to negotiate a peace settlement. The government allowed her to keep her plunder but executed some of her pirates while allowing others to join the Chinese army. Two days later, 17,382 pirates formally surrendered, and 226 junks were handed over to authorities.[49]

Although the large-scale threat was eliminated, local attacks remained a constant. In recent years, Chinese provincial officials were accused of being complicit in smuggling and theft, until the country's growing role in world trade led to an official crackdown in the 1990s.

But piracy remained acute in the strategic Strait of Malacca, where some 70,000 vessels each year transport half the world's oil and more than a third of its commerce, including supply ships heading to and from China and Japan.[50] Batam, an Indonesian island just across the Singapore Strait from Singapore, became a haven for criminals, including pirates.

In 1992, Indonesia, Malaysia and Singapore began aggressively patrolling the region, virtually eliminating piracy for a while. But due to the high cost, including air support and surveillance, they dropped the strategy after six months.[51]

By the early 2000s, the Malacca Strait was the world's piracy hot spot, giving rise to the brutal phenomenon of "phantom ship" piracy. Pirates would board vessels and kill or cast off the crews, stealing not just the cargo but the ships themselves. They would then repaint the ships and change their names and registries — creating "phantoms" that they used as mother ships.

By 2006, piracy in the region was so bad that many fishermen simply stayed home. Roughly half the 300 locals who fished off the coast of the Malaysian city of Melaka, for instance, refused to go out.[52]

To address the problem, the International Maritime Organization (IMO) instituted a unique ship-numbering system. Pirates also lost their markets for phantom ship

Crew members of the French tourist yacht Le Ponant prepare to board a French frigate after Somali pirates released them on April 11, 2008. The ship had been hijacked a week earlier in the Gulf of Aden. French commandos captured six of the pirates after the hostages were released.

AP Photo/French Defense Ministry

cargo when the Chinese government and customs agents began cracking down on the illicit trade. Equally important, smaller neighboring countries renewed their efforts at aggressive patrols after receiving prodding and funding from outside powers such as Japan and the United States.

Besides conducting joint patrols, the littoral states share data. Pirates who hijacked the tanker *MT Kraton* in September 2007 thought they could hide their deed by changing the ship's name to *Ratu*. But a new international database allowed Malaysian authorities to inform other countries about the name change. Using additional information from Singapore, the Indonesian navy intercepted the tanker off southern Johor and nabbed all 13 hijackers.[53]

According to the latest IMB annual report, there were only two pirate incidents in the Malacca Strait in 2008, down from 34 in 2004. And only 65 attacks occurred within all of Southeast Asia, compared with 187 in 2003. "If pirates here were to try a copycat attack like in Somalia, it won't be easy for them because the governments in this region won't hesitate to take action," said Noel Choong, head of the bureau's Malaysia-based Piracy Reporting Centre.[54]

Growth in Somalia

Most piracy experts agree that getting regional powers together to combat piracy around the Horn of Africa like they have in Southeast Asia won't happen anytime soon.

Romantic Pirate Lore Is Mostly Fiction

Aarrgh, but they did have parrots and peg legs.

By the early 19th century, piracy had been largely eliminated from the Atlantic and Mediterranean seas, but pirates lived on in the Western imagination as glamorous outlaws.

Like cowboys, pirates starred as highly romanticized heroes in movies and novels, such as Robert Louis Stevenson's 1883 classic, and heavily embroidered, *Treasure Island*. And as a result, much of what most people believe today about pirates isn't actually true.

"The effect of *Treasure Island* on our perception of pirates cannot be overestimated," writes David Cordingly, a former curator at England's National Maritime Museum. "Stevenson linked pirates forever with maps, black schooners, tropical islands and peg-legged seamen with parrots on their shoulders."[1]

Here's a brief guide to sorting out pirate fact and fiction:

- **Walking the plank — Myth.** Captain Hook may have planned to make the "Lost Boys" of J. M. Barrie's *Peter Pan* walk the plank, but real pirates rarely made time for such dastardly deeds. There is no mention of pirates making anyone walk the plank during the so-called Golden Age of Piracy, although an account from a later era survives. "However," writes Canadian journalist and author of a book about pirates Daniel Sekulich, "throwing individuals overboard is another thing altogether and a common enough occurrence in the annals of piracy."[2]
- **Treasure chests and maps — Myth.** Although 18th-century pirates certainly stole doubloons and pieces of eight when they could get them, their typical booty consisted of bales of silk and cotton, barrels of tobacco, spare sails, carpenters' tools and the occasional slave. And maps with an X marking the location of buried treasure were the invention of the illustrator of *Treasure Island*. Pirates usually spent their money in port on gambling, prostitutes and alcohol before they could bury it. The legend grew largely out of reports that Captain Kidd had buried gold and silver from a plundered ship near his home before he was arrested.

- **Peg legs, earrings and parrots — Fact.** "Pirates really did tie scarves or large handkerchiefs around their heads, and they did walk around armed to the teeth with pistols and cutlasses," Cordingly writes.[3] They also wore frock coats, which were typical of the Stuart period, when the Caribbean buccaneers were most active. Tricorn hats were also typical of the period, but skull-and-crossbones emblems were an embellishment added by Barrie in *Peter Pan*.

The common depiction of pirates wearing earrings is accurate. Many people at the time believed that wearing gold or silver in the earlobe improved eyesight or offered protection from drowning.[4] Expressions such as "Aarrgh," "avast" and "shiver me timbers" were part of the seafarers' vocabulary of the day.

As for the wooden legs and parrots, pirates were vulnerable to serious injury, and historical accounts describe several pirates who had lost limbs having replacements fitted by ship's carpenters. And seamen traveling in the tropics often picked up birds and animals as souvenirs. Parrots were popular because they commanded a good price in the London bird markets and were easier to keep on board than monkeys and other wild animals.

---

[1] David Cordingly, *Under the Black Flag* (1995), p. 7.
[2] Daniel Sekulich, *Terror on the Seas* (2009), p. 285.
[3] Cordingly, *op. cit.*, p. xiv.
[4] David Pickering, *Pirates* (2006), p. 160.

The IMO has been leading talks in the area for years, resulting in January in the adoption of a "code of conduct" by 17 nations regarding interdiction, investigation and prosecution of pirates, as well as the establishment of information and training centers.

But the lack of a functioning Somali government makes the country a "black hole," author Murphy says.

Coastal waters were already lawless before dictator Mohamed Siad Barre's regime collapsed in 1991. Reportedly the Somali National Movement — which eventually overthrew Barre — seized three ships as early as 1989.[55]

The first officially recorded modern Somali piracy incident, however, took place on Jan. 12, 1991, when

Should an international piracy court be established?

YES
Dr. Farish A. Noor
Peter Lehr
Lecturer, Terrorism Studies
University of St. Andrews, Scotland

Written for *CQ Global Researcher*, August 2009

Let's face it: Responding to piracy off the coast of Somalia took us quite a while. Now, relatively effective anti-piracy patrols have been established, acts of piracy foiled and scores of pirates arrested. But what should be done with them?

Most nations cannot legally try foreign nationals attacking crews and ships of another foreign country at a foreign location. In the absence of such laws, many pirates simply were disarmed and sent back to their own shores, in their own skiffs.

Since such a response to a serious crime is quite underwhelming, an agreement with Kenya was hastily cobbled together envisioning that pirates would have to stand trial in Mombasa and serve a prison sentence in a Kenyan prison — at least until the Somalian government could establish its own court. So, mission accomplished?

Legal experts in Germany and the Netherlands beg to differ. Since the 2007 post-election riots in Kenya, they point out, the Kenyan judiciary system has been overstretched, and, in any case, it does not meet Western standards. Thus, dumping Somali pirates on the already creaking Kenyan judicial system is hardly a long-term solution. And the Somalis do not have a monopoly on piracy — so an agreement with Kenya addresses only one part of global piracy.

Creating an international piracy tribunal would speed up proceedings and guarantee a fair and efficient trial matching Western standards. It would also solve jurisdictional problems that have marred too many piracy cases in the past.

The Netherlands and Russia are exploring the details of such a tribunal, and some German politicians suggest extending the brief of the Hamburg-based International Tribunal for the Law of the Sea (ITLOS). Hamburg has the facilities and experts for such trials and would thus be a good place.

Sentenced pirates could then serve their terms in states that have adopted the U.N. Convention on the Law of the Sea (which don't include the United States, by the way).

Setting up an international piracy tribunal will cost money, of course, but it's a better solution to a problem that won't go away any time soon. It is politically viable at the moment, and it most definitely is a much fairer solution in the long run than yet another quick fix in the shape of a kangaroo court.

NO
John Knott
Consultant
Holman Fenwick Willan LLP*
London, England

Written for *CQ Researcher*, July 9, 2009

Amid continuing pirate attacks off the coasts of Somalia and legal difficulties in prosecuting captured pirates, it is not surprising that an international piracy tribunal — similar to the International Criminal Court (ICC) at The Hague — has been proposed. While there are some superficial attractions in such a plan, an examination reveals it to be impractical.

Such tribunals take a long time to set up, are very expensive to run and their trials often last for years. The ICC was created by the Rome Statute of 1998 and took four years to become effective, when 60 states ratified it in 2002. That followed the many years it took to draft and negotiate the statute. Even so, the ICC does not include China, India, Russia or the United States. A solution is needed for dealing with Somali pirates that can be implemented much sooner.

A rather vague, hybrid proposal to establish a "regional tribunal" and "an international tribunal" in an unnamed country in the region was considered at a July 7 meeting at The Hague. But more focused, practical and simpler solutions are available.

For instance, the catchment area could be expanded for trials among the African and Arab nations that in January signed a regional Code of Conduct for repressing piracy. Early signatories were Djibouti, Ethiopia (the only non-coastal state), Kenya, Madagascar, the Maldives, the Seychelles, Somalia, Tanzania and Yemen. The code called for participating nations to review their legislation to ensure that adequate laws were in place to criminalize piracy and related crimes and that captured pirates would be treated with a degree of uniformity in the region.

To simplify prosecutions, law enforcement detachments from these countries could be stationed aboard warships operating in the region (under the auspices of NATO, the Combined Task Force 151 and Operation Atalanta) to serve as arresting officers and to ensure that a single legal system is applied throughout a pirate's captivity.

Another possibility: A Somali-constituted court could sit in another country (as did a Scottish court when dealing with the Lockerbie air disaster), and convicted pirates could be housed in special U.N.-funded piracy jails in Puntland and Somaliland. There would be clear advantages in encouraging Somalia to help solve its own problems in this way, while avoiding the need for an international court in any guise.

Copyright (c) John Knott, 2009

* The firm represented shipowners and underwriters in over 30 Somali hijacking cases last year.

United States Navy/SFC Eric L. Beauregard

A Singaporean Navy ship patrols Singapore harbor, which faces the busy Strait of Malacca. Half the world's oil supplies pass through the narrow strait, which until recently was a popular target of pirates. Officials fear the strategic waterway could become a target of terrorists seeking to cripple world shipping.

three boatloads of pirates attacked the Russian ship *MV Nauviluck*, killing three crew members and forcing the rest overboard. They were later rescued by a trawler.[56]

Somali piracy initially appealed to fishermen "fed up with the depletion of their fisheries" by big, foreign factory ships, says maritime security consultant Burnett, who served as a United Nations official in Somalia, in the 1990s. "The foreign fishing fleets were basically raping the Somali fishing grounds." Fishing within another country's territorial waters is illegal under international law but is a common problem off Africa's coasts.

"The foreign vessels gave no consideration to the welfare and future growth of the marine life," says Abdulkareem Jama, chief of staff for the newly elected Somali president, Sheikh Sharif Sheikh Ahmed.

The Somalis say Europeans were not only destroying their fishing grounds but were dumping a variety of toxic materials, including radioactive uranium, lead, cadmium and mercury and industrial, hospital and chemical wastes.

Somali regional administrators eventually authorized small groups of fishermen to capture and fine vessels caught illegally fishing or dumping wastes in Somali waters. "What started as law enforcement effort became a lucrative business for individuals and groups," says Jama. Soon, every ship that came near Somali waters was a target for ransom.

Some Somali pirates still fancy themselves as eco-warriors, guarding the coast for local fishermen and protecting it against international toxic-waste dumping.

But it's clear the area is now plagued by maritime criminals who are not above attacking ships bringing humanitarian food shipments to Somalia's starving millions.

The attacks — on everything from cruise ships and oil tankers to fishing vessels and container ships — began drawing serious attention from the world's great powers last year. Media attention and shipowners' pleas eventually triggered formation of an impressive armada — warships from NATO, the European Union, France, the United States, China, Russia, India and two-dozen other countries.

"All these powers are showing up for these guys with AK-47s and flip-flops," says Abukar Arman, a Somali journalist and activist based in Ohio.

CURRENT SITUATION

Organized Gangs

In the first six months of 2009, Somali pirates have been responsible for more than 60 percent of the world's attacks, 86 percent of the world's maritime hostage-takings and virtually all of the growth in piracy.[57]

The pirate gangs come alongside trawlers and merchant ships in fast-moving skiffs and scamper on board using ladders or grappling hooks. They are typically armed with rocket-propelled grenades and AK-47s. "All you need is three guys and a little boat, and the next day you're millionaires," said Adullahi Omar Qawden, a former captain in Somalia's long-defunct navy.[58]

Several pirate gangs operate in Somalia, undoubtedly with connections to politicians and organized criminal gangs. "Believe me, a lot of our money has gone straight into the government's pockets," Farah Ismail Eid, a captured pirate, told *The New York Times*.

He said his team typically gave 20 percent to their bosses and 30 percent to government officials, allocating 20 percent for future missions and keeping 30 percent for themselves.[59] Abdi Waheed Johar, director general of Puntland's fisheries and ports ministry, acknowledges that some government officials are working with the pirates.

When Somali pirates attacked the *MV Faina*, a Ukrainian ship carrying tanks and ammunition to Mombasa last September, "they knew the number of crew on board and even some names," says Somali journalist Arman. "These are illiterate people — they're being given information."

"Without any form of domestic law and order within Somalia, organized militia groups and pirate gangs have managed to fill this vacuum," says Sekulich, the Canadian journalist and author. "They have it all — command-and-control structures, logistics people, armories, financiers."

In a country with an average annual income of $600, pirates now drive the biggest cars, run many businesses and throw the best parties, sometimes with foreign bands brought in for the occasion. "Entire clans and coastal villages now survive off piracy," *The New York Times* reported in December, "with women baking bread for pirates, men and boys guarding hostages and others serving as scouts, gunmen, mechanics, accountants and skiff builders."[60]

Pirates are also the best customers for retailers. "They pay $20 for a $5 bottle of perfume," Leyla Ahmen, a shopkeeper in Xarardheere, a coastal Somali pirate hangout, told the *Times.*

The huge amounts of cash flooding northeastern Somalia have created serious inflation in the region and corrupts the morals of youths and women in the conservative Muslim society, says Somali presidential chief of staff Jama. "Young men started paying $100 for a cup of tea and telling the waiter to 'Keep the change,' " he explained. And some women have left their husbands for rich, young pirates. "These ill-gotten fast riches . . . are as damaging to the very fabric of the society onshore as it is damaging to international trade offshore."

While the pirates may move freely on land, their movements at sea are now being curtailed. The massive new international armada has captured dozens of pirates and deterred attacks on vessels carrying food aid. Stephen Mull, U.S. acting assistant secretary of State for political and military affairs, says nearly three times as many pirates were interdicted in the first four months of the year as in all of 2008. Under the new international agreements, many of the prisoners are now being sent to Kenya and other area countries for trial. (*See sidebar, p. 430.*)

But Burnett, author of *Dangerous Waters*, attributes the southwest monsoon season — which makes the water too rough for small boats — to a temporary reduction in piracy attacks this summer. The pirates will be back in force by October, he predicts.

Meanwhile, the United States recently sent 40 tons of weapons and ammunition to shore up Somalia's Transitional Federal Government (TFG) against the

A U.S. Navy SEAL trains Indonesian marines during joint anti-piracy exercises in 2006. Since Southeast Asian governments began coordinating their efforts in 2004, piracy has declined dramatically in the region.

AFP/Getty Images/Bay Ismoyo

Islamist al-Shabaab rebels who control much of southern Somalia. And the European Union is considering helping to train Somali police and create courts and other legal infrastructures.[61]

"We are not being utilized as much as we could be," Somali Prime Minister Omar Abdirashid Ali Sharmarke told the *Los Angeles Times* in April. "We need to fight pirates on land. We have information about how they function and who they are. The long-term objective should be to build institutions that will deal with pirates from inside the country."[62]

"The solution is easy if the will-power is there," says Jama. "If a team of 500 Somali soldiers are given special advanced training in, say, Djibouti or Uganda for three months and are given swift boats equipped with good firepower, GPS tracking and 10 helicopters, piracy can be eliminated or severely curtailed in 6 months.

AFP/Getty Images/Fred Vloo

Two dozen crew members were taken hostage when this Norwegian chemical tanker was hijacked off the Somali coast on March 26, 2009. Both the ship and crew were released on April 10 after a $2.6 million ransom was paid. Somali pirates are still holding 10 cargo ships.

"Only Somalis can deny pirates the land to use their ill-gotten loot," he continues. "The international community would be wise to try this solution with little to lose and much to gain. Insurance companies in the UK have offered to help fund a local solution. Other governments would be wise to join."

However, at the moment Sheikh Ahmed's fledgling government is fighting for its survival against foreign-funded extremists, Jama acknowledged.

The administration of President Sheikh Ahmed is the 16th government that has tried to control the country since the fall of Barre in 1991. And while the moderate cleric is regarded by many as one of the few men whose clan base and political skills might bring peace to the war-ravaged country, many foreign observers are skeptical about the TFG's chances of restoring law and order. Currently, the TFG only controls part of Mogadishu, the capital, and fighting breaks out there frequently.

Moreover, suggests terrorism lecturer Lehr of the University of St. Andrews, the summer lull in piracy due to the monsoon season has stalled momentum toward devising a regional anti-piracy strategy, which had garnered particular interest in nearby countries such as Oman and Saudi Arabia.

A better idea, Lehr says, would be to aid stable provincial governments in Puntland, a semi-autonomous region in northeastern Somalia — home to much of the

piracy problem — and neighboring Somaliland, a stable, democratically run state in northwestern Somalia that declared its independence in 1991. Although neither "republic" has received international recognition, they may be more capable of imposing law and order than the fragile central government in Mogadishu.

Puntland President Abdirahman Mohamed Farole may have been complicit in piracy at one time, says piracy author Murphy, of the Center for Strategic and Budgetary Assessments, but he now wants it stopped because the lawlessness and corruption could undermine his regime and make it more vulnerable to insurgencies such as al-Shabaab.

"The piracy is happening in Puntland, not Mogadishu," Murphy says. "We can't address it in Mogadishu." Puntland has already begun imposing 15- to 30-year prison sentences for piracy.

Supporting provincial efforts, Lehr says, "would be a much better option in the long run" and "would take the thunder out" of the Islamist movements, which denounce the presence of foreign navies offshore as Western militarism, he says.

"It would be cheaper and would regionalize the issue," he continues. "They should have a bigger interest in securing their own waters than we have."

Defensive Maneuvers

Although Somali pirates have garnered the most attention, piracy is a problem across the globe, from the Philippines to Peru. In West Africa, Nigerian rebel activity has spilled out of the Niger Delta into the Gulf of Guinea, where violent attacks on mariners occur almost weekly. Seaborne assaults on offshore oil facilities have cut Nigeria's oil exports by more than a quarter since 2006.[63]

In the Indian Ocean, pirates prey on Bangladeshi fishermen in the Ganges Delta and international ships anchored in Chittagong port in Bangladesh. And Somali pirates have extended their reach south along the East African coast to Kenya, Tanzania and the Seychelles.

Although worldwide piracy declined between 2003 and 2006, after Southeast Asian countries cracked down on regional piracy, it's been on the upswing since then, as pirates began ramping up activity in the Horn of Africa.[64] Maritime crimes largely stem from the inability of poor coastal nations to police their territorial waters.

As Murphy writes, "common piracy can be suppressed, or at least contained, by onshore police work supported by vigorous maritime patrolling."[65] But, he notes, the 1982 U.N. Law of the Sea Treaty gave countries greater jurisdiction over their territorial waters — extending jurisdiction 200 nautical miles out to sea, without regard to their ability to exercise authority over that expanded area. Shortly after the law was adopted, a Nigerian official said it "imposes on coastal states, regardless of their resources, an undue burden for providing security in long stretches of sea."[66]

While weak coastal states have allowed piracy to fester, the extent of the Somali piracy problem has forced larger nations to flex their naval muscles. Great Power politics are at work in the anti-piracy armada — a sort of dress rehearsal for further influence or combat in the Indian Ocean.

Japan, for instance, wants to escape the post-World War II constitutional constraints that limit its military posture to self-defense. On June 19, Japan's House of Representatives approved a bill authorizing the Self-Defense Forces to protect any commercial ships, regardless of nationality. Other countries, including China, are trying to determine which waters they may need to patrol to ensure oil shipments.

"They're learning the long-distance deployment ropes," says Murphy.

And the shipping industry is learning how better to defend itself. The International Maritime Organization now recommends ships stay at least 600 nautical miles off the coast of Somalia.

The U.S. Coast Guard issued new rules in May requiring U.S. ships plying pirate-infested waters to post lookouts and be ready to fend off pirates with water hoses and high-speed maneuvers.[67] "Anything over 14 or 15 knots tends to be fast, as far as the pirates are concerned," said Marcus Baker, managing director of the global marine practice at Marsh Ltd., an insurance broker in London.[68]

Many companies are fitting their ships with barbed wire and high-decibel long range acoustic devices — which are louder than standing behind a 747 jet during take-off and can be pointed at pirates up to 1,000 feet away. Some are stationing security guards on board for the most dangerous stretches of water.

"There's a bit of everything" being tried, says Wegener, the Norwegian Shipowners Association's security chief. "It does cost more, and so much more management time must be put into finding preventive measures."

A Somali fisherman hauls his catch to market in Mogadishu. Environmentalists and Somali officials say that after the government collapsed in 1991, foreign vessels illegally entered the country's territorial waters to exploit the rich fishing grounds or dump toxic wastes. Initially, the government encouraged Somali fishermen to collect fines from the foreign vessels, but those efforts soon morphed into full-blown piracy, the government says.

AP Photo/Mohamed Sheikh Nor

Most of the world's shippers — predominantly those with larger ships — are following "best practice" security guidelines, but smaller ships that account for two-thirds of the Somali attacks remain more vulnerable. "Shipping companies are also hit very hard by the economic downturn," says Lehr. "You can't make much money right now with cargo ships, so they're not very keen at throwing more money at security."

OUTLOOK
No Quick Fix

Although the recent surge in piracy has momentarily captured the world's attention, most maritime experts say sustained, concerted effort is needed over the long term.

"Piracy off the Horn of Africa is not a problem we will cure overnight, nor is there a single solution," Vice Admiral Winnefeld told the Senate Armed Services Committee in May.

Criminal activity that has long occurred on land in Somalia — kidnapping, roadblocks and violence — has migrated out to sea, so "something has to be done on land in Somalia," says Wegener. "They operate safe havens, and it's totally risk-free on the part of the pirates."

Although the Europeans and Americans recently have stepped up aid to Somalia, it remains to be seen whether external assistance will have much impact, given the long history of unsuccessful attempts to establish a functioning government.

Most observers expect it to take years for stability to come to Somalia. "That's a long-term endeavor, and a costly one," says RAND's Chalk.

"In Somalia, let us hope that in 10 years there is the beginning of some kind of solution ashore," says the International Maritime Bureau's Mukundan.

Somalia's internal problems create a particularly fertile breeding ground for maritime piracy, says Mukundan. So he doubts similar problems will arise elsewhere. But others aren't so sure.

"There is a risk of this being contagious, when criminals in other parts of the world see how profitable this can be," Wegener says.

For their part, the Somalis say if the international community were serious about halting piracy, foreign in the region would try to halt the illegal fishing or toxic dumping that triggered the upsurge in piracy in the first place. But that's not happening.

"It would be much cheaper to prevent these illegal activities and provide some basic support for the fishing villages and central government so they could deny the pirates land to operate from," says Somali presidential aide Jama.

It's also unclear how long the world's major powers will maintain their naval presence in the region. Historically, says Murphy — the author and Center for Strategic and Budgetary Assessments research fellow — it has taken decades to defeat piracy, using both political and economic measures.

Western nations must decide what level of piracy is tolerable. "None of the people I spoke to — shipping insiders, government officials, naval people — ever said that piracy could be completely eradicated," says author Sekulich. "The best you can do is to suppress and contain it. What's different now is a greater awareness of the economic impact that maritime piracy can have on the global community."

But if piracy is seen as mostly a nuisance, rich nations may decide it's not worth the expense to aggressively patrol for pirates. "Like most other crimes, piracy will not go away," says Ong-Webb, of the Centre for Defence and International Security Studies. "The question we need to answer is what levels of piracy we are prepared to live with."

It's important that the great powers continue to combat the problem, suggests Bainbridge of the International Transport Workers' Federation. "Piracy always has and always will be around," he says. "The trick is not to let the message out that it is easy and safe to do and highly profitable."

NOTES

1. Daniel Sekulich, *Terror on the Seas* (2009), p. 6.

2. www.eaglespeak.us/2009/04/somali-pirates-con voys-could-work.html.

3. "ICC-IMB Piracy and Armed Robbery Against Ships Report — Second Quarter 2009," ICC International Maritime Bureau, July 2009, pp. 5-6.

4. John S. Burnett, *Dangerous Waters* (2002), p. 9.

5. Sahal Abdulle and Rob Crilly, "Rich pickings for pirates hook fishermen," *The Times* (London), April 7, 2009, p. 33, www.timesonline.co.uk/tol/news/world/africa/article6045092.ece.

6. Sekulich, *op. cit.*, p. 80.

7. Elizabeth A. Kennedy, "Pirates Target, Vow to Kill U.S. Crews," The Associated Press, April 16, 2009, www.boston.com/news/world/africa/articles/2009/04/16/pirates_target_vow_to_kill_us_crews/.

8. "Over 5,000 pirates operate off Somali coast: Russian Navy," *Hindustan Times*, July 19, 2009, www.hindustantimes.com/StoryPage/StoryPage.aspx?sectionName=HomePage&id=adf76ecd-a7be-41ca-a08f-072def60b7e0&Headline='Over+5K+pirates+operate+off+Somali+coast.

9. Andy Crick, "Pirates," *The Sun* (England), June 8, 2009, p. 1, www.thesun.co.uk/sol/homepage/showbiz/tv/2468907/Ross-Kemps-yo-ho-no-go.html.

10. For background, see Jason McLure, "The Troubled Horn of Africa," *CQ Global Researcher*, June 2009, pp. 149-176.

11. "ICC-IMB Piracy and Armed Robbery Against Ships Report — Second Quarter 2009," *op. cit.*, p. 34.

12. Robert D. Kaplan, "Anarchy on Lands Means Piracy at Sea," *The New York Times*, April 12, 2009, p. WK9, www.nytimes.com/2009/04/12/opinion/12kaplan.html.

13. Ian Storey, "What's Behind Dramatic Drop in S-E Asian Piracy?" *The Straits Times* (Singapore), Jan. 19, 2009, http://app.mfa.gov.sg/pr/read_content.asp?View,11946,.

14. "Statement for the Record, Ms. Michèle Flournoy. Undersecretary of Defense (Policy) and Vice Admiral James A. Winnefeld, Director for Strategic Plans and Policy, Joint Chiefs of Staff," Senate Armed Services Committee, May 5, 2009, www.marad.dot.gov/documents/Flournoy-Winnefeld_05-05-09.pdf.

15. Katharine Houreld, "Navies ask: What do you do with a captured pirate?" The Associated Press, April 18, 2009, http://abcnews.go.com/US/wireStory?id=7365467.

16. His testimony is at http://foreign.senate.gov/testimony/2009/PhillipsTestimony090430p.pdf.

17. His testimony is at http://foreign.senate.gov/testimony/2009/ClanceyTestimony090430p.pdf.

18. Burnett, *op. cit.*, p. 85.

19. Peter Spiegel and Henry Chu, "Grappling With a Forgotten Scourge," *Los Angeles Times*, Nov. 20, 2008, p. A1, http://8.12.42.31/2008/nov/20/world/fg-highseas20.

20. Burnett, *op. cit.*, p. 88.

21. Lauren Ploch, *et al.*, "Piracy off the Horn of Africa," Congressional Research Service, April 21, 2009, p. 8, www.fas.org/sgp/crs/row/R40528.pdf.

22 Paul Alexander, "Boredom, Hunger and Fear for Pirates' Hostages," The Associated Press, April 19, 2009, http://abcnews.go.com/International/wireStory?id=7373830.

23. Ploch, *et al.*, *op. cit.*

24. Henry Samuel, "Pirates' Hostage 'Shot by French Rescuers,'" *The Daily Telegraph*, May 5, 2009, p. 15, www.telegraph.co.uk/news/worldnews/europe/france/5272730/French-skipper-held-hostage-by-pirates-shot-dead-by-special-forces.html.

25. "Trial of Somali pirates opens in Yemen," *RIA Novosti*, July 2, 2009, www.globalsecurity.org/military/library/news/2009/07/mil-090702-rianovosti05.htm.

26. Matthew Lynn, "Ignoring Piracy Poses Risk for World Economy," *Sydney Morning Herald*, Dec. 8, 2008, p. 45, www.bloomberg.com/apps/news?pid=newsarchive&sid=aRgDvDy5TQpU.

27. David Osler, "Preventing Piracy," *Lloyd's List*, May 28, 2009, p. 7.

28. Sharon Otterman, "Pirates Said to Ask for $25 Million Ransom," *The New York Times*, Nov. 20, 2008, www.nytimes.com/2008/11/21/world/africa/21pirates.html.

29. Mohamed Olad Hassan, "Five Pirates Drown With Share of $3 Million Ransom a Day After Freeing Saudi Tanker," The Associated Press, Jan. 10, 2009, www.cbsnews.com/stories/2009/01/10/world/main4711893.shtml.

30. Jean-Marc Mojon, "Ransom Payments: The Hole in Somali Pirates' Net," Agence France-Presse, Jan. 12, 2009, www.google.com/hostednews/afp/article/ALeqM5gGilBVHvFJS-ae2dlsyDb84aDiKg.

31. Burnett, *op. cit.*, p. 75.

32. Peter Earle, *The Pirate Wars* (2004), p. 20.

33. Sekulich, *op. cit.*, p. 33.

34. Martin P. Murphy, *Small Boats, Weak States, Dirty Money* (2009), p. 11.

35. David Cordingly, *Under the Black Flag* (1995), p. 203.

36. *Ibid.*, p. 277.

37. Colin Woodard, *The Republic of Pirates* (2007), p. 1.

38. Bill Weinberg, "Book Review: Jefferson's War: America's First War on Terror, 1801-1805," *Journal, Middle East Policy Council*, fall 2006, www.mepc.org/journal_vol13/0609_Weinberg2.asp.

39. Gerard W. Gawalt, "America and the Barbary Pirates: An International Battle Against an Unconventional Foe," The Thomas Jefferson Papers, Library of Congress, http://memory.loc.gov/ammem/collections/jefferson_papers/mtjprece.html.

40. Michael B. Oren, *Power, Faith and Fantasy* (2007), p. 35. Also see "Barbary Wars," U.S. Department of State, www.state.gov/r/pa/ho/time/jd/92068.htm.

41. Cordingly, *op. cit.*, p. xiii.

42 *Ibid.*, p. 96.

43. *Ibid.*, p. xx.

44. Murphy, p. 1.

45. *Ibid.*, p. 9.

46. *Ibid.*, p. 13.

47. *Ibid.*, p. 10.

48. Kaplan, *op. cit.*

49. Cordingly, *op. cit.*, p. 77.

50. Sean Yoong, "Pirate Abduction in Malacca Strait After Long Quiet," The Associated Press, Feb. 21, 2009, www.thejakartapost.com/news/2009/02/21/pirate-abduction-malacca-strait-after-long-quiet.html.

51. Murphy, *op. cit.*, p. 32.

52. Sekulich, *op. cit.*, p. 46.

53. K. C. Vijayan, "Data-Sharing System Boost for Malacca Strait Security," *The Straits Times* (Singapore), March 29, 2008, http://app.mfa.gov .sg/pr/read_content.asp?View,9678,.

54. Storey, *op. cit.*

55. See McLure, *op. cit.*

56. Murphy, *op. cit.*, p. 31.

57. "ICC-IMB Piracy and Armed Robbery Against Ships Report — Second Quarter 2009," *op. cit.*, p. 11.

58. Jeffrey Gettleman, "Somali's Pirates Flourish in a Lawless Nation," *The New York Times*, Oct. 31, 2008, p. A1, www.nytimes.com/2008/10/31/world/africa/31pirates.html.

59. *Ibid.*

60. Jeffrey Gettleman, "Pirates in Skiffs Still Outmaneuvering Warships Off Somalia," *The New York Times*, Dec. 16, 2008, p. A6, www.nytimes .com/2008/12/16/world/africa/16pirate.html.

61. Mary Beth Sheridan, "U.S. Has Sent 40 Tons of Munitions to Aid Somali Government," *The Washington Post*, June 27, 2009, p. A5, www.washington post.com/wp-dyn/content/article/2009/06/26/AR2009062604261.html.

62. Edmund Sanders, "Let Us Handle Pirates, Somalis Say," *Los Angeles Times*, April 15, 2009, p. A22, http://articles.latimes.com/2009/apr/15/world/fg-somalia-pirates15.

63. "A Clear and Present Danger," *The Economist*, April 18, 2009, www.economist.com/displaystory .cfm?story_id=13496711.

64. Peter Chalk, "The Maritime Dimension of International Security: Terrorism, Piracy and Challenges for the United States," RAND Corporation, 2008.

65. Murphy, *op. cit.*, p. 161.

66. *Ibid.*, p. 32.

67. "US Beefs Up Anti-Piracy Action for Ships," Agence France-Presse, May 13, 2009, www.blnz.com/news/2009/05/13/beefs_anti-piracy_action_ships_9407.html.

68. "Nigerian Pirates Blamed for Hike in Marine Premium," *Africa News*, June 30, 2009, http://allafrica.com/stories/200907010274.html.

BIBLIOGRAPHY

Books

Burnett, John S., *Dangerous Waters: Modern Piracy and Terror on the High Seas, Dutton,* **2002.**
After being robbed at sea, a former UPI reporter — now a marine security consultant — investigates the rise of modern piracy, talking with leading authorities and riding on board an oil tanker crossing the Indian Ocean.

Cordingly, David, *Under the Black Flag: The Romance and the Reality of Life Among the Pirates, Random House,* **1995.**
The former head of exhibitions at England's National Maritime Museum recounts the history of 17th- and 18th-century pirates and the legends they inspired.

Langewiesche, William, *The Outlaw Sea: A World of Freedom, Chaos, and Crime, North Point Press,* **2004.**
A writer for *The Atlantic* and *Vanity Fair* looks at the oceans post-9/11, finding that piracy and terror are symptomatic of the stateless, "inherently disorderly" nature of the seas, which are largely beyond the reach of nations and their laws.

Murphy, Martin N., *Small Boats, Weak States, Dirty Money: Piracy and Maritime Terrorism in the Modern World, Columbia University Press*, 2009.
A research fellow at King's College, London, thoroughly assesses piracy and terrorism, drawing careful distinctions between them but explaining how the two problems may overlap.

Sekulich, Daniel, *Terror on the Seas: True Tales of Modern-Day Pirates, Thomas Dunne Books*, 2009.
A Canadian journalist travels around the Indian Ocean, tracing the origins of contemporary piracy through interviews with experts and personal experiences.

Woodard, Colin, *The Republic of Pirates: Being the True and Surprising Story of the Caribbean Pirates and the Man Who Brought Them Down, Houghton Mifflin Harcourt*, 2007.
A journalist and author tells the story of the Caribbean pirates of the 18th century and the colonial governors and the former privateer who brought them to justice.

Articles

Alexander, Paul, "Boredom, Hunger and Fear for Pirates' Hostages," *The Associated Press*, April 19, 2009.
Hostages released by Somali pirates share accounts of fear and deprivation.

Bradsher, Keith, "Captain's Rescue Revives Debate Over Arming Crews," *The New York Times*, April 12, 2009, p. A8.
Amid growing calls for arming merchant ship crews against pirates, questions persist about whether it would escalate the level of violence.

Carney, Scott, "Cutthroat Capitalism," *Wired*, July 2009, www.wired.com/images/multimedia/magazine/1707/Wired1707_Cutthroat_Capitalism.pdf.
A graphics-heavy "economic analysis of the Somali pirate business model" examines the ratio of risk vs. rewards of attacking multiple ships when only a few pay off big. The package includes interviews with a pirate, a security contractor and a former hostage.

Gettleman, Jeffrey, "Rounding Up Suspects, the West Turns to Kenya as Piracy Criminal Court," *The New York Times*, April 24, 2009, p. A8.
Kenya will prosecute Somali pirates captured by the European Union, the United Kingdom and the United States.

Kaplan, Robert D., "Anarchy on Land Means Piracy at Sea," *The New York Times*, April 12, 2009, p. WK9.
Maritime piracy is a ripple effect of anarchy on land and could potentially serve as a platform for terrorism.

Storey, Ian, "What's Behind Dramatic Drop in S-E Asian Piracy," *The* [Singapore] *Straits Times*, Jan. 19, 2009.
Although worldwide piracy reached record levels in 2008, the number of regional incidents in Southeast Asia has dropped by two-thirds since 2003, thanks to improved security cooperation among Singapore, Indonesia and Malaysia.

Sudderuddin, Shuli, and Debbie Yong, "It's a Terrible Time to be a Seaman," *The* [Singapore] *Straits Times*, Nov. 23, 2008.
Seafarers describe being hijacked and held hostage by pirates.

Reports and Studies

Chalk, Peter, "The Maritime Dimension of International Security: Terrorism, Piracy and Challenges for the United States," *RAND Corporation*, 2008; available at www.rand.org/pubs/monographs/2008/RAND_MG697.pdf.
A policy analyst with the California think tank finds no nexus between maritime piracy and terrorism in the early years of this decade. Chalk does suggest, however, that the vulnerabilities that have encouraged piracy also apply to terrorism.

Ploch, Lauren, *et al.*, "Piracy off the Horn of Africa," *Congressional Research Service*, April 24, 2009, www.fas.org/sgp/crs/row/R40528.pdf.
The United Nations allows international ships to combat piracy in Somali waters, but anarchy in Somalia feeds the problem. U.S. officials pledge a more robust response.

For More Information

Congressional Research Service, 101 Independence Ave., S.E., Washington, DC 20540; (202) 707-7640; www.loc.gov. The research arm of the U.S. Congress that has produced detailed reports about maritime piracy and its effects on insurance.

International Maritime Bureau, 26 Wapping High Street, London E1W 1NG, United Kingdom; (44) 20 7423 6960; www.icc-ccs.org. A division of the International Chamber of Commerce that aims to identify and investigate fraud and other threats; manages the Piracy Reporting Centre in Kuala Lumpur, which issues warnings to shippers and reports pirate attacks to local law enforcement.

International Maritime Organization, 4, Albert Embankment, London SE1 7SR, United Kingdom; (44) 20 7735 7611; www.imo.org. A U.N. agency responsible for helping to improve the safety and security of international shipping.

International Shipping Federation, 12 Carthusian Street, London EC1M 6EZ, United Kingdom; (44) 20 7417 8844; www.marisec.org. The principal international shipowners organization.

International Transport Workers' Federation, 49-60 Borough Road, London, SE1 1DR, United Kingdom; (44) 20 7403 2733; www.itf.org.uk. A federation of 654 transport workers' unions, representing 4.5 million workers in 148 countries.

International Union of Marine Insurance, c/o Swiss Insurance Association, C.F. Meyer-Strasse 14, Postfach 4288, CH-8022 Zurich, Switzerland; (41) 1-208-2870; www.iumi.com. A professional association that provides a forum for exchanging information on issues of importance to the marine shipping and insurance sectors.

Nautilus International, 750-760 High Road, Leytonstone, London E11 3BB, United Kingdom; (44) 20 8989 6677; www.nautilusint.org. A union representing 25,000 seafarers and other workers employed by British and Dutch shipping companies.

RAND Corporation, 1776 Main Street, Santa Monica, CA 90401 USA; (310) 393-0411; www.rand.org. A think tank that has produced reports about piracy and maintains a comprehensive database of terrorism incidents worldwide.

Terrorism and the Internet

17

Should Web Sites That Promote Terrorism Be Shut Down?

Barbara Mantel

AP Photo/Ellis County Sheriff's Department

Hosam Maher Husein Smadi, a Jordanian teenager in the United States illegally, pleaded not guilty on Oct. 26 of trying to blow up a 60-story Dallas skyscraper. Smadi reportedly parked a vehicle in the building's garage on Sept. 24 hoping to detonate explosives with a cellphone. FBI agents, posing as al-Qaeda operatives, had been keeping tabs on Smadi after discovering him on an extremist Web site earlier this year where he stood out for "his vehement intention to actually conduct terror attacks in the United States."

From *CQ Researcher*, November 2009.

In March 2008 a participant on the pro al-Qaeda online forum ek-Is.org posted six training sessions for aspiring terrorists. The first was entitled: "Do you want to form a terror cell?" Using the name Shamil al-Baghdadi, the instructor described how to choose a leader, recruit members and select initial assassination targets. The second lesson outlined assassination techniques.[1]

"Although the first two training lessons often contain very basic instructions that may be less significant for experienced jihadis, they provide essential training for novices," said Abdul Hameed Bakier, a Jordanian terrorism expert who translated and summarized the training manual.[2]

The sessions then progressed to more sophisticated topics. Lesson three explained in more detail how to carry out assassinations, including: suicide attacks using booby-trapped vehicles or explosive belts; sniper attacks using Russian, Austrian and American rifles and direct attacks through strangling, poison and booby-trapped cellular phones.[3] Lesson four explained how to steal funds, and the final two lessons gave detailed instructions on how to conduct "quality terror attacks," including strikes against U.S. embassies.[4]

While this particular forum can no longer be accessed under its original domain name, Web sites controlled or operated by terrorist groups have multiplied dramatically over the past decade.

"We started 11 years ago and were monitoring 12 terrorist Web sites," says Gabriel Weimann, a professor of communication at Haifa University in Israel and a terrorism researcher. "Today we are monitoring more than 7,000."

Analysts say nearly every group designated as a foreign terrorist organization by the U.S. State Department now has an online presence, including Spain's Basque ETA movement, Peru's Shining Path, al Qaeda, the Real Irish Republican Army and others.[5] (*See list, p. 447.*)

The Internet appeals to terrorists for the same reasons it attracts everyone else: It's inexpensive, easily accessible, has little or no regulation, is interactive, allows for multimedia content and the potential audience is huge.[6] And it's anonymous.

"You can walk into an Internet café, enter a chat room or Web site, download instructions to make a bomb, and no one can find you," says Weimann. "They can trace you all the way down to the computer terminal, but by then you'll already be gone."

Terrorism on the Internet extends far beyond Web sites directly operated or controlled by terrorist organizations. Their supporters and sympathizers are increasingly taking advantage of all the tools available on the Web. "The proliferation of blogs has been exponential," says Sulastri Bte Osman, an analyst with the Civil and Internal Conflict Programme at Nanyang Technological University in Singapore. Just two years ago, Osman could find no extremist blogs in the two predominant languages of Indonesia and Malaysia; today she is monitoring 150.

The University of Arizona's "Dark Web" project, which tracks terrorist and extremist content in cyberspace, estimates there are roughly 50,000 such Web sites, discussion forums, chat rooms, blogs, Yahoo user groups, video-sharing sites, social networking sites and virtual worlds.[7] They help to distribute content — such as videos of beheadings and suicide attacks, speeches by terrorist leaders and training manuals — that may originate on just a few hundred sites.

Security experts say terrorist groups use the Internet for five general purposes:

- **Research and communication:** The Sept. 11, 2001, terrorists who attacked the World Trade Center and the Pentagon used the Internet to research flight schools, coordinate their actions through e-mail and gather flight information.[8]
- **Training:** Global Islamic Media Front, a propaganda arm of al Qaeda, issued a series of 19 training lessons in 2003 covering topics like security, physical training, weapons and explosives. The document was later found on a computer belonging to the terrorist cell responsible for the 2004 train bombings

in Madrid, Spain, that killed 191 people. But most material is posted by individuals who use the Internet as a training library.[9]

- **Fundraising:** In 1997 the rebel Tamil Tigers in Sri Lanka stole user IDs and passwords from faculty at Britain's Sheffield University and used the e-mail accounts to send out messages asking for donations.[10]
- **Media operations:** Before his death in 2006, Abu Musab al Zarqawi, the mastermind behind hundreds of bombings, kidnappings and killings in Iraq, posted gruesome videos of terrorist operations, tributes immortalizing suicide bombers and an Internet magazine offering religious justifications for his actions.[11]
- **Radicalization and recruitment:** In 2006, Illinois resident Derrick Shareef pleaded guilty to attempting to acquire explosives to blow up a mall in Rockford, Ill. Although not part of a terrorist organization, he was inspired in part by violent videos downloaded from a Web site linked to al Qaeda.[12]

The use of the Internet for recruitment and radicalization particularly worries some authorities. But experts disagree over the extent to which cyber content can radicalize and convert young men and women into homegrown supporters of — or participants in — terrorism.

The Internet is where "the gas meets the flame," says Evan F. Kohlmann, a senior investigator with the NEFA Foundation, a New York-based terrorism research organization.* "It provides the medium where would-be megalomaniacs can try and recruit deluded and angry young men . . . and magnify that anger to convince them to carry out acts of violence." The Internet replaces and broadens the traditional social networks of mosques and Arabic community centers, which have come under intense government scrutiny since 9/11, says Kohlmann.

A frequent expert witness in terrorism cases, Kohlmann says the Internet comes up in nearly every prosecution. For instance, Hamaad Munshi — a British national convicted in 2008 of possessing materials likely to be used for terrorism — participated in an online British extremist group that shared terrorist videos and used chat rooms to discuss its plans to fight overseas.[13] He was arrested at age 16.

The group's ringleader, then 22-year-old Aabid Khan, another Briton, used the chat rooms to incite Munshi to fight, Kohlmann says; the youth's grandfather also

---

* NEFA stands for "Nine Eleven Finding Answers."

Internet Offers Vast Potential for Spreading Terror

The Internet has opened global communication channels to anyone with computer access, creating a simple and cheap venue for spreading terrorist ideology. Interestingly, the regions with the largest concentrations of terrorist groups — the Middle East and Asia — have some of the lowest Internet usage rates. The highest rates are in developed countries, such as the United States, Canada, Australia and New Zealand.

World Internet Usage Rates, by Region

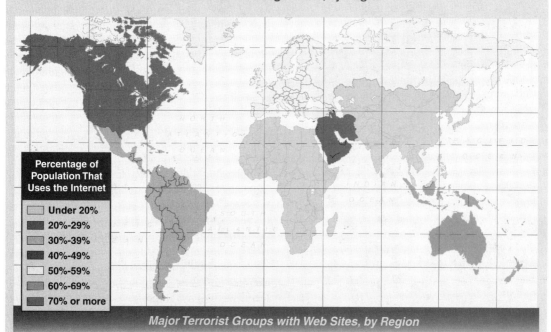

Percentage of Population That Uses the Internet

- Under 20%
- 20%-29%
- 30%-39%
- 40%-49%
- 50%-59%
- 60%-69%
- 70% or more

Major Terrorist Groups with Web Sites, by Region

Middle East: *Hamas, Lebanese Hezbollah, al-Aqsa Martyrs Brigades, Fatah Tanzim, Popular Front for the Liberation of Palestine, Palestinian Islamic Jihad, Kahane Lives Movement, People's Mujahidin of Iran, Kurdish Workers' Party, Popular Democratic Liberation Front Party, Great East Islamic Raiders Front*

Europe: *Basque Euskadi Ta Askatasuna, Armata Corsa, Real Irish Republican Army*

Latin America: *Tupac-Amaru, Shining Path, Colombian National Liberation Army, Armed Revolutionary Forces of Colombia, Zapatista National Liberation Army*

Asia: *Al Qaeda, Japanese Supreme Truth, Ansar al Islam, Japanese Red Army, Hizb-ul Mujahidin, Liberation Tigers of Tamil Eelam, Islamic Movement of Uzbekistan, Moro Islamic Liberation Front, Lashkar-e-Taiba, Chechnyan Rebel Movement*

Sources: "World Internet Penetration Rates by Geographic Region," Internet World Stats, June 30, 2009, www.internetworldststs.com/stats.htm; Gabriel Weimann, "Terror on the Internet," 2006

Terrorist Web Sites Have Proliferated

The number of Web sites run by terrorists or their supporters has grown since 1998 from a dozen to more than 7,000, with pro-jihad sites predominating, according to researcher Gabriel Weimann of Israel's Haifa University.

No. of Terrorist Web Sites

Source: Gabriel Weimann, Haifa University, Oct. 20, 2009

International Centre for the Study of Radicalisation and Political Violence at King's College in London. "In most cases, radicalization requires would-be terrorists to come in contact with social groups of people in the real world."

For instance, he pointed out, while much of Munshi's extremist activism took place online, "his radicalisation had been initiated in the 'real world.' " Through a friend at a local mosque, Munshi had met Khan, who spotted Munshi's computer expertise and groomed him to become a part of his online network. "It was the early meetings with Khan and some of his friends that helped turn a boy interested in religion into a young man dedicated to killing 'non-believers,' " according to Neumann.[15]

"There is anecdotal evidence out there, but no one has done a systematic study to show that radicalization via the Internet is a reality," says Maura Conway, a terrorism expert at Dublin City University in Ireland. Nevertheless, she adds, "governments are certainly acting as if radicalization through the Internet is possible, putting in place legislation that curbs how people can interact online."

As terrorists' presence on the Internet continues to grow, here are some of the questions being asked:

Should governments block terrorist Web sites?

Many of those who think the Internet is a major terrorist recruiting tool say authorities should simply shut down terrorists' sites.

Often the call comes from politicians. "It is shocking the government has failed to shut down a single Web site, even though Parliament gave them that power," Britain's opposition security minister, Baroness Pauline Neville-Jones, said last March. "This smacks of dangerous complacency and incompetence."[16]

In France, a minister for security said she wanted to stop terrorist propaganda on the Internet.[17] And a European Commission official called for a Europe-wide prohibition on Web sites that post bomb-making instructions.[18]

Although governments have shut down terrorist Web sites when they felt the information posted was too great a threat, some critics say such a move is legally complicated, logistically difficult and unwise.

Last year, three of the most important discussion forums used by Islamist terrorist groups disappeared from the Internet, including ek-Is.org, which had posted the six-part training manual. Jordanian terrorism expert

blamed the Internet. "This case demonstrates how a young, impressionable teenager can be groomed so easily through the Internet to associate with those whose views run contrary to true Muslim beliefs and values," Yakub Munshi said after the teen's conviction.[14]

But other researchers say online terrorism sites are largely about preaching to the choir and have limited influence on non-terrorists. "There has been very little evidence that the Internet has been the main or sole driver in radicalization," says Peter Neumann, director of the

Bakier says counterterrorism officials were so worried about the site that he "used to get requests from concerned agencies to translate the exact texts posted on ek-Is.org that were referenced in my articles. It was that serious."

"It is widely assumed that Western intelligence agencies were responsible for removing the three sites," and probably without the cooperation of the Internet service providers (ISPs) that host the sites, says Neumann, of King's College. "It would have required the cooperation of all the ISPs in the world," because those Web sites were not accessible at all, he explains. Instead, he thinks intelligence agencies may have launched so-called denial-of-service attacks against the sites, bombarding them with so many requests that they crashed. This September, one of the sites resurfaced; however, many experts believe it is a hoax.[19]

But government takedowns of terrorist sites — by whatever method — are not common, say many researchers. First, there are concerns about free speech.

"Who is going to decide who is a terrorist, who should be silenced and why?" asks Haifa University's Weimann. "Who is going to decide what kind of Web site should be removed? It can lead to political censorship."

Concern about free speech may be more acute in the United States than elsewhere. Current U.S. statutes make it a crime to provide "material support" — including expert advice or assistance — to organizations designated as terrorist groups by the State Department.[20] However, the First Amendment guarantee of free speech may trump the material support provisions.

"Exceptions to the First Amendment are fairly narrow" says Ian Ballon, an expert on Internet law practicing in California. "Child pornography is one, libelous or defamatory content another. There is no terrorism exception per se." Words that would incite violence are clearly an exception to the First Amendment, he says, "but there is a concept of immediacy, and most terrorism sites would not necessarily meet that requirement." A 1969 Supreme Court case, *Brandenburg v. Ohio*, held that the government cannot punish inflammatory speech unless it is inciting or likely to incite imminent lawless action.[21]

In Europe, where free-speech rights are more circumscribed than in the United States, the legal landscape varies. Spain, for instance, outlaws as incitement "the act of performing public ennoblement, praise and/or justification of a terrorist group, operative or act," explains

Tunisian Moez Garsallaoui, right, and his wife Malika El Aroud, the widow of an al-Qaeda suicide bomber, were convicted in Switzerland's first Internet terrorism trial of running pro-al-Qaeda Web sites that showed executions. Garsallaoui served three weeks in prison; El Aroud received no jail time. They are continuing their online work from Belgium, where El Aroud is described by Belgian State Security chief Alain Winants as a "leading" Internet jihadist.

British officials, including Prime Minister Gordon Brown, center right, visit a London cyber security firm on June 25 during the launch of a new government campaign to counter cyber criminals and terrorists.

Raphael Perl, head of the Action Against Terrorism Unit at the Organization for Security and Co-operation in Europe, a regional security organization with 56 member nations, based in Vienna, Austria. And the U.K. passed the Terrorism Acts of 2000 and 2006, which make it an

Southeast Asian Sites Now Espouse Violence

Extremist Web sites using the two main languages in Indonesia and Malaysia have evolved since 2006 from mostly propagandizing to providing firearm and bomb-making manuals and encouraging armed violence.

How the Sites Evolved

2006-July 2007	Posted al-Qaeda and Jemaah Islamiyah propaganda (videos, photographs, statements, etc.); articles about how Muslims are victimized and the necessity to fight back; celebrations of mujahidin victories; conspiracy theories; anger directed at the West; local grievances linked to global jihad; endorsements of highly selective Islamic doctrines
August 2007	First posting of manual on how to hack Web sites
February 2008	First posting of bomb-making manual and bomb-making video compilation in Arabic; emergence of a password-protected forum
April 2008	First posting of a firearm manual
Present	All of the above posted/available

Source: "Contents of Bahasa and Malay Language Radical and Extremist Web Sites, 2006 to 2009," in "Countering Internet Radicalisation in Southeast Asia," S. Rajaratnam School of International Studies, Singapore, and Australian Strategic Policy Institute, 2009

offense to collect, make or possess material that could be used in a terrorist act, such as bomb-making manuals and information about potential targets. The 2006 act also outlaws the encouragement or glorification of terrorism.[22] Human Rights Watch says the measure is unnecessary, overly broad and potentially chilling of free speech.[23]

Yet, it does not appear that governments are using their legal powers to shut down Web sites. "I haven't heard from any ISP in Europe so far that they have been asked by the police to take down terrorist pages," says Michael Rotert, vice president of the European Internet Service Providers Association (EuroISPA).

For one thing, says Rotert, there is no common, legal, Europe-wide definition of terrorism. "We are requesting a common definition," he says, "and then I think notice and takedown procedures could be discussed. But right now, such procedures only exist for child pornography."

But even if a European consensus existed on what constitutes terrorism, the Internet has no borders. If an ISP shuts down a site, it can migrate to another hosting service and even register under a new domain name.

Instead of shutting down sites, some governments are considering filtering them. Germany recently passed a filtering law aimed at blocking child pornography, which it says could be expanded to block sites that promote terrorist acts. And Australia is testing a filtering system for both child pornography and material that advocates terrorism.

The outcry in both countries, however, has been tremendous, both on technical grounds — filtering can slow down Internet speed — and civil liberties grounds. "Other countries using similar systems to monitor Internet traffic have blacklisted political critics," wrote an Australian newspaper columnist. "Is this really the direction we want our country to be heading? Communist China anyone? Burma? How about North Korea?"[24]

Ultimately, filtering just may not be that effective. Determined Internet users can easily circumvent a national filter and access banned material that is legal elsewhere. And filtering cannot capture the dynamic parts of the Internet: the chat rooms, video sharing sites and blogs, for instance.

Even some governments with established filtering laws seem reluctant to remove terrorist sites. The government owns Singapore's Internet providers and screens all Web sites for content viewed as " 'objectionable' or a potential threat to national security."[25] Yet Osman, of the Nanyang Technological University, says the government is not blocking Web sites that support terrorism. "I can still get access to many of them," she says, "so a lot of other people can, too."

In fact, counterterrorism officials around the world often prefer to monitor and infiltrate blogs, chat rooms, discussion forums and other Web sites where terrorists and sympathizers converse. If the sites remain active, they can be mined for intelligence.

"One reason [for not shutting down sites] is to take the temperature, to see whether the level of conversation is going up or down in terms of triggering an alert among security agencies," says Anthony Bergin, director of research at the Australian Strategic Policy Institute.

Another purpose is to disrupt terrorist attacks, says Bergin. Just recently, the violent postings of Texas resident Hosan Maher Husein Smadi to an extremist chat room attracted the attention of the FBI, which was monitoring the site. Agents set up a sting operation and arrested the 19-year-old Jordanian in late September after he allegedly tried to detonate what he thought was a bomb, provided by an undercover agent, in the parking garage beneath a Dallas skyscraper.[26]

Should Internet companies do more to stop terrorists' use of the Web?

Between 100 and 200 Web sites are the core "fountains of venom," says Yigal Carmon, president of the Middle East Media Research Institute, headquartered in Washington, D.C., with branch offices in Europe, Asia and the Middle East. "All the rest, are replication and duplication. You need to fight a few hundred sites, not thousands."

And many of these sites, he says, are hosted in the West. American hosting services, for instance, are often cheaper, have sufficient bandwidth to accommodate large video files and enjoy free-speech protection. But the companies often don't know they are hosting a site that, if not illegal, is perhaps violating their terms-of-service agreements.

Most Internet Service Providers, Web hosting companies, file-sharing sites and social networking sites have terms-of-service agreements that prohibit certain content. For instance, the Yahoo! Small Business Web hosting service states that users will not knowingly upload, post, e-mail, transmit or otherwise distribute any content that is "unlawful, harmful, threatening, abusive, harassing, tortious, defamatory, vulgar, obscene, libelous, invasive of another's privacy, hateful or racially, ethnically or otherwise objectionable."

It also specifically forbids users from utilizing the service to "provide material support or resources . . . to any organization(s) designated by the United States government as a foreign terrorist organization."

But Yahoo! also makes clear that it does not pre-screen content and that "You, and not Yahoo!, are entirely responsible for all Content that you upload, post, transmit, or otherwise make available."[27]

Some policy makers want Internet companies to begin screening the sites they host. Last year in the U.K., for instance, the House of Commons's Culture, Media and Sport Select Committee recommended that the "proactive review of content should be standard practice for sites hosting user-generated content."[28]

Internet companies, as well as civil libertarians and privacy advocates, disagree. "We do not think that ISPs should monitor anything since they are just in the business of transferring bits and bytes," says Rotert of EuroISPA. "We still believe in privacy laws."

David McClure, president and CEO of the U.S. Internet Industry Association, concurs. "If I'm a Web hoster, it is not my job to go snooping through the files and pages that people put on those Web sites," says McClure. "It's my job to keep the servers and the hosting service running." And, according to McClure, no U.S. law compels them to do more. Under the Telecommunications Act of 1996, McClure says, companies that host Web sites are not legally responsible for their content.

Still, ISPs and Web hosting companies do remove sites that violate their terms-of-service agreements, once they are aware of them. Since 9/11 a variety of private watchdog groups — like the SITE Intelligence Group and Internet Haganah — have made it their business to track jihadi Web sites.

Some anti-jihadist activists, like Aaron Weisburd — who created and runs Internet Haganah — have even contacted ISPs in an effort to shame them into taking down sites. Perhaps hundreds of sites have been removed with his help. "It is rare to find an Internet company that does not care or that actively supports the terrorist cause," he says.

Weisburd says some sites should be left online because they are good sources of intelligence, "while many other sites can — and arguably should — be taken down." He says the main reason to remove them is not to get them off the Internet permanently — which is extremely difficult to do — but to track individuals as they open new accounts in order to gather evidence and prosecute them.

Members of the Peruvian revolutionary movement Tupac Amaru flash victory signs after seizing the Japanese ambassador's residence in Lima in December 1996, along with hundreds of hostages. The morning after the seizure, the rebels launched a new era in terrorist media operations by posting a 100-page Web site, based in Germany. As the four-month siege dragged on, the group updated the site periodically, using a laptop and a satellite telephone. The hostages were eventually rescued in a raid by the Peruvian military.

But ISPs don't always follow through. "Even when you get a complaint about a Web site that may be violating the terms of service, many Web hosting services may be unlikely to pursue it," says McClure. Investigating complaints is time-consuming and expensive, he says, and "once you start pursuing each complaint, you are actively involved in monitoring, and the complaints will skyrocket."

To monitor how the big Internet platforms respond to user complaints, Neumann, of King's College, suggests forming an Internet Users Panel, which could name and shame companies that don't take users' complaints seriously. "We don't want the panel to be a government body," says Neumann. "We are proposing a body that consists of Internet users, Internet companies and experts." It could publicize best practices, he says, and act as an ombudsman of last resort. ISPs would fund the panel.

But Neumann's proposal does not sit well with the ISPs. "A lot of people propose that ISPs do a lot of things," says McClure, "and what they want is for ISPs to do a lot of work for nothing."

Carmon also objects to relying on ISPs and Web hosting companies to respond to user complaints. "It's a totally

untrustworthy system because you don't know who is making the complaint and why," Carmon says. "I issue a complaint against your Web site, but I may be settling an account against you, I may be your competitor in business." So ISPs must be very careful in evaluating complaints, which takes time, he says; ISPs don't want to be sued.

Instead, Carmon proposes creating what he calls a Civic Action Committee, based at an accredited research organization, which would monitor the Web and recommend sites that ISPs should consider closing. The committee would be made up of "intellectuals, writers, authors, people known for their moral standing, activists and legislators from different political parties," says Carmon.

Rotert is doubtful. "The ISPs in Europe would follow only government requests for notice and takedown procedures," he says, "because the ISPs know they cannot be held liable for destroying a business by taking down a site if the order came from the police."

Conway, of Dublin City University, has another objection to private policing of the Internet. "The capacity of private, political and economic actors to bypass the democratic process and to have materials they find politically objectionable erased from the Internet is a matter of concern," she said. Governments might want to consider legislation not just to regulate the Internet — "perhaps, for example, outlawing the posting and dissemination of beheading videos — but also writing into law more robust protections for radical political speech."[29]

Does cyberterrorism pose a serious threat?

Last year Pakistani President Asif Ali Zardari issued the following decree: "Whoever commits the offence of cyberterrorism and causes death of any person shall be punishable with death or imprisonment for life."[30]

In March India's cabinet secretary warned an international conference that cyber attacks and cyberterrorism are looming threats. "There could be attacks on critical infrastructure such as telecommunications, power distribution, transportation, financial services, essential public utility services and others," said K. M. Chandrasekhar. "The damage can range from a simple shutdown of a computer system to a complete paralysis of a significant portion of critical infrastructure in a specific region or even the control nerve centre of the entire infrastructure."[31]

Politicians, counterterrorism officials and security experts have made similarly gloomy predictions about cyberterrorism since 9/11 — and even before. But to date there have been no such attacks, although an ex-employee of a wastewater treatment plant in Australia used a computer and a radio transmitter to release sewage into parks and resort grounds in 2000.

Cyberterrorism is generally defined as highly damaging computer attacks by private individuals designed to generate terror and fear to achieve political or social goals. Thus, criminal hacking — no matter how damaging — conducted to extort money or for bragging rights is not considered cyberterrorism. (Criminal hacking is common. A year ago, for instance, criminals stole personal credit-card information from the computers of RBS WorldPay and then used the data to steal $9 million from 130 ATMs in 49 cities around the world.[32]) Likewise, the relatively minor denial-of-service attacks and Web defacements typically conducted by hackers aligned with terrorist groups also are not considered cyberterrorism.[33]

Skeptics say cyberterrorism poses only a slim threat, in part because it would lack the drama of a suicide attack or an airplane crash. "Let's say terrorists cause the lights to go out in New York City or Los Angeles, something that has already happened from weather conditions or human error," says Conway, of Dublin City University. "That is not going to create terror," she says, because those systems have been shown they can rapidly recover. Besides, she adds, terrorist groups tend to stick with what they know, which are physical attacks. "There is evolution but not sea changes in their tactics."

Even if terrorists wanted to launch a truly destructive and frightening cyber attack, their capabilities are very limited, says Irving Lachow, a senior research professor at the National Defense University in Washington, D.C. "They would need a multidisciplinary team of people to pull off a cyberterrorism attack," he says.

"A lot of these critical facilities are very complicated, and they have hundreds of systems," he continues. To blow up a power plant, for instance, a terrorist group would need an insider who knows which key computer systems are vulnerable, a team of experienced hackers to break into these systems, engineers who understand how the plant works so real damage can be done, a computer simulation lab to practice and lots of time, money and secrecy.

"At the end of the day, it's a lot easier just to blow something up," Lachow says.

But others fear that as governments continue to foil physical attacks, terrorists will expand their tactics to include cyberterrorism. Some analysts warn that terrorists could purchase the necessary expertise from cyber criminals. That, said Steven Bucci, IBM's lead researcher for cyber security, would be "a marriage made in Hell."[34]

According to Bucci, cybercrime is "a huge (and still expanding) industry that steals, cheats and extorts the equivalent of many billions of dollars every year." The most insidious threat, he said, comes from criminal syndicates that control huge botnets: worldwide networks of unwitting personal computers used for denial-of-service attacks, e-mail scams and distributing malicious software.[35]

The syndicates often rent their botnets to other criminals. Some analysts fear it's only a matter of time before a cash-rich terrorist group hires a botnet for its own use. "The cyber capabilities that the criminals could provide would in short order make any terrorist organization infinitely more dangerous and effective," said Bucci, and the permutations are "as endless as one's imagination." For example, terrorists could "open the valves at a chemical plant near a population center," replicating the deadly 1984 chemical accident in Bhopal, India.[36]

And a full-fledged cyberterrorism attack is not the only disturbing possibility, say Bucci and others. Perl at the Organization for Security and Co-operation believes terrorists are much more likely to use a cyber attack to amplify the destructive power of a physical attack. "One of the goals of terrorism is to create fear and panic," says Perl, "and not having full access to the Internet could greatly hamper governments' response to a series of massive, coordinated terrorist incidents." For example, terrorists might try to disable the emergency 911 system while blowing up embassies.

Some experts are particularly concerned that al Qaeda could launch a coordinated attack on key ports while simultaneously disabling their emergency-response systems, in order to immobilize the trade-dependant global economy. Al-Qaeda leaders have made it clear that destroying the industrialized world's economy is one of the group's goals.

But Dorothy Denning, a professor of conflict and cyberspace at the Naval Postgraduate School in Monterey, Calif., said, "Terrorists do not normally integrate

Governments Now Prosecute Suspected Online Terrorists

New laws apply to online activities.

Governments around the world have prosecuted suspected terrorists before they carry out acts of violence, but not many have been prosecuted solely for their alleged online activities in support of terrorism.

Those cases have been hampered by concerns about restricting free speech, the desire to monitor terrorist-linked sites for intelligence and the difficulty of identifying individuals online. Here are some examples of such cases:

Sami Al-Hussayen — A 34-year-old graduate student in computer science at the University of Idaho, Al-Hussayen was arrested in February 2003 and accused of designing, creating and maintaining Web sites that provided material support for terrorism. It was the U.S. government's first attempt at using statutes prohibiting material support for terrorism to prosecute activity that occurred exclusively online. The definition of "material support" used by the prosecutors had been expanded under the Patriot Act of 2001 to include "expert advice or assistance."

Al-Hussayen had volunteered to run Web sites for two Muslim charities and two Muslim clerics. But prosecutors alleged that messages and religious fatwas on the sites encouraged jihad, recruited terrorists and raised money for foreign terrorist groups. It didn't matter that Al-Hussayen had never committed a terrorist act or that he hadn't written the material. Prosecutors said it was enough to prove that he ran the Web sites and knew the messages existed.

Jurors were not convinced, however. They acquitted Al-Hussayen in June 2004. "There was no direct connection in the evidence they gave us — and we had boxes and boxes to go through — between Sami and terrorism," said one juror.[1]

The case attracted national attention, and according to University of Idaho law professor Alan Williams, "triggered a heated debate focused mainly on a key question: Were Al-Hussayen's Internet activities constitutionally protected free speech or did they cross the line into criminal and material support to terrorism?"[2]

The U.S. Supreme Court is scheduled to hear challenges to the material support statute — which critics complain is too vague — in two related cases this session.[3]

Younis Tsouli — In late 2005, British police arrested 22-year-old Tsouli, a Moroccan immigrant and student who prosecutors alleged was known online as "Irhaby 007" — or Terrorist 007. The government linked Tsouli and his accomplices Waseem Mughal and Tariq al-Daour to "the purchase, construction and maintenance of a large number of Web sites and Internet chat forums on which material was published which incited acts of terrorist murder, primarily in Iraq."[4]

Tsouli had been in active contact with al Qaeda in Iraq and was part of an online network that extended to Canada, the United States and Eastern Europe. In July 2007, Tsouli, Mughal and Al-Daour "became the first men to plead guilty to inciting murder for terrorist purposes" under the U.K.'s Terrorism Act of 2000.[5]

Samina Malik — In November 2007 the 23-year-old shop assistant became the first woman convicted of terrorism in the United Kingdom when she was found guilty of "possessing information of a kind likely to be useful to a person committing or preparing an act of terrorism."[6]

Malik had downloaded and saved on her hard drive *The Terrorist's Handbook*, *The Mujahideen Poisons Handbook* and other documents that appeared to support violent jihad.

multiple modes of attack." If coordinating cyber and physical attacks did become their goal, Denning would expect to see evidence of failed attempts, training, discussions and planning. "Given terrorists' capabilities today in the cyber domain, this seems no more imminent than other acts of cyberterror," she said. "At least in the near future, bombs remain a much larger threat than bytes."[37]

But that doesn't mean critical infrastructure is secure from cyber criminal syndicates or nation-states, which do have the technical know-how, funds and personnel to launch a damaging attack, Denning said. "Even if our critical infrastructures are not under imminent threat by terrorists seeking political and social objectives," she said, "they must be protected from harmful attacks conducted for other reasons, such as money, revenge, youthful curiosity and war."[38]

She had also written violent poems about killing nonbelievers. Her defense portrayed her as a confused young woman assuming a persona she thought was "cool."

Her conviction sparked public outrage. Muhammed Abdul Bari, secretary general of the Muslim Council of Britain, said, "Many young people download objectionable material from the Internet, but it seems if you are Muslim then this could lead to criminal charges, even if you have absolutely no intention to do harm to anyone else." An appeals court later overturned her conviction and clarified a new requirement that suspects must have a clear intent to engage in terrorism.[7]

Ibrahim Rashid — In 2007 German prosecutors charged the Iraqi Kurdish immigrant with waging a "virtual jihad" on the Internet. They argued that by posting al-Qaeda propaganda on chat rooms, Rashid was trying to recruit individuals to join al Qaeda and participate in jihad. It was Germany's first prosecution of an Islamic militant for circulating propaganda online.[8]

"This case underscores how thin the line is that Germany is walking in its efforts to aggressively target Islamic radicals," wrote Shawn Marie Boyne, a professor at Indiana University's law school. "While active membership in a terrorist organization is a crime . . . it is no longer a crime to merely sympathize with terrorist groups or to distribute propaganda."[9] Thus, the prosecution had to prove that Rashid's postings went beyond expressing sympathy and extended to recruiting. The court found him guilty in June 2008.

Saïd Namouh — On Oct. 1, the 36-year-old Moroccan resident of Quebec was convicted under Canada's Anti-Terrorism Act of four charges largely related to his online activities. In March 2007 he had helped publicize a video warning Germany and Austria that they would suffer a bomb attack if they didn't withdraw their troops from Afghanistan. He also distributed violent videos on behalf of Global Islamic Media Front, a propaganda arm of al Qaeda. Intercepted Internet chats revealed Namouh's plans to explode a truck bomb and die a martyr. "Terrorism is in

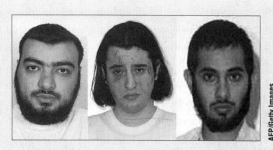

AFP/Getty Images

Tariq al-Daour, Younis Tsouli and Waseem Mughal (left to right), in 2007 became the first to plead guilty to inciting murder for terrorist purposes online under the U.K.'s Terrorism Act of 2000.

our blood, and with it we will drown the unjust," Namouh said online.[10]

— *Barbara Mantel*

[1] Maureen O'Hagan, "A terrorism case that went awry," seattletimes. com, Nov. 22, 2004, http://seattletimes.nwsource.com/html/local-news/2002097570_sami22m.html.

[2] Alan Williams, "Prosecuting Website Development Under the Material Support in Terrorism Statutes: Time to Fix What's Broken," *NYU Journal of Legislation & Public Policy*, 2008, p. 366.

[3] The cases are *Holder v. Humanitarian Law Project; Humanitarian Law Project v. Holder*, 08-1498; 09-89. See http://onthedocket.org/cases/2009.

[4] Elizabeth Renieris, "Combating Incitement to Terrorism on the Internet: Comparative Approaches in the United States and United Kingdom and the Need for an International Solution," *Vanderbilt Journal of Entertainment and Technology Law*, vol. 11:3:673, p. 698, 2009.

[5] *Ibid.*

[6] *Ibid.*

[7] *Ibid.*, pp. 699-700.

[8] Shawn Marie Boyne, "The Criminalization of Speech in an Age of Terror," working paper, June 12, 2009, p. 7, http://ssrn.com/abstract=1418496.

[9] *Ibid.*

[10] Graeme Hamilton, "Quebec terror plotter undone by online activities," *National Post*, Oct. 1, 2009, www.nationalpost.com/news/story .html?id=2054720.

BACKGROUND

Growth and Evolution

After seizing the Japanese embassy in Lima, Peru, on Dec. 17, 1996, the Tupac Amaru communist rebels "launched a new era in terrorist media operations," wrote Denning. The next morning the group had a Web site with more than 100 pages up and running out of

Germany, which it updated using a laptop and a satellite telephone.[39]

"For the first time, terrorists could bring their message to a world audience without mediation by the established press or interference by the government," Denning said. They could offer the first news accounts to the media, and they could use the Web site to communicate directly with their members and supporters. "The advantage the

CHRONOLOGY

1990s *Terrorist groups discover the Internet's usefulness for fundraising and publicity.*

1996 After seizing the Japanese embassy in Lima, Peruvian revolutionary movement Tupac Amaru creates a Web site to publicize its actions.

1997 Sri Lanka's Tamil Tigers use stolen Sheffield University faculty members' computer IDs and passwords to solicit donations.

1998 Researchers looking for online terrorism sites discover al Qaeda's Web site, www.alneda.com.

1999 Nearly all 30 U.S.-designated foreign terrorist organizations have an Internet presence.

2000-2005 *Extremist Web sites and discussion forums multiply; first prosecution of man accused of providing material online in support of terrorists fails.*

July 20, 2000 Terrorism Act of 2000 makes it illegal in the U.K. to collect, make or possess information likely to be used in terrorism.

2001 The 9/11 attackers use the Internet to research flight schools and flights and to coordinate their actions. On Oct. 26, 2001, President George W. Bush signs the USA Patriot Act, which prohibits "material support" for terrorists.

2003 Abdelaziz al-Muqrin, leader of al Qaeda in Saudi Arabia, pioneers several digital magazines, including *Sawt al-Jihad* (*The Voice of Jihad*).

2004 Video of the decapitation of kidnapped U.S. businessman Nicholas Berg is released on a Malaysian Web site. . . . University of Idaho graduate student Sami Omar al-Hussayen is acquitted of fostering terrorism online after his lawyers raise freedom of expression issues. Autobiography of Imam Samudra, mastermind of the 2002 Bali nightclub bombings that killed 202, promotes online credit-card fraud to raise funds. . . . Saudi Arabia launches the Sakinah Campaign, in which Islamic scholars steer religious questioners away from online extremists.

2005 YouTube, launched in February, quickly becomes repository for jihadist video content and commentary.

More than 4,000 Web sites connected to terrorist groups are on the Internet.

2006-Present *Governments reauthorize and expand antiterrorism laws; U.K. begins prosecuting those who use the Internet to "incite" others to commit terrorist acts.*

2006 President Bush reauthorizes Patriot Act. . . . U.K. passes Terrorism Act of 2006, outlawing encouragement or glorification of terrorism; civil libertarians raise concerns about free speech. . . . U.S. State Department creates Digital Outreach Team with two Arabic-speaking employees who converse online with critics of U.S. policies.

2007 EU police agency Europol begins "Check the Web" program, in which member states share in monitoring and evaluating terrorists' Web sites. . . . In July, U.K. resident Younis Tsouli pleads guilty to inciting terrorism after he and two associates used stolen credit cards to register Web site domains that promote terrorisim. . . . Samina Malik becomes the first woman convicted of terrorism in the U.K. for having documents that support violent jihad on her computer. A court of appeals later overturns her conviction, questioning her intent to engage in terrorism.

2008 Three important Islamist terrorist discussion forums disappear from the Internet; analysts assume counterterrorism agencies bombarded the sites with denial-of-service attacks. . . . On Nov. 6, Pakistan's president makes cyberterrorism punishable with death or life imprisonment. . . . In its first prosecution for promoting terrorism online, a German court finds Iraqi Kurdish immigrant Ibrahim Rashid guilty of waging a "virtual jihad" for attempting to recruit individuals online to join al Qaeda and participate in jihad.

2009 Canadian resident Saïd Namouh is convicted on Oct. 1 of planning terrorist acts and distributing jihadist propaganda via the Internet. . . . On Oct. 26 Jordanian teenager Hosam Maher Husein Smadi pleads not guilty of plotting to blow up a Dallas skyscraper on Sept. 24. FBI agents had been keeping tabs on Smadi after discovering him on an extremist Web site earlier this year. . . . Researchers are tracking more than 7,000 Web sites connected to terrorist groups and their supporters.

Web offered was immeasurable and recognized by terrorist groups worldwide."[40]

By the end of 1999, nearly all of the 30 organizations designated by the U.S. State Department as foreign terrorist organizations had a presence on the Internet. By 2005, there were more than 40 designated terrorist groups and more than 4,300 Web sites serving them and their supporters. Today, the number of such Web sites exceeds 7,000, according to Weimann, of Haifa University.[41]

Of these groups, Islamic terrorists have perhaps made the most use of the Internet. When al Qaeda suffered defeat in Afghanistan directly after 9/11, its recruiters in Europe "who had previously encouraged others to travel to mujahidin training camps in Afghanistan, Bosnia-Herzegovina and Chechnya began radically changing their message," wrote Kohlmann, of the NEFA Foundation. "Their new philosophy emphasized the individual nature and responsibility of jihad."[42] Recruits did not necessarily have to travel abroad; they could learn what they needed online.

Thus the Internet became a vital means for communication amid a global law enforcement clampdown on suspected terrorists.

Al Qaeda's first official Web site was the brainchild of a senior Saudi operative — and one-time Osama bin Laden bodyguard — Shaykh Youssef al-Ayyiri. The site contained audio and video clips of the al-Qaeda leader, justification for the 9/11 attacks and poetry glorifying the attackers and — on its English version — a message to the American people.[43]

After al-Ayyiri's 2003 death during a clash with Saudi security forces, his top lieutenant, Abdelaziz al-Muqrin, took control. He was a "firm believer in using the Web to disseminate everything from firsthand accounts of terrorist operations to detailed instructions on how to capture or kill Western tourists and diplomats," according to Kohlmann. Before he was killed by Saudi forces in 2004, al-Muqrin created several digital magazines, including *Sawt al-Jihad*, or *The Voice of Jihad*. The author of an article in its inaugural issue told readers, "The blood [of the infidels] is like the blood of a dog and nothing more."[44]

While al Qaeda's Saudi Arabian network pioneered the use of online publications, Kohlmann said, "The modern revolution in the terrorist video market has occurred in the context of the war in Iraq and under the watchful eye of Jordanian national Abu Musab al-Zarqawi." Until his death in 2006, Zarqawi led al Qaeda in Iraq and was known for "his penchant for and glorification of extreme violence

— particularly hostage beheadings and suicide bombings," many of them captured on video, including the murder of American civilian contractor Nicholas Berg.[45]

"Images of orange-clad hostages became a headline-news staple around the world — and the full, raw videos of their murders spread rapidly around the Web."[46]

Content on militant Islamist Web sites in Southeast Asia tends to "mimic the contents and features of their Arabic and Middle Eastern online counterparts," according to a study from the Australian Strategic Policy Institute. "Although they aren't yet on par in operational coordination and tradecraft, they are catching up."[47]

Between 2006 and July 2007, extremist content on radical Bahasa Indonesia (the official language of Indonesia) and Malay language Web sites consisted of propaganda from al Qaeda and the Indonesian jihadist group Jemaah Islamiyah. The sites celebrated mujahidin victories, aired local grievances linked to the global jihad and posted highly selective Koranic verses used to justify acts of terror. In August 2007, one of the first postings of instructions on computer hacking appeared, and in the first four months of 2008 the first bomb-making manual, bomb-making video and a password-protected forum emerged.[48] (*See box, p. 450.*)

Not all terrorist organizations use the Internet to showcase violence. Many, such as FARC (Revolutionary Armed Forces of Colombia), focus on human rights and peace. "In contrast to al Qaeda's shadowy, dynamic, versatile and often vicious Web sites," wrote Weimann, "the FARC sites are more 'transparent,' stable and mainly focused on information and publicity."

Established in 1964 as the military wing of the Colombian Communist Party, FARC has been responsible for kidnappings, bombings and hijackings and funds its operations through narcotics trafficking.[49] Yet there are no violent videos of these attacks. Instead, FARC Web sites offer information on the organization's history and laws, its reasons for resistance, offenses perpetrated by the Colombian and U.S. governments, life as a FARC member and women and culture. Weimann called the sophisticated FARC Web sites "an impressive example of media-savvy Internet use by a terrorist group."[50]

From Web 1.0 to 2.0

Terrorist content can now be found on all parts of the Internet, not just on official sites of groups like FARC and al Qaeda and their proxies. Chat rooms, blogs, social

'Terrorists Are Trying to Attract Young Recruits'

An interview with the director of the Dark Web project.

The University of Arizona's Dark Web project, funded by the National Science Foundation, studies international terrorism using automated computer programs. The project has amassed one of the world's largest databases on extremist/ terrorist-generated Internet content. Author Barbara Mantel recently interviewed Hsinchun Chen, the project's director.

CQ: What is the purpose of Dark Web?

HC: We examine who terrorists talk to, what kind of information they disseminate, what kind of new violent ideas they have, what kind of illegal activities they plan to conduct. We're looking at Web sites, forums, chat rooms, blogs, social networking sites, videos and virtual worlds.

CQ: How difficult is it to find terrorist content on the Web?

HC: From Google you can find some, but you won't be able to get into the sites that are more relevant, more intense and more violent.

CQ: So how do sympathizers find these sites?

HC: Typically people are introduced by word of mouth, offline. And there are different degrees of openness on these sites.

CQ: For example?

HC: There are many sites that require an introduction; they may require a password; moderators may also ask a series of questions to see if you are from the region, if you are real and if you are in their targeted audience.

CQ: How does the Dark Web project find these sites?

HC: We have been collaborating for six or seven years with many terrorism study centers all around the world, and they have been monitoring these sites for some time. So they know how to access these Web sites and whether they are legitimate forums. But most of them do not have the ability to collect all the content; they can do manual review and analysis.

So these researchers will give us the URLs of these sites, and they'll give us the user names and passwords they've been using to gain access. Once we get this information, we load it into our computer program, and the computers will spit out every single page of that site and download that into our database.

CQ: How much material are we talking about?

HC: The researchers we work with can analyze maybe hundreds or thousands of pages or messages, but we collect and analyze maybe half a million to 10 million pages easily.

CQ: How do you know that a site is actually linked to a terrorist group or supporter?

HC: Remember we start off with the URLs that terrorism researchers think are important. We also do "crawling" to find new sites. Any Web site will have links to other sites, and by triangulating those links from legitimate sites, we can locate other legitimate sites.

CQ: After finding the content, do you analyze it?

HC: Our claim to fame is analysis. We have techniques that look at social network linkages, that categorize the content into propaganda, training, recruiting, etc., and techniques that determine the sophistication of Web sites. We have a technique that looks at the extent of the violent sentiment in these sites and techniques that can determine authorship.

---

networking sites and user groups allow conversation and debate among a wide variety of participants.

"Yahoo! has become one of al Qaeda's most significant ideological bases of operations," wrote researchers Rita Katz and Josh Devon in 2003. "Creating a Yahoo! Group is free, quick and extremely easy. . . . Very often, the groups contain the latest links to jihadist Web sites, serving as a jihadist directory."[51] A Yahoo! user group is a hybrid between an electronic mailing list and a discussion forum. Members can receive posted messages and photos through e-mail or view the posts at the group's Web site.

While much of the original content on the terrorist-linked sites was text-based, videos began to play a much larger role after 2003, especially for militant Islamist organizations and their supporters. "Nevertheless, much of this video content remained quite difficult to access for Westerners and others, as it was located on Arabic-only Web sites" that were often frequently changing domain names and were therefore used "only by those who were strongly committed to gaining access," according to a study co-authored by Conway, of Dublin City University.[52]

CQ: None of this is done manually?

HC: Everything I talk about — almost 90 percent — is entirely automated.

CQ: What trends you are noticing?

HC: I'm not a terrorism researcher, but there are trends that we observe on the technology end. Terrorists are trying to attract young recruits, so they like to use discussion forums and YouTube, where the content is more multi-media and more of a two-way conversation. We also see many home-grown groups cropping up all over the world.

CQ: Do you share this information with government agencies?

HC: Many agencies — I cannot name them — and researchers from many countries are using the Dark Web forum portal.

CQ: How does the portal work?

HC: There is a consensus among terrorism researchers that discussion forums are the richest source of content, especially the forums that attract sometimes 50,000 members to 100,000 members. So we have created this portal that contains the contents from close to 20 different, important forums. And these are in English, Arabic and French. The French ones are found in North Africa.

We also embedded a lot of search, translation and analysis mechanisms in the portal. So now any analyst can use the content to see trends. For example, they can see what are the discussions about improvised explosive devices in Afghanistan, or they can look at who are the members that are interested in weapons of mass destruction.

CQ: Are these forums mostly extremist jihadi forums?

HC: Yes, they are. That's what analysts are primarily interested in. We are also creating another portal for multimedia content that will be available in another month or two. That would contain material from YouTube, for instance.

Hsinchun Chen oversees the University of Arizona's Dark Web project, which analyzes terrorists' online activities.

CQ: Do you collect information from U.S. extremist sites?

HC: We collect from animal-liberation groups, Aryan Nation and militia groups, but that is just for our research purposes. We don't make it available to outsiders. Government lawyers advise us against giving that kind of information out to them or to the outside world. It's a civil liberty issue.

CQ: Even if that material is open source material, available to anyone who finds their Web site?

HC: Even if it is open source.

But the advent of YouTube in 2005 changed the situation dramatically, Conway wrote, playing an increasing role in distributing terrorist content. Not only did YouTube become an immediate repository for large amounts of jihadist video content, but the social-networking aspects of the site allowed a dialogue between posters and viewers of videos.[53]

Terrorists-linked groups also have used mass e-mailings to reach broad audiences, according to Denning. "The Jihadist Cyber-Attack Brigade, for example, announced in May 2008 they had successfully sent 26,000 e-mails to 'citizens of the Gulf and Arab countries explaining the words of our leader Usama Bin Ladin.'"[54]

Terrorists and Cybercrime

Terrorists increasingly have turned to the Internet to raise funds, often through cybercrime. "We should be extremely concerned about the scope of the credit-card fraud problem involving terrorists," according to Dennis Lormel, a retired special agent in the FBI. Although there is "limited or no empirical data to gauge the extent

Political Change Is Main Attack Motivation

Four out of six types of cyber attacks or threats are politically motivated. Attackers typically use "malware," or malicious software that spreads viruses, or denial-of-service attacks to disrupt Web sites of individuals, companies, governments and other targets.

Cyber Threat	Motivation	Target	Method
Cyberterror	Political or social change	Innocent victims	Computer-based violence or destruction
Hacktivism*	Political or social change	Decision-makers or innocent victims	Web page defacements or denial of service
Black Hat Hacking**	Ego, personal enmity	Individuals, companies, governments	Malware, viruses, worms or hacking
Cybercrime	Economic gain	Individuals, companies	Malware for fraud or identity theft; denial of service for blackmail
Cyber Espionage	Economic or political gain	Individuals, companies, governments	Range of techniques
Information War	Political or military gain	Infrastructures, information-technology systems and data (private or public)	Range of techniques

Hacking to promote an activist's political ideology.

** *Hacking just for the challenge, bragging rights or due to a personal vendetta.*

Source: Franklin D. Kramer, Stuart H. Starr and Larry Wentz, eds., "Cyber Threats: Defining Terms," Cyberpower and National Security (2009)

of the problem . . . there are compelling signs that an epidemic permeates," he wrote.[55]

In his jailhouse autobiography, Imam Samudra — convicted of masterminding the 2002 nightclub bombings in Bali, Indonesia, that killed 202 people — includes a rudimentary outline of how to commit online credit-card fraud, or "carding."

"If you succeed at hacking and get into carding, be ready to make more money within three to six hours than the income of a policeman in six months," Samudra writes. "But don't do it just for the sake of money." Their main duty, he tells readers, is to raise arms against infidels, "especially now the United States and its allies."[56] Although Samudra's laptop revealed an attempt at carding, it's not clear he ever succeeded.

But others have. Younis Tsouli, a young Moroccan immigrant in London who made contact with al Qaeda online, and two associates used computer viruses and stolen credit-card accounts to set up a network of communication forums and Web sites that hosted "everything from tutorials on computer hacking and bomb making to videos of beheadings and suicide bombing attacks in Iraq," said Lormel.[57]

The three hackers ran up $3.5 million in charges to register more than 180 Web site domains at 95 different Web hosting companies and purchased hundreds of prepaid cellphones and more than 250 airline tickets. They also laundered money through online gaming sites.[58]

Even though both Samudra and Tsouli are in jail, "they left their successful tradecraft on Web pages and in chat rooms for aspiring terrorists to learn and grow from," noted Lormel.[59]

CURRENT SITUATION

Alternative Voices

Western governments and terrorism experts are concerned that the United States and other nations are not providing a counter message to online militant Islamists.

"The militant Islamist message on the Internet cannot be censored, but it can be challenged," says Johnny Ryan, a senior researcher at the Institute of International and European Affairs in Dublin, Ireland. But governments and societies, he says, for the most part, have ceded the dialogue in cyberspace to extremists, who are highly skilled at crafting their message.

That message "is mostly emotional," according to Frank Cilluffo, director of the Homeland Security Policy Institute at The George Washington University in Washington, D.C. It "uses images, visuals and music to tell a powerful story with clear-cut heroes and villains."

Societies interested in countering that message should not shy away from emotion either, he argues. "Who are the victims of al Qaeda?" Cilluffo asks, "and why don't we know their stories?" Western and Arab-Muslim media rarely reveal victims' names unless they are famous or foreign, he points out. Personal stories about victims "from the World Trade Center to the weddings, funerals, schools, mosques and hotels where suicide bombers have brought untold grief to thousands of families, tribes and communities throughout the Muslim world" could be told in online social networks, he suggested, "creating a Facebook of the bereaved that crosses borders and cultures."[60]

Raising doubts is "another powerful rhetorical weapon," says Ryan, who suggests exploiting the chat rooms and discussion forums frequented by prospective militants and sympathizers. Moderate Islamic voices should question the legitimacy of al Qaeda's offensive jihad, disseminate the arguments of Muslim scholars who renounce violence and challenge militant Islamists' version of historical relations between the West and Islam, according to Ryan.[61]

The U.S. Department of State has begun its own modest online effort. In November 2006 it created a Digital Outreach Team with two Arabic-speaking employees. The team now has 10 members who actively engage in conversations on Arabic-, Persian- and Urdu-language Internet sites, including blogs, news sites and discussion forums. Team members identify themselves as State Department employees, but instead of posting dry,

The Top 10 Jihadi Web Forums

The most influential jihadi online forums serve as virtual community centers for al Qaeda and other Islamic extremists, according to Internet Haganah — an online network dedicated to combating global jihad. Jihadi Web addresses, which are often blocked, change frequently.

 al-Faloja

Highly respected among terrorists; focuses on the Iraq War and the Salafi-jihadi struggle.

 al-Medad

Was associated with Abu Jihad al-Masri, the al-Qaeda propaganda chief killed in a U.S. missile strike in Pakistan on Oct. 30, 2008; disseminates Salafi-jihadi ideology.

 al-Shouaraa

Originally named el-Shouraa, it was blocked, but later reemerged with a new name; has North African influences; no longer active.

 Ana al-Muslm

Very active; was used by al Qaeda to communicate with Abu Musab al-Zarqawi (Osama bin Laden's deputy in Iraq) until he was killed by U.S. forces in 2006.

 al-Ma'ark

Has been slowly and steadily building an online following in recent years.

 al-Shamukh

Successor to al-Mohajrun, a militant Islamic organization that was banned in the U.K. in 2005; provides radio broadcasts.

 as-Ansar

Features English and German invitation-only spin-off sites; a favorite among Western jihadists.

 al-Mujahideen

Attracts a strong contingent of Hamas supporters, with an overall global jihad perspective; especially focused on electronic jihad.

 al-Hanein

Has a significant amount of jihadi content tinged by Iraqi, Egyptian and Moroccan nationalism.

 at-Tahaddi

Sunni jihadist; recruits from Somali, Taliban and other terrorist groups.

Source: "Top Ten List of Jihadi Forums," Internet Haganah, a project of The Society for Internet Research, Aug. 3, 2009, http://internethaganah .com/harchives/006545. html; Jamestown Foundation

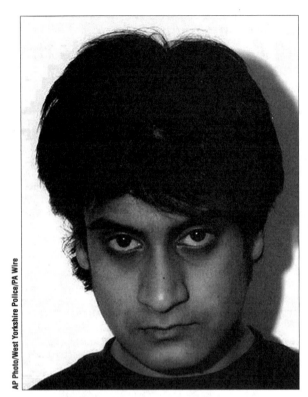

Hamaad Munshi — a British national convicted in 2008 of possessing materials likely to be used for terrorism — was 16 when he was arrested after participating in an online British extremist group. The trial revealed that Munshi had downloaded details on how to make napalm and grenades and wished to become a martyr by fighting abroad.

policy pronouncements they create "engaging, informal personas for [their] online discussions." The team's mission is "to explain U.S. foreign policy and to counter misinformation," according to the State Department.[62]

No one knows the full impact of the team's efforts, but the project has come in for criticism. "They should be larger," says Matt Armstrong, an analyst and government advisor who writes a blog on public diplomacy at mountainrunner.us, "and they should be coordinated to a much greater degree with the production side of the State Department." The team's Internet conversations should directly shape a post on the State Department Web site or on its radio program, he says.

But Duncan MacInnes, principal deputy coordinator at the State Department's Bureau of International Information Programs, says the scale of the Digital Outreach Team is about right, although it could use one or two more Persian speakers and possibly expand into more languages. "Having too many people blogging in a fairly small blogosphere would raise our profile, and we felt [it] would create a reaction against us. You don't want to overdo it." Also, he says, the team does not work in isolation. It writes a biweekly report about the issues, concerns and misunderstandings members encounter online, which goes to hundreds of people inside the State Department.

Others question whether the government should be the one to hold this dialogue. "The state is not in a position to be the primary actor here because it lacks credibility in online forums," says Ryan.

"The best approach is to provide young people with the information and the intellectual tools to challenge this material themselves on various Web forums," says Bergin, of the Australian Strategic Policy Institute. "It's got to be provided by stakeholders in the Muslim community themselves, from community workers, religious figures and parents."

The Sakinah Campaign

Many terrorism analysts cite Saudi Arabia's Sakinah Campaign as a model program. Internet use in the kingdom has grown rapidly since access first became available there 10 years ago. Since 2000, the kingdom's total number of Internet users has risen from roughly 200,000 to more than 7 million today, out of an overall population of nearly 29 million.[63]

Meanwhile, extremist Web sites in the kingdom have multiplied from 15 sites in 1998 to several thousand today, even though the Saudi government controls Internet access and blocks sites featuring gambling, pornography and drug and alcohol use, according to Christopher Boucek, a researcher at the Carnegie Endowment for International Peace. Extremist sites "often appear faster than they can be identified and blocked," said Boucek.[64]

Responding to that trend, the Sakinah Campaign since 2004 has used volunteer Islamic scholars "to interact online with individuals looking for religious knowledge, with the aim of steering them away from extremist sources." These scholars have "highly developed understandings of extremist ideologies, including the religious interpretations used

Is cyberterrorism a significant global threat?

YES

Mohd Noor Amin
Chairman, International Multilateral Partnership Against Cyber Threats Selangor, Malaysia

Written for *CQ Global Researcher*, November 2009

Alarm bells on cyberterrorism have been sounding for more than a decade, and yet, hacktivism aside, the world still has not witnessed a devastating cyber attack on critical infrastructure. Nothing has occurred that caused massive damage, injuries and fatalities resulting in widespread chaos, fear and panic. Does that mean the warnings were exaggerated?

On the contrary, the convergence of impassioned politics, hacktivism trends and extremists' growing technological sophistication suggests that the threat of cyberterrorism remains significant — if not more urgent — today. Although hacktivists and terrorists have not yet successfully collaborated to bring a country to its knees, there is already significant overlap between them. Computer-savvy extremists have been sharpening their skills by defacing and hacking into Web sites and training others to do so online. Given the public ambitions of groups like al Qaeda to launch cyber attacks, it would be folly to ignore the threat of a major cyber assault if highly skilled hackers and terrorists did conspire to brew a perfect storm.

Experts are particularly concerned that terrorists could learn how to deliver a simultaneous one-two blow: executing a mass, physical attack while incapacitating the emergency services or electricity grids to neutralize rescue efforts. The scenario may not be so far-fetched, judging from past cyber attacks or attempts, although a certain level of technical skill and access would be needed to paralyze part of a nation's critical infrastructure. However, as shown by an oft-cited 2000 incident in Australia, a single, disgruntled former employee hacked into a wastewater management facility's computer system and released hundreds of thousands of gallons of raw sewage onto Sunshine Coast resort grounds and a canal.

Vital industrial facilities are not impenetrable to cyber attacks and, if left inadequately secured, terrorists and hackers could wreak havoc. Similarly, the 2008 cyber attacks that caused multicity power outages around the world underscore the vulnerabilities of public utilities, particularly as these systems become connected to open networks to boost economies of scale.

If this past decade of terrorist attacks has demonstrated the high literacy level, technological capability and zeal of terrorists, the next generation of terrorists growing up in an increasingly digitized and connected world may hold even greater potential for cyberterrorism. After all, if it is possible to effect visibly spectacular, catastrophic destruction from afar and still remain anonymous, why not carry it out?

NO

Tim Stevens
Associate, Centre for Science and Security Studies, King's College London

Written for *CQ Global Researcher*, November 2009

Cyberterrorism is the threat and reality of unlawful attacks against computer networks and data by an individual or a non-governmental group to further a political agenda. Such attacks can cause casualties and deaths through spectacular incidents, such as plane crashes or industrial explosions, or secondary consequences, such as crippled economies or disrupted emergency services.

We have seen many attempts to disrupt the online assets of governments, industry and individuals, but these have mercifully not yet caused the mass casualties predicted by the term "cyberterrorism." The assumption that terrorists might use cyberspace in such attacks is not in question, but the potential threat that cyberterrorism poses is accorded disproportionate weight in some circles.

Cyberterrorism resulting in civilian deaths is certainly one possible outcome of the convergence of technology and political aggression. That it has not happened yet is a function of two factors. First, the ongoing vigilance and operational sophistication of national security agencies have ensured that critical infrastructure systems have remained largely unbreached and secure. And second, like all self-styled revolutionaries, terrorists talk a good talk.

Although a terrorist group might possess both the intent and the skill-sets — either in-house, or "rented" — there is little evidence yet that any group has harnessed both to serious effect. Most attacks characterized as "cyberterrorism" so far have amounted to mere annoyances, such as Web site defacements, service disruptions and low-level cyber "skirmishing" — nonviolent responses to political situations, rather than actions aimed at reaping notoriety in flesh and blood.

It would be foolish, however, to dismiss the threat of cyberterrorism. It would also be disingenuous to overstate it. Western governments are making strides towards comprehensive cyber security strategies that encompass a wide range of possible scenarios, while trying to overcome agency jurisdictional issues, private-sector wariness and the fact that civilian computer systems are now seen as "strategic national assets."

As it becomes harder to understand the complexities of network traffic, identify attack vectors, attribute responsibility and react accordingly, we must pursue integrated national and international strategies that criminalize the sorts of offensive attacks that might constitute cyberterrorism. But designating the attacks as terrorism is a taxonomic firewall we should avoid.

to justify violence and terrorism," according to Boucek.[65] The campaign is officially an independent, nongovernmental project, even though several government ministries encourage and support it.

According to Abdullah Ansary, a lawyer and former lecturer at King Abdul-Aziz University in Saudi Arabia, al Qaeda has issued several statements over the Internet cautioning their followers not to engage in dialogues with members of the Sakinah Campaign, a sign that the campaign is having an impact on al Qaeda's membership.[66] The campaign itself periodically releases the number of people it says it has turned away from extremism. In January 2008, it announced it had "convinced some 877 individuals (722 male and 155 female) to reject their radical ideology across more than 1,500 extremists Web sites."[67]

But in 2007, after the government arrested members of seven terrorist cells operating in the kingdom, several columnists complained that the Sakinah Campaign and other government supported programs trying to reform extremists were ineffective and not getting to the root of the problem. According to translations from the Middle East Media Research Institute, columnist Abdallah bin Bajad Al-'Utaibi wrote in the Saudi daily *Al-Riyadh*: "There are schoolteachers, imams in the mosques, preachers and jurisprudents who do nothing but spread hatred and *takfir** in our society. They should be prosecuted for their actions, which lay down the foundations for terrorism."[68]

Ansary said the government must make wider reforms if it wants to prevent young people from turning to extremism. The government must "speed up the process of political reform in the country, widening popular participation in the political process, improving communication channels of both the government and the public, creating effective communication among branches of government, continuing the efforts in overhauling the Saudi educational system and boosting the role of women in the society."[69]

In late 2006, the Sakinah Campaign expanded its role and created its own Web site designed to "serve as a central location for people to turn to online with questions about Islam."[70]

Government-funded Sites

Similar Web sites have been set up in other countries to offer alternative messages to terrorist propaganda.

---

* *Takfir* is the act of identifying someone as an unbeliever.

The Islamic Religious Council of Singapore — the country's supreme Islamic authority, whose members are appointed by the country's president — has several interactive Web sites to counter extremist strands of Islam. The sites feature articles, blogs and documentary videos targeted at young people and host an online forum where religious scholars answer questions about Islam. One site specifically challenges the ideology of Jemaah Islamiyah, the jihadist group responsible for the deadly 2002 nightclub bombing in Bali and the July 2009 bombings of the Marriott and Ritz Carlton hotels in Jakarta. The organization wants to establish a pan-Islamic theocratic state across much of Southeast Asia.[71]

But the effectiveness of such sites is difficult to gauge. "To a certain extent it is helping to drown out extremist voices online," says Osman, of Nanyang Technological University in Singapore, "but for those who are actively seeking extremist ideology, these kinds of Web sites don't appeal to them."

A similar project in the United Kingdom also meets with skepticism. On its Web site, the Radical Middle Way calls itself "a revolutionary grassroots initiative aimed at articulating a relevant mainstream understanding of Islam that is dynamic, proactive and relevant to young British Muslims."[72] It rejects all forms of terrorism, and its site has blogs, discussions, videos, news and a schedule of its events in the U.K. Its two dozen supporters and partners are mostly Muslim organizations as well as the British Home Office, which oversees immigration, passports, drug policy and counterterrorism, among other things.

"We are arguing that this is not money well spent," says Neumann of King's College. "The kind of money the government is putting into the Web site is enormous, and the site doesn't attract that much traffic."

The government money has also caused at least some young people to question the group's credibility. One blogger called the group "the radical wrong way" and wrote that "because the funding source is so well known, large segments of alienated British Muslims will not have anything to do with this group. . . . If anything, such tactics will lead to even further alienation of young British Muslims — who will rightly point out that this kind of U.S./U.K.-funded version of Islam is just another strategy in the ongoing war on Islam."[73]

Neumann and Bergin recommend instead that governments give out many small grants to different Muslim organizations with ideas for Web sites and see if any can grow to significance without dependence on government funds.

In the end, individual governments' direct role in providing an online alternative narrative to terrorist ideology may, out of necessity, be quite small because of the credibility issue, say analysts. Instead, they say, governments could fund Internet literacy programs that discuss hate propaganda, adjust school curriculums to include greater discussion of Islam and the West and encourage moderate Muslim voices to take to the Web. Cilluffo, of the Homeland Security Policy Institute, said the United Nations could lead the way, sponsoring a network of Web sites, publications and television programming.

"The United Nations can and should play a significant role," Cilluffo said, "bringing together victims to help meet their material needs and raising awareness by providing platforms through which to share their stories."[74]

OUTLOOK
Pooling Resources

Web sites that promote terrorism are here to stay, although governments and Internet companies will occasionally shut one down if it violates the law or a terms-of-service agreement. Such decisions can only be reached after prolonged monitoring and "must weigh the intelligence value against the security risk posed by the Web site," says Jordanian terrorism expert Bakier.

But monitoring the thousands of Web sites, discussion forums, chat rooms, blogs and other open sources of the Web requires trained personnel with expertise in the languages, cultures, belief systems, political grievances and organizational structures of the terrorist groups online. Because such personnel are scarce, most experts agree that nations should pool their resources. "It is hardly possible for one individual member state to cover all suspicious terrorism-related activities on the Internet," according to a European Union (EU) report.[75]

Good intentions aren't enough. "There are lots of conferences, lots of declarations, lots of papers, but in reality, you have different counterterrorism agencies not sharing information, competing, afraid of each other, sometimes in the same state and also across borders," says Haifa University's Weimann.

Above, an Internet café in Sydney. Many Australians oppose government plans to build what critics call the Great Aussie Firewall — a mandatory Internet filter that would block at least 1,300 Web sites prohibited by the government.

Europol, the EU police agency, began a program in 2007 called Check the Web, which encourages member nations to share in monitoring and evaluating open sources on the Web that promote or support terrorism. The online portal allows member nations to post contact information for monitoring experts; links to Web sites they are monitoring; announcements by the terrorist organizations they are tracking; evaluations of the sites being monitored and additional information like the possibility of legal action against a Web site.

Weimann, who calls the program a "very good idea and very important," says he cannot directly evaluate its progress, since access is restricted to a handful of counterterrorism officials in each member nation. But he does speak to counterterrorism experts at workshops and conferences, where he hears that "international cooperation — especially in Europe — is more theoretical than practical."

When asked if barriers exist to such cooperation, Dublin City University's Conway says, "Emphatically, yes! These range from protection-of-institutional-turf issues — on both a national and EU-wide basis — to potential legal constraints." For instance, she says, some member states' police are unsure whether or not they need a court order to monitor and participate in a Web forum without identifying themselves. Others disagree about the definition of a terrorist and what kinds of sites should be watched.

These barriers may not be the program's only problem. "It might be a disadvantage that so far just EU countries participate," according to Katharina von Knop, a professor of international politics at the University of the Armed Forces, in Munich, Germany, thus limiting the expertise available.[76]

NOTES

1. Abdul Hameed Bakier, "An Online Terrorist Training Manual — Part One: Creating a Terrorist Cell," Terrorism Focus, vol. 5, no. 13, The Jamestown Foundation, April 1, 2008. The ek-Is.org Web site has also gone under various other names, including ekhlass.org.

2. Ibid.

3. Bakier, op. cit., "Part Two: Assassinations and Robberies," vol. 5, no. 14, April 9, 2008.

4. Bakier, op. cit., "Part Three: Striking U.S. Embassies," vol. 5, no. 15, April 16, 2008.

5. Gabriel Weimann, Terror on the Internet, United States Institute of Peace Press (2006), p. 51.

6. Ibid., p. 30.

7. University of Arizona, "Artificial Intelligence Lab Dark Web Project," www.icadl.org/research/terror/.

8. "The 9/11 Commission Report," www.9-11commission.gov/report/index.htm.

9. Anne Stenersen, "The Internet: A virtual training camp?" Norwegian Defense Research Establishment, Oct. 26, 2007, p. 3, www.mil.no/multimedia/archive/00101/Anne_Stenersen_Manu_101280a.pdf.

10. Dorothy Denning, "Terror's Web: How the Internet Is Transforming Terrorism," Handbook on Internet Crime, 2009, p. 19, http://faculty.nps.edu/dedennin/publications/Denning-TerrorsWeb.pdf.

11. Ibid., p. 4.

12. "Violent Islamic Extremism, the Internet, and the Homegrown Terrorist Threat," U.S. Senate Committee on Homeland Security and Governmental Affairs, May 8, 2008, pp. 2, 13, http://hsgac.senate.gov/public/_files/IslamistReport.pdf.

13. "Safeguarding Online: Explaining the Risk Posed by Violent Extremism," Office of Security and Counter Terrorism, Home Office, Aug. 10, 2009, p. 2, http:// security.homeoffice.gov.uk/news-publications/publication-search/general/Officers-esafety-leaflet-v5.pdf?view=Binary.

14. Ibid.

15. Peter Neumann and Tim Stevens, "Countering Online Radicalisation: A Strategy for Action," The International Centre for the Study of Radicalisation and Political Violence, Kings College London, 2009, p. 14, www.icsr.info/news/attachments/1236768445ICSROnlineRadicalisationReport.pdf.

16. Clodagh Hartley, "Govt Can't Stop 'Web of Terror,'" The Sun (England), March 20, 2009, p. 2.

17. "Interview given by Mme. Michèle Alliot-Marie, French Minister of the Interior, to Le Figaro," French Embassy, Feb 1, 2008, www.ambafrance-uk.org/Michele-Alliot-Marie-on-combating.html.

18. Greg Goth, "Terror on the Internet: A Complex Issue, and Getting Harder," IEEE Computer Society, March 2008, www2.computer.org/portal/web/csdl/doi/10.1109/MDSO.2008.11.

19. Howard Altman, "Al Qaeda's Web Revival," The Daily Beast, Oct. 2, 2009, www.thedailybeast.com/blogs-and-stories/2009-10-02/is-this-al-qaedas-website.

20. Gregory McNeal, "Cyber Embargo: Countering the Internet Jihad," Case Western Reserve Journal of International Law, vol. 39, no. 3, 2007-08, p. 792.

21. Brandenburg v. Ohio, www.oyez.org/cases/1960-1969/1968/1968_492/.

22. "Safeguarding Online: Explaining the Risk Posed by Violent Extremism," op. cit., p. 3.

23. Elizabeth Renieris, "Combating Incitement to Terrorism on the Internet: Comparative Approaches in the United States and the United Kingdom and the Need for an International Solution," Vanderbilt Journal of Entertainment and Technology Law, vol. 11:3:673, 2009, pp. 687-688.

24. Fergus Watts, "Caught out by net plan," Herald Sun (Australia), Dec. 29, 2008, p. 20, www.heraldsun.com.au/opinion/caught-out-by-net-plan/story-6frfifo-1111118423939.

25. Weimann, op. cit., p. 180.

26. "Jordanian accused in Dallas bomb plot goes to court," CNN, Sept. 25, 2009, www.cnn.com/2009/CRIME/09/25/texas.terror.arrest/index.html.

27. http://smallbusiness.yahoo.com/tos/tos.php.

28. Neumann and Stevens, *op. cit.*, p. 32.

29. Maura Conway, "Terrorism & Internet Governance: Core Issues," U.N. Institute for Disarmament Research, 2007, p.11. www.unidir.org/pdf/articles/pdf-art2644.pdf.

30. Isambard Wilkinson, "Pakistan sets death penalty for 'cyber terrorism,'" *Telegraph.co.uk*, Nov 7, 2008, www.telegraph.co.uk/news/worldnews/asia/pakistan/3392216/Pakistan-sets-death-penalty-for-cyber-terrorism.html.

31. "Cyber attacks and cyber terrorism are the new threats," *India eNews*, March 26, 2009, www.indiaenews.com/print/?id=187451.

32. Linda McGlasson, "ATM Fraud Linked in RBS WorldPay Card Breach," Bank info Security, Feb. 5, 2009, www.bankinfosecurity.com/articles.php?art_id=1197.

33. Dorothy Denning, "A View of Cyberterrorism Five Years Later," 2007, pp. 2–3, http://faculty.nps.edu/dedennin/publications/Denning-TerrorsWeb.pdf.

34. Steven Bucci, "The Confluence of Cyber-Crime and Terrorism," Heritage Foundation, June 15, 2009, p. 6, www.heritage.org/Research/NationalSecurity/upload/hl_1123.pdf.

35. *Ibid.*, p. 5.

36. *Ibid.*, p. 6.

37. Dorothy Denning, *op. cit.*, p. 15.

38. *Ibid.*

39. Denning, "Terror's Web: How the Internet is Transforming Terrorism," *op. cit.*, p. 2.

40. *Ibid.*

41. Weimann, *op. cit.*, p. 15.

42. Evan Kohlmann, " 'Homegrown' Terrorists: Theory and Cases in the War on Terror's Newest Front," *The Annals of the American Academy of Political and Social Science*, July 2008; 618; 95. p. 95.

43. Denning, "Terror's Web: How the Internet is Transforming Terrorism," *op. cit.*, p. 3.

44. Kohlmann, *op. cit.*, p. 101.

45. *Ibid.*

46. David Talbot, "Terror's Server," *Technology Review.com*, Jan. 27, 2005, www.militantislammonitor.org/article/id/404.

47. Anthony Bergin, *et al.*, "Countering Internet Radicalisation in Southeast Asia," The Australian Strategic Policy Institute Special Report, March 2009, p. 5.

48. *Ibid.*, p. 6.

49. Weimann, *op. cit.*, pp. 75-76.

50. Weimann, *op. cit.*, p. 75.

51. Rita Katz and Josh Devon, "WWW.Jihad.com," *National Review Online*, July 14, 2003, http://nationalreview.com/comment/comment-katz-devon071403.asp.

52. Maura Conway and Lisa McInerney, "Jihadi Video & Auto-Radicalisation: Evidence from an Exploratory YouTube Study," 2008, p. 1, http://doras.dcu.ie/2253/2/youtube_2008.pdf.

53. *Ibid.*, p. 2.

54. Denning, "Terror's Web: How the Internet is Transforming Terrorism," *op. cit.*, p. 5.

55. Dennis Lormel, "Terrorists and Credit Card Fraud . . . A Quiet Epidemic," Counterterrorism Blog, Feb. 28, 2008, http://counterterrorismblog.org/2008/02/terrorists_and_credit_card_fra.php.

56. Alan Sipress, "An Indonesian's Prison Memoir Takes Holy War Into Cyberspace," *The Washington Post*, Dec. 14, 2004, p. A19, www.washingtonpost.com/wp-dyn/articles/A62095-2004Dec13.html.

57. Lormel, *op. cit.*

58. Dennis Lormel, "Credit Cards and Terrorists," Counterterrorism Blog, Jan. 16, 2008, http://counterterrorismblog.org/2008/01/credit_cards_and_terrorists.php.

59. Dennis Lormel, "Terrorists and Credit Card Fraud . . . ," *op. cit.*

60. Frank Cilluffo and Daniel Kimmage, "How to Beat al Qaeda at Its Own Game," *Foreign Policy*, April

2009, www.foreignpolicy.com/story/cms.php?story_id=4820.

61. Johnny Ryan, "EU must take its anti-terrorism fight to the Internet," *Europe's World*, Summer 2007, www.europesworld.org/EWSettings/Article/tabid/191/ArticleType/ArticleView/ArticleID/21068/Default.aspx.

62. Digital Outreach Team, U.S. Department of State, www.state.gov/documents/organization/116709.pdf.

63. "Middle East Internet Usage and Population Statistics," *Internet World Stats*, www.internetworldstats.com/stats5.htm.

64. Christopher Boucek, "The Sakinah Campaign and Internet Counter-Radicalization in Saudi Arabia," *CTC Sentinel*, August 2008, p. 2, www.carnegieendowment.org/files/CTCSentinel_Vol1Iss9.pdf.

65. *Ibid.*, p. 1.

66. Abdullah Ansary, "Combating Extremism: A brief overview of Saudi Arabia's approach," *Middle East Policy*, Summer 2008, vol. 15, no. 2, p. 111.

67. *Ibid.*

68. Y. Admon and M. Feki, "Saudi Press Reactions to the Arrest of Seven Terrorist Cells in Saudi Arabia," Inquiry and Analysis, no. 354, MEMRI, May 18, 2007.

69. Ansary, *op. cit.*, p. 111.

70. Boucek, *op. cit.*, p. 3.

71. Bergin, *op. cit.*, p. 19.

72. www.radicalmiddleway.co.uk.

73. "A radical wrong way," Progressive Muslims: Friends of Imperialism and Neocolonialism, Oct. 31, 2006, http://pmunadebate.blogspot.com/2006/10/radical-wrong-way.html.

74. Cilluffo and Kimmage, *op. cit.*

75. "Council Conclusions on Cooperation to Combat Terrorist Use of the Internet ("Check the Web")," Council of the European Union, May 16, 2007, p. 3, http://register.consilium.europa.eu/pdf/en/07/st08/st08457-re03.en07.pdf.

76. Katharina von Knop, "Institutionalization of a Web-Focused, Multinational Counter-Terrorism Campaign," *Responses to Cyber Terrorism* (2008), p. 14.

BIBLIOGRAPHY

Books

Jewkes, Yvonne, and Majid Yar, eds., *The Handbook on Internet Crime, Willan Publishing,* **2009.**
British criminology professors have compiled essays by leading scholars on issues and debates surrounding Internet-related crime, deviance, policing, law and regulation in the 21st century.

Kramer, Franklin D., Stuart H. Starr and Larry K. Wentz, eds., *Cyberpower and National Security, Potomac Books,* **2009.**
Experts write about cyber power and its strategic implications for national security, including an assessment of the likelihood of cyberterrorism.

Sageman, Marc, *Leaderless Jihad: Terror Networks in the Twenty-First Century, University of Pennsylvania Press,* **2008.**
A senior fellow at the Center on Terrorism, Counter-Terrorism, and Homeland Security in Philadelphia examines the impact of the Internet on global terrorism, including its role in radicalization, and strategies to combat terrorism in the Internet age.

Weimann, Gabriel, *Terror on the Internet, United States Institute of Peace Press,* **2006.**
A professor of communication at Haifa University in Israel explores how terrorist organizations exploit the Internet to raise funds, recruit members, plan attacks and spread their message.

Articles

Boucek, Christopher, "The Sakinah Campaign and Internet Counter-Radicalization in Saudi Arabia," *CTC Sentinel,* **August 2008.**
Saudi Arabia enlists religious scholars to engage in dialogue on the Internet with individuals seeking out religious knowledge in order to steer them away from extremist beliefs.

Cilluffo, Frank, and Daniel Kimmage, "How to Beat al Qaeda at Its Own Game," *Foreign Policy,* **April 2009, www.foreignpolicy.com.**

Two American terrorism experts recommend using Web sites, chat rooms, social networking sites, broadcasting and print to tell the stories of Muslim victims of militant Islamist terror attacks.

Goth, Greg, "Terror on the Internet: A Complex Issue, and Getting Harder," *IEEE Distributed Systems Online*, **vol. 9, no. 3, 2008.**
Counterterrorism agencies cringe when posturing by politicians leads to the dismantling of terrorist Web sites they've been monitoring.

Labi, Nadya, "Jihad 2.0," *The Atlantic Monthly*, **July/August, 2006.**
With the loss of training camps in Afghanistan, terrorists turned to the Internet to find and train recruits.

Talbot, David, "Terror's Server — How radical Islamists use Internet fraud to finance terrorism and exploit the Internet for Jihad propaganda and recruitment," *Technology Review.com*, **Jan. 27, 2008.**
Terrorists use the Internet for fundraising, propaganda and recruitment, but government and the Internet industry responses are limited by law and technology.

Reports and Studies

Bergin, Anthony, *et al.*, **"Countering Internet Radicalisation in Southeast Asia," Australian Strategic Policy Institute, March 2009.**
The director of research at the institute traces the evolution of extremist and terrorist-linked content from static Web sites to the more dynamic and interactive parts of the Internet.

Boyne, Shawn Marie, "The Criminalization of Speech in an Age of Terror," Indiana University School of Law-Indianapolis, working paper, June 12, 2009.
A law professor compares prosecution of incitement to terror in Germany, the U.K. and the United States.

Conway, Maura, "Terrorism & Internet Governance: Core Issues," *Disarmament Forum*, **2007.**
A terrorism expert at Dublin City University in Ireland explores the difficulties of Internet governance in light of terrorists' growing use of the medium.

Denning, Dorothy, "Terror's Web: How the Internet is Transforming Terrorism," *Naval Postgraduate School*, **2009.**
A professor of conflict and cyberspace discusses the implications of shutting sites down versus continuing to monitor sites or encouraging moderate voices to engage in dialogue online with terrorist sympathizers.

Neumann, Peter R., and Tim Stevens, "Countering Online Radicalisation: A Strategy for Action," *The International Centre for the Study of Radicalisation and Political Violence*, **2009.**
Shutting down terrorist sites on the Internet is expensive and counterproductive, according to the authors.

Renieris, Elizabeth, "Combating Incitement to Terrorism on the Internet," *Vanderbilt Journal of Entertainment and Technology Law*, **vol. 11:3:673, 2009.**
The author compares U.S. and U.K. laws used to prosecute incitement to terrorism on the Internet.

For More Information

Australian Strategic Policy Institute, 40 Macquarie St., Barton ACT 2600, Australia; (61) 2 6270 5100; www.aspi .org.au. Nonpartisan policy institute set up by the Australian government to study the country's defense and strategic policy choices.

EuroISPA, 39, Rue Montoyer, B-1000 Brussels, Belgium; (32) 2 503 2265; www.euroispa.org. World's largest association of Internet service providers.

Homeland Security Policy Institute, George Washington University, 2300 I St., N.W., Suite 721, Washington, DC 20037; (202) 994-2437; www.gwumc.edu/hspi. A think tank that analyzes homeland security issues.

Institute for International and European Affairs, 8 North Great Georges St., Dublin 1, Ireland; (353) 1 8746756; www.iiea.com. A think tank that analyzes how global and European Union policies affect Ireland.

International Centre for Political Violence and Terrorism Research, Nanyang Technological University, South Spine S4, Level B4, Nanyang Ave., Singapore 639798; (65) 6790 6982; www.pvtr.org. Studies threats and develops countermeasures for politically motivated violence and terrorism.

International Centre for the Study of Radicalisation and Political Violence, King's College London, 138-142 Strand, London, WC2R 1HH, United Kingdom; (44) 207 848 2098; http://icsr.info/index.php. A think tank set up by King's College London, the University of Pennsylvania, the Interdisciplinary Center Herzliya (Israel) and the Jordan Institute of Diplomacy.

Internet Haganah, http://internet-haganah.com/haganah/ index.html. Tracks, translates and analyzes extremist Islamic sites on the Web.

The Jamestown Foundation, 1111 16th St., N.W., Suite #320, Washington, DC 20036; (202) 483-8888; www .jamestown.org. Informs policy makers about trends in societies where access to information is restricted.

Middle East Media Research Institute, P.O. Box 27837, Washington, DC 20038-7837; (202) 955-9070; www.memri .org. Provides translations of Arabic, Persian, Turkish and Urdu-Pashtu media and analyses political, ideological, intellectual, social, cultural and religious trends in the Middle East.

NEFA Foundation, (212) 986-4949; www1.nefafoundation .org. Exposes those responsible for planning, funding and executing terrorist activities, with a particular emphasis on Islamic militant organizations.

Norwegian Defense Research Establishment, FFI, P.O. Box 25, NO-2027 Kjeller, Norway; (47) 63 80 70 00; www .mil.no/felles/ffi/english. The primary institution responsible for defense-related research in Norway.

Organization for Security and Co-operation in Europe, Action Against Terrorism Unit, Wallnerstrasse 6, 1010 Vienna, Austria; (43) 1 514 36 6702; www.osce.org/atu. Coordinates anti-terrorism initiatives among European nations.

18

Climate Change

*Will the Copenhagen Accord Slow
Global Warming?*

Reed Karaim

Erosion is washing away beachfront land in the Maldives. The island nation in the Indian Ocean faces possible submersion as early as 2100, according to some climate change predictions. President Mohamed Nasheed said the voluntary emission cuts goal reached in Copenhagen last December was a good step, but at that rate "my country would not survive."

From *CQ Global Researcher*,
February 2010.

I t was the global gathering many hoped would save the world. For two weeks in December, delegates from 194 nations came together in Copenhagen, Denmark, to hammer out an international agreement to limit global warming. Failure to do so, most scientists have concluded, threatens hundreds of millions of people and uncounted species of plants and animals.

Diplomatic preparations had been under way for years but intensified in the months leading up to the conference. Shortly before the sessions began, Yvo de Boer, executive secretary of the United Nations Framework Convention on Climate Change — the governing body for negotiations — promised they would "launch action, action and more action," and proclaimed, "I am more confident than ever before that [Copenhagen] will be the turning point in the fight to prevent climate disaster."[1]

But delegates found themselves bitterly divided. Developing nations demanded more financial aid for coping with climate change. Emerging economic powers like China balked at being asked to do more to limit their emissions of the greenhouse gases (GHGs) — created by burning carbon-based fuels — blamed for warming up the planet. The United States submitted proposed emissions cuts that many countries felt fell far short of its responsibility as the world's dominant economy. As negotiations stalled, frustration boiled over inside the hall and on the streets outside, where tens of thousands of activists had gathered to call world leaders to action. A historic opportunity — a chance to reach a global commitment to battle climate change — seemed to be slipping away.

Major Flooding, Drought Predicted at Century's End

Significant increases in runoff — from rain or melting snow and ice — are projected with a high degree of confidence for vast areas of the Earth, mainly in northern regions. Up to 20 percent of the world's population lives in areas where river flood potential is likely to increase by the 2080s. Rainfall and runoff are expected to be very low in Europe, the Middle East, northern and southern Africa and the western United States.

Projected Changes in Annual Runoff (Water Availability), 2090-2099
(by percentage, relative to 1980-1999)

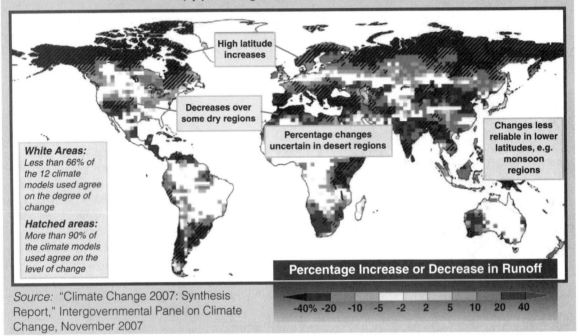

High latitude increases

Decreases over some dry regions

Percentage changes uncertain in desert regions

Changes less reliable in lower latitudes, e.g. monsoon regions

White Areas:
Less than 66% of the 12 climate models used agree on the degree of change

Hatched areas:
More than 90% of the climate models used agree on the level of change

Percentage Increase or Decrease in Runoff

-40% -20   -10   -5   -2   2   5   10   20   40

Source: "Climate Change 2007: Synthesis Report," Intergovernmental Panel on Climate Change, November 2007

Then, on Dec. 18 — the final night of the conference — leaders from China, India, Brazil, South Africa and the United States emerged from a private negotiating session with a three-page, nonbinding accord that rescued the meeting from being judged an abject failure.

But the accord left as much confusion as clarity in its wake. It was a deal, yes, but one that fell far short of the hopes of those attending the conference, and one largely lacking in specifics. The accord vowed to limit global warming to 2 degrees Celsius (3.6 Fahrenheit) above pre-Industrial Revolution levels, provide $30 billion in short-term aid to help developing countries cope with the effects of climate change — with more promised longer-term — and included significant reporting and transparency standards for participants, including emerging economic powers such as China and India.

The accord did not, however:

- Include earlier language calling for halving global greenhouse gas emissions by 2050;
- Set a peak year by which greenhouse gases should begin to decline;
- Include country-specific targets for emission reductions (signatories began filling in the numbers by the end of January) (*See Current Situation, p. 486*);
- Include a timetable for reaching a legally binding international treaty; or
- Specify where future financial help for the developing world to cope with climate change will come from.[2]

Called back into session in the early morning hours, delegates from much of the developing world reacted with dismay to a deal they felt left their countries vulnerable to catastrophic global warming.

"[This] is asking Africa to sign a suicide pact — an incineration pact — in order to maintain the economic dependence [on a high-carbon economy] of a few countries," said Lumumba Di-Aping, the Sudanese chair of the G77 group of 130 poor countries.[3]

British Prime Minister Gordon Brown, however, hailed the deal as a "vital first step" toward "a green and low-carbon future for the world."[4] A total of 55 countries, including the major developed nations, eventually signed onto the deal.

But at the Copenhagen conference, delegates agreed only to "take note" of the accord, without formally adopting it.

Since then, debate has raged over whether the accord represents a step backward or a realistic new beginning. "You had the U.S., China and India closing ranks and saying it's too hard right now to have a binding agreement," says Malini Mehra, an Indian political scientist with 20 years of involvement in the climate change debate. "It's really worse than where we started off."

Others are more upbeat. Michael Eckhart, president of the American Council on Renewable Energy, points out that the convention had revealed how unworkable the larger effort — with 194 participants — had become. "The accord actually sets things in motion in a direction that is realistic," he says. "To have these major nations signed up is fantastic."

Copenhagen clearly demonstrated how extremely difficult and complex global climate negotiations can be. Getting most of the world's nations to agree on anything is no easy task, but climate change straddles the biggest geopolitical fault lines of our age: the vast economic disparity between the developed and developing worlds, questions of national sovereignty versus global responsibility and differences in political process between democratic and nondemocratic societies.

Climate change also involves a classic example of displaced hardship — some of the worst effects of global warming are likely to be felt thousands of miles from

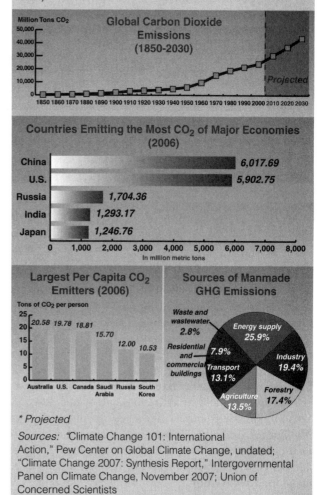

Carbon Emissions Rising; Most Come from China

Global emissions of carbon dioxide (CO_2) — the most common greenhouse gas (GHG) blamed for raising the planet's temperature — have grown steadily for more than 150 years. Since 1950, however, the increases have accelerated and are projected to rise 44 percent between 2010 and 2030 (top graph). While China emits more CO_2 than any other country, Australians produce the most carbon emissions per person (bottom left). Most manmade GHG comes from energy production and transportation (pie chart).

* Projected

Sources: "Climate Change 101: International Action," Pew Center on Global Climate Change, undated; "Climate Change 2007: Synthesis Report," Intergovernmental Panel on Climate Change, November 2007; Union of Concerned Scientists

those nations that are most responsible for the higher temperatures and rising seas, making it easier for responsible parties to delay action. Finally, tackling the problem is likely to take hundreds of billions of dollars.

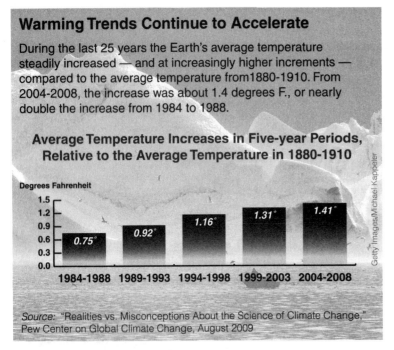

Warming Trends Continue to Accelerate

During the last 25 years the Earth's average temperature steadily increased — and at increasingly higher increments — compared to the average temperature from1880-1910. From 2004-2008, the increase was about 1.4 degrees F., or nearly double the increase from 1984 to 1988.

Average Temperature Increases in Five-year Periods, Relative to the Average Temperature in 1880-1910

Degrees Fahrenheit

1984-1988	0.75°
1989-1993	0.92°
1994-1998	1.16°
1999-2003	1.31°
2004-2008	1.41°

Source: "Realities vs. Misconceptions About the Science of Climate Change," Pew Center on Global Climate Change, August 2009

Getty Images/Michael Kappeler

None of this is comforting to those already suffering from climate change, such as Moses Mopel Kisosion, a Maasai herdsman who journeyed from Kenya to tell anyone who would listen how increasingly severe droughts are destroying his country's traditional way of life. (*See story on climate refugees, p. 480.*) But it does explain why reactions to the Copenhagen Accord — which even President Barack Obama acknowledged is simply a "beginning" — have varied so widely.[5]

For some U.S. environmental groups, the significance of the accord was in the commitment Obama secured from emerging economies to provide greater transparency and accountability, addressing one of the U.S. Senate's objections to earlier climate change proposals. The Senate never ratified the previous international climate agreement, known as the Kyoto Protocol.

Carl Pope, executive director of the Sierra Club, called the accord "historic — if incomplete," but said, "Now that the rest of the world — including countries like China and India — has made it clear that it is willing to take action, the Senate must pass domestic legislation as soon as possible."[6]

But to nongovernmental organizations focused on global poverty and economic justice, the accord represented an abdication of responsibility by the United States and other developed countries. Tim Jones, chief climate officer for the United Kingdom-based anti-poverty group World Development Movement, called the accord "a shameful and monumental failure that has condemned millions of people around the world to untold suffering."[7]

Easily lost in the heated rhetoric, however, is another part of the Copenhagen story: The conference illustrated how a consensus now unites most of the globe about the threat climate change poses. And although skeptics continue to speak out (*see p. 484*), the scientific community has overwhelmingly concluded that average global temperatures are rising and that manmade emissions — particularly carbon dioxide from burning coal, oil and other fossil fuels — are largely to blame. According to a comprehensive assessment released in June 2009 by the U.S. Global Change Research Program, "Observations show that warming of the climate is unequivocal."[8] The conclusion echoes earlier findings by the U.N.'s Intergovernmental Panel on Climate Change (IPCC).[9]

The costs of climate change, both economic and in human lives, already appear significant. Disasters tied to climate change kill around 300,000 people a year and cause roughly $125 billion in economic losses, according to the Global Humanitarian Forum, a Geneva-based think tank led by former U.N. Secretary General Kofi Annan.[10] Evidence widely cited during the conference strengthens the conclusion the world is heating up. The World Meteorological Organization (WMO) reported that the last decade appeared to be the warmest on record, continuing a trend. The years 2000 through 2009 were "warmer than the 1990s, which were warmer than the 1980s, and so on," said Michel Jarraud, the secretary general of the WMO, as Copenhagen got under way.[11] Other reports noted that sea levels appeared likely to rise higher than previously estimated by 2100, with one estimating seas could rise more than six feet by then. The Antarctic ice shelves and the Greenland ice sheet are also melting faster than the U.N. scientific body previously found.[12]

Copenhagen also provided evidence of a growing international political consensus about climate change. About 120 heads of state attended the final days of the conference, hoping to sign their names to an agreement, an indication of the seriousness with which the global community now views the issue.

"It was remarkable the degree to which Copenhagen galvanized the public," says David Waskow, Oxfam America's climate change policy adviser, who attended the conference. "That's true with the literally millions who came out to show their support for strong action on climate change around the world. It's true with the number of heads of state who showed up, and even in terms of the number of developing countries making substantial offers to tackle their emissions."

As observers try to determine where the world is headed on climate change and how the Copenhagen Accord helps or hinders that effort, here are some of the questions they are considering:

Is the Copenhagen Accord a meaningful step forward in the fight against global warming?

No one claims that a three-page accord that leaves out hard emission-reduction targets or a firm timetable is the final answer to global climate change. But does it bring the world closer to adequately addressing the problem?

Accord supporters range from the dutiful to the enthusiastic. But the unifying thread is a feeling that the accord is better than no deal at all, which is where the conference seemed to be headed until the 11th-hour negotiations.

"If the standard is — were we going to get a blueprint to save the world? The fact is, we were never going to meet it. None of the documents circulating were a feasible basis for agreement among the major players," says Michael A. Levi, director of the Program on Energy Security and Climate Change for the U.S. Council on Foreign Relations. "What we ended up with is something that can be useful if we use it the right way. It has pieces that empower all sorts of other efforts, like increased transparency, some measure of monitoring and reporting. It sets a political benchmark for financing. It can be a meaningful step forward."

Levi also notes that countries signing the accord agreed to fill in their targets for emissions cuts (as the

Protesters outside the U.N. Climate Change Conference in Copenhagen on Dec. 10, 2009, call for rich countries to take responsibility for their disproportionate share in global warming. Greenhouse gas emissions by industrial countries are causing climate changes in poor countries thousands of miles away. The nonbinding Copenhagen Accord calls for $10 billion a year for the next three years to help them deal with climate change.

Reuters/Christian Charisius

major signatories and other nations did at the end of January), addressing one of the main criticisms of the deal.

But the Indian political scientist Mehra says even if countries abide by their commitments to cut emissions, the accord will not meet its target of holding global warming to 2 degrees Celsius (3.6 degrees Fahrenheit), which U.N. scientists consider the maximum increase that could avoid the worst effects of climate change, including a catastrophic rise in sea levels and severe damage to world food production.

She cites an IPCC conclusion that says in order to meet the 2-degree goal industrialized countries must reduce their emissions to 25-40 percent of 1990 levels by 2020 and by 50 percent by 2050. "What we actually got in the various announcements from the developed nations are far below that, coming in at around 18 percent," Mehra says.

Indeed, research by Climate Interactive — a joint effort by academic, nonprofit and business entities to assess climate policy options — found that the countries' commitments would allow temperatures to rise about 3.9 degrees Celsius (7 degrees Fahrenheit) by 2100 — nearly twice the stated goal.[13] "If you're looking at an average of 3 to 4 degrees, you're going to have much higher rises in significant parts of the world. That's why so many of the African negotiators were so alarmed by this," says Mehra. "It's worse than where we started because it effectively sets in stone the lowest possible expectations."

But other analysts point out that President Obama and other leaders who backed the accord have acknowledged more must be done.[14] They add that focusing on the initial emissions goals ignores the areas where the deal breaks important ground. "A much bigger part of the story, I think, is the actual money the developed world is putting on the table, funds for mitigation and adaptation," says Mike Hulme, a professor at the University of East Anglia in Great Britain who has been studying the intersection between climate and culture. "This is as much part of the game as nominal reduction targets."

The accord calls for $10 billion a year to help poorer, more vulnerable countries cope with climate change over the next three years, rising to $100 billion a year by 2020. The money will come from "a wide variety of sources, public and private, bilateral and multilateral, including alternative sources of finance," according to the agreement.[15]

Equally important, say analysts, is the fact that the agreement sets new standards of participation and accountability for developing economies in the global warming fight. "The developing countries, particularly China, made a step forward and agreed not only to undertake some actions to reduce emissions, but to monitor and report those. I think that's significant," says Stephen Eule, a U.S. Chamber of Commerce climate expert and former George W. Bush administration climate official.

However, to many of the accord's critics, the accord mostly represents a failure of political leadership. "It was hugely disappointing. Watching world leaders lower expectations for three months coming into this, and then actually having them undershoot those expectations was unbelievable," says Jason Blackstock, a research scholar at the International Institute for Applied Systems Analysis in Austria, who studies the intersection of science and international affairs. He places some of the blame at the feet of President Obama: "This is clearly not one of his top issues, and that's disappointing."

But Thomas Homer-Dixon, who holds an international governance chair at the Balsillie School of International Affairs in Waterloo, Canada, and studies

climate policy, believes critics are underestimating the importance of leaders from around the globe sitting down face-to-face to tackle the problem. "Symbolically, that photograph of the leaders of those countries sitting around the table with their sleeves rolled up was enormous," he says. "All of a sudden we're having a direct conversation among the actors that matter, both in the developed and developing world."

He also credits the conference for tackling difficult questions such as how much money developed countries need to transfer to the developing world to fight climate change and how much countries have to open themselves up to international inspection. "There's been sort of an agreement not to talk about the hard stuff," he says, "and now, at Copenhagen, it was finally front and center."

But to those who believe that the time for talk is running out, the dialogue meant nothing without concrete results. "This [deal], as they themselves say, will not avert catastrophic climate change," said Kumi Naidoo, Greenpeace International's executive director. "That's the only thing on which we agree with them. Everything else is a fudge; everything else is a fraud, and it must be called as such."[16]

Is the U.N.'s climate change negotiating framework outdated?

Although delegations from most of the world's nations came to Copenhagen, the final deal was hammered out by the leaders of only five countries. Those nations — the United States, China, India, Brazil and South Africa — provide a snapshot of the changing nature of geopolitical power.

Although they had been involved in larger group discussions of about 30 nations, the traditional European powers and Japan were not involved in the final deal. The five key players represented the world's largest economy (the United States), the largest emitter of greenhouse gases and second-biggest economy (China) and significant emerging economies in South America (Brazil), Africa (South Africa) and India, with the world's second-largest population.

The five-nation gathering could be seen as an effort to fashion a thin cross-section of the global community. But the U.N.-sponsored Copenhagen conference was supposed to embody the entire world community. To some observers, the fact that the accord was fashioned outside the official sessions appeared to be an attempt to undermine the U.N. effort.

Anne Petermann, co-director of the Global Justice Ecology Project, an international grassroots organization, notes the Bush administration also worked outside the U.N., setting up a smaller meeting of major economies to discuss climate change. "It wasn't particularly surprising the U.S. negotiated an accord that was completely outside the process," she says. "This wasn't the first time that the U.S. had come in with a strategy of undermining the U.N. Framework Convention."

To other analysts, however, the ability of the small group of leaders to come together where the larger conference had failed shows that the U.N. effort no longer fits the crisis. "The Framework Convention is actually now an obstacle to doing sensible things on climate change," says East Anglia's Hulme. "Climate change is such a multifaceted problem that we need to find sub-groups, multiple frameworks and initiatives to address it."

To others, the U.N. effort remains both the best chance for the world to reach a binding climate change agreement and essential to proceeding. "Because you've really got to have a global solution to this problem, it's essential that all the interested parties, including the most vulnerable countries, be around the table," says Oxfam's Waskow. "There's no question the U.N. Framework Convention, which has been working on this for many years, is the right place for that."

But Homer-Dixon, of the Balsillie School of International Affairs, believes the U.N. Framework process "has too many parties." He expects that on the negotiating side "we're going to migrate to something like the G-20 [economic forum], which includes all the major emitters. It would make sense to have the G-20 responsible."

However, Kassie Siegel, the climate law expert for the Center for Biological Diversity, a U.S. environmental group, thinks critics underestimate the U.N. effort. "Both the U.N. Framework Convention and the Intergovernmental Panel on Climate Change have been building capacity since 1992," she says. "There's not any other institution that came close to their experience on this issue. The U.N. Framework process is the best and fastest way forward."

Supporters also note that the United States and other signatories to the Copenhagen Accord have called for efforts to continue toward reaching a binding agreement at the next U.N. climate gathering in Mexico City at the end of this year. "I don't think the U.N. negotiations are irrelevant because the U.S. is still engaged in the Framework Convention," says Nicola Bullard, a climate change analyst and activist with Focus on the Global South, a nongovernmental group in Bangkok, Thailand.

But Eckhart believes the results in Copenhagen mean that key countries will now focus most of their efforts outside the U.N. framework. "I doubt Mexico City is still relevant," he says. "What can they get done in Mexico City that they couldn't get done in Copenhagen?"

The relationship between the Copenhagen Accord and the U.N. Framework Convention is somewhat ambiguous. Jacob Werksman, a lawyer specializing in international environmental and economics law at the World Resources Institute, concludes the conference's decision to only "take note" of the accord means that some provisions, including the call for setting up a Copenhagen Green Climate Fund to manage billions of dollars in aid through the U.N. mechanism, cannot occur without a conference decision to accept the accord.

U.N. Secretary General Ban Ki-moon has called on all U.N. countries to back the accord.[17] (*See "At Issue," p. 488.*) But some analysts believe the U.N. Framework Convention can't legally adopt it until the Mexico City conference, which would push the Climate Fund and possibly other accord provisions down the road another year — a delay climate change activists say the world can't afford.

Would a carbon tax reduce emissions more effectively?

Obscured by the immediate furor over Copenhagen is a longer-term debate over whether the developed world is taking the right tack in its approach to reducing emissions.

The most popular approach so far has been the so-called cap-and-trade programs.[18] Progressively lower caps on overall emissions allow power companies and other entities to trade their emission quotas, creating a market-based approach to cutting greenhouse gases. Several European nations have embraced "cap-and-trade," and the climate change legislation that passed the U.S. House last June takes such an approach. But the system has been criticized for its complexity and susceptibility to manipulation and abuse.

Some analysts believe a carbon tax — a levy on carbon-emitting fuels, coupled with a system to rebate most

Residents grin and bear flooding in Jakarta, Indonesia, in December 2007. Similar scenes would be played out in coastal cities and communities around the world if climate change causes glaciers and polar ice caps to melt, which many researchers predict. Analysts say the worst effects of climate change are expected to be felt in Asia.

of the tax back to consumers, is a more straightforward and effective way to control emissions. Robert Shapiro, former undersecretary of commerce during the Clinton administration and chair of the U.S. Climate Task Force, advocates such a program and works to educate the public on the need for action on climate change.

Shapiro's plan would use 90 percent of the carbon tax revenue to cut payroll taxes paid by workers and businesses, with the remaining 10 percent going to fund research and development of clean energy technology. The tax would provide a price incentive for discouraging the use of carbon emitting fuels and encouraging the use of green energy, while the tax cut would keep the approach from unduly burdening lower-income Americans. "A carbon tax would both directly reduce greenhouse gas emissions and provide powerful incentives for technological progress in this area," Shapiro wrote. "It offers the best way forward in both the national and global debate over climate change."[19]

However, carbon tax opponents argue it would be no more effective than cap-and-trade and would lead to a huge expansion of government. Analysts at the Heritage Foundation, a conservative U.S. think tank, wrote that a carbon tax "would cause significant economic damage and would do very little to reduce global temperatures." Even coupling it with a payroll tax cut, they continue, "would do little to offset the high energy prices that fall

particularly hard on low-income households." The real agenda of a carbon tax, they charge, is "about raising massive amounts of revenue to fund a huge expansion in government."[20]

Several Scandinavian countries have adopted carbon taxes, with mixed results. Norway has seen its per capita CO_2 emissions rise significantly. But Denmark's 2005 emissions were 15 percent below what they were in 1990, and the economy still remained strong.[21]

But to Bullard, at Focus on the Global South, a carbon tax is the approach most likely to spur changes in personal behavior. "Reducing consumption is really important, reducing our own dependence on fossil fuels," she says. "I think it's very important to have a redistributive element so that working people and elderly people don't end up with a huge heating bill. But it's really a simpler and more effective route than a complicated solution like cap-and-trade."

However, Bill McKibben — an American environmentalist and the founder of 350.org, an international campaign dedicated to scaling back GHG emissions — says a carbon tax faces an almost insurmountable political hurdle in the United States. "Even I can't convince myself that America is going to sit very long with something called a carbon tax," he says.

McKibben thinks "cap and rebate" legislation recently introduced by Sens. Maria Cantwell, D-Wash., and Susan Collins, R-Maine, would be more palatable to voters. It would cap total emissions — a limit that would be tightened over time — with the government auctioning off available carbon credits. The money raised would be rebated to consumers to offset any higher energy bills. [22]

Congressional efforts, however, have focused on cap-and-trade. But as wariness grows in the U.S. Senate toward the ramifications of cap-and-trade, Shapiro believes a carbon tax could prove a more appealing option. "A real public discussion and debate about a carbon tax tied to offsetting cuts in payroll or other taxes," he said, "could be the best news for the climate in a very long time."[23]

BACKGROUND

Road to Copenhagen

The road to Copenhagen was a long one. In one sense, it began with the Industrial Revolution in the 18th and

19th century, which brought with it the increased burning of coal and the beginning of large-scale carbon dioxide emissions in Europe and America. It also started with scientific speculation in the 1930s that manmade emissions could be changing the planet's climate.

Those first studies were widely discounted, a reflection of the difficulty humanity has had coming to grips with the idea it could be changing the global climate. But by the mid-1980s, thanks in large part to the work of David Keeling at the Mauna Loa Observatory in Hawaii, the world had a nearly three-decade record of rising carbon dioxide levels in the atmosphere.[24] Scientists were also reporting an overall warming trend in the atmosphere over the last 100 years, which they considered evidence of a "greenhouse effect" tied to CO_2 and other manmade emissions.

Humankind began a slow, often painful struggle to understand and deal with a global challenge. From the beginning, there were doubters, some well intentioned, some with a vested interest in making sure that the world continued to burn fossil fuels. Even as the scientific consensus on climate change has grown stronger, and many nations have committed themselves to tackling global warming, the issue continues to provoke and perplex.

Climate and Culture

In her book *Field Notes from a Catastrophe, Man, Nature and Climate Change*, American writer Elizabeth Kolbert visits, among other spots, Greenland's ice fields, a native village in Alaska and the countryside in northern England, surveying how global warming is changing the Earth. In the opening section, she admits her choices about where to go to find the impact of climate change were multitudinous.

"Such is the impact of global warming that I could have gone to hundreds if not thousands of other places," Kolbert writes, "From Siberia to the Austrian Alps to the Great Barrier Reef to the South African *fynbos* (shrub lands)."[25]

Despite mounting evidence, however, climate change remains more a concept than a reality for huge parts of the globe, where the visible impacts are still slight or nonexistent. Research scholar Blackstock, whose work focuses on the intersection between science and international affairs, points out that for many people this makes the issue as much a matter of belief as of fact.

"It really strikes to fundamental questions on how we see the human-nature interface," he says. "It has cultural undertones, religious undertones, political undertones." Blackstock thinks many climate scientists have missed this multifaceted dimension to the public dialogue. "Pretending this is just a scientific debate won't work," he says. "That's important, but we can't have that alone."

The heart of the matter, he suggests, is how willing we are to take responsibility for changes in the climate and how we balance that with other values. This helps to explain the varying reactions in the United States, which has been reluctant to embrace limits on carbon emissions, and Europe, which has been more willing to impose measures. "You're seeing the cultural difference between Europe and America," Blackstock says, "the American values of individualism and personal success versus the communal and collective good, which Europe has more of a sense of being important."

Other analysts see attitudes about climate deeply woven into human culture. The University of East Anglia's Hulme, author of *Why We Disagree About Climate Change*, notes that climate and weather have been critical to humanity for most of its history. The seasons, rains and hot or cold temperatures have been so essential to life — to the ability to obtain food and build stable communities — that they have been attributed to deities and formed the basis for religious ceremonies. Even in the modern age, Hulme says, "People have an instinctive sense that weather and climate are natural phenomena, that they work at such scales and complexity that humans could not possibly influence them."

He points out that weather was once the realm of prophets, "and part of our population is still resistant to the idea that science is able to predict what the weather will be. This deep cultural history makes climate change a categorically different phenomenon than other scientifically observed data."

Climate is also often confused with weather. England, for example, has a temperate, damp climate, but can have dry, hot years. The human inclination is to believe what's before our eyes, so every cold winter becomes a reason to discount global warming.

Sander van der Leeuw, director of the School of Human Evolution and Social Change at Arizona State University in Tempe, Ariz., notes that facing climate change also means contemplating the costs of consumerism. "Those of us in

Climate Change Could Force Millions to Relocate

"Climate Refugees" from Africa to the Arctic could be affected.

Maasi herdsman Moses Mopel Kisosion had never been outside Kenya before. He'd never ridden on a plane. But he flew across parts of two continents to deliver a message to anyone who would listen at the Copenhagen climate conference in December.

Climate change, he believes, is destroying the ability of his people, the Kajiado Maasi, to make a living. "I am a pastoralist, looking after cattles, walking from one place to another looking for grass and pastures," Kisosion said. "And now, for four years, we have a lack of rain, so our animals have died because there's no water and no grass. . . . We are wondering how our life will be because we depend on them."[1]

The Maasi are hardly alone in worrying if they will be able to continue living where they are. From small South Pacific island nations to the Arctic, hundreds of millions of people might have to relocate to survive as a result of climate change. If global warming predictions prove accurate, some researchers believe the world could soon find itself dealing with a tidal wave of "climate refugees."

A study by the U.N. Office for the Coordination of Humanitarian Affairs and the Internal Displacement Monitoring Centre found that "climate-related disasters — that is, those resulting from hazards that are already being or are likely to be modified by the effects of climate change — were responsible for displacing approximately 20 million people in 2008."[2]

Norman Myers, a British environmentalist, sees the situation worsening as the effects of climate change grow. In a 2005 study, he concluded that up to 200 million people could become climate refugees.[3] But he recently revised his estimate significantly. "We looked at the best prognosis for the spread of desertification and sea level rise, including the associated tsunamis and hurricanes, and we meshed those figures with the number of people impoverished or inhabiting coastal zones," says Myers. "We believe we could see half a billion climate refugees in the second half of the century."

The human displacement is likely to take place over several decades, experts say, and determining who is a climate refugee and who is simply a political or economic refugee could be difficult. International organizations have just begun the discussion about their status and what kind of assistance they might require.

The European Commission is funding a two-year research project, "Environmental Change and Forced Migration Scenarios," based on case studies in 24 vulnerable countries.[4] An African Union Summit in Kampala, Uganda, also met last October to consider how it would address the growing number of displaced Africans.[5]

Wahu Kaara, a Kenyan political activist, says the need for action is pressing. Kenya has recorded four major droughts in the last decade, significantly higher than the average over the previous century. "Very many people are dislocated and have to move to where they can salvage their lives," she says. "We have seen people die as they walk from one place to another. It's not a hardship; it's a catastrophe. They not only have lost their animals, they have lost their lives, and the framework of their lives for those who survive."

While Africa already may be suffering population movement due to climate change, the worst consequences are likely to be felt in Asia, analysts say. Rising sea levels threaten low-lying coastal areas, which constitute only 2 percent of the land surface of the Earth but shelter

the developed world have the most invested in this particular lifestyle," he says. "If that lifestyle has to change, we'll be facing the most wrenching dislocations."

Van der Leeuw, who worked for the European Union on climate change issues in the 1990s, is actually optimistic about the progress the world has made on climate change in the face of these challenges. "It's a very long process," he says, "but I'm encouraged by my students. It's wonderful to see how engaged they are, how open to thinking differently on these issues. I know we have very little time, but history is full of moments where we've reacted in the nick of time."

However, there are still those who doubt the basic science of climate change.

The Doubters

To enter the world of the climate change skeptics is to enter a mirror reflection of the scientific consensus on the issue. Everything is backwards: The Earth isn't warming; it may be cooling. If it is warming, it's part of the

10 percent of its population. About 75 percent of the people living in those areas are in Asia.[6]

The Maldives, a nation of low-lying islands in the Indian Ocean that could be submerged if predictions prove accurate, has taken the lead in trying to organize smaller island nations in the global warming debate. President Mohamed Nasheed initially supported the Copenhagen Accord and its 2-degree Celsius target for limiting global warming as a beginning. But before the deal was struck, he declared, "At 2 degrees, my country would not survive."[7]

Rising sea levels threaten every continent, including the Americas. Until recently, Kivalina Island, an eight-mile-long barrier island in northern Alaska, had survived the punishing storms that blew in from the ocean because of ice that formed and piled up on the island.[8]

Inupiat hunters from the island's small village began noticing changes in the ice years ago, says the island's tribal administrator, Colleen Swan, but the change has accelerated in recent years. "In early September and October, the ice used to start forming, but now it doesn't form anymore until January and it's not building up," she says. "When that happened, we lost our barrier from fall sea storms, and our island just started falling apart. We started losing a lot of land beginning in 2004."

The U.S. Army Corps of Engineers is building a seawall to protect what's left of Kivalina, but Swan says it is expected to buy only 10 or 15 years. "People in the United States are still debating whether climate change is happening. The U.N. is focusing on the long-term problem of emissions," Swan says, "but we're in the 11th hour here. The bottom line is we need someplace to go."

— *Reed Karaim*

A house tumbles into the Chukchi Sea in Shishmaref, Alaska. Like other victims of climate change, residents may have to abandon the tiny community due to unprecedented erosion caused by intense storms.

official conference. It is available online at http://en.cop15.dk/blogs/view+blog?blogid=2929.

[2] "Monitoring disaster displacement in the context of climate change," the U.N. Office for the Coordination of Humanitarian Affairs and The Internal Displacement Monitoring Centre, September 2009, p. 12.

[3] Norman Myers, "Environmental Refugees, an Emergent Security Issue," presented at the 13th Economic Forum, Prague, May 2005.

[4] "GLOBAL: Nowhere to run from nature," IRIN, Nov. 9, 2009, www.irinnews.org/report.aspx?ReportId=78387.

[5] "AFRICA: Climate change could worsen displacement — UN," IRIN, Nov. 9, 2009, www.irinnews.org/report.aspx?ReportId=86716.

[6] Anthony Oliver-Smith, "Sea Level Rise and the Vulnerability of Coastal Peoples," U.N. University Institute for Environment and Human Security, 2009, p. 5, www.ehs.unu.edu/file.php?id=652.

[7] "Address by His Excellency Mohamed Nasheed, President of the Republic of Maldives, at the Climate Vulnerable Forum," Nov. 9, 2009, www.actforclimatejustice.org/2009/11/address-by-his-excellency-mohamed-nasheed-president-of-the-republic-of-maldives-at-the-climate-vulnerable-forum/.

[8] See John Schwartz, "Courts As Battlefields in Climate Fights," *The New York Times*, Jan. 26, 2010.

[1] Moses Mopel Kisosion spoke in a video blog from Kilmaforum09, the "people's forum" on climate change held in Copenhagen during the

---

planet's natural, long-term climate cycles. Manmade carbon dioxide isn't the heart of the problem; it's a relatively insignificant greenhouse gas. But even if carbon dioxide is increasing, it's beneficial for the planet.

And that scientific consensus? It doesn't exist. "What I see are a relatively small number, perhaps a few hundred at most, of extremely well-funded, well-connected evangelistic scientists doing most of the lobbying on this issue," says Bob Carter, a geologist who is one of Australia's more outspoken climate change skeptics.

Many scientists who take funds from grant agencies to investigate global warming, he says, "don't speak out with their true views because if they did so, they would lose their funding and be intimidated."

It's impossible to know if people are keeping views to themselves, of course. But professional science has a method of inquiry — the scientific method — and a system of peer review intended to lead to knowledge that, as much as possible, is untainted by prejudice, false comparison or cherry-picked data. The process isn't always

CHRONOLOGY

1900-1950s *Early research indicates the Earth is warming.*

1938 British engineer Guy Stewart Callendar concludes that higher global temperatures and rising carbon dioxide levels are probably related.

1938 Soviet researchers confirm that the planet is warming.

1957 U.S. oceanographer Roger Revelle and Austrian physicist Hans Suess find that the oceans cannot absorb carbon dioxide as easily as thought, indicating that manmade emissions could create a "greenhouse effect," trapping heat in the atmosphere.

1958 U.S. scientist David Keeling begins monitoring atmospheric carbon dioxide levels, creating a groundbreaking record of their increase.

1960s *Climate science raises the possibility of global disaster.*

1966 U.S. geologist Cesare Emiliani says ice ages were created by tiny shifts in Earth's orbit, backing earlier theories that climate reacts to small changes.

1967 Leading nations launch 15-year program to study the world's weather.

1968 Studies show Antarctica's huge ice sheets could melt, raising sea levels.

1970s-1980s *Research into climate change intensifies, and calls for action mount.*

1975 A National Aeronautics and Space Administration (NASA) researcher warns that fluorocarbons in aerosol sprays could help create a greenhouse effect.

1979 The National Academy of Sciences finds that burning fossil fuels could raise global temperatures 6 degrees Fahrenheit in 50 years.

1981 U.S. scientists report a warming trend since 1880, evidence of a greenhouse effect.

1985 Scientists from 29 nations urge governments to plan for warmer globe.

1988 NASA scientist James Hansen says global warming has begun; he's 99 percent sure it's manmade.

1988 Thirty-five nations form a global panel to evaluate climate change and develop a response.

1990s *As the world responds to global warming, industry groups fight back.*

1990 The carbon industry-supported Global Climate Coalition forms to argue that climate change science is too uncertain to take action.

1995 The year is the hottest since the mid-19th century, when records began being kept.

1997 More than 150 nations agree on the Kyoto Protocol, a landmark accord to reduce greenhouse gases. The U.S. signs but never ratifies it.

2000s *The political battle over climate change action escalates worldwide.*

2000 Organization of Petroleum Exporting Countries (OPEC) demands compensation if global warming remedies reduce oil consumption.

2006 National Academy of Sciences reports the Earth's temperature is the highest in 12,000 years, since the last Ice Age.

2007 A U.N. report concludes that global warming is "unequivocal" and human actions are primarily responsible.

2009 The 194 nations attending the Copenhagen Climate Change Conference cannot agree on a broad treaty to battle global warming. After two weeks of contentious discussion, five nations create a nonbinding climate change accord, which 55 nations eventually sign, but which falls far short of delegates' hopes.

2010 The U.N effort to get a global, legally binding climate change treaty is scheduled to continue in November-December in Mexico City.

perfect, but it provides our best look at the physical world around us.

In December 2004, Naomi Oreske, a science historian at the University of California, San Diego, published an analysis in *Science* in which she reviewed 928 peer-reviewed climate studies published between 1993 and 2003. She did not find one that disagreed with the general consensus on climate change.[26]

The U.S. National Academy of Sciences, the Royal Society of London, the Royal Society of Canada, the American Meteorological Society, the American Association for the Advancement of Science and 2,500 scientists participating in the IPCC also have concluded the evidence that humans are changing the climate is compelling. "Politicians, economists, journalists and others may have the impression of confusion, disagreement or discord among climate scientists, but that impression is incorrect," Oreske wrote, after reviewing the literature.[27]

The debate over climate change science heated up last fall, when, shortly before the Copenhagen conference, hackers broke into the University of East Anglia's computer network and made public hundreds of e-mails from scientists at the school's climate research center — some prominent in IPCC research circles. Climate change skeptics were quick to point to the "Climategate" e-mails as evidence researchers had been squelching contrary opinions and massaging data to bolster their claims.

Reviews by *Time*, *The New York Times* and the Pew Center on Climate Change, however, found the e-mails did not provide evidence to alter the scientific consensus on climate change. "Although a small percentage of the e-mails are impolite and some express animosity toward opponents, when placed into proper context they do not appear to reveal fraud or other scientific misconduct," the Pew Center concluded.[28]

Some skeptics are scientists, but none are climate researchers. Perhaps the most respected scientific skeptic is Freeman Dyson, a legendary 86-year-old physicist and mathematician. Dyson does not dispute that atmospheric carbon-dioxide levels are rapidly rising and humans are to blame. He disagrees with those who project severe consequences. He believes rising CO_2 levels could have some benefits, and if not, humanity could bioengineer trees that consume larger amounts of carbon dioxide or find some other technological solution. He is sanguine

about the ability of the Earth to adapt to change and is suspicious of the validity of computer models.

"The climate-studies people who work with models always tend to overestimate their models," Dyson has said. "They come to believe models are real and forget they are only models."[29]

Unlike Dyson, many climate change skeptics are connected to groups backed by the oil, gas and coal industries, which have worked since at least 1990 to discredit global warming theories. A 2007 study by the Union of Concerned Scientists found that between 1998 and 2005 ExxonMobil had funneled about $16 million to 43 groups that sought to manufacture uncertainty about global warming with the public.[30]

The tactics appear to be patterned after those used by the tobacco industry to discredit evidence of the hazards of smoking. According to the study, ExxonMobil and others have used ostensibly independent front groups for "information laundering," as they sought to sow doubts about the conclusions of mainstream climate science.

Several prominent climate change skeptics — including physicist S. Fred Singer and astrophysicists Willie Soon and Sallie Baliunas — have had their work published by these organizations, some of which seem to have no other purpose than to proliferate the information. "By publishing and re-publishing the non-peer-reviewed works of a small group of scientific spokespeople, ExxonMobil-funded organizations have propped up and amplified work that has been discredited by reputable climate scientists," the study concludes.[31]

Is the world cooling? Is global warming a natural phenomenon? Is more CO_2 really good for the planet? Science and media watchdog groups have published detailed rebuttals to the claims of climate change skeptics.[32] To cite one example, assertions that the Earth is actually cooling often use 1998 as the base line — a year during the El Niño weather system, which typically produces warmer weather. The Associated Press gave temperature numbers to four statisticians without telling them what the numbers represented. The scientists found no true declines over the last 10 years. They also found a "distinct, decades-long" warming trend.[33]

James Hoggan, a Canadian public relations executive who founded DeSmogblog to take on the skeptics, feels climate scientists have done a poor job of responding to the skeptics, too often getting bogged down in the minutiae of detail. "We need to start asking these so-called skeptics a number of basic questions," says Hoggan, the author of

Climate Scientists Thinking Outside the Box

"Geoengineering" proposes futuristic solutions that sound like science fiction.

Imagine: A massive squadron of aircraft spewing sulfur particles into the sky. An armada of oceangoing ships spraying sea mist into the air. A swarm of robotic mirrors a million miles out in space reflecting some of the sun's harmful rays away from the Earth. Thousands of giant, air-filtering towers girdling the globe.

The prospect of devastating global warming has led some scientists and policy analysts to consider the kind of planet-altering responses to climate change that were once the province of science fiction. The underlying concept, known as "geoengineering," holds that manmade changes in the climate can be offset by futuristic technological modifications.

That idea raises its own concerns, both about the possibility of unintended consequences and of technological dependence. But from an engineering perspective, analysts say the sulfur particle and sea vapor options — which would reflect sunlight away from the Earth, potentially cooling the planet — appear feasible and not even that expensive.

"Basically, any really rich guy on the planet could buy an ice age," says David Keith, a geoengineering expert at the University of Calgary, estimating that sulfur injection could cost as little as $1 billion or so a year. "Certainly, it's well within the capability of most nations."

"Technologically, it would be relatively easy to produce small particles in the atmosphere at the required rates," says Ken Caldiera, a climate scientist at the Carnegie Institution for Science's Department of Global Ecology in Stanford, Calif. "Every climate-model simulation performed so far indicates geoengineering would be able to diminish most climate change for most people most of the time."

To spread sulfur, planes, balloons or even missiles could be used.[1] For sea vapor, which would be effective at a lower altitude, special ships could vaporize seawater and shoot it skyward through a rotor system.[2]

A global program of launching reflective aerosols higher into the atmosphere would cost around $5 billion annually — still small change compared to the economic costs of significant global warming, says Caldiera. Other geoengineering options are considerably more expensive. The cost of launching the massive (60,000 miles by 4,500 miles) cloud of mirrors into space to block sunlight would cost about $5 trillion.[3] Building air-scrubbing towers would also be expensive and would require improved technology.[4]

Climate Cover-Up: The Crusade to Deny Global Warming. "The first one is, 'Are you actually a climate scientist?' The second one is, 'Have you published peer-reviewed papers on whatever claims you're making?' And a third one is, 'Are you taking money directly or indirectly from industry?'"

Untangling the Threads

Since nations first began to seriously wrestle with climate change, most of the effort has gone into fashioning a legally binding international treaty to cut greenhouse gas emissions while helping poorer nations cope with the effects of global warming.

The approach has a powerful logic. Climate change is a worldwide problem and requires concerted action around the planet. Assisting those most likely to be affected — populations in Africa and Asia who are among the poorest on the globe — is also a burden that is most equitably shared.

But the all-in-one-basket approach also comes with big problems. The first is the complexity of the negotiations themselves, which involve everything from intellectual-property rights to hundreds of billions of dollars in international finance to forest management. Global nations have been meeting on these issues for nearly two decades without a breakthrough deal.

Some observers believe the best chance for moving forward is untangling the threads of the problem. "We don't have to try to set the world to rights in one multilateral agreement," says East Anglia's Hulme. "It's not something we've ever achieved in human history, and I doubt we can. It seems more likely it's acting as an unrealistic, utopian distraction."

Analysts cite the 1987 Montreal Protocol, which phased out the use of chlorofluorocarbons that were damaging the ozone layer, as an example of a successful smaller-scale deal.

But cost is not what worries those studying geoengineering. "Everyone who's thinking about this has two concerns," says Thomas Homer-Dixon, a political scientist at Canada's Balsillie School of International Affairs in Waterloo, Ontario. "One is unintended consequences — because we don't understand climate systems perfectly — something bad could happen like damage to the ozone layer. The second is the moral-hazard problem: If we start to do this, are a lot of people going to think it means we can continue the carbon party?"

Keith thinks the consequences could be managed. "One of the advantages of using aerosols in the atmosphere is that you can modulate them," he says. "If you find it's not working, you can stop and turn the effect off." But he shares a concern with Caldeira and Homer-Dixon that geoengineering could be used as an excuse to avoid reducing carbon-dioxide emissions.

Geoengineering also raises geopolitical concerns, in part because it could be undertaken unilaterally. Unlike lowering greenhouse gas emissions, it doesn't require a global agreement, yet its effects would be felt around the planet — and not evenly.

That could aggravate international tensions: Any sustained bad weather in one nation could easily raise suspicion that it was the victim of climate modifications launched by another country. "If China, say, were to experience a deep drought after the deployment of a climate-intervention system," says Caldeira, "and people were starving as a result, this could cause them to lash out politically or even militarily at the country or countries that were engaged in the deployment."

Such scenarios, along with the fear of undercutting global negotiations to reduce emissions, make serious international consideration of geoengineering unlikely in the near term, says Homer-Dixon. But if the direst predictions about global warming prove accurate that could change. "You could see a political clamor worldwide to do something," he says.

Some scientists believe stepped-up geoengineering studies need to start soon. "We need a serious research program, and it needs to be international and transparent," says Keith. "It needs to start small. I don't think it needs to be a crash program, but I think there's an enormous value in doing the work. We've had enough hot air speculation. We need to do the work. If we find out it works pretty well, then we'll have a tool to help manage environmental risk."

— *Reed Karaim*

[1] Robert Kunzig, "A Sunshade for Planet Earth," *Scientific American*, November 2008.

[2] *Ibid.*

[3] *Ibid.*

[4] Seth Borenstein, "Wild ideas to combat global warming being seriously entertained," *The Seattle Times*, March 16, 2007, http://seattletimes.nwsource.com/html/nationworld/2003620631_warmtech16.html.

So far, the effort to control global warming has focused on limiting carbon-dioxide emissions from power plants and factories. But CO_2 accounts for only half of manmade greenhouse gas emissions.[34] The rest comes from a variety of sources, where they are often easier or cheaper to cut.

Black carbon, mainly produced by diesel engines and stoves that burn wood or cow dung, produces from one-eighth to a quarter of global warming.[35] Promoting cleaner engines and helping rural villagers move to cleaner-burning stoves would cut global warming gases, yet hardly requires the wrenching shift of moving from coal-fired electricity. Hydrofluorocarbons (HFCs) are more than a thousand times more potent as greenhouse gases than CO_2, but are used in comparably minuscule amounts and should be easier to limit.

"Why are we putting all the greenhouse gases into one agreement? CO_2 is very different from black soot, or methane or HFCs," Hulme says. "Tropical forests, why do they have to be tied to the climate agenda? They sequester carbon, yes, but they're also valuable resources in other regards."

Those who support negotiating a sweeping climate change accord believe that untangling these threads could weaken the whole cloth, robbing initiative from critical parts of the deal, such as assistance to developing countries. But Hulme believes the poorer parts of the world could benefit.

"We can tend to the adaptation needs of the developing world without having them hitched to the much greater complexity of moving the economy in the developed world away from fossil fuels," he says.

Other analysts, however, are unconvinced that climate change would be easier to deal with if its constituent issues were broken out. "There are entrenched interests on each thread," says Blackstock, at Austria's International Institute

Getty Images/Christopher Furlong

AP Photo/John Stanmeyer

Hunger and Thirst

A young Turkana girl in drought-plagued northern Kenya digs for water in a dry river bed in November 2009 (top). Momina Mohammed's 8-month-old son Ali suffers from severe malnutrition in an Ethiopian refugee camp in December 2008 (bottom). Food and water shortages caused by climate change are already affecting many countries in Africa. A Sudanese delegate to the Copenhagen Climate Change Conference called the nonbinding accord reached at the convention "an incineration pact" for poor countries.

in Applied Systems Analysis. "That's the real problem at the end of the day."

CURRENT SITUATION

Next Steps

The whole world may be warming, but as has been said, all politics is local — even climate change politics. "It's

still the legislatures of the nation states that will really determine the pace at which climate policies are driven through," notes the University of East Anglia's Hulme. "In the end, that's where these deals have to make sense."

Nations around the globe are determining their next steps in the wake of Copenhagen. Most greenhouse gases, however, come from a relative handful of countries. The United States and China, together, account for slightly more than 40 percent of the world's manmade CO_2 emissions.[36] If India and the European Union are added, the total tops 60 percent.[37] The post-Copenhagen climate change status is different for each of these major players.

China — China presents perhaps the most complex case of any of the countries central to climate change. It was classified as a developing country in the Kyoto Protocol, so it was not required to reduce carbon emissions.[38] But as the country's economy continued to skyrocket, China became the world's largest carbon dioxide emitter in 2006, passing the United States.[39] (*See graph, p. 473.*)

But with roughly 700 million poorer rural citizens, promoting economic growth remains the Chinese government's essential priority. Nevertheless, shortly before Copenhagen, China announced it would vow to cut CO_2 emissions by 40 to 45 percent *per unit of gross domestic product* below 2005 levels by 2020. The complicated formula meant that emissions would still rise, but at a slower rate. China subsequently committed to this reduction when confirming its Copenhagen pledge at the end of January.

U.N. climate policy chief de Boer hailed the move as a critical step. But the United States — especially skeptical members of the U.S. Congress — had hoped to see more movement from China and wanted verification standards.

Some participants say China's recalcitrance is why Copenhagen fell short. The British seemed particularly incensed. Ed Miliband, Great Britain's climate secretary, blamed the Chinese leadership for the failure to get agreement on a 50-percent reduction in global emissions by 2050 or on 80-percent reductions by developed countries. "Both were vetoed by China," he wrote, "despite the support of a coalition of developed and the vast majority of developing countries."[40]

But the Global Justice Ecology Project's Petermann places the blame elsewhere. "Why should China get involved in reducing emissions if the U.S. is unwilling to really reduce its emissions?" she asks.

Jiang Lin, director of the China Sustainable Energy Program, a nongovernmental agency with offices in Beijing and San Francisco, thinks China's leaders take the threat of climate change seriously. "There's probably a greater consensus on this issue in China than the United States," says Jiang. "The Chinese leadership are trained engineers. They understand the data."

Jiang points out that China already is seeing the effects predicted by climate change models, including the weakening of the monsoon in the nation's agricultural northwest and the melting of the Himalayan glaciers. "The Yellow River is drying up," he adds. "This is very symbolic for the Chinese. They consider this the mother river, and now almost half the year it is dry."

The Copenhagen Accord is not legally binding, but Jiang believes the Chinese will honors its provisions. "When they announce they're committed to something, that's almost as significant as U.S. law," he says, "because if they don't meet that commitment, losing facing is huge for them."

While attention has focused on international negotiations, China is targeting improved energy efficiency and renewable power. In 2005, China's National People's Congress set a goal of generating 20 gigawatts of power through wind energy by 2020. The goal seemed highly ambitious, but China expected to meet it by the end of 2009 and is now aiming for 150 gigawatts by 2020. The target for solar energy has been increased more than 10-fold over the same period.[41]

Coal still generates 80 percent of China's power, and the country continues to build coal-fired plants, but Chinese leaders clearly have their eyes on the green jobs that President Obama has promoted as key to America's future.[42] "Among the top 10 solar companies in the world, China already has three," says Jiang, "and China is now

More Countries Agree to Emissions Cuts

The nonbinding climate agreement reached in Copenhagen, Denmark, on Dec. 18 was originally joined by 28 countries, which were to send the United Nations by the end of January their individual goals for reducing carbon emissions by 2020. But other nations also were invited to sign on by submitting their own plans to cut emissions. On Feb. 1, the U.N. reported that a total of 55 nations had submitted targets for cutting greenhouse gases. Analysts say while these countries produce 78 percent of manmade carbon emissions, more cuts are needed. The U.N. will try to use the accord as a starting point for a binding treaty at the next international climate conference in Mexico City, Nov. 29-Dec. 10.

Key provisions in the Copenhagen Accord:

- Cut global greenhouse gas emissions so global temperatures won't rise more than 2 degrees Celsius above the pre-Industrial Revolution level.
- Cooperate in achieving a peak in emissions as soon as possible.
- Provide adequate, predictable and sustainable funds and technology to developing countries to help them adapt to climate change.
- Prioritize reducing deforestation and forest degradation, which eliminate carbon-consuming trees.
- Provide $30 billion in new and additional resources from 2010 to 2012 to help developing countries mitigate climate change and protect forests; and provide $100 billion a year by 2020.
- Assess implementation of the accord by 2015.

Sources: "Copenhagen Accord," U.N. Framework Convention on Climate Change, Dec. 18, 2009; "UNFCCC Receives list of government climate pledges," press release, United Nations Framework Convention on Climate Change, Feb. 1, 2010, http://unfccc.int/files/press/news_room/press_releases_and_advisories/application/pdf/pr_accord_100201.pdf

the largest wind market in the world. They see this as an industry in which China has a chance to be one of the leaders."

The United States — To much of the world, the refusal of the United States so far to embrace carbon emission limits is unconscionable. U.S. emissions are about twice Europe's levels per capita, and more than four times China's.

"The United States is the country that needs to lead on this issue," says Oxfam's Waskow. "It created a lot of problems that the U.S. wasn't able to come to Copenhagen with congressional legislation in hand."

In the Copenhagen Accord, President Obama committed the United States to reduce its carbon dioxide

Is the Copenhagen Accord a meaningful step forward in halting climate change?

YES Ban Ki-moon
Secretary-General, United Nations

NO Nnimmo Bassey
Chair, Friends of the Earth International

From opening remarks at press conference, U.N. Climate Change Conference, Copenhagen, Dec. 19, 2009

Written for *CQ Global Researcher*, February 2010

The Copenhagen Accord may not be everything that everyone hoped for. But this decision of the Conference of Parties is a new beginning, an essential beginning.

At the summit I convened in September, I laid out four benchmarks for success for this conference. We have achieved results on each.

- All countries have agreed to work toward a common, long-term goal to limit global temperature rise to below 2 degrees Celsius.
- Many governments have made important commitments to reduce or limit emissions.
- Countries have achieved significant progress on preserving forests.
- Countries have agreed to provide comprehensive support to the most vulnerable to cope with climate change.

The deal is backed by money and the means to deliver it. Up to $30 billion has been pledged for adaptation and mitigation. Countries have backed the goal of mobilizing $100 billion a year by 2020 for developing countries. We have convergence on transparency and an equitable global governance structure that addresses the needs of developing countries. The countries that stayed on the periphery of the Kyoto process are now at the heart of global climate action.

We have the foundation for the first truly global agreement that will limit and reduce greenhouse gas emission, support adaptation for the most vulnerable and launch a new era of green growth.

Going forward, we have three tasks. First, we need to turn this agreement into a legally binding treaty. I will work with world leaders over the coming months to make this happen. Second, we must launch the Copenhagen Green Climate Fund. The U.N. system will work to ensure that it can immediately start to deliver immediate results to people in need and jump-start clean energy growth in developing countries. Third, we need to pursue the road of higher ambition. We must turn our back on the path of least resistance.

Current mitigation commitments fail to meet the scientific bottom line.

We still face serious consequences. So, while I am satisfied that we have a deal here in Copenhagen, I am aware that it is just the beginning. It will take more than this to definitively tackle climate change.

But it is a step in the right direction.

The Copenhagen Accord is not a step forward in the battle to halt climate change. Few people expected the Copenhagen climate talks to yield a strong outcome. But the talks ended with a major failure that was worse than predicted: a "Copenhagen Accord" in which individual countries make no new serious commitments whatsoever.

The accord sets a too-weak goal of limiting warming to 2 degrees Celsius, but provides no means of achieving this goal. Likewise, it suggests an insufficient sum for addressing international solutions but contains no path to produce the funding. Individual countries are required to do nothing.

The accord fails the poor and the vulnerable communities most impacted by climate change. This non-agreement (it was merely "noted," not adopted, by the conference) is weak, nonbinding and allows false solutions such as carbon offsetting. It will prove completely ineffective. Providing some coins for developing countries to mitigate climate change and adapt to it does not help if the sources of the problem remain unchecked.

The peoples' demands for climate justice should be the starting point when addressing the climate crisis. Instead, in Copenhagen, voices of the people were shut out and peaceful protests met brutal suppression. Inside the Bella Center, where the conference took place, many of the poor countries were shut out of back-room negotiations. The accord is the result of this anti-democratic process.

The basic demands of the climate justice movement remain unmet. The U.N. climate process must resume, and it must accomplish these goals:

- Industrialized countries must commit to at least 40 percent cuts in emissions by 2020 by using clean energy, sustainable transport and farming and cutting energy demand.
- Emission cuts must be real. They cannot be "achieved" by carbon offsetting, such as buying carbon credits from developing countries or by buying up forests in developing countries so they won't be cut down.
- Rich countries must make concrete commitments to provide money for developing countries to grow in a clean way and to cope with the floods, droughts and famines caused by climate change. Funding must be adequate, not the minuscule amounts proposed in the accord.

Wealthy nations are most responsible for climate change. They have an obligation to lead the way in solving the problem. They have not done so with the Copenhagen Accord.

emissions to 17 percent below 2005 levels by 2020. That equates to about 4 percent below 1990 levels, far less stringent than the European and Japanese pledges of 20 percent and 25 percent below 1990 levels, respectively. However, Congress has not passed global warming legislation. Last year, the House of Representatives passed a bill that would establish a cap-and-trade system, which would limit greenhouse gases but let emitters trade emission allowances among themselves. The legislation faces stiff opposition in the Senate, however.

In 1997, after the Kyoto Protocol was adopted, the Senate voted 95-0 against signing any international accord unless it mandated GHG emission reductions by developing countries as well. Securing such commitments in Copenhagen — especially from China, along with improved verification — was considered critical to improving the chances a climate change bill would make it through the Senate.

Some analysts also blamed the lack of U.S. legislation for what was considered a relatively weak American proposal at Copenhagen. "Obama wasn't going to offer more than the U.S. Senate was willing to offer," says the International Institute for Applied System's Blackstock. "He could have done more and said, 'I cannot legally commit to this, but I'll go home and fight for it.' He didn't."

But Obama's negotiating effort in Copenhagen impressed some observers. "He could have stood back and worried about looking presidential," says the American Council on Renewable Energy's Eckhart. "He didn't. He rolled up his sleeves and got in there and tried to do good for the world."

Early reviews of the Copenhagen Accord were favorable among at least two key Republican senators, Lisa Murkowski of Alaska and Richard Lugar of Indiana. "Whenever you have developing countries, and certainly China and India stepping forward and indicating that they have a willingness to be a participant . . . I think that that is progress," said Murkowski.[43]

Still, analysts remain skeptical whether it will make a real difference on Capitol Hill. "I don't see Congress doing anything, even in line with the position in the Copenhagen Accord unless Obama makes it his 2010 priority," says 350.org's McKibben. "There's no question it's going to be hard because it's going to require real change."

The administration is planning to regulate some greenhouse gases through the Environmental Protection Agency (EPA). The Center for Biological Diversity has petitioned the EPA to make further use of regulation to reduce greenhouse emissions. "The president has the tools he needs. He has the Clean Air Act," says the center's Siegel. "All he has to do is use it."

However, some Senate Republicans are already calling for a resolution to undo the EPA's limited actions, and polls show a rising number of Americans skeptical about global warming, particularly Republicans.[44] Given the highly polarized nature of American politics, any significant move on climate change is likely to prove a bruising battle. President Obama has made promoting green energy jobs a priority, but with health care and joblessness still leading the administration's agenda, further action on climate change seems unlikely in the next year. Chances for major legislative action shrunk even further with the election of Republican Scott Brown, a climate change skeptic, to the Senate from Massachusetts. Brown's win ended the democrats' 60-vote, filibuster-proof majority.[45]

India — Although India's economy has grown almost as rapidly as China's in recent years, it remains a much poorer country. Moreover, its low coastline and dependence on seasonal monsoons for water also make it sensitive to the dangers of global warming. Jairam Ramesh, India's environment minister, said, "The most vulnerable country in the world to climate change is India."[46]

India's leaders announced recently they will pursue cleaner coal technology, higher emissions standards for automobiles and more energy-efficient building codes. Prior to Copenhagen, India also announced it would cut CO_2 emissions per unit of GDP from 2005 levels, but rejected legally binding targets.

After the negotiations on the accord, Ramesh told the *Hindustan Times* that India had "upheld the interest of developing nations."[47] But some analysts said India had largely followed China's lead, a position that could cost India some prestige with other developing nations, whose cause it had championed in the past.

"The worst thing India did was to align itself uncritically to China's yoke," says Indian political scientist Mehra, "because China acted purely in its own self interest."

The European Union — European leaders are calling for other countries to join them in backing the Copenhagen Accord, but they've hardly tried to hide their disappointment it wasn't more substantial. The European Union had staked out one of the stronger positions on emissions reductions beforehand, promising to cut emissions by 20 percent from 1990 levels to 2020, or 30 percent if other countries took similarly bold action. They also wanted rich nations to make 80 to 95 percent cuts in GHG emissions by 2050.[48]

Some national leaders also had expended political capital on global warming before the conference. French President Nicolas Sarkozy had announced a proposal to create a French "carbon tax" on businesses and households for use of oil, gas and coal. The proposal was blocked by the French Constitutional Council, but Sarkozy's party plans to reintroduce it this year.[49]

In the United Kingdom, Prime Minister Brown's government passed legislation committing to an 80 percent cut in U.K. greenhouse gas emissions by 2050.[50] Brown also pressed publicly for $100 billion a year in aid to the developing world to cope with climate change.

The European efforts were designed to lead by example. But analysts say the approach yielded little fruit in Copenhagen. "The European perspective that they could lead by example was the wrong strategy. This was a negotiation. Countries do not check their national interests at the door when they enter the U.N.," says the Chamber of Commerce's Eule, who worked on climate change in the Bush administration.

Although Europe's leaders finally backed the accord and formally pledged 20 percent emission reductions, they had only limited influence on the deal's final shape. "Europe finds itself now outside the driver's seat for how this is going to go forward," says Hulme at the University of East Anglia. "I think in Brussels [home of the E.U. headquarters], there must be a lot of conversations going on about where Europe goes from here." He believes Europe's stricter emissions regulations could now face a backlash.

Framework Conference chief de Boer, who is a citizen of the Netherlands, captured the resignation that seemed to envelope many European diplomats during his post-Copenhagen comments to the press. Before the climate conference kicked off, de Boer had predicted that Copenhagen would "launch action, action and more action" on climate change.

But in his December 19 press conference, when asked what he hoped could be accomplished in the year ahead, he responded, "Basically, the list I put under the Christ-mas tree two years ago, I can put under the Christmas tree again this year."

OUTLOOK

Too Late?

The world's long-term climate forecast can be summed up in a word: warmer. Even if the nations of the world were to miraculously agree tomorrow to reduce global greenhouse gas emissions, global warming could continue for some time because of the "lag" in how the climate system responds to GHG emission reductions.

In the last decade, researchers have poured a tremendous amount of effort into trying to foresee where climate change could take us. But the projections come with an element of uncertainty. Still, taken together, the most startling forecasts amount to an apocalyptic compendium of disaster. Climate change could:

- Lead to droughts, floods, heat waves and violent storms that displace tens of millions of people, particularly in Asia and sub-Saharan Africa (see "Climate Refugees," p. 480);
- Create a high risk of violent conflict in 46 countries, now home to 2.7 billion people, as the effects of climate change exacerbate existing economic, social and political problems;[51]
- Cause the extinction of about a quarter of all land-based plant and animal species — more than a million — by 2050;[52]
- Effectively submerge some island nations by 2100,[53] and create widespread dislocation and damage to coastal areas, threatening more than $28 trillion worth of assets by 2050; and[54]
- Cause acidification of the oceans that renders them largely inhospitable to coral reefs by 2050, destroying a fragile underwater ecosystem important to the world's fisheries.[55]

If temperatures climb by an average of 3.5 to 4 degrees Celsius (6.3 to 7.2 Fahrenheit) by the end of the century, as some projections predict, it would mean "total devastation for man in parts of the world," says the Global Justice Ecology Project's Petermann. "You're talking about massive glaciers melting, the polar ice caps disappearing. It would make life on this planet completely unrecognizable."

But some analysts, while endorsing the potential dangers of climate change, still back away from the view that it's a catastrophe that trumps all others. "The prospective tipping points for the worst consequences are just that, prospective tipping points, and they're resting on the credibility of scientific models," says East Anglia University's Hulme. "We should take them seriously. But they're not the Nazis marching across Belgium. We need to weigh our response within the whole range of needs facing the human race."

The critical question likely to determine the shape of the planet's future for the rest of this century and beyond is when humans will stop pouring greenhouse gases into the atmosphere. If done soon enough, most scientists say, climate change will be serious but manageable on an international level, although billions of dollars will be needed to mitigate the effects in the most vulnerable parts of the globe.

But if emissions continue to rise, climate change could be far more catastrophic. "It is critically important that we bring about a commitment to reduce emissions effectively by 2020," said IPCC Chairman Rajendra Pachauri, shortly before Copenhagen.[56]

To accomplish Copenhagen's goal of holding warming to 2 degrees Celsius, Pachauri said emissions must peak by 2015. The agreement, however, sets no peaking year, and the emission-reduction pledges by individual nations fall short of that goal, according to recent analysis by Climate Interactive, a collaborative research effort sponsored by the Sustainability Institute in Hartland, Vt.[57]

World leaders acknowledge they need to do more, and some observers remain hopeful the upcoming climate conference in Mexico City could provide a breakthrough that will avert the worst, especially if pressure to act continues to grow at the grassroots level. "Right now there is a massive gulf between where the public is and where the political process is," says India's Mehra. "But I think [in 2010] you will see government positions mature. And I think you will see more politicians who have the conviction to act."

Canadian political scientist Homer-Dixon considers bold action unlikely, however, unless the world's major emitting nations, including the United States and China, start suffering clearly visible, serious climate-change consequences.

"In the absence of those really big shocks, I'm afraid we're achieving about as much as possible," he

Getty Images/Christopher Furlong

AFP/Getty ImagesSTR

Causes of Climate Change

Rapidly industrializing China has surpassed the United States as the world's largest emitter of carbon dioxide — one of the greenhouse gases (GHG) responsible for rising world temperatures. Although most GHGs are invisible, air pollution like this in Wuhan, China, on Dec. 3, 2009 (above) often includes trapped greenhouse gases. The destruction of tropical rainforests decreases the number of trees available to absorb carbon dioxide. Palm oil trees once grew on this 250-acre plot being cleared for farming in Aceh, Indonesia (below).

says. "Because of the lag in the system, if you wait until the evidence is clear, it's too late."

NOTES

1. Yvo de Boer, the United Nation's Framework Convention on Climate Change video message before the opening of the Cop15 conference, Dec. 1, 2009, www.youtube.com/climateconference#p/u/11/ xUTXsdkinq0.

2. The complete text of the accord is at http://unfccc .int/resource/docs/2009/cop15/eng/l07.pdf.

3. John Vidal and Jonathan Watts, "Copenhagen closes with weak deal that poor threaten to reject," *The Guardian*, Dec. 19, 2009, www.guardian.co.uk/ environment/2009/dec/19/copenhagen-closes-weak-deal.

4. *Ibid.*

5. "Remarks by the President," The White House Office of the Press Secretary, Dec. 18, 2009, www .whitehouse.gov/the-press-office/remarks-president-during-press-availability-copenhagen.

6. http://action.sierraclub.org/site/MessageViewer? em_id=150181.0.

7. See Jones' complete comments at http://wdm .gn.apc.org/copenhagen-'deal'-'shameful-and-monumental-failure'.

8. Jerry Melillo, Karl Thomas and Thomas Peterson, editors-in-chief, "Global Climate Change Impacts in the United States," U.S. Global Change Research Program, executive summary, June 16, 2009, www .education-research-services.org/files/USGCRP_ Impacts_US_executive-summary.pdf.

9. Intergovernmental Panel on Climate Change staff, "Climate Change 2007: Synthesis Report," The U.N. Intergovernmental Panel on Climate Change, Nov. 17 2007, www.ipcc.ch/pdf/assessment-report/ ar4/syr/ar4_syr_spm.pdf.

10. "Climate Change responsible for 300,000 deaths a year," Global Humanitarian Forum, http://ghfge-neva.org/NewsViewer/tabid/383/vw/1/ItemID/6/ Default.aspx.

11. Andrew C. Revkin and James Kanter, "No Slowdown of Global Warming, Agency Says," *The New York Times*, Dec. 8, 2009, www.nytimes.com/2009/12/09/ science/earth/09climate.html.

12. "Key Scientific Developments Since the IPCC Fourth Assessment Report," in Key Scientific Developments Since the IPCC Fourth Assessment Report, Pew Center on Global Climate Change, June 2009.

13. "Final Copenhagen Accord Press Release," The Sustainability Institute, Dec. 19, 2009, http:// climateinteractive.org/scoreboard/copenhagen-cop15-analysis-and-press-releases.

14. "Remarks by the President," *op. cit.*

15. "Copenhagen Accord," draft proposal, United Nations Framework Convention on Climate Change, Dec. 18, 2009, p. 3. http://unfccc.int/ resource/docs/2009/cop15/eng/l07.pdf.

16. Kumi Naidoo, speaking at Copenhagen in a video blog posted by Greenpeace Australia, www.facebook .com/video/video.php?v=210068211237.

17. Ban Ki-moon, remarks to the General U.N. Assembly, Dec. 21, 2009, www.un.org/News/Press/ docs/2009/sgsm12684.doc.htm.

18. Jennifer Weeks, "Carbon Trading, Will it Reduce Global Warming," *CQ Global Researcher*, November 2008.

19. Robert Shapiro, "Addressing the Risks of Climate Change: The Environmental Effectiveness and Economic Efficiency of Emissions Caps and Tradable Permits, Compared to Carbon Taxes," February 2007, p. 26, http://67.23.32.13/system/files/carbon-tax-cap.pdf.

20. Nicolas Loris and Ben Lieberman, "Capping Carbon Emissions Is Bad, No Matter How You Slice the Revenue," Heritage Foundation, May 14, 2009, www.heritage.org/Research/Energyand Environment/wm2443.cfm.

21. Monica Prasad, "On Carbon, Tax and Don't Spend," *The New York Times*, March 25, 2008, www.nytimes .com/2008/03/25/opinion/25prasad.html.

22. "Cantwell, Collins Introduce 'Cap and Rebate' Bill," Clean Skies, Energy and Environment Network, Dec. 11, 2009, www.cleanskies.com/articles/ cantwell-collins-introduce-cap-and-rebate-bill.

23. Robert J. Shapiro, "Carbon Tax More Likely," *National Journal* expert blog, Energy and the Environment, Jan. 4, 2010, http://energy.national-journal.com/2010/01/whats-next-in-the-senate .php-1403156.

24. A concise history of Keeling and his work is at "The Keeling Curve Turns 50," Scripps Institution of Oceanography, http://sio.ucsd.edu/special/ Keeling_50th_Anniversary/.

25. Elizabeth Kolbert, *Field Notes from a Catastrophe: Man, Nature, and Climate Change* (2006), p. 2.

26. Naomi Oreskes, "Beyond the Ivory Tower: The Scientific Consensus on Climate Change," *Science*,

Dec. 3, 2004, www.sciencemag.org/cgi/content/full/306/5702/1686.

27. *Ibid.*

28. "Analysis of the Emails from the University of East Anglia's Climatic Research Unit," Pew Center on Global Climate Change, December 2009, www.pewclimate.org/science/university-east-anglia-cru-hacked-emails-analysis.

29. Quoted by Nicholas Dawidoff, "The Civil Heretic," *The New York Times Magazine*, March 23, 2009, p. 2, www.nytimes.com/2009/03/29/magazine/29Dyson-t.html?pagewanted=1&_r=1.

30. "Smoke, Mirrors & Hot Air: How ExxonMobil Uses Big Tobacco's Tactics to Manufacture Uncertainty on Climate Science," Union of Concerned Scientists, January 2007, p. 1, www.ucsusa.org/assets/documents/global_warming/exxon_report.pdf.

31. *Ibid.*

32. Many are summarized in a policy brief by the nonprofit Pew Center on Global Climate Change, "Realities vs. Misconceptions about the Science of Climate Change," August 2009, www.pewclimate.org/science-impacts/realities-vs-misconceptions.

33. Seth Borenstein, "AP IMPACT: Statisticians Reject Global Cooling," The Associated Press, Oct. 26, 2009, http://abcnews.go.com/Technology/wireStory?id=8917909.

34. "Unpacking the problem," *The Economist*, Dec. 5-11, 2009, p. 21, www.economist.com/special reports/displaystory.cfm?story_id=14994848.

35. *Ibid.*

36. It is important to note that if CO_2 emissions are calculated on a per capita basis, China still ranks far below most developed nations. The highest emitter on a per capita basis is Australia, according to the U.S. Energy Information Agency, with the United States second. See www.ucsusa.org/global_warming/science_and_impacts/science/each-countrys-share-of-co2.html.

37. A chart of the top 20 CO_2 emitting countries is at www.ucsusa.org/global_warming/science_and_impacts/science/graph-showing-each-countrys.html.

38. "China ratifies global warming treaty" CNN.com, Sept. 4, 2002, http://archives.cnn.com/2002/WORLD/africa/09/03/kyoto.china.glb/index.html.

39. "China overtakes U.S. in greenhouse gas emissions," *The New York Times*, June 20, 2007, www.nytimes.com/2007/06/20/business/worldbusiness/20iht-emit.1.6227564.html.

40. Ed Miliband, "The Road from Copenhagen," *The Guardian*, Dec. 20, 2009, www.guardian.co.uk/commentisfree/2009/dec/20/copenhagen-climate-change-accord.

41. "A Long Game," *The Economist*, Dec. 5-11, 2009, p. 18.

42. *Ibid.* Keith Bradsher, "China Leading Global Race to Make Clean Energy" *The New York Times*, Jan. 31, 2010, p. A1.

43. Darren Samuelsohn, "Obama Negotiates 'Copenhagen Accord' With Senate Climate Fight in Mind," *The New York Times*, Dec. 21, 2009, www.nytimes.com/cwire/2009/12/21/21climatewire-obama-negotiates-copenhagen-accord-with-senat-6121.html.

44. Juliet Elperin, "Fewer Americans Believe in Global Warming, Poll Shows," *The Washington Post*, Nov. 25, 2009, www.washingtonpost.com/wp-dyn/content/article/2009/11/24/AR2009112402989.html.

45. Suzanne Goldenberg, "Fate of US climate change bill in doubt after Scott Brown's Senate win," *The Guardian*, Jan. 20, 2010, www.guardian.co.uk/environment/2010/jan/20/scott-brown-climate-change-bill.

46. "India promises to slow carbon emissions rise," BBC News, Dec. 3, 2009, http://news.bbc.co.uk/2/hi/8393538.stm.

47. Rie Jerichow, "World Leaders Welcome the Copenhagen Accord," Denmark.dk, Dec. 21, 2009, www.denmark.dk/en/menu/Climate-Energy/COP15-Copenhagen-2009/Selected-COP15-news/World-leaders-welcome-the-Copenhagen-Accord.htm.

48. "Where countries stand on Copenhagen," BBC News, undated, http://news.bbc.co.uk/2/hi/science/nature/8345343.stm.

49. James Kantor, "Council in France Blocks Carbon Tax as Weak on Polluters," *The New York Times*, Dec. 31, 2009, www.nytimes.com/2009/12/31/business/energy-environment/31carbon.html.

50. Andrew Neather, "Climate Change could still be Gordon Brown's great legacy," *The London Evening*

Standard, Dec. 15, 2009, www.thisislondon.co.uk/standard/article-23783937-climate-change-could-still-be-gordon-browns-great-legacy.do.

51. Dan Smith and Janini Vivekananda, "A Climate of Conflict, the links between climate change, peace and war," *International Alert*, November 2007, www.inter-national-alert.org/pdf/A_Climate_Of_Conflict.pdf.

52. Alex Kirby, "Climate Risk to a Million Species," BBC Online, Jan. 7, 2004, http://news.bbc.co.uk/2/hi/science/nature/3375447.stm.

53. Adam Hadhazy, "The Maldives, threatened by drowning due to climate change, set to go carbon-neutral," *Scientific American*, March 16, 2009, www.scientificamerican.com/blog/post.cfm?id=maldives-drowning-carbon-neutral-by-2009-03-16.

54. Peter Wilkinson, "Sea level rise could cost port cities $28 trillion," CNN, Nov. 23, 2009, www.cnn.com/2009/TECH/science/11/23/climate.report.wwf.allianz/index.html.

55. "Key Scientific Developments Since the IPCC Fourth Assessment Report," *op. cit.*

56. Richard Ingham, "Carbon emissions must peak by 2015: U.N. climate scientist," Agence France-Presse, Oct. 15, 2009, www.google.com/hostednews/afp/article/ALeqM5izYrubhpeFvOKCRrZmWSYWCkPoRg.

57. "Final Copenhagen Accord Press Release," *op. cit.*

BIBLIOGRAPHY

Books

Hoggan, James, *Climate Cover-Up: The Crusade to Deny Global Warming*, Greystone Books, 2009.
A Canadian public relations executive who founded the anti-climate-skeptic Web site DeSmogblog takes on what he considers the oil and gas industry's organized campaign to spread disinformation and confuse the public about the science of climate change.

Hulme, Mike, *Why We Disagree About Climate Change: Understanding Controversy, Inaction and Opportunity*, Cambridge University Press, 2009.
A professor of climate change at East Anglia University in Great Britain looks at the cultural, political and scientific forces that come into play when we consider climate and what that interaction means for dealing with climate change today.

Kolbert, Elizabeth, *Field Notes from a Catastrophe: Man, Nature and Climate Change, Bloomsbury*, 2006.
A *New Yorker* writer summarizes the scientific evidence on behalf of climate change and looks at the consequences for some of the world's most vulnerable locations.

Michaels, Patrick J., and Robert C. Balling, *Climate of Extremes: Global Warming Science They Don't Want You to Know*, The Cato Institute, 2009.
Writing for a libertarian U.S. think tank, the authors argue that while global warming is real, its effects have been overstated and do not represent a crisis.

Articles

"Stopping Climate Change, A 14-Page Special Report," *The Economist*, Dec. 5, 2009.
The authors provide a comprehensive review of the state of global climate change efforts, including environmental, economic and political conditions.

Broder, John and Andrew Revkin, "A Grudging Accord in Climate Talks," *The New York Times*, Dec. 19, 2009.
The Times assesses the Copenhagen Accord and reports on the final hours of the climate change convention.

Kunzig, Robert, "A Sunshade for Planet Earth," *Scientific American*, November 2008.
An award-winning scientific journalist examines the various geoengineering options that might reduce global warming, their costs and possible consequences.

Schwartz, John, "Courts as Battlefields in Climate Fights," *The New York Times*, Jan. 26, 2009.
A reporter looks at environmental groups' and other plaintiffs' efforts to hold corporations that produce greenhouse gases legally liable for the effects of climate change on vulnerable areas, including Kivalina Island off the coast of Alaska.

Walsh, Bryan, "Lessons from the Copenhagen Climate Talks," *Time*, Dec. 21, 2009.
Time's environmental columnist provides predictions about the future of the climate change battle, based on the final Copenhagen Accord.

Walsh, Bryan, "The Stolen Emails: Has 'Climategate' Been Overblown?" *Time Magazine online*, Dec. 7, 2007. The stolen East Anglia University e-mails, the author concludes, "while unseemly, do little to change the overwhelming scientific consensus on the reality of man-made climate change."

Reports and Studies

"Climate Change 101: Understanding and Responding to Global Climate Change," *Pew Center on Global Climate Change*, January 2009. This series of reports aims to provide an introduction to climate change science and politics for the layman.

"World Development Report 2010: World Development and Climate Change," *World Bank*, November 2009, http://econ.worldbank.org/ WBSITE/EXTERNAL/EXTDEC/EXTRESEARCH/ EXTWDRS/EXTWDR2010/0,,contentMDK:21969 137~menuPK:5287816~pagePK:64167689~piPK:64 167673~theSitePK:5287741,00.html. This exhaustive, 300-page study examines the consequences of climate change for the developing world and the need for developed nations to provide financial assistance to avert disaster.

Bernstein, Lenny, *et al.*, "Climate Change 2007: Synthesis Report," *The Intergovernmental Panel of Climate Change*, 2007, www.ipcc.ch/pdf/assessment-report/ar4/syr/ar4_syr_spm.pdf. The international body tasked with assessing the risk of climate change caused by human activity gathered scientific research from around the world in this widely quoted report to conclude, "warming of the climate system is unequivocal."

Thomas, Karl, Jerry Melillo and Thomas Peterson, eds., "Global Climate Change Impacts in the United States," *United States Global Change Research Program*, June 2009, www.globalchange .gov/publications/reports/scientific-assessments/ us-impacts. U.S. government researchers across a wide range of federal agencies study how climate change is already affecting the United States.

For More Information

Cato Institute, 1000 Massachusetts Avenue, N.W., Washington D.C. 20001; (202) 842-0200; www.cato.org/ global-warming. A conservative U.S. think tank that maintains an extensive database of articles and papers challenging the scientific and political consensus on climate change.

Climate Justice Now; www.climate-justice-now.org. A network of organizations and movements from around the world committed to involving people in the fight against climate change and for social and economic justice at the grassroots level.

Climate Research Unit, University of East Anglia, Norwich, NR4 7TJ, United Kingdom; +44-1603-592722; www.cru .uea.ac.uk. Recently in the news when its e-mail accounts were hacked; dedicated to the study of natural and manmade climate change.

Greenpeace International, Ottho Heldringstraat 5, 1066 AZ Amsterdam, The Netherlands; +31 (0) 20 7182000; www.greenpeace.org/international. Has made climate change one of its global priorities; has offices around the world.

Intergovernmental Panel on Climate Change, c/o World Meteorological Organization, 7bis Avenue de la Paix, C.P. 2300 CH- 1211, Geneva 2, Switzerland; +41-22-730-8208; www.ipcc.ch. U.N. body made up of 2,500 global scientists; publishes periodic reports on various facets of climate change, including a synthesis report summarizing latest findings around the globe.

Pew Center on Global Climate Change, 2101 Wilson Blvd., Suite 550, Arlington, VA, 22201; (703) 516-4146; www.pewclimate.org. Nonprofit, nonpartisan organization established in 1998 to promote research, provide education and encourage innovative solutions to climate change.

United Nations Framework Convention on Climate Change, Haus Carstanjen, Martin-Luther-King-Strasse 853175 Bonn, Germany; +49-228-815-1000; http://unfccc.int/2860.php. An international treaty that governs climate change negotiations.

Confronting Rape as a War Crime

Will a New U.N. Campaign Have Any Impact?

Jina Moore

Kula, a 47-year-old victim of the mass rapes that occurred during Liberia's civil war, covers her face in shame as she tells counselors at a treatment center about her wartime trauma. While some experts say more men are needed in the fight for justice for war rape victims, women's advocates say local and international courts must prosecute rapists.

AP Photo/Ben Curtis

19

From *CQ Global Researcher*, May 2010.

Last fall in Guinea, soldiers killed 157 pro-democracy protestors in the capital city of Conakry. The horrific violence in and around the city's sports stadium was tragic but not unprecedented in West Africa. But then reports emerged that the soldiers also had raped at least 109 women in broad daylight. The conservative Muslim country — and the international community — were shocked by both the public nature and the sheer viciousness of the attacks.

In a deliberate attempt to engender public humiliation, the victims were often stripped on the streets and gang-raped in front of onlookers, some of whom recorded the attacks with cell phone cameras. Eyewitnesses and survivors told of women being raped with guns and then shot; of soldiers using knives to slice off women's clothing and then to sexually assault them. Some women reportedly were dragged into houses where they were held captive and gang-raped for days.

"It is simply horrifying. Women were raped, gang-raped in the open, in and around the stadium, in the cold light of day," one woman said. "I have never seen such violence in my life. I swear that this is the first time in Guinea that we have witnessed women's bodies being treated as if they were battlefields. It goes against our culture and traditions. . . . We're all horrified."[1]

Guinea's mass rapes were only the latest example of the strategic use of rape, a common wartime tactic that is now also increasingly used to spread terror and humiliation among political opponents. "A woman's place is in the home. If you want political rallies, we'll show you political rallies. We'll show you who's in command in this country," one Guinean woman remembered her attacker saying.[2]

Africa Hit Hardest by Wartime Sexual Violence

More than two dozen countries around the world suffered widespread or numerous rapes during civil wars between 1980 and 1999. Ten nations experienced widespread sexual violence during conflicts, including five in Africa.

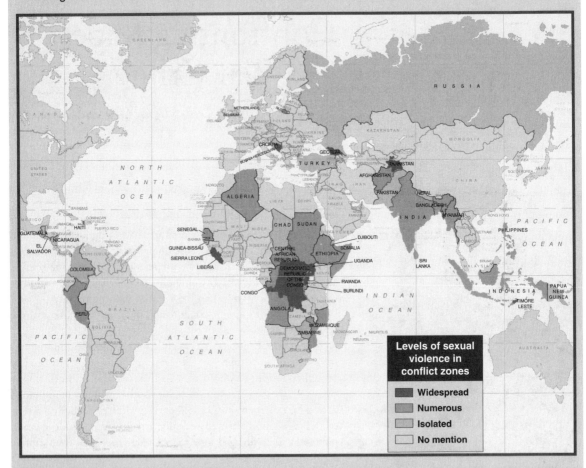

Source: Dara Kay Cohen, "The Causes of Sexual Violence by Insurgents During Civil War: Cross-National Evidence," University of Minnesota, 2009

The U.N. Security Council dispatched a commission of inquiry to Guinea to investigate the incidents. In December the panel reported that the rapes and massacre were ordered by the then-leader of Guinea's military, Moussa Dadis Camara, who had taken over the government in a coup d'etat nine months before the stadium massacre. Camara's government had tried to cover up the September massacre, the panel said, by denying victims medical treatment, sabotaging evidence and intimidating witnesses — actions not uncommon by governments after their soldiers commit mass rape.[3]

Rape in conflict zones is not new. As long as there has been war and conflict between men, soldiers have raped women. And wartime rape is not limited by time or geography. From World War II to the 1971 war in Bangladesh, from Latin America to the disputed Kashmir region claimed by India and Pakistan — rape as a war strategy exploded in the 20th century and continues today.

But as the mass rapes in Guinea exemplified, today's rape is often different — in its brutality, scope and goals. Women are no longer simply part of the spoils of war — "booty and beauty," as Gen. Andrew Jackson reportedly quipped, protesting the barbarity of the British during the War of 1812.[4] Neither is modern wartime rape an isolated occurrence perpetrated by rogue soldiers. In many conflicts, as in Guinea, mass rape has become an official strategy — a tactic premeditated at the highest levels of military and civilian leadership.

"In modern conflicts, rape is the front line of conflict. It is not a side effect," says Margot Wallström, appointed in February as the first special representative to the U.N. secretary-general for sexual violence. No one knows how many women are raped in conflicts each year; the number of rapes reported is believed to be low because many go unreported due to the stigma associated with rape. Survivors often don't speak up because they believe they will be ostracized for bringing shame to their families and communities.

Guinea is not the only place where mass rape has been used to spread terror among dissidents. More than 2,000 women and girls — allegedly associated with the opposition party — were raped leading up to and immediately after the disputed 2008 presidential elections in Zimbabwe.[5] Agents of President Robert Mugabe's ZANU-PF party fanned out across the country in a deliberate campaign of rape as political retribution against opposition supporters, according to an investigation by AIDS-Free World.[6] And in Kenya, up to 3,000 women were raped in the ethnic violence that erupted

---

Rape: A Weapon Used in War and Peace

Hundreds of thousands of women have been raped during modern conflicts — both military and political. The victims range from hundreds of thousands of Eastern Europeans raped by Soviet troops after World War II to the thousands raped in Zimbabwe, Kenya and Guinea during recent election or political violence.

Number of Victims in Selected Mass Rapes

Up to 80,000 — By Japanese occupiers in the Chinese city of Nanking during World War II (1937-38).

Up to 110,000 — By the Soviet Army in Berlin plus hundreds of thousands — some say as many as 2 million — across Eastern Europe at the end of the World War II (1945).

200,000-400,000 — During Bangladesh's "war of liberation" (1971).

20,000-50,000 — By Serbs during the war in Bosnia and Herzegovina (early 1990s).

250,000-500,000 — Tutsi women raped by Hutus over the three-month period of the Rwandan genocide (1994).

50,000-64,000 — Women and girls living in internal displaced persons camps during the civil war in Sierra Leone (1990s).

Up to 3,000 — Women attacked during post-election violence in Kenya (2008).

More than 2,000 — Females associated with the political opposition raped before and after the disputed presidential election in Zimbabwe (2008).

109 — Raped by government soldiers in Guinea in premeditated effort to terrorize dissidents (2009).

12,000-15,000 per year — Raped during the ongoing conflict in eastern Democratic Republic of the Congo (2000-present).

Sources: "Security Council Resolution 1820: Women, Peace and Security," U.N. Development Fund for Women; Iris Chang and Laura Flanders, in Anne L. Barstow, ed., *War's Dirty Secret* (2000); Conway W. Henderson, "The Political Repression of Women," *Human Rights Quarterly,* November 2004; Susanne Beyer, "German Woman Writes Ground-Breaking Account of WW2 Rape," *Der Spiegel,* Feb. 26, 2010

---

after the 2007 presidential elections.[7] Mass rape has also been used as a tool of ethnic cleansing or genocide in Bosnia and Herzegovina, Rwanda, Bangladesh and Darfur in western Sudan.

During the war in the Balkans in the early 1990s, an estimated 20,000 Muslim women were raped by Serb soldiers, some in "rape camps" set up expressly for that purpose.[8] The conflict led the United Nations to recognize rape as a tool of ethnic cleansing[9] and the International Criminal Tribunal for the former Yugoslavia to rule, for the first time in history, that rape is a crime against humanity.[10]

The International Criminal Tribunal for Rwanda in 1998 recognized rape as an act of genocide as committed during the 1994 Rwandan genocide, when machete-wielding extremist Hutu militias murdered up to 800,000 minority Tutsis and moderate Hutus and also raped 250,000-500,000 Tutsi women and girls. Their goal was to punish the women for their ethnic identity or to infect them with HIV/AIDS.[11]

More recently, roving *janjaweed* militias, mostly of Arab descent, have raped black Sudanese women in Darfur in what many say is a genocidal campaign. "They grabbed my donkey and my straw and said, 'Black girl, you are too dark. You are like a dog. We want to make a light baby,' " recalled 22-year-old Sawela Suliman. " 'You get out of this area and leave the child when it is made.' "[12]

And while the Guinean population was shocked by the sheer brutality of the mass rapes in Conakry, the level of violence was not uncommon, according to physicians and aid workers who minister to the victims. "A stick was pushed through the private parts of an 18-year-old pregnant girl and it appeared [through her abdomen]. She was torn apart," a Colombian woman told Amnesty International of a crime she had witnessed.[13]

Similarly horrific rapes have occurred during the ongoing conflict in eastern Democratic Republic of Congo (DRC). Denis Mukwege, a physician who specializes in treating rape victims at the Panzi Hospital in DRC, said, "When you talk about rape in New York or Paris everyone can always say, 'Yes we have rape here, too.' But it's not the same thing when a woman is raped by four or five people at the same time, when a woman is raped in front of her husband and children, when a woman is not just raped but then . . . her genitals are attacked with a gun, a stick, a torch or a bayonet. That's not what you see in New York. That's not what you see in Paris."[14]

On a recent trip to the DRC, Secretary of State Hillary Rodham Clinton — the first person in her post to visit since the fighting erupted there nearly 10 years ago — demanded accountability for the Congo rapes.

"We state to the world that those who attack civilian populations using systematic rape are guilty of crimes against humanity," she said.[15] Her comment reflects a new understanding that rape in conflict areas is about more than opportunity, or testosterone gone wild or the notion of spoils in war. Wartime rape is about terror, about targeting and about threatening whole communities by violating their women.

Another type of wartime rape has emerged: rape against men, which aid workers say has increased in the past year in eastern Congo.[16] Researchers also have documented rape against men in conflicts in Peru and El Salvador, among others. No one knows how many such crimes have occurred, however, because men and boys — facing perhaps even greater difficulty telling their stories than female rape victims — report the crime in far fewer numbers. And when they do, it often is not recorded as sexual violence.

Women's advocates say rape against men is too easily sensationalized and detracts attention from the much more pervasive problem of rape against women. But Yale University political science professor Elisabeth Jean Wood says to "really understand the different forms and settings where sexual violence occurs . . . we need to understand the patterns of sexual violence against men and boys as well."

Whether committed as an act of terror or genocide or as a crime of opportunity, wartime rape of women serves a unique function: It destroys communities. "This is certainly used as a way to intimidate women, as a way to break the backs of communities, to bring shames to communities," says Maryam Elahi, director of the International Women's Program at the Open Society Institute, a democracy-promoting organization financed by the George Soros Foundation in New York.

Desiree Zwanck agrees. She is a German expert on violence against women with the HEAL Africa hospital in Goma, in eastern DRC, where UNICEF has reported that more than 1,000 women are raped each month. [17] "They've been rejected by their husbands, by their families, even by entire communities, which basically don't want to be close to them or associated with them any more," she says.

Mukesh Kapila, a Sri Lankan physician, has worked in Rwanda, DRC and Darfur, where he was considered a "whistleblower" on rape and genocide. He points out that rape is also "a cheap way to prosecute a war," because it doesn't require guns or munitions to devastate the "morale . . . the very integrity of the society."

Nearly everyone agrees impunity contributes to the proliferation of the problem. Both international and domestic courts have been slow to prosecute wartime rapists. The Rome Statute, which delineates the crimes under the International Criminal Court's (ICC) jurisdiction, defines rape as both a crime against humanity and a war crime.[18] Established in 2002 to prosecute war crimes and crimes against humanity, the ICC has confirmed charges against only two defendants for rape or sexual violence charges, even though it has filed charges against 13 people for alleged war crimes in Sudan, the Central African Republic, the DRC and Uganda.[19] The court is investigating the political rapes in Guinea and Kenya, but no charges have been filed yet.[20] In eastern Congo, the government has prosecuted 27 soldiers — none of them high-level officers — for sexual violence in 2008, even though the United Nations documented nearly 8,000 new cases of rape committed by Congolese soldiers or by rebel or militia groups in the region.[21]

Still, some new precedents have been established. The Special Court for Sierra Leone, created in 2002 to prosecute atrocities committed during the country's civil war, ruled in 2008 that taking a woman as a "bush wife" — a kind of forced marriage of the battlefield — was a crime against humanity.[22] In the last two years, the Security Council passed two resolutions aimed at better protecting women in war zones. Resolution 1888, adopted in September 2009, established Wallström's post. (*See box, p. 510.*) A U.N. resolution in 2008 demanded an end to both sexual violence and impunity for perpetrators. (*See At Issue, p. 514.*)

But Kapila says it will take generations to curb wartime rape and its legacy. "The atmosphere, the feeling it leaves behind, the degradation of society as a whole, the relationships of men and women, the effect on children — it will be at least a couple of generations" before the crime is overcome, he says. "Violent societies beget violent societies."

As international organizations and governments around the world strive to end wartime rape and cope with the aftermath, here are some of the questions being asked:

Is rape an inevitable consequence of war?

For millennia, war and rape were thought to go hand in hand, and political and military leaders alike have long claimed it is impossible to rein in troops. A veteran journalist described the reaction as a "worldwide shrug, in effect saying rape is an unavoidable part of the battlefield."[23]

Some have argued that war gives men cover to commit violence against women, others that war whips men into a frenzy from which sex is a release. Often, wartime rape has been construed as an unfortunate consequence of circumstantial celibacy; both Japanese Gen. Matsui Iwane and American Gen. George S. Patton thought during World War II that men without wives or girlfriends needed prostitutes, and that the availability of sex workers might keep soldiers from raping civilians in the theater. Japan even went so far as to forcibly conscript up to 200,000 "comfort women" from among the populations of countries they occupied, primarily China, Korea and the Philippines.[24]

In his book examining biological explanations for war, British historian David Livingstone Smith argues that rape is necessarily intertwined with battle. "Warriors have a twofold sexual advantage," he writes. "They are especially attractive to women in their own communities . . . [and] they can also sexually coerce the wives and daughters of defeated enemies." Smith thinks this gave warriors a reproductive edge, resulting in successive generations inheriting "the war-like temperament" — and, presumably, instinct for rape —"of their fathers."[25]

Maurizia Tovo, a social protection specialist for Africa at the World Bank, thinks an element of mass psychology is at work. Particularly in Côte d'Ivoire (Ivory Coast), where rebels and government forces alike have used rape in an armed conflict dating back to 2002, rape is sometimes committed by "men who individually wouldn't do that," she says. "In a group, it becomes sort of a frenzy, or at least an acceptable thing to do. Inevitable may be a strong word, but it's close to it."[26]

But the Open Society Institute's Elahi says rape does not necessarily have to be the norm in conflict situations. "It's taken for granted that soldiers kill, loot and rape," she says. "That's a myth we have to start fighting against."

Indeed, in some conflicts at least one side has abstained from rape. For instance, very little rape occurred during ethnic and political violence in Indonesia from 1999 to 2002, in part because militia members'

Secretary of State Hillary Rodham Clinton speaks with U.N. peacekeepers during a trip to Goma in the Democratic Republic of Congo in August 2009. She demanded accountability for the thousands of rapes in the war-ravaged eastern part of the country, calling them "crimes against humanity."

communal traditions generally forbade the sexual assault of women.[27] In Guatemala, where the government violence against Mayans has been described as genocide, guerrilla fighters generally abstained from the use of rape.[28] So, too, did insurgents during the separatist conflict in Sri Lanka and in El Salvador's civil struggle in the 1970s and 1980s.[29]

Yale's Wood studies conflicts in which rape is not used as a tool of war. She attributes the abstention, in part, to the norms of behavior that govern the fighters. "Recruits come into an armed group with certain cultural norms about what kind of violence is appropriate against whom," she says. Leaders "build training camps and develop internal regulations to transform those cultural norms . . . into . . . norms that support the kinds of violence the armed group wants to engage in." In other words, the use of rape is a deliberate choice, often of the military elite who set the standards for acceptable behavior on and off the battlefield.

Sometimes, researchers say, rape is used asymmetrically. Michele Leiby, a researcher at the University of New Mexico, found that insurgents in Guatemala and El Salvador abstained from rape. In Sierra Leone, on the other hand, the rebel Revolutionary United Front engaged in widespread rape, and some of the perpetrators were women, either as accomplices in gang rape or as direct participants, using guns, bottles or both.[30]

Wood says the war experience may change the warriors, including those predisposed not to engage in rape. "Once in combat, wielding violence and seeing violence wielded and suffering violence, many combatants undergo some very profound psychological processes," she says. "Some become desensitized to violence; they tend to dehumanize those associated with the enemy and to [blame] . . . the civilians they're shooting at," individually or collectively. All of that can change the idea of acceptable behavior, she says.

Financial considerations may also motivate some officers to direct their troops to rape, since rape is a low-cost way to destroy an enemy society. "I don't think it is a consequence of a lack of discipline. These are acts of commission," says Kapila. "Very definitely, it appears orchestrated, that officers and those in command are using [rape] strategically."

If rape is a choice, say Kapila and others, it is not inevitable, and the key to its prevention may be changing that cost-benefit analysis: Making sexual violence an unappealing, costly option.

Can the global community stop strategic rape?

The international community has taken several steps recently to address the problem of wartime rape.

In February the U.N. appointed Wallström as special representative on sexual violence to report to U.N. Secretary-General Ban Ki-moon and the U.N. Security Council. Two earlier resolutions in 2000 and 2008 demanded the cessation of rape, promised punishment for perpetrators and encouraged women to get involved in negotiating peace and rebuilding nations and communities.[31]

But few feel resolutions alone can prevent strategic rape. "We need those expressions," says Kapila of the formal resolutions, if only to acknowledge that the rapes are occurring. "One of the things I remember from my own Darfur experience is that [women] felt that they were not [there]; there was a complicity of silence. But," he continues, "as always with such resolutions, it is the enforcement . . . that is necessary."

U.N. special representative Wallström took a similar point of view four months before her appointment. The resolutions "are excellent, they are very good texts," she said, "but the problem is implementation and enforcement, so very little has happened. I would say almost nothing."[32]

Today, she interprets her appointment as a call for implementation and enforcement, and she is optimistic about the U.N.'s ability to help prevent the ongoing use of rape. "There is a window of political opportunity at the moment, especially with me reporting directly to the Security Council," she says. "There is this chance of creating a political accountability, and I would say this is what I would have to use to the full."

Creating accountability is one solution, but the path to combating rape depends on the cause. If rape is a crime of opportunity, says Wallström, then opportunity must be eliminated. For instance, refugee camps can be designed in ways that minimize rape risk factors, such as reducing the distance women must travel to fetch firewood, a trip that can leave women and girls isolated, exposed and vulnerable to rapists. A U.N. peacekeeper in DRC suggested that governments could pay soldiers on time, eliminating the need for them to loot houses for food.

But where rape is used as a weapon, the calculus of the perpetrators must be changed, experts say. "Armed groups that are good at extracting resources, carrying out offensives and retreating should be able to apply those same military hierarchies to prohibiting sexual violence and other forms of violence against civilians if they have the right incentives to do so," says Yale's Wood.

Punishment, or at least legal accountability, should be the top priority among those incentives, many say. If perpetrators are never tried, in either local or international courts, then the crime is cost-free. Tovo, at the World Bank, says even one well-publicized trial could be helpful. "It would be good to have some symbolic [judicial] processes," she says. "If . . . the culprit is actually condemned, with a lot of publicity around it, it will send the message that

'This is not acceptable; it is not right; and if you do it you will be punished.'"

On the other hand, she says, making the cost of rape too high could have unintended consequences. "If you make a huge deal out of rape, and you put the person in prison for life, at this point the person may think he's better off after he rapes the woman to also kill her. He then limits the risk of being condemned, because there's no witness," she says.

Trials aren't the only way to send a signal to armed groups that rape has consequences. Dara Kay Cohen, an

Rapists Targeted Opponents in Zimbabwe Election

During the disputed 2008 presidential election in Zimbabwe, more than 2,000 women and girls were raped by agents of President Robert Mugabe's ZANU-PF party, according to AIDS-Free World. Some of the victims reportedly opposed Mugabe; others were married to opposition supporters. In some cases, the victims were taken to ZANU-PF camps in eastern Zimbabwe, the organization said.

Locations Where Rapes Were Documented in Zimbabwe, 2008

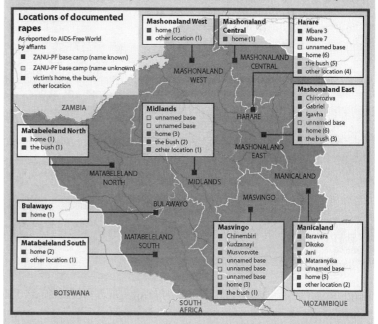

Source: "Electing to Rape: Sexual Terror in Mugabe's Zimbabwe," AIDS-Free World, December 2009

U.N. Recognizes Rape as War Tactic

The U.N. Security Council adopted Resolution 1820 in 2008, explicitly recognizing sexual violence as a tactic of war and giving the council authority to intervene when necessary to provide security to victims. It also demands that conflicting parties train troops and enforce military discipline in an effort to end sexual violence.

Key Elements of Resolution 1820

- Explicitly links sexual violence as a tactic of war with the maintenance of international peace and security. It will no longer be possible to portray rape in war as an issue that does not warrant the council's attention.

- Recognizes sexual violence as a security issue, thus justifying a security response. The council thus has a clear mandate to intervene, including through sanctions and empowering field staff.

- Requests a comprehensive report from the secretary-general on strategies for improving providing the council with better data to inform better responses.

- Demands that parties in armed conflicts adopt concrete protection/prevention measures to end sexual violence, including training troops, enforcing military discipline, upholding command responsibility and investigating past perpetrators.

- Asserts the importance of women's participation in all processes related to ending sexual violence in conflict, including peace talks.

Source: "Security Council Resolution 1820," U.N. Action Against Sexual Violence in Conflict

assistant professor at the University of Minnesota's Hubert H. Humphrey Institute of Public Affairs, has done extensive fieldwork talking to Sierra Leonean ex-combatants, including rapists, many of whom said they contracted sexually transmitted diseases after participating in gang rape. "It was not only unpleasant and uncomfortable but directly affected the ability of combatants to fight, to walk, to run, to urinate," Cohen says. That, in turn, led to concern about engaging in rape.

Sending signals from the international community may be less important than ensuring protection on the ground, says Doris Mpoumou, director of the International Coalition for the Responsibility to Protect, a New York based organization that advocates protection for civilians in conflict zones. She wants the U.N. to better prepare peacekeepers to protect women by including

rape prevention in the formal rules of engagement approved by the Security Council that set the scope of a peace-keeping mission.

"We've heard directly from the women in Bunia or in the Kivus [in eastern DRC] that some women can be raped in front of the blue berets [U.N. peacekeepers] and they don't even act, because it's not in their mandate, which is just ridiculous," Mpoumou says. "The mandate is key."

The U.N. mandate in the DRC does require its soldiers to "protect civilians under imminent threat of physical violence," but critics often charge that civilian protection clauses are vague, and unless they are translated into direct marching orders by commanders, soldiers often do not know when they should or shouldn't intervene.

Meanwhile, the U.N. itself has a spotty record when it comes to troop behavior. In 2009, the world body received more than 100 reports of sexual abuse or exploitation committed by its peacekeepers, the vast majority of them in the DRC. But only about a dozen reports received follow-up by the U.N. member states whose troops allegedly were involved.[33]

Does speaking out about strategic rape do more harm than good?

In March 2005, the Dutch branch of Médecins Sans Frontières, or Doctors Without Borders, published a report about rape in Darfur. The Sudanese government responded by arresting two of the organization's doctors and charging them with espionage. In 2006, the government effectively evicted the Norwegian Refugee Council for its report on gender-based violence in Darfur.[34]

"You can't even talk about" rape in Sudan, says Susannah Sirkin, deputy director of Physicians for Human Rights. Organizations have opted for euphemisms like "protection," but even those are becoming problematic. "The word 'protection' is dangerous because that implies people need to be protected," which might anger a government intent on denying the severity of the conflict. "So then it becomes 'services for support to women.' Those are necessary code words to talk about women who have been raped in war."

In both Sudan and the DRC, Sirkin says, perpetrators have begun creating obstacles to prevent women from accessing health services after they've been raped. In Sudan, President Omar al-Bashir evicted 13 aid organizations after the International Criminal Court indicted him for genocide. With their departure, services for survivors of rape and other gender-based violence (GBV) were cut back dramatically. As one aid worker put it, "After the expulsions, the message was clear — work on GBV, and you'll be kicked out."[35]

The chilling effect knows no borders. In Chad, Sudan's western neighbor, humanitarian organizations are reluctant to offer services to rape victims. And in Burma (also known as Myanmar), activists see the same hesitancy. "The international organizations I met with very informally in Burma are very fearful of doing anything, because they're afraid they'll be thrown out," says Jody Williams, the Nobel Peace Prize laureate for her work to ban land mines and chair of the Nobel Women's Initiative, an Ontario-based association of women Nobel laureates promoting gender rights and accountability for sexual violence around the world. "Sometimes we think, 'Do something. Be thrown out. You're not making any change!' "

Burmese women's activist Phyu Phyu Sann agrees. "I worked inside Burma. International organizations . . . fear. They become like the Burmese people," says Sann, now a researcher with the Center for Global Justice in New York. "They don't want to lose their projects. They don't want to lose their jobs."

Though the trade-off can be risky, not everyone agrees that silence is worth the price. Sann insists that speaking out in Burma is an obligation. "If you see it's injustice, that it's not right, at least we can put it in a report," she says.

Rape survivors also face the trade-off between speaking out and keeping silent. In many countries, women are blamed for the attack. "In some cases if a woman speaks up she is kicked out. She becomes ostracized, sometimes she is kicked out by the family, and sometimes by the whole village," says Tovo of the World Bank.

In many cases, women try to keep rape a secret. In Nepal, victims often are silenced by their husbands. "Sometimes the wife wants to talk about it, but the husband shuts her up, saying 'You better not talk about it or go any place to report about it, because I also feel ashamed that you've been raped,' " says Bandana Rana, president of the Kathmandu-based women's organization Saathi-Nepal.

Some rape victims may even be formally punished. "When I was eight months pregnant from the rape, the police came to my hut and forced me with their guns to go to the police station. They asked me questions, so I told them that I had been raped. They told me that as I was not married, I will deliver this baby illegally," a rape survivor in Sudan told Doctors Without Borders. She was beaten and imprisoned with other women who were also carrying children from rape. She was released after 10 days, but she had to pay a $65 fine for her "crime."[36]

On the other hand, in some countries the widespread nature of the crime can actually encourage women to speak out. "When rape is something so commonly experienced by victims, at least some of the stigma seems to be mitigated," as in Sierra Leone, says Cohen, of the University of Minnesota.

Indeed, after the war that created Bangladesh — in which 3 million people died and an estimated 200,000 women were raped — authorities declared rape victims national heroines, hoping to break through the stigma and urge husbands to take back their wives, no longer sinners but patriots.[37]

Tovo says getting survivors' stories into public discussion is the only way to change the status quo on both the individual and collective levels. The more women speak freely, she says, the less likely their communities will reject them. Meanwhile, growing public attention to the problem has resulted in better interventions. "It became more acceptable to talk about it, and therefore there are more . . . resources to help survivors, as they should be called," she says.

Tovo also thinks a healthy public discourse about rape may help prevent its recurrence. "I'm the mother of a boy, for example. I would hope my boy, the way he has been brought up, would never, ever dream of doing something like that," Tovo says. "If there is enough discussed in the culture, I would hope that at least in some cases, the discussion would act as a brake."

Helping Survivors Heal After War Rape

'Women have had enough of these things happening. They want this to end.'

The use of rape as a weapon of war may be global, but today the Democratic Republic of Congo (DRC) is often called the epicenter of the crisis. The eastern part of one of Africa's biggest countries has been the site of on-and-off fighting for the last 10 years. As peace talks come and go, violence ebbs and flows.

"We say the war has ended," said Denis Mukwege, a physician who treats rape victims in eastern Congo's South Kivu province. "But really it has not ended."[1]

The consequences of rape are many — physical, psychological, spiritual and social — and they linger. But intervention specialists, from doctors to gender advisers to lawyers, are trying to improve the situation for rape survivors in eastern Congo.

Their primary concern is the physical effect of rape. Eastern DRC has become infamous for the particularly traumatic physical consequences of some rapes there. The condition, known as fistula, occurs when the wall between the vagina and the rectum tears; it can happen in childbirth, as well, but it has lately been a consequence of rape in which foreign objects are used. Women who suffer from fistula can't control their excretions, and they are often isolated by their communities, left to suffer alone. They are, as one survivor described it, "not women anymore."[2]

Fistula can be fixed with surgery. And after recent international and national publicity about the dire situation for eastern Congo's rape victims, survivors have begun turning up to ask for the surgery. Doctors also are being trained in how to perform it.

HEAL Africa hospital in Goma, capital of DRC's North Kivu province, takes a more holistic and communal approach to rape and its consequences. It treats the physical and psychological needs of survivors and creates community outreach programs. "We try to help these women by having counselors on the ground," says Desiree Zwanck, the group's gender advisor, "When a woman comes back [from the hospital] to her community, we try to discuss it with the husbands and with the families and start a mediation process."

Zwanck has also found that giving returning survivors access to microcredit can improve their chances for acceptance in their homes and communities — and improve their own sense of self-respect.[3] "A lot of families here are in such dire need that they are actually more inclined to accept the woman back into the household when there is an economic incentive for it," she says. "When they are able to manage their own funds, their own livestock, their own little boutique, the family respects them more, and so does the community."

But HEAL Africa is also home to professionals who don't usually walk the hospital halls: legal advisors.

The American Bar Association (ABA) has a one-room office at the hospital. Flanked by offices for psychological and spiritual counseling, the offices are a "one-stop shop" for survivor services. The ABA helps women who want to press charges against the men who raped them. The choice is becoming more and more popular, says Mirielle Amani Kahatwa, an ABA program officer at the hospital. "Women have had enough of these things happening. They want this to end."

BACKGROUND

Spoils of War

There has always been rape during wartime. But today's strategic rape — in which rape becomes a weapon of war — is fundamentally different from the sexual assault perpetrated by an individual soldier against a vulnerable woman. Strategic rape is committed with a specific political intent.

It is "rape unto death, rape as massacre, rape to kill and to make the victims wish they were dead," wrote American human rights lawyer Catherine A. MacKinnon. "It is rape as an instrument of forced exile, rape to make you leave your home and never want to go back. It is rape to be seen and heard and watched and told to others: rape as spectacle. It is rape to drive a wedge through a community, to shatter a society, to destroy a people. It is rape as genocide."[38]

While there have been isolated examples of such intentional use of rape throughout history, the practice — on today's broad scale — is relatively new. In the 1975 book *Against Our Will*, the first comprehensive look at rape,

So they turn to the courts to fight against impunity, hoping that punishing some rapists might deter others. Since last September, the ABA has helped move 226 cases through local Congolese courts, resulting in 20 convictions.

Kahatwa says the process can be difficult: Not all perpetrators are known, and those who are can't always be found. And in some cases, like that of Marie Chantal Murakamanzi, the rapists are in positions of authority themselves.

Murakamanzi wears the brightly patterned *kitenge* fabric popular among Congolese women; a baby suckles at her breast. She has two other children, but she left them alone, without even a word, fleeing, as she tells it, for her life after a local police commander raped her.

The policeman controls her part of Masisi, in rural eastern Congo. He accused her and her brother of orchestrating a cattle theft the night before; her brother was tortured. She, too, was abused. "Then he said, 'If you don't agree to have sex with me, I will torture you more than your brother,'" she recalls, explaining that she knew she would not survive the torture. "I was obliged to agree."

She fled to Goma after the rape, hoping that if she reported it to the authorities they might free her brother and prosecute the commander. She was treated at HEAL Africa and reported the rape, but the ABA legal clinic hasn't been able to get the commander arrested: No one is willing to serve him with the papers. Murakamanzi, meanwhile, is afraid to go home. "I may be killed by him," she says.

That makes the risk of pursuing prosecution worth it, she says. "If he isn't arrested, his family could do its best to kill me" to make the allegation disappear, she says. "If he is arrested, I will feel secure. Everyone will see the greatness of the crime that he has done, and that will bring my family security."

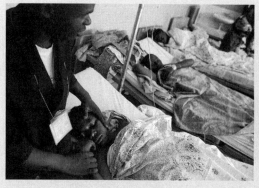

Father Samuel prays with a Congolese rape victim on Aug. 11, 2009, before she undergoes surgery at the Heal Africa clinic in Goma to repair severe physical damage caused to her internal organs by her brutal rape.

As Murakamanzi's story suggests, despite much progress in treating eastern Congo's rape victims, impunity is still widespread.

Kahatwa sees this, too. In fact, she says, impunity is an even bigger problem than war rape. "Before, it was like a gun in war. Today, things have cooled down," she says. "But the mind remains in people, especially in soldiers . . . and the perpetrators know they may rape with impunity."

— *Jina Moore*

[1] "Surgeon describes horrors that ensue when rape is a 'weapon of war,'" *Harvard Gazette*, April 17, 2008, http://news.harvard.edu/gazette/story/2008/04/surgeon-describes-horrors-that-ensue-when-rape-is-a-'weapon-of-war'/.

[2] Stephanie Nolen, "Congo's Rape Survivors," *Ms. Magazine*, Spring 2005, www.msmagazine.com/spring2005/congo.asp.

[3] For background, see Sarah Glazer, "Evaluating Microfinance," *CQ Global Researcher*, April 2010, pp. 79-104.

American feminist author Susan Brownmiller finds evidence of rape from the Homeric epics to the Crusades, from the American Revolution to Vietnam — but not always en masse or as a tactical tool of warfare.

"In the name of victory and the power of the gun, war provides men with a tacit license to rape," Brownmiller writes.[39] For instance, she concludes, the action in the first of Homer's two epic poems, *The Iliad*, is driven as much by warriors' "rights" to women as by battle necessity. It was, after all, the capture — and presumed rape — of Helen of Troy that proverbially launched a thousand ships.[40] In

Geoffrey Chaucer's *Canterbury Tales*, a knight — a symbol of the warrior class — rapes an elderly woman.

But sanctions against wartime rape also stretch back through time. In one of the earliest behavioral codes for soldiers in battle, Richard the II of England decreed in 1385 that no English soldier should "force any woman" — under penalty of death.[41]

Nevertheless, authorities historically have responded to rape by soldiers with the attitude that "boys will be boys."[42] Jonathan Gottschall — an English professor at Washington and Jefferson College in Washington, Pa., and author of *The*

AFP/Getty Images/Jay Directo

Japan forced up to 200,000 "comfort women" in occupied countries — primarily Korea, China, and the Philippines — to serve as sex slaves for Japanese soldiers. Aging survivors periodically hold protest rallies — like this one in front of the Japanese Embassy in Manila in 2007 — demanding that Japan apologize and pay them restitution.

Rape of Troy: Evolution, Violence, and the World of Homer — has crafted a list of wartime rape, often done en masse. In the 20th century alone, he finds rape committed by armed forces in 43 countries, in Europe, Asia, Latin and South America and Africa, but he insists the list is incomplete.[43] Such a list, though, obscures other relevant details — the scale or intensity of the rape, the perpetrating groups and the purpose.

Rape, both ancient and modern, also has been used as a collective punishment for the vanquished. The Old Testament book of Isaiah tells of a coming war with Babylon; Isaiah, the narrator, describes a vision of the battle in which, "Their infants will be dashed to pieces before their eyes; their houses will be looted and their wives ravished."[44]

Rape as punishment was practiced on an especially brutal scale during the Second World War. In the Asian theater, when the Japanese army invaded China, its horrific violence against civilians in Nanking became known as "the rape of Nanking." In the eight weeks following the city's surrender in 1937, the Japanese murdered an estimated 300,000 people, both military and civilian, and raped some 20,000-80,000 women.[45]

In her book *The Rape of Nanking*, the first to bring serious attention to Japan's wartime sexual violence,

journalist Iris Chang documented the stories of thousands of survivors — and some perpetrators. A former Japanese soldier told Chang, "No matter how young or old, [women] could not escape the fate of being raped." While rape technically violated Japan's military code of conduct, Chang's research convinced her that rape was an integral part of Japanese military culture.

Thus not only did the code not protect women from being raped, it gave soldiers an incentive to kill them. One confessed to Chang, "It would be all right if we only raped them. I shouldn't say alright. But we also stabbed and killed them. Because dead bodies don't talk."[46]

Ironically, the mass rape in Nanking led directly to the Japanese military's institution of "comfort women." Hundreds of thousands of women, mainly Korean, were captured and taken to Japanese military bases throughout the theater, where they were forced to become sex slaves for soldiers. The idea was to prevent a repetition of mass rape in conquered cities — and in part to protect soldiers from sexually transmitted diseases. The practice today is recognized as a crime against humanity.

Perhaps the most infamous mass rape in the European theater of World War II occurred in Berlin. When the German capital and its surroundings fell, victorious Soviet soldiers literally hunted down their female victims. Gabrielle Köpp, the first German woman to write a memoir about wartime rape under her own name, remembers Russians searching with flashlights for girls. In a single three-day span, Köpp, then 15, was raped five times, and later, "relentlessly, for two weeks."[47]

A Polish woman who experienced the brutality of the Soviets before they rolled into Berlin later described her encounter. "They beat on the door with their rifle butts until it was opened. Without any consideration for my mother and aunt, who had to get out of bed, we were raped by the Russians, who always held a machine pistol in one hand," she said. "They lay in bed with their dirty boots on, until the next lot came."[48]

These circumstances are not confined to World War II, nor to Asian or Eurasian perpetrators. During the so-called Winter Soldier Investigation, conducted by the Vietnam Veterans of America in 1971, U.S. veterans testified on atrocities they witnessed in Vietnam, telling repeated stories of rape, mass rape and other sexual violence by American soldiers. In her research, Brownmiller uncovered U.S. Army records showing that 86 soldiers were tried for rape or

CHRONOLOGY

1930s-1940s *Rape occurs on a massive scale during World War II.*

1937-1938 From 20,000-80,000 women are raped by Japanese soldiers in Nanking, China, in the infamous "rape of Nanking," which is virtually ignored for 50 years.

1945 Soviet army sweeps through Nazi-controlled Eastern Europe to Berlin; soldiers rape thousands of German women. . . . U.S.-backed courts in Nuremberg, Germany, and Tokyo, Japan, try Nazi and Japanese soldiers for war crimes. Despite mass rapes by both armies, no one is charged with sexual violence.

1970s-1980s *Rape is used during conflicts and civil wars from Indonesia to Guatemala.*

1971 About 200,000 women are raped in the war that establishes Bangladesh as a sovereign country.

1975 Indonesia annexes newly independent East Timor, beginning two decades of military rule that included civilian massacres and widespread rape.

1982 Guatemalan soldiers slaughter most inhabitants of the Mayan village of Rio Negro, raping many women before killing them. Such government-sponsored violence occurred throughout the country's 36-year civil war, in which an estimated 200,000 Mayans were killed.

1990s-2000s *Rape is used a tool of ethnic warfare in Bosnia and Rwanda; international tribunals determine that mass rape is a crime against humanity.*

1991 Indian soldiers gang-rape 23 women in Kunan, Kashmir, in a incident that became the symbol of the military's willingness to use rape to intimidate citizens in the disputed border region claimed by India and Pakistan.

1991-1993 Serb forces commit mass rape against Bosnian Muslims.

1993 International Criminal Tribunal for the former Yugoslavia enumerates rape as a crime against humanity,

paving the way for landmark prosecutions against perpetrators.

1994 An estimated half-million minority Tutsi women are raped during the Rwandan genocide.

1998 International Criminal Tribunal for Rwanda recognizes rape as an act of genocide. . . . Burma's junta forcibly relocates its ethnic minorities, raping many women in the process.

2001 International Tribunal for the former Yugoslavia secures its first conviction for rape as a crime against humanity.

2004 Initial reports emerge from Darfur about the use of rape as a tool of ethnic cleansing; Amnesty International's earliest report finds evidence of at least 500 rapes.

2008 In February, the Special Court for Sierra Leone finds that the use of "bush wives" — women forced to marry and have sexual intercourse with a soldier — is a crime against humanity. . . . Rape becomes notorious as a tool of warfare in the Democratic Republic of Congo (DRC). . . . U.N. Security Council passes Resolution 1820, demanding all armed groups cease using rape and other forms of sexual violence. Mass rapes occur in connection with elections in Kenya and Zimbabwe.

2009 In August, U.S. Secretary of State Hillary Rodham Clinton visits the DRC, and announces $17 million in U.S. funding to train female police officers and local doctors. . . . On Sept. 28, an estimated 107 women are raped in public by Guinean soldiers seeking to quell pro-democracy protests. . . . U.N. Security Council appoints a special representative on sexual violence. . . . U.N. task force on the Guinea violence says orders to kill protestors and rape women may have come from top military and government officials.

2010 Nobel Women's Initiative holds a proxy international tribunal in March about sexual assaults committed against Burmese women. . . . In April, U.N. Special Representative for Sexual Violence Margot Wallström visits the DRC, speaking with government leaders, peacekeepers and rape survivors.

U.N. Anti-Rape Czar: 'Mission Irresistible'

Rape is a security issue, not a gender issue, says Margot Wallström.

Margot Wallström was appointed the United Nations' Special Representative for Sexual Violence in February. Her assignment: to help reduce wartime rape worldwide. The week before her first trip to the Democratic Republic of Congo, she talked by phone with CQ Global Researcher reporter Jina Moore about her trip, which she called "not a mission impossible but a mission irresistible."

CQGR: You said that right now, you think there is a window of political opportunity for dealing with rape in war. What is unique about this moment?

MW: We have never before acknowledged this as a security problem to the extent that the most recent [U.N.] resolutions [have] expressed. So it has come to the very top of the economic development and security agenda, and I think that's what is different. Now it is acknowledged as an international crime.

Also, the agenda for fighting sexual violence is made more concrete. Everybody focuses on, of course, ending impunity, but also at the same time empowering women — protecting women but also empowering women.

CQGR: If we've only recently seen rape as a security problem, how were we looking at it before? What's changed?

MW: It was on the gender agenda. You can see that most men are not that interested, unfortunately, in the gender agenda. . . . It's easier to brush aside if they think this is feminism or something that only women care for. They say, 'It's a women's issue.' But this is a human rights issue; it's a

criminal issue. I have often quoted Madeline Albright, who says that [rape] 'is not cultural, it's criminal.' They have to realize that it is at the core of security policy, so that it comes to the attention of both men and women.

CQGR: How can the international community better protect women from rape?

MW: We have learned that from how you design setting up refugee camps to the daily patrolling or the way you define protection of civilians affects this problem. We had a few good examples where firewood patrols and the fact that they have constructed these fuel-efficient stoves has reduced the number of rapes.

If we can have more peacekeepers that are women that will also . . . help us. [These] can seem like very simple things, but they reflect this understanding of the problem. It has to be thought of from the very beginning.

CQGR: What about protecting women from rape as a deliberate strategy of armed groups?

MW: That is . . . very much linked to impunity. If the perpetrators go unpunished . . . then this will only get worse. I've been saying in my speeches that in modern conflicts, rape is the front line. It is not a side effect. That means that it requires also a security response. . . . It also has to be part of the peace negotiations. Amnesty is not an option.

CQGR: There is concern among Africans that their continent is singled out by the International Criminal Court, all of whose open cases are in Africa. And, of course, we hear a great deal about rape in Congo. What other regions might you be dealing with?

---

attempted rape and related crimes in Vietnam; 50 were convicted. But she warned, "As an indicator of the actual number of rapes committed by the American military in Vietnam, [the numbers] are practically worthless," as few are likely to have been reported to senior officers, let alone carried through to court-martial.[49]

Equally universal was the silence that fell on the victims and their stories after the conflicts had ended. The "Rape of Nanking" was among the charges brought forward at the Tokyo War Crimes Trial, a U.S.-backed tribunal held after the war. But the full scope of the crime did not

emerge, and the story gradually faded from view. By the time Chang published her book in 1997, Japan had omitted references to the violence in Nanking from its history textbooks.[50]

In Germany, talking about the Soviet rapes was taboo for more than half a century. One woman anonymously published her diary in Germany in the 1950s (it was reissued, still anonymously, in 2006). Then in March Köpp published her *Why Was I Born a Girl* — the first memoir about the Soviet rapes with a name and a face attached to it.

MW: I'm very clear about my team having to prioritize. . . . I think we will have to choose not only Africa but probably also choose one or two other places where we have rape in conflict or post-conflict [situations]. Of course a lot of people say Afghanistan; we will have to see what can realistically be done. . . . It is true that this is not only an African problem, although Congo is very much described as being the epicenter of sexual violence, but I think it's so important to recognize that this is unfortunately a global problem.

CQGR: There are also reports of sexual exploitation or abuse by U.N. peacekeepers. How will your office advocate for women in the face of those accusations?

MW: This is the first thing I hear very often: 'How can you be credible, if your own peacekeepers sexually exploit women on the ground, if they rape women as well?' This is extremely important, that we have the credibility of implementing the policy that has been introduced and we show that there is no impunity in our system. . . .

A lot has been done over the past couple of years, but it's a constant struggle. We have to do even more. . . . I will travel definitely to some of the big troop-contributing countries. I can go and talk to India, Pakistan or Bangladesh and make sure I engage with their governments.

CQGR: What might your position allow you to accomplish that hasn't happened before?

MW: For example, we have finalized a team of legal experts, we are recruiting the people to this team of legal experts. We think we will have six to eight, maximum, people on that team. The head of that team will be located with me, and I will be able, in my political context . . . to hopefully offer to governments [the team's] expertise to modernize and upgrade their legal frameworks for addressing all the problems that have to do with sexual violence.

Margot Wallström, the U.N.'s first special representative for sexual violence, says rape is the front line, not a side effect, of modern warfare.

It's very important to meet at the highest political levels to address this . . . but also to be interested in how it works operationally on the ground. And never to forget who you're working for. They are both the victims and the most important actors in society; as I say, what is an African village without the women?

— *Jina Moore*

Rape and Ethnic Cleansing

The final decade of the 20th century saw a brutal refinement of the use of rape in warfare. During the war in the Balkans in the early 1990s, the Serb army explicitly wielded rape as a tool of ethnic cleansing. Not only was rape widespread and systematic, experts say. It was also clearly Serb policy.

The policy took several forms, including the establishment of "rape camps" similar to the concentration camps of World War II. Muslim women were herded into the camps with the express intent of impregnating them with "Serb babies." Only about 20 percent of the women survived their detention.[51]

The imprisoned women were raped day and night by men, usually in groups. "The degradation and molestation of women was central to the conquest" in Bosnia, writes Roy Gutman, an American journalist who won a Pulitzer Prize for his reporting on the Balkan conflict.[52] In particular, he said, Serbs targeted single women, whom Muslim custom obliged to remain chaste until marriage.

A United Nations investigation in 1992 found that "sexual assault and rape have been carried out by some of

Demanding Long-Delayed Justice

"We demand punishment for war criminals" says a poster with a caricature of a blood-thirsty war criminal held by activists at a Bangladesh Independence Day celebration in Dhaka on March 26 (top). Bangladesh recently established a war crimes tribunal for the long-delayed trials of people accused of war crimes during the country's 1971 war of independence with Pakistan, when 200,000-400,000 women were reportedly raped. At the U.N. office in Sarajevo on July 18, 2008, Bosnian women protest a decision by a U.N. war crimes tribunal in the Netherlands not to prosecute two Bosnian Serb military leaders for organizing mass rapes of hundreds of Muslim women held in "rape camps" during the 1992-95 Bosnian war. The two men — Milan and Sredoje Lukic — were being prosecuted for other war crimes.

the parties so systematically that they strongly appear to be the product of policy;" a follow-up report clarified that it was indeed a policy of ethnic cleansing practiced by the Serbs.[53] The clarification was important. Local television in the Balkans was airing reports about rape — but in those reports the victims were said to be Serbs, the perpetrators Muslim. In fact, the Serbian propaganda campaign used footage of its own soldiers raping Muslim women but lied about the identities of victim and perpetrator.[54]

After the conflict, the International Criminal Tribunal for the former Yugoslavia (ICTY) — the U.N.-backed court established to try the war's most heinous crimes — for the first time recognized mass rape as a crime against humanity.

Shortly after the world was horrified by the images from the Balkans, attention shifted to the ongoing genocide in Rwanda, where the Hutu ethnic group set upon the Tutsis. In 100 days in the spring of 1994, Hutu soldiers and militiamen murdered some 800,000 Tutsis (and moderate Hutus) and raped thousands of Tutsi women.

The seeds of sexual violence were wrapped up in the nature of the genocide. Ever since Belgian colonists brought their notions of beauty and eugenics to Rwanda, the Tutsis, tall and slender with big eyes and narrow noses, were thought to be "superior" Africans. They looked more like the Belgians than did the Hutu, whom colonial literature describes as short and stout. A missionary described the Tutsi as "European[s] under black skin."[55]

Thus, explained a woman who survived the genocide, "Tutsi women have always been viewed as enemies of the state."[56] In the run-up to the genocide, Rwandan radio programs broadcast gender-based slanders about Tutsi women designed to incite the Hutu to hatred and violence.[57]

During the 100-day killing spree, Hutu men raped up to half a million Tutsi women and girls. The attacks were "part of a pattern in which Tutsi women were raped after they had witnessed the torture and killings of their relatives and the destruction and looting of their homes."[58] The pattern of rape was recognized by the International Criminal Tribunal for Rwanda (ICTR) in 1998 as an act of genocide.[59]

Political Rape

Rape is also used to spread terror during elections. Both before and during presidential elections in 2008, the party of Zimbabwe's President Mugabe reportedly used violence against his opponents and rape to intimidate opposition communities, according to the international organization AIDS-Free World. It investigated the use of rape in the lead-up and aftermath of the controversial election and found evidence of a coordinated rape campaign by the ZANU-PF, Mugabe's political party, to terrorize his opponents.

"Unless you love ZANU-PF, we are going to kill you because you don't listen. That is what we are raping you for," a survivor recalled her perpetrator as saying.[60]

Some of the women targeted, the organization found, were politically active. Others were simply married to activists and were raped to punish and terrorize their husbands for supporting the opposition. Sometimes, the rapes occurred in the women's villages; sometimes, the victims were taken to ZANU-PF camps in five provinces in the eastern part of the country.[61] (*See map, p. 503.*)

Similarly, rape was used after Kenya's controversial 2007 election. Kenyan police recorded 876 reports of rape, but since rape victims rarely report the crime, observers think the actual number is higher. Kenyan health clinics reported treating far more victims than the official number reported by police.[62] And most recently, rape was used for retribution against dissidents in the Guinean military junta's crackdown on democracy protesters in 2009. According to some reports, it was the first time rape had been used as a tactic of military oppression in Guinea.[63]

All Talk, No Action?

In the last 10 years, the U.N. Security Council has passed increasingly stringent resolutions about the treatment of women in war zones. The first, UNSC Resolution 1325, called for greater participation of women in peace negotiations and post-war peace building. Although largely focused on broad-based gender issues, the resolution also recognized that civilians generally — and women and children in particular — suffer the most from armed warfare and, increasingly, are targets of militants.[64]

The resolution helped pave the way for a tougher measure, passed by the Security Council in 2008, demanding that armed groups immediately stop using rape in conflict zones. Last September, three days after the Guinea rapes, the council passed a third resolution, establishing a special representative to help oversee and integrate U.N. resolutions and other efforts to prevent and punish rape in warfare.

"Really, the problem is the international community comes in almost when it's too late," says Mpoumou, of the International Coalition for the Responsibility to Protect. "It took the international community five years" to

A billboard in Monrovia, Liberia, encourages women who have been raped to seek treatment. The country's brutal civil war left hundreds of rape victims suffering in silent shame. But some are coming forward now to seek treatment for their physical, psychological and emotional wounds, which experts say can last a lifetime.

recognize the problem of sexual violence in the DRC, she points out.

But the world seems to have finally had enough of the rapes in Congo. In the lead-up to last September's resolution, U.S. Secretary of State Clinton visited the DRC, promising funds for, among other things, medical and legal aid for rape victims.

"We are raising this issue at the highest levels of [the Congolese] government," she told a group of civil society and public health organizations in Goma. "[T]hese crimes, no matter who commits them, must be prosecuted and punished. That is particularly important when those who commit such acts are in position of authority, including members of the Congolese military."[65]

CURRENT SITUATION
Demanding Accountability

Although recent international attention has focused on strategic rape in the DRC, some observers hope the publicity will catalyze awareness of other, lesser-known rape crises. They also hope attention from powerful political players will translate into better judicial accountability.

Will recent U.N. resolutions help protect women?

YES Kudakwashe Chitsike
Programme Manager
Women's Programme Research and
Advocacy Unit (RAU) Zimbabwe

Written for *CQ Researcher*, May 2010

The adoption of U.N. Resolutions 1820 and 1880 was welcomed. Finally the international community was recognizing the treatment of women during war and conflict. Women all over the world felt a sense of relief, albeit with a little apprehension.

The relief came from the fact that the world now realizes women suffer differently in wars than men. Women frequently are raped to dehumanize them and to punish the men to whom they are related. Often the women are even forced to bear the children of their violators. So they suffer not only for their own actions, but also for those of their men. The long-awaited resolutions also show that the international community now views sexual violence as a security issue that needs urgent attention.

The apprehension arises from concerns that the international community may not be prepared to respond to the issue. The world will have to look at the problems caused by sexual violence, including the fear instilled by the perpetrators, the stigma associated with reporting sexual violence and the cultural beliefs where the issue is reported. Resolutions are easy, but implementation can be enormously difficult, especially since protecting women's rights must inevitably confront patriarchal structures of society.

The international community has taken steps before to afford women necessary and special protection, such as setting up institutions to address gender-based violence. Because these instruments have not taken into consideration the situation on the ground, they have failed to make an impact on the very people they were attempting to serve.

Protection for women will only be achieved if there is no impunity for past offenders; if command responsibility is enforced and if there is training not only for troops but also for communities, including men and women, on the dangers and consequences of sexual violence. It is critical to remember that once violence is embedded in a culture it always makes women vulnerable, especially during periods of tension, and it constitutes a major obstacle to development, peace and security. It must be guaranteed that women are consulted and centrally involved in all processes that aim to end sexual violence. For the resolutions to offer protection there has to be zero tolerance for sexual violence by the U.N. as this will encourage more women to speak out where it occurs.

NO Rosebell Kagumire
Ugandan human rights journalist and blogger

Written for *CQ Global Researcher*, May 2010

In 2008, Major Gen. Patrick Cammaert — former U.N. force commander in eastern Democratic Republic of Congo (DRC) — told a U.N. Security Council meeting: "It is now more dangerous to be a woman than to be a soldier in modern conflict."

As the 20th century ended, wars had changed. Civil wars trapped civilians on undefined frontlines, and sexual violence was embraced as part of a military strategy to inflict fear and subjugate the "other."

Women in my country have not escaped mass sexual violence. For two decades the Lord's Resistance Army (LRA) has wreaked havoc in northern Uganda, DRC and Central African Republic, killing civilians and abducting women and girls as sex slaves. Most of the rapes are committed by "rebels" — young men abducted as children and forced into rebellion. The International Criminal Court has indicted LRA leaders for rape — but this has yet to stop them.

Thus, it seems unlikely that recent U.N. resolutions will translate into accountability and prevention of sexual violence. While the resolutions show the world is finally paying attention, ensuring protection for women in wartime still has a long way to go.

While such resolutions help build cases against leaders who perpetrate mass rape, they don't help to prevent sexual violations in areas where the security situation has disintegrated. To do that, governments must be held accountable for women's security. Countries must improve their judicial infrastructure. In Uganda, most rape victims cannot seek justice because of lengthy court procedures and expensive access to lawyers.

The political will to enforce accountability is also critical. The Ugandan government remains opposed to civil trials for soldiers in relation to the war in northern Uganda. While several reports indicate government soldiers have raped women, the army insists such cases have been tried in military courts, but there is no record of such trials.

Finally, sexual violence is not just a wartime problem. Even in peaceful regions of Uganda, women often must pay a police surgeon to get a medical check after a sexual offense. And women are still blamed for being raped. If we cannot protect vulnerable women in peacetime, how can we do it once countries have fallen into such lawlessness?

That could start in The Hague, where ICC Prosecutor Luis Moreno-Ocampo is pursuing sexual violence charges against eight of 14 defendants facing trial, including Sudanese President al-Bashir.[66] Among other charges, he has been indicted for genocide based on his support of alleged rape and sexual assault — the first time the ICC has used the precedent set by the tribunal for Rwanda.

Moreno-Ocampo also is investigating the post-election violence in Kenya in 2008, where, he said, rape allegations "will be central to the investigation."[67] Local human rights groups, meanwhile, say neither justice nor support services are forthcoming for the women, including those who testified at a Kenyan national commission that investigated the violence. "There is no support absolutely," said Kenyan human rights advocate Maina Kiai.[68]

In Guinea, progress in bringing perpetrators of last fall's mass rapes to justice has been slow. Although Secretary Clinton has called for the rapists to face justice, and ICC investigations are ongoing, but no indictments have been filed.[69]

Victims' Voices

In the DRC, radio journalist Chouchou Namegabe Dubuisson has co-founded, with three other women, the South Kivu Women's Media Association, known by its French acronym "AFEM." They collect rape survivors' stories and broadcast them for women in rural eastern Congo, along with information about women's health and human rights.

When the broadcasts began, the radio program faced "many cultural restrictions," Dubuisson recalls. "You couldn't talk about sex on the radio. We had to borrow a word from Tanzanian Swahili, *ubakaji*. . . . There are many local languages, but they didn't have a word to talk about it. They talked around it."

The journalists who work for AFEM began in 2003 as self-taught volunteers; four years later, they had a small studio and were broadcasting on six radio stations. At first, their work wasn't exactly welcome. "It was a scandal," she remembers. "People were saying, 'How can they talk widely about sex?!' " But as the programs continued, and humanitarian organizations in the region began their own outreach to combat the stigma associated with rape, the outrage abated.

Now, the community reacts differently to rape cases, Dubuisson says. "Before it was a shame. Victims were

Congolese gynecologist Denis Mukwege won the Olof Palme Prize for his aid to women victims of rape and war crimes in the Democratic Republic of Congo. One reason the world doesn't end wartime rape is that men are not the victims, he says. "Do we need men to start being killed so that other men will react?" he asks.

rejected," she remembers. "After we began, it changed. Victims say it's a first step to heal their internal wounds — to talk, to confide what happened to them."

In Burma (Myanmar), anti-rape activists have taken a different grassroots approach. In a country ruled by a notoriously cruel military junta that uses sexual violence to repress ethnic groups, rape is not discussed. "You can't talk about it," says Hseng Noung, a Burmese journalist and an advisory board member of the Women's League of Burma, an association of local organizations that operates clandestinely inside Burma. "There's nowhere for women, or anyone, to go and get justice."

So the league, along with the Nobel Women's Initiative — a network of female Nobel Peace Prize laureates, including Burmese democracy activist Aung San Suu Kyi — launched an international "tribunal" for Burma in

Two young rape victims being treated at Panzi hospital in Bukavu, Democratic Republic of the Congo, walk with their lawyer (center). Women's rights advocates say the problem of mass rape in wartime will only be solved when more perpetrators are brought to justice.

New York in March. The mock court process included testimony by Burmese women, some in person, some by video and some read aloud by proxy witnesses. Each account represented dozens more like it. "The testifiers are just one [person] — but there are so many, so many people like them," says Burmese refugee Phyu Phyu Sann, a researcher at the Center for Global Justice in New York.

Raising awareness about rape was only part of the goal, Sann says. She and other activists want Burma's case referred to the International Criminal Court for prosecution. But because Burma has not signed the treaty that established the court, the U.N. Security Council would have to vote to make the referral.

Williams, the 1997 Nobel Peace laureate for her work to ban land mines,[70] says the groups hope to shame the Security Council into making the referral. "The international community seems a little lame, if you will, on actual action," she says. "We decided if they couldn't do it, we'd do it and use that as an organizing tool."

Burma has been the subject of other Security Council resolutions recognizing the use of rape or sexual violence against women, but unless a case is sent to the ICC for prosecution, critics say the junta will continue to enjoy impunity.

Whatever the outcome of the campaign to pressure the Security Council, Sann says the people's tribunal brought Burmese women a different kind of relief. "My whole life, I saw everything, all the atrocities, and even me, I have held my tears," she says. "Here, I can speak up. Now we are hopeful. Here, the world is at least listening to us."

OUTLOOK

No End in Sight

Although the fight against rape as a weapon of war has made major strides — especially in the last two years — few observers think the problem will disappear anytime soon.

For all the recent publicity about rape in war zones, little is understood about "the context and conditions under which armed groups engage in sexual violence . . . and do not," says Wood of Yale. Experts lack evidence — both qualitative and quantitative — about why perpetrators engage in wartime rape. Researchers hope scholarly attention to the topic in the future will make "policy interventions," in Wood's words, "more sophisticated."

Special Representative Wallström is already thinking about how to make current humanitarian responses more sophisticated. Two innovations have helped reduce rape in Darfur, she says: fuel-efficient stoves, which allow female refugees and internally displaced persons to make fewer trips outside of the camps in search of firewood, and peacekeepers assigned to "firewood patrols," accompanying women as they forage for wood.

On her trip to Congo, Secretary Clinton expressed hope that other technological advances could help curb rape. She introduced a plan to give women in Congo video cameras, so they can document assaults. Critics responded that a lack of evidence wasn't the problem, and that the money could be better spent on other interventions.

Physician Mukwege at Panzi Hospital in DRC says one reason the world doesn't put an end to wartime rape is that men are not usually the victims. Although he has been working for more than a decade to bring attention to the plight of rape victims in Congo, "sometimes it seems that ears are closed. So we've been wondering: . . . Do we need men to start being killed so that other men will react?"[71]

Men are, however, getting involved in prevention. The organization Women for Women International has hired local men to reach out to other Congolese men, teaching them not to rape and not to blame their wives who become victims. As program director Cyprien Walupakah put it, "If men are not involved, it will not change."[72]

In fact, Sri Lankan physician Kapila thinks "men should be in leadership positions" in the effort to prevent wartime rape. "All these gender advisors are being appointed, and they're all women," he points out. "Women talking about women's problems to other women is only going to go so far. This is one area where we need reverse gender discrimination." He suggests that perhaps the next special representative should be a man or that powerful men should advocate more vocally for an end to sexual violence.

Female advocates, however, say having men in powerful positions has been part of the problem. In fact, women say they have spent years seeking support from powerful men in the international community. In Colombia, for example, women's groups, human rights organizations and female lawmakers say they have been demanding attention to the problem of sexual violence for the past 20 years. But their demands have fallen on deaf ears.[73]

In the end, it may take the passionate determination of women to end the practice of wartime rape. As a female doctor in Guinea insisted after last fall's attacks, "With the last breath in my body, I will fight to restore the dignity of our women. The soldiers may have beaten us, they may have raped us, but we will win the battle for decency, democracy and respect in Guinea."[74]

NOTES

1. Ofeibea Quist-Arcton, "Guinea Shaken By Wave Of Rapes During Crackdown," "All Things Considered," National Public Radio, Oct. 20, 2009, www.npr.org/templates/story/story.php?storyId=113966999.

2. *Ibid.*

3. Neil MacFarquhar, "U.N. Panel Calls for Prosecution of Guinea's Military Leaders Over Massacre," *The New York Times*, Dec. 22, 2009, p. A6, www.nytimes.com/2009/12/22/world/africa/22guinea.html.

4. Quoted in Susan Brownmiller, *Against Our Will: Men, Women and Rape* (1975), p. 37.

5. "Hear Us," May 2009, a video production of the Zimbabwean Research and Advocacy Unit and WITNESS, http://hub.witness.org/en/HearUs-ViolenceAgainstWomeninZimbabwe.

6. "Electing to Rape: Sexual Terror in Mugabe's Zimbabwe," AIDS-Free World, December 2009, p. 19, www.swradioafrica.com/Documents/23919945-Electing-to-Rape-Final.pdf.

7. Zoe Alsop, "Kenya's Rape Probe Falters after Lawyers Drop Out," Women's eNews, Dec. 14, 2008, www.womensenews.org/story/rape/081214/kenyas-rape-probe-falters-after-lawyers-drop-out.

8. "International Justice Failing Rape Victims," Institute for War and Peace Reporting, Feb. 15, 2010, www.iwpr.net/report-news/international-justice-failing-rape-victims.

9. Angela M. Banks, "Sexual Violence and International Criminal Law," Women's Initiatives for Gender Justice, September 2005, p. 21.

10. Barnaby Mason, "Rape: A crime against humanity," BBC, Feb. 22, 2001, http://news.bbc.co.uk/2/hi/europe/1184763.stm.

11. Judgment in *The Prosecutor vs. Jean Paul Akayesu*, International Criminal Tribunal for Rwanda, Case No. ICTR-96-4-T, Sept. 2, 1998.

12. Emily Wax, " 'We want to make a light baby': Arab militiamen in Sudan said to use rape as a weapon of ethnic conflict," *The Washington Post*, June 30, 2004, p. A1, www.washingtonpost.com/wp-dyn/articles/A16001-2004Jun29.html.

13. "Colombia: Scarred Bodies, Hidden Crimes," Amnesty International, p. 3 www.amnesty.org/en/library/asset/AMR23/040/2004/en/ec8e59b4-d598-11dd-bb24-1fb85fe8fa05/amr230402004en.pdf.

14. Jeb Sharp, "Healing the victims," Public Radio International, Jan. 8, 2008, www.pri.org/theworld/?q=node/15166.

15. "Secretary Clinton Tours Refugee Camp," U.S. Department of State press release, Aug. 11, 2009, www.state.gov/secretary/rm/2009a/08/127181.htm.

16. Jeffrey Gettleman, "Symbol of Unhealed Congo: Male rape victims," *The New York Times*, Aug. 5, 2009, www.nytimes.com/2009/08/05/world/africa/05congo.html.

17. Tanya Turkovich, "As DR Congo crisis persists, UN classifies rape as a weapon of war," UNICEF, June 24, 2008, www.unicef.org/infobycountry/drcongo_44598.html.

18. Rome Statute of the International Criminal Court, 1998, www2.ohchr.org/english/law/criminalcourt.htm.

19. Charges were also confirmed against a third defendant, who was ultimately released by the court. Brigid Inder, "Making a Statement: A Review of Charges and Prosecutions for Gender-based Crimes before the International Criminal Court," Women's Initiatives for Gender Justice, February 2010, pp. 10-13.

20. "Situations and Cases," International Criminal Court, www.icc-cpi.int/Menus/ICC/Situations+and+Cases/.

21. Sarah Childress, "Clinton Addresses War Crimes in Congo," *The Wall Street Journal*, Aug. 11, 2009, http://online.wsj.com/article/SB124993248728220321.html.

22. Jina Moore, "In Africa, justice for bush wives," *The Christian Science Monitor*, June 10, 2008, www.csmonitor.com/World/Africa/2008/0610/p06s01-woaf.html.

23. Thom Shanker, "Sexual Violence," in Crimes of War, www.crimesofwar.org/thebook/sexual-violence.html.

24. For background, see "Comfort Women: World War II Sex Slavery — Survivors continue to call for justice, compensation, apology from Japanese government," Women's U.N. Report Network, March 8, 2010, www.wunrn.com/news/2010/03_10/03_15_10/031510_comfort.htm.

25. David Livingstone Smith, *The Most Dangerous Animal: Human nature and the origins of war* (2007), p. 90.

26. "My Heart is Cut: Sexual Violence by Rebels and Pro-Government Forces in Côte d'Ivoire," Human Rights Watch, August 2007, p. 3, www.hrw.org/en/reports/2007/08/01/my-heart-cut.

27. Christopher Wilson, "Overcoming Violent Conflict, Volume 5: Peace and Development Analysis in Indonesia," United Nations Development Program, 2005, pp. 2, 50, www.internal-displacement.org/8025708F004CE90B/(httpDocuments)/AF478B69BD73D815C125724400378515/$file/Overcoming+violent+conflict+Vol5+Indonesia.pdf.

28. Michele Leiby, "Wartime Sexual Violence in Guatemala and Peru," *International Studies Quarterly*, vol. 43, 2009, p. 454.

29. Elisabeth Jean Wood, "Armed Groups and Sexual Violence: When is wartime rape rare?" *Politics and Society*, vol. 37, 2009, pp. 146.

30. Dara Kay Cohen, "Female Combatants and Violence in Armed Groups: Women and Wartime Rape in Sierra Leone (1991-2002)" Jan. 26, 2010.

31. Resolutions 1882 (2009), 1820 (2008) and 1325 (2000), U.N. Security Council.

32. Michele Keleman, "In war zones, rape is a powerful weapon," National Public Radio, Oct. 21, 2009, www.npr.org/templates/story/story.php?storyId=114001201.

33. Thalif Deen, "U.N. envoy to crack down on sexual violence," Inter Press Service, Feb. 2, 2010, http://ipsnews.net/news.asp?idnews=50198.

34. "Agency ends Darfur aid after obstruction," Reuters, Nov. 10, 2006, www.abc.net.au/news/newsitems/200611/s1786169.htm.

35. Rebecca Hamilton, "Left Behind," *The New Republic*, Oct. 14, 2009, www.tnr.com/article/world/left-behind.

36. "The Crushing Burden of Rape: Sexual Violence in Darfur," *Médecins Sans Frontiéres*, 2005, p. 5, www.doctorswithoutborders.org/publications/reports/2005/sudan03.pdf.

37. Brownmiller, *op. cit.*, pp. 78-80.

38. Quoted in "Rape as Genocide: Bangladesh, the Former Yugoslavia, and Rwanda," *New Political Science*, vol. 22, Issue 1, March 2000, p. 89.

39. Brownmiller, *op. cit.*, p. 33.

40. *Ibid.*, pp. 33-36.

41. *Ibid.*, p. 34.

42. See Myriam Miedzian, *Boys Will Be Boys: Breaking the Link Between Masculinity and Violence* (2002).

43. Jonathan Gottschall, *The Rape of Troy: Evolution, Violence and the World of Homer* (2008), p. 76.

44. Holy Bible, Isaiah 13:16.

45. Iris Chang, "The Rape of Nanking," in Anne Llewellyn Barstow, ed., *War's Dirty Secret: Rape, Prostitution and Other Crimes Against Women* (2001), p. 46.

46. *Ibid.*, pp. 46-49.

47. Susanne Beyer, "Harrowing Memoir: German Woman Writes Ground-breaking Account of WW2 Rape," Feb. 26, 2010," www.spiegel.de/international/germany/0,1518,680354,00.html.

48. Quoted in Brownmiller, *op cit.*, p. 69.

49. *Ibid.*, pp. 99-101.

50. Barstow, *op. cit.*, p. 46.

51. Todd Salzman, "Rape Camps, Forced Impregnation and Ethnic Cleansing," in Barstow, *ibid.*, p. 75; Kelly Dawn Askin, in "Rape: Weapon of Terror," *Aware*, 2001, p. 37.

52. Roy Gutman, "Foreward," in Alexandra Stiglmayer, ed., *Mass Rape: The War Against Women in Bosnia-Herzegovina* (1994), p. x.

53. Quoted in Salzman, *op. cit.*, p. 70.

54. *Ibid.*, p. 68.

55. Jina Moore, "From noses to hips, Rwandans redefine beauty," *The Christian Science Monitor*, July 18, 2008, www.csmonitor.com/World/Africa/2008/0718/p01s05-woaf.html.

56. Binaifer Nowrojee, "Shattered Lives: Sexual Violence During the Rwandan Genocide and its Aftermath," Human Rights Watch, 1996.

57. *Ibid.*

58. Nowrojee, *op. cit.*

59. Judgment in *The Prosecutor vs. Jean Paul Akayesu, op. cit.* Also see Laura Flanders, "Rwanda's Living Casualties," in *War's Dirty Secret, op. cit.*, p. 96.

60. "Electing to Rape: Sexual Terror in Mugabe's Zimbabwe," *op. cit.*

61. *Ibid.*, p. 25.

62. "Kenya: Post-election violence not spontaneous," *Daily Nation*, April 2, 2010, http://allafrica.com/stories/201004020934.html.

63. Adam Nossiter, "In a Guinea Seized by Violence, Women are Prey," *The New York Times*, Oct. 5, 2009, www.nytimes.com/2009/10/06/world/africa/06guinea.html.

64. U.N. Security Council Resolution 1325 (2000), Oct. 31, 2000, www.un.org/events/res_1325e.pdf.

65. U.S. Department of State release of remarks at HEAL Africa, Goma, DRC, Aug. 11, 2009, www.state.gov/secretary/rm/2009a/08/127171.htm.

66. Inder, *op cit.*

67. "ICC to probe Kenya post-election violence," The Associated Press, April 1, 2010, www.cbc.ca/world/story/2010/04/01/icc-kenya-investigation.html.

68. Caroline Wafula, "Rape victims awaiting justice," *Daily Nation*, March 8, 2010, http://multimedia.marsgroupkenya.org/?StoryID=283546&p=Gender+Commission.

69. Adam Nossiter, "US Envoy protests rape in Guinea," *The New York Times*, Oct. 9, 2009, www.nytimes.com/2009/10/07/world/africa/07guinea.html.

70. For background on land mines, see Robert Kiener, "Dangerous War Debris," *CQ Global Researcher*, March 2010, pp. 51-78.

71. Nergui Manalsuren, "How Many More Will Be Raped?" Inter Press Service, Feb. 12, 2009, http://ipsnews.net/africa/nota.asp?idnews=45751.

72. Matthew Clark, "Congo: Confronting rape as a weapon of war," *The Christian Science Monitor*, Aug. 4, 2009, www.csmonitor.com/World/Africa/2009/0804/p17s01-woaf.html.

73. Helda Martinez, "Colombia: Sexual violence as a weapon of war," Inter Press Service, Oct. 21, 2009, http://ipsnews.net/news.asp?idnews=48942.

74. Quist-Arcton, *op. cit.*

BIBLIOGRAPHY

Books

A Woman in Berlin: Eight Weeks in the Conquered City, translated by Philip Boehm, *Picador*, 2006.
This anonymous diary broke the silence about the rapes of German women by Soviet soldiers after the fall of Berlin in 1945.

Barstow, Anne Llewelyn, ed., *War's Dirty Secret: Rape, Prostitution and Other Crimes Against Women*, *Pilgrim Press*, 2000.
A former State University of New York professor of history has assembled expert essays about the use of rape in conflicts worldwide.

Shannon, Lisa, *A Thousand Sisters: My Journey Into the Worst Place on Earth to Be a Woman, Seal Press,* **2010.**
A former Portland, Ore., photographer who founded Run for Congo Women, an awareness and fundraising initiative for Congolese rape survivors, describes her year living in eastern Congo, helping and learning from the country's rape survivors.

Soh, C. Sarah, *The Comfort Women, University of Chicago Press,* **2009.**
A San Francisco State University professor of anthropology interviews surviving Korean "comfort women," who were forced into sexual slavery by the Japanese military in World War II.

Articles and Broadcasts

"Hear Us: Women Affected by Political Violence in Zimbabwe Speak Out," *WITNESS,* **2009.**
A human rights video organization presents the voices of opposition women raped by members of Zimbabwean President Robert Mugabe's ZANU-PF political party in what has been called an orchestrated campaign to intimidate voters through rape.

Hamilton, Rebecca, "Left Behind," *The New Republic,* **Oct. 14, 2009, www.tnr.com/article/world/left-behind.**
A former assistant to International Criminal Court Prosecutor Luis Moreno-Ocampo visits Darfur and finds that after the court indicted Sudanese president Omar al-Bashir for genocide, aid to rape survivors has been halted.

Hochschild, Adam, "Rape of the Congo," *The New York Review of Books,* **Aug. 13, 2009, www.nybooks .com/articles/archives/2009/aug/13/rape-of-the-congo/.**
The best-selling author of *King Leopold's Ghost,* a history of Belgian brutality in colonized Congo, visits the women of eastern Congo and tries to understand the circumstances that have victimized them.

Jackson, Lisa F., "The Greatest Silence," *Jackson Films with Fledgling Films and HBO Documentary Films,* **2008.**
An Emmy-Award-winning producer spends a year in eastern Congo talking to women, aid workers and peacekeepers about the rape epidemic.

Sharp, Jeb, "Congo Rape," *Public Radio International,* **January 2008.**

An award-winning two-part series about rape and its aftermath in Democratic Republic of Congo.

Reports and Studies

"Bloody Monday: The September 28 Massacre and Rapes by Security Forces in Guinea," *Human Rights Watch,* **Dec. 17, 2009, www.hrw.org/node/87190.**
This 108-page report describes the preplanned murders and sexual assaults at an opposition rally in and around a stadium in Conakry last September by Guinea's elite Presidential Guard.

"Characterizing Sexual Violence in the Democratic Republic of the Congo: Profiles of Violence, Community Responses, and Implications for the Protection of Women," *Harvard Humanitarian Initiative,* **August 2009.**
A team of doctors and public health specialists surveys women — and rapists — in Congo about the frequency and character of rape attacks.

"Making a Statement: Gender-based Crimes before the International Criminal Court," *Second Edition, Women's Initiatives for Gender Justice,* **February 2010.**
A Netherlands-based ICC watchdog summarizes the court's action on rape and related charges and suggests how the court can strengthen its investigations into sexual violence.

"My Heart Is Cut: Sexual Violence by Rebels and Pro-Government Forces in Côte d'Ivoire," *Human Rights Watch,* **Aug. 2, 2007, www.hrw.org/en/ reports/2007/08/01/my-heart-cut.**
A 135-page report based on interviews with more than 180 victims and witnesses documents women and girls being subjected to individual and gang rape, sexual slavery, forced incest and other sexual assaults during the five-year military-political crisis in the West African country.

Wood, Elisabeth Jean, "Armed Groups and Sexual Violence: When Is Wartime Rape Rare?" *Politics and Society,* **Vol. 37, 2009, pp. 131-161.**
A Yale University political scientist examines data from wars in which rape is not used as a weapon and suggests that military norms and enforcement prevent fighters from assaulting women.

For More Information

American Bar Association, 740 15th St., N.W., Washington, DC 20005-1019; (202) 662-1000; www.abanet.org/rol/africa/democratic_republic_congo.html. Sponsors a Rule of Law Initiative in the Democratic Republic of Congo that gives rape survivors access to lawyers and the ability to press charges against their perpetrators.

Avega Agahozo, P.O. Box 1535, Kigali, Rwanda; +250 516125; www.avega.org.rw/English.html. An association founded by 50 women widowed during the Rwandan genocide; provides fellowship, health support and trauma counseling for other female genocide survivors of all ages.

Friends of the Congo, 1629 K St., N.W., Suite 300, Washington, DC 20006; (202) 584-6512; www.friendsofthecongo.org. Led by the Congolese diaspora; tries to address the country's problems, including wartime rape, with special attention to solutions that involve and empower Congolese citizens.

HEAL Africa, Goma, Democratic Republic of Congo, and P.O. Box 147, Monroe WA 98272; www.healafrica.org. The primary hospital in North Kivu, epicenter of the rape epidemic in eastern Congo, which specializes in surgery and other medical services for rape survivors.

International Women's Program, Open Society Institute, 400 West 59th St., New York, NY 10019; (212) 548-0600; www.soros.org/initiatives/women?a. George Soros-funded initiative that focuses on reducing gender violence and discrimination, strengthening women's access to justice and increasing the number of women in leadership and decision-making roles.

Nobel Women's Initiative, 430-1 Nicholas St., Ottawa, Ontario K1N 7B7, Canada; +1 613 569 8400; www.nobelwomensinitiative.org. A partnership of female Nobel Peace Prize laureates dedicated to advancing women's rights worldwide; co-hosted the International Gender Justice Dialogue in Mexico in April.

Raise Hope for Congo, 1225 Eye St., N.W., Suite 307, Washington, DC 20005; (202) 682-1611; www.raisehopeforcongo.org. A campaign by the ENOUGH Project, which fights against genocide and mass atrocities, that uses social media, college networks and other outreach efforts to bring attention to the plight of Congo's rape victims and unite voices across America in a demand for the end to sexual violence.

Saathi, Kathmandu, Nepal; www.saathi.org.np/. A Nepali nongovernmental organization working to end violence against women and train more women as negotiators and decision-makers in post-conflict governance.

UNIFEM, 304 East 45th St., New York, NY 10017; (212) 906-6400; www.unifem.org. The U.N. Development Fund for Women; has been a leading advocate of ending violence against women in both wartime and times of peace; seeks prevent violence against women by tackling the problem of gender inequality worldwide.

Women's Initiatives for Gender Justice, Anna Paulownastraat 103, 2518 BC, The Hague, Netherlands; +31 (70) 302 9911; www.iccwomen.org. International organization that monitors action by the International Criminal Court on gender-related crimes and partners with women's organizations worldwide to advocate against impunity for rape and sexual violence in war zones.

Women's League of Burma, www.womenofburma.org. An association of grassroots women's and human rights organizations working clandestinely in Burma to unite and protect women suffering under the junta's repressive dictatorship.

Supporting researchers for more than 40 years

Research methods have always been at the core of SAGE's publishing program. Founder Sara Miller McCune published SAGE's first methods book, *Public Policy Evaluation*, in 1970. Soon after, she launched the *Quantitative Applications in the Social Sciences* series—affectionately known as the "little green books."

Always at the forefront of developing and supporting new approaches in methods, SAGE published early groundbreaking texts and journals in the fields of qualitative methods and evaluation.

Today, more than 40 years and two million little green books later, SAGE continues to push the boundaries with a growing list of more than 1,200 research methods books, journals, and reference works across the social, behavioral, and health sciences. Its imprints—Pine Forge Press, home of innovative textbooks in sociology, and Corwin, publisher of PreK–12 resources for teachers and administrators—broaden SAGE's range of offerings in methods. SAGE further extended its impact in 2008 when it acquired CQ Press and its best-selling and highly respected political science research methods list.

From qualitative, quantitative, and mixed methods to evaluation, SAGE is the essential resource for academics and practitioners looking for the latest methods by leading scholars.

For more information, visit **www.sagepub.com**.